Why do we continue to outperform every other middle grades American History program?

THE AMERICAN NATION
PRENTICE HALL

FEATURES NEW FULLY INTEGRATED TECHNOLOGY

The American Nation was developed for today's evolving middle grades approach.

Timely, up-to-date content.

Includes 1996 Presidential election results, updated charts and graphs reflecting recent changes in the world.

Student-centered, activity-based approach.

Look for hundreds of skill-based, student-centered activities throughout the text. Cooperative learning, linking past and present, critical thinking, learning styles, and alternative assessment.

Strong interdisciplinary connections.

In-text connections for every chapter link main ideas to six other disciplines. In addition, team teaching strategies and an Interdisciplinary Connections section of the Teaching Resources provide you with a wealth of materials to integrate other disciplines into your American History classroom.

Choose from **Survey** and **Beginnings to 1877** editions.

New
Fully Integrated Technology

Relevant and accessible narrative.

A lively, exceptionally clear narrative rich in primary sources and anecdotal material, spectacular visuals and maps, and strong links between past and present make the story of America exciting and memorable.

Widely acclaimed.

As always, the nation's #1 favorite offers a strong geography focus, connections to world events, up-to-date content, outstanding skill instruction, and a special Civics Overview chapter.

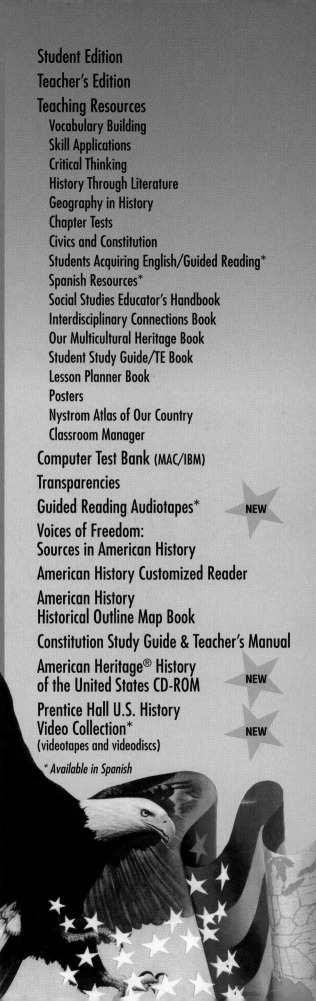

Student Edition

Teacher's Edition

Teaching Resources
  Vocabulary Building
  Skill Applications
  Critical Thinking
  History Through Literature
  Geography in History
  Chapter Tests
  Civics and Constitution
  Students Acquiring English/Guided Reading*
  Spanish Resources*
  Social Studies Educator's Handbook
  Interdisciplinary Connections Book
  Our Multicultural Heritage Book
  Student Study Guide/TE Book
  Lesson Planner Book
  Posters
  Nystrom Atlas of Our Country
  Classroom Manager

Computer Test Bank (MAC/IBM)

Transparencies

Guided Reading Audiotapes*   NEW

Voices of Freedom:
Sources in American History

American History Customized Reader

American History
Historical Outline Map Book

Constitution Study Guide & Teacher's Manual

American Heritage® History
of the United States CD-ROM   NEW

Prentice Hall U.S. History
Video Collection*   NEW
(videotapes and videodiscs)

* Available in Spanish

ANNOTATED TEACHER'S EDITION

THE AMERICAN NATION
PRENTICE HALL

James West Davidson
Michael B. Stoff

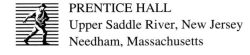

PRENTICE HALL
Upper Saddle River, New Jersey
Needham, Massachusetts

THE AMERICAN NATION
ANNOTATED TEACHER'S EDITION

ISBN 0-13-432212-6
1 2 3 4 5 6 7 8 9 10   01 00 99 98 97

PHOTO CREDITS   Page **T6** ©1993
Shadowfax Photography/Courtesy NMSA;
T8 William Dilillo/Courtesy Chris Stevenson;
T13 Paula Lerner/The Picture Cube;
T14 David W. Hamilton/The Image Bank;
T21-T22 Dean Abramson

PRENTICE HALL
Simon & Schuster Education Group
A VIACOM COMPANY

CONTENTS

Chapter Managers

UNIT 1 A Meeting of Different Worlds

UNIT 2 From Revolution to Republic

Civics Overview

UNIT 3 The New Republic

Middle Grades Educator's Handbook

*T*he middle grades classroom is the most rapidly evolving area in contemporary education. Research shows that in just a few years, middle grades teaching practices have substantially redefined themselves. Prentice Hall recognizes your changing needs and has developed this *new edition* of *The American Nation.* The *Middle Grades Educator's Handbook* has been created for the Annotated Teacher's Edition to help you understand key issues and trends in the middle grades classroom.

UNDERSTANDING THE MIDDLE GRADES PHILOSOPHY

Sue Swaim
Executive Director, National Middle School Association

> " The middle school concept is rooted entirely in the realities of human growth and development. "

Extensive discussions, debates, and assessments of public education throughout our country have brought us to the threshold of the twenty-first century with a resounding challenge and mandate to restructure our schools. It has become apparent that simply improving on what we currently do will not meet the needs of today's young adolescents or respond to the challenges of adequately preparing them for the demands of the twenty-first century.

Middle level schools, without a doubt, have been one of the focal points of these various discussions, for it is recognized that they have an especially critical role to play. The time for engaging in a thoughtful examination of the middle level curriculum is now. Putting into action a developmentally appropriate curriculum that is responsive to the 10- to 15-year-old learner's needs is a high priority on the education agenda of the United States.

The middle school concept is rooted entirely in the realities of human growth and development. Practices advocated, such as interdisciplinary instruction, cooperative learning, and a student-centered approach, are built upon our best holistic understanding of this particular age group and the principles of learning. The call for middle level educators to understand fully the developmental needs and characteristics of 10- to 15-year-olds is a major determinant of the ultimate success of our middle level schools.

Schools where educational opportunities and stimulating learning environments open the door to life-long learning as well as meet students' immediate needs are vital to the full development of young adolescents. Students must be given opportunities to develop their own agendas for learning, which can then be put into action through collaborative and self-directed developmental experiences. The academic rigor, which they deserve, and the humane curriculum, which they require, must be balanced and valued.

Established in 1973, the National Middle School Association stands for educational beliefs that are based on the needs of young adolescents. These beliefs provide the foundation for programmatic characteristics and instructional practices that NMSA believes are essential in a true middle school. It is the only educational association exclusively devoted to improving the educational experiences of young adolescents.

In fulfilling its mission as an international advocate for youngsters ages 10 to 15, the National Middle School Association has developed the following goals.

- To promote collaboration among all who contribute to the well-being of young adolescents.

- To promote an understanding of and a responsiveness to the developmental needs of young adolescents.

- To support middle level educators and others who impact the education of young adolescents.

- To promote appropriate curriculum, instruction, and assessment for young adolescents.

- To promote an understanding of and responsiveness to our increasingly diverse student population.

These are ambitious goals, yet we are committed to addressing them vigorously. It is our intent to forge educational partnerships with other professional organizations, private companies, and foundations with similar priorities to increase the research and resources available to middle level educators. We encourage active membership involvement in a variety of working committees such as the Curriculum Study Task Force to develop appropriate professional development activities, publications, and position statements geared to the needs of middle level professionals. Our annual conference, which brings together over 10,000 middle level professionals, is the premier networking opportunity for middle level educators.

National Middle School Association invites you to join in these efforts by taking a proactive role in achieving developmentally responsive educational experiences and an overall improvement in the quality of life for young adolescents. Whether you are a classroom teacher, administrator, other type of educator, parent, student, or someone interested simply in the education of young adolescents, we hope you will join in our quest to provide a brighter future for our youth. Working together, our common goals can be achieved.

> " . . . we hope you will join in our quest to provide a brighter future for our youth. "

From **Theory** to **Practice**

The American Nation

- provides strategies and resources for your growing middle grades needs

- provides family involvement ideas and letters, suggestions for community and home projects, and a directory of support organizations and hotlines for teens in The Middle Grades Experience booklet of the Social Studies Educator's Handbook within the *Chapter Resources* binder.

Successful Interdisciplinary Instruction

Chris Stevenson, Ph.D.
Associate Professor of Education
University of Vermont

An Invitation to Dance

Although adolescent culture has changed in many ways since we who are now teachers of young adolescents were teens ourselves, one event is ageless: the dance. The music has changed, students' fashions have changed, and their social protocol seems altogether different from what we knew. But the fact and the significance of the dance persist, still attracting young adolescents of diverse interests and lifestyles. The essence of the dance remains constant: social interchanges put to music and movement. Young people still come together, often around a theme, to physically respond to the rhythms of music and each other. The appeal of the dance transcends time.

For teachers, there are compelling lessons in the dance. Our students are usually well-acquainted with the Three Rs of Pedagogy: Read, Recite, and Regurgitate. Although some of them may have become compliant with this perspective on teaching, many more of them register indifference and even open resistance, often becoming cynical about education. Sadly, too many withdraw altogether from the quality of personal engagement that characterizes authentic learning—"the dance."

Learning that endures has its own purposes and rhythms, and it generates its own energy. It is also ex-pressive, creative, and joyous—an experience that affirms and empowers the individual in accord with his or her own priorities. Thus, authentic learning is a dance, not merely a march or drill across the parade grounds of subject matter. And as with learning to dance, authentic learning through interdisciplinary study often requires learning some new steps by teachers and students.

Authentic knowledge for young adolescents is always *integrative;* that is to say, it reflects structures of understanding that form connections between students' own perceptions, ideas, questions, values, and subject matter. It is each student's personalized inquiry and interpretation that will achieve the ultimate reward of relevance and meaning.

Perhaps the greatest challenge we face is that of engaging students' interest in curriculum they often regard as "boring" and "irrelevant." Our initial challenge is to establish a classroom climate that provokes genuine student interest and that invites their exploration. This climate constitutes a platform upon which students pursue enduring connections between their contemporary adolescent experience and our nation's history.

It is in the pedagogical music which teachers provide that students' interest and attitude toward inquiry can be salvaged. We can acknowledge diverse approaches to learning, and we can encourage correspondingly diverse pedagogy. When we encourage multiple approaches to learning, we affirm our students' individuality and their idiosyncratic approaches to "the dance."

Interdisciplinary studies must balance existing knowledge with students' individual and collective questions. This balance encourages a partnership—a relationship that is also defined by the dance. You might begin by asking general questions that invite students to reflect and then share what they already know. Ask questions such as "What is an American?" "What do Americans believe?" "How are they similar to and different from other people?" "What does all of this have to do with me? Their responses are a starting place for establishing topics for interdisciplinary units of study. These units will combine students' priorities with those of the teacher.

Next, the prudent teacher invites small groups of students to brainstorm such questions as "What do we already know?" "What do we want to find out?" "What else do we need to understand?"

Using large sheets of butcher paper and markers, small groups of students begin by building lists—a process that may continue for several class meetings. Teachers' functions are largely ones of facilitation and clarification, helping students articulate their interests and judiciously offering their own questions to complement students' ideas. The lists then need to be further classified to provide a working structure from which benchmarks for small group and whole group work are planned.

These benchmarks are the indications of students' readiness to pursue the questions.

Once priorities have been established, a variety of alternative teaching and learning strategies become available. Drawing, videotaping, mapping, designing, constructing, interviewing, simulating, calculating, and debating can be used to answer the questions students have listed.

With such a variety of activities taking place at once, it is impossible for a single teacher to know precisely what each student is doing. One of the great opportunities inherent in teaching young adolescents is their readiness to learn *how* to become more responsible for themselves and their own learning. The tasks of maintaining documentary records of their work and their use of time are well within their capabilities. Given clear examples and guidance, they can also learn to assess personal progress toward individual and group goals. It is in carrying out just such responsibilities that students learn the value of initiative and responsibility, essential dimensions of self-sufficiency.

Just as there are many different dances and idiosyncratic preferences for one step or another, so are there a variety of approaches. Every teacher is not equally confident about stepping onto the curriculum dance floor and spinning to the music. However, *what* we have to teach young adolescents depends heavily on *how we go about teaching them* and *how we present ourselves as learners*. This bid to the Integrated Curriculum Ball invites you to boogie to some new steps.

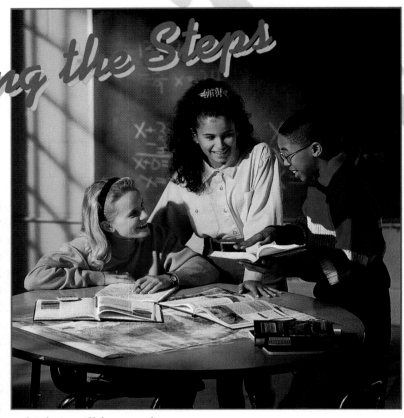

Following the Steps

First Steps

Choosing a Topic

The first step in planning an interdisciplinary unit of study is choosing a topic. The topic should be broad enough to encompass several disciplines. It should balance students' interests with their individual and collective questions. The topic should also be relevant to teachers and students in the setting in which it will be taught.

Once a topic for study has been chosen, a planning scheme will help both the teacher and student to begin moving to the same beat. The scheme should include all of the steps in the unit of study.

Defining the Scope

To help define the scope of a study, students create lists of what they already know or believe about the topic. Take, for example, the study of Americans already suggested. Small groups of students can generate responses to "What is an American?" Their discussions will help shape the direction of a subsequent question: "What are important questions about Americans?" or "What should Americans know about each other?"

Then the teacher and students compile the lists, classifying items by category and prioritizing what they wish to learn. Students should think about how they might explore the topic from the perspective of different disciplines. Their personal ideas and priorities become the reference points for subsequent planning and learning.

Next Steps

Implementing the Study

Just as a dance involves partners, so do interdisciplinary learning and teaching. A big part of the pleasure and effectiveness of interdisciplinary studies stems from student participation in day-to-day planning. The teacher should guide students in finding answers to the questions generated in their discussions. What resources are available? Where might students look? Students will also share in planning groups for different aspects of the unit. What size will the groups be? Who will handle which tasks?

Students should be prepared to explore and inquire about issues relevant to the entire class, as well as their personal interests. Their idea exchanges and their choices make the dance credible and appealing.

Planning a Culminating Event

To give structure to the interdisciplinary unit and to give students a goal to work toward, plan a culminating event for the study. Ideally, this should be a collective decision. First, the teacher and students pick a date for the event, then work backward to establish benchmarks for completing different phases of the unit of study.

It helps to think of closure in terms of three elements: student presentations of what they have produced and learned (e.g., a book, documentary, play/skit, display, debate, reenactment, video show, outing); recognition for students and others for initiative and particularly notable contributions to the study (certificates, ribbons, flowers, dedication); and refreshments to ensure a social dimension to the culminating event (adolescents love to decide about food).

Selecting Activities

The teacher's perspective and guidance are crucial to selecting the activities that will take place during the unit of study. He or she should provide many choices, both mandatory, teacher-directed activities and optional, student-directed activities.

The teacher's wider general experience, understanding of teaching and learning activities, and general expertise with learning and scholarship will help students identify realistic possibilities for their activities. He or she can guide them to rely not only on print resources immediately available but also on resources beyond the school. For example, activities such as collecting public opinion, interviewing, drawing and photographing, creating murals, constructing graphic and three-dimensional models, producing video documentations, and other hands-on activities are valuable learning experiences. On the other hand, reading analytically, expository writing, forming hypotheses, making comparisons and predictions, producing reviews and critiques, devising alternative solutions, creating detailed explanations, and debating are basic scholarly skills cultivated naturally according to the idiosyncrasies and skills of particular learners.

Understanding What Is Happening

Setting Standards

The teacher should set clearly defined standards by which students can evaluate their own work. Each student should keep a record of each day's work—including the original or a copy of each plan agreed upon and each piece of work produced. They should also keep a record of their daily work through personal reflections in a journal and critiques of particular pieces in their individual portfolios. Then the teacher can work with individuals and small groups largely in relationship to the contents of portfolios, thereby gaining a comprehensive grasp of the study.

Making Students Accountable

It is common to interdisciplinary studies that everyone is simultaneously involved in a variety of learning activities. Every student, therefore, should help set group and personal goals, plan and organize activities, carry out portions of the study, and evaluate their own and each other's work.

With so many different investigations and other activities taking place simultaneously, it is not possible for a single teacher to know everything that is happening at a particular moment. A special benefit of working with young adolescent students is their readiness and ability to take responsibility for documenting their work.

Publicizing the Study

The teacher and students should work together to publicize the ongoing unit. Students can provide copies of drawings and writings. Both students and teachers can write articles for newsletters and newspapers, as well as for national professional publications. Regular updates for parents and colleagues are important ways to show what students are accomplishing.

"Swing your partner!"

One of the distinct benefits of this kind of teaching is the spirit of fraternity that inevitably emerges as the study takes on its own life. Students talking and working together around common goals exude an irresistible authenticity. The teacher is not only a source of accurate information, but also a partner with students in exploring and learning. Priorities are negotiated rather than mandated. Where this kind of true partnership exists, learning is always occurring—not only by students but by teachers.

From Theory to Practice

The American Nation

- provides a Connections feature in each chapter that links a main idea to one of six subjects: the Arts, the Sciences, Geography, the World, Economics, and Civics. The *Interdisciplinary Connections* booklet in the Teaching Resources provides full-page interdisciplinary links between the main idea in each Connections feature and the other five subjects.

- provides students with choices for actively exploring an important idea from the chapter with an Interdisciplinary Activity in each Chapter Review

- illustrates major advances in technology with an Exploring Technology drawing in each unit and Exploring Technology transparencies in the *American History Transparencies*

- fosters an appreciation of literature with a History Through Literature selection at the end of each unit

- provides students with links between the student edition and *Prentice Hall Literature, Prentice Hall Science,* and fine art with Connections charts in the Reference Section

- helps you take advantage of team teaching with Team-Teaching notes in the *Annotated Teacher's Edition*

- helps you point out the connections between American history and other disciplines with interdisciplinary background and activity notes throughout the *Annotated Teacher's Edition*

- provides a series of high-interest, interdisciplinary units linking topics in American history to other major disciplines in the *Prentice Hall Interdisciplinary Explorations Series*

WORKING WITH BLOCK SCHEDULES

Consultants

Michael Rettig
Assistant Professor of Education
James Madison University, Virginia

Judith Cannizzaro
K–12 Social Studies Supervisor
Nashville, Tennessee

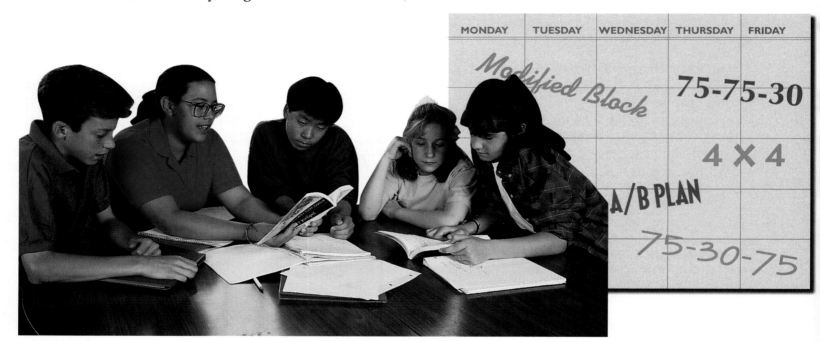

During the past ten years, American schools have been experimenting with a new kind of organization known as block scheduling. These schools have shifted from the traditional school day, organized into six, seven, or eight single class periods, to "block" schedules, in which students take fewer classes of longer duration daily.

Why Block Scheduling?

Teachers who are adopting block scheduling hope to ease a number of problems that they associate with the traditional school day. By introducing block scheduling, they say, schools will:

- reduce the number of students teachers must interact with each day and/or each term.
- reduce the number of courses teachers must prepare for each day and/or each term.
- reduce the number of classes students attend and prepare for each day and/or each term.
- provide teachers with blocks of teaching time that allow and encourage the use of active teaching strategies and greater student involvement.
- give teachers more planning time.
- provide students with variable amounts of time for learning, without lowering standards and without penalizing those who need more or less time to learn.
- reduce the number of class changes and the discipline problems that go along with them.
- give teachers the time to deal with discipline problems as they arise.

Going "On the Block"

Block scheduling can take a variety of forms. Some of the most popular forms are outlined below. It is important to select the one that is suitable for your school situation before going "on the block."

•Intensive Block Students on an intensive block schedule concentrate on one or two subjects at a time. The classic intensive block is the trimester plan, which has students completing two courses in 60 days, then moving on to two different courses. Advocates like the intensive block because they can concentrate on fewer students at a time. Critics, however, worry about students who transfer to or from schools on traditional schedules.

•4x4 Block Sometimes called the *accelerated block,* the 4x4 block allows students to take four subjects each semester in blocks of 85 to 100 minutes each. Because of the accelerated pace, students complete a year's work in a single semester. Again, many teachers and students are enthusiastic, but the schedule makes midyear transfers difficult.

•A/B Plan This model is often called the *alternating day schedule* or *block 8,* because students attend eight blocks of classes over a two-day period. A variation is to schedule six blocks over two days. The A/B Plan makes transfers easier because students complete courses at about the same pace as students on a traditional schedule.

•Modified Block Many different plans go by this name. At some schools, a modified block combines a 4x4 block four days a week with a traditional seven- or eight-period Friday devoted to electives. At others, students take two block courses and three single-period classes each day. The block courses end after a semester, but the single-period classes continue all year to accommodate music, foreign languages, and other courses that need daily sessions.

•Other Options The scheduling options multiply when schools combine various block modifications with different ways of dividing up the school year. One especially intriguing option is a 75-75-30 plan used in an Ohio middle school. The students have two 75-day block-scheduled semesters. Then, near the end of April, when "school's a bear," they get a fresh start with a short semester in which teachers offer specialty courses in their subject areas. In another variation, a California school is considering a 75-30-75 plan that would offer specialty courses in the middle of the year, the way many colleges do.

"We've never been able to graph the change in 'smiles per hundred students,' but if we could, I know we'd see a sizable increase. The block schedule has changed more than the timing of our bells; it has changed the entire culture of our school."

From **Theory** *to* **Practice**

The American Nation

■ provides hands-on activities appropriate for block schedules in chapter openers, section reviews, skill lessons, and Connections features in the student edition.

■ includes an Interdisciplinary Activity in each chapter of the student edition that encourages the exploration and presentation made possible by block scheduling.

■ presents activity and team-teaching suggestions in the *Annotated Teacher's Edition* that might be used as the basis for one or more extended class periods—or even for an entire block.

■ promotes in-depth exploration suitable for block schedules through a multidiscipline study of main chapter ideas in the *Interdisciplinary Connections* booklet in the Teaching Resources.

■ offers more than 100 fully developed cooperative-learning lesson plans in the *Lesson Planner* booklet in the Teaching Resources. These lesson plans help develop the group interaction and student exploration that are important goals of block scheduling.

■ features a Block Scheduling booklet in the *Social Studies Educator's Handbook* in the Teaching Resources. This booklet provides model pacing guides and extensive tips from experienced teachers.

■ features a wide variety of multimedia materials, including CD-ROMs, videodiscs, videotapes, and transparencies, that might be used to introduce a lesson segment, serve as a transition from one part of a lesson to another, or provide the focus of a wrap-up activity in a block schedule.

NEW TRENDS IN ASSESSMENT

Hannah Kruglanski
Director of Curriculum and Assessment,
Edunetics Corporation, Arlington, Virginia

When closely examining alternative assessments—tests that differ from the traditional multiple-choice, true-false, and matching assessments—social studies teachers usually find them both familiar and unfamiliar. The essays, presentations, constructions, and portfolios used in alternative assessments seem familiar because they have long been a part of the social studies classroom. They appear unfamiliar primarily because teachers are asked to use these activities in unaccustomed ways.

The Importance of Testing

We know that tests play a major role in the lives of students—and teachers. Tests signal to students what is important; students then make adjustments in their efforts to get the best possible grades. Tests determine students' placement in programs and "track" future schooling paths. Test scores affect schools as well by indicating the quality of programs to district administrators and legislators. Furthermore, tests communicate educational standards and signal to the community—students, teachers, parents—what the community considers important to teach and learn.

Too often the tests used in our schools reward only the memorization of facts. Thus, students gear their learning and teachers focus their instruction on learning the bits of information needed for the test. If we choose to emphasize reasoning, problem solving, and application of knowledge over memorization, we need to provide assessments that measure these outcomes and foster their learning. This goal—improving critical thinking and the ability to apply knowledge—is why the new forms of assessment are important.

What Is Alternative Assessment?

All forms of alternative assessment require students to construct answers, generate information, or create products in response to test assignments. These assessments tap higher-order thinking skills and challenge students to apply their knowledge in problem-solving situations that encourage active learning. The various forms of alternative assessments foster conceptual understanding and making connections to students' own lives. They frequently mirror the processes of learning by asking students to reflect on their work, periodically assess their knowledge, and seek feedback from peers and experts. Alternative assessments allow for a broader, more complete measurement of diverse learning experiences than the limited responses to standardized tests.

Teachers do not need to throw out the traditional tests when adopting alternative assessments. For subjects such as American history, in which the amassing of a knowledge base is an important instructional outcome, traditional tests offer a good measurement of this outcome. But students need to learn how to evaluate the knowledge they acquire—to apply it, use it to solve problems, and link their new knowledge to their old knowledge and their lives. Alternative assessments provide the means for meeting these goals.

How to Carry Out Alternative Assessments

The most frequently used forms of alternative assessments are performance, portfolio, essay, and exhibition. Examining performance assessment in more detail will provide examples of how to carry out alternative assessments in the classroom.

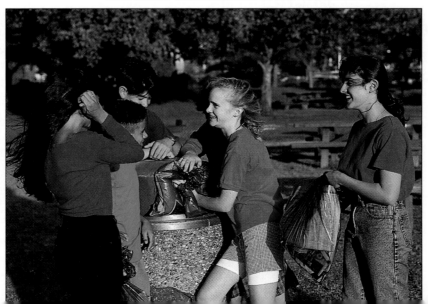

Performance Assessment

This method consists of open-ended and multistep tasks that are designed to demonstrate how students can apply and use their learning in solving problems and making decisions. The tasks usually reflect authentic, or real-life, problems and issues. They focus on the "big ideas" or important concepts. Student responses could be in the form of written or oral presentations or in visual forms such as videotapes or posters.

Social studies performance assessments could require students to analyze an issue, form an opinion, debate various points of view, or consider causes and effects. Performance assessment tasks link students' prior knowledge and provide opportunities for new connections to be made. Although tasks do not target facts or formulas, students are still expected to use and apply knowledge of facts when appropriate.

Portfolio Assessment

This assessment tool is designed to measure growth in student performance over time by keeping a systematic record of progress as demonstrated in samples of student work. Before students begin assembling portfolios, teachers should determine:

- **Its Purpose** Will it be used for instruction, assessment, or both?
- **How It Will Be Used** Will it be the sole measurement of student work for that course? Will it be used for the entire year or a specific time period?
- **The Criteria for Selection of Items** Will it be the students' best work, their typical work, or a combination?
- **Ownership** Who decides what goes in the portfolio—the teacher, the student, or both?
- **Scoring Criteria** Will the entire portfolio, the separate components, or a composite be scored?

Once these decisions have been made, the teacher should next focus on the contents of the portfolios. A valid portfolio includes a variety of evidence and a range of students' work. Evidence in a portfolio needs to relate directly to the outcomes it is intended to measure. Use the following guidelines to help ensure that portfolios meet these criteria:

- **Work Biographies** To demonstrate student development, collect samples of students' work from different points in time but on a specific topic or type of activity. For example, several drafts of a writing assignment constitute a work biography.
- **Range of Works** To demonstrate growth, collect samples of different types of work. For example, works from different areas of social studies constitute a range of works.
- **Self-Assessment** To show changes in student awareness about their performance and perspective in relation to their previous work, collect evidence that shows how students react to the content of their own portfolios.

Scoring Alternative Assessments

Alternative assessments are scored in a way that reflects the desired outcomes and that is closely linked with instruction. The procedure for scoring involves developing a rubric—preestablished criteria for a scoring scale and sample performances to illustrate each point on the scale. To begin developing the rubric, the teacher explains the characteristics of an outstanding performance; this is the top scoring point. The teacher then spells out the criteria for an unacceptable or limited performance; this is the bottom point on the scale. Generally, the rubric contains two scoring points between unacceptable and outstanding—one for an acceptable performance and one for an extensive, or commendable, performance.

There are several methods of scoring, the two major strategies being holistic and analytic.

- **Holistic Scoring** A strategy by which a task is rated on criteria and a single score is given for the overall quality of task. It provides general information about the performance.
- **Analytic Scoring** A strategy by which the task is rated by multiple criteria. Scores are given for each criterion, and they reflect the relative contribution of each criterion and can provide a diagnosis of the performance.
- **Modified Holistic Scoring** A strategy that combines elements from holistic and analytic. A single score is given but the relative contribution of each criterion can be isolated.

From *Theory* to **Practice**

The American Nation

- includes an Interdisciplinary Activity with each Chapter Review that is an ideal performance assessment opportunity
- presents a multitude of portfolio opportunities through a wide variety of activities, each accompanied by guided instruction
- provides an Alternative Assessment booklet in the Social Studies Educator's Handbook within the *Chapter Resources* binder that explains the varied assessment opportunities available in the program and includes rubrics for evaluating student work

Using Cooperative Learning

Prentice Hall interviews Robert Slavin

Cooperative learning is being used now more than ever before. But what is cooperative learning, and why should you incorporate it into your classroom activities? For a clearer picture, we talked to Robert Slavin, Director of the Johns Hopkins University Center for Social Organization of Schools and one of the nation's leading researchers on the use of cooperative learning in the classroom.

Q What are we talking about when we say "cooperative learning"?

A Cooperative learning actually refers to a wide range of different methods. What is common to all of them is the idea that kids of the same age are working together to help each other learn.

Q How does that happen? How does cooperative learning reinforce or expand learning?

A One of the things that cooperative learning does is motivate students to be concerned about each other's learning, so that students feel that their peers are supporting their learning efforts. Another thing is that students, in the process of discussing the material that the teacher has presented, get to voice their own current understanding, which helps them in the sense that people learn by teaching. Cooperative learning also helps other kids by filling in gaps. Explaining ideas to each other may help kids to grasp ideas that they may have only dimly understood at the end of the teacher's lesson.

Q Why should cooperative learning be used in the classroom? For example, what are its benefits?

A The main benefit of cooperative learning is that it improves student achievement. Many studies that have compared it to traditional learning have found that cooperative learning improves the achievement of high achievers, of average achievers, and of low achievers in many different circumstances. Cooperative learning also fosters improved intergroup relations, acceptance of mainstreamed, academically handicapped kids, and self-esteem. Because kids enjoy working cooperatively, I think they would feel good about a class in which they are able to work together in this way.

Q Are there any drawbacks to using cooperative learning?

A Well, I suppose some people would say that it's noisy. You've got to be prepared for some noise. Also, in many forms of cooperative learning there is scoring to be done, so there's some paperwork that may be involved, but not a great deal. Other than that, I'm not sure that there are any serious drawbacks.

Q Let's focus on the groups. What is the ideal group size for cooperative learning?

A I personally believe four is the ideal group size. It allows you to do some activities in pairs, and some activities as a total team. Of course, then, five, if you have left-over kids.

How It Works

To give you a wide range of options, many cooperative learning activities are provided in the *Annotated Teacher's Edition* of *The American Nation*. You are the best judge of which activities work best in your class. Use these guidelines when you decide to use a cooperate learning activity.

Group Size: 4–5 students.

Group Makeup: Combination of high, average, and low achievers, with a balance of sex, ethnicity, and personalities.

Duration of Groups: Change after about six weeks.

Frequency of Use: As often as practical; consistency is important.

Accountability: Group success should depend on individual learning—measured by one evaluation or by improvement over time.

Recognition: Just something small to show you value group success—praise and public recognition are often enough; bonus points or small prizes such as stickers or pins are good, too.

Q How should groups be assigned?

A I think they should be assigned by the teacher. Try to have a high achiever, a low achiever, and a couple of average achievers in each group, and be sure that there's some kind of balance of sex and ethnicity. The teacher should also take into account which kids are likely to work together— you know, which kids were dating but have now broken up, the personalities involved, et cetera.

Q Once students are assigned to a group, how are individual roles decided?

A Well, in our methods [at Johns Hopkins], there aren't individual roles. All the students have the same role, which is to be a learner and a teacher. In methods that do use roles, I think that they should be assigned randomly and then rotated over time.

Q How can cooperative learning be structured so that one student doesn't do all the work?

A There are many ways to do it. In our methods, the groups are working to earn certificates or other kinds of recognition based on the learning of all members of the group. . . . What this means is that the only way for the group to succeed is if everybody learns, so there's no way for one student to do all the work. You rarely want to give the group a single task, or a single activity that they all have to do, because then it is possible for one kid to do all the work.

Q You've said that group success should depend on individual learning. How does that work?

A If there's something that can be traced back to each individual student, then the sum of those individual assessments are used to determine teams that get certificates or special recognition or bonus points on their grades—something to indicate that the teacher values group performance. But the success of the group is dependent on things that show the individual learning or the individual participation of the student.

Q Some people are opposed to the idea of using rewards and certificates. How do you feel about that?

A I think there are some kinds of objectives for which they may not be necessary, such as composition, because kids enjoy that anyway; but for most school students, some kind of a group reward is necessary. It doesn't have to be big, just something to communicate to the kids that the activity is important and valuable. Because without that, the students don't see as clearly the need to help each other. There has to be something that they're trying to work toward as a group. Most often, simple recognition is sufficient to tell the group that its success matters.

Q How often should cooperative learning be used?

A It should be used pretty extensively. Even when you're using cooperative learning, the kids are not working in groups all day or all the time. There's a cycle of activities that includes instruction, individual assessment, and may include some individual work. I think that we certainly have many, many classrooms where cooperative learning is used essentially all year. But it also makes sense to use it for shorter periods, as long as you're not using it on, say, every other Thursday when it's raining. If you are going to use it, it's important to use it consistently for some period of time—maybe six weeks—rather than to do it just from time to time.

Q Should the groups be constant over that time period?

A We recommend changing them after every six weeks . . . we definitely recommend against the use of ad hoc groups, of just saying, "Everybody find a partner." There's a major benefit to having a group that kids really identify with and think is important. If you're changing groups every day, then that's not going to happen.

From **Theory** *to* **Practice**

The American Nation

- provides a multitude of activities in the student edition that are appropriate for cooperative learning
- includes cooperative learning activity suggestions throughout the *Annotated Teacher's Edition*
- provides for each section of every chapter a cooperative learning lesson plan in the *Lesson Planner* booklet in the Teaching Resources

Writing as a Process

Today we think of writing as a complex process that involves the application of a wide range of thinking skills and language abilities. Thinking of the process as a series of steps, we can focus on the techniques and tools writers need, the knowledge they must develop, and the choices they must learn to make at each of these steps. From this understanding of what writers must be able to do, we can begin to devise some instructional strategies and some direct activities to teach appropriate skills and knowledge.

The process theory proposes that writers practice very different skills and undertake very different activities at each of the following five productive stages:

Prewriting

Writers get warmed up, choose a focus, gather ideas and details, record, and begin to sort out their data, seeing how the data fit together in useful ways. This stage is a time of discovery and of invention. It is rich, productive, and extravagant.

Writing

Writers need to get their ideas recorded in some sort of tentative, first-draft shape as easily and as quickly as possible. Fluency with written English is critical at this stage, as is the knowledge of the choices that are available to writers and the factors that influence their judgment about these options. Therefore, writers must learn how to turn streams of thoughts and ideas into coherent, organized written streams, and they need to have a great deal of experience in making the choices and in having their judgments work effectively in the written piece.

Revising

From revision that is supported by the positive, informed response of outside readers and by the rethinking and revising by the writers themselves, writers learn that writing benefits from being scrutinized again (and again) after that first draft. This stage involves revising for sense and editing for word choice and sentence style. Writers must learn how to review a draft with an eye to revision; they must learn to be editors. In addition, they need to learn to proofread—to spot errors and make corrections in spelling, capitalization, punctuation, and grammar. These are complicated skills that require a great deal of learning and teaching.

Evaluating

After a student's final draft is turned in, there are still opportunities for teaching and learning to occur. Students may be involved in evaluating

---

From **Theory** to **Practice**

The American Nation

- provides opportunities for students to use the writing process in a Writing to Learn Activity in every Section Review
- offers a wide variety of activities that present students with writing opportunities
- includes many skill lessons that help develop writing skills, particularly Skill Lesson 26, Writing a Research Paper
- provides you with suggestions for evaluating student writing, including many sample evaluation forms in the Alternative Assessment booklet in the Social Studies Educator's Handbook within the *Chapter Resources* binder

their writing and the writing of others by using scoring sheets or rubrics and by emphasizing one of several different methods of scoring.

Publishing

Writers benefit when the classroom is a place where writing is valued, where it is honored, put on display, kept in a student file or portfolio, or presented in a classroom book. Yet although honoring student writing can be done quite simply, it seems to be overlooked in many classrooms. Publishing seeks to give credibility and value to the act of writing and to its product. As the final step in the writing process, it demonstrates to the student that the written piece (and indirectly its author) is valued by other people.

Benefits

Following these steps can involve students deeply in a process in which they have a good chance of success. The steps teach them how to make the process useful and operational in their own writing.

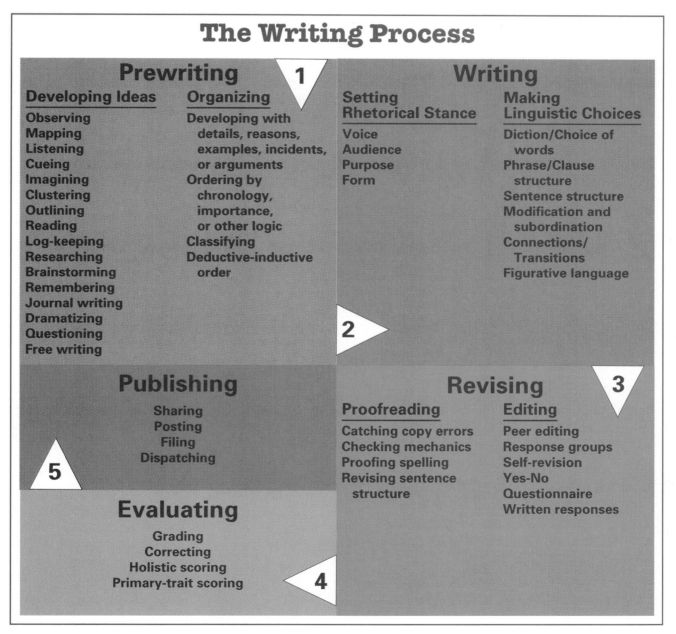

The Writing Process

Prewriting 1

Developing Ideas

Observing
Mapping
Listening
Cueing
Imagining
Clustering
Outlining
Reading
Log-keeping
Researching
Brainstorming
Remembering
Journal writing
Dramatizing
Questioning
Free writing

Organizing

Developing with
  details, reasons,
  examples, incidents,
  or arguments
Ordering by
  chronology,
  importance,
  or other logic
Classifying
Deductive-inductive
  order

Writing 2

Setting Rhetorical Stance

Voice
Audience
Purpose
Form

Making Linguistic Choices

Diction/Choice of
  words
Phrase/Clause
  structure
Sentence structure
Modification and
  subordination
Connections/
  Transitions
Figurative language

Revising 3

Proofreading

Catching copy errors
Checking mechanics
Proofing spelling
Revising sentence
  structure

Editing

Peer editing
Response groups
Self-revision
Yes-No
Questionnaire
Written responses

Publishing 5

Sharing
Posting
Filing
Dispatching

Evaluating 4

Grading
Correcting
Holistic scoring
Primary-trait scoring

Much of the information in "Writing as a Process" was adapted from *The Writing Process in Action: A Handbook for Teachers* by Jackie Proett and Kent Gill, University of California, Davis. Copyright 1986 by the National Council of Teachers of English. Reprinted with permission.

Addressing Individual Learning Styles and Special Needs

Take a look around your classroom. If it's anything like the vast majority of other American classrooms, it includes students from several different ethnic backgrounds and cultural groups. It may also include gifted students as well as students with learning disabilities, native speakers as well as students for whom English is a second language, and visual learners as well as verbal learners.

The range of abilities, languages, cultural perspectives, and learning styles found in the typical American classroom is enough to challenge even the most accomplished teacher. Yet it is imperative that today's teachers meet this challenge. They must provide meaningful instruction to all students *and* they must do so within the confines of the already-existing social studies curriculum.

How can teachers accomplish this? First, they must look to their diverse student populations as a source of tremendous opportunity. They must also take their students' differences into account and plan their curriculum accordingly. To help in this task, *The American Nation* contains several special features designed to address these challenges.

THE CHALLENGE
To accommodate students with individual learning styles.

THE SOLUTION
One of the more recent trends in education addresses the reality that students have different learning styles. Students in the same class often have different methods of absorbing information. An explanation of a concept may be clear to one student while it completely escapes another equally intelligent learner.

What this means for educators is that learning styles must be considered when lessons are planned and implemented. The simplest strategy for meeting this objective is to provide students with opportunities to work in ways that are most meaningful to them. In addition, realize that what may seem like a left-field question from a student may indeed be an attempt to fit the content being covered into a unique learning perspective. A class atmosphere that fosters tolerance for individual differences and focuses on strengths rather than on weaknesses is one in which the teacher as well as the students can grow and learn.

THE CHALLENGE
To provide meaningful and significant instruction that recognizes students' differing abilities.

THE SOLUTION
Students successfully complete the process of intellectual development and subject mastery when instruction makes sense to them. However, what makes sense to one student doesn't always make sense to another. For example, one student may grasp difficult and complicated concepts and learn very quickly while another may learn more slowly and thus require guided instruction and frequent opportunities for remediation. Still another student may have difficulty reading.

Offering a variety of activities geared to different ability levels helps teachers achieve a balance between the need for enrichment in students who are high achievers and the need for remediation in students who are low achievers. For students who need more intellectual stimulation, the presentation of more than one perspective increases the opportu-

LEARNING STYLES	
Style	**Learns Best By**
Auditory	Hearing words and sounds of people and objects, including different rhythms and melodies
Kinesthetic	Manipulating and moving objects that represent concepts
Visual	Reading and writing, seeing pictures, charts, tables, or other presentations that appeal to the sense of sight
Introverted	Working independently, researching and reporting in written form
Extroverted	Interacting with others in discussions, making presentations, performing

nities for the discovery of interrelationships. It also provides opportunities for the analysis and evaluation of information and multiple perspectives. For the student of slow to average ability, learning experiences should enhance his or her understanding of the key issues and facts.

THE CHALLENGE
To focus discussion in a manner that capitalizes on different cultural perspectives.

THE SOLUTION
The study of American history is in itself a way of focusing on different cultures. Certainly the history of the United States includes the contributions and achievements of the many diverse cultures that make up our population. If your class is fortunate enough to have students of diverse backgrounds and cultures, they can provide firsthand knowledge of their heritages.

THE CHALLENGE
To communicate content to students acquiring English.

THE SOLUTION
The greatest challenge in teaching students for whom English is a second language lies in the creation of materials and experiences that rely less heavily on the printed word. Often, these students have average or above average ability but lack the cultural background or the language skills necessary to build a framework for learning and for clearly expressing themselves.

Students acquiring English need assistance in overcoming the language barrier. Using visual cues to illustrate key points and reviewing the meaning of idiomatic phrases and words that may be unfamiliar to nonnative speakers often help them overcome this barrier. Providing background knowledge that may be missing from a student's personal experience also helps.

From *Theory* to *Practice*

The American Nation

- includes an Interdisciplinary Activity with each Chapter Review, which provides activities appropriate for students with varying learning styles

- provides a multitude of activities throughout the student text and in the *Annotated Teacher's Edition* that are designed for individual learning styles

- includes an activity-based lesson plan for every chapter, tailored for individual learning styles

- presents the rich cultural diversity of American history as an integral part of the narrative and through first-person accounts

- provides on-page teaching suggestions and activities in the *Annotated Teacher's Edition* that are specifically designed for assisting students acquiring English

- includes Guided Reading worksheets in the English Guided Reading section of the *Chapter Resources* binder to help SAE or reluctant readers master the basic content of each chapter

- provides Guided Reading worksheets in Spanish in the Spanish Resources section of the *Chapter Resources* binder to help Spanish-speaking students learn key terms introduced in the text and review the main ideas of each chapter

- provides Guided Reading Audiotapes, in English and Spanish, that can be used by aural learners, students who have difficulty reading, and students acquiring English

Putting Technology to Work in the Classroom

The most rewarding moments for any teacher are those in which the flicker of understanding and recognition registers on the student's face—those moments when the previously struggling student "gets it" for the first time. And as any teacher can confirm, there are few things more frustrating than the repeated failure to engage that student who just does not seem to be thriving on traditional pedagogical fare.

The challenge of achieving the rewards and overcoming the frustrations of teaching has never been greater. Yet at the same time, the tools with which teachers can approach this challenge have never been more potent. For with the help of the latest educational technologies, teachers can overcome the obstacles that stand in the way of learning and understanding. They can address the specific needs of students with different learning styles. Rather than being overwhelmed by the rapidity of change in knowledge and information, they can use that change as a device for inspiring and motivating their students.

Technological Solutions for the Teacher — and Student

Research tells us that different students have different learning styles. Some learners need to get a general overview of a topic before they can grasp its details; others need to build from a group of details to develop their own generalizations or to understand those that others make. Some learners need a structured approach to learning; other learners are restricted by such structure. Still others prefer group work, and some must verbalize their ideas to understand them or use hands-on learning in order to achieve a concrete understanding of an abstract idea.

Technology offers many ways to make issues in American history come alive and to engage students of different learning styles. Computers, CD-ROM, and other technologies place vast sources of information and information-processing capabilities at students' fingertips. Audiovisual tools such as television documentaries, cable news broadcasts, videodiscs, and the Internet help bring events to life by presenting images and sounds that command attention.

Such technologies offer students with varying learning styles an opportunity to interact with information on their own terms, in ways that enable them to utilize their particular intellectual strengths.

Keeping Pace in a Changing World

Another challenge of teaching today is the rapid pace of change in knowledge and information. This challenge is partially the result of technology that enables huge amounts of information to be transferred over vast distances in tiny fragments of time. Yet it is that same technology that will allow teachers to use that information to their advantage and to the advantage of their students.

Real-Life Learning

The lessons learned with the help of current and future technology promise to serve the student for a lifetime. Students who learn by using technology to present their own ideas will be those best prepared for their lives in the twenty-first century. Students who have experience working with networked computers, databases, and the Internet, as well as those who have learned how to work cooperatively, will enter the workplace of tomorrow with some of the requisite skills for success.

Perhaps there is also an even greater potential in technology—to equalize opportunity. Once information is freed from the control of a single individual, it becomes less authoritarian and prescriptive in its essence. Also, the technology itself becomes an aid to cooperation and collaboration as students learn to work interactively with information and with other people.

The Promise of Technology

When students use technology to learn, to share, and to express themselves, they become more actively involved in learning. Instead of merely receiving instruction, they can follow their own paths to discovery. Instead of relying on a single source or perhaps just a few sources for information, they can tap into huge reservoirs of information, playing ideas off other networked users, interacting with and communicating by new means, and sharing approaches to problem-solving.

Teachers, too, are empowered. The teacher is no longer the sole presenter of the information but the manager of a special learning environment. Instead of directing the experience, he or she needs only to help keep it smoothly on track. Many teachers report great personal satisfaction and a heightening of their own self-concept when they use various options in technology to solve problems and facilitate student learning.

Technology promises great rewards to both teacher and student. So invite technology into your classroom, and watch this new world unfold.

From Theory to Practice

The American Nation

- provides on-page bar codes in the *Annotated Teacher's Edition* for the dynamic videotape/videodisc program, *United States History Video Collection*

- includes on-page references in the *Annotated Teacher's Edition* for the *American Heritage*® History of the United States CD-ROM, an interactive companion to *The American Nation*

- provides practical advice for using the Internet to enhance the study of American History in the *Using the Internet* booklet in the Social Studies Educator's Handbook within the *Chapter Resources* binder

- includes valuable hints about using technology in the classroom in *Using Multimedia Technology* in the Social Studies Educator's Handbook within the *Chapter Resources* binder

- integrates the audiotape package *Listening to Literature, The American Experience,* with on-page references in the *Annotated Teacher's Edition*

- provides point-of-use references in the *Annotated Teacher's Edition* to a full-color package of *American History Transparencies*

Using *The American Nation* to Meet Middle Grades Needs

*P*rentice Hall recognizes that the needs of middle grades students are very special. That is why the new edition of *The American Nation* continues to provide students with a lively chronological history of the United States, from its beginnings to the present. The authors emphasize important issues—such as forging a national identity from a multicultural population, strengthening democratic institutions, building our economy, managing and respecting the environment, and developing a global perspective.

The middle grades classroom is the most rapidly evolving area in contemporary education. As a result, great care has been taken to create a truly *teachable* middle grades textbook. To that end, a broad range of ancillary components support the student edition of *The American Nation*:

Annotated Teacher's Edition

Teaching Resources

Computer Test Bank

American History Transparencies

Guided Reading Audiotapes (English and Spanish)

American History Customized Reader

Nystrom Atlas of Our Country

American History Historical Outline Map Book

Constitution Study Guide

Voices of Freedom: Sources in American History

Listening to Literature Audiocassettes, The American Experience

Prentice Hall Social Studies Update

United States History Video Collection (videodiscs and videotapes)

American Heritage® *History of the United States* CD-ROM

The Student Text

The American Nation is divided into 9 units and 30 chapters, covering the major periods and themes of American history. Chapter sections provide a manageable amount of material on specific topics. Each section can serve as the basis of a day's lesson. A Reference Section contains important material that students can use throughout their study.

Interdisciplinary Connections

▶ **Connections** feature in each chapter connects a main idea from the chapter to one of six subjects: the Arts, the Sciences, Geography, the World, Economics, or Civics.

▶ **Interdisciplinary Activity** in each Chapter Review actively explores an important idea from the chapter.

▶ **Fine Art** throughout the book helps students gain appreciation for the humanities.

▶ **Exploring Technology** drawing in each unit depicts a major advance in technology.

▶ **History Through Literature** selection from a well-known work of American literature appears at the end of each unit.

▶ **Connections Charts** in the Reference Section provide links to *Prentice Hall Literature, Prentice Hall Science,* and fine art.

A Student-Centered, Activity-Based Approach

▶ **Issues for Today: An Introduction** traces five important issues in American history. This highly visual presentation includes student art and helps students understand the relevance of studying American history.

▶ **Issues for Today: Getting Involved** gives students a chance to explore the five issues on their own. Case studies of student-directed activities show how students can get involved and make a difference in their communities.

▶ **Chapter Setting** at the beginning of each chapter includes a high-interest story that draws students into the narrative.

▶ **Activities** help students understand and respond to content. There is an activity with each Chapter Setting, Section Review, Connections, Skill Lesson, and History Through Literature selection.

▶ **Up Close** in each chapter offers students an exciting, in-depth look at a significant person or event in American history.

▶ **Picturing the Past** photo essays provide students with a glimpse of the lives of young Americans at different times in our history.

▶ **Linking Past and Present** picture pairs show students how important ideas and events from the past influence their lives today.

▶ **History and You** and **Linking Past and Present** extended footnotes highlight the connections between students' lives and events, ideas, and people from our past.

A Multicultural, Global Perspective

▶ **The narrative** presents our rich cultural diversity as an integral part of American history.

▶ **First-person accounts** throughout the text help students develop an appreciation of cultural diversity.

▶ **Art Gallery: Our Common Heritage** shows how contemporary artists of diverse cultural heritages have depicted events and people from the American past.

▶ **Our Common Heritage** extended footnotes highlight important people, ideas, and events from diverse cultures.

▶ **Time Lines** in every chapter opener include world events to help students develop a global perspective about American history.

Individual Learning Styles and Special Needs Opportunities

▶ **Three-step lesson format**—preview, read, and review—for each section ensures reading comprehension.

▶ **Vocabulary** and **key terms** are highlighted and defined where they first appear.

▶ **Maps, charts,** and **pictures** serve as learning tools. Captions provide valuable information, and questions help students use the illustration to better understand American history.

▶ **Causes and Effects** charts trace the causes and effects of a major event in each unit.

▶ **Skill Lessons** in each chapter provide step-by-step instruction for important map, graph, and chart, critical thinking, or research skills.

▶ **Chapter Reviews** contain a variety of questions that help students review main ideas and strengthen critical thinking and geography skills.

Strong Geography and Civics Skills Building

▶ **Geography opportunities** include Chapter One, Geography of the Americas, as well as more than 80 maps, several geography-related Skill Lessons, and geography questions in Chapter and Section Reviews. In the Reference Section, a Gazetteer, Fifty States chart, and Geographic Atlas reinforce the text.

▶ **Civics Overview** chapter, The Constitution at Work, introduces students to the goals and principles of our Constitution, the American form of government, and the rights and duties of American citizens. Because the Civics Overview stands on its own, you can use it at any time during the school year to introduce students to basic civics. To help students further, fully annotated texts of The Declaration of Independence and The Constitution of the United States, as well as the Presidents of the United States chart are in the Reference Section.

....

Annotated Teacher's Edition

The *Annotated Teacher's Edition* gives you a wrap-around format to help you easily manage all the components that support this program. On-page, in-depth background notes, activities, and lesson plans help meet your needs for cooperative learning, interdisciplinary instruction, multicultural education, linking past and present, critical thinking, limited English proficiency, learning styles, portfolios, and performance-based education. In addition, a chapter manager chart begins each chapter, giving you convenient planning information.

The Middle Grades Educators Handbook, located at the beginning of the *Annotated Teacher's Edition,* will help you address key issues and trends in middle grades education. Contributors include middle grades specialists Sue Swaim and Chris Stevenson.

Chapter Manager
A two-page chart preceding each chapter provides an overview of:

▶ **Learning Objectives** for each section.

▶ **Teaching Resources** materials you will need for each section. Resources include materials from the *Chapter Resources* binder; materials from the *Interdisciplinary Connections, Our Multicultural Heritage, Lesson Planner,* and *Student Study Guide* booklets; and the *Art Gallery: Our Common Heritage Posters.*

▶ **Multimedia Resources** you can use for each section. Resources include transparencies, videodiscs, videotapes, audiocassettes, and CD-ROMs.

▶ **Additional Resources** that are appropriate for each section. Resources listed include *Voices of Freedom,* the *American History Historical Outline Map Book,* the *American History Customized Reader,* and the *Interdisciplinary Explorations Series.*

- ▶ **Chapter-Level Resources** you will need for the chapter. The resources can be found in the *Chapter Resources* binder, the *Computer Test Bank,* the *Guided Reading Audiotapes,* and the *Constitution Study Guide.*

Side-Column Annotations

- ▶ **Bell Ringer** activities for each section get students thinking and writing at the beginning of the lesson.

- ▶ **Lesson Plans** for each section include three steps: focus, instruct, and close. An activity-based lesson plan for each chapter and a cooperative learning lesson plan for each section are provided in the *Lesson Planner* in the *Teaching Resources.*

- ▶ **Point-of-use references** for the chapter resources, multimedia resources, and additional resources appropriate for each section help you easily integrate all the components that support the program.

- ▶ **Guided Instruction** notes provide structure and guidance for every activity in the chapter.

- ▶ **Answers** for all map, chart, graph, and picture captions are provided.

Bottom-Box Annotations

- ▶ **Background** notes provide additional information, interdisciplinary connections, multicultural enrichment, and historical sidelights about important people, ideas, and events in the chapter.

- ▶ **Activity** notes provide a wide range of time-sensitive activities for teachers with different teaching styles and for students with different learning styles.

- ▶ **Team-Teaching Suggestions** help you to make connections between social studies and other content areas.

- ▶ **Answers** for all section review questions are provided.

··

Teaching Resources

With the Teaching Resources for *The American Nation,* you will discover a new world of instructional support. This is an integrated program of unique teaching materials, conveniently organized on a chapter-by-chapter basis and packaged in a handy three-ring binder. Additional resources contained in the package include the *Nystrom Atlas of Our Country,* as well as four booklets: *Interdisciplinary Connections, Lesson Planner, Our Multicultural Heritage,* and *Student Study Guide* (Teacher's Edition). Colorful and easy-to-read unit posters enhance student motivation.

Chapter Resources Binder

The *Chapter Resources* binder gives you literally hundreds of worksheets to choose from, organized by chapter.

- ▶ **Vocabulary Building** worksheets preview or test section vocabulary.

- ▶ **Skill Application** worksheets reteach and reinforce the skill taught in each chapter's Skill Lesson.

- ▶ **Critical Thinking** worksheets reteach and reinforce critical thinking skills.

- ▶ **History Through Literature** worksheets feature excerpts from classic works of American literature.

- ▶ **Geography in History** worksheets include essays and map activities to help students understand the role of geography in history.

- ▶ **Chapter Tests A and B** are two different reproducible tests for each chapter.

Our Multicultural Heritage

The *Our Multicultural Heritage* booklet highlights the contributions of many diverse cultures to American history. For each chapter, two biographies and one milestone focus on people, ideas, and events that have contributed to our rich multicultural society.

Lesson Planner

The *Lesson Planner* booklet provides you with hundreds of additional fully developed lesson plans. There is a **Cooperative Learning** lesson plan for each section and an **Activity-Based** lesson plan for each chapter.

Student Study Guide (Teacher's Edition)

The *Student Study Guide* (student editions are available for classroom use) helps your students to study and review what they have read in the text. The introduction provides a useful outline of good study habits. Study guide worksheets for each section and each chapter review key people, places, events, and ideas. The *Student Study Guide* also provides a biographical dictionary and a chart of key events in American history. An answer key appears in the Teacher's Edition.

▶ **Extra Unit Questions** can be used to create a unit, midterm, or final exam. Answers to the unit instructional materials and to all the blackline masters are included.

The *Chapter Resources* binder also provides several other classroom resources.

▶ **Social Studies Educator's Handbook** series of booklets provides valuable information for social studies educators. The booklets explore such timely topics as the special needs of middle grades students, block scheduling, how to use multimedia technology and the Internet, activities for teachers by teachers, and alternative assessment.

▶ **Civics and the Constitution** worksheets help students study the basic principles and parts of the United States Constitution.

▶ **English Guided Reading** worksheets provide vocabulary instruction, section summaries, and review questions for students acquiring English or students who have difficulty reading.

▶ **Spanish Resources** worksheets provide vocabulary practice, section summaries, and short quizzes for Spanish-speaking students.

Interdisciplinary Connections

The *Interdisciplinary Connections* booklet provides five additional full-page interdisciplinary links to the main idea explored in the Connections feature in each chapter.

Art Gallery: Our Common Heritage Posters

Nine full-color unit posters are enlarged versions of selected works that appear in the Art Gallery: Our Common Heritage art. Lesson suggestions for each poster are included in a Teacher's Guide.

Nystrom Atlas of Our Country

An up-to-date atlas of the United States includes national and regional maps, as well as hundreds of charts, graphs, and illustrations to bring geography to life for students.

Computer Test Bank

The *Computer Test Bank* book supplies you with copies of two different reproducible tests for each chapter. Each test contains four parts: Key People, Places, and Terms; Chapter Checkup; Using Your Skills; and Thinking About History. In addition, extra unit-level questions are included.

The *Computer Test Bank* enables you to create tests tailored to the needs of your class. You may order your Prentice Hall TEST GENERATOR software with the order form in the *Chapter Resources* binder or in the *Computer Test Bank* book. (IBM and Macintosh format available.) Or you may use DIAL-A-TEST, a free phone-in testing service.

Guided Reading Audiotapes

Guided Reading Audiotapes accompany *The American Nation.* These tapes provide section-by-section reading previews, summaries, and review questions. They can be used by the aural learner, the student who has difficulty reading, and the student acquiring English. The tapes can be used in conjunction with the Guided Reading worksheets in the English Guided Reading section of the *Chapter Resources* binder. The tapes are also available in Spanish. They can be used in conjunction with the Guided Reading worksheets in the Spanish Resources section of the *Chapter Resources* binder.

American History Transparencies

A new package of over 130 transparencies emphasizes such important themes as interdisciplinary connections, the multicultural heritage of the United States, fine art, historical sequence, relating causes and effects, political cartoons, development of technology, and the role of geography in American history. Detailed lesson suggestions for each transparency provide extensive background information plus at least two lesson ideas.

CD-ROM

The American Heritage® *History of the United States* CD-ROM, an interactive supplement to *The American Nation,* allows students to explore American history through its illustrated summary of main ideas, biographies of Presidents and history makers, examples of literature and music, and ready access to the Internet.

Videodiscs/Videotapes

Prentice Hall's United States History Video Collection gives students an up-close view of American history, with historical re-enactments, archival images, and interviews with historians. In 10 videodiscs or 20 videotapes, the collection spans the nation's history from the beginnings to modern times. The Spanish track on the videodiscs makes American history accessible for Spanish-speaking students.

American History Customized Reader

The American History Customized Reader service allows you to choose the content for a high-interest supplement that brings American history to life. It is a data bank of over 300 articles organized around two themes: Our Multicultural Heritage and Daily Life. You select articles from the data bank, creating a book of readings that meet your students' diverse interests and learning styles. Your 94-page Customized Reader is printed with a customized table of contents and bound with a customized cover. A sampler of the Customized Reader is included in the *Chapter Resources* binder.

Historical Outline Map Book

The *American History Historical Outline Map Book* contains 70 historical outline maps, 11 outline maps of current world regions, and 11 regional maps of the United States today. A Teacher's Edition provides lesson ideas for each of the 92 maps.

Constitution Study Guide

The *Constitution Study Guide* provides in-depth treatment of the Constitution through 15 easy-to-teach illustrated lessons. Four lively "You Are the Judge" features let students focus on constitutional issues that directly affect them. A Teacher's Manual provides lesson plans, activities, and more.

Voices of Freedom: Sources in American History

This valuable supplement gives students a fresh perspective on topics and events covered in *The American Nation*. The book contains 232 letters, poems, diary excerpts, songs, drawings, and other primary sources. Each reading is preceded by a vocabulary list and followed by critical thinking questions.

Listening to Literature Audiocassettes, The American Experience

Listening to Literature Audiocassettes help you enrich students' understanding and appreciation of the American experience. The cassettes feature poetry, fiction, and other literary works from periods of time throughout American history. In addition, they contain numerous, evocative samples of American music.

Prentice Hall Social Studies Update

Includes timely materials, such as current events units of study, a "hot-spot" map transparency, or a year-in-review poster, that you can use immediately in your classroom to help keep your classes current. Adopters of Prentice Hall Social Studies programs can receive the Prentice Hall Social Studies Update every fall and every January free of charge.

Classroom Manager

This booklet makes *The American Nation* all the more manageable, with an easy-to-use chart of program resources that are available to enrich your students' study of American history. A lesson plan for each section includes lesson objectives; focus, instruct, and close activities; and assessment suggestions.

THE AMERICAN NATION

James West Davidson
Michael B. Stoff

PRENTICE HALL
Upper Saddle River, New Jersey
Needham, Massachusetts

James West Davidson

James West Davidson is coauthor of *After the Fact: The Art of Historical Detection* and *Nation of Nations: A Narrative History of the American Republic.* Dr. Davidson has taught at both the college and high school levels and has consulted on curriculum design for American history courses.

Michael B. Stoff

Michael B. Stoff teaches history at the University of Texas at Austin. He is the author of *Oil, War, and American Security: The Search for a National Policy on Foreign Oil, 1941–1947,* and a coauthor of *Nation of Nations: A Narrative History of the American Republic.*

Staff Credits

Advertising and Promotion: Carol Leslie, Rip Odell, Rob Richman, Ann Shea
Art and Design: Eric Dawson, Annemarie Franklin, AnnMarie Roselli
Computer Test Bank Technology: Greg Myers, Cleasta Wilburn
Editorial: Jim Doris, Anne Falzone, Nancy Gilbert, Marion Osterberg, Kirsten Richert, Frank Tangredi
Manufacturing: Rhett Conklin, Loretta Moe
Marketing: Laura Asermily, Lynda Cloud
Media Resources: Martha Conway, Libby Forsyth, Maureen Raymond
Prepress Production: Carol Barbara, Kathryn Dix, Annette Simmons
Production: Margaret Antonini, Christina Burghard, Cathy Profitko
Text Permissions: Doris Robinson

ISBN 0-13-432204-5
1 2 3 4 5 6 7 8 9 10   01 00 99 98 97

PRENTICE HALL
Simon & Schuster Education Group
A VIACOM COMPANY

Historian Reviewers
Pedro Castillo, University of California, Santa Cruz, California
Judith Chesen, Wilberforce University, Wilberforce, Ohio
Robert H. Ferrell, Indiana University, Bloomington, Indiana
Stephen Middleton, North Carolina State University, Raleigh, North Carolina
John R. M. Wilson, Southern California College, Costa Mesa, California

Teacher Consultants and Reviewers
Jamie Braden, Bingham Middle School, Kansas City, Missouri
Sandra Eades, Ridgely Middle School, Lutherville, Maryland
Priscille Fontaine, B. F. Butler Middle School, Lowell, Massachusetts
Luther Ford, Kennedy-King Middle School, Gary, Indiana
Thomas P. Fusco, South Woods Middle School, Syosset, New York
Brian Gibson, Highland East Junior High School, Moore, Oklahoma
Rick Moulden, Chinook Middle School, Bellevue, Washington
Judy Myers, West Junior High School, Boise, Idaho
Marilyn Renger, Balboa Middle School, Ventura, California
Laura G. Rodriguez, Palmetto Middle School, Miami, Florida
Ron Sergent, Jefferson Junior High School, Columbia, Missouri

Reading Specialist
Barbara Mackie, Valley Stream Schools, K–12, Valley Stream, New York

Multicultural Consultants and Reviewers
David Beaulieu, Minnesota Department of Human Rights, St. Paul, Minnesota
Pedro Castillo, University of California, Santa Cruz, California
Judith Chesen, Wilberforce University, Wilberforce, Ohio
Charles Hancock, Ohio State University, Columbus, Ohio
Aida A. Joshi, University of San Francisco, San Francisco, Califorinia
Horacio D. Lewis, State Department of Public Instruction, Dover, Delaware
Cornel Pewewardy, Mounds Park All-Nations Magnet School, St. Paul, Minnesota

Accuracy Panel
Susan Smulyan, Brown University, Providence, Rhode Island
With Lucy Barber, Laura Briggs, Crista DeLuzio, Konstantin Dierks, Ruth Feldstein, Kathleen Franz, Carol Frost, Sarah Leavitt, Miriam Reumann

Acknowledgements and Illustration Credits begin on page 970.

UNIT 1

A Meeting of Different Worlds   1

An Expanding Nation 324

UNIT 5

The Nation Torn Apart 424

UNIT 6

Reshaping the Nation 504

SPECIAL FEATURES

CONNECTIONS

★ *Lively features connect main ideas of*
American history to other subject areas.

History Through LITERATURE

★ *Selections from well-known works of American literature provide insights into the past.*

Art Gallery OUR COMMON HERITAGE

★ *Present-day artists representing the nation's diverse cultural heritage depict major events and people in the American past.*

★ *In-depth stories offer a vivid close-up look at an important person or event.*

★ *Pairs of pictures show how important events and ideas from the past influence our lives today.*

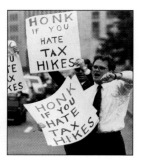

Picturing the Past

★ *Picture essays provide a glimpse of the daily life of young Americans at different times in our history.*

Geographic Atlas

CHARTS, GRAPHS, AND TIME LINES

Causes and Effects

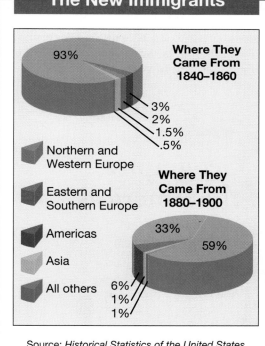

The New Immigrants

93%

Where They Came From 1840–1860

3%
2%
1.5%
.5%

Northern and Western Europe

Eastern and Southern Europe

Where They Came From 1880–1900

33%
59%

Americas

Asia

All others
6%
1%
1%

Source: *Historical Statistics of the United States*

The American Nation is organized into 9 units and 30 chapters, with Issues for Today sections at the front and the back of the book. The Table of Contents lists the titles of the units and chapters. It also lists Connections and other special features, skill lessons, interdisciplinary activities, maps, charts, graphs, and time lines. In addition, the Table of Contents provides a guide to the Reference Section at the back of the book.

Issues for Today

An Introduction   This introduction is a brief visual presentation of five important issues in American history: Multicultural Nation, Spirit of Democracy, Changing Economy, Environment, and Global Interdependence.

Getting Involved   Following the last chapter, this section revisits each of the five issues. Milestones—important events related to each issue—are provided. Case studies show how students took action to make a difference in their communities. Suggested activities help you get involved in your community.

In Each Unit

Unit Opener   Each unit opens with fine art that illustrates a major idea from the unit. The caption explains the connection between the artwork and the unit. In addition, a unit outline presents a brief description of each chapter.

History Through Literature   Each unit concludes with a two-page selection from a well-known work of American literature that relates to the time period. The literary selection provides additional insight into the past.

In Each Chapter

Chapter Opener   Each chapter begins with a Chapter Outline that lists the numbered sections of the chapter. An illustrated time line shows some of the main events that you will read about in the chapter, as well as important world events that occurred during the time period covered in the chapter. The Chapter Setting introduces the chapter. It includes a primary source that sets the tone for the material that follows.

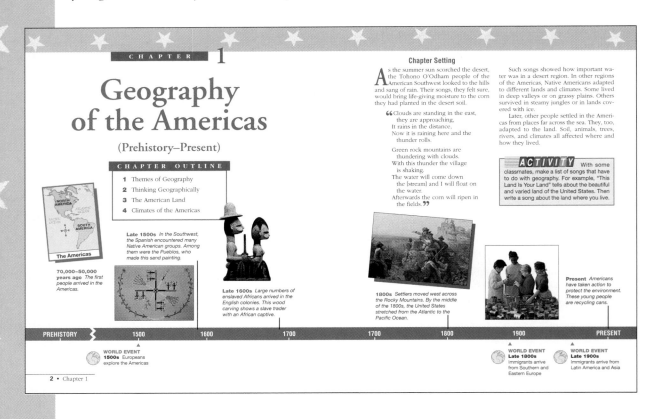

Activities   A wide variety of activities help you understand and respond to the chapter. The activities promote active learning and can be found in every Chapter Setting, Section Review, Connections, Skill Lesson, and History Through Literature.

To Help You Learn   Several features help you to read and understand the chapter:

★ *Find Out*   Questions at the beginning of each section guide your reading.

★ *Important Terms*   Vocabulary words are printed in blue type and are clearly defined the first time they are used. Important historical terms are printed in *dark slanted type.* Vocabulary words and many terms also appear in a Glossary.

★ *Section Reviews*   Questions at the end of each section test your understanding of what you have read and sharpen your critical thinking skills.

Skill Lesson   A step-by-step skill lesson in each chapter helps you to understand and practice important skills.

Illustrations   Pictures and other graphics help you to understand major events:

★ *Pictures*—works of fine art, photographs, cartoons, posters, and artifacts—bring history to life. Picture captions include a question that encourages you to explore major ideas of American history.

★ *Maps, Graphs, and Charts* help you to understand major historical developments. Captions provide important background information and also include questions to sharpen your map, graph, and chart skills.

Chapter Review   The Chapter Review provides a summary of the chapter and helps you review the main ideas and strengthen geography and critical thinking skills. The Chapter Review also includes the Interdisciplinary Activity:

★ *Interdisciplinary Activity* provides a variety of choices for actively exploring an important idea from the chapter.

Special Features

There are several kinds of special features throughout the book:

★ *Connections* is a lively full-page feature in each chapter that connects a main idea from the chapter to one of six subjects: the Arts, the Sciences, Geography, the World, Economics, and Civics.

★ *Up Close* provides a vivid, in-depth look at an interesting person or event in American history.

★ *Causes and Effects* charts are easy-to-read charts that trace the causes and effects of a major event in the unit.

★ *Picturing the Past* is a two-page photo essay that provides a glimpse of the lives of young Americans at different times in our history.

★ *Exploring Technology* is a detailed drawing of a major advance in technology.

★ *Linking Past and Present* pairs two pictures to show how ideas and events from the past influence our lives today.

★ *Art Gallery: Our Common Heritage* shows how present-day artists representing the nation's diverse cultural heritage have depicted major events and people from the American past.

★ *Extended Footnote* is a brief high-interest passage that highlights important people, ideas, and events. The footnotes are divided into three categories: Our Common Heritage, Linking Past and Present, and History and You.

Reference Section

At the back of the book, you will find a section of reference materials for use in the course. It includes a Geographic Atlas, charts with information about the 50 states and the Presidents, a Gazetteer of important places, a Glossary, charts that make connections between *The American Nation* and literature, science, and fine art, the Declaration of Independence, the Constitution of the United States, and an Index.

An Introduction

"Who cares about the past? I want to live in the present.**"** Many young people would probably agree with this statement. In fact, however, the present reflects the past. The actions of people long ago still affect our lives today. And the actions *we* take will affect the people of the future.

The study of history helps us to understand the relationship between past and present. Only by learning about the past can we truly understand the present. Only by learning about our nation's history can we understand what it means to be an American today—creating history for the Americans of tomorrow.

Threads of History

At first, history may seem like an unconnected mass of names, dates, and places. In truth, several issues serve as threads that tie the facts of American history together: Multicultural Nation, Spirit of Democracy, Changing Economy, Environment, and Global Interdependence.

The many faces of history. The United States was built by people from every part of the globe. In this book, you will read about Native Americans, who first arrived thousands of years ago. You will also learn the stories of the millions of others— Europeans, Africans, Asians, Latin Americans, and peoples from the Caribbean—who helped build our land. In a multicultural nation like ours, all these histories are important.

A democratic political system. Today, some quarter of a *billion* people live in the United States. They include farmers who plow fields and office workers who live in populous cities. Some Americans are recent immigrants to the United States. Others come from families who have been here for hundreds of years.

How can so many different peoples unite in a single nation? An important part of studying American history is learning about the government that holds the nation together. Americans often disagree with one another on important issues.

Issues for Today

Once, we even fought a civil war. Still, our democratic traditions have made this country a model for the rest of the world.

The lessons of economics. Economic history, too, is a part of our past. Blessed with abundant resources and a spirit of invention, Americans have built a thriving economy. At first, this economy revolved around the land and agriculture. In time, however, the focus shifted as Americans moved into "smokestack" industries and later into service and technology. Today, as you will learn, Americans face new challenges as we prepare to move into the global economy of the twenty-first century.

Our land and resources. Environment shapes our history, as well. How have we used our land in the past? What are we doing to ensure that we will preserve our resources for the future? In this book, you will discover how people's attitudes toward the environment have changed over time.

Links across the world. Our history links us with peoples and places all across the world. In both the American Revolution and the Civil War, we looked across the seas for allies. During the 1900s, thousands of Americans fought and died in overseas wars. In the 1970s, decisions made in desert kingdoms of the Middle East forced motorists in the United States to line up for hours at the gas pumps. Events thousands of miles away affect the history of Americans.

Your Role in History

You are about to begin a study of American history. As you read, keep in mind the major issues: Multicultural Nation, Spirit of Democracy, Changing Economy, Environment, and Global Interdependence. Try to discover how these issues helped to shape the lives of earlier Americans. Then make the connection to see how these same issues touch your life today. To help you get started, the picture essays on the following pages offer an overview of each issue.

At the end of the book, Issues for Today: Getting Involved helps you to trace the threads of American history from past to present. It also offers you an opportunity to make a difference for the future. Our history, after all, is far from complete. How Americans deal with the issues in the next hundred years is up to you.

Jim Davidson

Mike Stoff

Issues for Today • **xxiii**

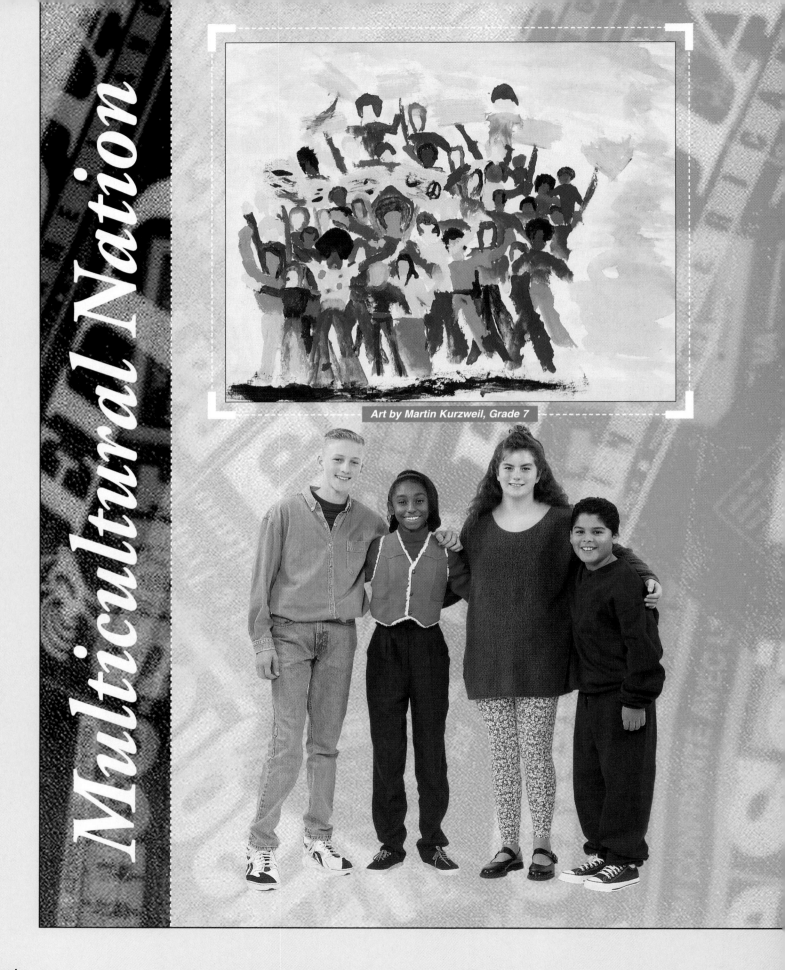

Multicultural Nation

Art by Martin Kurzweil, Grade 7

Interlocking hands

Flag of immigrant faces

Sign in many languages

IN 1 UUR KLAAR!

VOTRE FILM EN COULEUR
DÉVELOPPÉ ET TIRÉ
EN 1 HEURE

DEVELOPING AND PRINTING
OF YOUR COLOR FILMS
IN 1 HOUR

ENTWICKELN UND ABDRUCKEN
IHRER FARBFILME IN 60 MINUTEN
DIENST AM KUNDE IN 1 STUNDE

REVELAR Y IMPREMIR DE PELÍCULAS
EN COLOR ESTARÁN LISTAS
EN 1 HORA

Multicultural Nation

The United States is unique among nations. The people who make up our country represent hundreds of cultures, languages, and beliefs. This diversity poses a challenge. Americans must find ways to build unity while preserving their separate identities. At the same time, diversity provides the nation with its greatest strength. From food to fashion, from art to politics, American society is enriched by the talents, skills, and ideas of people from all parts of the world.

MEN'S SHOES
ONLY $19.99

SE HABLA ESPAÑOL
ON PARLE LE FRANÇAIS
SE FALA Portugues NO MUITO BUONO
מדברים עברית

Welcoming customers of many cultures

Spirit of Democracy

Art by Kathryn DePue, Grade 6

Student Council ★ Election ★

VOTE TODAY!

Ballot Box

Political convention

Campaign signs

"Now, you try to get a fire started while I draft a constitution."

Spirit of Democracy

Two hundred years ago, the United States set up a democratic government based on the ideals of liberty, justice, and equality. Ever since, each new generation of Americans has shaped democracy to reflect its times. Equality, for example, meant something very different to Americans in 1876 than it did to Americans in 1776. The process is never finished. Today, Americans are still struggling to perfect our democracy and to extend our ideals to include all the people in our land.

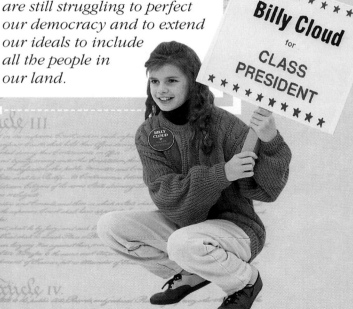

Campaign buttons forming an American flag

Issues for Today • **xxvii**

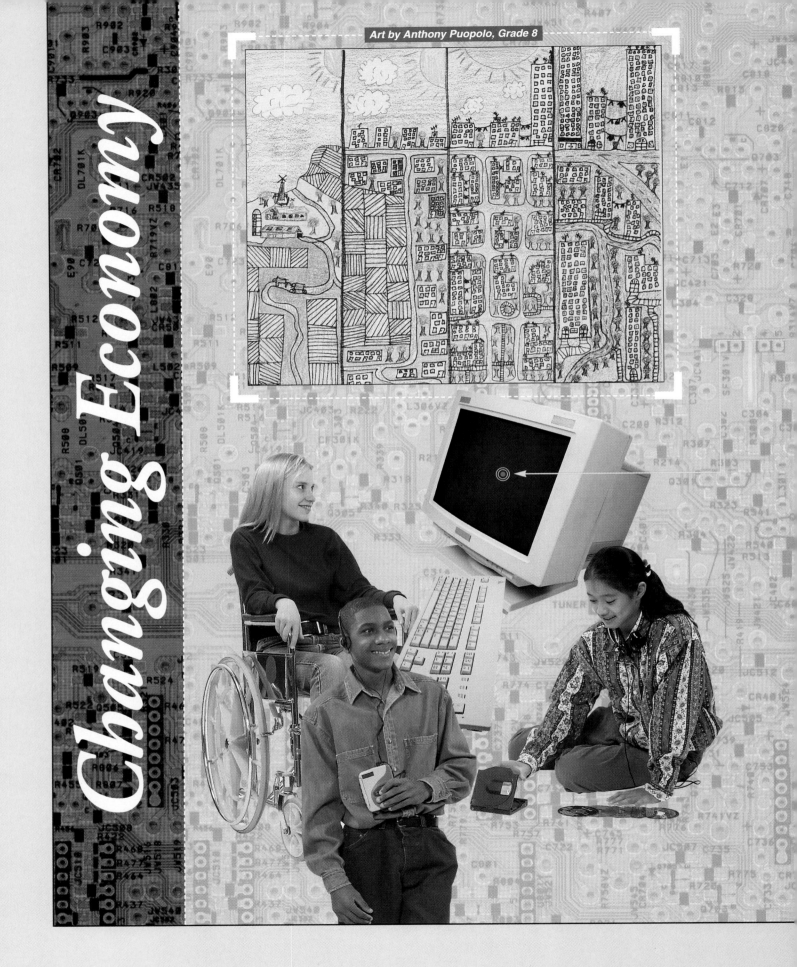

Changing Economy

Art by Anthony Puopolo, Grade 8

Computerized factory

"Oh, too bad, Mrs. Taporek, the computer just ate up all your money."

Changing Economy

When Native Americans first arrived in the Americas thousands of years ago, they lived by hunting and fishing and, in time, by growing crops. Early European settlers also lived off the land. Then in the 1800s, the economy began to change. By 1900, the United States was the leading industrial nation in the world. Today, the American economy has shifted once again. In the Computer Age, workers pursue the American dream not in local farms and factories but in "high tech" global industries that market goods and services around the world.

Computerized tag tracks a cow's diet

Environment

Art by Jennifer Hodgkins, Grade 7

"It's either a global warming trend or merely a fad."

Cleaning up the United States

Rescuing a bird after an oil spill

Environment

For most of our history, Americans have taken for granted the rich resources of our land. As we worked to create opportunity and abundance, we sometimes forgot that the minerals beneath our soil were not limitless. We neglected to take care of our rivers and streams. In recent years, however, Americans have shown a new concern for the environment. Working together, citizens, industries, and government are seeking to balance economic development with the need to preserve and protect the Earth on which we live.

Satellite map showing a hole in the ozone layer

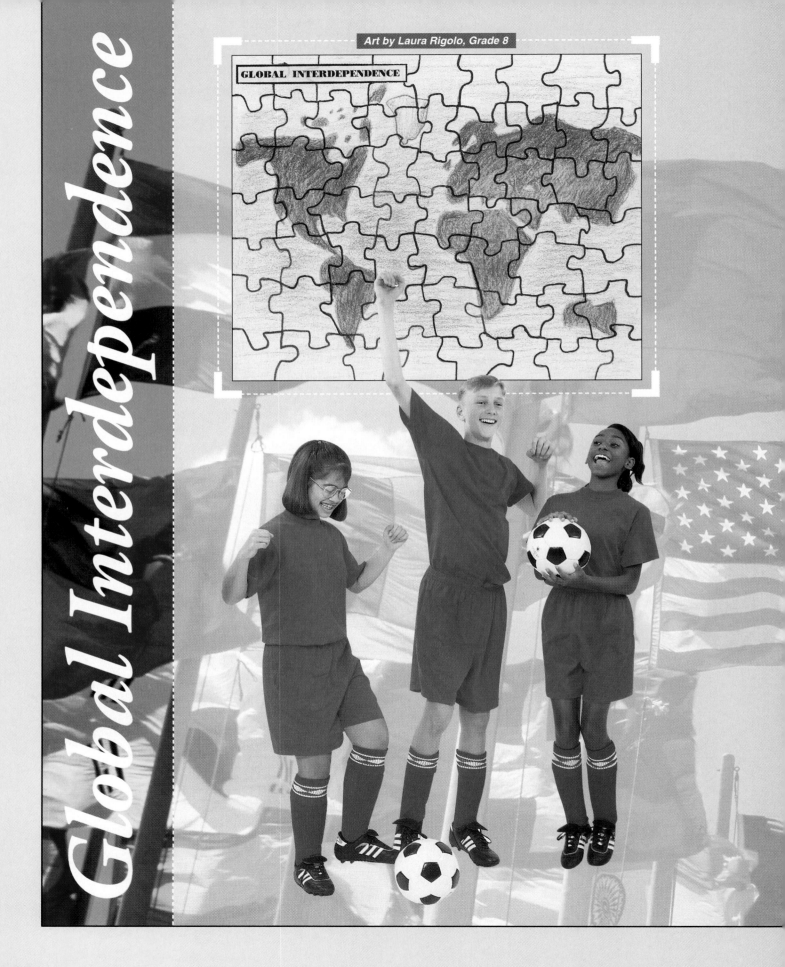

Global Interdependence

GLOBAL INTERDEPENDENCE

Art by Laura Rigolo, Grade 8

Athletes at the International Games for the Disabled

PAYS / COUNTRY   VENTE / SELL

U.S.A.	1.15750
GR. BRITAIN	2.01750
JAPAN	.00871
ITALY	. 0009
FRANCE	.20310
HOLLAND	.6062
GERMANY	.5861
SWISS	/2 390
MEXICO	.0404
AUSTRALIA	.92 46

CHEQUE$ CA$HED

Sign on a bank door

Global Interdependence

In 1796, George Washington, the nation's first President, cautioned Americans not to become involved in the affairs of foreign nations. For nearly 100 years, Americans heeded Washington's advice. Then, the United States began to look overseas. By the mid-1900s, it had become the world's leading political and economic power. Today, the communications revolution has shrunk the world. The United States, like all the world's nations, must learn how to compete—and cooperate—in the new "global village."

Computer image of the "global village"

Issues for Today • **xxxiii**

Unit 1
A Meeting of Different Worlds

Unit Focus

Have students examine the world map on these pages and read the caption that describes it. (You might also have them compare it with the modern world map on pages 890–891.) Ask: Which parts of this map are most accurate? What does that suggest about the Europeans of that era? As students consider that period, read aloud the four chapter summaries. Ask questions such as the following to stimulate discussion.

1. (a) Based on the map, what did this mapmaker know about the geography of the Americas? (b) What do you know about some of the geographical regions and/or climates in the Americas?
2. (a) How many Native American groups can you name? (b) What do you know about any of them?
3. The caption on page 1 mentions the year 1492. What important event took place in that year?
4. (a) Which American cities of the 1990s were also cities in the English colonies? (b) What do you know about life in colonial times?
5. Unit 1 is entitled A Meeting of Different Worlds. Based on the information in the four chapter summaries, what "worlds" met 500 years ago? Explain.

Connections With Art
Background

Many of the basic principles of cartography can be traced to Ptolemy, a Greek mathematician, astronomer, and geographer of the second century A.D. (A portrait of Ptolemy appears in the upper right-hand corner of the map.) Ptolemy's eight-volume *Geography* listed about 8,000 locations (giving the latitude and longitude of each), included several maps, and explained systems of map projection.

In the 1400s, Ptolemy's work was translated into Latin, and his methods were rediscovered.

UNIT 1

A Meeting of Different Worlds

CHAPTER 1
Geography of the Americas
(Prehistory–Present)

The varied geography of the Americas has affected their history.

....

CHAPTER 2
The First Americans
(Prehistory–1600)

Native Americans developed many different cultures.

....

CHAPTER 3
Europeans Reach the Americas
(1000–1650)

The Spanish, French, English, and Dutch competed for colonies in the Americas.

....

CHAPTER 4
The 13 English Colonies
(1630–1750)

Different ways of life grew up in the New England, Middle, and Southern colonies.

Building on that foundation, Gerardus Mercator (depicted in the lower left-hand corner of the map) created his own map projection and published his first map in 1537. In 1569, the first of a series of publications he called *Atlas* was published.

By the time the map on these pages appeared, measuring techniques had become more sophisticated. Further refinements came as Europeans explored other areas of the world.

Connections With Art
Activity

Ask questions such as the following to stimulate discussion about the world map.
1. If you were a sailor, what could you learn from this map?
2. How do you explain the fact that eastern Asia, the South Pacific, and northwestern North America are drawn so inaccurately?

3. Why do you think that many people today are so fascinated by old maps?
4. Notice that the borders of the map are filled with pictures and designs. What reason or reasons might there be for such decoration?

ORBIS GEOGRAPHICA AC HYDROGRAPHICA TABVLA. Auct: Henr: Hondio.

> **B**efore 1492, the people of the Americas had no lasting contact with the outside world. Then, Europeans arrived, seeking trade and wealth. The encounter between peoples of different worlds had effects that are still felt today. This map shows a European view of the world in 1630.

Bulletin Board Suggestion

Have students create a bulletin board display of a variety of Native American cultures. Sections of the display—which can include cultures from both North and South America—could deal with housing, clothing, family life, government, religion, food, crafts, and so on. Encourage students to incorporate in the design a depiction of the arrival of European explorers and colonists.

Art Gallery Posters

Mixed Kachina Dance, by Raymond Naha, is appropriate for Unit 1. Lesson suggestions for the poster appear in the *Art Gallery: Our Common Heritage Posters* Teacher's Guide. The art also appears in Chapter 2, page 41, of the student book.

CD-ROM

Time Tour Access A Meeting of Different Worlds from the American Heritage® *History of the United States* CD-ROM to accompany Unit 1.

Connections With the World
Activity

Have students preview the world events on the chapter time lines (pages 2–3, 30–31, 60–61, and 92–93). Call on volunteers to use the world map on pages 890–891 to locate each nation or area mentioned. Then ask the class: What was going on in the Americas at the same time as each world event? Which of the world events suggest "a meeting of different worlds"—not only between Europe and the Americas but also between other parts of the world? Explain.

Linking Past and Present
Activity

Have students expand on anything that they already have said about Native American cultures and/or about what the arrival of Europeans meant to those cultures. Ask: Are people today generally more aware of Native American history and culture than they used to be? Why or why not? If you wanted to learn more about a particular Native American group, how would you do so? Why might preserving Native American history and culture continue to be important?

Chapter 1 Geography of the Americas (Prehistory–Present), pp. 2–29

Lessons	Teaching Resources
1 Themes of Geography **Objectives** 1. Describe how geographers help historians understand the past. 2. Identify the five themes of geography. 3. Describe how geography influences the way people live.	**Lesson Planner** Cooperative Learning, p. 1 **Student Study Guide** Section 1 Study Guide, p. 31 **Our Multicultural Heritage** *Biography* Ellen Churchill Semple, Eminent Geographer, p. 1
2 Thinking Geographically **Objectives** 1. Describe the advantages that flat maps have over globes. 2. Identify two kinds of map projections. 3. Explain why the world is divided into time zones.	**Lesson Planner** Cooperative Learning, p. 2 **Student Study Guide** Section 2 Study Guide, p. 32 **Chapter Resources Binder, Unit 1** *Skill Application* The Parts of a Map, p. 2
3 The American Land **Objectives** 1. Identify the landforms found in North America and South America. 2. Identify the seven physical regions of North America. 3. Identify rivers and lakes that are important to the United States.	**Lesson Planner** Cooperative Learning, p. 3 **Student Study Guide** Section 3 Study Guide, p. 33 **Chapter Resources Binder, Unit 1** *Geography in History* Glaciers Reshape North America, pp. 5–6 *History Through Literature* Our Old Feuillage, p. 4 **Interdisciplinary Connections:** The American Land ■ *Arts* Landscapes on Canvas, p. 2 ■ *Geography* Glaciers on the Move, p. 3 ■ *World* Acid Rain and Killer Fog, p. 4 ■ *Economics* Mining and Minerals, p. 5 ■ *Civics* Kids Who Care, p. 6 **Our Multicultural Heritage** *Biography* John James Audubon, American Naturalist, p. 2 *Milestone* Environmental Treasures: Birds of the Americas, p. 3
4 Climates of the Americas **Objectives** 1. Identify the factors that influence climate. 2. Identify the major climates of North America. 3. Describe the climate of South America.	**Lesson Planner** Cooperative Learning, p. 4 **Student Study Guide** Section 4 Study Guide, p. 34 **Chapter Resources Binder, Unit 1** *Critical Thinking* Understanding Causes and Effects, p. 3

Multimedia Resources	Additional Resources	Chapter-Level Resources

		Lesson Planner
		Activity Based, pp. 5–6
		
		Student Study Guide
		Chapter 1 Study Guide,
		  pp. 35–36
		
		**Chapter Resources
		  Binder**
		Unit 1
		Vocabulary Building, p. 1
		Chapter Test A, pp. 7–9
		Chapter Test B, pp. 10–12
		Extra Unit Questions,
		  pp. 51–53
		English Guided Reading
		Guided Reading, pp. 1–2
		Spanish Resources
		
		Computer Test Bank
		Chapter Tests A and B
		Extra Unit Questions
		
		**Guided Reading
		  Audiotapes**
		Side 1

Transparencies
Interdisciplinary Connections Plate Collisions,
  p. B-33
Geography and History The United States,
  p. I-51; regional maps, pp. I-57, I-61, I-65,
  I-69, I-73, I-77, I-81, I-85
	Voices of Freedom
	America the Beautiful, p. 13
	A European View of North America,
	  pp. 14–15
	Historical Outline Map Book
	Physical Regions of the United States, p. 2
	Physical United States, p. 83
	Regional maps, pp. 86–92
	Customized Reader
	Exploring the Coast of Florida With John
	  Hawkins in 1565, article IB-2
	Interdisciplinary Explorations
	Where River Meets Sea: America's
	  Estuaries at Risk	

Transparencies
Geography and History The United States,
  p. I-51
	Voices of Freedom
	An Indian Prayer for the Sun, p. 16
	Historical Outline Map Book
	Climates of the United States, p. 3
	Customized Reader
	A Walk in the Desert, article XB-7
	A Fur Trader Describes
	  Southeastern Alaska, article IVB-5	

Lesson Planner

For a fully developed **Activity-Based** lesson plan for Chapter 1, see the *Lesson Planner,* pages 5–6.

 Chapter Resources

Vocabulary Building The Vocabulary Building worksheet for Chapter 1 from Unit 1, page 1, of the *Chapter Resources* binder can be used as a prereading activity or as a review of chapter vocabulary. (Reteaching/Easy)

 Student Study Guide

Chapter 1 Study Guide Refer students to pages 35–36 of the *Student Study Guide.* The study guide can be used for chapter review as well as for reteaching. (Reteaching/Average)

 Guided Reading Audiotapes

Students can use *Guided Reading Audiotapes,* Chapter 1, side 1, to listen to section previews, summaries, and review questions. The tapes might benefit students who are auditory learners, students who have trouble reading, or students acquiring English. Tapes are also available in Spanish. (Reteaching/Easy)

CHAPTER 1

Geography of the Americas

(Prehistory–Present)

CHAPTER OUTLINE

1 Themes of Geography

2 Thinking Geographically

3 The American Land

4 Climates of the Americas

The Americas

30,000–15,000 years ago *The first people arrived in the Americas.*

Late 1500s *In the Southwest, the Spanish encountered many Native American groups. Among them were the Pueblos, who made this sand painting.*

Late 1600s *Large numbers of enslaved Africans arrived in the English colonies. This wood carving shows a slave trader with an African captive.*

PREHISTORY	1500	1600	1700

 WORLD EVENT
1500s Europeans explore the Americas

2 • Chapter 1

Chapter Time Line
Activity

Divide students into four groups. Assign each group one event from page 2 and another from page 3 (for example, "Late 1500s" and "WORLD EVENT/Late 1900s"). Have each group create two collages—one for each event. Give each group two pieces of 11" x 17" posterboard; have someone in the group copy the note about each event onto the board. Students may surround that text in a variety of ways—for example, re-creating the art from the text or responding to the text through freewriting, poetry, or art. Encourage creativity. Each piece of surrounding art or text should be done on a separate page; then the group can work together to arrange, cut, and mount the pieces. You might use the eight finished collages to create a class time line, using construction paper for the time line itself.

Chapter Setting

As the summer sun scorched the desert, the Tohono O'Odham people of the American Southwest looked to the hills and sang of rain. Their songs, they felt sure, would bring life-giving moisture to the corn they had planted in the desert soil.

> 66 Clouds are standing in the east,
> they are approaching,
> It rains in the distance,
> Now it is raining here and the
> thunder rolls.
>
> Green rock mountains are
> thundering with clouds.
> With this thunder the village
> is shaking.
> The water will come down
> the [stream] and I will float on
> the water.
> Afterwards the corn will ripen in
> the fields. 99

Such songs showed how important water was in a desert region. In other regions of the Americas, Native Americans adapted to different lands and climates. Some lived in deep valleys or on grassy plains. Others survived in steamy jungles or in lands covered with ice.

Later, other people settled in the Americas from places far across the sea. They, too, adapted to the land. Soil, animals, trees, rivers, and climates all affected where and how they lived.

ACTIVITY With some classmates, make a list of songs that have to do with geography. For example, "This Land Is Your Land" tells about the beautiful and varied land of the United States. Then write a song about the land where you live.

1800s *Settlers moved west across the Rocky Mountains. By the middle of the 1800s, the United States stretched from the Atlantic to the Pacific Ocean.*

Present *Americans have taken action to protect the environment. These young people are recycling cans.*

1700	1800	1900	PRESENT

 WORLD EVENT
Late 1800s
Immigrants arrive from Southern and Eastern Europe

 WORLD EVENT
Late 1900s
Immigrants arrive from Latin America and Asia

Chapter Resources

English Guided Reading Duplicate and distribute to SAE students the Chapter 1 Guided Reading worksheet on pages 1–2 in the English Guided Reading section of the *Chapter Resources* binder. Students who have difficulty reading also might benefit from using this worksheet. Have students complete the worksheet before they begin reading. You might pair a more fluent student, or a student who is a stronger reader, with each SAE student to review. (Reteaching/Easy)

Spanish Resources See Spanish Resources section of the *Chapter Resources* binder.

ACTIVITY

Guided Instruction You might play a recording of "This Land Is Your Land" to begin this activity. Divide the class into groups of four and assign each group a geographic region of the United States. Have each group brainstorm for songs whose lyrics include geographic references and have them list specific descriptions found in the songs. They can use the list as a guide to create striking images that describe physical features found in their region. After students collaborate on drafting lyrics for their song, they can compose their own melody or adapt one from the songs discussed. Be prepared to offer assistance to students who need help fitting their lyrics to their melodies. Ask each group to sing its finished song for the class.

Students Acquiring English
Activity

To help SAE students master the chapter, you might have them use books in the library to copy a physical map of their native region, including as many key physical elements (rivers, mountains, plains, and so on) as possible. They should also include relative references (Equator, latitude, longitude, and so on). As terms are introduced, ask students to associate each term with its equivalent in their primary language; then help them write a brief definition in English. Students can use code letters (A, B, C, . . .) to cross-reference each term to a comparable feature on their maps. You might preview key abstract terms (such as *climate, precipitation, marine*) by discussing their definitions with students before beginning the chapter.

Linking Past and Present
Activity

Lead the class in an informal discussion of how people adapt to their environments. Ask: Do you think that people think about their environment today as they did centuries ago? Has technology affected the ways in which people adapt to different environments? Students should note that science and technology have eased adaptation but have also brought new environmental challenges.

Bell Ringer

Write the words *geography* and *history* on the chalkboard. Have students write down ways in which they think these two terms are related.

Lesson Plan

1. Focus To show the connections between geography and history, geographers use five themes. In this section, students examine those themes.

2. Instruct List the five themes on the chalkboard. Help students review the meaning of each and the differences among them. Then have students give examples of each, based on the geography of the local area or state.

3. Close To close the lesson, have the class come to a group definition for each of the five geographic themes. Encourage students to write the definitions for future reference—and to look for examples of the themes "at work" in the coming chapters.

Lesson Planner

For a developed **Cooperative Learning** lesson plan, see the *Lesson Planner,* page 1.

1
Themes of Geography

FIND OUT
- How do geographers help historians understand the past?
- What are the five themes of geography?
- How does geography influence the way people live?

VOCABULARY geography, history, latitude, longitude, irrigate

If you read almost any newspaper, you will find stories about the land around you. One story might argue that building a dam will be harmful to a river. Another might announce the discovery of oil. To understand these and other issues, we need to understand geography.

Geography is the study of people, their environments, and their resources. Geographers ask how the natural environment affects the way we live and how we, in turn, affect the environment. By showing how people and the land are related, geography helps to explain both the past and the present.

Geography is closely linked to history. **History** is an account of what has happened in the lives of different peoples. Both historians and geographers want to understand how the characteristics of a place affect people and events. They both ask the question, Why did this happen in this place?

To help show the connection between geography and history, geographers have developed five themes, or topics. The themes are location, place, interaction between people and their environment, movement, and region.

Location

Where did it happen? Both historians and geographers ask this question about an event. Finding out where something happened involves the geographic theme of location.

Exact location. As you study American history, you will sometimes need to know the absolute, or exact, location of a place. For example, where exactly is Washington, D.C., the nation's capital?

To describe the exact location of Washington, D.C., geographers use a grid of numbered lines on a map or globe that measure latitude and longitude. Lines of **latitude** measure distance north and south from the Equator. Lines of **longitude** measure distance east and west from the Prime Meridian, which runs through Greenwich (GREHN ihch), England. (You will read more about latitude and longitude later in this chapter. See page 11.)

The exact location of Washington, D.C., is 39 degrees (°) north latitude and 77 degrees (°) west longitude. In writing, this location is often shortened to 39°N/77°W. The Gazetteer in the Reference Section of this book provides the exact location of many important places in American history.

Relative location. Sometimes you might find it more useful to know the relative location of a place, or where it is located in relation to some other place. Is Washington, D.C., on the east coast or the west coast of the United States? Is it north or south of Richmond, Virginia? These questions involve relative location.

History and You
Geography affects the way people live. Name three ways in which the geography of your area influences your life.

Our Multicultural Heritage
Activity

Explain to students that folklore includes traditional customs, tales, sayings, and songs preserved among a people. Have students share examples from their own heritages of folklore that include geographic themes and references. SAE students might relate examples first in their primary language and then in English. Ask: What stories were you told as a child? What songs have you heard family members sing? What sayings give advice about behavior? What have you been told about the origins of family customs? As examples are given, have class members identify geographic references and list these on the chalkboard. Compare and contrast geographic themes found in each.

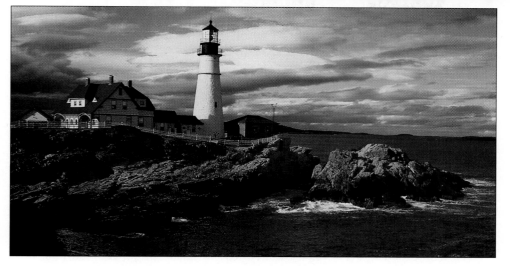

The Maine Coast *The physical and human features of a place are often closely related. The coastline of Maine has thousands of rock-bound bays and inlets. To guide ships through dangerous waters, residents built tall lighthouses.* **Economics** *How might people along the Maine coast earn their living?*

 Our Multicultural Heritage

Biography Have students read the biography, Ellen Churchill Semple, Eminent Geographer, on page 1 of the *Our Multicultural Heritage* booklet. (Enrichment/Average)

Relative location includes knowing how places are connected to one another. Is a place located near a lake, river, or other source of water and transportation? Is it in the interior or on the coast? Answers to these kinds of questions help explain why cities grew where they did. Chicago, Illinois, for instance, developed at the center of water, road, and railroad transportation in the Midwest.

Place

A second theme that geographers study is place. Geographers generally describe a place in terms of both physical and human features.

The physical features of a place include climate, soil, plant life, animal life, and bodies of water. For example, New England has a hilly terrain, a rock-bound coast, and many deep harbors. Because of these physical features, early Native Americans of the region turned to fishing for a living.

People help to shape the character of a place through their ideas and actions. The human features of a place include the kinds of houses people build as well as their means of transportation, ways of earning a living, languages, and religions.

Think of the human features of the American frontier. In the forests of the frontier, early settlers built log cabins. On the grassy plains, some settlers built their first homes out of sod.

Interaction Between People and Their Environment

A third theme of geography is interaction between people and their environment. Throughout history, people have adapted to and changed their natural environment.

Connections With Technology
Background

Native Americans who fished the Atlantic Coast interacted with their environment by using a variety of tools. In shallow water, they set traps and used barbed poles to spear fish. In deep waters, they cast nets from their canoes or used multipronged spears. They also found that a fire built on a clay hearth in the canoe not only allowed them to fish at night, but its light proved an effective fish lure!

Critical Thinking
Comparing and Contrasting

Pair students and have partners create a chart comparing and contrasting the physical features (climate, soil, plant life, animal life, and bodies of water) of any two states of their choice. Partners can take a closer look at the geographic theme of interaction by choosing two constructed features—such as dams, bridges, or highways—and adding these to their charts. Refer students to an encyclopedia or atlas for information. Ask sets of partners to exchange charts and comment constructively.

Answer to Caption

Possible Answers: air pollution, water pollution, destruction of forests and farmland

New Mexico Cotton Fields *In much of New Mexico, the average yearly rainfall is less than 10 inches. Yet irrigation has allowed farmers to grow a wide variety of crops. Irrigation canals, like these, bring water from the Rio Grande to desert farms.* **Geography** *What are some negative effects of interaction between people and their environment?*

For example, ancient hunters learned to grow food crops in the Americas. Later, Native Americans in the Southwest found ways to **irrigate,** or bring water to, the desert so that they could farm the land. In the 1860s, workers blasted through mountains and built bridges across rivers for railroads that linked the Atlantic and Pacific coasts.

Today, advanced technology allows people to alter their environment dramatically. People have invented ways to take oil from the ocean floor. They have cut down thick forests to build highways. They have wiped out pests that destroy food crops. Such changes have brought enormous benefits. But they have created new problems, such as air and water pollution.

Movement

A fourth geographic theme involves the movement of people, goods, and ideas. Movement occurs because people and resources are scattered unevenly around the globe. To get what they need or want, people travel from place to place. As they meet other people, they exchange ideas and technology as well as goods.

History provides many examples of the movement of people and ideas. The first

Connections With Local History
Activity

Have students research why successive groups of people came to and settled in their town, city, or region. Ask: Who were the first inhabitants? Who followed and when? What reasons did each group have for coming? What elements survive today? What has changed and how? Tell each student to write a brief report on his or her findings and present it to the class.

Connections With the World
Background

San Francisco's Chinatown (pictured on page 7) is the world's largest Chinese community outside Asia. Other similarly well-known regions in the United States are the Mexican community of Los Angeles, the Polish community of Chicago, the Cuban community of Miami, and the Italian and Greek communities of New York.

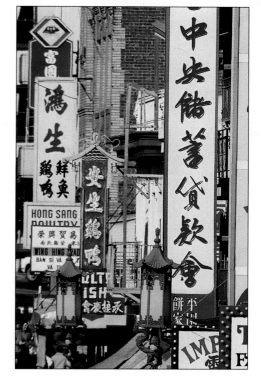

A Street in Chinatown *A region can be as small as a neighborhood. In the 1800s, Chinese immigrants began to form close-knit communities in cities along the Pacific coast. Today, some 30,000 Chinese Americans live in a 16-block area of San Francisco known as Chinatown.* **Multicultural Heritage** *What signs of cultural diversity can you find in your area?*

people who came to the Americas were hunters following animal herds. Much later, people from all over the world moved to the United States in search of political and religious freedom. These newcomers brought with them customs and beliefs that have helped shape American life.

Today, the movement of goods links the United States with all parts of the globe. American producers ship goods such as grain and computers to Europe and Africa,

for example. At the same time, we rely on materials such as oil and rubber from other parts of the world.

Region

Geographers study regions. A region is an area of the world that has similar, unifying characteristics. The characteristics of a region may be physical, such as its climate or landforms. For example, the Great Plains is a region because it has fairly level land, very hot summers, very cold winters, and little rainfall.

A region's characteristics may also be human and cultural. San Francisco's Chinatown is a region because Chinese Americans there have preserved their language and culture.

A region can be any size. It can be as large as the United States or as small as a neighborhood.

SECTION 1 REVIEW

1. **Define:** (a) geography, (b) history, (c) latitude, (d) longitude, (e) irrigate.
2. Why is geography important to the study of history?
3. Briefly describe the five themes of geography.
4. (a) Name two benefits of interaction between people and their environment. (b) Name two problems that can result when people make major changes in their natural environment.
5. **CRITICAL THINKING Synthesizing Information** Why do you think understanding movement is important to the study of history?

 Writing to Learn
Write a paragraph in which you apply the five themes of geography to a study of your town or city.

Chapter 1 • **7**

Bell Ringer

Ask: What kind of maps have you seen? Invite students to list the different kinds and write the kinds of information that are found on each.

Lesson Plan

1. Focus Maps are among the most important tools that geographers use to study the world. In this section, students compare different kinds of maps, map projections, and computer images.

2. Instruct Have students skim their texts and select three maps at random. Ask: What kind of map (for example, physical, population, and so on) is each? What geographic area does each show? What kinds of information does each give? Use responses as a stimulus for class discussion.

3. Close To close the lesson, review with students why globes are more accurate than maps and the distortions that map projections may introduce. Ask: How have satellite photos revolutionized cartography?

Lesson Planner

For a developed **Cooperative Learning** lesson plan, see the *Lesson Planner,* page 2.

2
Thinking Geographically

FIND OUT

■ What advantages do flat maps have over globes?

■ What are two kinds of map projections?

■ Why is the world divided into time zones?

VOCABULARY cartographer, map projection, hemisphere, standard time zone

In a tiny Indian fishing village in the early 1600s, a small group gathered around Samuel de Champlain. They watched closely as the French explorer pointed to the shore and then drew a sweeping line on a deerskin spread out on the ground. The line represented the coastline where they stood. Quickly, the Native American chief drew other lines on the informal map. A young man added piles of rocks to represent the village and nearby settlements.

Champlain and the Native Americans he met on Cape Ann in Massachusetts did not understand one another's languages. Yet they found a way to communicate. Together, they created a map of the local area. Champlain later used the map to aid him in exploring the Massachusetts coast. People today use maps, too, to help them locate places, judge distances, and follow routes.

Maps and Globes

To locate places, geographers use maps and globes. A map is a drawing of the Earth's surface. A globe is a sphere with a map of the Earth's landmasses and bodies of water printed on it. Because a globe is the same shape as the Earth, it shows sizes and shapes accurately.

Even though a globe has this advantage, geographers often use flat maps rather than globes. Unlike a globe, a flat map allows you to see all of the Earth's surface at one time. It also can show more detail. And it is easier to handle. Still, a flat map has the disadvantage that it distorts, or misrepresents, some part of the Earth.

Map Projections

Mapmakers, or **cartographers**, have developed dozens of map projections. **Map projections** are ways of drawing the Earth on a flat surface. Two map projections are shown on page 9.

Any given map projection has benefits and disadvantages. Some projections show the sizes of landmasses correctly but distort their shapes. Others give continents their true shapes but distort their sizes. Still other projections distort direction or distances.

Mercator projection. In 1569, Gerardus Mercator developed the Mercator projection, the best map in its day. For hundreds of years, sailors used the Mercator map. Mercator himself boasted of his map:

❝If you wish to sail from one port to another, here is a chart, and a straight line on it, and if you follow this line carefully you will certainly arrive at your destination.❞

A Mercator map shows the true shapes of landmasses, but it distorts size, especially for places that are far from the Equator. On a Mercator map, for example, Greenland appears as big as all of South America, even though South America is more than eight times larger!

Robinson projection. Today, many geographers use the Robinson projection. It

Learning Styles
Kinesthetic Learners

To illustrate how maps can distort geographic features, bring a globe to class. Have students use a piece of string to measure the distances between the North Pole and Miami and between Moscow and New York. Then have students calculate these distances using a classroom map.

Cooperative Learning
Activity

Divide the class into groups of five or six students each. Tell each group to imagine that they are cartographers who have been asked to create a map of the world. Have each group list what it would need to make an accurate map. As they examine the map projections shown in the text, have them list reasons for and against the three types of projections and decide which type they prefer.

M A P   S T U D Y

Map projections make it possible for mapmakers to show a round world on a flat map.
1. *Which projection would you use to compare the sizes of North America and Europe?*
2. *Where does the Mercator projection show the least distortion?*
3. **Comparing** *Compare the landmasses on the Mercator and Robinson projections. (a) How are they similar? (b) How are they different?*

Map Projections

Mercator Projection

Robinson Projection

shows the correct sizes and shapes of landmasses for most parts of the world. The Robinson projection also gives a fairly accurate view of the relationship between landmasses and water.

Kinds of Maps

Maps are part of our everyday lives. You have probably read road or bus maps. As a child, you may have drawn treasure maps. On television, you have seen weather maps and maps of places in the news.

As you study American history, you will use many other kinds of maps. Turn now to the Geographic Atlas in the Reference Sec-

tion of this book. There, you will find five different kinds of useful maps: political, physical, population, economic, and natural resource.

Each kind of map serves a specific purpose. A political map shows boundaries that people have set up to divide the world into countries and states. A physical map shows natural features, such as mountains and rivers. A population map lets you see how many people live in the various urban and rural areas. An economic map shows how people make a living in a given area. A natural resource map helps you understand the links between the resources of an area and the way people use the land.

Chapter 1 • **9**

Connections With Science
Background

Mercator thought of the Earth as shaped like an orange. The lines of longitude were like vertical cuts made in the rind of the orange. If the orange were peeled and the segments of rind were lined up side by side, the sphere could be flattened out. Because the tops and bottoms of the segments did not touch, Mer-

cator widened each section of his flattened globe at the top and bottom so that it formed a rectangle. By so doing, however, Mercator had to sacrifice accuracy at the areas around the poles, which accounts for the enlargement of the landmasses at the top and bottom of a Mercator projection.

Chapter Resources

Skill Application For additional practice, duplicate and distribute the worksheet, The Parts of a Map, from Unit 1, page 2, of the *Chapter Resources* binder. (Reteaching/Average)

Answers to Skill Lesson

1. (a) Today's Weather (b) green (c) diagonal lines   **2.** (a) about 2,500 miles (b) about 3,700 km **3.** (a) northwest (b) northeast

ACTIVITY

Guided Instruction If possible, obtain samples of floor plans from magazines or from a vocational education teacher. Display these visual aids on an overhead projector. Before students begin work, answer any questions concerning symbols, legends, point of view, and scale. Allow students to measure the dimensions of the classroom and selected objects.

Suggest that students first make a rough copy; then provide students with graph paper for their final maps. Between the rough draft and finished work, you might pair students who have good spatial relations skills with those who have difficulty in this area. Display completed room maps on a bulletin board, or encourage students to use them as a cover for a portfolio or other collection of original work.

MAP, GRAPH, AND CHART SKILLS
The Parts of a Map

Maps are important tools used by historians and geographers. They have many uses. They can show physical features such as lakes, rivers, and mountains. They can show where people live, how people use the land, and where events took place. Some maps, like the one below, show weather patterns for a given area.

To use a map, you need to be able to read its different parts. Most maps in this book have a title, key, scale, and directional arrow.

1. **Look carefully at the map to see what it shows.** The *title* tells you the subject of the map. The *key* explains the meaning of the colors or symbols. (a) What is the title of the map below? (b) What color shows places where the temperature is in the 50s? (c) How is rain shown on the map?

2. **Practice reading distances on the map.** The *scale* helps you read distances on the map in miles or kilometers. On a small-scale map, 1 inch (2.5 cm) might equal 500 miles (800 km). On a large-scale map, 1 inch might equal only 5 miles (8 km). The map below is a small-scale map. (a) What is the distance in miles from Washington, D.C., to Seattle? (b) In kilometers?

3. **Study the map to read directions.** The *directional arrow* shows which way is north, south, east, and west. Generally, north is toward the top of a map, and south is toward the bottom. East is to the right, and west is to the left. (a) In which direction would you travel to get from Miami to Los Angeles? (b) In which direction would you travel from El Paso to reach a place where it is snowing?

ACTIVITY
Make a map of your classroom using symbols for doors, windows, desks, chalkboard, and other features. Include a map key, a scale, and a directional arrow. Use your completed map to answer the following questions: (a) How far are the windows from the door? (b) In which direction would you travel to get from the chalkboard to your desk?

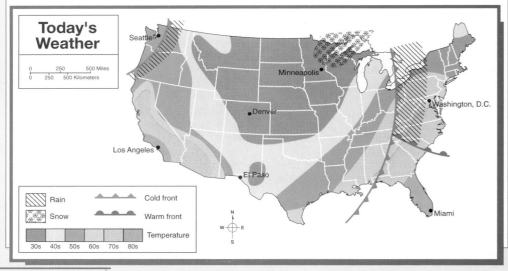

Students Acquiring English
Activity

SAE students might benefit by being paired with more advanced students to work on the skill lesson. Sample schematic plans may assist SAE students in understanding the nature of the skills activity.

Still other kinds of maps you will use this year include election maps, product maps, and battle maps. These maps also let you see the connections between geography and history.

Latitude and Longitude

Most maps and globes include lines of latitude and longitude. The lines form a grid, making it possible to locate places exactly. Each line on the grid is measured in degrees (°).

Latitude. Look at the map of the world, below. Notice that lines of latitude run east and west. As you have read, lines of latitude measure distances north and south from the Equator.

The **Equator** is an imaginary line that lies at 0° latitude. It divides the Earth into two halves, called **hemispheres.**

The Northern Hemisphere lies north of the Equator. In the Northern Hemisphere, lines of latitude are numbered from 1°N to 90°N, where the North Pole is located.

The Southern Hemisphere lies south of the Equator. There, lines of latitude are numbered from 1°S to 90°S, where the South Pole is located. On the map below, what continent lies mostly between 30°N and 30°S?

Longitude. Lines of longitude on a map or globe run north and south. They measure distances east and west from the **Prime Meridian,** which lies at 0° longitude.

Lines of longitude are numbered from 1° to 179° east or west longitude. The line of longitude at 180° lies directly opposite the Prime Meridian.

The circle formed by the Prime Meridian and 180° divides the Earth into the Eastern and Western hemispheres. The Eastern

MAP STUDY

Geographers use imaginary lines of latitude and longitude to locate places.
1. *What is the exact location of Beijing?*
2. *Which city is located at about 55°N/35°E?*
3. *Applying Information Which continents lie entirely north of the Equator?*

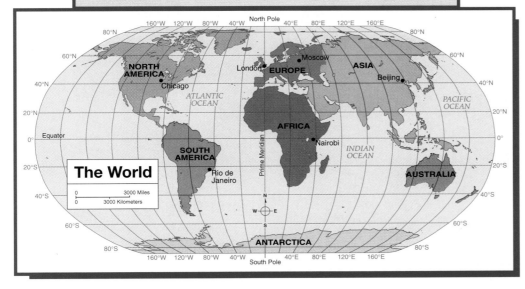

Connections With Science
Background

Most people remember Ptolemy (A.D. 90–168) for his mistakes. His belief that the sun and the planets revolved around the Earth (geocentrism) was disproved by Copernicus. A second belief—that most of the Earth's surface was dry land—was similarly erroneous. In spite of these errors, which were due mainly to lack of accurate informa-tion, Ptolemy made contributions to geography that are still relevant today. It was Ptolemy who popularized the terms *latitude* and *longitude.* (He even may have created the terms, but historians are not certain on this point.) He also established the practice of orienting maps with north at the top and east on the right.

Answers to Map Study

1. 2 P.M.   2. Moscow   3. Possible Answer: In some instances, natural boundaries such as mountain ranges divide populations, and time zones are set accordingly.

Hemisphere includes most of Europe, Africa, and Asia. The Western Hemisphere includes North America and South America. On the map, through what continent or continents does 90°W run?

Finding locations. To locate places, you need to combine latitude and longitude. Look at the map on page 11. The city of Chicago is located north of the Equator at about 42°N latitude. It lies west of the Prime

MAP STUDY

A system of 24 standard time zones allows business people and travelers to determine the time in different parts of the world. Airports, stock exchanges, and newspaper offices often have a series of clocks, like those below, that show the time in major cities.

1. *If it is 7 A.M. in Washington, D.C., what time is it in Cairo?*
2. *Where is it earlier: Beijing or Moscow?*
3. **Drawing Conclusions** *Why do you think that the boundaries of time zones are jagged lines?*

HONG KONG   TOKYO   NEW YORK   LONDON   PARIS

1 A.M. 2 A.M. 3 A.M. 4 A.M. 5 A.M. 6 A.M. 7 A.M. 8 A.M. 9 A.M. 10 A.M. 11 A.M. NOON 1 P.M. 2 P.M. 3 P.M. 4 P.M. 5 P.M. 6 P.M. 7 P.M. 8 P.M. 9 P.M. 10 P.M. 11 P.M. MIDNIGHT

World Time Zones

Not on standard time

Connections With the World
Background

The ancient Egyptians told time with a horizontal bar with a small T-shaped object at one end. The T cast a shadow on the bar, which was marked to indicate the hour. In the morning, the bar was set with the T facing east. At noon, the bar was reversed so that the T faced west. Of course, the device was useless at night; it did not even measure the hours at the beginning and end of the period of daylight.

A bowl of water with a hole in the bottom was used throughout the Roman world as a measure of time. Water-clock technology had a serious drawback. Water freezes. By the eighth century, sand-filled hourglasses began to replace water clocks. Since sand does not freeze, the devices worked in extreme cold—but they, too, were impractical at night. Mechanical timepieces did not appear until the fourteenth century.

Meridian at about 88°W longitude. In shortened form, its location is 42°N/88°W. Use the United States map in the Reference Section to find the exact location of the capital of your state.

Time Zones

Lines of longitude are also used to help us know what time it is around the world. When it is 11 A.M. in Miami, Florida, it is 8 A.M. in Portland, Oregon. In Lagos, Nigeria, it is 5 P.M.

Why does time differ from place to place? The answer is that the Earth rotates on its axis. As the Earth moves, the sun appears to rise in some places and to set in others. Throughout the world, people determine time by this rising and setting of the sun.

To make it easier to tell time around the world, a system of **standard time zones** was set up in 1884. Under this system, the world was divided into 24 time zones. Standard time is measured from the Prime Meridian, which runs through Greenwich, England.

Find Greenwich, England, on the map of world time zones on page 12. Notice that when it is noon in Greenwich, it is before noon (A.M.) in places west of Greenwich. It is after noon (P.M.) in places east of Greenwich. If you travel east from Greenwich across Europe, Africa, or Asia, you add one hour as you move through each time zone.

History and You
Today, we expect maps to be accurate. Early explorers, however, often used inaccurate maps. Imagine that you are making an automobile trip across the United States. What would happen if you did not have an accurate map?

If you travel west from Greenwich across the Atlantic Ocean and North America, you subtract one hour as you move through each time zone.

Making Accurate Maps

The oldest surviving map in the world today was created by an ancient cartographer on a clay tablet sometime around 2300 B.C. Ever since, geographers have worked to make maps more accurate.

Early mapmakers relied on information from sailors and travelers as well as legends to create maps of the world. As a result, their maps included many errors along with accurate information. Five hundred years ago, cartographers in Europe did not even know that North America and South America existed!

Since the 1500s, mapmaking has improved greatly. Daring sailors gained information about uncharted lands. Explorers studied ocean currents and wind patterns around the world. Scientists learned more about the Earth itself. Today, mapmakers take advantage of high-speed computers and space satellites to create maps that are more accurate than anyone ever believed possible.

Eye in the Sky

 One hundred miles above the Earth, Gordon Cooper was living a mapmaker's dream. It was May 1963, and "Gordo" was the sixth American astronaut to ride in space. His Mercury capsule orbited the Earth at 17,000 miles (27,000 km) an hour. Gordo was taking the mission calmly, pointing out the sights as he passed overhead.

An unexpected discovery. "Down there's the Himalayas," he told radio controllers as the world's highest mountain

---

Connections With Mathematics
Background

The Earth rotates on its axis, completing one full rotation each day. Astronomers divided each day into 24 equal periods called hours. Scientists used this calculation as a basis for dividing the Earth into 24 time zones. Because the Earth is turning, the sun is always "rising" and "setting" somewhere in the world. Whether you face toward or away from the sun during the rotation process determines if it is daylight or nighttime where you are.

The Earth is a circle measured in 360 degrees. Scientists determined how many degrees apart to place each time zone by dividing 360 degrees by 24 hours, resulting in 15 degrees in each time zone. There are four time zones in the contiguous (excluding Alaska and Hawaii) United States — Eastern, Central, Mountain, and Pacific.

Learning Styles
Visual Learners

Visual learners might benefit by seeing photographs of the tiny Mercury capsule in which Cooper circled the Earth and the huge Atlas rocket that launched it. Ask: What problems do you think Cooper may have experienced using a camera in such a confined area? Why do you think the capsule was so small and the rocket so gigantic?

range came into view. With his hand-held camera, Cooper took photographs of the peaks far below. His Oklahoma twang cut right through the static. "Ah-yuh...the Himalayas."

Later, passing over Tibet, Cooper reported that he saw individual houses and streets—100 miles (160 km) below! He made even wilder claims as he passed over the desert area of western Texas and Arizona. As he later recalled,

> **66**I saw what I took to be a vehicle along a road....I could first see the dust blowing off the road, then could see the road clearly, and when the light was right, an object that was probably a vehicle.**99**

The ground controllers scratched their heads. Was Gordo joking? True, Cooper had very good eyesight. He could see things from 20 feet away that most people would see only at 12 feet. Still, NASA scientists did not believe that anyone could see a moving vehicle from a distance of 100 miles!

NASA sent investigators to the Texas-Arizona desert. They learned that on the day of Gordo's mission, a large white-topped truck had indeed driven along the little-used desert highway. The truck had been on the highway at exactly the time when Cooper reported seeing a vehicle.

Later, other scientists examined Cooper's photographs. They saw mountains that had never appeared on any map. They found large lakes located miles from where existing maps said they should be.

These discoveries set scientists thinking: Could they use photographs from space to map the Earth? Space satellites had photographed clouds. Those pictures provided information about weather patterns. But no one had studied features on the ground from such a height.

Landsat maps. *Landsat 1,* the first satellite specially designed to study the Earth's surface from space, was launched in 1972. The unmanned butterfly-shaped spacecraft entered an orbit about 570 miles (900 km) above the Earth. It carried television cameras, a scanner that measured light, videotape recorders, and radio receivers and transmitters.

Landsat's orbit gave mapmakers every possible advantage. The spacecraft made a complete circle of the Earth every 103 minutes, 14 times a day. A single Landsat image showed an expanse of land that an airplane

A View From Outer Space *This photograph of the Mississippi River was taken by a Landsat satellite orbiting the Earth. The areas shown in blue are the river and some of its tributaries.* **Science and Technology** *How has Landsat photography changed mapmaking?*

---

would need 1,000 pictures to depict. Within two years, Landsat had photographed more than 80 percent of the Earth's land areas at least once.

Images from *Landsat 1* and later satellites were remarkable. They revealed uncharted islands and unmapped bends in rivers. They permitted scientists to see entire mountain ranges and drainage basins at a single glance. They allowed surveys of remote areas, such as the polar regions and oceans, that regular aircraft cannot reach. Based on these images, cartographers corrected old maps and mapped some places for the first time.

Landsat has transformed mapmaking. By taking photographs from high in space, Landsat satellites provide clues that no one on the ground can furnish. ■

SECTION 2 REVIEW

1. **Locate:** (a) Equator, (b) Prime Meridian.
2. **Define:** (a) cartographer, (b) map projection, (c) hemisphere, (d) standard time zone.
3. Why does a globe show the Earth more accurately than a flat map?
4. Name one advantage and one disadvantage of the Mercator projection.
5. What is the purpose of lines of latitude and longitude on maps and globes?
6. Why did people set up a system of standard time zones?
7. **CRITICAL THINKING Analyzing Information** Why is it important to have accurate maps?

ACTIVITY **Writing to Learn**
Write five questions that can be answered by using the time zone map on page 12. For example, If it is 3 P.M. in Los Angeles where you live, what time will it be where your friend lives in Buenos Aires, Argentina? Trade questions with a partner and answer your partner's questions.

3
The American Land

FIND OUT
■ What landforms are found in North America and South America?
■ What are the seven physical regions of North America?
■ What rivers and lakes are important to the United States?

VOCABULARY isthmus, mountain, elevation, relief, hill, plain, plateau, tributary

---

"**A**merica is so vast," observed the writer James Farrell, "that almost anything said about it is likely to be true, and the opposite is probably equally true." The Americas are truly a land of opposites. For example, one of the world's highest mountains, Mount Aconcagua, is in Argentina. Yet one of the lowest points on the Earth is in Death Valley, California. You will find many examples of contrast as you read more about the American land.

Where Are the Americas?

North America and South America are the world's third and fourth largest continents. These two continents plus the islands in the Caribbean Sea are the major lands in the **Western Hemisphere.**

As the World map in the Reference Section shows, the Atlantic Ocean washes the eastern shores of North America and South America. The Pacific Ocean laps at their western shores. Far to the north lies the ice-choked Arctic Ocean. Far to the south is the Strait of Magellan (muh JEHL uhn), a water passage between the Atlantic and Pacific oceans. Joining the continents of North

Chapter 1 • **15**

Student Study Guide

Section 2 Study Guide Have students use the Section 2 Study Guide on page 32 of the *Student Study Guide* to review and reinforce the content of this section. (Reteaching/Average)

ACTIVITY

Guided Instruction Before students write their questions, you might pair students and have partners locate the Prime Meridian and the longitudinal lines that separate time zones. Before partners exchange questions, have them verify direction east or west of Greenwich to check that addition or subtraction was used correctly.

Section 3
pp. 15–21

Bell Ringer

Have students complete the following sentence: "The most beautiful picture of a natural American setting that I've ever seen included _____."

Answers to Section 2 Review

1. See the map on p. 11.
2. (a) cartographer, p. 8, (b) map projection, p. 8, (c) hemisphere, p. 11, (d) standard time zone, p. 13
3. Because a globe is a sphere like the Earth, it can represent sizes and shapes accurately. A map always distorts part of the Earth.
4. The Mercator projection shows the true shape of landmasses, but it distorts their relative sizes.

5. The lines form a grid, making it possible to locate places exactly. Lines of longitude also help to mark time zones.
6. This system makes it easier to tell time around the world.
7. Possible Answer: Without accurate maps, travel between different locations might be more difficult and dangerous. Accurate maps also help scientists study weather patterns and remote regions.

Geographic Facts About the United States

Largest state, by area	Alaska	591,004 square miles
Smallest state, by area	Rhode Island	1,212 square miles
Largest state, by population (1990)	California	29,287,000
Smallest state, by population (1990)	Wyoming	468,000
Longest rivers	1. Mississippi 2. Missouri 3. Rio Grande	2,348 miles 2,315 miles 1,885 miles
Highest mountain	Mount McKinley (Alaska)	20,320 feet
Lowest point	Death Valley (California)	282 feet below sea level
Largest lake	Lake Superior*	31,820 square miles
Deepest lake	Crater Lake (Oregon)	1,932 feet
Rainiest spot	Mt. Waialeale (Hawaii)	460 inches rainfall per year
Highest recorded temperature	Death Valley (California)	134° Fahrenheit, on July 10, 1913

*Part of Lake Superior is located in Canada.
Sources: *Statistical Abstract of the United States;* National Geographic Society

CHART SKILLS *Everyone likes to know about extremes. What is the biggest? The smallest? The shortest? The longest? This chart shows some extremes in the geography of the United States. ● What is the longest river? The highest mountain? What was the highest temperature recorded in the United States?*

America and South America is an **isthmus** (IHS muhs), or narrow strip of land. It is called the ***Isthmus of Panama.***

Types of Landforms

North America and South America have many landforms, or natural features. There are high mountains, rolling hills, and long rivers. There are grassy plains, dense forests, and barren deserts. Within these different landscapes are four basic landforms: mountains, hills, plains, and plateaus (pla TOHZ).

Mountains are high, steep, rugged land. They rise to an **elevation,** or height, of at least 1,000 feet (300 m) above the surrounding land. Few people can live on the steep, rocky sides of high mountains. Yet people often settle in valleys that lie between mountains.

Geographers call the difference in height of land **relief.** In maps in this book, relief is shown by gray shading. For example, see the gray shading indicating mountains and valleys on the map on page 19.

Hills are also areas of raised land, but they are lower, less steep, and more rounded than mountains. More people live in hilly areas than on mountains because farming is possible there.

Plains are broad areas of fairly level land. Very few plains are totally flat. Most are gently rolling. Plains do not usually rise much above sea level. People often settle

---

1. Focus The Americas are vast and infinitely varied. In this section, students learn about the physical landscape of the Americas — their landforms, major physical regions, and major rivers and lakes.

2. Instruct Divide the class into groups of three or four students each. Assign each group one of the major physical regions of the United States. Have each group prepare a brief oral report describing the physical characteristics of its region.

3. Close To close the lesson, play a question-and-answer game in which you give students the names of various physical regions and have them provide details that describe the region.

 Lesson Planner

For a developed **Cooperative Learning** lesson plan, see the *Lesson Planner,* page 3.

Answers to Chart Skills

the Mississippi River; Mount McKinley; 134°F

Learning Styles
Kinesthetic Learners

To help students better comprehend the variety of landforms on the American continents, have them construct three-dimensional topographical maps. Divide the class into groups of four students each. Give half the groups photocopied relief maps of North America and the other half similar maps of South America. After gluing the maps to cardboard, they can use clay to build and shape the landforms. Each member should be responsible for creating one of the landforms on the group's model. When the clay has dried, members can paint their landscapes in green, brown, blue, and white. Depending upon students' abilities, you may encourage a more varied range of colors for varied landforms.

Pair groups completing North and South American maps to combine their projects for a complete topographical representation of the Western Hemisphere.

CONNECTIONS

ARTS | **SCIENCES** | **GEOGRAPHY** | **WORLD** | **ECONOMICS** | **CIVICS**

How the Rocky Mountains Were Formed

When we look at the soaring Rocky Mountains today, it is hard to believe they were not always there. In fact, the Rockies are young mountains. They were first formed only about 63 million years ago — not a very long time in terms of the Earth's 4-billion-year history.

How were the Rockies formed? The answer can be found in a theory scientists call plate tectonics.

Scientists believe that the Earth's outer surface, or crust, is made up of a number of rigid plates. These plates are always moving. Some plates are moving toward each other. Some are moving apart. As they move, major changes occur on the Earth's surface.

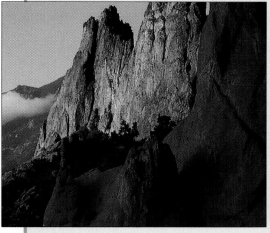

Peak in the Colorado Rockies

Mountains
Crust
Collision of two plates

About 63 million years ago, moving plates gave birth to the Rocky Mountains. Two huge plates — the North American plate and the Pacific plate — crashed head on into each other. In one great heave, the land rose up in jagged peaks. Over the next million or so years, other collisions caused the crust to crumple and push up more new mountains.

Today, the Rockies include some of the highest mountains in North America. But they are still growing and changing. In the next 50 million years, the tectonic plates will continue to move and grind and crash into each other. No one can predict for certain what the future size and shape of the Rocky Mountains will be.

■ How did plate movement form the Rocky Mountains?

ACTIVITY Form clay into two long rectangles and place them on a flat surface. Push the pieces of clay together. What happens to the clay? Use your model to explain how the Rocky Mountains were formed.

Chapter 1 • **17**

Answer to Connections

Shifting plates collided. At points of impact, the force of the collision pushed the land upward.

ACTIVITY

Guided Instruction Review movement of tectonic plates before providing clay. Discuss how mountains were formed over many centuries and under great pressure. Ask students to compare these factors with the time and pressure it takes them to complete this activity.

Transparencies

Interdisciplinary Connections Use the transparency Plate Collisions on page B-33 of *American History Transparencies* to illustrate the three types of plate collisions. Teaching suggestions can be found on page B-3. (Enrichment/Challenging)

Team-Teaching Suggestion
Science

You might work with a science teacher to present a lesson about the making and shaping of the Earth's crust. Discuss theories about supercontinents and continental drift. You might illustrate with maps of Pangaea, Laurasia, and Gondwanaland. Show how certain modern landmasses can fit together like pieces of a jigsaw puzzle.

Team-Teaching Suggestion
Language Arts

You might work with a language arts teacher to present a lesson about the keeping of diaries and scientific logs. Then have students imagine that they are watching the formation of the Rockies from outer space. Invite them to record several log entries, describing what they see over time and any other relevant impressions that they may have.

Chapter Resources

Geography in History Duplicate and distribute the worksheet, Glaciers Reshape North America, from Unit 1, pages 5–6, of the *Chapter Resources* binder. The worksheet allows students to apply each of the five themes of geography as they explore the results of glacial action. (Enrichment/Challenging)

Voices of Freedom

Primary Source You might assign selection 1-1, the lyrics to the song "America the Beautiful," or selection 1-2, A European View of North America, on pages 13 and 14–15 of *Voices of Freedom*. Have students compare and contrast the subject matter and point of view in the two works. (Enrichment/Easy)

Transparencies

Geography and History Use the transparency map set 1, The United States, on page I-51 of *American History Transparencies*. The base map and overlay 1 show the topography found within this country. Teaching suggestions can be found on page I-7. (Enrichment/Average)

---

on plains because it is easy to build farms, roads, and cities on the level land.

Plateaus are large raised areas of flat or gently rolling land. The height of plateaus may range from a few hundred to many thousand feet above sea level. With enough rain, plateaus can be good for farming. Mountains surround some plateaus. Such plateaus are called basins. Basins are often very dry because the mountains cut off rainfall.

Mountains, hills, plains, and plateaus are only a few of the special words that geographers use to describe the Earth. For definitions of these and other geographic terms, you may refer to the Dictionary of Geographic Terms on pages 26–27.

North America From West to East

The mountains, hills, plateaus, and plains of North America form seven major physical regions. The United States also includes an eighth region, the Hawaiian Islands, which lies in the Pacific Ocean. (See the map on page 19.)

The seven physical regions of North America offer great contrasts. In some regions, the land is fertile. There, American farmers plant crops and reap rich harvests. Other regions have natural resources such as coal and oil.

Pacific Coast. Beginning in the West, the first of the seven physical regions is the Pacific Coast. It includes tall mountain ranges that stretch from Alaska to Mexico. In the United States, some of these western ranges hug the Pacific Ocean. The Cascades and Sierra Nevada* stand a bit farther inland. Some important cities of the Pacific Coast are Seattle, Portland, and San Francisco.

Intermountain region. East of the coast ranges is the Intermountain region. It is a

---

*Sierra (see EHR uh) is the Spanish word for mountain range. Nevada is Spanish for snowy. Spanish explorers were the first Europeans to see these snow-covered mountains.

18 • Chapter 1

---

rugged region of mountain peaks, high plateaus, deep canyons, and deserts. The Grand Canyon, which is more than 1 mile (1.6 km) deep, and the Great Salt Lake are natural features of this region. Salt Lake City and Phoenix are among the few major cities of the Intermountain region.

Rocky Mountains. The third region, the Rocky Mountains, reaches from Alaska through Canada into the United States. In Mexico, the Rocky Mountains become the Sierra Madre (MAH dray), or mother range.

The Rockies include some of the highest peaks in North America. Many peaks are more than 14,000 feet (4,200 m) high. Throughout history, people have described their grandeur. A gold prospector wrote:

    " No, partner—if you want to see scenery see the Rockies: that's something to look at! Even the sea's afraid of them mountains—ran away from them: you can see 4,000 feet up where the sea tried to climb before it got scared! **"**

The Rockies were a serious barrier to European settlement of the United States. When settlers moved west in the 1800s, crossing the Rockies posed great hardships.

Interior Plains. Between the Rockies in the West and the Appalachians in the East is a large lowland area called the Interior Plains. The dry western part of the Interior Plains is called the Great Plains. The eastern part is called the Central Plains.

According to scientists, the Interior Plains were once covered by a great inland sea. Today, some parts are rich in coal and petroleum.* Other parts have fertile soil, making them rich farmlands. Chicago, St. Louis, and Dallas are in the Interior Plains.

Appalachian Mountains. The fifth region, the Appalachian Mountains, runs

---

*The Natural Resources map in the Reference Section shows where natural resources are located.

Connections With Geography
Background

In South Dakota, which is part of the Interior Plains, lies the Badlands—an area with very little drinkable water, shaped in unusual ways by wind and rain. In 1824, Jedediah Smith led an expedition to explore the Badlands. He described the area as a "tract of country where no vegetation of any kind existed, being worn into knobs and gullies."

Team-Teaching Suggestion
Science

You might work with a science teacher to present a lesson about timberlines, watersheds, and the ways in which altitude can affect species, adaptations, and growth of plants on mountains.

Connections With Geography
Background

The Great Salt Lake is actually an inland sea—a sea that is saltier than any ocean because its waters evaporate rather than run off into streams and rivers. Because its rate of evaporation varies, so does its size; but its average is about 75 miles (120 k) long and 30 miles (48 k) wide. In places, its salt content has varied from 5 to 27 percent salt.

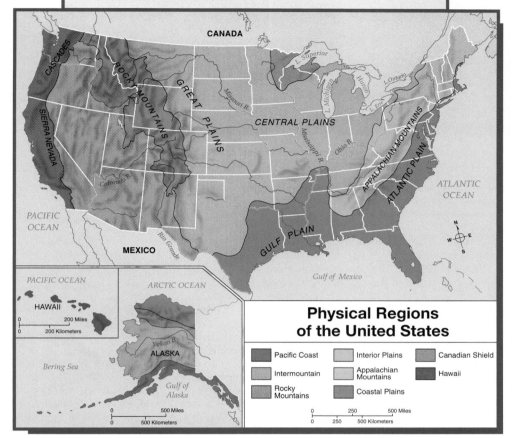

MAP STUDY

The United States can be divided into eight physical regions.
1. Which region borders the Intermountain region on the west?
2. Through which physical region does the Missouri River flow?
3. **Drawing Conclusions** Based on the map, would you describe the United States as a varied land? Explain.

Physical Regions of the United States

- Pacific Coast
- Intermountain
- Rocky Mountains
- Interior Plains
- Appalachian Mountains
- Coastal Plains
- Canadian Shield
- Hawaii

Answers to Map Study

1. Pacific Coast **2.** Interior Plains **3.** Yes; it has eight different physical regions, each with its own variety of landforms.

 Historical Outline Map Book

Historical Outline Maps Duplicate and distribute the maps, Physical Regions of the United States, and Physical United States, on pages 2 and 83 of the *American History Historical Outline Map Book.* Lesson ideas for these maps can be found on pages T1 and T25, respectively. (Reteaching/Average)

 Chapter Resources

History Through Literature To introduce students to a poetic view of America's varied landscapes, duplicate and distribute the worksheet, Our Old Feuillage, from Unit 1, page 4, of the *Chapter Resources* binder. (Enrichment/Challenging)

 Transparencies

Geography and History Use the transparency map sets 2–9, on pages I-57, I-61, I-65, I-69, I-73, I-77, I-81, and I-85 of *American History Transparencies.* The base maps and overlays illustrate the topography of the various regions of the United States. Teaching suggestions can be found on pages I-8, I-9, I-10, I-11, I-12, I-13, I-14, and I-15 respectively. (Enrichment/Easy)

---

along the eastern part of North America. The Appalachians have different names in different places. For example, the Green Mountains, Alleghenies, Blue Ridge, and Great Smokies are all part of the Appalachian Mountains.

The Appalachians are lower and less rugged than the Rockies. The highest Appalachian peak is Mt. Mitchell in North Car-

olina, which is 6,684 feet (2,037 m) high. Still, early European settlers had a hard time crossing these heavily forested mountains.

Canadian Shield. The sixth region is the Canadian Shield. It is a lowland area. Most of it lies in eastern Canada. The southern part extends into the United States. The region was once an area of high mountains. The mountains were worn away to low hills

Chapter 1 • **19**

Historical Sidelight
Background

Despite the presence of Native Americans, much of the Americas was not heavily populated. In the pre-Columbian forests, trees grew thick and tall, creating a canopy of leaves that spanned hundreds of thousands of acres along the east coast of what is now the United States. According to folklore, a squirrel could travel from tree to tree for hundreds of miles. Wild animals — including elk, deer, and buffalo — grazed in clearings.

Learning Styles
Auditory Learners

Invite students to plan an American vacation itinerary. Tell students to select a site in the Americas that they would like to visit by car. Explain that they must use a map to plan their travel route and schedule daily stops depending on distance. Ask: How far is your destination? How many days will it take you to travel? (Designate a standard legal speed

limit.) What physical regions will you pass through on your trip? What attractions will you see along the way and when you reach your destination?

After students have completed their plans, have each student give an oral presentation in the form of a travel guide that might convince others to take a similar vacation.

Contrasting Coastlines *American coastlines offer great contrasts in mood and beauty. At right, the still waters of the Gulf Coast in Florida take on a golden glow in the light of sunset. At left, waves crash against rugged rocks along the Pacific Coast.* **Geography** *What other coastal area is found in mainland United States?*

and plains. The Canadian Shield lacks topsoil for farming, but it is rich in minerals.

Coastal Plains. The seventh region is a lowland area called the Coastal Plains. Part of this region, the Atlantic Plain, lies between the Atlantic Ocean and the foothills of the Appalachians. It was once under water and is now almost flat. The Atlantic Plain is narrow in the North, where Boston and New York City are located. It broadens in the South to include all of Florida.

Another part of the Coastal Plain is the Gulf Plain, which lies along the Gulf of Mexico. The Gulf Plain has large deposits of petroleum. New Orleans and Houston are major cities of the Gulf Plain.

Hawaiian Islands. The eighth physical region of the United States is made up of the Hawaiian Islands. They lie far out in the Pacific, about 2,400 miles (3,860 km) west of California. There are eight large islands and many small islands.

The islands are the tops of volcanoes that erupted through the floor of the Pacific Ocean. Some volcanoes are still active. Mauna Loa on the island of Hawaii is an active volcano that rises 13,677 feet (4,169 m).

Rivers and Lakes

Great river systems crisscross North America. They collect the runoff from rains and melting snows and carry it into the oceans.

The mighty Mississippi. "What has four eyes and cannot see?" The Mississippi River, of course. You probably knew the answer to this favorite American riddle long before you knew the importance of the Mississippi to American geography and history.

The Mississippi and Missouri rivers make up the longest and most important river system in the United States. This river system flows through the Interior Plains into the Gulf of Mexico.

Many **tributaries,** or streams and smaller rivers, flow into the Mississippi-Missouri river system. Among these tributaries are the Ohio, Tennessee, Arkansas, and Platte rivers.

20 • Chapter 1

The Mississippi River carries moisture across the Interior Plains. It also serves as a means of transportation. Today, barges carry freight up and down the river. As in the past, people travel by boat on the river.

The mighty Mississippi has inspired many admiring descriptions. Among them is this one from the 1937 film *The River:*

> "From as far west as Idaho,
> Down from the glacier peaks of
>   the Rockies—
> From as far east as New York,
> Down from the turkey ridges of
>   the Alleghenies;
> Down from Minnesota, twenty
>   five hundred miles,
> The Mississippi River runs to
>   the Gulf.
> Carrying every drop of water,
>   that flows down two thirds
>   of the continent,
> Carrying every brook and rill,
>   rivulet and creek,
> Carrying all the rivers that run
>   down two thirds the continent.
> The Mississippi runs to the Gulf
>   of Mexico."

Borders between nations. The Rio Grande and the St. Lawrence River serve as political boundaries. They form parts of the borders between the United States and its neighbors, Mexico and Canada.

Five large lakes, called the *Great Lakes,* also form part of the border between the United States and Canada. The Great Lakes are Superior, Michigan, Huron, Erie, and

Our Common Heritage
Native Americans who live on the slopes of the Andes Mountains have hearts as much as 20 times larger than the average. Their large hearts help them make the most of the limited oxygen at such high altitudes.

Ontario. Today, canals connect the Great Lakes, forming a major inland waterway.

South American Landforms

Like North America, South America has a variety of landscapes. The Andes are a rugged mountain chain. They stretch along the western part of South America.

The tallest peaks of the Andes are much higher than those of the Rockies. The Andes plunge almost directly to the Pacific, leaving only a narrow coastal plain. Many people live in the high plateaus and valleys of the Andes.

To the east of the Andes is an interior plain. The plain is drained by three great river systems: the Orinoco, Amazon, and Paraguay-Paraná. The Amazon is the world's second longest river. It flows about 4,000 miles (6,500 km) from the Andes Mountains to the Atlantic Ocean.

SECTION 3 REVIEW

1. **Locate:** (a) North America, (b) South America, (c) Atlantic Ocean, (d) Pacific Ocean, (e) Sierra Nevada, (f) Rocky Mountains, (g) Interior Plains, (h) Appalachian Mountains, (i) Mississippi River.
2. **Identify:** (a) Western Hemisphere, (b) Isthmus of Panama, (c) Great Lakes.
3. **Define:** (a) isthmus, (b) mountain, (c) elevation, (d) relief, (e) hill, (f) plain, (g) plateau, (h) tributary.
4. (a) What are the eight physical regions of the United States? (b) Describe one feature of each.
5. Why are the Great Lakes important to the United States and Canada?
6. **CRITICAL THINKING Applying Information** What kinds of businesses might be likely to grow up along the Mississippi River?

 Writing to Learn
Write a poem about the American landscape.

 Our Multicultural Heritage

Biography Have students read the biography, *John James Audubon, American Naturalist,* on page 2 of the *Our Multicultural Heritage* booklet. (Enrichment/Average)
Milestone Have students read *Environmental Treasures: Birds of the Americas,* on page 3 of the *Our Multicultural Heritage* booklet. (Enrichment/ Easy)

Student Study Guide

Section 3 Study Guide Have students use the Section 3 Study Guide on page 33 of the *Student Study Guide* to help review and reinforce the content of this section. (Reteaching/Average)

ACTIVITY

Guided Instruction Before students begin writing their poems, have student volunteers share what they think makes a poem memorable. Encourage students to emphasize description in their poems and also to base their descriptions upon geographic features. If students express an interest in writing poems that rhyme, suggest that they use a rhyming dictionary to help them draft and revise their poems.

Answers to Section 3 Review

1. See the maps on pp. 11 and 19.
2. (a) Western Hemisphere, p. 15, (b) Isthmus of Panama, p. 16, (c) Great Lakes, p. 21
3. (a) isthmus, p. 16, (b) mountain, p. 16, (c) elevation, p. 16, (d) relief, p. 16, (e) hill, p. 16, (f) plain, p. 16, (g) plateau, p. 18, (h) tributary, p. 20
4. (a) Pacific Coast, Intermountain, Rocky Mountains, Interior Plains, Appalachian Mountains, Canadian Shield, Coastal Plains, Hawaiian Islands, (b) Pacific Coast—tall mountain ranges; Intermountain—high plateaus, deserts, and deep canyons; Rocky Mountains—high peaks that were a barrier to settlement; Interior Plains—large lowland area; Appalachian Mountains—lower and less rugged than the Rockies; Canadian Shield—lowland area rich in minerals; Coastal Plains—lowland area once under water; Hawaiian Islands—tops of volcanoes that lie on the floor of the Pacific Ocean
5. The Great Lakes form part of the border between Canada and the United States and are part of an important inland waterway.
6. Possible Answer: Businesses likely to grow up along the Mississippi River include trade, transportation, agriculture, and shipping.

Bell Ringer

Have students list and define in their own words terms they have heard on local TV or radio weather forecasts.

Lesson Plan

1. Focus Climate is another factor of geography that affects the way people live. In this section, students study the 10 major climates of North America and the main climates of South America.

2. Instruct Help the class plan and produce a "superstation" weather forecast in which studio anchors and field teams report conditions around the Americas on a given day and explain how those conditions are linked to the different climates.

3. Close To close the lesson, have students identify each of the 10 types of climate found in the United States based either on clues that you give them or clues that they provide to quiz each other.

Lesson Planner

For a developed **Cooperative Learning** lesson plan, see the *Lesson Planner,* page 4.

4
Climates of the Americas

FIND OUT
- What factors influence climate?
- What are the major climates of North America?
- What is the climate of South America like?

VOCABULARY weather, climate, precipitation, altitude

"**O**h, what a blamed uncertain thing
This pesky weather is;
It blew and snew and then it thew,
And now, by jing, it friz."

Those lines by the humorist Philander Johnson suggest our constant concern with weather. People worry about weather because it affects their lives. It affects jobs, leisure time activities, and the types of homes they build. Throughout history, people have adapted to different kinds of weather.

Factors That Affect Climate

Weather is the condition of the Earth's atmosphere at any given time and place. It may be hot or cold, rainy or dry, or something in between. **Climate** is the average weather of a place over a period of 20 to 30 years. Two main aspects of climate are temperature and **precipitation** (pree sihp uh TAY shuhn), or water that falls from the sky in the form of rain or snow.

Several factors affect climate. One factor is distance north or south from the Equator. Lands close to the Equator, such as Hawaii, usually are hot and wet all year. Lands near the North and South poles are cold all year.

A second factor that affects climate is **altitude,** or height above sea level. In general, highland areas are cooler than lowland areas.

Ocean currents, wind currents, and mountains also influence climate. When winds carrying moisture from the ocean strike the side of a mountain, the air rises and cools rapidly. As the air cools, it cannot hold as much moisture, and the water falls as rain or snow. Plenty of moisture falls on the side of the mountain closest to the body of water. The other side is usually quite dry because the winds have already dumped their moisture. The western sides of the Cascades, for example, get abundant precipitation, while the eastern slopes are dry.

North American Climates

Within North America, climate varies greatly. The United States has 10 major climates. Look at the map on page 23 and at the chart on page 25 to see where these climates are located and to learn about the conditions in each one.

Marine. The strip of land from southern Alaska to northern California is sometimes called the Pacific Northwest. This region has a mild, moist marine climate, with warm summers and cool winters. The Pacific Northwest has many forests that make it the center of a busy lumber industry.

Mediterranean. Most of California has a Mediterranean climate. Winters are mild and wet. Summers are hot and dry. In many areas, the soil is good, but plants need to be watered in the summer. Farmers and fruit growers must irrigate the land there.

Highland. In the Cascades, Sierra Nevada, and Rocky Mountains, a highland climate brings generally cooler temperatures. Exact conditions in a highland climate vary according to altitude. For example, Mount Rainier in the state of Washington, at over 14,000 feet (4,200 m) above sea level, is snow-capped all year.

---

22 • Chapter 1

Connections With Science
Background

Precipitation refers to any form of moisture that falls to the Earth. Rain and snow are the most common forms of precipitation, but hail and sleet also qualify. Although dew, frost, and fog are other forms of moisture in the atmosphere, they are not, technically, forms of precipitation.

Connections With Mathematics
Activity

Explain to students that temperature on Earth is usually measured on either of two scales, Fahrenheit or Celsius. Both scales are based on the boiling and freezing points of water. Students can convert temperature from one of these scales to the other by using the following formulas:

Fahrenheit = (Celsius x 9/5) + 32
Celsius = (Fahrenheit – 32) x 5/9

Ask: If the boiling point of water on the Celsius scale is 100 degrees, what is it on the Fahrenheit scale? (212 degrees) If the freezing point of water on the Fahrenheit scale is 32 degrees, what is it on the Celsius scale? (0 degrees)

Steppe. East of the Rockies are the Great Plains. They have a steppe climate with limited rainfall. Summers are hot and winters are cold. Huge herds of buffaloes once grazed on the short grasses of the Great Plains. In the 1800s, settlers brought cattle to graze on the plains. The popular song "Home on the Range" was set on the plains:

66 Oh, give me a home, where the buffalo roam,
Where the deer and the antelope play.
Where seldom is heard a discouraging word
And the skies are not cloudy all day. 99

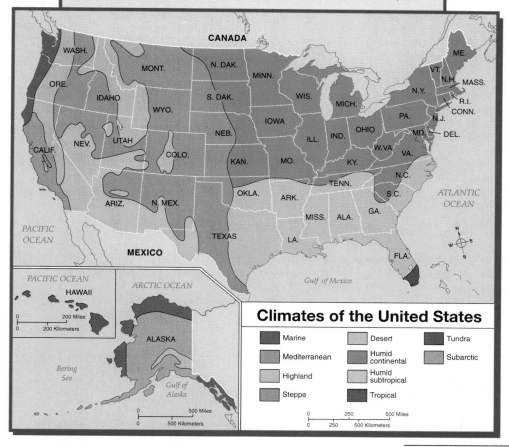

MAP STUDY

The United States is a land of many climates.
1. Name a state with a steppe climate.
2. What type of climate or climates are found in your state?
3. **Making Decisions** Which climate would you least like to live in? Why?

Climates of the United States

- Marine
- Mediterranean
- Highland
- Steppe
- Desert
- Humid continental
- Humid subtropical
- Tropical
- Tundra
- Subarctic

 Historical Outline Map Book

Historical Outline Map Duplicate and distribute the map, Climates of the United States, on page 3 of the *American History Historical Outline Map Book.* Lesson ideas for this map can be found on page T1. (Reteaching/Average)

 Transparencies

Geography and History Use transparency map set 1, The United States, on page I-51 of *American History Transparencies.* The base map and the overlay illustrate climatic conditions throughout the country. Teaching suggestions can be found on page I-7. (Reteaching/Average)

Cooperative Learning Activity

Divide the class into groups to play a game of Where Am I? Have each group choose three cities that appear on the United States map in the Reference Section. Next, ask each group to write a set of statements that describe the landforms and climate of each place they have chosen.

A sample set of statements for Duluth, Minnesota, might be the following: 1. I live in a place that has cold winters. 2. I live in a place that is near a large lake. 3. I live in a place with a humid continental climate. 4. I live in the Canadian Shield. Have groups compete to identify the city, giving 5 points for each identification after the first statement, 4 points after the second statement, and so on.

Team-Teaching Suggestion Science

You might work with a science teacher to present a lesson about the two absolute temperature scales, Kelvin (degrees Celsius + 273.15) and Rankine (degrees Fahrenheit + 459.67). Discuss why these scales would be more important than water-based scales in the design of weather satellites and in space exploration.

Varied Climates *American climates vary a great deal, as these two photographs show. At top, huge sand dunes reflect the desert climate of California's Imperial Valley. At bottom, ice breaks up during the spring thaw in Alaska's tundra climate.* **Daily Life** *How have people adapted to desert and tundra climates?*

Desert. On the eastern side of the Cascades and Sierra Nevada, the land has a desert climate, with hot days and cold nights. This dry region stretches as far east as the Rockies. In the deserts of Nevada, Arizona, and southeastern California, there is almost no rainfall. In many areas, people irrigate the land so that they can grow crops.

Humid continental. The Central Plains and the northeastern United States have a humid continental climate. This climate, with mild summers and cold winters, has more precipitation than the steppe. Tall prairie grasses once covered the Central Plains. Today, American farmers raise much of the world's food in this region.

At one time, forests covered much of the northeastern United States. Early European settlers cleared the forests to build settlements and to grow crops. But many forests remain, and the lumber industry thrives in some areas.

Humid subtropical. The southeastern United States has a humid subtropical climate. Warm temperatures and regular rainfall make this region ideal for growing crops such as cotton, tobacco, and peanuts.

Tropical. Southern Florida and Hawaii, located near the Equator, have tropical climates. The hot, humid conditions make these regions good for growing such crops as pineapples and citrus fruits.

Tundra and subarctic. Northern and western coastal regions of Alaska have a tundra climate. It is cold all year round. The rest of Alaska and northern Canada have a

24 • Chapter 1

Climates of the United States

Climate	Weather
Marine	Mild, rainy
Mediterranean	Mild; wet winters; sunny, dry summers
Highland	Seasons and rainfall vary with elevation
Steppe	Very hot summers; very cold winters; little rainfall
Desert	Hot days; cold nights; very little rainfall
Humid continental	Mild summers; cold winters; rainfall varies
Humid subtropical	Humid summers; mild winters
Tropical	Hot, rainy, steamy
Tundra	Very cold winters; very short summers
Subarctic	Very short summers; long, cold winters

CHART SKILLS *This chart shows the weather conditions in each climate of the United States. Compare the chart with the map on page 23.*
● *Describe the weather for your state.*

subarctic climate with long, cold winters and short summers. Few people live in these harsh climates.

South American Climates

South America has many climates. Some of the world's driest deserts and largest rain forests are found in South America.

The huge area drained by the Amazon River is largely tropical rain forest. With warm temperatures and abundant rainfall all year round, the rain forest is rich in a wide variety of vegetation. Today, developers are cutting down the rain forest to make room for farms and to harvest the valuable wood of the forest trees. Destruction of the rain forest is causing concern throughout the world.

A dry climate is found along much of the Pacific coastal plain. Indeed, in the middle of the plain is the Atacama Desert, one of the driest deserts in the world. Winds blowing across the cold currents that flow off western South America drop moisture into the ocean. Only dry winds reach the land, and a desolate wasteland is created.

Large parts of Brazil have a savanna climate. These areas have a short rainy season when huge amounts of rain fall. The rainy season is followed by a long dry season with no precipitation. Other countries in South America—such as Argentina, Uruguay, and Chile—have climates similar to those in the United States.

SECTION 4 REVIEW

1. **Define:** (a) weather, (b) climate, (c) precipitation, (d) altitude.
2. Name two factors that affect climate.
3. (a) List the 10 major climates of the United States. (b) Name two United States climates that are suitable for growing crops.
4. Describe two climates of South America.
5. **CRITICAL THINKING Synthesizing Information** Why do you think climate is important to people's lives?

 Writing to Learn
Use the map on page 23 and the chart on page 25 to choose one type of climate. Then write a short story set in that climate. Be sure to show how the climate affects the events of your story.

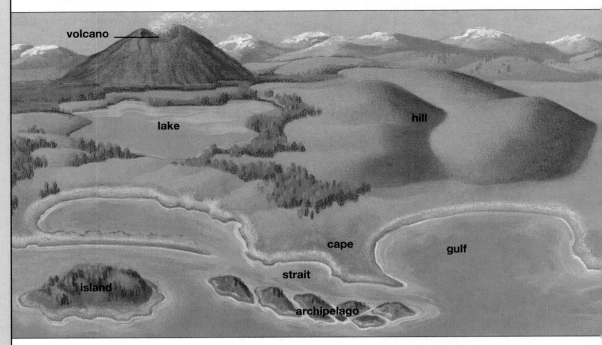

The list below includes important geographic terms and their definitions. Sometimes, the definition of a term includes an example in parentheses. An asterisk (*) indicates that the term is illustrated above.

altitude height above sea level.

***archipelago** chain of islands. (Hawaiian Islands)

basin low-lying land area that is surrounded by land of higher elevation; land area that is drained by a river system. (Great Basin)

***bay** part of a body of water that is partly enclosed by land. (San Francisco Bay)

canal waterway made by people that is used to drain or irrigate land or to connect two bodies of water. (Erie Canal)

***canyon** deep, narrow valley with high, steep sides. (Grand Canyon)

***cape** narrow point of land that extends into a body of water. (Cape Canaveral)

climate pattern of weather in a particular place over a period of 20 to 30 years.

***coast** land that borders the sea. (Pacific Coast)

coastal plain lowland area lying along the ocean. (Gulf Plain)

continent any of seven large landmasses on the Earth's surface. (Africa, Antarctica, Asia, Australia, Europe, North America, South America)

continental divide ridge along the Rocky Mountains that separates rivers that flow east from those that flow west.

***delta** land area formed by soil that is deposited at the mouth of a river. (Mississippi Delta)

desert area that has little or no moisture or vegetation. (Painted Desert)

directional arrow arrow on a map that always points north.

downstream in the direction of a river's flow; toward a river's mouth.

elevation the height above sea level.

fall line place where rivers drop from a plateau or foothills to a coastal plain, usually marked by many waterfalls and rapids.

foothills low hills at the base of a mountain range.

***gulf** arm of an ocean or sea that is partly enclosed by land, usually larger than a bay. (Gulf of Mexico)

hemisphere half of the Earth. (Western Hemisphere)

***hill** area of raised land that is lower and more rounded than a mountain. (San Juan Hill)

***island** land area that is surrounded by water. (Puerto Rico)

***isthmus** narrow strip of land joining two large land areas or

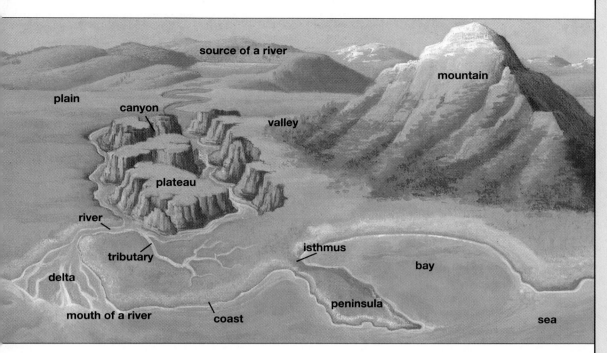

joining a peninsula to a mainland. (Isthmus of Panama)

*lake body of water surrounded by land. (Lake Superior)

latitude the distance in degrees north and south from the Equator.

longitude distance in degrees east or west from the Prime Meridian.

marsh lowland with moist soils and tall grasses.

*mountain high, steep, rugged land that rises sharply above the surrounding land. (Mount McKinley)

mountain range chain of connected mountains. (Allegheny Mountains)

*mouth of a river place where a river or stream empties into a large body of water.

ocean any of the large bodies of salt water on the Earth's surface. (Arctic, Atlantic, Indian, and Pacific oceans)

*peninsula piece of land that is surrounded by water on three sides. (Delmarva Peninsula)

piedmont area of rolling land along the base of a mountain range.

*plain broad area of fairly level land that is generally close to sea level.

*plateau large area of high, flat, or gently rolling land.

prairie large area of natural grassland with few or no trees or hills.

*river large stream of water that empties into an ocean or lake or another river. (Pecos River)

*sea large body of salt water that is smaller than an ocean. (Caribbean Sea)

sea level average level of the ocean's surface from which the height of land or depth of the ocean is measured.

*source of a river place where a river begins.

steppe flat, treeless land with limited moisture.

*strait narrow channel that connects two larger bodies of water. (Straits of Florida)

*tributary stream or small river that flows into a larger stream or river.

upstream in the direction that is against a river's flow; toward a river's source.

*valley land that lies between hills or mountains. (Shenandoah Valley)

*volcano cone-shaped mountain formed by an outpouring of lava—hot, liquid rock—from a crack in the Earth's surface. (Mount St. Helens or Mauna Loa)

weather condition of the air at any given time and place.

Chapter 1 • **27**

Cooperative Learning
Activity

Divide the class into groups of four or five students each. Appoint a student in each group to be the recorder. Have the recorders write the following terms across the top of an 8½" x 11" page that has been turned sideways: *bay, canal, desert, island, mountain.*

Have the students in each group take turns naming specific bays, canals, deserts, and so on, in the United States. Tell students that they may use maps in their textbooks, if necessary, but that they must not repeat the examples given in the listing above. Recorders should write each example given by their teammates under the appropriate heading on the paper.

After a suitable length of time, have the recorders share their charts with the class.

CHAPTER 1 REVIEW

Answers to Reviewing the Main Ideas

1. (a) location (b) Possible Answers: houses, transportation, ways of making a living, language, and religion

2. (a) Because globes are the same shape as the Earth, they show sizes and shapes accurately. (b) Maps can show all of the Earth's surface at one time, can show more detail than globes, and are easier to handle.

3. to determine exact locations of places; to set up standard time zones

4. (a) mountains, hills, plains, plateaus (b) mountains—high, steep, rugged; hills—raised, but lower, less steep, more rounded than mountains; plains—broad areas of fairly level land, mostly gently rolling; plateaus—large areas of high, flat, or gently rolling land

5. (a) Atlantic Plain and Gulf Plain (b) Atlantic Plain—lowland, lies between Atlantic Ocean and the Appalachian foothills, flat, broadens in the south to include all of Florida; Gulf Plain—lowland, lies along the Gulf of Mexico, rich in petroleum, major cities are New Orleans and Houston.

6. (a) the system formed by the Mississippi and Missouri rivers (b) These rivers and their tributaries cover a large part of the United States, providing moisture and transportation.

7. (a) tropical—hot and wet all year (b) tundra—long, cold winters; short summers

Answers to Thinking Critically

1. (a) Possible Answers: scheduling of transportation and meetings in various parts of the world, knowledge of exact dates, standardization of scientific observation; (b) Possible Answers: travel, telephone communications, taped versus live TV broadcasts

2. (a) Technology affects interaction by allowing people to alter their environment. It affects movement by making it easier for people and resources to move from place to place. (b) Possible Answer: The development of airplanes allowed people to move around the globe faster.

Summary

- Five themes help geographers study the Earth and its people: location, place, interaction between people and their environment, movement, and region.
- Maps and globes are among the most useful tools of geography.
- The United States has varied landforms and includes eight physical regions.
- North America has varied climates, depending on factors such as distance from the Equator, altitude, wind and ocean currents, and mountains.

Reviewing the Main Ideas

1. (a) Which theme of geography focuses on where an event happened? (b) What do the human features of a place include?

2. (a) What are the advantages of globes? (b) Of maps?

3. How do people use latitude and longitude?

4. (a) What are the four basic landforms in North and South America? (b) Describe each landform.

5. (a) What are the two parts of the Coastal Plains? (b) Describe one part.

6. (a) What is the most important river system in the United States? (b) Why is this river system important?

7. Describe the weather in the following climates: (a) tropical, (b) tundra.

Thinking Critically

1. Linking Past and Present (a) What problems might have arisen before the introduction of standard time zones? (b) How do time zones affect your life today?

2. Applying Information (a) How does technology affect both interaction and movement? (b) Give one example of the effect of technology on movement.

3. Asking Questions What questions would you ask to learn about your state's physical geography?

Applying Your Skills

1. Outlining An outline helps you summarize facts. It includes a list of topics, subtopics, and facts. See the sample below to outline the third section of Chapter 1. To begin, write the main topic—the numbered title on page 15. Below the topic, write the first subtopic—the subsection on page 15. Under the subtopic, write at least two facts. Complete the outline for the third section of Chapter 1.

I. The American Land (main topic)
   A. Where Are the Americas? (subtopic)
      1. Western Hemisphere
      2. Between Atlantic and Pacific oceans

2. Comparing When you compare two or more things, you need to look for ways they are similar and ways they are different. Compare Mercator projections with Robinson projections.

Thinking About Geography

Match the letters on the map with the following places: **1.** North America, **2.** South America, **3.** Atlantic Ocean, **4.** Pacific Ocean, **5.** Isthmus of Panama, **6.** Great Lakes. **Location** What ocean lies to the east of North and South America?

3. Possible Answers: What physical region is my state a part of? What rivers and mountains are in my state? What would a relief map of my state look like?

Answers to Applying Your Skills

1. Students should complete the outline with these subtopics: B. Types of Landforms, C. North America From West to East, D. Rivers and Lakes, and E. South American Landforms. At least two facts should be listed under each subentry.

2. Both projections allow the Earth to be presented on a flat surface. The Mercator projection was developed before the Robinson projection. A Mercator projection shows the true shapes of landmasses, but it distorts size, especially for places that are far from the Equator. A Robinson projection shows the correct sizes and shapes of landmasses for most parts of the world. It also gives a fairly accurate view of the relationship between landmasses and water.

Exploring American Rivers

Form into groups to review rivers in the Americas. Follow the suggestions below to write, draw, sing, or play music to show what you have learned about rivers. You may use the textbook, encyclopedias, atlases, or other materials in your classroom library to complete the tasks. Be able to name your sources of information when you have finished the activity.

"Flow Along River Tennessee"

CARTOGRAPHERS On a large sheet of paper, create a map of the United States. On the map:
- Draw the 50 states of the United States.
- Draw and label the Mississippi, Missouri, Ohio, Rio Grande, and St. Lawrence rivers.
- Label the states through which each river passes.

MATHEMATICIANS Learn the length of these rivers: Amazon, Orinoco, Mississippi, Missouri, Ohio, Rio Grande, and St. Lawrence. Create a graph comparing their lengths.

ARTISTS Find out about a bridge or a dam located on the Mississippi, Missouri, Ohio, Rio Grande, or St. Lawrence rivers—or on a river near your community. Draw a picture or build a model of the bridge or dam. Be prepared to explain how it makes a difference to people who live in the area.

"Across the Wide Missouri"

LANGUAGE EXPERTS Find out how these rivers got their names: Mississippi, Missouri, Ohio, Rio Grande, St. Lawrence. Display the information on a chart.

MUSICIANS Use the information in the chapter to list five facts about American rivers. Then write a song with a river theme.

★ Cut wavy edges along the top and bottom of a sheet of mural paper about 5 feet long. Post the completed activity from each group on the Exploring American Rivers mural.

Missouri River

Chapter 1 • 29

Answers to Thinking About Geography

1. B **2.** F **3.** C **4.** A **5.** D
6. E
Location: Atlantic Ocean

Assessment

Chapter Resources Binder For a more comprehensive evaluation of student understanding of this chapter, assign Chapter Tests A and B and/or Extra Unit Questions from Unit 1, pages 7–12 and 51–53.
Computer Test Bank You can use Chapter Tests and Extra Unit Questions to create your own tests for both testing and retesting.

Alternative Assessment

Chapter Resources Binder See the Alternative Assessment booklet in the *Social Studies Educator's Handbook* series.
Portfolio You might meet with students to choose appropriate work from the chapter for inclusion in their portfolios.

Learning Styles

The following chart indicates the activities appropriate for different learning styles.

Visual Learners
 Cartographers
 Mathematicians
 Language experts
 Artists

Auditory Learners
 Artists
 Musicians

Kinesthetic Learners
 Cartographers
 Mathematicians
 Language experts
 Artists
 Musicians

Evaluation

Cartographers Boundaries between states need not be exact but must reflect approximate shape and size in comparison with adjacent states. Rivers must flow through correct states. All pertinent information should be accurate.
Mathematicians Graphs must include the correct lengths (in miles and perhaps in kilometers) for all rivers; the comparisons between river lengths must be exact.
Artists Artistic ability need not be a criterion, but pictures or models should represent the design of the bridge or dam depicted. Presentations should be interesting and informative.
Language experts Information must be complete and accurate. Finished charts should be organized, legible, and neat.
Musicians Song lyrics should be original and should contain accurate facts. Do not judge performance on singing ability, but do note if the lyrics fit the melody of the tune selected or composed.

Lessons	Teaching Resources
1 Uncovering the American Past **Objectives** 1. Explain how people first reached the Americas. 2. Explain how archaeologists learn about the past. 3. Identify the Mound Builders. 4. Describe how early peoples in the Southwest adapted to the desert.	**Lesson Planner** Cooperative Learning, p. 7 **Student Study Guide** Section 1 Study Guide, p. 37 **Chapter Resources Binder, Unit 1** *Geography in History* Adapting to a Dry Climate, pp. 17–18 *History Through Literature* The Girl Who Hunted Rabbits, p. 16
2 The Peoples of North America **Objectives** 1. Describe the 10 major culture areas of North America. 2. Describe how Native Americans adapted to different environments. 3. Describe how religious beliefs affected people's daily lives.	**Lesson Planner** Cooperative Learning, p. 8 **Student Study Guide** Section 2 Study Guide, p. 38 **Chapter Resources Binder, Unit 1** *Critical Thinking* Comparing Information on a Chart, p. 15 **Our Multicultural Heritage** *Biography* Dekanawida, Iroquois Lawgiver, p. 4 *Milestone* The Iroquois False Face Society: A Healing League, p. 6 **Interdisciplinary Connections:** Native American Life ■ *Arts* Painting With Sand, p. 8 ■ *Sciences* Native American Medicine, p. 9 ■ *Geography* Cayuga Country, p. 10 ■ *World* Comparing Cultures, p. 11 ■ *Economics* A Word About Wampum, p. 12 **Posters** *Mixed Kachina Dance,* by Raymond Naha
3 Early Civilizations of the Americas **Objectives** 1. Identify the regions that the Mayas, Aztecs, and Incas influenced. 2. Describe how each civilization adapted to its environment. 3. Identify some major achievements of each civilization.	**Lesson Planner** Cooperative Learning, p. 9 **Student Study Guide** Section 3 Study Guide, p. 39 **Our Multicultural Heritage** *Biography* Topa Inca Yupanqui, Incan Emperor, p. 5
4 After 1492 **Objectives** 1. Explain how the 1492 encounter with Europeans affected Native Americans. 2. Explain how Native American cultures influenced peoples around the world after 1492.	**Lesson Planner** Cooperative Learning, p. 10 **Student Study Guide** Section 4 Study Guide, p. 40 **Chapter Resources Binder** *Skill Application* Reading a Line Graph, p. 14

Multimedia Resources	Additional Resources	Chapter-Level Resources

Videotapes/Videodiscs
United States History Video Collection
  The First Americans, Vol. 1, Ch. 7
	Historical Outline Map Book
	Hunters Reach America, p. 1
		Lesson Planner
		Activity Based, pp. 11–12
		
		Student Study Guide
		Chapter 2 Study Guide,
		  pp. 41–42
		
		Chapter Resources
		  Binder
		Unit 1
		Vocabulary Building, p. 13
		Chapter Test A, pp. 19–21
		Chapter Test B, pp. 22–24
		Extra Unit Questions,
		  pp. 51–53
		English Guided Reading
		Guided Reading, pp. 3–4
		Spanish Resources
		
		Computer Test Bank
		Chapter Tests A and B
		Extra Unit Questions
		
		Guided Reading
		  Audiotapes
		Side 1
		
		CD-ROM
		Time Tour The First
		  Americans in A Meeting
		  of Different Worlds

Transparencies
Fine Art Celestial Germinators, p. D-25
Fine Art Native American Handcrafts, p. D-27
Exploring Technology Native American
  Dwellings, p. H-23
Interdisciplinary Connections How a Bill
  Becomes a Law, p. B-35
Listening to Literature Audiocassettes
The American Experience Navajo Night
  Chant, side 1; From the Houses of Magic,
  side 1; Spring Song, side 1; Song
  Concerning a Dream of the Thunderbirds,
  side 1; From *The Walam Olum,* side 1
CD-ROM
Arts and Entertainment Books, Native
  American Storytelling
Virtual Buildings Iroquois Longhouse
	Voices of Freedom
	An Arapaho Legend, pp. 16–17
	Keeping a Heritage Alive, pp. 18–19
	Founding of the League of the Iroquois,
	  pp. 19–20
	Historical Outline Map Book
	Native American Cultures, p. 4
	Customized Reader
	When Grizzlies Walked Upright, article
	  IA-7
	The Good Twin and the Evil Twin, article
	  IA-6
	The Legend of Devil's Tower, article IA-5	

Transparencies *Time Lines* America and the World, 1300–1600, p. E-13	**Voices of Freedom** Farming Methods of the Incas, p. 21 **Historical Outline Map Book** Great Empires of the Americas, p. 5	

Transparencies
Time Lines America and the World,
  1300–1600, p. E-13
	Voices of Freedom
	Columbus Lands in America, pp. 24–26
	Customized Reader
	Viking Saga of the Discovery of Vinland,
	  article IB-6	

Lesson Planner

For a fully developed **Activity-Based** lesson plan for Chapter 2, see the *Lesson Planner,* pages 11–12.

Chapter Resources

Vocabulary Building The Vocabulary Building worksheet for Chapter 2 from Unit 1, page 13, of the *Chapter Resources* binder can be used as a prereading activity or as a review of chapter vocabulary. (Reteaching/Easy)

Student Study Guide

Chapter 2 Study Guide Refer students to pages 41–42 of the *Student Study Guide* for the Chapter 2 Study Guide. The study guide can be used for chapter review as well as for reteaching. (Reteaching/Average)

Guided Reading Audiotapes

Students can use *Guided Reading Audiotapes,* Chapter 2, side 1, to hear section previews, summaries, and review questions. The tapes might benefit students who are auditory learners, students who have trouble reading, or students acquiring English. Tapes are also available in Spanish. (Reteaching/Easy)

CHAPTER 2

The First Americans

(Prehistory–1600)

CHAPTER OUTLINE

1 Uncovering the American Past
2 The Peoples of North America
3 Early Civilizations of the Americas
4 After 1492

5000 years ago *People's lives changed when they learned to grow crops. These ears of corn were fashioned from bronze by an Incan metalworker.*

2000 years ago *The Mayas built a rich civilization in present-day Mexico and Guatemala. This vase shows an athlete playing a traditional Mayan ball game.*

1200s *The peoples known as Mound Builders left records of their culture in large burial mounds. This copper warrior's head was dug up in Oklahoma.*

PREHISTORY		1200	1300

WORLD EVENT
30,000–15,000 Years Ago
Hunters from Asia cross land bridge to the Americas

WORLD EVENT
1200–1400 West African kingdom of Mali reaches its height

30 • Chapter 2

Chapter Time Line
Understanding Chronology

Have students use notebook paper to create 10 time cards, labeling them as follows:
    5000 years ago
    2000 years ago
    1200s
    1300s
    1400s
    1570s

World Event/30,000–15,000 years ago
World Event/1200–1400
World Event/1300s
World Event/1492
Check students' understanding of chapter chronology by reading statements such as the following and having students raise the time card that places it correctly:

■ "I was a merchant in the kingdom of Mali." (World Event/1200–1400)
■ "My people were eager to join the Iroquois League." (1570s)
■ "How our lives changed when we started to grow our own food!" (5000 years ago)
Invite students to think of additional examples.

Chapter Setting

❝In the beginning the earth was covered with water, and all living things were below in the underworld. . . . But now the earth was all dry, except for the four oceans and the lake in the center. . . .

All the people came up [from the underworld]. They traveled east until they arrived at the ocean. Then they turned south until they came again to the ocean. Then they went west to the ocean, and then they turned north. And as they went, each tribe stopped where it wanted to.

But the [Apaches] continued to circle around the hole where they had come up from the underworld. Three times they went around it. . . .[Their god] became displeased and asked them where they wished to stop. They said, 'In the middle of the earth.' So he led them to a place [in New Mexico]. . . .There . . .the [Apaches] made their home.❞

For countless generations, a group of Native Americans known as the Apaches have handed down this story. Some people think that the Apaches were describing the settlement of North America.

Today, we know that the first humans to enter North and South America slowly spread across the land, much as the Apache legend says. We know this because early peoples left behind a trail of evidence, such as earthen burial mounds, stone cities, and pottery. By studying these physical remains, scientists are piecing together the story of the first Americans.

> **ACTIVITY** Imagine that you arrive in the United States in the year 3000 and find the following items dating from the 1990s: chicken bone, paper with writing on it, TV set, computer, guitar. Discuss what these items would tell you about American life in the 1990s.

1300s *The Aztecs built an empire in Mexico. This drawing celebrates the founding of the Aztec capital.*

1400s *The Incan empire arose in present-day Peru. Skilled artists made ceramic vases such as this one.*

1570s *Peoples of the Eastern Woodlands formed the Iroquois League to promote peace and cooperation.*

1300	1400	1500	1600

▲ **WORLD EVENT**
1300s Europeans seek trade with Asia

▲ **WORLD EVENT**
1492 Columbus reaches the Americas

Chapter 2 • **31**

 Chapter Resources

English Guided Reading Duplicate and distribute to SAE students the Chapter 2 Guided Reading worksheet on pages 3–4 in the English Guided Reading section of the *Chapter Resources* binder. Students who have difficulty reading also might benefit from using this worksheet. Have students complete the worksheet before they begin reading. You might pair a student who is more fluent or who is a stronger reader with one whose skills need improvement. (Reteaching/Easy)

Spanish Resources See Spanish Resources section of the *Chapter Resources* binder.

> **ACTIVITY**

Guided Instruction Explain that artifacts are objects made by people. Ask: Which of the items listed in the activity are artifacts? After pointing out that archaeologists are very careful about making assumptions, ask: What is it about the bone that might explain the chicken's role (e.g., if cooked, might it be food)? Note that archaeologists often find patterns among artifacts. Encourage groups to do the same (e.g., a TV set and a computer both require electricity).

CD-ROM

Time Tour Access The First Americans in A Meeting of Different Worlds on the American Heritage® *History of the United States* CD-ROM. (Enrichment/Average)

Students Acquiring English
Activity

Visual images of unfamiliar words may help SAE students grasp difficult concepts. You might have SAE students start a picture dictionary of words associated with Native American customs, artifacts, and buildings. Words from Sections 1 and 2 of this chapter include *adobe, pueblo, igloo, kayak, potlatch, kiva, hogan, tepee, travois, long house, sachem,* and *buffalo.* Students can use descriptions and context clues from the chapter, as well as from other reference books on Native Americans. By illustrating these nouns, students will gain a better understanding of their meanings and will create a reference product that could be part of the class library.

Linking Past and Present
Activity

Today's renewed interest in native peoples can lead to a lively discussion. Have students consider how their perception of Native Americans today compares with their views five years ago. Ask: What and how have you learned about various Native American peoples? How has that information changed your views?

32

Answer to Caption

Possible Answer: to allow them to strike at large, powerful animals from a distance

Section 1
pp. 32–37

Bell Ringer

Write the word *culture* on the chalkboard. Ask students to list words or phrases that they associate with modern American culture.

Lesson Plan

1. Focus In this section, students learn what archaeologists have discovered about the origins and cultures of the first Americans— in particular, those of the Mound Builders of the central and eastern United States and those of the farming societies of the Southwest.

2. Instruct On the chalkboard, record students' responses to the Bell Ringer activity under such headings as Food, Religion, Housing, Clothing, Customs, and so on. Then have students make their own charts to record information about the Native American cultures studied in this section.

3. Close To close the lesson, have students work as a class to identify the distinguishing characteristics of each culture.

1
Uncovering the American Past

FIND OUT
- How did people first reach the Americas?
- How do archaeologists learn about the past?
- Who were the Mound Builders?
- How did early peoples in the Southwest adapt to the desert?

VOCABULARY glacier, artifact, archaeology, culture, adobe, pueblo, drought

Crouched low, the small band of hunters crept slowly forward. Ahead, a herd of bison grazed at the edge of a swamp. At a signal, the hunters leaped up, shouting loudly. The startled herd stampeded into the swamp. As the bison struggled in the deep mud, the hunters hurled their spears, bringing down many beasts.

Scenes much like this one took place on the Great Plains more than 10,000 years ago. Skillful hunters were among the first people to settle the Americas. Over many thousands of years, their descendants spread out across two continents. In the process, they developed many different ways of life.

Woolly Mammoth Skeleton *Some 12,000 years ago, hunters of the Clovis culture stalked mammoth across what is now the southwestern United States. Archaeologists have found many Clovis spearheads mixed in with mammoth bones in Arizona.* **Science and Technology** *Why would it be important for early hunters to develop spears and arrows?*

32 • Chapter 2

The First Americans

Like other early peoples, the first Americans left no written records to tell us where they came from or exactly when they arrived in the Western Hemisphere. However, scientists have found evidence that suggests the first people reached the Americas sometime during the last ice age.

The land bridge. Between 100,000 and 10,000 years ago, thick sheets of ice, called **glaciers,** often covered much of the Earth. Because glaciers locked up water from the oceans, sea levels fell. As a result, land appeared that had once been covered by water. In the far north, a land bridge, now known as **Beringia,** joined Siberia in northeastern Asia to Alaska in North America. Today, this land is under the Bering Strait.

Scientists think that the first Americans were probably hunters. Traveling in small bands, they followed herds of woolly mam-

---

Thinking Critically
Comparing Information

Have students review the route of the Apaches described on page 31. Tell them to trace this route on the map of the Western Hemisphere on page 33. Ask students to compare this mythical route with what modern historians believe was the route followed by the first Americans.

Connections With Science
Background

The Asian origins of Native Americans was first suggested about 400 years ago by Father José de Acosta, a Jesuit scholar. He believed that the first Americans were Asians who had been stranded "by shipwracke and tempest of wether."

moth, bison, and other game across Beringia from Asia into North America. Some groups may have wandered along the southern coast of Beringia, catching fish and sea mammals.

Experts date the arrival of these first Americans anywhere from 30,000 to 15,000 years ago. Once they reached the Americas, the constant search for better hunting grounds led the newcomers across the land. Over thousands of years, they spread out through North America, Central America, and South America.

Global warming. About 12,000 years ago, temperatures rose around the globe. Glaciers melted, and water once more covered Beringia. At the same time, the woolly mammoths and mastodons died out.

The peoples of the Americas adapted to the new conditions. They hunted smaller game, gathered berries and grains, and caught fish.

Then, about 5,000 years ago, some people learned to grow crops such as corn, beans, and squash. Farming changed those people's lives. People who farmed no longer had to move constantly to find food. They built the first permanent villages in the Americas. As farming methods improved, villagers produced more food that, in turn, allowed populations to grow.

The Study of Early Peoples

Today, experts in many fields are working to develop a clearer picture of the first Americans. Some are studying the remains of ancient peoples of northeast Asia. They hope to learn how these Asian peoples might be related to the first Americans.

Other experts are analyzing the languages of Native Americans living today. *Native Americans* are descendants of the first people to reach the Americas thousands of years ago. Through the study of languages, scholars are trying to trace how these peoples spread out across the Americas.

MAP STUDY

The first Americans crossed into Alaska from Asia anywhere from 70,000 to 15,000 years ago. Over thousands of years, these hunters and their descendants populated two huge continents, North America and South America.

1. *About how many miles did glaciers stretch from north to south?*
2. *In which direction did early hunters travel to reach North America?*
3. **Drawing Conclusions** *Why do you think many of the first Americans continued to travel southward after crossing the land bridge?*

Hunters Reach the Americas

☐ Glaciers　▨ Land bridge　← Migration routes

0　1000　2000 Miles
0　1000　2000 Kilometers

 Lesson Planner

For a developed **Cooperative Learning** lesson plan, see the *Lesson Planner,* page 7.

Answers to Map Study

1. about 2,500 miles 2. east and south 3. Possible Answers: They followed the paths of animals; they sought better climates.

 Historical Outline Map Book

Historical Outline Map Duplicate and distribute the map, Hunters Reach America, on page 1 of the *American History Historical Outline Map Book.* Lesson ideas for this map can be found on page T1. (Reteaching/Average)

 Videotapes/ Videodiscs

United States History Video Collection Use the video segment "The First Americans" from Volume 1, *Three Worlds Meet,* to enhance students' understanding of Native Americans. Approx. running time 5:00 min. (Enrichment/Average) Vol. 1, Ch. 7

Chapter 7

Play

Linking Past and Present
Activity

Global warming dramatically affected history 12,000 years ago. Ask: What effects did this phenomenon have on landmasses, certain mammals, and the movement of people?

The possibility of renewed global warming is an issue of great concern today. Have students discuss what they have learned about this issue in science class or from other sources. Ask: Why are some people concerned about global warming? What factors are said to contribute to global warming? What do some scientists believe will happen to the environment if global warming takes place? What preventive measures are being suggested?

Still other scholars are examining stone tools, weapons, baskets, and carvings found throughout the Americas. These objects made by humans are called **artifacts** (AHRT uh faktz). They are the building blocks of **archaeology** (ahr kee AHL uh jee), the study of evidence left by early peoples.

Studying the evidence. By studying artifacts, archaeologists can learn much about early people. A finely carved arrowhead suggests that people knew how to make weapons and hunt. Woven plant fibers suggest that they were skilled basket makers.

Each object can provide valuable information. At the same time, each new find raises questions, such as, "When was it made?" and "Who made it?"

In laboratories, experts analyze new finds. By testing the level of carbon in a piece of pottery or bone, they can date it within a few hundred years. They might X-ray a bone to learn more about the animal it came from. They might study kernels of ancient corn through a microscope to discover the climate in which it grew. By piecing together a shattered pot, they can compare it to pots from other areas.

Forming theories about cultures. From artifacts and other evidence, archaeologists form theories about the culture of an ancient people. **Culture** is the entire way of life that a people has developed. It includes the behavior, customs, ideas, beliefs, and skills that a people teaches each new generation. It also includes their homes, clothes, and government.

Often, very little evidence survives about an ancient people. Still, each new find or new method of studying ancient artifacts helps to fill in the story of early Americans.

Protecting Native American burial grounds. In their search for evidence about the past, archaeologists often need to dig up ancient sites. In recent years, however, they have grown more aware of the need to respect Native American landmarks and traditions. Government officials, too, have become more respectful of Native American concerns. Some laws have been passed to protect Native American burial grounds.

The Mound Builders

Archaeologists have found a wealth of artifacts in thousands of earthen mounds in North America. The mounds are scattered across a region stretching from the Appalachian Mountains to the Mississippi Valley and from Wisconsin to Florida. Scholars call the peoples who built these earthworks *Mound Builders.* The Mound Builders belonged to various groups who lived from about 3,000 years ago until the 1700s. Among them were the Hopewell and Mississippian peoples.

Purpose of the mounds. The first mounds were burial grounds, probably for important leaders. Inside the mounds, archaeologists have found carved pipes and stone sculptures as well as copper weapons, tools, and ornaments. They have also found shells from the Gulf of Mexico and turquoise from the Southwest. This evidence shows that the Mound Builders traded with peoples from other parts of North America.

Some mounds were used for religious ceremonies. They are shaped like pyramids with flat tops. On the flat surfaces, the people built temples and homes for the ruling class.

More than 2,000 years ago, Hopewell builders created the twisting Great Serpent Mound. From above, it looks like a snake with a coiled tail. The meaning of this and other animal-shaped mounds remains a mystery.

A sprawling city. Some time between 700 and 1500, the Mississippians built a large city at Cahokia (kah HOH kee ah), in present-day Illinois. As many as 30,000 people may have lived there. Over the years, the people of Cahokia moved tons of soil, basket load by basket load, to build Monk's Mound. This vast platform mound covers

Team-Teaching Suggestion
Art

You might work with an art teacher to present a lesson about prehistoric art, such as the Lascaux cave paintings. Ask students to compare and contrast this art with the oral tradition in history. Have each student create a "cave painting" on paper that conveys information about one aspect of a culture discussed in this section.

Team-Teaching Suggestion
Science

You might work with a science teacher to present a lesson about Thomas Jefferson's accomplishments in the field of archaeology. Although Jefferson is best known as one of the founders of the American nation, scientists also consider him the founder of American archaeology because of his excavations and findings.

Burial Mounds *The Mound Builders left behind thousands of mounds. The Great Serpent Mound of Ohio, at right, twists across the land for more than 1,200 feet. The painting above shows workers excavating a much smaller, but higher, Mississippian burial mound.* **Linking Past and Present** *Why do you think archaeologists are eager to examine early burial mounds?*

Answer to Caption
Possible Answer: to learn more about the technology, daily life, or religious practices of early Americans

Chapter Resources

Geography in History Duplicate and distribute the worksheet, Adapting to a Dry Climate, from Unit 1, pages 17–18, of the *Chapter Resources* binder. This worksheet focuses on the Anasazis and their desert environment. (Enrichment/Average)

about 16 acres—equal to 14½ football fields! Hundreds of other smaller mounds stand nearby.

The Mississippians built a wooden fence around Cahokia. Beyond it, they placed circles of evenly spaced posts. Some archaeologists think the posts served as a kind of calendar. From the top of Monk's Mound, rulers could see the shadows cast by the posts. Shorter shadows announced the coming of spring. Longer ones showed that autumn was near. To farming people like the Mississippians, knowing when to plant and when to harvest crops was important.

Early Cultures of the Southwest

Through careful study, archaeologists have also learned much about early peoples of the American Southwest. This desert region may seem like a poor place to farm. Annual rainfall is only 5 to 10 inches (13 to 25 cm). Daytime temperatures can soar above 100° Fahrenheit (38°C). Cactus and sagebrush cover the desert floor. Still, at

least 3,000 years ago, people in the Southwest learned to grow crops such as corn. In time, several major farming societies, including the ***Hohokams*** (hoh HOH kahmz) and ***Anasazis*** (ah nuh SAH zeez), made their homes there.

The Hohokams lived in present-day southern Arizona. About 2,000 years ago, they developed ways to turn the desert into farmland. They dug a vast system of irrigation ditches. The ditches channeled water from the Salt and Gila rivers into fields that produced corn, squash, and beans.

In the late 1800s, archaeologists began to study thousands of abandoned stone buildings that dotted the Southwest. Most were built between 750 and 1300.

Who built these structures? When archaeologists asked the Navajos, the Native Americans who live in the region today, they replied, the Anasazis. In the Navajo language, Anasazi means "ancient one."

Anasazi pueblos. Like the Hohokams, the Anasazis farmed the desert by using irrigation. The Anasazis built large, multistoried

Chapter 2 • **35**

Connections With Civics
Background

From the artifacts found at the Mississippian Burial Mound, historians have concluded that the Mound Builders had a class system that included a ruling class (probably priests); an upper class; a warrior class; farmers, artists, traders; and slaves.

Linking Past and Present
Background

Historians and archaeologists believe that the modern Pima and Papago peoples are descendants of the Hohokams. Both peoples lived on the same land that the Hohokams had called home; both peoples also were farmers. Elements of their language and ceremonies suggest an ancient link with the Aztecs as well.

Chapter Resources

History Through Literature For an insight into another Native American culture of the Southwest, duplicate and distribute the worksheet, The Girl Who Hunted Rabbits, from Unit 1, page 16, of the *Chapter Resources* binder. (Enrichment/Average)

Student Study Guide

Section 1 Study Guide Have students use the Section 1 Study Guide on page 37 of the *Student Study Guide* to review and reinforce the content of this section. (Reteaching/Average)

ACTIVITY

Guided Instruction Before students write their questions, you might want to review the *Who, What, Where, When, Why,* and *How* technique used in journalism. Students might work with partners to formulate possible answers and develop an interview for presentation to the class.

houses. Walls were made of stone and sun-dried bricks, called **adobe.** When the Spanish explored the Southwest in the early 1500s, they called these houses that could shelter hundreds of families **pueblos** (PWEHB lohz), or villages.

At Pueblo Bonito, in New Mexico, a giant house, much like a modern-day apartment complex, was once home to 1,000 people. Its 800 rooms are tiny, but the Anasazis spent much of their time in sunny, outdoor courtyards. The house has no stairways or hallways. To reach rooms on the upper floors, people climbed ladders.

Cliff dwellers. Between 1000 and 1200, some Anasazis sought protection from warlike neighbors. To make their villages harder to attack, they built adobe houses along the faces of cliffs. Toeholds cut into the rock let the Anasazis climb up and down the cliff wall. On top of the cliff, they planted corn and other crops.

A network of roads connected Anasazi villages. Along these roads, traders carried cotton, sandals made from yucca leaves, and blankets woven from turkey feathers. Some Anasazi traders headed into present-day Mexico to trade with people there.

In the late 1200s, the Anasazis abandoned most of their villages. Archaeologists think that a **drought,** or long dry spell, hit the region. One legend recalls such a disaster:

> **66** Snow ceased in the north and the west; rain ceased in the south and the east; the mists of the mountains above were drunk up; the waters of the valleys below were dried up. . . . Our ancients who dwelt in the cliffs fled. . . when the rain stopped long, long ago. **99**

Later, some Anasazis may have returned to their homes. Most, however, became part of other cultures. Today, descendants of these early peoples preserve traditions of the ancient Anasazi culture.

Achievements of the Anasazis *Anasazi craftsworkers made fine objects of shell, bone, turquoise, and clay. These highly decorated mugs were found in the ruins of Pueblo Bonito, below.* **Geography** *Why do you think many early peoples made objects of clay?*

Connections With Science
Background

The ruins of Chaco Canyon are considered the greatest testimony to the skill of Anasazi architects and builders. Even here, though, there are a variety of architectural styles. The older buildings seem to have a unique local style. Some of the more recent buildings, however, suggest a Mexican influence. These features include round towers and colonnades, as well as walls that consist of two layers of stone with rubble sandwiched in between. Evidence even suggests that some Anasazis worshipped Quetzalcoatl, the feathered god of the Aztecs.

1. **Identify:** (a) Beringia, (b) Native Americans, (c) Mound Builders, (d) Hohokams, (e) Anasazis.
2. **Define:** (a) glacier, (b) artifact, (c) archaeology, (d) culture, (e) adobe, (f) pueblo, (g) drought.
3. Describe three kinds of evidence that archaeologists study.
4. What have archaeologists learned about the Mound Builders?
5. How did the Hohokams farm the desert?
6. **CRITICAL THINKING Formulating Questions** Suppose that you are an archaeologist studying an Anasazi ruin. What questions might you ask about Anasazi houses?

ACTIVITY Writing to Learn

Imagine that you are a television reporter. Write three questions you would ask the first people who traveled from Asia to the Americas.

2
The Peoples of North America

FIND OUT
- What are 10 major culture areas of North America?
- How did Native Americans adapt to different environments?
- How were religious beliefs important to people's daily lives?

VOCABULARY culture area, igloo, kayak, potlatch, kiva, hogan, tepee, travois, long house, sachem

---

When Christopher Columbus reached the Americas in 1492, he thought he had reached the East Indies. He called the peo-ple he met "los Indios," or Indians. Soon, all Europeans were calling the people of the Americas Indians. By the time they realized Columbus's error, they were used to the term.

The name Indian is misleading for another reason, too. Native Americans do not belong to a single group. In Columbus's time, as now, Native Americans included many different peoples with many distinct cultures. In North America alone, Native Americans spoke hundreds of languages. Their cultures also varied in other ways.

Culture Areas and Tribes

The map on page 42 shows 10 major culture areas of North America, north of Mexico. A **culture area** is a region in which people share a similar way of life.

Within each culture area, there were many different tribes. A tribe was a group of villages or settlements that shared common customs, language, and rituals. Members of a tribe saw themselves as a distinct people who shared the same origin. Throughout their history, tribal organizations have played an important role in Indian life.

Tribe members felt a strong bond with the land, plants, and animals in the region where they lived. As they hunted animals or raised crops or gathered wild plants for food, members of the tribe tried to maintain a balance with the forces of the natural world. Their religious ceremonies and daily customs were designed to help them maintain that balance.

Peoples of the North

Two culture areas, the Arctic and Sub-arctic, stretched across the northern part of North America. In both regions, people adapted to harsh climates. In the Arctic, winter temperatures drop to –30° Fahrenheit (–34° C). Snow stays on the ground much of the year.

Section 2
pp. 37–47

Bell Ringer

Using the map on page 42, have students choose one Native American culture area and freewrite for three minutes about what they might expect to find in that culture (for example, housing needs based on climate).

Lesson Plan

1. **Focus** Millions of people were already living in North America when Columbus arrived in 1492. These first Americans had learned to adapt to a variety of environments. This section introduces students to the cultures of various Native American groups.
2. **Instruct** Ask students to imagine that they are traveling across North America in 1491. As you progress through the lesson, have each student keep a journal record of the Native American groups that they meet. Encourage students to use a firsthand narrative style.
3. **Close** To close the lesson, have students play a Jeopardy!-like game. Choose several students to give information relating to various Native American groups. Call on volunteers to create corresponding questions.

Lesson Planner

For a developed **Cooperative Learning** lesson plan, see the Lesson Planner, page 8.

Answers to Section 1 Review

1. (a) Beringia, p. 32, (b) Native Americans, p. 33, (c) Mound Builders, p. 34, (d) Hohokams, p. 35, (e) Anasazis, p. 35
2. (a) glacier, p. 32, (b) artifact, p. 34, (c) archaeology, p. 34, (d) culture, p. 34, (e) adobe, p. 36, (f) pueblo, p. 36, (g) drought, p. 36
3. Evidence includes artifacts—such as weapons, tools, and carvings—which tell about a people's way of life; bones, which tell of a people's physical makeup and diet; examples of food, such as corn, that tell of an ancient people's diet and the climate of the time.
4. Archaeologists have learned that some mounds were built as burial grounds for important leaders and that others were used for religious ceremonies. Artifacts indicate that the Mound Builders traded with people from other parts of North America.
5. The Hohokams dug irrigation ditches to bring water from the Salt and Gila rivers to their fields.
6. Possible Answers: Why did the houses lack stairways and hallways? Why did the Anasazis build houses in the faces of cliffs? How were the houses built? Did each room have a specific purpose?

Arctic. Frozen seas and icy, treeless plains made up the world of the ***Inuits,*** the people of the Arctic.* The Inuits used all the limited resources of their environment. In summer, they collected driftwood from the ocean shores to make tools and shelters. In winter, they built **igloos,** or houses of snow and ice.

Because food was scarce, the Inuits could not live in the same place all year round. In winter, large bands set up camp at a favorite spot near the sea. There on the thick sea ice, they hunted for seals. In spring, they paddled **kayaks** (KĪ aks), or small skin boats, to spear seal, whale, and walrus. When summer came, they moved inland in smaller bands to hunt caribou or to fish on inland rivers and lakes.

Inuit religious beliefs reflected their close ties to the natural world. Inuits believed that each animal had a spirit. Before the hunt, they offered gifts to the animal they hoped to catch. After a successful hunt, they sang songs of praise and thanks to the animals.

Subarctic. Like their northern neighbors, the peoples of the Subarctic faced a severe environment. They, too, moved from place to place, hunting moose and caribou or fishing in rivers and oceans. They fashioned caribou and rabbit skins into robes and leggings. When Europeans arrived, many Subarctic peoples supplied furs to traders.

Peoples of the Northwest Coast

The peoples of the Northwest Coast enjoyed a favorable climate and abundant food supplies. They gathered rich harvests of fish from the sea. In autumn, the rivers were full of salmon. To show their gratitude, the people returned salmon skeletons to the water. They believed that the Salmon Beings would grow new bodies and continue to provide food.

The fishers of one Northwest Coast group, the Kwakiutls (kwah kee OOT 'lz), chanted this prayer when they caught their first fish of the year:

> 66 We have come to meet alive,
>   Swimmer,
>   do not feel wrong about what I
>   have done to you,
>   friend Swimmer,
>   for that is the reason why you
>   came,
>   that I may spear you,
>   that I may eat you,
>   Supernatural One, you, Long-
>   Life-Giver, you Swimmer.
>   Now protect us, me and my
>   wife. 99

---

*Inuit, meaning "humans," was the Arctic people's name for themselves. Neighboring people, the Crees, called the Inuits "Eskimos" or "Eaters of Raw Meat."

Basket From the Subarctic *Subarctic hunters moved across the land in search of food and furs. The decorations on this basket show some of the animals they hunted.* **The Arts** *Why do you think that animals such as bear and caribou were a popular subject of Subarctic craftsworkers?*

Mask of a Storyteller *The Kwakiutl people of the Northwest Coast used colorful masks in storytelling ceremonies. This bird's-head mask has a hinged beak. At the climax of the ceremony, the storyteller would throw open the beak to reveal the fiercely decorated human face underneath.* **Geography** *How did favorable geography allow people of the Northwest Coast to develop elaborate arts and ceremonies?*

The Northwest Coast peoples also benefited from the nearby forests. They cut down majestic cedar trees and floated the timber by water to their villages. There, they split the tree trunks into planks for houses and canoes. From the soft inner bark, they made rope, baskets, and clothes. The forests also were home to deer, moose, and bear that the people hunted for meat and hides.

With plenty of food, the peoples of the Pacific Northwest could stay in one place. They built permanent villages and prospered from trade with nearby groups.

Within a village, families gained status according to how much they owned. Families sometimes competed for rank. To improve their standing, they held a **potlatch,** or ceremonial dinner, to show off their wealth. The family invited many guests and gave everyone presents. The more the family gave away, the more it was respected. At one potlatch, which took years for the family to prepare, gifts included 8 canoes, 54 elk skins, 2,000 silver bracelets, 7,000 brass bracelets, and 33,000 blankets!

Other Peoples of the West

Climates and resources varied in other parts of the West. As people adapted to these environments, they developed very different cultures.

Great Basin. The Great Basin lies in the dry Intermountain region of the United States. With little water, few plants or animals survived. As a result, Great Basin peoples like the Utes (YOOTZ) and Shoshones (shoh SHOH neez) had to spend most of their time looking for food. They hunted rabbits or dug for roots in the desert soil.

Chapter 2 • **39**

Connections With Fine Arts
Background

Northwest Coast peoples are renowned for their magnificent totem poles. Historians have debated whether the people of the Northwest Coast developed the totem pole before or after they had contact with Europeans— for example, many claim that poles were carved with metal tools, which Native Americans probably obtained from Europeans. Point out that some poles that were made in the 1800s and early 1900s are still standing today.

Learning Styles
Kinesthetic Learners

Divide the class into several teams. Assign each team a different group of Native Americans without letting the other teams know which group is which. Each team should then act out one of that group's activities as described in the text. They may use pantomime or include dialogue. For example, the team representing the Kwakiutl people may act out a potlatch; the team representing the Inuits could mime building an igloo. Have the other teams try to determine each team's Native American group and activity. Conclude with a discussion of how various activities show the interaction of the Native Americans with their environment.

Voices of Freedom

Primary Source You might assign selection 2-1, An Arapaho Legend, on pages 16–17 of *Voices of Freedom.* This tale of the first buffalo hunt explains the animal's importance to this people. To reinforce this concept, you might also assign selection 2-3, Keeping a Heritage Alive, on pages 18–19. (Enrichment/Challenging)

Customized Reader

Primary Source For a captivating view of the creation stories of the Yumas, one of the California coastal peoples, order article IA-6, The Good Twin and the Evil Twin, from the *American History Customized Reader.* (Enrichment/Average)

Transparencies

Fine Art Use the transparency Celestial Germinators on page D-25 of *American History Transparencies.* This contemporary painting by Dan V. Lomahaftewa is based on one style of ancient Native American art. Teaching suggestions can be found on page D-3. (Enrichment/Easy)

Because the land offered so little, only a few related families traveled together in search of food. They had few possessions beyond digging sticks, baskets, and other tools or weapons needed to hunt. When they camped, they built shelters out of willow poles and reeds.

Plateau. The peoples of the Plateau lived between the Rocky Mountains to the east and the Cascades to the west. Their main source of food was fish from rivers like the Columbia and Fraser or from smaller streams. They also hunted and gathered roots, nuts, and berries. In winter, they lived in earth houses that were partly underground. In summer, they set up lodges, placing rush mats over cottonwood frames.

Some groups traded with the Northwest Coast peoples and were influenced by their way of life. Others, like the Nez Percés (NEHZ PER sihz), adopted customs from the peoples of the Great Plains.

California. Differences in climate and resources helped create diverse cultures in California. Coastal peoples fished in the ocean and rivers. In the northern valleys, other groups hunted deer, rabbits, and elk or collected berries and nuts. In the southeast desert, however, small bands lived much like the peoples of the Great Basin.

For many Californians, like the Pomos, acorns were the basic food. Women harvested the nuts in autumn and later pounded them into flour. Both women and men among the Pomos were skilled at weaving baskets, which they decorated with fine designs.

Peoples of the Southwest

The ***Pueblos,*** the Spanish name for peoples of the Southwest, were descended from the Anasazis. They included groups like the Hopis, Acomas, Zuñis, and Lagunas. By 1500, only the Hopis still farmed on clifftops as the Anasazis had done. Other groups lived in villages along the Rio Grande and its tributaries.

Farming, religion, and family life. Like their ancestors, the Pueblos built adobe houses and grew corn, beans, and squash. Their religious beliefs reflected the importance of farming. Most Pueblo villages had a **kiva,** or underground chamber where men held religious ceremonies. Through prayers and other rituals, they tried to please the spirits of nature, such as wind, rain, and thunder.

At planting or harvest time, the Hopis and Zuñis held other ceremonies. In the villages, cries rang out: "The kachinas are coming! The kachinas are coming!" The ***kachinas*** were masked dancers who represented the spirits. The Pueblos believed that the kachina ceremonies would ensure rainfall and good crops.

The Pueblos traced their family lines through the mother. This custom gave women special importance. When a man married, he went to live with his wife's family. Also, Pueblo wives owned most of the family property.

Hunters arrive. About 1500, two new groups reached the Southwest: the Apaches and the Navajos. Both groups lived as hunters but often raided Pueblo fields for food.

In time, the Navajos accepted many Pueblo ways. They began to farm and to build **hogans,** or houses made of mud plaster over a framework of wooden poles. The Apaches, however, continued to follow herds of buffalo and the other game they hunted. They traded dried buffalo meat and animal skins to the Pueblos for corn and cloth.

Peoples of the Great Plains

Centuries ago, vast grasslands extended across the Great Plains from the Rocky Mountains to the Mississippi River. As artist George Catlin observed in the early 1800s, "The meadows roll on for as far as the eye can see and thought can travel."

40 • Chapter 2

Our Multicultural Heritage
Activity

Invite students to research and read some of the folk tales or myths of a Native American group. Creation myths and myths about the stars offer many possibilities, as do the stories that feature Coyote, the trickster. Have each student prepare a brief report summarizing the tale or myth and explaining what it shows about the culture and environment of that group. For example, does the story express a respect for honesty or cleverness? What elements of nature are mentioned? What, if anything, does the story suggest about the people's belief in one or more gods? Ask students to compare and contrast these stories with myths and tales from their own heritage.

40

ART GALLERY: OUR COMMON HERITAGE

● **RAYMOND NAHA** *Mixed Kachina Dance, 1964* ●

Each June, the Hopi people of the Southwest gathered for the dance of the kachinas. The kachinas, masked dancers representing the spirits, performed the ancient ritual. If the dance was pleasing, the spirits would return as rain for the next season's crops. Raymond Naha, a modern Hopi painter, recreated this part of his Hopi heritage in his painting.
Linking Past and Present *How does Naha's painting help to preserve Hopi culture?*

Because there were few trees, Plains people built their homes of sod, or chunks of thickly matted grass. They also used buffalo hides to make cone-shaped tents called **tepees.**

Some Plains people farmed along riverbanks. In spring, women broke up the soft ground using hoes made from animal bones. They then planted corn, beans, squash, and sunflowers.

Chapter 2 • **41**

Audiocassettes

Listening to Literature Audiocassettes To introduce students to Native American poetry, play Navajo Night Chant (side 1, 0:40) and the Pima song from the Houses of Magic (side 1, 2:49) from *Listening to Literature Audiocassettes, The American Experience.* (Enrichment/Average)

Art Gallery Posters

Mixed Kachina Dance, by Raymond Naha, appears in poster form in the *Art Gallery: Our Common Heritage Posters.* Lesson Suggestions for the poster are available in the Teacher's Guide.

Answer to Art Gallery: Our Common Heritage

Possible Answer: He has made a permanent record of an important aspect of Hopi religious life.

Customized Reader

Primary Source For an explanation of the existence of Devil's Tower, order article IA-5, The Legend of Devil's Tower, from the *American History Customized Reader.* This exciting tale of two boys who encounter and outwit a bear is told by Lakota (Sioux) medicine man Lame Deer. (Enrichment/Easy)

Our Multicultural Heritage
Background

The Hopis believe that the kachinas were supernatural beings who lived among the first Hopis and taught them how to live in their new world. By making kachina dolls, the Hopis symbolize their belief in the gods (more than 250 of them) and share their beliefs with their children. The kachinas, then, are symbols of their faith and heritage.

The characters in a kachina dance might represent animals, forces of nature, or even clowns. One of the most popular kachina characters, in fact, is the Mudhead, a clown who amuses the crowds who gather for ceremonies by imitating visitors or other dancers and by staging balancing acts.

Audiocassettes

Listening to Literature Audiocassettes To provide students with a focus on the rhythm, repetition, and emotion found in Native American songs, play the Chippewa Spring Song (side 1, 0:10) and the Teton Sioux Song Concerning a Dream of the Thunderbirds (side 1, 0:34) from *Listening to Literature Audiocassettes, The American Experience.* See the Audiocassette Guide for previewing information and suggested activities. (Enrichment/Average)

Transparencies

Fine Art Use the transparency Native American Handcrafts on page D-27 of *American History Transparencies*. It shows two creations by Native American women—a buffalo-hide bag from the Plains and fur-lined mittens from the Subarctic. Teaching suggestions can be found on page D-4. (Enrichment/Average)

Large herds of animals grazed on the Plains, including buffalo, antelope, elk, deer, and bighorn sheep. Plains people hunted the animals on foot. In winter, men hunted near the village. In summer, however, they often traveled for miles in search of buffalo and other animals.

Each village had a ruling council that included the best hunters. The chief was respected by other council members because he spoke well and judged wisely.

Horses Come to the Plains

Until the 1500s, the peoples of North America had no horses. The only species of horse on the North

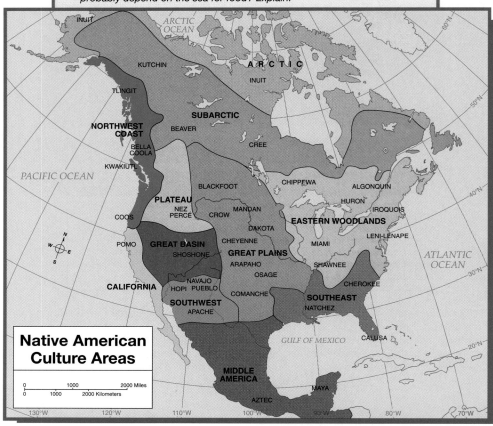

MAP STUDY

Historians estimate that by 1400, as many as 2 million Native Americans lived in North America north of Mexico. Historians group the Native Americans into major culture areas.
1. *Name two groups that lived in the Southeast culture area.*
2. *About how many miles north to south did the Great Plains culture area extend?*
3. **Analyzing Information** *In which culture areas could Native Americans probably depend on the sea for food? Explain.*

Native American Culture Areas

0   1000   2000 Miles
0   1000   2000 Kilometers

Cooperative Learning
Activity

Divide students into 10 groups. Assign each group a Native American society from one of the culture areas discussed in this section. Ask each group to imagine that its members are archaeologists working at an excavation site where artifacts of the Native American society assigned to them have been found. Have students do library research on the Native American culture assigned and then make drawings or clay models of pottery, fabric, tools, weapons, and eating utensils that might have been found at such a site.

Have each group display its "artifacts" for the class. Give class members an opportunity to make educated guesses as to origin, function, and so on. Afterward, have the "archaeologists" explain the part that each artifact played in the given culture.

American continent had died out thousands of years earlier. The Blackfeet, one group of Plains people, tell a story about how horses came to their land.

The Blackfoot story. Shaved Head was leading a band of Blackfeet in search of some Shoshone people. The Shoshones were hunting buffalo in Blackfoot territory. Shaved Head intended to stop them.

Before long, the Blackfeet came upon a Shoshone camp. There, they saw what to them looked like very large dogs. Blackfeet used dogs to haul skin lodges, cooking pots, and other gear on a *travois* (truh VOI), or sled. These "dogs" were different though. They were as tall as men and as broad as elk.

As the Blackfeet watched in awe, a band of Shoshones rode into camp on yet more of these dogs. With great ease, the riders halted the animals and slid off their backs. They removed pads of buffalo skin from the animals' backs and straps from their heads. Then they tied the animals to a post.

Shaved Head and his men decided to take these creatures to their people. Late at night, they slipped into the Shoshone camp, untied four horses, and led them away.

At a safe distance, a few Blackfeet mounted the animals. When the horses began to move, though, the men became frightened and jumped off. It would be easier, they decided, to lead the animals instead.

The Blackfeet long remembered the return of Shaved Head and his band:

❝When the people heard that Shaved Head had brought back a pack of 'big dogs,' they gathered around the strange animals and looked at them in wonder. They put robes on the horses, but when the animals began to jump, they ran. After a time a woman said, 'Let's put a travois on one of them just like we do on our small dogs.' They made a larger travois and attached it to one of the gentler horses. It didn't kick or jump. They led the horse around with the travois attached. Finally, a woman mounted the horse and rode it.❞

A new way of life. The Blackfeet handed down this story for generations. Although the details may not be exact, historians know that horses reached the northern

Warriors on Horseback *The use of horses transformed the way Plains people lived. They became better hunters and so raised fewer crops. Horses also changed the way Plains people waged war. Here, rival warriors on horseback engage in fierce battle on the Plains.* **Science and Technology** *What advantages would horses give to warriors in battle?*

Answer to Caption

Possible Answers: greater speed for escaping, ability to travel farther and to see farther (because the rider has a higher vantage point)

 CD-ROM

Arts and Entertainment Access the Books section on the American Heritage® *History of the United States* CD-ROM to find information about the Native American storytelling tradition. (Enrichment/Average)

Our Multicultural Heritage
Background

The first documentation of Native Americans on horseback comes from northern Mexico in the late 1500s. It is likely that the use of horses spread across the Plains as the result of trading among various groups of people.

Horses quickly became a valued commodity. Some peoples began to use horses as a measure of wealth—the more horses, the greater the prosperity. Some groups even used horses in reference to a specific period in time: Before the coming of the horse, the people lived in the "dog days" (the time when dogs were used to haul gear from one campsite to another).

Plains in the mid-1700s. The Spanish had brought horses to the Southwest 200 years earlier. From there, horses had spread to other areas.

In time, Plains people became skillful riders. Because they could travel farther and faster than before, they raised fewer crops and hunted more. They made larger tepees because horses could pull bigger travois. Slowly, horses transformed the Plains peoples' way of life. ■

Peoples of the Southeast

The Southeast was home to more Native Americans than any other region. A warm climate, fertile soil, and plentiful rain helped Southeast peoples produce good crops.

Most people lived in villages and farmed nearby land. They built houses from saplings, or young trees. They split the trees into strips and wove them to make a frame for walls. Then they plastered the walls with a mixture of clay and dry grass.

Farming and religion. Men and women had clearly defined roles in the community. Men cleared the land and hunted deer and other animals. Women planted, weeded, and harvested the crops. Among rows of corn, they planted beans that climbed up the cornstalks. They also grew squash, pumpkins, and sunflowers.

Most religious ceremonies were linked to farming. The most important, the Green Corn Ceremony, took place in midsummer,

⭐⭐
Our Common Heritage
The peoples of the Southeast played a game called istaboli, an early form of lacrosse. The object of the game was to heave a skin-covered ball into the opposing team's goal. Hitting, kicking, and tackling were permitted. To annoy their opponents, a team would make gobbling sounds like a turkey.

when the corn ripened. It marked the end of the year. Celebrations lasted several days. The highlight, on the last day, was the lighting of the sacred fire followed by a dance around its flames. With this event, the new year began.

Natchez society. One Southeast group, the *Natchez* (NACH ihz), hunted, fished, and farmed along the fertile Gulf Coast. They divided the year into 13 months. Each month was named after a food or animal the Natchez harvested or hunted. Names included Strawberry, Little Corn, Mulberry, Deer, Turkey, and Bear.

Natchez religious beliefs centered on worship of the sun. Priests kept a fire going day and night in a temple atop a great mound. The Natchez believed that fire came from the sun.

The Natchez ruler, the Great Sun, was worshipped as a god. He lived atop a giant pyramid mound. The Great Sun's feet never touched the ground. He either rode in a litter or walked on mats. Below the Great Sun were other members of his family, called Little Suns. Next came Nobles, then Honored People, and finally Stinkards, or commoners, who were the majority of the people.

Marriage laws ensured that membership in each class kept changing. By law, noble men and women had to marry Stinkards. Even the Great Sun chose a Stinkard as a wife. In this way, no one family could hold the position of Great Sun forever. In time, even descendants of a Great Sun became Stinkards.

Peoples of the Eastern Woodlands

Many groups lived in the Eastern Woodlands. In the forests and open lands, they hunted deer, moose, and other game. They also planted crops of corn, squash, and pumpkins.

The House Builders. The most powerful people of this region were the *Iroquois*

Historical Sidelight
Background

Each daybreak, the Great Sun went to the Temple to greet "the rising of his elder brother" (the sun). Little Suns held important positions in the Great Sun's village, or they were chiefs of other villages that owed allegiance to the Great Sun. The Great Sun was considered so important that at his death, his wife and servants were executed so that they might escort him into the afterlife.

Connections With Geography
Background

The Iroquois originally lived in southeastern North America. They migrated north around 1300 and drove out the area's Algonquin residents.

PUEBLO The walls are made of sandstone blocks plastered with adobe.

Kivas are rooms used for religious ceremonies.

Winter cooking room

Roofs are used as a center for work and socializing.

Storage room

Sleeping room

Ladder

Drainspouts and splash blocks keep moisture away from roofs and walls.

TEPEE

Lodge poles

Smoke flaps

Buffalo sinew

Inner lining

Buffalo hide

The entrance almost always faced the rising sun in the east.

Wooden stakes

LONG HOUSE

Storage shelves

The stockade provided protection from enemies.

Each fire was shared by two families on either side of the center aisle.

Sleeping benches

The support posts divided the long house into separate rooms.

Elm bark walls

Native American Dwellings *Native Americans developed a wide variety of dwellings to suit their different environments. Shown here are a pueblo from the Southwest, a tepee from the Great Plains, and a long house from the Eastern Woodlands.* **Geography** *How does each type of dwelling reflect the local environment?*

Chapter 2 • **45**

Answer to Exploring Technology

Possible Answer: Each type of dwelling makes use of local materials.

 Our Multicultural Heritage

Biography Have students read the biography, Dekanawida, Iroquois Lawgiver, on page 4 of the *Our Multicultural Heritage* booklet. (Enrichment/Average)

Milestone Have students read The Iroquois False Face Society: A Healing League, on page 6 of the *Our Multicultural Heritage* booklet. (Enrichment/Easy)

 Transparencies

Exploring Technology Use the transparency Native American Dwellings on page H-23 of *American History Transparencies*. Teaching suggestions can be found on page H-2. (Enrichment/Average)

CD-ROM

Virtual Buildings Access the Iroquois Longhouse on the American Heritage® *History of the United States* CD-ROM. (Enrichment/Average)

Connections With Architecture
Background

The cone shape of a tepee is practical—on a tepee there are no corners to catch the wind and no pockets to hold rainwater. The shape is not a symmetrical cone, however, for each tepee is tilted toward the entrance. The floor of a tepee, then, is egg shaped rather than circular; and the back of the tepee, with its lower ceiling, is a storage or sleeping area.

Most tepees were made and owned by women. Women chose campsites and raised or dismantled the tepees. They also arranged the furnishings—which they often had made, as well. The women in some Native American groups banded together to form guilds and even competed to display their homemaking skills.

Voices of Freedom

Primary Source You might assign selection 2-4, Founding of the League of the Iroquois, on pages 19–20 of *Voices of Freedom*. This selection relates Hiawatha's decision to organize the union of the five nations. (Enrichment/Average)

Chapter Resources

Critical Thinking Duplicate and distribute the worksheet, Comparing Information on a Chart, from Unit 1, page 15, of the *Chapter Resources* binder. The worksheets will allow students to learn more about the Iroquois, Inuits, and Pueblos. (Enrichment/Easy)

Student Study Guide

Section 2 Study Guide Have students use the Section 2 Study Guide on page 38 of the *Student Study Guide* to review and reinforce the content of this section. (Reteaching/Average)

ACTIVITY

Guided Instruction Have students prepare an outline before writing their speeches. Explain that the introduction should contain the topic sentence, the body should contain the supporting arguments, and the conclusion should restate the main idea.

(IHR uh kwoi). They lived in present-day New York State.

The Iroquois called themselves House Builders. They built **long houses** out of poles sided with bark. A typical long house was about 150 feet (46 m) long and 20 feet (7 m) wide. A hallway, with small rooms on either side, ran the length of the long house. Each room was home to one family. Families living across from each other shared a fireplace in the hallway.

Women had a special place among the Iroquois. They owned all the property in the long house. Also, they were in charge of planting and harvesting crops. Like a Pueblo man, an Iroquois man moved in with his wife's family when he married. Iroquois women also held political power because they chose the **sachems,** as the tribal chiefs were called.

Peace among nations. The Iroquois included five nations: the Mohawk, Seneca (SEHN ih kuh), Onondaga (ahn uhn DAW guh), Oneida (oh NĪ duh), and Cayuga (kay YOO guh). Each nation had its own ruling council.

The five nations fought constantly. According to legend, about 1570, a religious leader named Dekanawida (deh kan ah WEE dah) called for an end to the warfare. He inspired Hiawatha, a Mohawk, to organize a

The Hiawatha Belt *This beaded belt commemorates the founding of the Iroquois League. The four squares linked to the central tree stand for unity among the Iroquois nations.* **Citizenship** *Why was the Iroquois League set up?*

---

union of the five nations. The alliance was known as the ***League of the Iroquois.*** Later, a sixth nation, the Tuscarora (tuhs kuh ROR uh) joined the League.

According to legend, the founders of the League of the Iroquois made this promise:

> 66We bind ourselves together by taking hold of each other's hands. . . .Our strength shall be in union, our way the way of reason, righteousness, and peace. . . . Be of strong mind, O chiefs. Carry no anger and hold no grudges.99

A council of 50 members, chosen by women, made decisions for the League. Each nation had one vote. The council could take action only if all nations agreed.

SECTION 2 REVIEW

1. **Identify:** (a) Inuits, (b) Pueblos, (c) kachina, (d) Natchez, (e) Iroquois, (f) League of the Iroquois.
2. **Define:** (a) culture area, (b) igloo, (c) kayak, (d) potlatch, (e) kiva, (f) hogan, (g) tepee, (h) travois, (i) long house, (j) sachem.
3. List 10 major Native American culture areas of North America.
4. Give two examples of how climate and resources affected the kinds of houses Native Americans built.
5. How were farming and religion closely linked among Native American peoples like the Pueblos?
6. **CRITICAL THINKING Evaluating Information** Why do you think many peoples of the Plains developed stories about the arrival of horses?

ACTIVITY **Writing to Learn**

Imagine you are Hiawatha. Write a speech to convince the ruling councils of the five nations to join the League of the Iroquois.

Answers to Section 2 Review

1. (a) Inuits, p. 38, (b) Pueblos, p. 40, (c) kachina, p. 40, (d) Natchez, p. 44, (e) Iroquois, p. 44, (f) League of the Iroquois, p. 46

2. (a) culture area, p. 37, (b) igloo, p. 38, (c) kayak, p. 38 (d) potlatch, p. 39, (e) kiva, p. 40, (f) hogan, p. 40, (g) tepee, p. 41, (h) travois, p. 43, (i) long house, p. 46, (j) sachem, p. 46

3. Arctic, Subarctic, Northwest Coast, Great Basin, Plateau, California, Southwest, Great Plains, Southeast, Eastern Woodlands

4. Possible Answer: The Inuits of the Arctic built igloos, or houses of snow and ice. The

Pueblos of the Southwest built adobe houses from sun-baked clay bricks.

5. Through prayers and other rituals, the people tried to please the spirits of nature. At planting or harvest time, they held ceremonies to ensure rainfall and good crops.

6. Possible Answer: At first, horses were strange and fascinating. They later assumed great importance, revolutionizing the lives of the Plains peoples.

CONNECTIONS

How the Iroquois Governed Themselves

Among the Iroquois, the basic unit of society was the "fireside," or family, made up of a woman and all her children. A group of two or more families was known as a clan. Everyone in a clan considered the others in the clan to be relatives. Several clans lived together in a village.

The eldest women from each family chose the man who would serve as leader of the clan. Together, the clan leaders governed the village. If a clan leader did not do his job well, the women could remove him from the position. After the League of the Iroquois was formed in the late 1500s (see page 46), the women also named the 50 sachems, or peace chiefs, who made up the ruling council of the League.

The League council usually met each summer at the main village of the Onondagas. People spoke one at a time. No one was permitted to interrupt or shout, because the purpose of speaking was to persuade, not to argue. Every decision had to be agreed to by all.

The Iroquois thought of the League as an "extended lodge"—the long house of the family and clan extended to include all League members. In this way, the close family feelings shared by clan members came to include all the peoples of the six nations.

Decorative comb

■ What role did women play in the League of the Iroquois?

Staff used by Iroquois sachem

 ACTIVITY Plan a student government for your school. Make a chart showing how your government is to be organized.

Women collecting sap to make maple sugar

Interdisciplinary CONNECTIONS

For worksheets establishing connections between the Chapter 2 main idea, Native American cultures, and five other disciplines, see the *Interdisciplinary Connections* booklet. (Enrichment)

■ **Arts** Painting With Sand, page 8 (Easy)

■ **Sciences** Native American Medicine, page 9 (Average)

■ **Geography** Cayuga Country, page 10 (Challenging)

■ **World** Comparing Cultures, page 11 (Average)

■ **Economics** A Word About Wampum, page 12 (Average)

Answer to Connections

Women defined each family and chose the clan leaders; they also chose the ruling council.

ACTIVITY

Guided Instruction Have students work in groups. Members can brainstorm for official titles, roles within the political structure, and interrelationships. Some members can use artistic skills to design the chart. Prepare a display of the completed projects.

Transparencies

Interdisciplinary Connections Use the transparency How a Bill Becomes a Law on page B-35 of *American History Transparencies* to compare the Iroquois system of government with ours. Teaching suggestions can be found on page B-4. (Enrichment/Challenging)

Team-Teaching Suggestion
Science

You might work with a science teacher to present a lesson about the agricultural practices of the Iroquois and what Europeans learned from them. Discuss crops indigenous to the region, effects of climate and terrain on crop development, and the impact that this knowledge had on the survival of early colonies.

Team-Teaching Suggestion
Mathematics

You might work with a mathematics teacher to present a lesson about demographics. Include graphs comparing nations that comprised the League of the Iroquois in terms of population, the extent of land owned, and political influence in the council (equal).

Bell Ringer

Have students brainstorm and then discuss a variety of responses that would complete this statement: "When I call a place *civilized,* I mean that _____."

Lesson Plan

1. Focus Several great civilizations flourished in Central and South America. The Mayas, Aztecs, and Incas are the three most impressive examples. In this section, students read about the histories and cultures of these Native Americans.

2. Instruct Tell students that the Mayas, Aztecs, and Incas solved problems in ways considered advanced for their time. Divide the class into five groups. Assign each group one of the following problems:
(a) The Mayas settled in swampy land that bred mosquitoes and disease. (b) The Aztec capital was often in danger of attack. (c) The Incas needed a way to send messages to all parts of their empire. (d) Earthquakes posed a threat to Incan temples. (e) Incan farmers lived on steep slopes where rain could wash the land and crops away.

Have each group discuss the problem and ways it might be solved. Then lead a class discussion on how each problem actually was solved. Ask: What do the solutions tell us about these peoples?

3

Early Civilizations of the Americas

FIND OUT

- What region did the Mayas, Aztecs, and Incas influence?

- How did each civilization adapt to its environment?

- What were some major achievements of each civilization?

VOCABULARY civilization, hieroglyphics

Large canoes sped along the Caribbean coast of Mexico. Cutting swiftly through the blue waters, they were an impressive sight.

The canoes belonged to the Mayas, whose great cities flourished more than 1,500 years ago. At the height of Mayan culture, more than 4,000 canoes sailed the sea. Mayan traders carried jade statues, turquoise jewelry, parrot feathers, cocoa beans, and other goods across a wide area.

The Mayas were one of several Native American peoples who built great civilizations in the Americas. A **civilization** is an advanced culture. It usually includes cities, well-organized government, complex religion, social classes, specialized skills and jobs, and some method of keeping records.

The Mayas

Mayan civilization emerged about 3,000 years ago. It grew up in the rain forests of present-day southern Mexico and Guatemala. These rain forests were difficult and dangerous places to live. Poisonous snakes hung from trees. Jaguars prowled the forest floor. Disease-carrying insects infested the swamps.

From earlier peoples, the Mayas learned to grow corn and to build structures of stone. With much work, they cut down the trees and drained the swamps. On the cleared land, they grew corn to feed a growing population.

Large cities. Most Mayas lived in simple homes with mud walls and thatch roofs. Wealthy and powerful Mayas, however, lived in stone palaces in great cities like Tikal and Copán.

Our Multicultural Heritage
Background

Chocolate is made from the bean of the cacao tree, found in regions conquered by the Aztecs. The Aztecs prized chocolate so highly that they used it as a form of currency as well as a food. The drink they made from roasted cocoa beans, water, vanilla, and other herbs and spices was called xocoatl—"bitter water." Europeans later used milk and sugar to create a sweet chocolate drink. (In fact, King Ferdinand of Spain originally threatened the death penalty for anyone who disclosed the secret recipe for cocoa.) Chocolate candy was not created until the mid-1800s, far from Central America.

Mayan cities rose in many parts of Mexico and Central America. Each city controlled the surrounding area and had its own ruler. Although rival cities sometimes fought, they also enjoyed times of peaceful trade. Roads cut through the jungle, linking inland cities to the coast.

Towering above each city were huge stone pyramids. Atop the pyramid stood a temple. There, priests performed elaborate ceremonies to please the Mayan gods.

Because of their special knowledge, priests were at the top of Mayan society. Nobles, government officials, and warriors also enjoyed high rank. A visitor to a Mayan city could easily spot priests and nobles. They wore gold jewelry, fine headdresses, and colorful cotton garments.

Near the bottom of Mayan society were peasant farmers. Lowest of all were slaves, generally prisoners of war.

Mayan achievements. Mayan priests paid careful attention to time and to the pattern of daily events. By studying the heavens, they tried to predict the future. In that way, they could honor the gods who controlled events, including harvests, trade, and hunts.

Concern with time led the Mayas to learn much about astronomy and mathematics. They created an accurate 365-day calendar. They also developed an advanced number system that included the concept of zero.

To record their findings, Mayan priests invented a system of **hieroglyphics,** or writing that uses pictures to represent words and ideas. The Mayas carved their records on stone columns or painted them on paper made from bark.

About 850, the Mayas abandoned their cities, and the forests once more took over

Mayan Wall Painting *The Mayan city of Bonampak was noted for its superb frescoes. A fresco is a painting done in watercolor on wet plaster. This fresco shows the elaborate ceremony and carefully crafted headdresses of a Mayan procession.* **Daily Life** *What do you think the purpose of this procession might have been?*

3. Close To close the lesson, have students write three sentences that compare (a) the cities, (b) the class systems, and (c) the religions of the three great empires of Central and South America.

 Lesson Planner

For a developed **Cooperative Learning** lesson plan, see the *Lesson Planner,* page 9.

Answer to Caption

Possible Answers: part of a religious ceremony; celebration of a victory

Connections With Mathematics
Background

The Mayas were sophisticated mathematicians and astronomers. Their system of arithmetic had a base of 20 rather than a base of 10 (as in the European system). Mayan astronomers used observations of the moon, the sun, and Venus to create a calendar of the time. The Mayan calendar was divided into 19 months—18 months of 20 days each and 1 month of 5 days.

Team-Teaching Suggestion
Art

You might want to work together with an art teacher to present a lesson about hieroglyphics and pictographs. The art teacher might provide the students with calligraphy pens. Have each student write a simple sentence of his or her choice and then create hieroglyphics that might make the meaning of the sentence clear to a person unfamiliar with English.

Historical Outline Map Book

Historical Outline Map Duplicate and distribute the map, Great Empires of the Americas, on page 5 of the *American History Historical Outline Map Book.* Lesson ideas for this map can be found on page T2. (Reteaching/Average)

the land. We are unsure why the cities were left to decay. Perhaps peasants rebelled against their rulers. Maybe farming wore out the soil. Even though the cities declined, the Mayan people survived. Today, more than 2 million people speak Mayan languages.

The Aztecs

To the north of the Mayan cities, the Aztecs built a powerful empire. Until the 1300s, the Aztecs were wanderers, moving from place to place in search of food. Then, according to legend, a god told the Aztecs to look for a sign. Search for an eagle perched on a cactus with a snake in its beak, the god said. On that spot, the Aztecs

should build their capital. The Aztecs found the eagle in swampy Lake Texcoco (tay SKOH koh), in central Mexico.

A great capital. Following the god's instructions, the Aztecs built their capital, ***Tenochtitlán*** (tay noch tee TLAHN), on an island in Lake Texcoco. Engineers built causeways, or roads made of packed earth, to connect the island to the mainland.

Farmers dug canals and filled in parts of the lake to create farmland. With long stakes, they attached reed mats to the swampy lake bottom. Then they piled mud onto the mats and planted gardens. Farmers harvested as many as seven crops a year on these floating gardens.

In the 1400s, the Aztecs expanded their power by conquering neighboring peoples. They adopted many beliefs and ideas from these defeated peoples.

Riches from trade and conquest turned Tenochtitlán into a large, bustling city. City marketplaces offered an abundance of goods. "There are daily more than 60,000 people bartering and selling," wrote a Spanish visitor in the 1500s.

Aztec Education *Pictures in an Aztec book show how the Aztecs taught their children. At left, a father teaches his son how to gather firewood, canoe, and fish. The mother, at right, instructs her daughter in grinding grain and weaving cloth.* **Technology** *What items of Aztec technology are shown here?*

Connections With Economics
Activity

You might discuss with the class how a barter economy works. Ask: What advantages and disadvantages might there be to a barter economy? Divide the students into groups of three or four. Tell each group to assume that they are economists who have been hired to convert the U.S. economy from a monetary to a barter system. Explain that each group should brainstorm and list items frequently purchased, classifying the lists as either Needs or Wants. They should then assign relative values to each item, forming rates of exchange among the various goods. Have each group post its list on a bulletin board; then allow the groups to barter with each other. Remind them to consider the importance of needs and wants. Afterward, have students discuss what they learned about the relative values of various items.

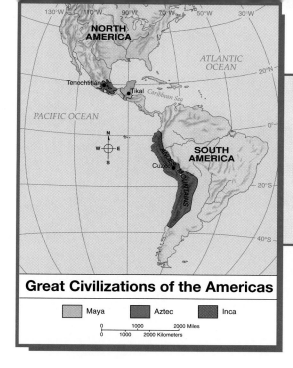

Great Civilizations of the Americas

Maya   Aztec   Inca

0   1000   2000 Miles
0   1000   2000 Kilometers

M A P   S T U D Y

The Mayas, Aztecs, and Incas built great civilizations in the Americas.
1. *Which civilization was farthest north?*
2. *What was the main city of the Mayan civilization?*
3. **Drawing Conclusions** *Why might the Incas have had trouble keeping their empire united?*

Canoes darted up the canals that crisscrossed the city. Soldiers and merchants trudged along the causeways between Tenochtitlán and the mainland. Drawbridges on the roads could be raised in case the city was attacked.

Aztec religion. Religion was central to Aztec life. Young men and women attended special schools where they trained to become priests and priestesses. Like the Mayas, Aztec priests studied the heavens and developed advanced calendars. They

---

Linking Past and Present
During an Aztec wedding ceremony, the priest tied together the clothing of the bride and the groom to symbolize the joining together of their two lives. The practice is still followed in some Mexican villages today.

---

used these calendars to determine when to plant or harvest and to predict future events. The priests divided the year into 18 months, and each month was governed by its own god. Aztec books contained knowledge about the gods as well as special prayers and hymns.

The sun god was especially important. Each day, the Aztecs believed, the sun battled its way across the heavens. They compared the sun's battles to their own, calling themselves "warriors of the sun." To ensure a successful journey across the sky, the sun required human sacrifices. The Aztecs sacrificed tens of thousands of prisoners of war each year to please their gods.

A powerful empire. By 1500, the Aztecs ruled millions of people from the Gulf of Mexico to the Pacific Ocean. The emperor had absolute power and was treated almost like a god. Servants carried him from place to place on a litter. If the emperor did walk,

Chapter 2 • **51**

Historical Sidelight
Background

Human sacrifice was not the only way in which the Aztecs honored their gods. During the course of each year, ceremonies with dances, songs, processions, offerings, and dramas were held. In addition, Aztec priests managed the temple lands and educated children. All these tasks were seen as methods of honoring the gods.

The Aztecs' ceremonial centers included a teocalli (a pyramidlike structure with a temple at its top), dwellings for the priests, and gardens. Many centers also included a playing court, on which athletes challenged each other in a game like basketball, using their knees and hips—but not their hands or feet—to pass a rubber ball through a hoop.

Voices of Freedom

Primary Source You might assign selection 2-5, Farming Methods of the Incas, on page 21 of *Voices of Freedom*. Garcilaso de la Vega describes methods that produced abundant food supplies and the enforcement of codes governing the use of food and clothing. (Enrichment/Average)

Our Multicultural Heritage

Biography Have students read the biography, Topa Inca Yupanqui, Inca Emperor, on page 5 of the *Our Multicultural Heritage* booklet. (Enrichment/Challenging)

Machu Picchu *High in the Andes Mountains lie the ruins of the ancient Incan city of Machu Picchu. The city contained a temple, a fortress, and a vast system of terraced gardens. It was abandoned hundreds of years ago, and the ruins remained undiscovered until 1911.* **Geography** *What problems might the Incas have faced in building Machu Picchu?*

nobles scattered flower petals in his path so that his feet never touched the ground. Ordinary people lowered their eyes when he passed.

Heavy taxes and the demand for human sacrifices fueled revolts among the neighboring peoples conquered by the Aztecs. Powerful Aztec armies, however, put down any uprising, taking even more prisoners to be sacrificed to the gods. One Aztec poet boasted, "Who could conquer Tenochtitlán? Who could shake the foundation of heaven?" As you will read in Chapter 3, enemies of the Aztecs would help bring about their defeat in the 1520s.

The Incas

Far to the south of the Aztecs, the Incas united the largest empire in the Americas. By 1492, the Incan empire stretched for almost 3,000 miles (4,800 km) along the western coast of South America. The Incan capital at Cuzco (KYOOS koh) was high in the Andes Mountains. From there, the Incas ruled more than 10 million people living in coastal deserts, lowland jungles, and high mountains.

Expert farmers. Like the Mayas and Aztecs, the Incas adapted customs and ideas from earlier cultures. Among them were the

52 • Chapter 2

Linking Past and Present
Background

The Incas drew conquered people into their empire. Settlers from older parts of the empire moved into the conquered areas and taught the official language, Quechua, to the new people. Twenty-eight languages of the Quechua family are still spoken by the Native American inhabitants of the Andean highlands.

Cooperative Learning
Activity

Divide students into groups of four, and tell each group to imagine that it is preparing a new museum exhibit. Have each group select one of the civilizations discussed in this chapter and create a detailed diagram or layout of a museum room that would focus on the culture and lifestyle of the people selected. Encourage groups to do further research before creating their exhibit plans. Have groups decide on the kinds of displays they would include. Possibilities include murals, glass cases with artifacts, illustrated time lines, touch talks, craft demonstrations, and maps. Ask groups to present and explain their layouts and exhibition plans to the class. Then, as a class, design a floor plan on the chalkboard for a Museum of Native American Culture, grouping related exhibits together and identifying where each exhibit would be located.

Moche, who lived along the Pacific coast between about 250 and 700, and the Chimu people, who came after them.

Expanding on farming methods of these early Andean peoples, the Incas carved terraces into the steep mountainsides. Sturdy stone walls kept rains from washing the soil off the terraces. Most gardens produced two crops a year, including more than 100 varieties of potatoes.

The emperor, known as the Sapa Inca, controlled all the land and riches of the empire. Officials kept records of what each family in the empire produced. The government stored surplus, or extra, food in warehouses owned by the Sapa Inca. Famine victims or the sick were given food from these warehouses.

Expert engineers. The Incas perfected highly advanced building techniques. Their huge stone temples and forts showed their expert engineering skills. With only human labor, ropes, and wooden rollers, the Incas moved huge stones weighing as much as 200 tons into place.

Stone masons chiseled each block so that it fit tightly to the next without any kind of cement. Even a knife blade could not fit between blocks. Incan buildings have survived hundreds of earthquakes. Some remain standing today.

Holding the empire together. To unite their sprawling empire, the Incas built a complex network of roads. More than 19,000 miles (30,000 km) of roads linked all parts of the empire. Incan engineers carved roads through rock mountains and stretched rope bridges across deep gorges.

Teams of runners carried royal commands and news quickly across the empire. A runner from Cuzco, for example, would carry a message to a nearby village. From there, another runner would race to the next relay station. Sometimes the runner might bring news of a revolt. Incan armies could move swiftly along the network of roads to crush it.

Achievements in medicine. Besides their success as farmers and engineers, the Incas made several important advances in medicine. They used quinine to treat malaria, performed successful brain surgery, and also discovered medicines to lessen pain.

Religious beliefs. Like the Aztecs, the Incas worshipped the sun. The emperor, they believed, was descended from the sun god. To honor the sun, the Incas lined the walls of palaces and temples with sheets of gold. They called gold "the sweat of the gods." Nobles and priests adorned themselves with gold ornaments.

Very little Incan gold has survived, however. In the 1530s, as you will read, the Spanish rode up Incan highways to the golden city of Cuzco. Weakened by civil war and disease, the Incas were unable to fight off the invaders. The newcomers melted down the riches of the Incan empire to send back to Europe.

SECTION 3 REVIEW

1. **Locate:** (a) Mexico, (b) Guatemala, (c) Tikal, (d) Tenochtitlán, (e) Andes Mountains, (f) Cuzco.
2. **Define:** (a) civilization, (b) hieroglyphics.
3. Where did the Mayas, Aztecs, and Incas build their civilizations?
4. Describe the farming methods of the following: (a) Mayas, (b) Aztecs, (c) Incas.
5. Describe two achievements of each of the following civilizations: (a) Mayas, (b) Aztecs, (c) Incas.
6. **CRITICAL THINKING   Applying Information** A Spanish soldier described the Aztec capital of Tenochtitlán as "something out of a dream." What might he have meant by this description?

ACTIVITY **Writing to Learn**
Imagine that you have visited the Andes. Write a postcard describing the engineering success of the Incas.

Student Study Guide

Section 3 Study Guide Have students use the Section 3 Study Guide on page 39 of the *Student Study Guide* to review and reinforce the concepts of this section. (Reteaching/Average)

ACTIVITY

Guided Instruction Before students begin writing postcards, have them use the reference section of the library to locate photographs and drawings that can inspire their descriptive writing. Encourage students to examine the pictures for interesting details and to record their feelings about each. As they revise, remind them to use transitional words and phrases to improve coherence. You might wish to provide each student with a blank file card. On one side, they can write their final note. On the other, they can draw a colorful picture illustrating their message.

Answers to Section 3 Review

1. See the map on p. 51 and the World Map in the Reference Section.
2. (a) civilization, p. 48, (b) hieroglyphics, p. 49
3. The Mayas lived in present-day southern Mexico and Guatemala; the Aztecs lived in present-day central Mexico; the Incas lived in the Andes Mountains, along the western coast of South America.
4. (a) The Mayas cut down trees and dug canals to drain swamps. (b) The Aztecs dug canals and filled in parts of the lake, and created floating gardens atop swampy lakes. (c) The Incas carved terraced gardens into the mountainside.
5. (a) The Mayas created an accurate 365-day calendar and developed an advanced number system that included the concept of zero. To record their findings, they invented a system of hieroglyphics, or picture writing. (b) The Aztecs built causeways connecting the island capital to the mainland and built drawbridges that could be raised in case of attack. (c) The Incas developed highly advanced building techniques and made startling medical discoveries.
6. Possible Answer: Tenochtitlán may have seemed like a dream because it was a "floating city" with canals instead of streets, raised roads that linked the city to dry land, and floating gardens. Nothing in Europe resembled the color and layout of Tenochtitlán.

Bell Ringer

Write the words *explore* and *colonize* on the chalkboard. Have students orally develop a working definition of each term.

Lesson Plan

1. Focus Columbus's arrival in 1492 began a series of encounters between Native Americans and Europeans that changed history. European exploration also started a tragic pattern of exploitation that ravaged Native American peoples. Elements of their culture, however, survived and continue to have influence today.

2. Instruct Preview the headings covered under Native American Influences by writing them for the class on the chalkboard. Have students create charts, placing information about which they have prior knowledge under appropriate headings. As each influence is discussed in class, have students confirm prior information and add new discoveries. Encourage students to discuss how exploitation diminished what could have been gained from the cultural exchanges.

3. Close To close the lesson, have students, as a class, choose the most important idea in each subsection. Have students copy the consensus ideas in a journal for later review.

4
After 1492

FIND OUT
- How did the 1492 encounter with Europeans affect Native Americans?
- How did Native American cultures influence peoples around the world after 1492?

For thousands of years, many different peoples lived in the vast land we now call the Americas. As you have read, they adapted to their environments and developed a rich variety of cultures. Yet despite great advances, they knew little about the world beyond their shores.

Then, in the late 1400s, strangers began to arrive from lands across the ocean. The first, Christopher Columbus, from a country called Spain, sailed into the Caribbean Sea in 1492. Other Europeans soon followed. At first, the native peoples greeted the newcomers warmly. Before long, however, they came to see these foreigners as invaders and a threat to their way of life.

Early Contacts

Christopher Columbus is the best known of the early voyagers. He and his crew, however, were not the first to land in the Americas. Others had come hundreds of years earlier.

Viking voyages. The *Vikings* were a bold, seafaring people from Scandinavia. In 1001, they settled briefly in North America, in a flat, wooded country they called Vinland. Today, archaeologists believe that the Viking settlement was located in present-day Newfoundland, in Canada.

The Vikings did not stay in Vinland for long. No one is sure why they left. Viking

stories, however, describe fierce battles with Skraelings, the Viking name for the Inuits.

Pacific voyages. There are many stories about seafaring peoples from Asia reaching the Americas. Most experts agree that such voyages were very rare, if they occurred at all. Still, some believe that even after the last ice age ended, people continued to cross the Bering Sea from Asia into North America. Others claim that fishing boats from China and Japan blew off course and landed on the western coast of South America.

Encounter in the Caribbean

If these early contacts did in fact take place, they had little impact either on Native Americans or the rest of the world. The encounter in 1492, however, changed history. Columbus's arrival in the Caribbean set off a chain of events whose effects are still felt throughout the world today. (You will read more about Christopher Columbus and other Europeans in Chapter 3.)

A tragic pattern. Columbus first landed in the Americas on a small Caribbean island. Friendly relations with the *Taínos* (tī nohz), the Native Americans he met there, did not last. Columbus and the Europeans who followed him had little respect for Native American culture. They claimed Taíno lands for themselves. They forced Taínos to work in gold mines, on ranches, or in Spanish households. Many Taínos died from harsh conditions. Others died from European diseases.

Within 100 years of Columbus's arrival, the Taíno population had been destroyed. The Taínos' experience with Europeans set a pattern that was repeated again and again throughout the Americas.

Cultural Exchange

The 1492 encounter between Native Americans and Europeans had other effects, too. It started an exchange of goods and

---

Connections With Science
Background

The Vikings believed that they discovered grapes in Vinland. Some historians doubt that grapes could have grown that far north. They think that the fruit actually may have been cranberries or gooseberries.

Team-Teaching Suggestion
Science

You might work with a science teacher to present a lesson on navigational methods. Include a discussion of techniques used by the early explorers and their reliance on astronomy. To link past and present, compare and contrast those methods with navigational technology in use today.

MAP, GRAPH, AND CHART SKILLS
Reading a Line Graph

Historians use graphs to present *statistics,* or number facts, in a visual way. The most commonly used graph is a line graph. Other kinds are circle and bar graphs.

A line graph has a grid that is made up of horizontal and vertical lines. A *horizontal axis* runs across the bottom of the grid. A *vertical axis* runs up and down one side of the grid. Information is put on the grid with points, or small dots. The points are then connected to make a *curve.* The curve shows changes that take place over a certain period of time.

Use the steps that follow to read the line graph at right.

1. **Identify the type of information shown on the line graph.** Most graphs have a title, a date, and a source. The title tells you what the subject is. The date tells you what time period is covered. The source tells you where the information was found. (a) What is the title of the graph? (b) What time period does the graph cover? (c) What is the source of the graph?

2. **Study the labels on the graph.** Both the horizontal axis and the vertical axis have labels. (a) What do the numbers on the horizontal axis show? (b) What do the numbers on the vertical axis show?

3. **Practice reading the graph.** The dates on the horizontal axis are spaced evenly. The numbers on the vertical axis are also spaced evenly. The words "in millions" in the label mean that you must add six zeroes to the numbers shown. (a) About how many Native Americans lived in central Mexico in 1520? (b) About how many lived there in 1540? (c) In 1600? (d) During which period did the population fall the most?

4. **Draw conclusions.** Use the graph and your reading in this chapter to answer the following questions: (a) What happened to the population of Native Americans living in central Mexico between 1520 and 1600? (b) Why do you think the Indian population of central Mexico declined so rapidly? (c) What effect do you think the death of so many people might have had on those people who survived? (d) Why do you think the rate of decline slowed down after 1560?

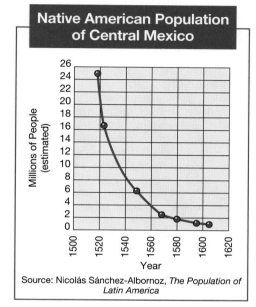

Native American Population of Central Mexico

Source: Nicolás Sánchez-Albornoz, *The Population of Latin America*

 Over a five-day period, keep track of the number of students in your social studies class who are wearing something green each day. Use your statistics to make a line graph.

 Lesson Planner

For a developed **Cooperative Learning** lesson plan, see the *Lesson Planner,* page 10.

Chapter Resources

Skill Application For additional practice, duplicate and distribute the worksheet, Reading a Line Graph, from Unit 1, page 14, of the *Chapter Resources* binder. (Reteaching/Average)

Answers to Skill Lesson

1. (a) Native American Population of Central Mexico (b) 1500–1620 (c) *The Population of Latin America,* by Nicolás Sánchez-Albornoz 2. (a) years, in 20-year increments (b) millions of people, in 2-million increments 3. (a) about 20 million people (b) about 9 million (c) about 1 million (d) 1520–1540 4. (a) It declined rapidly. (b) because of diseases introduced by the Spanish and because of fighting against the Europeans (c) It probably left them demoralized. (d) Possible Answers: The survivors had stopped fighting and were conquered by the Europeans; they had developed resistance to European diseases.

ACTIVITY

Guided Instruction As students plan their graphs, remind them to keep an accurate count each day and plot this information on graph paper. Display and discuss the line graph presentation of the statistics.

Students Acquiring English
Activity

SAE students might benefit by being paired with more advanced students to work on the skill lesson. Because of the highly visual nature of the material in this lesson, students should have little trouble with the basic concepts. Still, encourage students to ask questions about any directions that they do not completely understand.

Riches of the Caribbean *The waters and islands of the Caribbean provided a rich variety of foods. Here, the Caribs, an island people, spread their nets for a harvest of fish.* **Economics** *How did the products of the Caribbean spread throughout the world?*

Answer to Caption

European explorers and conquerors carried Caribbean products with them on their travels.

ideas that transformed people's lives around the globe. In this way, the meeting between two old, very different worlds—the Americas and Europe—led to the creation of one new world.

The exchange between Native Americans and Europeans covered a wide range of areas. It included food, medicine, government, technology, the arts, and language.

The exchange went both ways. Europeans learned much from Native Americans. At the same time, Europeans contributed in many ways to the culture of the Americas. For example, they introduced domestic animals such as chickens and goats and taught Native Americans how to use metals to make copper pots and iron knives. Unfortunately, Europeans also brought disease to the Americas. Millions of Native Americans died of European diseases to which they had no resistance.

Native American Influences

The 1492 encounter introduced Europeans to Native American cultures. Over time, elements of these cultures spread and enriched the entire world.

Food and farming. Over thousands of years, Native Americans had learned to grow a variety of crops. After 1492, Europeans learned of new foods such as corn, potatoes, beans, tomatoes, manioc (a root vegetable), squash, peanuts, pineapples, and blueberries. Today, almost half the world's food crops come from plants that first grew in the Americas.

Europeans carried the new foods around the world. Everywhere, people's diets changed and populations increased. In South Asia, people used American hot peppers and chilies to spice their curries, or stews. Millions of Chinese peasants began growing sweet potatoes. Italians made sauces from tomatoes. People in West Africa grew manioc and maize.

Language. Native American influences also show up in language. Europeans adopted Native American words for animals they had not known before, including moose, chipmunks, and raccoons. They wore Indian clothing, such as ponchos, moccasins, and parkas. They used Indian inventions like toboggans and hammocks. Europeans also learned about trees with Indian names, such as pecan and hickory.

History and You
English has more than 2,000 words taken from Indian languages. What place names in your area come from Native American words?

Connections With Geography
Activity

Discuss with the class the fact that many states—including Michigan, Iowa, and Tennessee—have names of Native American origin, as do cities such as Kalamazoo, Mich.; Ten Sheep, Wyo.; Walla Walla, Wash.; and Pawtucket, R.I. Divide students into pairs. Assign each pair a state or region of the United States (covering the entire country, if possible) and provide a map of the area assigned. Have partners locate three state, town, river, or other place names that they think might be of Native American origin. Have them use library reference sources to find the meanings of the names chosen and to identify the Native American group that gave it that name. Post a large outline map of the United States on a bulletin board. Ask students to write their place names on the map at the appropriate locations, along with the English translations.

In the United States and Canada, most states and provinces have Indian names. Alabama, Texas, Ontario, and Manitoba all are Indian words. Many rivers bear Indian names, including the Mississippi, Potomac, and Monongahela.

Technology. Native Americans helped European settlers survive in North America. Besides showing the newcomers how to grow foods such as corn, Indians taught them hunting skills. They led explorers on foot along Indian trails and paddled them up rivers in Indian canoes.

In the North, they showed Europeans how to use snowshoes and trap fur-bearing animals. Europeans also learned to respect Native American medical knowledge. Indians often treated the newcomers with medicines unknown to Europeans.

Other influences. Native American cultures have influenced the arts, sports, and even government. Today, Indian designs in pottery and leather work are highly prized. Americans play versions of such Indian games as lacrosse. Some early leaders of the United States studied Native American political structures. They saw the League of the Iroquois as a model and urged Americans to unite in a similar way.

In time, all Native Americans felt the effects of European conquest. Still, despite attacks on their cultures, Native Americans survived throughout the Americas. They preserved many traditions, including a respect for nature. Native Americans sought to live in harmony with the natural world. If that harmony was disrupted, they believed, misfortune would result. Today, many people share the same concern for the natural world.

Potato Farming *Andean people first raised potatoes about 2,000 years ago. The Spanish took this vegetable back to Europe. In time, potatoes became an important part of people's diets around the world.* **Geography** *What other food crops first grew in the Americas?*

SECTION 4 REVIEW

1. **Identify:** (a) Vikings, (b) Vinland, (c) Taínos.
2. How were Native Americans affected by the 1492 encounter with Europeans?
3. List three ways in which Native American cultures influenced peoples around the world.
4. **CRITICAL THINKING Analyzing Information** Some experts think that Asians explored the Americas years before Columbus arrived. What kinds of evidence might prove that these experts are correct?

ACTIVITY Writing to Learn
List five questions you would like to ask the Taínos about their encounter with Christopher Columbus. Then write a paragraph describing how your life would be different if that encounter had never occurred.

Connections With Sports
Background

Like many other cultures, Native Americans played ball games. These games ranged from the unstructured form of kickball played by the Inuits to the complex ceremonial games performed on elaborate stone courts by the Mayas. The Algonquins are generally credited with inventing lacrosse. The lacrosse ball was fashioned from tightly packed deerskin. In the version first observed by Europeans, as many as 700 players at a time were on the field.

Answers to Section 4 Review

1. (a) Vikings, p. 54, (b) Vinland, p. 54, (c) Taínos, p. 54
2. The 1492 encounter with Europeans set off a tragic chain of events in which Native American culture was treated with disrespect. Native Americans lost their lands, were used as forced labor, and in many cases lost their lives due to harsh conditions and European diseases.
3. food and farming, language, and technology
4. Possible Answer: Evidence might include artifacts found in Native American cultures whose similarity to Asian artifacts of the same period cannot be explained by any reason other than physical contact.

CHAPTER 2 REVIEW

Answers to Reviewing the Main Ideas

1. by studying artifacts that have survived from that time

2. The Anasazis built their homes in cliffs to make it more difficult for warlike neighbors to attack them.

3. (a) Northwest Coast—the abundance of fish and game encouraged the building of permanent villages and greater prosperity from trade; (b) Great Basin—meager natural resources forced them to travel in small nomadic bands in search of food; (c) Southeast—warm climate, fertile soil, and plentiful rain led to farming villages and close links between farming and religion.

4. The Mayas created an accurate 365-day calendar, invented hieroglyphics, and developed an advanced number system that included the concept of zero.

5. (a) The Aztecs often sacrificed captives. (b) They believed the sun god required human sacrifices to ensure success in its journey across the heavens.

6. The Incas carved terraces into the steep mountainsides and built sturdy stone walls to keep rain from washing away soil.

7. (a) food—corn; (b) language—place names; (c) technology—medical knowledge

Answers to Thinking Critically

1. Possible Answers: complex network of roads and bridges; messenger system with relay stations

2. Possible Answers: (a) obey laws protecting burial grounds; return the artifacts studied to their original sites for preservation after laboratory study; (b) These objects embody the customs, ideas, and beliefs of a culture.

Summary

● By studying physical remains and other evidence, archaeologists are piecing together the story of the first Americans.
● The peoples of North America developed varied ways of life based on their natural environments.
● The Mayas, Aztecs, and Incas developed complex civilizations with important achievements in farming, engineering, medicine, and mathematics.
● The encounter between Native Americans and Europeans that began in 1492 influenced the diet, languages, technology, and ideas of peoples around the world.

Reviewing the Main Ideas

1. How do experts learn about early peoples?
2. Why did the Anasazis build their homes in cliffs?
3. How did the need for food affect the way of life in the following culture areas: (a) Northwest Coast, (b) Great Basin, (c) Southeast?
4. Name three achievements of the Mayas.
5. (a) How did the Aztecs treat captured peoples? (b) Why?
6. What methods of farming did the Incas use?
7. Give one example of Native American influence in each of the following areas: (a) food, (b) language, (c) technology.

Thinking Critically

1. Evaluating Information What evidence shows that the Incas had a well-organized empire?
2. Linking Past and Present (a) What steps can archaeologists take to show respect for the peoples whose cultures they study? (b) Why is it important that they show respect?

Applying Your Skills

1. Outlining Review the outlining steps on page 28. Then outline the section Uncovering the American Past, which begins on page 32.

2. Understanding Sequence Place the following events in the correct order. Then write a few sentences explaining why they must have happened in that order. (a) Columbus reaches the Americas. (b) Italians begin to make tomato sauces. (c) Taínos live peacefully on their home island in the Caribbean..

3. Analyzing a Quotation "Who could conquer Tenochtitlán? Who could shake the foundation of heaven?" This quotation comes from the work of an Aztec poet. (a) What does it tell you about the Aztecs' view of their empire? (b) Why do you think they viewed their empire this way?

Thinking About Geography

Match the letters on the map with the following places: **1.** Mayan civilization, **2.** Aztec empire, **3.** Incan empire, **4.** Tenochtitlán, **5.** Tikal, **6.** Cuzco. **Interaction** How were the Aztecs able to grow crops on swampland?

Answers to Applying Your Skills

1. Outlines will vary; however, students should use the following basic format:

   1. Uncovering the American Past
     A. The First Americans
     B. The Study of Early Peoples
     C. The Mound Builders
     D. Early Cultures of the Southwest

Students should have at least two facts under each lettered item.

2. (c), (a), (b) is the correct sequence of events. Reasons explaining the sequence will vary but should be supported by information from the text, especially the fact that tomatoes were unknown in Europe before 1492.

3. Possible Answers: (a) Aztecs felt that their empire, like heaven, was impossible to destroy. (b) They believed in their gods and leaders.

Answers to Thinking About Geography

1. D **2.** B **3.** F **4.** A **5.** C
6. E
Interaction: by creating floating gardens

Visiting the Incas

Form into groups to explore the early Incan civilization in South America. Follow the suggestions below to write, draw, or build to show what you have learned about the Incas. You may use the textbook, encyclopedias, atlases, or other materials in your classroom library to complete the tasks. Be able to name your sources of information when you have finished the activity.

CARTOGRAPHERS   On a large sheet of paper, create a map of the Americas showing the location of the Incan empire.
On the map:
- Label important cities of the Incan empire.
- Label the Andes Mountains.
- Draw the borders of present-day countries within the Incan empire. Label each country.

SCIENTISTS   Draw a diagram of a terrace that the Incas constructed to farm steep hills. Include a paragraph explaining how the Incas used terraced farms to adapt to their environment.

ENGINEERS   Make a model or draw a picture of an Incan bridge, road, or building. Be prepared to explain how the Incas carried out these great engineering projects.

GOVERNMENT OFFICIALS   Find out how the Incan empire was governed. What was the leader called? Who helped the leader? How were government and religion related? How were royal commands communicated to the people? Make a chart showing the way in which the Incan government was organized.

ARCHAEOLOGISTS   Plan a museum exhibit of Incan artifacts. Decide what items will be included, and write a catalog for the exhibit. Illustrate and describe each item.

 Create a Visiting the Incas brochure that includes an example or summary from each group.

Gold Incan hands

Incan textile

Lessons	Teaching Resources
1 Europeans Look Overseas **Objectives** 1. Explain why Europeans looked beyond their borders. 2. Describe how attitudes toward learning changed during the Renaissance. 3. Describe how Portugal expanded its trade. 4. Identify the lands that Columbus reached.	**Lesson Planner** Cooperative Learning, p. 13 **Student Study Guide** Section 1 Study Guide, p. 43 **Our Multicultural Heritage** *Milestone* Ackee, Salt Fish, Rice, and Peas, p. 9 **Interdisciplinary Connections:** The Columbian Exchange ■ *Arts* New Styles for a New Land, p. 14 ■ *Sciences* The Tragedy of the Taínos, p. 15 ■ *Geography* Corn Across the Continents, p. 16 ■ *Economics* Bar Pricing, p. 17 ■ *Civics* El Día de la Raza, p. 18
2 Spain's Empire in the Americas **Objectives** 1. Describe how Spain conquered Native American empires. 2. Describe how Spain ruled its empires in the Americas. 3. Explain why the Spanish brought slaves from Africa. 4. Describe how Spanish and Native American ways helped shape the culture of New Spain.	**Lesson Planner** Cooperative Learning, p. 14 **Student Study Guide** Section 2 Study Guide, p. 44 **Chapter Resources Binder, Unit 1** *Geography in History* The Search for Golden Kingdoms, pp. 29–30 *Critical Thinking* Analyzing Information, p. 27 **Our Multicultural Heritage** *Biography* Doña Marina, Adviser to Cortés, p. 7
3 Staking Claims in North America **Objectives** 1. Identify the European nations that searched for a northwest passage. 2. Explain why the Protestant Reformation heightened rivalry among nations. 3. Describe how New France and New Netherland were founded. 4. Describe how the arrival of Europeans affected Native Americans in North America.	**Lesson Planner** Cooperative Learning, p. 15 **Student Study Guide** Section 3 Study Guide, p. 45
4 The First English Colonies **Objectives** 1. Explain how tobacco helped save the Jamestown Colony. 2. Describe how self-government began in Virginia. 3. Explain why the Pilgrims started a colony in North America. 4. Describe how Native Americans helped the Plymouth colonists.	**Lesson Planner** Cooperative Learning, p. 16 **Student Study Guide** Section 4 Study Guide, p. 46 **Chapter Resources Binder, Unit 1** *Skill Application* Understanding Causes and Effects, p. 26 *History Through Literature* Of Plymouth Plantation, p. 28 **Our Multicultural Heritage** *Biography* Pocahontas, Link Between Two Worlds, p. 8

Multimedia Resources	Additional Resources	Chapter-Level Resources
Transparencies *Time Lines* America and the World, 1300–1600, p. E-13 *Time Lines* America and the World, 1600–1800, p. E-15 *Cause and Effect* Exploration of the Americas, p. F-13 *Interdisciplinary Connections* Columbian Exchange, p. B-37 **CD-ROM** *History Makers* Christopher Columbus **Videotapes/Videodiscs** *United States History Video Collection* Europe, Vol. 1, Ch. 13; West Africa, Vol. 1, Ch. 10; The Columbian Exchange, Vol. 1, Ch. 19	**Voices of Freedom** Marco Polo on the Wealth of Asia, pp. 23–24 **Historical Outline Map Book** Voyages of Discovery, p. 8 Columbus Reaches America, p. 7 **Customized Reader** Columbus Lands in the Americas, article IB–3	**Lesson Planner** Activity Based, pp. 17–18 **Student Study Guide** Chapter 3 Study Guide, pp. 47–48 **Chapter Resources Binder** **Unit 1** Vocabulary Building, p. 25 Chapter Test A, pp. 31–33 Chapter Test B, pp. 34–36 Extra Unit Questions, pp. 51–53 **English Guided Reading** Guided Reading, pp. 5–6 **Spanish Resources** **Computer Test Bank** Chapter Tests A and B Extra Unit Questions **Guided Reading Audiotapes** Side 1 **CD-ROM** *Time Tour* Europeans Reach the Americas in A Meeting of Different Worlds
	Voices of Freedom Rescued by Indians, pp. 26–27 Hardships of the Atlantic Crossing, pp. 30–31 **Historical Outline Map Book** Spanish Explorers in North America, p. 9 Voyages of Discovery, p. 8 **Customized Reader** Montezuma, article IA-1 A Spanish Colony in Florida, article IB-7 The Founding of San Diego: California's First Mission, article IIA-17	
Transparencies *Political Cartoons,* When Worlds Collide, p. G-13 **Videotapes/Videodiscs** *United States History Video Collection* Europe and North America, Vol. 1, Ch. 25; Europe's North American Colonies, Vol. 2, Ch. 7	**Voices of Freedom** Marquette and Joliet, pp. 32–33 **Historical Outline Map Book** Search for a Northwest Passage, p. 10 **Customized Reader** Fort Beauharnois, article IIA-7 A Voyage Down the Mississippi, article IIA-8 Taking Possession of Louisiana, article IIA-6 Dutch Customs in Old New York, article IIA-15	
Transparencies *Cause and Effect,* Exploration of the Americas, p. F-13 **CD-ROM** *History Makers* Pocahontas; John Smith **Videotapes/Videodiscs** *United States History Video Collection* The English in the New World, Vol. 2, Ch. 10; Pilgrims and Puritans, Vol. 2, Ch. 13	**Voices of Freedom** Skills Needed in the New World, pp. 28–29 A Virginia Colonist's Despair, p. 34 Pilgrims and Indians Make Peace, pp. 35–36 **Customized Reader** Returning to Roanoak Colony, article IB-4	

Lesson Planner

For a fully developed **Activity-Based** lesson plan for Chapter 3, see the *Lesson Planner,* pages 17–18.

 Chapter Resources

Vocabulary Building The Vocabulary Building worksheet for Chapter 3 from Unit 1, page 25, of the *Chapter Resources* binder can be used as a prereading activity or as a review of chapter vocabulary. (Reteaching/Easy)

 Student Study Guide

Chapter 3 Study Guide Refer students to pages 47–48 of the *Student Study Guide* for the Chapter 3 Study Guide. The study guide can be used for chapter review as well as for reteaching. (Reteaching/Average)

Guided Reading Audiotapes

Students can use *Guided Reading Audiotapes,* Chapter 3, side 1, to hear section previews, summaries, and review questions. The tapes might benefit students who are auditory learners, students who have trouble reading, or students acquiring English. Tapes are also available in Spanish. (Reteaching/Easy)

CHAPTER 3

Europeans Reach the Americas

(1000–1650)

CHAPTER OUTLINE

1 Europeans Look Overseas

2 Spain's Empire in the Americas

3 Staking Claims in North America

4 The First English Colonies

1100s *The Anasazis built cliff dwellings in the dry, rugged deserts of the American Southwest.*

1300s *The Aztecs built a powerful empire in Mexico. This feather headdress belonged to the last Aztec ruler.*

1400s *The Incas of Peru built an advanced civilization. These gold ceremonial knives show the riches of their empire.*

1100	1200	1300	1400

 **WORLD EVENT
1100–1300**
Christians go on Crusades to Holy Land

**WORLD EVENT
1300s** Renaissance begins

Chapter Time Line
Critical Thinking

In Chapter 3, students will examine clashes between the culture of European explorers and that of the Native Americans they met. Have students examine the pictures that relate to the time line, looking for cultural differences (such as in styles of housing and decoration). Ask: If you were a Native American, what might you think about European fashions? If you were a European, what might you think about Native American fashions?

Students Acquiring English
Activity

It may be easier for SAE students to absorb key information in this chapter if it is organized on a chart. A sample chart might include the names of explorers; the nations they represented; the dates (in chronological order) of their voyages and discoveries; and the places they visited, claimed, or conquered. A final section of the chart might include space for students to make comments about the significance or results of a particular voyage. Preface the addition of each explorer to the chart with a discussion of the reasons or causes for a particular voyage.

Have students use the completed chart along with the relevant maps in the chapter.

Chapter Setting

In 1598, Juan de Oñate (oh NYAH tay) started north up the Rio Grande with about 400 men and several thousand cattle. Oñate's task was to set up the first Spanish colony north of Mexico. The land was rough, and travel was not easy. Along the way, the men stopped at several Pueblo Indian villages. Oñate described such a visit:

❝On August 3 we went to the great pueblo of the Jemez. . . . [T]he natives came out to meet us, bringing water and bread, at a most difficult hill, and they helped us to take up the cavalry armor and weapons. . . . On the 4th we went down to other Jemez pueblos. . . . The descent was so rough that three horses tumbled down the [cliff], and two of them were killed. Most of us who were on foot also fell.❞

After several months, Oñate reached a spot he thought suitable for settlement. Claiming the land for Spain, he set the men to work building a church. On September 8, they held a Roman Catholic service. The Spanish colony of New Mexico was formally founded.

Oñate's travels in the Southwest came at the end of a century of European exploration. Starting in the late 1400s, the nations of Portugal, Spain, England, and France all sent explorers to distant lands. At first, Europeans competed for trade in these new lands. After they reached the Americas, they also became rivals for colonies.

ACTIVITY List three reasons why you might be willing to risk a long, dangerous space journey to explore and settle a distant planet.

1500s After Christopher Columbus reached the West Indies in 1492, Spain set up a vast empire in the Americas. Columbus's ships are shown here.

1620 The Pilgrims sailed for the Americas in search of religious freedom. Here, they are signing the Mayflower Compact.

Late 1600s France's colonies grew slowly. This coat of arms was on the gates of Quebec, capital of New France.

| 1400 | 1500 | 1600 | 1700 |

WORLD EVENT
1400s Portuguese slave trade begins

WORLD EVENT
1500s Europeans seek Northwest Passage

Chapter 3 • **61**

Chapter Resources

English Guided Reading Duplicate and distribute to SAE students the Chapter 3 Guided Reading worksheet on pages 5–6 in the English Guided Reading section in the *Chapter Resources* binder. Students who have difficulty reading might also benefit from using this worksheet. Have students complete the worksheet before they begin reading. You might pair a more fluent student or a student who is a stronger reader with each SAE student to review. (Reteaching/Easy)

Spanish Resources See the Spanish Resources section in the *Chapter Resources* binder.

ACTIVITY

Guided Instruction You might have students brainstorm and list kinds of background experiences they know or think would be prevalent among astronauts (e.g., test pilot, scientist, military officer, teacher). Have them use the list as a prompt to determine reasons why people might undertake a journey into space. Then ask students to list some reasons why they themselves would risk this kind of trip. Conclude with a class discussion comparing and contrasting individual responses.

CD-ROM

Time Tour Access Europeans Reach the Americas in A Meeting of Different Worlds on the American Heritage® *History of the United States* CD-ROM. (Enrichment/Average)

Linking Past and Present
Activity

Before students begin reading the chapter, direct them to the World Map in the Reference Section. Focusing on Europe, Asia, and Africa, have students suggest routes that people in Europe might have used to reach China and India before 1500. Ask: What methods of transportation might Europeans have used at that time? How long might a trip to China or India have taken? Then have students suggest routes that Europeans might use today to reach the same destination. Ask: How easily can these trips be taken today? How has technology changed the methods of travel over long distances?

Answer to Caption

Possible Answers: People believed that the seas were full of monsters. Mapmakers did not make accurate maps. Daily life was hard, and the main concern of most people was survival. They did not have time to think about the outside world.

Section 1
pp. 62–70

Bell Ringer

Tell students to imagine that they are about to board the first space flight to travel beyond the solar system. Ask: What would your thoughts and feelings be? What might you encounter on the voyage?

Lesson Plan

1. Focus By the late 1400s, European travel and trade increased; Europeans began to expand their social, political, and economic horizons. In this section, students learn about life in the Middle Ages, the effects of the Crusades, and the Portuguese voyages to Africa. The section concludes with a discussion of the opening of the Americas to European trade—and conquest.

2. Instruct Before students read each subsection, preview key terms and ask students to suggest the importance of each. As students continue, have them confirm predictions, make ad-

1
Europeans Look Overseas

FIND OUT

■ Why did Europeans look beyond their borders?

■ How did attitudes toward learning change during the Renaissance?

■ How did Portugal expand its trade?

■ What lands did Columbus reach?

VOCABULARY feudalism, manor, serf, magnetic compass, astrolabe, caravel, colony

During the **Middle Ages,** a period from about 500 to 1350, many Europeans thought of the world as a disk floating on a great ocean. The disk was made up of three continents: Europe, Africa, and Asia.

Most Europeans knew little about the lands beyond their small villages. Even mapmakers called the waters bordering Europe the Sea of Darkness. Sailors who strayed into these waters often returned with tales

of monsters. "One of these sea monsters," swore one sailor, "has terrible tusks. Another has horns, flames, and huge eyes 16 or 20 feet across."

Were such tales true? The few people who wondered had no way of finding out. Besides, for most Europeans, daily life was hard, and their main concern was survival.

A Changing World

Toward the end of the Middle Ages, Europeans began to look beyond their borders. Religious wars and the lure of new products from faraway lands brought major changes in the way Europeans lived.

The Middle Ages. During the Middle Ages, weak European kings and queens divided their lands among powerful nobles. These nobles, or lords, had their own armies and courts but still owed loyalty to their king. This system of rule by lords who owe loyalty to a king is called **feudalism** (FYOOD 'l ihz uhm).

Most life in Europe revolved around manors of these powerful lords. The **manor** included the lord's castle, peasants' huts, and surrounding villages or fields. Most people on the manor were **serfs,** or peasants bound to the land for life. Serfs worked for

BIOGRAPHY Marco Polo in China *In 1271, at age 17, Marco Polo set out with his father and uncle from Venice, Italy, for lands in the East. He returned 24 years later. His tales of his travels made other Europeans eager to explore the world. This illustration shows the ruler of China receiving the Polo family.* **Geography** *Why did most Europeans in the Middle Ages know little about lands outside Europe?*

Connections With Economics
Background

Although serfs were bound to the land, they were not slaves. They could not be sold to other lords; and if the land itself were sold, serfs became the tenants of the new owner. Leaving the land usually required the payment of a fee—a fee that was higher than a serf could afford. Thus, many serfs were born, lived, and died in the same village. Their lives were shorter than our own, too—probably 40 years or less.

A typical feudal village consisted of more than the lord's manor and the serfs' homes and fields. Skilled workers—carpenters, blacksmiths, and millers, for example—were needed. They, too, rented land from the lord, but they had much more freedom than the serfs did. Most villages also had a priest and a church or chapel.

the lord and could not leave the manor without the lord's permission.

Under feudalism, there were few merchants and traders. Few roads or towns existed. The manor produced nearly everything people needed. Most manors even provided a place of worship, such as a church or small chapel. Here, serfs and lords heard teachings of the Roman Catholic Church.

Effects of the Crusades. During the Middle Ages, Christians in Western Europe belonged to the Roman Catholic Church. The Church had great influence. In time, Church teachings led Europeans to look beyond their manors.

Christians in Western Europe referred to the Middle East as the Holy Land because Jesus had lived and died there. The region was also sacred to Muslims. Their prophet, Muhammad, had also lived in the Holy Land. From about 1100 to 1300, the Roman Catholic Church fought a series of religious wars to gain control of the Holy Land from Turkish Muslims. The wars were known as the ***Crusades.***

Thousands of Christians from all across Europe joined the Crusades. Among them were kings and peasants, adults and children. Many Crusaders sewed a white cross on their shirts and on flags as a symbol of their cause.

The Crusaders did not regain the Holy Land. The Crusades did have lasting effects, however. For the first time, large numbers of Europeans traveled beyond their small towns. In the Middle East, they ate strange foods, such as rice, oranges, and dates. They tasted ginger, pepper, and other spices that both improved the taste of food and helped preserve it. From Arab traders, they bought shimmering silks and tightly woven, colorful rugs from lands to the east, known as Asia.

Italian merchants along the Mediterranean Sea saw that Europeans would pay handsome prices for these foreign goods.

They soon began a lively trade with Arab merchants in the Middle East.

Arabs taught Italian sailors how to use new instruments to navigate large bodies of water, such as the Mediterranean Sea. The **magnetic compass,** with a needle that always pointed north, helped ship captains sail a straight course. The **astrolabe** (AS troh layb) made it possible for sailors to measure the positions of stars and figure out latitude at sea. Both the magnetic compass and the astrolabe helped make sailing less frightening.

The Renaissance spirit. Increased trade and travel made Europeans curious about the wider world. Scholars translated the works of ancient Greeks, Romans, and Arabs. They then made discoveries of their own in fields such as medicine, astronomy, and chemistry. This burst of learning was called the ***Renaissance*** (REHN uh sahns), a French word meaning rebirth. It started in the late 1300s and continued until about 1600.

One invention that helped spread the spirit of the Renaissance was the printing press. It was invented during the mid-1400s by Johannes Gutenberg (GOOT uhn berg) of Germany. Before Gutenberg's invention, monks wrote out books by hand. As a result, only a few copies were available. With the printing press, large numbers of books could be printed at a low cost. As more books became available, more people learned to read. The more people read, the more they learned about the world.

> ***History and You***
> *During the Renaissance, a new ideal person emerged. To meet the ideal, a person had to master every area of learning and be expert in a wide range of skills. Who do you know today who might be considered a "Renaissance person"?*

Chapter 3 • **63**

justments, and add new information as necessary.
3. Close To close the lesson, ask students to vote on which developments they think were the most important and why.

Lesson Planner
For a developed **Cooperative Learning** lesson plan, see the *Lesson Planner,* page 13.

Videotapes/ Videodiscs
United States History Video Collection Use the video segment "Europe" from Volume 1, *Three Worlds Meet*, to enhance students' understanding of Europe in the fifteenth century. Approx. running time 5:00 min. (Enrichment/Average) Vol. 1, Ch. 13

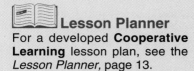

Chapter 13   Play

Connections With Civics
Background

Tell students that Richard the Lion-Hearted, king of England from 1189 to 1199, is a popular figure in the literature and lore of the Crusades. However, his frequent absences and constant demands for tax money to support his wars caused unrest at home. In 1215, unhappy nobles forced his successor, King John, to sign the Magna Carta (Great Charter). The Magna Carta contains many of the rights later incorporated into the U.S. Constitution.

Our Multicultural Heritage
Background

From the fall of Rome until the Renaissance, much of the learning of Europe was preserved by Arab scholars or by Christian and Jewish scholars working in Arab lands. Arab scholars made important advances in the fields of astronomy, mathematics, medicine, science, and philosophy.

Answer to Chart Skills

John Cabot and Henry Hudson; the east coast of North America and Hudson Bay, respectively

 Transparencies

Time Lines Use the transparencies, America and the World, 1300–1600, and America and the World, 1600–1800, on pages E-13 and E-15 of *American History Transparencies* for visual reference throughout this section. Teaching suggestions for these transparencies can be found on pages E-2 and E-3. (Enrichment/Average)

European Explorers

Explorer	Achievements
For Portugal	
Bartolomeu Dias 1487–1488	Sailed around the southern tip of Africa
Vasco da Gama 1497–1498	Sailed around Africa to India
Pedro Álvares Cabral 1500	Reached Brazil
For Spain	
Christopher Columbus 1492–1504	Explored the West Indies and the Caribbean
Vasco Núñez de Balboa 1513	Sighted the Pacific Ocean
Juan Ponce de León 1508–1509, 1513	Explored Puerto Rico Explored Florida
Ferdinand Magellan 1519–1522	Led first expedition to sail around the world
Pánfilo de Narváez/Cabeza de Vaca/Estevanico 1528–1536	Traveled in the Spanish borderlands
Francisco Coronado 1540–1542	Explored southwestern North America
Hernando De Soto 1516–1520, 1539–1542	Explored Central America Led expedition to the Mississippi River
Juan Cabrillo 1542–1543	Explored west coast of North America
For England	
John Cabot 1497–1501(?)	Explored east coast of North America
Henry Hudson 1610–1611	Explored Hudson Bay
For the Netherlands	
Henry Hudson 1609	Explored east coast of North America and the Hudson River
For France	
Giovanni da Verrazano 1524	Explored east coast of North America, including present-day New York harbor
Jacques Cartier 1534–1542	Explored St. Lawrence River
Samuel de Champlain 1603–1615	Explored St. Lawrence River valley Founded Quebec
Jacques Marquette/Louis Joliet 1673	Explored along the Mississippi River
Robert de La Salle 1679–1682	Explored Great Lakes Reached the mouth of the Mississippi River

CHART SKILLS *Starting in the late 1400s, five major European nations sent out expeditions to explore the world.* ● *Name two explorers who sailed for England. Which areas did they explore?*

Connections With Architecture
Activity

Have students look through travel books or magazines for evidence of Muslim influences on the architecture of Spain and Portugal. Point out that one excellent example is the Alhambra, a Moorish (North African Muslim) palace in the Granada region of Spain. Ask students to present their findings in oral reports supplemented by illustrations and/or drawings.

Team-Teaching Suggestion
Art

You might work with an art teacher to present a lesson about such great Renaissance artists as Michelangelo and Leonardo da Vinci. Display some examples of their creations and discuss the influence that the genius of each has had on the artistic world to this day.

Search for New Trade Routes

During the Renaissance, strong rulers slowly gained control over feudal lords. These kings and queens built the foundations of the nations we know today.

European nations seek trade. In England and France, rulers increased their power in a long series of wars. In Portugal and Spain, Christian rulers fought Arab Muslims who had conquered parts of those lands. By 1249, the Portuguese had captured the last Muslim stronghold in Portugal. In Spain, Arabs continued to control territory until 1492.

The new rulers of England, France, Portugal, and Spain all looked for ways to increase their wealth. They could make huge profits by trading with China and other lands in Asia. However, Arab and Italian merchants controlled the trade routes across the Mediterranean Sea. If they wanted a share of the trade, European rulers had to find another route to Asia.

Portugal takes the lead. The Portuguese turned to the Atlantic Ocean. In the early 1400s, Prince Henry, known as the Navigator, encouraged sea captains to sail south along the coast of West Africa. He founded an informal school to help sailors in their explorations.

Using a new type of ship known as a **caravel** (KAR uh vehl), the Portuguese sailed farther and farther south. The caravel's triangular sails and its steering rudder allowed it to sail against the wind. By 1498, the Portuguese sailor Vasco da Gama passed the southern tip of Africa and continued north and east to India. Later, other Portuguese ships pressed on to the East Indies, the source of trade in spices.

Using their new route, the Portuguese built a successful trading empire in Asia. Along the way, they came into contact with great kingdoms in Africa.

African Trading States

In the 1400s, Europeans knew little about Africa or the many peoples who lived there. A Spanish map, for example, showed an African ruler in the middle of the Sahara, a great desert. The caption read:

66 This Negro lord is called Musa Mali. So abundant is the gold in his country that he is the richest and most noble king in all the land. 99

Advances in Technology *New sailing instruments, such as the astrolabe at left, allowed Europeans to take longer, more hazardous sea voyages. The illustration at right shows Portuguese ships crossing the Atlantic Ocean.* **Science and Technology** *What other advances in technology encouraged European exploration?*

66— Voices of 99 Freedom

Primary Source You might assign selection 3-2, Marco Polo on the Wealth of Asia, on pages 23–24 of *Voices of Freedom.* This selection is from Marco Polo's personal accounts of his travels in Asia, which interested many Europeans in new—and possibly wealthy—lands. (Enrichment/Average)

Historical Sidelight
Background

Muslim armies crossed the Strait of Gibraltar into Spain in 711. They conquered the area quickly and ruled there for more than 700 years.

Christian rulers were able to regain some control. By 1400, the Iberian peninsula consisted of five kingdoms—the Christian kingdoms of Navarre, Aragon, Castile-León, and Portugal, and the Muslim (Moorish) kingdom of Granada. In 1469, Isabella of Castile-León and Ferdinand of Aragon were married, and together they went to war against the Moors. They captured Granada in 1492, the same year in which they sponsored Columbus's voyage. A few years later, they united the kingdoms of Navarre, Aragon, Castile-León, and Granada to form the nation of Spain as we know it today.

In fact, Musa Mali's real name was Mansa Musa. He ruled Mali, a kingdom in West Africa. Mali reached its height between 1200 and 1400. In 1324, Mansa Musa traveled from Mali across North Africa to Egypt and the Middle East. He so dazzled the Egyptians with his wealth that news of his visit reached Europe.

West Africa. Mali was only one of several advanced states that rose in West Africa. (See the map below.) In the late 1400s, Songhai (SAWNG hī) became the most powerful kingdom in West Africa. Timbuktu, located on the Niger River, was a thriving center of trade and learning.

Portuguese explorers did not visit these kingdoms inside Africa. They did, however, trade with Africans along the coast. Africans exchanged gold, ivory, and statues of polished teak wood for European weapons and other goods.

East Africa. The Portuguese found well-developed kingdoms along Africa's eastern coast. There, states like Mogadishu and

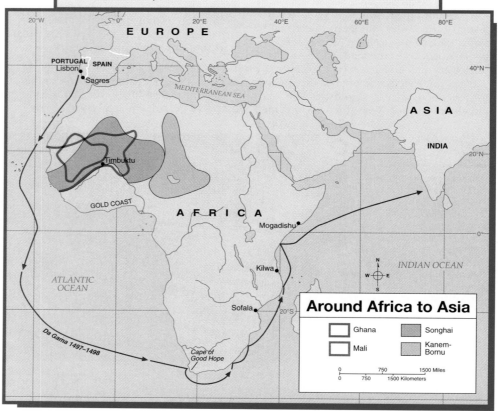

MAP STUDY

Portuguese sailors led the search for an all-water route to Asia.
1. Describe Da Gama's route from Portugal to India.
2. Which trading centers were on the east coast of Africa?
3. **Drawing Conclusions** Based on the map, why do you think Portugal was a leader in sea exploration?

Around Africa to Asia

Ghana · Songhai · Mali · Kanem-Bornu

Historical Sidelight
Background

The fabled city of Timbuktu was associated with both the Mali and Songhai empires. Under Mansa Musa, a strong believer in education and the arts, Timbuktu became a center of Muslim culture and learning. Scholars from northern Africa and the Middle East came to Timbuktu to study law, history, and religion at the university there.

Timbuktu's location—close to both the Niger River and the Sahara—led to its nickname as "the meeting point of camel and canoe." The city became rich through commerce, and its fame as a trading center for gold and salt spread to Europe during the Middle Ages. Before the invention of refrigeration, salt was one of the world's most important economic goods because of its use in preserving foods.

Kilwa prospered from trade with other ports along the Indian Ocean. Gold from Zimbabwe, a powerful inland state, made its way to the coastal city of Sofala. From there, ships carried the gold up the African coast as well as to India.

Portuguese slave trade. In 1441, the Portuguese raided an African village. They captured about a dozen Africans and sold them as slaves in Europe. By 1460, about 1,000 Africans were sold each year in Portugal. As the trade in slaves increased, Africans from kingdoms along the coast made raids into the interior seeking captives to sell to the Portuguese.

The Portuguese did not introduce slavery. Since ancient times, Europeans, Africans, Arabs, and Asians in many different regions had enslaved and sold people. However, the trade along the West African coast marked a turning point. Over the next 400 years, as many as 11 million Africans would be enslaved and sent across the Atlantic to the Americas.

Voyages of Columbus

As the Portuguese sailed east toward Asia, the Spanish watched with envy. They, too, wanted a share of the rich Asian trade. In 1492, King Ferdinand and Queen Isabella agreed to finance a voyage by Christopher Columbus, a bold Italian sea captain. Columbus planned to reach the East Indies, off the coast of Asia, by sailing west across the Atlantic.

Ivory Carving From West Africa *West African artists produced many fine carvings. This ivory salt cellar was probably carved to order for a European merchant.* **Culture** *What objects did the artist include to show that the man in the carving is European?*

The voyage west. In August 1492, Columbus set sail with three vessels and a crew of 90 sailors. As captain, he commanded the largest ship, the *Santa María*. The other ships were the *Niña* and the *Pinta*.

Fair winds sped the ships along. The crew saw no land for a month. Some of the less experienced sailors began to grumble. They had never been beyond the sight of land for so long. Still, Columbus sailed on.

On October 7, sailors saw flocks of birds flying southwest. Columbus changed course to follow the birds. A few days later, crew members spotted tree branches and flowers floating in the water. On the night of October 11, the moon shone brightly. At 2 A.M. on October 12, the lookout on the *Pinta* spotted white cliffs shining in the moonlight. "Tierra! Tierra!" he shouted. "Land! Land!"

At dawn, Columbus rowed ashore. He planted the banner of Spain in what he believed was the East Indies. In fact, as you have read in Chapter 2, he had reached the island home of the Taínos, in what are now known as the West Indies. Convinced he had reached the East Indies, Columbus called the Taínos Indians.

For three months, Columbus explored the West Indies. To his delight, he found signs of gold on the islands. Eager to report his success, he returned home.

From fame to disgrace. In Spain, Columbus presented King Ferdinand and Queen Isabella with gifts of pink pearls and brilliantly colored parrots. The royal couple listened intently to his descriptions of tobacco leaves, pineapples, and hammocks used for sleeping. Impressed, they agreed to finance future voyages.

Chapter 3 • **67**

LINKING PAST AND PRESENT

PAST

PRESENT

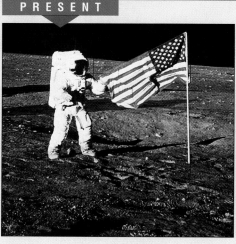

New Frontiers *Throughout history, people have explored the unknown. In the 1400s, Europeans dared to sail the world's uncharted oceans. At left, Christopher Columbus lands on the "New World" in 1492. Nearly 500 years later, Americans ventured into the uncharted seas of space. At right, an astronaut lands on another new world—the moon. • What qualities do you think Columbus and the astronaut had in common?*

Columbus made three more voyages to the West Indies. On his second voyage, in 1493, he founded the first Spanish colony in the Americas, on an island he called Hispaniola. A **colony** is a group of people who settle in a distant land and are ruled by the government of their native land.

Columbus proved to be a better explorer than a governor. During his third expedition, settlers at Hispaniola complained of his harsh rule. When Isabella sent an official to investigate, the official sent Columbus back to Spain in chains.

In the end, Isabella pardoned Columbus. He died in 1506, still convinced that he had reached Asia.

Columbus: Hero or Villain?

For years, Columbus has been remembered as the bold sea captain who "discovered America." In one sense, he deserves that honor. Europeans knew nothing of the Americas before Columbus brought them news of this "new world." Today, we recognize that other people "discovered" America long before Columbus. Still, his daring journey brought the peoples of Europe, Africa, and the Americas into lasting contact for the first time in history.

Native Americans, however, paid heavily for Columbus's voyage. Columbus and the Europeans who came after him forced

CONNECTIONS

ARTS SCIENCES GEOGRAPHY **WORLD** ECONOMICS CIVICS

The Columbian Exchange

Before 1492, a typical Aztec meal consisted of corn porridge, tortillas, beans, and tomato or pepper sauce. On the other side of the ocean, Europeans dined on dark bread, cabbage or turnip soup, and cheese. Neither knew the other existed. Neither imagined how their diet—and their entire world—would change after they met.

Then, Christopher Columbus arrived in the West Indies. His visit began an exchange of goods and ideas that transformed the world. Because it began with Columbus, this transfer is called the Columbian Exchange.

The Columbian Exchange involved hundreds of items. Besides foods, these items included peoples, plants, and animals. They also included diseases.

Native Americans taught Europeans to eat corn and potatoes. Easy to grow, these foods became staples in European, African, and Asian diets. At the same time, the introduction of livestock, wheat, bananas, and citrus fruit from Europe, Africa, and Asia changed the way Native Americans ate.

Sugar cane also traveled to the Americas from Europe, carried by Columbus on his second voyage. Soon, sugar was a thriving industry on the Caribbean islands. Europeans brought in millions of Africans to work as slaves in the sugar plantations.

Cattle and horses

Potato plant

Perhaps the most terrible item in the Columbian Exchange arrived as an invisible passenger on European ships. Native Americans had no resistance to "European" diseases such as measles, smallpox, or even the common cold. Scholars estimate that between 50 percent and 90 percent of Native Americans died of diseases introduced from Europe.

■ What were three effects of the Columbian Exchange?

Smallpox victim

ACTIVITY Make a map of the world that illustrates the flow of items in the Columbian Exchange.

Student Study Guide

ACTIVITY

Guided Instruction Remind students that an editorial uses logical arguments to convince readers to agree with the writer's opinion. Suggest that students state their opinion, provide supporting arguments, and conclude by restating their main idea. Ask students to present their editorials to the class. Have the class discuss which arguments (regardless of opinion) they thought were persuasive and why.

Section 2
pp. 70–77

Bell Ringer

Write the word *empire* on the chalkboard. Ask students to freewrite for 3 minutes about the images that the word brings to mind.

---

native peoples to work in mines or on farms raising sugar cane and cotton. Over the next 50 years, hundreds of thousands of Caribbean Indians died from harsh working conditions and European diseases.

"Discovery" also cost Native Americans their lands. Starting with Columbus, Europeans justified seizing Indian lands. Some believed they had the right to take the lands because Indians were not Christians.

For better or worse, the rise of powerful nations in Europe signaled a new era for the Americas. Curious Europeans wanted to know more about the lands across the Atlantic. They saw the Americas as a place where they could trade and grow rich. Once Columbus reached the Americas, nothing could stop the flood of explorers and settlers who followed him.

SECTION 1 REVIEW

1. **Locate:** (a) Europe, (b) Middle East, (c) Asia, (d) East Indies, (e) Mali, (f) West Indies.
2. **Identify:** (a) Middle Ages, (b) Crusades, (c) Renaissance, (d) Johannes Gutenberg, (e) Mansa Musa, (f) Queen Isabella.
3. **Define:** (a) feudalism, (b) manor, (c) serf, (d) magnetic compass, (e) astrolabe, (f) caravel, (g) colony.
4. What changes did the Crusades bring to Europe?
5. How did exploration help to expand Portugal's trade?
6. (a) Where did Columbus think he landed in 1492? (b) Where did he actually land?
7. **CRITICAL THINKING Analyzing Information** (a) How did Europeans view their arrival in the Americas? (b) How does this compare with the Native American view that you read about in Chapter 2?

ACTIVITY Writing to Learn
Should Americans celebrate Columbus's birthday? Write an editorial expressing your opinion.

2
Spain's Empire in the Americas

FIND OUT
- How did Spain conquer Native American empires?
- How did Spain rule its empire in the Americas?
- Why did the Spanish bring Africans as slaves to the Americas?
- How did Spanish and Indian ways help shape the culture of New Spain?

VOCABULARY conquistador, pueblo, presidio, mission, peninsulare, creole, mestizo, encomienda, plantation

"**W**hat a troublesome thing it is to discover new lands. The risks we took, it is hardly possible to exaggerate." So spoke Bernal Díaz del Castillo, one of the Spanish **conquistadors** (kahn KEES tuh dorz), or conquerors, who marched into the Americas. When asked why conquistadors traveled to the Americas, Díaz responded, "We came here to serve God and the king and also to get rich."

In their search for glory and gold, the conquistadors made Spain one of the richest nations in Europe. Before long, Spanish colonists had created a vast new empire in the Americas. But the arrival of Europeans meant suffering and even death for Aztecs, Incas, and other Native Americans.

Beyond the Caribbean

After Columbus reached the West Indies, the Spanish explored and settled other islands in the Caribbean Sea. By 1511, they

---

Answers to Section 1 Review

1. See the maps on pp. 66 and 72, and the World Map in the Reference Section.
2. (a) Middle Ages, p. 62, (b) Crusades, p. 63, (c) Renaissance, p. 63, (d) Johannes Gutenberg, p. 63, (e) Mansa Musa, p. 66, (f) Queen Isabella, p. 67
3. (a) feudalism, p. 62, (b) manor, p. 62, (c) serf, p. 62, (d) magnetic compass, p. 63, (e) astrolabe, p. 63, (f) caravel, p. 65, (g) colony, p. 68

4. The Crusades sparked an interest in goods from Asia. Italian merchants developed trade between the Middle East and Europe. Europeans learned about Arab sailing instruments, such as the astrolabe and the magnetic compass.
5. Explorers found new routes to Asia and came in contact with great kingdoms in Africa. These routes were later used to build Portuguese trade.

6. (a) East Indies (b) West Indies
7. Possible Answers: (a) Too often, Europeans viewed their arrival as an excuse to claim American lands as their own, as well as to trade, grow rich, and settle. (b) Native Americans felt that Europeans had little respect for their culture, stole their lands, and brought forced labor and diseases against which their people had no resistance.

had conquered Puerto Rico, Jamaica, and Cuba. They also explored the eastern coast of North America and South America. They were still seeking a western route to Asia, but these lands blocked their way.

Then in 1513, an adventurer named Vasco Núñez de Balboa (bal BOH uh) plunged into the jungles of the Isthmus of Panama. Native Americans had told him that a large body of water lay to the west. With a party of Spanish and Indians, Balboa reached the Pacific Ocean after about 25 days. In full armor, he stood in the crashing surf and claimed the sea for Spain.

The Spanish had no idea how wide the Pacific was until a sea captain named Ferdinand Magellan (muh JEHL uhn) sailed across it. The expedition set out from Spain in 1519. After much hardship, it rounded the stormy southern tip of South America and entered the Pacific Ocean. Crossing the vast Pacific, the sailors were forced to eat rats and sawdust when they ran out of food. Magellan himself was killed in a battle with the local people of the Philippine Islands off the coast of Asia.

Of five ships and about 250 crew members, only one ship and 18 sailors returned to Spain in 1522, three years after they set out. These survivors had found Spain's all-water route to Asia by sailing west. More important, their voyage around the world made Europeans aware of the true size of the Earth.

Conquest of the Aztecs and Incas

Meanwhile, Spanish colonists in the Caribbean began to hear rumors of gold and other riches in nearby Mexico. At the same time, the Aztecs there were hearing about the Spanish.

In 1518, messengers brought strange news to the Aztec emperor, Montezuma (mahn tuh ZYOO muh). They had seen a large house floating on the Gulf of Mexico. It was filled with white men with long, thick beards and clothing of many colors. The next year, Aztecs spotted even more bearded white men.

Were these strangers gods or men? Aztec sacred writings predicted that one day a powerful white-skinned god would return from the east to rule the Aztecs. These white strangers came from the east. And they were certainly powerful. They wore metal armor and had weapons that breathed fire and shattered trees into splinters. Could they be messengers of the Aztec god? Unsure, Montezuma invited them to enter the capital of his empire, Tenochtitlán.

Aztecs Battle the Spanish
Pedro de Alvarado was a conquistador in Mexico. This illustration shows Alvarado and his men retreating from a troop of Aztec soldiers.
Science and Technology
Based on this picture, what advantages did the Spanish have over the Aztecs?

Lesson Plan

1. Focus The European desire to conquer and colonize led to a treaty that divided the Americas between Spain and Portugal. In this section, students learn about the European discovery of the Pacific Ocean, the first Europeans to circle the globe, and the founding of a Spanish empire in the Americas.
2. Instruct Conduct a classroom trial focusing on this question: "Were the Spanish conquistadors justified in the way they treated the Aztecs and the Incas?" Let students representing the Native American empires bring charges against Cortés and Pizarro. Assign students to serve as judge, lawyers for each side, witnesses (including the defendants), and jury. After the evidence has been presented, have the jury deliberate in front of the class and then announce a verdict.
3. Close List the conquistadors discussed in this section on the chalkboard. For each, have students complete the following sentences: "I am proud that I . . ." and "I regret that I . . ."

 Lesson Planner

For a developed **Cooperative Learning** lesson plan, see the *Lesson Planner,* page 14.

Answer to Caption

Possible Answers: crossbows, rifles, suits of armor

Students Acquiring English
Activity

Note that the new vocabulary terms in this section are all words of Spanish origin. If the first language of any of your SAE students is Spanish, have them share with the class knowledge of pronunciation and background information. You might pair Spanish-speaking students with other SAE students or with students having difficulty with the concepts to assist in comprehension.

Connections With Geography
Background

In 1513, Spanish explorers led by Vasco Núñez de Balboa crossed the Isthmus of Panama and became the first Europeans to see the Pacific Ocean from American soil. Francisco Pizarro, who later conquered the Incas, was among them. Balboa called the ocean the "Great South Sea." It was Magellan, 7 years later, who called it *Pacific,* meaning "peaceful."

Learning Styles
Visual Learners

Visual learners might benefit if they trace Magellan's voyage on a globe to get a more comprehensive picture of how far his ships traveled.

Answers to Map Study

1. Viceroyalty of New Spain, Viceroyalty of Peru 2. Portugal 3. The Caribbean Sea provided the most direct sea route between New Spain and the Atlantic Ocean.

Historical Outline Map Book

Historical Outline Map Duplicate and distribute the map, Spanish Explorers in North America, on page 9 of the *American History Historical Outline Map Book*. In addition, have students refer to the map, Voyages of Discovery (previously distributed in Section 1), from page 8 of the *American History Historical Outline Map Book*. Lesson ideas for these maps can be found on page T2. (Reteaching/Average)

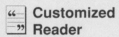

Customized Reader

Primary Source For a respectful account of Montezuma and a vivid description of the richness of his court, order article IA-1, Montezuma, from the *American History Customized Reader*. These observations were recorded by Bernal Díaz del Castillo, a Spanish conquistador who accompanied Cortés. (Enrichment/Average)

Our Multicultural Heritage

Biography Have students read the biography, Doña Marina, Adviser to Cortés, on page 7 of the *Our Multicultural Heritage* booklet. (Enrichment/Challenging)

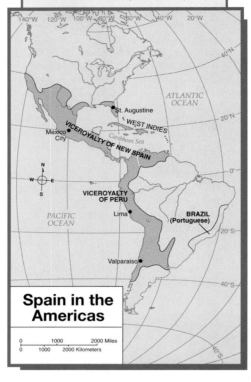

MAP STUDY

In the 1500s, Spain built a huge empire in the Americas.
1. *Into what two parts was Spain's American empire divided?*
2. *What other European nation set up colonies in South America?*
3. *Forecasting Why was control of the Caribbean Sea important to Spain?*

Spain in the Americas

St. Augustine
WEST INDIES
Mexico City
Caribbean Sea
VICEROYALTY OF NEW SPAIN
ATLANTIC OCEAN
VICEROYALTY OF PERU
Lima
BRAZIL (Portuguese)
PACIFIC OCEAN
Valparaiso

0   1000   2000 Miles
0 1000 2000 Kilometers

Two great empires fall. The Spanish leader, Hernando Cortés (kor TEHZ), accepted Montezuma's invitation. Like other conquistadors, Cortés wanted power and riches. An Indian woman the Spanish called Doña Marina had told Cortés about Aztec gold. With only about 600 soldiers and 16 horses, Cortés set out to defeat the Aztecs.

72 • Chapter 3

On November 8, 1519, Cortés marched into Tenochtitlán. For six months, he held Montezuma prisoner in his own city. Finally, the Aztecs attacked, driving out the Spanish. But Cortés soon returned. With the help of neighboring peoples the Aztecs had conquered, the Spanish captured and destroyed most of Tenochtitlán. The mighty Aztec empire had fallen.

A few years later, a conquistador named Francisco Pizarro (pee ZAR oh) matched Cortés's conquest. Sailing along the Pacific coast of present-day Chile, Pizarro invaded the Incan empire. In a surprise attack, he captured and later killed the Incan ruler, Atahualpa (at ah WAHL pah). By 1535, Pizarro controlled much of the Incan empire.

Reasons for the Spanish conquest. How did the conquistadors, with only a handful of soldiers, manage to conquer these two great empires? First, the Spanish fought with iron swords, guns, and cannons. The Native Americans fought with less powerful bows, arrows, and spears. Second, the Aztecs and Incas had never seen horses. They were frightened by the mounted Spanish knights.

Finally, the Indians had no resistance to European diseases. Large numbers of Indians died from chicken pox, measles, and influenza. Some historians believe that disease alone would have ensured Spanish victory over the Indians.

Aztec and Incan treasures made the conquistadors rich. Spain grew rich, too, especially after the discovery of gold and silver in Mexico and Peru. Spanish treasure ships laden with thousands of tons of gold and silver sailed regularly across the Atlantic.

The Spanish Borderlands

The Spanish search for treasure extended beyond Mexico and Peru. Moving north, conquistadors explored the area known as the **Spanish borderlands.** The borderlands

---

spanned the present-day United States from Florida to California.

To the east, Juan Ponce de León (PAWN suh day lay AWN) traveled through parts of Florida in 1513, looking for a Fountain of Youth. Indians claimed that anyone who bathed in this magical fountain would remain young forever. But Ponce de León found no fountain.

In 1539, Hernando De Soto arrived in Florida in search of gold and treasure. For the next few years, he explored the borderlands. In 1541, he reached the waters of the broad Mississippi River. De Soto died along the riverbanks, however, without finding the riches he sought.

In the meantime, a conquistador named Francisco Coronado (koh roh NAH doh) heard stories of seven cities of gold. Coronado led an expedition into the southwestern borderlands in 1540. Some of his party went as far as the Grand Canyon. Still, the Zuñi villages he visited had no golden streets.

Adventures in the Spanish Borderlands

One of the most remarkable journeys across the Spanish borderlands began with disaster. In 1528, the conquistador Pánfilo de Narváez (nar VAH ehs) landed in Florida with a few hundred men. Narváez unwisely attacked Native Americans and stole their food. The Indians struck back. The Spanish retreated west along the coast and then across the mouth of the Mississippi River. One stormy night, Narváez, in a small boat, was blown into the Gulf of Mexico, never to be seen again.

Four survivors. In the end, only four men from the expedition survived. Álvar Núñez Cabeza de Vaca became their leader. Estevanico (ehs teh vuh NEE koh), an enslaved African, became the group's transla-

tor and scout. Cabeza de Vaca recalled how desperate they were:

“[We] had lost everything. . . . It was November, bitterly cold, and we were in such a state that every bone could be counted. . . . We looked like death itself.”

The Charucco (chah ROO koh) Indians found the survivors and nursed them back to health. To the surprise of the Spanish, the Indians insisted that the men act as healers. "[The Charuccos] cure illness by breathing on the sick. . . and they ordered us to do the same," Cabeza de Vaca reported.

The survivors resisted at first but finally agreed to cooperate. "Our method," recalled Cabeza de Vaca, "was to bless the sick, breathing on them. . . praying with all earnestness to God our Lord that He would give health." When a number of the sick recovered, the Charuccos were impressed.

Estevanico *Between 1533 and 1536, a tiny band of shipwreck survivors wandered through the Spanish borderlands. Among them was a young African named Estevanico. He is pictured here in his finest clothes, after the journey.* **Daily Life** *What skills did Estevanico have that helped the group survive in the borderlands?*

Answer to Caption
Estevanico's skills as a translator and scout helped the four men survive.

Chapter Resources

Geography in History Duplicate and distribute the worksheet, The Search for Golden Kingdoms, from Unit 1, pages 29–30, of the *Chapter Resources* binder. This worksheet discusses some of the many explorers who set out for the Americas in the sixteenth century. (Enrichment/Average)

Linking Past and Present
Background

Before he searched for the Fountain of Youth, Ponce de León explored an island that Columbus had visited. Sighting a beautiful bay north of the island, he gave the site the name by which it is still known today—Puerto Rico, or "rich port." After putting down a rebellion by the Taínos, Ponce de León became the first European governor of Puerto Rico.

When Ponce de León made his quest in 1513, he was awed by the flower-filled peninsula that he found. He gave it a name that also has remained to this day—Florida.

Answer to Caption

Cannons posted around the walls of the fort were the chief means of defense.

Voices of Freedom

For nearly five years, the four men lived as slaves of the Charuccos. They ate mainly roots, spiders, worms, caterpillars, lizards, snakes, and ant eggs. Aside from healing the sick, the men were forced to gather and chop firewood. This labor left deep scars on their shoulders and chests.

A long journey. In 1533, the four men escaped their masters and set out in search of Spanish settlements to the west. Walking barefoot from Indian village to Indian village, they crossed the plains of Texas.

Throughout the journey, Estevanico acted as go-between with the Indians. According to Cabeza de Vaca, "He inquired about the road we should follow, the villages—in short, about everything we wished to know." Hundreds of Indians flocked around the four men, running ahead to the next village, bringing news of the great healers.

The journey continued across the Rio Grande and then south through the mountains and desert of Mexico. In 1536, the four men finally reached the Spanish settlement of Compostela (kahm poh STEH lah). It had been an astonishing journey of more than 1,000 miles (1,600 km). (See the map on page 75.) ■

Setting Up a Government

The Spanish expeditions into the borderlands met with little success. Faced with fierce Indian resistance in North America, Spain focused instead on bringing order to its empire to the south.

At first, Spain let the conquistadors govern its lands in the Americas. But the conquistadors proved to be poor rulers. When gold and silver began to flow into Spain from the Americas, the Spanish king decided to set up stronger, more stable governments there.

In 1535, the king divided his lands into New Spain and Peru. (See the map on page 72.) He put a viceroy in charge of each region to rule in his name.

Three kinds of settlements. The viceroy and other royal officials enforced a code of laws called the *Laws of the Indies.* These laws stated in detail how the colonies should be organized and ruled.

The Laws of the Indies provided for three kinds of settlements in New Spain. They were pueblos, presidios (prih SIHD ee ohz), and missions.

Pueblos were towns that were centers of farming and trade. In the middle of the town was a plaza, or public square. Here, townspeople and farmers gathered on important occasions. They also came to worship at the church. Shops and homes lined both sides of the plaza.

Presidios were forts with high adobe walls, where soldiers lived. Inside were

The Presidio at St. Augustine
The Spanish built a string of missions and presidios in the borderlands. This drawing, done in the late 1500s, shows a plan of the first presidio, built at St. Augustine, Florida. **Technology** *Based on this drawing, how did the Spanish defend the presidio?*

Conquistadors explored parts of North America in the 1500s. They mapped routes that Spanish missionaries and settlers later followed.
1. Which explorer was the first to visit Florida?
2. Which Spanish settlement was farthest east?
3. **Linking Past and Present** Based on the map, in what areas of the present-day United States would you expect to find Spanish influence?

The Spanish Borderlands

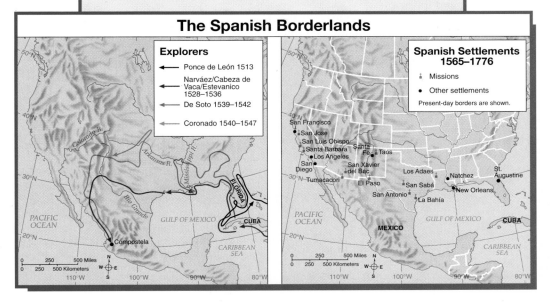

Explorers
→ Ponce de León 1513
→ Narváez/Cabeza de Vaca/Estevanico 1528–1536
→ De Soto 1539–1542
→ Coronado 1540–1547

Spanish Settlements 1565–1776
⚓ Missions
● Other settlements
Present-day borders are shown.

" " Customized Reader

Primary Source For a documented view of a Spanish colony in Florida between the years 1569 and 1576, order article IB-7, A Spanish Colony in Florida, from the *American History Customized Reader*. (Enrichment/Challenging)

" " Customized Reader

Primary Source For a firsthand view of Spanish missionaries' struggles to establish a mission in San Diego, order article IIA-17, The Founding of San Diego: California's First Mission, from the *American History Customized Reader*. Note that the letter, written in 1769 by Father Junípero Serra, reveals some lack of understanding and respect toward Native Americans. (Enrichment/Average)

shops, stables for horses, and storehouses for food. Most soldiers lived in large barracks. The farmers who settled around presidios felt safer knowing that military help was close by.

Missions were religious settlements run by Catholic priests and friars. Like other Europeans who settled in the Americas, the Spanish believed that they had a duty to convert Indians to the Christian religion. The missions throughout New Spain forced Indians to live and work on them. By setting up presidios and missions, the Laws of the Indies allowed Spain to rule the conquered Indians.

Missions in the borderlands. During their first hundred years in the Americas, the Spanish did not build settlements in the borderlands. The only exception was at *St. Augustine,* Florida, where a presidio was erected in 1565.

In time, however, Spanish interest in the borderlands grew. As you have read, in 1598, Juan de Oñate founded the colony of New Mexico. Later, Spanish missionaries moved into other areas of the American Southwest. The first mission in Texas was founded at El Paso in 1659.

Father Eusebio Francisco Kino (KEE noh) crossed into present-day Arizona in 1691. During the next 20 years, he set up 24 missions in the area. Missionaries also moved into California. By the late 1700s, a string of missions dotted the California coast from present-day San Diego to San Francisco. (See the map above.)

Chapter 3 • 75

Our Multicultural Heritage
Activity

Students may enjoy making a bulletin board display of Spanish influences on American culture. Students can begin by identifying Spanish words that have become a part of the English language, such as *alligator, cargo, cork, fiesta, lariat, lasso, mosquito, potato, ranch, rodeo, tobacco, tornado,* and *vanilla.* These and other Spanish words and phrases familiar to students might be defined and

illustrated along with their Spanish equivalents or root words.

Students can also identify foods such as tacos, tortillas, and fajitas that have become popular in the American diet. Have students make drawings or take photographs of buildings, clothing, footwear, and headgear that show Spanish influences.

A Class System

The Laws of the Indies divided the people in Spanish colonies into four social classes: peninsulares (puh nihn suh LAH rayz), creoles (KREE ohlz), mestizos (mehs TEE zohz), and Indians.

At the top of the social scale were the **peninsulares.** Born in Spain, the peninsulares were sent by the Spanish government to rule the colonies. They held the highest jobs in the colonial government and the Catholic Church. They also owned large tracts of land and rich gold and silver mines.

Next below the peninsulares were the **creoles.** Creoles were people born in the Americas to Spanish parents. Many creoles were wealthy and well educated. They owned farms and ranches, taught at universities, and practiced law. However, they could not hold the same jobs as peninsulares. This policy made the creoles resent the peninsulares.

Below the creoles were the **mestizos,** people of mixed Spanish and Indian background. Mestizos worked on farms and ranches owned by creoles. In the cities, they worked as carpenters, shoemakers, tailors, and bakers.

The lowest class in the colonies was the Indians. The Spanish treated them as a conquered people. Under New Spain's strict social system, Indians were kept in poverty for hundreds of years.

Native American and African Workers

The colonists who came to New Spain needed workers for their ranches and farms. The Spanish government helped by giving settlers **encomiendas** (ehn koh mee EHN dahz), or the right to demand labor or taxes from Native Americans living on the land. Indian labor became even more important after the Spanish found large veins of silver and gold in Mexico and Peru.

Indians in mines and on plantations. During the 1500s, Spanish mines in the Americas produced thousands of tons of silver. The mining center at Potosí, Peru, became larger than any city in the Americas or in Spain.

The Spanish forced Native American laborers to work in the mines. In flickering darkness, Indian workers climbed down rickety ladders to narrow tunnels where they hacked out the rich ore. Many died when tunnels caved in.

On the islands of the West Indies, the Spanish imported thousands of Indians to work on **plantations,** or large estates farmed by many workers. They grew sugar cane and tobacco, which plantation owners sold in Spain at a huge profit.

Las Casas seeks reform. Thousands of Native Americans died from overwork on plantations and in mines. As you have read, European diseases killed millions more. These harsh conditions led one priest, Bartolomé de Las Casas (day lahs KAH sahs), to plead for reform.

Traveling through New Spain, Las Casas saw Indians dying of hunger, disease, and mistreatment. In his own words:

66The Indians were totally deprived of their freedom. . . . Even beasts enjoy more freedom when they are allowed to graze in the field.99

Horrified, he journeyed to Spain and asked the king to protect the Indians. In the 1540s, the royal government did pass laws stating that Native Americans could not be enslaved. The laws also allowed Indians to own cattle and grow crops. Few officials in New Spain enforced the new laws, however.

Slaves from Africa. As more and more Native Americans died from disease and mistreatment, the Spanish looked for other workers. Bartolomé de Las Casas suggested that Africans be brought as slaves to replace Indian laborers. Unlike Indians, Africans did not catch European diseases, he said. Besides, they were used to doing hard farm work in their homelands.

76 • Chapter 3

Our Multicultural Heritage
Background

Before he became a priest, Las Casas had owned encomiendas in New Spain and the Indians who worked them. He was the first priest to be ordained in the Americas—and one of the first colonists to free his slaves.

In his crusade against enslavement, Las Casas told the story of Hatuey, a Native American who asked a monk if Spaniards could go to heaven: "The monk replied that it was [open] to those who were good. With no more thought, Hatuey said he had no mind to go to heaven, for fear of meeting with such cruel and wicked people as they were; he would much rather go to hell. This is the renown and honor that God and our religion have acquired."

BIOGRAPHY **Sor Juana** *Juana Inés de la Cruz was the most talented poet of New Spain. Refused admission to the university in Mexico City because she was a girl, she entered a convent at age 16. There, she devoted herself to studying and to writing poetry. She also wrote a spirited defense of women's right to education.* **Culture** *What obstacles did Sor Juana have to overcome?*

In 1517, colonists began importing Africans to labor as slaves in the Americas. By the time he died, Las Casas came to regret his suggestion. He saw that Africans suffered as much as Indians. By then, though, the plantation system had taken hold. In the years that followed, the African slave trade grew, not only in the Spanish colonies but elsewhere in the Americas.

A Blending of Cultures

By the mid-1500s, a new way of life had begun to take shape in New Spain. It blended Spanish and Indian ways.

Spanish settlers brought their own customs and culture to the colonies. They introduced their language, laws, religion, and learning. In 1539, a printer in Mexico City produced the first European book in the Americas. In 1551, the Spanish founded the University of Mexico.

Native Americans also influenced the culture of New Spain. As you have read in Chapter 2, colonists adopted many items of Indian clothing, such as the poncho, a coat-like blanket with a hole in the middle for the head. The Indians introduced Spanish colonists to new foods, including potatoes, corn, tomatoes, and chocolate. In time, Native American foods spread to Europe, Asia, and Africa, forever changing people's diets there.

Indian labor made it possible for Spanish settlers to build many fine libraries, theaters, and churches. The Indians worked with materials they knew well, such as adobe bricks. Sometimes, Spanish priests allowed Indian artists to decorate the church walls with paintings of harvests and local traditions.

SECTION 2 REVIEW

1. **Locate:** (a) Pacific Ocean, (b) Florida, (c) New Spain, (d) Peru, (e) St. Augustine.
2. **Identify:** (a) Vasco Núñez de Balboa, (b) Ferdinand Magellan, (c) Montezuma, (d) Hernando Cortés, (e) Francisco Pizarro, (f) Spanish borderlands, (g) Laws of the Indies.
3. **Define:** (a) conquistador, (b) pueblo, (c) presidio, (d) mission, (e) peninsulare, (f) creole, (g) mestizo, (h) encomienda, (i) plantation.
4. Why did Las Casas want colonists to bring Africans to labor as slaves in New Spain?
5. (a) How did the Spanish contribute to the culture of New Spain? (b) How did Native Americans contribute?
6. **CRITICAL THINKING Synthesizing Information** How did Cabeza de Vaca and his three companions survive for eight years in the Spanish borderlands?

ACTIVITY **Writing to Learn** Imagine that you are a messenger for Montezuma. Write a report to the emperor describing the arrival of Cortés.

Answers to Section 2 Review

1. See the maps on pp. 72 and 75.
2. (a) Vasco Núñez de Balboa, p. 71, (b) Ferdinand Magellan, p. 71, (c) Montezuma, p. 71, (d) Hernando Cortés, p. 72, (e) Francisco Pizarro, p. 72, (f) Spanish borderlands, p. 72, (g) Laws of the Indies, p. 74
3. (a) conquistador, p. 70, (b) pueblo, p. 74, (c) presidio, p. 74, (d) mission, p. 75, (e) peninsulare, p. 76, (f) creole, p. 76, (g) mestizo, p. 76, (h) encomienda, p. 76, (i) plantation, p. 76
4. He felt that Africans were more used to hard farm work and more resistant to European diseases.
5. (a) Spanish settlers introduced their customs and culture, including language, laws, religion, and learning. (b) Native Americans introduced clothing styles and new foods. Native American labor made it possible for Spanish settlers to build many fine libraries, theaters, and churches. They introduced adobe bricks as a building material.
6. Possible Answer: They survived with the help of various Native American tribes.

Section 3
pp. 78–83

Bell Ringer

Ask: Why do you think many American place names begin with the word *New*? Encourage students to suggest more than one reason.

Lesson Plan

1. Focus When news of Spain's success in the Americas reached other European nations, they sent their own expeditions. Some new explorers hoped to find a passage through or around North America. Others helped to establish colonies. In this section, students will learn about early French, Dutch, and English explorations in North America.

2. Instruct Have students create a classroom chart. Down the left side, they can write the names of the explorers covered in this section. Across the top, have them write: Nationality, Sponsor (Country), Area Explored, Dates of Exploration, Reason for Exploration, and Discoveries. Ask: Did any of these explorers visit our local area? If so, place a star beside that person's name.

3. Close Pair students. Have partners quiz each other. Allow students time to study the classroom chart; then remove it before they begin asking each other questions.

3
Staking Claims in North America

FIND OUT

■ What European nations searched for a northwest passage?

■ Why did the Protestant Reformation heighten rivalry among nations?

■ How were New France and New Netherland founded?

■ How did the arrival of Europeans affect Indians in North America?

VOCABULARY northwest passage, coureur de bois

In August 1497, the court of King Henry VII of England buzzed with excitement. Italian sea captain Giovanni Caboto and a crew of sailors from the port of Bristol, England, had just returned from a 79-day Atlantic voyage. Caboto, called John Cabot by the English, reported that he had reached a "new-found" island in Asia where fish were plentiful.

Cabot's voyage was one of many that Europeans made to North America in the late 1400s and early 1500s. England, France, and the Netherlands all envied Spain's new empire. They, too, wanted colonies. Soon, they were sending explorers across the Atlantic Ocean.

GEOGRAPHY AND HISTORY
Search for a Northwest Passage

Throughout the 1500s, European nations looked for a faster way to reach the riches of Asia. Magellan's route around South America took too long, they felt. They

78 • Chapter 3

searched for a **northwest passage,** or waterway through or around North America. (See the map on page 80.)

Cabot. John Cabot was confident he had found such a passage in 1497. He was mistaken. His "new-found" island off the Asian coast was in fact off North America. Today, it is called Newfoundland and is the most eastern province of Canada.

Verrazano and Cartier. Giovanni da Verrazano (vehr rah TSAH noh), another Italian captain, sailed for the French in 1524. Verrazano journeyed along the North American coast from the Carolinas to Canada.

During the 1530s, Jacques Cartier (KAR tee yay), also sailing for the French, spotted the broad opening where the St. Lawrence River flows into the Atlantic. Looking for a route to Asia, he sailed a good distance up the St. Lawrence.

Hudson. In 1609, the English sailor Henry Hudson sailed for the Dutch. His ship, the *Half Moon,* entered what is today New York harbor. Hudson continued some 150 miles (240 km) up the river that now bears his name.

The following year, Hudson made a voyage into the far north—this time for the English. After spending a harsh winter in what is now called Hudson Bay, Hudson's crew rebelled. They put Hudson, his son, and seven loyal sailors into a small boat and set it adrift. The boat and its crew were never seen again.

All these explorers failed to find a northwest passage to Asia. But in searching for

Our Common Heritage
Jacques Cartier used the Iroquois word kanata, meaning "settlement," to name the vast land in North America that he claimed for France. Today, our neighbor to the north still bears that Indian name, although its spelling is slightly different: Canada.

Critical Thinking
Analyzing Ideas

Marco Polo's tales describing the wonders and riches that he had seen on his overland trip by horse to China and back inspired the search for a northwest passage. Ask: What advantages (besides shorter distance) would ocean travel on a large boat have over Polo's method?

Historical Sidelight
Background

When Cabot first returned to England, an onlooker noted that on his next voyage, "Mr. Cabot . . . proposes to keep along the coast from the place at which he landed . . . until he reaches an island called [Japan]. Here he believes all the spices of the world have their origins, as well as jewels." When he set sail from England again in 1498, Cabot's five ships carried a supply of trade goods because the explorer felt confident that he would do business with the Great Khan of China.

As they explored the banks of the St. Lawrence River, Cartier and his men gathered barrels of what they believed were diamonds and gold. How disappointed they must have been when, upon their return to France, they found that their "treasure" consisted of quartz crystals and "fool's gold" (pyrite)!

78

one, they did something just as important. They mapped and explored many parts of North America. Now, rulers began thinking about how to profit from the region's rich resources. ■

Religious and Political Rivalries

As European nations raced to gain riches and trade, differences in religious beliefs heightened their rivalry. Until the 1500s, the Roman Catholic Church was the only church in western Europe. In 1517, however, a new reform movement arose that sharply divided Christians.

Catholics versus Protestants. In that year, a German monk named Martin Luther challenged many practices of the Catholic Church. Luther believed that the Church had become too worldly and greedy. He also objected to the Catholic teaching that believers needed to perform good works in order to gain eternal life. He argued that people could be saved only by their faith in God.

Luther's supporters became known as Protestants because of their protests against the Church. "Faith alone" became their rallying cry. The ***Protestant Reformation,*** as the new movement was known, sharply divided Christians in Europe. Within a short time, the Protestants also split, forming many different Protestant churches.

Rivalries in the Americas. When European states expanded to the Americas, they brought their religious and political rivalries with them. For example, in the late 1500s, Roman Catholic monarchs ruled Spain and France. England had a Protestant queen, Elizabeth. Elizabeth encouraged English adventurers to sail along the coasts of New Spain, raiding Spanish treasure fleets. England and France also were religious rivals. In North America, each tried to claim as much territory as possible.

Not all rivalries were religious, however. The Netherlands, like England, was a Prot-

Elizabeth I *Under Elizabeth I, England engaged in a bitter rivalry with Spain. The rivalry ended in 1588, when England defeated the Spanish Armada, the largest fleet in the world at the time. Here, Elizabeth is being carried by her courtiers.* **Daily Life** *How does the painting show the wealth of Elizabeth's court?*

estant nation. Yet Dutch and English merchant ships competed with each other for markets all over the world. Later, the Dutch and the English would be rivals in North America, as well.

Building New France

Early voyages of exploration convinced the French that they could not build an empire of gold in the Americas, as Spain had done. Instead, they profited from riches of the sea. Every year, French fishermen braved winter gales and dangerous icebergs to sail across the Atlantic. Off the coasts of Newfoundland, they pulled codfish from the sea in huge numbers.

French ships brought knives, kettles, cloth, and other items for trade with Native

Chapter 3 • **79**

 Lesson Planner

For a developed **Cooperative Learning** lesson plan, see the *Lesson Planner,* page 15.

Answer to Caption

Possible Answer: The presence of courtiers and the elaborate clothing show the wealth of the court.

Historical Outline Map Book

Historical Outline Map Duplicate and distribute the map, Search for a Northwest Passage, on page 10 of the *American History Historical Outline Map Book.* Lesson ideas can be found on page T3. (Reteaching/Average)

Linking Past and Present
Activity

The "birth" of Protestantism is often traced to October 31, 1517. On that day, Martin Luther nailed to the castle church door in Wittenberg, Germany, a list of 95 statements that challenged Church teachings and practices. The "95 Theses" created such a stir that a split with Catholicism became inevitable.

Point out the boldness of Luther's action. Then ask: What modern-day forms of protest help to gain attention for a cause?

Connections With the World
Background

In response to the Reformation, the Roman Catholic Church began its own period of reform in the 1500s and 1600s. This movement was called the Counter Reformation. A number of religious orders were founded, including the Jesuits, who became missionaries in the Americas and Asia. Jacques Marquette was a Jesuit.

Americans. In return, the French took home beaver skins. These furs sold for high prices in Europe.

In the early 1600s, the man who promoted French fur trade most was Samuel de Champlain (sham PLAYN). Champlain, an excellent sailor and mapmaker, founded the first permanent settlements in what became known as **New France.** The first colony took root at Port Royal, Nova Scotia, in 1605. Three years later, Champlain led another group of settlers along the route Cartier had pioneered. On a rocky cliff high above the St. Lawrence River, Champlain built a trading post known as Quebec (kwee BEHK).

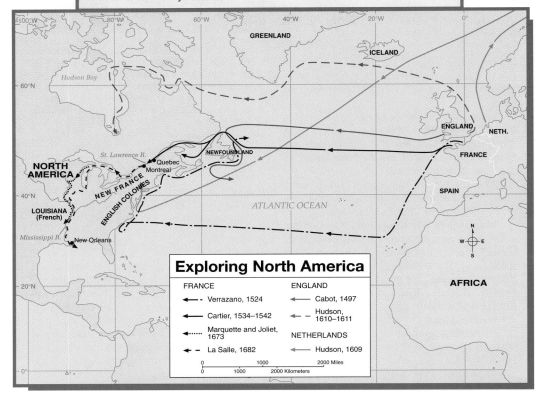

MAP STUDY

Explorers from many European nations traveled across North America.
1. For which nation was Hudson sailing when he entered Hudson Bay?
2. Name in order the bodies of water that La Salle traveled on or crossed over.
3. **Forecasting** *Explorers usually claimed lands for the nation that had outfitted their voyage. Name two areas of North America where conflicts over land claims were likely to arise.*

Exploring North America

FRANCE	ENGLAND
◄— Verrazano, 1524	◄— Cabot, 1497
◄— Cartier, 1534–1542	◄— Hudson, 1610–1611
◄····· Marquette and Joliet, 1673	NETHERLANDS
◄ – La Salle, 1682	◄— Hudson, 1609

0   1000   2000 Miles
0   1000   2000 Kilometers

Our Multicultural Heritage
Background

In the 1700s, many of the early French settlers in a section of Canada they called Acadia (known today as Nova Scotia or New Scotland) were forced to leave by the British, who had gained control of the area. They moved to Louisiana, which was still under French rule. There they kept many of their French customs and became known as "Cajuns." (*Cajun* is a corrupted form of *Acadian*.) *Evangeline,* a long narrative poem by the New England poet Henry Wadsworth Longfellow, is a sympathetic account of the Acadians' plight when deported from their northern homeland.

Claiming the Mississippi Valley *Frenchman Robert de La Salle explored the Mississippi River. In this painting, George Catlin shows the dramatic moment when La Salle claimed the Mississippi Valley for France.* **Multicultural Heritage** *How do you think La Salle's claim affected Native Americans, such as those in the painting?*

Trappers, traders, and missionaries. Most French colonists were trappers and traders. Because they lived in the woods, they became known as **coureurs de bois** (koo RYOOR duh BWAH), or runners of the woods.

Coureurs de bois learned from Native Americans how to trap and survive in the woods. Many married Indian women. Indians taught the French how to build and use canoes. Each fall, Indians and trappers paddled up the St. Lawrence to winter trapping grounds. In the spring, trappers loaded the furs they had collected into canoes for the trip back down the St. Lawrence.

Catholic missionaries often traveled with the fur traders. The missionaries were determined to convert Native Americans to Christianity. They set up missions, drew maps, and wrote about newly explored lands. Life was difficult, especially in winter.

One priest recalled traveling through deep snow using Indian snowshoes:

> 66 If a thaw came, dear Lord, what pain! . . . I was marching on an icy path that broke with every step I took; as the snow softened. . . we often sunk in it up to our knees and a few times up to the waist. 99

Reaching the "Father of the Waters." French trappers followed the St. Lawrence deep into the heart of North America. Led by Indian guides, they reached the Great Lakes. Here, Indians spoke of a mighty river, which they called Mississippi, or "Father of the Waters."

In 1673, a French missionary, Father Jacques Marquette (mar KEHT), and a fur trader, Louis Joliet (JOH lee eht), set out with Indian guides to reach the Mississippi. They followed the river for more than 700 miles

Chapter 3 • **81**

(1,100 km) before turning back. In 1682, another explorer, Robert de La Salle (lah SAHL), completed the journey to the Gulf of Mexico. La Salle named the region *Louisiana* in honor of the French king, Louis XIV.

To keep Spain and England out of Louisiana, the French built forts along the Mississippi. One fort, at the mouth of the river, was named New Orleans. New Orleans soon grew into a busy trading center. The French also built forts along the Great Lakes, in the north. Among them was Fort Detroit, built by Antoine Cadillac near Lake Erie.

Government of New France. New France was governed much like New Spain. The French king controlled the government directly, and people in settled areas had little freedom. A council appointed by the king made all decisions.

In the 1660s, to encourage farming, Louis XIV sent about a thousand farmers to the colony. The newcomers included many young women. Some were nobles. Others came from middle-class or peasant families. Most of the women were single, but they soon found husbands. Peasant women were in greatest demand because they were used to hard work.

Despite Louis's efforts, New France grew slowly. By 1680, only about 10,000 settlers lived in the colony. Of those, one third lived on farms along the St. Lawrence. Many more chose the life of the coureurs de bois, who lived largely free of government control.

Building New Netherland

At first, the Dutch paid little attention to Henry Hudson's reports about the river that now bears his name. Finally, in 1626, Peter Minuit (MIHN yoo wiht) led a group of Dutch settlers to North America. There, he bought Manhattan Island from local Indians. Minuit called his settlement New Amsterdam.

Other Dutch colonists settled farther up the Hudson River. The entire colony was known as *New Netherland.* In 1655, the Dutch enlarged New Netherland by taking over New Sweden. The Swedes had set up New Sweden along the Delaware River some 15 years earlier.

New Amsterdam *The Dutch founded New Amsterdam on the Hudson River. From 30 houses, it soon grew into a busy port where ships docked from all around the world. This painting of New Amsterdam was done about 1650.* **Geography** *How did its location on the Hudson River help New Amsterdam to thrive?*

Rivalry over furs. From the beginning, Dutch traders sent furs back to the Netherlands. The packing list for the first shipment included "the skins of 7,246 beaver, 853 otter, 81 mink, 36 cat lynx, and 34 small rats."

In the hunt for furs, the Dutch became fierce rivals of the French and their Indian allies, the Algonquins (al GAHN kwihnz). The Dutch made friends with the Iroquois, longtime enemies of the Algonquins. With Iroquois help, the Dutch brought furs down the Hudson to New Amsterdam. The French and Algonquins tried to block them. For many years, fighting raged among Europeans and their Indian allies.

Dutch ways in North America. By the mid-1600s, New Amsterdam had grown into a bustling port. The Dutch welcomed people of many nations and religions to their colony. One Dutch governor boasted that more than 15 languages could be heard in the streets of New Amsterdam.

The Dutch liked to ice-skate, and in winter the frozen rivers and ponds filled with skaters. Other Dutch customs also became part of American culture. For example, every year on Saint Nicholas's birthday, children put out their shoes to be filled with presents. Later, "Saint Nick" became Santa Claus, bringing gifts on Christmas Eve.

Some Dutch words entered the English language. A Dutch master was a "boss." The people of New Amsterdam sailed in "yachts." Dutch children munched on "cookies" and went for rides through the snow on "sleighs."

Impact on Native Americans

The coming of Europeans to North America brought major changes for Native Americans. As in New Spain, European diseases killed millions of Native Americans. Rivalry over the fur trade brought increased Indian warfare as European settlers encouraged their Indian allies to attack one another. The scramble for furs also led to overtrapping. By 1640, trappers had almost wiped out the beavers on Iroquois lands in upstate New York.

The arrival of European settlers affected Native Americans in other ways. Missionaries tried to convert Indians to Christianity. Indians eagerly adopted European trade goods, such as copper kettles and knives, as well as muskets and gunpowder for hunting. Alcohol sold by European traders had a harsh effect on Native American life.

The French, Dutch, and English all seized Indian lands. Indian nations that were forced off their lands moved westward onto lands of other Indians. At one time or another, each of these European nations also enslaved Native Americans and sold them to plantations in the West Indies. The conflict between Native Americans and Europeans would continue for many years.

SECTION 3 REVIEW

1. **Locate:** (a) Newfoundland, (b) St. Lawrence River, (c) Hudson Bay, (d) New France, (e) Quebec, (f) Louisiana.
2. **Identify:** (a) Henry Hudson, (b) Protestant Reformation, (c) Samuel de Champlain, (d) Robert de La Salle, (e) New Netherland.
3. **Define:** (a) northwest passage, (b) coureur de bois.
4. Why were Spain and England rivals in the late 1500s?
5. Why did settlers in New France prefer trapping to farming?
6. Name three ways Native Americans were affected by the arrival of Europeans.
7. **CRITICAL THINKING Comparing** (a) Name two ways in which New France differed from New Spain. (b) Name two ways in which they were similar.

 Writing to Learn

Imagine that you are a coureur de bois along the St. Lawrence River. Write a diary entry about a typical day.

Answers to Section 3 Review

1. See the map on p. 80.
2. (a) Henry Hudson, p. 78, (b) Protestant Reformation, p. 79, (c) Samuel de Champlain, p. 80, (d) Robert de La Salle, p. 82, (e) New Netherland, p. 82
3. (a) northwest passage, p. 78, (b) coureur de bois, p. 81
4. Spain was the most powerful Catholic nation in Europe; England was the most powerful Protestant nation.
5. Settlers preferred trapping to farming because trappers lived free of government control—and made more money.
6. Rivalry over the fur trade brought increased Native American warfare; alcohol had a harsh effect on their lives; settlers seized their lands.
7. Possible Answers: (a) New France was settled more slowly than New Spain; New France profited from the riches of the sea rather than from empires of gold; trapping and trading of furs for goods was prevalent in New France. (b) Both were controlled by governments at home in Europe, and missionaries in both settlements attempted to convert Native Americans (whom they often enslaved) to Roman Catholicism.

Section 4
pp. 84–89

Bell Ringer

Have the class brainstorm for and list rules they would enact if they were establishing a new colony.

Lesson Plan

1. Focus It was not until the late 1500s that some English explorers began establishing colonies as a means of laying permanent claim to land in the Americas. This section focuses on the "lost colony" of Roanoke, the Jamestown settlement, and the Plymouth colony. Students also learn about problems encountered by the Jamestown and Plymouth colonists, the help they received from Native Americans, and the establishment of representative governments in these two settlements.

2. Instruct Have students continue the classroom chart they began in Section 3, adding pertinent information about Roanoke, Jamestown, and Plymouth. (Tell them to research and find the names of leaders who helped establish Plymouth.)

4
The First English Colonies

FIND OUT
- How did tobacco help save the Jamestown Colony?
- How did self-government begin in Virginia?
- Why did the Pilgrims start a colony in North America?
- How did Native Americans help the Plymouth colonists?

VOCABULARY charter, burgess, representative government

"**I**f England possesses these places in America, Her Majesty will have good harbors, plenty of excellent trees for masts, good timber to build ships. . . all things needed for a royal navy, and all for no price."

Richard Hakluyt wrote these words to convince Queen Elizabeth I of England to set up colonies in North America. Hakluyt listed a total of 31 arguments in favor of settlement. "We shall," Hakluyt concluded, "[stop] the Spanish king from flowing over all the face. . . of America."

Hakluyt's pamphlet, written in 1584, appealed to English pride. England's rival, Spain, had built a great empire in the Americas. England was determined to win a place there, too.

Colony at Roanoke

The man who encouraged Hakluyt to write his pamphlet was Sir Walter Raleigh, a favorite of Queen Elizabeth. With the queen's permission, Raleigh raised money to outfit a colony in North America. In 1585, seven ships and about 100 men set sail across the Atlantic.

The expedition landed on Roanoke (ROH uh nohk), an island off the coast of present-day North Carolina. Within a year, colonists had run short of food and quarreled with neighboring Indians. When an English ship stopped in the harbor, the weary settlers climbed aboard and sailed home.

A second attempt. Among the original colonists was an artist, John White. In 1587, Raleigh asked White to return to Roanoke with another group of settlers. To help the settlers set up a farming community, Raleigh sent a number of women. In Roanoke, one woman, Ellinor Dare, gave birth to the first English child born in North America.

When supplies ran low, White returned to England. He left behind 117 colonists. Before sailing, White instructed the settlers carefully. If they moved to another place, they were to carve the name of their new location on a tree. If they were attacked, they were to draw a cross.

American Wildlife *John White made vivid drawings that gave many Europeans their first glimpse of the plants and animals of the Americas. Shown here are a sparrow eating corn, an alligator, and a box turtle.* **Geography** *Why would White's drawings be of value to Europeans who planned to settle in North America?*

Gone without a trace. White planned to return in a few months. In England, however, he found the whole nation preparing for war with Spain. It was three years before he could visit Roanoke again. When he rowed ashore, he found the settlement eerily quiet. Houses stood empty and vines twined through the windows. Pumpkins sprouted from the earthen floors.

Still, White had hope. No cross—the sign for an attack—was found. And the word CROATOAN, the name of a nearby island, was carved on a tree.

White was eager to investigate, but a storm was blowing up and his crew refused to make the trip. The next day, White stood sadly on board as the captain set sail for England. To this day, the fate of Roanoke's settlers remains a mystery.

Settlement at Jamestown

Nearly 20 years passed before England tried again to plant a colony. Then, in 1606, the Virginia Company of London received a charter from King James I. A **charter** is a legal document giving certain rights to a person or company.

The charter gave the Virginia Company the right to settle land to the north of Roanoke, between North Carolina and the Potomac River. The land was called Virginia. The charter guaranteed colonists of Virginia the same rights as English citizens.

Hard times. In the spring of 1607, 105 colonists arrived in Virginia. They sailed into Chesapeake Bay and began building homes along the James River. They named their tiny outpost Jamestown, after their king, James I.

BIOGRAPHY **Pocahontas** *Pocahontas, the daughter of Powhatan, brought food to the starving Jamestown settlers. She later married colonist John Rolfe. With him, she visited England, where an artist painted this portrait of her in English dress.* **Multicultural Heritage** *Why do you think later Americans have honored Pocahontas?*

Jamestown was located in a swampy area, however. The water was unhealthy, and mosquitoes spread malaria. Many settlers died from disease.

Governing the colony also proved difficult. The Virginia Company had chosen a council of 13 men to rule the settlement. Members of the council quarreled with each other and did little to plan for the colony's future. By the summer of 1608, the Jamestown colony was near failure.

Captain Smith takes charge. Captain John Smith, a swashbuckling soldier, saved the settlement. Smith had little patience with those who refused to plant crops. "No talk, no hope, nor work," he complained. People only wanted to "dig gold, wash gold, refine gold, load gold." But the colonists found no gold and soon ran out of food.

Smith visited nearby Indian villages to trade for food. Powhatan (pow uh TAN), the most powerful chief in the area, agreed to sell corn to the English. Back in Jamestown, Smith set up stern rules that forced colonists to work if they wished to eat.

Starvation and recovery. Life in the colony might have improved if Smith had remained in charge. In 1609, however, the

Ætatis suæ 21. Aᵒ. 1616.

Chapter 3 • **85**

3. Close To close, have students answer the *Who, What, Where, When, Why,* and *How* questions about the three colonies discussed in this section. Include questions about relationships between each group of colonists, Native Americans, and Africans.

 Lesson Planner

For a developed **Cooperative Learning** lesson plan, see the *Lesson Planner,* page 16.

Answer to Caption

Possible Answer: She helped Jamestown survive.

 Our Multicultural Heritage

Biography Have students read the biography, Pocahontas, Link Between Two Worlds, on page 8 of *Our Multicultural Heritage.* (Enrichment/Average)

 Voices of Freedom

Primary Source You might assign selection 3-6, Skills Needed in the New World, on pages 28–29 of *Voices of Freedom.* (Enrichment/Average)

CD-ROM

History Makers Access the biographies of Pocahontas and John Smith from the American Heritage® *History of the United States* CD-ROM. (Enrichment/Average)

Historical Sidelight
Background

Powhatan's actual name was Wahunsonacock, but English settlers referred to him by the name of his favorite village. The chief ruled an area—also known as Powhatan—of some 200 villages, all of which paid him "eight parts of ten tribute of all commodities which their country yieldth, as of wheat, pease, beanes . . . skyns, and furrs." The members of other Native American confederations had some independence, but Powhatan's villages united into a well-organized state.

Powhatan's agreement to sell corn to the English was not without problems. According to Smith's report, Powhatan complained, "My people dare not come to bring you corne, seeing you thus armed with your men. . . . What will it availe you to take that . . . you may quietly have with love, or to destroy them that provide you food?"

85

Customized Reader

Primary Source For John White's chilling report of his attempts to discover what happened to the colony at Roanoke, order article IB-4, Returning to Roanoke Colony, from the *American History Customized Reader*. (Enrichment/Challenging)

Voices of Freedom

Primary Source You might assign selection 4-4, A Virginia Colonist's Despair, on page 34 of *Voices of Freedom*. This indentured servant's letter to his parents describes the hardship of his life outside Jamestown in 1623. (Enrichment/Average)

Videotapes/ Videodiscs

United States History Video Collection Use the video segment "The English in the New World" from Volume 2, *The Era of Colonization*, to enhance students' understanding of the settlement at Jamestown. Approx. running time 4:00 min. (Enrichment/Average) Vol. 2, Ch. 10

Chapter 10	Play

---

captain badly injured his leg and had to return to England. For the next few years, the colony suffered terribly. Desperate settlers cooked "dogs, cats, snakes, [and] toadstools" to survive. To keep warm, they broke up houses to burn as firewood.

The economy of Jamestown improved when colonists began to grow tobacco after 1612. Europeans had learned about tobacco and pipe smoking from Native Americans. Although King James I considered smoking "a vile custom," the new fad caught on quickly. By 1620, England was importing more than 30,000 pounds (13,500 kg) of tobacco a year. At last, Virginians had found a way to make money.

The First Africans

In 1619, a Dutch ship landed in Jamestown with about 20 Africans. The Dutch sold the Africans to Virginians who needed laborers for growing tobacco. The colonists valued the farming skills that the Africans brought with them from their homeland.

Two of the Africans, Antoney and Isabella, married after they arrived in Virginia. In 1624, they had a son, William. He was the first child of African descent to be born in the English colonies.

Were the first Africans who came to Virginia treated as servants or as slaves? The records do not say. By 1644, about 300 Africans lived in Virginia. Some of them were slaves for life. Others worked as servants and expected one day to own their own farms. Some Africans were already free planters. In 1651, Anthony Johnson owned 250 acres of land and employed five servants to help him work it.

Later in the 1600s, Virginia would set up a system of laws allowing white colonists to enslave Africans. However, the legal system for slavery was not in place during Virginia's earliest years. For a time, some Africans who came to Virginia owned property, testified in court, and voted in elections.

Important Beginnings

The boom in tobacco saved Virginia's economy. Until 1619, however, the colony lacked a stable government. In that year, the Virginia Company sent a governor with orders to consult settlers on all important matters. Male settlers were allowed to elect **burgesses,** or representatives. The burgesses met in an assembly called the ***House of Burgesses.*** Together with the governor, they made laws for the colony.

Self-government takes root. The House of Burgesses marked the beginning of representative government in the English colonies. A **representative government** is one in which voters elect representatives to make laws for them.

The idea that people had political rights was not new to the English. In 1215, English nobles had forced King John to sign the ***Magna Carta,*** or Great Charter. This document said that the king could not raise taxes without first consulting the Great Council of nobles and church leaders. The Magna Carta showed that the king had to obey the law.

Over time, the rights won by nobles were extended to other English people. The Great Council grew into a representative assembly, called Parliament. By the 1600s, Parliament was divided into the House of Lords, made up of nobles, and an elected House of Commons. Only a few rich men had the right to vote. Still, the English had

Our Common Heritage
The first strike for civil rights may have taken place in Jamestown in 1619. Only English men could vote for the House of Burgesses. Polish settlers who had helped build the colony protested. "No vote, no work," they threatened. In the end, the Virginia Company gave the Poles the right to vote.

86 • Chapter 3

Critical Thinking
Applying Information

Representatives from Virginia and Massachusetts played leading roles in the framing of the U.S. Constitution. Ask: Which ideas found in this section do you think descendants of the Jamestown and Plymouth colonists would agree with? Which ideas might lead to disputes?

Connections With Civics
Background

King John had created a rebellion among his nobles by imposing upon them taxes that they considered unjust. This revolt was unusual, though, in that the nobles were not supporting a replacement for King John; rather, they were trying to reform the king that they had. Subsequent rulers swore to uphold the Magna Carta, thus cementing it into the English system of government.

established that their king or queen must consult Parliament on money matters and must respect the law.

At first, free Virginians had even greater rights than citizens in England. They did not have to own property in order to vote. In 1670, however, the colony restricted the vote to men who owned property.

As slavery grew, free Africans also lost rights. By 1723, even free African property owners could not vote. Women in Virginia were denied the right to vote throughout the colonial period.

Despite these limits, representative government remained important in Virginia. The idea took root that settlers should have a say in the affairs of the colony.

Women in Virginia. During the early years of the Jamestown Colony, only a few women chose to make the journey from England. The Virginia Company realized that if Jamestown were to last, there had to be more families. In 1619, the investors sent about 100 women to Virginia to help "make the men more settled." This first shipload of women quickly found husbands in Jamestown. Each man who married one of these women had to give the Virginia Company 150 pounds (68 kg) of tobacco.

Women did make the colony more settled. Still, life remained a daily struggle. Women had to make everything from scratch—food, clothing, even medicines. Hard work and childbirth killed many at a young age. Even so, settlers began to have hope that the colony might survive.

Pilgrims Seek Religious Freedom

In 1620, another band of English settlers, the **Pilgrims,** sailed for the Americas. Unlike the Virginians or the Spanish, these colonists sought neither gold nor silver. All they wanted was to practice their religion freely.

In England, the Pilgrims belonged to a religious group known as Separatists. They were called that because they wanted to sep-

arate from the official church, the Church of England. The English government bitterly opposed this. Separatists were fined, jailed, and sometimes even executed.

Leaving England. In the early 1600s, a group of Separatists left England for Leyden, a city in the Netherlands. The Dutch allowed the newcomers to worship freely. Still, the Pilgrims missed their English way

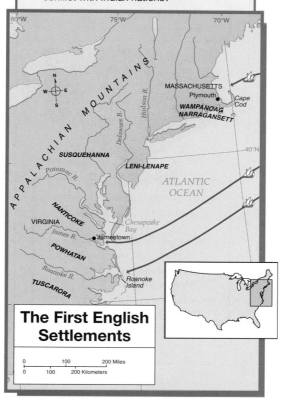

MAP STUDY

In the late 1500s and early 1600s, the English set up colonies in Roanoke, Jamestown, and Plymouth.

1. *Which of these colonies was farthest south?*

2. *The labels in dark capital letters are the names of Indian nations. Which Indians lived near the Plymouth colonists?*

3. *Forecasting Based on the map, why do you think the English settlers might come into conflict with Indian nations?*

The First English Settlements

 Videotapes/ Videodiscs

United States History Video Collection Use the video segment "Pilgrims and Puritans" from Volume 2, *The Era of Colonization,* to enhance students' understanding of the reasons the Pilgrims and the Puritans settled in Massachusetts. Approx. running time 5:00 min. (Enrichment/Average) Vol. 2, Ch. 13

Chapter 13   Play

Linking Past and Present
Activity

Explain that historical re-creations complete with actors portraying the people of the time are popular tourist attractions. Two examples are the "Lost Colony of Roanoke" in North Carolina and "Plymouth Plantation" in Massachusetts. If possible, obtain promotional literature from state tourist bureaus.

Have students design a similar attraction based on a settlement in their locale. Have

the class brainstorm and list ideas for setting, characters, costumes, activities, and so on. Have small groups of students develop specific ideas, but encourage an exchange of ideas among groups.

When planning is complete, help students prepare a proposal that can be presented to the principal for a school function with interdepartmental cooperation.

Chapter Resources

Skill Application For additional practice, duplicate and distribute the worksheet, Understanding Causes and Effects, on page 26 of the *Chapter Resources* binder. (Reteaching/Average)

Answers to Skill Lesson

1. (a) Students may list any two of the causes shown. (b) European trade with the Middle East increases; rulers of European nations seek ways to increase their wealth; European nations look for a new route to Asia. (c) Columbus reaches the Americas; exploration began as soon as Columbus reported his findings. **2.** (a) Students may list any two of the effects shown. (b) Millions of Native Americans die from "European" diseases. (c) Long-range effect; it took time for people to accept new foods. **3.** (a) Europeans were looking for a shortcut to the Middle East when they explored the Americas. (b) The slave trade grew over a long period of time.

Transparencies

Cause and Effect Use the transparency Exploration of the Americas on page F-13 of *American History Transparencies*. Teaching suggestions can be found on page F-2. (Enrichment/Average)

ACTIVITY

Guided Instruction Have students brainstorm for ideas about the Crusades. Suggest that they do additional research.

CRITICAL THINKING SKILLS
Understanding Causes and Effects

Every major event in history has both causes and effects. **Causes** are events or conditions that produced the major event. They explain why the event happened. **Effects** are events or conditions that resulted from the causes.

Causes can be immediate causes or long-range causes. Immediate causes take place shortly before the major event and help trigger it. Long-range causes are underlying causes that build up over time.

Effects can also be immediate or long range. Immediate effects take place shortly after the event. Long-range effects build up over time.

Historians sometimes give word clues for causes and effects. To signal causes, they use words such as *caused, led to,* and *brought about.* To signal effects, they use words such as *therefore, thus,* and *as a result.*

One major event that historians study is European exploration of the Americas. The chart at left lists some causes and effects of European exploration. The arrows show the order of events, from causes of the exploration to its effects.

The following steps will help you understand causes and effects. Use what you have read and the chart to answer the questions.

CAUSES

- European trade with the Middle East increases
- Europeans are curious about the world
- Rulers of European nations seek ways to increase their wealth
- European nations look for a new route to Asia
- Columbus reaches the Americas

EXPLORATION OF THE AMERICAS

EFFECTS

- Spain builds an empire in the Americas
- English, French, and Dutch set up colonies in North America
- Millions of Native Americans die from "European" diseases
- Slave traders bring enslaved Africans to the Americas
- New foods are introduced into people's diets around the world

1. **Study events that took place before the major event to find causes.** (a) What were two causes of exploration of the Americas? (b) Which causes of exploration were related to trade? (c) Which cause was most immediate? How do you know?

2. **Study events that took place after the major event to find effects.** (a) What were two effects of exploration of the Americas? (b) What was an effect of exploration on Native Americans? (c) Was the change in people's diets an immediate or a long-range effect? Explain.

3. **Analyze the causes and effects.** (a) Why was increased trade with the Middle East a cause of exploration of the Americas? (b) How was the enslaving of Africans a long-range effect?

ACTIVITY
Create a cause-and-effect chart for the Crusades. After you have made your chart, identify immediate causes and effects with an *I* and long-range causes and effects with an *L.*

Students Acquiring English
Activity

Understanding cause-and-effect relationships requires an awareness of some of the subtleties of language. Thus, SAE students might benefit by being paired with more advanced students to work on the skill lesson and activity. Encourage students to ask questions about concepts and directions that they do not understand.

of life. They also worried that their children were growing up more Dutch than English.

A group of Pilgrims returned to England. Along with some other English people, they won a charter to set up a colony in Virginia. In September 1620, more than 100 men, women, and children set sail aboard a small ship called the *Mayflower*. After a stormy two-month voyage, the Pilgrims landed on the cold, bleak shore of Cape Cod, in present-day Massachusetts. It was November 1620.

Mayflower Compact. Exhausted by the sea voyage, the Pilgrims decided to travel no farther. Their charter, however, was for a colony in Virginia, not Cape Cod. Before going ashore, they needed rules for their new home. Gathering together, the Pilgrims drew up the ***Mayflower Compact.*** The 41 men who signed it agreed to consult each other about laws for the colony and promised to work together to make the colony succeed:

66 We, whose names are underwritten... Having undertaken for the Glory of God, and Advancement of the Christian Faith... a voyage to plant the first colony in the northern parts of Virginia... do enact, constitute, and frame, such just and equal Laws... as shall be thought most [fitting] and convenient for the general Good of the Colony. 99

The Pilgrims named the colony Plymouth. During their first winter there, they had no time to build proper shelters. Most lived in sod houses quickly thrown together. Nearly half the settlers died of disease or starvation. The Pilgrims' religious faith was strong, however. They believed that it was God's will for them to remain in Plymouth.

Help from Native Americans. In the spring, the Pilgrims received help from neighboring Indians. A Pemaquid Indian, Samoset, had learned English from earlier explorers sailing along the coast. He intro-

duced the Pilgrims to Massasoit (MAS uh soit), chief of the local Wampanoag (wahm puh NOH ahg) Indians.

The Wampanoag who helped the Pilgrims most was named Squanto. Squanto brought the Pilgrims seeds of native plants—corn, beans, and pumpkins—and showed them how to plant them. He also taught the settlers to stir up eels from river bottoms and then snatch them with their hands. The grateful Pilgrims called Squanto "a special instrument sent of God."

In the fall, the Pilgrims had a good harvest. Because they believed that God had given them this harvest, they set aside a day for giving thanks. In later years, the Pilgrims celebrated each harvest with a day of thanksgiving. Americans today celebrate ***Thanksgiving*** as a national holiday.

SECTION 4 REVIEW

1. **Locate:** (a) Roanoke, (b) Jamestown, (c) Cape Cod, (d) Plymouth.
2. **Identify:** (a) Sir Walter Raleigh, (b) John White, (c) Virginia Company, (d) John Smith, (e) House of Burgesses, (f) Magna Carta, (g) Pilgrims, (h) Mayflower Compact, (i) Thanksgiving.
3. **Define:** (a) charter, (b) burgess, (c) representative government.
4. List three things that helped Jamestown to survive.
5. Why did the Pilgrims come to the Americas?
6. List two ways in which Squanto helped the Plymouth colonists.
7. **CRITICAL THINKING Comparing** How were the reasons for founding Jamestown different from the reasons for founding Plymouth?

 Writing to Learn
Imagine that it is 1620. Write an advertising pamphlet to attract settlers to Jamestown.

Chapter Resources

History Through Literature For a firsthand account of the Pilgrim settlement, duplicate and distribute the worksheet, Of Plymouth Plantation, from Unit 1, page 28, of the *Chapter Resources* binder. This is an account by William Bradford, first governor of the Plymouth Plantation. (Enrichment/Average)

Voices of Freedom

Primary Source You might assign selection 4-5, Pilgrims and Indians Make Peace, on pages 35–36 of *Voices of Freedom*. This selection contains two passages describing the first few weeks of the Pilgrims' life at Plymouth. (Enrichment/Average)

Student Study Guide

Section 4 Study Guide Have students use the Section 4 Study Guide on page 46 of the *Student Study Guide* to review and reinforce the content of this section. (Reteaching/Average)

ACTIVITY

Guided Instruction Before students begin writing advertisements, you might provide them with various travel brochures or the travel section of your local newspaper. Encourage students to draw colorful illustrations to accompany the text and to share their finished projects with the class.

Connections With Civics
Background

The signers of the Mayflower Compact included a few settlers who were not Pilgrims. However, no women signed this pact.

Answers to Section 4 Review

1. See the map on p. 87.
2. (a) Sir Walter Raleigh, p. 84, (b) John White, p. 84, (c) Virginia Company, p. 85, (d) John Smith, p. 85, (e) House of Burgesses, p. 86, (f) Magna Carta, p. 86, (g) Pilgrims, p. 87, (h) Mayflower Compact, p. 89, (i) Thanksgiving, p. 89
3. (a) charter, p. 85, (b) burgess, p. 86, (c) representative government, p. 86
4. growing tobacco, representative government, the arrival of women

5. The Pilgrims wanted the freedom to practice their religion freely.
6. Squanto brought the Pilgrims seeds of native plants and showed them how to grow them; he taught colonists how to catch eels.
7. Possible Answer: Jamestown was founded for profit; Plymouth was founded so that the Pilgrims could have religious freedom.

CHAPTER 3 REVIEW

Answers to Reviewing the Main Ideas

1. Possible Answers: new tastes and pleasures; an interest in trade; improvements in sailing; search for new routes to Asia

2. The Spanish had horses, iron swords, guns, and cannons. The Native Americans feared that the Spanish might be gods; they also had no resistance to European diseases.

3. (a) peninsulares, creoles, mestizos, Indians (b) The peninsulares held the highest jobs in the colonial government and the Roman Catholic Church. The creoles owned farms and ranches, taught at universities, and practiced law. The mestizos worked on creole-owned ranches; they were carpenters, shoemakers, tailors, and bakers in the cities. The Indians were used as forced labor.

4. Europeans hoped to find a northwest passage in or around North America that would provide a shorter route to Asia.

5. Possible Answers: European diseases killed thousands of Native Americans; European rivalry for the fur trade resulted in increased warfare; Europeans tried to convert Native Americans to Christianity; Native Americans gave up hunting with bows and arrows in favor of muskets and gunpowder; alcohol sold by European traders had a terrible effect on Native American life.

6. (a) a representative assembly that was elected to make laws for the Jamestown Colony (b) It marked the beginning of representative government in the English colonies.

7. The Pilgrims believed that it was God's will for them to remain at Plymouth.

Answers to Thinking Critically

1. Possible Answers: (a) foods like corn, potatoes, tomatoes, and chocolate (b) Spanish language, laws, and religion (c) St. Nicholas, the custom of exchanging gifts on his birthday, and many Dutch words that have remained a part of the English language (d) representative government (e) farming skills, words, music style.

Summary

- A growing interest in trade led European nations to explore the world beyond their borders.
- Spain built a large and powerful empire in the Americas.
- Throughout the 1500s, the English, French, and Dutch searched for a northwest passage to Asia.
- The first permanent English colonies in the Americas were founded at Jamestown and Plymouth.

Reviewing the Main Ideas

1. What were three results of the Crusades?

2. Why were the Spanish able to conquer the huge Aztec and Incan empires?

3. (a) What four social classes did the Laws of the Indies set up? (b) What did each group do for a living?

4. Why did Europeans send explorers to North America?

5. Name three ways in which the arrival of Europeans affected Native Americans in North America.

6. (a) What was the House of Burgesses? (b) Why was it important?

7. Why did the Pilgrims remain in Plymouth despite terrible hardships?

Thinking Critically

1. **Linking Past and Present** Identify one American tradition or idea that can be traced to each of the following: (a) Native Americans, (b) Spanish, (c) Dutch, (d) English, (e) Africans.

2. **Defending a Position** Do you agree or disagree with the following statement: In trying to help Native Americans, Bartolomé de Las Casas did more harm than good. Defend your position.

3. **Analyzing Information** Review the discussions of government in New Spain and Jamestown on pages 74–77 and 85–87. Which colony gave settlers more say in their government? Explain.

Applying Your Skills

1. **Ranking** Review the explorations of Columbus, Balboa, Magellan, Cartier, and Hudson. Then rank them according to which you think was most important. In a few sentences, explain your ranking.

2. **Making a Generalization** Review the descriptions of relations between Europeans and Native Americans on pages 76, 83, and 89. (a) Make a generalization about how Europeans treated Native Americans. (b) List at least three facts to support your generalization.

3. **Analyzing a Quotation** Review the excerpt from the Mayflower Compact on page 89. (a) Why did the Pilgrims want to set up a colony? (b) What kinds of laws did they plan to enact for the colony?

Thinking About Geography

Match the letters on the map with the following places: **1.** Africa, **2.** Asia, **3.** Europe, **4.** India, **5.** East Indies, **6.** West Indies, **7.** Mediterranean Sea. **Movement** Why did Europeans want to reach Asia?

2. Possible Answers: Students should recognize that, although Las Casas did help the Native Americans, he also unintentionally caused great suffering to the Africans.

3. Possible Answer: Settlers in Jamestown had more say in their government. Under New Spain's Laws of the Indies, only a small fraction of the population had a role in the lawmaking process. Under the original burgess system in Jamestown, all male settlers were allowed to elect their representatives. Even though voting rights later were restricted, Jamestown still had a higher proportion of its settlers involved in the lawmaking process.

Answers to Applying Your Skills

1. Rankings will vary, but Columbus and Magellan probably will be ranked very high. Students should support their reasons for ranking the individuals in the order chosen.

2. Possible Answers: (a) Most Europeans treated the Native Americans badly. (b) The Spanish forced Native Americans to work in mines and on plantations. Spanish, French, and Dutch settlers seized Native American lands. All the European nations with a presence in the Americas enslaved Native Americans and sold them to plantations in the West Indies.

Trading in New France

Form into groups to explore the life of trappers and traders in New France. Follow the suggestions below to write, draw, or dance to show what you have learned about French traders in New France. You may use the textbook, encyclopedias, atlases, or other materials in your classroom library to complete the tasks. Be able to name your sources of information when you have finished the activity.

WRITERS AND ARTISTS Make a list of goods that the French traded with Native Americans in the 1600s. Then create a sales catalog of these items. Describe and illustrate each one.

French trapper

SCIENTISTS Make a list of the animals whose pelts were prized in the fur trade. Then prepare a fact sheet for each animal. Include information such as what the animal eats, where it lives, type of home it builds, and natural enemies. Draw pictures or use pictures from old magazines to illustrate your fact sheets.

POETS AND DANCERS Form into pairs to create a poem and dance about the life of a coureur de bois. Present your poetry-dance recital to the class. Poets can read their poems aloud while dancers perform.

REPORTERS Conduct an interview with Samuel de Champlain. Cover such topics as Champlain's accomplishments as a sailor and mapmaker, his exploration and settlements in North America, and his role in the French fur trade. You might audiotape or videotape your interview to present it to the class as a radio or TV show.

CARTOGRAPHERS Draw a map of North America. On the map, draw the water routes that fur traders might have used to ship their furs to France. Label the waterways.

Powder horn showing route used in fur trade

 Prepare a Trading in New France bulletin board display on which each group presents or describes its completed activity.

Native American fur traders

Interdisciplinary ACTIVITY

Learning Styles

The following chart indicates the activities appropriate for different learning styles.

Visual Learners
Writers and artists
Scientists
Poets and dancers
Reporters
Cartographers

Auditory Learners
Poets and dancers
Reporters

Kinesthetic Learners
Writers and artists
Scientists
Poets and dancers
Reporters
Cartographers

Evaluation

Writers and artists The list of goods traded must include at least all those discussed in this chapter. Sales catalogs should be neat and well organized. Representative illustrations should be accompanied by clear, accurate descriptions.

Scientists Fact sheets must be legible and organized. Information should provide an overall picture of each animal's natural habitat and survival techniques. Illustrations should support information given. Any technical terms should be defined or used in context.

Poets and dancers Poems need not rhyme but should at least contain a rhythm based on the natural rise and fall of syllables. Dance ability need not be a criterion, but dances should creatively reflect facts suggested in the poems.

Reporters Interviews should cover all the suggested topics and should be organized in a coherent fashion. You may want to require that both questions and answers be complete sentences.

Cartographers Outline maps need not be exact but must be approximate and in perspective. Suggested water routes should follow main rivers and waterways. Labels must be accurate.

---

3. (a) The colony was to be for the glory of God and the advancement of Christianity. (b) They planned for just and equal laws that would promote the general good of the colony.

Answers to Thinking About Geography

1. D **2.** F **3.** E **4.** G **5.** B
6. A **7.** C
Movement: They wanted to increase their power and wealth through trade.

Assessment

Chapter Resources Binder For a more comprehensive evaluation of student understanding of this chapter, assign Chapter Tests A and B and/or Extra Unit Questions from Unit 1, pages 31 – 36 and 51 – 53.
Computer Test Bank You can use Chapter Tests and Extra Unit Questions to create your own tests for both testing and retesting.

Alternative Assessment

Chapter Resources Binder See the Alternative Assessment booklet in the *Social Studies Educator's Handbook* series.
Portfolio You might meet with students to choose appropriate work from the chapter for inclusion in their portfolios.

Lessons	Teaching Resources
1 The New England Colonies **Objectives** 1. Explain why the Puritans set up the Massachusetts Bay Colony. 2. Identify the founders of Connecticut and Rhode Island. 3. Describe how people in New England made a living.	**Lesson Planner** Cooperative Learning, p. 19 **Student Study Guide** Section 1 Study Guide, p. 49 **Chapter Resources Binder, Unit 1** *History Through Literature* Upon the Burning of Our House, p. 40 *Critical Thinking* Synthesizing Information, p. 39
2 The Middle Colonies **Objectives** 1. Describe William Penn's "holy experiment." 2. Explain why the Middle Colonies were known as the Breadbasket Colonies. 3. Identify the peoples who settled in the Middle Colonies. 4. Describe what life was like in the backcountry.	**Lesson Planner** Cooperative Learning, p. 20 **Student Study Guide** Section 2 Study Guide, p. 50 **Our Multicultural Heritage** *Biography* William Penn, Quaker Colonist, p. 10 *Milestone* The First Jewish Settlement in North America, p. 12
3 The Southern Colonies **Objectives** 1. Explain why each of the Southern Colonies was founded. 2. Identify Bacon's Rebellion. 3. Describe how geography helped to shape life in the Southern Colonies. 4. Identify the Middle Passage.	**Lesson Planner** Cooperative Learning, p. 21 **Student Study Guide** Section 3 Study Guide, p. 51 **Chapter Resources Binder, Unit 1** *Geography in History* Settling the Shenandoah Valley, pp. 41–42 **Our Multicultural Heritage** *Biography* Olaudah Equiano, Eyewitness to Slavery, p. 11
4 Ruling the Colonies **Objectives** 1. Explain why colonists resented the Navigation Acts. 2. Identify items that the colonies traded. 3. Identify the rights that colonists gained as a result of the Glorious Revolution. 4. Describe how self-rule was strengthened in the colonies.	**Lesson Planner** Cooperative Learning, p. 22 **Student Study Guide** Section 4 Study Guide, p. 52 **Chapter Resources Binder, Unit 1** *Skill Application* Using a Time Line, p. 38
5 The Colonies in 1750 **Objectives** 1. Explain how the Great Awakening increased religious tolerance. 2. Describe what life was like for women in the backcountry and in cities. 3. Describe how colonists educated their children. 4. Identify the Enlightenment.	**Lesson Planner** Cooperative Learning, p. 23 **Student Study Guide** Section 5 Study Guide, p. 53 **Interdisciplinary Connections: American Ingenuity** ■ *Arts* Pieces of the Past, p. 20 ■ *Geography* From House to House, p. 21 ■ *World* Come to North America!, p. 22 ■ *Economics* Indigo, p. 23 ■ *Civics* How Town Meetings Work, p. 24

Multimedia Resources	Additional Resources	Chapter-Level Resources
Transparencies *Time Lines* America and the World, p. E-15 *Geography and History,* p. I-57 *Fine Art* The Sargent Family, p. D-29 **CD-ROM** *History Makers* Anne Hutchinson; *Arts and Entertainment* Books **Videotapes/Videodiscs** *United States History Video Collection* The Religious Dissenters, Vol. 2, Ch. 16; The Indian Wars, Vol. 2, Ch. 19	**Voices of Freedom** A Slave's Ballad on an Indian Attack, pp. 37–38 **Historical Outline Map Book** The New England Colonies, p. 16 **Customized Reader** A Letter From a Massachusetts Settler, article IIB-11 The Examination and Trial of an Accused Witch, article IIB-9	**Lesson Planner** Activity Based, pp. 24–25 **Chapter Resources Binder** **Unit 1** Vocabulary Building, p. 37 Chapter Test A, pp. 43–45 Chapter Test B, pp. 46–48 Illustration Master, p. 49 Extra Unit Questions, pp. 51–53 **English Guided Reading** Guided Reading, pp. 7–8 **Spanish Resources**
Transparencies *Geography and History* Middle Atlantic States, p. I-61 *Our Multicultural Heritage* Ethnic Division of the Colonial Population, 1775, p. C-13 **CD-ROM** *History Makers* William Penn	**Historical Outline Map Book** The Middle Colonies, p. 17 **Customized Reader** William Penn's Regulations for Settlers in Pennsylvania, article IIB-14	**Student Study Guide** Chapter 4 Study Guide, pp. 54–55 **Computer Test Bank** Chapter Tests A and B Extra Unit Questions
Transparencies *Geography and History* Southeastern States, p. I-65 **Videotapes/Videodiscs** *United States History Video Collection* Enslaved Laborers, Vol. 3, Ch. 16; The Deep South, Vol. 3, Ch. 19	**Voices of Freedom** Bacon Rebels, pp. 41–42 **Historical Outline Map Book** The Southern Colonies, p. 18 **Customized Reader** Petition From North Carolina "Regulators," article IIB-8 **Interdisciplinary Explorations** The Wreck of the Henrietta Marie	**Guided Reading Audiotapes** Side 2 **CD-ROM** *Time Tour* The 13 English Colonies in A Meeting of Different Worlds
Transparencies *Geography and History* Thirteen Colonies, p. I-17 **Videotapes/Videodiscs** *United States History Video Collection* The Atlantic World, Vol. 3, Ch. 7; The Sugar Islands, Vol. 3, Ch. 10	**Historical Outline Map Book** The Thirteen Colonies, p. 15	
Transparencies *Our Multicultural Heritage,* p. C-13 *Interdisciplinary Connections* How Lightning Works, p. B-39 **CD-ROM** *Arts and Entertainment* Books *History Makers,* Benjamin Franklin **Videotapes/Videodiscs** *United States History Video Collection* Indentured Servants, Vol. 3, Ch. 13; The Great Awakening, Vol. 3, Ch. 28	**Voices of Freedom** A Critical View of Philadelphia, pp. 46–47 The Wisdom of Benjamin Franklin, pp. 50–51 **Customized Reader** Letter From an Indentured Servant to Her Father, article IIA-10	

Lesson Planner

For a fully developed **Activity-Based** lesson plan for Chapter 4, see the *Lesson Planner,* pages 24–25.

 Chapter Resources

Vocabulary Building The Vocabulary Building worksheet for Chapter 4 from Unit 1, page 37, of the *Chapter Resources* binder can be used as a prereading activity or as a review of chapter vocabulary. (Reteaching/Easy)

 Student Study Guide

Chapter 4 Study Guide Refer students to pages 54–55 of the *Student Study Guide* for the Chapter 4 Study Guide. The study guide can be used for chapter review as well as for reteaching. (Reteaching/Average)

 Guided Reading Audiotapes

Students can use *Guided Reading Audiotapes,* Chapter 4, side 2, to listen to section previews, summaries, and review questions. The tapes will benefit students who are auditory learners, students who have trouble reading, or students acquiring English. The tapes are also available in Spanish. (Reteaching/ Easy)

CHAPTER 4

The 13 English Colonies

(1630–1750)

CHAPTER OUTLINE

1 The New England Colonies
2 The Middle Colonies
3 The Southern Colonies
4 Ruling the Colonies
5 The Colonies in 1750

1630 *Puritans from England set up a colony in Massachusetts Bay. Here, settlers are building a home in Massachusetts.*

1670s *Relations between colonists and Native Americans ranged from friendly to hostile. This Bible in the Algonquian language was translated by a Puritan missionary.*

1682 *Pennsylvania was founded in 1682. Many settlers who came to Pennsylvania were skilled craftsworkers.*

| 1630 | 1650 | 1670 | 1690 |

WORLD EVENT
1660s England passes Navigation Acts

WORLD EVENT
1689 William and Mary sign English Bill of Rights

Chapter Time Line
Activity

Each illustration along the Chapter 4 time line suggests ownership. Have students choose and carefully examine an illustration that catches their interest. Then ask questions such as these:
■ If you owned the house under construction (1630), what would concern you about the future?
■ If you were planning to buy an African slave (1700s), how would you explain your decision to someone who disapproved of slavery?

■ If you were a wealthy member of London society, would you be excited about meeting Native Americans (1732)? What would you say to them?
Invite students to respond in writing.

Chapter Setting

On a warm May day in the 1750s, a parade made its way down a main street in Newport, Rhode Island. It was Negro Election Day.

Most of the city's Africans had turned out. Dressed in their finest clothes, they sang and played musical instruments as they marched. One resident later recalled:

> **❝**All the various languages of Africa, mixed with broken . . . English, filled the air, accompanied with the music of the fiddle, tambourine, the banjo, [and] drum.**❞**

Similar parades took place throughout New England in the mid-1700s. Each year, at about the time white New Englanders voted for their colonial government, Africans held their own elections. In Newport, African residents voted for a "governor." The winner presided over a grand feast. During the year, the governor settled court cases or disputes among black townspeople.

Negro Election Day was a truly American custom, blending traditions from different lands. In part, it was like festivals held by the Ashanti peoples of West Africa. Many Ashanti had been brought to the Americas as slaves. At the same time, it included elements of English election-day celebrations.

As the colonies grew in the 1600s and 1700s, they became home to peoples from many lands. These peoples brought their own customs and traditions. In time, they shaped these old ways into a new American culture.

ACTIVITY Write the following geography terms on a sheet of paper: rocky soil, fertile soil, mild winters, thick forests, long growing season, hilly land, good harbors. Brainstorm to decide how each might affect the way of life settlers developed in a new land.

1700s *Thousands of enslaved Africans arrived each year in the English colonies. This poster advertises a slave auction.*

1750s *New England merchants dominated colonial trade. This painting shows Moses Marcy, a wealthy "Yankee trader."*

1732 *James Oglethorpe founded the colony of Georgia. Here, he presents a group of Native Americans to Georgia's trustees in London.*

1690	1710	1730	1750

▲ **WORLD EVENT**
1700s Age of Enlightenment begins

▲ **WORLD EVENT**
1725 English Quakers speak out against slavery

Chapter 4 • **93**

Chapter Resources

English Guided Reading Duplicate and distribute to SAE students the Chapter 4 Guided Reading worksheet on pages 7–8 in the English Guided Reading section of the *Chapter Resources* binder. Students who have difficulty reading also might benefit from using this worksheet. Have students complete the worksheet before they begin reading. You might pair a more fluent student or a student who is a stronger reader with each SAE student to review. (Reteaching/Easy)

Spanish Resources See the Spanish Resources section of the *Chapter Resources* binder.

ACTIVITY

Guided Instruction Have students work with partners or in small groups to brainstorm. Encourage them to pretend that they are settlers who are faced with overcoming these geographic features or using them to their advantage. Ask students to consider positive as well as negative effects of each geographic feature; for example, a farmer must work hard to clear a field of rocks so that he or she can plow and grow crops, but rocks also are useful as building materials.

CD-ROM

Time Tour Access The 13 English Colonies in A Meeting of Different Worlds on the American Heritage® *History of the United States* CD-ROM. (Enrichment/Average)

Students Acquiring English Activity

Students with weak English reading skills can focus on key concepts more easily if material is presented orally. One way to accomplish this is to set up small collaborative learning groups in which students read aloud together selected sections of the text. The groups should include students whose first language is English as well as second-language learners.

Linking Past and Present Activity

The opening section of this chapter describes Negro Election Day in Newport, Rhode Island, in the 1750s. Suggest that students use this description, their own knowledge of election day activities, and other information from the chapter to create election day murals or montages showing colonial and modern election day celebrations.

Bell Ringer

Write the word *government* on the chalkboard. Have students list things for which they think the government of a new colony should be responsible.

Lesson Plan

1. Focus After Jamestown and Plymouth, the English founded more colonies. Puritans settled the Massachusetts Bay Colony in hopes of practicing their religious views freely. Colonists dissatisfied with the government in Massachusetts then set up colonies in Connecticut and Rhode Island. In this section, students learn about the New England Colonies.

2. Instruct Have the class conduct a panel discussion of New England colonists. Assign one student as moderator; have students take the roles of John Winthrop, Thomas Hooker, Roger Williams, and Anne Hutchinson. Remaining students can prepare questions for the panelists, focusing on the roles of government and religion in colonial life.

3. Close To close the lesson, have students describe the settlers in each New England colony and then name two facts about the colony that attracted—or troubled—the settlers.

1
The New England Colonies

FIND OUT

■ Why did Puritans set up the Massachusetts Bay Colony?

■ Who founded the colonies of Connecticut and Rhode Island?

■ How did people in New England make a living?

VOCABULARY toleration

April and May 1630 were cold, stormy months in the North Atlantic. Huddled below deck, colonists aboard the *Arbella* wondered if they had been foolish to sail to a new land. Their leader, John Winthrop, had no doubts. The new colony, he assured them, would set an example to the world:

> 66 The Lord will make our name a praise and glory, so that men shall say of succeeding [colonies]: 'The Lord make it like that of New England.' For we must consider that we shall be like a City upon a Hill. The eyes of all people are on us. 99

The passengers on the *Arbella* were among more than 1,000 men, women, and children who left England in 1630 to settle in the Americas. They set up their colony on Massachusetts Bay, north of Plymouth. Over the next 100 years, English settlers would build towns and farms throughout New England.

Puritans in Massachusetts

John Winthrop and his followers were part of a religious group known as ***Puritans.*** The Puritans wanted to reform the Church of England. They were different

from the Pilgrims, who had wanted to separate entirely from the English church. The Puritans called for simpler forms of worship. They wanted to do away with practices borrowed from Roman Catholics, such as organ music and special clothes for priests.

Reasons for leaving England. Puritans were a powerful group in England. Many were well-educated merchants or landowners. Some held seats in the House of Commons. However, Charles I, who became king in 1625, disliked their religious ideas. He took away many Puritan business charters and had Puritans expelled from universities. A few were even jailed.

Some Puritan leaders decided that England had fallen on "evil and declining times." In 1629, they convinced royal officials to grant them a charter to form the Massachusetts Bay Company. The company's bold plan was to build a new society in New England. The new society would be based on the laws of God as they appeared in the Bible. Far from the watchful eye of the king, Puritans would run their colony as they pleased.

Some people joined the colonists for economic rather than religious reasons. They were not Puritans escaping persecution but people looking for land. In England, the oldest son usually inherited his father's estate. Younger sons had little hope of owning land. For these people, Massachusetts Bay offered cheap land or a chance to start their own business.

Settling in. The Puritans sent a small advance party to North America in 1629. John Winthrop and his larger party of colonists arrived the following year. Winthrop was chosen as the first governor of the Massachusetts Bay Colony, as the Puritan settlement was called.

Once ashore, Winthrop set an example for others. Even though he was governor of the colony, he worked as hard as anyone to build a home, clear land, and plant crops. As one colonist wrote, "He so encouraged

---

94 • Chapter 4

Connections With Economics
Background

The United States has sometimes been called "a land of second sons" because so many of Europe's second sons immigrated in search of a better life. The reason for this relates to the idea of *primogeniture* — the right of the first-born (or oldest) son to inherit the family estate. But primogeniture was not the only economic reason people left England for America. In the 1700s, many small English farmers were the victims of the *enclosure movement.* As the value of farmland skyrocketed, wealthy landowners began fencing off or enclosing what previously had been open, or common, land. Unable to support themselves without land, small farmers and squatters who had lost their rights to the common property looked to America's abundant supply of inexpensive (and sometimes even free) farmland.

Connections With Civics
Background

The Puritans took their charter with them to Massachusetts, reasoning that this action would make it hard for Charles I to take it back. By writing their own system of rules for their government instead of accepting those set down by Charles I in the original charter, Thomas Hooker and other Connecticut colonists created the first constitution in the English colonies, the Fundamental Orders of Connecticut.

---

us that there was not an idle person to be found in the whole colony."

At first, Winthrop tried to govern the colony according to its charter. Under the charter, only stockholders who had invested money in the Massachusetts Bay Company had the right to vote. However, most settlers were not stockholders. They resented taxes and laws passed by a government in which they had no say.

Voters elect an assembly. Winthrop and other stockholders quickly realized that the colony would run more smoothly if other settlers could take part. On the other hand, the Puritan leaders were determined to keep non-Puritans out of government. As a result, they granted the right to vote for governor to all men who were church members. Later, male church members also elected representatives to an assembly called the *General Court.*

Under the leadership of Winthrop and other Puritans, the Massachusetts Bay Colony grew and prospered. Between 1629 and 1640, more than 20,000 men, women, and children journeyed from England to Massachusetts. This movement of people is known as the *Great Migration.* Many of the newcomers settled in Boston, which grew into the colony's largest town.

Settling Connecticut

In May 1636, about 100 settlers, led by a Puritan minister named Thomas Hooker, left Massachusetts Bay. Pushing west, they drove their cattle, goats, and pigs along Indian trails that cut through the forests. When they reached the Connecticut River, they built a town, which they called Hartford.

Hooker left Massachusetts Bay because he believed that the governor and other officials had too much power. He wanted to set up a colony in Connecticut with laws that set strict limits on government.

In 1639, the settlers wrote a plan of government called the *Fundamental Orders of*

The Puritan *Relying on faith and hard work, the Puritans built a thriving colony at Massachusetts Bay. Augustus Saint-Gaudens, the foremost American sculptor of the 1800s, captured the Puritan spirit in his powerful bronze statue* The Puritan. **American Traditions** *How did their religious beliefs help the Puritans succeed?*

Connecticut. The Fundamental Orders created a government much like that of Massachusetts. There were, however, two important differences. First, the Fundamental Orders gave the vote to all men who were property owners, including men who were not church members. Second, the Fundamental Orders limited the governor's power. In this way, the Fundamental Orders expanded the idea of representative government in the English colonies.

By 1662, 15 towns were thriving along the Connecticut River. In that year, Connecticut became a separate colony, with a new charter granted by the king of England.

 Lesson Planner

For a developed **Cooperative Learning** lesson plan, see the *Lesson Planner,* page 19.

Answer to Caption

Possible Answer: The Puritans felt that they were creating a society based on the laws of God. To achieve this goal, they were willing to work hard and to endure hardships.

 Transparencies

Time Lines Use the transparency, America and the World, 1600–1800, on page E-15 of *American History Transparencies,* to focus on domestic and worldwide events of this era. Teaching suggestions can be found on page E-13. (Enrichment/Average)

Chapter Resources

History Through Literature To give students a unique view of Puritan thought, duplicate and distribute the worksheet, Upon the Burning of Our House, from Unit 1, page 40, of the *Chapter Resources* binder. (Enrichment/Average)

Critical Thinking Duplicate and distribute the worksheet, Synthesizing Information, from Unit 1, page 39, of the *Chapter Resources* binder. The worksheet presents the views of two Puritans on the subject of accumulating wealth. (Reteaching/Average)

Our Multicultural Heritage
Background

John Winthrop, the son of a wealthy English landowner, had served as an attorney and government official. However, he lost his position as a result of the anti-Puritan policies of King Charles I. Winthrop was 42 years old when he sailed for the Massachusetts Bay Colony. During that voyage, he encouraged his fellow passengers with these words: "The Lord will make our name a praise and glory, so that men shall say of succeeding [colonies]: 'The Lord make it like that of New England.' For we must consider that we shall be like a City upon a Hill. The eyes of all people are on us."

It would be hard to overestimate Winthrop's influence upon the first colony in New England. Although he held very conservative religious views, he was much respected — enough so that he was elected governor of the colony 12 times.

Answers to Map Study

1. Massachusetts, New Hampshire, Connecticut, Rhode Island
2. cattle, grain, iron, ships **3.** New England had large supplies of lumber for building ships, as well as a long coastline with many good harbors.

 Transparencies

Geography and History Use the transparency set, New England States, on page I-57 of *American History Transparencies.* The base map and overlay 1 show students how geography influenced the area's history during the era of colonization and the American Revolution. Teaching suggestions can be found on page I-8. (Enrichment/Average)

 Historical Outline Map Book

Historical Outline Map Duplicate and distribute the map, The New England Colonies, on page 16 of the *American History Historical Outline Map Book.* Lesson ideas for this map can be found on page T5. (Reteaching/Average)

MAP STUDY

The New England Colonies were among the first colonies the English set up in North America. Major economic activities in the region included shipbuilding, fishing, and fur trapping.
1. *Name the four New England Colonies.*
2. *What products did Connecticut produce?*
3. **Understanding Causes and Effects** *How did New England's geography encourage the growth of shipbuilding?*

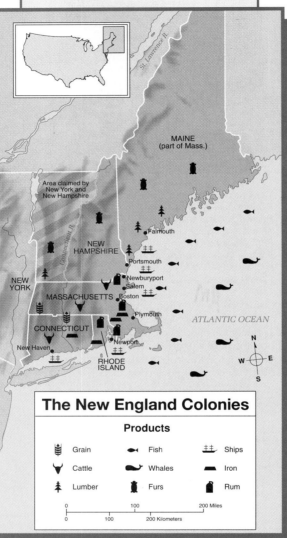

The New England Colonies

Products

Grain	Fish	Ships
Cattle	Whales	Iron
Lumber	Furs	Rum

Toleration in Rhode Island

Another Puritan who disagreed with the leaders of Massachusetts Bay was Roger Williams. A young minister in the village of Salem, Williams was gentle and good-natured. Most people, including Governor Winthrop, liked him. In 1635, however, Williams found himself in trouble.

Williams believed strongly that the Puritan church had too much power in Massachusetts. In Williams's view, the business of church and state should be completely separate. The state, said Williams, should maintain order and peace. It should not support a particular church.

Williams also believed in religious toleration. **Toleration** means a willingness to let others practice their own beliefs. In Puritan Massachusetts, non-Puritans were not permitted to worship freely.

Williams's ideas about these and other matters troubled Puritan leaders. In 1635, the Massachusetts General Court ordered him to leave the colony. Fearing that the court would send him back to England, Williams escaped to Narragansett Bay. He spent the winter with Indians there. In the spring, the Indians sold him land for a settlement. After several years, it became the English colony of Rhode Island.

In Rhode Island, Williams put into practice his ideas about religious toleration. He allowed complete freedom of religion for all Protestants, Jews, and Catholics. He did not set up a state church or require settlers to attend church services. He also gave all white men the right to vote. Before long, settlers who disliked the strict Puritan rule of Massachusetts flocked to Providence and other towns in Rhode Island.

⭐ **Linking Past and Present**
The first synagogue in the United States was built in Newport, Rhode Island, in 1763. The Touro Synagogue, designed by Peter Harrison, still stands today.

Connections With Civics
Background

Roger Williams wrote, "The government extends no further than over the bodies and goods of their subjects, not over their souls, and therefore they may not undertake to give laws unto the souls and consciences of men."

Our Multicultural Heritage
Background

In Newport, Rhode Island, Jewish immigrants from Spain and Portugal began meeting in 1658. For a century, the Jewish citizens of Newport worshipped in private homes. In 1759, however, they decided that the congregation was large enough and wealthy enough to build a house of worship. The result was Touro Synagogue, built in 1763. Now the oldest synagogue in the United States, it was named after Isaac Touro, the congregation's respected rabbi.

The Trial of Anne Hutchinson

One woman who found shelter in Rhode Island was Anne Hutchinson. Hutchinson and her husband, William, had settled in Boston in 1634. She worked as a midwife, helping to deliver babies. Hutchinson herself had 14 children.

Hutchinson was intelligent and God-fearing. Governor Winthrop called her "a woman of a ready wit and bold spirit." In time, however, her bold spirit got her into trouble with Puritan officials.

Forbidden meetings. Hutchinson often held Bible readings in her home. And after church, she and her friends gathered to discuss the minister's sermon. Sometimes, as many as 50 or 60 people flocked to her house to listen.

Anne Hutchinson Preaches at Home *Anne Hutchinson's independent views angered the Puritan leaders of Massachusetts Bay. In 1638, they ordered her to leave the colony. Here, Hutchinson defies Puritan leaders by preaching in her Boston home.* **Citizenship** *Why do you think Hutchinson moved to Rhode Island after leaving Massachusetts Bay?*

At first, Hutchinson merely related what the minister had said. Later, however, she expressed her own views. Often, she seemed to criticize the minister's teachings.

Puritan leaders grew angry. They believed that Hutchinson's opinions were full of religious errors. Even worse, Hutchinson was a woman. A woman did not have the right to explain God's law, they said. That job belonged to ministers. In November 1637, the General Court ordered Hutchinson to appear before it.

On trial. At her trial, Hutchinson answered all the questions put to her by Governor Winthrop and other members of the court. Time after time, she revealed weaknesses in their arguments. They could not prove that she had broken any Puritan laws or challenged any religious teachings. Winthrop was clearly annoyed. "Mrs. Hutchinson can tell when to speak and when to hold her tongue," he concluded sharply.

Then, after two days of questioning, Hutchinson made a serious mistake. She told the court that God spoke directly to her.

> *Hutchinson:* I bless the Lord. He hath let me see which was the [true] ministry and which [was] wrong. . . .
> *The court:* How do you know that it was God that did reveal these things to you?
> *Hutchinson:* By an immediate revelation.
> *The court:* How! An immediate revelation?
> *Hutchinson:* By the voice of his own spirit to my soul.

Members of the court were shocked. The Puritans believed that God spoke only through the Bible, not directly to individuals. The court declared that Hutchinson was "deluded by the Devil" and ordered her out of the colony.

Chapter 4 • **97**

Linking Past and Present
Activity

Voices of Freedom

Primary Source You might assign selection 5-12, A Slave's Ballad on an Indian Attack, on pages 37–38 of *Voices of Freedom.* The selection, adapted from a slave report, is in the form of a ballad. (Enrichment/Average)

Videotapes/ Videodiscs

United States History Video Collection Use the video segment "The Indian Wars" from Volume 2, *The Era of Colonization,* to enhance students' understanding of conflict between Native Americans and European settlers. Approx. running time 1:45 min. (Enrichment/Average) Vol. 2, Ch. 19

| Chapter 19 | Play |

CD-ROM

Arts and Entertainment Access the the Books segment on the American Heritage® *History of the United States* CD-ROM to find information about the literary traditions of the early English colonists. (Enrichment/Average)

In 1638, Hutchinson, along with her family and some friends, went to Rhode Island. The Puritan leaders had won their case against her. For later Americans, however, Hutchinson became an important symbol of the struggle for religious freedom. ■

Relations With Native Americans

From Massachusetts Bay, settlers fanned out across New England. Some built trading and fishing villages along the coast north of Boston. In 1680, the king of England made these coastal settlements into a separate colony called New Hampshire.

As more colonists settled in New England, they took over lands used by Native Americans for thousands of years. As a result, fighting often broke out between white settlers and Indian nations of the region.

The largest conflict came in 1675, when Wampanoag Indians, led by their chief, Metacom, attacked colonial villages throughout New England. Other Indian groups allied themselves with the Wampanoags. Fighting lasted 15 months. In the end, however, Metacom was captured and killed. The English sold his family and about 1,000 other Indians into slavery in the West Indies. Other Indians were forced from their homes. Many died of starvation.

The pattern of English expansion followed by war between settlers and Indians was repeated throughout the colonies. It would continue for many years to come.

Linking Past and Present
The biggest battle of the war between Metacom and New England settlers took place in a great swamp. Descendants of the Wampanoags have dedicated the spot as a shrine of brotherhood. Each September, they hold a ceremony at the monument that stands there.

BIOGRAPHY Metacom *Native Americans in New England watched with alarm as settlers moved onto Indian lands. More than 10,000 Indians joined the Wampanoag leader Metacom in a war against the New England Colonies.* ***Multicultural Heritage*** *Why do you think many Indians were willing to join Metacom?*

A Life of Hard Work

New England was a difficult land for colonists. But the Puritans believed that daily labor honored God as much as prayer. With hard work, they built a thriving way of life.

Farms, forests, and seas. New England's rocky soil was poor for farming. After a time, however, settlers learned to grow Native American crops, such as Indian corn, beans, squash, and pumpkins.

Although the soil was poor, the forests were full of riches. New Englanders hunted wild turkey and deer, as well as hogs that they let roam free in the woods. In the spring, colonists collected the sweet sap that dripped from gashes cut in sugar maple trees. Settlers also cut down trees and float-

Our Multicultural Heritage
Activity

Students will enjoy finding out about the Native Americans who were these colonists' neighbors. Divide the class into groups to research the peoples that make up the Iroquois nation, such as the Cayuga, Onondaga, Oneida, Mohawk, and Seneca. Each member of the group can investigate a different topic (for example, housing, food, clothing, communication, beliefs, art, and music). Encourage students to find information that will be interesting to their classmates; for example, a student interested in art might like to report about Native American painting, pottery, basketry, or even tattoos. After students share information within their groups, have each group pretend to be members of the tribe and have the rest of the class pretend to be reporters for a colonial newspaper. Have the reporters interview the tribe for a newspaper article.

ed them to sawmills near port cities such as Boston, Massachusetts, or Portsmouth, New Hampshire. Here, major shipbuilding centers grew.

Other New Englanders fished the coastal waters for cod and halibut. When the fish were running, fishers worked tirelessly, seldom taking time to eat or sleep. Shellfish in New England were especially large. Oysters sometimes grew to be a foot long. Lobsters stretched up to 6 feet. "Those a foot long," one host recommended, "are better for serving at a table." Larger ones hung off the edge!

In the 1600s, New Englanders also began to hunt whales. Whales supplied them with products such as oil for lamps and ivory. In the 1700s and 1800s, whaling grew into a big business.

Tightly knit towns and villages. Puritans believed that people should worship and take care of local matters as a community. For this reason, New England became a land of tightly knit towns and villages.

At the center of each village was the common, an open field where cattle grazed. Nearby stood the meetinghouse, where Puritans worshiped and held town meetings. Wooden houses with steep roofs lined both sides of the town's narrow streets.

The Puritans took their Sabbath, or holy day of rest, very seriously. On Sundays, no one was allowed to play games or visit taverns to joke, talk, and drink. The law required all citizens to attend church services.

In a New England Home Most New England homes had no fireplace in the bedroom. Colonists would fill a warming pan (left) with hot coals and slip it between the sheets to warm up the bed. Home furniture was sturdy and practical—like this oak chair that converted into a table. New England craftsworkers also produced fine pewter items, like the teapot at right. *Daily Life* How do these items reflect the geography of New England?

During the 1600s, women sat on one side of the church and men on the other. Blacks and Indians stood in a balcony at the back. Children had separate pews, where an adult watched over them. If they "sported and played" or made "faces [that] caused laughter," they were punished.

At town meetings, settlers discussed and voted on many issues. What roads should be built? What fences needed repair? How much should the schoolmaster be paid? Town meetings gave New Englanders a chance to speak their minds. This early experience encouraged the growth of democratic ideas in New England.

Puritan laws were strict, and lawbreakers faced severe punishment. About 15 crimes carried the death penalty. One crime punishable by death was witchcraft. In 1692, Puritans executed 20 men and women as witches in Salem Village, Massachusetts.

Student Study Guide

Section 1 Study Guide Have students use the Section 1 Study Guide on page 49 of the *Student Study Guide* to review and reinforce the content of this section. (Reteaching/Average)

Guided Instruction Before students write their dialogues, have them create "Problems to Be Solved" lists from the viewpoints of both Native Americans and settlers. Invite students to share their finished dialogues by reading them aloud with partners.

Section 2
pp. 100–105

Bell Ringer

As a whole-class activity, have students brainstorm for three to five minutes to develop a list of details that they associate with New York, New Jersey, Pennsylvania, and Delaware. You might keep the list on the chalkboard while discussing Section 2, encouraging students to look for the origins of the details they listed.

Lesson Plan

1. Focus The Middle Colonies were made up of settlements started by the Dutch, Swedish, and English for religious freedom. In this section, students learn about the growth of New York, New Jersey, Pennsylvania, and Delaware.

Home and family. The Puritans saw children as a blessing of God. The average family had seven or eight children. The good climate allowed New Englanders to live long lives. Many reached the age of 70. As a result, children often grew up knowing both their parents and their grandparents. This did much to make New England towns closely knit communities.

During the 1700s, the Puritan tradition declined. Fewer families left England for religious reasons. Ministers had less influence on the way colonies were governed. Even so, the Puritans stamped New England with their distinctive customs and their dream of a religious society.

SECTION 1 REVIEW

1. **Locate:** (a) New England Colonies, (b) Massachusetts, (c) Connecticut, (d) Rhode Island, (e) New Hampshire.
2. **Identify:** (a) John Winthrop, (b) Puritans, (c) General Court, (d) Great Migration, (e) Fundamental Orders of Connecticut, (f) Roger Williams, (g) Anne Hutchinson, (h) Metacom.
3. **Define:** toleration.
4. How did the Puritans govern the Massachusetts Bay Colony?
5. (a) Why did Thomas Hooker and Roger Williams leave the Massachusetts Bay Colony? (b) Where did each of them go?
6. How did New Englanders use the resources of the region to make a living?
7. **CRITICAL THINKING Linking Past and Present** (a) Why did the Puritan leaders see Anne Hutchinson as a threat to Massachusetts? (b) Do you think the government would see her as a threat today? Explain.

ACTIVITY Writing to Learn
Write a dialogue between a New England settler and a Wampanoag Indian in which they discuss tensions between their peoples in the mid-1600s.

2
The Middle Colonies

FIND OUT
- What was William Penn's "holy experiment"?
- Why were the Middle Colonies known as the Breadbasket Colonies?
- What peoples settled in the Middle Colonies?
- What was life like in the backcountry?

VOCABULARY patroon, proprietary colony, cash crop, backcountry

In the summer of 1744, a doctor from the colony of Maryland traveled north to Philadelphia. Doctor Hamilton was amazed at the variety of people he met in that city. Describing a meal he had there, he wrote:

❝I dined at a tavern with a very mixed company of different nations and religions. There were Scots, English, Dutch, Germans, and Irish. There were Roman Catholics, Church [of England] men, Presbyterians, Quakers, . . . Moravians, . . . and one Jew.❞

By the mid-1700s, England had four colonies in the region south of New England. Because of their location between New England and the Southern Colonies, they were known as the Middle Colonies. As Doctor Hamilton observed, the Middle Colonies had a much greater mix of peoples than either New England or the Southern Colonies.

New Netherland Becomes New York

As you have read in Chapter 3, the Dutch set up the colony of New Netherland

---

Answers to Section 1 Review

1. See the map on p. 96.
2. (a) John Winthrop, p. 94, (b) Puritans, p. 94, (c) General Court, p. 95, (d) Great Migration, p. 95, (e) Fundamental Orders of Connecticut, p. 95, (f) Roger Williams, p. 96, (g) Anne Hutchinson, p. 97, (h) Metacom, p. 98
3. toleration, p. 96
4. Under the Puritans' charter, only the stockholders could vote; later, they allowed all male church members to vote.
5. (a) Hooker left because he thought that the governor had too much power; Williams was

ordered to leave because of his opinions about religious toleration and the separation of church and state. (b) Hooker went to Connecticut; Williams went to Rhode Island.
6. They grew Native American crops, used the forests for hunting and lumber, and built ships for fishing in coastal waters and for whaling.
7. (a) Anne Hutchinson questioned the authority of the Puritan leaders to speak for God. (b) Possible Answer: No; today, there is more tolerance for religious differences.

along the Hudson River. In the colony's early years, settlers traded with Indians for furs and built the settlement of New Amsterdam into a thriving port.

Huge land grants. To encourage farming in New Netherland, Dutch officials granted large parcels of land to a few rich families. A single land grant could stretch for miles. Indeed, one grant was as big as Rhode Island! Owners of these huge estates, or manors, were called **patroons.** In return for the grant, each patroon promised to settle at least 50 European farm families on the land. However, patroons had great power and could charge whatever rents they pleased. Few farmers wanted to work for them.

BIOGRAPHY Peter Stuyvesant *As governor of New Netherland in the mid-1600s, Peter Stuyvesant held almost total power. He imposed heavy taxes and punished lawbreakers with public whippings. When colonists demanded a voice in government, he told them his authority came "from God." Stuyvesant had lost a leg fighting in the Caribbean.* **Citizenship** *What are some advantages and disadvantages of having a strong ruler like Stuyvesant?*

Most settlers lived in the trading center of New Amsterdam. They came from all over Europe. Many were attracted by the chance to practice their religion freely.

Freedom of religion. Most Dutch colonists were Protestants who belonged to the Dutch Reformed Church. They did, however, allow people of other religions—including Catholics, French Protestants, and Jews—to buy land. "People do not seem concerned what religion their neighbor is," wrote a shocked visitor from Virginia. "Indeed, they do not seem to care if he has any religion at all."

England takes over. In 1664, the rivalry between England and the Netherlands for trade and colonies led to war in Europe. English warships entered New Amsterdam's harbor and took over the city. King Charles II of England then gave New Netherland to his brother, the Duke of York. He renamed the colony New York in the duke's honor.

Founding New Jersey

At the time, New York stretched as far south as the Delaware River. The Duke of York realized that it was too big to govern easily. He gave some of the land to friends, Lord Berkeley and Sir George Carteret. They set up a proprietary (proh PRĪ uh tuhr ee) colony, which they called New Jersey.

In setting up a **proprietary colony,** the king gave land to one or more people, called proprietors. Proprietors were free to divide the land and rent it to others. They made laws for the colony but had to respect the rights of colonists under English law.

Like New York, New Jersey attracted people from many lands. English Puritans, French Protestants, Scots, Irish, Swedes, Dutch, and Finns mingled in the colony.

In 1702, New Jersey became a royal colony under control of the English crown. The colony's charter protected religious freedom and the rights of an assembly that voted on local matters.

Chapter 4 • **101**

2. Instruct Remind students that both the Puritans and the Quakers were Protestant reformers, but their beliefs and practices were quite different. Have students work in small groups to answer these questions: (a) How was the Puritan colony of Massachusetts Bay set up differently from the Quaker colony of Pennsylvania? (b) Which group was more tolerant of those with different beliefs? How did the group show its tolerance?

3. Close To close the lesson, have students answer *Who, What, Where, When, Why,* and *How* questions about the founding and early development of the Middle Colonies.

 Lesson Planner

For a fully developed **Cooperative Learning** lesson plan, see the *Lesson Planner,* page 20.

Answer to Caption

Possible Advantage: A strong ruler may be able to impose order on a society. Possible Disadvantage: A strong ruler might disregard the rights of citizens, as Stuyvesant did.

 Our Multicultural Heritage

Milestone Have students read The First Jewish Settlement in North America, on page 12 of the *Our Multicultural Heritage* booklet. (Enrichment/Easy)

Connections With Literature
Background

In the early 1800s, Washington Irving wrote many stories that had as their setting the Dutch settlements on the Hudson. He also popularized the figure of Diedrich Knickerbocker, an old Dutchman, as a symbol of New York. Suggest that students read "The Legend of Sleepy Hollow" or "Rip Van Winkle" to develop an appreciation of Irving's work.

Our Multicultural Heritage
Background

Protestants in France were known as Huguenots. Some Huguenots fled to America and founded the city of New Rochelle, north of New York City. The name honored the city of La Rochelle in France, which had fallen to the Catholics in 1628.

European Jews were often subject to persecution. During the Crusades, Christian mobs attacked many Jewish communities, and many towns passed laws forbidding Jews to own land. In the 1490s, Queen Isabella and King Ferdinand of Spain ordered all Jews as well as Muslims either to convert to Christianity or to leave the country. In the late 1800s, many Jewish families fled religious persecution in Russia and immigrated to the United States.

Answers to Map Study

1. New York, New Jersey, Pennsylvania, Delaware 2. the Delaware, the Susquehanna, and the Hudson 3. Possible Answer: It is located on a river and on an inlet of the Atlantic Ocean; it is at the eastern end of the Great Wagon Road.

 ### Transparencies

Geography and History Use the transparency set, Middle Atlantic States, on page I-61 of the *American History Transparencies* to show students how geography and topography influenced the area's history during the colonial period and the Revolutionary War. Teaching suggestions can be found on page I-9. (Enrichment/Average)

 ### Our Multicultural Heritage

Biography Have students read the biography, William Penn, Quaker Colonist, on page 10 of the *Our Multicultural Heritage* booklet. (Enrichment/Average)

 ### CD-ROM

History Makers Access the biography on William Penn from the American Heritage® *History of the United States* CD-ROM. (Enrichment/Average)

MAP STUDY

The Middle Colonies were set up south and west of New England.

1. *What were the four Middle Colonies?*
2. *Name three rivers that flowed through the Middle Colonies.*
3. **Analyzing Information** *Based on the map, why do you think Philadelphia would be a trading center?*

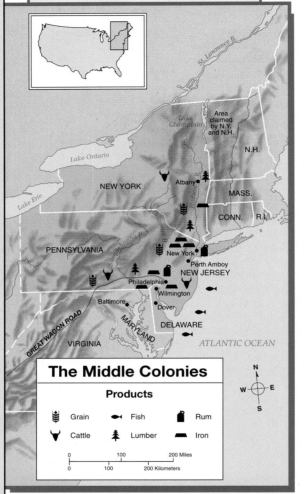

The Middle Colonies

Products

Grain	Fish	Rum
Cattle	Lumber	Iron

0   100   200 Miles
0   100   200 Kilometers

102 • Chapter 4

Pennsylvania Is Founded

South of New Jersey, another Englishman, William Penn, founded the colony of Pennsylvania. Penn came from a wealthy family. King Charles II was a personal friend. At age 22, however, Penn shocked family and friends by joining the **Quakers,** one of the most despised religious groups in England.

Quaker beliefs. Like Pilgrims and Puritans, Quakers were Protestant reformers. Their beliefs went further than those of other reformers, however. Quakers believed that all people—men and women, nobles and commoners—were equal in God's sight. They refused to bow or remove their hats in the presence of lords and ladies. They spoke out against war and refused to serve in the army.

To most English people, Quaker beliefs seemed wicked. In both England and New England, Quakers were arrested, fined, and even hanged for their beliefs. Penn became convinced that the Quakers must leave England. He turned for help to King Charles.

The king made Penn the proprietor of a large tract of land in North America. The king named the new colony Pennsylvania, or Penn's woodlands.

Penn's "holy experiment." William Penn thought of his colony as a "holy experiment." He wanted it to be a model of religious freedom, peace, and Christian living. Protestants, Catholics, and Jews went to Pennsylvania to escape persecution. Later, English officials forced Penn to turn away Catholic and Jewish settlers.

Penn's Quaker beliefs led him to speak out for fair treatment of Native Americans. Penn believed that the land belonged to the Indians. He said that settlers should pay for the land. Native Americans respected Penn for this policy. As a result, colonists in Pennsylvania enjoyed many years of peace with their Indian neighbors. As one settler remarked:

Critical Thinking
Analyzing Information

Have students imagine that they are counselors helping people to make choices about whether to immigrate to America and in which colony they will be most successful. Students can work in small groups, with partners, or individually to develop a list of questions to ask new immigrants before they leave Europe. The questions should be designed to give counselors the kind of information they can use to help guide the new immigrants. Then students can play the roles of counselor and potential immigrant; ask and answer the questions; and, depending upon the individual's answers, make decisions together about whether the individual should proceed to America and in which colony he or she should plan to live.

A Fair and Tolerant Leader *This painting shows William Penn greeting a Native American. Under Penn's leadership, Pennsylvania colonists enjoyed friendly relations with their Indian neighbors. Penn's tolerant policies also attracted settlers like the Pennsylvania Dutch. The pie plate, at right, came from a Pennsylvania Dutch home.* **Culture** *How did Penn's religious beliefs influence his treatment of people of diverse cultures?*

❝And as [Penn] treated the Indians with extraordinary humanity, they became very civil and loving to us. . . . As in other countries, the Indians were [angered] by hard treatment, which hath been the [cause] of much bloodshed, so the [opposite] treatment here hath produced love and affection.❞

Penn sent pamphlets describing his colony all over Europe. Soon, settlers from England, Scotland, Wales, the Netherlands, France, and Germany began to cross the Atlantic Ocean to Pennsylvania. Among the new arrivals were large numbers of German-speaking Protestants. They became known as **Pennsylvania Dutch** because people could not pronounce the word Deutsch (DOICH), which means German.

Most settlers landed at Philadelphia, the colony's capital along the Delaware River. Philadelphia grew quickly. By 1710, an English visitor wrote that it was "the most noble, large, and well-built city I have seen."

Delaware. For a time, Pennsylvania included some lands along the lower Delaware River. The region was known as Pennsylvania's Lower Counties. Settlers in the Lower Counties did not want to send delegates to a far-away assembly in Philadelphia. In 1701, Penn allowed them to elect their own assembly. Later, the Lower Counties broke away to form the colony of Delaware.

★★☆ **Our Common Heritage**
The Charter of Liberties that William Penn drew up for his colony specified that Native Americans charged with crimes should be tried by juries containing Native American members. This was a radical idea for the times.

Transparencies

Our Multicultural Heritage Use the transparency, Ethnic Division of the Colonial Population, 1775, on page C-13 of *American History Transparencies* to show the various ethnic groups that comprised the population of the 13 colonies in 1775. Teaching suggestions can be found on page C-2. (Enrichment/Average)

Customized Reader

Primary Source For a look at William Penn's outline for the organization of his colony, order article IIB-14, William Penn's Regulations for Settlers in Pennsylvania, from the *American History Customized Reader*. (Enrichment/Challenging)

Connection With Mathematics
Activity

Have students calculate distances between different places in the Middle Colonies — for example, between the Delaware border and Philadelphia or between New York and Philadelphia. Ask students how long they think it would take to travel each distance by as many different means of transportation they can think of that were available to people in the 1700s.

Learning Styles
Visual Learners

Students who learn visually and who like to create, draw, and design things will enjoy designing flags, currency, coins, passports, and/or seals for one of the Middle Colonies. Display students' designs after they are finished; have students explain the meaning behind each symbol in their designs.

Answer to Caption

Possible Answer: fertile soil and a mild climate

GEOGRAPHY AND HISTORY
A Land of Plenty

Farmers found more favorable conditions in the Middle Colonies than in New England. Unlike New England's thin and rocky soil, the broad Hudson and Delaware river valleys were rich and fertile. Winters were milder than in New England, and the growing season lasted longer.

Food to spare. On such promising land, farmers in the Middle Colonies produced surpluses of wheat, barley, and rye. These were **cash crops,** or crops that are sold for money on the world market. In fact, the Middle Colonies exported so much grain that they became known as the ***Breadbasket Colonies.***

Farmers of the Middle Colonies also raised herds of cattle and pigs. Every year, they sent tons of beef, pork, and butter to the ports of New York and Philadelphia. From there, the goods went by ship to New England and the South or to the West Indies, England, and other parts of Europe.

A center of manufacturing and crafts. Encouraged by William Penn, skilled German settlers set up shop in Pennsylvania. In time, the colony became a center of manufacturing and crafts. One visitor reported that workshops turned out "most kinds of hardware, clocks, watches, locks, guns, flints, glass, stoneware, nails, [and] paper."

To make household and farm tools, settlers in the Delaware River valley used rich deposits of iron ore. Heating the ore in furnaces, they purified it and then hammered it into nails, tools, and parts for guns. ■

Town and Country

Farms in the Middle Colonies were usually larger than those in New England. Because houses tended to be fairly far apart in the Middle Colonies, towns were less important.

Settling the Middle Colonies *The Middle Colonies attracted a wide variety of European settlers. The painting below shows the farming community of Bethlehem, Pennsylvania. It was founded by a group of Germans seeking religious freedom. The woman on the left is one of the many Irish Catholics who settled in New Jersey.* **Geography** *What attracted settlers to the Middle Colonies?*

The Conestoga Wagon *The Conestoga wagon originated in the Conestoga Creek region of Pennsylvania. Because its wheels did not sink easily into mud, the Conestoga wagon was well suited to the poor roads of the backcountry.* **Daily Life** *Why do you think many new settlers moved westward into the backcountry?*

Answer to Caption
Possible Answer: because most of the land in the coastal areas was already being farmed by earlier settlers

 Student Study Guide

Section 2 Study Guide Have students use the Section 2 Study Guide on page 50 of the *Student Study Guide* to review and reinforce the content of this section. (Reteaching/Average)

ACTIVITY

Guided Instruction Before students begin their letters, have them imagine some events that could have taken place either on the trip through the backcountry or after they arrived in their new homes. As students write, encourage them to describe at least one imagined event and tell of its effects. Invite students to exchange letters with a partner. Partners can select an interesting excerpt from the letter to read aloud.

Building homes. The different groups who settled the Middle Colonies had their own favorite ways of building. Swedish settlers introduced log cabins to the Americas. The Dutch used red bricks to build narrow, high-walled houses. German settlers developed a wood-burning stove that heated a home better than a fireplace, which let blasts of cold air leak down the chimney.

The backcountry. In the 1700s, thousands of German and Scotch-Irish settlers arrived in Philadelphia's booming port. From Philadelphia, they headed west into the **backcountry,** the area of land along the eastern slopes of the Appalachian Mountains. Settlers followed an old Iroquois trail that became known as the **Great Wagon Road.**

To farm the backcountry, settlers had to clear thick forests. From Indians, settlers learned how to use knots from pine trees as candles to light their homes. They made wooden dishes from logs, gathered honey from hollows in trees, and hunted wild animals for food. German gunsmiths developed a lightweight rifle for use in forests. Sharpshooters boasted that the "Pennsylvania rifle" could hit a rattlesnake between the eyes at 100 yards.

Many settlers arriving in the backcountry moved onto Indian lands. "The Indians. . . are alarmed at the swarm of strangers," one Pennsylvania official reported. "We are afraid of a [fight] between them for the [colonists] are very rough to them." On more than one occasion, disputes between settlers and Indians resulted in violence.

SECTION 2 REVIEW

1. **Locate:** (a) Middle Colonies, (b) New York, (c) New Jersey, (d) Pennsylvania, (e) Philadelphia, (f) Delaware.
2. **Identify:** (a) William Penn, (b) Quakers, (c) Pennsylvania Dutch, (d) Breadbasket Colonies, (e) Great Wagon Road.
3. **Define:** (a) patroon, (b) proprietary colony, (c) cash crop, (d) backcountry.
4. How did the land and climate of the Middle Colonies help farmers to prosper?
5. What groups of people settled the Middle Colonies?
6. **CRITICAL THINKING Comparing** (a) How was Penn's "holy experiment" like the Puritan idea of a "City upon a Hill"? (b) How was it different?

ACTIVITY **Writing to Learn**
Imagine that you moved to the backcountry with your family in the 1700s. Write a letter to a friend back in Philadelphia about your new life.

Answers to Section 2 Review

1. See the map on p. 102.
2. (a) William Penn, p. 102, (b) Quakers, p. 102, (c) Pennsylvania Dutch, p. 103, (d) Breadbasket Colonies, p. 104, (e) Great Wagon Road, p. 105
3. (a) patroon, p. 101, (b) proprietary colony, p. 101, (c) cash crop, p. 104, (d) backcountry, p. 105
4. Unlike New England's thin and rocky soil, the Hudson and Delaware river valleys were rich and fertile. Winters were milder than in New England, and the growing season lasted longer.
5. The Middle Colonies were settled by people from all over Europe, including Protestants, Catholics, and Jews from the Netherlands, France, Germany, Ireland, Sweden, Finland, England, Scotland, and Wales.
6. (a) William Penn and John Winthrop, leaders of the Puritans, both envisioned their colonies as models for others to follow. Both leaders intended for the colonies to separate entirely from the Church of England and to create a simpler form of worship. (b) In the Puritan colony, certain people (for example, the governor, the stockholders in the Massa- chusetts Bay Company, and male church members) were privileged. Because William Penn was a Quaker, however, he believed that all people were equal in God's sight. In his colony, he opposed deferential treatment of people just because they were powerful. Penn accepted Protestants, Catholics, and Jews, whereas the Puritans required people to live their lives exactly as the church decreed.

Section 3
pp. 106–112

Bell Ringer

Have students examine the map on page 109. Ask them to list any natural features they think would help or hinder settlers in the Southern Colonies.

Lesson Plan

1. Focus The prosperity of the Virginia colony encouraged other English settlers. As a result, the colonies of Maryland, North Carolina, South Carolina, and Georgia were formed. In this section, students focus on the similarities and differences among the Southern Colonies.

2. Instruct Make a chart on the chalkboard with three columns labeled Document, Colony, and Purpose. Under Document, list Fundamental Orders of Connecticut, Frame of Government, and Act of Toleration. As students complete the chart, discuss with them the significance of each document. When possible, have students link the documents to freedoms that they enjoy today.

3
The Southern Colonies

FIND OUT

- Why was each of the Southern Colonies founded?
- What was Bacon's Rebellion?
- How did geography help shape life in the Southern Colonies?
- What was the Middle Passage?

VOCABULARY slave code, racism

In 1763, two English mathematicians, Charles Mason and Jeremiah Dixon, began to survey the 244-mile boundary between Pennsylvania and Maryland. The boundary had been in dispute since 1681. For four years, Mason and Dixon carefully laid stone markers on the border between the two colonies. The sides of the markers facing Pennsylvania were inscribed with the letter P. The sides facing Maryland were inscribed with the letter M. In 1767, the two men completed the ***Mason-Dixon Line.***

The Mason-Dixon Line was more than just the boundary between Pennsylvania and Maryland. It also divided the Middle Colonies from the Southern Colonies. Below the Mason-Dixon Line, the Southern Colonies developed a way of life different in many ways from that of the other English colonies.

Lord Baltimore's Maryland

In 1632, Sir George Calvert convinced King Charles I to grant him land for a colony in the Americas. Calvert had ruined his career in Protestant England by becoming a Roman Catholic. Now, he planned to build a colony, Maryland, where Catholics could practice their religion freely. When Sir

---

George died, his son Cecil, Lord Baltimore, pushed on with the project.

Settling the colony. In the spring of 1634, 200 colonists landed along the upper Chesapeake Bay, across from England's first southern colony, Virginia. The land was rich and beautiful. In the words of one settler:

66 The soil is dark and soft, a foot in thickness, and rests upon a rich and red clay. Every where there are very high trees. . . . An abundance of springs afford water. . . . There is an [endless] number of birds. . . . There is not [anything] wanting to the region. 99

Maryland was truly a land of plenty. Chesapeake Bay was full of fish, oysters,

---

BIOGRAPHY Lord Baltimore *Cecil Calvert, the second Lord Baltimore, never visited Maryland. However, he influenced the life of the colony by supporting religious toleration for all Christians. This portrait shows Lord Baltimore with his grandson.* **American Traditions** *Why did Lord Baltimore support limited religious toleration?*

---

and crabs. Across the bay, Virginians were already growing tobacco for profit. Maryland's new settlers hoped to do the same.

Remembering the early problems at Jamestown, the newcomers avoided the swampy lowlands. They built their first town, St. Mary's, in a healthful location.

As proprietor of the colony, Lord Baltimore appointed a governor and a council of advisers. He gave colonists a role in government by creating an elected assembly. Eager to attract settlers to Maryland, Lord Baltimore made generous land grants to anyone who brought over servants, women, and children.

Women set up plantations. A few women took advantage of Lord Baltimore's offer of land. Two sisters, Margaret and Mary Brent, arrived in Maryland in 1638 with nine male servants. In time, they set up two plantations of 1,000 acres each. Later, Margaret Brent helped prevent a rebellion among the governor's soldiers. The Maryland assembly praised her efforts, saying that "the colony's safety at any time [was better] in her hands than in any man's."

Religious toleration. To ensure Maryland's continued growth, Lord Baltimore welcomed Protestants as well as Catholics to the colony. Later, he came to fear that Protestants might try to deprive Catholics of their right to worship freely. In 1649, he asked the assembly to pass an *Act of Toleration.* The act provided religious freedom for all Christians. As in many colonies, this freedom did not extend to Jews.

The Virginia Frontier

Meanwhile, many settlers had gone to Virginia, lured by the promise of profits from tobacco. Wealthy planters quickly took the best lands near the coast. Newcomers had to push inland, onto Indian lands.

Conflict with Indians. As in New England, conflict over land led to fighting between settlers and Indians. From time to time, Indian and white leaders met to restore peace. Still, new settlers continued to press inland. Indians, in turn, continued to attack these frontier plantations.

After several bloody clashes, settlers called on the governor to take action against Native Americans. The governor refused. He was unwilling to act in part because he profited from his own fur trade with Indians. Frontier settlers were furious.

Bacon's Rebellion. Finally, in 1676, Nathaniel Bacon, a young and ambitious planter, organized angry men and women on the frontier. He raided Native American villages. Then he led his followers to Jamestown and burned the capital.

The uprising, known as *Bacon's Rebellion,* lasted only a short time. When Bacon died suddenly, the revolt fell apart. The governor hanged 23 of Bacon's followers. However, he could not stop English settlers from moving onto Indian lands along the frontier.

The Carolinas

South of Virginia and Maryland, English colonists settled in a region called the Carolinas. Settlement took place in two separate areas.

The settlers. To the north, settlers were mostly poor tobacco farmers who had drifted south from Virginia. They tended to have small farms.

Farther south, a group of eight English nobles set up a larger colony. As proprietors, they received a grant of land from

> *Our Common Heritage*
> Groups of escaped slaves, called Maroons, established separate communities in Virginia as early as 1671. In time, there were more than 50 such communities. They were able to survive for years before they were hunted down by white settlers and troops.

3. Close To close the lesson, have students prepare a matching game in which details are linked with the appropriate Southern colony.

 Lesson Planner

For a developed **Cooperative Learning** lesson plan, see the *Lesson Planner,* page 21.

 Chapter Resources

Geography in History Duplicate and distribute the worksheet, Settling the Shenandoah Valley, from Unit 1, pages 41–42, in the *Chapter Resources* binder. (Enrichment/Challenging)

Voices of Freedom

Primary Source You might assign selection 5-4, Bacon Rebels, on pages 41–42 of *Voices of Freedom.* (Enrichment/Average)

Learning Styles
Kinesthetic Learners

Encourage kinesthetic learners to present a skit about the reason for Bacon's Rebellion and its results. The skit should include a jury that tries to decide what to do with the rebels. Some of the group should represent frontier settlers and coastal planters.

Team-Teaching Suggestion
Language Arts/Art

You might work with a language arts teacher and an art teacher to present this activity. Have students imagine that they work for a governor of a Southern colony who is eager to attract settlers to his colony. With the help of the other teachers, have students design an advertising campaign that will attract new settlers to the colony. For a comprehensive advertising plan, students also might want to include slogans or jingles, handbill or poster ads, employment opportunity ads, real estate opportunity ads, and feature stories that present the colony in a positive light for newspapers or magazines.

Answer to Caption

Oglethorpe founded Georgia as a haven for former debtors. These people had no money and no place to live, so they would be attracted by the promise of fertile soil and abundant food.

Transparencies

Geography and History Use the transparency set, Southeastern States, on page I-65 of *American History Transparencies*. The base map and overlay 1 show 10 states that comprise the southeastern United States and some of the topography. Teaching suggestions can be found on page I-10. (Enrichment/Average)

Customized Reader

Primary Source For a copy of a petition by poor farmers in western North Carolina, order article IIB-8, Petition From North Carolina "Regulators," from the *American History Customized Reader*. The petition outlines their grievances and demands. (Enrichment/Challenging)

King Charles II in 1663. The largest settlement, Charles Town, grew up where the Ashley and Cooper rivers met. Later, Charles Town was shortened to Charleston.

Most early settlers in Charleston were English people who had been living in Barbados, a British colony in the Caribbean. Later, other immigrants arrived, including Germans, Swiss, French Protestants, and Spanish Jews.

Carolina rice. Around 1685, a few planters discovered that rice grew well in the swampy lowlands along the coast. Before long, Carolina rice was a valuable crop traded around the world.

Carolina planters needed large numbers of workers to grow rice. At first, they tried to enslave local Indians. Many Indians died of disease or mistreatment, however. Others escaped into the forests. Planters then turned to slaves from Africa. By 1700, most people coming to Charleston were African men and women brought there against their will.

The northern area of Carolina had fewer slaves. Differences between the two areas led to division of the colony into North Carolina and South Carolina in 1712.

Georgia: A Haven for Debtors

The last of England's 13 colonies was carved out of the southern part of South Carolina. James Oglethorpe, a respected soldier and energetic reformer, founded Georgia in 1732. He wanted the colony to be a place where people jailed for debt in England could make a new start.

Under English law, the government could imprison debtors until they paid what they owed. If they ever got out of jail, debtors often had no money and no place to live. Oglethorpe offered to pay for debtors and other poor people to travel to Georgia. "In America," he said, "there are enough fertile lands to feed all the poor of England."

Early years. In 1733, Oglethorpe and 120 colonists built the colony's first settlement at Savannah, above the Savannah River. Oglethorpe set strict rules for the colony. Farms could be no bigger than 50 acres, and slavery was forbidden.

At first, Georgia grew slowly. Later, however, Oglethorpe changed the rules to allow large plantations and slave labor. After that, the colony grew more quickly.

Spanish and Indian neighbors. Spain and England both claimed the land between South Carolina and Florida. Spain, aided by Creek allies, tried to force the English out. But Oglethorpe and the Georgians held their ground.

A woman named Mary Musgrove greatly helped Oglethorpe during this time. The daughter of a Creek mother and an English father, Mary spoke both Creek and English. She helped to keep peace between the Creeks and the settlers in Georgia. Mus-

Founding the Colony of Georgia
James Oglethorpe was eager to attract settlers to his new colony. This illustration advertising the colony shows Georgia as a green, thriving land of fertile soil and ideal weather.
Economics *Why would a picture like this appeal to the kind of settlers Oglethorpe was trying to attract?*

Connections With Architecture
Background

During colonial times, the city of Charleston was noted for the beauty of its homes and the splendor of its social life. In 1749, the governor of the colony reported that colonists were importing the finest Dutch linens and "other East India goods, silk, gold, and silver laces. . . ." The governor warned that in their extravagant way of life, Carolinians resembled ancient Romans.

Historical Sidelight
Background

The English used an unusual event to justify their declaration of war on Spain. The Spanish had caught Robert Jenkins, an English sea captain, trading illegally with the Spanish colonies. As punishment, they cut off one of the captain's ears. Thus, the war became known as the War of Jenkins' Ear.

grove's efforts did much to allow the colony of Georgia to develop in peace.

Plantation Life

The Southern Colonies enjoyed warmer weather and a longer growing season than the colonies to the north. Virginia, Maryland, and parts of North Carolina all became major tobacco-growing areas. Settlers in South Carolina and Georgia raised rice and indigo, a plant used to make a blue dye.

Colonists soon found that it was most profitable to raise tobacco and rice on large plantations. Anywhere from 20 to 100 slaves did most of the work. Most slaves worked in the fields. Some were skilled workers, such as carpenters, barrelmakers, or blacksmiths. Still other slaves worked as cooks, servants, or housekeepers.

Location. Geography affected where southerners built plantations. Along the coastal plain, an area of low land stretched like fingers among broad rivers and creeks. Because the land was washed by ocean tides, the region was known as the ***Tidewater.*** The Tidewater's gentle slopes and rivers offered rich farmland for plantations.

Inland, planters settled along rivers. Rivers provided an easy way to move goods to market. Along the riverbanks, planters loaded their crops on ships bound for the West Indies and Europe. On the return trip, the ships carried English manufactured goods and other luxuries for planters and their families.

Most Tidewater plantations had their own docks, and merchant ships picked up crops and delivered goods directly to them. For this reason, few large seaport cities developed in the Southern Colonies.

Planters set the style. Only a small percentage of white southerners owned large plantations. Yet, planters set the style of life in the South. Life centered around the Great House, where the planter and his family lived. The grandest of these homes had

MAP STUDY

The Southern Colonies stretched from Maryland to Georgia. Farm products and lumber were important to the economy of the region.
1. Name the Southern Colonies.
2. What were the major products of the backcountry?
3. **Comparing** Compare this map with the map on page 102. (a) How were the products of the Southern Colonies similar to those of the Middle Colonies? (b) How were they different?

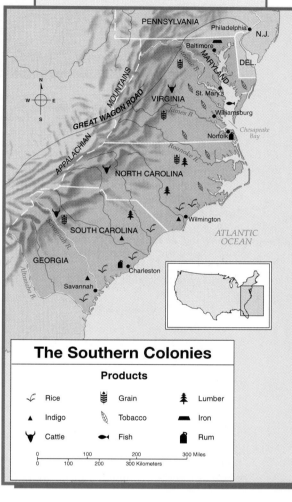

The Southern Colonies

Products

Rice	Grain	Lumber
Indigo	Tobacco	Iron
Cattle	Fish	Rum

Chapter 4 • 109

Answers to Map Study

1. Maryland, Virginia, North Carolina, South Carolina, Georgia **2.** cattle, grain, lumber **3.** (a) They both grew grain and lumber and raised cattle. (b) The Middle Colonies fished. The Southern Colonies grew rice, tobacco, and indigo.

Historical Outline Map Book

Historical Outline Map Duplicate and distribute the map, The Southern Colonies, on page 18 of the *American History Historical Outline Map Book*. Lesson ideas for this map can be found on page T6. (Reteaching/Average)

Historical Sidelight
Background

The southern Atlantic coast shaped the lives of Tidewater planters — but it also provided a haven for pirates. Shifting sandbars and shallow sounds provided effective hiding places for pirate ships.

The most famous pirate of the early 1700s was Edward Teach, more popularly known as Blackbeard. Blackbeard captured many trading ships in the waters off South Carolina.

When he ventured up the coast of Virginia, however, he ran into trouble. In November 1718, Virginians set off in two armed ships to find Blackbeard and get rid of him once and for all. Lieutenant Robert Maynard's ship finally trapped the pirate, killing him and many of his crew. Maynard and his men tied Blackbeard's head to the bow of their ship and sailed home in triumph.

A Tidewater Plantation *This painting shows a typical Tidewater plantation. The Great House of the planter and his family dominates the scene. Slave cabins, barns, and warehouses dot the hillside.* **Geography** *Why do you think the painting shows all roads leading to the river?*

elegant quarters for the family, a parlor for visitors, a dining room, and guest bedrooms.

In the growing season, planters decided which fields to plant, what crops to grow, and when to harvest the crops and take them to market. Planters' wives kept the household running smoothly. They directed house slaves and made sure daily tasks were done, such as milking cows.

The Backcountry

West of the Tidewater was very different. Here, at the base of the Appalachians, rolling hills and thick forests covered the land. As in the Middle Colonies, this inland area was called the backcountry. Attracted by rich soil, settlers followed the Great Wagon Road into the backcountry of Maryland, Virginia, and the Carolinas.

The backcountry was more democratic than the Tidewater. Settlers treated one another as equals. Men worked in their tobacco or corn fields or hunted game. Women

cooked meals and fashioned simple clothing out of wool or deerskins.

Life in the backcountry was not easy. Hardship, however, brought families closer. Families gathered to husk corn or help one another raise barns. Spread out along the edge of the Appalachians, these hardy families felled trees, grew crops, and changed the face of the land.

Growth of Slavery

The first Africans in the English colonies included free people and servants as well as slaves. In the early years, however, even those who were enslaved enjoyed some freedom. In South Carolina, for example, some enslaved Africans worked as cowboys, herding cattle to market.

African farming skills. On plantations throughout the Southern Colonies, enslaved Africans used farming skills they had brought from West Africa. They showed English settlers how to grow rice. They also knew how to use wild plants unfamiliar to the English. They made water buckets out of gourds, and they used palmetto leaves to make fans, brooms, and baskets.

By 1700, plantations in the Southern Colonies relied on slave labor. Slaves cleared the land, worked the crops, and tended the livestock.

To control the large number of slaves, colonists passed **slave codes.** These laws set out rules for slaves' behavior and denied slaves their basic rights. Slaves were seen not as humans but as property.

Attitudes toward slavery. Most English colonists did not question the justice of owning slaves. They believed that black Africans were inferior to white Europeans. The belief that one race is superior to another is called **racism.** Some colonists claimed that they were helping slaves by introducing them to Christianity.

A handful of colonists saw the evils of slavery. In 1688, Quakers in Germantown, Pennsylvania, became the first group of colonists to call for an end to slavery.

The Slave Trade

As demand for slaves grew, European slave traders set up posts along the African coast. They offered guns and other goods to African rulers who brought them slaves. They loaded the captives aboard Spanish, Portuguese, Dutch, English, and French ships headed for the Americas.

Most slave ships went to Brazil and the Caribbean. However, by the 1720s, between 2,000 and 3,000 Africans were arriving each year in North American English colonies.

The trip from Africa to the Americas was called the **Middle Passage.** Slaves were crammed into small spaces below deck. "Each had scarcely room to turn himself, [and the heat] almost suffocated us," recalled Olaudah Equiano (oh LAW dah ehk wee AH noh), an African who made the voyage.

The Middle Passage *Conditions on ships that carried enslaved Africans to the Americas were brutal. As the diagram shows, slave traders squeezed their human cargo into every available space. The painting was done by an English officer on a slave ship.* **Multicultural Heritage** *What qualities did Africans need to survive on slave ships?*

111

Answer to Caption

Possible Answers: physical strength, courage, determination to survive

Our Multicultural Heritage

Biography Have students read the biography, Olaudah Equiano, Eyewitness to Slavery, on page 11 of the *Our Multicultural Heritage* booklet. (Enrichment/Average)

Interdisciplinary Explorations

The Wreck of the Henrietta Marie Have students refer to the unit The Wreck of the Henrietta Marie to gain additional insight into conditions aboard a slave ship. (Enrichment/Challenging)

Our Multicultural Heritage
Background

The Middle Passage was so named because it fell between the First Passage, which was the slaves' journey from the interior of Africa to the coast as captives, and the Third Passage, which was the sale of slaves to their owners in the Americas.

Connections With Literature
Background

The Middle Passage has been the subject of numerous books and articles. Interested students might like to read about slave trading and the sea in a novel, *Middle Passage,* by Charles Johnson. The events of this adventure story take place primarily on board a slave ship, the *Republic.* The novel, published by Atheneum, won the National Book Award in 1990. Review material before assigning to students.

Student Study Guide

Section 3 Study Guide Have students use the Section 3 Study Guide on page 51 of the *Student Study Guide* to review and reinforce the content of this section. (Reteaching/Average)

ACTIVITY

Guided Instruction If students have difficulty thinking of appropriate adjectives, encourage them to imagine themselves being somewhere in the picture. Ask: If you were there, what would you hear, feel, smell, and see?

Section 4 pp. 112–117

 Bell Ringer

Write Philadelphia, Boston, Charleston, New York, and Newport on the chalkboard. After students locate these cities on a map, have them write two sentences telling what the cities have in common and what students think accounted for their growth in the 1700s.

Once or twice a day, the crew allowed the captives up on deck to eat and exercise.

Some Africans fought for their freedom during the trip. Others refused to eat. Equiano recalled:

> 66 One day...two of my wearied countrymen who were chained together...jumped into the sea; immediately another...followed their example.... Two of the wretches were drowned, but [the ship's crew] got the other, and afterwards flogged him unmercifully for thus attempting to prefer death to slavery. 99

Records of slave voyages show that about 10 percent of all Africans shipped to North America in the 1700s did not survive the Middle Passage. On some tragic voyages, the number of deaths was much higher.

SECTION 3 REVIEW

1. **Locate:** (a) Southern Colonies, (b) Maryland, (c) Virginia, (d) North Carolina, (e) South Carolina, (f) Georgia.
2. **Identify:** (a) Mason-Dixon Line, (b) Margaret Brent, (c) Act of Toleration, (d) Bacon's Rebellion, (e) James Oglethorpe, (f) Mary Musgrove, (g) Tidewater, (h) Middle Passage.
3. **Define:** (a) slave code, (b) racism.
4. Why did Lord Baltimore ask the assembly to pass the Act of Toleration?
5. What caused Bacon's Rebellion?
6. How did climate affect development of the Southern Colonies?
7. **CRITICAL THINKING Forecasting** Why do you think tensions might have developed between the backcountry and the Tidewater?

ACTIVITY Writing to Learn
Study the painting of the Middle Passage on page 111. Based on the painting, list five adjectives that describe conditions during the Middle Passage.

---

4 Ruling the Colonies

FIND OUT
- Why did colonists resent the Navigation Acts?
- What items did the colonies trade?
- What rights did colonists gain as a result of the Glorious Revolution?
- How was self-rule strengthened in the colonies?

VOCABULARY mercantilism, import, export, triangular trade, legislature

Philadelphia bustled with activity in 1750. Young men drove cattle, pigs, and sheep to market along narrow cobblestone streets. On the docks, sailors unloaded barrels of molasses from the West Indies, wines from Spain and Portugal, Dutch and English cloth, as well as spices, leather goods, tea, and coffee. "There is actually everything to be had in Pennsylvania that may be obtained in Europe," commented one German visitor.

Philadelphia was the largest and busiest seaport in the colonies. But by the 1700s, trade flourished all along the Atlantic coast. As trade increased, England began to take a new interest in its colonies.

England Regulates Trade

Like other European nations at the time, England believed that the purpose of colonies was to benefit the home country. This belief was part of an economic theory known as **mercantilism** (MER kuhn tihl ihz uhm). According to this theory, a nation became strong by building up its gold supply and expanding trade.

Answers to Section 3 Review

1. See the map on p. 109.
2. (a) Mason-Dixon Line, p. 106, (b) Margaret Brent, p. 107, (c) Act of Toleration, p. 107, (d) Bacon's Rebellion, p. 107, (e) James Oglethorpe, p. 108, (f) Mary Musgrove, p. 108, (g) Tidewater, p. 109, (h) Middle Passage, p. 111
3. (a) slave code, p. 111, (b) racism, p. 111
4. Lord Baltimore feared that Protestants might try to deprive Catholics of their right to worship freely, and he wanted to provide religious freedom for all Christians.

5. Settlers and Indians fought when settlers moved onto Indian land. Settlers rebelled when the governor refused to take action against Native Americans.
6. Because the weather was warm and the growing season longer than in the more northern colonies, the Southern Colonies were able to grow crops such as rice and tobacco for a profitable export market.
7. The plantation owners who lived in the Tidewater had access to an easier life, manufactured goods from England, and other luxuries that backcountry people were denied because of location and economics. Thus, backcountry people might have resented the people of the Tidewater, and the people of the Tidewater might have looked down on the people of the backcountry.

Founding of the Colonies

Colony/Date Founded	Leader	Reasons Founded
New England Colonies		
Massachusetts Plymouth/1620 Massachusetts Bay/1630	William Bradford John Winthrop	Religious freedom Religious freedom
New Hampshire/1622	Ferdinando Gorges John Mason	Profit from trade and fishing
Connecticut Hartford/1636 New Haven/1639	Thomas Hooker	Expand trade; religious and political freedom
Rhode Island/1636	Roger Williams	Religious freedom
Middle Colonies		
New York/1624	Peter Minuit	Expand trade
Delaware/1638	Swedish settlers	Expand trade
New Jersey/1664	John Berkeley George Carteret	Expand trade; religious and political freedom
Pennsylvania/1682	William Penn	Profit from land sales; religious and political freedom
Southern Colonies		
Virginia/1607	John Smith	Trade and farming
Maryland/1632	Lord Baltimore	Profit from land sales; religious and political freedom
The Carolinas/1663 North Carolina/1712 South Carolina/1712	Group of eight proprietors	Trade and farming; religious freedom
Georgia/1732	James Oglethorpe	Profit; home for debtors; buffer against Spanish Florida

CHART SKILLS *The 13 English colonies were founded for many different reasons. • Which colonies were founded by people seeking religious freedom? Which were founded by people seeking to expand trade?*

Trade takes place when goods are exchanged. **Imports** are goods brought into a country. **Exports** are goods sent to markets outside a country. Because exports help a country earn money, mercantilists thought that a country should export more than it imports.

New laws. Beginning in the 1650s, Parliament passed a series of laws to regulate trade between England and its colonies. The

Chapter 4 • **113**

Lesson Plan

1. Focus As trade expanded, the colonies grew and prospered. In this section, students learn how the 13 English colonies changed in the mid-1700s.
2. Instruct Tell the class that they will prepare a three-page colonial newspaper. Divide the class into three groups. One group should outline a page of articles about social, political, and economic events in the New England Colonies. The other two groups should similarly cover the Middle and Southern colonies.
3. Close To close the lesson, have students identify one effect for each of the following causes: (a) Roads were poor and there were few bridges. (b) An active trade along the coast developed.

 Lesson Planner

For a developed **Cooperative Learning** lesson plan, see the *Lesson Planner,* page 22.

Answer to Chart Skills

Religious Freedom: Massachusetts, Rhode Island, Connecticut, New Jersey, Pennsylvania, Maryland, the Carolinas; Expand Trade: New Hampshire, Connecticut, Virginia, New York, Delaware, New Jersey, the Carolinas

Connections With Geography
Activity

Help students create a map showing the expansion of trade among the colonies. First, draw or bring in a large outline map of the 13 colonies. Using information from this chapter, have students list products that were shipped among the colonies and then create a symbol for each product (for example, a tree for lumber, a sack for sugar, a keg for molasses, a leaf for tobacco). Have volunteers draw arrows showing the movement of goods; near each arrow, students can draw the symbols for the goods being traded. Invite students to comment on what the finished map suggests about the state of commerce in the colonies.

Answer to Caption

The economy of the colonies depended primarily on trade with England; cities developed around the natural ports through which goods passed.

Videotapes/ Videodiscs

United States History Video Collection Use the video segment "The Atlantic World" from Volume 3, *Slavery and Freedom*, to enhance students' understanding of mercantilism. Approx. running time 1:45 min. (Enrichment/Average) Vol. 3, Ch. 7

| Chapter 7 | Play |

United States History Video Collection Use the video segment "The Sugar Islands" from Volume 3, *Slavery and Freedom*, to enhance students' understanding of the triangular trade. Approx. running time 4:00 min. (Enrichment/Average) Vol. 3, Ch. 10

| Chapter 10 | Play |

laws were known as the ***Navigation Acts.*** Parliament passed the laws to ensure that only England benefited from trade with the colonies.

For example, under the new laws, only colonial or English ships could carry goods to and from the colonies. The Navigation Acts also listed certain products, such as tobacco and cotton, that colonial merchants could ship only to England. In this way, Parliament created jobs for English workers who cut and rolled tobacco or spun cotton into cloth.

Colonists react. In many ways, the Navigation Acts helped the colonies as well as England. The law that required the use of English or colonial ships encouraged colonists to build their own ships. New England became a prosperous center for shipbuilding. Moreover, because of the acts, colonial merchants did not have to compete with foreign merchants.

Still, many colonists resented the Navigation Acts. In their view, the laws favored English merchants. Colonial merchants often ignored the Navigation Acts or found ways to get around them.

Molasses, Rum, and Slaves

The colonies produced a wide variety of goods. Ships moved up and down the Atlantic coast in an active trade. Merchants from New England dominated colonial trade. They were known as ***Yankees,*** a nickname that implied they were clever and hard-working. Yankee traders earned a reputation for getting a good buy and profiting from any deal.

Trade routes. Colonial merchants developed many trade routes. One route was known as the **triangular trade** because the three legs of the route formed a triangle. On the first leg of the journey, ships from New England carried fish, lumber, and other goods to the West Indies. There, they bought sugar and molasses, a dark-brown syrup made from sugar cane. They then car-

---

A Flourishing City *Almost from its founding in 1682, Philadelphia was a thriving port. This painting shows the busy Philadelphia waterfront in 1720.* **Economics** *Why did ports become the major cities of the colonies?*

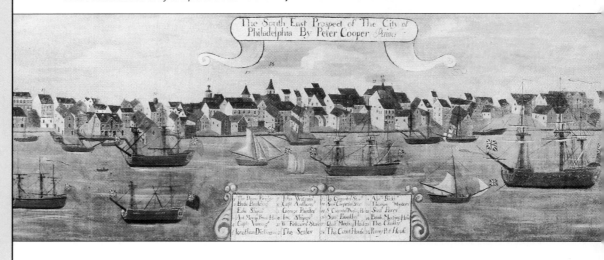

Our Multicultural Heritage
Background

The name *Yankee* probably derives from the Dutch language as a variation of the name *Jan Kees.* An Americanized version of this name, *John Cheese,* was a nickname generally used in colonial times for all Dutch and English settlers.

Critical Thinking
Classifying Information

Students can work in small groups to write the questions for several categories on a television game show devoted to the colonial period of American history. Questions can involve information about such categories as the people and governments of the New England, Middle, and Southern colonies; geographic features; economic development; and the colonists' relationships with England and other parts of the world.

ried the sugar and molasses back to New England, where colonists used them to make rum.

On the second leg, ships carried rum, guns, gunpowder, cloth, and tools from New England to West Africa. In Africa, merchants traded these goods for slaves. On the final leg, ships carried enslaved Africans to the West Indies. With the profits from selling the enslaved Africans, traders bought more molasses.

Breaking the law. Many New England merchants grew wealthy from the triangular trade. In doing so, they often disobeyed the Navigation Acts. Traders were supposed to buy sugar and molasses only from English colonies in the West Indies. However, the demand for molasses was so high that New Englanders bought from the Dutch, French, and Spanish West Indies, too. Although this trade was illegal, bribes made customs officials look the other way.

Travel and Communication

In the 1600s and early 1700s, travel in the colonies was slow and difficult. Roads were rough and muddy, and there were few bridges over streams and rivers. Most colonists stayed close to home.

Colonists set up a postal system, but it was slow. In 1717, it took one month for a letter to get from Boston to Williamsburg, Virginia. In winter, it took two months.

History and You

Settlers kept up a busy exchange of letters. Writing was a chore, however, done with goose quill pens that had to be dipped in ink every few moments. Why do you think people in colonial times went to so much trouble to write letters? Why do most people today write few personal letters?

Slowly, roads and mail service improved. Families built taverns along main roads and in towns and cities. Colorful signs attracted customers, who stopped to rest and to exchange news and gossip with local people.

Colonial printers spread news and ideas by publishing pamphlets and books. By 1750, most colonies published at least one weekly newspaper.

Rights of English Citizens

By the late 1600s, each colony had developed its own form of government. Still, the governments had much in common. In each colony, a governor directed the colony's affairs and enforced the laws. Usually, the governor was appointed by the king or the colony's proprietor. Rhode Island and Connecticut, though, elected their own governor.

Colonial assemblies. Each colony also had a legislature. A **legislature** is a group of people who have the power to make laws. In most colonies, the legislature had an upper house and a lower house. The upper house was also known as the governor's council. The council was made up of advisers appointed by the governor.

The lower house was an elected assembly. It approved laws and protected the rights of citizens. Just as important, it had the right to approve or disapprove any taxes the governor asked for. This "power of the purse," or right to raise or spend money, was an important check on the governor's power. Any governor who ignored the assembly risked losing his salary.

The right to vote. Each colony had its own rules about who could vote. By the 1720s, however, all the colonies had laws that restricted the right to vote to white Christian men over the age of 21. In some colonies, only Protestants or members of a particular church could vote. All voters had to own property. Colonial leaders believed

 Transparencies

Geography and History Use the transparency set, Thirteen Colonies, on page I-17 of *American History Transparencies.* The base map and overlay 1 show the location of the three groups of original colonies along the Eastern seaboard. Teaching suggestions can be found on page I-2. (Enrichment/Average)

Historical Outline Map Book

Historical Outline Map Duplicate and distribute the map, The Thirteen Colonies, on page 15 of the *American History Historical Outline Map Book.* Lesson ideas for this map can be found on page T4. (Reteaching/Average)

Connections With Technology
Background

The first postal route in the colonies was set up in 1672. It ran from New York to Hartford, Connecticut, to Boston. Part of this route is still known as the Boston Post Road. When Benjamin Franklin became Postmaster General for the colonies, he set up a relay system to move the mail more quickly. At relay stations along their routes, mail carriers exchanged tired horses for fresh ones.

Connections With Local History
Activity

Have students make a chart comparing a colonial government with their own state government. Students can develop their own points of comparison, including items such as structure and duties of government, voting requirements, and voting methods.

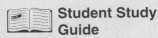
Student Study Guide

Section 4 Study Guide Have students use the Section 4 Study Guide on page 52 of the *Student Study Guide* to review and reinforce the content of this section. (Reteaching/Average)

ACTIVITY

Guided Instruction If a tape recorder is available, have students act out and tape a conversation between the two colonial merchants before they begin writing. Then, as they write, they can select portions of the tape to include in their dialogues. When students finish writing, have them read their dialogues with their partners and tape the reading. They then can compare the two tapes and identify the best features of each. If students think that they can improve either the writing or the delivery of their dialogues by emphasizing these positive features, allow students to tape another version.

that only property owners knew what was best for a colony.

On election day, voters and their families gathered in towns and villages. A buzz of excitement filled the air as people exchanged news and gossip. Smiling candidates shook hands with voters and slapped them heartily on the back. In some areas, they offered to buy them drinks. When things quieted down, the sheriff called the voters together. One by one, he read out their names. Everyone listened as each man announced his vote aloud:

> ❝*Sheriff:* Mr. Blair, whom do you vote for?
> *Mr. Blair:* John Marshall.
> *Mr. Marshall:* Your vote is appreciated, Mr. Blair.❞

Rights from the Glorious Revolution. Colonists took great pride in their elected assemblies. They also valued the rights the Magna Carta gave them as English subjects. (See page 86.) In 1689, colonists won still more rights as a result of the ***Glorious Revolution*** in England.

The Glorious Revolution began in 1688. Parliament removed King James from the throne and asked William and Mary of the Netherlands to rule. In return for Parliament's support, William and Mary signed the ***English Bill of Rights*** in 1689. It protected the rights of individuals and gave anyone accused of a crime the right to a trial by jury. Just as important, the English Bill

Our Common Heritage

In early Carolina, many people enjoyed the right to vote. In 1706, a citizen observed, "For this last election, Jews, Strangers, Sailors, Servants, Negroes, & almost every French Man in Craven & Berkly county came down to elect, & their votes were taken."

of Rights said that a ruler could not raise taxes or an army without the approval of Parliament.

Limited rights. The rights of English citizens did not extend to everyone in the colonies. Africans and Indians had almost no rights. Neither did women or servants.

Like women in Europe, colonial women had few legal rights. A woman's father or husband was supposed to protect her. A married woman could not start her own business or sign a contract unless her husband approved it. In most colonies, unmarried women and widows had more rights than married women. They could make contracts and sue in court. In Maryland and the Carolinas, women settlers who headed families could buy land on the same terms as men.

SECTION 4 REVIEW

1. **Identify:** (a) Navigation Acts, (b) Yankees, (c) Glorious Revolution, (d) English Bill of Rights.
2. **Define:** (a) mercantilism, (b) import, (c) export, (d) triangular trade, (e) legislature.
3. (a) List three ways the Navigation Acts helped England. (b) Why did colonists resent them?
4. What goods were included in the triangular trade?
5. How were colonial governments organized?
6. **CRITICAL THINKING Linking Past and Present** (a) Which rights granted by the English Bill of Rights are similar to rights Americans have today? (b) Why is each important?

ACTIVITY **Writing to Learn**

Write a dialogue between Yankee merchants in which they discuss their feelings about the Navigation Acts.

Answers to Section 4 Review

1. (a) Navigation Acts, p. 114, (b) Yankees, p. 114, (c) Glorious Revolution, p. 116, (d) English Bill of Rights, p. 116
2. (a) mercantilism, p. 112, (b) import, p. 113, (c) export, p. 113, (d) triangular trade, p. 114, (e) legislature, p. 115
3. (a) only English ships carried goods to and from the colonies; certain products, like tobacco and cotton, could be shipped only to England; there, manufacturing jobs such as

spinning cotton and rolling tobacco were created (b) Colonial merchants felt that the laws favored English merchants.
4. fish, lumber, sugar, molasses, rum, guns, gunpowder, cloth, tools, slaves
5. A governor directed the colony's affairs and enforced the laws. Each colony had a legislature to make laws. The legislatures usually had upper and lower houses.

6. (a) the right to a jury trial if accused of a crime, the right not to be taxed or drafted into the army without approval from Parliament (b) Each of these rights protects individuals against possible injustices from a powerful ruler by giving decision-making power to a group of citizens such as a jury or a legislature.

MAP, GRAPH, AND CHART SKILLS
Using a Time Line

Historians study events that happened in the past. They often look at these events in *chronological order,* or the order in which they occurred. In this way, they can judge whether or not events might be related.

A *time line* is one way to show the order in which events took place. A time line also shows the dates when events happened.

A time line appears at the beginning of each chapter in this book. These time lines are called horizontal time lines because they set out dates and events on a line from left to right.

Study the time line below. Then, use these steps to read the time line.

1. **Identify the time period covered in the time line.** (a) What is the earliest event shown on the time line below? (b) What is the latest event? (c) What is the period covered by this time line?

2. **Decide how the time line is divided.** Time lines are always divided into equal parts or time periods. Some time lines are divided into 10-year periods. A 10-year period is called a *decade*.

Some time lines are divided into 100-year periods, called *centuries.* The period from 1701 to 1800, for example, is called the eighteenth century. (a) List the dates that are marked off on the time line below. (b) How many years are there between each date? (c) What events occurred during the decade of the 1670s? (d) What century is shown on this time line?

3. **Study the time line to discover how events might be related.** Use your reading in this chapter and the time line to answer these questions. (a) When did the Glorious Revolution take place? (b) Was the English Bill of Rights passed before or after the Glorious Revolution? (c) Was there a relationship between these two events? Explain your answer.

4. **Draw conclusions.** Use your reading in the chapter and the time line to draw conclusions about the events taking place during this period. (a) What events took place in 1630, 1639, and 1689? (b) What do these events tell you about the growth of self-government in the colonies? Explain. (c) What events took place in 1675 and 1676? (d) Based on these events, what generalization can you make about relations between Native Americans and English settlers in the late 1600s?

 Make a time line of important events in your life.

1630 Puritans arrived in Massachusetts Bay.

1639 Settlers wrote the Fundamental Orders of Connecticut.

1675 Fighting broke out between New England settlers and the Wampanoag Indians.

1676 Angry settlers on the frontier took part in Bacon's Rebellion.

1688 The Glorious Revolution began in England.

1689 William and Mary signed the English Bill of Rights.

1630 | 1640 | 1650 | 1660 | 1670 | 1680 | 1690

Chapter Resources

Skill Application For additional practice, duplicate and distribute the worksheet, Using a Time Line, from Unit 1, page 38, of the *Chapter Resources* binder. (Reteaching/Average)

Answers to Skill Lesson

1. (a) 1630 (b) 1689 (c) 1630–1690 (60 years) **2.** (a) 1630, 1640, 1650, 1660, 1670, 1680, 1690 (b) 10 years (c) fighting between New England settlers and the Wampanoag Indians (1675); Bacon's Rebellion (1676) (d) the seventeenth century **3.** (a) 1688 (b) after (c) Yes. The Glorious Revolution put William and Mary in power, and they signed the English Bill of Rights to ensure Parliament's support. **4.** (a) Puritans arrived in Massachusetts Bay; settlers wrote the Fundamental Orders of Connecticut; William and Mary signed the English Bill of Rights. (b) Possible Answer: Both in the colonies and in England, dissatisfaction led to changes in government. (c) Fighting broke out between New England settlers and the Wampanoag Indians; angry settlers took part in Bacon's Rebellion. (d) Possible Answer: Relations were tense and easily erupted into violence.

ACTIVITY

Guided Instruction You might point out that some events that have had a major impact on students' lives might even have preceded their actual birthdates. After students have compiled a list of events, have them determine the time span involved and then calculate a practical measure.

Students Acquiring English
Activity

SAE students might benefit from using the information on their time lines to produce an oral report. Because they are better informed than their listeners about the personal content of their time lines, talking about the time lines offers SAE students a unique opportunity to produce an oral report without having the extra burden of being concerned about the accuracy of their information. Pair SAE students with English-proficient students; allow each partner to explain to the other why he or she has chosen each event on the time line.

Bell Ringer

Ask students to imagine their daily lives if they had lived in colonial times and to write a schedule of their activities for one day.

Lesson Plan

1. Focus The English colonists developed a culture that was distinct from the culture of England. In this section, students learn about the social system, the role of women, the influence of African cultures, and education in the colonies.

2. Instruct Write the following statements on the chalkboard: (a) Puritans wanted all people to be able to read the Bible. (b) A formal education was not considered as important for a girl as for a boy. (c) During the Great Awakening, preachers encouraged people to examine their lives. Have students explain how each of these attitudes affected life in colonial America.

3. Close To close the lesson, play a game in which students unscramble and explain key terms from Section 5—for example, *Tager Winganeka* for "Great Awakening" and *Melthetenning* for "Enlightenment."

Lesson Planner

For a developed **Cooperative Learning** lesson plan, see the *Lesson Planner,* page 23.

5
The Colonies in 1750

FIND OUT
- How did the Great Awakening increase religious tolerance?
- What was life like for women in the backcountry and in cities?
- How did colonists educate their children?
- What was the Enlightenment?

VOCABULARY gentry, indentured servant, public school, apprentice

In 1743, Benjamin Franklin, a leading citizen of Philadelphia, made a proposal to the English colonists. It began:

66 The first drudgery of settling new colonies... is now pretty well over, and there are many in every province... [who have time] to cultivate the finer arts, and improve the common stock of knowledge. 99

Franklin wanted colonists to put their spare time to good use. He invited them to join a society to promote "USEFUL KNOWLEDGE among British [colonies] in America." Thanks to Franklin's efforts, the American Philosophical Society was born.

Franklin's new society was only one sign that the English colonies were coming of age. By the mid-1700s, they had developed a culture quite different from that of England. Blending the traditions of Native Americans, Europeans, and Africans, this culture was truly new and American.

Social Classes

Colonists enjoyed more social equality than people in England did. Still, class differences existed.

At the top of society stood the **gentry.** The gentry included wealthy planters, merchants, ministers, successful lawyers, and royal officials. They could afford to dress in elegant clothes and follow the latest fashions from London.

Below the gentry was the middle class. The middle class included farmers who worked their own land, skilled craftsworkers, and some tradespeople. Nearly three quarters of all white colonists belonged to the middle class. They prospered because land in the colonies was plentiful and easy to buy. Also, laborers were in demand, and skilled workers received good wages.

The lowest social class included hired farmhands, indentured servants, and slaves. **Indentured servants** promised to work without wages for four to seven years for whomever would pay their ocean passage to the Americas. When their term of service was completed, indentured servants received "freedom dues": a set of clothes, tools, and 50 acres of land.

Women in the Colonies

Women throughout the colonies did many of the same tasks—whether they lived in Connecticut or Delaware or South Carolina. A woman took care of her household, husband, and family. By the kitchen fire, she baked squash or a kind of boiled corn known as hominy grits. She milked cows, watched the children, and made clothing.

Backcountry women often worked with their husbands in the fields at harvest time. There was too much to be done to worry about whether it was proper "woman's work." A visitor from the East was amazed by a backcountry woman's activities:

66 She will carry a gunn in the woods and kill deer, turkeys &c., shoot down wild cattle, catch and tye hoggs, knock down [cattle] with an ax, and perform the most manfull Exercises as well as most men. 99

Connections With Technology
Background

Benjamin Franklin considered all knowledge valuable — whether or not it had an immediate use. As he watched a balloon ascension in Paris one day, someone asked him what use this new toy could have. "What good," replied Franklin, "is a newborn baby?"

Some of Benjamin Franklin's experiments were dangerous. Once, Franklin tried to kill a turkey with an electric charge. As he put the electrodes on its wings, the turkey got away, and the electrodes slipped into Franklin's hands. He felt "a Universal blow throughout my whole body from head to feet." Franklin later remarked, "I meant to kill a turkey, and instead, almost killed a goose."

Colonial Women at Work *Women played a major role in the economic life of the colonies. The woman at left is spinning thread into cloth. The woman at right is making pins.* **Daily Life** *How did the lives of these women differ from those of women in the backcountry?*

In cities, women sometimes worked outside the home. A young single woman from a poorer family might work as a maid, a cook, or a nurse for one of the gentry. Other women were midwives, like Anne Hutchinson, delivering babies. Still others sewed fine hats, dresses, or cloaks to be sold to women who could afford them. Learning these skills required many years of practice and training.

Women sometimes learned trades from their fathers, brothers, or husbands. They worked as shoemakers, silversmiths, and butchers. Quite a few women became printers. Then, too, a woman might take over her husband's business when he died.

African Cultural Influences

By the mid-1700s, the culture of Africans in the colonies varied greatly. On rice plantations in South Carolina, slaves saw few white colonists. As a result, African customs remained strong. For example, parents often chose African names for their children, such as Quosh or Juba or Cuff. In some coastal areas, slaves spoke a distinctive combination of English and West African languages, known as Gullah.

The Southern Colonies. In Charleston and other South Carolina port towns, more than half the population was African. Many of them worked along the docks, making rope or barrels or helping to build ships. Skilled craftsworkers made fine wood cabinets or silver plates and utensils. Although most Africans in these towns were enslaved, many opened their own shops or stalls in the market.

★★★ *Our Common Heritage*
Elizabeth Timothy was the first woman publisher in the English colonies. She took over her husband's newspaper, the South Carolina Gazette, *after he died. In all, it is estimated that 30 colonial women published newspapers.*

Chapter 4 • **119**

Our Multicultural Heritage
Activity

Have students prepare biographical sketches about early women settlers such as Mary Tranton, Frances White, Winifred Seaborne, or Elizabeth Beach. Some students may prefer to synthesize their knowledge of the role of women in this period of American history by writing about a fictional woman. Suggest that students write a diary entry for their imaginary woman in response to a real historical event or development.

Connections With Fashion
Background

In 1711, the hoop skirt was introduced in England; it set the style of clothing for wealthy women for several decades, both in England and in the colonies. Explain to students that a hooplike framework of whalebone, wicker, or osier caused these skirts to bulge considerably. Some skirts were fully 18 feet wide!

MAP STUDY

New immigrants from Europe, as well as enslaved Africans, carried their own cultures to the American colonies.

1. Where did most enslaved Africans live?
2. Which group settled the farthest inland?
3. **Drawing Conclusions** (a) Which group settled in all the colonies? (b) How would you explain this?

Colonists From Many Lands

- English
- Scotch-Irish
- Scottish
- German
- French
- Dutch
- Swedish
- African (free and slave)

In Virginia and Maryland, African traditions were weaker. Africans in the Chesapeake region were less isolated from white farmers and planters. Also, by the 1750s, the number of new slaves arriving in the region each year had begun to decline. Even so, many old customs survived. One traveler observed an African-style funeral. Mourners took part in a ceremony to speed the dead to his home, which they believed was in Africa.

The Middle and New England colonies. Fewer Africans lived in the Middle Colonies and New England. Still, Africans arrived there in greater numbers after the 1740s. Most lived in such cities as Philadelphia, New York, and Newport. Often, the men outnumbered the women. As a result, the number of African families remained small.

A Renewal of Faith

In the 1730s and 1740s, a religious movement known as the **Great Awakening** swept through the colonies. Its drama and emotion touched people of all backgrounds.

A New England preacher, Jonathan Edwards, set off the Great Awakening in the colonies. Edwards called on colonists to examine their lives. In powerful sermons, he warned listeners that unless they heeded the Bible's teachings, they would be "sinners in the hands of an angry God," headed for the fiery torments of hell.

In 1739, when an English minister named George Whitefield arrived in the colonies, the movement spread like wildfire. Whitefield drew huge crowds to outdoor meetings from Massachusetts to Georgia. His voice rang with feeling as he called on sinners to reform. Jonathan Edwards's wife described the impact Whitefield had on his listeners:

❝[Whitefield] casts a spell over an audience. . . . I have seen upwards of a thousand people hang on his

African Crafts *African craftsworkers created much fine wooden furniture. Many of these works, such as this detail from a fireplace mantel, often had African-inspired designs.* **The Arts** *Compare this carving to the African carving shown on page 67. How are they similar?*

words with breathless silence, broken only by an occasional half-suppressed sob. **"**

The Great Awakening aroused bitter debate. People who supported it often split away from their old churches to form new ones. Opponents warned that the movement was too emotional. Still, the growth of so many new churches forced colonists to become more tolerant of people with different beliefs.

Concern With Education

Among the colonists, New Englanders were most concerned about education. Puritans believed that all people had a duty to study the Bible. If settlers did not learn to read, how would they fulfill this duty?

Public schools in New England. In 1647, the Massachusetts assembly passed a law ordering all parents to teach their children "to read and understand the principles of religion." Beyond that, they required all towns with 50 families to hire a schoolteacher. Towns with 100 families or more had to set up a grammar school that prepared boys for college.

In this way, Massachusetts set up the first **public schools,** or schools supported by taxes. Public schools were important because they allowed both rich and poor children to get an education.

The first New England schools had only one room for students of all ages. Parents paid the schoolteacher with corn, peas, or other foods. Each child was expected to bring a share of wood to burn in the stove. Students who forgot would find themselves seated in the coldest corner of the room!

Middle and Southern colonies. In the Middle Colonies, churches and individual families set up private schools. Pupils paid to attend. As a result, only wealthy families could afford to educate their children.

In the Southern Colonies, people lived too far apart to bring children together in one building. Some planters hired tutors, or private teachers. The wealthiest planters sent their sons to school in England. As a rule, slaves were denied education of any kind.

Learning by doing. Some children served as apprentices (uh PREHN tihs ehz). An **apprentice** worked for a master to learn a trade or a craft. For example, when a boy reached age 12 or 13, his parents might apprentice him to a master glassmaker. The young apprentice lived in the glassmaker's home for six or seven years. The glassmaker gave him food and clothing and treated him like a member of the family. He was also supposed to teach the boy how to read and write and provide him with religious training.

In return, the apprentice worked without pay in the glassmaker's shop and learned the skills he needed to become a

Chapter 4 • **121**

Critical Thinking
Evaluating Ideas

In 1671, Governor Berkeley of Virginia commented: "I thank God, there are no free schools nor printing [in Virginia] . . . for learning has brought disobedience, and heresy, and sects into the world, and printing has divulged them, and libels against the best government. God keep us from both!"

Ask students to reflect on Governor Berkeley's comments about education and communication. Have them first explain what they think he meant, then decide with which parts they agree or disagree. They should provide examples of how they think his ideas apply today.

CONNECTIONS

ARTS | **SCIENCES** | **GEOGRAPHY** | **WORLD** | **ECONOMICS** | **CIVICS**

Ben Franklin: Practical Inventor

Ben Franklin was always asking questions. To his restless mind, there was nothing that could not be learned; nothing that could not be improved.

One of Franklin's nagging concerns was fireplaces. The fireplace was the heart of the colonial home. But fireplaces of the day worked poorly. They spewed black smoke throughout the house and sent most of the heat up the chimney.

To solve these problems, Franklin invented the "Pennsylvania Fireplace." Set in the middle of the room, the fireplace gave off heat from three sides. Once cold air entered the fireplace, it was heated in an "air box." The heated air then rushed into the room through vents in the fireplace sides. As for smoke, a wall at the back of the fireplace forced smoke up a pipe, into the chimney, and out of the house.

The new fireplace saved money, too. As Franklin proudly pointed out, the "Franklin stove" made the room "twice as warm with a quarter of the wood."

The Pennsylvania Fireplace was only the first of Franklin's many inventions. During his long life, he designed a chair that turned into a step stool, a pole with "fingers" to reach books on high shelves, and a wind-

Franklin stove

mill to turn his meat roaster.

In his old age, Franklin grew tired of removing his reading glasses so that he could see things far away. To remedy this problem, he designed his own bifocal glasses. The top half of the lens was for distance vision, and the bottom half was for reading.

Ben Franklin

Franklin's inventions offered practical solutions to everyday problems. He probably could have become wealthy from them. He refused to patent his creations, however. "As we enjoy great advantages from the inventions of others," he wrote, "we should be glad of an opportunity to serve others by an invention of ours."

■ What were some of Franklin's inventions?

Scientific models for an experiment with lightning

ACTIVITY
Draw a plan for an invention that solves an everyday problem.

master glassmaker. He was then ready to start his own shop. Boys were apprenticed in many trades, including papermaking, printing, and leather tanning.

Education for girls. In New England, some girls attended dame schools, or private schools run by women in their own homes. Most schools in the colonies accepted only boys, however. Girls learned skills from their mothers, who taught them to spin wool, weave, and embroider. A few were also taught to read and write.

An Age of Reason

During the 1600s, European scientists tried to use reason and logic to understand the world. They developed theories and then performed experiments to test them. In doing so, they discovered many laws of nature. Isaac Newton, for example, explained how the force of gravity kept planets from flying out of their orbits.

European thinkers of the late 1600s and 1700s believed that the same methods could be applied to the study of society. They tried to discover the natural laws that governed human behavior. Because these thinkers believed in the light of human reason, the movement that they started is known as the *Enlightenment.*

Benjamin Franklin. The best example of the Enlightenment spirit in the colonies was Benjamin Franklin. Franklin was born in 1706, the son of a poor Boston soap and candle maker. A strong believer in self-improvement, Franklin worked his way from poverty to become an important colonial leader. Although he had only two years of formal schooling, he used his spare time to read and to study literature, mathematics, and foreign languages.

At age 17, Franklin ran away from Boston and made his way to Philadelphia. There, he built up a successful printing business. His most popular publication was *Poor Richard's Almanac.* Published yearly, it contained clever quotes, calendars, and other useful information.

Science and change. Franklin's many interests included science. In 1752, he proved that lightning was a form of electricity. To do this, he flew a kite during a thunderstorm. A bolt of lightning struck a wire fastened to the kite and caused an electric spark.

Like other Enlightenment thinkers, Franklin wanted to use reason to improve the world around him. Using what he learned about electricity, he invented the lightning rod to protect buildings from fire during thunderstorms.

Franklin convinced city officials to pave Philadelphia's streets and to organize a fire company. With his help, local leaders also set up the first lending library in the Americas. Ben Franklin's practical inventions and his public service earned him worldwide fame.

SECTION 5 REVIEW

1. **Identify:** (a) Great Awakening, (b) Jonathan Edwards, (c) George Whitefield, (d) Enlightenment, (e) Benjamin Franklin.
2. **Define:** (a) gentry, (b) indentured servant, (c) public school, (d) apprentice.
3. What were the results of the Great Awakening?
4. Why did the Puritans support public education?
5. List three contributions of Benjamin Franklin.
6. **CRITICAL THINKING Comparing** Compare the lives of women in the backcountry with those of women in cities.

ACTIVITY Writing to Learn

Imagine that you are an apprentice to a master craftsworker. Write a short story about life with your master.

Voices of Freedom

Primary Source You might assign selection 6-6, The Wisdom of Benjamin Franklin, on pages 50–51 of *Voices of Freedom.* The selection is an excerpt from Franklin's "The Way to Wealth." (Enrichment/Average)

CD-ROM

History Makers Access the biography on Benjamin Franklin from the American Heritage® *History of the United States* CD-ROM. (Enrichment/Average)

Student Study Guide

Section 5 Study Guide Have students use the Section 5 Study Guide on page 53 of the *Student Study Guide* to review and reinforce the content of this section. (Reteaching/Average)

ACTIVITY

Guided Instruction Encourage a variety of prewriting activities to help students choose the kinds of characters they want in their stories. Students can read drafts of their stories to partners, who can help them identify places to "show" instead of "tell."

Answers to Section 5 Review

1. (a) Great Awakening, p. 120, (b) Jonathan Edwards, p. 120, (c) George Whitefield, p. 120, (d) Enlightenment, p. 123, (e) Benjamin Franklin, p. 123
2. (a) gentry, p. 118, (b) indentured servant, p. 118, (c) public school, p. 121, (d) apprentice, p. 121
3. The Great Awakening created a greater sense of self-examination, caused new churches to form, and encouraged greater religious toleration in the colonies.
4. The Puritans believed that all people needed to learn to read so that they could study the Bible.
5. Possible Answers: invention of the lightning rod; *Poor Richard's Almanac*; encouragement of street paving, fire companies, and lending libraries
6. Women worked hard whether they lived in a city or in the backcountry. In addition to cooking and housework, women in the backcountry harvested crops, butchered cattle, and hunted. Women in the city also took care of homes and families and often worked outside the home as nurses, cooks, or maids. Some city women learned trades and ran businesses.

CHAPTER 4 REVIEW

Answers to Reviewing the Main Ideas

1. (a) to build a society based on the laws of God as they appear in the Bible (b) to provide a place where Catholics could practice their religion freely
2. Quakers believed that all people were equal in God's sight; from the beginning, therefore, William Penn accepted Protestants, Catholics, and Jews in his colony. He also spoke out for fair treatment of Native Americans.
3. As settlers fanned out from coastal settlements, taking over more and more Native American lands, fighting broke out between white settlers and local Native Americans.
4. Life in the Tidewater focused on large plantations, where planters and their families lived in elegance and where enslaved Africans did most of the work. The backcountry was more democratic because few people were rich and everyone worked hard, often helping one another.
5. Africans used their knowledge of farming to successfully plant and harvest crops. They worked inside the home as cooks, maids, seamstresses, and child-care workers. They worked as cowhands and in skilled crafts as carpenters, cabinetmakers, and silversmiths.
6. New England ships carried fish and lumber to the West Indies. They returned to New England with sugar and molasses. Colonists used the sugar and molasses to make rum. Ships took the rum, along with guns, gunpowder, cloth, and tools, to Africa to trade for slaves. The ships then took the slaves to the West Indies. The routes followed by these New England trading ships formed a triangle.
7. Benjamin Franklin wanted to use the light of human reason and logic to improve the world.

Answers to Thinking Critically

1. Answers may vary; however, students should note that a belief in African inferiority allowed Europeans to trade and own African slaves without feeling guilty.
2. Religious toleration was one of the major reasons people

Summary

- New England colonists were farmers, fishers, and merchants who lived in close-knit communities centered around the church.
- Blessed by rich land and mild climate, people from many lands enjoyed a prosperous way of life in the Middle Colonies.
- Two ways of life grew up in the South: plantation life, which relied on enslaved Africans, and the rougher life of the backcountry.
- Colonial governments included a governor and an elected assembly, which passed laws and protected citizens' rights.
- Despite differences, colonists developed a uniquely American culture by the mid-1700s.

Reviewing the Main Ideas

1. (a) Why did the Puritans start the Massachusetts Bay Colony? (b) Why was Maryland founded?
2. How did Quaker beliefs influence William Penn when he set up Pennsylvania?
3. Describe settlers' relations with Native Americans on the frontier in the late 1600s.
4. How was life in the Tidewater different from life in the backcountry?
5. What contributions did Africans make to the economies of the colonies?
6. Describe the triangular trade.
7. In what ways was Benjamin Franklin an example of the Enlightenment spirit?

Thinking Critically

1. Evaluating Information Do you think racism was a major or a minor factor in the growth of slavery? Explain.
2. Applying Information Why do you think there was greater social equality in the colonies than there was in England?

3. Linking Past and Present Review the description of early New England public schools on page 121. How do they compare with public schools today?

Applying Your Skills

1. Analyzing a Quotation James Oglethorpe believed that once debtors reached Georgia, they could work "in a land of liberty and plenty, where...they are unfortunate indeed if they can't forget their sorrows." What do you think he meant?
2. Constructing a Time Line Make a time line showing events related to religious toleration in the English colonies. Then draw at least one conclusion based on the time line you have made.
3. Using a Painting as a Primary Source Study the painting on page 110. (a) Which building do you think was the Great House? Why? (b) Which building or buildings were the slaves' houses? Why? (c) How do the hill and the houses on it show the different classes in the South?

Thinking About Geography

Match the letters on the map with the following places: **1.** New England Colonies, **2.** Middle Colonies, **3.** Southern Colonies, **4.** Massachusetts, **5.** Pennsylvania, **6.** Virginia. **Region** Name the five Southern Colonies.

came to America. Settlers learned to accept differences and to work together for the common good.
3. Early New England schools taught children to read and to understand the principles of Christianity. Today, it would be unlawful to teach religious doctrine in a public school. In the 1600s, children of all ages were taught in one room by a teacher who was often paid in crops. Today, instruction is designed for specific age groups and is usually taught in separate rooms—often in separate buildings.

Answers to Applying Your Skills

1. Oglethorpe meant that his colony offered freedom and opportunity to settlers, so that even debtors could improve their lives and put their troubles behind them.
2. Student time lines should span the years from 1630 to 1750 and may identify the following dates and events: 1630, Puritans establish Massachusetts Bay Colony; 1634, Colony for Roman Catholics established in Mary-

land; 1635, Roger Williams leaves Massachusetts and establishes a new colony in Rhode Island; 1636, Colony established in Connecticut; 1639, Fundamental Orders of Connecticut written; 1682, Pennsylvania founded by Quakers. Possible Conclusion: As new colonies were established, religious toleration and freedom grew.
3. (a) big house on top of the hill (b) houses on each side of the hill, going away from the Great House. They are much smaller. (c) The Great House was at the

INTERDISCIPLINARY ACTIVITY

Living in the English Colonies

Form into groups to review life in the English colonies. Follow the suggestions below to write, draw, build, or present a broadcast to show what you have learned about colonial life. You may use the textbook, encyclopedias, atlases, or other materials in your classroom library to complete the tasks. Be able to name your sources of information when you have finished the activity.

GOVERNMENT OFFICIALS Find out about government in the Massachusetts Bay Colony, Connecticut, Rhode Island, Pennsylvania, Maryland, and Georgia. Make a large wall chart comparing government in these colonies. Include information about the role of leaders, the legislature, voting, freedom of religion, and slavery.

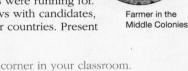
A colonial wedding

ECONOMISTS Make a chart showing the contributions slaves made to the economy of the Southern Colonies.

WRITERS Review the life of women in the backcountry and in cities. Write a story, dialogue, or play in which a city woman and a backcountry woman meet and compare their lives.

ARCHITECTS Find out about one type of house design in the English colonies, including materials used and special features. Make a diagram or build a model of the house. Be prepared to explain why colonists built houses in that way. For example, did available materials or climate conditions affect the design?

Farmer in the Middle Colonies

REPORTERS Prepare a newscast about election day in the colonies. Provide background information about who voted and what government offices the candidates were running for. Also include "person on the street" interviews with candidates, voters, other citizens, and visitors from other countries. Present your newscast to the class.

 Create a Living in the English Colonies corner in your classroom. Display or describe your completed activity there.

Iron garden tools made by enslaved Africans in the Southern Colonies

Chapter 4 • **125**

top of the hill, just as planters were at the highest level of society. Slaves were at the lowest level, and their houses were below the planter's house.

Answers to Thinking About Geography

1. A **2.** B **3.** C **4.** F **5.** E
6. D

Region: Maryland, Virginia, North Carolina, South Carolina, Georgia

Assessment

Chapter Resources Binder For a more comprehensive evaluation of student understanding of this chapter, assign Chapter Tests A and B and/or Extra Unit Questions from Unit 1, pages 43–48 and 51–53.
Computer Test Bank You can use Chapter Tests and Extra Unit Questions to create your own tests for both testing and retesting.

Alternative Assessment

Chapter Resources Binder See the Alternative Assessment booklet in the *Social Studies Educator's Handbook* series.
Portfolio You might meet with students to choose appropriate work from the chapter for inclusion in their portfolios.

Interdisciplinary ACTIVITY

Learning Styles
The following chart indicates the activities appropriate for different learning styles.

Visual Learners
Government officials
Economists
Architects

Auditory Learners
Writers
Architects
Reporters

Kinesthetic Learners
Government officials
Economists
Architects

Evaluation

Government officials Information must be complete, accurate, and organized into suitable categories. It should reflect an understanding of similarities and differences among the governments of the colonies. Finished charts should be legible and neat.
Economists Organization of charts must be visually clear. Information must be complete, concise, accurate, and organized into suitable categories.
Architects Diagrams or models should accurately represent the essential and special features of one type of colonial house, but artistic ability need not be a requirement. Conclusions must make sense when defended.
Writers Stories, dialogues, or plays should be original. They must contain accurate details that reflect an understanding of the similarities and differences in the characters' lives.
Reporters Broadcasts should be informative and lively. Individual reports and interviews must reflect knowledge about the structure of government and election issues in the colonies.

125

Jean Fritz was born in Hankow, China, in 1915. She has been a research assistant at a publishing company, a children's librarian, a teacher, and a book reviewer (for *The New York Times*). Her books center around the events of United States history, and she has a gift for making historical figures seem more human—and more remarkable—than most people realize. In such novels as *Brady; I, Adam;* and *Early Thunder,* Fritz depicts teenagers whose involvement in historic events brings history alive for modern readers.

Vocabulary

Ask students if they know the meaning of the word *drought*. Discuss the effects of drought on an agricultural community. Ask for volunteers to use the word in a sentence.

Prereading Focus

You might have students reread pages 85–86 in Chapter 3 to review what they have learned about the Jamestown colony and its relationship with Powhatan.

Motivation/Prior Knowledge

Have you ever thought of what daily life was like in North America before the Europeans came? What words would you use to describe the lifestyle of the Native Americans who lived along the eastern shores of this continent? Would you like to lead such a life? Why or why not?

Purpose-Setting Question

Why does Pocahontas think that Powhatan is the most important person in the world?

History Through LITERATURE

The Double Life of Pocahontas

Jean Fritz

Introduction Pocahontas was the daughter of Powhatan, leader of a powerful alliance of Indians in present-day Virginia. After the English established a colony at Jamestown, Pocahontas acted as a link between the Native Americans and the English. She befriended Captain John Smith and later married another English colonist. This excerpt is from a biography of Pocahontas written for young adults. It describes her life just before the arrival of the Jamestown colonists.

Vocabulary Before you read the selection, find the meaning of this word in a dictionary: **drought**

Pocahontas had every reason to be happy. It was the budding time of the year; who would not be happy? The world was new-green, cherry trees were afroth, and strawberries, like sweet red secrets, fattened on the ground. At first birdcall, Pocahontas would run splashing into the river, and along with the others in the village she would wait to greet the Sun as it rose.

Together they would watch the sky turn from gray to pink, to gold. Then suddenly they would shout. There it came! And was it not a wonder that always it returned again and yet again? All the people welcomed it, scattering sacred tobacco into a circle, lifting up their hands and singing to please their god, Okee, in the way their priests had taught them. One must not forget Okee, for it was He who held danger in his hands—lightning, floods, drought, sickness, war.

Indeed, Pocahontas could hardly help but be happy. At eleven, she was the right age for happiness. Still young enough to romp with the children, yet old enough to join the dance of unmarried girls. And how she danced—whirling and stamping and shouting until her breath was whisked into the wind, until she had grown wings like a bird, until she had become sister to the trees, until she was at one with everything that lived and grew. With the world itself, round like a plate under the sky. And in the center of the plate, there was her father, the great Chief Powhatan, seated high, twelve mats under him, raccoon robe around him with tails dangling. And beside him, there was Pocahontas herself, for was she not her father's favorite? Did he not say that Pocahontas was as dear to him as his own life? So of course Pocahontas was happy.

Around the edges of the world plate, Pocahontas knew, were unfriendly tribes. And somewhere on the far, far rim beyond the waters there were strangers from a land she could not picture at all.

Discussion Questions

1. What is the "budding time of the year"? (spring)
2. Pocahontas thinks of the world as a "round plate under the sky." How big does Pocahontas think the world is? (Pocahontas believed that the size of the world was very limited.)

Historical Sidelight

The Powhatan Confederacy was a group of 30 Eastern Woodland Indian tribes that lived along the shores of Virginia and Chesapeake Bay. Chief Powhatan, or Wahunsonacock, was the leader of the confederacy at the time Jamestown was settled. The English took its best land, which resulted in bad feelings between the confederacy and the newcomers. The marriage of Pocahontas to John Rolfe secured peace until 1622, when Powhatan's successor attacked the English settlement.

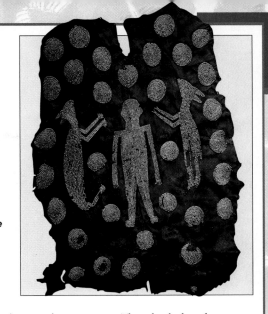

Powhatan's Cloak *This cloak belonged to Pocahontas's father, Powhatan. Made of buckskin and decorated with shells, it is one of the oldest surviving examples of Native American art.* **Culture** *How do the cloak and the excerpt reveal a close connection between Pocahontas's people and nature?*

Sometimes these strangers came to her father's kingdom, coat-wearing men with hair on their faces. The last time, these men had kidnapped a chief's son and killed a chief, but since then the geese had flown north three times and they had not come back. Perhaps they would not come again.

There was no way, of course, for Pocahontas to know that at that very moment three English ships with one hundred and four such coat-wearing men were approaching Chesapeake Bay. No one told these men that the land was taken, that this was Powhatan's kingdom, but even if they had, the English would not have cared. Naked savages, they would have said—they were like herds of deer. How could they legally own land? The world was made for civilized people, for people who wouldn't let the land go to waste, for people who knew the right way to live. In other words, for Christians.

The year, according to the Christian calendar, was 1607, and these Christians were here to stay. They had already named this place Virginia, and they meant to make it theirs.

Source: Jean Fritz, from *The Double Life of Pocahontas* (Grey Castle Press, Lakeville, Connecticut, 1983).

THINKING ABOUT LITERATURE

1. Why did Pocahontas and her people greet the sun each morning?
2. Why did Pocahontas have "every reason to be happy"?
3. CRITICAL THINKING **Recognizing Points of View** (a) Based on this excerpt, how did Pocahontas and her people view the English? (b) How did the English view Pocahontas's people?

ACTIVITY Imagine that you are Pocahontas. Based on this excerpt and what you have read in Chapter 3, create a picture book for a younger sister or brother about your life before and after the arrival of the English in Jamestown.

The beads that decorated this cape were probably made by hand from clamshells. The process of making beads was a painstaking one. Indians used a stone tool to remove unwanted portions of a shell. Then, while one person held the shell, another would rapidly rotate a slender drill to make a hole. Indians finished the bead by polishing the rough outer surface of the shell with sand. A similar technique was used by the Eastern Woodland Indians to make wampum, which was originally used as a gift on ceremonial occasions rather than as a medium of exchange.

You might wish to arrange with a language arts teacher to read this excerpt at the same time the students are reading Native American literature in their language arts class. The language arts teacher might want to discuss with students the similarity of the viewpoints of Jean Fritz's fictionalized Pocahontas and the viewpoint of actual Native American writers. Students might be asked to consider whether Fritz's Pocahontas is a believable representation of Native Americans of her time and place.

ACTIVITY

Guided Instruction You might wish to have students discuss the events of Pocahontas's life as a group. Have students create a story map, which you can write on the chalkboard. This will help them as they create their books.

Tell students that they may either draw all of the pictures in their books or they may use a combination of original drawings and illustrations cut from magazines.

When students have completed their books, tell them to read them with a younger child. As a follow-up for this activity, ask the students to share with the class the reactions and comments of the younger children.

Answers to Thinking About Literature

1. They regarded the sun as a blessing and a wonder. Their greeting was a part of their religion.
2. She was young enough to play with the children but old enough to join the unmarried girls in their dancing. She was the favorite child of Powhatan, who was the chief.

3. (a) Pocahontas and her people thought of the English as alien and violent. (b) The English thought the Indians were savages, like herds of deer. They believed the Indians could not legally own land.

Answer to Caption

Answers may vary. The materials used to create the cloak come directly from nature. Also, the figures of deer and the man on the cloak reveal a closeness to nature. In the excerpt, Pocahontas's greeting of the sun and the reasons to be happy also reveal a close connection to nature.

Unit 2
From Revolution to Republic

Unit Focus

Direct students' attention to the military flag depicted on these pages and to the caption that describes it. Ask: How would you feel about having this flag represent you? You might use questions such as the following to expand on students' responses and to stimulate discussion after students have read the three chapter summaries.

1. The caption on page 129 says that the eagle symbolizes "freedom and power." Why is that an appropriate symbol for a nation whose origins began with a revolution?

2. What kinds of tensions existed between Great Britain and its North American colonies before the American Revolution began?

3. When you think about the American Revolution, what names and images come to mind?

4. (a) What does the word *republic* mean? (b) Why do you think that a republic needs a constitution?

5. Notice the title of Unit 2 — From Revolution to Republic. (a) Based on the information in the three chapter summaries, how do you think the North American colonists felt about the experience of seeing their homeland go "from revolution to republic"? (b) Do you think that everyone felt the same way? Why or why not?

UNIT 2

From Revolution to Republic

CHAPTER 5
The Road to Revolution
(1745–1775)

After years of tension, colonists and British troops clashed in battle.

....

CHAPTER 6
The American Revolution
(1775–1783)

In a long, hard-fought war, Americans won independence from Britain.

....

CHAPTER 7
Creating a Republic
(1776–1790)

The new United States set up a government under the Constitution.

128 • Unit 2

Connections With Art
Background

The bald eagle is known around the world as a symbol of the United States. It became the national symbol in 1782, when it was used in the Great Seal of the United States. (You might display a picture of the Great Seal and invite students to compare the two.) The eagle was not widely used in military designs until the War of 1812. Nevertheless, the *Stan-dard of the Eagle* is the oldest United States regimental flag; it represents the U.S. 1st Infantry (also known as the "Trinity Church" regiment) and is dated between 1789 and 1791. The artwork shown on these pages is not the original flag itself; rather, it is a later watercolor of that flag. It was painted to better bring out the flag's detail.

Connections With Art
Activity

Ask questions such as the following to stimulate discussion.

1. (a) What is the eagle clutching in its talons? (b) What do you think those items represent?

2. (a) How many stars are on the flag? (b) What do the stars symbolize?

3. Notice the saying on the banner — E PLURIBUS UNUM. What does that mean?

4. The sunburst behind the eagle is called a "glory." Do you think that a member of the U.S. 1st Infantry in 1790 felt "glorious" as he looked at the flag? Why or why not?

128

*A*fter years of protesting British rule, the colonists won independence in the American Revolution. The eagle became a symbol of the freedom and power of the new nation.

Unit 2 • **129**

Have students create a bulletin board display of North American sites that were important during the Revolutionary Period. Students should begin by papering the bulletin board with a map showing the colonial United States and eastern Canada. Then have them mark several historic places with thumbtacks. (You might suggest the following places, to begin: Fort Duquesne, Plains of Abraham, Boston Common, Concord, Fort Ticonderoga, Trenton, Valley Forge, and Yorktown.) Have students prepare index cards that briefly describe the importance of each place, along with an illustration, if possible. Attach each card to the appropriate thumbtack with a length of yarn.

 Art Gallery Posters

Crossing the Delaware, by Oscar de Mejo, is appropriate for Unit 2. Lesson suggestions for the poster appear in the *Art Gallery: Our Common Heritage Posters* Teacher's Guide. The art also appears in Chapter 6, page 171, of the student book.

 CD-ROM

Time Tour Access the From Revolution to Republic section of the Time Tour on the American Heritage® *History of the United States* CD-ROM to accompany Unit 2.

Connections With the World
Activity

Have students preview European influences on the government of the United States by skimming the subsection Ideas That Shaped the Constitution on pages 199–201. Ask them to define *Enlightenment* and then list three ideas that Americans took from British and French philosophers. Ask students whether they agree or disagree with this statement: The first leaders of the United States were still European in many ways. Ask: How did Europe continue to influence the United States after the American Revolution?

Linking Past and Present
Activity

As you direct students' attention to the military flag, point out that the eagle was like a mascot for the troops that carried this flag. Ask: What qualities of the eagle do you think these troops admired? Then have students identify the mascot of your school and of other schools with which they are familiar. Ask: Why do you think the school chose that particular mascot? What characteristics of that mascot do you think should be admired or should become goals for the students of the school?

Chapter 5   The Road to Revolution (1745–1775), pp. 130–157

Lessons	Teaching Resources
1 **Rivalry in North America** **Objectives** 1. Identify the nations that were rivals for North America. 2. Describe how the French prevented expansion of the English colonies. 3. Explain why Native Americans became involved in the struggle between France and England.	**Lesson Planner** Cooperative Learning, p. 26 **Student Study Guide** Section 1 Study Guide, p. 56 **Chapter Resources Binder, Unit 2** *Geography in History* Riverways Through French North America, pp. 5–6 *Skill Application* Using a Primary Source, p. 2
2 **The French and Indian War** **Objectives** 1. Identify the causes of the French and Indian War. 2. Describe the advantages that each side had in the war. 3. Describe how the Treaty of Paris affected North America.	**Lesson Planner** Cooperative Learning, p. 27 **Student Study Guide** Section 2 Study Guide, p. 57 **Our Multicultural Heritage** *Biography* Jean Baptiste Pointe du Sable, Pioneer and Peacemaker, p. 13
3 **A Storm Over Taxes** **Objectives** 1. Explain why Britain issued the Proclamation of 1763. 2. Identify the steps that Britain took to raise money to repay its war debts. 3. Describe how colonists protested British taxes. 4. Explain why the Boston Massacre occurred.	**Lesson Planner** Cooperative Learning, p. 28 **Student Study Guide** Section 3 Study Guide, p. 58 **Our Multicultural Heritage** *Biography* Mercy Otis Warren, Patriot and Playwright, p. 14 **Interdisciplinary Connections:** Growing Tensions With Britain ▪ *Sciences* Tea Time, p. 26 ▪ *Geography* Secret Shipping, p. 27 ▪ *World* Reporting the Boston Massacre, p. 28 ▪ *Economics* Tariffs and Trade, p. 29 ▪ *Civics* Creating a Colonial Militia, p. 30
4 **To Arms!** **Objectives** 1. Explain why Britain passed the Tea Act. 2. Identify the Boston Tea Party. 3. Describe how colonists responded to the Intolerable Acts. 4. Identify "the shot heard 'round the world."	**Lesson Planner** Cooperative Learning, p. 29 **Student Study Guide** Section 4 Study Guide, p. 59 **Chapter Resources Binder, Unit 2** *Critical Thinking* Making Decisions, p. 3 *History Through Literature* Paul Revere's Ride, p. 4 **Our Multicultural Heritage** *Milestone* Moving Toward a Break With Britain, p. 15

Chapter Manager

Multimedia Resources	Additional Resources	Chapter-Level Resources
Transparencies *Geography and History* North Central States, p. I-73	**Customized Reader** A Prophetic Warning About the United States, article IIIA-1	**Lesson Planner** Activity Based, pp. 30–31 **Student Study Guide** Chapter 5 Study Guide, pp. 60–61 **Chapter Resources Binder** **Unit 2** Vocabulary Building, p. 1 Chapter Test A, pp. 7–9 Chapter Test B, pp. 10–12 Illustration Master, p. 13 Extra Unit Questions, pp. 43–45 **English Guided Reading** Guided Reading, pp. 9–10 **Spanish Resources**
Videotapes/Videodiscs *United States History Video Collection* The Colonial Wars, Vol. 2, Ch. 28; The French and Indian War, Vol. 2, Ch. 31; America in 1763, Vol. 2, Ch. 34	**Voices of Freedom** Washington Meets With the French, p. 54 Wolfe and Montcalm: The Last Battle, pp. 55–56 **Historical Outline Map Book** The French and Indian War, p. 21 North America in 1763, p. 22	
Transparencies *Cause and Effect* p. F-15 *Exploring Technology* p. H-29 *Interdisciplinary Connections* p. B-41 **Listening to Literature Audiocassettes** *The American Experience* Chester, side 2; Speech in the Virginia Convention, Patrick Henry, side 2 **CD-ROM** *History Makers* Abigail Adams *History Makers* Patrick Henry **Videotapes/Videodiscs** *United States History Video Collection* The People Get Political, Vol. 4, Ch. 7	**Voices of Freedom** Paul Revere on the Boston Massacre, pp. 57–58 **Customized Reader** "I Heard the Word 'Fire'": The Boston Massacre, article IIB-4	**CD-ROM** **Time Tour** The Road to Revolution in From Revolution to Republic **Computer Test Bank** Chapter Tests A and B Extra Unit Questions **Guided Reading Audiotapes** Side 2
Videotapes/Videodiscs *United States History Video Collection* The Boston Tea Party, Vol. 4, Ch. 13; The Shot Heard 'Round the World, Vol. 4, Ch. 16	**Historical Outline Map Book** Lexington and Concord, p. 23	

Lesson Planner

For a fully developed **Activity-Based** lesson plan for Chapter 5, see the *Lesson Planner,* pages 30–31.

 Chapter Resources

Vocabulary Building The Vocabulary Building worksheet for Chapter 5 from Unit 2, page 1, of the *Chapter Resources* binder can be used as a prereading activity or as a review of chapter vocabulary. (Reteaching/Easy)

 Student Study Guide

Chapter 5 Study Guide Refer students to pages 60–61 of the *Student Study Guide* for the Chapter 5 Study Guide. The study guide can be used for chapter review as well as for reteaching. (Reteaching/Average)

 Guided Reading Audiotapes

Students can use *Guided Reading Audiotapes,* Chapter 5, side 2, to listen to section previews, summaries, and review questions. The tapes will benefit students who are auditory learners, students who have trouble reading, or students acquiring English. Tapes are also available in Spanish. (Reteaching/ Easy)

CHAPTER 5

The Road to Revolution

(1745–1775)

CHAPTER OUTLINE

1 Rivalry in North America

2 The French and Indian War

3 A Storm Over Taxes

4 To Arms!

1740s *English settlers moved westward into the Ohio Valley. Here settlers clear the land.*

1759 *The battle for Quebec, shown here, was a turning point in the French and Indian War.*

1754 *As a young major, George Washington played an important role when fighting began in the French and Indian War.*

1745   1750   1755   1760

▲ **WORLD EVENT 1748** Britain and France fight for control of trade in India

▲ **WORLD EVENT 1756–1763** Seven Years' War is fought in Europe

Chapter Time Line
Understanding Chronology

After giving students the opportunity to examine and discuss the time line, play a game of Before and After to check students' understanding of chronology. Read statements such as the following and have students complete each statement correctly with *before* or *after*.

■ The Quebec Act was passed _____ the French and Indian War. (*after*)

■ Settlement of the Ohio Valley began _____ the Proclamation of 1763 was issued. (*before*)

■ Some 21 years _____ the American Revolution began, George Washington held the rank of major. (*before*)

Chapter Setting

"Yesterday Morning at break of day was discovered hanging upon a tree in the street of the town a [likeness]. . . of Mr. Andrew Oliver. . . . That night a mob carried the effigy to. . . Mr. Oliver's house where they burnt the effigy in a bonfire. . . . The mob finding the doors of the house [blocked]. . . beat in all the doors and windows. . . . As soon as they got possession they searched about for Mr. Oliver, declaring that they would kill him. "

In this letter, Massachusetts Governor Francis Bernard described an attack on Andrew Oliver by an angry Boston mob in 1765. Who was Andrew Oliver? What had stirred the mob's anger?

The mob unleashed its fury on Oliver because he was a tax collector for the English government. A series of wars had left England deeply in debt. To raise money to repay the debt, Parliament decided to tax the colonies. Colonists were outraged. They saw Parliament's action as an attack on their basic liberties.

As time went by, the colonists' anger grew. By early 1775, it became clear to many that only war could settle the quarrel with England.

ACTIVITY Brainstorm to identify a government policy that Americans today might consider unjust. Make a poster protesting that policy.

1763 Conflict with Native Americans, led by Chief Pontiac, convinced Britain to issue the Proclamation of 1763. It closed western lands to further settlement.

1765 To raise money from the colonies, Britain passed the Stamp Act. All items listed in the act had to carry a stamp, such as this one.

1775 The war for American independence began with shots fired in Lexington and Concord. This bronze statue honors the colonial minutemen.

1760   1765   1770   1775

WORLD EVENT
1763 Treaty of Paris ends French power in North America

WORLD EVENT
1774 Quebec Act guarantees religious freedom in Canada

Chapter 5 • **131**

131

Answer to Caption

The French received a profitable trade item; the Native Americans received goods that they could not make (or make as well) or that they could trade with other Native Americans.

Section 1
pp. 132–135

Bell Ringer

Write the term *property owner* on the chalkboard. Ask students what a person must do to prove his or her claim to a piece of land.

Lesson Plan

1. Focus In the 1700s, England, France, and Spain all claimed lands in North America. In this section, students learn about the growing conflicts over ownership of land, especially in the Ohio River valley, and how the conflicts affected Native Americans.
2. Instruct Write the following generalization on the chalkboard: "By the late 1740s, both the French and the British realized that a struggle for control of North America was inevitable." Ask students to list evidence from this section to support or refute this generalization. Have students decide as a class whether they agree or disagree with the generalization.
3. Close To close, ask students a series of *Who, What, Where, When, Why,* and *How* questions about the people and events in this section.

1
Rivalry in North America

FIND OUT
- What nations were rivals for North America?
- How did the French prevent expansion of the English colonies?
- Why did Native Americans become involved in the struggle between France and England?

In June 1749, the governor of New France sent a group of men to the Ohio Valley. The men traveled down the Ohio River. From time to time, they stopped to nail an engraved lead plate to a tree or to set one in the ground. These plates proclaimed that the land belonged to France.

About the same time, Christopher Gist, a Virginia fur trader working for the Ohio Company, roamed the Ohio Valley. King George II of England had given the Ohio Company a huge tract of land in the valley. The company sent Gist to find a good spot for settlement. He chose a site where the Ohio and Allegheny rivers meet. On a rock beside the water, he carved these words:

The Ohio Company
FEBy 1751
By Christopher Gist

The stage was set for a battle between France and England. At stake was more than control of the Ohio River valley. Each nation hoped to drive the other out of North America altogether.

Competing Claims

By the mid-1700s, the nations of Europe were locked in a worldwide struggle for empire. England, France, Spain, and the Netherlands were competing for trade and colonies in far-flung corners of the globe. The English colonies in North America soon became caught up in the contest.

Spanish claims. By the late 1600s, England had two rivals in North America: Spain and France. The major threat from Spain

Trading With North Americans *French traders exchanged a variety of goods with Native Americans in return for furs. In this painting, Native Americans inspect a blanket being offered in trade. Copper pots and pans, such as those shown below, were also popular trading items.* **Economics** *How did both sides benefit from this trade?*

Connections With the World
Background

Remind students that the rivalry between England and Spain was linked to the Protestant Reformation. Ask: Do you think that religion also may have played a role in the rivalry between England and Spain in North America?

Connections With Geography
Activity

Have students locate the Ohio Valley on an outline map of North America. Ask: Which two rivers meet to form the Ohio River at Pittsburgh? Into which river does the Ohio flow? Have students trace the Ohio River in red, the Allegheny in blue, the Monongahela in green, and the Mississippi in orange. Ask: Why do you think this river system was so important to the French? Students should note the system flows from near the Great Lakes to New Orleans.

was in the West Indies and along the border between Georgia and Spanish Florida. England and Spain clashed often in these areas.

Spain also had settlements in present-day New Mexico, Texas, and Arizona. However, these settlements lay far away from England's colonies on the Atlantic coast. As a result, the English paid little attention to them.

French claims. The threat from France was much more serious. France claimed a vast area in North America. French land claims stretched west from the St. Lawrence River all the way to the Great Lakes and south to the Gulf of Mexico. To protect their lands, the French built a system of forts. (See the map at right.)

Conflict in the Ohio Valley. At first, most English settlers were content to remain along the Atlantic coast. By the 1740s, however, traders from New York and Pennsylvania were crossing the Appalachian Mountains in search of furs. Pushing into the Ohio Valley, they tried to take over the profitable French trade with the Indians.

The French were determined to stop the English from intruding on their territory. The Ohio River was especially important to them because it provided a vital link between their lands in Canada and the Mississippi River. In 1751, the French government sent the following orders to its officials in New France:

❝Drive from the Ohio River any European foreigners, and do it in a way that will make them lose all taste for trying to return.❞

Native Americans Choose Sides

Native Americans had hunted animals and grown crops in the Ohio Valley for centuries. They did not want to give up the land to European settlers, French *or* English. One Native American protested to an English trader:

M A P   S T U D Y

In 1753, France and Spain claimed land to the north, south, and west of the English colonies in North America.
1. *Which nation claimed land along the Mississippi River?*
2. *Which nation controlled Florida?*
3. **Drawing Conclusions** *Notice the location of French forts in North America. Why do you think the French built forts at these places?*

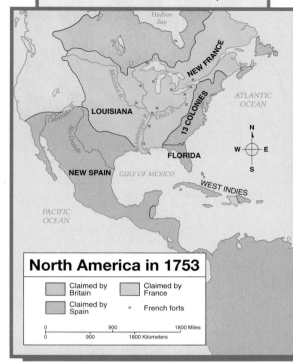

North America in 1753

- Claimed by Britain
- Claimed by Spain
- Claimed by France
- ■ French forts

0   900   1800 Miles
0   900   1800 Kilometers

❝You and the French are like the two edges of a pair of shears. And we are the cloth which is to be cut to pieces between them.❞

Some Native Americans decided that the only way to protect their way of life was to take sides in the struggle.

Competing for allies. Both France and England tried to make Indian allies because

 Lesson Planner

For a developed **Cooperative Learning** lesson plan, see the *Lesson Planner,* page 26.

Answers to Map Study

1. France **2.** Spain **3.** Possible Answer: They wanted to take advantage of waterways for transportation.

 Transparencies

Geography and History Use the transparency set, North Central States, on page I-73 of *American History Transparencies.* The base map and overlay 1 show the boundaries and topography of the North Central states. Teaching suggestions for this transparency can be found on page I-12. (Enrichment/Average)

Chapter Resources

Geography in History Duplicate and distribute the worksheet, Riverways Through French North America, from Unit 2, pages 5–6, of the *Chapter Resources* binder. The worksheet will help students understand the importance of waterways to trade, settlement, and military strength in New France. (Enrichment/Average)

Critical Thinking
Understanding Causes and Effects

The dim view of the English taken by many Native Americans in Ohio was based on their own history as well as their treatment at that time. In the late 1600s, the Iroquois claimed sovereignty over the Leni-Lenapes and began selling Leni-Lenape lands to English colonists. Dispossessed, many Leni-Lenapes moved from Pennsylvania to Ohio—much of which was unclaimed by any Native American group. When the Iroquois granted Ohio land to the English, many Native Americans remembered the past and welcomed French resistance to the English presence there.

BIOGRAPHY Joseph Brant *Joseph Brant, a Mohawk chief, helped persuade the Iroquois nations to side with the English in their struggle against the French. In later years, Joseph Brant became a Christian and helped translate the Bible into the Mohawk language.* **Multicultural Heritage** *How does the painting show that Brant combined Native American and English cultures?*

Indians controlled the fur trade in the heart of North America. The French expected the Indians to side with them. Most French in North America were trappers and traders, not farmers. They did not destroy hunting grounds by clearing forests for farms. Also, many French trappers married Native American women and adopted their ways.

In contrast, English settlers were mostly farm families. They ignored Indian rights when they cleared land for crops, and they did not respect Indian ways. Indians fought back as the English moved onto their lands.

Algonquins, Hurons, and Iroquois. In the end, both France and England found allies among Native Americans. The French gained the support of the Algonquins and Hurons. In time, the English won over the powerful Iroquois nations, who were old enemies of the Algonquins.

An English trader and official, William Johnson, helped gain Iroquois support for England. Johnson was one of the few English settlers who had an Indian wife. He was married to Molly Brant, sister of Joseph Brant, a Mohawk chief. The Iroquois respected Johnson, and they listened carefully when he urged them to side with the English.

Some Indians supported the English because they charged lower prices for trade goods than the French did. Many Indians began to buy goods from English rather than French traders. The loss of Indian trade angered the French, who were determined to defend their claims in the Ohio Valley.

SECTION 1 REVIEW

1. **Locate:** (a) Ohio River, (b) St. Lawrence River, (c) Great Lakes, (d) Gulf of Mexico, (e) Canada, (f) Mississippi River.
2. (a) Name three European nations that claimed lands in North America. (b) Where did conflict between these nations occur?
3. How did France protect its lands in North America?
4. (a) Which Indians sided with the English? (b) Why?
5. **CRITICAL THINKING Synthesizing Information** How did the rivalry between Spain, France, and England in North America relate to their worldwide struggle?

ACTIVITY Writing to Learn

Imagine that you are a Native American leader in the Ohio Valley in the 1750s. Would you support the French or the English? Write a speech urging other Native Americans to adopt your position.

CRITICAL THINKING SKILLS
Using a Primary Source

Historians use primary sources to learn about the past. A ***primary source*** is firsthand information about people or events. Letters, diaries, maps, drawings, and artifacts are all primary sources. The primary sources below are from speeches by Native Americans about English actions in the Ohio Valley in the 1760s.

1. **Identify the source.** (a) Who made these statements? (b) What are they about? (c) When were they made?

2. **Recognize the author's point of view.** Many eyewitnesses have a special reason for writing or speaking about an event. Often, they want to persuade the listener to share their views. When you read a primary source, you need to recognize the author's point of view. (a) What opinion did these Native Americans have of the English?

(b) What words or phrases show you how strongly they felt?

3. **Decide whether the source is reliable.** (a) Do you think these Native Americans gave an accurate view of the situation in the Ohio Valley in the 1760s? Why? (b) Have they left out any important information? (c) Would you say that these are reliable sources for learning about relations between the English and Native Americans in the mid-1700s? Explain.

ACTIVITY Prepare a document that would provide useful information to a future historian studying the 1990s. Your document can be a letter, a diary entry, a petition, or a speech describing the concerns of young Americans today. Trade documents with a classmate and determine whether each document is a reliable primary source.

A Seneca Chief, July 1761

"The English treat us with much disrespect, and we have the greatest reason to believe, by their behavior, they intend to cut us off entirely. They have possessed themselves of our country. It is now in our power to dispossess them and recover it, if we will but embrace the opportunity before they have time to assemble together and [strengthen] themselves. There is no time to be lost, let us strike immediately."

An Iroquois, August 1761

"We, your brethren of the several nations, are penned up like hogs. There are forts all around us, and therefore we are [fearful] that Death is coming upon us."

Pontiac, 1763

"The Great Spirit [told a Delaware Indian to] be seated, and thus addressed him:

'I am the Maker of heaven and earth, the trees, lakes, rivers, and all things else. I am the Maker of mankind; and because I love you, you must do my will. The land on which you live I have made for you, and not for others. Why do you suffer the white men to dwell among you? My children, you have forgotten the customs and traditions of your forefathers. Why do you not clothe yourselves in skins, as they did, and use the bows and arrows, and the stone-pointed lances, which they used. You have bought guns, knives, kettles, and blankets, from the white men, until you can no longer do without them; and what is worse, you have drunk the poison fire-water, which turns you into fools. Fling all these things away; live as your wise forefathers lived before you. And as for these English—these dogs dressed in red, who have come to rob you of your hunting-grounds, and drive away the game,—you must lift the hatchet against them.'"

Section 2
pp. 136–141

 Bell Ringer

Write the following headline on the chalkboard: "ENGLAND AND FRANCE AT WAR: Both Claim Right to Native American Lands." Have students write down their thoughts and feelings about this news. Ask: How might Native Americans react?

Lesson Plan

1. Focus Having fought three wars between 1689 and 1748, France and Britain entered a long conflict known in North America as the French and Indian War. In this section, students learn about the battles of the French and Indian War, the reactions of Native Americans to the struggle, and the treaty that gave Britain a vast new empire in North America.

2. Instruct Tell students to imagine that they are war correspondents writing for a newspaper in a neutral country. As you progress through the section, have them compose a headline and two narrative sentences that summarize the importance of each major event.

3. Close To close the lesson, have students reach a class consensus about the most important facts to remember from each subsection within Section 2.

2
The French and Indian War

FIND OUT

- What were the causes of the French and Indian War?
- What advantages did each side have in the war?
- How did the Treaty of Paris affect North America?

Captain Joncaire had just sat down to dinner on December 4, 1753, when a tall young man strode into the room. He introduced himself as Major George Washington. He said he had a letter from the English lieutenant governor of Virginia, Robert Dinwiddie, to the commander of the French forces in the Ohio Valley.

Joncaire told Washington where the commander could be found and then invited him to dine. As they ate, Joncaire boasted, "It is our absolute design to take possession of the Ohio, and by God, we will do it!" The remark made Washington pause. Dinwiddie's letter, he knew, warned the French to get out of the Ohio Valley. A conflict between England and France seemed certain.

Opening Shots

Three times between 1689 and 1748, France and Great Britain* had fought for power in Europe and North America. Each war ended with an uneasy peace. In 1754,

---

*In 1707, England and Scotland were officially joined into the united kingdom of Great Britain. After that date, the terms Great Britain and British were used to describe the country and its people. However, the terms England and English were still used throughout much of the 1700s.

136 • Chapter 5

---

fighting broke out again. The long conflict that followed was called the *French and Indian War.*

Major Washington. Scuffles between France and Britain in the Ohio River valley triggered the opening shots of the French and Indian War. Young Major Washington played an important part as fighting began.

George Washington had grown up on a plantation in Virginia, the son of wealthy parents. At age 15, he began work as a surveyor. His job took him to frontier lands in western Virginia. When Lieutenant Governor Dinwiddie wanted to warn the French in Ohio in 1753, Washington offered to deliver the message.

After Washington returned, Dinwiddie promoted him. He also sent the young man west again. This time, Dinwiddie ordered Washington to take 150 men and build a fort where the Monongahela and Allegheny rivers meet. (See the map on page 139.) The fort was to protect Virginia's land claims in the upper Ohio River valley.

Trapped at Fort Necessity. In April 1754, Washington and his party headed for Ohio country. Along the way, they heard disturbing news. The French had just completed Fort Duquesne (doo KAYN) at the fork of the Monongahela and Allegheny rivers. The fork was the precise spot where Washington was to build a British fort.

Determined to carry out his orders, Washington continued on. Indian allies revealed that a French scouting party was camped in the woods ahead. Marching quietly through the night, Washington surprised and scattered the French.

Washington's success was short-lived, however. Hearing that the French were planning to counterattack, he and his men quickly built a makeshift stockade. They named it *Fort Necessity.* A huge force of French and Indians surrounded the fort. Trapped and heavily outnumbered, the Virginians were forced to surrender. Soon after,

---

Connections With the World
Background

Three years before the French and Indian War began, young George Washington took his first and last trip outside the area that would later become the United States. In 1751, he accompanied his older half brother, Lawrence, on an ocean voyage to the Caribbean island of Barbados. They hoped that the tropical climate would cure Lawrence's tuberculosis.

Connections With Geography
Background

The site of Fort Necessity was poorly chosen. The fort was built on a soggy creek bottom. Even worse, it was surrounded on three sides by thickly wooded hills, making it easy for the French and Indians to attack.

136

Washington Meets With Iroquois Chiefs *Young George Washington played an important role in the opening skirmishes of the French and Indian War. Here, Washington confers with chiefs of the Iroquois nations.* **Geography** *What region was at the heart of the conflict that triggered the French and Indian War?*

the French released Washington, and he returned home to Virginia.

The British quickly saw the importance of the skirmish. "The volley fired by this young Virginian in the forests of America," a British writer noted, "has set the world in flames."

The Albany Congress

While Washington was defending Fort Necessity, delegates from seven colonies gathered in Albany, New York. The delegates met for two reasons. They wanted to persuade the Iroquois to help them against the French. They also wanted to plan a united defense.

Iroquois leaders listened patiently to the delegates, but they were wary of the request for help. The British and French "are quarreling about lands which belong to us," pointed out Hendrik, a Mohawk chief. "And such a quarrel as this may end in our destruction." The Iroquois left without agreeing to help the British. But they did not join the French either.

The delegates in Albany knew that the colonists needed to work together if they were to defeat the French. Benjamin Franklin, the delegate from Pennsylvania, proposed the *Albany Plan of Union.* The plan called for a Grand Council with representatives from each colony. The council would make laws, raise taxes, and set up the defense of the colonies.

The delegates voted to accept the Plan of Union. When the plan was submitted to the colonial assemblies, however, not one approved it. None of the colonies wanted to give up any of its powers to a central council. In the words of the disappointed Franklin:

Chapter 5 • **137**

66Everyone cries a union is necessary. But when they come to the manner and form of the union, their weak noodles are perfectly distracted.99

Early Years of the War

At the start of the French and Indian War, the French enjoyed several advantages over the British. Because the English colonies could not agree on a united defense, 13 separate colonial assemblies had to approve all decisions. New France, on the other hand, had a single government that could act quickly when necessary. Also, the French had the support of many more Indian allies than the British did.

Britain, however, also had strengths. The English colonies were clustered along the coast, so they were easier to defend than the widely scattered French settlements. At the same time, the population of the English colonies was about 15 times greater than that of New France. And although most Indians sided with the French, the British did have some Indian allies. Finally, the British navy ruled the seas.

"Bulldog" Braddock. In 1755, General Edward Braddock led British and colonial troops in an attack against Fort Duquesne. The general boasted that he would sweep the French from the Ohio Valley.

Braddock was a stubborn man, called "Bulldog" behind his back. He knew how to fight a war in the open fields of Europe. However, he knew little about how to fight in the wilderness of North America.

Braddock's men moved slowly because they had to clear a road through thick forests for their cannons and other heavy gear. George Washington, who went with Braddock, was upset by the slow pace. Indian scouts warned Braddock that he was headed for trouble. He ignored them.

Disaster for the British. As the British neared Fort Duquesne, the French and their Indian allies launched a surprise attack.

Sharpshooters hid in the forest and picked off British soldiers, whose bright-red uniforms made them easy targets. Braddock had five horses shot out from under him before he fell, fatally wounded. Washington was luckier. As he later reported, he "escaped without a wound, although I had four bullets through my coat."

Almost half the British were killed or wounded. Washington and other survivors returned to Virginia with news of Braddock's defeat. Washington was now put in command of a small force of men. For the rest of the war, he had the almost impossible task of guarding the long Virginia frontier against Indian attack.

During the next two years, the war continued to go badly for the British. British attacks against several French forts ended in failure. Meanwhile, the French won important victories, capturing Fort Oswego on Lake Ontario and Fort William Henry on Lake George. (See the map on page 139.) To English colonists, the situation looked grim. In the words of Massachusetts minister Jonathan Edwards:

66God indeed is remarkably frowning upon us every where; our enemies get up above us very high, and we are brought down very low: They are the Head, and we are the Tail. . . . What will become of us God only knows.99

A Bold Leader Takes Charge

In 1757, William Pitt became head of the British government. Pitt was a bold leader. "I believe that I can save this nation and that no one else can," he declared with great confidence.

Pitt set out to win the war in North America. Once that was done, he argued, the British could focus on victory in other parts of the world. Pitt sent Britain's best generals to North America. To encourage

---

Learning Styles
Kinesthetic Learners

You might have students select one of the battles listed in this section and create a three-dimensional terrain map of the battle site. Before they begin, students could do additional research on selected battles. When students have completed their projects, ask them to use their maps to demonstrate to the class how geographic features affected the outcome of the battle.

Connections With Mathematics
Activity

In 1754, the population of the English colonies was 15 times greater than that of New France. The population of New France was approximately 100,000. Ask: What was the population of the English colonies? (approximately 1,500,000)

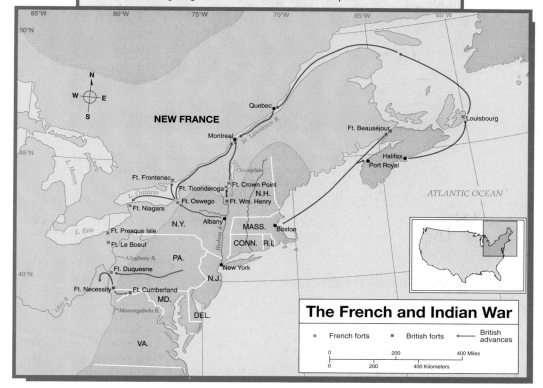

MAP STUDY

During the French and Indian War, Britain and France battled for control of North America.

1. *Which French forts were located on Lake Ontario?*
2. *About how many miles did advancing British troops travel from Louisbourg to Quebec?*
3. **Analyzing Information** *Based on the map, do you think naval power was important in fighting the French and Indian War? Explain.*

The French and Indian War

✕ French forts   ✕ British forts   ⟵ British advances

0   200   400 Miles
0   200   400 Kilometers

Answers to Map Study

1. Ft. Frontenac, Ft. Niagara, Ft. Oswego 2. about 800 miles (1,280 km) 3. Yes; most of the forts were located on water. Also, students should note that the British advances shown on the map usually took place along rivers, over lakes, or across the ocean.

colonists to support the war, he promised large payments for military services and supplies.*

---

*By 1756, fighting between the French and the British had broken out in Europe. There, it became known as the Seven Years' War. The British and the French also fought in India. In the early years of the war, the British suffered setbacks on every front.

Under Pitt's leadership, the tide of battle turned. In 1758, Major General Jeffrey Amherst captured ***Louisbourg,*** the most important fort in French Canada. That year, the British also won more Iroquois support.

The Iroquois persuaded the Delawares at Fort Duquesne to abandon the French. Without the Delawares, the French could no longer hold the fort. Acting quickly, the

Chapter 5 • **139**

Historical Sidelight
Background

William Pitt (1708–1778), the Earl of Chatham, has been called the "organizer of victory" for the way in which he turned around Britain's fortunes in the war. Pitt later became a great defender of the rights of American colonists.

Linking Past and Present
Background

Many modern midwestern cities began as forts to defend against Indian attack. The traders and trappers who built these forts picked sites that would have a "command of the rivers." Locations along major transportation routes helped cities develop and thrive, especially during and after the Industrial Revolution of the 1800s.

Answer to Caption

Louisbourg was at the entrance to the St. Lawrence River. By gaining control of Louisbourg, the British were able to block supplies and troops from reaching the French army in North America.

Voices of Freedom

Primary Source You might assign selection 7–3, Wolfe and Montcalm: The Last Battle, on pages 55–56 of *Voices of Freedom*. This selection discusses the battle on the Plains of Abraham. (Enrichment/Challenging)

Videotapes/ Videodiscs

United States History Video Collection Use the video segment "America in 1763" from Volume 2, *The Era of Colonization*, to enhance students' understanding of the effects of the French and Indian War on North America. Approx. running time 2:20 min. (Enrichment/Average) Vol. 2, Ch. 34

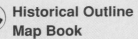

Chapter 34   Play

Historical Outline Map Book

Historical Outline Map Duplicate and distribute the map, North America in 1763, on page 22 of the *American History Historical Outline Map Book*. Lesson ideas can be found on page T7. (Reteaching/Average)

Battle of Louisbourg *The British capture of Louisbourg was a turning point in the French and Indian War. In this engraving, cannonballs fly as British ships shell the fort.* **Geography** *Locate Louisbourg on the map on page 139. Why do you think control of this fort was important?*

British seized Fort Duquesne, which they renamed **Fort Pitt.** The city of Pittsburgh later grew up on the site.

The Fall of New France

The British enjoyed even greater success in 1759. By summer, they had pushed the French from Fort Niagara, Crown Point, and Fort Ticonderoga (tī kahn duh ROH guh). Now, Pitt sent General James Wolfe to take *Quebec,* capital of New France.

Battle for Quebec. Quebec was vital to the defense of New France. Without Quebec, the French would be unable to supply their forts farther up the St. Lawrence River. But Quebec was well defended. The city sat atop a steep cliff above the St. Lawrence. An able French general, the Marquis de Montcalm, was prepared to fight off any British attack.

General Wolfe devised a bold plan. Late one night, he ordered British troops to move quietly in small boats to the foot of the cliff. Under cover of darkness, the soldiers swarmed ashore and scrambled to the top. The next morning, Montcalm awakened to see 4,000 British troops drawn up on the *Plains of Abraham,* a grassy field just outside the city.

Montcalm quickly marched out his own troops. A fierce battle followed. When it was over, both Montcalm and Wolfe were dead. Moments before Wolfe died, a soldier gave him the news that the British had won.

Linking Past and Present
The British commander who seized Fort Duquesne and rebuilt it as Pittsburgh was a Scotsman. He used the Scottish spelling "burgh" for the name, rather than the more common English "burg" or "boro." Later Pittsburghers resisted government efforts to make them drop the "h."

Cooperative Learning
Activity

Divide students into three groups. Tell one group that they are French soldiers during the French and Indian War. The second group will represent British soldiers; the third group, American colonists fighting alongside the British. Have each group collaborate to write diary entries showing that group's point of view about the following events: (a) General Braddock's attack on Fort Duquesne, (b) battle for Quebec, and (c) the British capture of Montreal. Remind students to include facts about each event as well as the feelings of the participants. Invite each group to share its diary with the class; compare the different points of view expressed.

MAP STUDY

The Treaty of Paris of 1763 greatly changed the map of North America.
1. Which countries shared control of North America in 1763?
2. Which country controlled the land west of the Mississippi?
3. **Comparing** Compare this map with the map on page 133. How was North America in 1763 different from North America in 1753?

North America in 1763

- Claimed by Britain
- Claimed by Spain
- Claimed by France
- Claimed by Russia, Spain, and Britain
- 13 Colonies
- Proclamation Line of 1763

0   900   1800 Miles
0   900   1800 Kilometers

Wolfe reportedly whispered, "Now, God be praised, I will die in peace."

Treaty of Paris. The fall of Quebec sealed the fate of New France. In 1760, the British took Montreal, and the war in North America ended. Fighting dragged on in Europe until Britain and France signed the *Treaty of Paris* in 1763.

The Treaty of Paris marked the end of French power in North America. Under the treaty, Britain gained Canada and all French lands east of the Mississippi River. France was allowed to keep a few sugar-growing islands in the West Indies. Spain, which had entered the war on the French side in 1762, gave up Florida to Britain. In return, Spain received all French land west of the Mississippi, as well as the city of New Orleans.

After years of fighting, peace returned to North America. But in a few short years, a new struggle would break out. This struggle would pit Britain against its own colonies.

SECTION 2 REVIEW

1. **Locate:** (a) Fort Necessity, (b) Louisbourg, (c) Fort Pitt, (d) Quebec.
2. **Identify:** (a) French and Indian War, (b) George Washington, (c) Albany Plan of Union, (d) Edward Braddock,

(e) James Wolfe, (f) Marquis de Montcalm, (g) Plains of Abraham, (h) Treaty of Paris.
3. Why did the British and French go to war in North America in 1754?
4. List two strengths of the British in the French and Indian War.
5. What lands did Britain gain under the Treaty of Paris?
6. **CRITICAL THINKING Evaluating Information** Under the Albany Plan of Union, the Grand Council could "draw on the fund in the Treasury of any Colony" during war. Why might colonial assemblies object?

 Writing to Learn

Write a short scene for a TV movie depicting the battle for Quebec.

Section 3
pp. 142–149

Bell Ringer

Ask students to complete this sentence in as many appropriate ways as they can: "A citizen is someone who _____." Discuss the various rights, privileges, and responsibilities suggested by students' responses.

Lesson Plan

1. Focus Even before its victory over France, Britain began to face new problems in its colonies. In this section, students learn how conflicts between the English and Native Americans erupted into war and how England's attempts to pay war debts by taxing the colonists led to bitter disputes.
2. Instruct Collaborate with students to create a classroom chart. On the chalkboard or a bulletin board, draw a chart with three columns, titled Act, Purpose, and Effect. Under Act, list Proclamation of 1763, Sugar Act of 1764, Stamp Act of 1765, and Townshend Acts. Call on volunteers to complete the chart.
3. Close To close the lesson, play a Jeopardy!-like game with students. Provide answers that identify important people, places, and events; have students prepare questions to which your information provides the answers.

3
A Storm Over Taxes

FIND OUT
- Why did Britain issue the Proclamation of 1763?
- What steps did Britain take to raise money to repay its war debts?
- How did colonists protest British taxes?
- Why did the Boston Massacre occur?

VOCABULARY boycott, repeal, writ of assistance, nonimportation agreement, committee of correspondence

As Britain celebrated the victory over France, a few officials in London expressed some of their concerns. Now that the French were no longer a threat, they wondered, would the 13 colonies become too independent? Might the colonies even unite one day against Great Britain? Benjamin Franklin, who was visiting London at the time, gave his opinion:

66 If [the colonies] could not agree to unite for their defense against the French and Indians, . . . can it reasonably be supposed there is any danger of their uniting against their own nation? . . . I will venture to say, a union amongst them for such a purpose is not merely improbable, it is impossible. 99

But Franklin misjudged the situation. After the French and Indian War, new British policies toward the colonies aroused angry cries from Massachusetts to Georgia. Despite their differences, colonists were moving toward unity.

142 • Chapter 5

New Troubles on the Frontier

By 1760, the British had driven France from the Ohio Valley. Their troubles in the region, however, were not over. For many years, fur traders had sent back glowing reports of the land beyond the Appalachian Mountains. With the French gone, English colonists eagerly headed west to farm the former French lands.

Relations with Indians worsen. Many Native American nations lived in the Ohio Valley. They included the Senecas, Delawares, Shawnees, Ottawas, Miamis, and Hurons. As British settlers moved into the valley, they often clashed with these Native Americans.

In 1762, the British sent Lord Jeffrey Amherst to the frontier to keep order. French traders had always treated Native Americans as friends, holding feasts for them and giving them presents. Amherst refused to do this. He raised the price of British goods traded to Indians. He also allowed English settlers to build forts on Indian lands.

Discontented Native Americans found a leader in Pontiac, an Ottawa chief who had fought with the French. An English trader remarked that Pontiac "commands more respect amongst these nations than any Indian I ever saw." In April 1763, Pontiac spoke out against the British, calling them "dogs dressed in red, who have come to rob [us] of [our] hunting grounds and drive away the game."

Fighting on the frontier. Soon after, Pontiac led an attack on British troops at Fort Detroit. Other Indians joined the fight, and in a few months they captured most British forts on the frontier. British and colonial troops struck back and regained much of what they had lost.

Pontiac's War, as it came to be called, did not last long. In October 1763, the French informed Pontiac that they had signed the Treaty of Paris. As you have read,

Our Multicultural Heritage
Background

Pontiac, the strong and proud leader of the Ottawas, was determined to hold the Ohio Valley against the British. Pontiac believed that the Native Americans could save their land only by returning to their old ways; he carried this message to his followers. A skillful organizer, Pontiac brought many Native American peoples together to fight the British.

Connections With Literature
Activity

Several excellent biographies of Pontiac have been written for young people. Among them are *Pontiac: Chief of the Ottawas* by Jane Fleischer and *Pontiac: Mighty Ottawa Chief* by Virginia Voight. Students can write brief profiles of Pontiac based on outside readings and read them to the class. Reports can focus on Pontiac's contributions to the Ottawas, the results of Pontiac's War, and Pontiac's later life.

Ottawa War Council *Chief Pontiac led Native Americans against the British in the Ohio Valley. Here, Pontiac addresses a war council in 1763.* **Economics** *For what uses did the British want Indian lands?*

the treaty marked the end of French power in North America. As a result, the Indians could no longer hope for French aid against the British. One by one, the Indian nations stopped fighting and returned home. "All my young men have buried their hatchets," Pontiac sadly observed.

Proclamation of 1763

Pontiac's War convinced the British to close western lands to settlers. To do this, the government issued the ***Proclamation of 1763.*** The proclamation drew an imaginary line along the crest of the Appalachian Mountains. Colonists were forbidden to settle west of the line. The proclamation ordered all settlers already west of the line "to remove themselves" at once. To enforce the law, Britain sent 10,000 troops to the colonies. Few troops went to the frontier, however. Most stayed in cities along the Atlantic coast.

The proclamation angered colonists. Some colonies, including New York, Pennsylvania, and Virginia, claimed lands in the West. Also, colonists had to pay for the additional British troops that had been sent to enforce the law. In the end, many settlers simply ignored the proclamation and moved west anyway.

Stamp Act Crisis

The French and Indian War had plunged Britain deeply into debt. As a result, the tax bill for citizens in Britain rose sharply. The British prime minister, George Grenville, decided that colonists in North America should help share the burden. After all, he reasoned, it was the colonists who had gained most from the war.

New taxes. Grenville persuaded Parliament to pass two new laws. The Sugar Act of 1764 placed a new tax on molasses. The ***Stamp Act*** of 1765 put a tax on legal documents such as wills, diplomas, and marriage papers. It also taxed newspapers, almanacs, playing cards, and even dice. All items named in the law had to carry a stamp showing that the tax had been paid. Stamp taxes were used in Britain and other countries to raise money. However, Britain had never used such a tax in its colonies.

When British officials tried to enforce the Stamp Act, they met with stormy protests. Riots broke out in New York City, Newport, and Charleston. Angry colonists threw rocks at agents trying to collect the unpopular tax. Some tarred and feathered the agents. In Boston, as you read, a mob burned an effigy, or likeness, of Andrew Oliver and then destroyed his home. As John Adams, a Massachusetts lawyer, wrote:

66 Our presses have groaned, our pulpits have thundered, our legislatures have resolved, our towns have voted, the crown officers everywhere trembled. 99

 Lesson Planner

For a developed **Cooperative Learning** lesson plan, see the *Lesson Planner,* page 28.

Answer to Caption

for settlement and farming

 Transparencies

Cause and Effect Use the transparency, The American Revolution, on page F-15 in *American History Transparencies.* The transparency shows the political steps that led to the American Revolution and its immediate aftermath. Teaching suggestions can be found on page F-3. (Enrichment/Average)

Learning Styles
Kinesthetic Learners

You might have students act out a conversation about the Proclamation of 1763 with the following characters taking part: a fur trapper, a farmer, a British official, and an Ottawa Indian. Students can work in groups of four to write appropriate dialogue and play the roles of the characters suggested.

Historical Sidelight
Background

Upon hearing of the Stamp Act, South Carolina legislators declared that "it is inseparably essential to the freedom of a people and the undoubted rights of Englishmen that no taxes be imposed upon them but by their own consent." Reaction in the Virginia legislature was so strong, and the language so inflammatory, that the Royalist editor of the Virginia *Gazette* refused to print a full account of the meeting.

No taxation without representation! The fury of the colonists shocked the British. After all, Britain had spent a great deal of money to protect the colonies against the French. Why, the British asked, were colonists so angry about the Stamp Act?

Colonists replied that the taxes imposed by the Stamp Act were unjust. The taxes, they claimed, went against the principle that there should be no taxation without representation. That principle was rooted in English traditions dating back to the Magna Carta. (See page 86.)

Colonists insisted that only they or their elected representatives had the right to pass taxes. Since the colonists did not elect representatives to Parliament, Parliament had no right to tax them. The colonists were willing to pay taxes—but only if the taxes were passed by their own colonial legislatures.

A call for unity. The Stamp Act crisis brought a sense of unity to the colonies. Critics of the law called for delegates from every colony to meet in New York City. There, the delegates would consider actions against the hated Stamp Act.

In October 1765, nine colonies sent delegates to what became known as the Stamp Act Congress. The delegates drew up petitions, or letters, to King George III and to Parliament. In these petitions, they rejected the Stamp Act and asserted that Parliament had no right to tax the colonies. Parliament paid little attention.

The colonists took other steps to change the law. They joined together to **boycott** British goods. To boycott means to refuse to buy certain goods and services. The boycott of British goods took its toll. Trade fell off by 14 percent. British merchants suffered.

LINKING PAST AND PRESENT

PAST   PRESENT

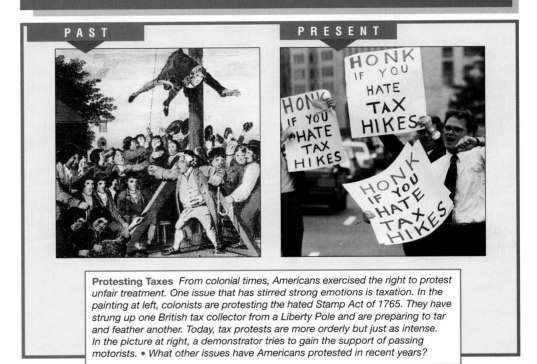

Protesting Taxes *From colonial times, Americans exercised the right to protest unfair treatment. One issue that has stirred strong emotions is taxation. In the painting at left, colonists are protesting the hated Stamp Act of 1765. They have strung up one British tax collector from a Liberty Pole and are preparing to tar and feather another. Today, tax protests are more orderly but just as intense. In the picture at right, a demonstrator tries to gain the support of passing motorists. • What other issues have Americans protested in recent years?*

Connections With Language Arts
Background

Although the colonists certainly boycotted British goods, they must have used another term to describe their action. Referring to the refusal to buy goods in protest as a *boycott* did not actually come into use until the late 1800s. Captain Charles Cunningham Boycott was a rent collector for an absentee landlord in County Mayo, Ireland. In 1880, he insisted upon full payment of the rents owed by Irish tenant farmers, despite the fact that their crops had failed and the farmers were impoverished. He threatened eviction if the rent was not paid. The tenants retaliated by trying to stop his supply of goods and by refusing any interaction with him. Boycott finally gave up and returned to England—but his name stayed on to describe the tenants' form of protest against him.

So, too, did British workers who made goods for the colonies. Finally, in 1766, Parliament **repealed,** or canceled, the Stamp Act.

More Taxes

In May 1767, Parliament continued the debate over taxing the colonies. In one especially fiery exchange, George Grenville, now a member of Parliament, clashed with Charles Townshend, who was in charge of the British treasury:

> **66** *Grenville:* You are cowards, you are afraid of the Americans, you dare not tax America!
> *Townshend:* Fear? Cowards? I dare tax America!
> *Grenville:* Dare you tax America? I wish I could see it!
> *Townshend:* I will, I will! **99**

The next month, Parliament passed the ***Townshend Acts,*** which taxed goods such as glass, paper, paint, lead, and tea. The taxes were low, but colonists still objected. The principle, they felt, was the same: Parliament did not have the right to tax them without their consent.

The Townshend Acts set up new ways to collect taxes. Using legal documents known as **writs of assistance,** customs officers could inspect a ship's cargo without giving a reason. Colonists protested that the writs violated their rights as British citizens. Under British law, an official could not search a person's property without a good reason for suspecting the owner of a crime.

Colonists Fight Back

The colonists' response to the Townshend Acts was loud and clear. From north to south, merchants and planters signed **nonimportation agreements.** In these agreements, they promised to stop importing goods taxed by the Townshend Acts. The colonists hoped that the new boycott would win repeal of the Townshend Acts.

Colonists supported the boycott in various ways. Men and women refused to buy cloth made in Britain. Instead, they wore clothes made of fabric spun at home, or homespun. A popular Boston ballad encouraged women to avoid British cloth and "show clothes of your own make and spinning." Harvard College printed its graduation program on coarse paper made in the colonies instead of buying British paper.

Some angry colonists joined the ***Sons of Liberty.*** This group was first formed during the Stamp Act crisis to protest British policies. Women set up their own group, known as ***Daughters of Liberty.***

In cities from Boston to Charleston, Sons and Daughters of Liberty placed lanterns in large trees. Gathering around these Liberty Trees, as they were called, they staged mock hangings of cloth or straw figures dressed like British officials. The hangings were meant to show tax collectors what might happen to them if they tried to collect the unpopular taxes.

Sons and Daughters of Liberty also used other methods to strengthen their cause. Some visited merchants to urge them to sign the nonimportation agreements. A few even threatened people who continued to buy British goods.

Leaders in the Struggle

During the struggle over taxes, leaders emerged in all the colonies. Men and women in the New England colonies and Virginia were especially active in the colonial cause.

History and You
Young colonial women considered it a great sacrifice to give up fine British cloth for rough "homespun." Would you be willing to give up wearing blue jeans to protest an injustice?

Chapter 5 • **145**

Audiocassettes

Listening to Literature Audiocassettes To introduce students to early patriotic music, play *Chester* (side 2, 1:43) from *Listening to Literature Audiocassettes, The American Experience.* The song, composed by William Billings in the 1700s, was one of the first and most influential songs to inspire American troops. See the Audiocassette Guide for previewing information and suggested activities. (Enrichment/Average)

Videotapes/ Videodiscs

United States History Video Collection Use the video segment "The People Get Political" from Volume 4, *The American Revolution,* to enhance students' understanding of actions the colonists took to protest taxation. Approx. running time 3:00 min. (Enrichment/Average) Vol. 4, Ch. 7

Chapter 7   Play

Critical Thinking
Synthesizing Information

Explain that *exports* are goods made in a country and sent elsewhere to be sold. *Imports* are goods made elsewhere and brought into a country to be bought. Ask: Why would the colonial merchants' refusal to buy the British goods listed in the nonimportation agreement hurt the British economy?

Team-Teaching Suggestion
Home Economics/Art

You might work with a home economics teacher and/or an art teacher to demonstrate some of the ways in which colonists supported the boycott of British goods. A home economics teacher might prepare samples of herbal tea or show how homespun cloth was made; an art teacher might demonstrate the art of papermaking.

Answer to Exploring Technology

Each letter had to be placed; the forms were inked by hand; one page was printed at a time and then hung up to dry.

Transparencies

Exploring Technology Use the transparency "Colonial Printing Press" on page H-29 of *American History Transparencies*. The transparency illustrates the time-consuming labor involved in producing colonial newspapers, letters, and pamphlets. Teaching suggestions can be found on page H-5. (Enrichment/Average)

⑤ The frisket kept the margins of the paper clean. It folded onto the tympan.

④ The form was inked with ink balls.

⑥ The tympan held the paper. It folded onto the form.

⑦ The form was slid under the platen.

⑧ The press bar was pulled to lower the platen.

① The type case held metal letters.

② Letters were placed in a composing stick to create lines of type.

③ Lines of type were locked in a form to create a sheet of text.

⑩ The printed page was removed and hung on a drying rack.

⑨ The platen pressed the inked form against the paper.

Colonial Printing Press *Colonial printers played an important role in uniting colonists against the British. Besides publishing newspapers and magazines, they also printed letters and pamphlets that kept colonists informed of anti-British activities. The drawing and photograph above are of a typical colonial printing press.* ***Science and Technology*** *Why would printing a document with this printing press be very time consuming?*

146 • Chapter 5

Cooperative Learning
Activity

Have students imagine that they are the family and fellow townspeople of the owner of a print shop in the 1760s. Discuss the issues that this printer might face. For example, would the printer be approached by customs officials to print writs of assistance, by merchants to print nonimportation agreements, or by both? Would the printer create materials for the Sons and Daughters of Liberty? Would the printer print pamphlets for use by the local committee of correspondence? How would the printer justify involvement in the growing Patriot cause? Appoint several students to record their classmates' responses. Then have students work in small groups to create a short play about this printer. Each group should be responsible for writing one scene. Work with representatives from the groups to ensure continuity. When the script is complete, cast the play; then, after sufficient rehearsal time, perform it for other classes.

The Mighty Pen *Colonial writers supported the cause of liberty. Samuel Adams (left) and Mercy Otis Warren (right) used their pens to stir feelings against the British—Adams with his letters, Warren with her plays. Both of these portraits were painted by John Singleton Copley, a leading artist of the period.* **Linking Past and Present** *How do writers influence public opinion today?*

In Massachusetts. Samuel Adams of Boston stood firmly against Britain. Sam Adams seemed an unlikely leader. He was a failure in business and a poor public speaker. But he loved politics. He was always present at Boston town meetings and Sons of Liberty rallies.

Adams worked day and night to unite colonists against Britain. He organized a **committee of correspondence**, which wrote letters and pamphlets reporting on events in Massachusetts. The idea worked well, and soon there were committees of correspondence in every colony. Adams's greatest talent was organizing people. He knew how to work behind the scenes, arranging protests and stirring public support.

Sam's cousin John was another important leader in Massachusetts. John Adams was a skilled lawyer. More cautious than Sam, he weighed evidence carefully before acting. His knowledge of British law earned him much respect.

Mercy Otis Warren also aided the colonial cause. Warren published plays that made fun of British officials. She formed a close friendship with Abigail Adams, who was married to John Adams. The two women used their pens to spur the colonists to action.

In Virginia. Virginia contributed many leaders to the struggle against taxes. In the House of Burgesses, George Washington joined other Virginians to protest the Townshend Acts.

A young firebrand, Patrick Henry, gave speeches that moved listeners to both tears and anger. In one speech, Henry attacked Britain with such fury that some listeners cried out, "Treason!" Henry boldly replied, "If this be treason, make the most of it!"

Centers of Protest

Port cities such as Boston and New York were centers of protest. In New York, a dispute arose over the **Quartering Act.** Under

 Our Multicultural Heritage

Biography Have students read the biography, Mercy Otis Warren, Patriot and Playwright, on page 14 of the *Our Multicultural Heritage* booklet. (Enrichment /Average)

 Audiocassettes

Listening to Literature Audiocassettes To help students understand Patrick Henry's power of oratory, play, Speech in the Virginia Convention, Patrick Henry (side 2, 7:36), from *Listening to Literature Audiocassettes, The American Experience.* See the Audiocassette Guide for previewing information and suggested activities. (Enrichment/Average)

 CD-ROM

History Makers Access the biography of Abigail Adams on the American Heritage® *History of the United States* CD-ROM. (Enrichment/Average)

History Makers Access the biography of Patrick Henry on the American Heritage® *History of the United States* CD-ROM. (Enrichment/Average)

Connections With Literature
Background

American drama developed slowly, partly because the Puritans considered the theater immoral. Before the mid-1700s, the few plays performed in the colonies were British. Not until 1767 was a play by an American-born author produced (in Philadelphia). In 1772, Mercy Otis Warren wrote her first play dealing with American and British relationships. In four more plays, she used humor to make the British look ridiculous. Warren's plays helped win support for the colonial cause. She also wrote a history of the struggle for independence. Titled *History of the Rise, Progress, and Termination of the American Revolution,* the three-volume work was published in 1805.

CONNECTIONS

ARTS	SCIENCES	GEOGRAPHY	WORLD	ECONOMICS	CIVICS

Paul Revere and the Boston Massacre

Coffins of massacre victims

Could a picture change history? Paul Revere's engraving of the Boston Massacre, below, may not have caused the American Revolution. But it played a major role in whipping up colonial fury against the British.

In the engraving, Revere purposely distorted events. At right, for example, is a British officer, Captain Thomas Preston. Sword raised, he orders his men to fire. At left, unarmed and orderly citizens look on helplessly. A few distressed Patriots pick up their dead.

This scene, however, did not really take place. According to eyewitnesses, Captain Preston never gave an order to shoot. The redcoats, faced by an unruly and threatening mob, acted on their own and opened fire. Revere altered other details, too. He set the bloody scene in front of a building labeled Butcher's Hall. In fact, the building was the Boston customs house. Finally, at the bottom of the engraving, Revere lists seven dead. In truth, five Patriots, not seven, were killed. Revere wrote a poem to go with the engraving. It, too, sought to stir anti-British sentiment. One stanza is reprinted below.

Within days, copies of Revere's engraving appeared on walls all over Massachusetts. The "Bloody Massacre," as the engraving was titled, aroused cries of rage. Revere's vivid but distorted portrayal created a rallying point for colonists who resented British rule.

■ Name three ways that Revere's engraving distorted events to stir up anti-British feeling.

ACTIVITY Create a poster to support a cause. Use words, pictures, or a combination of both.

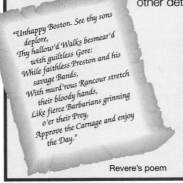

"Unhappy Boston. See thy sons deplore,
Thy hallow'd Walks besmear'd with guiltless Gore:
While faithless Preston and his savage Bands,
With murd'rous Rancour stretch their bloody hands,
Like fierce Barbarians grinning o'er their Prey,
Approve the Carnage and enjoy the Day."

Revere's poem

Paul Revere's engraving of the Boston Massacre

that law, colonists had to provide housing, candles, bedding, and beverages to British soldiers stationed in the colonies. New Yorkers saw the law as another way to tax them without their consent. The New York assembly refused to obey the law. As a result, in 1767, Britain dismissed the assembly.

Britain also sent two regiments of British soldiers to Boston to protect customs officers from local citizens. To many Bostonians, the soldiers' tents set up on Boston Common were a daily reminder that Britain was trying to bully them into paying unjust taxes. When British soldiers walked along the streets of Boston, they risked insults or even beatings. The time was ripe for disaster.

The Boston Massacre

On the night of March 5, 1770, a crowd gathered outside the Boston customs house. Colonists shouted insults at the "lobsterbacks," as they called the redcoated British who guarded the building. Then they began to throw snowballs, oyster shells, and chunks of ice at the soldiers.

The crowd grew larger and rowdier. Suddenly, the soldiers panicked. They fired into the crowd. When the smoke from the musket volley cleared, five people lay dead or dying. Among them was Crispus Attucks, a black sailor who was active in the Sons of Liberty.

Sam Adams quickly wrote to other colonists about the shooting, which he called the *Boston Massacre.* As news of the Boston Massacre spread, colonists' outrage grew.

The soldiers were arrested and tried in court. John Adams agreed to defend them, saying that they deserved a fair trial. He wanted to show the world that the colonists believed in justice, even if the British government did not. At the trial, Adams argued that the crowd had provoked the soldiers. His arguments convinced the jury. In the end, the British soldiers received very light sentences.

Repeal of the Townshend Acts

By chance, on the day of the Boston Massacre, Parliament voted to repeal most of the Townshend Acts. British merchants, hurt by the nonimportation agreements, had pressured Parliament to end the Townshend taxes. But King George III asked Parliament to keep the tax on tea. "There must always be one tax to keep up the right [to tax]," argued the king. Parliament agreed.

News of the repeal delighted the colonists. Most people dismissed the remaining tax on tea as not important and ended their boycott of British goods. For a few years, calm returned.

SECTION **3** REVIEW

1. **Locate:** Appalachian Mountains.
2. **Identify:** (a) Pontiac's War, (b) Proclamation of 1763, (c) Stamp Act, (d) Townshend Acts, (e) Sons of Liberty, (f) Daughters of Liberty, (g) Sam Adams, (h) Mercy Otis Warren, (i) Quartering Act, (j) Crispus Attucks, (k) Boston Massacre.
3. **Define:** (a) boycott, (b) repeal, (c) writ of assistance, (d) nonimportation agreement, (e) committee of correspondence.
4. What event convinced Britain to issue the Proclamation of 1763?
5. How did Britain try to raise money to repay its war debt?
6. (a) Why did colonists object to the Stamp Act? (b) What actions did colonists take to protest the Townshend Acts?
7. **CRITICAL THINKING Drawing Conclusions** Why do you think Pontiac felt he had to fight the British?

 Writing to Learn
Write an article for a colonial newspaper reporting the events of the Boston Massacre.

Answers to Section 3 Review

1. See the map on p. 19.
2. (a) Pontiac's War, p. 142, (b) Proclamation of 1763, p. 143, (c) Stamp Act, p. 143, (d) Townshend Acts, p. 145, (e) Sons of Liberty, p. 145, (f) Daughters of Liberty, p. 145, (g) Sam Adams, p. 147, (h) Mercy Otis Warren, p. 147, (i) Quartering Act, p. 147, (j) Crispus Attucks, p. 149, (k) Boston Massacre, p. 149
3. (a) boycott, p. 144, (b) repeal, p. 145, (c) writ of assistance, p. 145, (d) nonimportation agreement, p. 145, (e) committee of correspondence, p. 147

4. Pontiac's War
5. Parliament created taxes through the Sugar Act of 1764 and the Stamp Act of 1765.
6. (a) Colonists claimed that since they did not elect representatives to Parliament, Parliament had no right to tax them. (b) Merchants and planters signed nonimportation agreements and stopped importing taxed goods. Many colonists boycotted the taxed items and/or joined the Sons or Daughters of Liberty.

7. Possible Answer: The British generally did not treat Native Americans with respect or fairness. Pontiac realized that relations with British settlers were worsening. This became evident when Lord Amherst raised the price of British goods and allowed British settlers to build forts on Native American lands.

Bell Ringer

Guide students in formulating a working definition of *intolerable*. Have students name actions that they would find intolerable.

Lesson Plan

1. Focus In 1773, Britain passed another law that set off a chain of angry reactions and British counterreactions. In this section, students examine the events that made the battles of Lexington and Concord virtually inevitable.

2. Instruct Write the following quotation from John Adams on the chalkboard: " . . . the Revolution was in the minds of the people, and this was effected, from 1760 to 1775, in the course of fifteen years before a drop of blood was drawn at Lexington." Ask students to explain what Adams meant. Then have students list events and facts from this section that support Adams's claim.

3. Close To close the lesson, have students suggest a series of cause-and-effect statements about the events discussed in Section 4.

 Lesson Planner

For a developed **Cooperative Learning** lesson plan, see the *Lesson Planner,* page 29.

4
To Arms!

FIND OUT
■ Why did Britain pass the Tea Act?
■ What was the Boston Tea Party?
■ How did colonists respond to the Intolerable Acts?
■ What was the shot heard 'round the world?

VOCABULARY militia, minuteman

One night in July 1774, John Adams stopped at a tavern in eastern Massachusetts. After riding more than 30 miles (48 km), he was hot and dusty, and his body ached with fatigue. Adams asked the innkeeper for a cup of tea. He would have to drink coffee, she said. She did not serve tea. In a letter to his wife, Adams later praised the innkeeper's conduct. "Tea," he wrote, "must be . . . [given up]" by all colonists. He promised to break himself of the habit as soon as possible.

Why did colonists like John Adams give up tea? The answer was taxes. When Parliament decided to enforce a tea tax in 1773, a new crisis exploded. This time, colonists began to think the unthinkable. Perhaps the time had come to reject British rule and declare independence.

Uproar Over Tea

Tea became popular after it was brought to the colonies in the early 1700s. By 1770, at least one million Americans brewed tea twice a day. People "would rather go without their dinners than without a dish of tea," a visitor to the colonies noted.

Parliament passes the Tea Act. Most tea was brought to the colonies by the British East India Company. The company sold its tea to colonial tea merchants. The merchants then sold the tea to the colonists.

In the 1770s, however, the British East India Company found itself in deep financial trouble. More than 15 million pounds of its tea sat unsold in British warehouses. Britain had kept a tax on tea as a symbol of its right to tax the colonies. The tax was a small one, but colonists resented it. They refused to buy English tea.

Parliament tried to help the East India Company by passing the ***Tea Act*** of 1773. The act let the company bypass the tea merchants and sell directly to colonists. Although colonists would still have to pay the tea tax, the tea itself would cost less than ever before.

To the surprise of Parliament, colonists protested the Tea Act. Colonial tea merchants were angry because they had been cut out of the tea trade. If Parliament ruined tea merchants today, they warned, what would prevent it from turning on other businesses tomorrow? Even tea drinkers, who would have benefited from the law, scorned the Tea Act. They believed that it was a British trick to make them accept Parliament's right to tax the colonies.

Boycott the "accursed STUFF"! Once again, colonists responded with a boycott. One colonial newspaper warned:

❝Do not suffer yourself to sip the accursed, dutied STUFF. For if you do, the devil will immediately enter into you, and you will instantly become a traitor to your country.❞

Daughters of Liberty and other women led the boycott. They served coffee or made "liberty tea" from raspberry leaves. Sons of Liberty enforced the boycott by keeping the British East India Company from unloading cargoes of tea.

Connections With Literature
Background

A poem written in 1774 included these lines: "No more shall I dish out the once lov'd liquor. /Though now detestable, /Because I'm taught (and I believe it true)/Its use will fasten slavish Chains upon my Country, /And LIBERTY's the goddess I would choose/To reign triumphant in America."

Our Multicultural Heritage
Activity

Tea was a popular beverage in the colonies and in Britain, but its influence over the centuries has been worldwide. Students may be interested to research and report on the history of tea, kinds of tea and the ways in which they are processed, and the leading producers of tea around the world today.

Much early protest against the British occurred in the city of Boston. This map shows Boston in the 1770s.

1. (a) At which building did colonists gather before the Boston Tea Party? (b) On which street was it located?
2. In what part of Boston did the Boston Tea Party take place?
3. **Drawing Conclusions** Why would taxes on trade be especially unpopular in cities like Boston?

Boston in the 1770s

Answers to Map Study

1. (a) Old South Meeting House (b) Milk Street 2. Griffin's Wharf 3. Boston was a major port; its economy depended upon trade.

Chapter Resources

Critical Thinking Duplicate and distribute the worksheet, Making Decisions, from Unit 2, page 3, of the *Chapter Resources* binder. The worksheet will help students understand the problem-solution thinking that led to the Boston Tea Party. (Reteaching/Average)

Videotapes/ Videodiscs

United States History Video Collection Use the video segment "The Boston Tea Party" from Volume 4, *The American Revolution*, to enhance students' understanding of the causes and effects of the Boston Tea Party. Approx. running time 1:30 min. (Enrichment/Average) Vol. 4, Ch. 13

Chapter 13   Play

The Boston Tea Party

In late November 1773, three ships carrying tea arrived in Boston harbor. Governor Thomas Hutch- inson ordered the captain to pay the required taxes, unload, and sell the tea as usual. If the taxes were not paid within 20 days, he would seize the cargo and have it sold. The deadline was Thursday, December 16.

Chapter 5 • **151**

Historical Sidelight
Background

When faced with colonial resistance, most captains of tea-bearing ships either took the tea back to England or left it in warehouses under the watchful eye of colonists. Governor Hutchinson would not allow the captain to do this in Boston. His ultimatum and deadline set the scene for an action that would do more than any other single event before the American Revolution to unify Patriots in the colonies and solidify anticolonial feelings in Britain.

Team-Teaching Suggestion
Language Arts

You might work with a language arts teacher to present a lesson about literature connected with the start of the Revolution. Selections might include the full texts of Emerson's "Concord Hymn" and Longfellow's "Paul Revere's Ride"; students might also enjoy discussing the lyrics to popular Patriot (and Loyalist) songs of the era.

Answer to Caption

Under the Tea Act, the British East India Company could bypass the merchants and sell directly to colonists. The tea merchants were thus cut out of the tea trade.

A demand that the tea ships leave. All that day, Boston seethed with excitement. Townspeople roamed the streets, wondering what the Sons of Liberty would do. Farmers and workers from nearby towns joined the crowds. "Committee Men & Mob Men were buzzing about in Swarms, like Bees," reported a nephew of Governor Hutchinson.

By 10 A.M., thousands of people had made their way along Milk Street to the Old South Meetinghouse. Sam Adams was there, directing affairs. The wealthy merchant John Hancock was also present. At the meeting, colonists voted that the tea ships should leave Boston that afternoon—without unloading. Runners were sent to the customs house to voice the colonists' demand.

By afternoon, word came back. Customs officers would not act without the governor.

Messengers then set off to see Governor Hutchinson.

Nervously, Sam Adams waited. So did the 5,000 people who had gathered in and around the meetinghouse. Finally, the messengers returned. The governor would not let the ships sail. The crowd's angry roar echoed far down the streets of Boston.

"Boston harbor a teapot tonight!" Adams waved for silence. "This meeting can do nothing further to save the country," he announced. Suddenly, as if on cue, a group of men burst into the meetinghouse. Dressed like Mohawk Indians, they waved hatchets in the air. The crowd stirred. What was this? From the gallery above, voices cried, "Boston harbor a teapot tonight! The Mohawks are come!"

George Hewes was one of the "Mohawks" poised for action. He later reported:

The Boston Tea Party *British officials were outraged by the Boston Tea Party, shown here. One called it "the most wanton and unprovoked insult offered to the civil power that is recorded in history." John Adams, however, believed that many colonists wished that "as many dead Carcasses were floating in the Harbour, as there are Chests of Tea."* **Economics** *Why were colonial tea merchants angered by the Tea Act?*

Connections With Civics
Activity

One British official called the Boston Tea Party "the most wanton and unprovoked insult offered to the civil power that is recorded in history." Discuss with students why the official considered the event "wanton" and "unprovoked" and why he felt that the event was so significant.

Historical Sidelight
Background

As other tea-bearing ships were approaching the ports of New York, Philadelphia, and Charleston, Paul Revere was riding south from Boston with news of the Boston Tea Party. Sam Adams later wrote of the New Yorkers' response, noting that "immediately they became united and determined that [the tea] should not be landed. . . . The Ministry could not have devised a more effectual measure to unite the Colonies." Indeed, New Yorkers had their own tea party, dumping the cargo into the East River. Philadelphians had their tea unloaded—but then left it to rot in warehouses. Patriots in Charleston took that plan one step further: When the Revolution began, they opened the warehouses, auctioned off the tea, and used the proceeds to support the South Carolina militia.

"I [had] dressed myself in the costume of an Indian, equipped with a small hatchet after having painted my face and hands with coal dust in the shop of a blacksmith. . . . When I first appeared in the street after being thus disguised, I fell in with many who were dressed, equipped and painted as I was, and . . . marched in order to the place of our destination."

That place was Griffin's Wharf, where the tea ships lay at anchor. About 50 or 60 people disguised as Indians were there. Some were carpenters and barbers. Others were doctors and merchants. In the cold, crisp night, under a nearly full moon, the men worked quickly. They boarded the ships, split open the tea chests, and dumped the tea into the harbor. On shore, the crowd watched silently. The only sounds were the chink of hatchets and the splash of tea landing in the water.

By 10 P.M., the job was done. The **Boston Tea Party,** as it was later called, had ended. However, the effects would be felt for a long time to come. ■

Britain Strikes Back

Did Sam Adams organize the Boston Tea Party? Although he never said so publicly, he very likely knew that it was planned. Whoever led the tea party, however, made sure that the protest was orderly. Only tea was destroyed. No other cargo was touched. The Boston Tea Party was meant to show Britain that the colonists would act firmly.

Colonists had mixed reactions to the event. Some cheered the action. Others worried that it would encourage lawlessness in the colonies. Even those who condemned the Boston Tea Party were shocked at Britain's response to it.

Punishment for Massachusetts. The British were outraged by what they saw as Boston's lawless behavior. In 1774, Parliament, encouraged by King George III, acted to punish Massachusetts. First, Parliament shut down the port of Boston. No ship could enter or leave the harbor—not even a small boat. The harbor would remain closed until the colonists paid for the tea.

Second, Parliament forbade colonists to hold town meetings more than once a year without the governor's permission. In the past, colonists had called town meetings whenever they wished.

Third, Parliament provided for customs officers and other officials charged with major crimes to be tried in Britain instead of in Massachusetts. Colonists protested. They said that a dishonest official could break the law in the colonies and avoid punishment "by being tried, where no evidence can pursue him."

Fourth, Parliament passed a new Quartering Act. No longer would redcoats camp in tents on Boston Common. Instead, British commanders could force citizens to house troops in their homes. The colonists called these laws the ***Intolerable Acts*** because they were so harsh.

Colonists support Boston. The committees of correspondence spread news of the Intolerable Acts. People from other colonies responded quickly to help the people of Boston, who faced hunger while their port was closed.

British Grenadier *The Intolerable Acts forced Bostonians to open their homes to British soldiers, such as the one shown here.* **Citizenship** *What were the other provisions of the Intolerable Acts?*

Our Multicultural Heritage

Milestone Have students read Moving Toward a Break With Britain, on page 15 of the *Our Multicultural Heritage* booklet. (Enrichment/Easy)

Cooperative Learning
Activity

Divide students into three groups (Colonials, British, and Neutral). Have students imagine that it is 1774 and that the Intolerable Acts have just been passed. Ask: Can war be avoided?

Have the British and Colonial groups make two lists: (1) what each group has to gain from continued association with the other side; (2) the reasons for going to war. The Neutral group should list reasons why both sides should continue to seek peace. Then have British and Colonial groups write one-page proposals explaining how they think conflicts could be settled. The Neutrals will carry proposals and transmit responses or information on the progress of negotiations. Set a time limit for negotiations. See if groups can find a way to avoid armed conflict.

Carts rolled into the city with rice from South Carolina, corn from Virginia, and flour from Pennsylvania.

In the Virginia assembly, a young lawyer named Thomas Jefferson suggested that a day be set aside to mark the shame of the Intolerable Acts. The royal governor of Virginia rejected the idea and dismissed the assembly. But the colonists went ahead anyway. On June 1, 1774, church bells tolled slowly. Merchants closed their shops. Many colonists prayed and fasted all day.

The First Continental Congress

In response to the Intolerable Acts, colonial leaders called a meeting in Philadelphia. In September 1774, delegates from 12 colonies gathered in what became known as the ***First Continental Congress.*** Only Georgia did not send delegates.

After much debate, the delegates passed a resolution backing Massachusetts in its struggle against the Intolerable Acts. They agreed to boycott all British goods and to stop exporting goods to Britain until the harsh laws were repealed. The delegates also urged each colony to set up and train its own **militia** (muh LIHSH uh). A militia is an army of citizens who serve as soldiers during an emergency.

Before leaving Philadelphia, the delegates agreed to meet again the following May. Little did they know that by May 1775 an incident in Massachusetts would have changed the fate of the colonies forever.

The Shot Heard 'Round the World

In Massachusetts, newspapers called on citizens to prevent what they called "the Massacre of American Liberty." Volunteers

Redcoats at Concord *Minuteman Amos Doolittle made this engraving of two British commanders scouting the area around Concord. Brilliantly clad British troops are marching toward their battle with colonial minutemen. An engraving of a minuteman is shown at left.* **Citizenship** *Do you think that the fighting at Lexington and Concord could have been avoided? Explain.*

known as **minutemen** trained regularly. Minutemen got their name because they kept their muskets at hand, prepared to fight at a minute's notice. Meanwhile, Britain built up its forces. More troops arrived in Boston, bringing the total number in that city to 4,000.

Early in 1775, General Thomas Gage, the British commander, learned that minutemen had a large store of arms in Concord, a village about 18 miles (29 km) from Boston. General Gage planned a surprise march to Concord to seize the arms.

On April 18, about 700 British troops quietly left Boston under cover of darkness. The Sons of Liberty were watching. As soon as the British set out, they hung two lamps from the Old North Church in Boston as a signal that the redcoats were on the move.

Sounding the alarm. Colonists who were waiting across the Charles River saw the signal. Messengers mounted their horses and galloped through the night toward Concord. One midnight rider was Paul Revere. "The British are coming! The British are coming!" shouted Revere as he passed through each sleepy village along the way.

At daybreak on April 19, the redcoats reached Lexington, a town near Concord. There, waiting for them on the village green, were 70 minutemen commanded by Captain John Parker. The British ordered the minutemen to go home. Outnumbered, the colonists began to leave. A shot suddenly rang out through the chill morning air. No one knows who fired it. In the brief struggle that followed, eight colonists were killed and one British soldier was wounded.

The British pushed on to Concord. Finding no arms in the village, they turned back to Boston. On a bridge outside Concord, they met 300 minutemen. Again, fighting broke out. This time, the British were forced to retreat. As they withdrew, colonial sharpshooters took deadly aim at them from the woods and fields. By the time they reached Boston, the redcoats had lost 73 men. Another 200 were wounded or missing.

A turning point. News of the battles at Lexington and Concord spread swiftly. To many colonists, the fighting ended all hope of reaching an agreement with Britain. Only

★★★
★
Our Common Heritage
One colonist who heeded Paul Revere's call to action was a minuteman named Peter Salem. A former slave, Salem marched with his company to face the British at Concord. Armed with a flintlock musket, he kept firing until the redcoats retreated.

war would decide the future of the 13 colonies.

More than 60 years after the battles, a well-known New England poet, Ralph Waldo Emerson, wrote a poem about them. It begins:

> ❝By the rude bridge that arched
> the flood,
> Their flag to April's breeze un-
> furled,
> Here once the embattled farmers
> stood,
> And fired the shot heard round
> the world.❞

The "embattled farmers" faced long years of war. At the war's end, though, the 13 colonies would stand firm as a new, independent nation.

SECTION 4 REVIEW

1. **Locate:** (a) Boston, (b) Concord, (c) Lexington.
2. **Identify:** (a) Tea Act, (b) Boston Tea Party, (c) Intolerable Acts, (d) First Continental Congress, (e) Paul Revere.
3. **Define:** (a) militia, (b) minuteman.
4. (a) Why did Britain pass the Tea Act? (b) Why did the act anger colonists?
5. How did the Intolerable Acts help unite the colonies?
6. Describe the events that led to fighting at Lexington.
7. **CRITICAL THINKING Analyzing Information** Do you think that the organizers of the Boston Tea Party would have ended their protests against Britain if Parliament had repealed the tax on tea? Explain.

ACTIVITY **Writing to Learn**
Imagine that you are a writer for the Massachusetts committee of correspondence. Write a letter informing colonists about the Intolerable Acts.

Historical Outline Map Book

Historical Outline Maps Duplicate and distribute the map, Lexington and Concord, on page 23 of the *American History Historical Outline Map Book*. Lesson ideas for this map can be found on page T7. (Reteaching/Average)

Student Study Guide

Section 4 Study Guide Have students use the Section 4 Study Guide on page 59 of the *Student Study Guide* to review and reinforce the content of this section. (Reteaching/Average)

Guided Instruction Before students begin writing their letters, review the function of committees of correspondence as envisioned by Sam Adams. Discuss with students how this view should influence their reporting of events. Unlike the newspaper article in section 3, this letter will express a point of view that justifies opposition to British interference in colonial affairs. You might wish to review the format used in modern newsletters and encourage the use of attention-getting introductions. Have a volunteer collect and randomly deliver the "mail" to student colonists, who may offer comments.

Answers to Section 4 Review

1. See the maps on pp. 151 and 163.
2. (a) Tea Act, p. 150, (b) Boston Tea Party, p. 153, (c) Intolerable Acts, p. 153, (d) First Continental Congress, p. 154, (e) Paul Revere, p. 155
3. (a) militia, p. 154, (b) minuteman, p. 154
4. (a) Britain was trying to help the British East India Company by lowering the price of tea in the colonies, thus encouraging the colonists to buy more tea from the company. (b) Colonial tea merchants were cut out of the

tea trade; some people believed that the act was a British trick to make them accept Parliament's right to tax the colonies.
5. Colonists united to send food to the Bostonians, who faced hunger while their port was closed; delegates from 12 colonies met in Philadelphia to plan a united response to the Intolerable Acts.
6. British troops on the way to Concord to seize weapons reached Lexington at dawn, where they were met by a group of minute-

men. The minutemen refused to obey a British order to disband. Suddenly, a shot rang out; a struggle followed.
7. Possible Answer: No; most organizers opposed not only the taxes imposed on the colonies but also the concept of British rule in general.

CHAPTER 5 REVIEW

Answers to Reviewing the Main Ideas

1. Native Americans decided that participation was the only way to protect their way of life.

2. (a) to build a fort (b) It became the first battle of the French and Indian War.

3. (a) Pontiac fought because Lord Amherst had allowed English settlers to build forts on Native American lands and had raised the price of British goods traded to them. (b) As a result of Pontiac's War, Britain issued the Proclamation of 1763, which forbade colonists to settle western lands.

4. French power in North America was ended. Britain gained Canada and all French lands east of the Mississippi River.

5. (a) Sugar Act, Stamp Act, Townshend Acts (b) Colonists protested the Sugar and Stamp acts by destroying the homes of British officials, by boycotting British goods, and by petitioning the king and Parliament. In response to the Townshend Acts, merchants and planters signed nonimportation agreements. Some colonists joined the Sons or Daughters of Liberty.

6. (a) Dressed as Indians, a group of colonists boarded British ships in Boston harbor and dumped the cargo of tea overboard. (b) Britain passed the Intolerable Acts.

7. (a) to seize arms that he heard were stored there (b) They were greeted by 70 minutemen. The British ordered the minutemen to go home. The colonists refused, and a shot was fired. Eight colonists were killed and one British soldier was wounded.

Summary

- In the mid-1700s, rivalry between France and England in the Ohio Valley led to the French and Indian War.
- By 1763, Britain had driven France out of most of North America.
- Tensions between colonists and Britain grew when Parliament imposed new taxes to help repay Britain's huge war debts.
- The first armed clashes between minutemen and British troops took place at Lexington and Concord in April 1775.

Reviewing the Main Ideas

1. Why did Native Americans take sides in the struggle between France and Britain?
2. (a) Why did George Washington lead troops into the Ohio Valley in 1754? (b) Why was his clash with the French at Fort Necessity important?
3. (a) Why did Pontiac fight the British? (b) How did Pontiac's War affect British policy in the colonies?
4. What were the main results of the Treaty of Paris of 1763?
5. (a) List three ways Parliament tried to tax the colonies. (b) How did colonists respond to each?
6. (a) How did colonists protest the Tea Act? (b) What did Britain do in response?
7. (a) Why did General Gage send troops to Concord? (b) What happened when they reached Lexington?

Thinking Critically

1. **Linking Past and Present** How might your life be different if France, not England, had won the French and Indian War?
2. **Understanding Causes and Effects** Make a cause-and-effect chart about the Stamp Act. Use at least two causes and two effects.

3. Evaluating Information The dictionary defines a massacre as the cruel and violent killing of large numbers of people. Why do you think Sam Adams called the incident in Boston a massacre when only five people were killed?

Applying Your Skills

1. **Analyzing a Quotation** Review the following statement made by a Native American to an English trader in the mid-1700s: "You and the French are like the two edges of a pair of shears. And we are the cloth which is to be cut to pieces between them." (a) What did the speaker mean by these words? (b) Do you think he felt that Native Americans could hold out against the British and French? Explain.

2. **Ranking** List the events discussed in Sections 3 and 4. Then rank them in the order of their importance in bringing about war between the colonists and Britain.

Thinking About Geography

Match the letters on the map with the following places: **1.** Spanish lands in 1763, **2.** British lands in 1763, **3.** Original 13 English colonies, **4.** Mississippi River, **5.** Ohio River. **Location** What body of water formed the western boundary of British lands in North America in 1763?

Answers to Thinking Critically

1. Answers will vary. Students should recognize that many present-day practices and customs in the United States are of British origin. They might suggest that if the French had won, Americans might speak French, eat more French cuisine, or follow the French legal system and form of government.

2. Charts may vary. Possible causes include debt incurred from the cost of the French and Indian War and Grenville's belief that the colonists should share the burden because they had gained the most from the British victory. Possible effects include stormy protests, riots in major cities, and attacks on tax agents by colonists.

3. Possible Answer: to stir up feelings against the British and for the Patriot cause

Answers to Applying Your Skills

1. (a) Possible Answer: Britain and France were each fighting to win Native American allies. However, each was interested only in its own needs; as a result, together they would destroy the Native Americans. (b) He sounds hopeless about the Native American cause; by comparing the Native Americans to a piece of cloth between a pair of shears, he expresses the idea that the Native Americans were powerless in the hands of the French and the British.

2. Students should list some of the following: Proclamation of 1763, Stamp Act, Townshend Acts, Quartering Act, Boston Massacre, Boston Tea Party, Intolerable Acts. Ranking will vary but should show logic.

INTERDISCIPLINARY ACTIVITY

Protesting British Policies

Form into groups to review British policies toward the colonies after 1763. Follow the suggestions to write, draw, or perform to show what you have learned about the colonists' reaction to these policies. You may use the textbook, encyclopedias, atlases, or other materials in your classroom library to complete the tasks. Be able to name your sources of information when you have finished the activity.

Stamp Act riot

ECONOMISTS Review the taxes Britain imposed on the 13 English colonies in the 1760s and 1770s. Then create a Taxation Time Line showing the British tax acts. Illustrate your time line with drawings of your own or pictures cut from newspapers or old magazines.

ARTISTS Imagine that you live in one of the 13 English colonies after the French and Indian War. Draw a political cartoon expressing your reaction to British taxes.

Teapot protesting the Stamp Act

MUSICIANS List five reasons for the colonists' anger with Britain. Based on your list, write a song of protest against British treatment. You can make up your own melody or write new words to an existing tune. Sing or play your song for the class.

WRITERS In the 1760s and 1770s, colonists staged acts of protest against the British. Imagine that you are a movie director. Write a scene dramatizing the Boston Massacre for a movie titled "The Road to Revolution."

Tax stamp

CITIZENS Review the events of the Boston Tea Party. Make a chart with two columns. In one column, list reasons for colonists' support of the Boston Tea Party. In the other column, list reasons for condemning the event.

★ Publish a pamphlet titled "The Road to Revolution." Include the completed activity of each group.

"Song of Liberty"

The MASSACHUSETTS Song of LIBERTY.

Come swallow your bumpers, ye Tories, and roar, That the Sons of fair Freedom are hamper'd once more; But know that no Cut-throats our

---

Answers to Thinking About Geography

1. A **2.** D **3.** E **4.** B **5.** C
Location: the Mississippi River

Assessment

Chapter Resources Binder For a more comprehensive evaluation of student understanding of this chapter, assign Chapter Tests A and B and/or Extra Unit Questions from Unit 2, pages 7–12 and 43–45.
Computer Test Bank You can use Chapter Tests and Extra Unit Questions to create your own tests for both testing and retesting.

Alternative Assessment

Chapter Resources Binder See the Alternative Assessment booklet in the *Social Studies Educator's Handbook* series.
Portfolio You might meet with students to choose appropriate work from the chapter for inclusion in their portfolios.

Interdisciplinary ACTIVITY

Learning Styles

The following chart indicates the activities appropriate for different learning styles.

Visual Learners
Economists
Artists
Writers
Citizens

Auditory Learners
Musicians
Writers

Kinesthetic Learners
Economists
Artists
Musicians
Citizens

Evaluation

Economists All tax acts mentioned in this chapter must appear on the time line in chronological sequence and be labeled with the correct year. Illustrations should depict goods taxed and/or colonists' reactions to these acts.
Artists Artistic ability need not be a criterion, but cartoons should clearly depict and accurately state the opinions of British officials and the reactions of one or more colonists.
Musicians Musical ability need not be a criterion, but lyrics should be original, should mention several reasons for colonists' feelings, and should convey the mood of the colonists before the American Revolution.
Writers Events associated with the Boston Massacre should be in chronological order. Original dialogue should reflect the moods and feelings both of British soldiers and of colonists involved in the action.
Citizens Charts should be neat and well organized. Reasons for supporting and opposing the Boston Tea Party must be factual and clearly stated.

Lessons	Teaching Resources
1 Early Battles **Objectives** 1. Identify the actions that the Second Continental Congress took in 1776. 2. Identify the strengths and weaknesses of each side in the Revolution. 3. Explain how colonists forced the British to leave Boston.	**Lesson Planner** Cooperative Learning, p. 32 **Student Study Guide** Section 1 Study Guide, p. 62 **Our Multicultural Heritage** *Milestone* Delivering a Message to General Washington, p. 18 **Chapter Resources Binder, Unit 2** *History Through Literature* To His Excellency, General Washington, p. 18
2 Independence Declared **Objectives** 1. Describe how *Common Sense* influenced the colonists. 2. Identify the main ideas of the Declaration of Independence. 3. Describe how Americans responded to the Declaration of Independence.	**Lesson Planner** Cooperative Learning, p. 33 **Student Study Guide** Section 2 Study Guide, p. 63 **Chapter Resources Binder, Unit 2** *Critical Thinking* Distinguishing Fact From Opinion, p. 17 *Skill Application* Comparing Points of View, p. 16
3 Desperate Days **Objectives** 1. Identify the battles that were fought in the Middle States. 2. Explain why the Battle of Saratoga was important. 3. Describe how volunteers from other lands helped the Americans.	**Lesson Planner** Cooperative Learning, p. 34 **Student Study Guide** Section 3 Study Guide, p. 64 **Our Multicultural Heritage** *Biography* Juan de Miralles, Friend of the Revolution, p. 16 **Interdisciplinary Connections:** The American Revolution ■ *Arts* A Uniform Appearance, p. 32 ■ *Sciences* The Cost of War, p. 33 ■ *World* France and Spain Look On, p. 34 ■ *Economics* Financing a Revolution, p. 35 ■ *Civics* Enemies of the State?, p. 36 **Posters** *Crossing the Delaware,* by Oscar de Mejo
4 Other Battlefronts **Objectives** 1. Identify the role that Native Americans played in the Revolution. 2. Identify the battles that Americans won in the West and at sea. 3. Describe how African Americans and women contributed to the war.	**Lesson Planner** Cooperative Learning, p. 35 **Student Study Guide** Section 4 Study Guide, p. 65 **Our Multicultural Heritage** *Biography* Lydia Barrington Darragh, Revolutionary Heroine, p. 17
5 The World Turned Upside Down **Objectives** 1. Explain why fighting shifted to the South in 1778. 2. Describe how Washington forced the British to surrender at Yorktown. 3. Identify the terms of the Treaty of Paris.	**Lesson Planner** Cooperative Learning, p. 36 **Student Study Guide** Section 5 Study Guide, p. 66 **Chapter Resources Binder, Unit 2** *Geography in History* Battle for a Peninsula, pp. 19–20

Multimedia Resources	Additional Resources	Chapter-Level Resources
Transparencies *Fine Art* Battle of Bunker Hill, p. D-31 **Listening to Literature Audiocassettes** *The American Experience* To His Excellency, General Washington, side 2	**Historical Outline Map Book** The Revolutionary War: An Overview, p. 24 The Revolutionary War in the Northeast, p. 25 **Customized Reader** A Frontier Scout in Vermont During the Revolution, article IIIB-9	**Lesson Planner** Activity Based, pp. 37-38 **Student Study Guide** Chapter Study Guide, pp. 67-68 **Chapter Resources Binder** **Unit 2** Vocabulary Building, p. 15 Chapter Test A, pp. 21-23 Chapter Test B, pp. 24-26 Illustration Master, p. 27 Extra Unit Questions, pp. 43-45
Videotapes/Videodiscs *United States History Video Collection* The Declaration of Independence, Vol. 4, Ch. 19	**Voices of Freedom** How the Declaration Was Written, pp. 60-62 **Customized Reader** Diary of a Quaker and a Tory, article IIIA-6	**English Guided Reading** Guided Reading, pp. 11-12 **Spanish Resources** **CD-ROM** *Time Tour* The American Revolution in From Revolution to Republic
Transparencies *Geography and History* Middle Atlantic States, p. I-61 **CD-ROM** *Arts and Entertainment* Patriotic Songs **Videotapes/Videodiscs** *United States History Video Collection* The War for Independence, Vol. 4, Ch. 25	**Voices of Freedom** Lafayette's Impressions of America, p. 63	**Computer Test Bank** Chapter Tests A and B Extra Unit Questions **Guided Reading Audiotapes** Side 2
Transparencies *Geography and History* South Central States, p. I-69 *Geography and History* North Central States, p. I-73	**Historical Outline Map Book** The Revolutionary War in the West, p. 26 **Customized Reader** Nancy Ward, Beloved Woman of the Cherokees, article IIIA-11 A Black Man's Request for His Revolutionary War Pension, article IIIA-1 A Woman's Experience in the American Revolution, article IIIA-2	
Transparencies *Interdisciplinary Connections* The Battle of Yorktown, p. B-43 *Cause and Effect* The American Revolution **Videotapes/Videodiscs** *United States History Video Collection* Vol. 4, Chs. 28, 31	**Voices of Freedom** An Eyewitness at Yorktown, pp. 65-67 **Historical Outline Map Book** The Revolutionary War in the South, p. 27 North America in 1783, p. 28	

Lesson Planner

For a fully developed **Activity-Based** lesson plan for Chapter 6, see the *Lesson Planner,* pages 37–38.

 Chapter Resources

Vocabulary Building The Vocabulary Building worksheet for Chapter 6 from Unit 2, page 15, of the *Chapter Resources* binder can be used as a prereading activity or as a review of chapter vocabulary. (Reteaching/Easy)

 Student Study Guide

Chapter 6 Study Guide Refer students to pages 67–68 of the *Student Study Guide* for the Chapter 6 Study Guide. The study guide can be used for chapter review as well as for reteaching. (Reteaching/Average)

 Guided Reading Audiotapes

Students can use *Guided Reading Audiotapes,* Chapter 6, side 2, to listen to section previews, summaries, and review questions. The tapes might benefit students who are auditory learners, students who have trouble reading, or students acquiring English. Tapes are also available in Spanish. (Reteaching/Easy)

CHAPTER 6

The American Revolution

(1775–1783)

CHAPTER OUTLINE

1 Early Battles

2 Independence Declared

3 Desperate Days

4 Other Battlefronts

5 The World Turned Upside Down

1776 *The Declaration of Independence marked the colonists' formal break from Britain. Delegates used the pen and ink set shown here to sign the Declaration.*

1777 *American victory at the Battle of Saratoga convinced France to help the Patriot cause. The young Frenchman, the Marquis de Lafayette, fought with Washington's army.*

1779 *The Americans enjoyed their greatest naval victory when the Bonhomme Richard defeated the British warship Serapis.*

1775	1776	1777	1778	1779

 WORLD EVENT
1778 France recognizes American independence

158 • Chapter 6

Chapter Time Line
Critical Thinking

Write the following statement on the chalkboard: "Because of the way in which the British government responded to dissatisfaction in the colonies, Britain opened the door to almost a decade of trouble." Invite students to support that statement by referring to the time line. Students can find evidence both in World Event information (for example, "Spain declares war on Great Britain" [1779]) and in captions for the visuals (for example, "The Americans enjoyed their greatest naval victory when the *Bonhomme Richard* defeated the British warship *Serapis*" [1779]).

Chapter Setting

"Gentlemen may cry, 'Peace! peace!'—but there is no peace. The war is actually begun! . . . Our brethren are already in the field! Why stand we here idle? . . . Is life so dear, or peace so sweet, as to be purchased at the price of chains and slavery? Forbid it, Almighty God! I know not what course others may take; but as for me, give me liberty or give me death!"

Patrick Henry's words echoed through St. John's Church in Richmond, Virginia. By March 1775, the 13 colonies stood on the brink of war.

Delegates from across Virginia had gathered at the church to debate what action to take. Some wanted to give Britain one last chance to change its conduct toward the colonies. Others, like Henry, were ready to fight to protect their rights. "There is no longer any room for hope," cried Henry. "We have done everything that could be done to [prevent] the storm which is coming on us now."

Similar debates raged in other colonies. As the British sent more and more troops to Boston, colonists faced a hard decision: Should they accept British actions? Or should they fight for their liberties? In July 1776, colonial leaders took a fateful step. One by one, they voted to form a new nation, the United States of America. To make that nation free and independent, however, colonists had to fight a long, hard war.

ACTIVITY Stage a debate between English colonists in 1775 on the following question: Should the 13 English colonies fight to win independence from Britain?

1781 *The American Revolution ended with the Patriot victory at the Battle of Yorktown. This painting shows the surrender of the British.*

1783 *Britain signed the Treaty of Paris, recognizing the United States as an independent nation. This medal celebrated the coming of peace.*

1779	1780	1781	1782	1783

WORLD EVENT
1779 Spain declares war on Great Britain

WORLD EVENT
1783 Spain regains Florida in Treaty of Paris

Chapter 6 • **159**

Chapter Resources

English Guided Reading Duplicate and distribute to SAE students the Chapter 6 English Guided Reading worksheet on pages 11–12 in the English Guided Reading section of the *Chapter Resources* binder. Students who have difficulty reading also might benefit from using this worksheet. Have students complete the worksheet before they begin reading. You might pair a more fluent student or a student who is a stronger reader with each SAE student to review. (Reteaching/Easy)

Spanish Resources See the Spanish Resources section of the *Chapter Resources* binder.

CD-ROM

Time Tour Access The American Revolution section in From Revolution to Republic on the American Heritage® *History of the United States* CD-ROM. (Enrichment/Average)

ACTIVITY

Guided Instruction Before students plan their strategies, ask: What is the proposition? (The 13 English colonies should fight to win independence from Britain.) Divide students into two teams. One team should determine reasons that support the proposition; the other, opposing reasons. Each team should present its hypotheses, arguments, and conclusions using the formal rules of debate. You might invite language arts classes and/or the debate team to act as judges.

Students Acquiring English
Activity

Students who are learning English or who have weak language skills may have trouble understanding the quoted material in the text. Ask peers with strong language skills to work with SAE students as partners. Have each partner read the quotation aloud and then restate it in his or her own words. Remind peer partners to be alert for idiomatic or archaic expressions that may confuse SAE students. SAE students may copy unfamiliar words and phrases in a journal for review and future reference.

SAE students will also benefit from seeing suggested videotapes that are relevant to the chapter.

Linking Past and Present
Activity

Lead the class in a discussion about why Patrick Henry's rallying cry—"Give me liberty or give me death!" — has become one of the most famous quotations in American history. Ask: What modern patriotic comments might achieve the same kind of lasting fame? Why? Suggest that students begin a notebook listing patriotic expressions that they find inspirational; encourage them to use a dictionary of quotations.

Answer to Caption

Fort Ticonderoga controlled a key route into Canada across Lake Champlain.

Section 1
pp. 160–164

 Bell Ringer

Write the following on the chalkboard: "BRITISH SOLDIERS ATTACK NEW ENGLAND TOWNS: Residents Fight Back!" Have students write down their thoughts about this news. How might residents of other states (beyond New England) react?

Lesson Plan

1. Focus In 1775, the Second Continental Congress tried to prevent a break with Britain. At the same time, however, they established a Continental Army. In this section, students examine the advantages and disadvantages of each side and the early battles in the struggle for independence.
2. Instruct Have students create a chart on the chalkboard listing American and British strengths and weaknesses. When the class chart is completed, have students vote on what they think were the greatest strengths and weaknesses of each side.
3. Close To close the lesson, ask students to write one generalization about the strengths and another about the weaknesses of each side. They should use the chart that the class created during the lesson as a guide for their four statements.

1
Early Battles

FIND OUT
- What actions did the Second Continental Congress take in 1776?
- What were the strengths and weaknesses of each side in the Revolution?
- How did colonists force the British to leave Boston?

VOCABULARY blockade

As darkness fell, the redcoats limped into Boston from Lexington and Concord. All along the route, rebels had fired on them. The events of April 19, 1775, left the British stunned. How had a handful of rebels forced 700 redcoats to retreat? That night, British soldiers grew even more uneasy as they watched rebels set up campfires all around Boston.

In the weeks and months ahead, the campfires remained. They were a clear sign that the quarrel between Britain and its colonies had blazed into war. Many colonists clung to hopes for a peaceful solution to the crisis. The rebels outside Boston, however, were ready to fight.

The Green Mountain Boys

In 1775, the colonies did not have a united army—or even a united government. In each colony, rebels took daring action. Ethan Allen, a Vermont blacksmith known for his strength and fierce temper, flew into a rage when he learned of events in Massachusetts. "I read with horror," he later wrote, of the "bloody attempt at Lexington to enslave America."

Allen led a band of Vermonters, known as the *Green Mountain Boys*, in a surprise attack on Fort Ticonderoga. The fort was located at the southern tip of Lake Champlain. (See the map on page 163.) Allen knew that it had many cannons, which the colonists badly needed.

In early May, the Green Mountain Boys slipped through the morning mists at Fort Ticonderoga. They quickly overpowered the guard on duty and entered the fort. Allen rushed to the room where the British commander slept. "Come out, you old rat!" he shouted.

The commander demanded to know on whose authority Allen acted. "In the name

Ethan Allen Captures Ticonderoga
In May 1775, Ethan Allen and the Green Mountain Boys made a bold attack on Fort Ticonderoga. Here, Allen demands that the British commander surrender. **Geography** *Why was Fort Ticonderoga important?*

Historical Sidelight
Background

When he approached Fort Ticonderoga, Ethan Allen is said to have shouted to its commander, "Come out, you old rat!" Indeed, Allen so stole the spotlight in the capture of the fort that it is sometimes forgotten that he had help—namely, Colonel Benedict Arnold and his troops.

The victory also posed a problem: To whom did the fort now belong? Should it be claimed by New York, in which it was located? By Massachusetts, which had sponsored Arnold? By Connecticut or Vermont, which had sup-ported Allen? As the Second Continental Congress pondered the issue, some leaders even suggested returning the fort to British control. After the Battle of Bunker Hill, however, the lure of the fort's cannons proved too great. General Washington declared that "no Trouble or Expence must be spared to obtain them." Thus, under the supervision of bookseller Henry Knox, 59 guns from Ticonderoga were dragged over 300 miles of mountainous terrain to Boston.

Team-Teaching Suggestion
Language Arts

You might work with a language arts teacher (or a sponsor of the school newspaper) to present a lesson about objectivity in reporting. Then divide students into three groups. Have one group write an article about the surrender of Fort Ticonderoga for a pro-Patriot newspaper, have another group write about the same event for a newspaper in London, and have the third group write about the event in a very objective style. Ask: Which article seems most interesting? Which one seems most like an article that you would read in a newspaper today?

of the Great Jehovah and the Continental Congress!" Allen replied. The commander had no choice but to surrender the fort with its cannons and valuable supply of gunpowder. Allen's success gave the Americans control of a key route into Canada.

Last Efforts for Peace

While the Green Mountain Boys celebrated their victory, delegates from the colonies met at the Second Continental Congress in Philadelphia. Although fighting had begun, most delegates did not want to break with Britain. A few, however, including Sam and John Adams, secretly wanted the colonies to declare independence.

After much debate, the Continental Congress voted to patch up the quarrel with Britain. Delegates sent King George III the **Olive Branch Petition.** In it, they declared their loyalty and asked the king to repeal the Intolerable Acts.

At the same time, the Congress took a bold step. It set up the **Continental Army.** John Adams proposed George Washington of Virginia as commander:

> **❝**I [have] in my mind for that important command...a gentleman whose skill and experience as an officer, whose independent fortune, great talents, and excellent universal character would command the [approval] of all America. **❞**

Washington heard Adams's words. Embarrassed by the praise, he quietly slipped out of the room. In a vote, all delegates approved Washington as commander.

Strengths and Weaknesses

Without wasting any time, Washington left Philadelphia to take charge of the forces around Boston. He faced an uphill struggle. Colonial forces were untrained. They had few cannons, little gunpowder, and no navy.

The British, on the other hand, had highly trained, experienced troops. Britain's navy was the most powerful in the world. Its ships could move soldiers quickly up and down the Atlantic coast.

Still, Britain faced serious problems. Its armies were 3,000 miles (4,800 km) from home. News and supplies took months to travel from Britain to North America. Also, British soldiers risked attacks by colonists once they marched out of the cities into the countryside.

The Americans had certain advantages. They were fighting to defend their homes, farms, lands, and shops. Reuben Stebbins of Williamstown, Massachusetts, was typical of many farmers. When he heard that the British were nearby, he rode off to battle. "We'll see who's goin' t' own this farm!" he cried.

Although few Americans had military training, many owned rifles and were good shots. Also, the colonists had a brilliant leader in George Washington. He demanded—and received—respect from his troops.

Taking a Stand at Bunker Hill

While Washington was riding toward Boston, rebels tightened their circle around the city. The Americans wanted to keep the British from marching out of the city.

At sunset on June 16, 1775, Colonel William Prescott led 1,200 minutemen to take up a position on Bunker Hill in Charlestown, across the river from Boston.

History and You
Patriots used many different flags during the Revolution. Besides the familiar stars and stripes, flags featured a variety of symbols, including a pine cone and an eagle. What symbols would you use to represent the United States today?

 Lesson Planner

For a developed **Cooperative Learning** lesson plan, see the *Lesson Planner,* page 32.

Historical Outline Map Book

Historical Outline Map Duplicate and distribute the maps, The Revolutionary War: An Overview, and The Revolutionary War in the Northeast, on pages 24–25 of the *American History Historical Outline Map Book.* Lesson ideas for these maps can be found on pages T7–T8. (Reteaching/Average)

Critical Thinking
Comparing

Have students write essays in which they compare the First Continental Congress with the Second Continental Congress. Questions students should consider include (a) How were the situations facing the delegates to the two congresses different? (b) Why did the Second Continental Congress act more boldly?

Our Multicultural Heritage
Background

Continental soldiers from different colonies did not want to serve in the same regiments at first. New Englanders mistrusted Virginians, whom they called "buckskins" because General Daniel Morgan's recruits wore the fringed hunting shirts of the frontier. Pennsylvanians often were suspicious of "Yankees," or New England residents.

Battle of Bunker Hill *American forces fought fiercely but could not prevent the British from taking Bunker Hill. This painting by Winthrop Chandler gives a bird's-eye view of this first major battle of the Revolution.* **Geography** *Why did the Americans take up a position on a hill?*

From there, they could fire on British ships in Boston harbor.

"Dig, men, dig." Prescott soon saw that nearby Breed's Hill was a better position. He had his men dig trenches there. "Dig, men, dig," he urged. Prescott knew that the trenches must be ready before dawn. Otherwise, the British could force him off the hill.

At sunrise, the British general, William Howe, spotted the Americans. He ferried about 2,400 redcoats across the harbor to Charlestown. The British then had to cross rough fields and climb Breed's Hill. Each soldier carried a heavy pack that weighed about 125 pounds. It was hot, exhausting work, and the soldiers moved slowly.

From their trenches, the Americans watched the British approach. Because the colonists had very little gunpowder, their commanders warned, "Don't shoot until you see the whites of their eyes!"

The deadly attack. As the enemy advanced, "We gave them such a hot fire that they were obliged to retire nearly 150 yards before they could rally," recalled Colonel Prescott. Twice, the British advanced up the hill. Twice, they had to retreat under deadly fire.

On the third try, the British pushed over the top. By then, the colonists had run out of gunpowder. The British took both Bunker Hill and Breed's Hill. They paid a high price for their victory, however. "The day ended in glory," noted a British officer, "but the loss was uncommon in officers for the number engaged." More than 1,000 redcoats lay dead or wounded. American losses numbered 400.

The ***Battle of Bunker Hill*** was the first major battle of the Revolution. It proved that the Americans could fight bravely. It also showed that the British would not be easy to defeat.

162 • Chapter 6

Redcoats Leave Boston

Washington finally reached Boston in midsummer. There, he found about 16,000 troops camped in huts and tents at the edge of the city. Their weapons ranged from rifles to swords made by local blacksmiths.

General Washington quickly began to turn raw recruits into a trained army. His job was especially difficult because soldiers from different colonies mistrusted one another. "Connecticut wants no Massachusetts men in her corps," he wrote. And "Massachusetts thinks there is no necessity for a Rhode Islander to be introduced into her [ranks]." Slowly, Washington won the loyalty of his troops. They, in turn, learned to take orders and work together.

By January 1776, the Continental Army had a firm grip around Boston. From Ticonderoga, soldiers had dragged cannons on sleds across the mountains. Washington had the cannons placed on Dorchester Heights, overlooking Boston and its harbor. General Howe realized that he could not overpower the Americans. In March 1776, he and his troops sailed from Boston to Halifax, Canada.

Although the British left New England, they had not given up. King George III ordered a blockade of all colonial ports. A **blockade** is the shutting off of a port to keep people or supplies from moving in or out. The king also hired Hessian troops from Germany to help fight the colonists.

March on Canada

Some Americans wanted to attack the British in Canada. They hoped to win support from French Canadians, who were not happy under British rule.

In the fall of 1775, two American armies moved north into Canada. (See the map at right.) Richard Montgomery led one army from Fort Ticonderoga to Montreal. He seized that city in November 1775. He then moved toward the city of Quebec.

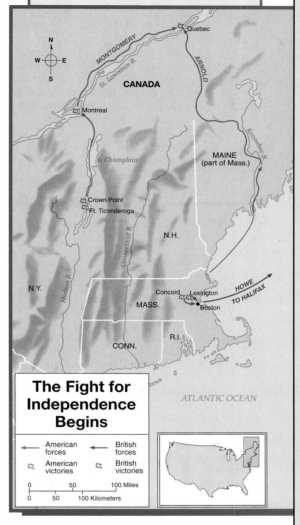

The Fight for Independence Begins

| American forces | British forces |
| ☆ American victories | ☆ British victories |

0   50   100 Miles
0 50 100 Kilometers

ATLANTIC OCEAN

Chapter 6 • **163**

MAP STUDY

The first clashes of the Revolution took place in the northern colonies and in Canada.

1. *In which direction did Benedict Arnold march to reach Quebec?*
2. *About how far did Montgomery have to travel from Fort Ticonderoga to Quebec?*
3. **Analyzing Information** *Based on the map, which American commander would have had a harder time reaching Quebec? Explain.*

Answers to Map Study

1. north to northwest **2.** about 250 miles (405 km) **3.** Arnold; Montgomery's forces took a route that paralleled the St. Lawrence River, but Arnold's forces made their way over land, through the Maine woods.

 Our Multicultural Heritage

Milestone Have students read Delivering a Message to General Washington, on page 18 of the *Our Multicultural Heritage* booklet. (Enrichment/Easy)

 Audiocassettes

Listening to Literature Audiocassettes Have students listen to the poem, To His Excellency, General Washington (side 2, 3:16), from *Listening to Literature Audiocassettes, The American Experience.* The selection expresses Phillis Wheatley's admiration for the hero of the Revolution. See the Audiocassette Guide for previewing information and suggested activities. (Enrichment/Challenging)

 Chapter Resources

History Through Literature To show students how Patriots often felt about George Washington — or to provide a text for the audiocassette named above — duplicate and distribute the worksheet, To His Excellency, General Washington, from Unit 2, page 18, of the *Chapter Resources* binder. (Enrichment/Challenging)

Connections With Geography
Activity

Have students do further research on the role that geography played in the capture of Fort Ticonderoga, the Battle of Bunker Hill, or the invasion of Canada. Students should describe the geographic features of the area and explain how geography affected the outcome of the event. Have them present their findings in brief reports, using maps to illustrate.

Connections With the World
Background

Because French Canadians were satisfied with the Quebec Act, they did not openly support the Americans. The Quebec Act was passed by Parliament in 1774, at the same time as the Intolerable Acts. However, the Quebec Act did not punish; instead, it protected the rights, religion, and language of the French who lived in this region of Canada.

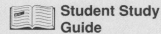
Section 1 Study Guide Have students use the Section 1 Study Guide on page 62 of the *Student Study Guide* to review and reinforce the content of this section. (Reteaching/Average)

Guided Instruction Before students write their diary entries, briefly review the concepts of purpose and audience. Remind them that Washington is writing a private journal; thus, he can be more candid about the problems that he envisions than if he were writing for publication. Encourage students to share their fictional diary entries.

Section 2
pp. 164–168

Bell Ringer

Ask students to explain what the term *human rights* means to them. Have the class brainstorm to compile a list of what they consider to be "reasonable" human rights.

Lesson Plan

1. Focus After war broke out, more and more Americans began to favor independence. The Continental Congress declared independence in 1776. In this section, students learn about the events leading up to the Declaration of Independence, the con-

---

Benedict Arnold led the second army north through Maine. He was supposed to join forces with Montgomery in Quebec.

Arnold and his troops had a terrible journey through the Maine woods in winter. Rainstorms followed by freezing nights coated their clothes with ice. Supplies ran so low that soldiers survived only by eating boiled bark and shoe leather. Finally, Arnold reached Quebec. He was disappointed, however. French Canadians did not support the Americans.

In a blinding snowstorm on December 31, 1775, the Americans attacked Quebec. Montgomery was killed, and Arnold was wounded. The Americans failed to take the city. They stayed outside Quebec until May 1776, when the British landed new forces in Canada. At last, weakened by disease and hunger, the Americans withdrew, leaving Canada to the British.

SECTION 1 REVIEW

1. **Locate:** (a) Fort Ticonderoga, (b) Boston, (c) Montreal, (d) Quebec.
2. **Identify:** (a) Ethan Allen, (b) Green Mountain Boys, (c) Olive Branch Petition, (d) Continental Army, (e) Battle of Bunker Hill, (f) Benedict Arnold.
3. **Define:** blockade.
4. Describe three actions taken by the Second Continental Congress.
5. What did the Battle of Bunker Hill reveal about each side?
6. **CRITICAL THINKING Comparing** Compare the strengths and weaknesses of the British and Americans at the start of the war.

ACTIVITY Writing to Learn

Imagine that you have George Washington's job at the beginning of the American Revolution. Write several diary entries describing the task you face as commander of the Continental Army.

2
Independence Declared

FIND OUT
- How did *Common Sense* influence the colonists?
- What are the main ideas of the Declaration of Independence?
- How did Americans respond to the Declaration of Independence?

VOCABULARY traitor

George III was furious when he heard about the Olive Branch Petition. The colonies, he raged, are in a "desperate [plot] to establish an independent empire!" He vowed to bring the rebels to justice.

Colonists learned of the king's response in November 1775. At first, most still hoped to patch up the quarrel with Britain. As the months passed, however, attitudes changed. More and more colonists spoke openly of breaking away from Britain.

Common Sense

In January 1776, a pamphlet appeared on the streets of Philadelphia. "I offer nothing more than simple facts, plain arguments, and common sense," said its author, Thomas Paine. The pamphlet, *Common Sense,* created a great stir. Paine's "plain arguments" boldly urged the colonies to declare their independence.

Paine had only recently arrived from England. Still, he shared the colonists' desire for liberty. In *Common Sense,* he showed how colonists had nothing to gain from staying under British rule. He pointed out that there were many disadvantages in their current situation:

Answers to Section 1 Review

1. See the map on p. 163.
2. (a) Ethan Allen, p. 160, (b) Green Mountain Boys, p. 160, (c) Olive Branch Petition, p. 161, (d) Continental Army, p. 161, (e) Battle of Bunker Hill, p. 162, (f) Benedict Arnold, p. 164
3. blockade, p. 163
4. The Second Continental Congress sent the Olive Branch Petition to George III, set up the Continental Army, and chose Washington as its commander.

5. It revealed that the Americans could fight bravely under fire, but it also showed that the British would not be easy to defeat.
6. Possible Answer: The British had an experienced, well-trained army and the world's most powerful navy. However, they were fighting a war in a hostile country 3,000 miles from home. The American troops were untrained and poorly supplied, but they were highly motivated and commanded by George Washington, who was a skilled leader.

"[It is foolish]. . . to be always running three or four thousand miles with a tale or petition, waiting four or five months for an answer, which when obtained requires five or six more to explain it in."

Since King George had just rejected the Olive Branch Petition, that argument made sense to many colonists.

Paine also attacked the idea of having kings and queens as rulers. One honest man, he insisted, was worth more "in the sight of God than all the crowned ruffians that ever lived."

In *Common Sense,* Paine's reasoning was so clear that he won many colonists to the idea of independence. In six months, more than 500,000 copies were printed and sold. "*Common Sense* is working a powerful change in the minds of men," George Washington observed. It even changed the general's own habits. Until 1776, Washington followed the custom of toasting the king at official dinners. After reading Paine's pamphlet, he ended this practice.

The Fateful Step

Common Sense affected members of the Continental Congress, too. In June 1776, Richard Henry Lee of Virginia offered a resolution saying that "these United Colonies are, and of right ought to be, free and independent States."

Delegates faced a difficult decision. There could be no turning back if they declared independence. If they fell into British hands, they would be hanged as traitors. A **traitor** is a person who betrays his or her country.

Writing the Declaration. The delegates took a fateful step. They chose a committee to draw up a declaration of independence. The committee included John Adams, Benjamin Franklin, Thomas Jefferson, Robert Livingston, and Roger Sherman. Their job was to tell the world why the colonies were

Down With the King! In July 1776, angry New Yorkers tore down a statue of King George III. Patriots, like Laura Wolcott (at right), used lead from the statue to make cartridges for Washington's army. **American Traditions** How did Thomas Paine's writings inflame American opinion against the king?

Chapter 6 • **165**

tent of the document, and colonial reactions to it.

2. Instruct Ask students to list reasons why the American colonies would want to separate from Britain, based on their study of Chapter 5. After they read this section, have students check their lists against the list of grievances in the Declaration of Independence.

3. Close To close the lesson, ask students the following questions about the Declaration of Independence: (a) What were the colonial grievances against the king? (b) What was the colonists' solution?

Lesson Planner

For a developed **Cooperative Learning** lesson plan, see the *Lesson Planner,* page 33.

Answer to Caption

Paine attacked the idea of rule by kings and queens, calling them "crowned ruffians." His common-sense arguments persuaded many colonists.

Chapter Resources

Critical Thinking Duplicate and distribute the worksheet, Distinguishing Fact From Opinion, from Unit 2, page 17, of the *Chapter Resources* binder. The worksheet allows students to examine in detail excerpts from *Common Sense.* (Enrichment/Average)

Connections With the World
Background

After the American Revolution, Thomas Paine spent 15 years in England and France. He wrote to persuade the British to change their government from a monarchy to a republic. He also wrote in support of the French Revolution (although he opposed the execution of the king). Paine returned to America in 1802 and died in New York City in 1809. In 1819, his remains were removed to his native England.

Critical Thinking
Analyzing Ideas

John Locke, a British philosopher of the late 1600s, wrote that oppressed people had the right to revolt against an unjust government. Have students find one or more passages in the Declaration of Independence that suggest Locke's influence on Jefferson's thinking. Encourage them to explain their choices.

Connections With Literature
Background

Congress opposed anything British. In fact, it once considered making Hebrew the official language of the new country. Hebrew was one of the main languages of the Bible (and the language of the Israelites, with whom many delegates felt a spiritual kinship), whereas English was the language of Britain.

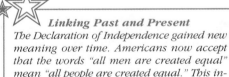

Declaring Independence *Thomas Jefferson labored many hours perfecting the Declaration of Independence. Here, Jefferson and other committee members present the Declaration to the Continental Congress. The delegates' signatures on the document appear at right.* **American Traditions** *What was the purpose of the Declaration of Independence?*

breaking away from Britain. The committee asked Jefferson to write the document.

Jefferson was one of the youngest delegates. A quiet man, he spoke little at formal meetings. But among friends, he liked to sprawl in a chair with his long legs stretched out and talk for hours. In late June, Jefferson completed the declaration, and it was read to the Congress.

The vote. On July 2, the Continental Congress voted that the 13 colonies were "free and independent States." Two days later, on July 4, 1776, the delegates accepted the ***Declaration of Independence.*** Since then, Americans have celebrated July 4th as Independence Day.

John Hancock, president of the Continental Congress, signed the Declaration first. He penned his signature boldly, in large,

clear letters. "There," he said, "I guess King George will be able to read that."

The Declaration

Across the colonies, people read the Declaration of Independence. The document has three main parts. (The complete Declaration

> *Linking Past and Present*
> The Declaration of Independence gained new meaning over time. Americans now accept that the words "all men are created equal" mean "all people are created equal." This includes women and African Americans, as well as minorities of all kinds.

of Independence is printed in the Reference Section.)

Basic rights. The first part of the Declaration describes the basic rights on which the nation was founded. In bold, ringing words, Jefferson wrote:

66 We hold these truths to be self-evident, that all men are created equal, that they are endowed by their Creator with certain unalienable rights, that among these are life, liberty, and the pursuit of happiness. 99

How do people protect these rights? By forming governments, the Declaration says. Governments can exist only if they have the "consent of the governed." If a government takes away its citizens' rights, then it is the people's "right [and] duty, to throw off such government, and provide new guards for their future security."

British wrongs. The second part of the Declaration lists the wrongs committed by Britain. Jefferson carefully showed how George III had abused his power. He condemned the king for disbanding colonial legislatures and for sending troops to the colonies in times of peace. He listed other wrongs to show why the colonists had the right to rebel.

An independent nation. The last part of the Declaration announces that the colonies had become "the United States of America." All ties with Britain were cut. As a free and independent nation, the United States could make alliances and trade with other countries.

Choosing Sides

John Dunlap of Philadelphia printed the Declaration of Independence on July 4, 1776. Later, Mary Katherine Goddard, a Baltimore printer, produced the first copies that included the names of all the signers. As colonists studied the document, they had to decide what course to take.

Opinion was divided. Some colonists were **Patriots,** people who supported independence. Others were **Loyalists,** people who remained loyal to Britain. Many families were split. Ben Franklin, for example, was a Patriot. His son, the royal governor of New Jersey, supported King George.

During the American Revolution, tens of thousands of people supported the British. Loyalists included wealthy merchants and former officials of the royal government. However, many farmers and craftsworkers were Loyalists, too. There were more Loyalists in the Middle States and the South than in New England.

Life was difficult for Loyalists everywhere. Patriots tarred and feathered people known to favor the British. Many Loyalists fled to England or Canada. Others found shelter in cities controlled by the British. Those who fled lost their homes, stores, and farms.

SECTION 2 REVIEW

1. **Identify:** (a) Thomas Paine, (b) Richard Henry Lee, (c) Thomas Jefferson, (d) Declaration of Independence, (e) Mary Katherine Goddard, (f) Patriot, (g) Loyalist.
2. **Define:** traitor.
3. What arguments did Thomas Paine offer in favor of independence?
4. Describe the three main parts of the Declaration of Independence.
5. Why was life difficult for Loyalists during the Revolution?
6. CRITICAL THINKING **Comparing** Compare the viewpoints of Patriots and Loyalists at the outbreak of the Revolution.

 Writing to Learn

Imagine that you are one of the delegates to the Continental Congress. Write a letter to a friend describing your feelings about signing the Declaration of Independence.

Answers to Section 2 Review

1. (a) Thomas Paine, p. 164, (b) Richard Henry Lee, p. 165, (c) Thomas Jefferson, p. 165, (d) Declaration of Independence, p. 166, (e) Mary Katherine Goddard, p. 167, (f) Patriot, p. 167, (g) Loyalist, p. 167
2. traitor, p. 165
3. It was foolish for Americans to remain connected to Britain because Britain was so far away; kings and queens had no right to rule ordinary people.
4. The first part explains the rights—to life, liberty, and the pursuit of happiness—on

which the nation is founded; it states that the government must protect those rights, or else the people have the right to rebel. The second part lists the reasons for the colonists' break from Britain. The third part declares the colonies to be an independent nation.
5. Possible Answers: Loyalists faced family conflicts with relatives who supported independence; anti-British feeling led to the tarring and feathering of some Loyalists and the confiscation of the property of those who fled.

6. Possible Answer: Patriots: The colonies had to break away because Britain had violated colonists' rights and therefore could not be trusted or expected to change. Loyalists: If colonists were willing to compromise, peace could be restored; besides, the colonies needed Britain.

Chapter Resources

Skill Application For additional practice, duplicate and distribute the worksheet, Using a Primary Source, from Unit 2, page 16, of the *Chapter Resources* binder. (Reteaching/Average)

Answers to Skill Lesson

1. (a) She wants him to make sure that women's rights are included in the laws that they are proposing. (b) Adams replies that he and his male associates are not about to loosen their political control. (c) women

2. (a) She believes that all men are potential tyrants. (b) Adams does not agree; he believes that men are masters in name only.

3. (a) Men held political power and were reluctant to grant women rights. At least some women opposed this injustice enough to put their feelings in writing. (b) Possible Answer: Yes; John and Abigail Adams had firsthand knowledge of the subject. While their views differ, they support their opinions with valid arguments.

ACTIVITY

Guided Instruction Before students begin writing their letters, have them brainstorm and list arguments supporting or opposing the idea of women in combat. Explain that the letters must state an opinion and support that opinion with relevant arguments. When revising, have students use the criteria for primary sources discussed in this feature to evaluate the reliability of their letters.

CRITICAL THINKING SKILLS
Comparing Points of View

A primary source, or firsthand account, reflects the author's point of view. Two people writing about the same subject can have different points of view.

The letters below were written by Abigail and John Adams. During the Revolution, John Adams was away from home for long periods. His wife, Abigail, wrote to him often. When the Continental Congress was preparing the Declaration of Independence, she wrote her husband the first letter reprinted below. The second letter is John Adams's reply.

1. Study the contents of each source. (a) What does Abigail Adams want her husband to do? (b) What is John Adams's response to her request? (c) Who is John Adams referring to with the words "another tribe, more numerous and powerful than all the rest"?

2. Compare the points of view. (a) What does Abigail Adams think men are like? (b) Does John Adams agree with his wife's view? Explain.

3. Evaluate the usefulness of the sources. (a) What do these letters tell you about American society in 1776? (b) Do you think these letters are a reliable source of information? Explain.

ACTIVITY
Write a letter expressing your views about whether women in the armed forces should be allowed to take part in combat. Would your letter be a reliable primary source 100 years from now? Explain.

Abigail Adams wrote:

❝I long to hear that you have declared independence. And by the way, in the new code of laws that I suppose you will make, I wish you would remember the ladies and be more generous and favorable to them than your ancestors. Do not put such unlimited power in the hands of husbands. Remember, all men would be tyrants if they could. If particular care and attention is not paid to the ladies, we are determined to stir up a rebellion and will not regard ourselves as bound by any laws in which we have had no voice or representation.❞

John Adams replied:

❝As to your extraordinary code of laws, I can't help laughing. We have been told that our struggle has loosened the bonds of government everywhere, that children and apprentices were disobedient, that schools and colleges had grown turbulent, that Indians slighted their guardians and negroes grow insolent to their masters. But your letter was the first hint that another tribe, more numerous and powerful than all the rest, had grown discontented.

Depend upon it, we know better than to repeal our masculine systems. Although they are in full force, you know they are little more than theory. . . . In practice, you know, we are the subjects. We have only the title of masters, and rather than give this up, which would subject us completely to the power of the petticoat, I hope General Washington and all our brave heroes would fight.❞

Students Acquiring English Activity

SAE students might benefit by being paired with more advanced students to work on the skill lesson and its activity. Partners might help SAE students to comprehend the complexity of the ideas expressed in the longer sentences. Discussion between the partners also could bring out the strength of the convictions that underlie the intimate, humorous tone of each letter.

3
Desperate Days

FIND OUT
- What battles were fought in the Middle States?
- Why was the Battle of Saratoga important?
- How did volunteers from other lands help the Americans?

VOCABULARY cavalry, neutral

One morning in late June 1776, rifleman Daniel McCurtin glanced out his window at New York harbor. A startling sight met his eyes. He saw "something resembling a wood of pine trees trimmed." As he watched, the forest moved across the water. Suddenly, he realized that the trees were the masts of ships!

❝I could not believe my eyes... when in about ten minutes, the whole bay was full of shipping as ever it could be. I declare that I thought all London was afloat.❞

By noon, a British fleet was anchored offshore. General Howe and his redcoats had arrived in force.

The arrival of the British fleet in New York marked a new stage in the war. Most early battles of the American Revolution were fought in New England. In mid-1776, the heavy fighting shifted to the Middle States. There, the Continental Army suffered through the worst days of the war.

Campaign in New York

Washington had expected Howe's attack and had led his forces south from Boston to New York City. His raw army, however, was no match for the British. Howe had about 34,000 troops and 10,000 sailors. He also had ships to ferry them ashore. Washington had fewer than 20,000 poorly trained troops. Worse, he had no navy.

Washington did not know exactly where Howe would land. He sent some forces to Long Island. Others he sent to Manhattan.

On the run. In August, Howe's army pushed ashore on Long Island. In the ***Battle of Long Island,*** more than 1,400 Americans were killed, wounded, or captured. The rest retreated to Manhattan. The British followed. To avoid capture, Washington hurried north.

Pursuing General Washington
In November 1776, the Continental Army retreated from New York into New Jersey. The British followed closely behind. This sketch shows British troops landing at Fort Lee, New Jersey. **Geography** *What river did the two armies have to cross to reach New Jersey?*

Chapter 6 • **169**

Section 3
pp. 169–174

Bell Ringer

Write the following statement on the chalkboard: "These are the times that try men's souls." Ask: What kinds of situations might make people wonder if they've made the right decision? How might they react?

Lesson Plan

1. Focus The early stages of the American Revolution included several major setbacks for American forces in the Middle Atlantic states. However, a victory at Saratoga marked a turning point in the war. In this section, students read about the war in the Middle States from 1776 to 1778.

2. Instruct On separate index cards, write the names of key persons and terms from this section. Be certain that there is one card for each class member. Distribute the cards and have each student describe that person or term on the other side of the card. Collect the cards; then divide the class into teams. Have a volunteer read the description from the top card. The first student who correctly identifies the term described wins 10 points for the team and reads the next description. Teams lose 5 points for incorrect answers. Continue until all cards have been correctly identified.

Historical Sidelight
Background

The beaten colonial forces withdrew first to Brooklyn Heights. Washington, however, felt that Howe's forces would press their advantage. Therefore, Washington rounded up every fishing boat, barge, and rowboat that he could find. On the night of August 29, during a heavy rain and under cover of fog, Washington's troops—a force of over 10,000— were ferried across the river to Manhattan.

Team-Teaching Suggestion
Music

You might work with a music teacher to present a lesson about the subject matter and morale-boosting effects that martial music can have on military units. Concentrate on colonial music that inspired the Patriots.

3. Close To close the lesson, have the class decide on the most important facts or ideas to remember from each subsection.

Lesson Planner

For a developed **Cooperative Learning** lesson plan, see the *Lesson Planner,* page 34.

Answers to Map Study

1. St. Leger's forces traveled southwest along the St. Lawrence River. They crossed Lake Ontario to Fort Oswego; then they headed east, past Fort Stanwix, and met Arnold's forces at Oriskany. **2.** the British **3.** The British gained control of Philadelphia in 1777, and Patriots may have feared harsh treatment at the hands of the British forces.

 Transparencies

Geography and History Use the transparency set, Middle Atlantic States, on page I-61 of *American History Transparencies.* The base map and overlay 1 illustrate the importance of topographic features of this region. Teaching suggestions can be found on page I-9. (Enrichment/Average)

 CD-ROM

Arts and Entertainment Access the Patriotic Songs section in Music on the American Heritage® *History of the United States* CD-ROM. (Enrichment/ Easy)

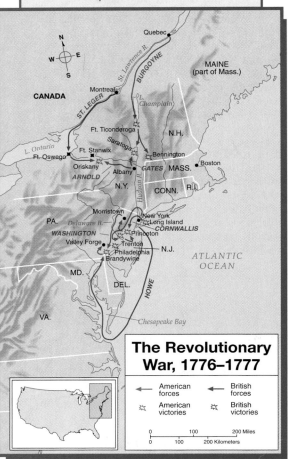

M A P   S T U D Y

In 1776 and 1777, American and British forces fought many battles over a large land area. An American victory at the Battle of Saratoga in October 1777 marked a major turning point of the war.
1. What route did St. Leger's army take after leaving Montreal?
2. Who won the Battle of Brandywine?
3. **Understanding Causes and Effects** Based on the map, why do you think many Patriots left Philadelphia in 1777?

The Revolutionary War, 1776–1777

← American forces   ← British forces
☆ American victories   ☆ British victories

0   100   200 Miles
0   100   200 Kilometers

Throughout the autumn, Washington fought a series of battles with Howe's army. In November, he crossed the Hudson River into New Jersey. Pursued by the British, the Americans retreated across the Delaware River into Pennsylvania. (See the map at left.)

Nathan Hale. During the campaign for New York, Washington needed information about Howe's forces. Nathan Hale, a young Connecticut officer, slipped behind British lines and returned with the details. Soon after, the British captured Hale. They tried and condemned him to death. As Hale walked to the gallows, he is said to have declared: "I only regret that I have but one life to lose for my country."

New Hope for Americans

Months of campaigning took a toll on the Continental Army. In December 1776, Washington described his troops as sick, dirty, and "so thinly clad as to be unfit for service." Every day, soldiers fled camp to return home. Washington wrote to his brother: "I am wearied to death. I think the game is pretty near up."

The Crisis. Thomas Paine had retreated with the army through New Jersey. Once again, he took up his pen. This time, he wrote *The Crisis,* urging Americans to support the army.

❝These are the times that try men's souls. The summer soldier and the sunshine patriot will, in this crisis, shrink from the service of his country; but he that stands it *now* deserves the love and thanks of man and woman.❞

Grateful for Paine's inspiring words, Washington had *The Crisis* read aloud to his troops.

A bold move. The Americans needed more than words to help their cause, how-

---

Team-Teaching Suggestion
Language Arts

You might work with a language arts teacher to present a lesson about the effective use of metaphors. Discuss Paine's use of metaphor in *The Crisis* (for example, "the *summer* soldier and the *sunshine* patriot"). Then have students create metaphors that can be applied to individuals or to events discussed in this section.

Historical Sidelight
Background

Nathan Hale, born in 1755, was barely out of his teens when he passed into American legend. He graduated from Yale in 1773 and taught school until fighting broke out; he then joined the Connecticut militia, followed by service in the Continental Army. According to the legend of his final mission, Hale was captured while returning from gathering information under the identity of a Dutch schoolteacher.

ever. General Washington decided on a bold move—a surprise attack on Trenton.

On Christmas night, Washington secretly led his troops across the icy Delaware River. Soldiers shivered as spray from the river froze on their faces. Once ashore, they marched through swirling snow. "Soldiers, keep by your officers," Washington urged.

Early on December 26, the Americans surprised the Hessian troops guarding Trenton and took most of them prisoner. An American summed up the **Battle of Trenton:** "Hessian population of Trenton at 8 A.M.— 1,408 men and 39 officers; Hessian population at 9 A.M.— 0."

Cheered by victory. British General Charles Cornwallis set out at once to retake Trenton and capture Washington. Late on January 2, 1777, he saw the lights of Washington's campfires. "At last we have run down the old fox," he said, "and we will bag him in the morning."

Washington fooled Cornwallis. He left the fires burning and slipped behind British lines to attack Princeton. There, the Continental Army won another victory. From Princeton, Washington moved to Morristown, where the army spent the winter. The victories at Trenton and Princeton gave the Americans new hope.

A New British Strategy

In London, British officials were dismayed by the army's failure to crush the rebels. Early in 1777, General John Burgoyne (buhr GOIN) presented George III with a new plan for victory. If British troops cut off New England from the other colonies, he argued, the war would soon be over.

Burgoyne wanted three British armies to march on Albany from different directions. They would crush American forces there. Then, in control of the Hudson River, the British could stop the flow of soldiers and supplies from New England to Washington.

ART GALLERY
OUR COMMON HERITAGE

OSCAR DE MEJO
Crossing the Delaware, 1986

On Christmas Eve 1776, Washington led his troops across the icy Delaware River to surprise Hessian troops dug in at Trenton, New Jersey. In this striking painting, Oscar de Mejo, an Italian-born American artist, captures the drama of Washington's crossing. De Mejo has a deep interest in American history and has painted many scenes from the nation's past. **The Arts** What impression does this painting give of George Washington?

Chapter 6 • **171**

Art Gallery Posters

Crossing the Delaware, by Oscar de Mejo, appears in poster form in the *Art Gallery: Our Common Heritage Posters.* Lesson Suggestions for the poster are available in the Teacher's Guide.

Answer to Art Gallery: Our Common Heritage

Possible Answer: It shows Washington as a bold, decisive leader. He is looking directly at the viewer, holding his sword in one hand and pointing with the other.

  ### Videotapes/ Videodiscs

United States History Video Collection Use the video segment "The War for Independence" from Volume 4, *The American Revolution*, to enhance students' understanding of military aspects of the Revolutionary War. Approx. running time 3:00 min. (Enrichment/Average) Vol. 4, Ch. 25

Chapter 25   Play

Critical Thinking
Understanding Causes and Effects

Have students imagine that they are Hessians who have just been captured in Trenton. Ask: How would you explain the fact that you were taken so easily? What do you think will happen to you as a captive—and when you are released?

Historical Sidelight
Background

General Burgoyne, nicknamed "Gentleman Johnny," was known for his sense of humor and his genuine concern for his troops. Another officer wrote that Burgoyne "engrossed their warmest attachment . . . idolized by the army, his orders appearing more like recommending subordination than enforcing it . . . he was the soldier's friend." Besides being a general, Burgoyne was also a playwright, socialite, and politician, having served in Parliament.

Brandywine and Germantown. Burgoyne's plan called for General Howe to march on Albany from New York City. George III, however, wanted Howe to capture Philadelphia first.

In July 1777, Howe sailed from New York to the Chesapeake Bay. (See the map on page 170.) Despite Washington's efforts to stop him, Howe captured Philadelphia. He then went on to defeat the Americans at the battles of Brandywine and Germantown. Howe now retired to comfortable quarters in Philadelphia for the winter. Washington retreated to Valley Forge, where he set up his own makeshift camp.

Meanwhile, two other British armies under Barry St. Leger (lay ZHAIR) and Burgoyne marched from Canada toward Albany. St. Leger tried to take Fort Stanwix. However, Benedict Arnold drove him back with a strong American army.

Success at Saratoga. Only Burgoyne was left to march on Albany. His army moved slowly because it had many heavy baggage carts to drag through the woods. To slow Burgoyne further, Patriots cut down trees to block the route and dammed up streams to create swampy bogs.

Burgoyne retook Fort Ticonderoga. He then sent troops into Vermont to find food and horses. Patriots attacked the redcoats. At the Battle of Bennington, they wounded or captured nearly 1,000 British.

Burgoyne's troubles grew. The Green Mountain Boys hurried into New York to help the American forces. At the village of Saratoga, the Americans surrounded the British. When Burgoyne tried to break free, the Americans beat him back. Realizing he was trapped, Burgoyne surrendered his army to the Americans on October 17, 1777.

A Powerful Ally

The American victory at the ***Battle of Saratoga*** was a turning point in the war. It ended the British threat to New England. It

also boosted American spirits at a time when Washington's army was suffering defeats in Pennsylvania. Most important, it convinced France to become an ally of the United States.

In 1776, the Continental Congress had sent Benjamin Franklin to Paris. His job was to persuade the French king, Louis XVI, to help the Americans with weapons and other badly needed supplies. The Congress also wanted France to declare war on Britain. France had a strong navy that could stand up to the British.

The French were still angry about their defeat by the British in the French and Indian War. But Louis XVI did not want to help the colonists openly unless he was sure they could win. Saratoga provided that proof.

In February 1778, France became the first nation to sign a treaty with the United States. In it, Louis XVI recognized the new nation and agreed to provide military aid.

Cold Winter at Valley Forge

French aid arrived too late to help Washington's ragged army at Valley Forge. During the long, cold winter of 1777–1778, the Continental Army suffered severe hardships in Pennsylvania.

American soldiers shivered in damp, drafty huts. Many slept on the frozen ground. They had little or no warm clothing. Some soldiers stood on guard wrapped only in blankets. Many had no shoes, and they wrapped bits of cloth around their feet. As the bitter winter wore on, soldiers suffered from frostbite and disease. An army surgeon from Connecticut wrote about the suffering:

66 There comes a Soldier, his bare feet are seen thro his worn-out stockings, his Breeches not sufficient to cover his nakedness. . . his whole appearance pictures a person forsaken & discouraged. 99

Cooperative Learning Activity

Tell students to imagine that it is the bitter winter of 1777–1778. George Washington, camped at Valley Forge, is desperately in need of new recruits. Divide students into groups of three or four; then have them create recruitment posters for a local regiment or for Washington's army at Valley Forge. Posters should focus on the benefits of service to the American cause, warn about the consequences of defeat, and/or describe the benefits of victory. Students may use one of the patriotic quotations in this chapter. Encourage students to do additional research to find ideas or information for their posters. You might work with students to prepare a display of the finished posters.

Our Multicultural Heritage Background

Lafayette was only 20 years old when he arrived in America. The French troops under his command included a force of 600 black Haitian soldiers.

The outgoing von Steuben wrote a book, *Regulations for the Order and Discipline of Troops of the United States.* It became the first official manual for the U.S. Army.

CONNECTIONS

ARTS   SCIENCES   **GEOGRAPHY**   WORLD   ECONOMICS   CIVICS

Through the Wilderness to Saratoga

The plan seemed simple. All General Burgoyne had to do was lead his men from Canada to Albany. There, they would meet up with two other British forces. They would take control of the Hudson River and drive a wedge between New England and the rest of the colonies. The rebellion, Burgoyne assured his superiors, would soon be over.

Burgoyne set out down Lake Champlain with 9,500 men in June 1777. He was sure he would be in Albany by the end of summer. He did not realize that his planned route of attack crossed lakes, swamps, mountains, and trackless forests. His splendidly equipped army was ill suited to fighting a war in a wilderness.

At first, things went well for the British. They captured Fort Ticonderoga with little opposition. Burgoyne was now supposed to continue southward by way of Lake George to the Hudson River. Instead, he chose to turn east and march overland to the Hudson. That proved a serious mistake.

Burgoyne's advance slowed to a crawl. The army took 24 days to cover 23 miles. Soldiers clothed in wool worked up to their chests in mud to build bridges across streams.

Mosquitoes and "punkies," tiny insects with needle-sharp bites, rose from the swamps to attack the men. The Americans slowed British progress even more by felling trees and rolling boulders across trails.

Burgoyne's forces finally broke out of the forests in late July. Weakened and short of supplies, they clashed with the Americans several times.

Burgoyne met the main body of the American forces in the area of Bemis Heights, near Saratoga. Outnumbered by more than three to one, Burgoyne surrendered on October 17, 1777. All that remained of his force—5,700 men—became prisoners of war.

Burgoyne's March to Saratoga

CANADA
Montreal
Ft. St. John
Richelieu R.
L. Champlain
VERMONT
Crown Point
Ft. Ticonderoga
L. George
NEW YORK
Hudson R.
Saratoga
Bemis Heights
Bennington
Albany
N W E S

■ How did Burgoyne's lack of knowledge about the American land help cause his defeat?

ACTIVITY Imagine that you are General Burgoyne. Write a series of telegrams to your superiors in London describing your trek through the wilderness.

British cannon

Interdisciplinary CONNECTIONS

For worksheets establishing connections between the Chapter 6 main idea, The American Revolution, and five other disciplines, see the *Interdisciplinary Connections* booklet. (Enrichment)

■ **Arts** A Uniform Appearance, page 32 (Average)
■ **Sciences** The Cost of War, page 33 (Challenging)
■ **World** France and Spain Look On, page 34 (Average)
■ **Economics** Financing a Revolution, page 35 (Easy)
■ **Civics** Enemies of the State?, page 36 (Average)

Answer to Connections

Burgoyne did not realize that his planned route of attack would force him to transport troops and supplies across lakes, swamps, mountains, and forests. His slow advance weakened his troops and allowed the American forces to gain the upper hand.

ACTIVITY

Guided Instruction You might have students work in pairs, asking and answering questions about Burgoyne. Remind students that telegrams use as few words as possible. Have students pay attention to geographic accuracy.

Team-Teaching Suggestion
Science

You might work with a science teacher to present a lesson about illnesses transmitted by insects. Discuss allergic reactions, the symptoms associated with more serious diseases, and the treatments required. Relate the discussion to conditions that Burgoyne's troops might have experienced and to medical knowledge of that time.

Team-Teaching Suggestion
Art

You might work with an art teacher to present a lesson about art in colonial America. Include paintings (portrait, landscape, and historic), engravings, and folk art. Discuss the important artists of this era and the techniques associated with each art form.

Biography Have students read the biography, *Juan de Miralles, Friend of the Revolution*, on page 16 of the *Our Multicultural Heritage* booklet. (Enrichment/Average)

Student Study Guide

Section 3 Study Guide Have students use the Section 3 Study Guide on page 64 of the *Student Study Guide* to review and reinforce the content of this section. (Reteaching/Average)

ACTIVITY

Guided Instruction Before students begin their articles, create a class list of the major battles in the American Revolution. Ask each student to select one battle from the list. You might provide students with sample newspaper articles written by war correspondents for guidance in drafting their own accounts. When revising, suggest that they use the *Who, What, Where, When, Why,* and *How* strategy to check that they have reported the facts fully and accurately.

When Americans learned about conditions at Valley Forge, they sent help. Women collected food, medicine, warm clothes, and ammunition for the army. They raised money to buy other supplies. Some women, like Martha Washington, wife of the commander, went to Valley Forge to help the sick and wounded.

Help From Abroad

Throughout the war, volunteers from Europe arrived to join the American cause. The Marquis de Lafayette (lah fee YEHT), a young French noble, brought trained soldiers to the United States. He fought at Brandywine and became one of Washington's most trusted friends.

Two Polish officers joined the Americans. Thaddeus Kosciusko (kahs ee UHS koh), an engineer, helped build forts and other defenses. Casimir Pulaski trained **cavalry,** or troops on horseback.

Bernardo de Gálvez. Help for the Americans came from New Spain, too. At first, Spain was **neutral**—it did not take sides in the war between Britain and its colonies. But Bernardo de Gálvez, governor of Spanish Louisiana, favored the Patriots. He secretly supplied medicine, cloth, muskets, and gunpowder to the Americans. He also sent cattle from Texas to feed the Continental Army.

Spain entered the war against Britain in 1779. Gálvez then seized British forts along the Mississippi and Gulf of Mexico. He also drove the British out of West Florida.

A Prussian officer. Friedrich von Steuben (STOO buhn) from Prussia helped train Continental troops. Von Steuben had served in the Prussian army, considered the best in Europe. A lively man, Von Steuben kept everybody in good spirits. At the same time, he taught American soldiers skills, such as how to use bayonets. Until then, many soldiers had used their bayonets to roast meat over a fire!

Although Von Steuben spoke little English, he drilled troops and taught them to march. He ordered each soldier to put his left hand on the shoulder of the man in front of him. Then, Von Steuben called out in his German accent: "Forward march! One, Two, Three, Four!"

Growing confidence. By spring 1778, the army at Valley Forge was more hopeful. A New Jersey soldier observed:

&&The army grows stronger every day. The troops are instructed in a new and so happy a method of marching that they will soon be able to advance with the utmost regularity, even without music and on the roughest grounds.&&

While soldiers drilled, Washington and his staff planned new campaigns against the British.

SECTION 3 REVIEW

1. **Locate:** (a) New York, (b) Delaware River, (c) Princeton, (d) Albany, (e) Saratoga, (f) Valley Forge.
2. **Identify:** (a) Battle of Long Island, (b) Nathan Hale, (c) Battle of Trenton, (d) John Burgoyne, (e) Battle of Saratoga, (f) Marquis de Lafayette, (g) Thaddeus Kosciusko, (h) Friedrich von Steuben.
3. **Define:** (a) cavalry, (b) neutral.
4. Why did many Patriots feel discouraged from late 1776 to early 1778?
5. Describe three results of the Battle of Saratoga.
6. Why was an alliance with France important to Americans?
7. **CRITICAL THINKING Analyzing Ideas** Why do you think that people from other lands—such as Lafayette, Pulaski, and Gálvez—were willing to risk their lives for the American cause?

ACTIVITY Writing to Learn

Write a newspaper article about a battle of the American Revolution.

Answers to Section 3 Review

1. See the map on p. 170.
2. (a) Battle of Long Island, p. 169, (b) Nathan Hale, p. 170, (c) Battle of Trenton, p. 171, (d) John Burgoyne, p. 171, (e) Battle of Saratoga, p. 172, (f) Marquis de Lafayette, p. 174, (g) Thaddeus Kosciusko, p. 174, (h) Friedrich von Steuben, p. 174
3. (a) cavalry, p. 174, (b) neutral, p. 174
4. The Continental Army suffered many defeats and lacked food, clothing, and medicine.

5. This battle ended the British threat to New England, boosted American spirits, and convinced France to sign a treaty with the United States.
6. The French would be able to help the Americans get needed supplies and could threaten British control of the seas.
7. Possible Answer: Foreigners admired Americans and were impressed by the goals of the Revolution, as set out in the Declaration of Independence; they disliked the British.

4
Other Battlefronts

FIND OUT
- What role did Native Americans play in the Revolution?
- What battles did Americans win in the West and at sea?
- How did African Americans and women contribute to the war?

Flying Crow, a Seneca chief, looked sternly at the British officers who were seated before him. "If you are so strong, Brother, and they but a weak boy, why ask our assistance?"

Like many Native American leaders, Flying Crow did not want to become involved in a war between the "weak boy"—the United States—and Britain. Yet Native Americans could not avoid the struggle. Fighting took place not only in the East but also on or near Indian lands in the West. The war was also fought at sea.

Fighting on the Frontier

During the war, white settlers continued to push west of the Appalachians. In Kentucky, newcomers named a settlement Lexington, after the first battle of the Revolution. They called another wilderness settlement Louisville, in honor of the new American ally, Louis XVI of France. In the West, settlers clashed with Native Americans, whose lands they were invading.

Native Americans choose sides. When the Revolution began, most Indians tried to stay neutral. "It is a family affair," said an Iroquois chief. He told whites that he preferred "to sit still and see you fight it out."

As the war spread, some Indians did take sides. The Six Nations of the Iroquois were divided, although most helped the British. In Massachusetts, the Algonquins supported the Patriots. In the West, many Indians joined the British to protect their lands from American settlers.

In Tennessee, most Cherokees were at first neutral or even favored the Patriots. Nancy Ward, a Cherokee leader, warned American settlers of a raid planned by a small group of Cherokees. Settlers responded by attacking all the Cherokees. This betrayal of trust led the Cherokees to join the British.

Victory at Vincennes. In 1778, George Rogers Clark led Virginia frontier fighters against the British in the Ohio Valley. With

MAP STUDY

In 1778 and 1779, American and British forces fought for control of lands west of the Appalachian Mountains.
1. Along which river did Clark's men travel after setting out from Fort Pitt?
2. Which British forts did Clark capture?
3. **Applying Information** Why was control of lands west of the Appalachians important to Americans?

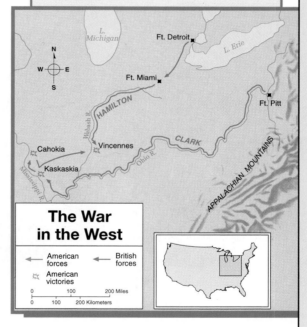

The War in the West

- ← American forces
- ← British forces
- ☆ American victories

0   100   200 Miles
0 100 200 Kilometers

Section 4
pp. 175–179

Bell Ringer

Have the class brainstorm a list of activities—besides the act of combat itself—that are important to winning a war.

Lesson Plan

1. **Focus** In this section, students read about the progress of the American Revolution in the West and the war at sea. They also study the roles played in the war by African Americans, Native Americans, and women.
2. **Instruct** Write the following statements on the chalkboard: (a) Native American groups found it easy to remain neutral. (b) Brilliant leadership allowed American forces to defeat larger British forces. (c) Neither the British nor the Patriots won support of African Americans. (d) Women made important contributions to the Patriot cause. Have students decide which generalizations are valid.
3. **Close** To close the lesson, give students the names of important people and events in this section and have them identify each.

Critical Thinking
Defending a Position

To help students understand the issues of alliance that Native Americans faced, ask groups of students to imagine that they are Native Americans sitting in council. Have each group debate the advantages or disadvantages of allying with the British or the Patriots—or of staying neutral. Have group representatives report to the class on the results.

Our Multicultural Heritage
Background

From the Iroquois nations, the Oneidas and Tuscaroras sided with the Americans. The Mohawks under Thayendanegea (also known as Joseph Brant) fought with the British, as they had in the French and Indian War.

Answer to Caption

in response to the British policy of offering freedom to any male slave who served the king

 Historical Outline Map Book

Historical Outline Map Use the map, The Revolutionary War in the West, on page 26 of the *American History Historical Outline Map Book.* Lesson ideas for this map can be found on page T8. (Reteaching/Average)

 Customized Reader

Primary Source For an account of the struggles between Cherokees and white settlers, order article IIIA-11, Nancy Ward, Beloved Woman of the Cherokees, from the *American History Customized Reader.* Ilene J. Conwell's biographical essay relates Ward's accomplishments. (Enrichment/Challenging)

help from Miami Indians, Clark captured the British forts at Kaskaskia and Cahokia. (See the map on page 175.)

Clark then plotted a surprise winter attack on the British fort at Vincennes. He led a small band 150 miles (240 km) through heavy rains, swamps, and icy rivers. When they reached the fort, they spread out through the woods to make their numbers appear greater than they really were. The strategy worked. The British commander thought it was useless to fight so many Americans. He surrendered Vincennes in February 1779.

A Victory at Sea

The Americans could do little against the powerful British navy. British ships blockaded American ports. From time to time, however, a bold American captain captured a British ship.

The most daring American captain was John Paul Jones, who raided the English coast. In his most famous battle, in September 1779, Jones commanded the *Bonhomme*

Richard. He was sailing in the North Sea near Britain when he spotted 39 enemy merchant ships. They were guarded by a single warship, the *Serapis.* The *Serapis* was larger than the *Bonhomme Richard,* but Jones attacked it.

In a furious battle, cannonballs ripped through the *Bonhomme Richard,* setting it on fire. The British commander called on Jones to surrender. "I have not yet begun to fight!" Jones replied.

Jones sailed close to the *Serapis* so that his sailors could board the enemy ship. In hand-to-hand combat, the Americans defeated the British. Jones earned a hero's welcome on his return home.

African Americans in the Battle for Freedom

At the outset of the Revolution, more than a half million African Americans lived in the colonies. At first, the Continental Congress refused to let African Americans, whether free or enslaved, join the army. The British, however, offered freedom to any

African Americans in the Revolution *Many African Americans contributed to the Revolution. Peter Williams, at right, risked his life to save an outspoken Patriot clergyman from British officers. Agrippa Hull, at left, served for four years under the Polish war hero Thaddeus Kosciusko.* **Citizenship** *Why did Washington decide to allow free African Americans to serve in the Continental Army?*

Connections With Economics
Background

American ships, called privateers, roamed the seas attacking British ships. Privateers were owned by private citizens, who were allowed to keep anything they seized.

Connections With Technology
Background

The first known instance of a submarine used to attack a surface vessel occurred during the American Revolution. David Bushnell invented the *Turtle,* which was designed to accommodate only one person. It had no engine. Bushnell steered the *Turtle* by hand underwater to reach the British ship, the *Eagle,* anchored in New York harbor. Then

he tried to drill a hole in the *Eagle*'s hull to place an explosive charge with a timed detonator inside. Unable to pierce the copperlined hull, he set the explosive off beside the ship. The *Eagle* was not damaged, but the alarmed captain moved his ship farther out to sea.

The Home Front *Americans on the home front played an important role. This printed handkerchief shows three sisters who took charge of the family farm when their husbands joined the fighting.* **American Traditions** *In what other ways did women on the home front aid the Continental Army?*

male slave who served the king. In response, Washington changed his policy and allowed free African Americans to enlist.

Comrades in arms. About 5,000 African Americans fought against the British. At least nine black minutemen saw action at Lexington and Concord. One of them, Prince Estabrook, was wounded. Two others, Peter Salem and Salem Poor, went on to fight bravely at Bunker Hill.

Some African Americans formed special regiments. Others served in white regiments as drummers, fifers, spies, and guides. Thousands of black sailors also served on American ships. Whites recognized the courage of their African American comrades, as this eyewitness account shows:

66Three times in succession, [African American soldiers] were attacked... by well-disciplined and veteran [British] troops, and three times did they successfully repel the assault, and thus preserve our army from capture.99

"All men are created equal." Black Patriots hoped that the Revolution would bring an end to slavery. After all, the Declaration of Independence proclaimed that "all men are created equal." In Massachusetts and elsewhere, enslaved African Americans sent petitions to lawmakers asking for freedom.

Some white leaders also hoped the war would end slavery. James Otis wrote that "the colonists are by the law of nature free born, as indeed all men are, white or black."

By the 1770s, slavery was declining in the North, where a number of free African Americans lived. During the Revolution, several states moved to outlaw slavery, including Vermont, Massachusetts, New Hampshire, and Pennsylvania. Other states debated the issue.

Women in the War

Women also helped in the struggle for independence. When men went off to war, women took on added work. They planted and harvested the crops that fed the Continental Army. They made guns and other weapons. One woman, known as "Handy Betsy the Blacksmith," was famous for supplying cannons and guns to the army.

Women made shoes and wove cloth for blankets and uniforms. Betsy Ross of Philadelphia sewed flags for Washington's army. Legend claims that Washington asked her to make the first American flag of stars and stripes. But the story cannot be proved.

Many women also joined their soldier-husbands at the front. There, they washed clothes, cooked, and cared for the wounded. Martha Washington joined her husband whenever she could.

A few women took part in battle. During the Battle of Monmouth in 1778, Mary Ludwig Hays carried water to her husband and

Chapter 6 • 177

Answer to Caption

Quaker religious beliefs forbade fighting in any war.

Customized Reader

Primary Source For a firsthand account of a civilian's service with the Continental Army, order article IIIA-2, *A Woman's Experience in the American Revolution*, from the *American History Customized Reader*. In this selection, Sarah Osborn, a cook and washerwoman, recounts the uproar over Benedict Arnold's treason, a meeting with General Washington, and the final surrender at Yorktown. (Enrichment/Average)

Student Study Guide

Section 4 Study Guide Have students use the Section 4 Study Guide on page 65 of the *Student Study Guide* to review and reinforce the content of this section. (Reteaching/Average)

other soldiers. The soldiers called her Moll of the Pitcher or Molly Pitcher. When her husband was wounded, she took his place, loading and firing a cannon. Deborah Sampson of Massachusetts dressed as a man and fought in several battles. Later, she wrote about her life in the army.

A Young Girl's War

Most colonists saw little actual fighting. For them, daily life went on much as usual. But when armies marched through an area, no one escaped the effects of war.

For 16-year-old Sally Wister of Philadelphia, the war brought both excitement and fear. In 1777, Sally and her family fled when the British approached Philadelphia. The Wisters were Quakers and opposed fighting. Still, they favored the Patriot cause. They settled behind American lines, in a country house outside Philadelphia.

A house full of officers. One autumn day, two Patriot officers rode up to the house to warn the Wisters of British troops nearby. "About seven o'clock we heard a great noise," Sally reported in her diary.

> 66 To the door we all went. A large number of waggons, with about three hundred of the Philadelphia Militia [were outside]. They begged for drink, and several pushed into the house. 99

Even though the men were Patriots, Sally rushed out the back door, "all in a shake with fear; but after a while, seeing the officers appear gentlemanly. . . my fears were in some measure dispelled, tho' my teeth rattled, and my hand shook like an aspen leaf."

For a time, Patriot General William Smallwood and his officers made the Wister home their headquarters. "How new is our situation!" Sally wrote. "I feel in good spirits, though surrounded by an Army, the house

A Quaker Aids the Patriots *Even though they did not take part in the fighting, many Quakers helped the Patriot cause. Here, a young Quaker woman gives news of British troop movements to one of General Washington's aides.* **Multicultural Heritage** *Review page 102. Why did Quakers refuse to serve in the army?*

full of officers, the yard alive with soldiers— very peaceable sort of men, tho'."

Many Patriot officers came from other colonies. Sally "took great delight in teasing" two Virginians about their accents. They, in turn, told her about life at home and "how good turkey hash and fryed hominy is."

Handsome Major Stoddert. Sally's favorite soldier was 26-year-old Major Benjamin Stoddert. But the handsome young man from Maryland was "vastly bashful" at first. He said little to her except "Good morning," and "Your servant, madam."

One night, Major Stoddert stood by the dining room table, holding a candle so that General Smallwood could read his newspaper. Sally managed to strike up a conversation. "We talked and laughed for an hour. He is very clever, amiable, and polite. He has the softest voice, never pronounces the *R* at all."

Historical Sidelight
Background

Laura Wolcott was a 15-year-old who lived in Litchfield, Connecticut, with her Patriot parents. In July 1776, New Yorkers tore down a statue of King George III. Pieces of lead from the statue were sent to Litchfield. Women used them to make cartridges for Washington's army. Wolcott herself made at least 4,250 cartridges.

Historical Sidelight
Background

Sally Wister may never have seen Major Stoddert again, but the young officer survived the war and went on to bigger things. He became Secretary of the Navy during the administration of President John Adams.

Before long, the militia—and Major Stoddert—had to move on. "Good-bye, Miss Sally," he said, in a voice so "very low" that Sally guessed he was sorry to leave her.

A month later, Major Stoddert returned. He could "scarcely walk," reported Sally, and "looked pale, thin, and dejected." He had caught a fever. The Wisters looked after him until he recovered. Then he was off to war once more. Sally never saw him again.

Back home. Sally Wister's experience of war was like that of many Americans. At times, armies marched and drilled nearby while musket and cannon fire sounded in the distance. Then life returned to normal.

In mid-1778, the British left Philadelphia. Sally Wister returned to the city and "the rattling of carriages over the streets." By then, the fighting had shifted from the Middle States to the South. ■

SECTION 4 REVIEW

1. **Locate:** (a) Kaskaskia, (b) Cahokia, (c) Vincennes.
2. **Identify:** (a) Nancy Ward, (b) George Rogers Clark, (c) John Paul Jones, (d) Peter Salem, (e) Mary Ludwig Hays, (f) Deborah Sampson.
3. Why did Native Americans in the West help the British?
4. Why was John Paul Jones a hero to Americans?
5. How did women help in the struggle for independence?
6. **CRITICAL THINKING Linking Past and Present** Suppose that you were living in a country at war today. Would your experience be similar to that of Sally Wister during the American Revolution? Explain.

ACTIVITY **Writing to Learn**
Imagine that you are a free African American man in New England during the Revolution. Write a paragraph explaining why you either will or will not join the Continental Army.

5
The World Turned Upside Down

FIND OUT
■ Why did fighting shift to the South in 1778?
■ How did Washington force the British to surrender at Yorktown?
■ What were the terms of the Treaty of Paris?

VOCABULARY ratify

Thomas Young was only 16 years old when he set out with 900 other Patriots to capture King's Mountain in South Carolina. Although most of the Patriots were barefoot, they moved quickly up the wooded hillside, shouldering their old muskets. The Patriots were determined to take the mountain from the Loyalists dug in at the top.

Whooping and shouting, Young and his comrades dashed from tree to tree, dodging bullets as they fired their own weapons. Suddenly, Thomas heard the cry "Colonel Williams is shot!"

❝I ran to his assistance for I loved him as a father. He had ever been kind to me and almost always carried a cake in his pocket for me and his little son Joseph. They . . . sprinkled some water in his face. He revived, and his first words were, 'For God's sake boys, don't give up the hill!'. . . I left him in the arms of his son Daniel, and returned to the field to avenge his fate.❞

The Patriots captured King's Mountain on October 7, 1780. The victory boosted morale after a string of Patriot defeats in the South.

Chapter 6 • **179**

ACTIVITY
Guided Instruction Before students choose a persona for their writing, encourage them to create a chart listing the advantages and disadvantages that an African American might associate with supporting the Revolution. Suggest that students use their lists to decide which position they will take. You might use the completed paragraphs as the basis for a class debate.

Section 5
pp. 179–183

 Bell Ringer

Tell students to imagine that they command an army. Ask: What circumstances might lead you to decide that it would be better to surrender than to continue fighting?

Lesson Plan

1. Focus After the French entered the war, the British concentrated their efforts in the South. Though at first they were able to seize Savannah and Charleston, American forces began to turn the tide. The British finally surrendered at Yorktown. In this section, students learn about the last battles of the war, the treaty that ended the war, and Washington's farewell to his officers.

Answers to Section 4 Review

1. See the map on p. 175.
2. (a) Nancy Ward, p. 175, (b) George Rogers Clark, p. 175, (c) John Paul Jones, p. 176, (d) Peter Salem, p. 177, (e) Mary Ludwig Hays, p. 177, (f) Deborah Sampson, p. 178
3. to protect their lands from American settlers
4. Jones raided the English coast and seized British merchant ships.
5. Women took on additional responsibilities in running homes, farms, and businesses. Some women joined their husbands at the front; there, they washed clothes, cooked, cared for the wounded, and occasionally even participated in battle.
6. Answers will vary, but students should suggest that with modern technology and communication, they probably would know more about what was happening and would be more greatly affected by the war.

War in the South

Scattered fighting had taken place in the South from the start of the Revolution. In February 1776, North Carolina Patriots defeated a Loyalist army at the **Battle of Moore's Creek Bridge.** This battle is sometimes called the Lexington and Concord of the South.

After France entered the war, the British focused their efforts on the South. They counted on the support of Loyalists there. Greatly outnumbered, the Patriots suffered many setbacks. In December 1778, the British seized Savannah, Georgia. They later took Charleston, South Carolina. "I have almost ceased to hope," wrote Washington when he learned of the losses.

An American traitor. In September 1780, Washington received more bad news. Benedict Arnold, one of his best generals, had joined the British. Arnold had fought bravely in many battles. One soldier recalled that Arnold always led—never followed—his men into battle. "It was 'Come on, boys!' not 'Go on, boys!' He didn't care for nothin'. He'd ride right in."

Washington had put Arnold in command of the key fort at West Point. But Arnold was angry. He felt he had not received enough credit for his victories. He also needed money. He secretly offered to turn over West Point to the British. By chance, a Patriot patrol captured the messenger carrying Arnold's offer. Although Arnold escaped to join the British, West Point was saved.

The Patriots rally. The victory at King's Mountain in October 1780 helped rally Patriots. Slowly, the tide turned in their favor.

Several Patriots made hit-and-run attacks on the British. Francis Marion of South Carolina led a small band of men who slept by day and traveled by night. Marion was known as the Swamp Fox. He would ap-

---

The "Swamp Fox" and His Men *Francis Marion, known as the "Swamp Fox," kept the British off guard in South Carolina. This painting by William Ranney shows Marion and his rough band of men setting out on a raid.* **Geography** *How did Marion use the geography of South Carolina to surprise the British and avoid capture?*

---

pear suddenly out of the swamps, attack the British, and then retreat into the swamps. His attacks kept the British off balance.

Two American generals, Daniel Morgan and Nathanael Greene, won victories in the South. Morgan was a big, bull-necked man. His company of Virginia Riflemen had served well in the Battle of Saratoga. In January 1781, he defeated the British at the Battle of Cowpens in South Carolina.

Like Marion, General Greene used hit-and-run tactics. Even though Greene won few battles, his attacks wore down the British. Raids by bands of fierce backcountry Patriots, who struck often and without warning, also took their toll. The harassed British general, Charles Cornwallis, decided to move his army north into Virginia in the spring of 1781.

Victory at Last

Cornwallis set up camp at Yorktown, on a strip of land that juts into the Chesapeake Bay. He felt safe there, knowing that British ships could supply his troops from the sea.

Washington knew the area well. He realized that he could trap Cornwallis at Yorktown. While a French fleet under Admiral de Grasse sailed toward the Chesapeake, Washington prepared to march south from New York. French troops under the Comte de Rochambeau (roh shahm BOH) had landed in Rhode Island the previous year. Now, they joined Washington, and the combined forces rushed toward Virginia.

Meanwhile, De Grasse's fleet kept British ships out of the Chesapeake. Cornwallis was cut off. He could not get supplies. And he could not escape by sea.

Cornwallis held out for three weeks before he surrendered his army on October 17, 1781. Two days later, the defeated British turned their weapons over to the Americans. A British army band played the tune "The World Turned Upside Down."

MAP STUDY

The final battles of the Revolution were fought in the South. The Americans suffered a string of defeats between 1778 and 1780, but the tide slowly turned. Finally, trapped at Yorktown in 1781, the British surrendered.
1. *Name three British victories in the South.*
2. *(a) Who commanded American troops at Yorktown? (b) Who commanded British troops?*
3. **Analyzing Information** *How did the French fleet contribute to the American victory at Yorktown?*

The War in the South

| American and French forces | British forces |
| American victories | British victories |

0   100   200 Miles
0   100   200 Kilometers

Answers to Map Study

1. Camden, Charleston, Savannah **2.** (a) Washington and Rochambeau (b) Cornwallis **3.** The French fleet took Chesapeake Bay, cutting off British supplies to Yorktown—and cutting off a British escape route.

 Transparencies

Interdisciplinary Connections Use the transparency The Battle of Yorktown on page B-43 of American History Transparencies. It illustrates the importance of geography in the battle. Teaching suggestions can be found on page B-8. (Enrichment/Average)

Chapter Resources

Geography in History Duplicate and distribute the worksheet, Battle for a Peninsula, from Unit 2, page 19, of the *Chapter Resources* binder. This worksheet focuses on the strategic value of Yorktown. (Enrichment/Challenging)

Voices of Freedom

Primary Source You might assign selection 8-7, An Eyewitness at Yorktown, on pages 65–67 of *Voices of Freedom.* This selection comes from Dr. James Thacher's diary, which recounts the Massachusetts doctor's service as a surgeon in the Continental Army. (Enrichment/Challenging)

Learning Styles
Kinesthetic Learners

You might have kinesthetic learners write and perform a skit depicting the events leading up to and including Cornwallis's surrender at Yorktown. The skit should include the following characters: Lafayette, Admiral de Grasse, Comte de Rochambeau, George Washington, Cornwallis, and several British and American soldiers. Writers might consider these questions when drafting the script:

What might the British have said to each other when they felt safe? What comments might the French and Americans have made to each other upon meeting? What reactions might the British have had when they realized that surrender was inevitable? How might the Americans and their allies have reacted when they realized that they had won? Actors should rehearse before presenting the skit.

Historical Outline Map Book

Historical Outline Map Use the map, North America in 1783, on page 28 of the *American History Historical Outline Map Book*. Lesson ideas can be found on page T9. (Reteaching/Average)

Videotapes/ Videodiscs

United States History Video Collection Use the video segment "The World Turned Upside Down" from Volume 4, *The American Revolution.* Approx. running time 3:00 min. (Enrichment/Average) Vol. 4, Ch. 28

| Chapter 28 | Play |

United States History Video Collection Use the video segment "Winners and Losers" from Volume 4, *The American Revolution.* Approx. running time 5:05 min. (Enrichment/Average) Vol. 4, Ch. 31

| Chapter 31 | Play |

Making Peace

Americans rejoiced when they heard the news from Yorktown. In London, however, the defeat shocked the British. "It is all over," cried the British prime minister, Lord North. Left with no other choice, he agreed to peace talks.

The talks began in Paris in 1782. Congress sent Benjamin Franklin and John Adams, along with John Jay of New York and Henry Laurens of South Carolina, to work out a treaty. Because Britain was eager to end the war, the Americans got most of what they wanted.

Under the **Treaty of Paris,** the British recognized the United States as an independent nation. The borders of the new nation extended from the Atlantic Ocean to the Mississippi River. The southern border stopped at Florida, which was returned to Spain.

On their part, the Americans agreed to ask state legislatures to pay Loyalists for property they lost in the war. In the end, however, most states ignored the Loyalist claims.

On April 15, 1783, Congress **ratified,** or approved, the Treaty of Paris. It was almost eight years to the day since the battles of Lexington and Concord.

Washington's Farewell

The Revolution had been a long and difficult struggle for the Americans. They fought a much more powerful nation that had better-armed and better-trained soldiers.

MAP STUDY

Under the Treaty of Paris of 1783, Britain recognized the United States as an independent nation.

1. *Which nation held land west of the new United States?*
2. *What natural feature formed the western border of the United States?*
3. **Comparing** *Compare this map with the map on page 141. (a) According to the maps, what was the major difference between North America in 1783 and in 1763? (b) Name one way in which North America was the same in 1783 and in 1763.*

North America in 1783

■ United States	■ Spanish colonies
■ British colonies	■ Disputed territory
■ French colony	

0   900   1800 Miles
0   900   1800 Kilometers

★★★ ***Our Common Heritage***
Almost 100,000 Loyalists fled the United States after the Revolution. Among them were more than 10,000 African Americans who had supported Britain in hopes of winning freedom. They moved to Canada, England, Spanish Florida, Jamaica in the West Indies, and Sierra Leone in Africa. There, they lived as free men and women.

Connections With the World Background

King George III regretted the loss of the American colonies but tried to make the best of the situation. In a letter, he wrote: "I should be miserable indeed if I did not feel that . . . knavery seems to be so much a striking feature of [the colonies'] inhabitants that it may not in the end be an evil that they will become aliens to this kingdom."

Cooperative Learning Activity

Have students compile a *Who's Who in the American Revolution.* First have them nominate people, both British and American, to include. Then assign each group one part of the list, making sure that each has both major and secondary figures. Tell each group to prepare a short biographical entry for each person on its list. Encourage the addition of art. After the groups have finished their entries, compile the *Who's Who* for class reference.

In the end, money, arms, and soldiers from France helped the Americans win the war. But the strength and courage of leaders like Washington played a major role in the American victory.

In December 1783, General Washington bid farewell to his officers at Fraunces' Tavern in New York City. Colonel Benjamin Tallmadge recalled the event:

66Such a scene of sorrow and weeping I had never before witnessed. . . . The simple thought that we were then about to part from the man who had conducted us through a long and bloody war, and under whose conduct the glory and independence of our country had been achieved, and that we should see his face no more in this world, seemed to me utterly [unbearable].99

All along Washington's route home to Mount Vernon, Virginia, crowds cheered the hero of American independence. The new nation faced difficult days ahead. Before long, Americans would again call on Washington to lead them.

CAUSES

- Proclamation of 1763 stops colonists from moving west
- Parliament taxes the colonies to pay British war debts
- Intolerable Acts set up harsh rule in Massachusetts

THE AMERICAN REVOLUTION

EFFECTS

- Colonies declare independence
- Britain recognizes United States independence
- United States borders extend to Florida and to the Mississippi River
- George Washington emerges as a leader

Understanding Causes and Effects
In the 1770s, protests against British colonial rule quickly turned into armed resistance, then war. List two effects of the American Revolution.
- *What effects do you think a British victory might have had?*

SECTION 5 REVIEW

1. **Locate:** (a) King's Mountain, (b) Savannah, (c) Charleston, (d) Cowpens, (e) Yorktown.
2. **Identify:** (a) Battle of Moore's Creek Bridge, (b) Benedict Arnold, (c) Francis Marion, (d) Daniel Morgan, (e) Nathanael Greene, (f) Admiral de Grasse, (g) Comte de Rochambeau, (h) Treaty of Paris.
3. **Define:** ratify.
4. Why did Britain focus its efforts on the South after 1778?
5. Why was Cornwallis forced to surrender at Yorktown?
6. What were the boundaries of the United States in 1783?
7. **CRITICAL THINKING Analyzing Ideas** Why do you think the British played "The World Turned Upside Down" when they surrendered at Yorktown?

 Writing to Learn
Imagine that you are General Cornwallis. In a letter to George III, describe the events at Yorktown.

CHAPTER 6 REVIEW

Answers to Reviewing the Main Ideas

1. (a) Washington had military experience, an excellent character, and the support of many Americans. (b) Washington's army was a poorly trained and disorganized militia, and there was no navy.

2. *Common Sense* helped to persuade many colonists, including the delegates to the Continental Congress, to support independence.

3. The battle boosted morale and ended the British threat to New England; by proving that the British could be defeated, it convinced France to sign a treaty of alliance with the Americans.

4. (a) The Patriots had lost several battles, including Brandywine and Germantown; the Continental Army faced severe hardships at Valley Forge, while the British were comfortable in Philadelphia. (b) Soldiers were hungry, had little clothing, lived in makeshift huts, slept on frozen ground, and suffered from frostbite and disease.

5. (a) Gálvez secretly supplied medicine, cloth, muskets, and gunpowder to the Americans. (b) Ward warned Patriot settlers of a Cherokee raid. (c) Clark captured the British fort at Vincennes. (d) Salem fought at Lexington and Concord and at Bunker Hill. (e) Hays carried water to her husband and other soldiers at the Battle of Monmouth.

6. French ships under Admiral de Grasse drove the British navy from the Chesapeake, cutting off Cornwallis's supplies and escape route. French troops under Comte de Rochambeau joined Washington, helping him to trap Cornwallis.

7. Britain recognized the United States as an independent nation, with borders extending from the Atlantic Ocean to the Mississippi River and to Florida; the United States agreed to ask state legislatures to pay Loyalists for property lost in the war.

Answers to Thinking Critically

1. (a) The Declaration guarantees equality, life, liberty, and the pursuit of happiness. (b) Possible

---

Summary

- When the American Revolution began in 1775, Americans faced an uphill struggle.
- The Declaration of Independence set out the basic ideas on which the United States was founded and explained why the colonies were breaking away from Britain.
- The American victory at Saratoga marked a turning point in the war.
- Native Americans, African Americans, and women made important contributions to the war effort.
- After Cornwallis surrendered at Yorktown in 1781, Britain recognized the United States as an independent nation.

Reviewing the Main Ideas

1. (a) Why did John Adams think George Washington was a good choice for commander of the Continental Army? (b) What problems did Washington face in 1775?

2. How did the pamphlet *Common Sense* influence colonists?

3. Why was the Battle of Saratoga a turning point in the American Revolution?

4. (a) Why was the winter of 1777–1778 a bad time for the Americans? (b) Describe conditions at Valley Forge.

5. How did each of the following people help the Patriot cause: (a) Bernardo de Gálvez, (b) Nancy Ward, (c) George Rogers Clark, (d) Peter Salem, (e) Mary Ludwig Hays?

6. How did France help the Americans win the Battle of Yorktown?

7. Describe the major points of the Treaty of Paris of 1783.

Thinking Critically

1. Linking Past and Present Review the Declaration of Independence in the Reference Section. (a) What basic rights does the Dec-

---

laration guarantee? (b) Do Americans today enjoy these rights? Explain.

2. Defending a Position After the Declaration of Independence was issued, enslaved Africans sent petitions to state legislatures asking for freedom. How might they have used the Declaration of Independence to support their position?

Applying Your Skills

1. Comparing Points of View Read about the Olive Branch Petition on pages 161 and 164. (a) What was the subject of the Olive Branch Petition? (b) How do you think colonists viewed the petition? (c) How did King George III respond to the petition? (d) What arguments might each side have used to defend its point of view?

2. Analyzing a Quotation Reread the quotation from *The Crisis* on page 170. (a) What did Paine mean by the words, "These are the times that try men's souls"? (b) What are "sunshine patriots"? (c) What do you think Washington's soldiers thought about Paine's words?

Thinking About Geography

Match the letters on the map with the following places: **1.** Bunker Hill, **2.** Trenton, **3.** Saratoga, **4.** Vincennes, **5.** Cowpens, **6.** Savannah, **7.** Yorktown. **Movement** Why was British control of the Chesapeake Bay important to Cornwallis at Yorktown?

Answers to Applying Your Skills

Answers: Yes, because the federal government still protects those rights; no, because poverty and discrimination prevent some people from fully enjoying these rights.

2. Possible Answer: They could cite the first part, in which Jefferson wrote that "all men are created equal" and endowed with "certain inalienable rights," one of which was liberty.

1. (a) colonists' loyalty to the king and a request for the repeal of the Intolerable Acts (b) Many colonists probably felt that the petition was a reasonable request. (c) with anger (d) Colonists: The Intolerable Acts and other British actions were unfair; the petition was a reasonable alternative to a violent response. George III: Colonists were British subjects; their questioning of his decisions was treason.

2. (a) The difficulties facing the colonists were a test of strength, courage, and endurance. (b) people who were Patriots only when they weren't suffering because of it (c) Possible Answer: They would have been glad that their sacrifices were recognized.

Fighting With the Continental Army

Form into groups to learn more about the American Revolution. Follow the suggestions below to write, dance, draw, or talk to show what you have learned about the Continental Army during the Revolution. You may use the textbook, encyclopedias, atlases, or other materials in your classroom library to complete the tasks. Be able to name your sources of information when you have finished the activity.

CARTOGRAPHERS On a large sheet of paper, about 3 feet by 5 feet, draw a map of North America. On the map, show the major battles of the American Revolution. Mark each battle with a symbol to show which side won. Create a map key explaining the symbols you used. Leave space on the map for a battle chart created by class mathematicians.

Flag of a Pennsylvania regiment

MATHEMATICIANS Compile statistics on the major battles of the American Revolution. Include the dates on which the battles were fought, the number of soldiers who fought in each, the number of soldiers killed, and how long the battle lasted. Put your information in chart form, and display it on the battle map created by class cartographers.

Flag of a Massachusetts regiment

DANCERS Review what you learned about Molly Pitcher. Then create a dance portraying her actions at the Battle of Monmouth.

WRITERS Imagine that you are a soldier with Washington's army at Valley Forge. Write a letter to your family describing conditions in the camp. What are your feelings about the chances of winning the war?

ARTISTS Locate a painting in your textbook or in another book showing a scene from the American Revolution. Plan a brief talk describing the picture and giving background information about the scene depicted.

★ Hold a Fighting With the Continental Army press conference at which each group presents or describes its completed activity.

Continental Army medicine chest

Continental Army musket

Chapter 6 • **185**

Answers to Thinking About Geography

1. A **2.** C **3.** B **4.** G **5.** E
6. F **7.** D
Movement: Cornwallis was relying on the British navy in the Chesapeake to supply his troops at Yorktown and to provide a means of escape.

Assessment

Chapter Resources Binder For a more comprehensive evaluation of student understanding of this chapter, assign Chapter Tests A and B and/or Extra Unit Questions from Unit 2, pages 21–26 and 43–45.
Computer Test Bank You can use Chapter Tests and Extra Unit Questions to create your own tests for both testing and retesting.

Alternative Assessment

Chapter Resources Binder See the Alternative Assessment booklet in the *Social Studies Educator's Handbook* series.
Portfolio You might meet with students to choose appropriate work from the chapter for inclusion in their portfolios.

Lessons	Teaching Resources
1 A Confederation of States **Objectives** 1. Identify the kinds of government that the states set up. 2. Identify the problems that the nation faced in the early years. 3. Describe how the Northwest Ordinance provided for growth in the United States. 4. Identify the causes and results of Shays' Rebellion.	**Lesson Planner** Cooperative Learning, p. 39 **Student Study Guide** Section 1 Study Guide, p. 69 **Chapter Resources Binder, Unit 2** *Critical Thinking* Solving Problems, p. 31 *History Through Literature* Paul Bunyan of the North Woods, p. 32 *Geography in History* Surveying the Public Lands, pp. 33–34 **Interdisciplinary Connections:** Western Lands ■ *Arts* Appalachian Crafts, p. 38 ▨ *Sciences* Surveying for Settlement, p. 39 ■ *Geography* The Wilderness Road, p. 40 ■ *World* River Rights, p. 41 ■ *Civics* The State of Franklin, p. 42
2 A Grand Convention **Objectives** 1. Explain why the Constitutional Convention met in secret. 2. Describe how the delegates settled the question of representation. 3. Identify other issues that the Convention resolved.	**Lesson Planner** Cooperative Learning, p. 40 **Student Study Guide** Section 2 Study Guide, p. 70 **Our Multicultural Heritage** *Biography* Paul Cuffe, Fighter for the Right to Vote, p. 19
3 A More Perfect Union **Objectives** 1. Explain how Enlightenment ideas influenced the Constitution. 2. Describe how power was divided between the federal government and the states. 3. Explain how the framers of the Constitution limited the powers of government.	**Lesson Planner** Cooperative Learning, p. 41 **Student Study Guide** Section 3 Study Guide, p. 71
4 Ratifying the Constitution **Objectives** 1. Explain how the views of Federalists and Antifederalists differed. 2. Describe how the Constitution can be amended. 3. Identify the rights that the Bill of Rights protects.	**Lesson Planner** Cooperative Learning, p. 42 **Student Study Guide** Section 4 Study Guide, p. 72 **Our Multicultural Heritage** *Biography* Ann Lee, Mother of the Shakers, p. 20 *Milestone* A Victory for Freedom of the Press, p. 21 **Chapter Resources Binder, Unit 2** *Skill Application* Finding Main Ideas, p. 30

*C*hapter *M*anager

Multimedia Resources	Additional Resources	Chapter-Level Resources
Transparencies *Time Lines* The United States and the World, 1775–1825, p. E-17 *Geography and History* Expansion of the United States, p. I-25 *Political Cartoons* The Need for Order, p. G-15 *Interdisciplinary Connections* Barter on the Western Frontier, p. B-45 **Videotapes/Videodiscs** *United States History Video Collection* Birth of a New Government, Vol. 5, Ch. 7; Shays' Rebellion, Vol. 5, Ch. 13	**Voices of Freedom** Articles of Confederation, pp. 67–68 **Historical Outline Map Book** Western Land Claims, p. 29	**Lesson Planner** Activity Based, pp. 43–44 **Student Study Guide** Chapter 7 Study Guide, pp. 73–74 **Chapter Resources Binder** **Unit 2** Vocabulary Building, p. 29 Chapter Test A, pp. 35–37 Chapter Test B, pp. 38–40 Illustration Master, p. 41 Extra Unit Questions, pp. 43–45 **English Guided Reading** Guided Reading, pp. 13–14 **Spanish Resources** **CD-ROM** *Time Tour* Creating a Republic in From Revolution to Republic **Computer Test Bank** Chapter Tests A and B Extra Unit Questions **Guided Reading Audiotapes** Side 3
CD-ROM *Face the Issues* The Great Compromise of the Constitutional Convention **Videotapes/Videodiscs** *United States History Video Collection* The Constitutional Convention, Vol. 5, Ch. 16; Am I Not a Man and Brother, Vol. 5, Ch. 19	**Voices of Freedom** Franklin Asks Support for the Constitution, p. 69	
Videotapes/Videodiscs *United States History Video Collection* Liberty, Fraternity, Equality!, Vol. 5, Ch. 31		
Videotapes/Videodiscs *United States History Video Collection* The Promise of Freedom, Vol. 5, Ch. 25	**Voices of Freedom** A Farmer Speaks Out for the Constitution, pp. 70–71 An Antifederalist Argues His Case, p. 71	

Lesson Planner

For a developed **Activity-Based** lesson plan for Chapter 7, see the *Lesson Planner,* pages 43–44.

 Chapter Resources

Vocabulary Building The Vocabulary Building worksheet for Chapter 7 from Unit 2, page 29, of the *Chapter Resources* binder can be used as a prereading activity or as a review of chapter vocabulary. (Reteaching/Easy)

 Student Study Guide

Chapter 7 Study Guide Refer students to pages 73–74 of the *Student Study Guide* for the Chapter 7 Study Guide. The study guide can be used for chapter review as well as for reteaching. (Reteaching/Average)

 Guided Reading Audiotapes

Students can use *Guided Reading Audiotapes,* Chapter 7, side 3, to listen to section previews, summaries, and review questions. The tapes will benefit students who are auditory learners, students who have trouble reading, or students acquiring English. Tapes are also available in Spanish. (Reteaching/Easy)

CHAPTER 7

Creating a Republic

(1776–1790)

CHAPTER OUTLINE

1 A Confederation of States

2 A Grand Convention

3 A More Perfect Union

4 Ratifying the Constitution

1778 *The winter at Valley Forge was a low point for Washington's army, but by spring 1778 Americans became more hopeful.*

1783 *The Treaty of Paris formally ended the American Revolution. John Adams used this seal at the signing of the treaty.*

1777 *While Americans fought for independence, the Continental Congress completed the Articles of Confederation.*

1776   1780   1784

WORLD EVENT
1778 British Captain Cook becomes first European to reach Hawaii

186 • Chapter 7

Chapter Time Line
Activity

Divide the class into groups of three or four students each. Have each group choose one of the illustrations or World Events entries. (You can avoid duplication by assigning a number to each event and then having a representative from each group pull a numbered slip of paper from a container.) Allow the groups time to discuss why the event happened and what its results were. Student responses can be based upon what they have learned thus far. At the end of Chapter 7, have the groups reconvene to discuss the questions again and to compare their responses.

186

Chapter Setting

❝The American war is over: but this is far from being the case with the American revolution. On the contrary, nothing but the first act of the great drama is closed. It remains yet to establish and perfect our new forms of government.❞

Those words, spoken by Dr. Benjamin Rush in January 1787, reflected the feelings of many Americans after the Revolution. They knew that winning the war against Britain had been only a beginning.

Rush was a respected doctor. In Philadelphia, he set up the nation's first free medical clinic. At the University of Pennsylvania, he taught the latest medical theories.

Rush had been an outspoken Patriot. In 1775, he urged Thomas Paine to write a pamphlet in favor of independence and suggested the title *Common Sense*. As a member of the Continental Congress, Rush signed the Declaration of Independence.

With his fellow Patriots, he celebrated the signing of the Treaty of Paris in 1783.

Now, however, Rush was worried about the health of the nation. Could the United States succeed in its bold experiment at self-government? During the war, Americans had set up their first government. Rush believed that the government was too weak to hold the 13 states together. Others agreed. In May 1787, a special convention met in Philadelphia. There, the curtain rose on the next act of the American Revolution.

> ## ACTIVITY
> Imagine that you live in the United States after the Revolution. Design a coat of arms for your new nation. Include elements that make the nation special. Under the coat of arms, list three problems that you think a new nation might face.

1787 *The Northwest Ordinance set up a way to admit new states to the United States. This map shows the Northwest Territory.*

1788 *The Constitution united the country under a strong central government.*

1791 *The Bill of Rights guaranteed individual rights and freedoms.*

1784   1788   1792

WORLD EVENT
1787 Sierra Leone founded as settlement for free slaves

WORLD EVENT
1789 French Revolution begins

Chapter 7 • **187**

Answer to Caption

Answers will vary, but students should understand that towns and states rely on the federal government for many things, such as funding for schools, roads, and pollution control.

Section 1
pp. 188–194

Bell Ringer

Write this question on the chalkboard: Which is more important, state government or the national government? Have students freewrite a response.

Lesson Plan

1. Focus During the Revolution, each state government had its own constitution. At the same time, the Continental Congress wrote a constitution for the nation that set up a weak central government. In this section, students examine early problems in governing and extending the new nation.

2. Instruct Have students consider how the early problems of the United States illustrate the problems of a democracy. Ask: How would a monarchy have helped avoid these problems? Why, then, were Americans generally unwilling to accept a monarchy?

3. Close To close the lesson, have students create and answer at least one question about each subsection heading.

1
A Confederation of States

FIND OUT

- What kinds of government did the states set up?
- What problems did the nation face in the early years?
- How did the Northwest Ordinance provide for growth of the United States?
- What were the causes and results of Shays' Rebellion?

VOCABULARY constitution, execute, bill of rights, economic depression

One afternoon in January 1776, a Patriot mob aimed a cannon at the home of John Wentworth, governor of New Hampshire. Wentworth, a Loyalist, did not wait to find out what the mob would do. He scurried to safety in a nearby British fort.

When the war broke out, royal officials throughout the colonies fled. "The sudden and abrupt departure of our late Governor," announced the New Hampshire assembly, "creates the necessity of establishing a [new] form of government."

In May 1776, the Continental Congress asked each colony to set up a government to protect "the lives, liberties, and properties" of its citizens. In July, the Congress set about the more difficult task of organizing a new national government.

State Constitutions

During the Revolution, most states wrote their own constitutions. A **constitution** is a document that sets out the laws and principles of a government. States wanted written constitutions for two reasons. First, a written constitution would spell out the rights of all citizens. Second, it would set limits on the power of government.

In writing their constitutions, states often followed the basic form of their old colonial charters. These, in turn, were based on English law. Some states simply kept the charters but struck out all mention of the king. Others wrote new constitutions, which voters approved.

Dividing power. Colonists were concerned about putting too much power in the hands of a few people. To avoid this, they divided the power of state governments between a legislature and an executive.

Every state had a legislature that passed laws. Lawmakers were elected by voters. Power within the legislature was divided between an upper house, called a senate, and a lower house. All states except Pennsylva-

A New England Town *Exeter, New Hampshire, shown here in the late 1700s, had its own way of doing things. Few Americans wanted to give control to a national government.* **Linking Past and Present** *Do you think towns like Exeter could manage today without help from the national government? Explain.*

Connections With Civics
Background

According to legend, Fisher Ames, a member of Congress from Massachusetts, provided a popular description of the new democracy after the Revolution. Monarchy, he said, was like "a full-rigged ship, trim and beautiful, with all hands at their stations and the captain at the helm. It executes its maneuvers sharply and operates with the greatest efficiency, but if it hits a rock, the frail hull is crushed and the vessel sinks. Democracy is like a raft — hard to navigate, impossible to keep on course, and distressingly slow. If it runs onto a rock, it simply careens off and takes a new course."

Critical Thinking
Understanding Causes and Effects

Have students write one cause and one effect for each of the following: (a) Each of the new states wrote its own constitution. (b) The Articles of Confederation created a weak central government. (c) Virginia gave up its claim to western lands.

nia had a governor, who **executed**, or carried out, the laws.

Protecting freedoms. Virginia further limited the power of government by including a bill of rights in its constitution. A **bill of rights** lists freedoms that the government promises to protect. In Virginia, the bill of rights protected freedom of religion and freedom of the press. Citizens also had the right to a trial by jury. Other states followed Virginia's example and included bills of rights in their own constitutions.

Expanding the right to vote. Under state constitutions, more people had the right to vote than in colonial times. To vote, a citizen had to be a white male and be over age 21. He had to own a certain amount of property or pay a certain amount of taxes. For a time, some women in New Jersey could vote. In a few states, free black men could vote. Enslaved African Americans could not vote in any state.

Forming a National Government

Although the states had formed 13 separate governments, the Continental Congress drafted a plan for the nation as a whole. Delegates believed that the colonies could not succeed in their struggle for independence unless they were united by a national government.

The first national constitution. Writing a constitution that all the states would approve was difficult. In 1776, few Americans thought of themselves as citizens of one nation. Instead, they felt loyal to their own states. "Virginia, Sir, is my country," said Thomas Jefferson. "Massachusetts is our country," John Adams told a friend.

The states were unwilling to turn over power to the national government. They did not want to replace the "tyranny" of British rule with another strong government. In 1777, after much debate, the Continental Congress completed the first American constitution, the ***Articles of Confederation.***

Women at the Polls *For a brief time, from 1790 to 1807, the state of New Jersey let women vote. This picture shows New Jersey women at the polls.* **Citizenship** *What other people were denied the right to vote after the Revolution?*

The Articles of Confederation created a "firm league of friendship" among the 13 states. The states agreed to send delegates to a Confederation Congress. Each state had one vote in Congress.

Congress could pass laws, but at least 9 of the 13 states had to approve a law before it would go into effect. Congress could not regulate trade between states or even between states and foreign countries. Nor could it pass any laws regarding taxes. To raise money, Congress had to ask the states for it. No state, however, could be forced to contribute.

Under the Articles, Congress could declare war, appoint military officers, and coin money. Congress was also responsible for foreign affairs. However, these powers were few compared with those of the states.

A loose alliance. The Articles created a loose alliance among the 13 states. The national government was weak. The Articles did not provide for a president to carry out laws. It was up to the states to enforce laws passed by Congress.

Chapter 7 • **189**

 Lesson Planner

For a developed **Cooperative Learning** lesson plan, see the *Lesson Planner,* page 39.

Answer to Caption

all slaves, most free African Americans, men without property, men below the age of 21

 Chapter Resources

Critical Thinking Duplicate and distribute the worksheet, Solving Problems, from Unit 2, page 31, of the *Chapter Resources* binder. The worksheet gives students the chance to negotiate a compromise among the delegates to the Continental Congress. (Enrichment/Average)

 Voices of Freedom

Primary Source You might assign selection 9-1, Articles of Confederation, on pages 67–68 of *Voices of Freedom.* This first constitution defined the powers of the states and those of the new national government. (Enrichment/Challenging)

 Transparencies

Political Cartoons Use the transparency The Need for Order on page G-15 of *American History Transparencies.* This contemporary cartoon shows the urge to create a government as a basic human need. Teaching suggestions can be found on page G-3. (Enrichment/Average)

Connections With the World
Background

Britain also had a constitution; but instead of a single document, it was made up of written and unwritten laws, traditions, and customs. The part of the law based on traditions and customs is referred to as "common law."

Since Americans did not want an aristocratic class, Benjamin Franklin and others felt that there should be only one house in each legislature, instead of an upper and a lower house, as in the British Parliament. John Adams, however, felt that the legislatures should have an upper house, in which those of superior talent, birth, and wealth could limit the moves of the masses. He persuaded every state but Pennsylvania to create a two-house legislature.

Answers to Map Study

1. Virginia 2. New Hampshire, Rhode Island, New Jersey, Pennsylvania, Maryland, Delaware 3. He believed that it was more important to have a national government than for Virginia to have more territory.

Videotapes/ Videodiscs

United States History Video Collection Use the video segment "Birth of a New Government" from Volume 5, *A New Nation (1776–1815).* Approx. running time 2:00 min. (Enrichment/Average) Vol. 5, Ch. 7

| Chapter 7 | Play |

Transparencies

Time Lines Use the transparency, The United States and the World, 1775–1825, on page E-17 of *American History Transparencies.* Teaching suggestions can be found on page E-14. (Enrichment/Average)

Historical Outline Map Book

Historical Outline Map Duplicate and distribute the map, Western Land Claims, on page 29 of the *American History Historical Outline Map Book.* Lesson ideas for this map can be found on page T-9. (Reteaching/Average)

Despite these weaknesses, the Articles might have worked if the states could have agreed about what needed to be done. Many disputes arose, however. And there was no way of settling them because the Articles did not set up a system of courts. As

MAP STUDY

By 1783, a number of states claimed lands west of the Appalachians.
1. *Which state claimed land directly south of Lake Superior?*
2. *Which states had no claims to western lands?*
3. **Solving Problems** *Why did Thomas Jefferson, a Virginian, persuade Virginia to give up its claims to western lands?*

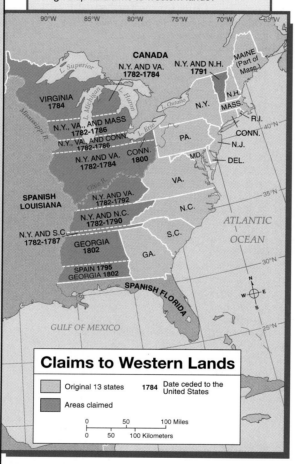

Claims to Western Lands

| | Original 13 states | **1784** Date ceded to the United States |
| | Areas claimed | |

0   50   100 Miles
0   50   100 Kilometers

Noah Webster, a teacher from New England, warned:

66So long as any individual state has power to defeat the measures of the other twelve, our pretended union is but a name, and our confederation, a cobweb.99

Disputes Over Western Lands

The first dispute between the states arose even before the Articles of Confederation went into effect. Most states quickly ratified the Articles. Maryland, however, refused to ratify. It would not sign, it said, until all lands between the Appalachian Mountains and the Mississippi River were turned over to Congress.

Virginia and several other states claimed lands in the West. (See the map at left.) As a small state, Maryland worried that states such as Virginia would become too powerful if they were allowed to keep the western lands. Also, what if Virginia sold its western lands to gain income? Then, Virginia would not need to tax its citizens. What would prevent people and businesses in Maryland from flocking to Virginia to escape taxes?

At first, the "landed" states rejected Maryland's demand. One by one, however, all the states except Virginia agreed to give up their claims. In Virginia, Thomas Jefferson and other leaders strongly believed that a national government was needed. Finally, they convinced state lawmakers to give up Virginia's claims to western lands. In 1781, Maryland ratified the Articles of Confederation, and the first American government went into effect.

Serious Challenges for the Articles of Confederation

By 1783, the United States had won independence. The new nation faced many problems, however. From 1783 to 1787,

---

Linking Past and Present
Activity

Have students speculate about how the United States government today might be different if the Articles of Confederation had been adopted as the final constitution. Ask: What problems might the new national government have faced under the Articles of Confederation? How could such a government try to solve those problems? Under what conditions might this form of government have succeeded? Could a modern national government get along without a chief executive? Why or why not? Could it get along without a strong legislative branch? Why or why not?

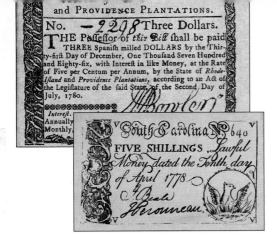

and PROVIDENCE PLANTATIONS.

No. — 2208 Three Dollars.
THE Possessor of this Bill shall be paid
ty-first Day of December, One Thousand Seven Hundred
and Eighty-fix, with Interest in like Money, at the Rate
of Five per Centum per Annum, by the State of *Rhode-Island* and *Providence Plantations*, according to an Act of
the Legiflature of the faid State, of the Second Day of
July, 1780.

Interest.
Annually
Monthly

South Carolina 640
FIVE SHILLINGS *Lawful
Money dated the Tenth day
of April 1778*

State Bank Notes *After the Revolution, each state issued its own money. The bills pictured here were issued by Rhode Island and South Carolina.* **Economics** *Give an example of how your life would be affected if each state issued its own money today.*

Americans had reason to doubt whether their country could survive.

Troubles with money and trade. Perhaps the biggest problem the nation faced was money. As a result of borrowing during the Revolution, the United States owed millions of dollars. But it had no way to repay its debts. Under the Articles of Confederation, Congress could ask the states for money. The states, however, had the right to turn down Congress's request. Often, they did.

During the Revolution, the Continental Congress solved the problem of raising funds by printing paper money. With the crank of a printing press, plain paper was turned into Continental dollars. Without gold or silver to back up the paper money, however, it had little value. Before long, Americans began to describe any useless thing as "not worth a Continental."

As Continental dollars became worthless, states printed their own paper money. This caused confusion. How much was a

North Carolina dollar worth? Was a Virginia dollar as valuable as a Maryland dollar? Most states refused to accept the money of other states. As a result, trade between states became difficult.

Other troubles. The new nation faced other troubles. New Hampshire and New York both claimed Vermont. Under the Articles of Confederation, these states had no way to settle their dispute.

Foreign countries took advantage of the new government's weakness. Britain, for example, refused to withdraw its troops from the Ohio Valley, as it had agreed to do under the Treaty of Paris. Spain, too, challenged the United States. It closed its port in New Orleans to American farmers in the western lands. This was a serious blow to the farmers, who needed the port to ship their products to markets in the East.

GEOGRAPHY AND HISTORY

A Farsighted Policy for Western Lands

Settlers in the western lands posed still another problem. The Articles of Confederation said nothing about admitting new states to the United States. Some settlers in the West took matters into their own hands. For example, in eastern Tennessee, people set up a government called the State of Franklin and applied for admission to the United States.

Congress realized it needed to provide for local governments in the western lands. Thousands of settlers lived in these lands, and every year many more headed west.

To meet the challenge, Congress passed two laws. Both concerned the Northwest Territory, the name used for lands lying north of the Ohio River and east of the Mississippi. (See the map on page 192.) The principles set out in the two laws were later applied to other areas of settlement.

Answers to Map Study

1. Ohio, Michigan, Indiana, Illinois, Wisconsin **2.** (a) 36 square miles (b) 1 square mile **3.** The income from one section in each township was reserved to support schools.

Chapter Resources

Geography in History Duplicate and distribute the worksheet, Surveying the Public Lands, from Unit 2, pages 33–34, of the *Chapter Resources* binder. This worksheet is a description of the different surveying systems used to divide the land in Ohio and Louisiana. (Enrichment/Average)

Townships and sections. The first law, the *Land Ordinance of 1785,* set up a system for settling the Northwest Territory. The law called for the territory to be surveyed and then divided into townships.

Each township would have 36 sections. A section was 1 square mile and contained 640 acres. (See the diagram below.) Congress planned to sell sections to settlers for $640 each. One section in every township was set aside to support public schools.

A plan for new states. The second law, passed in 1787, was the *Northwest Ordinance.* It set up a government for the Northwest Territory and outlawed slavery there. It also provided for the vast region to be divided into three to five separate territories in the future.

When the settlers of a territory numbered 60,000 free settlers, they could ask Congress to admit the territory as a new state. The newly admitted state would be

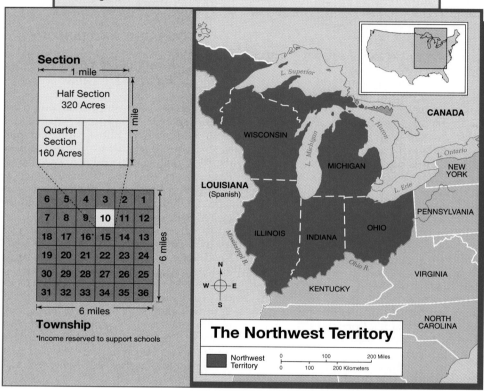

MAP STUDY

In the 1780s, Congress set up a system for settling and governing the Northwest Territory.
1. Which states were carved out of the Northwest Territory?
2. What was the size of (a) a township? (b) a section?
3. **Analyzing Information** How does the chart of a township show that Congress was concerned about education?

The Northwest Territory

Connections With Civics
Background

The Land Ordinance of 1785 enabled Congress to raise money and encouraged the orderly settlement of the new territory.

Originally, it was proposed that in addition to setting aside one section in every township to support public schools a second section be set aside to support the religion of the majority of the township's white male settlers. That proposal was defeated.

Critical Thinking
Analyzing Ideas

Explain that the Northwest Ordinance also called for religious freedom and the fair treatment of Native Americans. Share with them this quotation from the document that established the Northwest Territory: ". . . religion, morality, and knowledge being necessary to good government and the happiness of mankind, schools and the means of education shall forever be encouraged." Ask: How does this goal match a goal of the Land Ordinance of 1785? What subjects do you think would be taught in a school with this goal?

CONNECTIONS

ARTS | SCIENCES | GEOGRAPHY | WORLD | **ECONOMICS** | CIVICS

Barter on the Western Frontier

Few people had money on the American frontier. Pioneers traveled west with the clothes on their backs, a wagon, perhaps a horse and a cow, and a little seed corn. If they needed anything else once they reached their new home, they got it through barter. That is, they exchanged something they could do or shoot or grow or make for the items they needed.

Skins and furs were among the most common barter items. As one pioneer noted, "Furs and [pelts] were the people's money. They had nothing else to give in exchange for rifles, salt, and iron."

Making cloth

Milling grain into flour was strictly a barter business on the frontier. The young man of the family carted the grain to the local mill. There, he waited his turn, often overnight, to have the grain ground into flour. For this service, he paid the miller a portion of the flour, usually one eighth of it.

Women on the frontier produced a variety of goods for barter. A woman might raise a few pounds of cotton each year, spin it, and then weave it into cloth. Seven yards of cotton cloth could be traded for a pig. Nine yards might bring a calf in exchange.

Device for broiling meat

As frontier communities became more settled, their economies changed. After a few years, families produced more than they needed for themselves. They entrusted the surplus to merchants, who shipped it to markets to be sold for cash. In this way, a cash economy slowly replaced the barter system on the frontier.

■ How did the barter system work on the frontier?

> **ACTIVITY** Draw a picture of two items you might offer for barter if you were a pioneer on the frontier. Then hold a barter session to trade for items that you need.

Device for toasting bread

Answer to Connections

People exchanged things that they could grow or shoot or items that they could make for items that they needed.

Transparencies

Interdisciplinary Connections Use the transparency Barter on the Western Frontier on page B-45 of *American History Transparencies*. Teaching suggestions can be found on page B-9. (Enrichment/Average)

ACTIVITY

Guided Instruction Discuss why students feel that certain objects or services would be valuable in a barter economy. When students have completed their two pictures, hold a barter session to see which items are most popular and which items go for the highest "price."

Team-Teaching Suggestion
Economics

You might work with an economics teacher or a teacher known for being active in community service to present a lesson about how bartering works in today's economy. Students could explore the possibilities of bartering networks in their own areas and compare the economics of bartering today with bartering on the western frontier.

Team-Teaching Suggestion
Music

You might work with a music teacher to present a lesson about the uniquely American styles of music created during the settlement of the western frontier. Students can become familiar with specific pieces of music that have become classics of the period and can investigate some of the unusual types of instruments for making music that were available to settlers. You could support this lesson with the Arts Connection worksheet, Appalachian Crafts, on page 38 of the *Interdisciplinary Connections* booklet.

Videotapes/Videodiscs

United States History Video Collection Use the video segment "Shays' Rebellion" from Volume 5, *A New Nation (1776–1815)*, to enhance students' understanding of the causes of Shays' Rebellion and its effects. Approx. running time 2:00 min. (Enrichment/Average) Vol. 5, Ch. 13

Chapter 13 | Play

 Student Study Guide

Section 1 Study Guide Have students use the Section 1 Study Guide on page 69 of the *Student Study Guide* to review and reinforce the content of this section. (Reteaching/Average)

 ACTIVITY

Guided Instruction Before students begin writing their letters, have them discuss what they consider to be weaknesses in the Articles of Confederation. You might want to keep a class list on the board for reference. As they write, encourage students to focus their comments on one or two of the major issues they have discussed. As time permits, you also might have students suggest specific changes. Allow students to exchange letters and compare their ideas.

"on an equal footing with the original states in all respects whatsoever."

The Northwest Ordinance was the finest achievement of the national government under the Articles of Confederation. It provided a way to admit new states to the United States. It guaranteed that new states would be treated the same as the original 13 states. In time, five states were carved from the Northwest Territory: Ohio, Indiana, Illinois, Michigan, and Wisconsin. ■

A Farmers' Revolt

After the Revolution, the nation suffered an **economic depression.** An economic depression is a period when business activity slows, prices and wages fall, and unemployment rises.

Hard times for farmers. The depression hit farmers especially hard. During the Revolution, the demand for farm products had been high. Eager to produce more food, farmers borrowed money for land, seed, animals, and tools. Now, as soldiers returned to their home states, demand for farm goods fell. Many farmers could not repay their loans.

In Massachusetts, matters were made even worse when the state raised farmers' taxes. The courts seized the farms of people who could not pay their taxes or loans. Angry farmers protested what they considered unfair treatment.

Rebellion in Massachusetts. In 1786, discontent flared into rebellion. Daniel Shays, a Massachusetts farmer who had fought at Bunker Hill and Saratoga, was determined to save his debt-ridden farm.

Shays gathered a force of nearly 2,000 farmers. The ragged band traveled around the state, attacking courthouses and preventing the sale of property as payment for debts. When they tried to raid a warehouse full of rifles and gunpowder, the Massachusetts legislature sent the militia to drive them off. This ended ***Shays' Rebellion.***

Time for action. Shays' Rebellion worried many Americans. They saw it as a sign that the Articles of Confederation did not work. George Washington shared their concern. He felt that a desperate crisis was in store for the nation:

66 No day was ever more clouded than the present. . . . I predict the worst consequences from a half-starved, limping government, always moving upon crutches and tottering at every step. 99

Leaders from several states called for a convention to discuss ways to revise the Articles of Confederation. They decided to gather in Philadelphia in May 1787. The action they took when they met, however, went far beyond what many had imagined.

SECTION 1 REVIEW

1. **Locate:** Northwest Territory.
2. **Identify:** (a) Articles of Confederation, (b) Land Ordinance of 1785, (c) Northwest Ordinance, (d) Shays' Rebellion.
3. **Define:** (a) constitution, (b) execute, (c) bill of rights, (d) economic depression.
4. Why did states want written constitutions?
5. (a) What were the terms of the Northwest Ordinance? (b) Why was it important?
6. **CRITICAL THINKING Analyzing Ideas** "I like a little rebellion now and then," wrote Thomas Jefferson when he heard about Shays' Rebellion. "The spirit of resistance to government is so valuable on occasion that I wish it to be always kept alive." Do you think Shays' Rebellion was good for the United States? Explain.

ACTIVITY Writing to Learn

Imagine that you live in the United States under the Articles of Confederation. Write a letter to a friend explaining why the Articles should be revised.

Answers to Section 1 Review

1. See the map on p. 192.
2. (a) Articles of Confederation, p. 189, (b) Land Ordinance of 1785, p. 192, (c) Northwest Ordinance, p. 192, (d) Shays' Rebellion, p. 194
3. (a) constitution, p. 188, (b) execute, p. 189, (c) bill of rights, p. 189, (d) economic depression, p. 194
4. to spell out the rights of citizens and to limit the powers of government
5. (a) The Northwest Ordinance set up a government for the Northwest Territory, outlawed slavery there, divided the region into three to five separate future territories, and provided a way for new areas to become states. (b) The document made it possible for new states to be admitted on an equal footing with the original 13 states.
6. Possible Answer: Shays' Rebellion helped focus attention on the nation's serious problems and therefore encouraged Americans to solve them. On the other hand, the rebellion was a threat to peace at a time when Americans were trying to build a new, strong nation.

2
A Grand Convention

FIND OUT
- Why did the Constitutional Convention meet in secret?
- How did the delegates settle the question of representation?
- What other issues did the Convention resolve?

VOCABULARY *legislative branch, executive branch, judicial branch, compromise*

An air of mystery hung over the Pennsylvania State House in Philadelphia during the summer of 1787. Philadelphians watched as the nation's greatest leaders passed in and out of the building. Eleven years earlier, some of the same men had signed the Declaration of Independence there. What was going on now? Susannah Dillwyn wrote her father about the excitement:

66 There is now sitting in this city a grand convention, who are to form some new system of government or mend the old one. I suppose it is a body of great consequence, as they say it depends entirely upon their pleasure whether we shall in the future have a congress. 99

What would this "grand convention" decide? No one knew. For almost four months, Americans waited for an answer.

The Priceless Notebook

The *Philadelphia Flier* came to a halt in the center of town. The coach's passengers climbed slowly down, stiff and weary. Jammed together on hard, backless benches, they had endured a long, bruising ride to Philadelphia.

Among the passengers was a short, thin young man. Picking up his bags, he headed to a nearby boarding house. His mind was not on the journey, however. He was thinking of the convention set to begin on May 14, only 11 days away.

Madison the delegate. At age 36, James Madison was one of the youngest delegates to the ***Constitutional Convention.*** He also was the best prepared.

For months, Madison had secluded himself on his father's plantation in Virginia. There, he read stacks of books on history, politics, and commerce. During the night, he would rise at odd hours to read more or to write notes. He arrived in Philadelphia with a case bulging with research.

BIOGRAPHY James Madison *James Madison's careful notes at the Constitutional Convention provided a valuable record for future generations of Americans.* **Citizenship** *Why was it important for later Americans to know how the framers of the Constitution made their decisions?*

Answer to Caption
Possible Answer: If the constitutionality of a matter were later questioned, one could go back and determine the original intent.

Section 2
pp. 195–199

Bell Ringer

Ask students to compare the two houses of Congress by answering the following questions: Which house represents each state equally? Which house represents the state according to the size of its population? Why do you think Congress was set up this way?

Lesson Plan

1. Focus Delegates to the Constitutional Convention voted to write a new Constitution. In this section, students learn about the two plans that were discussed, the objections that were raised to each, and the compromises that allowed the delegates to agree on a new Constitution.
2. Instruct Have two groups of students re-create the debate at the Constitutional Convention over representation. One group can support the Virginia Plan and another the New Jersey Plan.
3. Close To close the lesson, have students compare the New Jersey and Virginia plans. Then ask them to describe the Great Compromise and the Three-Fifths Compromise.

Linking Past and Present
Activity

Believing that drafting a new form of government would be a delicate matter, Convention delegates agreed to keep their proceedings a secret. Have students in small groups discuss the issue of government secrecy and openness in a democracy. Ask them to consider the following questions, noting those items on which they can reach a consensus and those on which they cannot.

1. Do you agree or disagree with the secrecy decision of the delegates at the Constitutional Convention? Why or why not? In what ways was the decision fair to the American people? In what ways was it unfair?
2. Would such an agreement be possible today? Why or why not?
3. In what situations today is government secrecy appropriate? Why do you think so?

Connections With Civics
Background

Delegates to the Constitutional Convention included important leaders such as Benjamin Franklin, Alexander Hamilton, George Washington, and James Madison. Other leaders, however, declined to attend. John Adams and Thomas Jefferson were in Europe. Patrick Henry and Sam Adams suspected that the Convention would weaken the powers of the individual states. Indeed, Henry said that he "smelt a rat."

On May 14, Madison eagerly walked the few blocks to the State House. Only the delegates from Virginia and Pennsylvania were there, however. Madison was deeply disappointed. Without representatives from at least seven states, the work of the Convention could not start.

Madison waited impatiently for more than a week. One by one, delegates braved the spring rains, flooded streams, and muddy roads to reach Philadelphia. At last, on May 25, there were enough delegates for the Convention to begin.

Madison the historian. Madison watched as delegates greeted one another and began taking their seats. He did not want to miss a thing.

> **❝**I chose a seat in front of the presiding member, with the other members on my right and left hand.... I was not absent a single day nor more than a fraction of an hour in any day so that I could not have lost a single speech, unless a very short one.**❞**

Each night, by candlelight, he filled in from memory any gaps in his notes. Surely, he reasoned, future Americans would want to know how the delegates arrived at their decisions.

During the weeks that followed, Madison kept a full and clear record of the proceedings. Madison was a wise man, however. He knew that the delegates needed to speak freely. Often, they made statements or took positions that some people might not understand. He decided that his account should not become public so long as a single delegate was still alive.

The notes are published. As it turned out, Madison himself was the last surviving delegate. But even then, he turned down requests to publish his notes. Only in 1840, four years after his death, was Madison's record of the Constitutional Convention printed. At last, Americans learned how, during the hot summer of 1787, the framers of the Constitution created a strong and enduring government. ■

The Delegates Begin

The 55 delegates who gathered in Philadelphia were a remarkable group. Every state except Rhode Island sent representatives. At age 81, Benjamin Franklin was the oldest. He was wise in the ways of government and human nature. George Washington, like Madison, was a delegate from Virginia. Washington was so well respected that the delegates at once elected him president of the Convention.

Other delegates were young men in their twenties and thirties. Among them was Alexander Hamilton of New York. During the Revolution, Hamilton had served for a time as Washington's private secretary. Hamilton made no secret of his dislike for the Articles of Confederation. "The nation," he wrote, "is sick and wants powerful remedies." The powerful remedy he prescribed was a strong national government.

Delegates decided to keep their talks secret so that they could speak their minds freely. To ensure secrecy, guards stood at the door. The windows were left closed to keep passersby from overhearing the debates. The closed windows made the room very hot, however. The summer of 1787 was the hottest in many years.

> ### History and You
> *The delegates to the Constitutional Convention believed that they had two loyalties: to their state and to a national government. Do you consider yourself more a citizen of your town, your state, or the whole country? Explain your answer.*

Learning Styles
Kinesthetic Learners

Have each student choose a delegate to the Constitutional Convention to research. Students should relate what they find out about their subjects' backgrounds to their subjects' personal views about the Convention. Each student can report about his or her subject by pretending to be that person. Allow students to use simple props and/or costumes to enhance their reports.

Connections With Art
Background

Among the many decisions made at the Constitutional Convention was that of a national symbol. Not everyone favored the powerful bald eagle. Ben Franklin argued that the turkey was a more appropriate symbol: "For my own part, I wish the bald eagle had not been chosen as the representative of our country; he is a bird of bad moral character; he does not get his living honestly; you may have seen him perched on some dead tree, where too lazy to fish for himself, he watches the labor of the fishing-hawk; and, when that diligent bird has at length taken a fish, and is bearing it to his nest for the support of his mate and young ones, the bald eagle pursues him and takes it from him. . . . In truth, the turkey is in comparison a much more respectable bird, withal a true original native of America."

Hopelessly Divided

Soon after the meeting began, delegates decided to do more than revise the Articles of Confederation. They chose instead to write an entirely new constitution for the nation. They disagreed, however, about what form that government should take.

Virginia makes a proposal. Early on, Edmund Randolph and James Madison, both from Virginia, put forward a plan for the new government. It became known as the *Virginia Plan.* In the end, much of the plan was included in the new constitution.

The Virginia Plan called for a strong national government with three branches: the legislative, the executive, and the judicial. In general, the **legislative branch** of government passes the laws. The **executive branch** carries out the laws. The **judicial branch,** or system of courts, decides if laws are carried out fairly.

The Virginia Plan also called for a two-house legislature. Seats in both houses would be awarded to each state on the basis of population. Thus, in both houses, larger states would have more representatives than smaller ones. This differed from the Articles of Confederation, which gave every state, regardless of population, one vote in Congress.

Small states object. Small states objected strongly to the Virginia Plan. They feared that the large states could easily outvote them. Supporters of the Virginia Plan responded that it was only fair for a state with more people to have more representatives.

After two weeks of debate, William Paterson of New Jersey presented a plan that had the support of the small states. The *New Jersey Plan* also called for three branches of government. However, it provided for a legislature that had only one house. Each state, no matter what the size of its population, would have one vote in the legislature.

African Americans in the New Nation *The Constitutional Convention made many decisions affecting African Americans. African Americans, however, had no representation at the Convention. Leaders such as Absalom Jones formed the Free African Society to work for their rights.* ***Citizenship*** *What other groups would not have been represented at the Convention?*

Breaking the Deadlock

The two sides deadlocked. With tempers flaring, it seemed that the Convention would fall apart without adopting any plan. Finally, Roger Sherman of Connecticut worked out a compromise between the large and small states. A **compromise** is a settlement in which each side agrees to give up some of its demands.

Sherman's compromise called for a legislature with a lower and an upper house. Members of the lower house, known as the House of Representatives, would be chosen by all men who could vote. Seats in the lower house would be awarded to each

 Our Multicultural Heritage

Biography Have students read the biography, Paul Cuffe, Fighter for the Right to Vote, on page 19 of the *Our Multicultural Heritage* booklet. (Enrichment/Average)

Connections With Civics
Background

A one-house legislature was not the only feature that distinguished the New Jersey Plan from the Virginia Plan. The New Jersey Plan called for an executive branch of more than one person (although, like the Virginia Plan, it proposed that the executives be chosen by the federal legislature) to make sure that no one person became too powerful in the new government. Furthermore, the New Jersey Plan called for a national judiciary that would be appointed by the executive branch, whereas the Virginia Plan had proposed that the judiciary be appointed by the legislative branch. The New Jersey Plan was basically an attempt to revise rather than replace the Articles of Confederation, and it was debated for only four days in the Convention. When the Virginia Plan was adopted on June 19 (by a vote of 7 to 3) the Convention committed itself to establishing a new plan for a federal government.

state according to its population. This idea, which resembled the Virginia Plan, was popular with the larger states.

Members of the upper house, called the Senate, would be chosen by state legislatures. Each state, no matter what its size, would have two senators. This part of Sherman's compromise appealed to the smaller states.

On July 16, the delegates narrowly approved Sherman's plan. It became known as the *Great Compromise.* Each side gave up some demands to preserve the nation as a whole.

Compromises Between North and South

The Great Compromise raised another thorny issue. Would slaves be counted as part of a state's population? The answer to this question was important because it affected the number of votes a state would have in the House of Representatives.

Should slaves be counted? The question of slavery led to bitter arguments between the North and the South. Southerners wanted to include slaves in the population count even though they would not let slaves vote. Northerners protested. If slaves were counted, southern states would have more representatives than northern states. Northerners argued that since slaves could not vote, they should not be counted.

Once again, the delegates compromised. They agreed that three fifths of the slaves in any state would be counted. In other words, if a state had 5,000 slaves, 3,000 of them would be included in the state's population count. This agreement became known as the *Three-Fifths Compromise.*

The slave trade. Northerners and southerners also disagreed over another issue related to slavery. By 1787, some northern states had banned the slave trade within their borders. They wanted the new Congress to ban the slave trade in the entire nation. Southerners warned that such a ban would ruin their economy.

In the end, the two sides compromised. Northerners agreed that Congress could not outlaw the slave trade for at least 20 years. After that, Congress could regulate the trade if it wished. Northerners also agreed that no state could stop a fugitive slave from being returned to an owner who claimed him.

Signing the Constitution *On September 17, 1787, the work of the Constitutional Convention was done. Here, George Washington looks on as delegates sign the new Constitution of the United States.* **Citizenship** *Why was it important that delegates to the Constitutional Convention were willing to compromise?*

Signing the Constitution

As summer drew to a close, the weary delegates struggled with other difficult questions. How many years should the President, head of the executive branch, serve? How should the courts be organized? Would members of Congress be paid?

Finally, on September 17, 1787, the Constitution was ready. Gathering for the last time in the State House, delegates listened quietly as the final document was read aloud. Then, one by one, delegates came forward to sign the document. They had done something truly remarkable. In just a few months, they had set up the framework for a lasting government.

SECTION 2 REVIEW

1. **Identify:** (a) James Madison, (b) Constitutional Convention, (c) Virginia Plan, (d) New Jersey Plan, (e) Roger Sherman, (f) Great Compromise, (g) Three-Fifths Compromise.
2. **Define:** (a) legislative branch, (b) executive branch, (c) judicial branch, (d) compromise.
3. (a) How did the Virginia Plan arrange for seats to be awarded in the legislature? (b) Why did small states object to this arrangement?
4. (a) What compromises did the North and South reach? (b) Why were these compromises necessary?
5. **CRITICAL THINKING Defending a Position** James Madison said that "no Constitution would ever have been adopted by the Convention if the debates had been made public." Do you agree or disagree? Explain.

ACTIVITY Writing to Learn
Write a dialogue between a delegate from a large state and a delegate from a small state about the best plan for allotting seats in the legislature.

---

3 A More Perfect Union

FIND OUT
- How did Enlightenment ideas influence the Constitution?
- How was power divided between the federal government and the states?
- How did the framers of the Constitution limit the power of government?

VOCABULARY republic, separation of powers, federalism, electoral college, checks and balances, bill, veto, override, impeach

---

As the Constitutional Convention ended, a woman rushed up to Benjamin Franklin. "Well, Doctor," she asked, "what have we got, a republic or a monarchy?" "A republic," he replied. "If you can keep it."

A **republic** is a nation in which voters elect representatives to govern them. "We the people of the United States," the preamble, or introduction, to the Constitution begins. Those words make clear that the power of government comes from the people. As Franklin pointed out, it was up to the people to make their new government work.

Ideas That Shaped the Constitution

Americans were the first people to write a constitution setting up a government. Yet many ideas in the Constitution had come from other sources.

League of the Iroquois. Many early American leaders admired the Iroquois system of government. They considered the League of the Iroquois as a model for the

---

Answers to Section 2 Review

1. (a) James Madison, p. 195, (b) Constitutional Convention, p. 195, (c) Virginia Plan, p. 197, (d) New Jersey Plan, p. 197, (e) Roger Sherman, p. 197, (f) Great Compromise, p. 198, (g) Three-Fifths Compromise, p. 198
2. (a) legislative branch, p. 197, (b) executive branch, p. 197, (c) judicial branch, p. 197, (d) compromise, p. 197
3. (a) The Virginia Plan called for a two-house legislature, with seats in both houses to be awarded to each state on the basis of population. (b) Small states felt that large states would be able to outvote them.
4. (a) The two compromises reached by the North and South were the Three-Fifths Compromise, which allowed three fifths of the slaves in any state to be counted for representation in the House of Representatives and the agreement that slave trade could continue for at least 20 years, after which Congress could regulate the trade if it wished. (b) Possible Answer: If no one had been willing to compromise, the Union might not have survived.
5. Possible Answer: Secrecy allowed delegates to take positions that they might not have taken if debate were public; it also allowed them to change their minds without losing face. Nevertheless, secrecy meant that the general public was not allowed to offer suggestions or to make any changes in the Constitution.

1. Focus The new Constitution organized the United States as a republic. In this section, students learn how the powers of the national government were delegated. They also study the relationships among the three branches of government.

2. Instruct Have students find as many facts as they can to support the following generalizations: (a) Under the Constitution, the national government became more powerful than it had been under the Articles of Confederation. (b) Each branch of the federal government has some power over the other branches. (c) The framers of the Constitution did not want the President to be elected directly by the voters.

3. Close To close the lesson, have students create and play a matching game in which students link details about the Constitution's origins and its contents.

Lesson Planner

For a developed **Cooperative Learning** lesson plan, see the *Lesson Planner,* page 41.

Answer to Caption

It makes laws and provides a justice system so that all people can receive fair and equal treatment.

idea of unity. In the League, member nations governed their own affairs but joined together for defense. When Benjamin Franklin urged a similar union of colonies in 1754, he pointed to the League's success:

> 66The strength of the League . . . has bound our Friends the Iroquois together in a common tie which no crisis, however grave, since its foundation, has managed to disrupt.99

John Rutledge also admired the Iroquois union. At the Constitutional Convention, Rutledge read to delegates from an Iroquois treaty, which began, "We, the people, to form a union, to establish peace, equity and order." The framers used similar language when they wrote the preamble of the United States Constitution.

Ideas from Europe. Ideas in the Constitution also came to the United States from Europe. The idea of limiting the power of the ruler, for example, was included in England's Magna Carta. (See page 86.) From England, too, came the idea of representative government. Since the mid-1200s, representatives in Parliament had made laws for the country. Since 1689, the English Bill of Rights had protected the rights of individuals. (See page 116.)

The Constitution reflects ideas from the Enlightenment, too. During the Enlightenment, thinkers believed that people could improve society through the use of reason. Many of the Constitution's framers had read the works of Enlightenment thinkers, such as John Locke and the Baron de Montesquieu (MOHN tehs kyoo).

John Locke. In 1690, John Locke published *Two Treatises on Government.* In it, he stated two important ideas.

First, Locke declared that all people had natural rights to life, liberty, and property. Second, he suggested that government is an agreement between the ruler and the ruled. The ruler must enforce the laws and protect the people. If a ruler violates the people's

The Scales of Justice *In this tavern sign of the late 1700s, a woman holds the scales of justice. Americans valued the idea of justice, and they made establishing justice a goal of the Constitution.* **Linking Past and Present** *In what ways does the government establish justice today?*

natural rights, the people have a right to rebel.

Locke's ideas were popular among Americans. The framers of the Constitution wanted to protect the natural rights of the people and limit the power of government. They drew up the Constitution as a contract between the people and their government.

Montesquieu. In 1748, the French thinker Montesquieu published *The Spirit of the Laws.* In it, he urged that the power of government be divided among three separate branches: the legislative, executive, and judicial. Such a division was designed to keep any person or group from gaining too much

Team-Teaching Suggestion
Language Arts

You might work with a language arts teacher to have students create a fictional correspondence based on the important ideas and the historical events surrounding the drafting of the Constitution. Have each student imagine that he or she is the son or daughter of one of the framers of the Constitution. The student can write a series of letters representing a correspondence with his or her father during the period that he is in Philadelphia. Each letter can contain some personal and family news in addition to a discussion of some of the important ideas being considered for inclusion in the Constitution. Help students construct the letters so that an actual correspondence appears to be taking place.

power. This idea became known as the **separation of powers.**

Montesquieu stressed the importance of the rule of law. The powers of government, he said, should be clearly defined. This would prevent individuals or groups from using government power for their own purposes. In the Constitution of the United States, the framers set out the basic laws of the nation, defining and limiting the powers of the government.

A Federal System

The need to limit government power was only one of the issues Americans debated in 1787. Just as important, they had to decide how to divide power between the national government and the states.

Under the Articles of Confederation, the states had more power than Congress. The new Constitution changed that. Under the Constitution, the states delegated, or gave up, some of their powers to the national government. At the same time, the states reserved, or kept, other powers. This division of power between the states and the national government is called **federalism.** (See the chart on page 221 in the Civics Overview.)

Federalism has given Americans a flexible system of government. The people elect both national and state officials. The federal, or national, government has the power to act for the nation as a whole. At the same time, the states have power over many local matters.

History and You

Is there a division of powers in the running of events at your school? Which activities are planned and controlled by leaders of the student council or various clubs? What powers are reserved by the school administration?

What powers does the federal government have? The Constitution spells out the powers of the federal government. For example, only the federal government can coin money or declare war. The federal government can also regulate trade between the states and with other countries.

What powers do states have? Under the Constitution, states have the power to regulate trade within their borders. They decide who can vote in state elections. They also have power to establish schools and local governments.

In addition, the Constitution says that powers not given to the federal government belong to the states or the people. This point pleased people in small states, who were afraid that the federal government might become too powerful.

What powers are shared? The Constitution lists some powers that are to be shared by federal and state governments. Both governments, for example, can build roads and raise taxes.

"The supreme law of the land." The framers of the Constitution had to decide how the states and the federal government would settle disagreements. They did so by making the Constitution "the supreme law of the land." In other words, in any dispute, the Constitution is the final authority.

Separation of Powers

The Constitution set up a strong federal government. To keep the government from becoming too powerful, the framers relied on Montesquieu's idea of separation of powers. In the Constitution, they created three branches of government and then defined the powers of each. (See the chart on page 202.)

The legislative branch. Congress is the legislative branch of government. It is made up of the House of Representatives and the Senate. Members of the House are elected for two-year terms. Senators are elected for

Historical Sidelight
Background

Charles de Secondat, the Baron de la Brède et de Montesquieu (1689–1755), frequently critiqued his own French government. When he lived in England from 1729 to 1731, he became a supporter of the British political system.

Montesquieu believed that all things run according to laws that can be discovered through experimentation. If a nation knew those laws, he felt, it could improve life for its citizens. *The Spirit of the Laws,* his most important work, influenced the constitutions of many countries besides the United States.

Connections With Local Geography
Activity

Using local road maps, have students identify roads built by state governments and those built by the federal government.

Answer to Chart Skills

The President heads the executive branch. The legislative branch passes laws.

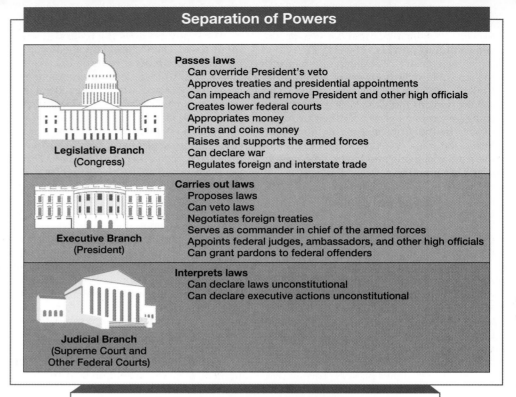

Separation of Powers

Legislative Branch (Congress)

Passes laws
- Can override President's veto
- Approves treaties and presidential appointments
- Can impeach and remove President and other high officials
- Creates lower federal courts
- Appropriates money
- Prints and coins money
- Raises and supports the armed forces
- Can declare war
- Regulates foreign and interstate trade

Executive Branch (President)

Carries out laws
- Proposes laws
- Can veto laws
- Negotiates foreign treaties
- Serves as commander in chief of the armed forces
- Appoints federal judges, ambassadors, and other high officials
- Can grant pardons to federal offenders

Judicial Branch (Supreme Court and Other Federal Courts)

Interprets laws
- Can declare laws unconstitutional
- Can declare executive actions unconstitutional

CHART SKILLS *The Constitution set up three branches of government. Each has its own powers.* ● *Who heads the executive branch? What is the role of the legislative branch?*

six-year terms. The main function of Congress is to make laws.

Under the Constitution, voters in each state elect members of the House of Representatives. Delegates to the Constitutional Convention wanted the House to represent the interests of ordinary people. At first, the Constitution provided for senators to be chosen by state legislatures. In 1913, this was changed. Today, senators are elected in the same way as House members.

Article 1 of the Constitution sets out the powers of Congress. These include the power to collect taxes and to regulate foreign and interstate trade. In foreign affairs,

Congress has the power to declare war and to "raise and support armies."

The executive branch. Some delegates in Philadelphia objected to the idea of a strong executive branch. They remembered the power that King George III had exercised over the colonies. Madison argued, however, that a strong executive was needed to balance the legislature. Otherwise, a headstrong Congress might pass "tyrannical laws" and then execute them "in a tyrannical way." His arguments prevailed.

Article 2 of the Constitution sets up the executive branch of government. It is headed by the President. The executive branch

202 • Chapter 7

Linking Past and Present
Activity

Have students clip articles that illustrate federalism, separation of powers, and/or checks and balances from current newspapers and magazines. (Examples of topics might include a congressional debate over a program proposed by the President, a state decision to make a change in the curriculum of its public schools, a congressional vote on a trade bill, or a conference between the President and state governors.) Students can prepare explanations of how their articles show the Constitution at work. Students may choose to present their explanations orally; alternatively, you may wish to work with them to prepare a bulletin board display that presents both the original articles and students' explanatory paragraphs.

also includes the Vice President and any advisers appointed by the President. The President and Vice President serve four-year terms.

The President is responsible for carrying out all laws passed by Congress. The President is also commander in chief of the armed forces and is responsible for foreign relations.

The judicial branch. Article 3 of the Constitution calls for a Supreme Court. This article also allowed Congress to set up other federal courts. The Supreme Court and other federal courts hear cases that involve the Constitution or any laws passed by Congress. They also hear cases arising between two or more states.

Electing the President

Delegates took great pains to ensure that the President would not become too strong. Some delegates feared that if the President were elected directly by the people, he might become too independent of Congress and the states.

The delegates had another worry. In the late 1700s, news traveled slowly. How would voters get to know a candidate who lived outside their area? New Englanders would probably know little about a candidate from the South. A candidate from Pennsylvania might be unknown to voters in Massachusetts or South Carolina.

To solve these problems, delegates set up the **electoral college.** The electoral college would be made up of electors from every state. Every four years, the electors would meet as a group and vote for the President and Vice President of the United States.

The framers of the Constitution expected that the electors would be well-informed citizens who were familiar with the national government. They believed that such men would choose a President and Vice President wisely.

A System of Checks and Balances

The Constitution set up a system of **checks and balances.** Under this system, each branch of the federal government has some way to check, or control, the other two branches. The system of checks and balances is another way in which the Constitution limits the power of government. (See the chart on page 223.)

Checks on Congress. The system of checks and balances works in many ways. For example, to do its work, Congress passes **bills,** or proposed laws. A bill then goes to the President to be signed into law. (See the chart on page 223.)

The President can check the power of Congress by **vetoing,** or rejecting, a bill. Congress can then check the President by **overriding,** or overruling, the President's veto. To override a veto, two thirds of both houses of Congress must vote for the bill again. In this way, a bill can become law without the President's signature.

Checks on the President. Congress has other checks on the President. The President appoints officials such as ambassadors to foreign countries and federal judges. However, the Senate must approve these appointments. The President can negotiate treaties with other nations. But a treaty becomes law only if two thirds of the Senate approves it.

Congress also has the power to remove a President from office if it finds the President guilty of a crime or serious misbehavior. First, the House of Representatives must **impeach,** or bring charges against, the President. A trial is then held in the Senate. If two thirds of the senators vote for conviction, the President must leave office.

Checks on the courts. Congress and the President have checks on the power of the courts. The President appoints judges, who must be approved by the Senate. If judges misbehave, Congress may remove them from office.

Connections With Civics
Background

Andrew Johnson was the only President ever impeached; only one vote kept him from being convicted in 1868. The House of Representatives was preparing to vote on whether to impeach Richard Nixon when he resigned in 1974.

Our Multicultural Heritage
Activity

Tell students that showing an understanding of how the federal government works is an important step for immigrants who want to become U.S. citizens. Have students work with partners. One student can pretend that he or she has just moved to the United States from another country. The partner explains to the "new immigrant" the different powers of the three branches of government and how the system of checks and balances works.

The "new immigrant" can ask questions to clear up any details that might be confusing. If time allows, reverse roles and repeat the activity.

Members of the class who actually have come from other countries may volunteer to explain how the American system of checks and balances is similar to or different from government practices in their countries of origin.

Answers to Chart Skills

(a) Articles: a one-house Congress; Constitution: a two-house Congress (b) Articles: no executive branch; Constitution: an executive branch, headed by a President, that carries out laws (c) Articles: only states have the power to tax; Constitution: Congress and the states have the power to tax.

Student Study Guide

Section 3 Study Guide Have students use the Section 3 Study Guide on page 71 of the *Student Study Guide* to review and reinforce the content of this section. (Reteaching/Average)

ACTIVITY

Guided Instruction Before students begin writing, have them list the pictures that their books will include and decide which feature of the Constitution each picture will illustrate. Offer assistance as students consider appropriate vocabulary sentence structures and as they revise their drafts. Encourage students to share their completed books with younger students.

The Articles of Confederation and the Constitution

The Articles	The Constitution
1. Legislative branch: Congress is made up of one house	1. Legislative branch: Congress is made up of two houses—Senate and House of Representatives
2. Each state has one vote in Congress	2. Each state has two votes in Senate; each state has one or more votes in House of Representatives, depending on population
3. At least 9 of 13 states must approve a law	3. A majority of each house must approve a law
4. No executive branch	4. Executive branch, headed by President, carries out laws
5. No judicial branch	5. Judicial branch, headed by Supreme Court, interprets laws
6. Only states can tax	6. Congress can tax
7. Each state can coin its own money	7. Only Congress can coin money
8. Each state can regulate trade with other states	8. Only Congress can regulate trade between states
9. Each state can act independently	9. States accept Constitution as supreme law of land

CHART SKILLS *The Constitutional Convention met to revise the Articles of Confederation. Instead, the delegates wrote a completely new document—the United States Constitution.* ● *Compare the way the two documents treat each of the following: (a) the legislative branch, (b) the executive branch, (c) the power to tax.*

A Living Document

The Constitution carefully balances power among three branches of the federal government and between the states and the federal government. This system has been working for more than 200 years, longer than any other written constitution in the world. The Constitution has lasted because it is a living document. As you will read in this and later chapters, it can be changed to meet new conditions in the United States.

SECTION 3 REVIEW

1. **Identify:** (a) John Locke, (b) Baron de Montesquieu.

2. **Define:** (a) republic, (b) separation of powers, (c) federalism, (d) electoral college, (e) checks and balances, (f) bill, (g) veto, (h) override, (i) impeach.
3. Name two Enlightenment ideas that influenced the Constitution.
4. Why did the framers of the Constitution set up a system of federalism?
5. **CRITICAL THINKING Applying Information** How did the following ideas limit government: (a) separation of powers, (b) checks and balances?

 Writing to Learn

Write the text for a picture book describing the main features of the Constitution.

Answers to Section 3 Review

1. (a) John Locke, p. 200, (b) Baron de Montesquieu, p. 200
2. (a) republic, p. 199, (b) separation of powers, p. 201, (c) federalism, p. 201, (d) electoral college, p. 203, (e) checks and balances, p. 203, (f) bill, p. 203, (g) veto, p. 203, (h) override, p. 203, (i) impeach, p. 203
3. Natural rights to life, liberty, and property—as discussed by Locke—are protected in the Constitution; Locke's idea that government is a contract between the people and their government is the basis of the Constitution; Montesquieu's principle of separation of powers is found in the system of three branches of government set up by the Constitution.
4. to resolve the problem of how to divide power between the states and the federal government
5. Possible Answers: (a) Since power is divided among the three branches of government, no one branch can gain too much power. (b) Since each branch has a check on the other two, the power of all three is limited.

4
Ratifying the Constitution

FIND OUT

■ How did the views of Federalists and Antifederalists differ?

■ How can the Constitution be amended?

■ What rights does the Bill of Rights protect?

VOCABULARY amend, due process

At home and in town squares, Americans discussed the new Constitution. Many supported it. Many others did not. Its critics especially worried that the Constitution had no bill of rights. In Virginia, Patrick Henry sounded the alarm:

❝Show me an age and country where the rights and liberties of the people were placed on the sole chance of their rulers being good men, without a consequent loss of liberty!❞

Was a bill of rights needed? Did the Constitution give too much power to the federal government? In the fall of 1787, citizens debated the document sentence by sentence. The Convention had done its work. Now the states had to decide whether or not to ratify the new frame of government.

A Vigorous Battle

The framers of the Constitution sent the document to Congress along with a letter from George Washington. "In our deliberations," wrote Washington, "we kept steadily in view. . . the greatest interests of every true American." He then called on Congress to support the plan.

The framers had set up a process for the states to decide on the new government. At least 9 of the 13 states had to ratify the Constitution before it could go into effect. In 1787 and 1788, voters in each state elected delegates to special state conventions. These delegates then met to decide whether or not to ratify the Constitution.

Heated debate. In every state, heated debates took place. Supporters of the Constitution called themselves *Federalists.* They called people who opposed the Constitution *Antifederalists.*

Federalists favored a strong national government. Among the best-known Federalists were James Madison, Alexander Hamilton, and John Jay. They wrote a series of essays, called *The Federalist Papers,* defending the Constitution. They used pen names, but most people knew who they were.

Antifederalists opposed the Constitution for many reasons. They felt that it made the national government too strong and left the states too weak. They thought that the Constitution gave the President too much power. Most people expected George Washington to be elected President. Antifederalists admired him. They worried, however, about future Presidents who might lack Washington's honor and skill.

Need for a bill of rights. The chief argument used by Antifederalists against the Constitution was that it had no bill of rights. Americans had just fought a revolution to protect their freedoms. They wanted a bill of rights in the Constitution that spelled out those basic freedoms.

Federalists replied that the Constitution protected citizens very well without a bill of rights. Anyway, they argued, it was impossible to list all the natural rights of people. Antifederalists responded that if rights were not written into the Constitution, it would be easy to ignore them. Several state conventions refused to ratify the Constitution unless they received a firm promise that a bill of rights would be added.

Bell Ringer

Have students suggest several ways to complete this sentence: "A law needs to be amended when _____."

Lesson Plan

1. Focus Before the Constitution was ratified, there was much debate between the Federalists, who supported the Constitution, and the Antifederalists, who opposed it. In this section, students learn about the debate, about the amendment process, and about the Bill of Rights.

2. Instruct Have students imagine that they are delegates to a state convention, trying to decide whether to ratify the Constitution. One group can represent the Federalists; another, the Antifederalists; and a third, the undecided delegates. The first two groups should prepare arguments to persuade the undecided delegates, while the undecided delegates prepare questions to ask each faction. Conclude by taking a vote on ratification.

3. Close To close the lesson, have students summarize the arguments over ratification.

 Lesson Planner

For a developed **Cooperative Learning** lesson plan, see the *Lesson Planner,* page 42.

Voices of Freedom

Primary Source You might assign selection 9-4, A Farmer Speaks Out for the Constitution, on pages 70–71 of *Voices of Freedom*. You also might assign selection 9-5, An Antifederalist Argues His Case, on page 71. Ask students to compare and contrast the two points of view. (Enrichment/Challenging)

The states vote to ratify. One by one, states voted to ratify. In June 1788, New Hampshire became the ninth state to ratify the Constitution. Now the new government could go into effect.

Still, the future of the United States remained in doubt. New York and Virginia, two of the largest states, had not yet ratified the plan. In both states, Federalists and Antifederalists were closely matched.

In Virginia, Patrick Henry strongly opposed the Constitution. "There will be no checks, no real balances in this government," he cried. In the end, however, Washington, Madison, and other Virginia Federalists prevailed. In late June, Virginia approved the Constitution.

In New York, the struggle went on for another month. At last, in July 1788, the state convention voted to ratify. North Carolina ratified in November 1789. Rhode Is-

land was the last state to approve the Constitution, finally doing so in May 1790.

"We Have Become a Nation"

Throughout the land, Americans celebrated the news that the Constitution was ratified. Philadelphia set its festival for July 4, 1788. At sunrise, church bells rang. In the harbor, the ship *Rising Sun* boomed a salute from its cannons.

A festive parade filed along Market Street, led by soldiers who had fought in the Revolution. Thousands cheered as six colorfully outfitted horses pulled a blue carriage shaped like an eagle. Thirteen stars and stripes were painted on the front, and the Constitution was raised proudly above it.

That night, even the skies seemed to celebrate. The northern lights, vivid bands of

Americans Celebrate the Constitution *When the Constitution was ratified, celebrations and huge parades, such as this one in New York City, were held across the nation.* **United States and the World** *Why do you think many newly formed nations have used the United States Constitution as a model for their own?*

Linking Past and Present
Activity

Ask students to bring in articles or pictures from newspapers and magazines that illustrate the different rights protected by the Bill of Rights. Students can explain to the class how their clippings represent specific amendments, or they can write explanatory paragraphs to be displayed alongside their clippings as part of a Bill of Rights bulletin board.

Connections With Civics
Background

The original Constitution did not specifically protect religious freedom. After George Washington became President in 1789, several religious groups wrote to him. Baptists, Quakers, Jews, Presbyterians, Catholics, and others expressed hopes that he would safeguard their religious freedom. Washington responded with a promise of support for religious freedom: "Every man . . . ought to be protected in worshipping the Deity according to the dictates of his own conscience."

color, lit up the sky above the city. Benjamin Rush wrote to a friend: "'Tis done. We have become a nation."

Americans voted in the first election under the Constitution in January 1789. As expected, George Washington was elected President. John Adams was chosen Vice President. The first Congress was made up of 59 representatives and 22 senators. It met in New York City, the nation's first capital.

Adding a Bill of Rights

The first Congress quickly turned its attention to adding a bill of rights to the Constitution. The framers had set up a way to amend, or change, the Constitution. They wanted the Constitution to be able to change as times changed. They did not want people to make changes lightly, however. So they made the process of amending the Constitution fairly difficult.

The amendment process. To start the amendment process, an amendment must be proposed. This can be done in two ways. Two thirds of both houses of Congress can vote to propose an amendment. Or two thirds of the states can request special conventions to propose amendments.

Next, the amendment must be ratified. Three fourths of the states must vote for the amendment before it becomes part of the Constitution.

In the more than 200 years since the Constitution was adopted, only 27 amendments have been approved. Ten of these amendments were added in the first years after the Constitution was ratified.

Columbia *Americans felt great pride in their new Constitution. Columbia, shown here, became a symbol of the new nation.* **Citizenship** *What symbols represent the United States today?*

Ten amendments. The first Congress proposed a series of amendments to the Constitution in 1789. By December 1791, three fourths of the states had ratified ten amendments. Those ten amendments became known as the ***Bill of Rights.***

James Madison, who wrote the amendments, insisted that the Bill of Rights does not *give* Americans any rights. People already have the rights listed in the amendments. They are natural rights, said Madison, that belong to all human beings. The Bill of Rights simply prevents the government from taking away these rights.

Protecting individual rights. The First Amendment guarantees freedom of religion, freedom of speech, freedom of the press, freedom of petition, and freedom of assembly, or the right to meet in groups. The next three amendments came out of the colonists' struggle with Britain. For example, the Third Amendment prevents Congress from forcing citizens to quarter, or house, troops in their homes. Before the Revolution, you will remember, Parliament tried to make colonists house and feed British soldiers.

> ***Linking Past and Present***
> *Over the years, many constitutional amendments have been proposed but few were ratified. In the 1970s, for example, Congress proposed the Equal Rights Amendment, designed to promote equal opportunity for women and men. After 10 years of debate, the amendment failed to receive the support of enough states to be ratified.*

Student Study Guide

Section 4 Study Guide Have students use the Section 4 Study Guide on page 72 of the *Student Study Guide* to review and reinforce the content of this section. (Reteaching/Average)

ACTIVITY

Guided Instruction Before students begin writing their editorials, have them list at least three reasons that support their positions. Then, as they write, encourage students to develop each reason into a paragraph. Have them add introductory and concluding paragraphs to complete the editorials. Students might have a peer reader proofread their work.

Freedom of Religion *The Bill of Rights guaranteed Americans the right to worship as they choose. Richard Allen, at right, founded the Bethel Church, shown here, one of the nation's first African American churches.* **Multicultural Heritage** *Why might Allen have felt that African Americans needed their own church?*

Amendments 5 through 8 protect citizens accused of crimes and brought to trial. Every citizen has the right to due process of law. **Due process** means that the government must follow the same fair rules in all cases brought to trial. Among these rules are the right to trial by jury, the right to be defended by a lawyer, and the right to a speedy trial. The last two amendments limit the powers of the federal government to those that are specifically granted in the Constitution.

With the Bill of Rights in place, the new framework of government was complete. Over time, the Constitution became a living document that grew and changed along with the nation.

208 • Chapter 7

SECTION 4 REVIEW

1. **Identify:** (a) Federalist, (b) Antifederalist, (c) Bill of Rights.
2. **Define:** (a) amend, (b) due process.
3. Why were Antifederalists opposed to the Constitution?
4. How can the Constitution be amended?
5. **CRITICAL THINKING Making Decisions**
   (a) List five rights protected by the Bill of Rights. (b) Which do you think is most important? Explain.

ACTIVITY Writing to Learn

Write a newspaper editorial taking a stand for or against ratifying the Constitution.

CRITICAL THINKING SKILLS
Finding Main Ideas

Each paragraph or group of paragraphs in this book has a main idea and supporting details. Finding the main idea is an important skill. It helps you to understand what you have read.

The main idea usually appears in a topic sentence. The topic sentence is often the first sentence of the paragraph. However, a topic sentence may also be at the beginning or at the end of the paragraph.

Read the essay below, and follow the steps to find the main ideas.

1. **Identify the main idea of each paragraph.** (a) What is the main idea of the first paragraph? (b) Which sentence best expresses the main idea? (c) Which sentence in the second paragraph states the main idea?

2. **Identify supporting details.** (a) What is the main idea of the third paragraph? (b) What two details support this main idea? (c) What are the supporting details in the fourth paragraph?

3. **Determine the main idea of the essay.** The main idea or ideas of the essay is the sum of the main ideas of the paragraphs. The main ideas of the paragraphs serve as supporting details for the main idea of the essay. (a) What is the main idea of "Religion and the Bill of Rights"? (b) What details support this main idea?

 Select a subsection of this chapter. Find the main ideas and supporting details. Present them in a concept map.

Religion and the Bill of Rights

Many Americans in 1789 worried that the new Constitution contained no protection of religious freedom. Without such written protection, they feared, their freedom to worship would not be secure. They called on the new government to adopt a bill of rights that would guarantee freedom of religion.

Religious leaders joined the battle for a bill of rights. Among them was Moses Brown, a Quaker leader from Rhode Island. Brown refused to support ratification of the Constitution until he received a promise that a bill of rights would be added. Baptist minister John Leland of Virginia and Bishop John Carroll of Maryland made similar stands in their states.

President Washington supported the efforts of these leaders. He wrote, "Every man...ought to be protected in worshipping the Deity according to the dictates of his own conscience." He promised that the new government would support religious freedom.

Religious freedom became law in 1791. In that year, the Bill of Rights was added to the Constitution. The First Amendment guaranteed religious freedom by stating, "Congress shall make no law respecting an establishment of religion, or prohibiting the free exercise thereof."

Chapter Resources

Skill Application For additional practice, duplicate and distribute the worksheet, Finding Main Ideas, from Unit 2, page 30, of the *Chapter Resources* binder. (Reteaching/Average)

Answers to Skill Lesson

1. Possible Answers: (a) Americans felt that it was very important to guarantee religious freedom in the new Constitution. (b) the first sentence (c) the first sentence
2. (a) George Washington supported a constitutional guarantee of religious freedom. (b) Washington put his opinion in writing; he also promised that the new government would support religious freedom. (c) The Bill of Rights was added to the Constitution; the First Amendment guaranteed religious freedom.
3. Possible Answers: (a) A strong desire to protect religious freedom sped the creation of the Bill of Rights and shaped one of its amendments. (b) Without a bill of rights, Americans worried that religious freedom would not be guaranteed. Religious leaders joined the battle for a bill of rights. President Washington supported their efforts. In 1791, religious freedom became law as a part of the Bill of Rights.

ACTIVITY

Guided Instruction Suggest that students begin by scanning subsection titles. From these titles, students can synthesize a main idea. You might suggest that students use a rough outline form to record their responses.

Students Acquiring English
Activity

Because this Skill Lesson and its Activity depend heavily upon a good grasp of English, SAE students might benefit from working in discussion groups of three. They can take turns summarizing their chosen subsections of the chapter. These summaries can be built upon the main ideas and supporting details they identified. Encourage students to help each other, as needed, to clarify or correct their summaries.

CHAPTER 7 REVIEW

Answers to Reviewing the Main Ideas

1. Nine states had to approve any law passed by Congress; Congress had no power to regulate trade or to raise taxes.

2. The New Jersey Plan called for a one-house legislature, with each state having one vote; the Virginia Plan called for a two-house legislature, with representation in both houses based on population.

3. the sharing of power between the states and the national government

4. (a) legislative, executive, judicial (b) The legislative branch makes the laws; the executive branch carries out the laws; the judicial branch interprets the laws.

5. Possible Answer: The President can check Congress by vetoing a bill; Congress can check the President by overriding his veto.

6. At least 9 of the 13 states had to ratify the Constitution before it could take effect.

7. The Bill of Rights guarantees the right to trial by jury, the right to be defended by a lawyer, and the right to a speedy trial.

Answers to Thinking Critically

1. (a) representation of states in the legislature; counting slaves as part of the population (b) Without compromises, the Convention would have ended in a stalemate; there would have been no agreement on a new constitution. (c) Possible Answers: the death penalty, gun control, abortion

2. Possible Answers: Under the Articles of Confederation, Congress could ask the states for money but could not force them to contribute; the Constitution gave Congress the power to collect taxes. Under the Articles of Confederation, the national government was too weak to hold the nation together; the Constitution provided a strong federal government but prevented tyranny by leaving some powers to the states and by limiting the power of each branch of government.

Summary

- Under the Articles of Confederation, the nation faced serious problems involving money, trade, and disputes between states.
- At the Constitutional Convention, leaders wrote a new Constitution.
- The Constitution divides power between the states and the federal government. It limits the government through separation of powers and through a system of checks and balances.
- After much debate, the states ratified the Constitution. Soon after, a Bill of Rights was added.

Reviewing the Main Ideas

1. How was the power of Congress limited under the Articles of Confederation?
2. Compare the Virginia Plan with the New Jersey Plan.
3. What is federalism?
4. (a) List the three branches of government under the Constitution. (b) What is the main job of each?
5. Give one example of how the legislative and executive branches of the federal government can check each other's power.
6. What process did the framers set up for ratifying the Constitution?
7. How does the Bill of Rights protect citizens who are accused of crimes?

Thinking Critically

1. **Linking Past and Present** (a) Name two issues on which the Constitutional Convention compromised. (b) Why were those compromises important? (c) Describe one local or national issue today that you think requires compromise.
2. **Synthesizing Information** How did the system of federalism help to solve some of

the problems the government faced under the Articles of Confederation?

3. **Understanding Causes and Effects** How do you think the experience of many Americans under British rule influenced the kind of government they set up under the Constitution?

Applying Your Skills

1. **Reading a Diagram** Study the diagram on page 192 that shows a township and section in the Northwest Territory. (a) How large is a township? (b) How many sections are there in a township? (c) How large is a section? (d) Can a section be subdivided? Explain.
2. **Exploring Local History** The Pennsylvania State House, where the Constitutional Convention took place, is a national historic landmark today. What historic buildings are located in your community or state?
3. **Analyzing a Quotation** Reread the exchange between Benjamin Franklin and an unidentified woman on page 199. What do you think Franklin was trying to say with his remark?

Thinking About Geography

Match the letters on the map with the following places: **1.** Original 13 states, **2.** Northwest Territory, **3.** Spanish Louisiana, **4.** Spanish Florida, **5.** Canada. **Movement** Why did settlers travel to the Northwest Territory?

ATLANTIC OCEAN

3. Possible Answer: Americans felt that the British government had abused its power so Americans wanted to avoid making their own government too powerful. Also, partly because of British abuses, Americans wanted to spell out the rights of citizens as well as the powers of government.

Answers to Applying Your Skills

1. (a) 36 square miles (b) 36 (c) 1 square mile (d) Yes; a section can be divided into half sections or quarter sections.
2. Answers will vary. Individual states often publish a listing of historic buildings and sites. Students may be able to find such a listing in the school or in the local library.

3. Franklin was saying that the strength of a republic depends upon the continued interest and involvement of its citizens.

Answers to Thinking About Geography

1. B 2. C 3. E 4. D 5. A
Movement: to find land to farm

Covering the Constitutional Convention

Form into groups to explore the Constitutional Convention. Follow the suggestions below to write, draw, or perform to show what you have learned about the Convention. You may use the textbook, encyclopedias, atlases, or other materials in your classroom library to complete your task. Be able to name your sources of information when you have completed the activity.

LANGUAGE EXPERTS Use your textbook to draw up a list of constitutional terms, such as legislative, executive, judicial, separation of powers, checks and balances, ratify, and amend. Define the terms, using a separate sheet of paper for each. Illustrate the definitions with pictures from newspapers or old magazines. Finally, compile definitions and illustrations in a Constitution Dictionary.

Pennsylvania
State House

ACTORS What was it like to be an ordinary citizen in Philadelphia at the time of the Constitutional Convention? With your group, prepare a skit in which citizens discuss what could be going on behind the closed doors of the Convention. Perform your skit for the class.

ARTISTS Express a point of view about the Constitutional Convention in one of the following ways:
- Draw a political cartoon.
- Design a stamp to commemorate the event.
- Create a button or badge that a street vendor might sell outside the State House where delegates are meeting.

Symbols of the
United States

CITIZENS Select one of the compromises made by Convention delegates. Write a letter to a newspaper explaining why this compromise is important to the success of the Convention.

HISTORIANS Create a TV program explaining the ideas that helped shape the Constitution. Use a large wall chart showing the main ideas to illustrate your talk. Interview a Convention delegate to explore how these ideas influenced the form of government the framers set up.

 Design a bulletin board display on which each group presents or describes its coverage of the Constitutional Convention.

Preamble to the
Constitution

We the People of the United States, in order to form a more perfect Union, establish Justice, insure domestic Tranquility, provide for the common defence, promote the general Welfare, and secure the Blessings of Liberty to ourselves and our Posterity, do ordain and establish this Constitution for the United States of America.

Author Note

Esther Forbes In 1943, Esther Forbes (1891–1967) won the Pulitzer Prize for *Paul Revere and the World He Lived In,* an adult biography. During her research, she became fascinated by the lives of apprentices in Boston, and she decided to write about them next. The result was *Johnny Tremain,* which in 1944 won the highest honor for children's books, the Newbery Medal.

Vocabulary

Have students look up and discuss the words *stealthily, billeted, spire, sufficient,* and *piteous* before they read the passage. Students might check their understanding of these words by giving a synonym for each one. Ask: Why would *stealthily* be a good word to describe some of the events just before the American Revolution? How do you think a *spire* might be involved in a story that features Paul Revere?

Prereading Focus

You might have students reread The Shot Heard 'Round the World on pages 154–155 in Chapter 5 to review what they learned about the events that led to the fighting at Lexington and Concord.

Motivation/Prior Knowledge

Have students list several famous Bostonians of this time. Ask: How would you feel about working side by side with these people?

Purpose-Setting Question

Read aloud the introduction to the excerpt. Then ask: How can one person change history?

Discussion Questions

1. Why did Doctor Warren want to speak with Paul Revere? (For some reason, more British troops than usual were gathering; perhaps an attack on the Patriots in

History Through
LITERATURE

Johnny Tremain
Esther Forbes

Introduction   *Johnny Tremain* is a historical novel about a teenage boy in Boston just before the American Revolution. As a member of the Sons of Liberty, Johnny comes in contact with Patriot leaders such as John Hancock and Paul Revere. He also takes part in important events such as the Boston Tea Party. As this excerpt begins, Johnny rushes to warn Paul Revere of British plans to march on Lexington and Concord.

Vocabulary   Before you read the selection, find the meaning of these words in a dictionary: stealthily, billeted, spire, sufficient, piteous

"It is tonight all right," Johnny said to Doctor Warren, "and Colonel Smith will command." He went on to tell what he had found out from Dove. That the expedition would start tonight and that Lexington and Concord were the likely objects, the men sitting about in Warren's surgery had already guessed. . . .

Outside the closed window on Tremont Street a small group of soldiers were marching stealthily toward the Common. These were the first they heard. But soon another group marched past, then another. A man whose duty it was to watch the British boats at the foot of the Common came in to say he had actually seen the men getting into the boats, heading for Cambridge.

Doctor Warren turned to Johnny. . . . "Go to North Square. I've got to talk to Paul Revere before he starts. . . . "

Johnny ran toward North Square. This he found crowded with light infantry and grenadier companies, all in full battle dress. They got in his way and he in theirs.

One of the men swore and struck at him with his gun butt. The regulars were getting ugly. He could not get to the Reveres' front door, but by climbing a few fences he reached their kitchen door, and knocked softly. Paul Revere was instantly outside in the dark with him.

"Johnny," he whispered, "the *Somerset* has been moved into the mouth of the Charles. Will you run to Copp's Hill and tell me if they have moved in any of the other warships? I think I can row around one, but three or four might make me trouble."

"I'll go look."

"Wait. Then go to Robert Newman— you know, the Christ's Church sexton. He lives with his mother opposite the church."

"I know."

"They have British officers billeted on them. *Don't rap at that door.* Take this stick. Walk by the house slowly, limping, tapping with the stick until the light in an upper window goes out. Then go 'round to the alley behind the house. Tell Newman the lanterns are to be hung now. Two of them. He knows what to do."

As Johnny stood among the graves of lonely Copp's Hill looking across the broad mouth of the Charles, he could see lights

Lexington and Concord was being planned.)
2. Why might Paul Revere need the help of a teenage boy? (Johnny had proven his devotion to the Patriot cause. Furthermore, Paul Revere was a well-known figure around Boston, whereas Johnny could go about without being noticed.)
3. Why was the *Somerset* the only British boat on the Charles River? (It was a large, powerful warship; the British must have

thought that no Patriots could stand up to it — or elude it.)
4. Why did Robert Newman discover Johnny before the redcoats did? (Apparently he had been watching for news about the signal that he was to send.)

Historical Sidelight

At the beginning of the excerpt, Johnny is with a man named Doctor Warren. Warren, like Paul Revere, was a real person. In ad-

dition to being a physician, Joseph Warren was a leading Massachusetts statesman and Patriot. He spoke and wrote many times for the colonial cause after 1765. In 1775, Warren was selected president of the Provincial Assembly. He was also elected major general in the Massachusetts forces. Warren fought in the Battle of Bunker Hill, where he was among the first to die for the Patriot cause.

Paul Revere's Ride *In April 1775, Paul Revere, as shown in this painting by Grant Wood, galloped across the countryside, alerting Patriots of the British advance.* **American Traditions** *What do you think would have happened if Revere had been unable to make his ride?*

in the houses of Charlestown. And over there he knew men were watching Boston, watching Christ's lofty spire—waiting for the signal. And as soon as they saw it, the best and fastest horse in Charlestown would be saddled and made ready for Paul Revere, who had himself promised to get over—if possible. Ride and spread the alarm. Summon the Minute Men. He watched the riding lights on the powerful sixty-four-gun *Somerset*. The British had evidently thought her sufficient to prevent boats crossing the river that night. She was alone. . . .

Salem Street, where the Newmans lived, like North Square, was filled with soldiers. The redcoats were assembling here, getting ready to march down to the Common—and they would be a little late. Their orders were to be ready by moon-rise. A sergeant yelled at Johnny as he started to limp past them, but when he explained in a piteous whine that his foot had been squashed by a blow from a soldier's musket and all he wanted was to get home to his mama, an officer said the men were to let "the child" pass. Johnny was sixteen, but he could pull himself together and play at being a little boy still.

Downstairs in the Newman house he could look in and see a group of officers as usual, almost as always, playing at cards. Their jackets were unbuttoned, their faces flushed. They were laughing and drinking. There was on the second floor one light. Johnny couldn't believe anyone up there could hear him tapping in the street below. Instantly the light went out. He had been heard.

Newman, a sad-faced young man, got out at a second-story window in back, ran across a shed roof, and was in the alley waiting for Johnny.

"One or two?" he whispered.

"Two."

That was all. Robert Newman seemed to melt away in the dark. Johnny guessed what the little tinkle was he heard. New-man had the keys to Christ's Church in his hand.

THINKING ABOUT LITERATURE

1. What did Revere ask Johnny to do?
2. How did Johnny fool the sergeant on the street where Newman lived?
3. **CRITICAL THINKING Analyzing Information** Why did the British want to leave Boston secretly?

ACTIVITY Imagine that you are a news reporter assigned to interview Paul Revere just after he returns from warning Patriots at Lexington and Concord. Based on this excerpt and the information in Chapter 5, write 10 questions that you would ask Revere.

Answers to Thinking About Literature

1. Revere asked Johnny to see how many warships were at the mouth of the Charles River; he then was to visit Robert Newman without being detected and to instruct the Christ's Church sexton to hang two lanterns.
2. Johnny pretended to be a younger boy, hurt by a soldier and crying for his mother. The sergeant was eager to get such a whining "child" out of the area quickly.
3. Possible Answer: As "the men sitting about in Warren's surgery had already guessed," General Gage was taking the soldiers to Concord, where a large store of arms was said to be under control of the minutemen. Gage hoped to seize the arms in a surprise raid.

Lessons	Teaching Resources
1 The Goals of the Constitution **Objectives** 1. Describe how the national government helps to unify the nation. 2. Explain why a national system of courts is necessary. 3. Describe how the Constitution protects the rights of the people.	**Chapter Resources Binder** *Civics and the Constitution* Preamble, pp. 21–22 *Civics and the Constitution* Goals of the Constitution, p. 1
2 Five Principles of the Constitution **Objectives** 1. Identify popular sovereignty. 2. Identify limited government. 3. Explain how federalism divides power. 4. Explain how the separation of powers limits government. 5. Explain how the system of checks and balances prevents abuse of power.	**Chapter Resources Binder** *Civics and the Constitution* Principle of Popular Sovereignty, pp. 7–8 *Civics and the Constitution* Principle of Limited Government, pp. 9–10 *Civics and the Constitution* Principle of Federalism, pp. 11–12 *Civics and the Constitution* Article 4: Relations Among the States, pp. 29–30 *Civics and the Constitution* Principle of Separation of Powers, pp. 13–14 *Civics and the Constitution* Principle of Checks and Balances, pp. 15–16 *Civics and the Constitution* Five Principles of the Constitution, p. 2
3 A Living Constitution **Objectives** 1. Describe how the Constitution can be formally changed. 2. Explain the purpose of the Bill of Rights. 3. Identify informal changes that have been made in the Constitution.	**Chapter Resources Binder** *Civics and the Constitution* Articles 5–7: Amending the Constitution/National Supremacy/Ratification, pp. 31–32 *Civics and the Constitution* The Bill of Rights, p. 3 *Civics and the Constitution* Amendments 1–10: The Bill of Rights, pp. 33–34 *Civics and the Constitution* Amendments 11–27, pp. 35–36 *Civics and the Constitution* Protection of Individual Liberties, pp. 17–18 *Civics and the Constitution* Changing the Constitution, p. 19–20
4 The National Government at Work **Objectives** 1. Explain why Congress has set up committees. 2. Identify the roles that the President plays. 3. Describe how the federal court system is organized.	**Chapter Resources Binder** *Civics and the Constitution* Article 1: The Legislative Branch, pp. 23–24 *Civics and the Constitution* Congress in Action, pp. 4–5 *Civics and the Constitution* Article 2: The Executive Branch, pp. 25–26 *Civics and the Constitution* Article 3: The Judicial Branch, pp. 27–28
5 Citizenship at Work **Objectives** 1. Describe how the Fourteenth Amendment helped to expand rights. 2. Identify the responsibilities of citizens.	**Chapter Resources Binder** *Civics and the Constitution* Are You an Informed Citizen?, pp. 39–40 *Civics and the Constitution* You and Your Community, pp. 41–42 *Civics and the Constitution* Voter Turnout, p. 6 *Civics and the Constitution* Self-Test on the Constitution, pp. 37–38

Multimedia Resources	Additional Resources	Chapter-Level Resources
Transparencies *Time Lines* The United States and the World, 1775–1825, p. E-17 **Videotapes/Videodiscs** *United States History Video Collection* We the People, Vol. 5, Ch. 22		**Constitution Study Guide** Chapters 1–5
Videotapes/Videodiscs *United States History Video Collection* The Promise of Freedom, Vol. 5, Ch. 25		

Civics Overview
pp. 214–239

Vocabulary

As part of a vocabulary-building program, you may want to review the following terms with students before they begin the chapter. The number in parentheses refers to the text page on which the word first appears: ensure (216), secure (216), ordain (216), framer (216), regulate (216), dispute (216), verging (217), enforce (217), maintain (217), entitled (218), responsible (218), safeguard (218), sovereignty (219), check (219), concurrent (221), administer (221), branch (222), negotiate (223), confirm (223), propose (223), principle (224), alter (225), agenda (226), flexible (227), house (228), staggered (230), version (230), executive (232), diplomat (232), agency (233), commission (234), corporation (234), district (234), abuse (236), petition (236).

The Constitution at Work

OUTLINE

1 The Goals of the Constitution

2 Five Principles of the Constitution

3 A Living Constitution

4 The National Government at Work

5 Citizenship at Work

1788 Americans ratified the Constitution. Here, crowds in Washington, D.C., celebrate the 200th anniversary.

1791 The Bill of Rights was ratified. These first 10 amendments to the Constitution guaranteed Americans certain basic rights.

| 1700 | 1750 | 1800 | 1850 |

WORLD EVENT
1700s Age of Enlightenment

WORLD EVENT
1789 French Revolution begins

Chapter Time Line
Critical Thinking

You might check students' understanding of the time line captions by comparing and contrasting the information provided. Begin with the following questions; then you or the students might think of others.

- How are the events of 1893 and 1920 similar?
- How does the event of 1870 differ from that of 1920? How are the events similar?
- What similarities might exist between the events of 1870 and 1992?

- What detail is similar about the events of 1788 and 1971? How do the events differ?

Alternatively, invite students to make inferences about each illustration and caption. Questions such as the following might prompt inferences:

- How do you think American women reacted to the 1893 event?
- What do you know about the voters in the illustration for the 1920 event?

214

Overview Setting

Imagine what your life might be like if there were no Constitution. For example, suppose you wanted to visit a neighboring state. Without the Constitution, you might need a passport. Or the state might deny you entry because of your religion or race.

Now suppose that you were to send a letter to the local newspaper criticizing the governor. Without the Constitution, the newspaper might ignore your letter because it must print only what the state government approves. Perhaps the governor might even order your arrest and imprisonment without a trial.

As you can see, the Constitution affects you personally. Under its protection, you are free to express your opinions. It also guarantees you equal opportunity under the law—whatever your religion, sex, race, or national origin. Most important, the Constitution allows you to make your own choices about how to live your life.

The Constitution has remained as the framework of our government for more than 200 years. It endures in part because it guarantees people their rights. At the same time, it has allowed the people to further define and extend those rights.

ACTIVITY Imagine that you and your classmates are stranded on a desert island. Write five laws for governing the group.

1870 The Fifteenth Amendment extended the right to vote to African American men. Here, a voter in New York signs in on election day.

1920 The Nineteenth Amendment gave women the right to vote. Here, a woman registers to vote in Florida.

1971 The Twenty-sixth Amendment extended the vote to Americans 18 years or older. This change gave millions of young Americans a voice in government.

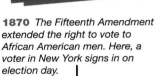

| 1850 | 1900 | 1950 | Present |

▲
WORLD EVENT
1893 New Zealand is first nation to give vote to women

▲
WORLD EVENT
1994 All races in South Africa vote for the first time

Bell Ringer

Ask students to define the term *unconstitutional* and discuss examples of actions that they would consider unconstitutional.

Lesson Plan

1. Focus The Preamble to the Constitution sets out the goals that the framers had for the new nation. In this section, students examine the six goals of the Constitution.

2. Instruct Divide the class into six groups. Have each group design a poster or collage to illustrate one of the six goals of the Constitution. As each group presents its poster, have members explain the pictures or symbols used.

3. Close To close the lesson, provide examples of the six goals of the Constitution. Have students identify the specific goal being discussed.

1
The Goals of the Constitution

FIND OUT
- How does the national government help to unify the nation?
- Why is a national system of courts necessary?
- How does the Constitution protect the rights of the people?

VOCABULARY justice, domestic tranquillity, general welfare, liberty

"We the people of the United States, in order to form a more perfect Union, establish justice, ensure domestic tranquillity, provide for the common defense, promote the general welfare, and secure the blessings of liberty to ourselves and our posterity, do ordain and establish this Constitution for the United States of America."

Those words make up the **Preamble,** or opening statement, of the Constitution. In the Preamble, the people proudly announce that they have established the Constitution. They have done so, they declare, to achieve certain goals. As you read about these goals, think about their importance to you.

Form a More Perfect Union

What do the words "my country" mean to you? You probably will say the United States. If you lived in the 1780s, however, you probably would have answered Virginia, Massachusetts, or whatever state you came from.

Indeed, under the Articles of Confederation, the United States was a loose alliance of independent, quarreling states. Many states acted like separate nations. The framers of the Constitution, however, saw the need for states to work together as part of a single, united nation.

How does the Constitution attempt to achieve "a more perfect union"? It provides the national government with the powers needed to unify and strengthen the nation.

For example, Congress—one part of the national government—has powers important to a healthy national economy. It can raise taxes and regulate trade between the states. It also has the sole power to coin and print money.

Other parts of the national government also have powers that help to unify the nation. The President is responsible for carrying out all the laws of the nation. National courts ensure fair treatment of all people under one system of law.

Establish Justice

A second goal of the Constitution is to establish **justice,** or fairness. The Constitution gives this task to a national system of courts.

The national courts deal with a broad range of cases. They hear cases involving the Constitution, national laws, treaties, foreign ambassadors, and ships at sea. They also decide disputes between individuals, between individuals and the national government, and between the states.

When the national courts decide cases, they often interpret, or explain, the law. The Supreme Court, the highest court in the land, can rule that a law is not permitted by the Constitution.

Why is a national system of courts necessary? Without it, the state or local courts would interpret national laws. Judges in some states might refuse to act on laws they did not like. Disputes about the meaning of

---

Connections With Local History
Activity

If your school is located in a state that was one of the original 13 states, have the students find out the names of that state's delegates to the Constitutional Convention. If your state was not one of the original 13, have students select one that was. Then ask each student to write short biographical sketches of the delegates from that state. Compile the sketches into a *Who Was Who at the Constitutional Convention.*

Historical Sidelight
Background

To illustrate the goal of creating a single, united nation, the United States adopted as one of its mottoes the Latin phrase, *e pluribus unum,* which means "out of many, one." This motto appears on the Great Seal of the United States, which students can find on the back of the one-dollar bill. The motto also appears on the back of U.S. coins.

Critical Thinking Activity
Analyzing Ideas

Ask students to discuss the meaning of the statement, "Freedom of speech does not give a person the right to shout 'Fire!' in a crowded theater." Relate the discussion to the balance between constitutional guarantees and civic responsibility. Ask students to suggest other examples of speech that they do not believe would be protected by the Constitution.

certain laws would remain unsettled. The result would be confusion and injustice.

Ensure Domestic Tranquillity

In 1786, Daniel Shays marched on a Massachusetts courthouse with nearly 1,200 other protesters. Upon hearing about Shays' Rebellion, George Washington warned, "We are fast verging to [absence of government] and confusion!" The uprising made it clear that the national government must have the means to ensure **domestic tranquillity,** or peace at home.

The Constitution allows for means to keep the peace. State and local governments have the power to use their own police to enforce national laws. When crime crosses state borders, however, national police agencies can step in to help protect life and property.

Have you ever watched a news broadcast about a civil emergency, such as a riot or a flood? If so, you probably saw members of the National Guard keeping the peace. The President can summon such aid if a state or local community cannot or will not respond to the emergency.

Provide for the Common Defense

After the American Revolution, the United States could not defend its new borders. Without a national army, it could not force British troops to leave the frontier. Lacking a navy, it was unable to prevent Spain from closing part of the Mississippi River to American trade.

The framers of the Constitution realized that strong armed forces are important to a nation's foreign policy. Military power helps not only to prevent attack by other nations but also to protect economic and political interests.

The Constitution gives Congress the power to "raise and support Armies" and to "provide and maintain a Navy." Today, the

Contents of the Constitution

CHART SKILLS *The Constitution includes a preamble, 7 articles, and 27 amendments. To find where they appear in this book, see the page numbers in the chart.* ● *On what pages will you find the Bill of Rights?*

Answer to Chart Skills

pages 943–945

 Videotapes/ Videodiscs

United States History Video Collection Use the video segment "We the People" from Volume 5, *A New Nation (1776–1815),* to enhance students' understanding of the Constitution. Approx. running time 2:30 min. (Enrichment/Average) Vol. 5, Ch. 22

Chapter 22	Play

Chapter Resources

Civics and the Constitution Duplicate and distribute the worksheet, Preamble, on pages 21–22 of the Civics and the Constitution section of the *Chapter Resources* binder. The worksheet will help the students better comprehend the specific language, vocabulary, and main ideas of the Preamble. (Reteaching/Average)

Team-Teaching Suggestion
Language Arts

You might want to work with a language arts teacher to present a lesson about the Latin origin of many words used in the Constitution and in legal terminology. Include as background the fact that Latin is a "dead language." As a result, the meanings of words do not change as they do with "living languages." Discuss why this constancy is important to the interpretation and application of laws.

Connections With Civics
Background

Because of their experience with England, many Americans in the late 1700s distrusted strong, centralized government. The Articles of Confederation established a Congress with one representative from each state. The Congress, however, had very little authority. Real power rested with the states, which often did not agree. Many Americans realized that the Articles had to be revised. In 1786, they approved a "Philadelphia Convention" to be attended by representatives from each state. However, these delegates were not authorized to draft a new constitution. The Convention was convened for "the sole and express purpose of revising the Articles of Confederation." By exceeding their powers and drafting a new constitution that established a strong, central government, the delegates created the United States from a loose alliance.

armed forces include the army, navy, air force, marine corps, and coast guard.

Promote the General Welfare

The Constitution gives the national government the means to promote the **general welfare**, or well-being of all the people. The national government has the power to collect taxes. It also has the power to set aside money for programs that will benefit the people.

In the workplace. The workplace provides many examples of how the national government—often in cooperation with state governments—has acted to promote the general welfare. Factory owners are required to meet safety standards for work areas. Workers who are disabled or unemployed receive financial support. Thanks to the Social Security system, all workers are entitled to income upon retirement.

In the school. Another area in which the national government helps to promote the general welfare is education. Education helps to prepare people to become responsible citizens. It also provides tools and training for employment.

Support for education takes many forms. The national government pays for school nutrition programs in local school districts. Many students receive money to help pay the costs of a college education.

In the laboratory. The national government supports scientific research and development to improve the quality of life. For example, researchers at the National Institutes of Health lead the fight against many diseases. Scientists at the Department of Agriculture help farmers to improve their crops and develop better livestock.

Secure the Blessings of Liberty

Protection of liberty was a major reason that colonists fought the American Revolution. It is no wonder, then, that the framers of the Constitution made securing liberty a major goal. **Liberty** is the freedom to live as you please, as long as you obey the laws and respect the rights of others.

One way that the Constitution ensures liberty is to limit the powers of government. For example, the **Bill of Rights,** the first 10 amendments to the Constitution, lists the liberties that Americans have. The amendments present these liberties as basic rights and freedoms that the government may not take away.

The Constitution provides yet another safeguard of liberty—the right to vote. The people can select the leaders who make the laws. At the same time, they can remove from office those leaders who have done a poor job.

The "blessings of liberty" have been extended to more Americans since the Constitution was written. Changes in the Constitution have been made to ensure that all

Government-Sponsored Research *The government supports a variety of scientific research. Here, two scientists use advanced equipment to study the human leg.* **Science and Technology** *Do you think the government should spend tax money on scientific research? Explain.*

Voting to Protect Liberty *The ballot box has long been a symbol of liberty. Through the vote, Americans have a say in government decisions and are able to safeguard their rights.* **Citizenship** *How does the Bill of Rights protect the "blessings of liberty" for Americans?*

Americans—no matter what sex or race—have the same rights regarding voting, education, housing, employment, and other choices in life.

SECTION 1 REVIEW

1. **Identify:** (a) Preamble, (b) Bill of Rights.
2. **Define:** (a) justice, (b) domestic tranquillity, (c) general welfare, (d) liberty.
3. List two powers of the national government that help to form a more perfect union.
4. Why would confusion and injustice result without a national court system?
5. List two ways in which the national government helps workers.
6. **CRITICAL THINKING Evaluating Information** Which goal of the Constitution do you think is most important? Explain.

ACTIVITY Writing to Learn
Create a crossword puzzle using the vocabulary words listed at the beginning of this section.

2
Five Principles of the Constitution

FIND OUT
- What is popular sovereignty?
- What is limited government?
- How does federalism divide power?
- How does the separation of powers limit government?
- How does the system of checks and balances prevent abuse of power?

VOCABULARY representative government, ratify, tyranny, federal, veto, override, bill, unconstitutional

The Constitution sets up a strong national government. At the same time, it safeguards the liberty of the people. Five basic principles, or rules, support this delicate balance. They are popular sovereignty, limited government, federalism, separation of powers, and checks and balances. In large part, the framers drew on European ideas for these principles. (See Chapter 7, pages 200 to 201.) As you read about the basic principles of the Constitution, think about how they help to protect you.

Popular Sovereignty Means the People Rule

The first three words of the Constitution, "We the people," express the principle of popular sovereignty. According to this principle, the people rule. They hold the final authority, or ruling power, in government.

A contract with the government. The Constitution is a contract, or formal, written

Civics Overview • **219**

 Chapter Resources

Civics and the Constitution Duplicate and distribute the worksheet, Goals of the Constitution, on page 1 of the Civics and the Constitution section of the *Chapter Resources* binder. The worksheet will guide students to consider ways in which each goal of the Constitution might be achieved. (Reteaching/Average)

ACTIVITY

Guided Instruction You might review some guidelines for crossword-puzzle format before students begin. Also, remind students that clues must be clear and concise. When the puzzles are completed, have students exchange them with a partner and try to solve them.

Section 2 pp. 219–224

 Bell Ringer

Ask the students to identify by name as many elected officials as they can. Then ask: "Who is their boss?" Point out that all are accountable to the people who elected them.

Answers to Section 1 Review

1. (a) Preamble, p. 216, (b) Bill of Rights, p. 218
2. (a) justice, p. 216, (b) domestic tranquillity, p. 217, (c) general welfare, p. 218, (d) liberty, p. 218
3. raise taxes, regulate trade between states, coin and print money, set up national courts
4. Without it, state and local courts would interpret national law; judges in some states might refuse to act on laws they disliked; disputes about certain laws would remain unsettled.

5. It sets safety standards and provides financial support for the disabled, the unemployed, and the retired.
6. Possible Answer: To "secure the blessings of liberty" is the most important goal, because it affects all citizens every day. On the other hand, the "common defense" is the goal that is most needed in order to protect all the other goals.

Lesson Plan

1. Focus The framers of the Constitution had to find a way to set up a strong government without threatening individual liberties or the powers of the states. In this section, students examine the five basic principles that underlie this constitutional system.

2. Instruct Work with students to create a chart on the chalkboard that lists the five principles upon which the Constitution is based. Label the columns: Principle, Definition, Examples. As students fill in the information — through class discussion and through restating the information in the chart on page 224 in their own words — make sure that they consider what each principle means and how it operates.

3. Close To close the lesson, play a Jeopardy!-like game with the students. Provide key facts from the section, and have students create appropriate questions.

Answer to Chart Skills

white men over age 21 who met property requirements; all citizens over age 18; Amendment 19

---

agreement, between the people and their government. In it, the people grant the government the powers it needs to achieve its goals. At the same time, they limit the power of government by spelling out what the government may not do.

The people vote. How does popular sovereignty work? In a large society, people cannot always take part directly in government. Instead, they exercise their ruling power indirectly. The people elect public officials to make laws and other government decisions for them. This practice is called **representative government.**

The people elect public officials by voting in free and frequent elections. Americans today have the constitutional right to vote for members of the House of Representatives (Article 1, Section 2) and for members of the Senate (Amendment 17). The people also elect the members of the electoral college, who, in turn, choose the President (Article 2, Section 1).

The right to vote has been gradually expanded over time. When the Constitution was **ratified,** or approved, only white men over age 21 who owned property could vote. As the chart at right shows, other Americans have won the right to vote since then. Today, if you are a citizen, you are eligible to vote at age 18.

The Government's Power Should Be Limited

The framers of the Constitution remembered well the harsh rule of the British king. Like most Americans, they feared **tyranny,** or cruel and unjust government. However, the failures of the Articles of Confederation made it clear that the national government had to be strong.

How could the framers strike a balance between too much government and too little government? The answer was limited government, or a government by law. According to this principle, the government

---

The Right to Vote

Year	People Allowed to Vote
1789	White men over age 21 who met property requirements (state laws)
Early 1800s–1850s	All white men over age 21 (state laws)
1870	Black men (Amendment 15)
1920	Women (Amendment 19)
1961	People in the District of Columbia in presidential elections (Amendment 23)
1971	People over age 18 (Amendment 26)

CHART SKILLS *The right to vote has expanded since the Constitution first went into effect.*
• *Who could vote in 1789? In 1971? Which amendment granted women the right to vote?*

does not have complete power. It has only the powers that the people grant it.

Limits on power. The Constitution states the powers of the national government. You and every other citizen can tell what powers Congress, the President, and the courts have. The Constitution also states what powers the government does not have. This list of denied powers puts still more limits on the government.

Guarantees to the people. The most important limits on government are set out in the Bill of Rights. In these amendments, the Constitution guarantees the individual freedoms of the people. One of the 10 amendments states that the people have other rights in addition to those listed in the Constitution (Amendment 9). In other words,

---

Historical Sidelight
Background

The system of representative, or republican, government was first developed by the ancient Romans around the year 500 B.C. The Roman Republic lasted almost 500 years.

The framers of the United States Constitution were well educated in the history of the Roman Republic. James Madison of Virginia, in particular, was a brilliant scholar who had studied many forms of government, ancient

and modern. Madison was one of the principal architects of the Constitution. He played such a leading role in its drafting and ratification that he is often referred to as "the father of the Constitution." Madison took careful notes on all the proceedings of the convention. These notes were later published in three volumes by order of Congress. They are one of the great primary sources in American history.

Linking Past and Present
Activity

Have students do research to find out how voting is conducted in your area today. Encourage them to find out where and how one registers to vote. Also have them identify several polling places in the area. You might also have them find out how votes are cast — for example, by machine or by a punched ballot. Alternatively, invite a member of the local Board of Elections to talk to the class about these things.

the rights of the people cannot be limited to those in the Constitution. Still another amendment gives the states or the people any powers not granted to the national government (Amendment 10).

Limited government is also known as the "rule of law." The Constitution is the law of the land. No person—not you, not the highest government official—is above it.

Federalism Results in a Sharing of Power

The framers of the Constitution faced a difficult conflict. They saw the need for a strong national government. At the same time, they did not want to take away all power from the states. Like most Americans, they believed that state governments would better understand the special needs and concerns of their citizens.

The framers choose federalism. The framers solved this conflict by basing the government on the principle of federalism.

Under federalism, power is divided between the federal, or national, government and the state governments. The national government has the power to deal with national issues. The states have the power to meet local needs.

A division of power. The Constitution delegates, or assigns, certain powers to the national government. Other powers are reserved, or left, to the states. Still other powers, sometimes called concurrent powers, are shared by the national and state governments. The chart below shows how powers are divided under federalism.

The powers of the states. The Constitution does not clearly list the powers of the states. Instead, it says that all powers not specifically granted to the national government are reserved to the states (Amendment 10). At the same time, it makes clear exactly what powers are denied to the states (Article 1, Section 10).

Besides reserved powers, the Constitution makes other guarantees to the states.

The Federal System

Powers Delegated to National Government

- Regulate interstate and foreign trade
- Set standard weights and measures
- Create and maintain armed forces
- Make copyright and patent laws
- Establish postal offices
- Establish foreign policy
- Create federal courts
- Coin money
- Declare war
- Admit new states

Powers Shared by National and State Governments

Provide for public welfare
Administer criminal justice
Charter banks
Raise taxes
Borrow money

Powers Reserved to States

- Create corporation laws
- Regulate trade within state
- Establish and maintain schools
- Establish local governments
- Make laws about marriage and divorce
- Conduct elections
- Provide for public safety

CHART SKILLS The system of federalism divides power between the national government and the state governments. ● Name two powers reserved to the states. Who has the power to raise taxes?

Connections With the World
Background

It is often said that Great Britain has an "unwritten constitution." This phrase refers to the fact that there is no single document that can be pointed to as "the Constitution." The written laws of England are contained in various charters, significant laws or acts of Parliament, and court decisions. Examples include the Magna Carta, the Petition of Right of 1628, the Bill of Rights of 1689, and the Representation of Peoples Act of 1969, which lowered the voting age. Furthermore, customs and usages that arose over time, called conventions, make up the unwritten part of the British constitution. For example, there is no law that states that Parliament will hold a session each year, but it does. Lack of a written constitution means that changes can be made easily by a majority vote of Parliament. It also means that hasty and ill-conceived changes could be made.

Chapter Resources

Civics and the Constitution Duplicate and distribute the worksheets, Principle of Federalism, and Article 4: Relations Among the States, on pages 11–12 and 29–30 of the Civics and the Constitution section of the *Chapter Resources* binder. The worksheets explain how federalism results in the sharing of power between the national and state governments and explore the privileges and guarantees afforded the states under the Constitution. (Reteaching/Average)

Public Schools *The power to establish and maintain schools is reserved to the states. Although the federal government provides funds, Americans exercise local control over schools.* **Citizenship** *Why do you think Americans want to keep local control over education?*

All states must be treated equally in matters of trade (Article 1, Section 9). Each state must respect the laws of the others (Article 4, Section 1). Perhaps most important of all, states are given representation in the national government.

National supremacy. Federalism creates a working partnership between the national government and the state governments. However, when a dispute arises between them, there is no doubt where the final authority lies. The Constitution is the "supreme law of the land" (Article 6, Section 2). Only national courts can settle the dispute.

Separation of Powers Further Limits the Government

In 1787, nearly every government in Europe was a monarchy. The king or queen made and enforced the laws and appointed judges to interpret the laws. This system was dangerous. It put all political power in the hands of a few people.

Three branches of government. In the United States, the Constitution prevents one person or group from having all the power. It separates the national government into three branches: the legislative, the executive, and the judicial. Each branch has its own powers and responsibilities. This division of the national government is known

as separation of powers. (See the chart in Chapter 7 on page 202.)

The legislative branch. Article 1 of the Constitution sets up the legislative branch. This branch, called Congress, makes the laws. It has two houses: the House of Representatives and the Senate. Its many powers include the power to tax, to coin money, and to declare war.

The executive branch. Article 2 describes the executive branch, which carries out the laws. The President heads the executive branch and appoints advisers and other officials to assist him.

The executive branch plays an important role in foreign affairs. As commander in chief, the President has broad military powers. The President also can make treaties.

The judicial branch. Article 3 creates the Supreme Court to head the judicial branch. This branch interprets and explains the laws. Congress may set up lower courts as necessary.

Checks and Balances Prevent Abuse of Power

The Constitution divides the powers of government among the three branches. But how does it prevent one branch of government from having too much power? The answer lies in a system of checks and bal-

222 • Civics Overview

System of Checks and Balances

Executive Branch (President carries out laws)	Checks on the Legislative Branch	Checks on the Judicial Branch
	Can propose laws Can veto laws Can call special sessions of Congress Makes appointments Negotiates foreign treaties	Appoints federal judges Can grant pardons to federal offenders
Legislative Branch (Congress makes laws)	Checks on the Executive Branch	Checks on the Judicial Branch
	Can override President's veto Confirms executive appointments Ratifies treaties Can declare war Appropriates money Can impeach and remove President	Creates lower federal courts Can impeach and remove judges Can propose amendments to overrule judicial decisions Approves appointments of federal judges
Judicial Branch (Supreme Court interprets laws)	Check on the Executive Branch	Check on the Legislative Branch
	Can declare executive actions unconstitutional	Can declare acts of Congress unconstitutional

CHART SKILLS *Through the system of checks and balances, each branch of government has checks, or controls, on the power of the other branches.* • *Name one check that the President has on Congress. How can the Supreme Court check Congress?*

ances. Each branch can check, or control, the power of the other two branches.

How does the system of checks and balances work? The chart above shows some of the checks that Congress, the President, and the Supreme Court have on each other.

Checks on Congress. Congress has the power to pass laws. However, the President can check Congress by **vetoing,** or rejecting, a proposed law. Congress, in turn, can check the President by **overriding,** or setting aside, a presidential veto. In this way, a **bill,** or proposed law, can become a law without the signature of the President.

The Supreme Court also can have a say in lawmaking. It can declare a law passed by Congress **unconstitutional,** or not permitted by the Constitution. That law then cannot take effect.

Checks on the President. The President has broad powers, especially in matters of foreign policy. As the chart shows, however, Congress has several checks on these powers.

For example, the President has the power to make treaties with foreign nations. However, the Senate must ratify treaties. Also, the President is commander in chief of the

Possible Answer: The President can veto laws; the Supreme Court can declare acts of Congress unconstitutional.

Chapter Resources

Civics and the Constitution Duplicate and distribute the worksheets, Principle of Separation of Powers, and Principle of Checks and Balances, on pages 13–14 and 15–16 of the Civics and the Constitution section of the *Chapter Resources* binder. The worksheets will help students understand how the separation of powers limits the national government and how checks and balances prevent abuses of power. (Reteaching/Average)

Connections With Civics
Background

The decision to declare a law unconstitutional is the result of a process known as *judicial review.* (Students will learn more about judicial review in the next section.) The first time that the Supreme Court declared a law unconstitutional was in the case of *Marbury* v. *Madison* (1803). Since then, the Supreme Court has been the final decision maker about the constitutionality of laws.

Judicial review is a tradition that has stirred great controversy. Up through the time of the Civil War, a belief in "constitutional supremacy" held sway. According to that view, each branch of government acts on the basis of its own interpretation of the Constitution, and the Supreme Court's interpretation affects only the cases that come before it. Presidents Jefferson, Jackson, and Lincoln are

among those who felt that they did not have to follow the Court's decisions. Since the Civil War, however, the feeling has grown that respect for the Court's decisions is a sign of stable government. Today, there is a stronger (though not universal) belief in "judicial supremacy"—the view that the Court's decisions are binding in all branches of government.

Chapter Resources

Civics and the Constitution Duplicate and distribute the worksheet, Five Principles of the Constitution, on page 2 of the Civics and the Constitution section of the *Chapter Resources* binder. The worksheet will reinforce students' understanding of the five principles by applying what they have learned about each principle to actual situations. (Reteaching/Average)

ACTIVITY

Guided Instruction Before students begin writing their public service announcements, suggest that they ask the questions *What?*, *Why?*, and *How?* about the topic. They can use the answers as a rough draft for their announcements. Invite students to exchange and comment on each other's announcements; you might also tape and play back the announcements for the class.

Principles of the Constitution

Principle	Definition
Popular sovereignty	Principle of government in which the people hold the final authority or power
Limited government	Principle that the government is not all powerful but can do only what the people say it can do
Federalism	Division of power between the national government and the state governments
Separation of powers	Division of the operations of the national government into three branches, each with its own powers and responsibilities
Checks and balances	Means by which each branch of the national government is able to check, or control, the power of the other two branches

CHART SKILLS *The Constitution is based on five principles.*
● *According to the principle of limited government, what can the government do? Which principle calls for dividing power between the national government and the state governments?*

armed forces. However, Congress, not the President, holds the power to declare war.

The President also faces possible checks by the Supreme Court. The Court has the power to declare that an act of the President is unconstitutional.

Checks on the courts. Both the President and Congress have several checks on the power of the judiciary. The President appoints all federal judges. However, the Senate must approve the President's appointments. In addition, Congress can remove federal judges from office if they are found guilty of wrongdoing. Congress may also propose a constitutional amendment to overrule a judicial decision.

SECTION 2 REVIEW

1. **Define:** (a) representative government, (b) ratify, (c) tyranny, (d) federal, (e) veto, (f) override, (g) bill, (h) unconstitutional.

2. According to the principle of popular sovereignty, who holds the final ruling power?
3. Why is limited government known as the "rule of law"?
4. How does the system of federalism divide power?
5. (a) List the three branches of government. (b) Name one power of each.
6. How can Congress check the President's power to make treaties?
7. **CRITICAL THINKING Analyzing Ideas** Explain the following statement: The Constitution sets up a government of law, not of people.

ACTIVITY Writing to Learn

Imagine that your local radio station is broadcasting public service announcements about the Constitution. Write a brief announcement describing the system of checks and balances and explaining its importance.

Connections With Civics
Background

Judges have the power to fine or imprison people. Some English kings used judges to punish enemies. For this reason, the framers of the Constitution took special care to protect the independence of the judicial branch. Unlike members of the executive and legislative branches, federal judges are not elected to a term in office. Supreme Court Justices are appointed for life. Judges can be removed only by impeachment for wrongdoing.

Answers to Section 2 Review

1. (a) representative government, p. 220, (b) ratify, p. 220, (c) tyranny, p. 220, (d) federal, p. 221, (e) veto, p. 223, (f) override, p. 223, (g) bill, p. 223, (h) unconstitutional, p. 223
2. the people
3. because no one, including government officials, is above the law
4. Under federalism, power is divided between the federal (national) government and the state governments.

5. (a) legislative, executive, and judicial (b) The legislative branch can coin money and declare war; the executive branch has the power to make treaties; the judicial branch has the power to interpret laws.
6. by refusing to ratify a treaty that the President has made
7. Possible Answer: Even the highest government officials are subject to the law.

3
A Living Constitution

FIND OUT
- How can the Constitution be formally changed?
- What is the purpose of the Bill of Rights?
- What informal changes have been made in the Constitution?

VOCABULARY amendment, precedent, Cabinet, judicial review

"**I** do not think we are more inspired, have more wisdom, or possess more virtue than those who will come after us," said George Washington. The framers of the Constitution agreed with Washington. Like him, they realized that the nation would grow and change. As a result, they provided future Americans with a living Constitution—one that could be adapted and altered to meet new conditions and challenges.

The Constitution Provides for Formal Changes

The Constitution allows **amendments**, or formal written changes, to the Constitution. Amending the Constitution is not easy, however. The process requires two difficult steps: proposal and ratification. (See the chart below.)

Proposing an amendment. Article 5 describes two methods for proposing amendments. Two thirds of each house of Congress can vote to propose an amendment. Or, two thirds of the state legislatures can demand that Congress summon a national "convention for proposing amendments."

So far, only the first method—a vote by Congress—has been used. As experts have pointed out, the Constitution does not give

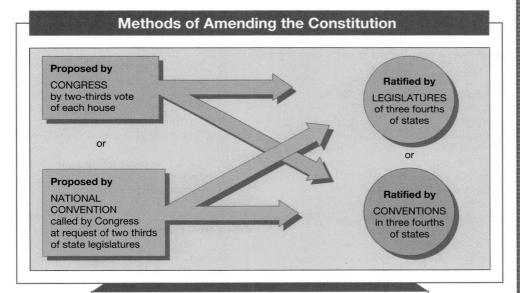

Methods of Amending the Constitution

Proposed by
CONGRESS
by two-thirds vote
of each house

or

Proposed by
NATIONAL
CONVENTION
called by Congress
at request of two thirds
of state legislatures

Ratified by
LEGISLATURES
of three fourths
of states

or

Ratified by
CONVENTIONS
in three fourths
of states

CHART SKILLS *The amendment process requires proposal and ratification. • Name one way to propose an amendment. Name one way to ratify an amendment.*

Section 3
pp. 225–228

Bell Ringer
Write the following sentence on the chalkboard: "Reasonable people can disagree." Discuss with the class how this concept applies to constitutional law and how it can lead to battles over the interpretation of various sections of the Constitution.

Lesson Plan

1. Focus The framers of the Constitution built into it a way to change the document to meet changing times. In this section, students examine formal and informal methods of amending the Constitution.

2. Instruct Have students review the amendments to the Constitution. Then ask students to list ways in which American life might be different today if there were no way to amend the Constitution. Ask: Do you think the framers were wise to include a process for changing the Constitution? Should it be easier to make amendments? Why or why not?

3. Close To close the lesson, have students explain the difference between formal and informal procedures for changing the Constitution.

Our Multicultural Heritage
Background

Many historians believe that the League of the Iroquois was one model for the federal system of the United States Constitution. The two systems are similar in philosophy, and Benjamin Franklin, who first proposed the Albany Plan of Union — a confederation of the colonies—was evidently familiar with the Native American confederacy from his job as official printer of Pennsylvania. His printing of the records and speeches of Native American assemblies and treaty negotiations led him to study Native American culture. Franklin was also present at the Constitutional Convention.

Citizens Exercise Their Rights *Constitutional amendments protect many individual rights. At left, members of the Gray Panthers, a group that promotes the needs of older citizens, exercise their right to assemble in a peaceful protest. At right, an 18-year-old exercises his right to vote.* **Citizenship** *Which amendments protect the rights shown in these pictures? Explain.*

guidelines for a national convention. Who should set the agenda? How should delegates be selected? Those and other questions probably would cause much delay and confusion.

Ratifying an amendment. Article 5 also outlines two methods of ratifying a proposed amendment. Either three fourths of the state legislatures, or three fourths of the states meeting in special conventions, must approve the amendment.

Congress decides which method of ratification to use. Until now, only the Twenty-first Amendment was ratified by special state conventions. All other amendments have been ratified by state legislatures.

In recent years, Congress has set a time limit for ratification of amendments. The time limit today is seven years, but it may be extended.

The Constitution Has 27 Amendments

As you can see, the amendment process is a difficult one. Since 1789, more than 9,000 amendments have been introduced in Congress. Yet only 27 amendments have been ratified.

Bill of Rights. The original Constitution did not list basic freedoms of the people. In fact, several states refused to approve the Constitution until they were promised that a bill of rights would be added. Those states wanted to ensure that the national government would not be able to take away basic freedoms.

The Bill of Rights includes the first 10 amendments to the Constitution. It was ratified in 1791. See the chart on page 217 for a list of the 10 amendments in the Bill of Rights.

You will easily recognize many of the freedoms in the Bill of Rights. For example, the First Amendment protects your right to worship freely, to speak freely, to write freely, to hold peaceful meetings, and to ask the government to correct wrongs. The Fourth Amendment protects you from "unreasonable" search and seizure of your home and property. The Sixth Amendment guarantees you the right to a trial by jury and to a lawyer.

Amendments 11 through 27. Only 17 amendments have been ratified since 1791. Several of these amendments reflect changing ideas about equality.

Connections With Civics
Background

Remind students that a main purpose of the First Amendment is to protect unpopular opinions. Oliver Wendell Holmes, who served as a Supreme Court Justice from 1902 to 1932, was a vigorous defender of First Amendment rights. The son of a poet, Holmes is remembered for the literary quality and memorable phrasing of his legal opinions. Referring to the First Amendment, Holmes wrote that the Constitution guaranteed "the principle of free thought—not free thought for those who agree with us but freedom for the thought we hate." His forceful opinions, which opposed many of the majority decisions of the Supreme Court, gained him a reputation as "the great dissenter."

Cooperative Learning
Activity

Students might collaborate in researching and reporting on the history of one amendment to the Constitution adopted after the Bill of Rights. Divide the class into groups of three or four students each, and assign each group a different amendment. Explain that each group should determine who originally supported the amendment and why, how it was proposed and ratified, and what its results were.

Amendments 13 through 15—the so-called Civil War amendments—were passed to protect the rights of former slaves. The Thirteenth Amendment ended slavery. The Fourteenth Amendment guaranteed citizenship and constitutional rights to African Americans. The Fifteenth Amendment guaranteed African Americans the right to vote.

Equality was also the goal of two later amendments. The Nineteenth Amendment gave women the right to vote. The Twenty-sixth Amendment set age 18 as the minimum voting age.

The chart on page 217 lists Amendments 11 through 27. For more information about the amendments, refer to the Constitution printed in the Reference Section.

Language and Tradition Allow Informal Changes

The language of the Constitution provides a general outline rather than specific details about the national government. Over time, this flexible language has allowed each branch of government to fulfill its role and meet the changing needs of the nation.

"Necessary and proper." The framers knew that they could not foresee the future. To deal with this problem, Article 1, Section 8, Clause 18, gives Congress the power to make all laws that shall be "necessary and proper" to carry out the powers of the national government. This so-called *Elastic Clause* has allowed Congress to stretch its power to pass laws.

"Regulate commerce." Still another clause of the Constitution has allowed Congress to extend its powers. Article 1, Section 8, Clause 3, gives Congress the power to "regulate" trade with other nations and between the states.

Armed with the *Commerce Clause* and the Elastic Clause, Congress has been able to keep pace with change. For example, it has passed laws that regulate the airline industry, television, nuclear energy, and genetic engineering.

A more powerful executive branch. The Constitution does not describe in detail the powers of the President. Some Presidents, however, have taken actions or made decisions that set a precedent, or example, for later Presidents.

George Washington set one such precedent. The Constitution does not state that the President may appoint a Cabinet, or group of close advisers. President Washington assumed the power to do so on his own. Every President since then has followed his lead.

In national emergencies, Presidents have expanded their constitutional role. During the Great Depression, President Franklin

Controlling Pollution *The flexible language of the Constitution has allowed the government to keep up with changing needs. It set up the Environmental Protection Agency to deal with hazards such as automobile emissions.* **Citizenship** *What clauses of the Constitution have allowed Congress to expand its powers?*

Critical Thinking
Analyzing Information

You might distribute copies of the following passage to the class:

"The framers of the Constitution set no rules on how long a President could remain in office. However, George Washington, the first President, left office after two terms. For the next 144 years, every President followed Washington's example until Franklin Roosevelt ran for a third term in 1940 and a fourth term in 1944. In 1947, Congress passed the Twenty-second Amendment, which limited a President to two terms. The amendment was ratified in 1951."

Ask: How do these events illustrate an informal precedent at work? How do these events illustrate formal changing of the Constitution?

ACTIVITY

Guided Instruction Before students choose an amendment and draft their paragraphs, you might have them freewrite about a few amendments. Encourage students to give their explanations a logical order, but do not over-stress formality in this piece of personal writing.

Section 4
pp. 228–235

Bell Ringer

Write on the chalkboard in random order the names of the current President, Vice President, your senators, representatives, and the Chief Justice of the Supreme Court. Have students identify each name and classify him or her as a member of the legislative, executive, or judicial branch.

Roosevelt expanded the size and power of the executive branch to propose and carry out programs that would restore the national economy.

A broader role for the judiciary. The Supreme Court can decide whether acts of a President or laws passed by Congress are unconstitutional. This power is known as **judicial review.**

The Constitution does not list judicial review as a power of the judicial branch. Like the unstated powers of the President, judicial review is implied in the words and structure of the Constitution. In the case of *Marbury* v. *Madison,* an early Supreme Court decision interpreted Article 3, Section 2, to mean that the Supreme Court has the right to decide whether a law violates the Constitution.

SECTION 3 REVIEW

1. **Identify:** (a) First Amendment, (b) Sixth Amendment, (c) Thirteenth Amendment, (d) Fourteenth Amendment, (e) Fifteenth Amendment, (f) Nineteenth Amendment, (g) Twenty-sixth Amendment, (h) Elastic Clause, (i) Commerce Clause, (j) *Marbury* v. *Madison.*
2. **Define:** (a) amendment, (b) precedent, (c) Cabinet, (d) judicial review.
3. Describe the amendment process.
4. List four rights protected by the Bill of Rights.
5. (a) How did George Washington expand the powers of the President? (b) How did Franklin Roosevelt expand the role of the President during the Great Depression?
6. **CRITICAL THINKING Drawing Conclusions** Why have there been more informal changes than formal changes in the Constitution?

ACTIVITY **Writing to Learn**
Which amendment is most important in your life? Write a paragraph explaining your choice.

4
The National Government at Work

FIND OUT
■ Why has Congress set up committees?
■ What roles does the President play?
■ How is the federal court system organized?

VOCABULARY appropriate, standing committee, joint committee, impeach, constituent, executive agreement, jury, appeal

---

The Constitution sets up three branches of government, each with its own clearly defined powers. The three branches work together to accomplish the same goal: a government of laws. Together, they make, carry out, and interpret the laws of the United States.

The Legislative Branch Makes the Laws

Congress, the legislative branch of government, is made up of two houses: the House of Representatives and the Senate. Together, the two houses have the power to make the laws that govern all 50 states. At the same time, the states have a say in making those laws.

House of Representatives. The larger house, the House of Representatives, seats 435 members. Representatives serve two-year terms and are elected on the basis of a state's current population. The more people that live in a state, the greater its number of representatives. Each state, however, is guaranteed at least one representative.

Answers to Section 3 Review

1. (a) First Amendment, p. 226, (b) Sixth Amendment, p. 226, (c) Thirteenth Amendment, p. 227, (d) Fourteenth Amendment, p. 227, (e) Fifteenth Amendment, p. 227, (f) Nineteenth Amendment, p. 227, (g) Twenty-sixth Amendment, p. 227, (h) Elastic Clause, p. 227, (i) Commerce Clause, p. 227, (j) *Marbury* v. *Madison,* p. 228
2. (a) amendment, p. 225, (b) precedent, p. 227, (c) Cabinet, p. 227, (d) judicial review, p. 228

3. The amount of detail may vary, but students' descriptions should include proposal (by Congress or by national convention) and ratification (by state legislatures or by state conventions).
4. Students might list freedom of speech, freedom of worship, freedom to hold peaceful meetings, protection from unreasonable search and seizure, right to trial by jury, or others.

5. (a) by selecting a Cabinet (b) by expanding the executive branch to carry out economic programs
6. Possible Answer: The formal process for proposing and ratifying an amendment is often long and unsure.

MAP, GRAPH, AND CHART SKILLS
Reading a Flowchart

A flowchart gives a lot of information in a simple, easy-to-understand way. It shows a process or development step by step. For example, under the Constitution, Congress can pass a bill and the President can sign it into law. Over the years, a complicated process has developed whereby a bill actually becomes a law.

1. **Identify the parts of the flowchart.** (a) What is the title of the flowchart? (b) What does each of the four columns show? (c) What do the red arrows show? (d) What color shows House action? Senate action?

2. **Practice reading the flowchart.** (a) Where is a bill usually introduced? (b) What happens to a bill after it has been introduced?

(c) What happens after the House and Senate have both passed their own forms of a bill? (d) What is the last step a bill goes through before it becomes a law?

3. **Evaluate the information shown on the flowchart.** During every two-year term, about 10,000 bills are introduced in Congress. Only about 1,000 ever make it through the many steps to become a law. (a) Why do you think House and Senate committees hold hearings on bills that have been introduced? (b) Using the flowchart, why do you think only a few bills actually become laws?

ACTIVITY Construct a flowchart that shows the step-by-step process you follow to get to school.

How a Bill Becomes a Law

Introduction	Committee Action	Floor Action		Enactment Into Law
Introduced in House	Referred to House committee	House debates and passes its form of bill	House and Senate members confer, reach compromise on single form of bill	
Introduced in Senate	Referred to Senate committee	Senate debates and passes its form of bill		
			House and Senate approve compromise	President signs bill into law
Most bills begin as similar proposals in House and Senate	Committee holds hearings, makes changes, recommends passage	All bills must go through both House and Senate before reaching President		

A Vote in the House *An electronic voting board keeps track of the votes cast by members of the House of Representatives. A bill passes if the majority of the representatives vote yes.* **Citizenship** *Who else must approve the bill before it becomes a law?*

Senate. In contrast to the House, the Senate has only 100 members. Each state has two senators, no matter how large or small the population of the state. Senators serve for six-year terms. The terms are staggered, however. As a result, one third of the Senate is up for election every two years.

Power to spend money. The chief purpose of Congress is to make the nation's laws. Congress has another important power. It decides what laws or programs will receive funds.

The federal government cannot spend money unless Congress has **appropriated** it, or set aside the money for a special purpose. In this way, Congress controls how much money the government spends on military aircraft, school lunches, national highways, and other programs.

How a bill becomes a law. A bill is a proposal for a new law. It must be passed by both houses of Congress and signed by the President to become law. The chart on page 229 shows the steps a bill must pass through before becoming a law.

Congress Relies on Committees

During the first session of Congress, 31 bills were proposed by both houses. Today, thousands of bills are introduced every year in Congress.

It would be impossible for each of the 535 members of Congress to study and make recommendations about every bill. This job is reserved for committees, or special groups, that work on legislation.

Committees in each house. The House of Representatives and the Senate each have **standing committees,** or permanent committees. These committees study special issues such as agriculture, labor, and energy. They are often broken up into subcommittees that study certain problems in depth.

Committees of both houses. Congress sometimes creates **joint committees,** or groups made up of both House and Senate members. One of the most important kinds of joint committee is the conference committee. Its task is to settle differences between the House and the Senate versions of

Connections With Civics
Background

Since the entire House of Representatives comes up for election every two years, congresses are numbered by these two-year terms. The Congress that met in 1789 through 1790 is called the First Congress. In modern times, national elections are always held in November of an even-numbered year (for example, 1994). Those elected, however, do not take office for about two months, or until January of the following odd-numbered year (for example, 1995). As a result, the tenure of any numbered Congress starts and ends with odd-numbered years. The Congress that was elected in November 1990 and met from January 1991 to January 1993 was called the One Hundred and Second Congress.

Historical Sidelight
Background

Joint committees may be created for a variety of purposes. In December 1861, with the country in the grip of the Civil War, the House and Senate agreed to establish a Joint Committee on the Conduct of the War. Its purpose was to be a watchdog over President Lincoln and the Union army. Maine Senator William Pitt Fessenden declared, "I hold it to be our bounden duty to keep an anxious watchful eye over all the executive agents who are carrying on the war at the direction of the people."

ISSUE FOR TODAY

The Federal Deficit

The federal government spends more money each year than it earns in taxes and other revenue. The difference between this spending and income is called the federal deficit. To make up the difference between spending and income, the government must

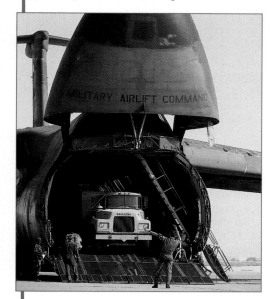

borrow money. The interest that the government pays on the borrowed money increases the deficit even further.

Most Americans believe that the deficit should be reduced. Deciding how to do so, however, often stirs fierce debate.

One way that the federal government can reduce the deficit is by raising taxes. However, Americans argue over how much taxes should be raised and who should pay more taxes.

Another way the government can reduce the deficit is to cut spending. Some people want to eliminate government departments, such as Commerce. Others favor cutbacks in programs such as foreign aid or health care.

In 1995, the President and Congress agreed to eliminate the deficit and balance the budget by 2002. The government faces difficult choices in trying to reach this goal.

■ What can the federal government do to reduce the deficit?

ACTIVITY Conduct a poll about the deficit among five adults you know. Ask them what steps they think the government should take to reduce the deficit. Organize the responses in a chart.

Answer to Issue for Today
cut spending or raise taxes

ACTIVITY

Guided Instruction You might allow students to work in pairs or small groups for this activity, but instruct all students to keep careful records. As students share the results of their polls, encourage students to note and comment on any responses that do not fit the two categories discussed in the feature.

the same bill. Members of a conference committee try to find a middle ground and to agree on the language of the bill. Very often, compromise is difficult.

Passing a bill requires the cooperation of many individuals. For example, a recent trade bill was 1,000 pages long. It required the efforts of 200 members of Congress, working in 17 subcommittees, to get it passed. Most bills introduced in Congress do not meet with such success. In fact, more than 90 percent of all the bills introduced are defeated in committees.

Congress Plays Other Roles

Members of Congress have duties other than serving on committees and making laws. They also guard the public trust and respond to the special needs of their states.

A "watchdog." For example, the House of Representatives can **impeach**, or bring a

Civics Overview • **231**

Connections With Local Civics
Activity

From the Issue for Today feature, students understand that trying to reduce the federal deficit is a difficult but vital task. Have students find out whether deficit problems exist in the government of your state, county, and/or town. If so, have them discuss the seriousness of the problem and what is being done to resolve it.

Connections With Civics
Background

In 1921, Congress created the General Accounting Office (GAO) to act as its watchdog in supervising the activities of the executive branch. The GAO is an independent agency that undertakes special projects and reports directly to Congress.

Congress also may act as a watchdog over itself. Members of Congress can vote to censure, or formally condemn, another member for wrongdoing. Each house of Congress also may expel one of its members by a two-thirds vote. In over 200 years, only four members of the House of Representatives have been expelled.

Office	Number	Term	Selection	Requirements
Representative	At least 1 per state; based on population	2 years	Elected by voters of congressional district	Age 25 or over Citizen for 7 years Resident of state in which elected
Senator	2 per state	6 years	Original Constitution—elected by state legislature Amendment 17—elected by voters	Age 30 or over Citizen for 9 years Resident of state in which elected
President and Vice President	1	4 years	Elected by electoral college	Age 35 or over Natural-born citizen Resident of U.S. for 14 years
Supreme Court Justice	9	Life	Appointed by President	No requirements in Constitution

CHART SKILLS *The Constitution details the number, length of term, methods of selection, and requirements for officeholders in the three branches of government.* ● *What are the requirements for the President? For a senator?*

formal charge of wrongdoing, against the President or another federal official. The Senate acts as a court to try the accused. Congress also acts as a "watchdog" by supervising the way the executive branch carries out the laws.

The people "back home." Responsible representatives and senators must remember their **constituents,** or the people who elected them. Therefore, members of Congress actively support bills that have a direct impact on the people "back home." Such bills might include promoting new post offices, improving highways, and helping pay for local education programs.

The President Has Several Roles

The framers created an executive branch to carry out the laws. However, they left out details about the President's powers. Over the years, the powers of the President have been increased or decreased, depending on the needs of the time. Still, Americans expect the President to fill certain roles.

Chief executive. The main role of the President is to carry out the nation's laws. As chief executive, the President oversees the many departments, agencies, and commissions that help to accomplish this task.

Chief of state. The President is the living symbol of the nation. In this role, the President represents all American citizens at many occasions. For example, the President greets visiting foreign leaders and gives medals to national heroes.

Chief diplomat. The President directs the nation's foreign policy. Three important powers allow the President to influence relations with other countries. They are the powers to appoint ambassadors, make treaties, and enter into executive agreements. **Executive agreements** are informal agreements with other heads of state, usually dealing with trade. Unlike treaties, they do not require Senate approval.

232 • Civics Overview

Connections With Civics
Background

The President decides whether to recognize or establish diplomatic relations with another government. Acting as the chief executive, the President also signs treaties on behalf of the United States. Between 1980 and 1985, for example, Presidents Carter and Reagan signed 101 treaties. During the same period, they entered into 1,940 executive agreements.

The Constitution assigns only one regular duty to the Vice President: to preside over the Senate. Recent Presidents, however, have given their Vice Presidents additional responsibilities, such as meeting with foreign officials or serving on the National Security Council.

Connections With Art
Activity

You might have students work in groups to create posters about one of the branches of government. Explain that groups may use current newspaper headlines and photographs to illustrate its branch at work. For example, the poster of Congress could feature material on current legislation, watchdog hearings, local projects championed by members of Congress, and so on. Select one member of each group to discuss the features illustrated on its poster.

Commander in chief. The President is the highest-ranking officer in the armed forces. As commander in chief, the President can appoint and remove top military commanders. The President may also use the armed forces to deal with crises both at home and abroad.

Chief legislator. The President suggests new laws and works for their passage. In this role, the President often meets with members of Congress to win their support. Sometimes, the President campaigns for public support through television or radio speeches and press conferences.

The President also can use persuasion to oppose a bill. In this case, however, the President's most powerful weapon is the power to veto a bill.

The President Carries Out the Laws

The nation's laws cover a broad range of concerns—defense, housing, crime, and pollution, to name a few. To carry out these laws and to perform other duties, the Presi-

dent needs the help of millions of government workers. These workers make up five major groups.

Executive Office. One group of assistants, the Executive Office, includes many agencies and individuals. They range from the Vice President to the Office of Management and Budget, which prepares the total budget of the United States. In all, the Executive Office has about 1,600 workers.

Executive departments. The President's Cabinet, called secretaries, are the heads of executive departments. President Washington had only four departments. Today, the President relies on 14 executive departments—among them, the Departments of Defense, Commerce, Justice, Labor, and Energy. Each department has many concerns. For example, the Department of Agriculture deals with food quality, crop improvement, and nutrition.

Independent executive agencies. More than 30 independent executive agencies also help the President carry out duties. For example, the Central Intelligence Agency

Presidents at Work *The President serves as both chief diplomat and commander in chief. At left, President Bill Clinton meets with Prime Minister Benazir Bhutto of Pakistan at the White House. At right, President George Bush greets American troops in the Middle East.* **Citizenship** *Describe two other roles of the President.*

Chapter Resources

Civics and the Constitution Duplicate and distribute the worksheet, Article 2: The Executive Branch, on pages 25–26 of the Civics and the Constitution section of the *Chapter Resources* binder. The worksheet will help students expand their knowledge of how the Constitution provides for the election of a President and Vice President in addition to establishing the roles and responsibilities of these leaders. (Reteaching/Average)

Connections with Civics
Background

The President's role as commander in chief also means that in time of war, the President, with authorization from Congress, has special authority to take actions at home that are in support of the war effort. President Franklin D. Roosevelt put this role to work during the years that the United States was involved in World War II. As commander in chief, he enacted rationing, limits on prices, and other policies considered necessary to conducting the war.

Connections With Civics
Activity

Explain that one way in which Congress has had a role in the executive branch of government is by determining the line of succession if the President leaves office. Many students may know that the President is succeeded by the Vice President and then by the Speaker of the House; they probably do not realize how far that line of succession extends. Have them find out the line of succession and the name of the person who currently holds each position.

(CIA) provides the President with secret information about the world's trouble spots. The National Aeronautics and Space Administration (NASA) is in charge of the nation's space program.

Independent regulatory commissions. The fourth group of workers, 11 independent regulatory commissions, enforce national laws. They set down specific rules, rates, and standards for trade, business, science, and transportation. For example, a law of Congress forbids "false or misleading advertising." It was the Federal Trade Commission (FTC), however, that ruled that cigarettes may not be advertised as "kind" to your throat.

Government corporations. There are at least 60 government corporations today. They include the United States Postal Service, the Tennessee Valley Authority, and Amtrak.

The Judicial Branch Interprets the Laws

Article 3 of the Constitution gives the judicial power of the United States to the Supreme Court and to lower courts that Congress may set up. Under the Judiciary Act of 1789, Congress created the system of federal courts that still operates today.

District courts. Most federal cases begin in the district courts. These courts are placed in more than 90 districts around the country. Cases brought to these courts may involve matters of criminal law, such as kidnapping and murder, or matters of civil law, such as bankruptcy and divorce. In district courts, decisions are made by either a judge or a **jury**, which is a panel of citizens.

Circuit courts. Every citizen has the right to **appeal** a decision, or ask that it be reviewed by a higher court. These higher courts of appeal are called circuit, or appellate, courts. The United States has 13 circuit courts of appeal.

Circuit courts operate differently from district courts. A panel of three judges reviews each case. The judges decide if rules of trial procedure were followed in the original trial. If errors did occur, the circuit court may reverse, or overturn, the original decision. Or it may send back the case to the district court for a new trial.

Supreme Court. The Supreme Court is the highest court in the United States. It is made up of a Chief Justice and eight Associate Justices.

Only two kinds of cases can begin in the Supreme Court. The first kind involves disputes between states. The second involves foreign ambassadors.

The Supreme Court *The Chief Justice and eight Associate Justices of the Supreme Court interpret the laws according to the Constitution. A majority of five Justices can determine a Supreme Court decision.* **Citizenship** *What kinds of cases does the Supreme Court hear?*

Connections With Language Arts
Activity

Have students use an almanac or other reference to find the names and purposes of other independent executive agencies. Then have students write a letter to an agency of their choice (for example, the National Science Foundation, the Commission on Civil Rights, or the Environmental Protection Agency). The letters may ask a question, request information, or describe a problem, but they should demonstrate the writers' understanding of that agency's responsibilities.

Connections With Civics
Background

The federal court system includes several "special courts" that hear only particular kinds of cases. For example, the United States Tax Court hears only cases involving tax laws, whereas someone suing the federal government might bring a case to the United States Claims Court. Other "special courts" include the Court of Military Affairs, which hears cases involving members of the armed forces who have been convicted of breaking military law, and the Courts of the District of Columbia, the judicial system for Washington, D.C.

Otherwise, the Supreme Court serves as a final court of appeals. It hears cases that have been tried and appealed as far as law permits in federal and state courts.

The Supreme Court hears only issues about the Constitution, federal law, or treaties. It selects only about 120 cases from the 4,000 or more requests it receives each year. Most of the cases involve laws written in unclear language. The Court must decide what each law means, whom it affects, and whether it is constitutional.

A Supreme Court decision rests on a simple majority vote of at least five Justices. It is a final decision. There are no other courts of appeal. If Congress strongly disagrees with a Supreme Court decision, however, it can take other action. It can pass a modified version of the law, or it can propose an amendment to the Constitution.

SECTION 4 REVIEW

1. **Identify:** (a) House of Representatives, (b) Senate, (c) Supreme Court.
2. **Define:** (a) appropriate, (b) standing committee, (c) joint committee, (d) impeach, (e) constituent, (f) executive agreement, (g) jury, (h) appeal.
3. Name three programs for which Congress might appropriate money.
4. (a) What duties does the President perform as chief executive? (b) As chief legislator?
5. (a) What is the role of circuit courts? (b) What is the role of the Supreme Court?
6. **CRITICAL THINKING Analyzing Ideas** Why is it important for Congress to approve the President's choices for Supreme Court Justices?

ACTIVITY **Writing to Learn**
Imagine that you are the President of the United States. Write a diary entry that describes your activities for the past week.

Citizenship at Work

FIND OUT
■ How did the Fourteenth Amendment help to expand rights?
■ What responsibilities do citizens have?

VOCABULARY due process of law

The Constitution and its amendments guarantee rights to you and every other American citizen. Along with these rights of citizenship, however, come responsibilities.

Citizens Have Rights

Americans first proclaimed their rights in the Declaration of Independence. "All men are created equal," the Declaration states, and they have "certain unalienable rights," including "life, liberty, and the pursuit of happiness." Since the birth of the nation, Americans have struggled to reach this ideal of basic rights for all citizens.

The first step. The original Constitution protected some individual rights by limiting government actions. For example, Article 6, Section 3, prevents government from making religion a requirement for public service. Also, Article 1, Section 9, forbids passing any law that makes someone guilty of a crime without a trial.

Bill of Rights. As you have read, many Americans demanded a more specific list of rights. The first 10 amendments to the Constitution further spell out rights. For example, the First Amendment forbids government actions that limit freedom of religion, speech, press, assembly, and petition. (See the chart on page 236.)

The Bill of Rights, however, applied only to the national government. It did not affect

Civics Overview • **235**

Section 5
pp. 235–237

ACTIVITY
Guided Instruction Before students begin writing their diary entry, briefly review the role and responsibilities of the President. Remind them to organize the entries sequentially by day and chronologically for each day. Suggest that they watch the nightly news for inspiration. Encourage students to include activities that illustrate as many aspects of the position as possible.

🔔 **Bell Ringer**

Write the following sentence on the chalkboard. "Every right carries with it a responsibility." Ask students to discuss the meaning of this concept.

Lesson Plan

1. Focus In this section, students look at the rights given to all Americans by the Constitution. They also examine the responsibilities of citizenship.
2. Instruct Remind the class that many Americans think that the duties of citizenship are a nuisance. Divide the class into groups of three or four. Have each group write a skit showing a conflict between citizens who fulfill their duties and those who do not. (You might assign each group a different topic, such as voting, staying well informed, or serving on a jury.) Conclude by leading a discussion on the meaning of citizenship.

Critical Thinking
Analyzing Information

Have students list two or three facts to support each of the following generalizations: (a) It is very difficult for a bill to pass through Congress unchanged. (b) The President relies on many people to fulfill the constitutional duties of the office. (c) The decisions of a few Supreme Court Justices can affect everyone in the country.

Answers to Section 4 Review

1. (a) House of Representatives, p. 228, (b) Senate, p. 230, (c) Supreme Court, p. 234
2. (a) appropriate, p. 230, (b) standing committee, p. 230, (c) joint committee, p. 230, (d) impeach, p. 231, (e) constituent, p. 232, (f) executive agreement, p. 232, (g) jury, p. 234, (h) appeal, p. 234
3. Possible Answers: military aircraft, school lunches, national highways
4. (a) oversees executive departments, agencies, and commissions (b) suggests new laws, works for their passage, vetoes bills

5. (a) Circuit courts review the decisions of the lower courts to make sure that the rules of trial procedure were correctly followed. (b) The Supreme Court serves as the final court of appeals in cases that deal with the Constitution, federal law, or treaties.
6. Possible Answer: Congressional confirmation is one way of checking the power of the President and maintaining the balance of power.

3. Close To close the lesson, call on students to identify a right and name a corresponding responsibility.

Liberties Protected by the First Amendment

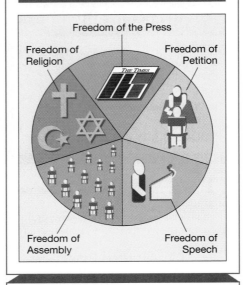

CHART SKILLS *The First Amendment to the Constitution guarantees some basic individual liberties.* • *Name two freedoms it protects. Which freedom allows you to hold and attend meetings?*

the actions of state governments. As a result, states were able to limit or deny basic rights of many Americans, including African Americans, Asian Americans, and women. The federal government sometimes restricted basic rights, too, through laws and in court decisions.

Fourteenth Amendment. An amendment passed in 1868 paved the way for a major expansion of rights. The Fourteenth Amendment states that persons born or naturalized in the United States are citizens of both the nation and their state. No state, the amendment says, may limit the rights of citizens or deny citizens **due process of law,** or a fair hearing or trial. States are also forbidden to deny citizens "equal protection of the laws."

Court decisions. Over the years, the Supreme Court has decided that the Four-

teenth Amendment's guarantee of due process and equal protection includes rights listed in the Bill of Rights. For example, in the 1960s, the Court ruled that due process of law includes the Sixth Amendment rights to a speedy trial by jury and to a lawyer. States cannot deny citizens the protections of the Bill of Rights.

Ideas of liberty grow. As the Ninth Amendment states, the people have rights beyond those described in the Constitution. Americans still strive to define and guarantee those rights. Many believe that their rights include the opportunity to pursue a good education, to find a job, and to live in decent housing.

Citizens Have Responsibilities

You and every other citizen must do your part to safeguard your rights. That role includes responsibilities.

Learn about your rights. You cannot protect your rights unless you know what they are. Books, government pamphlets, and groups such as the League of Women Voters, the National Association for the Advancement of Colored People (NAACP), and the Legal Aid Society can give you information about your rights and the law.

Respect the rights of others. Your rights are only as safe as your neighbor's. If you abuse or allow abuse of another citizen's rights, your rights may be at risk someday.

Express your views. The First Amendment guarantees you the freedom to speak, write, sign petitions, and meet with others freely. You can use those freedoms not only to defend your rights but also to take a stand on political and community issues. It is important to remember that such expressions should be truthful and peaceful.

Learn about community and national issues. As a responsible citizen, keep informed about issues critical to the nation and to your community. Besides reading newspapers and magazines, attend local

236 • Civics Overview

Historical Sidelight
Background

When discussing the constitutional right to due process, note that in 1963, the Supreme Court heard an appeal in the case of *Gideon* v. *Wainwright*. A poor Florida man had been convicted of breaking and entering. The Florida judge hearing the case had refused the defendant's request for a lawyer. The Supreme Court overturned the conviction, ruling that a state court must appoint a lawyer for any defendant who cannot afford to hire one.

Critical Thinking
Defending a Position

Explain that only 55 percent (or slightly more than one half) of eligible Americans bothered to vote in the 1992 presidential election. Even so, this low voter turnout was actually the highest since 1972. Have each student select a position—pro or con—on the following proposition: "Individuals who fail to vote in two successive presidential elections should lose their right to vote in the next two presidential elections." Have each student write and read aloud a short paragraph defending his or her position. Use the paragraphs as a basis for class discussion.

Critical Thinking
Analyzing Ideas

When discussing the concept of respect for the rights of others, you might have the class analyze the following statement: "Your right to swing your fist ends where my nose begins." Students should relate the idea expressed to respecting the rights of others and give concrete examples of its application in daily life.

meetings. At a town council meeting, for example, you might learn about proposed solutions to pollution problems. Or the League of Women Voters might offer a debate by candidates for political office.

Vote. Good government depends on good leaders. Therefore, citizens have the responsibility to exercise their right to vote and to select the best candidate. If citizens have studied the candidates and the issues in an election, they will be able to make responsible decisions.

Obey laws. Citizens enter into a contract with the government. They give the government the power to make certain laws. In return, they expect government to protect the health and well-being of society. As part of this contract, the government has the power to set penalties if laws are broken.

Like other citizens, you have a responsibility to obey the laws that safeguard your rights and the rights of others. For example, you should not steal, damage the property of others, or harm someone physically.

Serve on juries. The Bill of Rights guarantees citizens the right to a trial by jury. Every citizen, in turn, has the responsibility to serve on juries when called.

Serving on a jury is a serious duty. Jurors must take time out from their work and personal life. Deciding the guilt or innocence of the accused can be difficult.

Volunteer. Responsible citizens offer their time and talents to help others and to improve the community. For example, you can join or start a group to clean up parks or to serve food to senior citizens. You can also take part in a walk-a-thon or bike-a-thon to raise money for a worthy cause.

Defend the nation. At age 18, all young men must report their name, age, and address to the government. In time of war, the government may draft, or choose, them to serve in the armed forces. Some young citizens feel the duty to enlist in, or join, the military on their own.

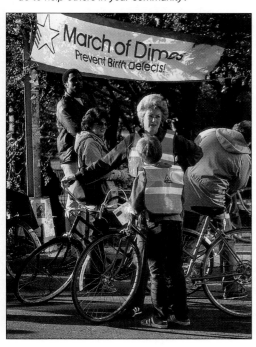

Biking for the March of Dimes *Responsibilities of citizens include helping others. Here, volunteers take part in a bike-a-thon to raise money for medical research.* **Citizenship** *What can you do to help others in your community?*

SECTION 5 REVIEW

1. **Define:** due process of law.
2. What are the five basic freedoms guaranteed by the First Amendment?
3. What does the Fourteenth Amendment guarantee?
4. List three responsibilities of citizenship.
5. CRITICAL THINKING **Applying Information** Why has the Fourteenth Amendment been called the "nationalization" of the Bill of Rights?

ACTIVITY **Writing to Learn**
Select an issue in the news today. Write a newspaper editorial taking a position on that issue.

Connections With the World
Background

Anyone born in the United States or born abroad to an American citizen is automatically an American citizen by birth. Persons may also become citizens through naturalization. Remind students that naturalized citizens have the same rights and duties as citizens by birth, except that they cannot become President.

Answers to Section 5 Review

1. due process of law, p. 236
2. freedoms of religion, speech, press, assembly, and petition
3. No state may limit the rights of citizens or deny its citizens "due process of law" and "equal protection of the law."
4. Possible Answers: to learn about one's rights, to respect the rights of others, to express one's views, to learn about community and national issues, to vote, to obey the laws, to volunteer
5. Possible Answers: The Fourteenth Amendment enlarged the protection of the Bill of Rights to cover all Americans.

CIVICS REVIEW

Answers to Reviewing the Main Ideas

1. Possible Answers: To form a more perfect union, Congress can regulate trade between the states; to ensure justice, the government sets up a national system of courts; to ensure domestic tranquillity, national police agencies can take action when crime crosses state borders or during a civil emergency such as a riot or a flood; to provide for the common defense, the government maintains the army, navy, and other armed services; to promote the general welfare, the government can designate money for programs to benefit people.

2. The legislative branch makes the laws; the executive branch carries out the laws; the judicial branch interprets the laws.

3. The President can veto a proposed law; the Supreme Court can declare a law unconstitutional.

4. Two thirds of each House vote to propose an amendment; two thirds of the state legislatures request that Congress call a convention.

5. The Elastic Clause gives Congress the power to make all laws that are "necessary and proper" to carry out the powers of the government; the Commerce Clause has allowed Congress to extend its power to regulate trade.

6. (a) Standing committees are permanent committees in the Senate and House that study special subjects; joint committees are made up of members of both houses. (b) to settle differences between House and Senate versions of the same bill

7. powers to appoint ambassadors, make treaties, and enter into executive agreements with other heads of state

8. The Fourteenth Amendment ensured that all states must guarantee the Bill of Rights to all citizens; the Fifteenth Amendment extended the vote to African Americans.

Summary

- The people have established the Constitution to achieve five major goals: form a more perfect union, establish justice, ensure domestic tranquillity, provide for the common defense, and promote the general welfare.
- The Constitution is based on five important principles that support a strong but limited national government.
- The Constitution is a living document that has been adapted to changes in the nation through formal and informal methods.
- The three branches of the national government work together to achieve a government of laws.
- The Constitution extends basic rights to all citizens, but citizens must assume responsibilities to safeguard their rights.

Reviewing the Main Ideas

1. List two goals of the Constitution. Describe one way that the national government helps to achieve each goal.
2. List the branches of the national government. Describe the role of each branch.
3. How can the President and the Supreme Court check the power of Congress to pass laws?
4. Describe two methods of proposing an amendment to the Constitution.
5. Describe two ways that the nonspecific language of the Constitution has allowed informal changes.
6. (a) Describe standing committees and joint committees. (b) What task does a conference committee have?
7. What three powers enable the President to direct foreign policy?
8. How did the Fourteenth and Fifteenth amendments pave the way for a major expansion of individual rights?

Thinking About the Constitution

1. **Linking Past and Present** Are the goals of the nation today the same as those set out in the Preamble? Explain.
2. **Synthesizing Information** How are the principles of popular sovereignty and limited government related?
3. **Defending a Position** Do you think the amendment process should be made simpler? Explain your answer.
4. **Analyzing Information** Former Chief Justice Hughes said, "We are under a Constitution, but the Constitution is what the judges say it is." What do you think Hughes meant?
5. **Comparing** Describe the differences between district courts and circuit courts. Which are the higher courts?
6. **Evaluating Information** What are the advantages and disadvantages of the process that a bill must go through to become a law?

Applying Your Skills

1. **Outlining** Review the outlining steps you learned on page 28. Then outline the section Five Principles of the Constitution, which begins on page 219.
2. **Reading a Chart** Review the chart on page 221. (a) Name three powers delegated to the national government. (b) Name three powers shared by the national government and state governments.
3. **Reading a Chart** Review the chart on page 232. Write a paragraph about Supreme Court Justices based on information in the chart.
4. **Ranking** Review the subsection The President Has Several Roles, beginning on page 232. List the roles of the President. Then rank the roles in order of importance. Explain your ranking.

238 • Civics Overview

Answers to Thinking About the Constitution

1. Possible Answer: The government still establishes justice by maintaining the court system. It still provides for the common defense by maintaining an army.

2. Possible Answer: If the powers of government were unlimited, the people would lose their power over the government.

3. Answers will vary. Students may suggest that the complexity of the system ensures that amendments are carefully considered before being enacted.

4. Possible Answer: Hughes meant that judges, especially Supreme Court Justices, have the power to interpret the Constitution. Students should recognize that the Supreme Court has interpreted the Constitution in different ways at different times.

5. There are more than 90 district courts and 12 circuit courts. Decisions in district courts are made by a judge or jury; circuit court decisions are made by a panel of three judges. Circuit courts review the decisions made by district courts and may overturn those decisions.

6. Possible Answer: The advantages relate to the fact that the bill is given a thorough review; the disadvantages relate to the facts that it may take a long time for a bill to work through the process and that many bills may be weakened in the review and compromise processes.

Participating in Democracy

Form into groups to review the Constitution. Follow the suggestions below to write, draw, or perform to show what you have learned about the government that the Constitution set up. You may use the textbook, encyclopedias, atlases, or other materials in your classroom library to complete the tasks. Be able to name your sources of information when you have finished the activity.

ARTISTS Review the discussion of the national government in the Civics Overview. Then create a comic book for younger students explaining the three branches of government set up by the Constitution. Be sure to include information about the separation of powers and the system of checks and balances.

GOVERNMENT LEADERS Organize a debate on a proposal for a new constitutional amendment. You might examine the idea of limiting the President to a single six-year term, or you may choose a proposal of your own.

ACTORS Find out more about what happens in a federal court trial. Then conduct a mock trial. Assign students to play the parts of attorneys, judge, members of the jury, witnesses, and so on.

WRITERS Write a short story about what might happen if people had no political rights. You might set the story in an imaginary place or in the United States in the future.

CITIZENS Exercise your rights and responsibilities by writing a letter to a representative in Congress about a national issue on which you have strong feelings.

Voting

 Hold a class Participating in Democracy workshop. Use your completed projects as the focus of the event.

Celebrating the Constitution

Answers to Applying Your Skills

1. Check students' outlines for accuracy of format and completeness of content.
2. (a) regulate interstate and foreign trade, set standard weights and measures, create and maintain armed forces, make copyright and patent laws, establish postal offices, establish foreign policy, create federal courts, coin money, declare war, admit new states (b) provide for public welfare, administer criminal justice, charter banks, raise taxes, borrow money
3. Paragraphs will vary but should include information about the number of Justices, their term, their method of selection, and the requirements for their office.
4. Check students' lists for accuracy. Rankings and explanations will vary.

Unit 3
The New Republic

The New Republic

Unit Focus

Discuss with students the painting on these pages—*Junction of the Erie and Northern (Champlain) Canals,* by John Hill. Ask: Does this scene make you think of an established, prospering nation? Explain. As students consider the United States in that way, call on volunteers to read aloud the chapter summaries. Ask questions such as the following to stimulate discussion.

1. Do you think that the people in this painting often recalled the Revolutionary years? Why or why not?

2. (a) Who were some of the first Presidents of the United States? (b) What do you know about any of them?

3. The caption on page 241 says that the United States made "a good showing" in the War of 1812, which was another war with Great Britain. (a) What does that expression mean? (b) Why was it important for the United States to have a "good showing" in that war?

4. What items did the first factories produce?

5. The New Republic is the title of this unit. Based on the information in the chapter summaries, how do you think most Americans felt about their new republic?

CHAPTER **8**
The New Government Begins
(1789–1800)

The first Presidents helped shape the new nation.

....

CHAPTER **9**
The Jefferson Era
(1801–1816)

The early 1800s saw the nation double in size and fight its first foreign war.

....

CHAPTER **10**
Years of Growth and Expansion
(1790–1825)

The growth of factories in the East and farms in the West inspired new confidence in the nation.

Connections With Art
Background

The attention to detail in *Junction of the Erie and Northern (Champlain) Canals* can be traced to John Hill's (1770–1850) career as a respected engraver in London. Hill came to the United States in 1816. He settled first in Philadelphia, then in New York City, and finally on a farm in West Nyack, New York. Hill is remembered for his landscape engravings and aquatints (a technique related to etching). His son (John William Hill) and his grandson (John Henry Hill) became landscape artists as well.

Hill completed *Junction of the Erie and Northern (Champlain) Canals* in 1835. Today, the work is part of the collection of the New York Historical Society.

Connections With Art
Activity

Ask questions such as the following to stimulate discussion about the painting.

1. If you could use only three words to describe this scene, which words would you choose?

2. Look at the map on page 308. Where could you go by traveling on the Erie Canal?

3. Study the boats in the painting. What types of people do you think would use a waterway like this?

4. Do you think that scenes like this were common in Europe? Explain.

240

The new republic faced many challenges. However, economic and political growth and a good showing in the War of 1812 gave Americans a sense of national pride. Here, boats move along the new Erie Canal.

Connections With the World
Activity

Have students preview the map on page 315 and list five nations that won independence from Spain during this period. Remind students that in 1825 the United States was still a young nation, with less military and naval strength than the European powers. Ask: Do you think that the United States was glad to see Latin American countries gain independence? Why? How do you think the nations of Europe felt about this push for independence—and about the United States?

Linking Past and Present
Activity

Explain that in the 1960s several European colonies in Africa gained their independence and became new nations. (Examples include Botswana [1966]; the Central African Republic and Chad [both 1960]; Gambia [1965]; Kenya [1963]; Nigeria, Somalia, and Mali [all 1960]; and Uganda [1962]). Also point out that many of these new countries faced severe problems. Ask: Based on the early history of the United States, what advice might you offer the leaders of a newly independent nation today?

Lessons	Teaching Resources
1 **Organizing the New Government** **Objectives** 1. Explain why Washington's actions as President were important to the future of the United States. 2. Describe how Hamilton proposed to pay government debts and strengthen the economy. 3. Explain why some groups opposed Hamilton's economic plans.	**Lesson Planner** Cooperative Learning, p. 45 **Student Study Guide** Section 1 Study Guide, p. 75 **Chapter Resources Binder, Unit 3** *Geography in History* The Changing Center of Population, pp. 5–6 **Interdisciplinary Connections:** Inventing a Nation ■ *Arts* American Spelling, p. 44 ▪ *Sciences* Patents and Progress, p. 45 ■ *Geography* A Capital Idea, p. 46 ■ *World* The French Revolution, p. 47 ■ *Economics* The New Nation's Coins, p. 48
2 **War Clouds** **Objectives** 1. Describe how Americans responded to the French Revolution. 2. Identify the purpose of the Neutrality Proclamation. 3. Explain why fighting erupted in the Northwest Territory. 4. Identify the main ideas of Washington's Farewell Address.	**Lesson Planner** Cooperative Learning, p. 46 **Student Study Guide** Section 2 Study Guide, p. 76 **Our Multicultural Heritage** *Biography* Eleuthère Irénée du Pont, Refugee to Manufacturer, p. 22
3 **Rise of Political Parties** **Objectives** 1. Explain why political parties formed in the United States. 2. Describe how Hamilton and Jefferson differed on major issues. 3. Describe how newspapers influenced the growth of political parties. 4. Explain why the election of 1796 increased political tensions.	**Lesson Planner** Cooperative Learning, p. 47 **Student Study Guide** Section 3 Study Guide, p. 77 **Chapter Resources Binder, Unit 3** *Skill Application* Distinguishing Fact From Opinion, p. 2 **Our Multicultural Heritage** *Biography* Benjamin Nones, the "Jewish Lafayette," p. 23
4 **John Adams as President** **Objectives** 1. Explain why many Americans wanted to declare war on France. 2. Explain why Adams lost the support of Federalists. 3. Identify the Alien and Sedition acts.	**Lesson Planner** Cooperative Learning, p. 48 **Student Study Guide** Section 4 Study Guide, p. 78 **Chapter Resources Binder, Unit 3** *History Through Literature* Letter to Her Daughter From the New White House, p. 4 *Critical Thinking* Understanding Causes and Effects, p. 3 **Our Multicultural Heritage** *Milestone* Gabriel Prosser's Rebellion, p. 24

Multimedia Resources	Additional Resources	Chapter-Level Resources
Transparencies *Interdisciplinary Connections* Martha Washington, First Lady p. B-47 **CD-ROM** *Presidents* George Washington *History Makers* Alexander Hamilton *History Makers* Benjamin Banneker **Videotapes/Videodiscs** *United States History Video Collection* Divisions Within the Government, Vol. 5, Ch. 28		**Lesson Planner** Activity Based, pp. 49–50 **Student Study Guide** Chapter 8 Study Guide, pp. 79–80 **Chapter Resources Binder** **Unit 3** Vocabulary Building, p. 1 Chapter Test A, pp. 7–9 Chapter Test B, pp. 10–12 Extra Unit Questions, pp. 41–43 **English Guided Reading** Guided Reading, pp. 15–16 **Spanish Resources** **Computer Test Bank** Chapter Tests A and B Extra Unit Questions **Guided Reading Audiotapes** Side 3 **CD-ROM** *Time Tour* The New Government Begins in The New Republic
	Voices of Freedom Washington Advises Neutrality, pp. 73–74 **Customized Reader** Fur Trade With the Ojibway, article IIIA-10	
Videotapes/Videodiscs *United States History Video Collection* The Many or the Few?, Vol. 5, Ch. 34	**Voices of Freedom** Jefferson Opposes the National Bank, pp. 74–75 Hamilton Supports the Bank, pp. 76–77	
CD-ROM *Presidents* John Adams **Videotapes/Videodiscs** *United States History Video Collection* The Revolution of 1800, Vol. 5, Ch. 37	**Voices of Freedom** A Song to Unite Americans, p. 77	

Lesson Planner

For a fully developed **Activity-Based** lesson plan for Chapter 8, see the *Lesson Planner,* pages 49–50.

 Chapter Resources

Vocabulary Building The Vocabulary Building worksheet for Chapter 8 from Unit 3, page 1, of the *Chapter Resources* binder can be used as a prereading activity or as a review of chapter vocabulary. (Reteaching/Easy)

 Student Study Guide

Chapter 8 Study Guide Refer students to pages 79–80 of the *Student Study Guide* for the Chapter 8 Study Guide. The study guide can be used for chapter review as well as for reteaching. (Reteaching/Average)

 Guided Reading Audiotapes

Students can use *Guided Reading Audiotapes,* Chapter 8, side 3, to listen to section previews, summaries, and review questions. The tapes will benefit students who are auditory learners, students who have trouble reading, or students acquiring English. Tapes are also available in Spanish. (Reteaching/Easy)

CHAPTER **8**

The New Government Begins

(1789–1800)

CHAPTER OUTLINE

1 Organizing the New Government

2 War Clouds

3 Rise of Political Parties

4 John Adams as President

1789 *George Washington, hero of the Revolution, was inaugurated as the first President of the United States.*

1791 *The Bank of the United States was set up to handle the finances of the new nation.*

1788	1790	1792	1794

 WORLD EVENT
1789 French Revolution begins

WORLD EVENT
1794 Thaddeus Kosciusko leads Polish uprising

242 • Chapter 8

Chapter Time Line
Understanding Chronology

Although Chapter 8 covers only an 11-year span, it focuses on an eventful period that shaped the new nation. Check students' grasp of the sequence of these events by copying each time-line caption—without the date—onto an index card and having students order the cards chronologically.

Students Acquiring English
Activity

Students who are learning English as a second language need to make extensive use of context clues to understand unfamiliar vocabulary. To help SAE students focus on this strategy, write the following sentence on the chalkboard and draw students' attention to the word *backcountry.* "In the backcountry, far from good roads or cities, corn was too bulky to haul to markets in the East." Point out the phrase "far from good roads or cities" and explain that it gives the reader a good clue to the meaning of "backcountry." Have students find their own examples—in this book and others—of context clues that suggest the meanings of unfamiliar words. Students can collect a variety of examples for a language arts Context Clues bulletin board.

Chapter Setting

To most Americans, George Washington was a great hero. After all, he had led the nation to independence. Americans welcomed his election as their first President. In a biography of Washington, Mason Weems describes the excited crowds that greeted Washington as he rode to New York City to take the oath of office:

❝As soon as it was officially notified to him, in the spring of 1789, that he was unanimously elected President of the United States. . .he set out for [New York]. Then all along the roads where he passed . . .it was only said, 'General Washington is coming.'. . .The inhabitants all hastened from their houses to the highways, to get a sight of their great countryman; while the people of the towns, hearing of his approach, sallied out. . .to meet him. In eager throngs, men, women and children pressed upon his steps.❞

As President, Washington faced difficult tasks both at home and abroad. In all recorded history, no republican form of government had survived for long. Washington and other American leaders knew that the odds of creating a successful republic were against them. Washington was the first President of a new nation that many people—especially the British—thought would fail.

The decisions made by the country's first two Presidents, George Washington and John Adams, set the young nation on a firm foundation. Thanks in part to their actions, the United States would become a strong republic and a model for nations around the world.

ACTIVITY

Imagine that George Washington was planning to visit the United States today. Prepare a short skit to show him some major differences between life in his time and life today.

1794 *Government troops defeated Native Americans at the Battle of Fallen Timbers. The army used hand cannons like this one.*

1798 *The XYZ Affair sparked anti-French feeling. This cartoon shows France as a many-headed monster demanding bribe money.*

1801 *Thomas Jefferson became the nation's third President.*

| 1794 | 1796 | 1798 | 1800 |

WORLD EVENT
1797 Talleyrand becomes French foreign minister

WORLD EVENT
1800 Spain secretly gives Louisiana Territory to France

Linking Past and Present
Activity

The leaders who organized the first federal government held strong opinions. They offered George Washington and the Congress many different ideas about how to solve problems faced by the country during the first administration. If these same leaders could be consulted today, what opinions might they have about the problems facing the United States? What advice might they offer the leaders of our present government? Have students choose one leader who was active in George Washington's administration to "interview." They can work with partners to write or tape the interview, covering at least three government issues of importance today.

Answer to Caption

Possible Answer: As commander of American troops in the Revolution, he was the nation's greatest hero, respected and loved by Americans from all parts of the country.

Section 1
pp. 244–250

Bell Ringer

Have students make a list of as many positions and officeholders in the current President's Cabinet as they can.

Lesson Plan

1. Focus President Washington worked with the first Congress to organize the daily operation of the new national government. In this section, students read how members of the Cabinet were chosen, how a federal court system was set up, and how plans for paying the national debt and strengthening the nation's finances were created.

2. Instruct Have students work in small groups to prepare the following: (a) a dialogue between Alexander Hamilton and James Madison on paying national and state debts; (b) a dialogue between Hamilton and a southern member of Congress on passing a tariff; (c) a dialogue between Hamilton and George Washington on dealing with the leaders of the Whiskey Rebellion.

1
Organizing the New Government

FIND OUT

- Why were Washington's actions as President so important to the future of the United States?

- How did Hamilton propose to pay government debts and strengthen the economy?

- Why did some groups oppose Hamilton's economic plans?

VOCABULARY precedent, Cabinet, bond, national debt, speculator, tariff, protective tariff

When Congress met for the first time in the spring of 1789, Vice President John Adams brought up a curious question. How should people address the President of the United States?

For weeks, members of Congress debated the issue. Some felt the title "President Washington" was just fine. Others thought it lacked dignity. They tried out titles like "His Elective Highness" or "His Highness the President of the United States and Protector of the Rights of the Same."

The debate ended when Washington let Congress know he was content with "President of the United States." The lawmakers had taken three weeks to settle this small issue. They intended to carefully examine each of their actions as the new government took shape.

President Washington

George Washington took the oath of office as President on April 30, 1789. He looked "grave, almost to sadness," reported one witness. Washington no doubt was feeling the awesome weight of office. Americans looked to him to make the new government work.

Setting an example. As the first President, Washington knew he was setting an example for future generations. "There is scarcely any part of my conduct," he said, "which may not hereafter be drawn into precedent." A **precedent** (PREHS uh dehnt) is an act or decision that sets an example for others to follow.

During his two terms in office, Washington set many precedents. In 1796, he decided not to run for a third term. His refusal to seek a third term set a precedent that later Presidents followed until 1940.

The First President Crowds cheered George Washington as he arrived in New York City to be inaugurated as the nation's first President. The button above was issued to celebrate the inauguration. **Citizenship** Why did Americans have confidence in President Washington?

The first Cabinet. The Constitution said little about how the executive branch should be organized. It was clear, however, that the President needed people to help him carry out his duties. When the first Congress met in 1789, it created five executive departments. They were the departments of State, Treasury, and War and the offices of Attorney General and Postmaster General.

Washington chose well-known leaders to head these departments. He appointed Thomas Jefferson as Secretary of State and Alexander Hamilton as Secretary of the Treasury. Henry Knox served as Secretary of War. The Attorney General was Edmund Randolph, and Samuel Osgood became Postmaster General. These department heads made up the President's **Cabinet.** Members of the Cabinet gave Washington advice and directed their departments.

The federal court system. The Constitution called for a Supreme Court. Congress, however, had to organize the federal court system. In 1789, Congress passed the ***Judiciary Act.*** It called for the Supreme Court to have one Chief Justice and five Associate Justices.* Washington named John Jay as the first Chief Justice of the Supreme Court.

The Judiciary Act also set up district courts and circuit courts across the nation. Decisions made in these lower courts could be appealed to the Supreme Court, the highest court in the land.

Hamilton and the National Debt

As Secretary of the Treasury, Alexander Hamilton wanted to build a strong economy. He faced many major problems, however. Among the most pressing was the large government debt.

Government bonds. During the Revolution, both the national government and the individual states needed money to pay

---

*Today, the Supreme Court has eight Associate Justices.

soldiers and buy supplies. They borrowed money from foreign countries and ordinary citizens.

Then, as now, governments borrowed money by issuing bonds. A **bond** is a certificate that promises to repay the money loaned plus interest on a certain date. For example, if a person buys a bond for $100, the government agrees to pay back $100 plus interest in five or ten years. The total sum of money a government owes is called the **national debt.**

By 1789, most southern states had paid off their debts from the Revolution. Other states and the federal government had not. Hamilton insisted that all these debts be repaid. After all, he said, who would lend money to the United States in the future if the country did not pay its old debts?

Plan for repayment. Hamilton developed a plan to repay both the national and state debts. He wanted to buy up all bonds issued by the national and state governments before 1789. He planned to sell new bonds to pay off those old debts. When the economy improved, the government would be able to pay off the new bonds.

Opposition to Hamilton's Plan

Many people, including bankers and investors, welcomed Hamilton's plan. Others attacked it.

Linking Past and Present
Early in his first term, Washington went to the Senate to gain approval of a treaty with the Creek Indians. After a brief debate, the senators set up a committee to study the issue. Washington returned in a few days, and the senators debated again. Disgusted, Washington never returned to the Senate chamber. Instead, he sent written messages—a precedent that still guides Presidents today.

---

3. Close To close the lesson, have the class make a group decision on the most important fact or concept to remember for each subsection of Section 1.

 Lesson Planner

For a developed **Cooperative Learning** lesson plan, see the *Lesson Planner,* page 45.

 Chapter Resources

Geography in History Duplicate and distribute the worksheet, The Changing Center of Population, from Unit 3, pages 5–6, of the *Chapter Resources* binder. This worksheet presents a study of the U.S. census, which began in 1790, and shows how population patterns have changed. (Enrichment/Average)

CD-ROM

Presidents Access the biography of George Washington on the American Heritage® *History of the United States* CD-ROM. (Enrichment/Average)
History Makers Access the biography of Alexander Hamilton on the American Heritage® *History of the United States* CD-ROM. (Enrichment/Average)

Cooperative Learning
Activity

One of the ways in which Washington's government raised money was by issuing bonds. Today, the federal government as well as state and municipal governments still issue bonds. Have students find out about the government's savings bond program. They can begin their research by finding answers to the following questions: What is the minimum amount a person can invest in government bonds? How long does it take for a government bond to mature? What is the current rate of interest? For an investor, what are the advantages of government bonds? What are the disadvantages?

Interdisciplinary CONNECTIONS

For worksheets establishing connections between the Chapter 8 main idea, Inventing a Nation, and five other disciplines, see the *Interdisciplinary Connections* booklet. (Enrichment)

■ **Arts** American Spelling, page 44 (Easy)
■ **Sciences** Patents and Progress, page 45 (Challenging)
■ **Geography** A Capital Idea, page 46 (Average)
■ **World** The French Revolution, page 47 (Challenging)
■ **Economics** The New Nation's Coins, page 48 (Average)

Answer to Connections

She believed her main job was to serve as hostess for the President. She also felt that she should work for a public cause.

 Transparencies

Interdisciplinary Connections Use the transparency Martha Washington, First Lady on page B-47 of *American History Transparencies*. Teaching suggestions can be found on page B-10. (Enrichment/Average)

ACTIVITY

Guided Instruction Students may want to explore a particular subject or theme associated with the First Lady. Encourage students to use photos, quotations from the First Lady, quotations about the First Lady, and general commentary about the First Lady, her activities, and her ideas.

CONNECTIONS

ARTS **SCIENCES** **GEOGRAPHY** **WORLD** **ECONOMICS** **CIVICS**

First Lady of the Land

The people do not elect them. The Constitution does not define their job. Yet more than 30 women have served the United States in this crucial position. They are the First Ladies.

When Martha Washington became the first First Lady, no one knew exactly what she should do. There had never been a First Lady before. What should she be called, Americans wondered. "The Presidentress"? "Lady President"? "Lady Washington"? All of these were tried. It was not until nearly a century later that "First Lady" came into common use.

Martha Washington decided that her main job as First Lady was to serve as hostess for the President. She regularly entertained guests at dinners and afternoon gatherings. She kept these affairs formal. She wanted guests, especially Europeans, to take the new country and its President seriously. Entertaining foreign leaders and other important people remains an important task of the First Lady today.

Martha Washington

Martha Washington also believed that the First Lady should serve the public in some way. She took up the cause of needy veterans of the Revolution. In later years, First Ladies continued to work for causes, such as the environment, education, or health care.

Each First Lady has brought her own interests and personality to the job. Some enjoyed the excitement of the position. Others became important advisers to their husbands in office. All of them helped to define the position that has been called "the most demanding unpaid, unelected job in America."

■ How did Martha Washington view her responsibility as First Lady?

Martha Washington's slippers

Greeting guests at a reception

ACTIVITY Make a list of questions that you would like to ask the current First Lady. Then collect information about her from newspapers and magazines to answer your questions. Organize your findings into a collage.

246 • Chapter 8

Team-Teaching Suggestion
Music

You might work with a music teacher to present a lesson on the role that music played in life at the White House. Students could research to find out the musical talents and tastes associated with different First Families; they might also find information about musicians who have performed at the White House and unusual concerts that have taken place there.

Team-Teaching Suggestion
Civics

You might work with a civics teacher to present a lesson about the work that First Ladies have done for specific public causes. Each student might research the interests and work of one First Lady and present his or her findings to the class.

Madison leads the opposition. James Madison led the opposition to Hamilton's plan. Madison argued that the plan was unfair because it would reward speculators. A speculator is someone willing to invest in a risky venture in the hope of making a large profit.

During the Revolution, the government had paid soldiers and citizens who supplied goods with bonds. Many of these bondholders needed cash to survive. They sold their bonds to speculators. Speculators paid only 10 or 15 cents for bonds that had an original, or face, value of one dollar.

If the government repaid the bonds at face value, speculators stood to make great fortunes. Madison thought that speculators did not deserve to make such profits.

Hamilton disagreed. The country must repay its bonds in full, he said, to gain the trust and help of investors. The support of investors, he argued, was crucial for building the new nation's economy. After much debate, Hamilton convinced Congress to accept his plan of repaying the national debt.

As a southerner, Madison also led the fight against another part of Hamilton's plan. It called for repaying state debts. But many southern states had already paid their debts. They thought other states should also pay for their own debts. So they bitterly opposed Hamilton's proposal.

Hamilton's compromise. To win support for his plan, Hamilton suggested a compromise. He knew that many southerners wanted to move the nation's capital from New York to the South. He offered to persuade his northern friends to vote for a capital in the South if southerners supported the repayment of state debts.

Madison and other southerners accepted this compromise. In July 1790, Congress passed bills taking over state debts and providing for a new capital city.

The capital would not be part of any state. Instead, it would be on land along the Potomac River between Maryland and Virginia. Congress called the area the District of Columbia. Today, it is known as Washington, D.C. Congress hoped the new capital

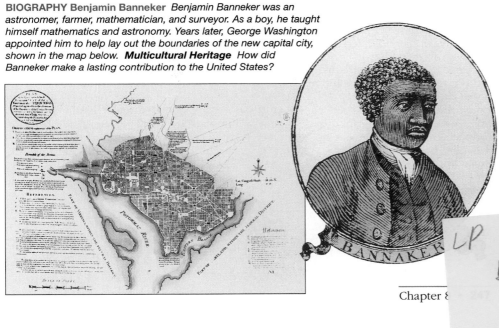

BIOGRAPHY **Benjamin Banneker** *Benjamin Banneker was an astronomer, farmer, mathematician, and surveyor. As a boy, he taught himself mathematics and astronomy. Years later, George Washington appointed him to help lay out the boundaries of the new capital city, shown in the map below.* **Multicultural Heritage** *How did Banneker make a lasting contribution to the United States?*

Chapter 8 • 247

Benjamin Banneker

LP 1

Connections With Architecture

Background

Washington, D.C., was originally called Federal City. The chief planner of the city was a French architect, Pierre L'Enfant. Benjamin Banneker, a free black from Maryland, served on the commission that surveyed and laid out the street plan. However, after less than a year on the job, L'Enfant was fired, and the surveyors, including Banneker, reproduced his original plan as best they could remember. L'Enfant later asked Congress for payment of

$95,500 for his work, but Congress voted to give him only $2,500.

L'Enfant fought in the American Revolution. His other designs include Federal Hall, New York City, where George Washington was inaugurated.

The Executive Mansion, or the White House, was designed by Irish American architect James Hoban.

would be ready by 1800. Meanwhile, the nation's capital was moved to Philadelphia.

Strengthening the Economy

Hamilton had resolved the problem of the national debt. Now he took steps to build up the new nation's economy.

A national bank. Hamilton called on Congress to set up a national bank. In 1791, Congress passed a bill setting up the ***Bank of the United States.*** The government deposited the money it collected in taxes in the Bank. The Bank, in turn, issued paper money. The government used the paper money to pay its bills. The Bank also made loans to farmers and businesses, helping them to expand.

Protecting the nation's industries. Hamilton also wanted to give American manufacturing a boost. He proposed that Congress pass a **tariff**, or tax, on all foreign goods brought into the country. Hamilton called for a very high tariff. He wanted to make imported goods more expensive to buy than goods made in the United States. Because such a tariff would protect American industry from foreign competition, it was called a **protective tariff.**

In the North, where factories were growing, many people supported Hamilton's plan. Southern farmers, however, bought more imported goods than northerners did. They did not want a tariff that would make these goods more expensive.

In the end, Congress did pass a tariff bill. However, it was meant to raise money for operating the government, not to protect American industries. For this reason, it was much lower than the protective tariff called for by Hamilton.

The Whiskey Tax

New taxes also created tensions in the backcountry. In 1791, Congress taxed all liquor made and sold in the United States. Settlers in the backcountry exploded in anger.

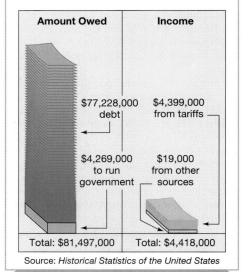

Money Problems of the New Nation, 1789–1791

Amount Owed	Income
$77,228,000 debt	$4,399,000 from tariffs
$4,269,000 to run government	$19,000 from other sources
Total: $81,497,000	Total: $4,418,000

Source: *Historical Statistics of the United States*

CHART SKILLS *As Secretary of the Treasury, Alexander Hamilton had to set up a plan for the government to meet its expenses.* • *What was the government's income in 1789? How much did it owe?*

Like many Americans, backcountry farmers grew corn. Corn was bulky to haul over rough backcountry roads. Instead, farmers turned their corn into whiskey, which they could easily ship in barrels to markets in the East.

Backcountry farmers loudly protested the whiskey tax. They compared it to the hated taxes Britain had forced on the colonies in the 1760s. Many refused to pay the tax. A backcountry poet wrote:

66 Some chaps whom freedom's
spirit warms
Are threatening hard to take up
arms. . . .
Their liberty they will maintain,
They fought for't, and they'll fight
again. 99

Connections With Economics
Background

In April 1792, Congress set up a mint to make gold and silver coins. Jefferson and Hamilton established the system of coins still used today. The first American coins were made of silver, gold, and copper.

Historical Sidelight
Background

George Washington was an all-around sportsperson. He especially liked fox hunting, for which he had hounds with names such as Tipsy, Harry's Drunkard, and Sweetlips. Washington also liked to dance. Once, he reportedly danced for three hours without stopping, doing such dances as the "High Betty Martin" and "Leather-the-strap."

The Whiskey Rebellion

When tax collectors appeared in western Pennsylvania to enforce the new law, they faced angry farmers. Some tax collectors, like John Neville, were treated harshly.

One spring morning, Neville and his wife were heading home from Pittsburgh. Mrs. Neville's saddle began to slip off her horse. Neville stopped to adjust it. Behind him, he heard the clip-clop of an approaching horse. A voice called out:

"Are you Neville, the tax collector?"

Still busy with his wife's saddle, Neville replied without turning round. "Yes, I'm Neville," he said.

"Then I must give you a whipping!" shouted the stranger. He grabbed Neville by the throat. The two men struggled. Finally, Neville threw his attacker to the ground and frightened him into running off. The incident showed Neville just how unpopular he was.

William Miller receives a summons. If the farmers refused to pay the whiskey tax, they were required to appear in distant federal courts. William Miller, a farmer who distilled whiskey, learned the hard way about the heavy hand of the law.

One hot July day in 1794, a stranger appeared at William Miller's door. The man said he was a sheriff from Philadelphia. He had come to serve legal papers on Miller. Next to the sheriff stood the hated tax collector, John Neville.

Miller read the summons. It ordered him to set aside "all manner of business and excuses" and appear before the court in little more than a month. To obey, Miller would have to make a long journey east. Even worse, the court papers seemed to say that he owed the government a tax of $250, a huge sum in those days. Later, Miller recalled his anger:

> ❝I felt myself mad with passion. I thought $250 would ruin me; and to have to go [to] the federal court at Philadelphia would keep me from going to Kentucky this fall [as I had planned]. . . . I felt my blood boil at seeing General Neville along to pilot the sheriff to my very door.❞

Farmers rebel. News quickly spread that a sheriff had come to take Miller to Philadelphia. Before long, angry farmers set out to find Neville and the sheriff. Some had muskets. Others had pitchforks. The sheriff and Neville fled.

Washington Reviews the Troops *When Pennsylvania farmers rioted against the whiskey tax, President Washington called out the state militias to restore order.* **Citizenship** *What role of the President does this painting illustrate?*

Connections With Language Arts
Background

A tax on certain goods, such as whiskey, made and sold within a country is called an excise tax. Current examples of excise taxes include gasoline and cigarette taxes.

Learning Styles
Visual Learners

Students can work in groups to make Major Events charts for the time period encompassing George Washington's presidency. Each group should reach a consensus as to which events will be included on the chart. Finished charts can show the events, categorized by labels such as Economic, Cultural, Political, and so forth, or arranged so that cause-and-effect relationships are easily recognizable.

Section 1 Study Guide Have students use the Section 1 Study Guide on page 75 of the *Student Study Guide* to review and reinforce the content of this section. (Reteaching/Average)

ACTIVITY

Guided Instruction Students might also enjoy taping their descriptions of Washington's inauguration as if they were reporters for radio or TV news shows. Encourage students to include enough sensory details so that their readers or listeners can experience the event as if they themselves were present.

Section 2
pp. 250–253

Bell Ringer

Write the word *neutrality* on the chalkboard. Have students define the word and identify examples of conflicts on which a person might take a position of neutrality.

Lesson Plan

1. Focus The new American nation faced many challenges. In this section, students explore Washington's presidency, with its problems of keeping peace at home and neutrality abroad.

Next day, farmers and Neville met head-on. This time, Neville fired, killing a man. Several others were wounded.

Mobs formed elsewhere. Thousands of farmers marched through Pittsburgh. They set up Liberty Trees, sang Revolutionary songs, and tarred and feathered tax officials.

Government response. News of the *Whiskey Rebellion* spread quickly. Alexander Hamilton called the revolt "treason against society, against liberty, against everything that ought to be dear to a free, enlightened, and prudent people." President Washington quickly responded to this challenge to authority. He called up the militia in several states.

When the rebels heard that troops were coming, they scattered. The government's show of strength worked. The President's quick response to the Whiskey Rebellion proved to Americans that their new government would act firmly in times of crisis. ∎

SECTION 1 REVIEW

1. **Identify:** (a) Judiciary Act, (b) Bank of the United States, (c) Whiskey Rebellion.
2. **Define:** (a) precedent, (b) Cabinet, (c) bond, (d) national debt, (e) speculator, (f) tariff, (g) protective tariff.
3. Describe a precedent set by Washington.
4. Why did Hamilton want to repay the national and state debts?
5. Describe two of Hamilton's ideas for strengthening the economy.
6. Why did some Americans oppose a protective tariff?
7. **CRITICAL THINKING Analyzing Ideas** Why do you think some Americans who had fought in the Revolution looked on the Whiskey Rebellion as "treason"?

ACTIVITY Writing to Learn

Imagine that you attended Washington's inauguration. Write a description of the event.

2
War Clouds

FIND OUT
- How did Americans respond to the French Revolution?
- What was the purpose of the Neutrality Proclamation?
- Why did fighting erupt in the Northwest Territory?
- What were the main ideas of Washington's Farewell Address?

Late in 1789, French ships arriving at American ports brought startling news. On July 14, a mob in Paris, France, had destroyed the Bastille (bahs TEEL), a huge fort that was used as a prison. The attack on the Bastille marked the beginning of the *French Revolution.*

The French Revolution broke out a few years after Americans won independence. Like the Americans, the French fought for liberty and equality. As the French Revolution grew more violent, however, it ignited political quarrels that had been smoldering in the United States.

Upheaval in France

The French had many reasons to rebel against their king, Louis XVI. Peasants and the middle class paid heavy taxes, while nobles paid none. Reformers called for a constitution to limit the power of the king. They also wanted a guarantee of rights like that in the American Constitution.

Americans support the revolution. At first, most Americans welcomed the French Revolution. They knew what it meant to struggle for liberty. Then, too, France had been America's first ally in the war against

---

Answers to Section 1 Review

1. (a) Judiciary Act, p. 245, (b) Bank of the United States, p. 248, (c) Whiskey Rebellion, p. 250
2. (a) precedent, p. 244, (b) Cabinet, p. 245, (c) bond, p. 245, (d) national debt, p. 245, (e) speculator, p. 247, (f) tariff, p. 248, (g) protective tariff, p. 248
3. Possible Answer: Washington served as President for only two terms—he refused to seek a third term.

4. Hamilton wanted to gain the trust and support of investors, which he felt was crucial to building the nation's future economy.
5. Hamilton wanted to set up a national bank in which to deposit tax monies and to issue paper money to pay the government's bills; he also proposed tariffs on foreign goods to protect American industry.

6. The tariff increased the price of imported goods, which southerners used more than northerners did.
7. Possible Answer: The Whiskey Rebellion, unlike the American Revolution, was a revolt against a law made by an elected government.

The French Revolution *At first, Americans supported the French Revolution, but the violence split public opinion. Here, a group of French women march toward the palace of the king.* **United States and the World** *Why would the French expect Americans to support their revolution?*

Great Britain. Many Americans felt that they should rally behind the Marquis de Lafayette, a leading French reformer. After all, Lafayette had fought with them in the American Revolution.

In the 1790s, however, the French Revolution entered a very violent stage. A radical group gained power. In 1793, they beheaded Louis XVI and his family. During a "reign of terror" that swept the country, tens of thousands of French citizens were executed.

Violence divides opinion. The violence in France divided Americans. Thomas Jefferson and others condemned the killings. Still, they felt that the French people had the right to use violence to win freedom. Later, Jefferson even said that he was willing to see "half the earth devastated" in order to win the "liberty of the whole."

Alexander Hamilton, John Adams, and others disagreed. They thought the French Revolution was doomed to fail. The French could no more create a democracy in that way, claimed Adams, "than a snowball can exist in the streets of Philadelphia under a burning sun."

A Policy of Neutrality

The French Revolution shocked rulers and nobles across Europe. They feared the spread of revolutionary ideas to their own lands. With this in mind, Britain, Austria, Prussia, the Netherlands, and Spain sent armies to overpower the revolutionaries in France. Europe was soon plunged into a war that continued on and off from 1792 to 1815.

The war in Europe threatened to involve the United States. In 1778, the United States and France signed a treaty that allowed French ships to use American ports. Now, the French wanted to use American ports to supply their ships and attack British ships.

Washington faced a difficult decision. He wanted to remain neutral. "It is the sincere wish of United America," said the President, "to have nothing to do with. . .the squabbles of European nations." How could the United States honor its treaty with France and still avoid war?

That question deepened divisions within Washington's Cabinet. Both Hamilton and

Chapter 8 • **251**

2. Instruct Divide the class into groups. Assign one of the following statements to each group: (a) "We are Americans who support the French Revolution." (b) "We are French citizens who believe that the United States should let us use its ports to attack the British." (c) "We are advisers to George Washington who want the United States to remain neutral." Have each group prepare a list of reasons for its assigned point of view.

3. Close To close the lesson, have students answer *Who, What, When, Where, Why,* and *How* questions about the people and events in Section 2.

 Lesson Planner

For a developed **Cooperative Learning** lesson plan, see the *Lesson Planner,* page 46.

Answer to Caption

The French had been inspired by the ideals of the American Revolution. Also, France had aided the Patriot cause during the American Revolution.

 Our Multicultural Heritage

Biography Have students read the biography, *Eleuthère Irénée du Pont, Refugee to Manufacturer,* on page 22 of the *Our Multicultural Heritage* booklet. (Enrichment/Average)

Critical Thinking
Recognizing Points of View

Divide the chalkboards (or provide large pieces of paper or posterboard) so that students have space to create graffiti reflecting different points of view about the French Revolution. Allow students to imagine membership in one of the following groups: (a) U.S. citizens sympathetic to the French Revolution, (b) French sailors in an American port, (c) British sailors in an American port, (d) European nobles visiting the United States, (e) U.S. citizens opposed to violence, (f) American merchants eager to trade with all European nations. Students can discuss the feelings and attitudes of their groups in reaction to the events of the French Revolution before creating graffiti appropriate to the groups.

Connections With the World
Background

The wars in Europe ended with the decisions issued by the Congress of Vienna in 1815. These decisions made the Europe of 1815 look very different from the Europe of today. For example, Finland and most of Poland were given to Russia, parts of Italy were given to Austria, and Norway was given to Sweden.

Voices of Freedom

Primary Source You might wish to assign selection 10-2, Washington Advises Neutrality, on pages 73–74 of *Voices of Freedom.* The selection, from George Washington's Farewell Address, makes it clear that Washington supported the policy of neutrality in foreign affairs for future generations. (Enrichment/Average)

Customized Reader

Primary Source For a historian's discussion of the fur trade between Europeans and Native Americans, order article IIIA-10, Fur Trade With the Ojibway, from the *American History Customized Reader.* Bruce M. White's article describes trading customs of the eighteenth century and the effects of competition between rival trading companies. (Enrichment/Challenging)

Jefferson wanted to avoid war. They disagreed, however, about how to do this.

After much debate, Washington issued the ***Neutrality Proclamation*** in April 1793. It stated that the United States would not support either side in the war. It also forbade Americans to aid either Britain or France in any way.

An Unpopular Treaty

Declaring neutrality was easier than enforcing it. American merchants wanted to trade with both Britain and France. However, those warring nations ignored the rights of neutral ships. They seized American cargoes headed for each other's ports.

In 1793, the British captured more than 250 American ships trading in the French West Indies. Americans clamored for war. Washington, however, knew that the United States was too weak to fight. He sent Chief Justice John Jay to Britain for talks.

Jay worked out a treaty. It called for Britain to pay damages for American ships seized in 1793. At the same time, Americans had to pay debts to British merchants, owed from before the Revolution. Britain agreed to give up forts it still held in the Ohio Valley. The treaty did not, however, protect the rights of neutral American ships to trade where they wanted.

Jay's Treaty sparked a storm of protest. Many Americans felt they were giving up more than Britain was. After a furious debate, the Senate finally approved the treaty in 1795. Washington accepted the treaty because he wanted to avoid war. "Such is the popularity of the President," noted Jefferson, "that the people will support him in whatever he will do."

War in the West

On the western frontier, the President faced another crisis. Thousands of white settlers moved into the Northwest Territory in the 1790s. The newcomers ignored treaties

the United States had signed with the Indian nations of that region. They simply took over Indian lands.

Spreading conflict. Native Americans responded to the invasion by attacking settlers and traders. White settlers took revenge. Often, they killed Indians who had not taken part in the attacks. The violence soon spread.

In 1791, the Miamis in Ohio joined with other Indian nations. Little Turtle, a skilled fighter, led the Miami nation. Armed with muskets and gunpowder supplied by the British, the Miamis drove white settlers from the area.

President Washington sent an army under General Arthur St. Clair to Ohio. Little Turtle and the Miamis defeated St. Clair's army. Frustrated, Washington replaced St. Clair with General Anthony Wayne.

Battle of Fallen Timbers. In 1794, Wayne marched a well-trained army into Miami territory. Blue Jacket, a Shawnee leader who served under Little Turtle, gathered the Native American forces at Fallen Timbers. Blue Jacket thought that Wayne would have trouble fighting there because the land was covered with fallen trees. But Wayne's forces pushed through the tangle of logs and defeated the Indians.

In 1795, the Miamis and 11 other Indian nations signed the ***Treaty of Greenville*** with the United States. In it, they gave up land that would later become the southern half of Ohio. In return, the Indian nations received $20,000 and the promise of more money if they kept the peace.

> ***Our Common Heritage***
> *Although they were defeated at Fallen Timbers, the Miami Indians are honored in southwestern Ohio. Miami County, the city of Miamisburg, the town of New Miami, and Miami University were named for them.*

Our Multicultural Heritage
Background

Native American peoples who fought in the Northwest Territories included the Miami, Shawnee, Ottawa, Potawatomi, Ojibway, Fox, and Sauk. They felt that no one "owned" the land; therefore, no one could sell it, give it away, or—as settlers did—take it.

Fallen Timbers, where the decisive battle took place between General Anthony Wayne's troops and Blue Jacket's forces, is near the present-day site of Toledo, Ohio.

Historical Sidelight
Background

General Anthony Wayne was nicknamed "Mad Anthony" because of his reckless bravery. At Fallen Timbers, he commanded a force of about 1,000 against Blue Jacket's force of about 2,000. In the year of peace negotiations that followed, Wayne was instructed by Timothy Pickering of the Cabinet, "Let them feel that they are at perfect liberty to speak their sentiments, and to sign or refuse to sign such a treaty as you are now authorized to negotiate. . . . One great principle ought to govern all public negotiations—*a rigid adherence to truth. . . .*"

Treaty of Greenville *In the Treaty of Greenville, Native Americans agreed to give up the southern half of present-day Ohio for about ⅛ cent per acre. Here, Indian leaders meet with General Wayne to discuss the terms of the treaty, shown at right.* **Linking Past and Present** *How do you think future generations of Indians viewed the terms of the treaty?*

Washington Retires

By 1796, Washington had weathered many crises. He had kept the nation out of war and set it on a path of growth. That year, he published his *Farewell Address.* In it, he announced he would retire. He urged that the United States remain neutral in its relations with other countries:

> 66 Observe good faith and justice toward all nations. Cultivate peace and harmony with all. . . . Nothing is more essential than that permanent, [habitual hatred] against particular nations and passionate attachments for others should be excluded. 99

Washington warned Americans to avoid becoming involved in European affairs. " 'Tis our true policy to steer clear of permanent alliances with any portion of the foreign world," said the retiring President. Such alliances, he felt, would pull the United States into war. That advice guided American foreign policy for many years.

Washington further called on Americans to avoid political parties. During his years in office, rival groups had grown up around Hamilton and Jefferson. Americans in different regions had diverse interests. Once Washington left office, those differences began to grow.

SECTION 2 REVIEW

1. **Identify:** (a) French Revolution, (b) Neutrality Proclamation, (c) Jay's Treaty, (d) Treaty of Greenville, (e) Farewell Address.
2. Why were Americans divided in their reaction to the French Revolution?
3. Why did Washington issue the Neutrality Proclamation?
4. How did Britain and France respond to the Neutrality Proclamation?
5. What events led to the Battle of Fallen Timbers?
6. **CRITICAL THINKING Analyzing Information** How did location help the United States to "steer clear of permanent alliances" with European nations for many years?

ACTIVITY **Writing to Learn**
Write a series of five headlines that highlight the crises Washington faced in the 1790s.

Answers to Section 2 Review

1. (a) French Revolution, p. 250, (b) Neutrality Proclamation, p. 252, (c) Jay's Treaty, p. 252, (d) Treaty of Greenville, p. 252, (e) Farewell Address, p. 253
2. Americans condemned the violence of the French Revolution but wanted to support the French struggle for freedom because France had been America's first ally against Britain during the American Revolution.
3. to keep the United States out of the wars in Europe
4. Britain and France ignored it and seized the cargoes of American ships.
5. Settlers took Indian lands that had been protected by treaty; Native Americans responded with violence. The violence grew on both sides; ultimately, a united force of Indians under Little Turtle defeated General St. Clair's troops.
6. Possible Answer: The Atlantic Ocean formed a natural barrier between Europe and the United States.

Section 3
pp. 254–258

Bell Ringer

To prepare for the section focus on the "image" that a political party tries to represent, have students freewrite for three minutes each about the images that *Democrat* and *Republican*—referring to today's political parties—bring to mind.

Lesson Plan

1. Focus The first political parties developed during Washington's presidency. In this section, students learn how the new parties supplied candidates for the 1796 presidential election and how newspapers influenced the growth of the parties.

2. Instruct Have students outline or draft editorials that might have appeared in 1796 in the *Gazette of the United States* and in the *National Gazette.* Use the editorials as a springboard for discussion about the differences between the Federalists and the Democratic Republicans. Students may want to save their notes for the Writing to Learn activity in the Section Review.

3. Close To close the lesson, play a Jeopardy!-like game. Provide answers and have students create the questions.

Lesson Planner

For a developed **Cooperative Learning** lesson plan, see the *Lesson Planner,* page 47.

3
Rise of Political Parties

FIND OUT
- Why did political parties form in the United States?
- How did Hamilton and Jefferson differ on major issues?
- How did newspapers influence the growth of political parties?
- Why did the election of 1796 increase political tensions?

VOCABULARY unconstitutional

Divisions in Congress worried Thomas Jefferson in the 1790s. Backers of Hamilton argued with supporters of Jefferson and James Madison. Jefferson described the unpleasant mood:

66 Men who have been [friends] all their lives cross streets to avoid meeting, and turn their heads another way, lest they should be obliged to touch their hats. 99

The split had occurred gradually since 1789. When Washington first took office, the country had no political parties. By the time he retired, there were two parties competing for power.

A Distrust of Political Parties

Most Americans distrusted political parties. They had seen how political parties worked in Britain. There, party members were more interested in personal gain than in the public good.

Americans also saw parties as a threat to unity. They agreed with George Washington, who warned that parties would lead to "jealousies and false alarms."

254 • Chapter 8

Despite the President's warning, parties grew up around two of his advisers: Alexander Hamilton and Thomas Jefferson. The two men differed in looks and personality as well as in politics. Hamilton was of medium height and slender. He dressed in fine clothes and spoke forcefully. Energetic, brilliant, and restless, Hamilton enjoyed political debate.

Jefferson was tall and a bit gawky. Although he was a wealthy Virginia planter, he dressed and spoke informally. As one senator recalled:

66 His clothes seem too small for him. He sits in a lounging manner, on one hip commonly, and with one of his shoulders elevated much above the other. His face has a sunny aspect. His whole figure has a loose, shackling air. . . . He spoke almost without ceasing. [His conversation] was loose and rambling; and yet he scattered information wherever he went. 99

Differing Views

Hamilton and Jefferson did not agree on many issues. At the root of their quarrels were different views about what was best for the country.

Manufacturing or farming? Hamilton thought the United States should model itself on Britain. He wanted the government

History and You
During recent elections, candidates for President and Vice President have tried to win the support of young voters by appearing for interviews on a music video television network. What are some other ways in which political parties could capture your support for their candidates?

Connections With the World
Background

Political parties emerged in England in the late 1600s. The Whigs, who were wealthy landowners, wanted laws limiting royal power. They upheld the rights of parliament over those of the monarchy. The Tories were smaller landowners who usually favored laws defending royal power. (In the 1830s, an American political party also took the name Whigs.)

Critical Thinking
Analyzing Ideas

Have students discuss the following quotations:

1. "All communities divide themselves into the few and the many. The first are rich and well-born; the other, the mass of the people who seldom judge or determine the right. Give therefore to the first class a distinct, permanent share in the government."

2. "I persuaded myself that the good sense of the people will always be found to be the best army. They may be led astray for a mo-ment, but will soon correct themselves. The people are the only censors of their governors."

Ask students which statement was made by Thomas Jefferson (the second) and which by Alexander Hamilton (the first). Then ask: How did Hamilton's view of people differ from Jefferson's? How did this difference influence the kind of government that each leader favored?

A Nation of Farmers *Thomas Jefferson believed the nation's strength rested with small, independent farmers, such as those in this painting by Edward Hicks.* **Citizenship** *How did this differ from Hamilton's vision of the nation?*

to encourage trade and manufacturing. He also favored the growth of cities.

Jefferson believed that farmers were the backbone of the new nation. "Cultivators of the earth," he wrote, "are the most valuable citizens." He feared that a manufacturing economy would corrupt the United States. "Let our workshops remain in Europe," Jefferson urged. "The mobs of the great cities add just so much to the support of pure government, as sores do to the strength of the human body."

Federal or state governments? Hamilton and Jefferson disagreed about the power of the federal government. Hamilton wanted the federal government to have more power than state governments. Jefferson thought the opposite. He feared that the federal government might take over powers that the Constitution gave to the states.

Strict or loose interpretation? The two leaders also clashed over the Bank of the United States. Jefferson opposed Hamilton's plan for the Bank. He said it gave too much power to the federal government and the wealthy investors who helped run it. Jefferson said that the law creating the Bank was **unconstitutional**, that is, not permitted by the Constitution.

Jefferson objected to the Bank because he interpreted the Constitution very strictly. Nowhere did the Constitution give Congress the power to create a Bank, he argued. He thought that any power not specifically given to the federal government belonged to the states.

Hamilton interpreted the Constitution more loosely. The Constitution gave Congress the power to make all laws "necessary and proper" to carry out its duties. Hamilton argued that the Bank was necessary for the government to collect taxes and pay its bills.

Britain or France? Finally, Hamilton and Jefferson had different ideas about foreign policy. Hamilton wanted to form close ties with Britain, an important trading partner.

Answer to Caption
Hamilton believed in a strong central government; he also favored cities and manufacturing.

 Voices of Freedom

Primary Source You might assign selection 10-3, Jefferson Opposes the National Bank, and selection 10-4, Hamilton Supports the Bank, on pages 74–75 and 76–77 of *Voices of Freedom.* (Enrichment/Challenging)

 Videotapes/ Videodiscs

United States History Video Collection Use the video segment "The Many or the Few?" from Volume 5, *A New Nation (1776–1815),* to enhance students' understanding of Hamilton's and Jefferson's interpretations of the Constitution. Approx. running time 3:30 min. (Enrichment/Average) Vol. 5, Ch. 34

Chapter 34   Play

Our Multicultural Heritage
Background

In 1791, Benjamin Banneker, the surveyor whom President Washington appointed to lay out the boundaries of the District of Columbia, wrote a letter to Thomas Jefferson, then a slave owner: "How pitiable . . . that although you were so fully convinced of the benevolence of [God] . . . that you should at the same time counteract his mercies, in detaining by fraud and violence, so numerous a part of my brethren under groaning captivity and cruel oppression."

Chapter Resources

Answers to Skill Lesson

1. (a) Possible Answer: Freneau, the present publisher of the *National Gazette,* was a known Antifederalist. At the time that he started his paper, he was also a clerk in the Department of State. (b) The accuracy of these statements can be checked.
2. (a) Possible Answer: "They are motivated by views that, in my judgment, will undermine the principles of good government and are dangerous to the peace and happiness of the country." "They have a womanish attachment to France and a womanish resentment against Great Britain." (b) Each statement reflects Hamilton's beliefs and judgments.
3. (a) a weak and dependent attachment to France and an unforgiving and vengeful resentment against Britain (b) Yes; Jefferson favored France. (c) Britain (d) Possible Answer: Hamilton was writing a letter, and including opinions in personal letters is appropriate.

ACTIVITY

Guided Instruction To help students' analyses, you may want to obtain editorials on the same issue from different points of view. After students identify the opinions and facts in the editorials, they can compare their findings.

CRITICAL THINKING SKILLS
Distinguishing Fact From Opinion

Primary sources—such as letters, diaries, and speeches—often express the opinions of the people who wrote them. Therefore, when historians study primary sources, they have to distinguish fact from opinion. A *fact* is something that can be proved or observed. An *opinion* is a judgment that reflects a person's beliefs or feelings. It may not always be true.

In the letter below, Alexander Hamilton writes about political differences between himself and the party led by James Madison and Thomas Jefferson. Like many writers, Hamilton combines fact and opinion. Read the letter, and distinguish fact from opinion.

1. **Determine which statements are facts.** Remember that facts can be proved. Use your reading in this chapter to help answer these questions. (a) Find two statements of fact in Hamilton's letter. (b) How can you prove that each statement is a fact?
2. **Determine which statements are opinions.** Writers often show that they are expressing an opinion by saying "in my view" or "I think" or "I believe." (a) Find two statements in which Hamilton gives his opinion. (b) How can you tell that each is an opinion?
3. **Determine how a writer mixes fact and opinion.** Reread the last sentence of the letter. (a) What did Hamilton mean by a "womanish attachment to France and a womanish resentment against Great Britain"? (b) Is it true that Jefferson supported France and opposed Britain? (c) What country did Hamilton want the United States to support? (d) Why do you think Hamilton mixed fact and opinion in the statement?

ACTIVITY Select an editorial from a recent newspaper. List the opinions expressed in the editorial. Underline the words that tell you these are opinions. Then, under each opinion list the facts the writers used to support it.

Alexander Hamilton wrote:

❝It was not until the last session of Congress that I became completely convinced that Mr. Madison and Mr. Jefferson are at the head of a faction that is hostile toward me. They are motivated by views that, in my judgment, will undermine the principles of good government and are dangerous to the peace and happiness of the country.

Freneau, the present publisher of the *National Gazette,* was a known Antifederalist. It is certain that he was brought to Philadelphia by Mr. Jefferson to be the publisher of a newspaper. At the same time as he was starting his paper, he was also a clerk in the Department of State. His paper is devoted to opposing me and the measures that I have supported. And the paper has a general unfriendly attitude toward the government of the United States.

On almost all questions, great and small, which have come up since the first session of Congress, Mr. Jefferson and Mr. Madison have been found among those who want to limit federal power. In respect to foreign policy, the views of these gentlemen are, in my judgment, equally unsound and dangerous. They have a womanish attachment to France and a womanish resentment against Great Britain.❞

Jefferson favored France, the first ally of the United States and a nation struggling for its own liberty.

Party Rivalry

At first, Hamilton and Jefferson clashed in private. When Congress began to pass Hamilton's programs, Jefferson and James Madison decided to organize public support for their views. They turned first to important New York leaders, including Governor George Clinton and Aaron Burr.

Republicans and Federalists. Soon, leaders in other states began to side with either Hamilton or Jefferson. Jefferson's supporters called themselves *Democratic Republicans.* They often shortened the name to Republicans.* Republicans included small farmers, craftsworkers, and some wealthy planters.

Hamilton and his supporters were called *Federalists* because they wanted a strong federal government. Federalists drew support from merchants and manufacturers in cities such as Boston and New York as well as from some southern planters. See the chart at right.

Newspapers begin to take sides. In the late 1700s, the number of American newspapers more than doubled—from about 100 to more than 230. They grew to meet the demand for information. A visitor from Europe noted with surprise that so many Americans could read.

❝The common people [there] are on a footing, in point of literature with the middle ranks of Europe. They all read and write, and understand arithmetic; almost every little town now furnishes a circulating library.❞

---

*Jefferson's Republican party was not the same as today's Republican party. In fact, his party later grew into the Democratic party.

The First Political Parties

Federalists	Republicans
1. Led by A. Hamilton	1. Led by T. Jefferson
2. Wealthy and well educated should lead nation	2. People should have political power
3. Strong central government	3. Strong state governments
4. Emphasis on manufacturing, shipping, and trade	4. Emphasis on agriculture
5. Loose interpretation of Constitution	5. Strict interpretation of Constitution
6. Pro-British	6. Pro-French
7. Favored national bank	7. Opposed national bank
8. Favored protective tariff	8. Opposed protective tariff

CHART SKILLS By the 1790s, two political parties had formed—the Federalist party and the Republican party. ● Who led each party? What were two ways in which the parties differed on economic issues?

Newspaper publishers lined up behind the parties. In the *Gazette of the United States,* publisher John Fenno backed Alexander Hamilton. Thomas Jefferson's friend Philip Freneau (frih NOH) started a rival paper, the *National Gazette.* He vigorously supported Republicans.

Newspapers had great influence on public opinion. In stinging language, they raged against opponents. Often, articles mixed rumor and opinion with facts. Emotional attacks and counterattacks fanned the flames of party rivalry. Yet, they also kept people informed and helped shape public opinion.

Chapter 8 • **257**

Connections With Literature
Background

Philip Freneau, publisher of the *National Gazette,* was one of the first important poets of the new nation. His most famous poem, "The Indian Burying Ground," was one of the first to idealize Native Americans.

Cooperative Learning
Activity

Divide students into groups. Tell the groups that they are media consultants for the Federalists and the Democratic Republicans. Discuss with the class the types of media used by politicians in the new nation (letters, newspapers, pamphlets, speeches, sideboards, town criers). Then assign each group, or allow it to choose, a party to represent and have each group create a button, print advertisement, and a one-minute political announcement for its party. In planning media campaigns, groups should think about the positions that each party has taken on such issues as the national bank, protective tariffs, interpretation of the Constitution, and the role of the federal government. Campaign advertising should highlight differences between the parties or explain why one party's positions on issues are better for the country.

A Slim Victory

Political parties played an important part in choosing George Washington's successor. In 1796, Republicans backed Thomas Jefferson for President and Aaron Burr for Vice President. Federalists supported John Adams for President and Thomas Pinckney for Vice President.

The election had an unexpected outcome, which created new tensions. Under the Constitution, the person with the most electoral votes became President. The person with the next highest total was made Vice President. John Adams, a Federalist, won office as President. The leader of the Republicans, Thomas Jefferson, came in second and became Vice President.

With the President and Vice President from different parties, political tensions remained high. Events would fuel the distrust between the two men. Meanwhile, Adams took office in March 1797 as the second President of the United States.

SECTION 3 REVIEW

1. **Identify:** (a) Democratic Republicans, (b) Federalists.
2. **Define:** unconstitutional.
3. Why did many Americans distrust political parties?
4. On what four issues did Hamilton and Jefferson disagree?
5. How did newspapers contribute to rivalry between the two parties?
6. What role did political parties play in the election of 1796?
7. **CRITICAL THINKING** **Drawing Conclusions** Why do you think political parties emerged even though many Americans opposed them?

ACTIVITY **Writing to Learn**

Write a campaign slogan for each of the candidates in the 1796 election.

John Adams as President

4

FIND OUT
- Why did many Americans want to declare war on France?
- Why did Adams lose the support of Federalists?
- What were the Alien and Sedition acts?

VOCABULARY alien, sedition, nullify

Late in life, John Adams wrote his autobiography. He knew that Washington, Franklin, and Jefferson were more widely admired than he was. To counter this, he wrote proudly of his work:

> ❝I have done more labor, run through more and greater dangers, and made greater sacrifices than any · man...living or dead, in the service of my country.❞

Still, Adams found it hard to boast of his achievements. In the end, he concluded: "I am not, never was, and never shall be a great man."

Neither statement was completely true. Although he was not a popular hero, Adams was an honest, able leader. As President, he tried to act in the best interests of the nation, even if it hurt him politically.

The XYZ Affair

No sooner did Adams take office than he faced a crisis with France. The French objected to Jay's Treaty between the United States and Britain. In 1797, French ships began to seize American ships in the West Indies, as the British had done.

The XYZ Affair *The French demand for tribute outraged Americans. In the cartoon above, grinning French agents rob "Madame Amerique" and even pluck the feathers from her hat. Despite the furor over the XYZ Affair, President John Adams, at right, resisted demands to go to war with France.* **United States and the World** *What events led to the XYZ Affair?*

Once again, Americans called for war—this time against France. Adams tried to avoid war by sending diplomats to Paris to discuss the rights of neutrals.

"Not a sixpence!" The French foreign minister, Charles Maurice de Talleyrand, would not deal directly with the Americans. Instead, he sent three secret agents to offer the Americans a deal.

"You must pay money," the agents said. "You must pay a great deal of money." Before Talleyrand would begin talks, he wanted $250,000 for himself and a loan to France of $10 million. "Not a sixpence!" replied one of the American diplomats.

The diplomats informed the President about the bribe. Adams, in turn, told Congress. He did not reveal the names of the French agents, referring to them only as X, Y, and Z.

When Americans heard about the ***XYZ Affair*** in 1798, they were outraged. They took up the slogan, "Millions for defense, but not one cent for tribute!" They were willing to spend money to defend their country, but they refused to pay a bribe to another nation.

Adams avoids war. Despite growing pressure, Adams refused to ask Congress to declare war on France. He did, however, strengthen the American navy. Shipyards built frigates—fast-sailing ships with many guns. This show of strength convinced France to stop attacking American ships. Talleyrand also assured Adams that he would treat American diplomats with respect.

The Federalist Party Splits

Many Federalists, led by Alexander Hamilton, criticized Adams's peace policy. They hoped a war would weaken Jefferson and the Republicans, longtime friends of France. War would also force the United States to build up its army and navy. A stronger military would mean increased federal power, which was a major Federalist goal.

Although John Adams was a Federalist, he would not give in to Hamilton. Their disagreement created a split in the Federalist

259

party. Hamilton and his supporters were called ***High Federalists.***

Over Hamilton's opposition, Adams again sent diplomats to France. When they arrived, they found a young army officer, Napoleon Bonaparte, in charge. Napoleon was eager to expand French power in Europe. He did not have time for a war with the United States. Napoleon signed the ***Convention of 1800.*** In this agreement, he promised to stop seizing American ships in the West Indies.

Like Washington, Adams kept the nation out of war. His success, however, cost him the support of many Federalists.

Alien and Sedition Acts

During the crisis with France, High Federalists pushed through several laws in Congress. Passed in 1798, the laws were known as the Alien and Sedition acts.

The ***Alien Act*** allowed the President to expel any alien, or foreigner, thought to be dangerous to the country. Another law made it harder for people to become citizens. Before, white people could become citizens after living in the United States for 5 years. Now, they had to wait 14 years. This law was meant to keep new arrivals from voting—often for Republicans.

Republican anger grew when Congress passed the ***Sedition Act.*** Sedition means stirring up rebellion against a government. Under this law, citizens could be fined or jailed if they criticized the government or its officials.

Republicans protested that the Sedition Act violated the Constitution. After all, the First Amendment protected freedom of speech and the press. The new law would make it a crime "to laugh at the cut of a congressman's coat, [or] to give dinner to a Frenchman," said one Republican.

Under the new law, several Republican newspaper editors, and even members of Congress, were fined and jailed for their opinions. Jefferson warned that the new laws threatened American liberties:

> ❝If this goes down, we shall immediately see attempted another act of Congress, declaring that the President shall continue in office during life, and after that other laws giving both the President and the Congress life terms in office.❞

The Rights of States

Republicans believed that the Alien and Sedition acts were unconstitutional. They did not turn to the Supreme Court, however, because most justices were Federalists.

Instead, Jefferson urged the states to act. He argued that the states had the right to nullify, or cancel, a law passed by the federal government. In this way, states could resist the power of the federal government.

Helped by Jefferson and Madison, Kentucky and Virginia passed resolutions in 1798 and 1799. The ***Kentucky and Virginia resolutions*** claimed that each state "has an equal right to judge for itself" whether a law is constitutional. If a state decides a law is unconstitutional, it can nullify that law within its borders.

The Kentucky and Virginia resolutions raised a difficult question. Did a state have the right to decide on its own that a law was unconstitutional?

The question remained unanswered in Jefferson's lifetime. Before long, the Alien and Sedition acts were changed or dropped. But the issue of a state's right to nullify federal laws would come up again.

Linking Past and Present
In 1800, the United States took its second census. The total population numbered 5,308,483—less than the population of New York City today.

Historical Sidelight
Background

As if to signal the passage of the United States into a new political era, George Washington died in 1799. On December 13, the ailing Washington called for his last will and testament, which provided for his family's welfare and the eventual freeing of his slaves. He told his doctor, "I die hard, but I am not afraid to go." The next day, saying, " 'tis well," he died.

In a December 26 service, General Henry "Light Horse Harry" Lee eulogized the late President as "first in war, first in peace, first in the hearts of his countrymen."

Election of 1800

By 1800, the fear of war with France had faded. As the election approached, Republicans hoped to sweep the Federalists from office. They focused on two issues. First, they attacked the Federalists for raising taxes to prepare for war. Second, they opposed the unpopular Alien and Sedition acts.

Republicans chose Jefferson to run for President and Aaron Burr for Vice President. Adams was the Federalist candidate.

A deadlock. In the race for President, the Republicans won. But when the electoral college voted, Jefferson and Burr each received 73 votes.

Under the Constitution, the House of Representatives decides an election in case of a tie vote. The House was evenly split. It voted 35 times. Each time, the vote was a tie.

The voting went on for four days. As an observer noted:

66 The scene was ludicrous. Many had sent home for nightcaps and pillows, and wrapped in shawls and great-coats, lay about the floor of the committee-rooms, or sat sleeping in their seats. 99

Finally, the tie was broken. The House chose Jefferson as President. Burr became Vice President.

Congress then passed the Twelfth Amendment. It required electors to vote separately for President and Vice President. The states ratified the amendment in 1804.

Federalists lose favor. Jefferson's election marked the end of the Federalist era. After 1800, Federalists won fewer seats in Congress. In 1804, the Federalist leader, Alexander Hamilton, was killed in a duel with Aaron Burr.

Although it declined, the Federalist party had helped shape the new nation. President Adams kept the country out of war. Also, over time, Republican Presidents kept most of Hamilton's economic programs.

Victory Flag for Jefferson *The election of Thomas Jefferson in 1800 marked the end of the Federalist era. This hand-painted flag celebrates Jefferson's victory.* **Citizenship** *Why did American voters reject the Federalists in 1800?*

SECTION 4 REVIEW

1. **Identify:** (a) XYZ Affair, (b) High Federalists, (c) Convention of 1800, (d) Alien Act, (e) Sedition Act, (f) Kentucky and Virginia resolutions.
2. **Define:** (a) alien, (b) sedition, (c) nullify.
3. Why did many Americans want war with France in 1797?
4. What caused the split between Adams and High Federalists?
5. Why did Republicans oppose the Sedition Act?
6. **CRITICAL THINKING Applying Information** How did the Kentucky and Virginia resolutions reflect Jefferson's views on government?

ACTIVITY **Writing to Learn**
Choose new titles for Section 4 and its subsections. Write a sentence explaining each of your choices.

Answers to Section 4 Review

1. (a) XYZ Affair, p. 259, (b) High Federalists, p. 260, (c) Convention of 1800, p. 260, (d) Alien Act, p. 260, (e) Sedition Act, p. 260, (f) Kentucky and Virginia resolutions, p. 260
2. (a) alien, p. 260, (b) sedition, p. 260, (c) nullify, p. 260
3. French ships had begun to seize American ships in the West Indies; and Talleyrand, the French foreign minister, would not meet directly with American diplomats until the American government gave money to him and a loan to France.

4. The High Federalists wanted war with France, but Adams refused to ask Congress to declare war.
5. Republicans argued that the Sedition Act violated the First Amendment's guarantee of freedom of speech.
6. Possible Answer: The resolutions reflected Jefferson's belief that state governments should have more power than the federal government.

Picturing the Past

Art Note

Art and Artifacts This feature illustrates the two main visual methods of capturing history before the invention of photography—through artwork and through artifacts. Today, one can use an old woodcut, valentine, sampler, or doll to learn about the past, while appreciating the beauty of the item. Students may have imagined that the term *artifact* refers only to such things as bones or broken pottery; encourage them to consider the items depicted here as artifacts as well.

Previewing Focus

Perhaps what comes across most strongly through the art and artifacts in this feature is that life before 1800 meant no conveniences—technology as students think of it today. Remind students that it once took weeks, not hours, to cross the Atlantic Ocean; that a family's diet once depended largely upon what could be grown or hunted locally; and that mass-produced items did not exist.

Point out that the feature also depicts a time that in many ways was simpler than our own. Ask: If you could choose to live in that time period, would you do it? If so, what kinds of adjustments might you have to make?

Historical Sidelight
Background

The *New England Primer* contained the alphabet, with each letter illustrated by a woodcut and a religious or moral teaching. It also contained questions and answers about Bible teachings, other moral guides, and the prayer "Now I lay me down to sleep." The first edition, compiled and printed by Benjamin Harris, probably appeared in 1683; with its subsequent editions, the *New England Primer* is estimated to have sold more than 5,000,000 copies.

Education and Religion in New England *In Massachusetts, religion and education dominated the lives of young people. This painting shows young Pilgrims on their way to church. Children learned to read from the primer above.*

A Pause in the Day's Work *For enslaved African Americans, free time was rare. Here, a group of slaves enjoy a pause in the day's labor.*

Be My Valentine *Young people found some time for courtship. Many of the symbols on this valentine, such as hearts and Cupids, are still popular today.*

Apprentices at Work *Being an apprentice was hard work. For many boys, however, it was the only way to learn a craft or trade.*

Linking Past and Present
Activity

After students discuss the reading primer, ask them to think about the books they enjoyed when they were learning to read. (If possible, display a few such easy-to-read books and perhaps a first-grade reading text.) Ask: How do today's books that encourage children to read differ from the primer? Why might children today have so many more choices in their reading material?

Historical Sidelight
Background

It is difficult to be certain of the identity of the historical St. Valentine. Christian church history reveals two martyrs with that name, both of whom were executed on February 14. According to one legend, Valentine was an early Christian who was a special friend to children. When he was imprisoned by the Romans for his faith, the children would slip notes of love and support into his cell—the first "valentines."

Discussion Questions

1. Why do you think the Pilgrims are carrying guns? (Possible Answer: as protection from wild animals or from Native Americans)
2. What is the purpose of a sampler, such as the one that Abigail Purintunn made? (Possible Answer: It displays the needleworker's skill at having mastered a variety of stitches.)
3. Of all the people shown, who do you think had the hardest life? Why? (Answers will vary. Students may suggest, justifiably, that slaves had the hardest life; remind them, however, that the Pilgrims faced severe hardships at first and that apprentices were not protected by any labor laws.)

Answer to Picturing the Past

Possible Answers: I would spend much more time at tedious work that helped keep the household running; I would not be able to amuse myself with technological entertainment (such as the radio or video games).

Games of the Eastern Woodlands *Young Native Americans amused themselves with a variety of games. At right, two young Indians play "cat's cradle." The bowl and peach pits below were used for another game of skill, played by the Iroquois.*

Sewing Sampler *Girls began learning skills such as needlecraft at a very early age. Young Abigail Purintunn spent many hours embroidering this finely detailed sampler.*

Picturing the Past
Young Americans Before 1800

For people of all ages, life before 1800 tended to be a daily round of hard work. Like adults, young Americans did a variety of chores, such as churning butter, planting crops, and hunting wildlife. As for leisure, young Americans relied on their imagination for amusement, along with a variety of simple, often homemade, games and toys.
■ *Describe two ways your life would be different if you were growing up before 1800.*

A Doll *It is hard to tell whether this doll was meant to be a child or an adult. Generally, the clothing worn by colonial children was just a smaller version of what their parents wore.*

Chapter 8 • **263**

Cooperative Learning
Activity

Divide the class into seven groups; have each group select one of the seven topics depicted in the feature. Then have the members of each group work together to write a first-person narrative relating to the topic—for example, a teen recalling how he learned to read from the primer, a young woman describing the first valentine that she received, an adult slave recounting the day's work, a young apprentice reflecting upon the proverbs depicted in the art, an Iroquois teen describing his victory in a game of skill, Abigail Purintunn describing her thoughts while embroidering the sampler shown, and a grandmother reflecting upon the doll with which she played as a child. As groups prepare to write their pieces, encourage them to use a variety of formats—for example, personal letter, interview, dramatic monologue, and so on. Have each group present its complete narrative to the class.

CHAPTER 8 REVIEW

Answers to Reviewing the Main Ideas

1. (a) Hamilton wanted to gain the trust and help of investors. (b) The bank could issue money, pay off government debts, and make loans to help new businesses grow. (c) Protective tariffs would encourage Americans to buy less expensive American-made goods.

2. When Congress passed a tax on whiskey, backcountry farmers, who made their corn into whiskey for sale, grew angry and rebelled.

3. Washington's declaration that the United States would not become involved in the war between Britain and France

4. (a) White settlers took over Indian land. (b) In signing the Treaty of Greenville, Indian nations gave up the land that would later become the southern half of Ohio.

5. (a) As the clash between Jefferson and Hamilton grew stronger, supporters rallied to each point of view. (b) merchants, manufacturers, and some southern planters (c) small farmers, craftsworkers, and some wealthy planters

6. Some Americans wanted war with France; the American navy was strengthened.

7. whether a state had the power to nullify a federal law that it felt was unconstitutional

Answers to Thinking Critically

1. (a) that the nation stay out of European affairs (b) Possible Answers: No; the United States is too affected by what goes on in other parts of the world to stay uninvolved. Yes; problems in the United States could be solved more easily if the nation were not involved abroad.

2. Some students may say that the acts were unconstitutional and that the Federalists were more interested in keeping power than in protecting the nation. Other students may find that the possibility of war with France made these laws necessary.

3. Students might list the following problems: building confidence in the national government and

Summary

- As the nation's first President, George Washington worked with Congress to organize the new government.
- The French Revolution divided public opinion, but Washington kept the United States out of war.
- Two political parties formed in the 1790s, representing opposing views on the economy, foreign policy, and the role of the federal government.
- The Federalist party split because President John Adams refused to declare war against France.

Reviewing the Main Ideas

1. Why did Alexander Hamilton support each of the following: (a) repayment of national and state debts, (b) national bank, (c) protective tariff?

2. What caused the Whiskey Rebellion?

3. What was the Neutrality Proclamation?

4. (a) What was one cause of the war in the Northwest Territory in the 1790s? (b) What was one result?

5. (a) How did political parties develop? (b) Who supported the Federalists? (c) Who supported the Republicans?

6. Describe two results of the XYZ Affair.

7. What important issue was raised by the Kentucky and Virginia resolutions?

Thinking Critically

1. Linking Past and Present (a) What advice did Washington give in his Farewell Address? (b) Do you think Americans today would agree with Washington? Explain your answer.

2. Defending a Position Do you think the Alien and Sedition acts were necessary to protect the nation? Explain.

3. Synthesizing Information What problems did the first Presidents face?

Applying Your Skills

1. Skimming a Chapter Skimming is reading quickly for the general idea. To skim a chapter in this book, first look at the list of section titles in the Chapter Outline. Next, look at the blue and boldface headings that show the main topics in each section. Finally, quickly read the first and last sentence of each paragraph.

Skim the first half of Chapter 8 (pages 242–253). (a) What does the Chapter Outline tell you about chapter content? (b) List the main topics in the section War Clouds. (c) What do you think is the main idea of this section? Explain.

2. Analyzing a Quotation After George Washington became President, he said, "There is scarcely any part of my conduct which may not hereafter be drawn into precedent." What do you think Washington meant by this statement?

Thinking About Geography

Match the letters on the map with the following places: **1.** New York City, **2.** Philadelphia, **3.** Washington, D.C., **4.** Virginia, **5.** Kentucky. **Location** On what river is Washington, D.C., located?

respect for the office of the President, organizing the executive branch, choosing the Supreme Court, putting down rebellions, building relations with foreign nations while avoiding war, and improving relations between Native Americans and white settlers.

Answers to Applying Your Skills

1. (a) The chapter will cover events from Washington's first administration through Adams's presidency. (b) Upheaval in France, A Policy of Neutrality, An Unpopular Treaty, War in the West, Washington Retires (c) Possible Answer: The United States avoided participating in wars by remaining neutral during international conflicts and by signing a treaty that ended the fighting with Native Americans in the Northwest Territory.

2. Nearly everything that Washington did would set an example for future Presidents.

Answers to Thinking About Geography

1. E **2.** D **3.** C **4.** B **5.** A
Location: the Potomac

Election of 1800

Form into groups to review the election of 1800. Follow the suggestions below to write, draw, sing, or act to show what you have learned about this election. You may use the textbook, encyclopedias, atlases, or other materials in your classroom library to complete the tasks. Be able to name your sources of information when you have finished the activity.

WRITERS Form into two groups— *National Gazette* (Republicans) and *Gazette of the United States* (Federalists). Work with your group to prepare an issue of your newspaper. Your issue should include news articles, editorials, cartoons, and advertisements related to the election of 1800.

Newspaper mastheads

ECONOMISTS Make a chart comparing Federalist and Republican views about the nation's economy. Then make a list of questions you would ask each candidate about his economic views and how they would affect the nation.

ACTORS Review how the election of 1800 was finally decided after four days and 35 tie votes. Then prepare a skit about the voting in the House of Representatives. Representatives should present arguments to persuade other House members to support the candidate of their choice.

John Adams on a ceramic jar

ARTISTS Study the pictures on pages 244 and 261 to get an idea of how artists showed support for a political figure in the late 1700s and early 1800s. Then design a poster or a flag to support one of the candidates for President in the 1800 election.

MUSICIANS List the important issues in the election of 1800. Then make up a campaign song based on these issues. You may use a familiar tune or one you have composed. Perform your song for the class.

 Plan an election rally in which each group presents or describes its completed activity.

Thomas Jefferson

Assessment

Chapter Resources Binder For a more comprehensive evaluation of student understanding of this chapter, assign Chapter Tests A and B and/or Extra Unit Questions from Unit 3, pages 7–12 and 41–43.

Computer Test Bank You can use Chapter Tests and Extra Unit Questions to create your own tests for both testing and retesting.

Alternative Assessment

Chapter Resources Binder See the Alternative Assessment booklet in the *Social Studies Educator's Handbook* series.

Portfolio You might meet with students to choose appropriate work from the chapter for inclusion in their portfolios.

Interdisciplinary ACTIVITY

Learning Styles

The following chart indicates the activities appropriate for different learning styles.

Visual Learners
Writers
Economists
Actors
Artists

Auditory Learners
Actors
Musicians

Kinesthetic Learners
Writers
Economists
Artists
Actors
Musicians

Evaluation

Writers Newspaper articles, editorials, cartoons, and advertisements should contain accurate details that reflect an understanding of the issues in the election of 1800. Newspapers should be visually pleasing and should be free of spelling, punctuation, and grammar errors.

Economists Information should be organized so that similarities and differences between the views are quickly apparent. Questions should require detailed responses and an understanding of cause-and-effect relationships.

Actors Skits should be lively and informative, with participants interacting as they argue for candidates. Speeches should be organized, convincing, and based on accurate information. The style of delivery can be either impassioned or reasonable, but it should be audible and clear.

Artists Designs for flags and posters should be based on accurate information about the candidate. They should be visually pleasing and exhibit originality.

Musicians Song lyrics should be original, fit the melody of the music, and contain accurate facts. Singing ability should not be a criterion, but performances should be audible and clear.

Lessons	Teaching Resources
1 Republicans in Power **Objectives** 1. Identify the steps that Jefferson took to limit government power. 2. Explain why the Federalists controlled the federal courts. 3. Explain the importance of *Marbury* v. *Madison.*	**Lesson Planner** Cooperative Learning, p. 51 **Student Study Guide** Section 1 Study Guide, p. 81 **Chapter Resources Binder, Unit 3** *Critical Thinking* Comparing Information on a Chart, p. 15
2 The Louisiana Purchase **Objectives** 1. Explain why the Mississippi River was important to western farmers. 2. Describe how the United States gained Louisiana. 3. Identify the purpose of the Lewis and Clark expedition.	**Lesson Planner** Cooperative Learning, p. 52 **Student Study Guide** Section 2 Study Guide, p. 82 **Chapter Resources Binder, Unit 3** *Geography in History* New Orleans, Then and Now, pp. 17–18 *Skill Application* Following Routes on a Map, p. 14 **Interdisciplinary Connections:** The Louisiana Purchase ■ *Arts* That Creole Flavor, p. 50 ▨ *Sciences* Recording the Wilderness, p. 51 ■ *Geography* A Big Part for a Big River, p. 52 ■ *World* A French Expansionist, p. 53 ■ *Civics* Expansion and the Constitution, p. 54
3 Protecting American Neutrality **Objectives** 1. Describe how overseas trade grew in the early 1800s. 2. Explain why British warships seized American sailors. 3. Explain why the Embargo Act was unpopular.	**Lesson Planner** Cooperative Learning, p. 53 **Student Study Guide** Section 3 Study Guide, p. 83
4 The Road to War **Objectives** 1. Explain why the South and the West wanted war with Britain. 2. Describe how the Prophet and Tecumseh tried to stop white settlement. 3. Explain why President Madison agreed to war with Britain.	**Lesson Planner** Cooperative Learning, p. 54 **Student Study Guide** Section 4 Study Guide, p. 84 **Our Multicultural Heritage** *Biography* Tecumseh, Champion for Indian Unity, p. 25 *Milestone* The Shawnees Defend Their Land, p. 27
5 The War of 1812 **Objectives** 1. Describe how Americans prepared for the War of 1812. 2. Describe the role of Native Americans in the fighting. 3. Explain the outcome of the war.	**Lesson Planner** Cooperative Learning, p. 55 **Student Study Guide** Section 5 Study Guide, p. 85 **Chapter Resources Binder, Unit 3** *History Through Literature* Old Ironsides, p. 16 **Our Multicultural Heritage** *Biography* Dolley Madison, a Gallant First Lady, p. 26

Multimedia Resources	Additional Resources	Chapter-Level Resources
CD-ROM *Presidents* Thomas Jefferson *History Makers* John Marshall **Videotapes/Videodiscs** *United States History Video Collection* The Marshall Court, Vol. 5, Ch. 40	**Voices of Freedom** The First Republican President, pp. 78–79	**Lesson Planner** Activity Based, pp. 56–57 **Student Study Guide** Chapter 9 Study Guide, pp. 86–87 **Chapter Resources Binder** **Unit 3** Vocabulary Building, p. 13 Chapter Test A, pp. 19–21 Chapter Test B, pp. 22–24 Illustration Master, p. 25 Extra Unit Questions, pp. 41–43 **English Guided Reading** Guided Reading, pp. 17–18 **Spanish Resources** **Computer Test Bank** Chapter Tests A and B Extra Unit Questions **Guided Reading Audiotapes** Side 4 **CD-ROM** *Time Tour* The Jefferson Era (1801–1816) in The New Republic
Transparencies *Geography and History* Expansion of the United States, p. I-25 *Fine Art* The Indian Council, p. D-37 *Interdisciplinary Connections* Lewis and Clark With Sacajawea, p. B-49 **CD-ROM** *History Makers* Meriwether Lewis *History Makers* William Clark **Videotapes/Videodiscs** *United States History Video Collection* The Louisiana Purchase, Vol. 6, Ch. 7; The Western Nations, Vol. 6, Ch. 10	**Voices of Freedom** The Shoshones Meet Lewis and Clark, pp. 79–80 **Historical Outline Map Book** Exploring the Louisiana Purchase, p. 30 **Customized Reader** The Lewis and Clark Expedition Meets With a Sioux Tribe, article IIIB-4	
CD-ROM *Presidents* James Madison	**Voices of Freedom** Sympathy for Impressed Americans, pp. 80–81	
Transparencies *Geography and History* Land Lost by Indians, p. I-39 **CD-ROM** *History Makers* Tecumseh	**Voices of Freedom** Henry Clay Defends War With Britain, pp. 82–83 Tecumseh Protests Land Sale, pp. 81–82 **Historical Outline Map Book** Land Acquired From Native Americans to 1810, p. 31	
CD-ROM *Arts & Entertainment* Music **Videotapes/Videodiscs** *United States History Video Collection* The War of 1812, Vol. 6, Ch. 13	**Historical Outline Map Book** The War of 1812, p. 32 **Customized Reader** The Inspiration for "The Star-Spangled Banner," article IIIB-7	

Lesson Planner

For a fully developed **Activity-Based** lesson plan for Chapter 9, see the *Lesson Planner,* pages 56–57.

 Chapter Resources

Vocabulary Building The Vocabulary Building worksheet for Chapter 9 from Unit 3, page 13, of the *Chapter Resources* binder can be used as a prereading activity or as a review of chapter vocabulary. (Reteaching/Easy)

 Student Study Guide

Chapter 9 Study Guide Refer students to pages 86–87 of the *Student Study Guide* for the Chapter 9 Study Guide. The study guide can be used for chapter review as well as for reteaching. (Reteaching/Average)

 Guided Reading Audiotapes

Students can use *Guided Reading Audiotapes,* Chapter 9, side 4, to listen to section previews, summaries, and review questions. The tapes will benefit students who are auditory learners, students who have trouble reading, or students acquiring English. Tapes are also available in Spanish. (Reteaching/Easy)

CHAPTER 9

The Jefferson Era

(1801–1816)

CHAPTER OUTLINE

1 Republicans in Power

2 The Louisiana Purchase

3 Protecting American Neutrality

4 The Road to War

5 The War of 1812

1804 *Lewis and Clark set out to explore the Louisiana Purchase. Clark used this compass to guide him during the journey.*

1805–1807 *The British navy seized thousands of American sailors and forced them to serve on British ships. Americans were enraged by this violation of their rights.*

| 1800 | 1802 | 1804 | 1806 | 1808 |

 WORLD EVENT
1800 France regains Louisiana Territory in treaty with Spain

 WORLD EVENT
1803 France and Britain go to war

Chapter Time Line
Activity

Have students identify the date and time line event that relates to each of the following statements:

■ "As a new settler, I was concerned when Tecumseh spoke to me." (1810; Tecumseh warns settlers against taking over Indian lands.)

■ "Because of our activity, President Jefferson worried that Napoleon might cross the Atlantic." (1800; France regains Louisiana Territory from Spain.)

■ "What right did the British have to make me a captive sailor?" (1805–1807; British navy seizes American sailors.)

Encourage students to create additional statements to exchange and solve.

Chapter Setting

"Educate and inform the whole mass of the people. Enable them to see that it is their interest to preserve peace and order, and they will preserve them. . . . They are the only [ones to rely on] for the preservation of our liberty. . . . This reliance cannot deceive us, as long as we remain [good]; and I think we shall . . . as long as agriculture is our principal object. . . . When we get piled up on one another in large cities, as in Europe, we shall become corrupt as in Europe, and go to eating one another as they do there."

In this letter to James Madison, Thomas Jefferson expressed his faith in the American people. At that time, nearly nine out of ten Americans were farmers. This fact gave Jefferson confidence in the nation's future.

Jefferson, himself, came from a wealthy family. But he was convinced that ordinary people, especially farmers, would best preserve the nation's peace, order, and liberty.

As President, Jefferson sought to protect and expand the rights of these ordinary citizens. The Federalists, he believed, had worried too much about the wealthy few. Jefferson wanted to represent the farmers who formed the backbone of the nation. As he pursued this goal, Jefferson turned the nation in a new direction.

ACTIVITY List the ways in which power might pass from one government to another. Then discuss why the peaceful passing of power from the Federalists to the Republicans was important to the future of the nation.

1810 *Shawnee leader Tecumseh, at right, warned settlers against taking over Indian lands.*

1812 *The Leni-Lenape, who fought on the American side in the War of 1812, received this pipe in recognition of their support.*

1815 *Andrew Jackson led the Americans to victory in the Battle of New Orleans.*

1808	1810	1812	1814	1816

WORLD EVENT
1814 Britain defeats France

Chapter 9 • **267**

Chapter Resources

English Guided Reading Duplicate and distribute to SAE students the Chapter 9 Guided Reading worksheet on pages 17–18 in the English Guided Reading section of the *Chapter Resources* binder. Students who have difficulty reading also might benefit from using this worksheet. Have students complete the worksheet before they begin reading. You might pair a more fluent student or a student who is a stronger reader with each SAE student to review. (Reteaching/Easy)

Spanish Resources See the Spanish Resources section of the *Chapter Resources* binder.

CD-ROM

Time Tour Access The Jefferson Era (1801–1816) section in The New Republic on the American Heritage® *History of the United States* CD-ROM (Enrichment/Average)

ACTIVITY

Guided Instruction As an introductory or follow-up activity, have students examine the chart in the Reference Section that shows all the Presidents and their political parties, from George Washington to the present. Ask students to determine the first time political power changed peacefully from one party to another and the number of times it has done so since.

Students Acquiring English
Activity

To help SAE students master the chapter, you might introduce the large cast of characters featured in it. Include Thomas Jefferson, John Marshall, James Madison, William Marbury, Meriwether Lewis, William Clark, Thomas Pinckney, Napoleon Bonaparte, Toussaint L'Ouverture, Maurice de Talleyrand, James Monroe, Robert Livingston, Sacajawea, Zebulon Pike, Stephen Decatur, Henry Clay, Tenskwatawa, Tecumseh, William Henry Harrison, Isaac Hull, William Hull, Andrew Jackson, Dolley Madison, and Francis Scott Key. Have students list these names in a journal, skipping three to four lines between each entry. As they encounter each name in the chapter, help students write a brief identification of that person and the events with which he or she was connected. Suggest that students use their completed lists to review chapter content.

Linking Past and Present
Activity

Have students work with partners or in small groups to write letters to historical figures prominent in this chapter. The letters can bring these leaders up to date as to the influence that their actions have had on the course of modern American life.

Section 1
pp. 268–270

Bell Ringer

Have students spend two or three minutes freewriting the thoughts and images that they associate with the word *democratic*. As they work through Section 1, they can compare their responses to the meaning of the word as interpreted by Thomas Jefferson.

Lesson Plan

1. Focus As President, Thomas Jefferson promised to make government more responsive to ordinary citizens. In this section, students learn about Jefferson's programs and his attitudes toward several Supreme Court decisions.

2. Instruct Have students list Jefferson's views and personal characteristics, as noted in this section and earlier chapters. Then have them do the same for Washington, Adams, and Hamilton. Guide students in classifying the items on their lists as more democratic or less democratic.

3. Close To close the lesson, have students decide the most important fact or concept to remember for each subsection.

1
Republicans in Power

FIND OUT

- What steps did Jefferson take to limit government power?
- Why did Federalists control the federal courts?
- Why was *Marbury* v. *Madison* important?

VOCABULARY democratic, laissez faire, judicial review

In 1801, Thomas Jefferson became the first President to be inaugurated in Washington, D.C., the nation's new capital. The city was located on swampy land near the Potomac River. Dense forests surrounded the area, and travel there was difficult.

Many visitors to Washington complained about its muddy streets and unfinished buildings. President Jefferson, however, was happy with the new capital. He believed that the success of the American republic signaled the dawning of a new age. It was only fitting, he thought, that the young nation should carve its new capital out of the wilderness.

A New Style of President

Jefferson brought new ideas to the capital. He strongly believed in the good sense of ordinary people, and he promised to make the government more democratic. **Democratic** means ensuring that all people have the same rights.

An informal air. Jefferson's personal style matched his democratic beliefs. The new President preferred quiet dinners to the formal parties that had been given by Washington and Adams. He wore casual clothes

and greeted people by shaking hands instead of bowing. With his informal manner, Jefferson showed that the President was an ordinary citizen.

Easing Federalist fears. Some Federalists worried about how Jefferson would govern. In his inaugural address, he tried to quiet their fears. As a minority, Federalists "possess their equal rights, which equal laws must protect," he told the nation. He called for an end to the bitter political quarrels of past years. "We are all Republicans, we are all Federalists," the President said.

Republican changes. Jefferson had no plan to punish Federalists. He did, however, want to change their policies. In his view, the Federalists had made the national

---

BIOGRAPHY Thomas Jefferson *Thomas Jefferson, third President of the United States, was a man of wide-ranging talents and interests. An avid reader, Jefferson designed the revolving book stand, below, to hold as many as five books at once.* **Citizenship** *What were Jefferson's goals for the government?*

Connections With Architecture
Background

Jefferson had many interests, including architecture. He spent 25 years planning and building his landmark home, Monticello, in Virginia. Nearly all the basic materials—stone, lumber, brick, nails—were found or made on the estate. Later, Jefferson fell into debt, and he died nearly bankrupt. Monticello passed into other hands; eventually, however, it became the property of a foundation that restored it. Monticello is now open to the public.

In addition to being an architect, Jefferson was a scholar, scientist, and inventor. He invented a polygraph machine, a dumbwaiter, a swivel chair, and a new type of plow.

Our Multicultural Heritage
Background

Although Jefferson sought to protect and expand the rights of ordinary citizens, including the Federalists, these protections under the law did not extend to African Americans. For example, in 1800, Ohio passed a law limiting the rights and movements of African Americans.

government too large and too powerful. To reduce government power, Jefferson wanted to cut the federal budget and lower taxes.

Jefferson believed in an idea known as **laissez faire** (lehs ay FAYR), from the French term for "let alone." According to laissez faire, government should play as small a role as possible in economic affairs. Laissez faire was very different from the Federalist idea of government. Alexander Hamilton, you recall, wanted government to promote trade, commerce, and manufacturing.

A Small and Simple Government

Jefferson chose a Cabinet that would help him reach his goals. He appointed Albert Gallatin as Secretary of the Treasury. A wizard at finances, Gallatin helped Jefferson cut government expenses.

For Secretary of State, Jefferson chose James Madison, his friend and Virginia neighbor. Madison had helped Jefferson build the Republican party. Like Jefferson, he believed that under the Federalists the national government had taken on powers that belonged to the states.

Limiting federal power. As President, Jefferson tried to reduce the role of government in people's lives. He decreased the size of government departments and cut the federal budget. With the approval of Congress, he reduced the size of the army and navy and halted construction of new naval ships. He also asked Congress to repeal the unpopular whiskey tax.

Linking Past and Present
When Thomas Jefferson became President in 1801, there were fewer than 1,000 federal employees. Today, the United States government employs more than 2 million people— not counting those in the armed services.

The Sedition Act had expired the day before Jefferson took office. Jefferson had hated the law, and he quickly pardoned those few men who were still in jail as a result of it. He also asked Congress to restore the five-year waiting period for foreign-born people who wanted to become citizens of the United States.

Some Federalist policies remain. Jefferson did not discard all Federalist programs, however. Secretary of the Treasury Gallatin convinced the President to keep the Bank of the United States. The federal government also continued to pay off state debts that it had taken over when Washington was President.

A Stronger Supreme Court

The election of 1800 had given Republicans control of Congress. Federalists, however, remained powerful in the courts.

Three months passed between election day and Jefferson's inauguration on March 4, 1801. During that time, Federalists in the old Congress passed a law increasing the number of federal judges. President Adams then appointed Federalists to fill these new positions.

John Marshall. Among the judges that Adams had appointed was John Marshall, Chief Justice of the Supreme Court. In some ways, Marshall was like Thomas Jefferson. He was a rich Virginia planter with a brilliant mind. Unlike Jefferson, however, Marshall was a staunch Federalist. He wanted to make the federal government stronger.

The framers of the Constitution expected the federal courts to balance the powers of the President and Congress. Yet John Marshall found the courts to be the weakest branch of government. In his view, it was not clear what powers the federal courts had. In 1803, Marshall decided a case that increased the power of the Supreme Court.

 Lesson Planner

For a developed **Cooperative Learning** lesson plan, see the *Lesson Planner,* page 51.

 Chapter Resources

Critical Thinking Duplicate and distribute the worksheet, Comparing Information on a Chart, from Unit 3, page 15, of the *Chapter Resources* binder. The worksheet asks students to compare Jefferson's actions with those of other Presidents.

Voices of Freedom

Primary Source You might assign selection 11-1, The First Republican President, on pages 78–79 of *Voices of Freedom.* In it, Thomas Jefferson describes essential principles of the federal government. (Enrichment/Challenging)

CD-ROM

Presidents Access the biography of Thomas Jefferson on the American Heritage® *History of the United States* CD-ROM. (Enrichment/Average)
History Makers Access the biography of John Marshall on the American Heritage® *History of the United States* CD-ROM. (Enrichment/Average)

Connections With Economics
Background

Adam Smith, a Scottish economist and philosopher, published *The Wealth of Nations* in 1776. In this work, he set out the principle of laissez-faire economics. Market forces, operating without government interference, would naturally work for self-interest and therefore for the good for all.

Cooperative Learning
Activity

Divide the class into groups of four or five students each to investigate Supreme Court cases decided during the time that Chief Justice John Marshall presided over the Court. Each group should choose one case to research. They can begin by reading encyclopedia entries about Chief Justice John Marshall and the important cases of his time. Students then can choose a case on which to focus and divide further research assignments among members of the group. Ask each group to prepare an oral report for the class on their case, providing information about both the plaintiff and the defendant. Students can summarize arguments for both sides and can identify the effects that their case has on the lives of Americans today.

Answer to Caption

It established the right of the Court to review any law made by Congress and to decide on its constitutionality.

Videotapes/ Videodiscs

United States History Video Collection Use the video segment "The Marshall Court" from Volume 5, *A New Nation (1776–1815)*, to enhance students' understanding of Marshall's role in creating a stronger Supreme Court. Approx. running time 1:45 min. (Enrichment/Average) Vol. 5, Ch. 40

Chapter 40

Guide
dents ◌
them lis◌
uations i◌
sonal st◌
negative ◌◌◌ ◌◌dents can
then deve◌◌p a description of
each situation and their reaction
to it into a paragraph for the letter.

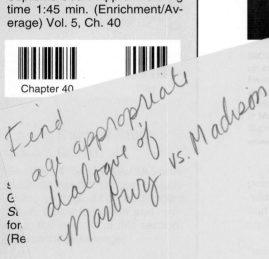

Find appropriate age appropriate dialogue of Marbury vs. Madison

BIOGRAPHY John Marshall *John Marshall grew up in frontier Virginia and served in the American Revolution. Under his strong leadership as Chief [Justice,] the Supreme Court gained prestige and [power.] Citizenship How did Marshall's decision in Marbury v. Madison strengthen the power of the Supreme Court?*

A "midnight judge." Another judge appointed by Adams was William Marbury. Adams made the appointment on his last night as President. But before Marbury could take office, Adams's term ended.

The Republicans refused to accept this "midnight judge." They accused Federalists of using unfair tactics to keep control of the courts. Jefferson ordered Secretary of State Madison not to deliver the official papers confirming Marbury's appointment.

Marbury v. Madison. Marbury sued Madison. According to the Judiciary Act of 1789, only the Supreme Court could decide a case brought against a federal official. The case, therefore, was tried before the Supreme Court.

In the case of **Marbury v. Madison,** the Supreme Court ruled against Marbury. Chief Justice Marshall wrote the decision. He stated that the Judiciary Act was unconstitutional. Nowhere, he continued, did the Constitution give the Supreme Court the right to decide cases brought against federal officials. Therefore, Congress could not give the Court that power by passing the Judiciary Act.

The Supreme Court's decision in *Marbury* v. *Madison* set an important precedent. It gave the Supreme Court the power to decide whether laws passed by Congress were constitutional. This power of the Court is called **judicial review.**

Jefferson was displeased with the decision. It gave more power to the Supreme Court, where Federalists were still strong. Even so, the President and Congress accepted the right of the Supreme Court to overturn laws. Today, judicial review is one of the most important powers of the Supreme Court.

SECTION 1 REVIEW

1. **Identify:** (a) Albert Gallatin, (b) John Marshall, (c) *Marbury* v. *Madison.*
2. **Define:** (a) democratic, (b) laissez faire, (c) judicial review.
3. (a) Name two Federalist policies that Jefferson changed. (b) Name two Federalist policies he allowed to continue.
4. How did Federalists keep control of the courts?
5. What precedent did *Marbury* v. *Madison* set?
6. **CRITICAL THINKING Analyzing a Quotation** "We are all Republicans, we are all Federalists." What did Jefferson mean by this statement?

ACTIVITY Writing to Learn

Imagine that you are an adviser to President Adams. Write a letter to a friend describing your reactions to Jefferson as President.

Answers to Section 1 Review

1. (a) Albert Gallatin, p. 269, (b) John Marshall, p. 269, (c) *Marbury* v. *Madison,* p. 270
2. (a) democratic, p. 268, (b) laissez faire, p. 269, (c) judicial review, p. 270
3. (a) He repealed the whiskey tax, stopped prosecutions under the Sedition Act, and restored the five-year waiting period for immigrants to become citizens. (b) He kept the Bank of the United States and let the federal government keep paying state war debts.
4. Before the new Republican Congress met, Federalists passed a bill creating more judges for the federal courts; Adams appointed Federalists to fill those positions.
5. The case established the practice of judicial review, or the Supreme Court's right to review any law made by Congress and decide on its constitutionality.
6. Possible Answer: Being an American is more important than being a member of a particular political party.

2

The Louisiana Purchase

FIND OUT
- Why was the Mississippi River important to western farmers?
- How did the United States gain Louisiana?
- What was the purpose of the Lewis and Clark expedition?

VOCABULARY continental divide

One day during his second term of office, President Jefferson received several packages. Inside, he found hides and skeletons of various animals, horns of a mountain ram, and a tin box full of insects. There were also cages of live birds and squirrels, as well as gifts from the Mandan and Sioux Indians.

The packages were from Meriwether Lewis and William Clark. Jefferson had sent the two men to explore the vast lands west of the Mississippi. Almost two years before, Jefferson had boldly purchased the territory for the United States. The packages confirmed his belief that the new lands were a valuable addition to the nation.

New Orleans and the Mississippi River

By 1800, almost one million Americans lived between the Appalachians and the Mississippi River. Most were farmers.

There were only a few roads west of the Appalachians. Western farmers relied on the Mississippi River to ship their wheat and corn to markets in the East. First, they shipped their goods down the Mississippi to New Orleans. There, the goods were stored in warehouses. Finally, the goods were loaded onto ships and carried to the Atlantic coast.

From time to time, Spain threatened to close the port of New Orleans to Americans. In 1795, President Washington sent Thomas Pinckney to find a way to keep the port open. In the **Pinckney Treaty,** Spain agreed to let Americans ship their goods down the Mississippi and store them in New Orleans.

Shortly afterward, Spain signed a secret treaty with Napoleon Bonaparte, the ruler of France. The treaty gave Louisiana back to France. President Jefferson was alarmed. Napoleon had already set out to conquer Europe. Jefferson feared that Napoleon might now attempt to build an empire in North America.

Market Day in New Orleans *In the bustling port of New Orleans, people from a wide variety of cultures met to do business. The traders shown here included African Americans from the South and the Caribbean, as well as many creoles—descendants of French and Spanish settlers.* **Geography** *Why was New Orleans important to the United States?*

Section 2 pp. 271–278

Bell Ringer

Have students locate New Orleans on a map. Then ask: Why would a country be so interested in a city that was so far away from its own major cities?

Lesson Plan

1. Focus Control of the Mississippi River and the port of New Orleans was important to western farmers. In this section, students learn how the Louisiana Purchase was accomplished. They also study how explorers mapped it and found a route to the Pacific Ocean.

2. Instruct Have students create a cause-and-effect chart for the Louisiana Purchase. Draw a blank chart on the chalkboard and title it Louisiana Purchase. Ask students to list, on their own pages, as many causes for the purchase as they can think of. Then help them select and order the ones to be included on the Causes section of the chart. Follow the same procedure for the Effects section.

Connections With Geography
Activity

Have students refer to a physical map of the United States to explain why the Mississippi River was the best route for sending goods to the east coast. Then ask students to list the states that now exist between the Appalachians and the Mississippi River and note when each joined the Union. Finally, have students list the states that were eventually carved out of the Louisiana Purchase and note the year in which each joined the Union.

Connections With Music
Background

New Orleans is considered to be the birthplace of jazz, the most original American form of music. The city is still famous for its jazz clubs.

New Orleans had been founded in 1718 and was the capital of the French colony of Louisiana from 1722 until the time of the Louisiana Purchase.

Revolt in Haiti

Jefferson had good reason to worry. Napoleon wanted to grow food in Louisiana and ship it to the French islands in the West Indies. However, events in Haiti thwarted his plan.

Haiti was the richest French colony in the Caribbean. There, enslaved Africans worked sugar plantations that made French planters wealthy. During the French Revolution, slaves in Haiti were inspired to fight for their liberty. Toussaint L'Ouverture (too SAN loo vehr TYOOR) led the revolt. By 1801, Toussaint and his followers had nearly forced the French out of Haiti.

Napoleon sent troops to recapture Haiti. He expected his army to win easily, but the Haitians fought back fiercely. Although the French captured Toussaint, they did not regain control of the island. In 1804, Haitians declared their independence. Haiti became the second republic in the Americas, after the United States.

Toussaint L'Ouverture *A self-educated former slave, Toussaint L'Ouverture led slaves in Haiti in a revolt against French rule. For enslaved African Americans, Toussaint became a symbol of the struggle for liberty.* **United States and the World** *Why would President Jefferson be concerned about the revolt in Haiti?*

The Nation Doubles in Size

About the time that Haiti forced out the French, President Jefferson decided to try to buy New Orleans from Napoleon. Jefferson wanted to be sure that American farmers would always be able to ship their goods through the port of New Orleans. The President appointed Robert Livingston and James Monroe to negotiate with the French. He instructed them to buy New Orleans and West Florida for $2 million—a sum that Congress had set aside for that purpose. If necessary, Jefferson said, they could offer as much as $10 million.

A surprising proposal. Livingston and Monroe talked to Talleyrand, the French foreign minister. At first, Talleyrand showed little interest in the offer. Then, events quickly changed.

Napoleon's dream of an empire in the Americas ended when the French lost con-

trol of Haiti. Also, Napoleon needed money to finance his wars in Europe. Talleyrand now asked Livingston an unexpected question: "What will you give for the *whole* of Louisiana?"

Livingston was shocked and delighted. France was willing to sell all of Louisiana, not just New Orleans. Livingston offered $4 million.

"Too low!" said Talleyrand. "Reflect, and see me tomorrow."

Livingston and Monroe debated the matter. They had no authority to buy all of Louisiana. They knew, however, that Jefferson wanted control of the Mississippi. They agreed to pay the French $15 million. Neither the French nor the Americans consulted the various Indian nations in Louisiana about the purchase.

Was the purchase constitutional? Jefferson was pleased by the news from France. But did the Constitution give him

272 • Chapter 9

---

3. Close To close the lesson, have students explain how the United States purchased Louisiana and why the Lewis and Clark expedition was important.

 Lesson Planner

For a developed **Cooperative Learning** lesson plan, see the *Lesson Planner,* page 52.

Answer to Caption

Napoleon's plans for an empire in the Americas threatened the United States. If the French recaptured Haiti, Napoleon would have been on his way to achieving his goal.

 Transparencies

Geography and History Use the transparency map set, Expansion of the United States, on page I-25 of *American History Transparencies.* Teaching suggestions can be found on page I-3. (Enrichment/Average)

 Videotapes/ Videodiscs

United States History Video Collection Use the video segment "The Louisiana Purchase" from Volume 6, *Expansionism,* to enhance students' understanding of the significance of the Louisiana Purchase. Approx. running time 5:00 min. (Enrichment/Average) Vol. 6, Ch. 7

Chapter 7   Play

Connections With the World
Background

The American purchase of Louisiana involved some juggling of claims. In October 1800, France acquired the territory from Spain. When Americans took possession of Louisiana in 1803, however, they found that St. Louis, in "Upper Louisiana," was still controlled by the Spanish. To make sure that the territory changed hands properly, Captain Amos Stoddard, an American, took command of St. Louis on March 9, 1804, as an agent for France. On the following day, he transferred the territory to himself, acting as an agent for the United States.

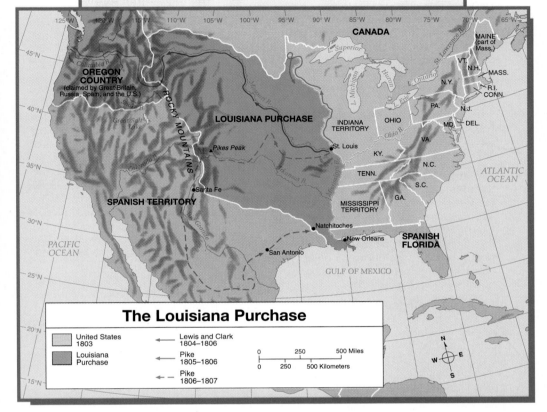

After buying Louisiana in 1803, Thomas Jefferson was eager to have it explored and mapped. Eventually, many new states were carved from the Louisiana Purchase.

1. *What rivers flowed across the Louisiana Territory?*

2. *What are the longitude and latitude of Pike's Peak?*

3. Forecasting *Judging from this map, in what territory would you expect the United States to become involved in future disputes with another country? Explain.*

The Louisiana Purchase

☐ United States 1803	← Lewis and Clark 1804–1806
☐ Louisiana Purchase	← Pike 1805–1806
	←- Pike 1806–1807

0   250   500 Miles
0   250   500 Kilometers

Answers to Map Study

1. the Missouri and the Arkansas
2. about 38°N/105°W **3.** Oregon Country, because the area was claimed by four different countries

Chapter Resources

Geography in History Duplicate and distribute the worksheet, New Orleans, Then and Now, from Unit 3, pages 17–18, of the *Chapter Resources* binder. The worksheet traces the history of the key port of which the United States took possession in 1803. (Enrichment/Challenging)

CD-ROM

History Makers Access the biographies of Meriwether Lewis and William Clark on the American Heritage® *History of the United States* CD-ROM. (Enrichment/Average)

---

the power to buy land? Jefferson had always insisted that the federal government had only those powers spelled out in the Constitution. The document said nothing about a President's power to purchase territory.

After much thought, Jefferson decided that he could buy Louisiana. The Constitution, he reasoned, allowed the President to make treaties. At his request, the Senate quickly approved a treaty making the ***Louisiana Purchase.*** In 1803, the United States took control of the vast lands west of the Mississippi.

Lewis and Clark's Assignment

The United States now owned Louisiana. However, few Americans knew anything

Chapter 9 • **273**

Connections With Civics
Background

In making his decision, Jefferson considered two main factors. First, the offer of the Louisiana Territory might not always be available — especially if Napoleon were replaced. Second, if the United States turned down the offer, the French might decide to settle — and expand — the territory. If that happened, the United States would be competing with the French for control of North America.

The Senate approved the treaty on October 20 by a vote of 24 to 7. On October 31, a special courier, carrying the documents for the transfer, left Washington. He was greeted in New Orleans by General James Wilkinson and C. C. Claiborne, who officially took possession of the Louisiana Territory for the United States.

Voices of Freedom

Primary Source You might assign selection 11-2, The Shoshones Meet Lewis and Clark, on pages 79–80 of *Voices of Freedom.* (Enrichment/Average)

Transparencies

Fine Art Use the transparency The Indian Council on page D-37 of *American History Transparencies.* Teaching suggestions can be found on page D-9. (Enrichment/Easy)

Customized Reader

Primary Source For a firsthand account of Lewis and Clark's tense meeting with the Sioux, order article IIIB-4, The Lewis and Clark Expedition Meets With a Sioux Tribe, from the *American History Customized Reader.* (Enrichment/Challenging)

Videotapes/ Videodiscs

United States History Video Collection Use the video segment "The Western Nations" from Volume 6, *Expansionism,* to enhance students' understanding of the Native American nations in the Louisiana Territory. Approx. running time 2:15 min. (Enrichment/Average) Vol. 6, Ch. 10

| Chapter 10 | Play |

about the territory. In 1803, Congress provided money for a team of explorers to study the new lands. Jefferson chose Meriwether Lewis, his private secretary, to head the expedition. Lewis asked William Clark, another Virginian, to join him. About 50 men made up their band.

Detailed instructions. Jefferson gave Lewis and Clark careful instructions. "Your observations are to be taken with great pains and accuracy," the President said. He even reminded them to write neatly so that others could read their notes. Jefferson asked the men to map a route to the Pacific Ocean.

Jefferson instructed the explorers to study the climate, wildlife, soil, and mineral resources of the new lands. The President requested a report on the following:

> ❝Climate as characterized by the thermometer, by the proportion of rainy, cloudy, and clear days, by lightning, hail, snow, ice...by the winds prevailing at different seasons, the dates at which particular plants put forth or lose their flower, or leaf, times of appearance of particular birds, reptiles or insects. ❞

Friendship with Native Americans. Jefferson also wanted Lewis and Clark to learn about the many Indian nations who lived in the Louisiana Purchase. For decades, these Native Americans had carried on a busy trade with English, French, and Spanish merchants. Jefferson hoped that the Indians

History and You

Among the supplies that Lewis and Clark took on their journey were 15 guns, a chronometer for calculating longitude, and 193 pounds of soup concentrate. Imagine that you are planning a cross-country camping trip today. What items would you take along?

274 • Chapter 9

could be convinced to trade with Americans instead. For this reason, he urged Lewis and Clark to tell the Indians of "our wish to be neighborly, friendly, and useful to them."

GEOGRAPHY AND HISTORY
The Expedition Begins

In May 1804, Lewis and Clark started up the Missouri River from St. Louis. In time, their trip would take them to the Pacific Ocean. (Follow their route on the map on page 273.)

At first, their progress was slow as they traveled against the Missouri's swift current. One night, the current tore away the riverbank where they were camping. The party scrambled into boats to avoid being washed downstream.

As they traveled, the expedition met people from various Indian nations. Lewis and Clark had brought many presents for Native Americans. They carried medals stamped with the United States seal, mirrors, beads, knives, and blankets, as well as more than 4,000 sewing needles and some 3,000 fishhooks.

As winter approached, the explorers arranged to stay with the Mandans near present-day Bismarck, North Dakota. The Mandan villages had been major trading centers for hundreds of years. (See Connections at right.)

Over the Rockies

Lewis and Clark planned to continue up the Missouri in the spring. But they worried about how they would cross the steep Rocky Mountains.

Luckily, a Shoshone woman, Sacajawea (sahk uh juh WEE uh), was also staying with the Mandans that winter. The Shoshones (shoh SHOH neez) lived in the Rockies, and Sacajawea knew the region well. She offered to guide the explorers across the mountains. She would also translate for

Our Multicultural Heritage
Activity

Sacajawea was 18 years old when she joined Lewis and Clark. Her husband, Toussaint Charbonneau, was a guide and interpreter. The couple brought their newborn baby along on the expedition. Discuss with students why Sacajawea's help was so important to Lewis and Clark.

If any students in the class speak more than one language, have them conduct a conversation through translators. Discuss the special challenge of translation.

Linking Past and Present
Background

A river, a peak, and a mountain pass have been named in honor of Sacajawea. Monuments to her also exist in Oregon, Montana, North Dakota, and Idaho.

CONNECTIONS

Mandan Traders

Lewis and Clark were lucky to meet up with the Mandans during the winter of 1804. The Mandans were a prosperous people, with a rich and ancient culture. Living in neatly laid out villages high above the Knife River, they grew corn and other crops. They also hunted the game that roamed the surrounding hills. Most important, however, they engaged in trade.

Since prehistoric times, the Mandans had been at the center of a vast trading network. They controlled the trade in Knife River flint, a hard, glassy stone prized for making strong tools and weapons. Native Americans from far and wide gave the Mandans exotic items such as shells and copper in return for the precious flint. As their farming prospered, the Mandans also traded surplus crops to wandering peoples for buffalo skins, dried meat, and other items.

In the 1600s, European goods entered the trading network. The Mandans proved themselves shrewd traders in these products as well. They acted as agents for exchanges between Europeans and other Native Americans. By the mid-1700s, Crows, Assiniboines, Cheyennes, Arapahoes, and Kiowas all traveled to the Mandans' Knife River villages to exchange horses

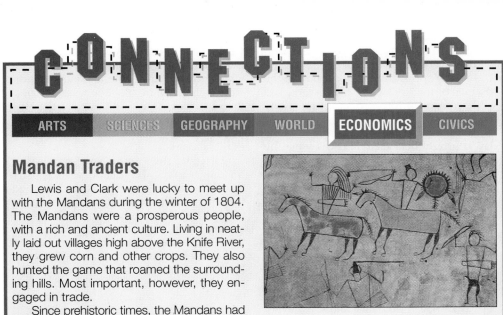

Mandan battle scene

for European guns, metal pots, hatchets, and knives.

■ What was the most important part of the Mandan economy?

ACTIVITY Create an advertisement for Mandan goods and services. Use words, pictures, or a combination of both.

A Mandan village

Interdisciplinary CONNECTIONS

For worksheets establishing connections between the Chapter 9 main idea, The Louisiana Purchase, and five other disciplines, see the *Interdisciplinary Connections* booklet. (Enrichment)

■ **Arts** That Creole Flavor, page 50 (Easy)
■ **Sciences** Recording the Wilderness, page 51 (Challenging)
■ **Geography** A Big Part for a Big River, page 52 (Average)
■ **World** A French Expansionist, page 53 (Average)
■ **Civics** Expansion and the Constitution, page 54 (Average)

Answer to Connections

trade

 Transparencies

Interdisciplinary Connections Use the transparency Lewis and Clark With Sacajawea on page B-49 of *American History Transparencies*. Teaching suggestions can be found on page B-11. (Enrichment/Average)

ACTIVITY

Guided Instruction Have students create a list of Mandan goods and services based on what they have read. Allow groups to brainstorm ideas for advertising. The group can assign a different task to each member. Have students prepare a bulletin board displaying the finished advertisements.

Team-Teaching Suggestion
Science

You might work with a science teacher to present a lesson about the plant and animal life described in Lewis and Clark's journals. Use the Sciences Connection worksheet, Recording the Wilderness, on page 51 of the *Interdisciplinary Connections* booklet as a springboard.

Team-Teaching Suggestion
Music

You might work with a music teacher to present a lesson about New Orleans and the creation of jazz music. You could support this lesson with the Arts Connection worksheet, That Creole Flavor, on page 50 of the *Interdisciplinary Connections* booklet.

Answer to Caption

She guided them across the Rocky Mountains, acted as an interpreter, found food, and provided medical care.

Historical Outline Map Book

Historical Outline Map Use the map, Exploring the Louisiana Purchase, on page 30 of the *American History Historical Outline Map Book*. Lesson ideas for this map can be found on pages T9 – T10. (Reteaching/Average)

them with different Native American groups. Sacajawea's French Canadian husband would travel with them, too.

In early spring, the party set out. In the foothills of the Rockies, the landscape and wildlife changed. Bighorn sheep ran along the high hills. The thorns of prickly pear cactus jabbed the explorers' moccasins. One day, a grizzly bear chased Lewis while he was exploring alone.

Sacajawea contributed greatly to the success of the expedition. She gathered wild vegetables and advised the men where to fish and hunt game. She knew about the healing qualities of different herbs, so the expedition relied on her for medical help.

When the party reached the mountains, Sacajawea recognized the lands of her people. One day, Lewis met several Shoshone leaders and invited them back to camp. Sacajawea began "to dance and show every mark of the most extravagant joy." One of the men, she explained, was her brother.

Sacajawea persuaded her Shoshone relatives to supply the expedition with the food and horses it needed to continue. The Shoshones advised Lewis and Clark about the best route to take over the Rockies.

Reaching the Pacific

As they crossed the Rockies, the explorers noted that the rivers flowed west,

Peace Medals *During their journey through the West, the Lewis and Clark expedition gave out peace medals as a token of friendly relations between Native Americans and the United States government.* **Multicultural Heritage** *How did Sacajawea help create good relations between Native Americans and the Lewis and Clark expedition?*

276 • Chapter 9

toward the Pacific Ocean. They had crossed the continental divide. A **continental divide** is a mountain ridge that separates river systems. In North America, the continental divide is located in the Rocky Mountains. Rivers east of the divide flow into the Mississippi, which drains into the Gulf of Mexico. West of the divide, rivers flow into the Pacific Ocean.

Entering the Pacific Northwest. After building canoes, Lewis and Clark's party floated down the Columbia River. It carried them into the Pacific Northwest. There, they met the Nez Percé Indians.

Lewis and Clark wanted to learn about the Nez Percés. However, every question had to be translated four times. First, their English words were translated into French for Sacajawea's husband. He then translated the French into Mandan. Sacajawea translated the Mandan into Shoshone. Then, a Shoshone who lived with the Nez Percés translated the question into Nez Percé. Each answer went through the same process in reverse.

A view of the west coast. On November 7, 1805, Lewis and Clark finally reached their goal. Lewis wrote in his journal: "Great joy in camp. We are in view of the ocean, this great Pacific Ocean which we have been so long anxious to see." On a nearby tree, Clark carved, "By Land from the U. States in 1804 & 5."

The return trip to St. Louis took another year. In 1806, Americans celebrated the return of Lewis and Clark. The explorers brought back much useful information about the Louisiana Purchase. Except for one small battle, their relations with Native Americans had been peaceful.

Pike Explores the West

Before Lewis and Clark returned, another explorer set out from St. Louis. From 1805 to 1807, Zebulon Pike explored the upper

---

Our Multicultural Heritage Background

The Nez Percés were expert horse breeders and riders who bred appaloosa horses— small brown horses, each with a large white patch and black spots on its rump.

Critical Thinking Analyzing Information

When Lewis and Clark and their party returned, they brought with them Chief Big White and his wife Yellow Corn. The Mandan couple later visited President Jefferson in Washington. Ask: Why do you think it would be valuable to have Big White and Yellow Corn come east?

MAP, GRAPH, AND CHART SKILLS
Following Routes on a Map

Every map tells a story. Some maps in this book tell the story of explorers moving across the land and the seas. Other maps show the movements of troops or ships during a war. The map below shows the route that Lewis and Clark followed as they crossed the Continental Divide.

1. **Study the map to see what it shows.** (a) What is the subject of the map? (b) What symbol shows their route? (c) What symbol shows Lewis and Clark campsites? (d) How does the map show Indian nations? (e) What types of landforms did Lewis and Clark travel through?

2. **Practice reading directions on the map.** To follow a route on a map, you need to determine in which direction or directions the route goes. Find the directional arrow that shows N, S, E, and W. Sometimes you need to combine directions. For example, when explorers travel in a direction be-tween north and east, they are said to be traveling northeast (NE). They could also travel northwest (NW), southeast (SE), or southwest (SW). (a) In which direction did Lewis and Clark travel after they crossed the Continental Divide? (b) In which direction did they travel after they left the campsite at Traveller's Rest?

3. **Describe movements on a map in terms of direction.** Maps like this one show movement. (a) Describe the movements of Lewis and Clark as they traveled from Great Falls to the Continental Divide. (b) Why do you think they took this route to cross the Continental Divide?

ACTIVITY Make a map that shows the route you take to get to school from your home. Give your map a title and a key that explains the symbols and colors you used. Include a scale and a directional arrow. In which directions do you travel on your way to school?

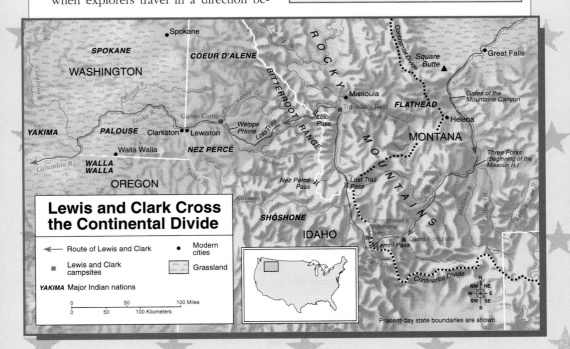

Lewis and Clark Cross the Continental Divide

Route of Lewis and Clark
Lewis and Clark campsites
YAKIMA Major Indian nations
Modern cities
Grassland

0   50   100 Miles
0   50   100 Kilometers

Present-day state boundaries are shown.

Chapter Resources

Skill Application For additional practice, duplicate and distribute the worksheet, Following Routes on a Map, from Unit 3, page 14, of the *Chapter Resources* binder. (Reteaching/Average)

Answers to Skill Lesson

1. (a) the route traveled by Lewis and Clark (b) a red line with occasional arrowheads (c) a small red square (d) by printing the name of the nation in small italic capital letters. (e) through mountains and other highlands; through grasslands
2. (a) north (N) (b) west (W)
3. (a) They followed the Missouri River southwest to its source, which took them to the continental divide and a pass in the Rocky Mountains. (b) Possible Answer: Along the Rocky Mountains, Spanish-held territory extended quite far north. Lewis and Clark probably wanted to stay within territory held by the U.S.

ACTIVITY

Guided Instruction Encourage students to use color on their maps for functional as well as design reasons. Alternately, students may want to include a specific number of purposeful errors in their maps for their classmates to discover. If they create a "Map of Errors," students should indicate how many items are wrong.

Students Acquiring English
Activity

SAE students might benefit from asking for and giving oral directions to local public places. As they become adept at giving directions, they can widen their focus to places of interest beyond their own local areas. Encourage SAE students to help each other to clarify and/or correct the directions, as needed.

Section 2 Study Guide Have students use the Section 2 Study Guide on page 82 of the *Student Study Guide* to review and reinforce the content of this section. (Reteaching/Average)

ACTIVITY

Guided Instruction Encourage students to describe the events of a specific but fictional situation in which Sacajawea translates for Lewis and Clark. In their diary entries, students can relate what happened and then explain Sacajawea's feelings about the events. Remind students that because they will be writing from Sacajawea's point of view, they should use the pronoun I.

Section 3
pp. 278–281

 Bell Ringer

Briefly discuss activities that students feel could be classified as terrorism. Ask: Has terrorism been going on for a long time? When do you think terrorism against the United States began? See if students change their minds after reading this section.

Mississippi River, the Arkansas River, and parts of present-day Colorado and New Mexico. On Thanksgiving Day in 1806, Pike saw a mountain peak rising above the Colorado plains. Today, this mountain is known as Pikes Peak. (See the map on page 273.)

The journeys of Lewis and Clark and Zebulon Pike excited Americans. It was a number of years, however, before settlers moved into the rugged western lands. As you will read, they first settled the region closest to the Mississippi River. Within a short time, the area around New Orleans had a large enough white population for the settlers to apply for statehood. In 1812, this area entered the Union as the state of Louisiana. ■

SECTION 2 REVIEW

1. **Locate:** (a) Mississippi River, (b) New Orleans, (c) Haiti, (d) St. Louis, (e) Missouri River, (f) Rocky Mountains, (g) Pikes Peak.
2. **Identify:** (a) Pinckney Treaty, (b) Toussaint L'Ouverture, (c) Louisiana Purchase, (d) Lewis and Clark, (e) Sacajawea, (f) Zebulon Pike.
3. **Define:** continental divide.
4. Why was New Orleans important to many American farmers?
5. Why did France offer to sell Louisiana to the United States?
6. (a) What did Jefferson instruct Lewis and Clark to do on their expedition? (b) What did Lewis and Clark accomplish?
7. **CRITICAL THINKING Analyzing Information** Was Jefferson's decision to purchase Louisiana based on a strict or a loose interpretation of the Constitution? Explain.

ACTIVITY Writing to Learn

Imagine that you are Sacajawea. Write a diary entry about the problems of translating for Lewis and Clark.

3
Protecting American Neutrality

FIND OUT
■ How did overseas trade grow in the early 1800s?
■ Why did British warships seize American sailors?
■ Why was the Embargo Act unpopular?

VOCABULARY impressment, embargo

The letter had been smuggled off a British ship and carried to the United States. The handwritten message described the desperate situation of a young American sailor, James Brown:

❝Being on shore one day in Lisbon, Portugal, I was [seized] by a gang and brought on board the [British ship] *Conqueror,* where I am still confined. Never have I been allowed to put my foot on shore since I was brought on board, which is now three years.❞

Brown's situation was not unusual. The British forced thousands of American sailors to serve on their ships in the early 1800s. This was only one of many dangers that Americans faced as their sea trade began to thrive.

Trading Around the World

After the Revolution, American overseas trade grew rapidly. Ships sailed from New England ports on voyages that sometimes lasted three years. Everywhere they went, Yankee captains kept a sharp lookout for

---

Answers to Section 2 Review

1. See the maps on pp. 273, 277, and the World Map in the Reference Section.
2. (a) Pinckney Treaty, p. 271, (b) Toussaint L'Ouverture, p. 272, (c) Louisiana Purchase, p. 273, (d) Lewis and Clark, p. 274, (e) Sacajawea, p. 274, (f) Zebulon Pike, p. 276
3. continental divide, p. 276
4. The cheapest way for farmers to ship their goods east was through New Orleans.
5. Defeats in Haiti ended Napoleon's dream of an empire in North America, and he needed money to fight his wars in Europe.

6. (a) They were to map the territory; learn about its inhabitants; and study its climate, wildlife, soil, and mineral resources. (b) They accomplished all the things that Jefferson had instructed them to do; in addition, they found a route to the Pacific Ocean.
7. Possible Answer: The decision was based on a loose interpretation, since the Constitution says nothing specific about buying land.

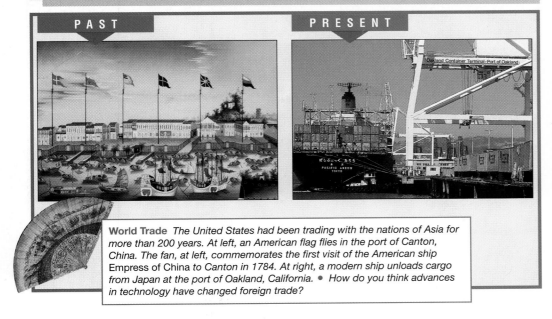

PAST   PRESENT

World Trade *The United States had been trading with the nations of Asia for more than 200 years. At left, an American flag flies in the port of Canton, China. The fan, at left, commemorates the first visit of the American ship* Empress of China *to Canton in 1784. At right, a modern ship unloads cargo from Japan at the port of Oakland, California.* • *How do you think advances in technology have changed foreign trade?*

Lesson Plan

1. Focus The growth of American trade during Jefferson's presidency brought both benefits and problems. In this section, students learn about the war with Tripoli and attempts to stop British and French attacks.
2. Instruct Divide the class into six groups of news reporters. Have each group write an interview with one of the following people affected by the Embargo Act: President Jefferson, an American sailor, a British merchant, an American farmer, a southern cotton grower, a Boston shipbuilder, and an American consumer (man or woman). Pairs of volunteers can present their interviews aloud.
3. Close To close the lesson, have students answer *Who, What, Where, When, Why,* and *How* questions about the war with Tripoli and about the Embargo and Nonintercourse acts.

Lesson Planner

For a developed **Cooperative Learning** lesson plan, see the *Lesson Planner,* page 53.

Answer to Linking Past and Present

Possible Answers: Boats now can carry more cargo and transport it faster. Some cargo can be shipped by airplane rather than by boat.

new goods to trade and new markets in which to sell. One clever trader cut up winter ice from New England ponds, packed the slabs deep in sawdust, and transported them to India. There, he traded the ice for silks and spices.

Yankee merchants. Yankee merchants sailed up the Pacific coast of North America in the 1790s. In fact, Yankee traders visited the Columbia River more than 10 years before Lewis and Clark. Indeed, so many traders from Boston visited the Pacific

Linking Past and Present
Yankee ships carried on a profitable trade in ginseng—a plant that grew wild in New England and that was used by the Chinese to make medicine. Ginseng is still used today as a medicine and as a tonic to maintain shiny hair and a clear complexion.

Northwest that Native Americans called every white man "Boston." Traders bought furs from Native Americans. Then they sold the furs for large profits in China.

To make a good profit, American traders ran great risks, especially in the Mediterranean Sea. For many years, pirates from nations along the coast of North Africa attacked vessels from Europe and the United States. The North African nations were called the ***Barbary States.*** To protect American ships, the United States paid a yearly tribute, or bribe, to the rulers of the Barbary States.

War with Tripoli. In the early 1800s, the ruler of Tripoli, one of the Barbary States, demanded a larger bribe than usual. When President Jefferson refused to pay, Tripoli declared war on the United States. In response, Jefferson ordered the navy to blockade the port of Tripoli.

During the blockade, the American ship *Philadelphia* ran aground near Tripoli. Pirates boarded the ship and hauled the crew

Chapter 9 • **279**

Connections With the World
Background

In 1784, the *Empress of China* became the first American ship to trade with China. Other New England traders followed and built a profitable China trade. Yankee ships traded ginseng for Chinese tea and silks.

Between 1787 and 1790, Captain Robert Gray of the *Columbia* accomplished the first circumnavigation of the globe by an American ship.

Linking Past and Present
Activity

Explain to students that the Barbary States are now the general area of Tunisia, Libya, Algeria, and Morocco. Have students choose one country and research its relations with the United States since 1805. The report may take the form of a brief paper, a time line, or a map with captions as well as a legend.

Answers to Map Study

1. Mediterranean Sea, Atlantic Ocean **2.** about 4,000 miles (6,500 km) **3.** Traders might have traveled around Africa to the Middle East and Asia or to northern Europe and then overland. Advantage: American ships would have avoided contact with the Barbary States. Disadvantage: Using these routes would have taken much longer and probably would have been more costly.

The Barbary States

Barbary States

0   1000   2000 Miles
0 1000 2000 Kilometers

M A P   S T U D Y

President Jefferson wanted to end the practice of paying tribute to the Barbary States.

1. *What bodies of water bordered the Barbary States?*

2. *About how far from the United States were the Barbary States?*

3. Making Decisions *Use this map and the World map in the Reference Section to describe routes American traders might have used to avoid the Barbary States. What advantage would these routes have? What disadvantage?*

to prison. The pirates planned to use the *Philadelphia* to attack other ships.

Stephen Decatur, an officer in the United States Navy, took action. Very late one night, Decatur and his crew quietly sailed a small ship into Tripoli harbor. When they reached the captured ship, they set it on fire so that the pirates could not use it.

In the meantime, a force of American marines landed in North Africa. The marines marched 500 miles (805 km) to launch a surprise attack on Tripoli. The war with Tripoli lasted until 1805. In the end, the ruler of Tripoli signed a treaty promising not to interfere with American ships.

Attacks on American Ships

In 1803, Britain and France went to war again. As in the 1790s, the European war gave a boost to American trade. British and French ships were so busy fighting that they could not carry trade goods. American merchants made profits trading with both sides.

Violating American neutrality. Of course, neither Britain nor France wanted the United States to sell supplies to its enemy. As in the 1790s, they ignored American claims of neutrality. Each tried to cut off American trade with the other. Napoleon seized American ships bound for England, and the British stopped Yankee traders on their way to France. Between 1805 and 1807, hundreds of American ships were captured.

Seizing American sailors. Britain did more than take American ships. The British navy also kidnapped American sailors and forced them to serve on British ships. This practice of forcing people into service, called **impressment,** was common in Britain. For centuries, impressment gangs had raided villages and forced young men to serve in the navy.

To fight France, the British navy needed more men than ever before. British warships even stopped and searched American vessels. If a British officer found British sailors on an American ship, he forced them off the ship. Even worse, the British impressed thousands of American sailors.

A Ban on Trade

Americans were furious with the British for attacking their ships and impressing their sailors. Many wanted to go to war with

280 • Chapter 9

Connections With the World
Background

When Britain and France had signed their 1802 peace treaty, Napoleon's empire stretched far beyond the boundaries of present-day France. Under his rule, the French people experienced peace, stability in government, and economic prosperity. Across the English Channel, however, Britain worried. Word came that Napoleon had started to train more troops. Additional strength could secure Napoleon's empire, damaging British trade. Even worse, it could mean that Napoleon was planning an invasion of Britain. As an intended invasion became more and more apparent, Britain declared war on France in 1803.

Critical Thinking
Comparing

Label two columns—Embargo Act and Nonintercourse Act—on the chalkboard. Have students fill in the chart by listing similarities and differences between the two acts. Conclude by leading a class discussion on whether these two laws were a good way for the United States to deal with its problems with England and France.

Britain. But Jefferson, like Washington and Adams, hoped to avoid war. He knew that the small American fleet was no match for the powerful British navy. Also, budget cuts had weakened the American navy.

A total ban. Jefferson convinced Congress to pass the Embargo Act in 1807. An embargo is a ban on trade with another country. The ***Embargo Act*** forbade Americans to export or import goods. Jefferson hoped that the embargo would hurt France and Britain by cutting off needed supplies. "Our trade is the most powerful weapon we can use in our defense," one Republican newspaper wrote.

The embargo hurt Britain and France. Americans, however, suffered even more.

Exports dropped from $108 million in 1807 to $22 million in 1808. American sailors had no work. Farmers lost money because they could not ship wheat overseas. Docks in the South were piled high with cotton and tobacco. The Embargo Act hurt New England merchants most of all, and they protested loudly.

A limited ban. After more than a year, Jefferson admitted that the Embargo Act had failed. In 1809, Congress voted to end the embargo. They passed the ***Nonintercourse Act*** in its place. Less severe than the embargo, this act allowed Americans to trade with all nations except Britain and France.

The Embargo Act was the most unpopular measure of Jefferson's years in office. Still, the Republicans remained strong. In 1808, Jefferson followed the precedent set by Washington and refused to run for a third term. James Madison, his fellow Republican, ran and easily won. When Madison took office in 1809, he hoped that Britain and France would soon agree to stop violating American neutrality.

American Foreign Trade 1800–1812

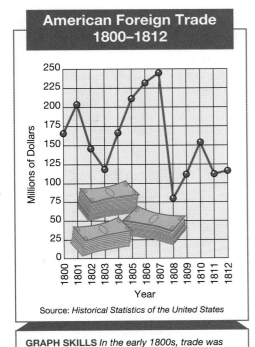

Source: *Historical Statistics of the United States*

GRAPH SKILLS *In the early 1800s, trade was important to the new nation, especially to New Englanders.* • *Why do you think trade decreased sharply between 1807 and 1808?*

SECTION 3 REVIEW

1. **Locate:** Tripoli.
2. **Identify:** (a) Barbary States, (b) Embargo Act, (c) Nonintercourse Act.
3. **Define:** (a) impressment, (b) embargo.
4. Why did the United States and Tripoli go to war?
5. How did renewed war in Europe affect American overseas trade?
6. (a) What was the purpose of the Embargo Act? (b) Why did it fail?
7. **CRITICAL THINKING Linking Past and Present** How would an embargo affect the economy of the United States today?

 Writing to Learn
Imagine that it is 1807 and you are a Yankee trader. Write a letter to President Jefferson protesting the Embargo Act.

Lesson Plan

1. Focus Despite his wish to avoid war, President Madison faced strong pressures from the War Hawks. In this section, students focus on the demands of the War Hawks and the beginning of open conflict with Native Americans and with the British.

2. Instruct Have students work in pairs to outline an agreement or disagreement with the following statement: "Tecumseh and the Prophet were justified in trying to unite Native Americans against white settlers." Have volunteers share their responses; use the responses as a springboard for class discussion.

3. Close To close the lesson, have students list the causes that led Madison into conflicts that he had hoped to avoid.

Lesson Planner

For a developed **Cooperative Learning** lesson plan, see the *Lesson Planner,* page 54.

4
The Road to War

FIND OUT

■ Why did the South and the West want war with Britain?

■ How did the Prophet and Tecumseh try to stop white settlement?

■ Why did President Madison agree to war with Britain?

VOCABULARY nationalism

James Madison was a quiet, scholarly man. Like Presidents who came before him, he wanted to avoid war.

Many Americans, however, felt that Madison's approach was too timid. They argued that the United States must stand up to foreign countries. How could the nation win respect if it allowed Britain and France to seize American ships? The cost of war might be great, said one member of Congress. But, he continued, who would count in money "the slavery of our impressed seamen"?

In time, this kind of talk aroused the nation. By 1812, Americans were clamoring for war.

War Hawks

In 1810, President Madison tried a new plan. If either Britain or France would stop seizing American ships, he said, the United States would halt trade with the other nation. Seizing the chance, Napoleon quickly announced that France would respect American neutrality. As promised, Madison declared that the United States would continue to trade with France but stop all shipments to Britain.

The President did not want war. Other Americans were less cautious, however. Ex-

cept in New England, where merchants wanted to restore trade with Britain, anti-British feeling ran strong. Members of Congress from the South and the West clamored for war with Britain. They were known as *War Hawks.*

War Hawks had a strong sense of nationalism. **Nationalism** is pride in or devotion to one's country. War Hawks felt that Britain was treating the United States as if it were still a British colony. "If we submit [to Britain]," warned one War Hawk, "the independence of this nation is lost."

Henry Clay of Kentucky was the most outspoken War Hawk. Clay wanted war for two reasons. He wanted revenge on Britain for seizing American ships. He also wanted an excuse to conquer Canada. "The militia of Kentucky are alone [able] to place Montreal and Upper Canada at your feet," Clay boasted to Congress. Canadians, Clay believed, would be happy to leave the British empire and join the United States.

War Hawks saw other advantages of war with Britain. South of the United States, Florida belonged to Spain, Britain's ally. If Americans went to war with Britain, War Hawks said, the United States could seize Florida from Spain.

Conflicts in the West

War Hawks had yet another reason to fight Britain. They claimed that Britain was arming Native Americans on the frontier and encouraging them to attack settlers. In fact, the British, who held military forts in Canada, tried to take advantage of troubles along the frontier.

Settlers push west. An important reason for frontier troubles was increasing settlement. As you have read, in 1795 the Treaty of Greenville forced Native Americans to sell much of their land in Ohio. (See page 252.) Ohio joined the Union in 1803. By then, thousands of settlers were pushing beyond Ohio into Indiana Territory.

Historical Sidelight
Background

Napoleon may have only pretended to cooperate with American neutrality in order to reestablish trade with the United States. In 1812, Britain also agreed to respect the rights of the United States, but this decision came too late to prevent war.

Cooperative Learning
Activity

Have students work as a class to prepare a propaganda leaflet taking the side of the War Hawks. The leaflet can include political cartoons as well as informational and persuasive articles.

As settlers moved west, they took over Native American lands.
1. *Which Indian groups lost their lands between 1784 and 1810?*
2. *When did the Natchez lose their land?*
3. **Forecasting** *Notice the areas of the map shaded tan. Based on what you have learned, what do you think happened to Indian lands in these areas after 1810? Explain.*

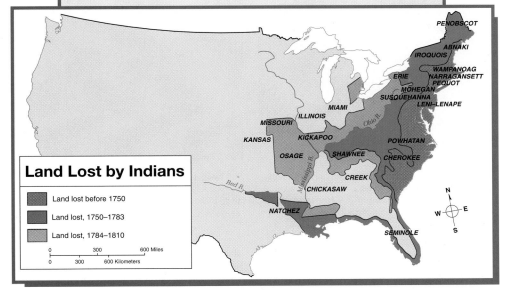

Land Lost by Indians

Land lost before 1750

Land lost, 1750–1783

Land lost, 1784–1810

The flood of settlers created big problems for Native Americans. Settlers built farms on land reserved for Indians. They hunted deer and birds that Indians depended on for food. "Stop your people from killing our game," Shawnee chiefs told the federal government. "They would be angry if we were to kill a cow or hog of theirs. The little game that remains is very dear to us."

Native Americans resist. Sometimes, Indian nations protested to the federal government about the new settlements. Other times, small bands attacked settlers to drive them off the land. Native Americans found it difficult to unite to oppose settlement, however. Indians who had once been enemies did not easily become allies.

During the same years that Americans considered war with Britain, many Native Americans determined to halt the flow of settlers. They were led by two Shawnee brothers, the Prophet and Tecumseh.

Two Shawnee Brothers Seek Unity

One winter evening in 1804, a 30-year-old Shawnee sat before a blazing campfire. Lifting a burning stick, he lit his long pipe. Suddenly, he gasped and fell to his side as if dead.

A journey to the spirit world. Families from the other lodges came running. They wanted to know what had happened to Tenskwatawa (ten SKWAH tah wah), as the dead man was called. Imagine their amazement when the dead man sat up.

Chapter 9 • **283**

Shawnee Leaders *Tecumseh, left, and the Prophet, right, believed that the land belonged to all Indians. No nation had the right to sell any part of it unless all agreed.* **Multicultural Heritage** *What message did the Prophet include in his teachings?*

At last, Tenskwatawa was able to speak. He reported that he had had a strange vision. His soul, he said, had taken a journey to the spirit world. There, he learned the path that all Indians must take if they were to live happily.

In the weeks that followed, Tenskwatawa repeated his experiences to all who came to listen. They began to call him the Prophet.

The Prophet's message. According to the Prophet, Native Americans must give up white ways. From settlers, Indians learned about the white people's way of life. Many Native Americans had come to depend on trade goods from the East, such as muskets, cloth, iron cooking pots, and whiskey. The Prophet said Native Americans must no longer trade for white goods. If Indians returned to the old ways, he believed, they would gain power to resist the settlers.

In 1808, the Prophet built a village for his followers along Tippecanoe Creek in In-

diana Territory. From as far away as Missouri, Iowa, and Minnesota, Indians traveled to hear his message. His teachings brought hope to many.

Tecumseh (tih KUHM suh), the Prophet's older brother, visited other Indian nations. Tall, handsome, and energetic, Tecumseh organized many Native Americans into a confederation, or league. Although the Prophet was the spiritual leader of the confederation, Tecumseh became its spokesperson. He said all Indians must unite "in claiming a common right in the land."

In 1809, William Henry Harrison, governor of the Indiana Territory, signed a treaty with several Indian leaders. The leaders gave up 3 million acres of Indian land for less than half a cent an acre. Tecumseh was enraged. He said that the chiefs who signed the treaties had no right to sell the land. The land belonged to all Native Americans, he said.

Tecumseh's message. In the summer of 1810, Tecumseh decided to deliver a firm

284 • Chapter 9

message to Governor Harrison. He and 75 warriors marched to Vincennes, in Indiana Territory. Awaiting their arrival, Governor Harrison arranged chairs on his front porch for the meeting. Tecumseh objected. He insisted that they meet on the grass of the forest—on Indian ground.

Tecumseh impressed Harrison. "He is one of those uncommon geniuses which spring up occasionally to produce revolutions and overturn the established order of things," Harrison commented.

As Tecumseh addressed the governor, he warned of the need for change:

66 You are continually driving the red people [from their land], when at last you will drive them into the [ocean] where they can't either stand or work. Brother, you ought to know what you are doing with the Indians. . . . It is a very bad thing and we do not like it. 99

Tecumseh insisted that Harrison give his message to President Madison. The governor agreed, but he warned that it was not likely to change Madison's mind. Tecumseh stared grimly. He knew that if whites did not stop moving onto Indian land, war would surely come. ■

Showdown at Tippecanoe

Old rivalries among Indian nations kept Tecumseh from uniting Native Americans east of the Mississippi River. Still, white settlers were alarmed at his success. "I am inclined to believe that a crisis is fast approaching," said Governor Harrison.

In 1811, Harrison decided to march with 1,000 soldiers to Prophetstown, on Tippecanoe Creek. He knew that Tecumseh was organizing Indians in the South. While he was away, the Prophet was in charge.

The Prophet learned of Harrison's approach. He decided to meet the danger with a surprise night attack on Harrison's troops.

In the battle that followed, neither side won a clear victory. Still, whites in the East celebrated the **Battle of Tippecanoe** as a major victory.

Congress Declares War

The Battle of Tippecanoe marked the beginning of a long and deadly war on the frontier. Fighting between Native Americans and settlers spurred the War Hawks to call even louder for war with Britain. Convinced that the British were arming the Indians, one newspaper called the war "purely BRITISH."

President Madison at last gave in to war fever. In June 1812, he asked Congress to declare war on Britain. The House voted 79 to 49 in favor of war. The Senate vote was 19 to 13. Americans soon discovered, however, that winning the war would not be as easy as declaring it.

SECTION 4 REVIEW

1. **Locate:** (a) Canada, (b) Spanish Florida, (c) Ohio, (d) Indiana Territory.
2. **Identify:** (a) War Hawks, (b) Henry Clay, (c) the Prophet, (d) Tecumseh, (e) Battle of Tippecanoe.
3. **Define:** nationalism.
4. Why did Henry Clay and other War Hawks want to fight the British?
5. How did the increased number of settlers affect Native Americans?
6. Why did President Madison ask Congress to declare war on Britain?
7. **CRITICAL THINKING Comparing** How was the Prophet's message different from Tecumseh's?

ACTIVITY **Writing to Learn**
Imagine that you are publishing a newspaper about the events discussed in this section. Write four headlines for the front page.

Chapter 9 • **285**

Answers to Section 4 Review

1. See the map on p. 273.
2. (a) War Hawks, p. 282, (b) Henry Clay, p. 282, (c) the Prophet, p. 284, (d) Tecumseh, p. 284, (e) Battle of Tippecanoe, p. 285
3. nationalism, p. 282
4. They wanted revenge on Britain for attacking American ships and an excuse to conquer Canada; they also claimed that Britain was arming Indians against settlers on the frontier.
5. White settlers built farms on Indian lands and killed Indian game; Indians came to depend on white trade goods and gave up many of their old ways.

6. The War Hawks had stepped up their pressure, saying that the United States must defend its rights at sea and end impressment. Madison finally gave in to the pressure and asked Congress to declare war.
7. Possible Answer: The Prophet urged Indians to give up the ways of white men, whereas Tecumseh wanted to unite all Indians to resist whites. Both wanted to resist white settlers, but Tecumseh saw direct action as the first step.

Bell Ringer

Ask students to jot down as many facts as they know about "The Star-Spangled Banner," including any lyrics they can remember. Then, if possible, play a recording of the national anthem.

Lesson Plan

1. Focus The War of 1812 divided Americans, yet it failed to resolve conflicts that caused the war. In this section, students examine the major battles of the war, the burning of the nation's capital, and the Treaty of Ghent.
2. Instruct Write the following statements, which could have been made by Americans during the War of 1812, on the chalkboard. Have students label each statement as Fact or Opinion, supply supporting evidence for each fact, and decide who might have held each opinion and why. (1) "This is entirely Mr. Madison's War." (2) "The British can't win; they're too tied up with the war in Europe." (3) "This war is hurting the merchants of New England." (4) "The delegates to the Hartford Convention are traitors."
3. Close To close the lesson, play a Jeopardy!-like game with students. Provide information from Section 5 as the answers and have students create appropriate questions.

5
The War of 1812

FIND OUT
- How did Americans prepare for the War of 1812?
- What part did Native Americans play in the fighting?
- What was the outcome of the war?

Many Republicans welcomed the news of war with Britain. In some cities, they fired cannons and guns and danced in the streets. One New Jersey man wrote a song calling for a swift attack on Canada:

> **"**On to Quebec's embattled halls!
> Who will pause, when glory calls?
> Charge, soldiers, charge, its lofty walls.
> And storm its strong artillery.**"**

Other Americans were less enthusiastic. New Englanders, especially, talked scornfully of "Mr. Madison's war." In fact, before the war ended, some New Englanders would plot to leave the Union and make a separate peace with Britain.

Preparing for War

The United States was not ready for war. The navy had only 16 ships to fight against the huge British fleet. The army was small and ill equipped. Moreover, many of the officers knew little about the military. "The state of the Army," commented a member of Congress, "is enough to make any man who has the smallest love of country wish to get rid of it."

Since there were few regular troops, the government relied on volunteers to fight the war. Congress voted to give them $124 and 360 acres of land for their service. The mon-

ey was high pay at the time—equal to a year's salary for most workers.

Lured by money and the chance to own their own farm, young men eagerly enlisted. They were not trained, however, and did not know how to be good soldiers. Many deserted after a few months. Others would not fight unless they were paid. One officer complained that his men "absolutely refused to march until they had [received] their pay."

Fighting at Sea

The American declaration of war took Britain by surprise. The British were locked in a bitter struggle with Napoleon. They could not spare troops to fight the United States. The powerful British navy, however, blockaded American ports.

The American navy was too small to break the blockade. Yet several sea captains won stunning victories. One famous battle took place early in the war, in August 1812. Sailing near Newfoundland, Isaac Hull, captain of the *Constitution,* spotted the British frigate *Guerrière* (gai ree AIR). For close to an hour, the two ships jockeyed for position. The *Guerrière* fired on the *Constitution* several times. Captain Hull ordered his cannons to hold their fire.

At last, Hull felt he was close enough to the enemy. Bending over, he shouted to the sailors on the deck below: "Now, boys, you may fire!" The cannons on the *Constitution* roared. They tore holes in the sides of the *Guerrière* and shot off both masts.

When the smoke cleared, Hull asked the British captain if he had "struck" his flag—that is, lowered his flag in surrender. "Well, I don't know," replied the stunned British captain. "Our mizzenmast is gone, our mainmast is gone. And, upon the whole, you may say we *have* struck our flag."

American sea captains won other victories at sea. But although these victories cheered Americans, they did little to win the war.

Our Multicultural Heritage
Background

Few African Americans fought in the War of 1812. Most free blacks lived in the North, where the war was unpopular, and so these states sent smaller contingents of soldiers than the South and the West. In states where slavery was practiced, enslaved African Americans were not eligible to serve in the armed forces.

Among the American troops at the battle of New Orleans were two battalions of black soldiers. Jackson singled them out for exceptional bravery during the battle. He issued a proclamation in praise of these soldiers on December 18, 1814: "TO THE MEN OF COLOR—Soldiers! . . . You surpass my hopes. I have found in you that noble enthusiasm which impels to great deeds."

"Old Ironsides" *In this painting by famed marine artist Thomas Birch, the U.S.S.* Constitution *levels a broadside blast at the British frigate* Guerrière. *After its remarkable victory against the* Guerrière, *the* Constitution *won the nickname "Old Ironsides."* **Geography** *What was the goal of the British navy during the War of 1812?*

War in the West

As you have read, one goal of the War Hawks was to conquer Canada. They were sure that Canadians would welcome the chance to throw off British rule.

Americans invade Canada. William Hull led American troops into Canada from Detroit. The Canadians had only a few untrained troops to fight the invasion. But General Isaac Brock tricked the Americans.

First, Brock paraded his soldiers in red cloaks to make it appear that well-trained British redcoats were helping the Canadians. Brock also let a false "secret" message fall into Hull's hands. It said that more than 5,000 Indians were fighting on Brock's side. The real number was much smaller. Brock's ally, Tecumseh, staged raids on the Americans that seemed to confirm the message.

Brock's strategy worked. Hull retreated from Canada. The invasion of Canada had failed.

Tecumseh's last battle. In September 1813, the tide turned when the Americans gained control of Lake Erie. William Henry Harrison, veteran of Tippecanoe and now a general in the army, invaded Canada in search of Tecumseh and the British. The Americans won a decisive victory at the ***Battle of the Thames.***

Tecumseh died in the fighting. For Native Americans, his death was a great loss. Without Tecumseh's leadership, the Indian confederation he had worked so hard to form fell apart.

Chapter 9 • **287**

Historical Sidelight
Background

When Hull retreated from Canada, the British followed him and captured Detroit. The Americans were unable to retake Detroit because the British controlled Lake Erie.

In 1813, the Americans set out to win control of Lake Erie. Captain Oliver Hazard Perry, who had no fleet, designed and built his own ships; in September of that year, he sailed his tiny fleet against the British. During the battle, Perry's own ship was battered by the British and left helpless. Perry took his flag down and rowed to another American ship, where he again raised the colors and continued to fight. The battle ended with an American victory. Perry announced this now-famous message of victory: "We have met the enemy and they are ours."

287

Answers to Map Study

1. the Thames, Ft. Mackinac, Frenchtown, Lundy's Lane, Chippewa, Lake Erie. 2. (a) any two of the following: Plattsburgh, Baltimore, the Thames, Lake Erie, Chippewa, Pensacola, New Orleans, Horseshoe Bend (b) any two of the following: Ft. Mackinac, Frenchtown, Lundy's Lane, Washington, D.C. 3. Possible Answer: They were similar. In both cases, the United States invaded Canada, thinking that Canadians would welcome them. Each time, the Americans were defeated and forced to retreat.

Historical Outline Map Book

Historical Outline Map Use the map, The War of 1812, on page 32 of the *American History Historical Outline Map Book*. Lesson ideas for this map can be found on pages T10–T11. (Enrichment/Average)

MAP STUDY

The War of 1812 was fought on several fronts.
1. What battles took place in or near Canada?
2. (a) Name two American victories shown on the maps. (b) Name two British victories.
3. **Comparing** Compare the American invasion of Canada in the Revolution with the invasion of Canada in the War of 1812. (See pages 163–164.) Were they similar or different? Explain.

The Creeks surrender. The Creeks, Tecumseh's allies in the South, were divided over what to do. Some wanted to keep fighting the bloody war against the settlers. Andrew Jackson, a Tennessee officer, took command of the American troops in the Creek War.

In 1814, Jackson led American troops into battle. With the help of the Cherokees, Jackson won a decisive victory at the **Battle of Horseshoe Bend**. The leader of the Creeks walked alone into Jackson's camp to surrender:

> I am in your power. Do unto me as you please. . . . If I had an army I would yet fight, and contend to the last. . . . But your people have destroyed my nation.

For the time being, the fighting ended. Once again, Native Americans were forced to give up land to whites.

288 • Chapter 9

Critical Thinking
Synthesizing Information

Help students create a chart of major battles of the War of 1812. Draw a blank chart on the chalkboard with columns labeled Battle, Date, Place, Winner, Importance. Have students fill in the chart with information from the text. Ask: Which battle was the greatest triumph for the United States? The greatest defeat?

Historical Sidelight
Background

Samuel Wilson, who was called "Uncle Sam," supplied meat to the American army. The barrels containing the meat were marked *U.S.,* for *United States,* but many assumed that the initials stood for *Uncle Sam.* Soon, "Uncle Sam" became a nickname for the government of the United States—a name that remains today.

The British Burn Washington

In 1814, Britain and its allies defeated France. Now, Britain could send its troops and ships to the United States.

March on the capital. That summer, British ships sailed into Chesapeake Bay. Soldiers came ashore about 30 miles (48 km) from Washington, D.C. Americans tried to stop the British at Bladensburg, Maryland. President Madison himself rode out to watch the battle. To Madison's dismay, the battle-hardened British quickly scattered the untrained Americans and continued their march to the capital.

In the President's mansion, Dolley Madison waited for her husband to return. Hastily, she scrawled a note to her sister:

> 66 Will you believe it, my sister? We have had a battle or skirmish near Bladensburg and here I am still within sound of the cannon! Mr. Madison comes not. May God protect us. Two messengers covered with dust come bid me fly. But here I mean to wait for him. 99

Soon after, British troops marched into the capital. Dolley Madison gathered up important papers of the President's and a portrait of George Washington. Then, she fled south. She was not there to see the British burn the President's mansion and other buildings.

Bombardment of Baltimore. From Washington, D.C., the British marched north to-

BIOGRAPHY Dolley Madison *As First Lady, Dolley Madison was best known for her skill at smoothing over quarrels between politicians. But when British troops burned Washington, D.C., Madison showed that she was also a woman of determination and courage.* **American Traditions** *How did Dolley Madison help to preserve the nation's heritage?*

ward Baltimore. The key to Baltimore's defense was Fort McHenry. From evening on September 13 until dawn on September 14, British rockets bombarded the harbor. When the early morning fog lifted, the "broad stripes and bright stars" of the American flag still waved over Fort McHenry. The British gave up the attack. Soon after, Francis Scott Key wrote a poem about the bombardment. Years later, "The Star-Spangled Banner" was set to music and adopted as the national anthem of the United States.

 Our Multicultural Heritage

Biography Have students read the biography, Dolley Madison, a Gallant First Lady, on page 26 of the *Our Multicultural Heritage* booklet. (Enrichment/Average)

Customized Reader

Primary Source For a copy of Francis Scott Key's own account of the experience that resulted in "The Star-Spangled Banner," order article IIIB-7, The Inspiration for "The Star-Spangled Banner," from the *American History Customized Reader*. (Enrichment/Average)

 CD-ROM

Arts & Entertainment Access the Patriotic Songs segment in Music on the American Heritage® *History of the United States* CD-ROM. (Enrichment/Easy)

Linking Past and Present
When Americans rebuilt Washington, D.C., after the War of 1812, they gave the President's mansion a coat of whitewash to cover the charred wood. Ever since, it has been called the White House.

Connections With Civics
Background

Dolley Madison influenced the social life of Washington for almost 50 years. Her career there began when James Madison became Jefferson's Secretary of State. When James Madison was elected President, Dolley Madison planned the first inaugural ball. Dolley Madison returned to the capital after the British burned it. Many times, her social skills helped to defuse quarrels between political leaders.

Connections With Music
Background

The flag that flew at Fort McHenry was made by Mary Young Pickersgill. It was 42 feet long and 30 feet wide, with each of the 15 stars measuring 2 feet from point to point. The original "star-spangled banner" is now preserved at the Smithsonian Institution in Washington, D.C.

Answer to Caption

Control of New Orleans would allow the British to sail up the Mississippi River.

Jackson Defends New Orleans

Meanwhile, the British prepared to attack New Orleans. From there, they hoped to sail up the Mississippi.

Andrew Jackson was waiting for the British. Jackson's forces included thousands of frontiersmen, many of them expert riflemen. Hundreds of African Americans from New Orleans as well as a group of Filipino Americans also volunteered to defend their city.

Jackson's troops dug trenches to defend themselves. On January 8, 1815, the British tried to overrun Jackson's line. Again and again, British soldiers charged the American trenches. More than 2,000 British fell. Only seven Americans died.

All over the United States, Americans celebrated their victory at the ***Battle of New Orleans.*** Overnight, Andrew Jackson became a national hero, second only to George Washington.

Jackson's fame did not dim even when Americans later learned that the long and bloody battle could have been avoided. The Battle of New Orleans took place two weeks after the United States and Britain had signed a peace treaty in Europe ending the war.

Peace at Last

News took weeks to cross the Atlantic Ocean in the early 1800s. By late 1814, Americans knew that peace talks had begun. But they did not know how they were progressing or how long they would last. While Jackson was preparing to fight the British at New Orleans, New Englanders were meeting to protest "Mr. Madison's war."

New Englanders protest. Delegates from around New England met in Hartford, Connecticut, in December 1814. Most were Federalists. They disliked the Republican President and the war.

The British blockade had hurt New England's sea trade. Also, many New Englanders felt that the South and the West had more to gain if the United States won land in Florida and Canada. If new states were carved out of these lands, New England would lose influence.

Delegates to the ***Hartford Convention*** threatened to leave the Union if the war continued. However, while the delegates debated what to do, news of the peace treaty arrived. The Hartford Convention ended quickly. With the war over, the protest was meaningless. The Federalist party died out completely with the end of the war.

The Battle of New Orleans *In this engraving, Andrew Jackson, at right, spurs the Americans on to victory in the Battle of New Orleans. Neither side, however, knew that the war was already over.* **Geography** *Why did the British want to gain control of New Orleans?*

"Our Flag Was Still There" *Rockets lit up the night sky as the British bombarded Fort McHenry. But when dawn came, the American flag, right, still flew over the fort. The event inspired Francis Scott Key to write "The Star-Spangled Banner."* **American Traditions** *Why is a national anthem important to citizens?*

"Nothing was settled." Peace talks had been held in Ghent, Belgium. The ***Treaty of Ghent*** was signed on December 24, 1814. John Quincy Adams, one of the Americans at Ghent, summed up the treaty in one sentence: "Nothing was adjusted, nothing was settled."

Both sides agreed to return matters to the way they had been before the war. The treaty said nothing about impressment or American neutrality. Since Britain was no longer at war with France, these conflicts had faded. Other issues were settled later. In 1818, the two countries agreed to set much of the border between Canada and the United States at 49°N latitude.

Looking back, some Americans believed that the War of 1812 had been a mistake. Others argued that Europe would now treat the young republic with more respect. The victories of Isaac Hull and Andrew Jackson had given Americans new pride in their country. In the words of one Republican, "The people are now more American. They feel and act more as a nation."

SECTION 5 REVIEW

1. **Locate:** (a) Detroit, (b) Chesapeake Bay, (c) Washington, D.C., (d) Baltimore.
2. **Identify:** (a) Battle of the Thames, (b) Battle of Horseshoe Bend, (c) Dolley Madison, (d) Andrew Jackson, (e) Battle of New Orleans, (f) Hartford Convention, (g) Treaty of Ghent.
3. What problems did Americans face in preparing for war?
4. What part did Tecumseh play in the War of 1812?
5. What were the terms of the Treaty of Ghent?
6. **CRITICAL THINKING Analyzing Information** Why do you think the War of 1812 has been called the Second War of American Independence?

ACTIVITY Writing to Learn

List the reasons why the delegates to the Hartford Convention opposed the War of 1812. Use the list to write a petition to Congress calling for an end to the war.

CHAPTER 9 REVIEW

Answers to Reviewing the Main Ideas

1. Jefferson believed in laissez faire, in which the government plays as small a role as possible in economics. The Federalists, however, wanted the government to promote trade, commerce, and manufacturing.

2. (a) The Court decided that Marbury could not become a judge and that the Judiciary Act, passed by Congress, was unconstitutional. (b) The decision set an important precedent in that the Supreme Court established a right to review any law made by Congress and to decide on its constitutionality.

3. (a) Farmers living between the Appalachians and the Mississippi depended on the river to send goods to market. (b) French defeats in Haiti ruined Napoleon's plan to build an empire in America.

4. (a) Trade grew rapidly, with Yankee captains sailing all over the world. (b) The blockade was a response to Tripoli's demand for a larger bribe to ensure protection from pirates.

5. The War Hawks wanted revenge on Britain for attacking American ships; an excuse to conquer Canada; a way to stop Britain from arming Indians against white settlers; and possession of Florida, which was held by Spain, Britain's ally.

6. Old rivalries among Indian nations made unity difficult.

7. The War of 1812 gave Americans a new pride in their country; it made separate states, or areas of the country, feel like part of one nation.

Answers to Thinking Critically

1. (a) The Louisiana Purchase doubled the size of the United States. (b) It proved that the Louisiana Territory was large and rich in resources. (c) Possible Answer: Americans felt that the new territory offered economic opportunities.

2. (a) They threatened to leave the Union. (b) Today, state representatives debate the issues and try to pass laws that will bring about change.

292

Summary

- President Jefferson worked to limit the power of the federal government and to make the nation more democratic.
- The Louisiana Purchase doubled the size of the United States.
- To protect American neutrality, Congress passed the Embargo Act, banning all foreign trade.
- Giving in to the War Hawks, in 1812 the United States declared war on Britain.
- Neither the United States nor Britain won the War of 1812, but Americans gained a new sense of national pride.

Reviewing the Main Ideas

1. How did Jefferson's economic policies differ from those of the Federalists?

2. (a) What did the Supreme Court decide in *Marbury* v. *Madison*? (b) Why was the decision important?

3. (a) Why did Americans want to control the Mississippi River? (b) How did the revolt in Haiti influence Napoleon's decision to sell Louisiana?

4. (a) How did American overseas trade grow after the Revolution? (b) Why did Jefferson blockade Tripoli?

5. Why did the War Hawks want war?

6. Why was Tecumseh unable to unite all Native Americans east of the Mississippi River?

7. How did the War of 1812 affect Americans?

Thinking Critically

1. Synthesizing Information (a) How did the Louisiana Purchase affect the size of the United States? (b) What did the journey of Lewis and Clark prove? (c) How might these two events have affected the view Americans had of their country?

292 • Chapter 9

2. Linking Past and Present Reread the paragraphs on page 290 about the Hartford Convention. (a) What did the delegates threaten to do if the war continued? (b) How do state representatives today protest government actions?

Applying Your Skills

1. Skimming a Chapter Review the steps on skimming a chapter on page 264. Then skim Chapter 9. (a) What are the main topics? (b) What is the main idea of the section Republicans in Power?

2. Following Routes on a Map Study the map on page 273. (a) How does the map show Pike's route during 1805 and 1806? (b) During 1806 and 1807? (c) In which directions did Pike travel in 1805 and 1806? (d) In which direction was Pike headed when he crossed the Rio Grande?

3. Analyzing a Quotation What did Tecumseh mean when he said that Native Americans must unite in "claiming a common right to the land"?

Thinking About Geography

Match the letters on the map with the following places: **1.** Canada, **2.** Battle of the Thames, **3.** Battle of Horseshoe Bend, **4.** Battle of New Orleans, **5.** Baltimore, **6.** British blockade. **Movement** How did the British blockade hurt the United States?

Answers to Applying Your Skills

1. (a) Republicans in Power, The Louisiana Purchase, Protecting American Neutrality, The Road to War, The War of 1812 (b) Possible Answer: Jefferson's principles of government differed from the Federalists, so he kept some Federalist programs but changed others.

2. (a) solid blue line (b) broken blue line (c) north and south (d) northeast

3. Possible Answer: All Native Americans must acknowledge and defend their equal right to the land that whites claimed.

Answers to Thinking About Geography

1. E **2.** B **3.** C **4.** D **5.** A **6.** F

Movement: The blockade kept Americans from trading with other countries.

INTERDISCIPLINARY ACTIVITY

Exploring With Lewis and Clark

Form into groups to think about the Lewis and Clark expedition. Follow the suggestions below to write, draw, or perform to show what you have learned about the expedition. You may use the textbook, encyclopedias, atlases, or other materials in your classroom library to complete the tasks. Be able to name your sources of information when you have finished the activity.

GEOGRAPHERS On a large sheet of paper, create a map of the United States in 1803. On the map:
- Draw the route of the Lewis and Clark expedition.
- Show the climate in the areas visited by the expedition.
- Show at least five plants and animals found in the areas visited by Lewis and Clark.

MATHEMATICIANS Create a bar graph comparing the land area of the United States before and after the Louisiana Purchase.

ACTORS Find out the details of an interesting incident during the Lewis and Clark expedition. Prepare a skit about the incident. Assign roles to group members, and perform the skit for the class.

ARTISTS, POETS, AND MUSICIANS Find out about the Native Americans who lived in the territory of the Louisiana Purchase. How did they feel about the arrival of the explorers on their land? Share your findings in a drawing, poem, or song.

REPORTERS Review President Jefferson's instructions to Lewis and Clark. Then write a letter or videotape a message to the explorers explaining why the task they are about to perform is important for the country.

★ Create an Exploring With Lewis and Clark corner in the classroom, and display your completed activity there.

Clark's sketch of a salmon

Lewis and Clark and Sacajawea greet a group of Indians

Clark's sketch of a bird

Chapter 9 • **293**

Assessment

Chapter Resources Binder For a more comprehensive evaluation of student understanding of this chapter, assign Chapter Tests A and B and/or Extra Unit Questions from Unit 3, pages 19–24 and 41–43.
Computer Test Bank You can use Chapter Tests and Extra Unit Questions to create your own tests for both testing and retesting.

Alternative Assessment

Chapter Resources Binder See the Alternative Assessment booklet in the *Social Studies Educator's Handbook* series.
Portfolio You might meet with students to choose appropriate work from the chapter for inclusion in their portfolios.

Interdisciplinary ACTIVITY

Learning Styles

The following chart indicates the activities appropriate for different learning styles.

Visual Learners
Geographers
Mathematicians
Actors
Artists, poets, and musicians
Reporters

Auditory Learners
Actors
Artists, poets, and musicians
Reporters

Kinesthetic Learners
Geographers
Mathematicians
Actors
Artists, poets, and musicians
Reporters

Evaluation

Geographers Maps should reflect appropriate shapes and sizes of states and territories relative to other states. Major rivers should be indicated correctly. Maps may include legends designating climatic features, flora, and fauna.
Mathematicians Finished bar graphs should be neat and visually understandable, with intervals that are equal and practical. Students may use standard or metric units of measure, or both.
Actors Skits should be entertaining (though not necessarily humorous) and informative, reflecting their historical basis.
Artists, poets, and musicians Artistic ability need not be a major criterion, but drawings, poems, and songs should display some originality and depth of feeling about the subject matter. Presentations should be interesting and informative. All pertinent information must be accurate.
Reporters Letters or videotapes should reflect an understanding of the unprecedented journey upon which Lewis and Clark embarked. Explanations should be based on accurate information and logical thinking.

Lessons	Teaching Resources
1 The Industrial Revolution **Objectives** 1. Describe how the early Industrial Revolution changed people's lives. 2. Identify the inventions that led to the Industrial Revolution. 3. Describe how the Industrial Revolution reached the United States.	**Lesson Planner** Cooperative Learning, p. 58 **Student Study Guide** Section 1 Study Guide, p. 88
2 From Workshops to Factories **Objectives** 1. Describe how the War of 1812 helped American manufacturers. 2. Describe how Lowell was a model community. 3. Describe what working conditions were like in early factories. 4. Identify the advantages and disadvantages of city life in the early 1800s.	**Lesson Planner** Cooperative Learning, p. 59 **Student Study Guide** Section 2 Study Guide, p. 89 **Our Multicultural Heritage** *Biography* P. T. Barnum, Great American Showman, p. 29 **Chapter Resources Binder, Unit 3** *Skill Application* Using a Concept Map, p. 28
3 Americans on the Move **Objectives** 1. Describe how settlers traveled west. 2. Identify the steps that Americans took to improve roads. 3. Describe how steamboats and canals changed transportation.	**Lesson Planner** Cooperative Learning, p. 60 **Student Study Guide** Section 3 Study Guide, p. 90 **Chapter Resources Binder, Unit 3** *Geography in History* Building a Waterway to the West, pp. 31–32 **Interdisciplinary Connections:** The Erie Canal ■ *Sciences* Packet Boats, p. 56 ■ *Geography* Construction Obstructions, p. 57 ■ *World* The Canals of Britain, p. 58 ■ *Economics* Canal Fever, p. 59 ■ *Civics* De Witt Clinton and the Canal, p. 60 **Posters** *My Ancestors Coming to America,* by Joan Landis Bahm
4 Building National Unity **Objectives** 1. Identify the Era of Good Feelings. 2. Describe how Congress tried to strengthen the national economy. 3. Identify Henry Clay's American System.	**Lesson Planner** Cooperative Learning, p. 61 **Student Study Guide** Section 4 Study Guide, p. 91 **Chapter Resources Binder, Unit 3** *Critical Thinking* Analyzing Information, p. 29 *History Through Literature* Letters From an American Farmer, p. 30
5 Neighboring Nations Gain Independence **Objectives** 1. Describe how Canada achieved self-rule. 2. Describe how revolutions changed Latin America. 3. Explain why the United States issued the Monroe Doctrine.	**Lesson Planner** Cooperative Learning, p. 62 **Student Study Guide** Section 5 Study Guide, p. 92 **Our Multicultural Heritage** *Biography* Joseph Marion Hernández, Florida Statesman and Soldier, p. 28 *Milestone* Changes for the Seminoles, p. 30

Chapter Manager

Multimedia Resources	Additional Resources	Chapter-Level Resources
Transparencies *Cause and Effect* The Industrial Revolution in the United States, p. F-17 *Exploring Technology* Spinning Mill, p. H-31		**Lesson Planner** Activity Based, pp. 63–64 **Student Study Guide** Chapter 10 Study Guide, pp. 93–94 **Chapter Resources Binder** **Unit 3** Vocabulary Building, p. 27 Chapter Test A, pp. 33–35 Chapter Test B, pp. 36–38 Illustration Master, p. 39 Extra Unit Questions, pp. 41–43 **English Guided Reading** Guided Reading, pp. 19–20 **Spanish Resources**
Transparencies *Cause and Effect* The Industrial Revolution in the United States, p. F-17	**Voices of Freedom** Pros and Cons of Factory Life, pp. 83–84 **Interdisciplinary Explorations** Mill Life in the 1840s: Roots of American Industry	**Computer Test Bank** Chapter Tests A and B Extra Unit Questions
Transparencies *Fine Art* Fur Traders Descending the Missouri, p. D-35 *Interdisciplinary Connections* Erie Canal, p. B-51 **CD-ROM** *History Makers* Daniel Boone **Videotapes/Videodiscs** *United States History Video Collection* The Move West, Vol. 6, Ch. 22	**Voices of Freedom** Mark Twain on the Lure of Steamboats, p. 85 **Historical Outline Map Book** The United States in 1824, p. 34 Transportation to the West, p. 33 **Customized Reader** Frontier Doctors, article IIIB-5 A Frontier Conversion, article IIIB-8	**Guided Reading Audiotapes** Side 4 **CD-ROM** *Time Tour* Years of Growth and Expansion (1790–1825) in The New Republic
CD-ROM *History Makers* Henry Clay	**Voices of Freedom** A Southerner Objects to the Tariff, pp. 86–87 Americans Sing Praises of Home, p. 88	
CD-ROM *Presidents* James Monroe **Videotapes/Videodiscs** *United States History Video Collection* Expansion and the Monroe Doctrine, Vol. 6, Ch. 16	**Voices of Freedom** Monroe Doctrine Declared, pp. 87–88 **Historical Outline Map Book** New Nations in Latin America, p. 35	

Lesson Planner

For a fully developed **Activity-Based** lesson plan for Chapter 10, see the *Lesson Planner,* pages 63–64.

 Chapter Resources

Vocabulary Building The Vocabulary Building worksheet for Chapter 10 from Unit 3, page 27, of the *Chapter Resources* binder can be used as a prereading activity or as a review of chapter vocabulary. (Reteaching/Easy)

 Student Study Guide

Chapter 10 Study Guide Refer students to pages 93–94 of the *Student Study Guide* for the Chapter 10 Study Guide. The study guide can be used for chapter review as well as for reteaching. (Reteaching/Average)

 Guided Reading Audiotapes

Students can use *Guided Reading Audiotapes,* Chapter 10, side 4, to listen to section previews, summaries, and review questions. The tapes might benefit students who are auditory learners, students who have trouble reading, or students acquiring English. Tapes are also available in Spanish. (Reteaching/Easy)

CHAPTER 10

Years of Growth and Expansion

(1790–1825)

CHAPTER OUTLINE

1 The Industrial Revolution

2 From Workshops to Factories

3 Americans on the Move

4 Building National Unity

5 Neighboring Nations Gain Independence

1700s Many enslaved African Americans fled to Spanish Florida. Some, like this young man, joined the Seminole Indians.

1790 Samuel Slater opened the first water-powered spinning mill in the United States.

1790s The Lancaster Turnpike was built in Pennsylvania. Better roads made stagecoach travel faster.

| 1785 | 1790 | 1795 | 1800 | 1805 |

WORLD EVENT
1700s The Industrial Revolution begins in Britain

 WORLD EVENT
1802 Child labor law enacted in Britain

294 • Chapter 10

Chapter Time Line
Critical Thinking

As you discuss the time line illustrations and captions, ask students to explain how various ones relate to either of the following statements:

■ The United States was showing its independence in many ways.

■ The United States was eager to develop. Then point out the World Event entries. Have students explain how each one was either a cause or an effect of events in the United States.

Students Acquiring English
Activity

To help SAE students access the information in this chapter, have them work in small collaborative groups or with a native English-speaking partner. Explain to SAE students that they should interview their partner or group members about the chapter content. Suggest that students use the Find Out items at the beginning of each section and the Section Reviews as a guideline for the interviews. This peer group strategy gives SAE students an opportunity to increase comprehension through oral language summaries. As the content becomes familiar to them, they can switch roles with their classmates and be interviewed.

Chapter Setting

Clang-clang-clang-clang! At dawn each day, the factory bell woke 11-year-old Lucy Larcom. Rising quickly, she ate breakfast and hurried off to work. Lucy worked in a factory in Lowell, Massachusetts. The factory turned raw cotton into cloth. Years later, Lucy described her workplace:

66 I never cared much for machinery. The buzzing and hissing and whizzing of pulleys and rollers and spindles and flyers around me often grew tiresome. . . .

The last window in the row behind me was filled with flourishing houseplants. . . . Standing before that window, I could look across the room and see girls moving backwards and forwards among the spinning frames, sometimes stooping, sometimes reaching up their arms, as their work required. . . .

On the whole, it was far from being a disagreeable place to stay in. . . . [But] in the sweet June weather I would lean far out of the window, and try not to hear the unceasing clash of sound inside. Looking away to the hills, my whole stifled being would cry out, 'Oh, that I had wings!' 99

A growing number of Americans, like Lucy Larcom, took jobs in the factories that were built in the early 1800s. As factories sprang up, cities grew up around them. Most Americans still lived in rural areas. Yet changes were underway that would transform life in the United States.

ACTIVITY
Imagine that you are a worker in the mill at Lowell, Massachusetts. Write a song about your average workday.

1807 *The launching of the* Clermont *ushered in the steamboat era. This riverboat is on the Mississippi River near St. Louis.*

1821 *The Boston Associates built a factory town in Massachusetts. The women who worked in the mills published their own magazine.*

1825 *This plate celebrates the opening of the Erie Canal, which linked the Great Lakes with the Hudson River.*

1805	1810	1815	1820	1825

WORLD EVENT
1810 Mexico and South America begin struggles for independence

WORLD EVENT
1821 Mexico, Guatemala, and Peru win independence from Spain

Chapter Resources

English Guided Reading Duplicate and distribute to SAE students the Chapter 10 Guided Reading worksheet on pages 19–20 in the English Guided Reading section of the *Chapter Resources* binder. Students who have difficulty reading also might benefit from using this worksheet. Have students complete the worksheet before they begin reading. You might pair a more fluent student or a student who is a stronger reader with each SAE student to review. (Reteaching/Easy)

Spanish Resources See the Spanish Resources section of the *Chapter Resources* binder.

CD-ROM

Time Tour Access the Years of Growth and Expansion (1790–1825) section in The New Republic on the American Heritage® *History of the United States* CD-ROM. (Enrichment/Average)

ACTIVITY

Guided Instruction You might discuss the use of a refrain to state and restate the central theme in a song. Suggest that students might want to include onomatopoeic words that imitate factory sounds (such as *hiss* or *crunch*) and a last line that expresses the singer's feelings. Stanzas preceding and following the refrain should describe typical workday activities. Collect the works and compile a songbook to share with other classes or to contribute to the school library.

Linking Past and Present
Activity

Lead the class in a discussion of the role that manufacturing played in the growth of American cities in the nineteenth century. Note that factories provided jobs for townspeople, attracted new residents, and helped the town to grow. On the negative side, manufacturing made cities noisier, dirtier, and more crowded. Then play a recording of the song "My Home Town" by Bruce Springsteen.

Have students paraphrase the lyrics. Ask: What effects do you think manufacturing has had on American cities in the late 1900s? Students should note that the closing of factories has hurt the economic health of cities in which manufacturing once flourished; as a result, there has been a population decline in many of these cities.

295

Bell Ringer

Ask: What advantages could be gained by building a factory close to a river?

Lesson Plan

1. Focus In the 1800s, the Industrial Revolution began to change the way in which goods were produced and the way in which many Americans worked and lived. In this section, students examine the effects of new inventions and new sources of power in the early 1800s.

2. Instruct Ask students to imagine that they live in a rural area in 1820. A factory for spinning thread and weaving cloth has just been built in a nearby town. Divide the class into seven groups: wool growers, spinners of thread, people without jobs, landowners, capitalists, merchants, and town officials. Have each group discuss ways this change will affect their lives. Have a volunteer from each group present the group's view to the class.

3. Close To close the lesson, ask students to explain (1) how manufacturing moved from homes to factories and (2) how the Industrial Revolution reached the United States.

1

The Industrial Revolution

FIND OUT
- How did the early Industrial Revolution change people's lives?
- What inventions led to the Industrial Revolution?
- How did the Industrial Revolution reach the United States?

VOCABULARY spinning jenny, cotton gin, capitalist, factory system

Shortly before his death in 1790, Benjamin Franklin wrote to a friend:

66I wished it had been my destiny to have been born two or three centuries [later]. For invention and improvement are everywhere. The present progress is nothing less than astounding.**99**

Franklin died just before a new revolution swept the United States. Unlike the revolution against British rule, this one had no battles and no fixed dates. Instead, it was a long, slow process that completely changed the way goods were produced.

New Ways to Produce Goods

The revolution in the way goods were produced is known as the *Industrial Revolution.* Before the Industrial Revolution, most goods were produced by hand at home or in workshops. Most people were farmers and lived in rural areas. As the Industrial Revolution got underway, machines replaced hand tools. At the same time, new sources of power, such as steam and electricity, replaced human and animal power.

The Industrial Revolution generated widespread changes. The economy shifted

from farming to manufacturing. As a result, people moved from farms to cities.

New technology. The Industrial Revolution began in Britain in the mid-1700s. There, inventors developed new technologies that transformed the textile industry.

In 1764, James Hargreaves developed a machine he called the spinning jenny. With a **spinning jenny,** a worker could spin several threads at once—not just one thread as on a spinning wheel. Richard Arkwright took the process a step further. In 1769, he invented a machine that could hold 100 spindles of thread. Because the machine was too heavy to be operated by hand, it required water power to turn its wheels. As a result, it became known as the water frame.

Other inventions speeded up the process of weaving thread into cloth. In the 1780s, Edmund Cartwright built a loom powered by water. Using this power loom, a worker could produce 200 times more cloth in a day than was possible before.

In 1793, Eli Whitney, an American, gave a further boost to the textile industry. Whitney invented the **cotton gin,** a machine that speeded up the process of cleaning cotton fibers. (You will read more about effects of the cotton gin in Chapter 13.)

Birth of the factory. Machines like the water frame had to be set up near rivers. Water flowing rapidly downstream or over a waterfall turned a water wheel that produced the power to run the machines.

Our Common Heritage
One byproduct of the Industrial Revolution was a rise in immigration to the United States. Between 1815 and 1818, for example, more than 15,000 Irish immigrants came to the United States. Many were skilled weavers and artisans who found work in American mills and factories.

Critical Thinking
Comparing

Before the Industrial Revolution, most workers were self-employed. They set their own hours, worked in their own homes, and were paid by the number of items they produced. Tell students to imagine themselves as early nineteenth-century cloth weavers who have gone to work in a textile factory. Have them write two journal entries in which they compare their life as an independent worker with their life as a factory worker.

Connections With Technology
Background

Inventor Samuel Crompton used aspects of both Hargreaves's spinning jenny and Arkwright's water frame to develop the spinning mule in 1779. It increased the speed of cotton thread production.

A Changing Landscape *The Industrial Revolution changed the face of the nation. This painting shows an early factory set among the church spires and green fields of a New England town.* ***Daily Life*** *How do you think the factory affected the life of the townspeople?*

The new machines were expensive and had to be housed in large buildings. Most were owned by **capitalists,** people with capital, or money, to invest in business to make a profit. Early capitalists built spinning mills and hired hundreds of workers to run the machines.

The spinning mills led to a new system of production in Britain. Instead of spinning and weaving in their homes, people went to work in factories. The new **factory system** brought workers and machines together in one place to produce goods. In factories, everyone had to work a certain number of hours each day. Workers were paid daily or weekly wages.

A Secret Crosses the Atlantic

Britain tried to keep its inventions secret. It did not want rival nations to copy the new machines. To protect national interests, the British Parliament passed a law forbidding anyone to take plans of Arkwright's water frame out of the country. It also forbade factory workers to leave Britain.

Samuel Slater's memory. Samuel Slater soon showed that the law could not be enforced. Slater was a skillful mechanic in one of Arkwright's mills. When he heard that Americans were offering large rewards for plans of British factories, he decided to leave England.

In 1789, Slater boarded a ship bound for New York. He knew that British officials often searched the baggage of passengers sailing to the United States. To avoid getting caught, he memorized the design of the machines in Arkwright's mill. He even used a false name when he traveled.

In New York, Slater learned that Moses Brown, a Quaker merchant, wanted to build a spinning mill in Rhode Island. Slater wrote confidently to Brown:

Chapter 10 • **297**

 Lesson Planner

For a developed **Cooperative Learning** lesson plan, see the *Lesson Planner,* page 58.

Answer to Caption

Possible Answer: The factory provided work for townspeople and helped the town to grow, but it also may have made the town noisier, dirtier, and more crowded.

Historical Sidelight
Background

Some historians believe that slavery in the South might have died out if Eli Whitney had not invented the cotton gin. Before the gin, growing cotton was becoming unprofitable, and southerners were looking for new ways to make money. The gin resulted in increased cotton production and created a need (from the planters' viewpoint) for more slaves to work in the fields.

The cotton gin's success was so overwhelming that Whitney's company lacked the technological ability to keep pace with demand. Consequently, many imitations were manufactured and sold by patent violators. Disgusted with fighting constant legal battles over royalty payments, Whitney turned to the manufacture of firearms.

EXPLORING TECHNOLOGY

⑧ Wagons carry spun thread to weavers who use it to make cloth.

⑦ Spinning frames twist combed and drawn cotton strands into thread and wind them onto a bobbin.

⑥ Drawing machines pull the combed cotton fibers into ropelike strands.

⑤ Carding machines comb the raw cotton fiber.

④ The main shaft drives pulleys, which turn belts that drive the mill machinery.

① Wagons bring raw cotton to the mill to be spun into thread.

② Fast-moving water causes the water wheel to turn.

③ The turning water wheel powers the mill's main shaft.

Spinning Mill *The swift-moving streams of New England provided power for the nation's first factories. As shown here, rapidly moving water turned a water wheel that produced the power to run the machines.* **Local History** *Would your town or community have been a suitable place for a water-powered spinning mill? Why or why not?*

298 • Chapter 10

Answer to Exploring Technology

Answers will vary, depending upon local geography. The location would have to have a fast-moving water source to be a suitable location for such a mill.

 Transparencies

Cause and Effect Use the transparency, The Industrial Revolution in the United States, on page F-17 of *American History Transparencies*. The chart highlights some of the causes that led to the Industrial Revolution in the United States and three subsequent effects of this industrialization upon American society. Teaching suggestions can be found on page F-4. (Enrichment/Average)

Exploring Technology Use the transparency Spinning Mill on page H-31 of *American History Transparencies*. The diagram shows how an early factory used water power to turn raw cotton into thread. Teaching suggestions can be found on page H-6. (Enrichment/Average)

 Student Study Guide

Section 1 Study Guide Have students use the Section 1 Study Guide on page 88 of the *Student Study Guide* to review and reinforce the content of this section. (Reteaching/Average)

Cooperative Learning
Activity

Divide students into groups. Have each group select a product or process discussed in this lesson, such as the spinning jenny, water frame, cotton gin, factory system, or interchangeable parts. Tell students that they will be writing an "autobiography" of the product or process that they have chosen. In its "autobiography," the invention should describe how and when it was created, by whom, how it contributed to the Industrial Revolution, and the details of its later life. In discussing its later life, the invention can indicate whether it is still used in industry today. If it is not, groups might do research and briefly mention the invention or process that has replaced it. Groups may be asked to illustrate their presentations with a "self-portrait" of the invention by the author of the "autobiography."

Linking Past and Present
Activity

The computer explosion of the 1970s and 1980s has been referred to as a high-tech revolution. Challenge students to research and then lead a class discussion on the similarities and differences between the Industrial and high-tech revolutions. Have them conclude with a discussion of this question: Which had a greater impact on everyday life?

"If I do not make as good yarn as they do in England, I will have nothing for my services, but will throw the whole of what I have attempted over the bridge."

Brown replied at once: "If thou canst do what thou sayest, I invite thee to come to Rhode Island."

The first American mill. By December 1790, Slater and Brown were ready to start production in their spinning mill. On a bitter cold morning, Slater chopped ice off the water wheel. As Brown looked on, the machinery cranked into motion. Soon the 2 water frames and 72 spindles were turning out cotton thread.

In 1793, the two men built an improved mill. Hannah Slater, wife of Samuel, discovered how to make thread stronger so that it would not snap on the spindles. Before long, other American manufacturers began to build mills using Slater's ideas.

SECTION 1 REVIEW

1. **Identify:** (a) Industrial Revolution, (b) Samuel Slater, (c) Moses Brown.
2. **Define:** (a) spinning jenny, (b) cotton gin, (c) capitalist, (d) factory system.
3. What are four ways in which the Industrial Revolution changed daily life?
4. (a) Name two inventions of the Industrial Revolution. (b) How did each change the way goods were produced?
5. How did Samuel Slater bring Arkwright's ideas to the United States?
6. **CRITICAL THINKING Linking Past and Present** What present-day inventions do you think would astonish Benjamin Franklin most?

ACTIVITY Writing to Learn
Write an article for a Rhode Island newspaper about the opening of the mill built by Slater and Brown.

2
From Workshops to Factories

FIND OUT
- How did the War of 1812 help American manufacturers?
- How was Lowell a model community?
- What were working conditions like in early factories?
- What were the advantages and disadvantages of city life in the early 1800s?

VOCABULARY interchangeable parts

The Constitution gave Congress the authority "to promote science and useful arts." To achieve that goal, Congress passed the Patent Act in 1790. The new law protected the rights of inventors.

Mary Kies of Connecticut was the first woman to take out a patent. In 1809, she patented a new weaving process for straw hats. Kies's invention gave a major boost to the New England hat industry.

Mary Kies was just one of many inventors working in the United States in the early 1800s. Inventors and other bold thinkers transformed American manufacturing.

The Lowell Experiment

Before the Revolution, colonists imported most manufactured goods from Britain. After independence, Americans were eager to build their own industries. For many years, however, progress was slow.

Britain's blockade of the United States during the War of 1812 provided a boost to American industries. Cut off from foreign

ACTIVITY

Guided Instruction Before students write their newspaper articles, you might suggest that they ask *Who, What, Where, When, Why,* and *How* questions. Remind students that they will be reporting on something that many of their readers have never seen. Consequently, their descriptions of the mill and its components must be precise and vivid. Suggest that students draw illustrations to accompany their articles. Encourage students to share their finished articles in small groups or with the entire class.

Section 2
pp. 299–303

Bell Ringer

Have students imagine that they could go to work—right now—and make a living in a factory. Ask: What might interest you in that opportunity? Can you see any disadvantages?

Lesson Plan

1. **Focus** Francis Lowell and his partners built a factory to spin thread and weave cloth in one building. In this section, students learn about Lowell, about Eli Whitney's invention of interchangeable parts, and about how the growth of factories led to the growth of cities.

Answers to Section 1 Review

1. (a) Industrial Revolution, p. 296, (b) Samuel Slater, p. 297, (c) Moses Brown, p. 297
2. (a) spinning jenny, p. 296, (b) cotton gin, p. 296, (c) capitalist, p. 297, (d) factory system, p. 297
3. Most goods were produced in factories instead of at home; machines replaced hand tools; steam and electricity replaced human and animal power; many people became factory workers rather than farmers.
4. (a) spinning jenny, water frame, power loom, cotton gin, (b) The spinning jenny made it possible to spin several threads at once; the water frame held 100 spindles of thread; the power loom enabled a worker to produce 200 times more cloth in a day than on a hand loom; the cotton gin speeded up the process of cleaning cotton fibers.
5. Samuel Slater, a British mechanic, memorized the design of Arkwright's mill before sailing for New York.
6. Possible Answers: airplanes, computers, movies, nuclear reactors, satellites

2. Instruct Write the following headings across the top of the chalkboard: Francis Lowell Forms the Boston Associates; Eli Whitney Invents Interchangeable Parts; and Cities Grow. Have students brainstorm a list of effects that each of these developments had. Ask students to list these effects in chronological order under the proper heading.

3. Close To close the lesson, have students turn the headings of the subsections into questions and then answer them.

 Lesson Planner

For a developed **Cooperative Learning** lesson plan, see the *Lesson Planner*, page 59.

 Interdisciplinary Explorations

Mill Life in the 1840s Have students refer to the unit Mill Life in the 1840s: Roots of American Industry in the *Prentice Hall Interdisciplinary Exploration Series* to learn more about the rise of mill towns and about what it was like to live and work in a mill town. (Enrichment/Challenging)

Answer to Caption

It allowed them to bring workers and machines together under one roof, saving time and money.

Textile Workers *In the 1820s, the town of Lowell, Massachusetts, became a leading center of the American textile industry. Many of the machines in the Lowell mills were operated by women, as shown above.* **Economics** *How did the factory system benefit capitalists?*

suppliers, Americans had to produce more goods themselves.

Francis Cabot Lowell. As in Britain, early advances occurred in the textile industry. A Boston merchant, Francis Cabot Lowell, had toured British textile mills. There, he saw how one factory spun thread while another wove it into cloth. Lowell had a better idea. Why not combine spinning and weaving under one roof?

To finance his project, Lowell joined with several partners to form the **Boston Associates** in 1813. They built a textile mill in Waltham, Massachusetts. The factory had all the machines needed to turn raw cotton into finished cloth. The machines were powered by water from the nearby Charles River.

A model community. Lowell died in 1817, but the Boston Associates continued. In time, they took on a more ambitious project. They built an entire factory town on the Merrimack River. They named the new town after Francis Lowell.

In 1821, Lowell, Massachusetts, was a village of five farm families. By 1836, it boasted more than 10,000 people along

300 • Chapter 10

with factories, banks, schools, stores, a library, and a church. Visitors flocked to this showplace of American industry. One left this description:

❝There are huge factories, five, six or seven stories high, each capped with a little white belfry...which stands out sharply against the dark hills on the horizon. There are small wooden houses, painted white, with green blinds, very neat, very snug, very nicely carpeted, and with a few small trees around them.❞

"Lowell girls." The Boston Associates hired young women from nearby farms to work in the mills. Usually, the "Lowell girls," as they were called, worked for a few years in the mills. Then they returned home to marry. Most sent their wages home to their families. Some saved part of their wages to help set up their own homes.

At first, parents hesitated to let their daughters work in the mills. To reassure parents, the Boston Associates built boarding houses for their workers. They hired housemothers to manage the houses. The company also built a church and made rules to protect the young women.

At Work in the Mills

In Lowell and elsewhere, mill owners mostly hired women and children. They did this because they could pay women and

History and You
It is hard to go to school and work at the same time. Massachusetts passed a law in 1837 prohibiting children from being employed more than nine months a year so that they could attend school for at least three months. Have you ever held a job during the school year? What type of work did you do and for how many hours each day?

Historical Sidelight
Background

Under the Patent Act of 1790, the Secretary of State, the Secretary of War, and the Attorney General personally examined all patent applications. (Only three patents were issued in 1790.) This time-consuming personal examination was discontinued in 1793. The number of patents granted each year then rose steadily—in 1825, 304 were issued.

Connections With Economics
Background

Married women who worked were expected to turn their pay over to their husbands, who could spend it as they wished. This injustice was one of many against which the women's movement fought later in the century.

In 1821, employees of the Boston Manufacturing Company (a Boston Associates mill) struck when their wages were cut. This was

the first strike by female workers against an American company. By the 1830s and 1840s, conditions had worsened in Lowell. In 1844, a group of Lowell workers, led by Sarah Bagley, organized the Lowell Female Labor Reform Association. The union could not attract enough workers, however, and it disbanded within two years.

children half of what they would have had to pay men.

Child labor. Children as young as 7 years of age worked in the mills. Because they were quick and small, they could squeeze around large machines to change spindles. Such children were called "doffers." They doffed, or took off, full spindles of thread and replaced them with empty ones. "I can see myself now," recalled a woman who had worked in a mill as a child, "carrying in front of me a [spindle] bigger than I was."

For many years, Americans have looked on child labor as cruel. Yet in the 1800s, farm boys and girls also worked long hours. Most people did not see much difference between children working in a factory or on a farm. Often, a child's wages were needed to help support the family.

Long hours. Working hours in the mills were long—12 hours a day, 6 days a week. True, farmers also put in long hours. But farmers worked shorter hours in winter. Mill workers, by contrast, worked the same hours all year round.

At first, conditions in American mills were better than in most European factories at the time. As industries grew, however, competition increased. As a result, employers took less interest in the welfare of their workers. Conditions worsened and wages fell.

Eli Whitney

Manufacturers benefited from the pioneering work of Eli Whitney. In the early 1800s, skilled workers made goods by hand. A gunsmith, for example, spent days making the stock, barrel, and trigger for a musket. Each musket differed a bit from the next because the parts were handmade. If a part broke, a gunsmith had to fashion a new part to fit that gun.

Whitney wanted to speed up the making of guns by having machines manufacture each part. Machine-made parts would all be

---

CAUSES

- British ideas of a spinning mill and power loom reach the United States
- Eli Whitney invents the cotton gin
- War of 1812 prompts Americans to make their own goods
- Eli Whitney introduces the idea of interchangeable parts

THE INDUSTRIAL REVOLUTION IN THE UNITED STATES

EFFECTS

- Factory system spreads
- Young women and children from nearby farms work in mills
- Growing cities face problems of fire, sewage, garbage, and disease

CHART SKILLS *The Industrial Revolution was a period of great change.* ● *What inventions and ideas helped to produce the Industrial Revolution? Do you think the effects of the Industrial Revolution were positive or negative? Explain.*

---

alike. Stocks would be the same size and shape. Barrels would be the same length. Whitney's idea of **interchangeable parts** would save time and money.

Because the government bought many guns, Whitney took his idea to Washington. At first, officials laughed at his plan. Whitney paid them no attention. Carefully, he sorted parts for 10 muskets into separate piles. He then asked an official to choose one part from each pile. In minutes, the first musket was assembled. Whitney repeated the process until 10 muskets were complete.

Chapter 10 • **301**

Shopping *In the early 1800s, most Americans depended on door-to-door peddlers for ready-made goods. In the growing cities, however, people could do their shopping in stores, like the one shown here.* **Daily Life** *What advantages can you see in each form of shopping?*

Onlookers, reported one observer, responded with "sheer amaze-nent."

The idea of interchangeable parts spread rapidly. Inventors designed machines to produce parts for locks, knives, and many other goods. With such machines, small workshops grew into factories.

Growing Cities

As factories grew, so did the towns and cities where they were located. By today's standards, these cities were small. A person could walk from one end of any American city to the other end in 30 minutes.

Hazards. Cities had many problems. Dirt and gravel streets turned into mudholes when it rained. Cities had no sewers, and people threw garbage into the streets. An English visitor to New York reported:

66 The streets are filthy, and the stranger is not a little surprised to meet the hogs walking about in them, for the purpose of devouring the vegetables and trash thrown into the gutter. 99

In these dirty, crowded conditions, disease spread easily. Yellow fever and cholera (KAHL er uh) epidemics raged through cities, killing hundreds.

Fire posed another threat. If a sooty chimney caught fire, the flames quickly spread from one wooden house to the next. Many cities had volunteer fire companies. Often, rival companies competed to get to a blaze first. Sometimes, companies fought each other instead of the fire!

Attractions. Cities had attractions, too. Circuses, racetracks, plays, and museums created an air of excitement. In New York, P. T. Barnum made a fortune exhibiting rare animals at his American Museum.

Cities also had fine stores that sold the latest fashions. Some offered modern "ready-to-wear" clothing. A New York store boasted that "gentlemen can rely upon being as well fitted from the shelves as if their measures were taken." Women still sewed most of their own clothes, but they enjoyed visiting china shops, "fancy-goods" stores, and shoe stores.

SECTION 2 REVIEW

1. **Identify:** (a) Francis Cabot Lowell, (b) Boston Associates, (c) Eli Whitney.
2. **Define:** interchangeable parts.
3. How did the War of 1812 help the growth of American industry?
4. How did the Boston Associates make the Lowell mills attractive to workers?
5. Why did mill owners hire women and children?
6. **CRITICAL THINKING Understanding Causes and Effects** How did industrial development help to bring about social change in the United States in the 1800s?

ACTIVITY Writing to Learn

Write a help-wanted ad to attract young women to work at the Lowell mills.

CRITICAL THINKING SKILLS
Using a Concept Map

A concept map is a way to organize ideas visually. Using a concept map is similar to taking notes. It helps you to keep track of the main ideas and supporting details as you read.

A concept map is made up of connected circles. In the center is the general topic. The general topic is often the same as the heading or title. The main ideas and supporting details are arranged around the general topic. Lines connect main ideas with their supporting details.

Study the concept map below. It shows the ideas in the subsection Growing Cities, on page 302.

1. **Identify the general topic.** (a) What is the general topic of the subsection? (b) How do you know that it is the general topic?

2. **Identify the main ideas.** The main ideas are connected with lines to the general topic. (a) How many main ideas are there in the subsection? (b) What are the main ideas of the subsection?

3. **Find the supporting details.** Two of the main ideas have one or more supporting details. (a) What are the supporting details for the main idea "Hazards"? (b) How do you know that these are supporting details? (c) What supporting details are connected to the main idea "Attractions"?

4. **Use the concept map to see how events and ideas are related.** (a) Why were people attracted to city life? (b) What were the hazards of city life?

ACTIVITY

Locate a brief newspaper or magazine article about the economy or city life today. Circle the main idea or ideas in the article. Draw a square box around the supporting details. Then make a concept map using the information you have highlighted in the article.

Chapter Resources

Skill Application For additional practice, duplicate and distribute the worksheet, Using a Concept Map, from Unit 3, page 28, of the *Chapter Resources* binder. (Reteaching/Average)

Answers to Skill Lesson

1. (a) Growing Cities, (b) It is located in the center of the map.
2. (a) two, (b) Hazards; Attractions
3. (a) disease, fire, filthy streets, no sewers, garbage, (b) They are connected to the main idea "Hazards." (c) stores selling the latest goods; circuses, racetracks, plays, museums
4. (a) Cities had stores selling the latest goods, and amusements such as circuses, racetracks, plays, and museums. (b) Hazards included disease, fire, filthy streets, no sewers, and garbage.

ACTIVITY

Guided Instruction Before students begin the construction of their concept maps using the information that they have highlighted in the article, have them review the design and features of the sample map. When evaluating, be certain students have included all supporting details required.

Students Acquiring English
Activity

Although concept maps are visual representations, they do require students to isolate and summarize information. SAE students, therefore, might benefit by being paired with more advanced students to work on the Skill Lesson and its Activity. Partners might help SAE students with complex ideas, unfamiliar or specialized vocabulary, and specific supporting references.

As students look at the map on page 306, have them imagine taking a 500-mile trip by wagon over unpaved roads and by raft down rivers. Then allow students to freewrite for three minutes, jotting down their thoughts about such a trip.

Lesson Plan

1. Focus The West attracted thousands of new settlers in the early 1800s. Settlers' dreams of new lands and new beginnings led to the development of better ways to travel and to transport goods. In this section, students learn about turnpikes and other road improvements, the development of the steamboat, and the building of canals.

2. Instruct Have students work in three groups—one group representing a manufacturer of steamboats, another group representing a road-building company, the third group representing a canal-digging company. Tell the class that you are the governor of an eastern state in the year 1820 and that you are accepting bids on a transportation project. You wish to make it easier for settlers to establish farms in the western part of your state and to ship their produce back east. It is up to each group to develop a plan that will convince you to hire them to complete the project. Tell them to be sure to include the benefits and superiority of their method of transportation.

3

Americans on the Move

FIND OUT

■ How did settlers travel west?

■ What steps did Americans take to improve roads?

■ How did steamboats and canals change transportation?

VOCABULARY turnpike, corduroy road, canal

An Irish visitor described a stagecoach trip through Maryland:

> 66 The driver frequently had to call to the passengers in the stage, to lean out of the carriage first at one side, then at the other, to prevent it from oversetting in the deep ruts with which the road abounds: 'Now gentlemen, to the right,'. . . 'Now gentlemen, to the left,' and so on. 99

In the 1790s, travel was as difficult as it had been in colonial times. Most roads were mud tracks. River travel could be difficult, too, when boats had to push upstream against the current. As the young nation grew, Americans saw the need to improve transportation.

GEOGRAPHY AND HISTORY
Heading West

In the early 1800s, thousands of settlers headed west, to the land between the Appalachians and the Mississippi. "Old America seems to be breaking up and moving westward," noted a visitor. By 1820, so many people had moved west that the population in some of the original 13 states had actually declined.

Western routes. Settlers took a number of routes west. One well-traveled path was the Great Wagon Road across Pennsylvania. Colonists had pioneered it years before. (See page 105.) Some settlers continued south and west along the trail opened by Daniel Boone before the Revolution. Called the Wilderness Road, it led through the Cumberland Gap into Kentucky.

Other settlers pushed west to Pittsburgh. There, they loaded their animals and wagons onto flatboats and journeyed down the Ohio River into Indiana, Kentucky, and Illinois. Flatboats were well suited to the shallow waters of the Ohio. Even with heavy loads, these raftlike barges rode high in the water.

Pioneers from Georgia and South Carolina followed other trails west. Enslaved African Americans helped to carve plantations in the rich, fertile soil of Alabama and Mississippi.

New Englanders, "Yorkers," and Pennsylvanians pushed into the Northwest Territory. Some traveled west from Albany, New York, along the Mohawk River and across the Appalachians. Some settlers then followed Indian trails around Lake Erie. Others sailed across the lake into Ohio.

New states. With the flood of settlers, there were enough people in some western lands to apply for statehood. Between 1792 and 1819, eight states joined the Union: Kentucky (1792), Tennessee (1796), Ohio (1803), Louisiana (1812), Indiana (1816), Mississippi (1817), Illinois (1818), and Alabama (1819).

Better Roads

Settlers faced a rough journey. Many roads were narrow trails that were barely wide enough for a single wagon. One pioneer wrote of "rotten banks down which horses plunged" and streams that "almost drowned them." The nation badly needed better roads.

Connections With Technology
Background

Early roads were so bad that stagecoach drivers had to tell the passengers to lean to the left or to the right to keep from tipping over on bad stretches. Stagecoaches tried to keep to schedules, stopping every 20 miles for a change of horses and covering up to 60 miles a day. Some early maps showed where blacksmiths were located. Since there was no way to make reservations at inns, travelers often had to share rooms with several strangers.

One passenger, remarking on the ride, complained about "the noise of the wheels, the tremble of a coach, . . . the jerking of the bad roads," and "the most detestable stagecoach that ever a Christian built to dislocate the joints of his fellow man."

Connections With Mathematics
Activity

Have students connect the information given about new states with what they have already learned. Ask: By 1819, how many states were part of the Union? (22)

ART GALLERY: OUR COMMON HERITAGE

JOAN LANDIS BAHM
My Ancestors Coming to America, 1990

In this quilt, Joan Landis Bahm records the journeys of her ancestors from Switzerland to the United States in the 1700s and 1800s. The symbols that border the quilt—steamships, canal barges and mules, covered wagons—indicate the many types of transportation that the settlers used in their new land. **Geography** *Locate the Erie Canal on the quilt. What form of transportation does Bahm show there?*

Turnpikes and covered bridges. Probably the best road in the United States was the ***Lancaster Turnpike.*** It was built in the 1790s by a private company. The road linked Philadelphia and Lancaster, Pennsyl- vania. Because the road was set on a bed of gravel, water drained off quickly. It was topped with smooth, flat stones.

Private companies built other gravel and stone roads. To pay for these roads, the

3. Close To close the lesson, have the class decide on the most important fact or idea to re- member from each subsection.

 Lesson Planner

For a developed **Cooperative Learning** lesson plan, see the *Lesson Planner,* page 60.

 Art Gallery Posters

My Ancestors Coming to Ameri- ca, by Joan Landis Bahm, ap- pears in poster form in the *Art Gallery: Our Common Heritage Posters.* Lesson Suggestions for the poster are available in the Teacher's Guide.

Answer to Art Gallery: Our Common Heritage

a mule-pulled canal boat or barge

 CD-ROM

History Makers Access the bi- ography of Daniel Boone on the American Heritage® *History of the United States* CD-ROM. (Enrich- ment/Average)

Learning Styles
Auditory Learners

After students have read and discussed pages 305–306, have them apply the infor- mation by creating a conversation between a wagon driver and a pike keeper. The wagon driver might talk about the journey in general, and the convenience of the Lancaster Turn- pike in particular; the pike keeper might pass along local news.

Connections With Art
Background

The quilt by Joan Landis Bahm is an example of an appliquéd quilt, in which cutout designs (in this case, ships, people, houses, and so on) are sewn onto a large piece of cloth. Stu- dents may be more familiar with pieced quilts, in which the top layer consists of pieces of cloth that are stitched together to make a de- sign. Both kinds of quilts consist of two layers of cloth that are stitched to an interlining.

305

Answers to Map Study

1. Maryland, Virginia, Pennsylvania, Ohio, Indiana, Illinois 2. Mohawk Turnpike 3. Possible Answer: As thousands of settlers headed west, there was an increased demand for new roads.

Customized Reader

Primary Source For an account of the experiences of frontier doctors, order article IIIB-5, Frontier Doctors, from the *American History Customized Reader*. In this article, Marilyn Van Voorhis Wendler describes the training of and the work performed by frontier doctors. (Enrichment/Challenging)

Primary Source For a frontier preacher's narrative of his own religious awakening, order article IIIB-8, A Frontier Conversion, from the *American History Customized Reader*. (Enrichment/Challenging)

Videotapes/ Videodiscs

United States History Video Collection Use the video segment "The Move West" from Volume 6, *Expansionism*, to enhance students' understanding of how settlers traveled west. Approx. running time 4:00 min. (Enrichment/Average) Vol. 6, Ch. 22

| Chapter 22 | Play |

companies collected tolls. At various points along the road, a pike, or pole, blocked the road. After a wagon driver paid a toll, the pike keeper turned the pole aside. These toll roads became known as **turnpikes.**

In swampy areas, roads were made of logs. These roads were called **corduroy roads** because the lines of logs looked like corduroy cloth. Corduroy roads kept wagons from sinking into the mud, but they made for a bumpy ride.

Bridges carried travelers across streams and rivers. Stone bridges were costly to build, but wooden ones rotted quickly. A clever Massachusetts carpenter designed a wooden bridge with a roof to protect it from the weather. Covered bridges lasted much longer than open ones.

The National Road. In 1806, Congress approved spending for the ***National Road.*** It was to run from Cumberland, Maryland, to Wheeling, in western Virginia. Work began in 1811 and was completed in 1818. Later, the road was extended across Ohio and Indiana into Illinois.

Increased traffic. Better roads helped not only travelers but also freight haulers. Heavy wagons pulled by eight or ten hors-

MAP STUDY

In the early 1800s, settlers took new roads to the West. Some were turnpikes built by private companies. Others were built by states or the national government.
1. Through which states did the National Road run?
2. Which road connected Albany and Buffalo?
3. **Synthesizing Information** Why were so many new roads built in the early 1800s?

Early Roads West

— Main roads

0   100   200 Miles
0   100   200 Kilometers

Connections With Local History
Activity

The early turnpikes often were privately financed by capitalists. The development of steam railroads caused many of them to fail financially by 1850. Ask students if any turnpikes exist in their local area. If so, have them find the answers to these questions: Who operates the turnpike(s)? Who provides financing for maintenance and improvements? How is the revenue from tolls used?

Historical Sidelight
Background

George Washington conceived the building of a National Road to the West. His experience as a surveyor in western Virginia may have inspired this vision. One advantage of the National Road was that it could withstand the weight of wagons loaded with as many as 20 passengers. Still, there were hazards. In Indiana, for example, it was legal to leave stumps up to 15 inches high on public roads, including the National Road.

es rumbled along the roads. Small farm wagons drawn by one or two horses also plodded along. All wagons moved aside when stagecoaches sped recklessly past.

From October to December, roads were filled with animals being driven to market. Herders, called drovers, used dogs to keep hogs, cattle, sheep, and even turkeys moving along. ■

Steam Transport

When possible, travelers and freight wagons used river transportation. Floating downstream on a flatboat was faster, cheaper, and more comfortable than bumping along rutted roads.

River travel had its problems, too. Moving upstream was difficult. To travel upstream, people used paddles or long poles to push boats against the current. Sometimes, they hauled boats from the shore with ropes. Both methods were slow. A boat could travel downstream from Pittsburgh to New Orleans in six weeks. The return trip upstream took at least 17 weeks!

Fitch and Fulton. Progress in river travel came from a new invention—the steam engine. In 1787, John Fitch showed members of the Constitutional Convention how a steam engine could propel a boat. Soon after, Fitch opened a ferry service on the Delaware River. Few people used his ferry, however, and Fitch went out of business.

Robert Fulton succeeded where Fitch had failed. Fulton had probably seen Fitch's steamboat in Philadelphia. In 1807, Fulton launched his own steamboat, the *Clermont,* on the Hudson River. On its first run, the *Clermont* carried passengers from New York City to Albany and back. The 300-mile (480-km) round trip took just 62 hours—a record at the time. Within three months, Fulton was making a profit on this run.

The age of steamboats. Fulton's success ushered in the age of steamboats. Soon, steamboats were ferrying passengers up and down the Atlantic coast. More important, they revolutionized travel in the West. Besides carrying people, steamboats on the Mississippi, Ohio, and Missouri rivers gave farmers and merchants a cheap means of moving goods.

Because western rivers were shallow, Henry Shreve designed a flat-bottomed steamboat. It could carry heavy loads without getting stuck on sandbars.

"Floating palaces." By the 1850s, some western steamboats had become "floating palaces." Wealthy passengers strolled on vessels that had three decks and a saloon for eating. Along the walls of the saloon were double-decker berths, where men slept. Women had a separate "ladies' parlor." They entered the saloon only for meals. The poor traveled in less comfort on boats with leaky roofs. They slept on pillows stuffed with corn husks.

Steamboat travel could be dangerous. Sparks from smokestacks could kindle fires. Steamboats used high-pressure boilers to make steam. As steamboat captains raced each other along the river, boilers sometimes exploded. Between 1811 and 1851, 44 steamboats collided, 166 burned, and more than 200 exploded.

The Canal Boom

Steamboats and better roads brought some improvements. But they did not help western farmers get their goods directly to markets in the East. To meet this need, Americans built canals. A **canal** is a channel dug by people, then filled with water to allow boats to cross a stretch of land.

The first canals were only a few miles long. Often, they were dug to get around waterfalls. Others linked a river to a nearby lake. By the early 1800s, Americans were building longer canals.

"Little short of madness." Some New Yorkers had a bold idea. They wanted to build a canal linking the Great Lakes with

 Transparencies

Fine Art Use the transparency, Fur Traders Descending the Missouri, on page D-35 of *American History Transparencies.* The painting is George Caleb Bingham's depiction of a typical frontier scene in St. Louis. Teaching suggestions can be found on page D-8. (Enrichment/Average)

Historical Outline Map Book

Historical Outline Maps Use the map, The United States in 1824, on page 34 of the *American History Historical Outline Map Book.* Lesson ideas for this map can be found on page T11. (Reteaching/Average)

 Voices of Freedom

Primary Source You might assign selection 12-2, Mark Twain on the Lure of Steamboats, on page 85 of *Voices of Freedom.* In this selection, Twain describes the fascination that steamboats held for him and his hometown neighbors. (Enrichment/Average)

Connections With Science
Background

Among the inventions that fascinated Benjamin Franklin was John Fitch's steamboat. Franklin, however, was too ill in 1787 to join the crowds along the Delaware River to watch Fitch stoke his ship's boiler. Steam poured from the boiler into the engine's pistons. Then, the machinery turned oars on each side of the boat, moving it forward.

In 1786, a 22-year-old artist named Robert Fulton had sailed for England. He intended to study portrait and landscape painting with another American, Benjamin West. While there, however, he met Scottish engineer James Watt, the inventor of the steam engine. This encounter changed his life.

Historical Outline Map Book

Historical Outline Maps Use the map, Transportation to the West, on page 33 of the *American History Historical Outline Map Book*. Lesson ideas for this map can be found on page T11. (Reteaching/Average)

Chapter Resources

Geography in History Duplicate and distribute the worksheet, Building a Waterway to the West, from Unit 3, pages 31–32, of the *Chapter Resources* binder. The worksheet encourages students to explore the importance of the Erie Canal and the canals that followed. (Enrichment/Average)

Transparencies

Interdisciplinary Connections Use the transparency Erie Canal on page B-51 of *American History Transparencies*. Teaching suggestions can be found on page B-12. (Enrichment/Average)

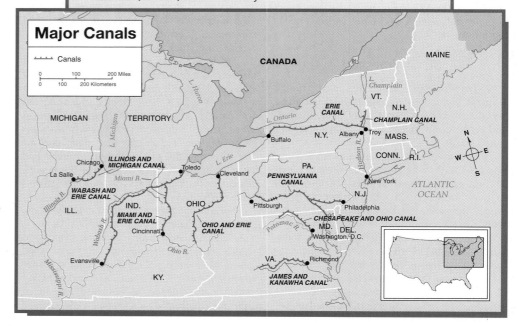

MAP STUDY

The success of the Erie Canal, completed in 1825, set off an age of canal building.
1. *About how long was the Erie Canal?*
2. *What two bodies of water were linked by the Ohio and Erie Canal?*
3. **Synthesizing Information** *Use the map to describe an all-water route from Evansville, Indiana, to New York City.*

the Mohawk and Hudson rivers. The canal would let western farmers ship their goods to the port of New York. It would also bring business to towns along the route.

To many people, such a canal seemed farfetched. When President Jefferson heard about it, he exclaimed:

❝Why, sir, you talk of making a canal 350 miles through the wilderness—it is little short of madness to think of it at this day!❞

Digging the waterway. Governor De Witt Clinton of New York disagreed. He convinced state lawmakers to provide money for the project.

Work on the ***Erie Canal*** began in 1817. At first, workers dug the waterway by hand. To speed up progress, inventors developed new equipment. One machine, a stump-puller, could pull out nearly 40 tree stumps a day. In two places, the canal had to cross over rivers. Workers built stone bridges to carry the canal over the rivers.

By 1825, the immense job was finished. On opening day, a cannon fired a volley in Buffalo, New York. When the sound got to the next town along the route, it, too, fired a cannon. Town after town fired their cannons—all the way to New York City. The thunderous salute took 80 minutes to complete.

308 • Chapter 10

Historical Sidelight
Background

During his long and varied public career, De Witt Clinton championed many unpopular causes. He fought for free public education and against slavery. He worked to improve conditions for the poor and called for an end to the practice of jailing debtors. Support for the Erie Canal, however, was Clinton's biggest battle. The potential of such a canal fascinated him; and when he became governor of New York in 1817, he devoted himself to making the canal a reality.

Eight years later, his dream came true. As he was towed through New York harbor aboard the canal boat *Seneca Chief,* Clinton poured a small keg of fresh Lake Erie water into the salty Atlantic Ocean. At this "wedding of the waters," he declared, "may the God of the heavens and the earth smile . . . on this work and [make it serve] the best interests of the human race."

CONNECTIONS

ARTS | SCIENCES | GEOGRAPHY | WORLD | ECONOMICS | CIVICS

Along the Erie Canal

"Low Bridge!" rang out the cry. What canal boat passenger would dare ignore the warning? A low bridge could bring a mighty crack in the head. Unheeding passengers might even be swept overboard.

"Low bridge, everybody down" begins the refrain of just one of the many songs that celebrate life along the Erie Canal. Each verse reveals more about the work of the mule drivers on the canal. Plodding slowly along the tow path, these "canal boys" led the animals that pulled the canal boats and barges. Like laborers everywhere, they eased the monotony of their work with songs about their jobs.

> ❝I've got a mule and her name
> is Sal,
> Fifteen miles on the Erie Canal.
> We've hauled some barges in
> our day
> Filled with lumber, coal, and hay,
> And we know every inch of
> the way
> From Albany to Buffalo. ❞

Erie Canal

Refrain:

> ❝Low bridge, everybody down!
> Low bridge! We're a-coming to
> a town.
> You'll always know your
> neighbor,
> You'll always know your pal
> If you've ever navigated on the
> Erie Canal. ❞

There are many versions of "The Erie Canal." Although they began along the canal, they soon passed by word of mouth far beyond its banks. In time, many were written down. Today, we treasure folk songs such as "The Erie Canal" for the glimpses they give us of the past.

Sheet music

LOW BRIDGE EVERYBODY DOWN
(OR FIFTEEN YEARS ON THE ERIE CANAL)

HAVILAND

THOS. S. ALLEN

■ What can you learn about the Erie Canal from the song?

ACTIVITY Based on the song, create a comic strip in which you show events that might happen during a canal boy's 15-mile stretch along the Erie Canal.

Chapter 10 • **309**

Interdisciplinary CONNECTIONS

For worksheets establishing connections between the Chapter 10 main idea, The Erie Canal, and five other disciplines, see the *Interdisciplinary Connections* booklet. (Enrichment)

- ■ **Sciences** Packet Boats, page 56 (Challenging)
- ■ **Geography** Construction Obstructions, page 57 (Easy)
- ■ **World** The Canals of Britain, page 58 (Average)
- ■ **Economics** Canal Fever, page 59 (Average)
- ■ **Civics** De Witt Clinton and the Canal, page 60 (Average)

Answer to Connections

Mules pulled the barges from Albany to Buffalo. The cargo included lumber, coal, and hay. To avoid injuries, mule drivers warned passengers as the barge approached low bridges.

ACTIVITY

Guided Instruction Provide sample comic strips for students to examine. Suggest that they list characters, including the mule(s), that will be featured and the personality traits of each. Each panel should show an event, and the strip should follow a logical sequence. Have students share their works with the class.

Team-Teaching Suggestion
Science

You might work with a science teacher to present a lesson about the history of and principles involved in the construction of canals. Include a discussion of barge canals for inland navigation and ship canals for use by seagoing vessels. If possible, work with students to create a working model of a canal lock.

Team-Teaching Suggestion
Music

You might work with a music teacher to present a lesson about folk music that developed during the Industrial Revolution. Include songs about the sea and inland waterways, as well as those associated with mill work and other industries. Discuss how the rhythmic patterns in work songs enhanced teamwork by establishing a beat on which regularly recurring tasks were performed by the work group.

309

Section 3 Study Guide Have students use the Section 3 Study Guide on page 90 of the *Student Study Guide* to review and reinforce the content of this section. (Reteaching/Average)

ACTIVITY

Guided Instruction As students consider their newspaper reports, you might provide sample newspaper accounts of historic events and gala festivities. Discuss the techniques and style used in reporting such events in newspapers and magazines, as well as in TV accounts. Suggest that students include not only comments by public figures of the time but also the thoughts of average Americans (both native New Yorkers and tourists). Before revising, students could exchange papers with a partner and offer each other constructive criticism. Compile an Erie Canal Retrospective from the individual accounts.

Section 4
pp. 310–314

 Bell Ringer

Have the students discuss the term *national economy*. Ask: What do you think this term means? What have you read or heard about the national economy today?

An instant success. The Erie Canal was an instant success. In a single day, more than 50 canal boats might be seen moving along its length. Standing on a bridge above the canal, one eyewitness described the scene:

&6It is an impressive sight to gaze up and down the canal. In either direction, as far as the eye can see, long lines of boats can be observed. By night, their flickering head lamps give the impression of swarms of fireflies.99

The Erie Canal brought many benefits. It reduced travel time and lowered the cost of shipping goods. Goods sent from Buffalo to New York by canal now took less than 20 days. The canal also helped to make New York City a center of commerce.

The success of the Erie Canal led other states to build canals. These canals created vital economic links between western farms and eastern cities.

SECTION 3 REVIEW

1. **Locate:** (a) National Road, (b) Erie Canal.
2. **Identify:** (a) Lancaster Turnpike, (b) Robert Fulton, (c) *Clermont,* (d) Henry Shreve, (e) De Witt Clinton.
3. **Define:** (a) turnpike, (b) corduroy road, (c) canal.
4. What different means of transportation did settlers use to move west?
5. (a) How did road travel improve in the early 1800s? (b) How did river travel change?
6. **CRITICAL THINKING Understanding Causes and Effects** (a) Describe two immediate effects of the Erie Canal. (b) Describe two long-range effects.

ACTIVITY **Writing to Learn**

Write a newspaper report about opening day on the Erie Canal.

4
Building National Unity

FIND OUT
■ What was the Era of Good Feelings?
■ How did Congress try to strengthen the national economy?
■ What was Henry Clay's American System?

VOCABULARY dumping

The Marquis de Lafayette made a triumphal tour of the United States in 1824. Everywhere, crowds cheered the hero who had helped Americans win independence more than 40 years earlier. Lafayette visited New Orleans. He traveled up the Mississippi by steamboat. He saw Cincinnati, a city that had not existed a few years before.

At the end of his trip, Lafayette spoke to Congress. He admired the "immense improvements" he saw everywhere. Lafayette praised "all the grandeur and prosperity of these happy United States, which. . . reflect on every part of the world the light of a far superior political civilization."

By the 1820s, Americans were feeling confident. After the War of 1812, the country grew and expanded. New lands opened to settlers with improved transportation. New industries appeared. In Congress, political leaders sought to direct this growth and expansion.

An Era of Good Feelings

In 1816, the Republican candidate for President, James Monroe, easily defeated the Federalist, Rufus King. Once in office, Monroe spoke of a new sense of national unity.

Answers to Section 3 Review

1. See the maps on pp. 306 and 308.
2. (a) Lancaster Turnpike, p. 305, (b) Robert Fulton, p. 307, (c) *Clermont,* p. 307, (d) Henry Shreve, p. 307, (e) De Witt Clinton, p. 308
3. (a) turnpike, p. 306, (b) corduroy road, p. 306, (c) canal, p. 307
4. overland by wagon, down rivers by flatboat
5. (a) New routes were opened; turnpikes and the National Road were built. (b) Steamboats were introduced, making river travel faster and easier; canals such as the Erie Canal were built to link bodies of water.
6. Possible Answers: (a) The Erie Canal made travel between New York and the West faster and cheaper; it also reduced the cost of shipping goods. (b) The Erie Canal encouraged the building of other canals, made New York a center of commerce, and improved travel in general across the nation.

In 1817, Monroe made a goodwill tour of the country. Not since George Washington had a President made such a tour. In Boston, crowds welcomed this tall, dignified man in his old-fashioned clothes and three-cornered hat.

Boston newspapers expressed surprise at the warm welcome. After all, Boston had been a Federalist stronghold. Monroe was a Republican from Virginia. One newspaper wrote that the United States was entering an "Era of Good Feelings." The bitter disputes between Republicans and Federalists had begun to fade.

When Monroe ran for a second term in 1820, no one opposed him. By then, the Federalist party had disappeared.

Three Political Giants

Although conflict between political parties declined, disputes between different sections of the nation sharpened. In Congress, three ambitious young men took center stage. They were John C. Calhoun of South Carolina, Daniel Webster of Massachusetts, and Henry Clay of Kentucky.

All three played key roles in Congress for more than 30 years. Each represented a different section of the country.

John C. Calhoun. Calhoun spoke for the South. He had grown up on a farm on the South Carolina frontier. Later, he went to Yale College in Connecticut. Slim and handsome, Calhoun had deep-set eyes, a high forehead, and immense energy. His way of speaking was so intense that some people felt uncomfortable in his presence.

Daniel Webster. Webster spoke for the North. With dark hair and flashing eyes, Webster was an impressive sight in Congress. When he spoke, he stood straight as a ramrod, with shoulders thrown back. The hall would fall silent. "He will not be outdone by any man, if it is within his power to avoid it," observed a friend. Webster served first in the House and later as a senator from Massachusetts.

A New Generation of Leaders *Three young politicians rose to prominence in the early 1800s. Both Daniel Webster, left, and Henry Clay, right, urged the government to take a larger role in developing the nation's economy. John C. Calhoun, center, had fears of making the central government too powerful.* **Citizenship** *How did sectional politics play a role in the rise of Calhoun, Webster, and Clay?*

Lesson Plan

1. Focus The presidency of James Monroe marked a hopeful period in American life. However, there also were internal conflicts and changes. In this section, students look at the decline of the Federalists and the rise of new leaders in Congress. They also study how protective tariffs angered the South.

2. Instruct Divide the class into three groups—one each to represent the North, the South, and the West. Have each group prepare arguments for or against the Tariff of 1816 and Clay's American System. Each group should then elect a person to play Webster (North), Calhoun (South), or Clay (West) and present that leader's views to the class. The class, acting as Congress, can vote on the measures. (You may want to use this activity to introduce the Activity in the Section Review.)

3. Close To close the lesson, have students summarize the growing differences among the sections of the nation.

 Lesson Planner

For a developed **Cooperative Learning** lesson plan, see the *Lesson Planner,* page 61.

Answer to Caption

Each politician represented the interests of a different section of the country: Calhoun, the South; Clay, the West; Webster, the North.

Historical Sidelight
Background

When James Monroe took the oath of office on March 4, 1817, the Capitol was still a burned-out building. Congress was meeting in temporary quarters opposite the Capitol.

In his first inaugural address, Monroe declared, "Possessing as we do all the raw materials, the fruit of our own soil and industry, we ought not to depend in the degree we have done on supplies from other countries. . . . If we look to the history of other nations, ancient or modern, we find no example of a growth so rapid, so gigantic, of a people so prosperous and happy. In contemplating what we have still to perform, the heart of every citizen must expand with joy when he reflects how near our Government has approached to perfection, that in respect to it we have no essential improvement to make; [and] that the great object is to preserve it in the essential principles and features which characterize it. . . ."

Team-Teaching Suggestion
Language Arts

You might work with a language arts teacher to create and present a lesson about the tall tale and the use of exaggeration for humorous effect in American literature. Use Stephen Vincent Benet's short story *The Devil and Daniel Webster* as an example of a twentieth-century work in this tradition. Also discuss the use of irony in the reasons that the devil gives for his right to claim American citizenship.

Voices of Freedom

Primary Source You might assign selection 12-3, A Southerner Objects to the Tariff, on pages 86–87 of *Voices of Freedom*. This selection is from a fiery speech made by Virginia congressman John Randolph against the Tariff of 1816. (Enrichment/Challenging)

Henry Clay. From the West came Henry Clay. He had grown up on a backcountry farm. He was a man of action who had been a War Hawk in 1812. (See page 282.) As a young lawyer, Clay was once fined for brawling with an opposing lawyer. Usually, however, Clay charmed both friends and rivals. He enjoyed staying up late to discuss politics or to play cards. Like Calhoun and Webster, Clay could move people to laughter or tears with his speeches.

A New National Bank

After the War of 1812, a major problem facing leaders like Calhoun, Webster, and Clay was the nation's economic weakness. The problem was due in part to the lack of a national bank.

The charter for the first Bank of the United States ran out in 1811. Without the Bank to lend money and regulate the nation's money supply, the economy suffered. State banks made loans and issued money. Often, they put too much money into circulation, causing prices to rise rapidly.

In the nation's early years, Republicans, like Jefferson and Madison, had opposed a national bank. By 1816, however, many Republicans saw that a bank was needed. They supported a law to charter the second Bank of the United States. By lending money to individuals and restoring order to the money supply, the Bank helped American businesses grow.

Competition From Abroad

Another problem the nation faced after the War of 1812 was foreign competition, especially from Britain. In the early 1800s, the Embargo Act and then the War of 1812 kept most British goods out of the United States. In response, ambitious Americans, like Samuel Slater and Francis Cabot Lowell, set up mills and factories.

Effect of a Protective Tariff

In the United States

American-made cloth sells for $6 per roll

In Britain

British-made cloth sells for $5 per roll

Shipped to America

Add 25% tariff of $1.25 per roll

British-made cloth sells for $6.25 per roll

CHART SKILLS *In 1816, the government passed a protective tariff to help American factory owners. As this chart shows, the tariff made British goods more expensive than American goods.* ● *Why did southerners object to the tariff?*

A flood of British goods. In 1815, British goods again poured into the United States. The British could make and sell goods more cheaply than Americans, who had to pay for building their new factories.

Sometimes, British manufacturers sold cloth for less than it cost to make. The practice of selling goods in another country at very low prices is called **dumping.** Through dumping, British manufacturers hoped to put American rivals out of business.

Congress acts. Dumping caused dozens of New England businesses to fail. Angry factory owners asked Congress for a protective tariff on all goods imported from Europe. As you recall, a protective tariff is meant to protect a country's industries from foreign competition. (See the diagram at left.)

Congress responded by passing the Tariff of 1816. It greatly raised tariffs on imports. This increase made imported goods far more expensive than American-made goods.

Southerners protest. Higher tariffs led to angry protests, especially from southerners. The South had few factories to benefit from the tariff. Also, southerners had long been buying British goods. The new tariff forced them to buy costly American-made goods. Southerners saw the tariff as a law that made northern manufacturers rich at the expense of the South.

Henry Clay's American System

The bitter dispute over tariffs reflected the growing importance of sectional interests. Americans identified themselves as southerners, northerners, and westerners. In Congress, clashes occurred between representatives from different sections.

Henry Clay wanted to promote economic growth for all sections. He set out a program that became known as the ***American System.*** It called for high tariffs on imports, which would help northern factories. With wealth from industry, northerners would buy farm products from the West and the South. High tariffs would also reduce American dependence on foreign goods.

Clay also hoped to boost the national economy by calling for internal improvements—the building of roads, bridges, and canals. He urged Congress to use money from tariffs on such improvements. A better transportation system, he believed, would make it easier—and cheaper—for farmers in the West and the South to ship goods to city markets.

Clay's American System never went into effect. Tariffs remained high, but Congress spent little on internal improvements. Southerners especially disliked Clay's plan. The South had many fine rivers to transport goods. Many southerners opposed paying for roads and canals that brought them no direct benefits.

Improving Travel *Many Americans argued that improved transportation was vital to the growth of the nation. Here, the Paragon, one of Robert Fulton's boats, steams up the Hudson River.* **Geography** *Why did many southerners oppose spending money for internal improvements?*

 Chapter Resources

Critical Thinking Duplicate and distribute the worksheet, Analyzing Information, from Unit 3, page 29, of the *Chapter Resources* binder. It gives students the chance to analyze an early tariff law.

Answer to Caption

They did not want to spend money on improvements for the benefit of the North and West.

 Voices of Freedom

Primary Source You might assign selection 12-5, Americans Sing the Praises of Home, on page 88 of *Voices of Freedom.* Early American songs often praised the virtues of simple, familiar things. "Home, Sweet Home" was a great favorite. (Enrichment/Average)

 CD-ROM

History Makers Access the biography of Henry Clay on the American Heritage® *History of the United States* CD-ROM. (Enrichment/Average)

 Chapter Resources

History Through Literature To give students one European's view of Americans at this time, duplicate and distribute the work sheet, Letters From an American Farmer, from Unit 3, page 30, of the *Chapter Resources* binder. (Enrichment/Average)

Connections With Economics
Activity

The practice of dumping remains an economic issue today. Have students check the *Readers' Guide to Periodical Literature* or *Facts on File* (or a computerized file, such as *Infotrac*) and make a list of articles during the past two years that deal with dumping. Encourage each student to select one article to review and present a synopsis to the class.

Connections With Economics
Background

In addition to a high protective tariff and federal funding for transportation projects, Clay's American System also called for a national bank, which would be owned jointly by the government and by private stockholders; and for a plan under which public lands in the West would be sold rather than given outright to settlers, with the proceeds being used for education and "internal improvements."

The program later became part of the political philosophy of the Whig party, which unsuccessfully supported Clay in the presidential elections of 1832 and 1844.

Even though the American System never went into effect as Clay had envisioned it, many of its principles eventually became part of government policy.

313

Guided Instruction Before students select two of the three "political giants" studied in this section, have them review the positions that each leader took on the possible topics for discussion. You might wish to have students review writing and punctuating dialogue, or you might give students the option of preparing the dialogue in the form of a script. When they revise, students might work with a partner to check for factual accuracy and to evaluate the realism of the dialogue.

Section 5
pp. 314–319

🔔 Bell Ringer

Have students brainstorm to create a class list of countries that are located in the Western Hemisphere. Ask: Which nations governed these countries before they became independent?

SECTION 4 REVIEW

1. **Identify:** (a) John C. Calhoun, (b) Daniel Webster, (c) Henry Clay, (d) American System.
2. **Define:** dumping.
3. Why were the years after Monroe became President known as the Era of Good Feelings?
4. Explain how Congress tried to solve each of the following problems: (a) the money supply, (b) dumping.
5. How did the tariff debate reflect sectional differences?
6. **CRITICAL THINKING Defending a Position** Do you think that Clay's American System was a good plan for the nation? Explain.

ACTIVITY Writing to Learn

Write a dialogue between two of the "political giants" in this section. Topics can include the tariff, national bank, and American System.

5
Neighboring Nations Gain Independence

FIND OUT
■ How did Canada achieve self rule?
■ How did revolutions change Latin America?
■ Why did the United States issue the Monroe Doctrine?

In 1812, a rebel army gathered in Caracas, in present-day Venezuela. For two years, they had been fighting to free their land from Spanish rule. Victory seemed near.

Then, on Thursday, March 26, the earth trembled and rolled. Buildings housing the rebel troops collapsed, killing thousands.

Only a few miles away, the Spanish Army was untouched. Simón Bolívar (see MOHN boh LEE vahr), a young rebel officer, leaped onto the rubble, crying: "If Nature thwarts us and our plans, we shall fight against her, and make her obey."

Throughout Latin America,* Spanish-ruled colonies fought long wars for independence in the early 1800s. Elsewhere in the hemisphere, Canada won self-rule largely through peaceful means.

Self-Government for Canada

In the early 1800s, Canada had a diverse population. Canadians included French and English settlers as well as Native Americans. Indian nations controlled much of what is today northern and western Canada.

Two cultures. In 1763, the British had won control of Canada. (See page 141.) The British conquest left Canada a troubled land. French Canadians and English Canadians distrusted one another. The two groups spoke different languages and practiced different religions. Most English settlers were Protestants. Most French settlers were Roman Catholics.

During and after the American Revolution, more than 40,000 Loyalists fled north to Canada. Many settled in Nova Scotia, New Brunswick, Prince Edward Island, and the area north of the Great Lakes. Among the newcomers were more than 3,000 enslaved African Americans who sought freedom in Canada.

Two Canadas. As Canada's population grew, Britain decided to rule the two groups separately. In 1791, it divided Canada into Upper and Lower Canada. Upper Canada included the area around the Great Lakes settled by English-speaking people. Lower

---

*Latin America refers to the parts of the Western Hemisphere where Latin-based languages such as Spanish, French, and Portuguese are spoken. It includes Mexico, Central and South America, and the West Indies.

Answers to Section 4 Review

1. (a) John C. Calhoun, p. 311, (b) Daniel Webster, p. 311, (c) Henry Clay, p. 312, (d) American System, p. 313
2. dumping, p. 312
3. This era seemed to mark the end of bitter disputes between political parties.
4. (a) Congress set up the Second National Bank to restore order to the money supply. (b) Congress passed the Tariff of 1816, raising tariffs on imported goods and thus making these products more expensive than American-made goods.
5. Northerners wanted high tariffs to protect their industries; however, southerners, who had few factories, did not want to pay high prices for northern goods or for imported products.
6. Possible Answer: The plan was a good idea because tariffs would have helped to develop industry, and internal improvements would have helped farmers get their goods to market. On the other hand, protective tariffs would have forced people to buy expensive American-made goods instead of inexpensive imports, and states or local communities were responsible for internal improvements.

Canada included lands along the lower St. Lawrence River settled by the French. Each province had its own government, but Britain made all important decisions.

By the early 1800s, most Canadians were pressing for change. They called for self-rule. They also wanted to reduce the power of a few wealthy families who controlled the government.

In 1837, uprisings occurred in both Upper and Lower Canada. The British had learned from their experience in the American Revolution. Faced with bands of armed patriots, they looked for peaceful solutions.

Britain sent Lord Durham to Canada to decide "the form and future government" of the provinces. Durham urged Britain to give Canadians control over local affairs. He also called for Upper and Lower Canada to be united. The Durham Report became the basis for Canadian self-rule.

The Dominion of Canada. Canadians slowly moved toward self-government. In 1867, the provinces of Nova Scotia, New Brunswick, Ontario, and Quebec joined to form the ***Dominion of Canada.*** Later on, Prince Edward Island, Manitoba, Alberta, Saskatchewan, and British Columbia also joined the Dominion.

By slow and generally peaceful means, Canada gained self-rule. Its government was similar to Britain's. Canada had an elected parliament and a prime minister. A governor general represented the British ruler but had little power.

Upheavals in Latin America

In the early 1800s, revolutions broke out in Spain's colonies in Latin America. Discontent was widespread. Most people had no say in government. Some were inspired by the French and American revolutions to seek self-rule. The poor hoped to end the harsh laws that ruled their lives.

Since the 1500s, Spain had put down many revolts. In Mexico and Peru, Indians

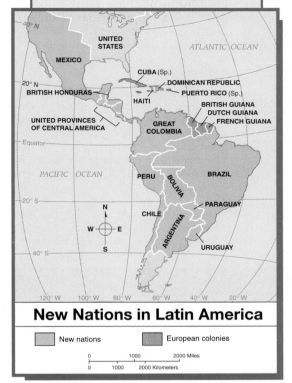

M A P   S T U D Y

The wars of independence in Latin America led to the creation of many new nations.
1. Which new nation was farthest north?
2. Which places remained European colonies?
3. **Linking Past and Present** Use the world map in the Reference Section to name the nations that were eventually carved out of the United Provinces of Central America.

New Nations in Latin America

New nations   European colonies

0   1000   2000 Miles
0   1000   2000 Kilometers

had resisted Spanish control. In the late 1700s, unrest among Spanish settlers also grew.

The early rebellions mostly involved Indians and mestizos. Creoles took no part in the uprisings. Without support from the creoles, the rebels could not succeed.

Chapter 10 • 315

Lesson Plan

1. Focus As the Industrial Revolution and westward expansion slowly changed the United States, its neighbors struggled toward independence. In this section, students examine the events that led to independence for Canada and Latin America, the treaty that gave Florida to the United States, and the Monroe Doctrine.
2. Instruct Have students reread the passage from the Monroe Doctrine on page 319. Ask: What were the reasons for the Monroe Doctrine? What did Monroe and John Quincy Adams fear? What does this passage show about how the United States felt about the Americas? After students discuss these questions, have each student write a paragraph that summarizes the meaning of the passage.
3. Close To close, play a Jeopardy!-like game with students. Have students select information from Section 5 and challenge each other to create appropriate questions.

Lesson Planner

For a developed **Cooperative Learning** lesson plan, see the *Lesson Planner,* page 62.

Answers to Map Study

1. Mexico **2.** Cuba, British Honduras, Puerto Rico, British Guiana, Dutch Guiana, French Guiana **3.** Guatemala, El Salvador, Honduras, Nicaragua, Costa Rica

Connections With Mathematics
Activity

The border between the United States and Canada is the longest unfortified border in the world. Have students locate this border on a map; then, using the scale on the map, have them estimate its length in miles or kilometers.

Connections With Civics
Background

Canada's rich natural resources attracted industries; in turn, industries attracted immigrants seeking citizenship. Between 1884 and 1914, Canada received more than three million immigrants, bringing the country's total population to more than seven million.

Connections With the World
Background

Tupac Amaru II, said to be a descendant of an Incan emperor, launched a rebellion against the Spanish in Peru in 1780. His capture and brutal murder ignited a widespread revolt against Spanish rule. In two years of war, which resulted in the crushing of the rebellion, about 80,000 Indians and Spaniards died.

Historical Outline Map Book

Historical Outline Maps Use the map, New Nations in Latin America, on page 35 of the *American History Historical Outline Map Book.* Lesson ideas for this map can be found on pages T11–T12. (Reteaching/Average)

Independence for Mexico

One Sunday in September 1810, the church bell of the village of Dolores rang longer than usual. Hurrying to the square, people found their priest, Father Miguel Hidalgo (mee GEHL ee DAHL goh), making a stirring speech. No one knows the exact words, but Mexicans remembered his message:

❝My children....Will you free yourselves? Will you recover the lands stolen 300 years ago from your forefathers by the hated Spaniards? We must act at once.... Long live our Lady of Guadalupe! Death to bad government!❞

Grito de Dolores. Father Hidalgo's message became known as the ***Grito de Dolores,*** or Cry of Dolores. It sounded the call to revolution. Thousands of Mexicans responded and joined Hidalgo.

The rebels won control of several Mexican provinces before Father Hidalgo was captured. In 1811, he was executed by troops loyal to Spain.

Another priest, José Morelos (hoh ZAY moh RAY lohs), took up the fight. Morelos proclaimed that all races should be treated equally. He called for a program to give land to peasants. Wealthy creoles opposed him. Before long, he, too, was captured and killed by the Spanish.

Success at last. Slowly, creoles began to support the revolution. In 1821, an army led by a creole officer, Agustín de Iturbide (ah goos TEEN day ee toor BEE day), won control of Mexico. After 300 years of Spanish rule, Mexicans won independence. A few years later, Mexico became a republic with its own constitution.

The Liberator

While Mexicans fought for freedom, people elsewhere in Latin America sought independence. Among the heroes of the wars of independence was Simón Bolívar. Because he fought so long and hard, Bolívar became known as the Liberator.

Bolívar came from a wealthy creole family in Venezuela. As a young man, he took up the cause of independence, vowing:

❝I will never allow my hands to be idle, nor my soul to rest until I have broken the shackles which chain us to Spain.❞

The Triumph of Mexico *This painting uses symbols to tell the story of Mexico's struggle for independence. Father Miguel Hidalgo, at left, places a victory wreath on the head of a woman representing Mexico. The feathers in her crown symbolize the nation's Indian heritage.* **The Arts** *Who do you think the man in the lower left represents?*

Connections With the World
Background

In far-off Spain, French forces took King Ferdinand VII prisoner in 1807. The political instability that resulted was felt in Spain's colonies; it provided an opportunity for revolution. The uprising that followed the *Grito de Dolores* involved mainly Indians and mestizos. Because so few creoles backed the revolt, and because the rebels' violent ways cost the cause even more support, Hidalgo had to retreat from some of his early victories.

His forces were also no match for the well-trained, well-equipped Spanish troops.

Ironically, when Ferdinand returned to power, he decided that taxing the creoles would show his strength. Instead, it pushed them into the independence movement.

In present-day Mexico, the president reads the *Grito de Dolores* in Mexico City each September 15. The next day, the people celebrate Mexico's Independence Day.

Critical Thinking
Comparing

Simón Bolívar was so highly regarded in Latin America that the nation of Bolivia was named in his honor. He has sometimes been called "the George Washington of South America." Have students find out more about the career of Bolívar. Then have them prepare brief essays or oral presentations in which they compare and contrast the achievements of Bolívar and Washington. They should especially consider the qualities that these two men shared.

Bolívar visited France and the United States. He admired the military genius of the French leader Napoleon Bonaparte. He also admired the republican form of government of the United States.

Back in Venezuela, Bolívar headed the struggle against Spain. In a bold move, he led an army from Venezuela over the ice-capped Andes Mountains into Colombia. There, he took Spanish forces by surprise and defeated them in 1819.

Soon after, Bolívar became president of the independent Republic of Great Colombia. It included the present-day nations of Venezuela, Colombia, Ecuador, and Panama.

Other New Nations

Other independent nations emerged in Latin America. José de San Martín (san mahr TEEN) led Argentina to freedom in 1816. Like Bolívar in the north, San Martín also led an army on a dangerous march across the Andes. He then helped the peoples of Chile, Peru, and Ecuador to win their freedom.

In 1821, the peoples of Central America declared independence from Spain. Two years later, they formed the United Provinces of Central America. It included the present-day nations of Nicaragua, Costa Rica, El Salvador, Honduras, and Guatemala. By 1825, Spain had lost all its colonies in Latin America except Puerto Rico and Cuba.

The Portuguese colony of Brazil won independence without a battle. Prince Pedro, son of the Portuguese king, ruled the colony. The king had advised his son, "If Brazil

> ***Our Common Heritage***
> *George Washington and Simón Bolívar each helped their nations win independence. Their nations honored them in similar ways. Each man has a state, a tall mountain, and many towns, streets, squares, and buildings in his country named for him.*

demands independence, proclaim it yourself and put the crown on your own head." In 1822, Brazilian patriots demanded freedom. Pedro agreed and had himself crowned emperor of the new nation.

The New Republics

The new republics modeled their constitutions on that of the United States. Yet their experience after independence was very different from that of their neighbor to the north.

Unlike the people of the 13 British colonies, the peoples of Latin America did not unite into a single country. Instead, they set up many different nations. In part, geography made unity difficult. Spain's American lands had covered a huge area. Mountains like the high, rugged Andes were a serious barrier to travel and communication.

The new nations had a hard time setting up stable governments. Under Spanish rule, the colonists had little experience in self-government. Deep divisions between social classes and economic problems increased discontent. Powerful leaders took advantage of the turmoil to seize control. As a result, the new republics were often unable to achieve their goal of democratic rule.

Showdown in Spanish Florida

Change was also taking place in Spanish Florida. For more than 100 years, Florida had been a refuge for many enslaved African Americans. During the 1700s, Spanish officials protected slaves who fled from plantations in Georgia and South Carolina. Seminole Indians allowed African Americans to live near their villages. In return, these "black Seminoles" gave the Indians a share of the crops they raised every year.

The black Seminoles adopted many Indian customs. They lived in houses with roofs thatched of palmetto leaves. They wore moccasins, colorful hunting shirts, and brightly colored turbans around their heads.

The Negro Fort. After the War of 1812, about 300 African Americans occupied a fort built by the British on the Apalachicola River. They invited runaway slaves from all across Florida to settle nearby. Runaways from the United States also found a welcome in the Florida fort.

Soon, some 1,000 African Americans lived on the banks of the Apalachicola. For 50 miles (80 km) along the river, they set up farms and began planting corn, sweet potatoes, melons, and beans. The Negro Fort, as it became known, provided them with protection.

American gunboats attack. General Andrew Jackson, himself a slave owner, demanded that Spain demolish the Negro Fort. When the Spanish governor refused, Jackson sent in American troops. They were to destroy the fort, Jackson insisted, "regardless of the ground it stands on."

Jackson's gunboats invaded Spanish territory in 1816, sailing up the muddy Apalachicola River. On a bluff above the river, they spotted the Negro Fort. Above the fort, a red flag fluttered.

Inside the fort, a force of about 300 free African Americans waited, their muskets loaded and cannons aimed. The red flag was a symbol of their defiance. Many of the fort's defenders had once been slaves—or their parents had. They knew that the Americans had come to return them to slavery. "Most of them determined never to be taken alive," commented one soldier.

Fighting for freedom. A seasoned fighter named Garcia commanded the Negro Fort. When the Americans demanded his surrender, he replied that he would sink any gunboat that tried to pass. Garcia's followers

"Black Seminoles" *This drawing shows an African American with Seminole Indians in Florida. Many "black Seminoles" spoke English, Spanish, and Indian languages. This gave them great influence as advisers and interpreters for the Seminoles.* **Multicultural Heritage** *Why did many African Americans go to Florida?*

cheered loudly and then fired their cannons at the ships.

The Americans returned fire. Even the ship's heaviest cannonballs thudded harmlessly into the fort's thick earthen walls. Then the sailing-master had an idea. He ordered a cannonball to be heated red-hot in the cook's galley. Sailors loaded the cannon, aimed carefully, and fired.

The heated ball screamed over the fort's wall. The ball landed in the magazine where the fort's gunpowder was stored. With a deafening roar and a huge orange flash, the magazine exploded. Within seconds, the entire fort was destroyed. The few defenders who remained alive surrendered.

With the fort destroyed, black settlers along the Apalachicola were forced to flee. Many joined Seminole Indians along the nearby Suwanee River. But the showdown at the Negro Fort had demonstrated how strongly African Americans were willing to fight for their freedom. Along with the Seminoles, they continued to resist American raids into Florida. ■

Historical Sidelight
Background

Years before Florida was officially ceded to the United States, President Madison had claimed part of the region. In 1810, American settlers revolted against Spanish rule. They captured the fort at Baton Rouge in the area known as West Florida (today's southern regions of Mississippi, Alabama, and Louisiana) and proclaimed the independence of the Republic of West Florida. President Madison quickly annexed the area, making it part of Orleans Territory.

After the cession of Florida in 1821, Andrew Jackson became its territorial governor, and he moved his family from just outside Nashville (an estate known as the Hermitage) to Pensacola. His wife, Rachel, was horrified at the rowdy behavior of the townspeople. She urged Jackson to pass an order that would keep things quiet on Sundays; but she was still unhappy: "I am not at rest, nor can I be, in this heathen land." Before the year ended, the Jacksons went back to Tennessee.

Spain Cedes Florida to the United States

In 1818, Jackson was determined once and for all to destroy the Seminole and African American forces in Florida. Commanding an army of over 3,000, he headed south again. President Monroe did not give Jackson formal permission to invade Spanish territory. He did not stop Jackson, either.

Jackson captured several Spanish towns. Although Spain protested, it was busy fighting rebels in Latin America. It could not risk war with the United States.

In the end, Spain agreed to peace talks. John Quincy Adams, the Secretary of State, worked out a treaty with Spain. The ***Adams-Onís Treaty*** took effect in 1821. In it, Spain gave Florida to the United States and received $5 million in exchange.

The Monroe Doctrine

Americans welcomed the Adams-Onís Treaty. They also cheered the success of Latin American nations in winning independence. The actions of European powers, however, worried American officials.

In 1815, Russia, Prussia, Austria, and France seemed ready to help Spain regain its colonies in Latin America. In addition, Russia claimed lands on the Pacific coast of North America.

The British, too, were concerned about other European nations meddling in the Western Hemisphere. They spoke of issuing a joint statement with the United States. It would guarantee the freedom of the new nations of Latin America.

President Monroe decided to act without the British. In 1823, he made a statement on foreign policy that is known as the ***Monroe Doctrine.*** The United States, he said, would not interfere in the affairs of European nations or European colonies in the Americas. At the same time, he warned European nations not to interfere with the newly independent nations of Latin America. He stated:

> **❝**The American continents...are henceforth not to be considered as subjects for future colonization by any European powers.... We should consider any attempt on their part to extend their system to any portion of this hemisphere as dangerous to our peace and safety.**❞**

The Monroe Doctrine showed that the United States was determined to keep European nations from recolonizing the Americas. The United States did not have the power to enforce the Monroe Doctrine. Britain, however, supported the statement. With its strong navy, it could stop Europeans from interfering in the Americas.

SECTION 5 REVIEW

1. **Locate:** (a) Mexico, (b) Great Colombia, (c) Argentina, (d) United Provinces of Central America, (e) Brazil.
2. **Identify:** (a) Dominion of Canada, (b) Miguel Hidalgo, (c) *Grito de Dolores,* (d) Simón Bolívar, (e) José de San Martín, (f) Adams-Onís Treaty, (g) Monroe Doctrine.
3. (a) Why did rebellions break out in Canada in 1837? (b) What recommendations did Lord Durham make?
4. What Latin American nations won independence from Spain in the early 1800s?
5. Why did the United States issue the Monroe Doctrine?
6. **CRITICIAL THINKING Drawing Conclusions** How would the defenders of the Negro Fort inspire enslaved Africans in the United States?

ACTIVITY Writing to Learn
Write a series of headlines that newspapers in the United States might have run before, during, and after General Jackson's invasion of Florida.

Answers to Section 5 Review

1. See the map on p. 315.
2. (a) Dominion of Canada, p. 315, (b) Miguel Hidalgo, p. 316, (c) *Grito de Dolores,* p. 316, (d) Simón Bolívar, p. 316, (e) José de San Martín, p. 317, (f) Adams-Onís Treaty, p. 319, (g) Monroe Doctrine, p. 319
3. (a) Reformers were upset that a few wealthy families controlled Canadian affairs. (b) He recommended that Canadians be given complete control over local affairs and that Upper and Lower Canada be united.
4. Mexico, Venezuela, Colombia, Ecuador, Panama, Argentina, Chile, Peru, Nicaragua, Costa Rica, El Salvador, Honduras, Guatemala
5. to stop Spain from trying to regain its colonies in Latin America; to keep other European nations from making attempts to establish other colonies and/or meddling in American affairs
6. Possible Answer: The defenders of the Negro Fort were willing to give their lives to keep their freedom. This action could have inspired enslaved Africans to attempt to gain and keep their freedom.

Answers to Reviewing the Main Ideas

1. Samuel Slater came to the United States with memorized designs for Arkwright's textile mill.
2. Lowell combined spinning and weaving under one roof.
3. Goods could be made more rapidly and repaired more easily.
4. Turnpikes, corduroy roads, and the National Road were built; covered bridges were invented; canals were built; and steamboats came into use.
5. (a) It protected them from competition from British imports. (b) Southerners had few factories. A higher tariff forced them to pay more for goods.
6. After Jackson invaded Spanish Florida, John Quincy Adams negotiated the Adams-Onís Treaty. Spain ceded Florida to the United States for $5 million.
7. (a) Russia, Prussia, Austria, and France seemed ready to help Spain regain its colonies. (b) The United States did not have the power to enforce the Monroe Doctrine by itself.

Answers to Thinking Critically

1. (a) risk of fire, dirt, disease, (b) jobs and entertainment not found in the country, (c) Possible Answer: Yes; cities today have problems such as overcrowding, poor housing conditions, and violence, but they are healthier places in which to live than cities in the 1800s were, and they still offer similar advantages.
2. (a) Travelers had to cross mountains or travel upstream on rivers, cross bodies of water, and travel on roads that were little more than muddy trails. (b) They discovered gaps in the mountains, built steamboats, built bridges, built canals, and built roads of stone and gravel or logs.
3. (a) Canada gained independence slowly and peacefully through legislative changes, whereas the Spanish colonies fought wars of independence. (b) Britain wanted to avoid another revolution like the one fought with the 13 colonies, so the British worked with Canadians to bring about self-government. Spain, on the other hand, was determined

---

Summary

- By the early 1800s, the Industrial Revolution that had started in Britain was spreading to the United States.
- The War of 1812 spurred the growth of industry in the United States.
- New roads, canals, and steamboats helped improve transportation.
- During the Era of Good Feelings, conflict between political parties declined, but sectional differences emerged.
- Canada and the nations of Latin America achieved independence.

Reviewing the Main Ideas

1. How did the Industrial Revolution come to the United States?
2. What new idea did Francis Cabot Lowell introduce to the textile industry?
3. Describe how interchangeable parts improved the way goods were produced.
4. Describe three ways that transportation improved in the early 1800s.
5. (a) Why did northern manufacturers want a protective tariff? (b) Why did southerners oppose the tariff?
6. How did Florida become part of the United States?
7. (a) Why did the United States fear that European nations might interfere in the Western Hemisphere? (b) Why was British support of the Monroe Doctrine important?

Thinking Critically

1. Linking Past and Present (a) What were the problems of city life in the early 1800s? (b) What advantages did cities offer? (c) Do cities today still have the same problems and advantages? Explain.
2. Analyzing Information (a) How did geography make travel to the West difficult? (b)

How did Americans overcome these travel problems?
3. Comparing (a) Compare the way Canada won its independence with the way the Spanish colonies won theirs. (b) Suggest two reasons why their experiences were different.

Applying Your Skills

1. Analyzing a Quotation Reread the quotation on page 295. (a) What did Lucy Larcom dislike about factory life? (b) Why did Lucy Larcom enjoy looking out the window? (c) Did Lucy think factory life was completely bad? Explain.
2. Making a Review Chart Make a review chart with three vertical columns. Label the columns Inventor, Invention, and Importance. Then use the information in the chapter to complete the chart.
3. Identifying the Main Idea Reread "The New Republics" on page 317. (a) What is the main idea of the subsection? (b) What facts support the main idea?

Thinking About Geography

Match the letters on the map with the following places: **1.** Wheeling, Virginia, **2.** New York City, **3.** Cumberland Gap, **4.** Lancaster Turnpike, **5.** National Road, **6.** Erie Canal. **Interaction** What obstacles did Americans overcome in building the Erie Canal?

---

to keep its Latin American colonies, so the Spanish used force to resist movements for independence there.

Answers to Applying Your Skills

1. (a) Larcom did not care much for machinery; constant motion and noise made her tired. (b) She could focus on something besides the noise of the machines inside. (c) No; she said that factory life was not completely "dis-agreeable" most of the time; still, when the weather was nice, she wished to get away outdoors.
2. Inventor James Hargreaves; Richard Arkwright; Edmund Cartwright; Eli Whitney; Hannah Slater, Mary Kies; Francis Cabot Lowell; John Fitch and Robert Fulton
Invention spinning jenny; water frame; power loom; cotton gin, interchangeable parts; stronger thread; weaving process for straw hats; new kind of textile mill; steamboat (improved)
Importance made it possible to spin several threads at once; held 100 spindles of thread at once; produced 200 times more cloth per worker per day; speeded up process of cleaning cotton fibers; saved time and money; kept thread from snapping on spindles; strengthened New England hat industry; combined spinning and weaving under one roof; improved travel, especially in the West
3. (a) Possible Answer: New Latin American nations found

Investigating the Industrial Revolution

Form into groups to review inventions and industry in the early 1800s. Follow the suggestions below to write, draw, interview, or perform to show what you have learned. You may use the textbook, encyclopedias, atlases, or other materials in your classroom library to complete the tasks. Be able to name your sources of information when you have finished the activity.

HISTORIANS Create a time line of inventions for the period 1790–1825. Be prepared to explain the importance of each item on the time line.

CITIZENS Make a chart showing the positive effects and the negative effects of the inventions in the historians' time line.

SCIENTISTS Draw a diagram or prepare a demonstration to show how early factories harnessed the force of water to create power to run machines.

Fulton's design for a steamboat engine

REPORTERS Conduct an interview with a traveler on a Mississippi River steamboat. Ask questions to find out about the kinds of cargo on board, the hazards and thrills of steamboat travel, and the traveler's purpose and destination.

DANCERS AND POETS Review the descriptions of working conditions in mills and factories. Form into pairs to create a dance and poem that portray a day in the life of a worker. Poets might read their poems aloud while dancers perform in a recital for the class.

★ Set up an Industrial Revolution display in your classroom. Have each group present or describe its completed activity.

Interchangeable parts for a revolver

Factory town in New England

---

self-government difficult. (b) Their geography hindered communication; new leaders had little experience with government; class struggles and economic problems continued.

Answers to Thinking About Geography

1. F **2.** B **3.** E **4.** C **5.** D **6.** A **Interaction:** the lack of equipment often meant digging by hand; the need to carry the canal over rivers required the building of stone bridges

Assessment

Chapter Resources Binder For a more comprehensive evaluation of student understanding of this chapter, assign Chapter Tests A and B and/or Extra Unit Questions from Unit 3, pages 33–38 and 41–43.

Computer Test Bank You can use Chapter Tests and Extra Unit Questions to create your own tests for both testing and retesting.

Alternative Assessment

Chapter Resources Binder See the Alternative Assessment booklet in the *Social Studies Educator's Handbook* series.

Portfolio You might meet with students to choose appropriate work from the chapter for inclusion in their portfolios.

History Through Literature

James Lincoln Collier and Christopher Collier The Collier brothers have written several novels together; perhaps best known is their Newbery Honor Book, *My Brother Sam Is Dead.* Other historical novels include *The Bloody Country* and *The Winter Hero. Who Is Carrie?* continues the saga of the Arabus family, begun in *War Comes to Willy Freeman* and *Jump Ship to Freedom.*

Vocabulary

There is no unusual vocabulary in this passage; however, you might suggest that students check their understanding of the words *note* (with its specifically financial meaning), *bushel,* and *reckon.* Alternatively, you might check students' spelling of such familiar words as *frequent, pieces, government, naturally, gamble, potatoes, percent,* and *chance.*

Prereading Focus

You might have students reread pages 245–248 in Chapter 8 to review what they have learned about the problem of repaying war debts.

Motivation/Prior Knowledge

Most students know what it is like to lend something and not get it back. Ask: How would you feel if someone was slow about repaying you money that you needed?

Purpose-Setting Question

Read the introductory note aloud. Then ask: If you were Dan, how would you feel about owning the notes?

Discussion Questions

1. Why were people so unsure about what the notes were worth? (The federal government had not yet decided whether to pay off government- and state-issued notes at face value — if at all.)

2. How much were Dan's notes worth? ($600 at face value; about $300 at the current, speculative rate of exchange)

3. Why has Dan decided not to sell the notes? (He wants to buy freedom for himself and his mother. With $600, he could do that; with $300, he could buy only his own freedom. It would take at least 10 years to earn enough to buy his mother's freedom; but if he kept the notes and then the government repaid them at face value, he would have the full amount quickly.)

History Through LITERATURE

Who Is Carrie?

James Lincoln Collier and *Christopher Collier*

Introduction The new United States government faced a difficult problem. It had to find a way to repay bonds, or notes, used to pay soldiers and purchase supplies during the Revolution. *Who Is Carrie?* is a historical novel about an enslaved teenage girl in New York City. Her friend Dan, also a slave, owns hundreds of dollars worth of the notes. In this excerpt, Carrie and Dan wonder how and if the government will repay the bonds.

Dan's notes were pretty confusing, and as frequent as he'd explained it to me, I never did understand the ins and outs of it all. What happened was Dan's father, who was Jack Arabus, fought in the Revolution right next to General Washington. He got free for fighting and a whole lot of money, too. Only it wasn't real money. It was just pieces of paper called notes that said the government owed you some money.

Well, of course Dan's daddy got drowned, and after that the notes belonged to Dan. . . .

The thing was, nobody knew if the notes would be worth real money. It was up to the government to decide if they would pay them off or not. And on top of it, the states had put out their own notes, too, which people had taken instead of real money, and nobody knew if they'd be worth anything, either.

So naturally, while everybody was waiting to see if the states could get together and make themselves into one big country, some people was going around buying other people's notes for a cheap price. Say, if your notes was worth a hundred dollars, somebody might give you a dollar, or ten dollars or something for them on the gamble that the states would be able to get themselves together. And finally they did get themselves together and made the United States of America; and people who owned these notes was mighty cheered up, because they figured that the government would pay them off. Maybe they wouldn't pay them off a hundred percent, but they might declare that your hundred-dollar note was worth fifty dollars or some such.

But then it come out that *maybe* the government would pay off the notes and *maybe* they wouldn't. And it also come out that *maybe* they would pay off the states' notes for them, too, and *maybe* they wouldn't. The whole thing was as full of maybes as a bushel of potatoes, and it was making people like Dan, who'd got notes, just wild crazy. . . .

And for Dan it wasn't just the money. It was freedom, because if they paid off the notes a hundred percent, he'd have six hundred dollars, and maybe more, which

---

Historical Sidelight

In 1790, around the time this selection takes place, African Americans comprised one fifth of the total population of the United States. The overwhelming majority of African Americans, about 90 percent, lived in southern states from Maryland to Georgia and worked as slaves on plantations.

Of the 750,000 African Americans, about 59,000 were free. The ideals of liberty fostered by the Revolution had helped to increase the number of free African Americans. In fact, relative to the total African American population, the free black population in 1790 was larger than at any time before the Civil War.

Under My Wings, Everything Prospers
Americans faced many challenges as they built their new nation. Despite problems, however, they looked forward to the future with hope and confidence. **Citizenship** *What problem did the new government face in repaying its debts from the Revolution?*

would be enough to buy his freedom, and his Ma's, too. But if they decided the other way, the notes wouldn't be worth nothing, and Dan and his Ma would have to stay slaves and work for Captain Ivers the rest of their lives.

"What are they worth now, Dan?" I said.

"Right now about half," Dan said. "People are buying them for half, because now that there's a government and a president and all, they figure there's a good chance that Congress will vote to pay them off. My notes is worth three hundred dollars, I reckon."

"That's a powerful lot of money," I said. "I'd sell them. I wouldn't risk waiting around. I'd sell them quick."

"It's a powerful lot," he said, "but it ain't enough to buy both me and Ma off. Captain Ivers, he said, if I gave him the notes he'd set me free, but that would leave Ma stuck."

"You know what I'd do," I said. "I'd grab the money and buy myself free and then work and save up money until I had enough to get my Ma free."

Dan shook his head. "I thought about that. I reckoned it up. It would take me near ten years to save up three hundred dollars. That's a powerful lot of money for anyone to save, and worse for a black man who don't get paid the same as whites.". . .

"What are you going to do?"

"Chance it," he said. "Chance it that the new government will pay off the notes a hundred percent."

THINKING ABOUT LITERATURE

1. How did Dan get the notes?
2. What did Dan hope to do with the money he received for his notes?
3. **CRITICAL THINKING Analyzing Information** How would the American people and other governments view the United States government if it decided *not* to repay the notes?

ACTIVITY Imagine that you are a writer for a television series based on *Who Is Carrie?* Write the dialogue for a scene in which Captain Ivers tries to convince Dan to give him the notes in exchange for Dan's freedom.

Unit 4
An Expanding Nation

Unit Focus

Direct students' attention to the painting on these pages — *The Rocky Mountains, Lander's Peak,* by Albert Bierstadt. Explain that this scene is typical of the West during the first half of the nineteenth century. As students consider the United States of that era, read aloud the four chapter summaries. Ask questions such as the following to stimulate discussion.

1. Based on this painting, what do you think that Americans in the East thought about the western part of the continent?

2. Many of the Americans of this era were the children and grandchildren of those who had lived through the American Revolution. How do you think descendants of Patriots felt about their country? Explain.

3. How do you think the lives of Americans in the North, the South, and the West differed?

4. (a) What kinds of social reform do people work for today? (b) Which of those issues might have existed 150 years ago?

5. Unit 4 is entitled An Expanding Nation. Based on the information in the chapter summaries, what kinds of "growing pains" do you think the nation experienced during this time?

Connections With Art
Background

Albert Bierstadt (1830–1902), a German immigrant, traveled throughout the West with a surveying team in 1859. His drawings and photographs from that trip were the sources for his later paintings. For many years, Bierstadt was one of the most popular landscape painters in the United States. One of his paintings sold for $25,000, which was the highest price ever paid for an American painting at that time. Bierstadt is best known for large, panoramic scenes with dramatic lighting. (The art on these pages

is a detail from a panorama measuring approximately 6 feet tall and 10 feet wide.)

The Rocky Mountains, Lander's Peak was first exhibited in 1864 as part of a fund-raiser for the Sanitary Commission — the forerunner of the Red Cross. Today, the painting is part of the collection of the Metropolitan Museum of Art in New York City.

UNIT 4
An Expanding Nation

CHAPTER 11
The Jackson Era
(1824–1840)

A new democratic spirit gave more Americans a voice in government.

....

CHAPTER 12
From Sea to Shining Sea
(1820–1860)

Thousands of Americans moved west, and by the 1850s the nation stretched from the Atlantic to the Pacific.

....

CHAPTER 13
The Worlds of North and South
(1820–1860)

The industrial North and the agricultural South developed two distinct ways of life.

....

CHAPTER 14
A Reforming Age
(1820–1860)

In the mid-1800s, Americans worked for reform in many areas.

Connections With Art
Activity

Ask questions such as the following to stimulate discussion about the painting.

1. Using just one sentence, how would you describe this scene?

2. What can you assume about the lives of this Native American group, based on the painting?

3. Compare this with the painting by William Richardson Tyler on page 419. In what ways are the paintings similar? How do they differ?

4. Would this scene and the people in it be threatened by "an expanding nation"? Explain.

*A*mericans worked to build a more democratic society. At the same time, they moved steadily westward—often onto Indian lands. Here, Native Americans are shown in their Rocky Mountain home.

Bulletin Board Suggestion

Have students create a bulletin board display illustrating some of the concurrent unit themes— prosperity, technological advancement, expansion, social reform, and democracy in the Jackson Era. Sections of the display could deal with key figures and illustrations or collages that represent key places such as a northern factory, a southern plantation, Texas, California, and the Great Plains.

 ## Art Gallery Posters

Cherokee Trail of Tears, by Chris Wolf Edmonds, is appropriate for Unit 4. Lesson suggestions for the poster appear in the *Art Gallery: Our Common Heritage Posters* Teacher's Guide. The art also appears in Chapter 11, page 339, of the student book.

 ## CD-ROM

Time Tour Access the Time Tour An Expanding Nation on the American Heritage® *History of the United States* CD-ROM to accompany Unit 4. (Enrichment/ Average)

Connections With the World
Activity

Have students preview the world events on the chapter time lines (pages 326–327, 348–349, 376–377, and 400–401). Call on volunteers to use the world map on pages 890–891 to locate each nation or area mentioned. Then ask the class: What was going on in the United States at the same time as each world event? In which of the world events do you think that the citizens of "an expanding nation" would have been most interested? Why?

Linking Past and Present
Activity

Have students examine the painting, commenting on the natural beauty of this Rocky Mountain landscape. Ask: Would you and/or your friends like to visit or even live in such a place even if it has no electricity or modern conveniences? Why or why not?

Do you think that many places like this still exist in the United States today? What are private organizations and government agencies doing to preserve such places? What can you do to help?

Lessons	Teaching Resources
1 **Champion of the People** **Objectives** 1. Explain why the election of 1824 was disputed. 2. Identify the policies that John Quincy Adams supported. 3. Describe how the country became more democratic in the 1820s.	**Lesson Planner** Cooperative Learning, p. 65 **Student Study Guide** Section 1 Study Guide, p. 95 **Our Multicultural Heritage** *Biography* Anne Newport Royall, Journalist, p. 31 *Biography* Ira F. Aldridge, Shakespearean Actor, p. 32 **Interdisciplinary Connections:** A Struggle for Democracy ■ *Arts* Politics in Paint, p. 62 ■ *Sciences* A New Knife, p. 63 ■ *Geography* The Attraction of the Wilderness, p. 64 ■ *World* American Ideals in Europe, p. 65 ■ *Economics* A Trail of Tears, p. 66
2 **Jackson in the White House** **Objectives** 1. Identify the qualities that helped Jackson succeed. 2. Explain why Jackson replaced many officeholders. 3. Explain why Jackson made war on the Bank of the United States.	**Lesson Planner** Cooperative Learning, p. 66 **Student Study Guide** Section 2 Study Guide, p. 96 **Chapter Resources Binder, Unit 4** *Critical Thinking* Synthesizing Information, p. 3
3 **A Strong President** **Objectives** 1. Describe how tariffs led to the Nullification Crisis. 2. Explain why South Carolina threatened to withdraw from the Union. 3. Explain why Native Americans were forced off their lands.	**Lesson Planner** Cooperative Learning, p. 67 **Student Study Guide** Section 3 Study Guide, p. 97 **Chapter Resources Binder, Unit 4** *Geography in History* A Forced Move West, pp. 5–6 **Our Multicultural Heritage** *Milestone* A Cherokee Plea, p. 33 **Posters** *Cherokee Trail of Tears,* by Chris Wolf Edmonds
4 **Jackson's Successors** **Objectives** 1. Identify the economic problems that Martin Van Buren faced. 2. Describe how William Henry Harrison campaigned for President. 3. Explain why Tyler had little success as President.	**Lesson Planner** Cooperative Learning, p. 68 **Student Study Guide** Section 4 Study Guide, p. 98 **Chapter Resources Binder, Unit 4** *History Through Literature* Johnny Appleseed, p. 4 *Skill Application* Reading a Circle Graph, p. 2

Multimedia Resources	Additional Resources	Chapter-Level Resources
Transparencies *Interdisciplinary Connections* Civil Rights, p. B-53 **CD-ROM** *Presidents* John Quincy Adams **Videotapes/Videodiscs** *United States History Video Collection* New Day Dawning, Vol. 7, Ch. 10; The Age of Jackson, Vol. 7, Ch. 13	**Customized Reader** On the Campaign Trail in Indiana, article IVB-12	**Lesson Planner** Activity Based, pp. 69–70 **Student Study Guide** Chapter 11 Study Guide, pp. 99–100 **Chapter Resources Binder** **Unit 4** Vocabulary Building, p. 1 Chapter Test A, pp. 7–9 Chapter Test B, pp. 10–12 Illustration Master, p. 13 Extra Unit Questions, pp. 57–59 **English Guided Reading** Guided Reading, pp. 21–22 **Spanish Resources** **Computer Test Bank** Chapter Tests A and B Extra Unit Questions **Guided Reading Audiotapes** Side 4 **CD-ROM** *Time Tour* The Jackson Era (1824–1840) in An Expanding Nation
Transparencies *Political Cartoons* Jackson, Man of the People, p. G-17 **CD-ROM** *Presidents* Andrew Jackson	**Voices of Freedom** A Mother Advises a Future President, p. 9	
CD-ROM *History Makers* Sequoyah *Arts & Entertainment* Books	**Voices of Freedom** Webster's Defense of National Supremacy, pp. 91–92 Jackson Warns the Seminoles, pp. 93–94 **Historical Outline Map Book** Indian Removal, 1830–1842, p. 37	
CD-ROM *Presidents* Martin Van Buren *Presidents* William Henry Harrison *Presidents* John Tyler *Virtual Buildings* Log Cabin	**Voices of Freedom** A Campaign Song, pp. 94–95	

Lesson Planner

For a fully developed **Activity-Based** lesson plan for Chapter 11, see the *Lesson Planner*, pages 69–70.

Chapter Resources

Vocabulary Building The Vocabulary Building worksheet for Chapter 11 from Unit 4, page 1, of the *Chapter Resources* binder can be used as a prereading activity or as a review of chapter vocabulary. (Reteaching/Easy)

Student Study Guide

Chapter 11 Study Guide Refer students to pages 99–100 of the *Student Study Guide* for the Chapter 11 Study Guide. The study guide can be used for chapter review as well as for reteaching. (Reteaching/Average)

Guided Reading Audiotapes

Students can use *Guided Reading Audiotapes,* Chapter 11, side 4, to listen to section previews, summaries, and review questions. The tapes might benefit students who are auditory learners, students who have trouble reading, or students acquiring English. Tapes are also available in Spanish. (Reteaching/Easy)

CHAPTER **11**

The Jackson Era

(1824–1840)

CHAPTER OUTLINE

1 Champion of the People
2 Jackson in the White House
3 A Strong President
4 Jackson's Successors

1820s *The right to vote was extended to almost all white men. Here, two voters discuss the issues of the day.*

1828 *Andrew Jackson was elected President. Many Americans considered his election a victory for the common people.*

1830 *Congress passed the Indian Removal Act, which forced Native Americans to move west of the Mississippi River. This painting shows Indians on the "Trail of Tears."*

| 1824 | 1826 | 1828 | 1830 | 1832 |

WORLD EVENT
1824 Simón Bolívar becomes President of Peru

WORLD EVENT
1829 Swiss adopt universal male suffrage, freedom of the press, and equality before the law

326 • Chapter 11

Chapter Time Line
Understanding Chronology

To help students check their understanding of the sequence of events in the time line, begin by writing the following dates on the chalkboard:

1830
1837
1824
1840
1829
1832
1828

Then ask questions such as these:

- Which two time line events are taking place in 1824? (Simón Bolívar becomes President of Peru; the vote is extended to almost all white men.) In 1837? (Canadian colonists revolt; Seminole War is waged.)
- Which U.S. Presidents are associated with this time line? (Jackson, Harrison)

After students have answered your questions, have them identify the events associated with the remaining dates.

Chapter Setting

❝ Yesterday the President's house was open at noon.... The old man stood in the center of a little circle...and shook hands with anybody that offered.... There was a throng of apprentices, boys of all ages, men not civilized enough to walk about the rooms with their hats off; the vilest...[group] that ever [gathered] in a decent house; many of the lowest gathering around the doors, pouncing...upon the wine and refreshments, tearing the cake ...all fellows with dirty faces and dirty manners; all the [trash] that Washington could turn forth from its workshops and stables. ❞

George Bancroft described this scene at the White House in 1831. Bancroft, who came from an old, wealthy family, did not like what he saw. In his opinion, the President should not welcome roughnecks to the White House. To Andrew Jackson, however, these workers and simple frontier folk were the backbone of America.

Jackson reflected the democratic spirit sweeping the country. In the early 1800s, more and more white men gained the right to vote. In 1828, the new voters helped send Jackson, a popular frontier hero, to Washington. Both supporters and critics knew that Jackson would usher in a new era.

ACTIVITY
Based on George Bancroft's description, draw a picture showing the scene at the White House in 1831. Then hold a discussion about whether or not the President should welcome ordinary people to the White House.

1832 *President Jackson vetoed the charter of the Bank of the United States. A cartoon of the time shows Jackson boxing with the Bank's president.*

1835–1842 *Seminole forces battled the United States Army in the Seminole War. Chief Osceola, shown here, led the Seminoles in their fight.*

1840 *William Henry Harrison was elected President. The log cabin used as a symbol of Harrison's campaign was meant to show that he was a "man of the people."*

| 1832 | 1834 | 1836 | 1838 | 1840 |

WORLD EVENT
1832 Reform Act doubles number of eligible voters in Britain

WORLD EVENT
1837 Canadian colonists revolt, demanding democratic reform

Chapter Resources

English Guided Reading Duplicate and distribute to SAE students the Chapter 11 Guided Reading worksheet on pages 21–22 in the English Guided Reading section of the *Chapter Resources* binder. Students who have difficulty reading also might benefit from using this worksheet. Have students complete the worksheet before they begin reading. You might pair a more fluent student or a student who is a stronger reader with each SAE student to review. (Reteaching/Easy)

Spanish Resources See the Spanish Resources section of the *Chapter Resources* binder.

CD-ROM

Time Tour Access The Jackson Era (1824–1840) section in An Expanding Nation on the American Heritage® *History of the United States* CD-ROM. (Enrichment/Average)

ACTIVITY

Guided Instruction Allow students to use a variety of materials to create their drawings—chalk, markers, colored pencils, paint, and so forth. Some students may wish to work together to create a mural of the scene. They could divide the work so that students with drawing ability could create the outlines, others could color them in, and a third group might paint the background.

Linking Past and Present
Activity

Andrew Jackson began his administration with a reception in the White House. There have been significant changes to the White House since Andrew Jackson occupied it. Have students research and report on how the White House appeared during Jackson's time, which Presidents made alterations to the White House, and why the changes were made.

Students Acquiring English
Activity

SAE students may not be familiar with the technique of asking *Who, What, Where, When, Why,* and *How* questions as a means of ensuring comprehension of chapter content. You might model this approach on the chalkboard, using information from the subsection A Disputed Election on pages 328–329: *Who?* John Quincy Adams, Henry Clay, Andrew Jackson, and William Crawford *What?* Ran for President *When?* 1824 *Where?* United States *Why?* Each drew support from people in a different part of the country who wanted to be represented in the White House. *How?* The House of Representatives had to choose from among the three top candidates because no one won the majority of electoral votes.

Section 1
pp. 328–332

Bell Ringer

Write the expression *common people* on the chalkboard. Ask students to describe the kinds of people to whom these words might apply.

Lesson Plan

1. Focus The election of 1824 brought John Quincy Adams to the presidency and caused a split in the Republican party. In this section, students focus on the democratic spirit that swept Adams out of office and brought Andrew Jackson to the forefront of American politics.
2. Instruct Have students label each of the following statements as fact or opinion. Ask students to give supporting evidence for each fact and tell why they agree or disagree with each opinion. (a) The 1824 election was decided by a "corrupt bargain." (b) The 1828 election was filled with personal attacks and name-calling. (c) Andrew Jackson's election in 1828 was a victory for the common people. (d) Nominating conventions were a fairer way of choosing candidates than caucuses.

1
Champion of the People

FIND OUT
■ Why was the election of 1824 disputed?

■ What policies did John Quincy Adams support?

■ How did the country become more democratic in the 1820s?

VOCABULARY suffrage, caucus, nominating convention

Harry Ward, a New England schoolteacher, visited Cincinnati, Ohio, during the 1824 election campaign. Writing to a friend, he described how Ohioans felt about Andrew Jackson, who was running for President. "Strange! Wild! Infatuated! All for Jackson!" he observed.

On election day, more people voted for Andrew Jackson than for the other candidates. Oddly enough, Jackson did not become President that year.

A Disputed Election

There were four candidates for President in 1824. Each had support in different parts of the country. John Quincy Adams was strong in New England. Henry Clay and Andrew Jackson had support in the West. William Crawford was favored in the South but became too ill to campaign.

The candidates. John Quincy Adams came from a famous New England family. As the son of Abigail and John Adams, he had been close to national affairs since birth. He was a talented diplomat, and he served as Secretary of State under President Monroe. People admired Adams for his intelligence and high morals. Yet to many, he seemed hard and cold.

Henry Clay, by contrast, was charming. A Kentuckian, Clay was a shrewd politician who had become Speaker of the House of Representatives. In Congress, Clay proved to be a skillful negotiator. He worked out several key compromises. Despite his abilities, Clay was less popular than the other candidate from the West, Andrew Jackson.

To most Americans, Andrew Jackson was the "Hero of New Orleans." (See page 290.) They also saw him as a man of the people. Although Jackson owned land and slaves, he had started life poor.

The "corrupt bargain." In the election, Jackson won a majority of the popular vote. But no candidate won a majority of electoral votes. As a result, the House of Representatives had to choose the President from among the top three candidates. Clay, who finished fourth, was out of the running. As

---

BIOGRAPHY John Quincy Adams *President John Quincy Adams had great plans for improving the nation. He lacked the political skill, however, to win support for his programs.* **Citizenship** *Why did Americans oppose Adams's projects?*

Connections With the World
Background

Of all the candidates in the 1824 election, Adams had the best record in foreign service. He had been minister to the Netherlands (1794–1796), to Prussia (1797–1801), to Russia (1809–1815), and to Great Britain (1815–1817). He then served as President Monroe's Secretary of State (1817–1825).

Connections With Civics
Activity

Review the description of the 1824 election on pages 328–329. Explain to students that when an election is decided in the House, each state has only one vote, so the representatives from each state must agree on one of the candidates. Lead a class discussion on this question: When an election is passed into the House, should representatives be required to vote for the candidate with the highest electoral vote? How would this requirement have changed the results of the 1824 election? Encourage students to support their positions with information from the text.

Speaker of the House, though, he could influence the results.

Clay urged his supporters in the House to vote for Adams. After Adams won, he made Clay his Secretary of State. Jackson and his backers were furious. They accused Adams and Clay of making a "corrupt bargain" and stealing the election from Jackson.

An Unpopular President

Adams knew that the election had angered many Americans. To "bring the whole people together," he pushed for a program of internal improvements. His plan backfired, however, and opposition to him grew.

Promoting economic growth. Like Alexander Hamilton, Adams thought that the federal government should promote economic growth. He called for the government to pay for new roads and canals. These internal improvements would help farmers to transport goods to market.

Adams wanted the United States to back national projects like governments in Europe did. He suggested building a national university and an observatory for astronomers. He also backed projects to promote farming, manufacturing, science, and the arts.

As Adams discovered, most Americans objected to spending money on such programs. In part, they feared that the federal government would become too powerful. In the end, Congress approved money for a national road and some canals. It turned down most of Adams's other programs.

A bitter campaign. In 1828, Adams was facing an uphill battle for reelection. This

MAP STUDY

In the election of 1828, Andrew Jackson ran against President John Quincy Adams.

1. *Who won the election?*
2. *(a) In which three states was the vote split between Jackson and Adams? (b) How did the mapmaker show this information?*
3. **Analyzing Information** *Judging from this map, do you think regional differences played a role in the election of 1828? Explain.*

Election of 1828

Andrew Jackson

John Quincy Adams

Linking Past and Present
Politicians today often complain that reporters will do anything to get a story. Determined reporters, however, are nothing new. In the summer of 1828, for example, a reporter, Anne Royall, spied John Quincy Adams swimming in the Potomac River. Royall set herself down on Adams's clothes on the riverbank and refused to budge until, neck deep in water, he gave her an interview.

Chapter 11 • **329**

Lesson Planner

For a developed **Cooperative Learning** lesson plan, see the *Lesson Planner,* page 65.

Answers to Map Study

1. Andrew Jackson **2.** (a) Maine, New York, and Maryland (b) Both colors—Jackson's and Adams's —are shown in these states. **3.** Possible Answer: Yes; although the Northeast supported Adams (who was a northerner), Jackson had support in the South (where he had been born) and in the West.

CD-ROM

Presidents Access the biography of John Quincy Adams on the American Heritage® *History of the United States* CD-ROM. (Enrichment/Average)

Our Multicultural Heritage

Biography Have students read the biography, Anne Newport Royall, Journalist, on page 31 of the *Our Multicultural Heritage* booklet. (Enrichment/Average)
Biography Have students read the biography, Ira F. Aldridge, Shakespearean Actor, on page 32 of the *Our Multicultural Heritage* booklet. (Enrichment/Average)

Historical Sidelight
Background

Commenting on Adams in 1826, Senator John Randolph of Virginia complained, "This is the first Administration that has openly run the principle of patronage against that of patriotism, that has unblushingly avowed, aye, and executed its purpose, of buying us up with our own money." A year later, Representative Samuel D. Ingram of Pennsylvania noted that Adams "was educated as a monarchist, has always been hostile to popular government, and particularly to its great bulwark, the right of suffrage, . . . he affected to become a Republican only to pervert and degrade the Democratic party; and to pave the way for such a change in the Constitution as would establish the United States as an aristocratical and hereditary government."

Connections With Mathematics
Activity

Have students make a line graph using the following data. Percentage of adult white males voting: 1824, 27 percent; 1828, 56 percent; 1832, 55 percent; 1836, 55 percent; 1840, 78 percent; 1844, 75 percent. Ask: What conclusions can you draw from the graph?

time, Andrew Jackson was Adams's only opponent.

The campaign turned into a bitter contest. Jackson supporters renewed charges of a "corrupt bargain" following the 1824 election. They attacked Adams as an aristocrat, or member of the upper class. Adams supporters replied with similar attacks. They dubbed Jackson a "military chieftain." If Jackson were to be elected, they warned, he could become a dictator like Napoleon Bonaparte.

Jackson won the election easily. His supporters cheered this victory for the common people. By common people, they meant farmers in the West and South and urban workers in the East. A disappointed Adams supporter warned that Jackson had been swept into office by "the howl of raving Democracy."

New Views of Democracy

During the 1820s, the United States was growing rapidly. New states had been admitted to the Union. As a result, the number of voters increased.

New voters. Many new voters lived in the western states between the Appalachians and the Mississippi. Frontier life encouraged a democratic spirit. Many frontier people were poor. Through hard work, some prospered. They respected others who succeeded on their own. In the western states, any white man over age 21 could vote.

In the eastern states, reformers fought to end the requirement that voters own land. In the 1820s and 1830s, they succeeded. Except for Rhode Island, every eastern state extended **suffrage,** or the right to vote, to all white men.

Limits on suffrage. Despite these reforms, large numbers of Americans did not have the right to vote. They included women, Native Americans, and most African Americans. Slaves had no political rights.

In fact, while more white men were winning suffrage, free African Americans were losing this right. Most northern states had allowed free African Americans to vote in the early 1800s. In the 1820s, many of these states took away that right. By 1830, only a few New England states allowed African Americans to vote.

New Political Practices

In the 1830s, new political parties were taking shape. They grew out of the conflict between John Quincy Adams and Andrew Jackson.

Two new parties. People who supported Adams and his programs for national growth called themselves National Republicans. In 1834, they became known as **Whigs.** Whigs wanted the federal government to spur the economy. Whigs included most eastern business people, some southern planters, and former Federalists.

Jackson and his supporters called themselves **Democrats.** Today's Democratic party traces its roots to Andrew Jackson's time. Democrats included frontier farmers as well as factory workers in the East.

New ways to choose candidates. Political parties developed new ways to choose candidates for President. In the past, powerful members of each party held a **caucus,** or private meeting. There, they chose their candidate. Critics called the caucus system undemocratic because so few people took part in it.

In the 1830s, both parties began to hold **nominating conventions.** At a convention, delegates from the states chose the party's candidate for President. Nominating conventions gave people a more direct voice in choosing future leaders. Today's political parties still hold nominating conventions.

As parties took shape, a new figure emerged—the professional politician. These people organized campaigns and worked to get out the vote.

330 • Chapter 11

Connections With the World
Background

The idea of democracy was expanding elsewhere. In 1829, Great Britain passed the Catholic Emancipation Act, allowing British Catholics most of their rights, including freedom of worship. Daniel O'Connell, an Irish landowner and lawyer, was instrumental in its passage.

Linking Past and Present
Activity

When Andrew Jackson arrived at the Capitol to be sworn in as President, an enormous crowd blocked his path. The President-elect had to climb over a wall and enter the building through the basement. Then, a wild inauguration party brought such a crowd to the White House that Jackson's friends feared he would be crushed. They hurried him out of the White House, and he spent his first night as President sleeping in a hotel. Have students compare these notes about Jackson's inauguration and the description on page 332 with their own memories of the most recent presidential inaugural festivities.

CONNECTIONS

No Democracy for African Americans

There were 320,000 free African Americans living in the United States in the early 1830s. Some saved money to buy their freedom. Some had earned freedom as a reward, such as the slave who saved the Georgia capital from burning down. Others ran away or were freed on their master's death.

What did freedom mean for an African American at that time? It was not the same as the freedom enjoyed by whites. During the Jackson era, white men made important democratic gains. African Americans, meanwhile, lost ground. As one northerner commented, "The policy and power of the national and state governments are against them. . . .Their prospects. . .are dreary."

Northerners capture a freedman

From a high point at the time of the American Revolution, the rights of African Americans steadily declined. By the mid-1830s, every southern state had laws that barred African Americans—slave or free—from voting. In the North, African Americans could vote on equal terms with white males only in

five New England states. In New York, African American males had to own property in order to vote. White males did not.

Wherever they lived, African Americans lacked basic civil rights. By 1835, most southern states and several northern states restricted or forbade the entry of free African Americans. In Pennsylvania, for example, African Americans had to post a $500 bond for "good behavior" to stay in the state. This sum was beyond the means of most Americans of any race at that time.

A barber at work

The 1830s also was a time of increased violence against free African Americans. White mobs attacked African Americans and burned their property in New York City, Philadelphia, Cincinnati, and Pittsburgh. Whether they were in the South or the North, free African Americans were not really free. Instead, they might more accurately have been called "slaves without masters."

■ How were the rights of free African Americans limited in the 1830s?

ACTIVITY Draw a political cartoon showing how the rights of free African Americans were limited in the 1830s.

On the Campaign Trail *A democratic spirit swept the nation during the Jackson era. This painting by popular artist George Caleb Bingham shows a political candidate campaigning for votes on the frontier.* **Linking Past and Present** *How do candidates campaign for votes today?*

Growing Spirit of Equality

The spirit of democracy affected American attitudes toward one another. Americans no longer felt that the rich deserved special respect. "Does a man become wiser, stronger or more virtuous and patriotic because he has a fine house?" asked a Democrat.

European visitors were surprised that servants expected to be treated as equals. Butlers and maids refused to be summoned with bells, as in Europe. A coach driver complained that his employer "had had private meals every day and not asked him to the table."

Andrew Jackson's inauguration in 1829 reflected this spirit of equality. For the first time, thousands of ordinary people flooded the capital to watch the President take the oath of office. They then followed Jackson to a reception at the White House. The behavior of the "common people" shocked an onlooker:

&&A rabble, a mob, of boys, negros, women, children, scrambling, fighting, romping. What a pity, what a pity! No arrangements had been made, no police officers on duty, and the whole house had been [filled] by the rabble mob.&&

The President, he continued, was "almost suffocated and torn to pieces by the people in their eagerness to shake hands." Critics said the scene showed that "King Mob" was ruling the nation. Amos Kendall, a Jackson supporter, disagreed: "It was a proud day for the people. General Jackson is *their own* President."

SECTION 1 REVIEW

1. **Identify:** (a) John Quincy Adams, (b) Henry Clay, (c) Whigs, (d) Democrats.
2. **Define:** (a) suffrage, (b) caucus, (c) nominating convention.
3. Why was the outcome of the election of 1824 a bitter blow to Andrew Jackson?
4. Why did most Americans reject Adams's programs for national growth?
5. (a) How did the United States become more democratic in the 1820s and 1830s? (b) Which groups did not benefit from increased suffrage?
6. **CRITICAL THINKING Applying Information** "Does a man become wiser, stronger or more virtuous and patriotic because he has a fine house?" How might a Jackson supporter have responded to this question?

ACTIVITY **Writing to Learn**

Write a dialogue in which John Quincy Adams and Andrew Jackson discuss the election of 1824.

2
Jackson in the White House

FIND OUT
- What qualities helped Jackson succeed?
- Why did Jackson replace many officeholders?
- Why did Jackson make war on the Bank of the United States?

VOCABULARY spoils system, pet bank

Dozens of stories about Andrew Jackson made the rounds during the 1828 election. Like the one that follows, they often showed Jackson's courage and grit.

Years before he ran for President, Jackson was a judge in Tennessee. One day, a disorderly lawbreaker, Russell Bean, refused to appear before the court. Bean scared off the sheriff, but not Andrew Jackson. The story tells how Jackson strode out of the courthouse. "Surrender, you infernal villain," he roared, "or I'll blow you through." Bean looked into Jackson's blazing eyes and quietly surrendered. The iron will that made Bean surrender also made Jackson a powerful President.

Tough as Hickory

Like many of the people who admired him, Jackson was born in a log cabin on the frontier. His parents had left Ireland to settle on the Carolina frontier. Both had died before Jackson was 15. Young Andrew had to grow up quickly.

"He would never stay throwed." By his teens, Jackson could defend himself. Even though he had a slight build, he was strong and determined. A friend who wrestled with him recalled, "I could throw him three times out of four, but he would never stay throwed."

Jackson showed his toughness during the American Revolution. At age 13, he joined the Patriots but was captured by the British. When a British officer ordered the young prisoner to clean his boots, Jackson refused. The officer slashed the boy's hand and face with a sword. Jackson bore the scars of that attack all his life.

A self-made man. As a young man, Jackson studied law in North Carolina. Later, he moved to Tennessee, where he set up a law practice. He became wealthy by buying and selling land. While still in his twenties, he was elected to Congress.

Jackson won national fame during the War of 1812. As you have read, he commanded American forces at New Orleans. To settlers on the frontier, Jackson was already well known. He had defeated the Creek Indians at Horseshoe Bend and forced them to give up vast amounts of land in Georgia and Alabama.

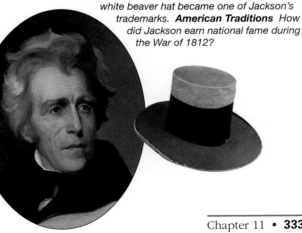

BIOGRAPHY Andrew Jackson *Andrew Jackson was a strong, self-confident man, as the portrait shows. As President, he greatly increased the prestige and power of the national government. The white beaver hat became one of Jackson's trademarks.* **American Traditions** *How did Jackson earn national fame during the War of 1812?*

Jackson's nicknames told something about his character. The Creeks called him Sharp Knife. His own men gave him another name—*Old Hickory.* To them, he was hard and tough as the wood of a hickory tree. The name stuck even after he became President.

The Spoils System

In 1828, President Jackson knew that Americans wanted change. "The people expected reform," he said. "This was the cry from Maine to Louisiana."

Reward for victory. After taking office, Jackson fired many federal employees. He replaced them with his own supporters. Although most other Presidents had done the same, Jackson did it on a larger scale.

Critics complained that Jackson was rewarding Democrats who had helped elect him. He was not choosing qualified and ex-

---

A Meeting of the Kitchen Cabinet *President Jackson relied for advice on an informal group of advisers known as the kitchen cabinet. This cartoon gives one artist's view of Jackson's kitchen cabinet.* **Citizenship** *What do you think was the cartoonist's opinion of Jackson's kitchen cabinet? Explain.*

perienced men, they said. Jackson replied that he was fulfilling a goal of democracy by letting more citizens take part in government. He felt that ordinary Americans could fill government jobs. "The duties of all public officers are...so plain and simple that men of intelligence may readily qualify themselves for their performance," he said.

A Jackson supporter explained the system another way. "To the victor belong the spoils," he declared. Spoils are profits or benefits. From then on, the practice of rewarding supporters with government jobs became known as the **spoils system.** In the years ahead, the spoils system grew.

An unofficial Cabinet. Jackson rewarded some supporters with Cabinet jobs. Only Secretary of State Martin Van Buren was truly qualified for his position.

Jackson seldom met with his official Cabinet. Instead, he relied on advice from Democratic leaders and newspaper editors. These men had a good sense of the nation's mood. Because Jackson met with them in the White House kitchen, the group became known as the ***kitchen cabinet.***

The Bank War

President Jackson waged war on the Bank of the United States. Like many westerners, he disliked the Bank. He thought that it was too powerful.

Mr. Biddle's bank. From the first, the Bank of the United States had been a subject of dispute. (See page 255.) The Bank had great power because it controlled loans made by state banks. When the Bank's directors thought that state banks were making too many loans, they limited the amount these banks could lend. The cutbacks angered farmers and merchants who borrowed money to buy land or finance new businesses.

Jackson and other Democrats saw the Bank as undemocratic. Although Congress had created the Bank, it was run by private

---

bankers. Jackson especially disliked Nicholas Biddle, president of the Bank since 1823.

Biddle came from a wealthy Philadelphia family. He was well qualified to run the bank, but he was also an arrogant, vain man. Jackson believed that Biddle used the Bank to benefit only the rich. He also resented Biddle's influence over certain members of Congress.

The war begins. Biddle and other Whigs worried that the President might try to destroy the Bank. Two Whig senators, Henry Clay and Daniel Webster, thought of a way to save the Bank and defeat Jackson at the same time.

The Bank's charter was not due for renewal by Congress until 1836. But Clay and Webster wanted to make the Bank an issue in the 1832 election. They convinced Biddle to apply for renewal early.

The Whigs believed that most Americans supported the Bank. If Jackson vetoed the bill to renew the charter, they felt sure that he would anger voters and lose the election.

Clay pushed the charter renewal bill through Congress in 1832. Jackson was sick in bed when he heard that Congress had renewed the Bank's charter. "The Bank...is trying to kill me," he fumed, "but I will kill it!"

Jackson's veto. In an angry message to Congress, Jackson vetoed the Bank bill. Nicholas Biddle compared the President's veto message to "the fury of a chained panther biting the bars of his cage."

Linking Past and Present

A supporter of Andrew Jackson started a tradition when he handed his baby to the President for a kiss. Unlike most modern politicians, however, Jackson declined to kiss the child. Instead, he handed him to Secretary of War John Eaton to do the honors.

King Andrew the First *To his opponents, Andrew Jackson's veto of the Bank bill was an abuse of presidential power. This Whig cartoon from the 1830s shows Jackson as a tyrant trampling on the Constitution.* **Citizenship** *Did Jackson as President have the right to go against the will of Congress?*

Jackson gave two reasons for his veto. First, he declared the Bank unconstitutional, even though the Supreme Court had ruled in the Bank's favor. Jackson believed that only states, not the federal government, had the right to charter banks. Second, Jackson felt that the Bank was a monster that helped the rich at the expense of the common people. He warned:

❝When the laws undertake...to make the rich richer and the potent more powerful, the humble members of society—the farmers, mechanics, and laborers—who have

---

Section 3
pp. 336–341

Bell Ringer

Ask: Whom do you think Jackson supported in the conflicts between white settlers and Native Americans? Why do you think so?

Lesson Plan

1. Focus In his second term, Andrew Jackson faced new crises. In this section, students read about the debates over tariffs and states' rights, as well as the tragic results of Jackson's policy toward Native Americans.

2. Instruct Have students work in small groups to prepare a television news magazine on the presidency of Andrew Jackson. Segments could include a brief biography of Jackson; a report on major events during Jackson's term of office; interviews about Jackson with such figures as John Quincy Adams, Nicholas Biddle, John C. Calhoun, and Chief Osceola; and a closing commentary. Assign two students to act as anchors to coordinate the segments.

---

neither the time nor the means of securing like favors to themselves, have a right to complain of the injustice of their government. **"**

As planned, the Whigs made the Bank a major issue in the election of 1832. They chose Henry Clay to run against Andrew Jackson. When the votes were counted, Jackson won a stunning victory. The common people had supported Jackson and rejected the Bank.

The Bank closes. Without a new charter, the Bank would have to close in 1836. Jackson did not want to wait. He ordered Secretary of the Treasury Roger Taney to stop putting government money in the Bank. Instead, Taney deposited federal money in state banks. They became known as **pet banks** because Taney and his friends controlled many of them.

The loss of federal money crippled the Bank of the United States. Its closing in 1836 would contribute to an economic crisis, as you will read.

SECTION 2 REVIEW

1. **Identify:** (a) Old Hickory, (b) kitchen cabinet, (c) Nicholas Biddle, (d) Roger Taney.
2. **Define:** (a) spoils system, (b) pet bank.
3. List three qualities that helped make Andrew Jackson a powerful national figure.
4. Why did critics object to the spoils system?
5. Why did Jackson dislike the Bank of the United States?
6. **CRITICAL THINKING Defending a Position** Do you think that the spoils system furthers democracy? Why or why not?

ACTIVITY **Writing to Learn**

Write the script for a television talk show in which Andrew Jackson and Nicholas Biddle discuss the Bank of the United States.

336 • Chapter 11

3
A Strong President

FIND OUT
- How did tariffs lead to the Nullification Crisis?
- Why did South Carolina threaten to withdraw from the Union?
- Why were Native Americans forced off their lands?

VOCABULARY nullification, states' rights, secede

The war on the Bank made Jackson more popular than ever among certain Americans. "The Jackson cause is the cause of democracy," boasted one Democrat. Another praised the President's strong stand:

"Who but General Jackson would have had the courage to veto the bill rechartering the Bank of the United States, and who but General Jackson could have withstood the overwhelming influence of that corrupt Aristocracy?**"**

In his second term of office, Jackson would face new tests of strength. To achieve his goals, he would extend the powers of the Chief Executive.

The Tariff of Abominations

Early in Jackson's second term, a crisis over tariffs threatened to split the nation. In 1828, Congress passed the highest tariff in the nation's history. Southerners called it the *Tariff of Abominations.* An abomination is something that is hated.

Like earlier tariffs, the new law benefited northern manufacturers by protecting them from foreign competition. Southern planters, however, were hurt by the tariff.

They sold their cotton in Europe and bought European goods in return. The high tariff meant that southerners had to pay more for these imported goods.

Calhoun for states' rights. Vice President John C. Calhoun led the South's fight against the tariff. He used an argument that Thomas Jefferson had made in the Kentucky and Virginia resolutions. (See page 260.) Like Jefferson, Calhoun claimed that a state had the right to nullify, or cancel, a federal law that it considered unconstitutional. The idea of a state declaring a federal law illegal is called **nullification.**

Calhoun raised a serious issue. Did states have the right to limit the power of the federal government? Or did the federal government have final power? Calhoun supported **states' rights,** the right of states to limit the power of the federal government. As he pointed out, the states had created the national government. Therefore, the states had final authority.

Webster for the Union. Daniel Webster disagreed. In 1830, he made a speech in the Senate attacking the idea of nullification. The Constitution, he said, united the American people, not just the states. If states had the right to nullify federal laws, the nation would fall apart. Webster ended his speech with stirring words: "Liberty and Union, now and forever, one and inseparable."

The Vice President Resigns

Calhoun and other southerners expected Jackson to support their view. After all, Jackson had been born in the South and had lived in the West. Both sections supported states' rights.

The President's stand soon became clear. In 1830, a group of states' rights supporters invited both Jackson and Vice President Calhoun to dinner. Several guests made toasts in favor of states' rights. Finally, Jackson rose. The room fell silent. Old Hickory raised his glass, looked straight at the

The Tariff of Abominations *The 1828 tariff divided the nation, as this cartoon shows. The figure on the left represents the South, carrying the burden of the tariff. The well-fed figure on the right represents the prosperous North.* **Economics** *Why did the tariff have different effects on the North and the South?*

Vice President, and declared, "Our Federal Union—it must be preserved!"

The drama continued. Calhoun raised his glass and answered the President's challenge with his own: "The Union—next to our liberty, most dear." To him, the liberty of a state was more important than the Union.

The debate over states' rights would rage for years. Because Calhoun disagreed with Jackson, he resigned from the office of Vice President. He was then elected senator from South Carolina. Martin Van Buren became Jackson's Vice President in 1833.

Challenge From South Carolina

As anger against the tariff grew in the South, Congress took action. In 1832, it passed a new tariff that lowered the rate slightly. South Carolina was not satisfied. It passed the Nullification Act, declaring the new tariff illegal. At the same time, it threatened to **secede,** or withdraw, from the Union if challenged.

Jackson was furious when he heard the news. He knew that nullification could destroy the nation. "It leads directly to civil war and bloodshed," he declared. In private, he raged:

> 66 If one drop of blood be shed there in defiance of the laws of the United States, I will hang the first man of them I can get my hands on to the first tree I can find. 99

Publicly, the President was more practical. He supported a compromise tariff proposed by Henry Clay. The bill would lower tariffs. At the same time, Jackson asked Congress to pass the Force Bill. It allowed him to use the army, if necessary, to enforce the tariff in South Carolina.

Faced with Jackson's firm stand, no other state supported South Carolina. Calhoun gave in and agreed to Clay's compromise tariff. South Carolina repealed the Nullification Act.

The **Nullification Crisis** passed. However, sectional tensions between the North and South would increase.

New Threats to Native Americans

Jackson took a firm stand on another key issue. It affected the fate of Native Americans. For more than 300 years, Europeans had been pushing Native Americans off their land. In the United States, white settlers had forced Indians to move west. Indian leaders like Pontiac and Tecumseh had tried to stop the invasion. But their efforts had ended in defeat.

Indian nations in the Southeast. By the 1820s, only about 125,000 Indians still lived east of the Mississippi. Many belonged to the Creek, Chickasaw, Cherokee, Choctaw, and Seminole nations. They lived on the fertile lands of the Southeast.

The Indians wanted to live in peace with their white neighbors. Their land, however, was ideal for growing cotton. To the land-hungry settlers, the Indians stood in the way of progress.

Like earlier Presidents, Jackson sided with the white settlers. At his urging, the government set aside lands beyond the Mississippi and then persuaded or forced Indians to move there. Jackson believed that such a policy would open up land to white settlers. It would also protect Native Americans from destruction.

The Cherokee nation. Few Indians wanted to move. Some, like the Cherokee nation, had adapted to the customs of white settlers. The Cherokees lived in farming villages. They had a constitution that set up a republican form of government.

Sequoyah (sih KWOI uh), a Cherokee, created a written alphabet for his people. Using Sequoyah's letters, Cherokee children

---

BIOGRAPHY Sequoyah *Sequoyah adapted Greek, Hebrew, and English letters to create the 86 symbols of his Cherokee alphabet. The Cherokee nation used Sequoyah's alphabet to write its constitution.* **Multicultural Heritage** *Why do you think Sequoyah wanted to create a written alphabet for the Cherokee language?*

Our Multicultural Heritage
Background

Sequoyah's alphabet had 86 symbols and used Greek, English, and Hebrew letters. The newspaper using Sequoyah's alphabet was called the *Cherokee Phoenix.*

John Ross, part Cherokee and part Scot, led the fight against Native American removal (see page 339). When the Cherokees were forced to leave, he led them to Oklahoma and became chief of the united Cherokee nation. About 1,000 Cherokees fled to the mountains of North Carolina. The federal government later set up a reservation for them, where the Cherokees still live.

After the Seminoles lost the war (see page 341), most of them relocated to Oklahoma; however, some Seminoles held out in the Everglades, where their descendants still live. Chief Osceola died in prison at Fort Moultrie, South Carolina.

learned to read and write. The Cherokees used their alphabet to publish a newspaper.

A legal battle. In 1828, Georgia claimed the right to make laws for the Cherokee nation. The Cherokees went to court to defend their rights. They pointed to their treaties with the federal government that protected their rights and property. Led by Chief Justice John Marshall, the Supreme Court ruled in favor of the Cherokees. It declared Georgia's action unconstitutional.

Jackson then stepped in. In the Nullification Crisis, he defended the power of the federal government. In this case, he backed states' rights. Georgia had the right to extend its authority over Cherokee lands, he said. The federal government could not stop this action.

The President refused to enforce the Court's decision. "John Marshall has made his decision," Jackson reportedly said. "Now let him enforce it."

A Tragic March

In 1830, Jackson supporters in Congress pushed through the **_Indian Removal Act._** Under it, Native Americans were forced to sign treaties agreeing to move west of the Mississippi. Whites thought the region was a vast desert. They did not mind turning it over to Indians.

Forced to leave. The Cherokees held out longest. Then in 1838, the United States Army forced them to leave at gunpoint.

Our Common Heritage

Like the United States Constitution, the Cherokee constitution established a legislature with two houses; an executive branch, consisting of a principal chief and vice principal chief; and a judicial branch. It also denied the vote to women and descendants of enslaved African Americans.

ART GALLERY
OUR COMMON HERITAGE

CHRIS WOLF EDMONDS
Cherokee Trail of Tears, 1979

In 1838, soldiers drove more than 15,000 Cherokees on a westward march to Oklahoma. On the 116-day journey, more than one out of every four Indians died from illness or exhaustion. The Cherokees called the westward route Nuna-da-ut-sun'y—"The Trail Where They Cried." Some 140 years later, Chris Wolf Edmonds created this quilt as a memorial to the Cherokee Trail of Tears. **_Linking Past and Present_** _Why do you think artists portray events from the past?_

Critical Thinking
Evaluating Information

Draw a chart on the chalkboard with four columns labeled Event, Jackson's Action, Democratic or Undemocratic? and Constitutional or Unconstitutional? In the first column, write Spoils System, Kitchen Cabinet, Bank Veto, Nullification Crisis, and Indian Removal Act. Have students fill in the remainder of the chart. Then, using the chart as a guide, have students write an essay stating whether they think Andrew Jackson was an effective President. They should consider why it is important for a President to act firmly, as well as the dangers that may result when a President takes too strong an action.

Answers to Map Study

Answers to Map Study

1. Seminole, Choctaw, Creek, Cherokee, Chickasaw **2.** about 750 miles (1,200 km) **3.** Possible Answer: They believed that Indian Territory was a vast desert and thus worthless.

Voices of Freedom

Primary Source You might assign selection 13-5, Jackson Warns the Seminoles, on pages 93–94 of *Voices of Freedom.* The selection is a letter from President Jackson advising the Seminoles to go west voluntarily. In the letter, Jackson hints at the measures that he is prepared to take if they do not heed his advice. (Enrichment/Average)

Student Study Guide

Section 3 Study Guide Have students use the Section 3 Study Guide on page 97 of the *Student Study Guide* to review and reinforce the content of this section. (Reteaching/Average)

MAP STUDY

In the 1830s, some 100,000 southeastern Indians were driven from their homes and forced to march to Indian Territory, west of the Mississippi.
1. What five southeastern nations marched to Indian Territory?
2. How many miles (km) did the Cherokees travel on this Trail of Tears?
3. **Drawing Conclusions** Why were many Americans willing to give Native Americans the land called Indian Territory?

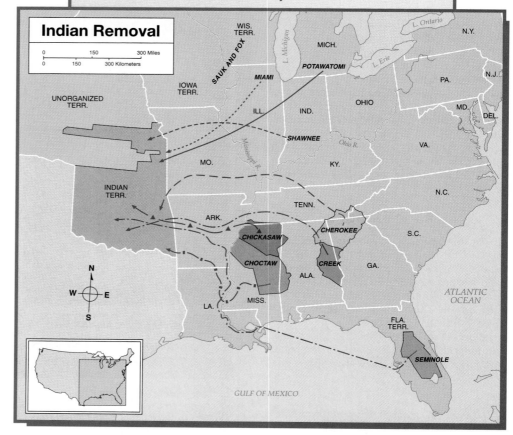

The Cherokees trekked hundreds of miles into lands they had never seen before. (See the map above.) They had little food or shelter. Thousands perished during the march, mostly children and the elderly. In all, about one fourth of the Indians died.

The Cherokees' long, sorrowful journey west became known as the **Trail of Tears.** An eyewitness described the suffering:

❝The Cherokees are nearly all prisoners. They had been dragged from

340 • Chapter 11

Our Multicultural Heritage
Activity

Divide students into five groups. Ask each group to design a historical marker for the routes taken by the five southeastern Indian nations who were forced west along the Trail of Tears. Encourage the use of encyclopedias and other reference books on North American Indians for information about each of the southeastern nations: Cherokee, Choctaw, Chickasaw, Creek, and Seminole. Markers or monuments might consist of a symbol of the culture of the specific Indian nation and an explanation of what happened to its people after the Trail of Tears. Have students decide at which present-day site along the Trail of Tears they would like to construct their marker.

their homes and encamped at the forts and military places, all over the nation. In Georgia especially, multitudes were allowed no time to take anything with them except the clothes they had on. . . . The property of many has been taken and sold before their eyes for almost nothing. **99**

The Seminoles resist. In Florida, the Seminole Indians resisted removal. Led by Chief Osceola (ahs ee OH luh), they fought the United States Army. The *Seminole War* lasted from 1835 to 1842. It was the costliest war waged by the government to gain Indian lands. In the end, the Seminoles were defeated. By 1844, only a few thousand Native Americans remained east of the Mississippi River.

SECTION 3 REVIEW

1. **Locate:** (a) South Carolina, (b) Georgia, (c) Mississippi River.
2. **Identify:** (a) Tariff of Abominations, (b) Nullification Crisis, (c) Sequoyah, (d) Indian Removal Act, (e) Trail of Tears, (f) Seminole War.
3. **Define:** (a) nullification, (b) states' rights, (c) secede.
4. (a) How did northerners benefit from tariffs? (b) Why did southerners oppose tariffs?
5. How did Jackson respond to the Nullification Crisis?
6. (a) How did the Cherokees try to protect their lands? (b) Why did they fail?
7. **CRITICAL THINKING Analyzing Information** Why do you think Andrew Jackson supported states' rights in the Cherokee case but not in the Nullification Crisis?

ACTIVITY **Writing to Learn**
Imagine that you are a Cherokee on the Trail of Tears. Write a brief story about your experiences.

4
Jackson's Successors

FIND OUT
- What economic problems did Martin Van Buren face?
- How did William Henry Harrison campaign for President?
- Why did Tyler have little success as President?

A weary Andrew Jackson retired from office after two terms. Americans then sent Martin Van Buren, Jackson's friend and Vice President, to the White House.

As Van Buren took the oath of office in March 1837, Jackson stood at his side. Onlookers watched the retiring President, not Van Buren. As Old Hickory left the platform, the crowd cheered. They had nothing but respect for the outgoing leader.

An Economic Crisis

Martin Van Buren was very different from Jackson. He was a politician, not a war hero. Davy Crockett, a member of Congress from Tennessee, once described Van Buren as "an artful, cunning, intriguing, selfish, speculating lawyer." As President, Van Buren needed more than sharp political instincts. Two months after taking office, he faced the worst economic crisis the nation had known. It was called the *Panic of 1837*.

The panic begins. The panic had several causes. During the 1830s, the government sold millions of acres of public land in the West. Farmers bought some land, but speculators bought even more. To pay for the land, speculators borrowed money from state banks, especially western banks. After the Bank of the United States closed, state banks could lend money without limit.

Chapter 11 • **341**

ACTIVITY
Guided Instruction Encourage students to tell their stories from the point of view of one character and perhaps to explore one crucial or severe incident. Suggest that students include dialogue between the important characters in their stories.

Section 4
pp. 341–345

Bell Ringer

Have students write answers to these questions: Do politicians still try to appear like one of the "common people"? What are some tactics that politicians today use to win votes?

Lesson Plan

1. **Focus** The Presidents who followed Andrew Jackson faced economic and political problems that caused them to lose support. In this section, students learn about Presidents Van Buren, Harrison, and Tyler.
2. **Instruct** After dividing the class into five groups, have each group write a paragraph summarizing the Up Close feature, The Log Cabin Campaign. Have each group read its summary aloud and have the class decide whether it accurately reflects the feature. Conclude by helping students formulate a sentence that expresses the main point of the Up Close feature.

Answers to Section 3 Review

1. Refer to the map on p. 340.
2. (a) Tariff of Abominations, p. 336, (b) Nullification Crisis, p. 338, (c) Sequoyah, p. 338, (d) Indian Removal Act, p. 339, (e) Trail of Tears, p. 340, (f) Seminole War, p. 341
3. (a) nullification, p. 337, (b) states' rights, p. 337, (c) secede, p. 338
4. (a) They protected northern manufacturers from foreign competition. (b) Southerners sold their cotton in Europe and bought European goods in return; high tariffs made the European goods more expensive.
5. He compromised and supported a lower tariff bill; he had Congress pass the Force Bill, which allowed him to enforce the tariff.
6. (a) They brought their case to the Supreme Court, which upheld their right to keep the land. (b) Jackson refused to use his power to carry out the Court's decision.
7. Possible Answer: Jackson probably supported western expansion and did not see the Cherokee case as a threat to the Union, but he did view the Nullification Crisis as a national threat.

3. Close To close the lesson, have students summarize the reasons for the Panic of 1837 and describe Harrison's campaign strategy in the election of 1840.

Lesson Planner

For a developed **Cooperative Learning** lesson plan, see the *Lesson Planner,* page 68.

CD-ROM

Presidents Access the biography of Martin Van Buren on the American Heritage® *History of the United States* CD-ROM. (Enrichment/Average)

Answer to Caption

Speculators bought land on borrowed money. Banks issued paper money that was not backed by gold or silver. When Jackson ordered that public land had to be bought with silver or gold, people rushed to the banks. The banks did not have enough gold or silver, however, and they were forced to close.

To meet the demand for loans, state banks printed more and more paper money. Often, the paper money was not backed by gold or silver. Paper money had value only if people had trust in the banks that issued it.

Before leaving office, Jackson had become alarmed at the wild speculation in land. To slow it down, he ordered that anyone buying public land had to pay for it with gold or silver. Speculators and others rushed to state banks to exchange their paper money for gold and silver. Many banks did not have enough gold and silver and had to close.

Banks fail. The panic spread. More and more people hurried to banks to trade in their paper money. In New York, one bank "was jammed with depositors crying 'Pay, pay!'" reported a witness. Hundreds of banks failed, leaving depositors empty-handed.

The panic worsened when cotton prices went down because of an oversupply. Cotton planters often borrowed money, which they repaid when they sold their crop. With cotton prices low, planters could not repay the loans. As a result, more banks failed. Business slowed, and the nation plunged into a deep economic depression.

Tough Times

In the worst days of the depression, 90 percent of the nation's factories were closed. Thousands of people were out of work. In

History and You
One of the causes of the Panic of 1837 was that banks allowed people to borrow more money than they could repay. Today, many people use credit cards when they shop. If you had a credit card, what limits would you put on your spending to make sure that you are able to pay for what you buy?

The Long Bill *Ordinary people suffered greatly in the Panic of 1837. People had bought on credit, sure that they could pay later. Now, many people, like the customer shown here, faced a "long bill" that they could not pay.* **Economics** *How did the sale of western lands contribute to the Panic of 1837?*

some cities, hungry crowds broke into warehouses and stole food.

Van Buren's response. The panic was not Van Buren's fault, but he was blamed for it. Once it began, he took little action. "The less the government interferes with private pursuits," he said, "the better for the general prosperity."

Van Buren did try to set up a more stable banking system, but with limited success. He also cut back on expenses at the White House. Guests, for example, were served simple dinners. As the depression dragged on, support for the President fell. Even so, the Democrats chose Van Buren to run for reelection.

The hero of Tippecanoe. In 1840, the Whigs saw a chance to win the White House. Learning from the Democrats, they chose a candidate who would appeal to the common people. He was William Henry

---

Connections With Economics
Activity

Have students research Gresham's law and the principle of supply and demand. Then have them write a paragraph defining each of these terms and another paragraph explaining how these principles apply to the Panic of 1837. Alternatively, have students create a cause-and-effect chart about the Panic of 1837. Remind students that causes and effects can be short or long term.

It is not only in the Panic of 1837 that President Van Buren failed to take decisive action. He was well known for being more of a listener than a talker — and for saying very little about his own opinions when he did talk. A colleague characterized him as someone who "rowed to his object with muffled oars." Nicknames such as the "Red Fox of Kinderhook" and the "Little Magician" also pointed to his evasiveness.

Even before he became President, Van Buren had this reputation. A popular story in

Historical Sidelight
Background

Washington told of a U.S. senator who made a bet that he could get Van Buren to take a definite stand on some issue. He went to Van Buren and said, "Mat, it's been rumored that the sun rises in the East. Do you believe it?" Van Buren reportedly replied, "Well, Senator, I understand that's the common acceptance, but as I never get up till after dawn, I can't really say."

Harrison of Ohio. Harrison was known as the hero of the Battle of Tippecanoe. (See page 285.) To run for Vice President, the Whigs chose John Tyler.

The Log Cabin Campaign

 Harrison's campaign reflected a new sort of politics that was emerging. Politicians made speeches, and candidates campaigned at rallies and banquets. Political parties competed for votes by offering exciting entertainment.

A war hero and man of the people. Most Americans knew little about William Henry Harrison's stand on the issues. To appeal to voters, the Whigs focused on his war record. "Tippecanoe and Tyler too" became their campaign slogan.

They also created an image for Harrison as a "man of the people." They presented him as a humble Ohio farmer who had been born in a log cabin. In fact, Harrison was a wealthy, educated man from Virginia whose family had owned a large estate.

Still, the Whigs made the log cabin their campaign symbol. In a typical Whig cartoon, Harrison stands outside a log cabin, greeting Van Buren and his aides:

66 Gentlemen, . . . If you will accept the [simple food] of a log cabin, with a western farmer's cheer, you are welcome. I have no champagne but can give you a mug of good cider, with some ham and eggs, and good clean beds. I am a plain backwoodsman. I have cleared some land, killed some Indians, and made the Red Coats fly in my time. 99

Attacks on Van Buren. The Whigs also attacked Van Buren. They blamed "Martin Van Ruin" for the economic depression. "King Mat," they sneered, was a "democratic peacock, plumed, perfumed, and strutting around the White House." Daniel Webster charged that the Democrats had replaced "Old Hickory" Jackson with "Slippery Elm" Van Buren.

Both parties used name-calling, half-truths, and lies. A Whig newspaper falsely reported that Van Buren spent "thousands of the people's dollars" to install a bathtub in the White House.

On the campaign trail. Harrison campaigned across the land, making speeches and greeting voters. Along the campaign trail, Whigs built log cabins to use as their headquarters. They even set up log cabins in large cities such as New York. Parades

Log Cabin Politics
The log cabin was the symbol of William Henry Harrison's campaign. Whigs sang the "Log Cabin March" and drank cider out of log cabin bottles. **Linking Past and Present** *Could the techniques of the Harrison campaign be used today? Explain.*

Chapter 11 • **343**

CD-ROM

Presidents Access the biographies of William Henry Harrison and John Tyler on the American Heritage® *History of the United States* CD-ROM. (Enrichment/Average)

Student Study Guide

Section 4 Study Guide Have students use the Section 4 Study Guide on page 98 of the *Student Study Guide* to review and reinforce the content of this section. (Reteaching/Average)

ACTIVITY

Guided Instruction Students can write entirely new lyrics for a popular melody, or they might change only some key words and phrases to give new political meaning to a well-known lyric. Some musically talented students may want to create both music and lyrics. Allow students to perform their songs in groups or individually.

---

featured log cabins carried on wagons. And at every stop, Whigs served plenty of free cider.

Ordinary citizens joined in the rallies. They gave speeches, marched in parades, and sang campaign songs like this one:

❝ The times are bad, and want
    curing;
They are getting past all
    enduring;
So let's turn out Martin Van
    Buren
And put in old Tippecanoe! ❞

"Keep the ball rolling." In towns across the United States, Harrison supporters rolled huge balls down the streets. The balls were 12 feet in diameter, made of twine, and covered with slogans. "Keep the ball rolling," people chanted as they marched.

Enterprising merchants sold campaign souvenirs. They offered badges, handkerchiefs, and even containers of shaving cream with the Tippecanoe slogan. A popular item was a bottle shaped like a log cabin.

Although women could not vote, they campaigned for Harrison. Women wrote pamphlets, sewed banners, rode on floats, and paraded with brooms to "sweep" the Democrats out of office. Young women's sashes proclaimed, "Whig husbands or none."

A Whig victory at last. The Democrats responded to Whig attacks with their own name-calling. "Granny Harrison, the Petticoat General," they revealed, had resigned from the army before the War of 1812 ended. They accused "General Mum" of not speaking out on the issues.

"Should Harrison be elected?" they asked voters. "Read his name spelled backwards," they advised. "No sirrah."

Harrison won the election easily, forcing the Democrats out of the White House for the first time in 12 years. "We have taught them how to conquer us!" lamented one Democrat. "We've been sung down," another complained. ■

Whigs in the White House

The Whigs had a clear-cut program. They wanted to create a new Bank of the United States and improve roads and canals. Also, they wanted a high tariff.

Whig hopes were soon dashed. Just weeks after taking office, President Harrison died of pneumonia. John Tyler became the first Vice President to succeed a President who died in office.

President Tyler disappointed the Whigs. He had once been a Democrat and opposed the Whig plan to develop the economy. When the Whigs in Congress passed a bill to recharter the Bank of the United States, Tyler vetoed it.

In response, Tyler's entire Cabinet resigned, except for Daniel Webster. The Whigs then threw Tyler out of their party. Democrats welcomed the squabbling. "Tyler is heartily despised by everyone," reported an observer. "He has no influence at all." With few friends in either party, Tyler could do little during his term in office.

SECTION 4 REVIEW

1. **Identify:** Panic of 1837.
2. How did Jackson's policies contribute to the Panic of 1837?
3. How did the oversupply of cotton deepen the depression?
4. Why did the Whigs back William Henry Harrison for President in 1840?
5. How did John Tyler disappoint the Whigs?
6. CRITICAL THINKING **Synthesizing Information** Why was the log cabin a successful campaign symbol for Harrison in 1840?

ACTIVITY **Writing to Learn**

Write the words for a song that one of the candidates might have used in the election campaign of 1840.

Critical Thinking
Asking Questions

Ask students to pretend that they are reporters at a debate between Martin Van Buren and William Henry Harrison during the 1840 presidential campaign. Have students write a series of questions that they would ask each candidate.

Answers to Section 4 Review

1. Panic of 1837, p. 341
2. Because of Jackson's veto, there was no national bank to limit lending or to slow down wild land speculation. Jackson also ordered that public land had to be purchased with gold or silver, causing a run on the state banks.
3. The price of cotton fell, and when planters who had borrowed money could not repay their loans, more banks failed and businesses slowed.
4. Harrison was a popular war hero.
5. Tyler disagreed with Whig plans for developing the economy and reviving the national bank.
6. Possible Answer: The symbol of the log cabin appealed to farmers, workers, and frontierspeople, who had humble homes.

MAP, GRAPH, AND CHART SKILLS
Reading a Circle Graph

Circle graphs are one method of showing statistics in a visual way. (See Skill Lesson 2 on page 55 to review what you have learned about reading a line graph.) A circle graph is sometimes called a pie graph because it is divided into wedges, like a pie. Each wedge, or part, can be compared to every other wedge, or part.

A circle graph shows the relationship between each of the parts and the whole. To compare information over a period of time, two circle graphs can be used.

1. **Identify the information shown on the graphs.** (a) What year does the circle graph on the left show? (b) What year does the circle graph on the right show? (c) What do the colors on the circle graphs represent?

2. **Practice reading the graphs.** In a circle graph, you can compare any part with every other part or with the whole graph. The graph shows each part as a percentage of the whole. The whole graph is 100 percent. (a) What percentage of the electoral vote did the Whigs get in 1836? In 1840? (b) What percentage of the electoral vote did the Democrats get in 1836? In 1840? (c) Which party got a greater percentage of the electoral vote in 1840? (d) Did the independent party affect the outcome of the election in 1836? Explain.

3. **Interpret the information shown on the graphs.** Compare the two graphs. (a) How did the Whig electoral vote in 1836 compare with the Democratic electoral vote in 1836? (b) Based on the graphs, draw a conclusion about the popularity of the two political parties. (c) Based on your reading in the chapter, what reasons might you give to explain the changes in each party's popularity?

ACTIVITY

Construct a circle graph that shows the percentage of students in your class whose last names begin with a letter in the following groups: A–H, I–P, Q–Z. What percentage of names falls in each group?

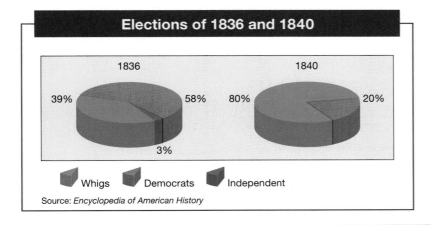

Elections of 1836 and 1840

1836
39% 58%
3%

1840
80% 20%

Whigs   Democrats   Independent

Source: *Encyclopedia of American History*

 Chapter Resources

Skill Application For additional practice, duplicate and distribute the worksheet, Reading a Circle Graph, from Unit 4, page 2, of the *Chapter Resources* binder. (Reteaching/Average)

Answers to Skill Lesson

1. (a) 1836, (b) 1840, (c) political parties
2. (a) 39 percent; 80 percent, (b) 58 percent; 20 percent, (c) Whigs, (d) No; the Democrats, with Martin Van Buren as Jackson's successor, took the clear majority of the vote.
3. (a) Possible Answer: The Whig vote was smaller but not so small as to allow the Democrats to ignore it. (b) Possible Answer: In just four years, the Whig party grew to greatly overshadow the Democrats. (c) Possible Answer: the Panic of 1837, for which Van Buren was blamed; a forceful campaign for Harrison

ACTIVITY

Guided Instruction Students can use proportional equations to figure out percentages and number of degrees for their circle graphs. For example, if the class has a total of 32 students, with 8 students in the A–H category, the equation would be as follows:

$$\frac{8}{32} = \frac{x}{100\%} \qquad \frac{25\%}{100\%} = \frac{x}{360°}$$

$$32x = 800\% \qquad 100x = 9000°$$

$$x = 25\% \qquad x = 90°$$

25% of students with last names in the A–H category
25% = 90°

Students Acquiring English
Activity

SAE students may become confused about the pronunciation of some numbers. For example, as they discuss their circle graphs, they may not be able to discriminate between the pronunciation of *fifty percent* and *fifteen percent*. Make sure that students can clearly pronounce each of the percentages on their circle graphs and the number of degrees in each of the various sections.

CHAPTER 11 REVIEW

Answers to Reviewing the Main Ideas

1. (a) He wanted the government to pay for new roads, canals, a national university, an observatory for astronomers, and projects to improve farming, manufacturing, science, and the arts. (b) People objected to the expense and feared that the federal government would become too powerful.

2. (a) Whigs, Democrats (b) Whigs: business people in the East and large planters in the South; Democrats: frontier farmers in the West and craftsworkers and factory workers in the East

3. Jackson said that he was fulfilling a goal of democracy by letting more citizens take part in government.

4. (a) Clay helped convince Biddle to apply for renewal early and pushed the recharter through Congress. (b) Biddle applied for early renewal of the Bank's charter. (c) Jackson vetoed the recharter bill and later stopped the deposit of government money in the Bank.

5. (a) South Carolina declared the tariffs of 1828 and 1832 illegal and threatened to secede from the Union. (b) Jackson supported lower tariffs as a compromise and got Congress to pass his Force Bill, allowing him to use the army, if necessary, to enforce the law in South Carolina.

6. (a) to defend its rights when the state of Georgia claimed control over Cherokee lands (b) Jackson backed states' rights and refused to enforce the Supreme Court's decision in favor of the Cherokees.

7. (a) Banks did not have enough gold and silver to exchange for paper money, so many banks failed. More banks failed when cotton planters could not repay loans. (b) People blamed Van Buren for the financial crisis and voted for Harrison.

Answers to Thinking Critically

1. (a) white men over the age of 21 (b) Possible Answers: women, African Americans, and Native Americans (c) Possible Answers: African Americans, Native Americans, Hispanics

346

Summary

● By the late 1820s, the growing spirit of democracy resulted in more and more white men getting the right to vote.

● As President, Andrew Jackson rewarded supporters with government jobs and fought against the national Bank.

● Jackson was a strong President who supported states' rights in the policy of Indian removal but not in the Nullification Crisis.

● President Van Buren did little to end the economic depression that started with the Panic of 1837, and William Henry Harrison defeated his bid for reelection in 1840.

Reviewing the Main Ideas

1. (a) What were President John Quincy Adams's programs for national growth? (b) Why did Americans reject his programs?

2. (a) What were the major political parties in the 1830s? (b) Who supported each party?

3. How did Jackson defend the spoils system?

4. Identify the role each of the following men played in the battle over the Bank of the United States: (a) Henry Clay, (b) Nicholas Biddle, (c) Andrew Jackson.

5. (a) What was the Nullification Crisis? (b) How was it resolved?

6. (a) Why did the Cherokee nation go to court? (b) How did President Jackson respond to the Supreme Court's decision in the Cherokee case?

7. (a) What were the causes of the Panic of 1837? (b) What was its effect?

Thinking Critically

1. Linking Past and Present (a) What group of Americans gained more rights in the 1820s? (b) What groups have gained more rights since then? (c) What groups are seeking more rights today?

---

2. Synthesizing Information Why was Andrew Jackson considered the people's President? Explain.

Applying Your Skills

1. Reading a Political Cartoon Study the cartoon on page 335. (a) Who is pictured in the cartoon? (b) What symbols does the cartoonist use? (c) What do you think the cartoonist thought of President Jackson? Explain.

2. Making a Review Chart Prepare a chart with two columns and three rows. Label the columns John Quincy Adams and Andrew Jackson. Label the rows Family, Education, Experience in Public Life. Fill out the chart. (a) What were the differences between Adams and Jackson? (b) How do the differences reflect the changes in American politics in the 1820s?

3. Understanding Sequence (a) When was the Tariff of Abominations passed? (b) When did South Carolina pass the Nullification Act? (c) What is the relationship between the two events?

Thinking About Geography

Match the letters on the map with the following places: **1.** Indian Territory, **2.** Chickasaw, **3.** Choctaw, **4.** Creek, **5.** Cherokee, **6.** Seminole. **Place** Why did settlers want Cherokee lands in the Southeast?

---

2. Jackson rose from poverty to become a lawyer and landowner; he fought for the United States; while President, he greeted the common people at the White House, rewarded his supporters with government jobs, and fought the Bank because he thought that it helped the rich and powerful.

Answers to Applying Your Skills

1. (a) Andrew Jackson (b) a crown, a royal scepter, the Con-stitution (c) Possible Answer: The cartoonist was unhappy with Jackson because the President was so quick to assert his will over Congress.

2. Have students use both the text and an encyclopedia to fill in the chart. Possible Answers: (a) Adams came from a wealthy New England family and was the son of John Adams, the second President; Jackson's parents were Irish immigrants who lived in a log cabin on the Carolina frontier. Adams was educated at Har-vard; Jackson did not have a formal education. Adams had experience as Secretary of State; Jackson had experience as a general and as a member of Congress. (b) Jackson's popularity reflected the democratic spirit that swept the nation in the 1820s.

3. (a) 1828 (b) 1832 (c) Southern planters were hurt by the high tariffs, so they claimed that a state could nullify any federal law the state considered unconstitu-tional.

Painting a Portrait of Andrew Jackson

Form into groups to explore the life of Andrew Jackson. Follow the suggestions below to write or draw to show what you have learned about Jackson. You may use the textbook, encyclopedias, atlases, or other materials in your classroom library to complete the tasks. Be able to name your sources of information when you have finished the activity.

HISTORIANS Research the major events and issues related to Andrew Jackson's life and career. Then create an Andrew Jackson board game. The game should trace Jackson's rise from poor beginnings on the western frontier to popular military hero and President. You might ask the class artists to help you design and construct your game.

ARTISTS Select an issue or incident related to Andrew Jackson's presidency. Then create a political cartoon based on your selection. Remember that political cartoonists represent a point of view in their work.

ECONOMISTS Review what you have read about Andrew Jackson and the Bank of the United States. Also review the cause-and-effect charts in this book. Then create a chart showing the causes and effects of the dispute over the Bank.

ACTORS AND DANCERS Review what you have read about the Indian Removal Act, and study the quilt portraying the Trail of Tears on page 339. Then prepare a presentation dramatizing this event.

CITIZENS List the events in which states clashed with the federal government during Jackson's years in office. Then make a chart showing these issues and explaining why they were important.

★ Create an Andrew Jackson bulletin board display. Include the completed works in the display.

Andrew Jackson

Comb with Jackson image

Political cartoon

Chapter 11 • **347**

Lessons	Teaching Resources
1 Oregon Fever **Objectives** 1. Explain why the United States and Britain agreed to share Oregon Country. 2. Explain why Mountain Men went to the Far West. 3. Identify the hardships that travelers faced on the Oregon Trail.	**Lesson Planner** Cooperative Learning, p. 71 **Student Study Guide** Section 1 Study Guide, p. 101 **Chapter Resources Binder, Unit 4** *Geography in History* Conquering the Oregon Trail, pp. 19–20 *Skill Application* Using a Diary as a Primary Source, p. 16
2 A Country Called Texas **Objectives** 1. Explain why Mexico wanted Americans to settle in Texas. 2. Describe how the Republic of Texas was set up. 3. Explain why the United States refused to annex Texas.	**Lesson Planner** Cooperative Learning, p. 72 **Student Study Guide** Section 2 Study Guide, p. 102 **Our Multicultural Heritage** *Biography* Lorenzo de Zavala, Texan Patriot, p. 34 **Chapter Resources Binder, Unit 4** *History Through Literature* Davy Crockett, p. 18
3 Manifest Destiny **Objectives** 1. Identify the first white settlers in New Mexico and California. 2. Describe what mission life was like for Native Americans. 3. Identify what Americans meant by Manifest Destiny.	**Lesson Planner** Cooperative Learning, p. 73 **Student Study Guide** Section 3 Study Guide, p. 103
4 The Mexican War **Objectives** 1. Describe how the United States gained Oregon. 2. Identify the events that led to war with Mexico. 3. Identify the lands that the United States gained from the Mexican War. 4. Describe how Spanish and Indian traditions blended in the new lands.	**Lesson Planner** Cooperative Learning, p. 74 **Student Study Guide** Section 4 Study Guide, p. 104
5 Surge to the Pacific **Objectives** 1. Describe how the Mormons set up a successful community in Utah. 2. Describe how the discovery of gold affected life in California. 3. Identify the mix of peoples who helped California grow and prosper.	**Lesson Planner** Cooperative Learning, p. 75 **Student Study Guide** Section 5 Study Guide, p. 105 **Our Multicultural Heritage** *Biography* Fatt Hing, Chinese Pioneer, p. 35 *Milestone* Legacy of the Golden Mountain, p. 36 **Chapter Resources Binder, Unit 4** *Critical Thinking* Drawing Conclusions, p. 17 **Interdisciplinary Connections:** The California Gold Rush ■ *Arts* Mining Music, p. 68 ■ *Sciences* Improved Methods of Mining, p. 69 ■ *Geography* The Road to Gold, p. 70 ■ *Economics* Women and the Gold Rush, p. 71 ■ *Civics* Miners and the Law, p. 72

Multimedia Resources	Additional Resources	Chapter-Level Resources
Transparencies *Time Lines* The United States and the World, 1820–1860, p. E-19 *Cause and Effect* Westward Movement, p. F-19 *Geography and History* Pacific Coast States, p. I-81	**Voices of Freedom** Camp Life in the Rockies, pp. 95–96 **Historical Outline Map Book** Trails to the West, p. 40 Oregon Country, p. 38 **Customized Reader** A Woman Missionary, article IVA-15 **Interdisciplinary Explorations** Wagons West: Exploring the Oregon Trail	**Lesson Planner** Activity Based, pp. 76–77 **Student Study Guide** Chapter 12 Study Guide, pp. 106–107 **Chapter Resources Binder** **Unit 4** Vocabulary Building, p. 15 Chapter Test A, pp. 21–23 Chapter Test B, pp. 24–26 Illustration Master, p. 27 Extra Unit Questions, pp. 57–59 **English Guided Reading** Guided Reading, pp. 23–24 **Spanish Resources** **Computer Test Bank** Chapter Tests A and B Extra Unit Questions **Guided Reading Audiotapes** Side 5 **CD-ROM** *Time Tour* From Sea to Shining Sea (1820–1860) in An Expanding Nation
Transparencies *Fine Art* Dancing on the Veranda, p. D-39 **CD-ROM** *History Makers* Sam Houston	**Historical Outline Map Book** Independence for Texas, p. 39 **Customized Reader** Tejanos' Petition to the Mexican Government, article IVA-12 "A Hard Lot": Texas Women in the Runaway Scrape, article IVA-2 A Mexican Account of the Alamo, article IVA-8	
CD-ROM *Presidents* James K. Polk	**Voices of Freedom** America's Manifest Destiny, pp. 98–99 **Customized Reader** The Founding of San Diego: California's First Mission, article IIA-17 Life at San Gabriel Mission, article IIIA-15	
Transparencies *Geography and History* South Central States, p. I-69; Expansion of the United States, p. I-25 **Videotapes/Videodiscs** *United States History Video Collection* The Southern Frontier, Vol. 6, Ch. 28; The Mexican-American War, Vol. 6, Ch. 31	**Voices of Freedom** Black Opposition to the Mexican War, pp. 99–100 **Historical Outline Map Book** War With Mexico, 1846–1848, p. 41 Growth of the United States to 1853, p. 42	
Transparencies *Cause and Effect* Westward Movement, p. F-19 *Interdisciplinary Connections* Forty-Niners, p. B-55 **Videotapes/Videodiscs** *United States History Video Collection* California Gold Rush, Vol. 6, Ch. 34	**Voices of Freedom** Louise Clappe Strikes Gold, pp. 100–101 **Customized Reader** A Mormon Village in the Early 1900s, article VIA-12 Discovering Gold at Sutter's Mill, article IVB-9 The Pioneer Chinese, article IVA-3	

Lesson Planner

For a fully developed **Activity-Based** lesson plan for Chapter 12, see the *Lesson Planner*, pages 76–77.

Chapter Resources

Vocabulary Building The Vocabulary Building worksheet for Chapter 12 from Unit 4, page 15, of the *Chapter Resources* binder can be used as a prereading activity or as a review of chapter vocabulary. (Reteaching/Easy)

Student Study Guide

Chapter 12 Study Guide Refer students to pages 106–107 of the *Student Study Guide* for the Chapter 12 Study Guide. The study guide can be used for chapter review as well as for reteaching. (Reteaching/Average)

Guided Reading Audiotapes

Students can use *Guided Reading Audiotapes,* Chapter 12, side 5, to listen to section previews, summaries, and review questions. The tapes might benefit students who are auditory learners, students who have trouble reading, or students acquiring English. Tapes are also available in Spanish. (Reteaching/Easy)

CHAPTER 12

From Sea to Shining Sea

(1820–1860)

CHAPTER OUTLINE

1 Oregon Fever

2 A Country Called Texas

3 Manifest Destiny

4 The Mexican War

5 Surge to the Pacific

1821 *The first American traders arrived in Santa Fe, New Mexico. Goods were loaded on mules and transported along the Santa Fe Trail.*

TEXAS!!

Emigrants who are desirous of assisting Texas at this important crisis of her affairs may have a free passage and equipments, by applying at the **NEW-YORK and PHILADELPHIA HOTEL,** On the Old Levee, near the Blue Stores.

Now is the time to ensure a fortune in Land: To all who remain in Texas during the War will be allowed 1280 Acres. To all who remain Six Months, 640 Acres. To all who remain Three Months, 320 Acres. And as Colonists, 4600 Acres for a family and 1470 Acres for a Single Man.

New Orleans, April 23d, 1836.

1836 *The Republic of Texas was formed. An advertisement offered free land to anyone who would help Texans fight for independence.*

1820	1825	1830	1835	1840

WORLD EVENT
1821 Mexico wins independence from Spain

WORLD EVENT
1833 Santa Anna comes to power in Mexico

Chapter Time Line
Activity

Point out that the events on the time line focus on movement to four western areas: New Mexico, Texas, Oregon, and California. After they study the illustrations and captions, have students choose one of these areas. Have them use the relevant illustration as a springboard to write a letter by a traveler to that area. Invite students to share their letters and review them as they learn more factual information in Chapter 12.

Students Acquiring English
Activity

Students learning English will often have difficulty with their writing as well as their reading. In teaching SAE students, understand why they make certain errors. For example, the consonant blend /st/ does not occur in the final position in Spanish, so these students may omit the "t" when writing a word such as *manifest* and instead write *manifes.* Likewise, /st/ does not exist in many Asian languages, so these students also may misspell words with -*est* endings. Use student writing relevant to this chapter to teach a mini-lesson on this problem. Words students might be called on to use in Section 1 include *manifest, first, forest, west, outpost,* and *biggest.*

Chapter Setting

"Last spring, 1846, was a busy season in the city of St. Louis. Not only were emigrants from every part of the country preparing for the journey to Oregon and California, but an unusual number of traders were making ready their wagons and outfits for Santa Fe. The hotels were crowded, and the gunsmiths and saddlers were kept constantly at work in providing arms and equipments for the different parties of travellers. Steamboats were leaving the [dock] and passing up the Missouri, crowded with passengers on their way to the frontier."

As American historian Francis Parkman noted in this passage from *The Oregon Trail,* St. Louis bustled with activity in the spring of 1846. Like Parkman, thousands of Americans had gathered in the city, ready to head west.

Moving west was not new to the people of the United States. The nation had begun as a string of colonies dotting the Atlantic coast. As the nation grew, pioneers moved inland, across the Appalachians to the Mississippi River.

By the 1830s, Americans were looking for new frontiers. Hardy settlers pushed west once more, into Texas, New Mexico, California, and Oregon. By 1850, the United States had expanded its borders until they reached "from sea to shining sea."

 ACTIVITY Use your five senses to imagine what moving west in the mid-1800's must have been like. Then complete the following sentences: Moving west looks like _____. Moving west feels like _____. Moving west smells like _____. Moving west tastes like _____. Moving west sounds like _____.

1843 *Wagon trains began taking thousands of Americans to Oregon Country. Space was limited, and settlers crammed whatever they could into trunks.*

1846 *Americans in northern California declared independence from Mexico. Their new nation was known as the Bear Flag Republic.*

1860 *A mix of peoples contributed to California's rich culture. Here, Mexican American settlers enjoy a celebration known as a fiesta.*

1840	1845	1850	1855	1860

▲
WORLD EVENT
1840 Britain recognizes Texas as an independent nation

Chapter 12 • **349**

 Chapter Resources

English Guided Reading Duplicate and distribute to SAE students the Chapter 12 Guided Reading worksheet on pages 23–24 in the English Guided Reading section of the *Chapter Resources* binder. Students who have difficulty reading also might benefit from using this worksheet. Have students complete the worksheet before they begin reading. You might pair a more fluent student or a student who is a stronger reader with each SAE student to review. (Reteaching/Easy)

Spanish Resources See the Spanish Resources section of the *Chapter Resources* binder.

CD-ROM

Time Tour Access the From Sea to Shining Sea (1820–1860) section in An Expanding Nation on the American Heritage® *History of the United States* CD-ROM. (Enrichment/ Average)

ACTIVITY

Guided Instruction Before students complete the sentences, have them consider specific sights, tactile sensations, smells, tastes, and sounds to use as details. Encourage the use of vivid adjectives. You might have each student select one sentence from his or her work to be included in a class list arranged by sense and titled *Moving West: The Sights, The Sounds,* and so on.

Linking Past and Present
Activity

Explain that pioneers traveling the old Oregon Trail usually did not leave Missouri before late spring, when there was enough grass on the prairie for the livestock to eat. They tried to reach Oregon before winter storms blocked the mountain passes. Have students compare this method of resettlement with modern relocation. Ask: What kinds of vehicles are used to move today? What conveniences are found now that did not exist then?

Approximately how long would a similar move take today? Students should note the use of cars, trucks, and planes; the existence of interstate transportation systems; and conveniences such as restaurants and motels. Encourage students to see that the trip today would be much shorter, but that modern travelers would not see the natural splendor or experience the sense of community, adventure, and accomplishment.

349

Bell Ringer

Have the class brainstorm for a list of equipment and supplies that they think they would need to travel across or live in the wilderness.

Lesson Plan

1. Focus In the 1820s, Americans began hearing about the rich lands and forests of the Oregon Country. This area of the Pacific Northwest had been claimed by four nations and was by that time occupied jointly by the United States and Britain. "Oregon Fever" drew missionaries and other settlers to join the hardy trappers who were already there. In this section, students learn about the pioneers who traveled to Oregon Country.

2. Instruct As students progress through this section, have them keep a "pioneer journal" in which they record important facts and observations about a trek west. Tell them to include sights they would see, adventures they would experience, hazards they would overcome, and people whom they would encounter.

3. Close To close the lesson, have students use the headings for the subsections to form questions and then answer them.

1
Oregon Fever

FIND OUT

- Why did the United States and Britain agree to share Oregon Country?
- Why did Mountain Men go to the Far West?
- What hardships did travelers face on the Oregon Trail?

VOCABULARY rendezvous

In 1846, Horace Greeley, a New York newspaper editor, published an article titled "To Aspiring Young Men." In it, Greeley offered the following advice:

&6&If you have no family or friends to aid you,...turn your face to the great West and there build up your home and fortune.&9&

Greeley's advice exactly suited the spirit of the times. Before long, his statement was shortened to four simple words: "Go West, young man." Thousands of Americans rallied to the cry "Westward Ho!"

GEOGRAPHY AND HISTORY
Oregon Country: A Varied Land

By the 1820s, white settlers occupied much of the land between the Appalachians and the Mississippi River. Families in search of good farmland continued to move west. Few, however, settled on the Great Plains between the Mississippi and the Rockies. Instead, they were drawn to lands in the Far West.

Americans first heard about Oregon Country in the early 1800s. **Oregon Country** was the huge area beyond the Rockies. To-day, this land includes Oregon, Washington, Idaho, and parts of Wyoming, Montana, and Canada. (See the map on page 353.)

The land that early settlers called Oregon Country has a varied geography. Along the Pacific coast, the soil is fertile and rainfall is plentiful. Temperatures are mild all year round. Early white settlers found fine farmland in the Willamette River valley and the lowlands around Puget Sound. Trappers were lured by beaver that filled the dense forests of coastal mountains farther inland.

Between the coastal mountains and the Rockies is a high plateau. This Intermountain region is much drier than the coast and has some desert areas. Temperatures are also more extreme here.

The Rocky Mountains formed the eastern boundary of Oregon Country. As in the coastal range, beaver and other fur-bearing animals roamed the Rockies. As a result, trappers flocked to the area. ■

Competing Claims

In the early 1800s, four countries had competing claims to Oregon. They were the United States, Great Britain, Spain, and Russia. Of course, Native Americans had lived in Oregon for thousands of years. The land rightfully belonged to them. But the United States and competing European nations gave little thought to Indian rights.

The United States based its claim to Oregon on several expeditions to the area. For example, Lewis and Clark had journeyed through the area in 1805 and 1806.

The British claim to Oregon dated back to a visit by Sir Francis Drake in 1579. Also, Fort Vancouver, built by the British, was the only permanent outpost in Oregon Country.

In 1818, the United States and Britain reached an agreement. The two countries would occupy Oregon jointly. Citizens of each nation would have equal rights in Oregon. Spain and Russia had few settlers in the area and agreed to drop their claims.

Historical Sidelight
Background

Greeley, as founder of the *New York Tribune* in 1841, had a large audience for his ideas. The many causes that Greeley supported included organized labor, temperance, women's rights, a homestead law, and abolition of slavery.

Connections With Economics
Background

John Jacob Astor, a German immigrant, founded the American Fur Company in 1808. In 1811, he sent a shipload of men and supplies around South America to Oregon. The men built the town of Astoria at the mouth of the Columbia River. They worked the northern plains in conjunction with two Canadian fur producers, the North West Company and the Michilimackinac Company.

An 1816 act of Congress that excluded foreigners from the fur trade gave Astor a virtual monopoly. The income from his fur trade, along with his income from trade in China and the interest on loans that he made to the government of the United States during the War of 1812, made him rich. In fact, when he retired in 1834, Astor was the richest man in the United States.

Fur Trappers in the Far West

At first, the only Europeans or Americans who settled in Oregon Country were a few hardy trappers. These adventurous men hiked through Oregon's vast forests, trapping animals and living off the land. They were known as **Mountain Men.**

Lives filled with danger. Mountain Men could make a small fortune trapping beaver in Rocky Mountain streams. They led dangerous lives, however. Bears, wildcats, and other wild animals lurked in the thick forests where they hunted. And the long, cold mountain winters demanded special survival skills.

Mountain Men wore shirts and trousers made of animal hides and decorated with porcupine quills. Their hair reached to their shoulders. Pistols and tomahawks hung from their belts. Around their necks dangled a "possibles sack," filled with a pipe, some tobacco, a mold to make bullets, and other items of "possible" use.

Living off the land. In warm weather, when game was plentiful, Mountain Men gorged themselves with food. During lean times, however, trappers ate almost anything. "I have held my hands in an anthill until they were covered with ants, then greedily licked them off," one Mountain Man recalled.

Trappers often spent winters in Native American villages. In fact, they learned many of their trapping skills and survival methods from Indians. Relations with Native Americans were not always friendly, however. Indians sometimes attacked Mountain Men who trapped on Indian hunting grounds without permission.

Trading furs. During the fall and spring, Mountain Men tended their traps. Then in July, they tramped out of the wilderness, ready to meet the fur traders. They headed to a place chosen the year before, called the **rendezvous** (RAHN day voo). Rendezvous is a French word meaning get-together.

For trappers, the first day of the rendezvous was a time to have fun. A visitor to one rendezvous captured the excitement:

> 66[The trappers] engaged in contests of skill at running, jumping, wrestling, shooting with the rifle, and running horses.... They sang, they laughed, they whooped; they tried to out-brag and out-lie each other in stories of their adventures and achievements. Here the... trappers were in all their glory.99

After the "laughing and whooping" were done, trappers and traders settled down to bargain. Because beaver hats were in great demand in the East and in Europe, Mountain Men got a good price for their furs. "With their hairy bank notes, the beaver skins, they can obtain all the luxuries of the mountains, and live for a few days like lords," one visitor said of the trappers.

By the late 1830s, the fur trade was dying out. Trappers had killed so many beavers that the animals had grown scarce. Also, beaver hats went out of style. Even so, the Mountain Men's skills were still in demand.

BIOGRAPHY **James Beckwourth** *One of the most daring Mountain Men was James Beckwourth. The son of an enslaved Virginian, Beckwourth went west as a young man. He discovered a pass in the Sierra Nevada that became a major route to California.* **Linking Past and Present** *Why are mountain passes less important to travelers today than in the 1800s?*

Chapter 12 • **351**

Our Multicultural Heritage
Background

James Beckwourth's mother was of African and Native American ancestry; his father was white. Beckwourth, born in 1798, was thrilled to hear stories of his father's exploits as a major in the American Revolution. At the age of 20, yearning for adventures of his own, Beckwourth set out for the West.

Beckwourth became a skilled Mountain Man. At times, he worked as a guide for wagon trains traveling west; he was also a fur trapper and trader. Along with some other traders, Beckwourth was taken captive by the Crow Indians. They became friends, however; the Crows called him "Morning Star" and made him one of their leaders. Beckwourth lived among the Crows for about 10 years.

In the 20 years after that, Beckwourth was active in California; his jobs included scouting for the U.S. Army, carrying mail, stealing horses (which many Mountain Men did), running a hotel and trading post in Beckwourth Valley, and dictating his memoirs. He later returned to the Crows and died among them in 1866 or 1867.

Heading for the Rendezvous *The yearly rendezvous was a chance both to have fun and to make a profit. This painting shows Mountain Men and Native Americans on their way to a rendezvous.* **United States and the World** *How did European fashions affect the American fur trade?*

Some took on a new job—leading settlers across the rugged trails into Oregon.

Mountain Men Explore New Lands

In their search for furs, Mountain Men explored new territory in the West. They followed Indian trails across the Rockies and through mountain passes. Later, they showed these trails to settlers moving west.

One Mountain Man, Jedediah Smith, led white settlers across the Rockies through South Pass, in present-day Wyoming. Manuel Lisa, a Spanish American fur trader, led a trip up the Missouri River in 1807. He founded Fort Manuel, the first outpost on the upper Missouri.

At least one Mountain "Man" was a woman. Marie Dorion, an Iowa Indian, first went to Oregon with fur traders in 1811. She won fame for her survival skills.

Missionaries in Oregon

The first white Americans to build permanent homes in Oregon Country were missionaries. Among them were Marcus and Narcissa Whitman. The couple married in 1836 and set out for Oregon, where they planned to convert local Native Americans to Christianity.

Arriving in Oregon, the Whitmans built their mission near the Columbia River. They set out to work with the Cayuse (kī yoos) Indians. Soon, other settlers joined the Whitmans. They took over Indian lands for their houses and farms.

Missionaries like the Whitmans helped stir up interest in Oregon Country. Eager to have others join them, the missionaries sent back glowing reports about the land. People throughout the nation read these reports. By 1840, more and more Americans were ready to make the long and difficult journey to Oregon.

Wagon Trains West

Throughout the 1840s, the settlement in Oregon grew. Back in the United States, farmers marveled at stories of wheat that grew taller than a man and Oregon turnips 5 feet around. "Oregon Fever" broke out. Soon, pioneers clogged the trails west. Beginning in 1843, wagon trains left every spring for Oregon following the **Oregon Trail.** (See the map at right.)

Leaving from Independence. Families planning to go west met at Independence, Missouri, in the early spring. When enough families had gathered, they formed a wagon train. Each group elected leaders to make decisions along the way.

The Oregon-bound pioneers hurried to leave Independence in May. Timing was important. Travelers had to reach Oregon by early October, before snow began to fall in the mountains. This meant that pioneers had to cover 2,000 miles (3,200 km) on foot in five months!

Life on the trail. Once on the trail, pioneer families woke to a bugle blast at dawn. Each person had a job to do. Young girls helped their mothers prepare breakfast. Men and boys harnessed the horses and oxen. By 6 A.M., the cry of "Wagons Ho!" rang out across the plains.

Wagon trains stopped for a brief meal at noon. Then it was back on the trail until 6 or 7 P.M. At night, wagons were drawn up in a circle to keep the cattle from wandering.

Most pioneer families set out on the journey west with a lot of heavy gear. When it came time to cross rivers and scale mountains, however, many possessions were left behind to lighten the load. Soon, the Oregon Trail was littered with junk. One traveler found the trail strewn with "blacksmiths' anvils, ploughs, large grind-stones, baking ovens, kegs, barrels, harness [and] clothing."

Rain, snow, and disease. The long trek west held many dangers. During spring rains, travelers risked their lives floating wagons across swollen rivers. In summer, they faced blistering heat on the treeless plains. Early snowstorms often blocked passes through the mountains.

The biggest threat was sickness. Cholera and other diseases could wipe out whole wagon trains. Because the travelers lived so close together, germs spread quickly.

MAP STUDY

Oregon Country was the first area in the Far West to draw settlers from the United States.
1. *What two rivers did the Oregon Trail follow as it wound into Oregon Country?*
2. *What line of latitude marked the northern boundary of Oregon Country?*
3. **Analyzing Information** *Why do you think the Oregon Trail often followed the course of a river?*

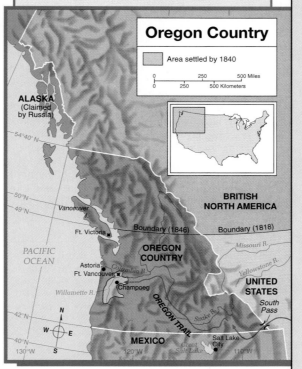

Oregon Country

Area settled by 1840

0   250   500 Miles
0   250   500 Kilometers

ALASKA
(Claimed by Russia)

54°40'N

50°N
49°N

Vancouver

Ft. Victoria

PACIFIC OCEAN

Astoria
Ft. Vancouver
Columbia R.
Champoeg

Willamette R.

42°N

40°N
130°W

BRITISH NORTH AMERICA

Boundary (1846)   Boundary (1818)

Missouri R.

OREGON COUNTRY

Yellowstone R.

UNITED STATES

South Pass

OREGON TRAIL

Snake R.

MEXICO   Salt Lake City

Great Salt Lake

120°W   110°W

Answers to Map Study

1. The Snake and Columbia rivers **2.** 54°40'N **3.** Possible Answer: Rivers provided one of the easiest means of travel at this time. Furthermore, because these rivers are west of the continental divide, they flowed westward.

Transparencies

Geography and History Use the transparency map set, Pacific Coast States, on page I-81 of *American History Transparencies.* The maps can help students understand the area's historical development, economy, and population distribution. Teaching suggestions can be found on page I-14. (Enrichment/Average)

Chapter Resources

Geography in History Duplicate and distribute the worksheet, Conquering the Oregon Trail, from Unit 4, pages 19–20, of the *Chapter Resources* binder. The worksheet focuses on the natural hazards of the trip from Missouri to Oregon's Willamette Valley. (Enrichment/Challenging)

Interdisciplinary Explorations

Wagons West Have students refer to the unit Wagons West: Exploring the Oregon Trail in the *Prentice Hall Interdisciplinary Exploration Series* to learn more about the challenges nineteenth-century pioneers encountered on their journey west. (Enrichment/Challenging)

Connections With Geography
Activity

Have students find a map of the Pacific Northwest today and compare it to the map on this page. Have them answer the following questions: (a) Which states contain land that was once part of Oregon Country? (b) Where is the boundary between the United States and Canada in the Pacific Northwest? (c) Which major cities emerged along the Oregon Trail? (d) Which cities now exist in the area that had been settled by 1840? (e) Are any cities or geographic features named after people mentioned in this section?

Linking Past and Present
Activity

In the 1800s, the Pacific Northwest was the site of competing claims among different nations. Today, it is the focus of a dispute between the logging groups and environmental groups. Have students research and prepare an oral report. They should define the problem, outline each party's position, and propose a balanced solution that might address each side's concerns.

Student Study Guide

Section 1 Study Guide Have students use the Section 1 Study Guide on page 101 of the *Student Study Guide* to review and reinforce the content of this section. (Reteaching/Average)

Guided Instruction Before students write their songs, have them list details about the lifestyle and behavior that they will include in the song. Remind them, too, that Mountain Men tried to "out-brag" and "out-lie" each other; therefore, exaggeration in the spirit of fun is encouraged. Ask each to select a lighthearted, familiar tune for which original lyrics might be written. Have students sing their songs to the class; record the performances.

On the Trail *Wagon trains crowded the trails to the West in the mid-1800s. Here, travelers listen closely as a guide tells them what lies ahead.* **Geography** *What hardships did travelers face on the trail?*

Trading with Native Americans. As they moved west toward the Rockies, pioneers often saw Indians. The Indians seldom attacked the whites trespassing on their land. A guidebook published in 1845 warned that pioneers had more to fear from their own guns than from Indians: "We very frequently hear of emigrants' being killed from the accidental discharge of firearms; but we very seldom hear of their being killed by Indians."

Many Native Americans traded with the wagon trains. Hungry pioneers were grateful for food the Indians sold. "Whenever we camp near any Indian village," a traveler said, "we are no sooner stopped than a whole crowd may be seen coming galloping into our camp. The [women] do all the swapping."

Oregon at last! Despite the many hardships, more than 50,000 people reached Oregon between 1840 and 1860. Their wagon wheels cut so deeply into the plains that the ruts can still be seen today.

By the 1840s, Americans greatly outnumbered the British in parts of Oregon. As you have read, the two nations agreed to occupy Oregon jointly in 1818. Now, many Americans began to feel that Oregon should belong to the United States alone.

Our Common Heritage

Pioneer women on the Oregon Trail had to be resourceful to feed their families. One trick that many learned was to use the rocking of the wagons on the rough trail to churn their butter.

SECTION 1 REVIEW

1. **Locate:** (a) Oregon Country, (b) South Pass, (c) Oregon Trail, (d) Independence.
2. **Identify:** (a) Mountain Man, (b) Jedediah Smith, (c) Manuel Lisa, (d) Marie Dorion, (e) Marcus and Narcissa Whitman.
3. **Define:** rendezvous.
4. What agreement did the United States and Britain reach about Oregon Country?
5. How did Mountain Men help open the Far West?
6. Why did settlers pour into Oregon Country?
7. **CRITICAL THINKING** **Analyzing Information** What qualities do you think Mountain Men needed to survive in the wilderness?

ACTIVITY **Writing to Learn**
Write lyrics to a song that Mountain Men might have sung during a rendezvous.

Answers to Section 1 Review

1. See the maps on pp. 353 and 361.
2. (a) Mountain Man, p. 351, (b) Jedediah Smith, p. 352, (c) Manuel Lisa, p. 352, (d) Marie Dorion, p. 352, (e) Marcus and Narcissa Whitman, p. 352
3. rendezvous, p. 351
4. In 1818, the United States and Britain agreed to a joint occupation of Oregon Country.
5. As they hunted for furs, Mountain Men explored much new territory, often following Native American trails across the Rockies and through mountain passes; later, they showed these trails to settlers moving west.
6. Stories about the fabulous farmlands there caused thousands to head west.
7. Possible Answer: good health, knowledge of survival techniques, skill at handcrafting tools and other necessary items

CRITICAL THINKING SKILLS
Using a Diary as a Primary Source

A diary is a useful primary source because it tells what the writer saw, heard, said, thought, and felt. It gives firsthand information about people, places, and events. Because diaries are private, writers often say what they honestly think.

The excerpts below are taken from a diary that was kept by Amelia Stewart Knight. With her husband and children, Knight traveled west along the Oregon Trail in 1853. Her diary tells about the hardships the family faced on their way to a new life in Oregon Country.

1. **Identify the primary source.** (a) Who wrote the diary? (b) In what year was the diary written? (c) Under what conditions was it written? (d) Why do you think the writer wrote it?

2. **Analyze the information in the primary source.** Study the diary for information about how the writer lived. (a) What evidence supports the claim that life on the Oregon Trail was hard? (b) Describe the geography of the area the Knight family traveled through. (c) What chores did Amelia Knight do? (d) What chores did the children do?

3. **Draw conclusions about the writer's point of view.** Decide how the writer felt about making the journey west. (a) How do you think Knight felt about the hardships of the journey? (b) How might keeping the diary have helped her face these hardships? (c) What personal qualities did a person need to make the journey to Oregon County?

ACTIVITY Keep a diary for a week. Then study your entries. Will your diary serve as a reliable primary source for someone trying to find out about life in the 1990s? Why or why not?

Amelia Stewart Knight's Diary

"*Monday, April 18th* Cold; breaking fast the first thing; very disagreeable weather; wind east cold and rainy, no fire. We are on a very large prairie, no timber to be seen as far as the eye can reach. Evening—Have crossed several bad streams today, and more than once have been stuck in the mud.

Saturday, April 23rd Still in camp, it rained hard all night, and blew a hurricane almost. All the tents were blown down, and some wagons capsized. Evening—It has been raining hard all day; everything is wet and muddy. One of the oxen missing; the boys have been hunting him all day. (Dreary times, wet and muddy, and crowded in the tent, cold and wet and uncomfortable in the wagon. No place for the poor children.)

I have been busy cooking, roasting coffee, etc. today, and have come into the wagon to write this and make our bed.

Friday, May 6th We passed a train of wagons on their way back, the head man had drowned a few days before, in a river called the Elkhorn, while getting some cattle across. With sadness and pity I passed those who a few days before had been well and happy as ourselves.

Friday, August 19th After looking in vain for water, we were about to give up, when husband came across a company of friendly Cayuse Indians, who showed him where to find water. The men and boys have driven the cattle down to water and I am waiting to get supper. We bought a few potatoes from an Indian, which will be a treat for our supper."

Section 2
pp. 356 – 360

 Bell Ringer

Have the class brainstorm for and list on the chalkboard characteristics that they associate with the state of Texas.

Lesson Plan

1. Focus In the early 1800s, Texas was still a province of Mexico. However, some Americans were allowed to build a colony after agreeing to become Mexican citizens and Catholics. As the American colony grew, conflicts with the Mexican government developed. In this section, students focus on the events leading to the establishment of the Republic of Texas.

2. Instruct Have students develop time lines on which they list in chronological order the major events covered in this section. Use this as a basis for discussion.

3. Close To close the lesson, ask students a series of rapid-fire *Who, What, When, Where, Why,* and *How* questions about the founding of the Republic of Texas.

2
A Country Called Texas

FIND OUT

■ Why did Mexico want Americans to settle in Texas?

■ How was the Republic of Texas set up?

■ Why did the United States refuse to annex Texas?

VOCABULARY annex

In late 1835, the word spread: Americans in Texas had rebelled against Mexico! Joseph Barnard, a young doctor, recalled:

> ❝I was at Chicago, Illinois, practicing medicine, when the news of the Texan revolt from Mexico reached our ears, in the early part of December, 1835. They were in arms for a cause that I had always been taught to consider sacred, [that is,] Republican principles and popular institutions. ❞

Dr. Barnard took a steamship down the Mississippi and made his way to Texas. Like hundreds of other Americans, he wanted to help Texans fight for independence.

Americans in Mexican Texas

Since the early 1800s, American farmers had looked eagerly at the vast region called Texas. At the time, Texas was part of the Spanish colony of Mexico.

At first, Spain refused to let Americans move into the region. Then in 1821, Spain gave Moses Austin a land grant in Texas. Austin died before he could set up a colony. His son Stephen took over the project.

Meanwhile, Mexico had won its independence from Spain. (See page 316.) The new nation agreed to let Stephen Austin lead settlers into Texas. Only about 4,000 Mexicans lived there. Mexico hoped that the Americans would help develop the area and control Indian attacks.

Mexico gave Stephen Austin and each settler a large grant of land. In return, the settlers agreed to become citizens of Mexico, obey its laws, and worship in the Roman Catholic Church. In 1821, Austin and 300 families moved to Texas. The colony grew under Austin's leadership. By 1830, about 20,000 Americans had resettled in Texas.

Mexico Tightens Its Laws

Stephen Austin and his settlers had agreed to become Mexican citizens and Catholics. However, Americans who later flooded into Texas felt no loyalty to Mexico. They spoke only a few words of Spanish,

A Texan Ranch *In the 1820s, thousands of Americans poured into Texas. They built prosperous farms and ranches, such as the one shown here.* **United States and the World** *Why do you think Mexicans might have been concerned about the arrival of so many Americans in Texas?*

Historical Sidelight
Background

Stephen Austin, whom Sam Houston would one day eulogize as the "father of Texas," committed himself fully to Mexican citizenship. When Mexico won independence from Spain, Austin traveled to Mexico City. He reconfirmed his father's land grant and met with the new government leaders. Austin returned to Texas with near-dictatorial authority over the area.

In the next few years, Austin's diplomatic skills were put to the test as he tried to hold American settlers in check while assuring Mexico City that Texas was not about to be annexed. His 1833 request that Texas be granted Mexican statehood, however, resulted in his imprisonment. When he was released in 1835, he briefly took command of

the Texan army and then went to the United States for funding and supplies for the rebels.

When Texas became a republic, Austin ran against Houston for president. Houston won but made Austin his secretary of state. Austin hoped for the annexation of Texas, but he died before it came to pass. Today, the capital of Texas is named in his honor.

the official language of Mexico. Also, most of the Americans were Protestants. Conflict soon erupted between the newcomers and the Mexican government.

In 1830, Mexico passed a law forbidding any more Americans to move to Texas. Mexico feared that the Americans wanted to make Texas part of the United States. This fear had some basis. The United States had already tried to buy Texas, once in 1826 and again in 1829.

Mexico also decided to make Texans obey Mexican laws that they had ignored for years. One law banned slavery in Texas. Another required Texans to worship in the Catholic Church. Texans resented the laws and the Mexican troops who came north to enforce them.

In 1833, General Antonio López de Santa Anna came to power in Mexico. Two years later, Santa Anna threw out the Mexican constitution. Rumors spread wildly. Santa Anna, some said, intended to drive all Americans out of Texas.

Texans Take Action

Americans in Texas felt that the time had come for action. In this, they had the support of many *Tejanos* (teh HAH nohs), Mexicans who lived in Texas. The Tejanos did not necessarily want independence from Mexico. But they hated General Santa Anna, who ruled as a military dictator. They wanted to be rid of him.

Fighting begins. In October 1835, Texans in the town of Gonzales (gahn ZAH lehs) clashed with Mexican troops. (See the map at right.) The Texans defeated the Mexicans, forcing them to withdraw. Inspired by the victory, Stephen Austin and other Texans aimed to "see Texas forever free from Mexican domination."

Two months later, Texans stormed and took San Antonio. Santa Anna was furious. Determined to stamp out the rebellion, he marched north with a large army.

Declaring independence. While Santa Anna massed his troops, Texans declared their independence from Mexico on March 2, 1836. They set themselves up as a new nation called the *Republic of Texas* and appointed Sam Houston as commander of their army. The army drew volunteers of all

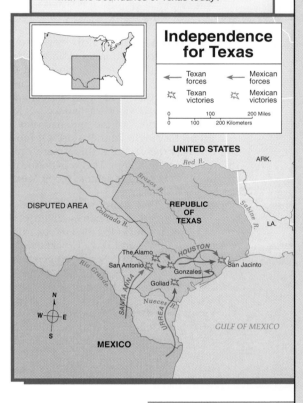

MAP STUDY

The Texan war for independence was brief but bloody.
1. Where did Santa Anna's army first fight the Texans?
2. Who won the battle at Gonzales?
3. **Comparing** Refer to the map of the United States in the Reference Section. How do the boundaries of the Republic of Texas compare with the boundaries of Texas today?

Independence for Texas

← Texan forces   ← Mexican forces
☆ Texan victories   ☆ Mexican victories

UNITED STATES
Red R.   ARK.
Brazos R.
DISPUTED AREA   REPUBLIC OF TEXAS
Colorado R.   Sabine R.   LA.
The Alamo   HOUSTON
San Antonio   Gonzales   San Jacinto
Rio Grande   Goliad
SANTA ANNA
Nueces R.
URREA
GULF OF MEXICO
MEXICO

Chapter 12 • **357**

Lesson Planner

For a developed **Cooperative Learning** lesson plan, see the *Lesson Planner,* page 72.

Answers to Map Study

1. San Antonio 2. Texans 3. The disputed area on the map showing the Republic of Texas is now part of the state of Texas.

Customized Reader

Primary Source For a copy of the Tejanos' request for relaxation of immigration policies in Texas, order article IVA-12, Tejanos' Petition to the Mexican Government, from the *American History Customized Reader.* The petition describes difficulties faced by the Tejanos, particularly attacks by Native Americans. (Enrichment/Challenging)

Our Multicultural Heritage

Biography Have students read the biography, Lorenzo de Zavala, Texan Patriot, on page 34 of the *Our Multicultural Heritage* booklet. (Enrichment/Challenging)

Connections With Geography
Activity

Have students use a map of the United States to locate the original 13 colonies and trace their outline on paper. Then have them locate and trace Texas. Tell them to cut out the colonies and place these outlines on the map of Texas. Ask: How does the size of Texas compare to the combined landmass of the original colonies? How do you think this might have affected American attitudes toward Texas in the 1830s?

Our Multicultural Heritage
Background

Sam Houston was born in Virginia of Scotch-Irish descent. In 1808, at the age of 15, he struck out on his own, and for three years lived with the Cherokees of East Tennessee. In 1827, he was elected governor of Tennessee. In 1829, he resigned from office and went again to live with the Cherokees, who formally adopted him as a member of their nation. Because of his dark hair and eyes, his adoptive family called him The Raven. In 1830 and 1832, he went to Washington, D.C., to protest abuses against Native Americans by government agents. As governor of the Republic and senator from the state of Texas, Houston often defended the rights of Native Americans.

races and nationalities. Free blacks, slaves, and Tejanos, as well as other people of many nationalities, joined to fight for Texan independence.

By the time Santa Anna arrived in San Antonio, many of the Texans who had taken the city had drifted away. Fewer than 200 Texans remained as defenders. Despite the odds against them, the Texans refused to give up. Instead, they retired to an old Spanish mission called the ***Alamo***.

Remember the Alamo!

The Spanish had built the Alamo in the mid-1700s. It was like a small fort, surrounded by walls 12 feet high and 3 feet thick. The Alamo, said an observer, was "a strong place."

Ill prepared to fight. However, Texan defenders who gathered in the Alamo in the winter of 1835–1836 were ill prepared to fight. Supplies of ammunition and medicine were low. Food consisted of some beef and corn, and access to water was limited. As for warm clothing, many of the men had only a blanket and a single flannel shirt! Of most concern was the fact that there were only 187 Texans in the Alamo. This was not nearly enough to defend it against 6,000 Mexican troops.

William Travis—hardly more than a boy—commanded the Texans. Volunteers inside the mission included the famous frontiersmen Jim Bowie and Davy Crockett. Several Tejano families, two Texan women, and two young male slaves were also present. They later helped to nurse the sick and wounded.

"Victory or Death!" On February 23, 1836, a Texan lookout spotted the gleam of swords in the sunlight. Santa Anna's army had arrived!

The first shots from the Alamo were rapid and deadly and took the Mexicans by surprise. Commander Travis had three or four rifles placed by each man's side. In that way, a Texan could fire three or four shots in the time it took a Mexican to fire one.

Still, Travis knew that unless he received help, he and his men were doomed. On February 24, he sent a Texan through the Mexican lines with a message. It was addressed "to the People of Texas and all the Americans in the World":

> 66Fellow Citizens and Compatriots—I am besieged by a thousand or more of the Mexicans under Santa Anna. I have sustained a continual bombardment for 24 hours and have not lost a man. The enemy have demanded a surrender. . . . I have answered the demand with a cannon shot and our flag still waves proudly from the walls.
>
> *I shall never surrender or retreat.*
>
> I call on you in the name of Liberty, of patriotism, and of everything dear to the American character to come to our aid with all dispatch. The enemy are receiving reinforcements daily. . . . If this call is neglected, I am determined to sustain myself as long as possible & die like a soldier who never forgets what is due to his own honor or that of his country. *Victory or Death!*
>
> W. Barret Travis99

Travis also sent scouts to seek additional soldiers and provisions. About 60 men were able to sneak through enemy lines and join the fighters in the Alamo. However, no large force ever arrived.

The final siege. Daily, the Mexicans bombarded the Alamo. For 12 days, the defenders bravely held them off. Then, at dawn on March 6, 1836, Mexican cannon fire broke through the Alamo walls. Thousands of Mexican soldiers poured into the mission. When the bodies were counted,

---

Connections With Science
Background

Alamo is from the Spanish word for cottonwood. The mission was built beside a grove of cottonwood trees. The cottonwood is one of about 30 species of the poplar tree, a group that grows in many areas of the United States. Pioneers found many uses for the fast-growing cottonwood tree, including lumber, fuel, and shade.

Critical Thinking
Analyzing a Primary Source

Have students reread William Travis's message "to the People of Texas and all the Americans in the World." Then discuss his message, considering questions such as the following: Why did Travis want this message sent? Why do you think it affected Americans so strongly? What does it reveal about Travis as a person?

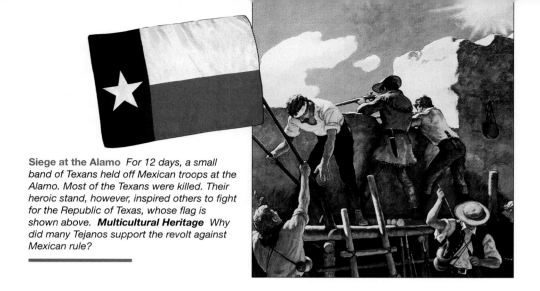

Siege at the Alamo *For 12 days, a small band of Texans held off Mexican troops at the Alamo. Most of the Texans were killed. Their heroic stand, however, inspired others to fight for the Republic of Texas, whose flag is shown above.* **Multicultural Heritage** *Why did many Tejanos support the revolt against Mexican rule?*

Answer to Caption
They wanted to be rid of Santa Anna, who ruled Mexico as a military dictator.

 Historical Outline Map Book

Historical Outline Map Use the map, Independence for Texas, on page 39 of the *American History Historical Outline Map Book.* Lesson ideas for this map can be found on page T13. (Reteaching/Average)

 Customized Reader

Primary Source For a Mexican officer's view of the battle at the Alamo, order article IVA-8, A Mexican Account of the Alamo, from the *American History Customized Reader.* (Enrichment/Challenging)

 Videotapes/ Videodiscs

United States History Video Collection Use the video segment "The Southern Frontier" from Volume 6, *Expansionism,* to enhance students' understanding of the Texas war for independence. Approx. running time 2:00 min. (Enrichment/Average) Vol. 6, Ch. 28

Chapter 28   Play

183 Texans and almost 1,500 Mexicans lay dead. The five Texan survivors, including Davy Crockett, were promptly executed at Santa Anna's order.

The slaughter at the Alamo angered Texans and set off cries for revenge. The fury of the Texans grew even stronger three weeks later, when Mexicans killed several hundred Texan soldiers at Goliad after they had surrendered. Volunteers flooded into Sam Houston's army. Men from the United States also raced south to help the Texan cause. ■

Texan Independence

While the Mexicans were busy at the Alamo, Sam Houston organized his army. Six weeks later, on April 21, 1836, Houston decided that the moment had come to attack.

Santa Anna was camped with his army near the San Jacinto (jah SEEN toh) River. With cries of "Remember the Alamo!" the Texans charged the surprised Mexicans. The Battle of San Jacinto lasted only 18 minutes. Although they were outnumbered, Texans killed 630 Mexicans and captured 700 more.

The next day, Texans captured Santa Anna himself. They forced the general to sign a treaty granting Texas its independence.

The Lone Star Republic

In battle, Texans had carried a flag with a single white star. After winning independence, they nicknamed their nation the *Lone Star Republic.* They drew up a constitution based on the Constitution of the United States and elected Sam Houston as their president.

History and You
Have you ever been fooled by false advertising? Many Americans in 1837 were persuaded by newspaper ads to buy land in a "booming new metropolis" in Texas called Houston. On arrival, they discovered just a small, rough settlement. Most stayed, however, and helped to build the city. Today, Houston is the fourth largest city in the United States.

Chapter 12 • **359**

Linking Past and Present
Background

One story about the origin of the slogan "Remember the Alamo!" is that it was the headline of a newspaper published by Gail Borden. Borden was a friend of Sam Houston and a pioneer in making maps of Texas. He is better known as the inventor of condensed milk and founder of what became and still is one of the nation's largest food companies.

Our Multicultural Heritage
Background

During the war for Texas independence, Juan Seguín, a good friend of Stephen Austin (and who, at the age of 18, had been elected mayor of San Antonio), served in the Texas cavalry, often behind enemy lines. His wife Josefa helped train soldiers. After independence, Seguín was put in command of San Antonio.

Many other people worked in supporting roles. Giuseppe Cassini, an Italian merchant, provided supplies for the Texan volunteers who eventually retook San Antonio. William Goyens, an African American businessman in Nacogdoches, served as a translator between Sam Houston and several Native American groups. As a result, the Cherokees promised to remain neutral. Moses Levy, a Jewish doctor, came to Texas from Virginia "with both scalpel and sword." Dr. Levy's untiring work on the battlefield saved countless Texan lives.

359

Section 3
pp. 360–363

 Bell Ringer

On the chalkboard, write the terms *America* and *United States*. Ask: Are these terms synonymous? Why or why not?

Lesson Plan

1. Focus Spanish explorers in the Southwest and California were followed by ranchers and missionaries. The transfer of these lands to Mexico opened up the West to American traders and settlers. In this section, students learn about the inhabitants of the West and the growth of the idea of Manifest Destiny.

The new country faced huge problems. First, Mexico refused to accept the treaty signed by Santa Anna. Mexicans still claimed Texas as part of their country. Second, Texas was nearly bankrupt. Most Texans thought that the best way to solve both problems was for Texas to become part of the United States.

In the United States, Americans were divided about whether to annex Texas. To **annex** means to add on. Most white southerners favored the idea. Many northerners, however, were against it. At issue was slavery.

Antislavery feelings were growing in the North in the 1830s. Knowing that many Texans owned slaves, northerners did not want to allow Texas to join the Union. President Andrew Jackson also worried that annexing Texas would lead to war with Mexico. As a result, the United States refused to annex Texas.

SECTION 2 REVIEW

1. **Locate:** (a) Mexico, (b) Gonzales, (c) San Antonio, (d) Republic of Texas.
2. **Identify:** (a) Stephen Austin, (b) Antonio López de Santa Anna, (c) Tejano, (d) Sam Houston, (e) Alamo, (f) Lone Star Republic.
3. **Define:** annex.
4. (a) Who were the first settlers from the United States to move into Texas? (b) Why did Mexico encourage Americans to settle in Texas?
5. Why did northerners and southerners disagree about annexing Texas?
6. **CRITICAL THINKING Analyzing Information** How was the defeat at the Alamo also a victory for Texans?

ACTIVITY Writing to Learn

Imagine you are a Texan in the 1830s. Write a letter to Americans stating your views on independence from Mexico.

3
Manifest Destiny

FIND OUT
- Who were the first white settlers in New Mexico and California?
- What was mission life like for Native Americans?
- What did Americans mean by Manifest Destiny?

In 1819, John Quincy Adams expressed the belief that the United States had the right to all of North America. He wrote:

❝[The world has to accept] the idea of. . . the continent of North America as our proper dominion. From the time we became an independent nation, it was as much a law of nature that this would become our claim as that the Mississippi should flow to the sea.❞

By the 1840s, many Americans agreed. They looked with interest toward California and New Mexico. Like Adams, they felt it was the "destiny" of the United States to expand all the way to the Pacific Ocean.

New Mexico Territory

The entire Southwest belonged to Mexico in the 1840s. This huge region was called **New Mexico Territory.** It included most of the present-day states of Arizona and New Mexico, all of Nevada and Utah, and parts of Colorado. The capital of New Mexico Territory was Santa Fe.

Much of the Southwest is hot and dry. In some areas, thick grasses grow. There are also desert and mountain areas. Before the arrival of the Spanish, Pueblo and Zuñi Indians irrigated and farmed the land. Other

---

Answers to Section 2 Review

1. See the map on p. 357.
2. (a) Stephen Austin, p. 356, (b) Antonio López de Santa Anna, p. 357, (c) Tejano, p. 357, (d) Sam Houston, p. 357, (e) Alamo, p. 358, (f) Lone Star Republic, p. 359
3. annex, p. 360
4. (a) a group of 300 families led by Stephen Austin, (b) The Mexican government hoped that the Americans would help develop the province and control raids by Native Americans.
5. Northerners did not want to add a slaveholding area to the United States.
6. Possible Answer: It angered Texans and made them more determined than ever to win independence from Mexico; it brought a flood of Texan and American volunteers to Houston's army.

Americans followed a number of trails to the West.
1. *Which trails ended in cities in California?*
2. *About how long was the Mormon Trail?*
3. *Analyzing Information (a) What would be the best route for a pioneer family to take from Independence, Missouri, to Sutter's Fort, California? (b) What mountains would they cross? (c) In which town might they seek shelter along the way?*

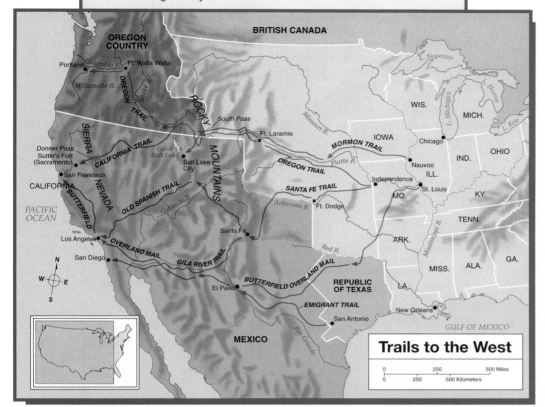

Trails to the West

2. **Instruct** Ask students to define Manifest Destiny in their own words and explain how it affected the North American continent. Use the following questions as the basis for a class discussion: Why did many Americans think the nation must expand? Why do you think the idea of Manifest Destiny appealed to many Americans? How might this idea lead to racism?

3. **Close** To close the lesson, play a Jeopardy!-like game with students. Provide key facts from the section and then have students create appropriate questions.

 Lesson Planner

For a developed **Cooperative Learning** lesson plan, see the *Lesson Planner,* page 73.

Answers to Map Study

1. California, Old Spanish, Butterfield Overland Mail, Gila River
2. about 1,100 miles (1,760 km)
3. (a) the Oregon Trail, to the California Trail, to Sutter's Fort, (b) the Rocky Mountains and the Sierra Nevada, (c) Fort Laramie

Native Americans, such as the Apaches, lived by hunting.

Santa Fe. As you have read, the explorer Juan de Oñate claimed the territory of New Mexico for Spain in 1598. In the early 1600s, the Spanish built Santa Fe as the capital of the territory.

Under the Spanish, Santa Fe grew into a busy trading town. But Spain refused to let

Americans settle in New Mexico. Only after Mexico won its independence in 1821 were Americans welcome in Santa Fe.

The first Americans arrive. William Becknell, a merchant and adventurer, was the first American to head for Santa Fe. In 1821, Becknell led a group of traders on the long trip from Franklin, Missouri, across the plains. When they reached Santa Fe, they

Chapter 12 • **361**

Connections With the World
Background

The United States was not the only expansionist power of the era. During the 1800s, the British expanded their empire in India, taking Sind and the Punjab. At the same time, France also began to create colonial empires in Africa and Asia.

Connections With Geography
Activity

Have students use a map of the United States to locate and define the New Mexico Territory in terms of longitude and latitude. Ask: Which states were originally part of this territory?

Connections With Economics
Background

Each year trading caravans went south from the United States to Mexico and returned laden with goods from Spain's far-flung empire—Europe, Asia, the Philippines, and South America. Santa Fe was a hub for this trade.

found Mexicans eager to buy their goods. Other Americans soon followed Becknell's route. It became known as the ***Santa Fe Trail***. (See the map on page 361.)

Early Years in California

California, too, belonged to Mexico in the early 1840s. Spain had claimed the region 100 years before English colonists built homes in Jamestown. In the years that followed, Spanish and Native American cultures shaped life in California.

A land of contrasts. California is a land of dramatic contrasts. Two tall mountain ranges slice through the region. One range hugs the coast. The other sits inland on the border of Nevada and Arizona. Between these two ranges is California's fertile Central Valley.

Northern California receives plenty of rain. But in the south, water is scarce and much of the land is desert. California enjoys mild temperatures all year, except for areas high in the mountains.

A string of missions. As you have read, Spanish soldiers and priests built the first European settlements in California. In 1769, Captain Gaspar de Portolá led a group of soldiers and missionaries up the Pacific coast. The chief missionary was Father Junípero Serra (hoo NEE peh roh SEHR rah).

Father Serra built his first mission at San Diego. He went on to build 20 other missions along the California coast. (See the map on page 75.) Each mission claimed the surrounding land and soon took care of all its own needs. Spanish soldiers built forts near the missions. The missions supplied meat, grain, and other foods to the forts.

Mission life for Native Americans. California Indians lived in small, scattered groups. They were generally peaceful people. They did not offer much resistance to soldiers who forced them to work for the missions.

Native Americans herded sheep and cattle and raised crops for the missions. In return, they lived at the missions and learned about the Catholic religion. But mission life

A California Mission *The Spanish forced many West Coast Indians into missions. This picture shows Native Americans at a mission in northern California.* **Daily Life** *Study the picture. What seems to be the main building? Where on the mission grounds did Native Americans live?*

Connections With Geography
Background

The major reason that Native Americans in California lived in small, scattered groups was the terrain. The many river valleys and mountains cut groups off from one another.

Our Multicultural Heritage
Activity

Have students research and present brief oral reports on the controversy that has arisen over honoring Father Serra and others who were indirectly responsible for the mistreatment of Native Americans at the Spanish missions.

was hard for Native Americans. Thousands died from overwork and diseases.

After Mexico won its independence, conditions for Native Americans grew even worse. The new Mexican government offered mission land to ranchers. Some of the ranchers cruelly mistreated the Indians. One American reported:

> 66 The natives [in California] . . . are in a state of absolute [slavery], even more degrading, and more oppressive than that of our slaves in the South. 99

These harsh conditions had a deadly effect. Between 1770 and 1850, the Native American population of California declined from 310,000 to 100,000.

Expansion: A Right and a Duty

As late as the mid-1840s, only about 700 people from the United States lived in California. Every year, however, more and more Americans looked toward the West.

The nation's destiny. Many Americans saw the culture and the democratic government of the United States as the best in the world. They believed that the United States had the right and the duty to spread its rule all the way to the Pacific Ocean.

In the 1840s, a New York newspaper coined a phrase for this belief. The phrase was ***Manifest Destiny.*** Manifest means clear or obvious. Destiny means something that is sure to happen. Americans who believed in

Our Common Heritage
When Spanish missionaries arrived in California, Native Americans there spoke more than 100 different languages. Within a few generations, however, most of those languages died out. The Indian children were taught only Spanish in the missions.

Manifest Destiny thought that the United States was clearly meant to expand to the Pacific.

Manifest Destiny had another side, too. Many Americans believed that they were better than Native Americans and Mexicans. For these Americans, racism justified taking over lands belonging to Indians and Mexicans whom they considered inferior.

Election of 1844. Manifest Destiny played an important part in the election of 1844. The Whigs nominated Henry Clay for President. Clay was a respected national leader. The Democrats chose a little-known man named James K. Polk.

Voters soon came to know Polk as the candidate who favored expansion. Polk demanded that Texas and Oregon be added to the United States. He made Oregon a special campaign issue. Polk insisted on the whole region for the United States—all the way to its northern border at latitude 54°40'N. "Fifty-four forty or fight!" cried the Democrats. On election day, Americans showed that they favored expansion by electing Polk President.

SECTION 3 REVIEW

1. **Locate:** (a) Santa Fe, (b) Santa Fe Trail, (c) San Diego.
2. **Identify:** (a) New Mexico Territory, (b) William Becknell, (c) Junípero Serra, (d) Manifest Destiny, (e) James K. Polk.
3. How did mission life affect Native Americans in California?
4. Why did Americans elect James Polk President in 1844?
5. **CRITICAL THINKING Analyzing Information** How do you think missionaries justified forcing Indians to live and work in missions?

ACTIVITY Writing to Learn
Write a dialogue between a Mexican and an American about Manifest Destiny.

CD-ROM

Presidents Access the biography of James K. Polk on the American Heritage® *History of the United States* CD-ROM. (Enrichment/Average)

Student Study Guide

Section 3 Study Guide Have students use the Section 3 Study Guide on page 103 of the *Student Study Guide* to review and reinforce the content of this section. (Reteaching/Average)

ACTIVITY

Guided Instruction Before students begin writing, have them create two lists. On the first list, they should indicate thoughts that a Mexican might have about Manifest Destiny. On the other, they should do the same for an American. Students might work with a partner to present their dialogues to the class in a format similar to a televised public affairs discussion.

Connections With the World
Background

For some of its supporters, the idea of Manifest Destiny extended beyond the Pacific Coast of North America. In 1842, the United States declared that it would not tolerate the annexation of Hawaii by another nation. In 1854, the United States itself attempted to annex the islands but ended negotiations when the Hawaiian king suddenly died.

Answers to Section 3 Review

1. See the map on p. 361.
2. (a) New Mexico Territory, p. 360, (b) William Becknell, p. 361, (c) Junípero Serra, p. 362, (d) Manifest Destiny, p. 363, (e) James K. Polk, p. 363
3. Thousands of Native Americans died of overwork and disease. After Mexican independence, conditions were even worse, with ranchers cruelly mistreating Native Americans.

4. Polk campaigned in favor of Manifest Destiny, saying that Texas and Oregon should belong to the United States. His view reflected and suited the feeling of the era.
5. Possible Answer: The missionaries believed that they were saving the souls of the Native Americans by converting them to Catholicism.

Answer to Caption

Houston pretended that Texas might become an ally of Britain if the Senate refused to ratify the annexation treaty.

Section 4
pp. 364–368

Bell Ringer

Write the following on the chalkboard: "UNITED STATES AND MEXICO AT WAR." Ask students to imagine that this was the headline in the morning paper. Have them freewrite about their thoughts and feelings.

Lesson Plan

1. Focus With the election of President James Polk, American expansionists pushed to expand their ambitions. In this section, students learn about the annexation of Texas, the compromise with Britain in Oregon, and the war with Mexico that brought vast new lands under American control. They also study the influence of Mexican, Spanish, and Native American traditions in shaping the culture of the West.

2. Instruct On separate index cards, write the name of a key person or term from this section. Distribute the cards and ask each student to write a description of that person or term on the reverse side. Collect the cards and divide the class into teams. Shuffle the cards and read the descriptions in order. The first student who correctly identifies

4
The Mexican War

FIND OUT
- How did the United States gain Oregon?
- What events led to war with Mexico?
- What lands did the United States gain from the Mexican War?
- How did Spanish and Indian traditions blend in the new lands?

VOCABULARY cede

In 1845, President Polk rode into the White House on a wave of popular support. Americans eagerly endorsed his promise to expand the United States from sea to sea.

Fulfilling that promise was a difficult task. First, the new President faced a showdown with Britain over the issue of Oregon. Happily for the nation, he resolved this issue peacefully. However, Polk also was determined to add Texas to the United States. To fulfill this dream, he led the United States into a bloody war with Mexico.

Annexing Texas

The United States refused to annex Texas in 1836. By 1844, many Americans had changed their minds. As Polk's election showed, expansionist feelings were strong in the United States.

In 1844, Sam Houston, the president of Texas, signed a treaty of annexation with the United States. The Senate refused to ratify the treaty. Senators feared that annexing Texas would cause a war with Mexico.

Sam Houston did not give up. To persuade Americans to annex Texas, he pretended that Texas might become an ally of Britain. The trick worked. Americans did not want Europe's greatest power to gain a foothold on their western border. In 1845, Congress passed a joint resolution admitting Texas to the Union.

Annexing Texas led at once to a dispute with Mexico. Texas claimed that its southern border was the Rio Grande. Mexico argued that it was the Nueces (noo AY says) River. The Nueces was some 200 miles (320 km) north of the Rio Grande. (See the map on page 365.) The United States supported Texan claims. Trouble with Mexico seemed likely.

Dividing Oregon

The quarrel over Texas was not the only problem Polk faced when he took office in March 1845. Acting on a campaign promise, he moved to gain control of Oregon. It seemed that Britain and the United States would go to war.

Despite his expansionist beliefs, President Polk did not really want a war with Britain. In 1846, he agreed to a compromise. Oregon was divided at latitude 49°N. Britain got the lands north of the line, and the United States got the lands south of the line. The

BIOGRAPHY Sam Houston *While a teenager, Sam Houston lived for three years among the Cherokee Indians. Later, he helped protect the Cherokees against fraud by government agents.* **Citizenship** *What role did Houston play in getting the United States to annex Texas?*

Historical Sidelight
Background

Polk's inaugural address made his position on the annexation of Texas clear: "I regard the question of annexation as belonging exclusively to the United States and Texas. . . . Foreign powers do not seem to appreciate the true character of our Government. Our Union is a confederation of independent States, whose policy is peace with each other and all the world. To enlarge its limits is to extend the dominions of peace over additional territories and increasing millions. . . . Foreign powers should therefore look on the annexation of Texas to the United States not as the conquest of a nation seeking to extend her dominions by arms and violence, but as the peaceful acquisition of a territory once her own, by adding another member to our confederation, with the consent of that member, thereby diminishing the chances of war and opening to them new and ever-increasing markets for their products."

The city of Dallas, Texas, was named for George Mifflin Dallas, Polk's Vice President.

Connections With Civics
Background

When the United States annexed Texas, it also gained the Public Land Strip. This later became a part of Oklahoma. With Texas and Florida admitted as states in 1845, there were more slave states than free states. However, Iowa was admitted in 1846 and Wisconsin in 1848 as free states.

United States named its portion the Oregon Territory. The states of Oregon (1859), Washington (1889), and Idaho (1890) were later carved out of the Oregon Territory.

War With Mexico

Meanwhile, the United States and Mexico stood on the brink of war. Mexico had never accepted the independence of Texas. Now, the annexation of Texas made Mexi- cans furious. They also were concerned that the example set by Texas would encourage Americans in California and New Mexico to rebel.

Americans, in turn, were angry with Mexico. President Polk offered to pay Mexico $30 million for California and New Mexico. However, Mexico strongly opposed any further loss of territory and refused the offer. Many Americans felt that Mexico stood in the way of Manifest Destiny.

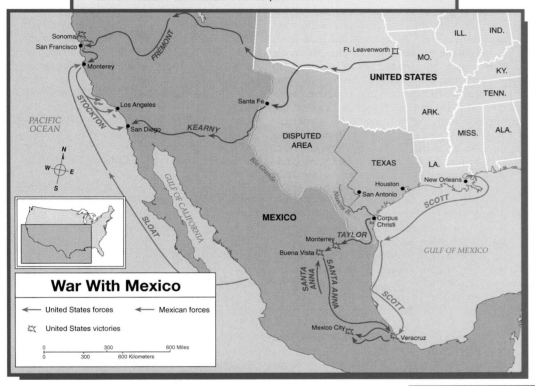

MAP STUDY

Fighting on the Texan border triggered the Mexican War.
1. *What two rivers border the area disputed by the United States and Mexico at the start of the war?*
2. *Which American commanders fought in the war?*
3. **Analyzing Information** *Based on the map, was sea power important to the United States in the Mexican War? Explain.*

War With Mexico

← United States forces   ← Mexican forces

☆ United States victories

0   300   600 Miles
0   300   600 Kilometers

Chapter 12 • 365

 Lesson Planner

For a developed **Cooperative Learning** lesson plan, see the *Lesson Planner,* page 74.

the subject wins 10 points for the team. Award 5 bonus points for an additional pertinent fact about the subject.
3. Close To close the lesson, have students summarize the reasons for the Mexican War and indicate on a map the territory that the United States received to fulfill its "Manifest Destiny."

 Lesson Planner

For a developed **Cooperative Learning** lesson plan, see the *Lesson Planner,* page 74.

Answers to Map Study

1. the Nueces River and the Rio Grande **2.** Scott, Taylor, Sloat, Stockton, Frémont, and Kearny **3.** Yes; Scott attacked the coast of Mexico by sea, and Sloat and Stockton attacked the coast of California by sea.

 Transparencies

Geography and History Use the transparency set, South Central States, on page I-69 of *American History Transparencies.* The base map and overlay 1 show the boundaries and topography of the South Central states. Teaching suggestions can be found on page I-11. (Enrichment/Average)

Critical Thinking
Understanding Causes and Effects

Have students brainstorm a list of causes for the Mexican War. Be certain that students include events from earlier sections, especially Section 2. After the list is completed, assist students in dividing the list into long-term and short-term causes. Have each student decide which cause was the most important. Use students' decisions as the basis for a class discussion.

Connections With Literature
Activity

Explain that American writer Henry David Thoreau spent a night in jail for refusing to pay taxes to support the Mexican War. Have students read sections of Thoreau's *Civil Disobedience* and discuss in class why Thoreau took this stand.

Sparking the war. In January 1846, Polk ordered General Zachary Taylor to cross the Nueces River and set up posts along the Rio Grande. Polk knew that Mexico claimed this land and that the move might spark a war. In April 1846, Mexican troops crossed the Rio Grande and fought briefly with the Americans. Soldiers on both sides were killed.

President Polk claimed that Mexico had "shed American blood upon the American soil." At his urging, Congress declared war on Mexico. Americans were divided over the war. Many people in the South and West wanted more land and so were eager to fight. Northerners, however, opposed the war. They saw it as a southern plot to add slave states to the Union.

Still, many Americans joined the war effort. Since the army was small, thousands of volunteers were needed. When the call for recruits went out, the response was overwhelming, especially in the South and West.

Fighting in Mexico. As the *Mexican War* began, the United States attacked on several fronts. General Zachary Taylor crossed the Rio Grande into northern Mexico. There, he won several battles against the Mexican army. In February 1847, he defeated General Santa Anna at the Battle of Buena Vista. (See the map on page 365.)

Meanwhile, General Winfield Scott landed another American army at the Mexican port of Veracruz. After a long battle, the Americans took the city. Scott then marched west toward the capital, Mexico City. He followed the same route taken by Hernando Cortés 300 years earlier.

Rebellion in California. A third army, led by General Stephen Kearny, captured Santa Fe without firing a shot. Kearny hurried on to San Diego. After several battles, he took control of southern California early in 1847.

Americans in northern California had risen up against Mexican rule even before hearing of the Mexican War. Led by John Frémont, the rebels declared California an independent republic on June 14, 1846. They called their new nation the *Bear Flag Republic.* Later in the war, Frémont joined forces with the United States Army.

A Nation's Dream Comes True

By 1847, the United States controlled all of New Mexico and California. Meanwhile, General Scott had reached the outskirts of the Mexican capital, Mexico City. There his troops faced a fierce battle. Young Mexican soldiers made a heroic last stand at Chapultepec (chah POOL tuh pehk), a fort just outside Mexico City. Like the Texans who died at the Alamo, the Mexicans at Chapultepec fought to the last man. Today, Mexicans honor these young men as heroes.

Peace with Mexico. With the American army in Mexico City, the Mexican government had no choice but to make peace. In 1848, Mexico signed the Treaty of Guadalupe Hidalgo (gwah duh LOOP ay ih DAHL goh). Under the treaty, Mexico was forced to **cede,** or give, all of California and New Mexico to the United States. These lands were called the *Mexican Cession.* (See the map on page 367.) In return for these lands, the United States paid Mexico $15 million. Americans also agreed to respect the rights of Spanish-speaking people in the Mexican Cession.

A final addition. A few years after the Mexican War, the United States completed its expansion across the continent. In 1853, it agreed to pay Mexico $10 million for a strip of land in present-day Arizona and New Mexico. The land was called the *Gadsden Purchase.* Americans rejoiced. Their dream of Manifest Destiny had come true.

A Rich Heritage

Texas, New Mexico, and California added vast new lands to the United States. In these lands, Americans found a rich culture

---

By 1848, the United States stretched all the way from the Atlantic Ocean to the Pacific Ocean.

1. What area on this map was the last to be added to the United States?
2. How did Oregon Country become part of the United States?
3. **Analyzing Information** Refer to the United States map in the Reference Section. When and in what way did your state become part of the United States?

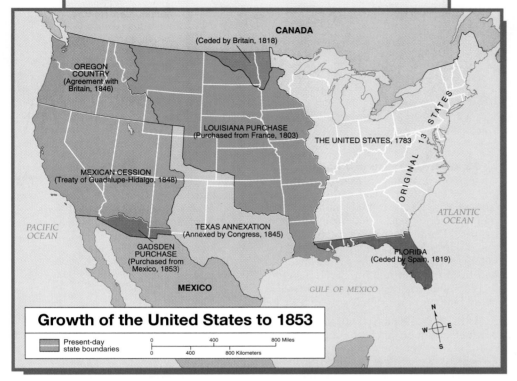

Growth of the United States to 1853

CANADA (Ceded by Britain, 1818)

OREGON COUNTRY (Agreement with Britain, 1846)

LOUISIANA PURCHASE (Purchased from France, 1803)

THE UNITED STATES, 1783

ORIGINAL 13 STATES

MEXICAN CESSION (Treaty of Guadalupe-Hidalgo, 1848)

PACIFIC OCEAN

ATLANTIC OCEAN

TEXAS ANNEXATION (Annexed by Congress, 1845)

GADSDEN PURCHASE (Purchased from Mexico, 1853)

FLORIDA (Ceded by Spain, 1819)

MEXICO

GULF OF MEXICO

Present-day state boundaries

0   400   800 Miles
0   400   800 Kilometers

that blended Spanish and Native American traditions.

A mix of cultures. English-speaking settlers poured into the Southwest bringing their own culture with them, including their ideas about democratic government. At the same time, they learned a great deal from the older residents of the region. Mexican Americans taught the newcomers how to irrigate the soil. They also showed them how to mine silver and other minerals. Many

Spanish and Indian words became part of the English language. Among these words were stampede, buffalo, soda, and tornado.

Americans kept some Mexican laws. One law said that a husband and wife owned property together. In the rest of the United States, married women could not own property. Another Mexican law said that landowners could not cut off water to their neighbors. This law was important in the Southwest, where water was scarce.

Chapter 12 • **367**

Student Study Guide

Section 4 Study Guide Have students use the Section 4 Study Guide on page 104 of the *Student Study Guide* to review and reinforce the content of this section. (Reteaching/Average)

ACTIVITY

Guided Instruction To introduce this activity, you might provide examples of editorials from a local newspaper. When students revise their writing, suggest that they use order of importance to defend their view. Also remind them that the conclusion should restate or summarize the position. As students share their editorials, have them note which arguments are used most frequently.

Fandango in Texas *Spanish traditions were strong in the Southwest. In this painting, couples enjoy a traditional Spanish dance. The brooch, right, also shows Spanish influence.* **Multicultural Heritage** *What other groups influenced the culture of the Southwest?*

Mexican Americans and Indians. Newcomers often treated Mexican Americans and Indians poorly. The earlier residents struggled to protect their traditions and rights. When Mexican Americans went to court to defend their property, they found that judges rarely upheld their claims. The family of Guadalupe Vallejo (vah YAY hoh) had lived in California for decades before the English-speaking settlers arrived. Vallejo noted bitterly:

66 In their dealings with the rancheros, [Americans] took advantage of laws which they understood, but which were new to the Spaniards, and so robbed the latter of their lands. 99

Our Common Heritage
Southwestern cooking reflects many of the cultures that have merged in the region. Popular foods include corn meal and chili peppers of Native American origin, cinnamon brought from Spain, and combinations of tortillas and ground beef developed by Mexicans.

SECTION 4 REVIEW

1. **Locate:** (a) Rio Grande, (b) Nueces River, (c) Buena Vista, (d) Mexico City, (e) Mexican Cession, (f) Gadsden Purchase.
2. **Identify:** (a) Sam Houston, (b) Zachary Taylor, (c) Mexican War, (d) Stephen Kearny, (e) John Frémont, (f) Bear Flag Republic, (g) Chapultepec.
3. **Define:** cede.
4. What event sparked the beginning of the Mexican War?
5. What were the terms of the Treaty of Guadalupe Hidalgo?
6. (a) Name two things that English-speaking settlers learned from Mexican Americans in the Southwest. (b) Name one tradition that English-speaking settlers brought to the Southwest.
7. CRITICAL THINKING **Drawing Conclusions** Why do you think the United States was willing to make a boundary compromise with Britain but not with Mexico?

ACTIVITY Writing to Learn
Write an editorial defending the right of the United States to expand to the Pacific Ocean.

Answers to Section 4 Review

1. See the maps on pp. 365 and 367.
2. (a) Sam Houston, p. 364, (b) Zachary Taylor, p. 366, (c) Mexican War, p. 366, (d) Stephen Kearny, p. 366, (e) John Frémont, p. 366, (f) Bear Flag Republic, p. 366, (g) Chapultepec, p. 366
3. cede, p. 366
4. Polk ordered the army to cross the Nueces and set up posts along the Rio Grande; Mexico responded by sending troops to fight the Americans. Saying that Mexico had shed American blood, Polk asked Congress to declare war.
5. Mexico gave California and New Mexico to the United States. In return, the United States paid Mexico $15 million and agreed to respect the rights of Spanish-speaking peoples in the new land.
6. (a) how to irrigate the soil; how to mine silver and other minerals, (b) Possible Answer: ideas about democratic government
7. Possible Answer: Britain was a much more powerful nation than Mexico. Furthermore, as a former British colony, the United States had cultural ties to Britain that might have made war more difficult.

5
Surge to the Pacific

FIND OUT
- How did the Mormons set up a successful community in Utah?
- How did the discovery of gold affect life in California?
- What mix of peoples helped California to grow and prosper?

VOCABULARY forty-niner, vigilante

In 1848, James Marshall was helping John Sutter build a sawmill on the American River, north of Sacramento, California. On the morning of January 24, Marshall set out to inspect a ditch his crew was digging. He later told a friend what he saw that day:

> 66 It was a clear, cold morning; I shall never forget that morning. As I was taking my usual walk, . . . my eye was caught with the glimpse of something shining in the bottom of the ditch. There was about a foot of water running then. I reached my hand down and picked it up; it made my heart thump, for I was certain it was gold. 99

Word of Marshall's find spread like wildfire. From all over the nation, thousands of prospectors flocked to California to seek their fortunes. The California Gold Rush had begun!

Gold was not the only thing that attracted settlers to the West in the mid-1800s. California, New Mexico, Oregon, Texas—all were now part of the United States. Restless pioneers, always eager to try something new, headed into these lands to build homes and a new way of life.

Mormons Seek Refuge in Utah

The largest group of settlers to move into the Mexican Cession were the **Mormons.** Mormons belonged to the Church of Jesus Christ of Latter-day Saints. The church was founded by Joseph Smith in 1830. Smith, a farmer who lived in upstate New York, attracted many followers.

Troubles with neighbors. Smith was an energetic and popular man. His teachings, however, angered many non-Mormons. For example, Mormons at first believed that property should be owned in common. Smith also said that a man could have more than one wife. Angry neighbors forced the Mormons to leave New York for Ohio. From Ohio, they were forced to move to Missouri, and from there to Illinois. In the 1840s, the Mormons built a community called Nauvoo in Illinois.

Before long, the Mormons again clashed with their neighbors. In 1844, an angry mob killed Joseph Smith. The Mormons chose Brigham Young as their new leader.

Brigham Young realized that the Mormons needed a home where they would be safe. He had read about a valley between the Rocky Mountains and the Great Salt Lake in Utah. Young decided that the isolated valley would make a good home for the Mormons.

A difficult journey. To move 15,000 men, women, and children from Illinois to Utah in the 1840s was an awesome challenge. Relying on faith and careful planning, Brigham Young achieved his goal.

In 1847, Young led an advance party into the Great Salt Lake valley. Wave after wave of Mormons followed. For the next few years, Mormon wagon trains struggled across the plains and over the Rockies to Utah. When they ran short of wagons and oxen, thousands made the long trip pulling their gear in handcarts.

The Mormons prosper in the desert. In Utah, the Mormons had to survive in a harsh

Bell Ringer

Write the following headline on the chalkboard: "GOLD DISCOVERED IN CALIFORNIA: Gold Fever Spreading Across the Land!" Have students write their thoughts and feelings about this news. Ask: How would people you know react?

Lesson Plan

1. Focus In the second half of the 1800s, Americans began to populate western lands. In this section, students examine the Mormon settlement of Utah, the Gold Rush in California, and the mixture of peoples in California.

2. Instruct Draw a blank chart on the chalkboard, with two columns labeled Utah and California and six rows labeled Years of American Settlement, Types of Settlers, Reasons for Settlement, Type of Settlement, Problems Encountered, and Year of Statehood. Help the class fill out the chart using information from the text.

3. Close To close the lesson, review the chart. Discuss similarities and differences between settlement of the two areas.

Lesson Planner

For a developed **Cooperative Learning** lesson plan, see the *Lesson Planner,* page 75.

Our Multicultural Heritage
Background

In addition to the Mormon settlement, other religious communities emerged in the 1800s. One was the Amana Church Society, a group of seven villages in Iowa founded by members of a German sect. The members farmed 25,000 acres and believed in cooperation and communal sharing.

Linking Past and Present
Background

Today, the state bird of Utah is the sea gull, which goes back to the days of Utah's settlement by Mormons. In the late 1840s, farmers in north-central Utah were plagued by grasshoppers, and complete destruction of the crops seemed inevitable. Then flocks of sea gulls flew in from the Great Salt Lake, devouring the insects—and saving the farmers.

Traveling to Utah *"This is the place," said Brigham Young when he and a small band of Mormons reached the Great Salt Lake in Utah. Other groups of Mormons, like the ones shown here, soon followed.* **American Traditions** *What other states were settled by people seeking religious freedom?*

desert climate. Once again, Young proved to be a gifted leader. He planned an irrigation system to bring water to farms. He also drew up plans for a large city, called **Salt Lake City,** to be built in the desert.

The Mormon settlement in Utah grew quickly. Like other whites, Mormons took over thousands of acres of Native American land, usually paying nothing for it.

Congress recognized Brigham Young as governor of the Utah Territory in 1850. Trouble later broke out when non-Mormons moved to the area. In the end, peace was restored, and Utah became a state in 1896.

Gold in California!

While the Mormons trekked to Utah, thousands of other Americans were racing to California. They all had a single objective: Gold!

Sutter's Mill. As you have read, James Marshall found gold at Sutter's Mill in California in January 1848. In a few days, word of the gold strike spread to San Francisco. Carpenters threw down their saws. Bakers left bread in their ovens. Schools emptied as teachers and students joined the rush to the gold fields.

The news spread outward from San Francisco. Thousands of Americans caught gold fever. People in Europe and South America joined the rush as well. More than 80,000 people made the long journey to California in 1849. They became known as **forty-niners.**

In the gold fields. The first miners needed little skill. Because the gold was near the surface of the Earth, they could dig it out with knives. Later, the miners found a better way. They loaded sand and gravel from the riverbed into a washing pan. Then, they held the pan under water and swirled it gently. The water washed away lighter gravel, leaving the heavier gold in the pan. This process was known as "panning for gold."

Only a few miners struck it rich. Most went broke trying to make their fortunes. Still, although many miners left the gold fields, they stayed in California.

A new state. The Gold Rush brought big changes to life in California. Almost overnight, San Francisco grew from a sleepy town to a bustling city.

Greed turned some forty-niners into criminals. Murders and robberies plagued many mining camps. To fight crime, miners formed vigilance committees. **Vigilantes** (vihj uh LAN teez), self-appointed law enforcers, dealt out punishment even though they had no legal power to do so. Sometimes an accused criminal was lynched, or hanged without a legal trial.

Californians realized they needed a government to stop the lawlessness. In 1849, they drafted a state constitution. They then asked to be admitted to the Union. Their request caused an uproar in the United States. Americans wondered whether or not the new state would allow slavery. As you will read in Chapter 15, after a heated debate, California was admitted to the Union in 1850 as a free state.

California's Unique Culture

Most mining camps included a mix of peoples. One visitor to a mining town met runaway slaves from the South, Native Americans, and New Englanders. There were also people from Hawaii, China, Peru, Chile, France, Germany, Italy, Ireland, and Australia.

Most of the miners, however, were white Americans. During the wild days of the Gold Rush, they often ignored the rights of other Californians.

Native Americans. Indians fared worst of all. Many Native Americans were driven

off their lands and later died of starvation or diseases. Others were murdered. In 1850, about 100,000 Indians lived in California. By the 1870s, there were only 17,000 Indians left in the state.

Mexican Americans. In many instances, Mexican Americans lost land they had owned for generations. Still, they fought to

CAUSES

- Oregon has fertile land
- Texas is ideal for raising cattle and growing cotton
- Many Americans believe in Manifest Destiny
- Mormons seek a safe home
- Gold is discovered in California

WESTWARD MOVEMENT

EFFECTS

- United States annexes Texas
- Britain and the United States divide Oregon
- United States gains the Mexican Cession after the Mexican War
- United States makes the Gadsden Purchase
- United States stretches from sea to sea
- Cotton Kingdom spreads

CHART SKILLS *Westward movement increased in the mid-1800s.* • *List two attractions that drew Americans west. According to this chart, was Manifest Destiny successful? Explain.*

Answer to Chart Skills

Possible Answers: fertile land in Oregon and gold in California; yes, because as a result of westward movement, the United States stretched from sea to sea.

 Transparencies

Cause and Effect Use the transparency Westward Movement on page F-19 of *American History Transparencies*. Teaching suggestions can be found on page F-5. (Enrichment/Average)

 Voices of Freedom

Primary Source You might assign selection 14-6, Louise Clappe Strikes Gold, on pages 100–101 of *Voices of Freedom*. (Enrichment/Average)

 Customized Reader

Primary Source For an account of the journey of a Chinese pioneer to California, order article IVA-3, The Pioneer Chinese, from the *American History Customized Reader*. (Enrichment/Average)

 Chapter Resources

Critical Thinking Duplicate and distribute the worksheet, Drawing Conclusions, from Unit 4, page 17, of the *Chapter Resources* binder. The worksheet traces the growth of the 10 largest cities in the United States between 1820 and 1860. (Enrichment/Average)

Learning Styles
Kinesthetic Learners

You might have students work in small groups of three or four to prepare and perform brief skits based on the settlement of Utah and California. Scenes could include an encounter between Mormons and non-Mormons in the East; the arrival of a Mormon family in Utah; a gold strike in California; a meeting of a vigilance committee in a mining town; or scenes involving the different cultural groups in California.

Historical Sidelight
Background

Blue jeans, probably the best-known and most popular item of American clothing, were first worn during the Gold Rush. Immigrant Levi Strauss arrived in California hoping to sell canvas to miners. Other merchants were selling tent material, so Strauss used canvas to make trousers and later made them from denim. When miners complained that the pockets tore open, Strauss had a blacksmith rivet the pockets on. The Levi Strauss Company still makes jeans.

Linking Past and Present
Activity

Mormons, Mexicans, Native Americans, African Americans, and Chinese all faced discrimination during the 1840s. Have students write a brief essay answering this question: Do religious and cultural differences cause similar problems for any groups today? Remind students to support their answers with specific examples.

Our Multicultural Heritage

Biography Have students read the biography, Fatt Hing, Chinese Pioneer, on page 35 of the *Our Multicultural Heritage* booklet. (Enrichment/Challenging)

Milestone Have students read Legacy of the Golden Mountain, on page 36 of the *Our Multicultural Heritage* booklet. (Enrichment/Easy)

Student Study Guide

Section 5 Study Guide Have students use the Section 5 Study Guide on page 105 of the *Student Study Guide* to review and reinforce the content of this section. (Reteaching/Average)

ACTIVITY

Guided Instruction Before students begin writing their journal entries, have them review the subsection Gold in California! Remind students that the entries should include those events that would have seemed noteworthy to the prospector at the end of the day. Invite several volunteers to read their entries to the class.

Prospecting for Gold *The lure of gold drew thousands of prospectors to California. These miners are using a wooden sluice to wash the lighter gravel away from the heavier gold.*
Linking Past and Present *How did the Gold Rush contribute to California's unique culture?*

preserve the customs of their people. José Carrillo (cah REE yoh) was from one of the oldest families in California. In part through his efforts, the state's constitution was written in both Spanish and English.

Chinese Americans. Attracted by the tales of a "mountain of gold," thousands of Chinese began arriving in California in 1848. Since California needed workers, the Chinese were welcomed at first. When the Chinese staked claims in the gold fields, how-

Linking Past and Present

California continues to attract newcomers in record numbers. In fact, in 1993, almost 30 percent of the immigrants coming to the United States settled in California. The largest group were those from Asia.

372 • Chapter 12

ever, white miners often drove them off. Still, many Chinese Americans stayed in California and helped the state to grow. They farmed, irrigated, and reclaimed vast stretches of land.

African Americans. Free blacks, like other forty-niners, rushed to the California gold fields hoping to strike it rich. Some did become wealthy. By the 1850s, in fact, California had the richest African American population of any state. Yet African Americans were also denied certain rights. For example, California law denied blacks and other minorities the right to testify against whites in court. After a long struggle, blacks gained this right in 1863.

In spite of these problems, California thrived and grew. Settlers continued to arrive in the state. By 1860, it had 100,000 citizens. The mix of peoples in California gave it a unique culture.

SECTION 5 REVIEW

1. **Locate:** (a) Sacramento, (b) Nauvoo, (c) Salt Lake City, (d) San Francisco.
2. **Identify:** (a) Mormons, (b) Joseph Smith, (c) Brigham Young.
3. **Define:** (a) forty-niner, (b) vigilante.
4. Why did Brigham Young lead the Mormons to Utah?
5. What problems did Californians face because of the Gold Rush?
6. Explain the problems that each of the following faced in California: (a) Native Americans, (b) Mexican Americans, (c) Chinese Americans, (d) African Americans.
7. **CRITICAL THINKING Comparing** Compare the settling of Utah with the settling of California.

ACTIVITY Writing to Learn

Imagine that you are a gold prospector in California in 1850. Write a journal entry describing a typical day.

CONNECTIONS

A Mountain of Gold

The penalty for trying to leave China in the 1800s was harsh and sure—a swift beheading. Yet, between 1848 and 1851, 25,000 Chinese risked the executioner's ax to sail 7,000 miles (11,265 km) to California. Oddly, almost all of these people came from the Toishan district of southern China.

Why did the people of Toishan risk death to leave China? The answer: hunger and poverty. Located in the mountains, Toishan was rocky and barren. Even with hard work, its people could grow only enough to feed themselves four months of the year. Life was a daily struggle for survival.

In 1848, exciting news reached Toishan. Mountains of gold had been discovered in a place called California. It was there just for the digging!

Wooden rocker for washing away gravel

Leaving their families behind, the men of Toishan rushed to the nearby port of Hong Kong. There, they crowded into ships for the three-month journey east to California.

Few of the Toishanese got rich in the California gold fields. Most found jobs, however, and many sent money back home. In fact, the money they sent to Toishan helped transform it into a prosperous, well-fed community. In this small way, California had fulfilled its promise as a "mountain of gold."

■ Why did many Chinese travel to California after 1848?

Mining tools

Chinese immigrant

ACTIVITY

Create a storybook for younger children about the people of Toishan and the "mountain of gold." Illustrate your book with colorful pictures and a map showing the journey to California.

Chapter 12 • **373**

CHAPTER 12 REVIEW

Answers to Reviewing the Main Ideas

1. (a) They heard that Oregon had fine farmland. (b) by wagon train along the Oregon Trail
2. (a) Mountain Men explored much new territory and later showed these trails to settlers moving west. (b) Missionaries were the first to establish permanent homes. (c) The forty-niners who came in search of gold stayed and helped develop the natural resources of California.
3. He threw out the Mexican constitution.
4. Soldiers forced Native Americans to work for the missions; in return, they lived at the mission and learned the Catholic religion; thousands died from overwork and disease.
5. It helped Polk win the election; he supported Manifest Destiny, demanding that the United States annex Texas and Oregon.
6. (a) survival in a desert environment, (b) He planned an irrigation system to bring water to farms.
7. The population rapidly increased; violence was evident in many mining camps; Californians realized that they needed a central government to control the lawlessness.

Answers to Thinking Critically

1. (a) a dispute over the southern border of Texas, (b) Mexicans were angry over the annexation of Texas by the United States and feared that California and New Mexico might rebel as Texas had done. Americans were angry over Mexico's refusal to sell California and New Mexico to the United States.
2. Possible Answer: War might have been avoided if the United States had given up the disputed territory, but expansionists wanted war and might have used some other pretense.
3. (a) They saw the Gold Rush as a once-in-a-lifetime chance to make a quick fortune. (b) Possible Answer: People hoping to make a fortune take risks by investing in the stock market, by speculating in real estate, or by gambling. Risks today are more likely to involve money than personal safety.

Summary

- Thousands of settlers traveled to Oregon Country along the Oregon Trail.
- Americans in Texas declared their independence from Mexico in 1836.
- Americans believed it was their Manifest Destiny to expand to the Pacific.
- The United States gained California and New Mexico after the Mexican War.
- The Mormons set up a successful community in Utah, while thousands of people rushed to California in search of gold.

Reviewing the Main Ideas

1. (a) What attracted settlers to Oregon Country in the mid-1800s? (b) How did they travel there?
2. Describe how each of the following groups helped to open the West: (a) Mountain Men, (b) missionaries, (c) forty-niners.
3. What action by Santa Anna convinced Texans to fight for independence?
4. Describe the life of Native Americans on missions in California.
5. What role did the idea of Manifest Destiny play in the election of 1844?
6. (a) What problem did the Mormons face in Utah? (b) How did Brigham Young help the Mormons to solve this problem?
7. How did the discovery of gold change life in California?

Thinking Critically

1. **Understanding Causes and Effects** Review the events leading up to the Mexican War. (a) What was the immediate cause of war with Mexico? (b) What were the long-range causes?
2. **Solving Problems** Do you think that the United States could have avoided war with Mexico in 1846? Explain.

3. **Linking Past and Present** (a) Why do you think forty-niners risked their savings and lives looking for gold in California? (b) Can you think of people today who take risks to earn great wealth? Explain.

Applying Your Skills

1. **Making a Review Chart** Make a chart with four columns and two rows. Title the chart American Expansion. Label the columns Oregon, Texas, Mexican Cession, Gadsden Purchase. Label the rows Date Added, How Added. Use the material in the chapter to complete the chart.
2. **Using a Primary Source** This excerpt is from the diary of a Mormon woman traveling to Utah: "To start out on such a journey in the winter and in our state of poverty, it would seem like walking into the jaws of death. But we put our trust in [our heavenly father], feeling that we were his chosen people." (a) What does the writer think the trip will be like? Explain. (b) Why is she willing to face the hardships of the trip?

Thinking About Geography

Match the letters on the map with the following places: **1.** Louisiana Purchase, **2.** Gadsden Purchase, **3.** Oregon Country, **4.** Florida, **5.** The United States, 1783, **6.** Texas Annexation, **7.** Mexican Cession. **Location** At what latitude did the United States and Britain agree to divide Oregon?

---

2. Possible Answer: War might have been avoided if the United States had given up the disputed territory, but expansionists wanted war and might have used some other pretense.
3. (a) They saw the Gold Rush as a once-in-a-lifetime chance to make a quick fortune. (b) Possible Answer: People hoping to make a fortune take risks by investing in the stock market, by

Answers to Applying Your Skills

1. Check student charts for accuracy.
2. (a) like walking into the jaws of death: they are starting out in the winter and in a state of poverty, (b) because she trusts God, believing that she is one of His chosen people

Answers to Thinking About Geography

1. B **2.** G **3.** E **4.** C **5.** A **6.** D **7.** F

Location: 49°N

Traveling Along the Oregon Trail

Form into groups to review life along the Oregon Trail. Follow the suggestions below to research, write, sing, or act to show what you have learned about this subject. You may use the textbook, encyclopedias, atlases, or other materials in your classroom library to complete the tasks. Be able to name your sources of information when you have finished the activity.

Pioneer's herbal medicine kit

GEOGRAPHERS Prepare fact sheets on the landforms, climate, animals, and vegetation that travelers might encounter along the Oregon Trail.

MUSICIANS Review what you have read about traveling west on the Oregon Trail. Then make up a song that pioneers might sing about life on the trail. Fit your words to a familiar tune or write a new one.

HISTORIANS Create a time capsule about life on the Oregon Trail. Use an empty coffee can as your time capsule. Put sketches, words, phrases, and "artifacts" into your time capsule to illustrate geography, people, and events along the trail. Seal your capsule and decorate the outside to identify the contents. Plan to open it at the end of the school year.

ARTISTS Choose a painting from the chapter that shows pioneers traveling west. Then find another painting showing a similar subject. Give a talk about the two paintings. What do the paintings tell you about the journey west? Are the two paintings similar? If they are different, how do you explain the differences? What are the artists trying to say in the paintings?

ACTORS Review the selections from Amelia Stewart Knight's diary on page 355. Prepare a dramatic reading of her diary. One member of the group can read from the diary while other members act out the story.

Butter churn

 Make an audiotape or videotape about Traveling Along the Oregon Trail. Tape each group that performs or presents its assignment.

Crossing the Platte River

Chapter 12 • **375**

Lessons	Teaching Resources
1 **The Growth of Industry in the North** **Objectives** 1. Identify the new inventions that changed farming in the North. 2. Describe how the telegraph helped business. 3. Describe how steam power and railroads helped industry grow.	**Lesson Planner** Cooperative Learning, p. 78 **Student Study Guide** Section 1 Study Guide, p. 108
2 **Life in the Industrial North** **Objectives** 1. Describe how working conditions changed in factories and shops. 2. Explain why skilled workers formed unions. 3. Identify the newcomers who arrived in the United States in the mid-1800s. 4. Describe what life was like for African Americans in the North.	**Lesson Planner** Cooperative Learning, p. 79 **Student Study Guide** Section 2 Study Guide, p. 109 **Our Multicultural Heritage** *Biography* Norbert Rillieux, Engineer and Inventor, p. 38 **Chapter Resources Binder, Unit 4** *Skill Application* Synthesizing Information, p. 30 *Critical Thinking* Comparing Points of View, p. 31
3 **Cotton Becomes King** **Objectives** 1. Describe how the cotton gin affected the growth of slavery. 2. Explain why cotton planters moved westward. 3. Explain why the South had less industry than the North.	**Lesson Planner** Cooperative Learning, p. 80 **Student Study Guide** Section 3 Study Guide, p. 110 **Chapter Resources Binder, Unit 4** *Geography in History* The Cotton Kingdom, pp. 33–34
4 **Life in the Cotton Kingdom** **Objectives** 1. Identify the three groups that made up white society in the South. 2. Describe how southerners treated free African Americans. 3. Describe what life was like for enslaved African Americans on plantations.	**Lesson Planner** Cooperative Learning, p. 81 **Student Study Guide** Section 4 Study Guide, p. 111 **Our Multicultural Heritage** *Biography* Prudence Crandall, Crusader for Black Education, p. 37 *Milestone* A Distinctly Southern Literature, p. 39 **Chapter Resources Binder, Unit 4** *History Through Literature* Go Down, Moses, p. 32 **Interdisciplinary Connections:** African American Contributions ■ *Arts* Spirituals, p. 74 ▨ *Sciences* A Refining Refinement, p. 75 ■ *World* Other Effects of Slavery, p. 76 ■ *Economics* The Goals of Paul Cuffe, p. 77 ■ *Civics* The A.M.E. Church, p. 78

Multimedia Resources	Additional Resources	Chapter-Level Resources
Transparencies *Exploring Technology* The Plow, p. H-37 **Videotapes/Videodiscs** *United States History Video Collection* The Industrial North, Vol. 8, Ch. 7	**Voices of Freedom** At Work on a Clipper, pp. 101–102 **Historical Outline Map Book** The Northern States, p. 43 **Customized Reader** Chicago in 1833, article IVB-18	**Lesson Planner** Activity Based, pp. 82–83 **Student Study Guide** Chapter 13 Study Guide, pp. 112–113 **Chapter Resources** **Binder** **Unit 4** Vocabulary Building, p. 29 Chapter Test A, pp. 35–37 Chapter Test B, pp. 38–40 Illustration Master, p. 41 Extra Unit Questions, pp. 57–59 **English Guided Reading** Guided Reading, pp. 25–26 **Spanish Resources** **Computer Test Bank** Chapter Tests A and B Extra Unit Questions **Guided Reading** **Audiotapes** Side 5 **CD-ROM** **Time Tour** The Worlds of North and South (1820–1860) in An Expanding Nation
Transparencies *Interdisciplinary Connections* American Labor Force, p. B-57	**Voices of Freedom** Life in a Mill in 1832, pp. 102–103 A Violent Reaction to Foreign-Born Voters, pp. 103–104 **Customized Reader** A Swiss Family's Immigration to the United States, article IVA-13	
Transparencies *Exploring Technology* Cotton Gin, p. H-33 **Videotapes/Videodiscs** *United States History Video Collection* The Agricultural South, Vol. 8, Ch. 10	**Voices of Freedom** Inventing the Cotton Gin, pp. 104–105 **Historical Outline Map Book** The Southern States, p. 44 **Customized Reader** A Ship's Captain Describes the Illegal African Slave Trade, article IVB-10	
Listening to Literature Audiocassettes *The American Experience* Swing Low Sweet Chariot, side 5; Go Down, Moses, side 5 **Videotapes/Videodiscs** *United States History Video Collection* The Slave South, Vol. 8, Ch. 13; Slave Life and Revolt, Vol. 8, Ch. 16	**Customized Reader** Traveling Through the Carolinas in 1828, article IVB-19 Life in Natchez, Mississippi, article IVA-19 African Americans Recall Their Lives as Slaves, article IVA-7 A Slave Auction, article IVB-11 A Cheerful View of Slavery, article IVB-13 Henry "Box" Brown Mails Himself to Freedom, article IVA-11	

Lesson Planner

For a fully developed **Activity-Based** lesson plan for Chapter 13, see the *Lesson Planner*, pages 82–83.

 Chapter Resources

Vocabulary Building The Vocabulary Building worksheet for Chapter 13 from Unit 4, page 29, of the *Chapter Resources* binder can be used as a prereading activity or as a review of chapter vocabulary. (Reteaching/Easy)

 Student Study Guide

Chapter 13 Study Guide Refer students to pages 112–113 of the *Student Study Guide* for the Chapter 13 Study Guide. The study guide can be used for chapter review as well as for reteaching. (Reteaching/Average)

 Guided Reading Audiotapes

Students can use *Guided Reading Audiotapes,* Chapter 13, side 5, to listen to section previews, summaries, and review questions. The tapes might benefit students who are auditory learners, students who have trouble reading, or students acquiring English. (Reteaching/Easy)

CHAPTER 13

The Worlds of North and South

(1820–1860)

CHAPTER OUTLINE

1 The Growth of Industry in the North

2 Life in the Industrial North

3 Cotton Becomes King

4 Life in the Cotton Kingdom

1830s *The first commercial railroads in the United States went into service. Here, an early steam locomotive pulls into a station in Maryland.*

Early 1800s *Slavery ended in the North. Many free African Americans, such as this news vendor, found work in the nation's cities.*

Growth of Slavery

Thousands of Slaves

4,000
3,500
3,000
2,500
2,000
1,500
1,000
500
0

1800 1810 1820 1830 1840 1850 1860
Year

1840s *A cotton boom in the South led to the expansion of slavery, as this graph shows.*

1820   1825   1830   1835   1840

WORLD EVENT
1840 World Anti-Slavery Convention held in Great Britain

Chapter Time Line
Critical Thinking

Discuss with students the time line illustrations and captions. Draw particular attention to what the information suggests about differing lifestyles in the North and South; you might ask students to classify each picture on that basis. Discuss each World Event entry, as well. Ask students to speculate as to whether each event had a greater impact on the North or on the South.

Then have students create cause-and-effect statements based on the time line. Model these examples and invite students to create others:

■ Because of the invention of labor-saving machines, _____.

■ One result of _____ was the movement of many African Americans into northern cities.

Have students test the accuracy of their statements as they work through Chapter 13.

Chapter Setting

"I was born in 1844.... First [thing] I remember was my ma and us [children] being sold off the [auction] block to Mistress Payne. When I was... too little to work in the field, I stayed at the big house most of the time and helped Mistress Payne feed the chickens, make scarecrows to keep the hawks away and put wood on the fires. After I got big enough to hoe, I went to the field same as the other[s].... In the summer after the crop was laid by I helped to cut wood for winter, build fences, cut bushes.... I never earned any money for myself.... I didn't hardly know what money looked like."

In this excerpt, Jack Payne recalls his life as an enslaved person in Texas. Payne was only one of millions of African Americans throughout the South who suffered the anguish of slavery. Toiling from dawn till dusk, they had neither freedom nor rights.

By the 1840s, cotton was the South's major cash crop. Cotton plantations and slavery spread from the east coast to the Mississippi River and beyond. From plantations worked by enslaved African Americans, hundreds of thousands of cotton bales were shipped to the North.

In the North, new machines and inventions triggered the growth of factories and cities. Workers toiled long hours at low wages to make cotton into thousands of rolls of cloth. So it was that the North and South, very different in ways of life, were linked by cotton—and the evils of slavery.

 ACTIVITY Study the pictures, maps, and graphs in this chapter. Then make a list of words or phrases that describe life in the North and the South in the mid-1800s. After you have read the chapter, review your list to see if you wish to make any changes.

Mid-1800s *Labor-saving machines—such as this sewing machine—changed the way goods were made. These new inventions helped northern industry to grow.*

1850s *A wave of immigrants came from Ireland and Germany. Many of these new Americans found jobs in northern factories.*

1840	1845	1850	1855	1860

 WORLD EVENT
1845 Potato famine begins in Ireland

 WORLD EVENT
1848 Revolutions in Germany

Chapter 13 • **377**

Bell Ringer

Have the class brainstorm and list on the chalkboard any inventions that they feel changed the American way of life.

Lesson Plan

1. Focus The Industrial Revolution greatly affected the economy of the North. Inventions and improved methods of transportation supported a factory system that produced goods more quickly and cheaply. In this section, students learn about the machines, railroads, and ships that helped industries and trade in the North expand.

2. Instruct Pair students and have partners alternately role-play an interview with an inventor from this section. Have the interviewer ask the inventor for a description of the invention, how it works, and the ways in which it will revolutionize American life. You might videotape and play selected interviews for the class.

3. Close To close the lesson, name an invention discussed in this section. Have students identify the invention and explain its significance.

 Lesson Planner

For a developed **Cooperative Learning** lesson plan, see the *Lesson Planner,* page 78.

FIND OUT

- What new inventions changed farming in the North?
- How did the telegraph help business?
- How did steam power and railroads help industry grow?

VOCABULARY telegraph, clipper ship

In 1846, Elias Howe made a bold claim. He had built a machine, he said, that could sew a piece of clothing faster than five seamstresses combined. Scoffing at Howe's claim, a Boston clothing maker arranged a contest.

During the competition, Howe sat at a small table, calmly pumping the foot pedal that drove his machine. Nearby, the seamstresses worked feverishly with needle and thread. In the end, all agreed that Howe had won.

Soon, clothing makers had bought hundreds of Howe's sewing machines. Workers could now make dozens of jackets faster than a tailor could sew one by hand. The cost of clothing dropped. Many tailors had to find new ways to earn a living. The sewing machine was one of many new inventions that changed life in the North after 1820.

Farming Inventions

In the 1800s, the North was a seedbed for new inventions. "In Massachusetts and Connecticut," a French visitor exclaimed, "there is not a laborer who has not invented a machine or a tool."

Several inventions made work easier for farmers. John Deere invented a lightweight plow made of steel. Earlier plows made of heavy iron or wood had to be pulled by slow-moving oxen. A horse pulling a steel plow could prepare a field for planting much faster.

In 1847, Cyrus McCormick opened a factory in Chicago that manufactured mechanical reapers. The reaper was a horse-drawn machine that mowed wheat and other grains. McCormick's reaper could do the work of five people using hand tools.

The reaper and the steel plow helped farmers raise more grain with fewer hands. As a result, thousands of farm workers left the countryside. Some went west to start farms of their own. Others found jobs in new factories in northern cities.

The Telegraph

In 1844, Samuel F.B. Morse received a patent for a "talking wire," or telegraph. The **telegraph** was a device that sent electrical signals along a wire. The signals were based on a code of dots, dashes, and spaces. Later, this code became known as the Morse code.

Congress gave Morse funds to run wire from Washington, D.C., to Baltimore. On May 24, 1844, Morse set up his telegraph in the Supreme Court chamber in Washington. He tapped out a short message: "What hath God wrought!" A few seconds later, the operator in Baltimore tapped back the same message. The telegraph worked!

Morse's invention was an instant success. Telegraph companies sprang up everywhere and strung thousands of miles of wire. Newspaper reporters wired their stories in. Businesses especially gained from being able to find out instantly about supply, demand, and prices of goods in different areas. For example, western farmers might learn of a wheat shortage in New York and ship their grain east to meet the demand.

Historical Sidelight
Background

Tailors made clothes to fit the specific requirements and measurements of individual customers. With the invention of the sewing machine, someone with fewer skills could follow a pattern for average sizes. Garments would not fit perfectly but would be close to the size requirements. This innovation was the beginning of ready-to-wear clothes as we know them.

Critical Thinking
Applying Information

Tailor-made clothing still costs more than ready-to-wear apparel. Ask: Why would tailor-made clothes in the mid-1800s (as well as today) be more expensive than ready-to-wear clothing?

Linking Past and Present
Background

The basic elements of McCormick's reaper—such innovations as the guards, platform, reciprocating knife, and reel—are still the basic components of modern harvesting machines. Interestingly, McCormick was aided in developing his reaper by Jo Anderson, a slave.

Railroads and Industry *The railroad was a key to the growth of industry in the North. Here, a freight train delivers ore to a foundry, where it will be turned into steel.* **Daily Life** *What other effects do you think the growth of railroads had on northern life?*

The First Railroads

A further boost to the economy came as transportation improved. Americans continued to build new roads and canals. The greatest change, however, came with the railroads.

The first railroads were built in the early 1800s. Horses or mules pulled cars along wood rails covered with strips of iron. Then, in 1829, an English family developed a steam-powered engine to pull rail cars. The engine, called the *Rocket,* barreled along at 30 miles (48 km) per hour, an amazing speed at the time.

In the United States, some people laughed at the noisy clatter of these "iron horses." Others watched in horror as sparks flew from the smokestack, burning holes in passengers' clothing and setting barns on fire.

Many Americans believed that horse-drawn rail cars were safer and faster than trains pulled by a steam engine. In 1830, a crowd gathered in Baltimore to watch a horse-drawn rail car race the *Tom Thumb,* a steam-powered engine. At first, the horse struggled to keep up with the steam engine. Suddenly, *Tom Thumb* broke down, leaving the horse-drawn car to cross the finish line first.

The defeat of *Tom Thumb* did not mean the end of the steam engine. Engineers soon designed better engines and rails. Private companies began to build railroads, sometimes with help from state governments. By the 1850s, railroads linked eastern cities to Cincinnati and Chicago in the Midwest. Cities at the center of railroad hubs grew rapidly.

Yankee Clippers

Railroads boosted business inside the United States. At the same time, trade also increased between the United States and other nations. At seaports in the Northeast, captains loaded their ships with cotton, fur, wheat, lumber, and tobacco. Then they sailed to the four corners of the world.

Speed was the key to successful trade at sea. In 1845, an American named John Griffiths launched the *Rainbow,* the first of the **clipper ships.** These sleek vessels had tall

Linking Past and Present
The development of speedy clipper ships led to a new sport for the very rich—yachting. In 1851, a clipper ship named America *won a highly promoted race in England. The winning trophy became known as the America's Cup. American yachts have won 28 of 30 America's Cup challenges since the first race in 1851.*

Answer to Caption
Possible Answer: faster transport of manufactured goods and mail; growth of cities

 Transparencies

Exploring Technology Use the transparency The Plow on page H-37 of *American History Transparencies.* Teaching suggestions can be found on page H-9. (Enrichment/Average)

Historical Outline Map Book

Historical Outline Map Use the map, The Northern States, on page 43 of the *American History Historical Outline Map Book.* Lesson ideas for this map can be found on page T14. (Reteaching/Average)

 Customized Reader

Primary Source For a Scottish farmer's observations of Chicago while visiting the United States, order article IVB-18, Chicago in 1833, from the *American History Customized Reader.* Patrick Shirreff records his impressions of a treaty celebration, with descriptions of Native Americans, a grand fair, and his hotel accommodations. (Enrichment/Average)

Connections With the World
Background

The first successful underwater telegraph cable was laid under the English Channel in 1851. It connected the British city of Dover and the French city of Calais. In 1858, Cyrus Field made the first attempt to connect the United States and Britain by transatlantic telegraph cable. He finally succeeded in 1866.

Historical Sidelight
Background

In 1817, engineers who were building the first railway suspension bridge between the United States and Canada faced a problem: How would they get the first cable across Niagara Falls? The answer came from 13-year-old Homan Walsh. Walsh tied a light rope to his kite and sailed it across the gorge; once that rope was secured, stronger ropes and then cables were pulled across. Walsh won a $10 prize for his solution.

Voices of Freedom

Primary Source You might assign selection 15-1, At Work on a Clipper, on pages 101–102 of *Voices of Freedom.* This selection is a sea chantey sung by sailors on board clippers to pass the time while they worked and to keep their movements in rhythm. (Enrichment/Average)

Videotapes/ Videodiscs

United States History Video Collection Use the video segment "The Industrial North" from Volume 8, *Causes of the Civil War,* to enhance students' understanding of the importance of industry to the economy of the North. Approx. running time 2:00 min. (Enrichment/Average) Vol. 8, Ch. 7

| Chapter 7 | Play |

masts and huge sails that caught every gust of wind. Their narrow hulls clipped swiftly through the water.

In the 1840s, American clipper ships broke every speed record. One clipper sped from New York to Hong Kong in 81 days, flying past older ships that took five months to reach China. The speed of the clippers helped the United States win a large share of the world's sea trade in the 1840s and 1850s.

The golden age of the clipper ship was brief. In the 1850s, Britain launched the first oceangoing steamships. These sturdy iron vessels carried more cargo and traveled even faster than clippers.

The Northern Economy Expands

In 1834, a young French engineer, Michel Chevalier, toured the North. He was most impressed by the burst of industry

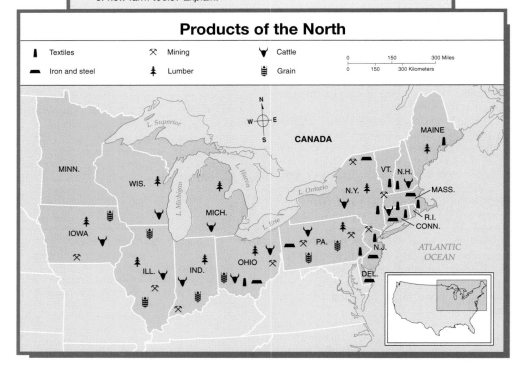

MAP STUDY

Farming remained vital to the northern economy, but industry grew in importance every year.
1. Which states produced textiles?
2. What products did Ohio produce?
3. **Applying Information** Which states were probably helped by the invention of new farm tools? Explain.

Products of the North

Textiles	Mining	Cattle	
Iron and steel	Lumber	Grain	

Cooperative Learning Activity

Divide the students into groups of three or four. Assign each group one of the inventions or innovations discussed in this section. Have each group prepare a TV commercial for its topic—for example, a commercial selling a McCormick reaper to farmers, offering telegraph service to business people in a large city, or praising the benefits of the clipper-ship trade to merchants. Commercials should show how the customer's life would be made easier by using this invention or service. Encourage the groups to present their commercials to the class. You might wish to videotape their performances and share them with other social studies classes.

Learning Styles Kinesthetic Learners

Have students play a game of historical charades. On 3" x 5" cards, write the names of the inventors and innovations discussed in this section. Invite volunteers to select a card and act out the topic for the class to guess.

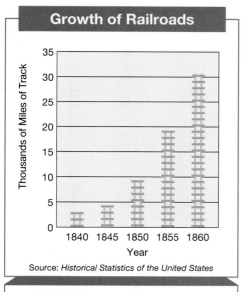

Growth of Railroads

Thousands of Miles of Track

35
30
25
20
15
10
5
0

1840 1845 1850 1855 1860
Year

Source: *Historical Statistics of the United States*

GRAPH SKILLS *Railroads expanded rapidly after 1840. Most new railroad track was laid in the North and the Midwest.* • *According to the graph, what five-year period saw the greatest growth in railroads?*

there—the textile factories, shipyards, and iron mills. He wrote:

> 66 Everywhere is heard the noise of hammers, of spindles, of bells calling the hands to their work, or dismissing them from their tasks. . . . It is the peaceful hum of an industrious population, whose movements are regulated like clockwork. 99

Northern industry did, in fact, grow steadily in the mid-1800s. That growth was largely due to new methods, inventions, and developments.

Advances in technology. By the 1830s, factories began to use steam power instead of water power. Machines driven by steam were powerful and cheap to run. Also, the use of steam power allowed factory owners

to build factories almost anywhere they wanted, not just alongside swift-flowing rivers.

At the same time, new machines made it possible to produce goods for less. These lower-priced goods attracted eager buyers. Families no longer had to make clothing and other goods in their homes. Instead, they could buy factory-made products.

Railroads. Railroads allowed factory owners to ship raw materials and finished goods cheaply and quickly. Also, as railroads stretched across the nation, they linked distant towns with cities and factories. These towns became new markets for factory goods.

Railroads also affected northern farming. New England farmers could not compete with cheap grains and other foods that the railroads brought from the West. Many left their farms to find new jobs as factory workers, store clerks, and sailors. More and more, New Englanders turned to manufacturing and trade.

SECTION 1 REVIEW

1. **Identify:** (a) Elias Howe, (b) John Deere, (c) Cyrus McCormick, (d) Samuel F.B. Morse, (e) John Griffiths.
2. **Define:** (a) telegraph, (b) clipper ship.
3. What new inventions made work easier for farmers?
4. How did many businesses benefit from the telegraph?
5. Explain how each of the following helped industry grow: (a) steam power, (b) new machines, (c) railroads.
6. **CRITICAL THINKING Forecasting** How do you think the growth of industry affected the daily lives of people in the North?

ACTIVITY Writing to Learn

Imagine that you are a newspaper reporter. Write an eyewitness description of the race between *Tom Thumb* and the horse-drawn railroad car.

Bell Ringer

Write the terms *Skilled Worker* and *Unskilled Worker* on the chalkboard. Have the class brainstorm for jobs that can be listed under each.

Lesson Plan

1. Focus Increasing numbers of people flocked to towns and cities, seeking jobs in factories. In this section, students examine the factory conditions that led workers to organize, and they study the special problems faced by women, immigrants, and free African Americans in the North.

2. Instruct Ask students to draft statements by each of the following groups, describing their views of life in the North in the mid-1800s: skilled workers, unskilled workers, women workers, factory owners, Irish immigrants, German immigrants, nativists, African Americans. Use volunteers' statements as a springboard for class discussion.

3. Close To close the lesson, have students turn the subsection headings in Section 2 into questions and answer them.

 Lesson Planner

For a developed **Cooperative Learning** lesson plan, see the *Lesson Planner,* page 79.

2
Life in the Industrial North

FIND OUT
- How did working conditions change in factories and shops?
- Why did skilled workers form unions?
- What newcomers arrived in the United States in the mid-1800s?
- What was life like for African Americans in the North?

VOCABULARY skilled worker, trade union, strike, unskilled worker, immigrant, famine, nativist, discrimination

---

Alzina Parsons never forgot her thirteenth birthday. The day began as usual, with work in the local spinning mill. Suddenly, Alzina cried out. She had caught her hand in the spinning machine, badly mangling her fingers. The foreman summoned the factory doctor. He cut off one of the injured fingers and sent the girl back to work.

In the early 1800s, such an incident probably would not have happened. Factory work was hard, but mill owners treated workers like human beings. By the 1840s, however, there was an oversupply of workers. Many factory owners now treated workers like machines.

Factory Conditions Worsen

Factories of the 1840s and 1850s were very different from earlier mills. They were larger, and they used steam-powered machines. More laborers worked longer hours for lower wages.

Cities where factories were located also changed. Factory owners no longer built planned villages with boarding houses and parks. Instead, workers lived in dark, dingy houses in the shadow of the factory.

Families in factories. The demand for workers increased as more factories sprang up. Owners hired entire families. In some cases, a family signed a contract to work for one year. If even one family member broke the contract, the entire family might be fired.

The factory day began early. A whistle sounded at 4 A.M. Father, mother, and children dressed in the dark and headed off to work. At 7:30 A.M. and at noon, the whistle announced breakfast and lunch breaks. The workday did not end until 7:30 P.M., when a final whistle sent workers home.

Hazards at work. On the job, factory workers faced discomfort and danger. Few factories had windows or heating systems. In summer, the heat and humidity were stifling. In winter, the cold chilled workers' bones and contributed to frequent sickness.

The factory's machines had no safety devices, and accidents were common. Owners ignored the hazards. There were no laws regulating factory conditions. Injured workers often lost their jobs.

Workers as machines. In 1855, a visitor to a textile mill in Fall River, Massachusetts, asked the manager of the mill how he treated his workers. The manager's reply was harsh but honest:

> **"**I regard people just as I regard my machinery. So long as they can do my work for what I choose to pay them, I keep them, getting out of them all I can.**"**

Despite the long hours and dangers, factory workers in America were better off than those in Europe. American workers could find jobs and earn regular wages. European workers often had no work at all.

Factories Replace Workshops

For skilled workers, the spread of factories changed the nature of work. **Skilled**

Connections With Geography
Activity

Ask students to list examples of the ways in which geography affected the growth of industry in the North. Use these lists as a basis for class discussion. Help the students discover the relationships between climate, terrain, natural resources, and industrial and technological developments.

Connections With Music
Background

In the 1850s, many songs were published that praised the life of a factory worker. One song began: "Oh, sing me a song of the Factory Girl/ So merry and glad and free / The bloom in her cheeks, of health how it speaks, / Oh! a happy creature is she!" Factory owners used such songs to recruit workers.

CRITICAL THINKING SKILLS
Synthesizing Information

To make the best use of historical evidence, you must be able to synthesize. That is, you must put pieces of evidence together to form conclusions.

Synthesizing often requires the analysis of different types of evidence, such as graphs, pictures, and primary sources. The more evidence you examine and synthesize, the more accurate will be your impression of a certain period of history.

Study the 1830 factory work rules and the picture of the 1854 shoe factory workers below. Then follow the steps to synthesize the information.

1. **Identify key facts and ideas in each piece of evidence.** (a) When does the workday begin for workers in Amasa Whitney's mill? (b) Are workers in Amasa Whitney's mill allowed to talk while they work?

(c) Who supervised the work of the boys in the shoe factory?

2. **Compare the pieces of evidence.** (a) To what type of workplace does each piece of evidence relate? (b) Which piece of evidence provides more information? (c) Which piece of evidence gives information about the exact hours of work? (d) Which piece shows working conditions?

3. **Synthesize the evidence in order to draw conclusions.** Use both sources to draw conclusions. What do the two pieces of evidence show about life for factory workers in the mid-1800s?

ACTIVITY Look through magazines that are meant for your age group. List the subjects of the articles and the advertisements. Synthesize the information you have gathered, and draw some conclusions about young people today.

Rules & Regulations
TO BE OBSERVED BY ALL PERSONS EMPLOYED IN THE FACTORY OF
AMASA WHITNEY

Rule 1. The Mill will be put in operation 10 minutes before sunrise at all seasons of the year. The gate will be shut 10 minutes past 8 from the 20th of March to the 20th of September; at 30 minutes past 8 from the 20th of September to the 20th of March; Saturdays at sunset.

2nd. It will be required of every person employed, that they be in the room in which they are employed, at the time mentioned above for the mill to be in operation.

3rd. Anything tending to impede the progress of manufacturing in working hours, such as unnecessary conversation, reading, eating fruit, etc, etc., must be avoided.

Chapter Resources

Skill Application For additional practice, duplicate and distribute the worksheet, Synthesizing Information, from Unit 4, page 30, of the *Chapter Resources* binder. (Reteaching/Average)

Answers to Skill Lesson

1. (a) 10 minutes before sunrise, (b) No unnecessary conversation is allowed. (c) an adult male
2. (a) The rules and regulations relate to Whitney's factory; the picture relates to a shoe factory. (b) the rules and regulations, (c) the rules and regulations, (d) the picture
3. Possible Answer: Conditions were harsh, and workers were pressured to concentrate only on the task at hand.

ACTIVITY

Guided Instruction Before students begin gathering and synthesizing their information, brainstorm and list magazines that might serve as good source materials for their research. You might schedule a class in the reference section of the school library for students to locate appropriate articles and advertisements. Use students' conclusions as a basis for a class discussion about similarities and differences between generations.

Students Acquiring English
Activity

SAE students should understand the picture fairly easily. They may have trouble, however, with the rules and regulations; the document not only consists entirely of text, but the style of writing is somewhat dated. Encourage students to work through the Skill Lesson and its Activity with partners who are more fluent, but be prepared to offer help as students read the complex sentence structures of the document.

Chapter Resources

Critical Thinking Duplicate and distribute the worksheet, Comparing Points of View, from Unit 4, page 31, of the *Chapter Resources* binder. The worksheet presents two accounts of factory conditions—one from a British social worker and the other from a factory employee. (Enrichment/Challenging)

Voices of Freedom

Primary Source You might assign selection 15-2, Life in a Mill in 1832, on pages 102–103 of *Voices of Freedom*. This selection is from an address Seth Luther gave in 1832 regarding the worsening conditions in cotton mills. (Enrichment/Average)

Transparencies

Interdisciplinary Connections Use the transparency American Labor Force on page B-57 of *American History Transparencies*. Teaching suggestions can be found on page B-15. (Enrichment/Average)

---

workers are people who have learned a trade, such as carpentry or shoemaking.

The nature of work changes. In the past, a typical shoemaker had several young apprentices. The shoemaker taught the apprentices how to make shoes. After they became expert shoemakers, the apprentices would then open their own shops.

By the 1830s, the shoe trade had changed completely. Apprentices no longer learned to make an entire shoe. Instead, workers did only one part of the job. One worker sewed the sole, for example, while another tacked on the heel. The workers did not work in a shop but were crowded together in a small factory.

Other trades also changed. Shop owners saw that they could produce goods more cheaply if they hired workers with fewer skills and paid them lower wages. More and more, laborers rather than skilled workers produced clocks, barrels, and other goods.

Skilled workers unite. Skilled workers had always taken pride in their skills and independence. The factory system threatened to rob them of both. By the 1830s, skilled workers in many trades were uniting to form **trade unions.**

The unions called for a shorter workday, higher wages, and better working conditions. Sometimes, unions pressed their demands by going on strike. In a **strike,** union workers refuse to do their jobs.

At the time, strikes were illegal in the United States. Strikers faced fines or jail sentences. Strike leaders often were fired.

Workers make progress. Slowly, however, workers made progress. In 1840, President Van Buren approved a 10-hour workday for government employees. Other workers pressed their demands until they won the same hours as government workers. Workers celebrated another victory in 1842 when a Massachusetts court declared that they had the right to strike.

Skilled workers won better pay because factory owners needed their skills. Unskilled

workers, however, were unable to bargain for better wages. **Unskilled workers** held jobs that required little or no training. Because these workers were easy to replace, employers did not listen to their demands.

Women Workers Organize

The success of trade unions encouraged unskilled workers to organize. Workers in New England textile mills especially were eager to protest cuts in wages and unfair work rules. Many of these workers were women.

Women workers faced special problems. First, they had always earned less money than men did. Second, most union leaders did not want women in their ranks. Like many people at the time, they believed that women should not work outside the home. In fact, the goal of many unions was to raise men's wages so that their wives could leave their factory jobs.

Despite the problems, women organized. They staged several strikes at Lowell, Massachusetts, in the 1830s. In the 1840s, Sarah Bagley organized the Lowell Female Labor Reform Association. The group gathered signatures for a petition to the state legislature demanding a 10-hour day.

Millions of New Americans

By the late 1840s, many workers in the new factories of the North were immigrants. An **immigrant** is a person who enters a new country in order to settle there. In the 1840s and 1850s, about 4 million immigrants arrived in the United States. They supplied much of the unskilled labor that helped to build the nation's growing industries.

The Irish. In the 1840s, a disease destroyed the potato crop across Europe. The loss of the crop caused a **famine,** or severe food shortage, especially in Ireland. Between 1845 and 1860, over 1.5 million Irish fled to the United States.

Our Multicultural Heritage
Background

Later in the century, the manufacturing of shoes by mass production was further enhanced by the invention of a machine to attach soles to shoes. The inventor, Jan Matzeliger, was an African American who was born in Dutch Guiana but emigrated to Massachusetts, where he learned his trade in a shoe factory. He perfected his machine in 1877 and patented it in 1883. It increased worker productivity by about 500 percent; it is still used in shoe factories today.

Our Multicultural Heritage
Background

It was the potato famine that spurred the great wave of Irish immigration, but Irish immigrants were not new to this country's shores. In 1776, approximately 40,000 American colonists were Irish, and Irish soldiers filled Washington's army. The Declaration of Independence was first published by John Dunlap, an Irish printer. An Irish sailor accompanied Henry Hudson; a Jamestown colonist was Irish—and one member of Columbus's crew was William Ayers, from Galway.

On Strike *Unskilled women workers organized to gain better treatment. Here, shoemakers in Lynn, Massachusetts, march to protest unfair work rules.* **Economics** *Why are employers less likely to respond to the demands of unskilled workers?*

Most of the Irish immigrants were too poor to buy farmland. They settled in the cities where their ships landed. In New York and Boston, thousands of Irish crowded into poor neighborhoods. They took any job they could find.

The Germans. Another wave of immigrants came from Germany. Nearly one million Germans arrived between 1850 and 1860. Revolutions had broken out in several parts of Germany in 1848. The rebels fought for democratic government. When the uprisings failed, thousands had to flee. Many other Germans came simply to make a better life for themselves. Those with enough money often bought farms in the Midwest. Others settled in eastern cities.

Imprint on American life. Newcomers from many lands helped the American economy grow. In New England, Irish men and women took factory jobs. Coal miners and iron workers from Britain and Germany brought useful skills to American industry.

Each group left an imprint on American life. The Irish brought lively music and dances. Germans brought the custom of decorating trees at Christmas. Immigrants from Norway, Sweden, and other countries also enriched the United States with their language, food, and customs.

A Reaction Against Immigrants

Not everyone welcomed the flood of newcomers. One group of Americans, called nativists, wanted to preserve the country for native-born, white citizens. Using the slogan "Americans must rule America," they called for laws to limit immigration. They also wanted to keep immigrants from voting until they had lived in the United States for 21 years. At the time, newcomers could vote after only 5 years in the country.

Some nativists protested that newcomers "stole" jobs from native-born Americans by working for lower pay. Others blamed immigrants for crime in the growing cities. Still others mistrusted the many Irish and German newcomers because they were Catholics. Until the 1840s, nearly all Americans were Protestants.

In the 1850s, nativists formed a new political party. It was called the ***Know-Nothing party*** because members answered, "I know nothing," when asked about the party. Many meetings and rituals of the party were kept secret. In 1856, the Know-Nothing candidate for President won 21 percent of the popular vote. Soon after, however, the party died out. Still, many Americans continued to blame the nation's problems on immigrants.

Chapter 13 • **385**

Connections With Civics
Background

Millard Fillmore, President from 1850 to 1853, accepted the nomination of the American, or Know-Nothing, party in 1856. However, Fillmore downplayed the party's anti-immigrant and anti-Catholic message; he tried instead to heal the growing sectional divisions that he feared would destroy the Union. After the election, he was "a little mortified" at having been "so unanimously rejected."

Critical Thinking
Concept Mapping

Have students create concept maps to support each of the following generalizations: (a) Factory workers led difficult lives. (b) Workers faced opposition when they tried to organize. (c) The United States was considered a land of freedom and opportunity by many Europeans. (d) Immigrants and free African Americans faced prejudice in the 1800s.

BIOGRAPHY **William Whipper** *William Whipper grew wealthy as the owner of a lumber yard in Pennsylvania. He devoted much time and money to help bring an end to slavery.* **Citizenship** *Why did many free blacks work to end slavery?*

African Americans in the North

In the nation's early years, slavery was legal in the North. By the early 1800s, however, all the northern states had outlawed slavery. As a result, thousands of free African Americans lived in the North.

Denied equal rights. Although they were free, African Americans in the North still faced discrimination. **Discrimination** is a policy or an attitude that denies equal rights to certain groups of people. One writer pointed out that African Americans were denied "the ballot-box, the jury box, the halls of the legislature, the army, the public lands, the school, and the church."

Even skilled African Americans had trouble finding decent jobs. One black carpenter was turned away by every furniture maker in Cincinnati. At last, he found someone willing to hire him. But when he entered the shop, the other workmen threw down their tools. Either he must leave or they would, they declared. Similar experiences occurred throughout the North.

Successful careers. Some free African Americans became wealthy businessmen. James Forten, for example, ran a successful sailmaking business in Philadelphia. Paul Cuffe went to sea at age 16. Later, he grew wealthy as a shipbuilder and owner of a small fleet of trading vessels in New Bedford, Massachusetts. Both Cuffe and Forten used the money they earned to help other African Americans gain freedom.

African Americans also made their mark in other fields. John Rock, a Massachusetts lawyer and judge, presented cases to the Supreme Court. Ira Aldridge became one of the most acclaimed actors in the world.

SECTION 2 REVIEW

1. **Identify:** (a) Know-Nothing party, (b) Sarah Bagley, (c) James Forten, (d) John Rock.
2. **Define:** (a) skilled worker, (b) trade union, (c) strike, (d) unskilled worker, (e) immigrant, (f) famine, (g) nativist, (h) discrimination.
3. How did working conditions in factories worsen in the 1840s and 1850s?
4. Name two groups of immigrants who arrived in the 1840s and 1850s.
5. (a) What problems did free African Americans face in the North? (b) What successes did they enjoy?
6. **CRITICAL THINKING Linking Past and Present** Why do you think hundreds of thousands of immigrants still come to the United States every year?

🅰️🅲🆃🅸🆅🅸🆃🆈 Writing to Learn

Imagine that you are a shoemaker in the early 1830s. Write an ad for your shoes. Tell why they are better than factory-made shoes.

3

Cotton Becomes King

FIND OUT
- How did the cotton gin affect the growth of slavery?
- Why did cotton planters move westward?
- Why did the South have less industry than the North?

In 1827, an Englishman, Basil Hall, traveled through much of the South aboard a riverboat. He complained that southerners were interested in only one thing—cotton:

66All day and almost all night long, the captain, pilot, crew and passengers were talking of nothing else; and sometimes our ears were so wearied with the sound of cotton! cotton! cotton! that we gladly hailed fresh...company in hopes of some change—but alas!...'What's cotton at?' was the first eager inquiry.99

Cotton became even more important to the South in the years after Hall's visit. Even though southerners grew other crops, cotton was the region's leading export. Cotton plantations—and the slave system they depended on—shaped the way of life in the South.

The Cotton Gin

New Englanders built the first American textile mills in the 1790s. These mills, along with mills in Great Britain, used raw cotton to manufacture cloth.

At first, southern planters could not keep up with the demand. They could grow cotton easily because the South's soil and climate were ideal. Removing the seeds

from the raw cotton, however, was a slow process. Planters needed a better way to clean the cotton.

In 1793, Eli Whitney, a young Connecticut schoolteacher, was traveling to Georgia. He was going to be a tutor on a plantation. When Whitney learned of the problem facing planters, he decided to build a machine to clean cotton.

In only 10 days, Whitney came up with a model. His cotton engine, or gin, had two rollers with thin wire teeth. The teeth separated the seeds from the fibers, leaving the cotton ready to be spun. (See Exploring Technology on page 388.)

The cotton gin was simple, but its effects were enormous. A worker using a gin could do the work of 50 people cleaning cotton by hand. Because of the gin, planters could now grow cotton at a huge profit.

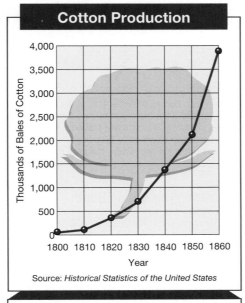

Cotton Production

Thousands of Bales of Cotton

4,000
3,500
3,000
2,500
2,000
1,500
1,000
500
0

1800 1810 1820 1830 1840 1850 1860
Year

Source: *Historical Statistics of the United States*

GRAPH SKILLS *Use of the cotton gin led to a cotton boom in the South.* • *How much did production increase between 1800 and 1860?*

Answer to Graph Skills
by almost 4 million bales

Section 3
pp. 387–390

🔔 **Bell Ringer**

Have students brainstorm for and list on the chalkboard cotton or cotton-blend items that they might find in a shopping mall.

Lesson Plan

1. Focus Unlike the North, the South depended mainly on one crop and the slave system for economic growth. Other industries and cash crops were secondary to the production of cotton, which left the South dependent on the North and Europe for finished goods. In this section, students examine the growth of the Cotton Kingdom and learn how one invention created a boom that changed the economy of the South and the nation.
2. Instruct Tell students to imagine that they are reporters who are preparing to interview Eli Whitney about the cotton gin and its effects on the South. Have the class suggest questions that they would like to ask Whitney. Then have students speculate on what Whitney's answers might have been.
3. Close To close the lesson, have students list and rank in order of importance the facts and concepts presented in each subsection.

Historical Sidelight
Background

Many southerners thought that as the world's main supplier of cotton they had an invulnerable economic advantage over the North. In 1858, South Carolina senator James Henry Hammond summarized this sentiment when he said: "Cotton is king. You dare not make war on cotton! No power on earth dares make war upon it. Cotton is king."

Critical Thinking
Drawing Conclusions

Explain that the North was one of the world's major market suppliers of wheat. Ask: Why do you think Hammond and the believers in "King Cotton" may have overestimated the South's economic advantage?

② As the handle is turned, the cylinder and brushes rotate.

① Cotton bolls, made up of fiber and seeds, are fed into the cotton gin. The red arrows show the path of the cotton through the gin.

③ Wire teeth catch the cotton bolls and pull them through narrow wire slots.

⑤ Rotating brushes pull cleaned cotton fiber from the wire teeth and sweep it out of the gin.

④ The seeds are too large to pass through the slots. They fall to the bottom of the gin.

Cotton Gin *Before the invention of the cotton "gin," or engine, cotton seeds had to be separated from the fibers by hand. It was a slow, time-consuming process, and a person could clean only a few pounds of cotton a day. A worker using the gin, however, could clean up to 50 pounds of cotton in a single day!* **Economics** *How did the cotton gin encourage the growth of slavery?*

The Cotton Boom

Planters soon found that soil wore out if planted with cotton year after year. They needed new land to cultivate. After the War of 1812, cotton planters began to move west. By the 1850s, the Cotton Kingdom extended in a wide band from South Carolina through Alabama and Mississippi to Texas.

As plantations spread across the South, cotton production increased rapidly. In 1792, cotton planters grew only 6,000 bales of cotton a year. By 1850, the figure was over 2 million bales.

The cotton boom had a tragic side, too. As the Cotton Kingdom spread, so did slavery. Even though cotton could now be cleaned by machine, it still had to be planted and picked by hand. The result was a cruel cycle. Slaves grew and picked the cotton that brought profits to planters. Planters used the profits to buy more land and more slaves.

The United States had made the slave trade with Africa illegal after 1807. As a result, planters in the new cotton regions bought slaves from planters in southeastern states. In many cases, these sales broke up slave families.

No Place for Industry

Cotton was the South's biggest cash crop. Tobacco, rice, and sugar cane also made money for planters. Southerners raised much of the nation's livestock, too.

Slaves rather than factories. Some southerners wanted to encourage industry in the South. William Gregg, for example, modeled his cotton mill in South Carolina on the mills in Lowell, Massachusetts. Gregg built houses and gardens for his workers and schools for their children.

Even so, the South lagged behind the North in manufacturing. Rich planters invested their money in land and slaves rather than in factories. Also, slavery reduced the demand for goods in the South. In the North, most people had enough money to buy manufactured goods. In the South, however, millions of slaves could not buy

MAP STUDY

By the mid-1800s, cotton had become king in the South. It overshadowed other important products, such as tobacco, rice, and livestock.
1. *To what areas did cotton growing spread between 1840 and 1860?*
2. *What were the main products of Virginia?*
3. **Comparing** *Compare this map with the map on page 380. (a) What products did both the North and South produce? (b) What products did the South alone produce? Explain.*

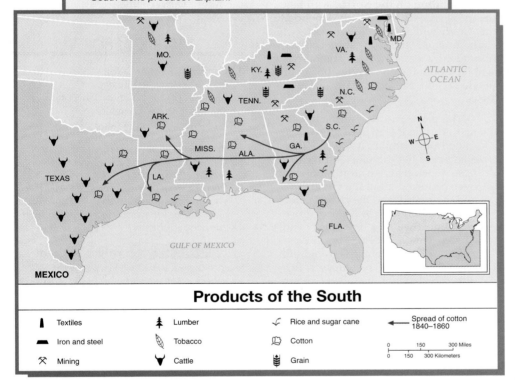

Products of the South

Symbol	Product		
Textiles	Lumber	Rice and sugar cane	Spread of cotton 1840–1860
Iron and steel	Tobacco	Cotton	
Mining	Cattle	Grain	0 150 300 Miles / 0 150 300 Kilometers

Historical Outline Map Book

Historical Outline Map Use the map, The Southern States, on page 44 of the *American History Historical Outline Map Book*. Lesson ideas for this map can be found on page T14. (Reteaching/Average)

Chapter Resources

Geography in History Duplicate and distribute the worksheet, The Cotton Kingdom, from Unit 4, pages 33–34, of the *Chapter Resources* binder. The worksheet traces the economic history of the South, focusing on a product map. (Enrichment/Challenging)

Answers to Map Study

1. westward into Alabama, Mississippi, Arkansas, Louisiana, and Texas 2. mining products, cattle, textiles, lumber, and tobacco 3. (a) textiles, iron and steel, mining products, lumber, cattle, and grain, (b) rice, sugar cane, cotton, and tobacco. These crops would grow only in the South's warmer climate.

Connections With Music
Background

"Amazing Grace," one of the best-known hymns in Christianity, had its roots in the slave trade. Its lyrics were written by John Newton, a British sea captain. Before his conversion to Christianity, Newton was a slave trader, and so despised by his own crew that once, when he fell overboard, they threw a harpoon at him. Newton later denounced his promotion of slavery.

Critical Thinking
Forecasting

Point out that the North and the South fought the Civil War in the 1860s. Refer students to the map on this page and ask: Why would the westward expansion of southern interests increase tensions between proslavery and antislavery forces? Then ask the class to forecast from this section and Section 1 what advantages the North would have in a war with the South. List student inferences on the chalkboard and have them copy the list for future reference.

The Business of Cotton *The French artist Edgar Degas painted this scene of merchants in a New Orleans cotton market. Cotton was the South's leading export in the mid-1800s.* **Economics** *What other products were important in the southern economy?*

anything. This greatly reduced the number of products used in the South and hurt southern industry.

Depending on the North. With little industry of its own, the South depended on the North and Europe for goods such as cloth, furniture, and tools. Many southerners resented this situation. One southerner described a burial to show how the South depended on the North for many goods in the 1850s:

66 The grave was dug through solid marble, but the marble headstone came from Vermont. It was in a pine wilderness but the pine coffin came from Cincinnati. An iron mountain overshadowed it but the coffin nails and the screws and the shovel came from Pittsburgh.... A hickory grove grew nearby, but the pick and shovel handles came from New York.... That country, so rich in underdeveloped resources, furnished nothing for the funeral except the corpse and the hole in the ground. 99

Still, most southerners were proud of their booming cotton industry. As long as cotton remained king, southerners looked to the future with confidence.

SECTION 3 REVIEW

1. **Locate:** (a) South Carolina, (b) Alabama, (c) Mississippi, (d) Texas.
2. **Identify:** (a) Eli Whitney, (b) Cotton Kingdom, (c) William Gregg.
3. What effect did the cotton gin have on the southern economy?
4. Why did cotton planters move west?
5. Why did the South lag behind the North in manufacturing?
6. **CRITICAL THINKING Forecasting** How do you think southerners in the 1800s would have reacted if someone had threatened the cotton industry?

 Writing to Learn

Imagine that you own thousands of acres of wilderness in Mississippi in the 1840s. Write an advertisement to attract planters to buy your land.

Life in the Cotton Kingdom

FIND OUT

■ What three groups made up white society in the South?

■ How did the South treat free African Americans?

■ What was life like for enslaved African Americans on plantations?

VOCABULARY extended family

Solomon Northup first learned to pick cotton at age 32. Northup was born a free African American in New York. In 1841, two white men kidnapped him and sold him as a slave in the South. For the next 12 years, Northup worked on a plantation in Louisiana. Like other enslaved African Americans, he toiled in the fields from "can see to can't see," or from dawn to dusk. For supper, he ate cold bacon and corn meal. His bed was a "plank twelve inches wide and ten feet long."

Northup was not the only free African American to be captured and sold into slavery. He was fortunate, however, to be one of the few who escaped. His book *12 Years a Slave* gave northerners a first-hand look at the slave system.

White Southerners

The Old South is often pictured as a land of vast plantations worked by hundreds of slaves. Such grand estates did exist in the South. However, most white southerners were not rich planters. In fact, most whites owned no slaves at all.

The "cottonocracy." A planter was someone who owned at least 20 slaves. In 1860, there were about 2 million white families in the South. Of them, only 1 in 40, or a total of about 50,000, were families of planters. These wealthy families were called the "cottonocracy" because they made their money from cotton. Even though they were few in number, their views and way of life dominated the South.

The richest planters built elegant homes and filled them with fine European furniture. They entertained lavishly, dressing and behaving very much like European nobility.

Planters had their responsibilities, too. Because of their wealth and influence, many planters became political leaders. They devoted many hours to local, state, and national politics. To run day-to-day affairs on their plantations, planters hired overseers to manage the work of slaves.

Small farmers. Most southern whites were small farmers. These "plain folk" owned the land they farmed and perhaps

---

A Plantation Mistress *The wife of a planter enjoyed wealth and social position. She also had many duties, including nursing the sick and overseeing the work of house slaves.* **Economics** *Why were wealthy southern families called the "cottonocracy"?*

Answer to Caption

because they made their money from growing cotton

Section 4
pp. 391–397

Bell Ringer

Have the students draw pictures or bring to class magazine photographs depicting life as they imagine it was lived in the South of the mid-1800s.

Lesson Plan

1. Focus The economy of the South was based on the enslavement of African Americans. It also created three classes of white southerners. In this section, students learn about the lives of planters, small farmers, and poor whites. They then study how the slave system led to resistance, revolt, and slave codes.

2. Instruct Divide the students into groups of three or four. Have each team research the life of an important African American from this period, such as Frederick Douglass, Denmark Vesey, or Nat Turner. Each group should then present a short dramatic episode from that person's life.

3. Close To close the lesson, have students summarize the class structure in the Cotton Kingdom.

Connections With Literature
Background

Students have already encountered the best-known early slave narrative—that told by Olaudah Equiano in 1790. It was so well received in Britain, in fact, that it went through eight printings in five years.

In the 1840s and 1850s, slave narratives were very popular in the United States. Abolitionist publications encouraged former slaves to recount their experiences; William Lloyd Garrison's *Liberator* printed more than 300 such accounts. Some slave narratives, such

as that of Solomon Northup, were published as books. Perhaps the greatest and most influential of all slave narratives was *My Bondage and My Freedom,* Frederick Douglass's autobiography, published in 1855. In it, Douglass not only recounts his years in slavery but also discusses what slavery meant in the minds of African Americans and whites alike. William Wells Brown, another former slave, wrote a slave narrative, a novel (*Clotel*), and a play (*The Escape*).

Connections With Language Arts
Background

The Greek root -*cracy* means "rule" or "strength." The Greek root *demos* means "people." *Democracy,* then, means "rule by the people." Cottonocracy means "government ruled by cotton," or government ruled by those who have wealth and political power because they grow cotton. The term also speaks of the power that cotton itself wielded over the economy and lifestyle of the South.

Lesson Planner

For a developed **Cooperative Learning** lesson plan, see the *Lesson Planner,* page 81.

Answer to Caption

Possible Answer: Cotton drove the economy of the South, especially in creating a justification for slavery.

Customized Reader

Primary Source For a British naval officer's account of his travels from Virginia to South Carolina, order article IVB-19, Traveling Through the Carolinas in 1828, from the *American History Customized Reader.* Captain Basil Hall describes the country and the people he encountered while traveling by stagecoach. (Enrichment/Challenging)

Primary Source For a free African American barber's description of his day-to-day life in the South, order article IVA-19, Life in Natchez, Mississippi, from the *American History Customized Reader.* The entries provide a unique perspective on life in the South and illuminate the complexity of the slavery issue. (Enrichment/Challenging)

one or two slaves. Unlike planters, plain folk worked alongside their slaves in the cotton fields.

Small farmers in the South were not as well off as those in the North. As a result, they often helped each other out. "People who lived miles apart counted themselves as neighbors," wrote a farmer in Mississippi. "And in case of sorrow or sickness, there was no limit to the service neighbors provided."

Poor whites. At the bottom of the social ladder was a small group of poor whites. They did not own the land they farmed. Instead, they rented it, often paying the owner with part of their crop. Many barely kept their families from starving.

Poor whites often lived in the hilly, wooded areas of the South. They planted crops such as corn, potatoes, and other vegetables. They also herded cattle and pigs. Yet despite their hard lives, poor whites enjoyed rights denied to all African Americans, enslaved or free.

African Americans in the South

Both free and enslaved African Americans lived in the South. Although legally free, free African Americans faced harsh discrimination. Enslaved African Americans had no rights at all.

Free blacks. Most free African Americans were descendants of slaves freed during and after the American Revolution. Others had bought their freedom. In 1860, over 200,000 free African Americans lived in the South. Most lived in Maryland and Delaware, where slavery was in decline. Others lived in cities such as New Orleans, Richmond, and Charleston.

Slave owners did not like free African Americans living in the South. They feared that free African Americans set a bad example, encouraging slaves to rebel. Also, slave owners justified slavery on the basis that African Americans could not take care of themselves. Free African American workers proved this idea wrong.

Hauling in Cotton *For African Americans living under slavery, life was a constant round of hard work. This picture shows enslaved African Americans hauling in cotton from the fields.* **Economics** *What role did cotton play in the economy of the South?*

Historical Sidelight
Background

In addition to renting farmland, poor white southerners often bought seed, tools, and supplies from the owner. Many times, these farmers could not repay the owner in full; thus, they went deeper into debt with each growing season. This was the beginning of sharecropping—a system that would come to hold both poor whites and freed African Americans in virtual slavery after the Civil War.

Connections With Civics
Background

Free African Americans in the North were not enslaved, but they were discriminated against. They could not vote, serve on juries, or hold public office. In many places, they were required to live in segregated areas and use separate sections in restaurants, hospitals, churches, and schools—if they were allowed to enter at all. In the South, free blacks had to carry papers proving that they were free, and any white person could ask to see proof that an African American was not a slave.

To discourage free African Americans, southern states passed laws that made life even harder for them. Free African Americans were not allowed to vote or travel. In some southern states, they either had to move out of the state or allow themselves to be enslaved.

Despite these limits, free African Americans made valuable contributions to southern life. For example, Norbert Rillieux (RIHL yoo) invented a machine that revolutionized sugar making. Henry Blair patented a seed planter.

Enslaved African Americans. Enslaved African Americans made up one third of the South's population by 1860. Most worked as field hands on cotton plantations. Both men and women cleared new land and planted and harvested crops. Children helped by pulling weeds, collecting wood, and carrying water to the field hands. By the time they were teenagers, they too worked between 12 and 14 hours a day.

On large plantations, some African Americans became skilled workers, such as carpenters and blacksmiths. A few worked in cities and lived almost as if they were free. Their earnings, however, belonged to their owners.

Older slaves, especially women, worked as house servants on big estates. They cooked, cleaned, and took care of children under the direction of the planter's wife.

Slave Codes

Southern states passed laws known as slave codes to keep slaves from either running away or rebelling. (See page 111.) Under the codes, enslaved African Americans were forbidden to gather in groups of more than three. They could not leave their owner's land without a written pass. They were not allowed to own guns.

Slave codes also made it a crime for slaves to learn how to read and write. Owners believed that without education enslaved African Americans would find it hard to escape. If they did not know how to read, owners reasoned, runaway slaves could not use maps or read train schedules. They would not be able to find their way north.

Some laws were meant to protect slaves, but only from the worst forms of abuse. Even so, enslaved African Americans did not have the right to testify in court. As a result, they were not able to bring charges against owners who abused them.

Chapter 13 • **393**

 Customized Reader

Primary Source For examples of differing points of view regarding slavery, order the following articles from the *American History Customized Reader:* article IVA-7, African Americans Recall Their Lives as Slaves (Enrichment/Challenging); article IVB-11, A Slave Auction (Enrichment/Average); and article IVB-13, A Cheerful View of Slavery (Enrichment/Average).

 Our Multicultural Heritage

Biography Have students read the biography, Prudence Crandall, Crusader for Black Education, on page 37 of the *Our Multicultural Heritage* booklet. (Enrichment/Challenging)
Milestone Have students read A Distinctly Southern Literature, on page 39 of the *Our Multicultural Heritage* booklet. (Enrichment/Average)

 Videotapes/ Videodiscs

United States History Video Collection Use the video segment "The Slave South" from Volume 8, *Causes of the Civil War*, to enhance students' understanding of the impact of slavery on the South. Approx. running time 4:00 min. (Enrichment/Average) Vol. 8, Ch. 13

Chapter 13   Play

Our Multicultural Heritage
Activity

Interested students may wish to research and report on inventions by other African Americans. These inventors represent only some of the possibilities:

Lewis H. Latimer
Garrett A. Morgan
Lewis Temple
Granville T. Woods

Critical Thinking
Evaluating Ideas

At this time, becoming a teenager generally meant assuming many responsibilities of an adult. Even in poor white farming families, teenage boys worked in the fields—plowing, planting, and harvesting—while teenage girls did domestic chores—cooking, cleaning, sewing, and milking. On plantations, however, teenage girls were generally sent to work in the fields along with teenage boys and their elders. Discuss with students why plantation owners often disregarded the domestic tradition for teenage girls.

393

Enslaved African Americans had only one real protection against mistreatment. Owners looked on their slaves as valuable property. Most wanted to keep this human property healthy and productive.

Life Without Freedom

The life of African Americans varied from plantation to plantation. Some owners made sure their slaves had decent food, clean cabins, and warm clothes. Other planters spent as little as possible on their slaves.

"Work, work, work." Even the kindest owners insisted that slaves work long, hard days. Slaves worked all year round, up to 16 hours a day. Frederick Douglass, who escaped slavery, recalled:

66 We were worked in all weathers. It was never too hot or too cold; it could never rain, blow, hail, or snow too hard for us to work in the field. Work, work, work. 99

Owners and overseers whipped slaves to get a full day's work. However, the worst part of slavery was not the beatings. It was the complete loss of freedom. "It's bad to belong to folks that own you soul an' body," one slave said.

Family life. It was hard for enslaved African Americans to keep families together. Southern laws did not recognize slave mar-

History and You
Enslaved African Americans passed down family history and traditions to their children and grandchildren in oral rather than written form. What stories about your family's past have your grandparents or parents passed on to you orally? Are there some special family traditions that you hope to pass along to your children?

riages. Owners could sell a husband and wife to different buyers. Children were taken from their parents and sold.

On large plantations, many enslaved families did manage to stay together. For those African Americans, the family provided strength, pride, and love. Grandparents, parents, children, aunts, uncles, and cousins formed a close-knit group. This idea of an **extended family** had its roots in Africa.

Enslaved African Americans preserved other traditions as well. Parents taught their children traditional African stories and songs. Many African cultures used folk tales as a way to pass on their history and moral beliefs.

Religion offers hope. By the 1800s, many enslaved African Americans were devout Christians. Planters often arranged for white ministers to preach to their slaves.

African Americans also had their own preachers and beliefs. These emphasized hope in the future. The moving spirituals sung by enslaved African Americans reflected this strong hope. Like the one below, many spoke of a coming day of freedom:

66 Old Satan thought he had me fast,
Broke his old chain and free at last. 99

In later years, much popular American music would develop from African American spirituals. Jazz, blues, and rock 'n' roll all have their roots in the songs enslaved African Americans sang as they worked in the cotton fields.

Resisting Slavery

Enslaved African Americans struck back against the system that denied them both freedom and wages. Some broke tools, destroyed crops, and stole food.

Many enslaved African Americans dared to run away. Most runaways wanted to reach the North. In the end, very few of

Critical Thinking
Recognizing Point of View

Have students read excerpts from a slave narrative. Based on their reading, have students answer the following questions for a brief oral report. What attitude did the writer have toward slavery? How did he or she show this attitude? Students should support their opinions with quotations from the slave account.

Connections With the World
Activity

Have students do research into the history of the country of Haiti. Encourage them to find out and report on the importance of slavery to the colonial economy, the contribution of slaves to the colony's establishment as an independent nation, and aspects of Haitian culture that can be traced to its past as a center of slavery.

Team-Teaching Suggestion
Literature

You might work with a literature teacher to present a lesson about how the African culture used folk tales as a way to pass on history and moral beliefs. Read several examples to the class. Then suggest that interested students locate a collection of African folk tales and report to the class on the subject matter, story line, and the purpose of the tales.

CONNECTIONS

ARTS SCIENCES **GEOGRAPHY** WORLD ECONOMICS CIVICS

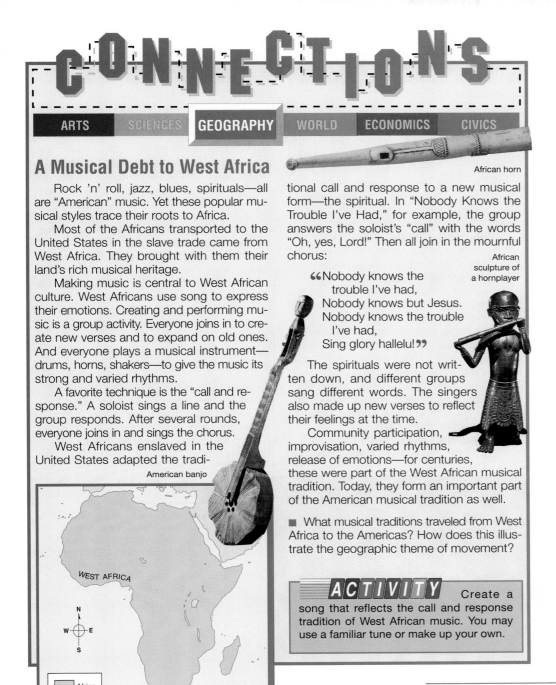

A Musical Debt to West Africa

Rock 'n' roll, jazz, blues, spirituals—all are "American" music. Yet these popular musical styles trace their roots to Africa.

Most of the Africans transported to the United States in the slave trade came from West Africa. They brought with them their land's rich musical heritage.

Making music is central to West African culture. West Africans use song to express their emotions. Creating and performing music is a group activity. Everyone joins in to create new verses and to expand on old ones. And everyone plays a musical instrument—drums, horns, shakers—to give the music its strong and varied rhythms.

A favorite technique is the "call and response." A soloist sings a line and the group responds. After several rounds, everyone joins in and sings the chorus.

West Africans enslaved in the United States adapted the tradi-

American banjo

African horn

tional call and response to a new musical form—the spiritual. In "Nobody Knows the Trouble I've Had," for example, the group answers the soloist's "call" with the words "Oh, yes, Lord!" Then all join in the mournful chorus:

African sculpture of a hornplayer

❝Nobody knows the
    trouble I've had,
Nobody knows but Jesus.
Nobody knows the trouble
    I've had,
Sing glory hallelu!❞

The spirituals were not written down, and different groups sang different words. The singers also made up new verses to reflect their feelings at the time.

Community participation, improvisation, varied rhythms, release of emotions—for centuries, these were part of the West African musical tradition. Today, they form an important part of the American musical tradition as well.

■ What musical traditions traveled from West Africa to the Americas? How does this illustrate the geographic theme of movement?

ACTIVITY Create a song that reflects the call and response tradition of West African music. You may use a familiar tune or make up your own.

them made it to freedom. The journey was long and dangerous. Every county had slave patrols and sheriffs ready to question an unknown black person. It took courage and a great deal of luck to make it through.

Flight for Freedom

What was it like to run away from slavery? The runaway in the following account was not a real person. The description of his flight is based on reports of real runaways who made their way to freedom.

Slipping away in the dark. In the dark, on an early Sunday morning, 20-year-old Jesse Needham slipped out of his shabby cabin into the nearby cotton fields. Sunday was the best day to escape. Slaves did not work on Sunday, and there was a chance he would not be missed for 24 hours.

In an extra shirt, Jesse carried a chunk of bacon and some cornbread, stolen from the cook house. Not much food for the 300-mile journey ahead, Jesse worried.

When he reached the edge of his master's land, Jesse crossed into the woods beyond. As he well knew, without a pass, he had already broken the law.

Finding courage. By dawn, Jesse was 8 miles from the plantation. Traveling by day-

light was easier, but it was too risky. He curled up under an old spruce tree to sleep.

But his mind would not rest. When dogs began barking at a nearby plantation, Jesse leaped to his feet. His heart pounded and his knees buckled. He was sure that the slave patrol's hounds had picked up his scent. To his relief, no one came.

At dusk, Jesse set out again. The countryside was becoming more and more unfamiliar. Jesse had never been so far from the plantation before. Making his way through the moonlit woods, he thought about life on the plantation—the weariness, the hunger, his bed of straw and rags. He would never go back, he vowed—never.

Thinking things through. Stopping under a tree to rest, Jesse thought about the men who would soon be hunting him. Today or tomorrow, newspapers would announce his escape. Handbills with his description would be posted and slave patrols alerted. Jesse could read—just a little—and he remembered a newspaper ad for a runaway slave:

66 TWENTY DOLLARS REWARD—the slave HERCULES. 36 years old, 5 feet 7 or 8 inches high, badly scarred with the whip. I will pay the reward if delivered to me, or lodged in jail, so that I get him. 99

Running Away *Each year, thousands of African Americans fled north to escape slavery. In this painting by Thomas Moran, two fugitives are pursued by bloodhounds through a swamp.* **Daily Life** *In what other ways did African Americans resist slavery?*

His mind racing, Jesse tried to form a plan. Perhaps he could steal some corn and roast it. No, he decided, a fire might draw attention. He had better eat the corn uncooked. Maybe other African Americans would give him food. He quickly reminded himself that going near slave quarters was a sure way to get caught. Patrols usually kept a close eye on the quarters.

The way north. As Jesse plotted, he remembered the words of a spiritual he often sang: "Follow the North Star, up to the land of freedom." Jesse looked up. There was nothing but clouds. Cold, alone, and helpless, he wondered if he was walking in a circle.

Moving on, Jesse soon spied a rutted country lane. He would leave the woods and follow it, he decided. After all, there probably would be few travelers at that hour. At every sound, Jesse ducked back into the woods, trembling.

Dawn was breaking as Jesse came to a crossroads. There, he spelled out a milestone: Richmond 27 miles. His master's brother lived in Richmond, Jesse recalled. Jesse took a deep breath. He was, indeed, headed north.

As the sun rose, Jesse returned to the woods. Kneeling at a stream, he washed and took a long drink. Then, looking up at the bright sky, he folded his hands and prayed that Jesus would help him find his way to freedom.

Did Jesse make it to the North? Like many other runaways, he was captured and returned to his owner. Now considered a troublemaker, he was sold to another owner. Other Jesses, however, would run from slavery. Despite the nearly hopeless odds, they would risk all to reach freedom. ■

Revolts Against Slavery

A few African Americans used violence to resist the brutal system they faced. Denmark Vesey, a free African American, planned a revolt in 1822. Vesey was betrayed before the revolt began. He and 35 other people were executed.

In 1831, an African American preacher named Nat Turner led a major revolt. Turner led his followers through Virginia, killing more than 57 whites. Terrified whites hunted the countryside for Turner. They killed many innocent African Americans before catching and hanging him.

Nat Turner's revolt increased southern fears of an uprising of enslaved African Americans. Revolts were rare, however. Since whites were cautious and well armed, a revolt had almost no chance of success.

As slavery grew, the economic ties between North and South became stronger. Northern mill owners needed southern cotton. Southerners relied on the goods from northern factories. Yet Americans in both regions knew that the North and the South had very different ways of life. The key difference seemed to be slavery.

SECTION 4 REVIEW

1. **Identify:** (a) Norbert Rillieux, (b) Henry Blair, (c) Denmark Vesey, (d) Nat Turner.
2. **Define:** extended family.
3. Describe the classes that made up white society in the South.
4. Why did slave owners discourage free African Americans from living in the South?
5. How did African culture and religion help enslaved African Americans endure the hardships of plantation life?
6. **CRITICAL THINKING Analyzing Information** What concerns did runaway slaves like Jesse Needham have in their flight to freedom?

ACTIVITY Writing to Learn
Imagine that you are an enslaved African American on a southern plantation. Write the words for a spiritual about the coming of freedom.

Chapter 13 • **397**

Student Study Guide

Section 4 Study Guide Have students use the Section 4 Study Guide on page 111 of the *Student Study Guide* to review and reinforce the content of this section. (Reteaching/Average)

ACTIVITY

Guided Instruction Before students begin writing their spirituals, you might play several well-known examples that exemplify the rhythmic patterns associated with this folk medium. In the prewriting stage, suggest that students create clusters of nouns and adjectives that they associate with freedom. Next, they can decide which words would be most fittingly adapted to a lyrical rhyme scheme. Students might work with partners to revise their spirituals and present their songs to the class.

Historical Sidelight
Background

Fear of slave revolts made for tension in the North as well as in the South long before the mid-1800s. In 1741, Mary Burton, a white indentured servant in New York City, claimed that a series of suspicious fires had been set by slaves. As she gained a hearing, she elaborated on her story of a slave plot to burn the city and slaughter its citizens. By the time the panic subsided, 31 slaves had been hanged.

Answers to Section 4 Review

1. (a) Norbert Rillieux, p. 393, (b) Henry Blair, p. 393, (c) Denmark Vesey, p. 397, (d) Nat Turner, p. 397
2. extended family, p. 394
3. planters who owned at least twenty slaves; small farmers who owned their land and perhaps one or two slaves; poor whites who rented land and barely grew enough food to feed their families
4. Slave owners were afraid that free African Americans were an encouragement to slave rebellion; furthermore, their freedom dispelled the idea that slaves could not care for themselves.
5. Slaves found security in African customs, such as the extended family, and in stories and songs that passed on African history and moral beliefs. Religion offered slaves hope of a better life and of freedom.
6. Possible Answer: food, slave patrols, finding the way north

397

CHAPTER 13 REVIEW

Answers to Reviewing the Main Ideas

1. Farmers did not need as many workers, so people moved to cities and factory towns to find jobs.

2. Clipper ships were much faster than ships of competing nations.

3. to reduce working hours, raise wages, and improve working conditions

4. Irish immigrants came because of the potato famine of the 1840s; Germans came after revolutions in 1848 failed, to avoid political repression and to make a better life.

5. Planters reinvested in land and slaves rather than investing in factories; slaves had no money to buy manufactured goods.

6. (a) Rich planters lived luxurious lifestyles: they entertained in their mansions, traveled extensively, and oversaw their business holdings, but they had slaves perform all physical labor. (b) If small farmers owned one or two slaves, they worked alongside them in the fields and at home; they developed a sense of community with other farm families. (c) Poor whites had little money, rented farm land, and barely raised enough food to feed their families.

7. (a) Enslaved African Americans were forbidden to gather in groups of three or more, could not leave their owner's land without written permission, were forbidden to own guns, and faced criminal charges if they learned to read or write. (b) Some broke tools, destroyed crops, and stole food; others successfully ran away to the North, where they could gain freedom.

Answers to Thinking Critically

1. Possible Answer: Computers, microwave ovens, cellular phones, and VCRs have changed American life, much as the earlier inventions did.

2. Possible Answer: Farmers could ship grain to eastern cities and buy manufactured goods from eastern cities; new shops and businesses would grow; as the town prospered, the popula-

tion would increase and so would the supply and demand for goods.

3. Possible Answer: Only planters had the time and money for politics; small farmers probably admired the wealth and power of rich planters and hoped to be planters themselves someday.

Answers to Applying Your Skills

1. Possible Answer: Hours were longer and wages were lower,

whole families sometimes worked in factories, and factories were uncomfortable and even dangerous. Factory conditions were badly in need of reform.

2. Possible Answer: The South depended on the North or on Europe for manufactured goods, but the North manufactured much of what its people needed.

3. (a) Cotton production rose dramatically. (b) The number of slaves grew dramatically. (c) Possible Answer: Yes; the rise in cotton production required a greater

number of workers; and in the South, where cotton was grown, that meant slaves.

Answers to Thinking About Geography

1. E **2.** F **3.** A **4.** B **5.** D **6.** C

Region: (a) industry, (b) agriculture (cotton)

Summary

- Inventions and advances in technology helped the northern economy to grow.
- Factory conditions worsened in the 1830s, and workers organized to win better working conditions.
- The cotton gin boosted cotton production and encouraged the spread of slavery.
- Southern society was made up of rich planters, small farmers, poor whites, free African Americans, and enslaved African Americans.

Reviewing the Main Ideas

1. How did the invention of labor-saving devices for farmers help spur the growth of industry?

2. How did clipper ships help the United States capture sea trade?

3. What goals did early trade unions have?

4. Why did large numbers of Irish and German immigrants come to the United States in the 1840s and 1850s?

5. Why was industry slow to grow in the South?

6. Describe the way of life of each of the following in the South: (a) rich planters, (b) small farmers, (c) poor whites.

7. (a) How did slave laws restrict the freedom of African Americans? (b) How did enslaved African Americans resist slavery?

Thinking Critically

1. Linking Past and Present Review the description of inventions on pages 378–379. What recent inventions have changed American life?

2. Understanding Causes and Effects How do you think life might have changed in a small Ohio town after a railroad linked it to New York City in the 1840s?

3. Drawing Conclusions Few southerners were planters. Why do you think this small group was able to dominate the political and social life of the South?

Applying Your Skills

1. Making a Generalization List three facts from Factory Conditions Worsen, on page 382. Then make a generalization about factory conditions in the mid-1800s.

2. Analyzing a Quotation In the 1840s, a southerner wrote this description of a southern gentleman: "See him with northern pen and ink, writing letters on northern paper, and sending them away in northern envelopes, sealed with northern wax, and impressed with a northern stamp." What point about the South do you think the writer was making?

3. Reading Graphs Study the graphs on pages 376 and 387. (a) Describe the trend in cotton production between 1800 and 1860. (b) Describe the trend in slave population between 1800 and 1860. (c) Are the two trends related? Explain.

Thinking About Geography

Match the letters on the map with the following places: **1.** Northern states, **2.** Southern states, **3.** Massachusetts, **4.** New Hampshire, **5.** Alabama, **6.** Mississippi. **Region** (a) What was the basis of the North's economy? (b) Of the South's economy?

Living in the Cotton Kingdom

Quilt made by an enslaved woman

Form into groups to review life in the South in the 1800s. Follow the suggestions below to make, write, draw, or sing to show what you have learned about the Cotton Kingdom. You may use the textbook, encyclopedias, atlases, or other materials in your classroom library to complete the tasks. Be able to name your sources of information when you have finished the activity.

HISTORIANS AND ARTISTS Create a chart showing the social groups that made up southern society in the mid-1800s. Include a description of each class and its way of life. Illustrate the chart with original drawings or pictures cut from old magazines.

WRITERS Study the drawing and photograph of a cotton gin on page 388. Then write a description for younger readers of how a cotton gin worked. Write three questions for your readers to test whether they understand the description.

SCIENTISTS Make a museum display about growing cotton. Include facts about the soil, climate, when to plant, insect pests, harvesting, and cleaning. Include a map showing where cotton was grown in the United States in the mid-1800s. Decorate your display with samples of raw cotton, cotton cloth, and pictures of cotton growing.

A slave's wedding dress

ECONOMISTS AND HISTORIANS Review the positive and negative effects of cotton on life in the South. Then make a concept map to show these effects.

MUSICIANS Learn the words and music to a spiritual sung by enslaved African Americans in the 1800s. Possible songs are "Go Down, Moses," "Deep River," and "Swing Low, Sweet Chariot." Perform the spiritual for the class and then explain what the words mean. Make an audiotape of your performance to include in the Living in the Cotton Kingdom bulletin board display.

 Create a Living in the Cotton Kingdom bulletin board display. Have each group include its completed activity.

Loading cotton in New Orleans

Assessment

Chapter Resources Binder For a more comprehensive evaluation of student understanding of this chapter, assign Chapter Tests A and B and/or Extra Unit Questions from Unit 4, pages 35–40 and 57–59.
Computer Test Bank You can use Chapter Tests and Extra Unit Questions to create your own tests for both testing and retesting.

Alternative Assessment

Chapter Resources Binder See the Alternative Assessment booklet in the *Social Studies Educator's Handbook* series.
Portfolio You might meet with students to choose appropriate work from the chapter for inclusion in their portfolios.

Interdisciplinary ACTIVITY

Learning Styles
The following chart indicates the activities appropriate for different learning styles.

Visual Learners
Historians and artists
Writers
Scientists
Economists and historians

Auditory Learners
Musicians

Kinesthetic Learners
Historians and artists
Scientists
Musicians

Evaluation

Historians and artists Artistic ability need not be a criterion, but charts should be well organized, and descriptions should include all pertinent facts discussed in Section 4.
Writers Establish an age range for which the descriptions are to be written; text and questions about the descriptions should be written at the established levels. Auditory learners might enjoy reading to and testing a sample audience of younger students.
Scientists Museum displays should contain charts or other visual aids explaining the facts requested; they should be interesting, well organized, and easy to comprehend.
Economists and historians Concept maps should contain relevant and factual information about both the positive and negative effects of the cotton-centered culture of the South during this era.
Musicians Singing ability need not be a criterion, but performances should capture the mood and sentiment of the inspirational lyrics. Explanations should be clear and concise.

Lessons	Teaching Resources
1 Liberty for All **Objectives** 1. Identify the roots of the antislavery movement. 2. Describe what reformers did to fight against slavery. 3. Describe how Americans reacted to the antislavery movement.	**Lesson Planner** Cooperative Learning, p. 84 **Student Study Guide** Section 1 Study Guide, p. 114 **Chapter Resources Binder, Unit 4** *Critical Thinking* Making Decisions, p. 45 *Geography in History* Pathway to Freedom, p. 47–48 *History Through Literature* Harriet Tubman: Conductor of the Underground Railroad, p. 46 *Skill Application* Using the Card Catalog, p. 44
2 Women Are Created Equal **Objectives** 1. Describe how the antislavery crusade helped spur the women's rights movement. 2. Identify the demands of the Seneca Falls Convention. 3. Describe how opportunities for women improved in the mid-1800s.	**Lesson Planner** Cooperative Learning, p. 85 **Student Study Guide** Section 2 Study Guide, p. 115 **Our Multicultural Heritage** *Biography* Sojourner Truth, Passionate Voice of Freedom, p. 40 **Interdisciplinary Connections:** Reform ■ *Arts* The Shaker Style, p. 80 ■ *Geography* The "Tracks" of the Underground Railroad, p. 81 ■ *World* A New Home in Liberia, p. 82 ■ *Economics* Success in Oneida, p. 83 ■ *Civics* Aid to Urban Children, p. 84
3 Reform Sweeps the Country **Objectives** 1. Identify the reforms that Dorothea Dix sought. 2. Describe how Americans improved public education in the mid-1800s. 3. Explain why some Americans wanted to ban the sale of alcohol.	**Lesson Planner** Cooperative Learning, p. 86 **Student Study Guide** Section 3 Study Guide, p. 116 **Our Multicultural Heritage** *Milestone* Philadelphia: A Reforming City, p. 42
4 New Voices, New Visions **Objectives** 1. Identify some of the writers and artists of the 1800s. 2. Describe how American writers expressed the unique spirit of the nation. 3. Identify the styles that American painters developed.	**Lesson Planner** Cooperative Learning, p. 87 **Student Study Guide** Section 4 Study Guide, p. 117 **Our Multicultural Heritage** *Biography* Ralph Waldo Emerson, New England Individualist, p. 41

Chapter Manager

Multimedia Resources	Additional Resources	Chapter-Level Resources

CD-ROM
History Makers Frederick Douglass
History Makers Harriet Tubman
Videotapes/Videodiscs
United States History Video Collection
  The Abolition Movement, Vol. 8, Ch. 19;
  The Argument for Slavery, Vol. 8, Ch. 22
	Voices of Freedom
	A Daring Escape to Freedom, pp. 106–107
	The Case for Slavery, p. 108
	Customized Reader
	Opposing Views of the African Colonization
	  Movement, article IIIA-12
	A "Conductor" on the Underground Railroad,
	  article IVA-10
		Lesson Planner
		Activity Based, pp. 88–89
		
		Student Study Guide
		Chapter 14 Study Guide,
		  pp. 118–119
		**Chapter Resources
		  Binder**
		Unit 4
		Vocabulary Building, p. 43
		Chapter Test A, pp. 49–51
		Chapter Test B, pp. 52–54
		Illustration Master, p. 55
		Extra Unit Questions,
		  pp. 57–59
		English Guided Reading
		Guided Reading, pp. 27–28
		Spanish Resources
		
		Computer Test Bank
		Chapter Tests A and B
		Extra Unit Questions
		
		**Guided Reading
		  Audiotapes**
		Side 5
		
		CD-ROM
		Time Tour A Reforming
		  Age (1820–1860) in
		  An Expanding Nation

Transparencies
Interdisciplinary Connections Bloomers,
  p. B-59
CD-ROM
History Makers Elizabeth Cady Stanton
	Voices of Freedom
	A New Approach to Raising Girls, p. 109
	Customized Reader
	Two Letters, article IVA-4
	New York's First African American Woman
	  Doctor, article VA-1	

Videotapes/Videodiscs
United States History Video Collection
  Cages, Closets, and Cellars, Vol. 7,
  Ch. 25; Awake My Soul, Vol. 7, Ch. 16;
  Demon Rum, Vol. 7, Ch. 19
	Customized Reader
	An Appeal to Improve Care for
	  the Mentally Ill, article IVA-9
	A Plea for Humane Treatment of
	  the Sick and Poor, article IVA-18	

Transparencies
Fine Art Landscape, p. D-33
CD-ROM
History Makers Emily Dickinson
Listening to Literature Audiocassettes
The American Experience Bonnets of Blue,
  from *New Cotillions*, side 3; Northfield,
  from *The Carmina Sacra*, side 4;
  Thanatopsis, side 3; The Raven, side 3
	Voices of Freedom
	A Plea for Simplicity, p. 111	

Chapter 14
pp. 400–421

 Lesson Planner

For a fully developed **Activity-Based** lesson plan for Chapter 14, see the *Lesson Planner,* pages 88–89.

 Chapter Resources

Vocabulary Building The Vocabulary Building worksheet for Chapter 14 from Unit 4, page 43, of the *Chapter Resources* binder can be used as a prereading activity or as a review of chapter vocabulary. (Reteaching/Easy)

 Student Study Guide

Chapter 14 Study Guide Refer students to pages 118–119 of the *Student Study Guide* for the Chapter 14 Study Guide. The study guide can be used for chapter review as well as for reteaching. (Reteaching/Average)

 Guided Reading Audiotapes

Students can use the *Guided Reading Audiotapes,* Chapter 14, side 5, to listen to section previews, summaries, and review questions. The tapes might benefit students who are auditory learners, students who have trouble reading, or students acquiring English. (Reteaching/Easy)

CHAPTER **14**

A Reforming Age
(1820–1860)

CHAPTER OUTLINE

1 Liberty for All

2 Women Are Created Equal

3 Reform Sweeps the Country

4 New Voices, New Visions

Early 1800s *A powerful religious movement swept the nation. Religious leaders urged their followers to take up reform.*

1820s *Northern states began requiring every town to build a grade school. This painting shows a typical schoolhouse of the period.*

1831 *William Lloyd Garrison founded the Liberator, an antislavery newspaper. Garrison called for an immediate and total end to slavery.*

| 1820 | 1825 | 1830 | 1835 | 1840 |

 WORLD EVENT
1822 Liberia set up in western Africa

 WORLD EVENT
1837 First kindergarten opens in Germany

400 • Chapter 14

Chapter Time Line
Activity

After a brief discussion of the illustrations and World Event entries on the time line, have each student choose one event or item on which to focus. Invite students to write a poem based on their choice of style; for example, a free-verse personal reflection from Harriet Tubman, a haiku about the Hudson River landscape, or a rhymed poem set in a schoolhouse of the early 1800s. Encourage students to share the results; you also might use the poems as the focal point of a bulletin board display.

Students Acquiring English
Activity

SAE students will benefit from a close look at word relationships; for example, SAE students may not realize that the word *abolish* is related to *abolitionist* or that *debt* is related to *debtor.* Discuss the following words from the chapter: *colony/colonize, liberty/Liberia/liberator, educate/education/educator,* and *crime/criminal.* Encourage students to use each form in a sentence relating to the chapter content.

400

Chapter Setting

"We are all a little wild here with numberless projects for social reform," wrote the New England author and philosopher Ralph Waldo Emerson in 1840. "But," Emerson continued, "what is man born for but to be a Re-former, a Re-maker of what man has made . . . a restorer of truth and good?"

Many other Americans in the mid-1800s shared Emerson's feelings. They were proud of what the United States had accomplished. But they believed that much remained to be done to fulfill the ideals on which the nation was founded.

The years between 1820 and 1860 were a period of great idealism in the United States. Countless reform movements sprang up to cure the nation's ills. Reformers worked to end slavery, win equal rights for women, and ensure kind treatment of prisoners and the mentally ill. They battled the evils of alcohol and fought to improve education for the nation's children. By the time this age of reform was over, Americans had worked to change every aspect of society. "Our ultimate aim," said newspaper editor Charles A. Dana, "is nothing less than Heaven on Earth."

ACTIVITY What do you think an "ideal" society would be like? Brainstorm to make a list of reforms that you think are needed in American society today.

Mid-1800s *American artists developed their own style. One group, the Hudson River School, specialized in landscapes of New York State.*

1850 *Harriet Tubman made the first of 19 trips to the South to lead slaves to freedom. In time, she helped more than 300 enslaved African Americans to escape.*

| 1840 | 1845 | 1850 | 1855 | 1860 |

WORLD EVENT
1840 World Antislavery Convention held in London

WORLD EVENT
1848 First women's college in Great Britain opens

Chapter 14 • **401**

Chapter Resources

English Guided Reading Duplicate and distribute to SAE students the Chapter 14 Guided Reading worksheet on pages 27–28 in the English Guided Reading section of the *Chapter Resources* binder. Students who have difficulty reading also might benefit from using this worksheet. Have students complete the worksheet before they begin reading. You might pair a more fluent student or a student who is a stronger reader with each SAE student to review. (Reteaching/Easy)

Spanish Resources See the Spanish Resources section of the *Chapter Resources* binder.

CD-ROM

Time Tour Access A Reforming Age (1820-1860) in An Expanding Nation on the American Heritage® *History of the United States* CD-ROM. (Enrichment/Average)

ACTIVITY

Guided Instruction If they wish, allow students to work with partners or in small groups to brainstorm their list of reforms. Groups can read their lists aloud to the class so that other groups can compare their work, make suggestions for additional reforms, or make additions to their own lists. When each group has finalized its list, have students order the list according to which reforms need attention first, second, and so forth.

Linking Past and Present
Activity

On the chalkboard, list several reform issues of the 1800s. Next to this list, have students make a list of the reform issues of the 1990s. Ask: Which of the issues of the 1800s are still important today? After a brief comparison of these time periods, have students choose one issue that appears on both lists.

Next, tell students to imagine that in the mid-1800s, there were public service announcements similar to those on radio and television today. Have students create such an announcement for the issue they have selected that would appeal to a mid-1800s audience and another one that would appeal to a modern audience. Their announcements should provide information about why the issue is important to the listener and what they want the listener to do. Volunteers can present both of their announcements to the class for discussion.

Section 1
pp. 402–407

Bell Ringer

Ask students to define the word *reformer*. Have the class brainstorm for qualities that they think a reformer opposed to slavery might have.

Lesson Plan

1. Focus The spirit of reform in the early 1800s found its strongest expression in the antislavery movement. In this section, students learn about abolitionists who protested slavery, about the colony of freed slaves in Liberia, about the underground railroad, and about the widening split between the North and South.

2. Instruct Divide the class into groups to produce their own antislavery newspaper. Groups might prepare articles about the history of slavery in the United States, firsthand accounts of slave life, successes of the underground railroad, or attacks on abolitionists. Others can write editorials, letters, or articles from the viewpoints of abolitionists mentioned in this section.

3. Close To close the lesson, play a Jeopardy!-like game with students. Provide key facts from the section and have students create appropriate questions.

1
Liberty for All

FIND OUT
- What were the roots of the antislavery movement?
- What did reformers do to fight against slavery?
- How did Americans react to the antislavery movement?

VOCABULARY abolitionist, underground railroad

"**S**ome people of color say that they have no home, no country. I am not among that number.... America is my home, my country.... I love every inch of soil which my feet pressed in my youth, and I mourn because the accursed shade of slavery rest[s] upon it. I love my country's flag, and I hope that soon it will be cleansed of its stains, and be hailed by all nations as the emblem of freedom and independence."

Henry Highland Garnet, an African American minister and escaped slave, spoke these emotional words at a meeting of women reformers in 1848. At the time, some African Americans were beginning to lose hope of ever winning full equality in the United States.

Garnet was one of a growing number of Americans—black and white—who spoke out against slavery in the mid-1800s. Like Garnet, these Americans loved their country but wanted to make it better. Only by ending slavery, they believed, would the United States fulfill its promise to provide liberty, justice, and equality for all people.

402 • Chapter 14

The Issue of Slavery

The election of Andrew Jackson in 1828 unleashed a wave of democratic change in the United States. Americans pointed proudly to the growth of democracy. More people could vote and take part in government than ever before.

Yet some Americans felt that democracy was far from complete. After all, would a democracy allow people to own slaves? An English visitor summed up the American dilemma: "You will see [Americans] with one hand hoisting the cap of liberty, and with the other flogging their slaves."

A spirit of democracy. The idea that slavery was wrong had two separate elements. One element was political. The other was religious.

The political reasons for opposing slavery went back to the American Revolution. In the Declaration of Independence, Thomas Jefferson wrote that "all men are created equal." Yet many white Americans, including Jefferson himself, did not think that the statement applied to enslaved African Americans. Reformers in the 1800s disagreed.

A spirit of revival. The second reason for opposing slavery was religious. Since colonial times, Quakers had spoken out against slavery. All men and women were equal in the eyes of God, they said. It was a sin for one human being to own another.

Other religious groups also began to speak out against slavery. In the early 1800s, a powerful religious movement known as the ***Second Great Awakening*** swept the nation. One of its leaders was a minister named Charles Grandison Finney.

At first, Finney asked the faithful to give up sin and "walk with God." Later, he urged his followers to broaden their outlook and take up the banner of reform. He especially called on Christians to join a crusade to stamp out the evil of slavery:

Linking Past and Present
Activity

One basis of the reform of this era could be called democratic idealism—that is, the belief that if democracy were to work, people had to become as educated and morally upright as possible. Many Americans at the time believed that people, and thus society as a whole, could be perfected. They felt that God wanted people to work to perfect themselves and the nation. Have students compare this idea of personal and national perfection with how people think and feel about democracy today. Students can work in small groups to reach a consensus on the answers to these questions: What effects do education and morality have on the ability of democracy to survive and prosper today? Is perfection an important goal for individuals and society today? Why or why not? What are some other worthwhile goals for individuals today? For the nation?

Historical Sidelight
Background

Charles Grandison Finney created a new public role for women by allowing them to pray aloud, a practice banned in many Christian churches of the time. The revival movement spawned by Finney and others encouraged women to act according to their "inner voices," or consciences.

The debate over the role of women split the antislavery movement in the 1840s. Most male abolitionists opposed the idea of women's rights. William Lloyd Garrison was an exception.

Slave Auction *Despite growing antislavery feeling, a brisk trade in slaves continued. At auctions such as the one shown here, enslaved African Americans were sold to the highest bidder.* **Citizenship** *How do you think people justified the sale of human beings?*

66Let Christians of all denominations meekly but firmly come forth . . . and wash their hands of this thing. Let them give forth and write on the head and front of this great [evil], SIN.99

Slavery ends in the North. The campaign against slavery succeeded in the North. By 1804, all states from Pennsylvania north had promised to free their slaves. Of course, there were only 50,000 slaves in the North in 1800, compared to nearly 1 million in the South.

A Colony in Africa

The ***American Colonization Society,*** founded in 1817, proposed to end slavery by setting up a colony in Africa for freed slaves. In 1822, President Monroe helped the society establish the nation of ***Liberia*** in western Africa. The name Liberia comes from the Latin word meaning free.

Many white southerners supported the colonization movement. They were pleased that the society did not call for an end to slavery. Instead, it promised to pay slave owners who freed their slaves.

> ***Our Common Heritage***
> *If you visited Liberia today, you would find many reminders of the United States. You could visit two cities, Monrovia and Buchanan, that are named after American Presidents. You could buy things with Liberian dollars and speak English, the official language.*

For a developed **Cooperative Learning** lesson plan, see the *Lesson Planner,* page 84.

Answer to Caption

Possible Answer: Some whites felt that African Americans were not equal beings and thus did not deserve better treatment; other people justified slavery as an economic necessity.

 Customized Reader

Primary Source For examples of differing opinions of the African colonization movement, order article IIIA-12, Opposing Views of the African Colonization Movement, from the *American History Customized Reader.* The selection consists of a published protest and a letter. (Enrichment/Challenging)

 Chapter Resources

Critical Thinking Duplicate and distribute the worksheet, Making Decisions, from Unit 4, page 45, of the *Chapter Resources* binder. The worksheet asks students to consider a major issue connected with promotion of colonization of Liberia. (Enrichment/Average)

Our Multicultural Heritage
Background

Many people did not see the American Colonization Society as an attempt to create a home for freed slaves; rather, they viewed it as white society's attempt to end the "Negro problem" by expelling African Americans. The first organized opposition to the American Colonization Society, from free blacks in Philadelphia, argued: "Whereas our ancestors (not of choice) were the first successful cultivators of the Wilds of America, we, their descendants, feel entitled to participate in the blessings of her soil, which their blood and sweat [enriched]." They went on to say that their participation in the American Revolution and the War of 1812 proved their American citizenship.

Abolitionist William Lloyd Garrison favored colonization at first, but in time he became a staunch anticolonizationist. His *Liberator* newspaper ran articles, letters, and editorials against colonization; Garrison also published an anticolonization tract, *Thoughts on Colonization* (1832), which was widely read.

403

Voices of Freedom

Primary Source You might assign selection 16-1, A Daring Escape to Freedom, on pages 106–107 of *Voices of Freedom*. The selection describes the daring escape of a young slave couple who posed as master and slave, traveling from Georgia to Philadelphia. (Enrichment/Average)

History Makers Access the biography of Frederick Douglass on the American Heritage® *History of the United States* CD-ROM. (Enrichment/Average)

African Americans, on the other hand, had mixed feelings. Some, like Paul Cuffe, thought African Americans should go to Africa because they would never have equal rights in the United States. Cuffe spent $4,000 of his own money to help settle 38 free African Americans in western Africa.

Most African Americans, however, opposed colonization. They wanted to stay in the United States. After all, nearly all American blacks—slave and free—had been born in the United States, and it was their homeland. In the end, only a few thousand free African Americans settled in Liberia.

A Call to End Slavery

Supporters of colonization did not attack slavery directly. But another group of Americans did. They were **abolitionists**—people who wanted to end slavery in the United States.

Some abolitionists supported a gradual end to slavery. They thought slavery would die out if it were kept out of the western territories. Other abolitionists demanded that slavery end everywhere, and at once.

African American abolitionists. From the start, African Americans played an important part in the abolitionist movement. Some African Americans tried to end slavery through lawsuits and petitions. In the 1820s, Samuel Cornish and John Russwurm set up an antislavery newspaper, *Freedom's Journal.* They hoped to turn public opinion against slavery by printing stories about the brutal treatment of enslaved African Americans. James Forten and other wealthy African Americans gave generously to the paper as well as to other antislavery efforts.

In 1829, David Walker, one of the most outspoken African American abolitionists, published *Appeal to the Colored Citizens of the World.* In it, he blasted the idea of slavery and called on enslaved African Americans to free themselves by any means necessary.

Frederick Douglass speaks out. The best-known African American abolitionist was Frederick Douglass. Douglass was born into slavery in Maryland. As a child, he defied the slave codes and taught himself to read. Because enslaved African Americans could not own books, the young Douglass often picked through "the mud and filth of the gutter" to find discarded newspapers.

In 1838, Douglass escaped and made his way to Boston. One day at an antislavery

404 • Chapter 14

Two Fiery Abolitionists *In their fight against slavery, both Frederick Douglass (below) and William Lloyd Garrison (left) were willing to face danger. Douglass risked recapture by publicly revealing that he was an escaped slave. Garrison was almost killed by an anti-abolition mob in Boston.* **Citizenship** *What actions did Douglass and Garrison take to win support for abolition?*

---

meeting, he felt a powerful urge to speak. Rising to his feet, he talked about the sorrows of slavery and the meaning of freedom. The audience was moved to tears. Soon, Douglass was traveling throughout the United States and Britain, lecturing against slavery. In 1847, he began publishing an antislavery newspaper, the *North Star.*

The *Liberator.* The most outspoken white abolitionist was a fiery young man named William Lloyd Garrison. Garrison launched his antislavery paper, the *Liberator,* in 1831. In it, he proclaimed that slavery was an evil to be ended immediately. On the first page of the first issue, Garrison revealed his commitment:

> **❝**I will be as harsh as truth, and as uncompromising as justice. . . . I am in earnest. . . . I will not excuse—I will not retreat a single inch—and I WILL BE HEARD.**❞**

A year after starting his paper, Garrison helped to found the ***New England Anti-Slavery Society.*** Members included Theodore Weld, a young minister connected with Charles Grandison Finney. Weld brought the energy of a religious revival to antislavery meetings.

The Grimké sisters. Women also played an important role in the abolitionist cause. Angelina and Sarah Grimké were the daughters of a wealthy slaveholder in South Carolina. They came to hate slavery and moved to Philadelphia to work for abolition. Their lectures about the evils of slavery drew large crowds.

Some people, including other abolitionists, objected to women speaking out in public. But the Grimkés defended their right to do so. "To me," said Sarah, "it is perfectly clear that whatsoever it is morally right for a man to do, it is morally right for a woman to do." This belief led the Grimkés and others to start a crusade for women's rights. (See pages 408–409.)

Railroad to Freedom

Most abolitionists pursued their goals through the press and through public debate. But some risked prison and even death by helping enslaved African Americans escape from the South.

These bold men and women formed the underground railroad. This was not a real railroad. The **underground railroad** was a network of abolitionists that secretly helped runaway slaves reach freedom in the North and in Canada.

Whites and free blacks served as "conductors" on the underground railroad. They guided runaway slaves to "stations" where they could spend the night. Some stations were houses of abolitionists. Others were churches, or even caves. Conductors sometimes hid runaways in wagons with false bottoms and under loads of hay.

One daring conductor, Harriet Tubman, was an escaped slave herself. Slave owners offered $40,000 for Tubman's capture. But Tubman paid no heed. Risking her freedom and her life, Tubman returned to the South 19 times. She conducted more than 300 slaves to freedom. On one of her last trips, Tubman led her aged parents out of slavery.

The Nation Reacts

Abolitionists like Douglass and Garrison made enemies in both the North and the South. Northern mill owners, bankers, and merchants depended on cotton from the South. They saw attacks on slavery as a threat to their livelihood.

Northern workers oppose abolition. Some northern workers also opposed the abolitionists. They feared that if slavery ended, free African Americans would come north and take their jobs by working for low pay. Henry Highland Garnet condemned northerners who "admit that slavery is wrong in the abstract, but when we ask them to help us overthrow it, they tell us it would make them beggars!"

Customized Reader

Primary Source For Quaker abolitionist Laura Haviland's account of how she and the director of the underground railroad in Ohio guided three runaway slaves to Canada, order article IVA-10, A "Conductor" on the Underground Railroad, from the *American History Customized Reader.* (Enrichment/Easy)

Chapter Resources

Geography in History Duplicate and distribute the worksheet, Pathway to Freedom, from Unit 4, pages 47–48, of the *Chapter Resources* binder. The worksheet traces several "lines" of the underground railroad. (Enrichment/Challenging)

History Through Literature To provide an up-close look at the most famous "conductor" of the underground railroad, duplicate and distribute the worksheet, Harriet Tubman: Conductor of the Underground Railroad, from Unit 4, page 46, of the *Chapter Resources* binder. (Enrichment/Average)

CD-ROM

History Makers Access the biography of Harriet Tubman on the American Heritage® *History of the United States* CD-ROM. (Enrichment/Average)

Historical Sidelight
Background

In December 1833, Garrison and other abolitionists met in Philadelphia and founded the American Anti-Slavery Society. Men and women, black and white, were delegates to that meeting. There, racial prejudice and slavery were condemned, and nonviolent methods of achieving antislavery goals were endorsed.

In the next few years, divisions within the society grew. In particular, many abolitionists objected to Garrison's support of women's rights and his view that women should have political equality in the organization. In 1840, two new abolitionist groups—the American and Foreign Anti-Slavery Society and the political Liberty party—resulted from a split in Garrison's organization. The short-lived Liberty party was not successful on the national level. In many local elections, however, the presence of Liberty party candidates forced other candidates to take a clear stand for or against slavery.

Connections With Music
Background

The slave song "Go Down, Moses," with its famous refrain "Let my people go," was about Harriet Tubman. Tubman was nicknamed "Moses" after the biblical figure who led the Hebrews out of slavery in Egypt. During the Civil War, Tubman served as a nurse and a spy for the Union. After the war, she raised money to build schools for African Americans in New York State.

Voices of Freedom

Primary Source You might assign selection 16-2, The Case for Slavery, on page 108 of *Voices of Freedom*. (Enrichment/Average)

Videotapes/Videodiscs

United States History Video Collection Use the video segment "The Argument for Slavery" from Volume 8, *Causes of the Civil War*. Approx. running time 2:10 min. (Enrichment/ Average) Vol. 8, Ch. 22

| Chapter 22 | Play |

Student Study Guide

Section 1 Study Guide Have students use the Section 1 Study Guide on page 114 of the *Student Study Guide* to review and reinforce the content of this section. (Reteaching/Average)

Guided Instruction Have students read their questions aloud. Classmates can react by identifying the questions that they think would elicit the most interesting information.

A Time of Violent Feelings *The* Liberator *and other abolitionist newspapers stirred strong emotions. Here, an angry band of slavery supporters destroys an abolitionist printing press.* **Economics** *Why did some northerners oppose abolition?*

In New York and other northern cities, mobs sometimes broke up antislavery meetings and attacked the homes of abolitionists. At times, the attacks backfired and won support for the abolitionists. One night, a Boston mob dragged William Lloyd Garrison through the streets at the end of a rope. A doctor who saw the scene wrote, "I am an abolitionist from this very moment."

Southerners defend slavery. The antislavery movement failed to gain a foothold in the South. In fact, many slave owners reacted to the crusade by defending slavery even more. One slave owner wrote that if slaves were well fed, well housed, and well clothed, they would "love their master and serve him cheerfully, diligently, and faithfully." Other owners argued that slaves were better off than northern workers—whom they called wage slaves—who worked long hours in dusty, airless factories.

Even some southerners who owned no slaves defended slavery. To them, slavery was essential to the southern economy. Many southerners exaggerated the extent of northern support for the antislavery movement. They began to believe that northerners wanted to destroy their way of life.

SECTION 1 REVIEW

1. **Locate:** Liberia.
2. **Identify:** (a) Henry Highland Garnet, (b) Second Great Awakening, (c) American Colonization Society, (d) Frederick Douglass, (e) William Lloyd Garrison, (f) New England Anti-Slavery Society, (g) Theodore Weld, (h) Angelina and Sarah Grimké, (i) Harriet Tubman.
3. **Define:** (a) abolitionist, (b) underground railroad.
4. Give two reasons why some Americans opposed slavery.
5. Why did most African Americans oppose the colonization movement?
6. How did the abolitionist movement affect the way the South viewed northerners?
7. **CRITICAL THINKING Analyzing Information** Why do you think it was easier to end slavery in the North than in the South?

ACTIVITY Writing to Learn

Imagine that you are a reporter interviewing a slave who escaped to freedom on the underground railroad. Write five questions you would ask about the journey.

Answers to Section 1 Review

RESEARCH SKILLS
Using the Card Catalog

You will sometimes need to research information using books in the library. Most libraries have a card catalog. The card catalog helps you find the books you need.

1. **Study the parts of the card catalog.** The *card catalog* is a set of drawers holding small cards. The cards are in alphabetical order. Every nonfiction, or factual, book has at least three cards. The *author card* lists the book by the author's last name. The *title card* lists the book by its title. The *subject card* lists it by its subject.

    You can tell what kind of card it is by reading the top line. The top line will show either the author's last name, the title of the book, or the subject heading. Sometimes, author and title cards are kept together in one set of drawers and the subject cards are kept in a separate set of drawers.

    Look at Card A. (a) Is this an author, title, or subject card? (b) Who is the author of the book? (c) What is its title?

2. **Practice using the call number.** Every card for a nonfiction book has a number in the top left corner. This is the call number of the book. The *call number* tells you where you will find the book on the library shelves. Each nonfiction book has its call number printed on the spine, or narrow back edge. The letters after the number are the first letters of the author's last name. Look at Card A. (a) What is the call number of the book? (b) What do the letters printed below the call number mean?

3. **Use other cards in the card catalog.** Look at Cards B and C. (a) Is Card B an author, title, or subject card? (b) Is Card C an author, title, or subject card? (c) Why do Cards A, B, and C all have the same call number?

ACTIVITY Make up author, title, and subject cards for three books in your classroom library.

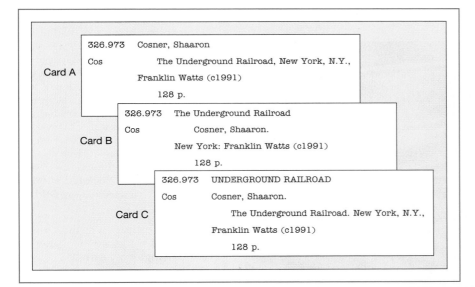

Card A
326.973   Cosner, Shaaron
Cos   The Underground Railroad, New York, N.Y.,
          Franklin Watts (c1991)
                 128 p.

Card B
326.973   The Underground Railroad
Cos   Cosner, Shaaron.
          New York: Franklin Watts (c1991)
                 128 p.

Card C
326.973   UNDERGROUND RAILROAD
Cos   Cosner, Shaaron.
                 The Underground Railroad. New York, N.Y.,
          Franklin Watts (c1991)
                 128 p.

Section 2
pp. 408–411

Bell Ringer

Challenge students to name occupations open to women today that would probably have shocked people in the 1800s.

Lesson Plan

1. Focus The antislavery movement awakened many women to their own lack of social and political rights. In this section, students examine the beginnings of the women's rights movement.

2. Instruct Have the class create a time line entitled "United States Women's History, 1800–1860." Have students draw a time line divided into five-year intervals. Ask students to plot on the time line key events from the text. Next, have the class research achievements by American women to place along the line. Students can briefly explain the importance of each entry. You might suggest they use references such as *America in Time* and *Notable American Women* for their research.

3. Close To close the lesson, have students turn the headings within the section into questions and then answer them.

2
Women Are Created Equal

FIND OUT
- How did the antislavery crusade help spur the women's rights movement?
- What did the Seneca Falls Convention demand?
- How did opportunities for women improve in the mid-1800s?

In 1840, a group of Americans sailed to London to attend the World Antislavery Convention. Among them were two young women: Lucretia Mott and Elizabeth Cady Stanton. Once they arrived in London, however, the convention refused to let women

---

BIOGRAPHY Elizabeth Cady Stanton *When Elizabeth Cady Stanton was growing up, clerks in her father's law office teased her by reading her laws that denied basic rights to women. This teasing helped make Stanton a lifelong foe of inequality.* **Citizenship** *How were women's rights limited in the mid-1800s?*

take an active part in the proceedings. Convention officials even forced female delegates, including Mott and Stanton, to sit behind a curtain, hidden from view.

Mott and Stanton stayed in London for several weeks. At their hotel each evening, they debated the issue of women's rights. "[We] agreed to hold a women's rights convention," Stanton later recalled. "The men . . . had [shown] a great need for some education on that question."

An Uphill Struggle

The treatment that Mott and Stanton faced in London was not unusual for the mid-1800s. Women had few political or legal rights at the time. They could not vote or hold office. When a woman married, her husband became owner of all her property. If a woman worked outside the home, her wages belonged to her husband. A husband also had the right to hit his wife as long as he did not seriously injure her.

"Unnatural" women. Many women had joined the abolitionist movement. As these women worked to end slavery, they became aware that they lacked full social and political rights themselves. Among the first to speak out were Angelina and Sarah Grimké.

As you have read, the boldness of the Grimkés' antislavery activities shocked audiences in the North. In a newspaper editorial, a group of New England ministers scolded the sisters. "When [a woman] assumes the place and tone of a man as a public reformer," they wrote, "her character becomes unnatural."

The Grimkés and other women reformers rejected such ideas. More determined than ever, they continued their crusade. Now, however, they lectured about women's rights as well as abolition. Said Angelina Grimké:

  66The investigation of the rights of the slave has led me to a better understanding of my own.99

"Ain't I a woman?" African American women joined the struggle for women's rights. Sojourner Truth was born into slavery in New York. She was freed by a New York law that banned slavery. Truth became active in the crusade against slavery.

Truth was a spellbinding speaker. At a meeting in 1851, she listened to a minister speak about women's need to be protected. When he was done, Truth leaped to her feet with this stinging reply:

> 66 The man over there says women need to be helped into carriages and lifted over ditches, and to have the best place everywhere. Nobody ever helps me into carriages, or over puddles, or gives me the best place. And ain't I a woman? I have ploughed and planted and gathered into barns. . . . And ain't I a woman? . . . I have borne thirteen children, and seen most of 'em sold into slavery, and when I cried out with my mother's grief, none but Jesus heard me! And ain't I a woman? 99

Others call for equal rights. After returning home from London, Lucretia Mott and Elizabeth Cady Stanton took up the cause of women's rights with new zeal. Mott was a Quaker minister and the mother of five children. A quiet speaker, she won the respect of many listeners with her logic.

Elizabeth Cady Stanton was the daughter of a well-known New York judge. Growing up, she became keenly aware that the laws denied basic rights to women.

Another tireless organizer was Susan B. Anthony. Even when audiences heckled her and threw eggs, Anthony always finished her speech. Lucy Stone and Abby Kelley also gave their energies to the movement.

A Historic Meeting

In 1840, Lucretia Mott and Elizabeth Cady Stanton decided to hold a convention

BIOGRAPHY Sojourner Truth *Born into slavery, Isabella Baumfree became one of the most powerful voices for abolition and women's rights. Taking a new name—Sojourner Truth—she "sojourned," or traveled, "up and down the land," declaring "the truth unto people."* **Daily Life** *What arguments did Truth use to show that women are as capable as men?*

to draw attention to the problems women faced. Eight years later, in 1848, in Seneca Falls, New York, that convention finally took place.

Linking Past and Present
Like many women today, Lucy Stone continued to use her own name after she married. "A wife should no more take her husband's name than he should hers," she said. Other women who kept their own names became known as "Lucy Stoners."

409

 Lesson Planner

For a developed **Cooperative Learning** lesson plan, see the *Lesson Planner,* page 85.

Answer to Caption

She pointed out that she herself had survived a harsh life without any help from men. She moved independently from place to place, did heavy farm work, and lived through the grief of losing children.

 Voices of Freedom

Primary Source You might assign selection 16-3, A New Approach to Raising Girls, on page 109 of *Voices of Freedom.* The selection is from a speech given by Elizabeth Cady Stanton to a women's convention in Akron, Ohio. She proposes a very different approach to raising girls. (Enrichment/Average)

 Our Multicultural Heritage

Biography Have students read the biography, Sojourner Truth, Passionate Voice of Freedom, on page 40 of the *Our Multicultural Heritage* booklet. (Enrichment/Challenging)

 CD-ROM

History Makers Access the biography of Elizabeth Cady Stanton on the American Heritage® *History of the United States* CD-ROM. (Enrichment/Average)

Our Multicultural Heritage
Background

After the Civil War, Sojourner Truth worked for universal suffrage. In 1867, she urged women to push hard "while things are stirring; because if we wait till it is still, it will take a great while to get things going again."

Cooperative Learning
Activity

Have the class plan a museum exhibit on the women's rights movement of the 1800s. Divide the class into groups. Give each group a large sheet of poster paper to draw a floorplan of their exhibit and sketches of the items it would include. First have students list the events and people that they think should be included in the exhibit. Then have students brainstorm specific items that they would include to illustrate the events and to represent the lives and contributions of the various people. If students have trouble getting started, the class might brainstorm a list of the kinds of items they have seen at historical or natural history museums: dioramas, photographs, artifacts, drawings, time lines, letters, and documents, such as the Declaration of Sentiments. After students have completed the sketches of their exhibit, they can write captions or explanations for each of the items.

For worksheets establishing connections between the Chapter 14 main idea, Reform, and five other disciplines, see the *Interdisciplinary Connections* booklet. (Enrichment)

- **Arts** The Shaker Style, page 80 (Easy)
- **Geography** The "Tracks" of the Underground Railroad, page 81 (Average)
- **World** A New Home in Liberia, page 82 (Average)
- **Economics** Success in Oneida, page 83 (Challenging)
- **Civics** Aid to Urban Children, page 84 (Average)

Answer to Connections

Heavy dresses and tight corsets made breathing difficult. A tightly laced corset could squeeze internal organs, narrow the pelvis, crush the rib cage, and cause the lungs to collapse.

 Transparencies

Interdisciplinary Connections Use the transparency Bloomers on page B-59 of *American History Transparencies*. Teaching suggestions can be found on page B-16. (Enrichment/Easy)

ACTIVITY

Guided Instruction Allow students to browse through magazines and catalogs for inspiration. Students who would prefer not to draw might cut out and trace around a picture of a person from a magazine or catalog.

CONNECTIONS

ARTS · **SCIENCES** · **GEOGRAPHY** · **WORLD** · **ECONOMICS** · **CIVICS**

Fashion and Women's Health

Thud! There was a faint ripple in the back of the theater as an unconscious woman was carried out. "She needs air. Give her air," the usher cried.

The scene was not unusual. Like many women of her time, this theatergoer was dressed in a tightly laced corset designed to make her waist as small as possible. On top of the corset, she wore layers of heavy, stiff petticoats, reaching to the ground. Over all this was a full-length gown. The entire outfit weighed 12 pounds (5 kg). Normal breathing was difficult.

Women reformers protested that such fashions were a threat to women's health. Doctors supported their claims. "Tight-lacers," they said, squeezed the internal organs and narrowed the pelvis. They could crush the rib cage and cause the lungs to collapse.

Elizabeth Smith Miller decided to do something about the problem. It was a spring day. Dressed in corset and petticoats, Miller struggled to bend as she planted her garden. Surely, she thought, there must be a better way for women to dress.

Miller designed a new fashion. It featured a more loosely cut top, shorter skirt, and full trousers gathered at the ankles. Trying on the new outfit, one thankful woman commented that she felt "like a captive set free from his ball and chain."

Reformer and publisher Amelia Bloomer promoted the new fashion in her journal for women. She wore it herself at public meetings. Soon, the outfit became known as "bloomers."

The new fashion did not catch on widely. Critics made fun of women who wore bloomers. They claimed the trousers were too "masculine."

Bloomers soon disappeared from the fashion scene. According to reformer Lucy Stone, they "suffered the usual fate of anything that is forty years ahead of its time."

Woman wearing bloomers

■ How did fashions in the mid-1800s threaten women's health?

ACTIVITY

Select an activity that you do every day, such as attending school, doing chores, playing ball, or working. Design an outfit that would be suitable to wear during that activity.

Team-Teaching Suggestion
Art

You might want to work with an art teacher to present a lesson on the form and function of Shaker furniture. Perhaps the art teacher can display other pictures of Shaker furniture or crafts. Students might create their own furniture designs.

About 200 women and 40 men attended the ***Seneca Falls Convention***. At the meeting, leaders of the women's rights movement presented a Declaration of Sentiments. Modeled on the Declaration of Independence, it proclaimed, "We hold these truths to be self-evident: that all men and women are created equal."

The women and men at Seneca Falls voted for resolutions that demanded equality for women at work, at school, and in church. All the resolutions passed without opposition except one. It demanded that women be allowed to vote in elections. Even the bold women at Seneca Falls hesitated to take this step. In the end, the resolution passed by a slim majority.

The Seneca Falls Convention marked the start of an organized women's rights movement. In the years after 1848, women worked for change in many areas. They won additional legal rights in some states. For example, New York State passed laws allowing women to keep property and wages after they married. Progress was slow, however. Many men and women opposed the goals of the women's rights movement. The struggle for equal rights would last many years.

New Opportunities for Women

The women at Seneca Falls believed that education was a key to equality. At the time, women from poor families had little hope of learning even to read and write. And while young middle-class women were often sent to school, they were taught dancing and drawing rather than mathematics and science, like their brothers. After all, people argued, women were expected to devote themselves to marriage and children. Why did they need an education?

Reformers, like Emma Willard and Mary Lyon, worked to improve education for women. Willard opened a high school for girls in Troy, New York. Here, young wom-en studied "men's subjects," such as mathematics, physics, and philosophy.

Mary Lyon spent years raising money for Mount Holyoke Female Seminary in Massachusetts. She did not call the school a college because she knew that many people thought it was wrong for women to attend college. In fact, Mount Holyoke, which opened in 1837, was the first women's college in the United States.

At about the same time, a few men's colleges began to admit women. As women's education improved, women found jobs teaching, especially in grade schools.

A few women tried to enter fields such as medicine. Elizabeth Blackwell attended medical school at Geneva College in New York. To the surprise of school officials, she graduated first in her class. Women had practiced medicine since colonial times, but Blackwell was the first woman in the United States with a medical degree. She later set up the first nursing school in the nation.

SECTION 2 REVIEW

1. **Identify:** (a) Lucretia Mott, (b) Elizabeth Cady Stanton, (c) Sojourner Truth, (d) Susan B. Anthony, (e) Seneca Falls Convention, (f) Emma Willard, (g) Mary Lyon, (h) Elizabeth Blackwell.
2. What rights were denied to women in the early 1800s?
3. What issues did delegates at Seneca Falls vote on?
4. What type of education did most women receive in the mid-1800s?
5. **CRITICAL THINKING Understanding Causes and Effects** How was the women's rights movement a long-range effect of the antislavery movement?

 Writing to Learn

Imagine that you are Lucretia Mott or Elizabeth Cady Stanton. Prepare a flier announcing the women's rights convention you are organizing.

Customized Reader

Primary Source For a copy of two letters written by Elizabeth Cady Stanton describing the purpose of the women's rights movement and her despair over her father's and husband's disapproval of her work, order article IVA-4, Two Letters, from the *American History Customized Reader.* (Enrichment/Challenging)

Primary Source You might wish to order article VA-1, New York's First African American Woman Doctor, from the *American History Customized Reader.* This article describes the life and times of Dr. Susan McKinney Steward. (Enrichment/Average)

Student Study Guide

Section 2 Study Guide Have students use the Section 2 Study Guide on page 115 of the *Student Study Guide* to review and reinforce the content of this section. (Reteaching/Average)

ACTIVITY

Guided Instruction To begin work on their fliers, students might list participants at the convention. Students then can write one sentence describing the background of each participant and a statement or question summarizing the issues about which each participant will speak. Volunteers can share their finished convention fliers with other members of the class.

Answers to Section 2 Review

1. (a) Lucretia Mott, p. 408, (b) Elizabeth Cady Stanton, p. 408, (c) Sojourner Truth, p. 409, (d) Susan B. Anthony, p. 409, (e) Seneca Falls Convention, p. 411, (f) Emma Willard, p. 411, (g) Mary Lyon, p. 411, (h) Elizabeth Blackwell, p. 411

2. Women could not vote or hold office; married women's property and earnings belonged to their husbands; husbands could hit their wives as long as they did not injure them badly.

3. The Seneca Falls delegates drafted a Declaration of Sentiments, which contained res-olutions demanding equality for women at school, work, and in church; a slim majority of the delegates demanded the right to vote.

4. Most poor women did not learn to read or write. Young middle-class women were taught subjects such as drawing and dancing but not "men's" subjects, such as mathematics and science.

5. Possible Answer: The antislavery movement made women aware of their own lack of social and political rights. Many leaders of the women's rights movement got their start in the antislavery movement.

Section 3
pp. 412–415

Bell Ringer

Repeat the following statement to the class: In 1850, free public education stopped after the eighth grade. Have students briefly speculate about how their lives would be different if this fact were still true today.

Lesson Plan

1. Focus In the mid-1800s, a variety of problems drew the attention of reformers. In this section, students learn about Dorothea Dix's reform efforts. They also examine efforts to improve education and to curb alcohol abuse.
2. Instruct Divide the class into four teams. Have each team present a brief TV news magazine segment on reforms or reformers mentioned in this section. Sample topics might include educational reform, prison reform, an interview with Dorothea Dix, and the temperance movement.
3. Close To close the lesson, have students answer a series of *Who, What, Where, When, Why,* and *How* questions about the goals of reformers in the mid-1800s.

 Lesson Planner

For a developed **Cooperative Learning** lesson plan, see the *Lesson Planner,* page 86.

3
Reform Sweeps the Country

FIND OUT

- What reforms did Dorothea Dix seek?
- How did Americans improve public education in the mid-1800s?
- Why did some Americans want to ban the sale of alcohol?

VOCABULARY temperance movement

In the mid-1800s, the spirit of reform led Americans to work for change in many areas. They took to heart the words of a poem they had learned in school:

> Beautiful hands are they that do
> Deeds that are noble, good, and true;
> Beautiful feet are they that go
> Swiftly to lighten another's woe.

Some reformers turned their attention to what one minister called the "outsiders" in American society—criminals and the mentally ill. One of the most vigorous of these reformers was a Boston schoolteacher, Dorothea Lynde Dix.

Dorothea Dix: Helping the Helpless

 Dorothea Dix was born on the Maine frontier in 1802. At age 12, her parents sent her to live with her grandmother in Boston. There, Dorothea attended school to become a teacher.

An energetic teacher. After completing eighth grade, Dix was considered qualified to teach by the standards of the time. At age 14, she opened her own grade school. A few years later, she opened another, larger school, which was a free school for poor children.

Dix amazed people with her energy and hard work. She rose each day at 4 or 5 A.M. She read, wrote, and studied until well after midnight. When the available textbooks did not provide enough material on history and science, Dix wrote her own book. Teachers throughout the nation were soon using it.

A new mission. One day in March 1841, Dix got an urgent message. A young Harvard University student had been asked to set up a Sunday School class for women in the jail at Cambridge, near Boston. The young man could not keep order among the prisoners. Did Dix know anyone who could help?

Dix took the job herself. At the Cambridge jail, she found 20 women prisoners. Some were there for stealing, others for drunkenness. But the prisoners who caught Dix's attention were those who had committed no crime. These women had been jailed because they were mentally ill.

The jailer locked the mentally ill prisoners in small, dark cells at the rear of the jail. There was no heat in the cells, and the women were half frozen. Dix demanded to know why these women were treated so cruelly. The jailer replied that "lunatics" did not feel the cold.

That moment changed Dix's life forever. By the time she left the jail, she knew she had to take action.

A shocking report. During the next 18 months, Dix visited every jail, poorhouse, and hospital in Massachusetts. Her detailed report shocked state legislators:

> I proceed, gentlemen, briefly to call your attention to the present state of Insane Persons confined within this Commonwealth, in cages, closets, cellars, stalls, pens! Chained, naked, beaten with rods, and lashed into obedience.

412 • Chapter 14

Historical Sidelight
Background

Dorothea Dix was responsible for starting state-supported hospitals for the insane in 15 states. In 1843, there were 13 in the United States; by 1880, there were 123. She also took her campaign to Canada and England, where she convinced officials to start similar programs. By the 1850s, Dix had earned an international reputation.

Dix never became involved in the women's movement. She often apologized to audiences for speaking publicly, knowing that this was an unusual act for a woman.

Among other reformers of the period was Richard Martin, who started a worldwide movement in 1824 to stop cruelty to animals. He influenced Henry Bergh (1811–1888), who founded the American Society for the Prevention of Cruelty to Animals (ASPCA) in 1866.

BIOGRAPHY Dorothea Dix *The sight of "harmless lunatics" locked in a cold, dark cell prompted Dorothea Dix to action. Largely through Dix's efforts, 28 states had established special hospitals for the care of the mentally ill by 1860.* **Citizenship** *How did Dix go about the task of achieving reform?*

Still, the legislators hesitated to raise taxes to build a new mental hospital. Dix offered her report to the newspapers. In the end, the legislature voted for the hospital.

Dix's work was not done. She inspected jails and poorhouses in Vermont, Connecticut, and New York. In time, she traveled as far as Louisiana and Illinois. In North Carolina, an angry official told Dix that "nothing can be done here." She replied, "I know no such word." In nearly every state, her reports convinced legislatures to treat the mentally ill as patients, not criminals.

Reforming prisons. Dix also spoke out against conditions in the prisons. Men, women, and children were often crammed into cold, damp rooms. If food was in short supply, prisoners went hungry unless they had money to buy meals from jailers.

In the early 1800s, five out of six people in northern jails were debtors. To Dix, jailing debtors made no sense. How could people earn money to pay back debts when they were behind bars?

Dix and others called for changes in the prison system. As a result, some states built prisons with only one or two inmates to a cell. Cruel punishments were banned, and people convicted of minor crimes received shorter sentences. Slowly, states stopped treating debtors as criminals. ∎

Educating a Free People

In 1816, Thomas Jefferson wrote, "If a nation expects to be ignorant and free, it expects what never was and never will be." Jefferson knew that a democracy needed educated citizens. Reformers agreed. As more men won the right to vote in the 1820s, reformers acted to see that they were well informed.

Before the 1820s, few American children attended school. Public schools were rare. Those that did exist were usually old and run down. Teachers were poorly trained and ill paid. Students of all ages crowded together in a single room.

New public schools. New York State led the way in reforming public education. In the 1820s, the state ordered every town to build a grade school. Before long, other northern states required towns to support public schools.

In Massachusetts, Horace Mann led the fight for better schools. Mann became head of the state board of education in 1837. For 12 years, he hounded legislators to provide more money for education. Under his leadership, Massachusetts built new schools, extended the school year, and gave teachers higher pay. The state also opened three colleges to train teachers.

Reformers in other states urged their legislatures to follow the lead of Massachusetts and New York. By the 1850s, most northern states had set up free tax-supported elementary schools. Schools in the South improved more slowly. In both the North and

Answer to Caption

She detailed hospital and jail conditions. When legislators did not respond, she took her report to the newspapers.

Customized Reader

Primary Source For a copy of Dorothea Dix's report to the Massachusetts legislature, order article IVA-9, An Appeal to Improve Care for the Mentally Ill, from the *American History Customized Reader.* Although sympathetic to their plight, she refers to the mentally ill as idiots, lunatics, madwomen, and madmen. (Enrichment/Easy)

Primary Source You might order article IVA-18, A Plea for Humane Treatment of the Sick and Poor, from the *American History Customized Reader.* In this letter, Mary Mann expresses her concern for the treatment of the sick, mentally ill, and poor. (Enrichment/Average)

Videotapes/ Videodiscs

United States History Video Collection Use the video segment "Cages, Closets, and Cellars" from Volume 7, *Democracy and Reform*, to enhance students' understanding of how the mentally ill were treated in the mid-1800s. Approx. running time 2:05 min. (Enrichment/Average) Vol. 7, Ch. 25

Chapter 25   Play

Connections With Local History
Activity

Have interested students research the history of public education in your community or state. Students should find out when the first public elementary and high schools were opened, how they were funded, and what type of education was available to African Americans and children with disabilities at that time. Have students present their findings in the form of short oral reports.

Our Multicultural Heritage
Background

As early as 1816, Boston educators experimented with "infant schools," attended by children age four and under. Later, Americans adopted the idea of kindergartens from the Germans. The first kindergarten in the United States was set up in 1856 in Watertown, Wisconsin, by German immigrants.

African Americans achieved some important educational firsts in the mid-1800s. In New York City in 1837, James M. Smith became the first African American to receive a medical degree. In Maine in 1844, Macon B. Allen became the first African American attorney.

One-Room Schoolhouse *Many Americans in the 1800s received their education in one-room schoolhouses, such as the one in this painting by Winslow Homer. The single room housed all grades, and older students helped younger ones with their lessons.* **Citizenship** *Why is education important in a democracy?*

South, schooling ended in the eighth grade. There were few public high schools.

Education for African Americans. In most areas, free African Americans had little chance to attend school. A few cities, like Boston and New York, set up separate schools for African American students. However, these schools received less money than schools for white students did.

Some African Americans went on to higher education. They attended private colleges such as Harvard, Dartmouth, and Oberlin. In the 1850s, several colleges for African Americans opened in the North. The first was Lincoln University, in Pennsylvania.

Special schools. Some reformers took steps to improve education for people with disabilities. In 1817, Thomas Gallaudet (gal uh DEHT) set up a school for people who are deaf, in Hartford, Connecticut. A few years later, Samuel Gridley Howe became director of the first American school for people who are blind. Howe invented a way to print books with raised letters. Blind students could read the letters with their fingers.

Battling "Demon Rum"

In 1854, Timothy Shay Arthur published a book called *Ten Nights in a Barroom and What I Saw There*. It told the story of how an entire village was destroyed by "demon rum." A play based on the novel followed.

History and You

The first public schools went through only the eighth grade. If your education stopped at eighth grade, what subjects would you not learn? What types of skills would you have to learn outside of school? Which careers would it be difficult for you to pursue?

Today, the play seems somewhat silly, but it addressed a serious problem of the 1800s. Alcohol abuse was widespread at the time. At political rallies, weddings, and funerals, men, women, and sometimes even children drank heavily. Craftsworkers and apprentices often drank alcohol in their workshops. In cities, men could buy a glass of whiskey in grocery stores, candy stores, and barber shops as easily as at taverns.

Reformers linked abuse of alcohol to crime, the breakup of families, and mental illness. In the late 1820s, reformers began a campaign against drinking. It was known as the **temperance movement.** Some temperance groups tried to persuade people to drink less. Others demanded that states ban the sale of alcohol.

In the 1850s, temperance groups won a major victory when Maine banned the sale of alcohol. Eight other states soon passed "Maine laws." Many Americans resented the laws, and most states later repealed them. Still, temperance crusaders pressed on. They gained new strength in the late 1800s.

SECTION 3 REVIEW

1. **Identify:** (a) Dorothea Dix, (b) Horace Mann, (c) Thomas Gallaudet, (d) Samuel Gridley Howe.
2. **Define:** temperance movement.
3. Why did Dorothea Dix decide to reform Massachusetts prisons?
4. What improvements were made in public education after the 1820s?
5. Why did temperance groups want to end the drinking of alcohol?
6. **CRITICAL THINKING Understanding Causes and Effects** How would lack of educational opportunities for African Americans contribute to prejudice against them?

ACTIVITY Writing to Learn
Write the script for a TV documentary exposing one of the abuses you read about in this section.

LINKING PAST AND PRESENT

PAST

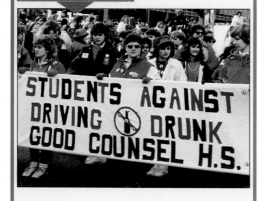
PRESENT

Fight Against Alcohol *Americans have long been concerned about the dangers of drinking alcohol. In the 1800s, temperance leaders warned that alcohol was destroying homes and families. In the 1854 engraving at top, a father is led home by his daughter after spending his pay in a saloon. Today, much of the debate about alcohol centers on drunken driving. At bottom, members of Students Against Driving Drunk (SADD) express their concern. ● How does your community fight drunken driving?*

Answer to Linking Past and Present

Possible Answer: drunken driving laws, organizations like SADD or MADD

 Videotapes/ Videodiscs

United States History Video Collection Use the video segment "Demon Rum" from Volume 7, *Democracy and Reform,* to enhance students' understanding of the temperance movement. Approx. running time 3:05 min. (Enrichment/Average) Vol. 7, Ch. 19

Chapter 19   Play

Student Study Guide

Section 3 Study Guide Have students use the Section 3 Study Guide on page 116 of the *Student Study Guide* to review and reinforce the content of this section. (Reteaching/Average)

ACTIVITY

Guided Instruction Students can expand on the topic they chose for the TV news segments described in the Lesson Plan, or they can focus on a different topic. Suggest that students list a series of film segments to show examples of an abuse. Then have them write narration for transitions between the film segments, an introduction, and a conclusion.

Connections With Local History
Activity

Have students find out about the state and local laws governing the sale and consumption of alcohol. Where, for example, can alcohol be sold? What is the legal drinking age? How severely are drunk-driving offenses judged? Students might also do research to see if these laws have been changed in the past 10 to 15 years, and if so, why.

Answers to Section 3 Review

1. (a) Dorothea Dix, p. 412, (b) Horace Mann, p. 413, (c) Thomas Gallaudet, p. 414, (d) Samuel Gridley Howe, p. 414
2. temperance movement, p. 415
3. Dix discovered that prisoners were crammed into cold, damp cells and often went hungry; she also saw that the mentally ill were housed with criminals and treated brutally.
4. Northern states began requiring towns to build and support public elementary schools.
5. Alcohol abuse was widespread in the mid-1800s; even children sometimes drank heavily; temperance groups felt that alcohol abuse led to crime, mental illness, and the breakup of families.
6. Possible Answer: A lack of education can limit a person's ability to get a good job and to stay informed about public issues. These limitations could lead to a public image of such people as lazy and/or ignorant.

Bell Ringer

Have students name an American artist for each of the following categories: painter, novelist, poet, playwright, and composer. Invite students to comment about anything they know about the artists whom they have named.

Lesson Plan

1. Focus In the 1800s, instead of copying European traditions, American writers and artists sought themes and styles deeply rooted in the American experience. In this section, students will examine the writers and artists who began the development of a distinctly American artistic culture.

2. Instruct Divide the class into small groups. Assign each group one of the American writers discussed in this section. For novelists, have groups act out scenes from the writers' most famous works. For poets, have groups select some short poems or one longer poem to read aloud. Discuss how American writers of the 1800s dealt with topics and themes that are distinctly American.

3. Close To close the lesson, have the class play a matching game in which they link key names and titles with defining details.

4
New Voices, New Visions

FIND OUT
- Who were some of the writers and artists of the 1800s?
- How did American writers express the unique spirit of the nation?
- What styles did American painters develop?

In 1820, a Scottish minister named Sydney Smith blasted the lack of culture in the United States:

> **"**In the four quarters of the globe, who reads an American book? Or goes to an American play? Or looks at an American picture or statue? What does the world yet owe to Americans?**"**

Any American artist or writer of worth, Smith went on, had been trained in the studios of Europe. The best the United States could offer, he said, was "a galaxy . . . of newspaper scribblers."

Even as Smith wrote these scornful words, a group of American writers and artists was breaking free of European traditions. These men and women created a voice and a vision that were truly American.

American Storytellers

Until the early 1800s, most American writers depended on Europe for their ideas and inspiration. In the 1820s, however, Americans began to write stories with American themes.

Washington Irving. One of the most popular American writers of the early 1800s was Washington Irving, a New Yorker. Irving first became known for *The Sketch Book,*

a collection of tales published in 1820. Two of the best-loved tales are "Rip Van Winkle" and "The Legend of Sleepy Hollow."

Irving's stories amused people. They also gave Americans a sense of the richness of their past. Irving's appeal went beyond the United States, however. Irving was the first American writer to enjoy fame in Europe as well as at home.

James Fenimore Cooper. James Fenimore Cooper, another New Yorker, also published novels set in the past. In *The Deerslayer* and *The Last of the Mohicans,* Cooper gave a romantic, or idealized, view of relations between whites and Native Americans on the frontier. The stories were so full of exciting adventures, however, that few readers cared whether or not they were true to life.

Later writers. Nathaniel Hawthorne drew on the history of Puritan New England to create his novels and short stories. The Puritan past fascinated Hawthorne. *The Scarlet Letter,* his best-known novel, was published in 1850. It explores the forces of good and evil in Puritan New England.

In 1851, Herman Melville published *Moby Dick.* In this novel, Melville takes the reader on a wild voyage aboard the whaling ship *Pequod.* The crazed captain, Ahab, has vowed revenge against the white whale that years earlier bit off his leg. *Moby Dick* had only limited success when it was first published. Today, however, critics rank *Moby Dick* among the finest American novels ever written.

William Wells Brown published *Clotel,* a novel about slave life, in 1853. Brown was the nation's first published African American novelist and the first African American to earn his living as a writer.

Women Writers

By the mid-1800s, a growing number of women were publishing books. Margaret Fuller wrote *Woman in the Nineteenth Cen-*

Historical Sidelight
Background

Mark Twain cared very much that Cooper's tales were not true to life. He wrote of *The Deerslayer:* "A work of art? It has no invention; it has . . . no life-likeness, no thrill, no stir, no seeming of reality; its characters are confusedly drawn; its . . . humor is pathetic; its pathos is funny; its conversations are—oh! indescribable; its love-scenes odious; its English a crime against the language. Counting these art, what is left is Art. I think we must all admit that."

Connections With Literature
Background

The term *romantic* applied to the literature and art of the few decades before the Civil War has little to do with falling in love. Rather, it refers to a philosophy that turned away from the restrictions of the past and glorified the power of the human imagination. Thus, works that are considered *romantic* may praise individualism while taking a dim view of society, or they may look for a symbolic or spiritual interpretation of events.

tury. The book was an important influence on the movement for women's rights.

Many of the best-selling novels of the period were written by women. These novels often told about young women who gained wealth and happiness through honesty and self-sacrifice. Some novels were more true to life. They showed the hardships faced by widows and orphans.

Few of these novels are read today. However, writers such as Catharine Sedgwick and Fanny Fern earned far more money than Nathaniel Hawthorne or Herman Melville. In fact, Hawthorne complained bitterly about the success of women writers. "America is now wholly given over to a . . . mob of scribbling women," he once said.

Poetic Voices

John Greenleaf Whittier, a Quaker from Massachusetts, wanted to write poems about the colonial past. But his friend William Lloyd Garrison, the abolitionist, urged him to use his pen to serve the antislavery cause. In many poems, Whittier sought to make his readers aware of the evils of slavery.

The favorite poet of Americans in the mid-1800s was Henry Wadsworth Longfellow. Longfellow based many of his poems on events from the nation's past. Perhaps his best-known poem is "Paul Revere's Ride." Today, many Americans can still recite the opening lines:

> **❝**Listen, my children, and you
> shall hear
> Of the midnight ride of Paul
> Revere,
> On the eighteenth of April in
> Seventy-five;
> Hardly a man is now alive
> Who remembers that famous day
> and year.**❞**

Walt Whitman published only one book of poems, *Leaves of Grass*. However, he

Women Writers
This poster shows a gathering of notable American writers of the mid-1800s. Among them are Harriet Beecher Stowe, author of Uncle Tom's Cabin, *and Julia Ward Howe, who wrote the lyrics to "The Battle Hymn of the Republic."* **Linking Past and Present** *What women writers are popular today?*

added to it over a period of 27 years. Whitman had great faith in the common people. His poetry celebrated democracy and the diverse people who made the nation great.

Some of the best poems of the period were written by Emily Dickinson. Dickinson wrote more than 1,700 poems, but only 7 were published in her lifetime. She called her poetry "my letter to the world." Today, Dickinson is considered one of the nation's greatest poets.

Emerson and Thoreau: Following the "Inner Light"

The American writer who probably had the greatest influence in the mid-1800s was Ralph Waldo Emerson. People flocked to hear him read his essays stressing the importance of the individual. Each person,

Chapter 14 • **417**

 Lesson Planner

For a developed **Cooperative Learning** lesson plan, see the *Lesson Planner*, page 87.

Answer to Caption

Possible Answer: Toni Morrison, Amy Tan, Virginia Hamilton, Nikki Giovanni

Audiocassettes

Listening to Literature Audiocassettes Play Frank Johnson's jig "Bonnets of Blue" from *New Cotillions* (side 3, 1:16), from *Listening to Literature Audiocassettes, The American Experience*. (Enrichment/Easy)
Listening to Literature Audiocassettes To offer students an example of hymns from this era, play "Northfield" from *The Carmina Sacra* (side 4, 1:17), from *Listening to Literature Audiocassettes, The American Experience*. (Enrichment/Easy)

Our Multicultural Heritage

Biography Have students read the biography, Ralph Waldo Emerson, New England Individualist, on page 41 of the *Our Multicultural Heritage* booklet. (Enrichment/Challenging)

CD-ROM

History Makers Access the biography of Emily Dickinson on the American Heritage® *History of the United States* CD-ROM. (Enrichment/Average)

Team-Teaching Suggestion
Literature

You might want to work with a literature teacher to present a lesson on the life and poetry of Emily Dickinson. After reading and discussing a selection of Dickinson's poems, students can compile and illustrate their own book of favorite Dickinson poems. Encourage students to memorize several of their choices.

Connections With Literature
Background

Walt Whitman worked as a carpenter, a reporter, and a nurse in a Civil War hospital. His poems, though largely ignored in his lifetime, revolutionized modern American poetry. Whitman wrote, "The old and motheaten systems of Europe have had their day. Here we have planted the standard of freedom, and here we will test the capacities of men for self-government."

Other famous poets of this period included William Cullen Bryant, James Russell Lowell,

Oliver Wendell Holmes, and Edgar Allan Poe. Poe also wrote such famous horror short stories as "The Pit and the Pendulum" and "The Tell-Tale Heart," as well as the first detective story, "The Gold Bug."

The most prominent black abolitionist poet was Frances Watkins Harper. Born to a free family in Baltimore, she also wrote fiction and was a lecturer for the Anti-Slavery Society. Her poems include "Bury Me in a Free Land."

Answer to Caption

Possible Answer: By celebrating Americans of all kinds, Whitman showed that every individual had value. The poems supported the idea of a nation where each individual had a voice.

Voices of Freedom

Primary Source You might assign selection 16-5, A Plea for Simplicity, on page 111 of *Voices of Freedom*. This selection is taken from Thoreau's *Walden,* in which he urged Americans not to get caught up in the growing complexities of life. (Enrichment/Average)

Audiocassettes

Listening to Literature Audiocassettes To give students a general lesson about oral interpretation of poetry, have them listen to "Thanatopsis" (side 3, 4:47) and "The Raven" (side 3, 10:16) from *Listening to Literature Audiocassettes, The American Experience.* (Enrichment/Easy)

BIOGRAPHY Walt Whitman *"I hear America singing,"* wrote Walt Whitman. In his poems, Whitman celebrated Americans of all kinds—from carpenters to seamstresses to runaway slaves. This portrait of Whitman was done by Thomas Eakins, one of the great American portrait painters. **Culture** How did Whitman's poetry support the ideals of democracy?

Emerson said, has an "inner light." He urged people to use this inner light to guide their lives.

Henry David Thoreau (thuh ROW), Emerson's friend and neighbor, believed that the growth of industry and the rise of cities were ruining the nation. Thoreau tried to live as simply as possible. A person's wealth, he said, is measured by the number of things he or she can do without.

Thoreau's best-known work is *Walden.* In it, he tells of a year spent alone in a cabin on Walden Pond in Massachusetts. Like Emerson, Thoreau believed that each person must decide what is right or wrong:

66 If a man does not keep pace with his companions, perhaps it is because he hears a different drummer.

Let him step to the music he hears. 99

Thoreau's "different drummer" told him that slavery was wrong. He was a fierce abolitionist and served as a conductor on the underground railroad.

American Landscapes

Before the 1800s, American painters traveled to Europe to study art. Benjamin West of Philadelphia, for example, settled in London. In 1772, he was appointed historical painter to King George III.

Many American painters journeyed to London to study with West. They included Charles Willson Peale, Gilbert Stuart, and John Singleton Copley, among the best American portrait painters of the time. Both Peale and Stuart painted well-known pictures of George Washington.

By the mid-1800s, American artists began to develop their own style. The first group to do so became known as the *Hudson River School* because they painted landscapes of New York's Hudson River region. Two of the best-known painters of the Hudson River School were Thomas Cole and Asher B. Durand. In his murals, African American artist Robert S. Duncanson also reflected the style of this school.

Other American artists painted scenes of hard-working farm families and country people. George Caleb Bingham was inspired by his native Missouri. His paintings

Linking Past and Present
Stuart's portraits of Washington are among the most familiar images of the first President. In fact, you probably see a Stuart portrait of Washington every day—on the one-dollar bill.

Connections With Art
Background

In the early 1800s, American artists such as Washington Allston, John Vanderlyn, and Samuel F.B. Morse, who were dedicated to the European tradition of art, rejected contemporary subjects and painted only noble and spiritual subjects of the past, which had little relevance to American life. Strangely enough, it was an immigrant, Thomas Cole, born and raised in England, who captured the beauty of the American landscape on canvas and delighted other artists and art lovers native to America. Artists at that time were often paid in goods rather than in money; Thomas Cole once received a saddle for a fine portrait he painted in America.

Shortly thereafter, the old European-style paintings fell out of favor, and the artists who painted in that style could no longer sell their works. Samuel F.B. Morse began concentrating on scientific projects instead of art. The result was the telegraph.

Connections With Art
Activity

Have interested students research paintings done by artists mentioned in this section. Students can bring to class copies of the artist's work from art books, museum print collections, or library picture collections, to discuss the following questions: Does the painting reflect a particular school of painting? What does the painting show about the daily life of the period? What is the theme of the painting?

Catskill Scene *Artists of the Hudson River School captured the gentle beauty of New York's Catskill Mountain region. This painting,* View of Troy, New York, *is by William Richardson Tyler.* **The Arts** *How did painters of the mid-1800s differ from earlier American painters?*

show frontier life along the rivers that feed the great Mississippi.

Several painters tried to capture the culture of Native Americans on canvas. George Catlin and Alfred Jacob Miller traveled to the Far West. Their paintings record the daily life of Indians on the Great Plains and in the Rocky Mountains.

Artists of the 1800s celebrated the vast American landscape. They expressed confidence in Americans and their future. This confidence was shared by reformers in the East and by the thousands of Americans opening up new frontiers in the West.

SECTION 4 REVIEW

1. **Identify:** (a) Washington Irving, (b) Nathaniel Hawthorne, (c) Herman Melville, (d) William Wells Brown, (e) Henry Wadsworth Longfellow, (f) Hudson River School, (g) George Catlin.
2. List the important themes that each of the following stressed in his work: (a) John Greenleaf Whittier, (b) Walt Whitman, (c) Ralph Waldo Emerson, (d) Henry David Thoreau.
3. Describe the works of each of the following: (a) Margaret Fuller, (b) Emily Dickinson.
4. What subjects did some artists paint in the 1800s?
5. **CRITICAL THINKING Drawing Conclusions** Why do you think artists and writers did not develop a unique American style until the mid-1800s?

 Writing to Learn

Imagine that you are an art critic. Write a paragraph summarizing your reaction to the painting above.

Answers to Section 4 Review

CHAPTER 14 REVIEW

Answers to Reviewing the Main Ideas

1. belief in the ideal that "all men are created equal," as set forward in the Declaration of Independence; belief that it was sinful to own another human being
2. (a) Many northern mill owners, bankers, and merchants did business with the South and viewed attacks on slavery as a threat to their livelihood; some northern workers feared that if slavery ended, free blacks would come north and take their jobs by working for lower wages. (b) Some southern planters argued that slaves were better off than factory workers in the North; others defended slavery as an essential part of their economy.
3. equality for women at work, school, and church; the right to vote
4. (a) Sojourner Truth used her power as a speaker to argue for women's rights. (b) Stanton helped to organize the Seneca Falls Convention. (c) Lyon worked to improve women's education and founded Mount Holyoke, the first college for women.
5. New York and Massachusetts, followed by other northern states, set up free, tax-supported elementary schools; extended the school year; and raised teachers' salaries.
6. American writers began to write stories about American life using American themes.
7. Themes included landscapes of New York's Hudson River region, frontier life, and the daily life of Native Americans.

Answers to Thinking Critically

1. (a) Abolitionists printed articles and made speeches about the brutal treatment of slaves. They also held antislavery meetings at which former slaves vividly described their lives. (b) Possible Answer: They use television and radio as well as the print medium to influence public opinion.
2. Possible Answer: No one could speak about the horrors of slavery with better authenticity than a former slave.

3. (a) Possible Answer: Without education, women could not hope to compete with men for good jobs or to take part successfully in public debate. (b) Possible Answer: Newly educated women took a more active role in American life and used their writing skills to promote the women's rights movement.
4. Possible Answer: Early colonists and pioneers in the West had to be self-reliant and independent in order to succeed. Because American writers wrote about the lives of these people, the stories naturally reflected the same themes.

Answers to Applying Your Skills

1. Possible Answer: I am an American, and I love my country. Still, I hope that my country will soon rid itself of the shame of slavery.
2. Answers will vary. Students should recognize that abolitionists and women's rights leaders had not achieved many of their goals by the mid-1800s.

Answers to Thinking About Geography

1. B 2. D 3. F 4. E 5. C
6. A
Region: South Carolina, Maryland

Summary

- In the mid-1800s, many Americans worked to end slavery in the United States.
- Women gained opportunities in education and other areas.
- The spirit of reform led Americans to call for better prison conditions, improvements in education and health care, and a ban on alcohol.
- American writers and artists began to use American themes in the 1800s.

Reviewing the Main Ideas

1. What were the political and religious ideas behind the antislavery movement?
2. (a) Why were some northerners opposed to the antislavery movement? (b) How did some southerners justify slavery?
3. What did women at the Seneca Falls Convention demand?
4. State the role each of the following played in the movement for women's rights: (a) Sojourner Truth, (b) Elizabeth Cady Stanton, (c) Mary Lyon.
5. How did American public schools improve in the mid-1800s?
6. How did American writers of the mid-1800s break free of European traditions?
7. What themes did American painters select in the mid-1800s?

Thinking Critically

1. **Linking Past and Present** (a) What did abolitionists do to win public support? (b) How do reform leaders today try to win support for their causes?
2. **Understanding Causes and Effects** Why do you think former slaves were especially effective speakers for the abolitionist cause?
3. **Drawing Conclusions** (a) Why do you think leaders in the women's rights move-

ment believed that education was a key to winning equality? (b) What effect do you think the opening of schools for women had on the women's rights movement?
4. **Analyzing Information** American writers in the 1800s stressed the importance of the individual. How did the writers' emphasis on the individual reflect the events and themes of American history?

Applying Your Skills

1. **Finding the Main Idea** Reread the statement by Henry Highland Garnet on page 402. Then write one or two sentences summarizing the main idea.
2. **Making a Review Chart** Make a review chart with five columns and three rows. Label the columns Abolition, Women's Rights, Care for the Mentally Ill, Prison Reform, Education Reform. Label the rows Problems to Solve, Leaders, Achievements. Then complete the chart. Which movement do you think achieved the most? Explain.

Thinking About Geography

Match the letters on the map with the following places: **1.** Massachusetts, **2.** New York, **3.** South Carolina, **4.** Maryland, **5.** Connecticut, **6.** Maine. **Region** Which states identified by letters on the map were part of the slaveholding region?

420 • Chapter 14

INTERDISCIPLINARY ACTIVITY

Traveling on the Underground Railroad

Form into groups to review the underground railroad. Follow the suggestions below to write, draw, dance, or give an oral presentation to show what you have learned about this famous escape route. You may use the textbook, encyclopedias, atlases, or other materials in your classroom library to complete the tasks. Be able to name your sources of information when you have finished the activity.

Harriet Tubman, at left, with people she led to freedom

CARTOGRAPHERS Create a map showing the routes taken by the underground railroad. The routes should start in the slave states of the South and extend to free states in the North as well as to Canada. Include a scale and a directional arrow.

MATHEMATICIANS Based on the map created by the cartographers, calculate the distances that escaping slaves had to travel along the different routes of the underground railroad. Then, based on people being able to walk about 10 miles a day, calculate how long it took to escape along each route. Make a chart of your statistics.

On the way to freedom

HISTORIANS Prepare brief profiles of these abolitionists: Frederick Douglass, William Lloyd Garrison, Angelina and Sarah Grimké, Sojourner Truth, Harriet Tubman, and John Greenleaf Whittier. Present your profiles in writing or as oral histories.

ARTISTS Design a mural depicting the flight of slaves on the underground railroad.

DANCERS Create a dance showing an escape along the underground railroad. Have dancers represent the "conductor" and the various escaping slaves, including mothers and children. Your dance should dramatize incidents along the escape route, as well as the feelings of the escaped slaves when they reached freedom.

"Station" on the underground railroad

★ Organize a Traveling on the Underground Railroad Day and have each group present its activity to the rest of the school.

Interdisciplinary ACTIVITY

Learning Styles

The following chart indicates the activities appropriate for different learning styles.

Visual Learners
  Cartographers
  Artists
  Mathematicians
  Dancers

Auditory Learners
  Historians

Kinesthetic Learners
  Dancers

Evaluation

Cartographers Map backgrounds should be approximately correct, with major bodies of water and mountain ranges correctly placed. Information concerning the routes of the underground railroad should be accurate.

Mathematicians Calculations should be accurate; charts should be organized into meaningful categories, with statistics recorded neatly.

Historians Written and oral profiles should present a clear, organized, and accurate summary of the important aspects of the subject's life. In addition, the profiles should discuss the subject's contribution to the antislavery movement.

Artists Murals should reflect an understanding of the events, emotions, and issues related to the flight from slavery. Artistic ability need not be a criterion, but murals should tell a story and/or represent a theme.

Dancers Dance interpretations or dramatizations should exhibit originality. They should tell a story and/or represent a theme. They might also reflect an understanding of the emotional impact the flight from slavery had on various people along the route of the underground railroad.

Assessment

Chapter Resources Binder For a more comprehensive evaluation of student understanding of this chapter, assign Chapter Tests A and B and/or Extra Unit Questions from Unit 4, pages 49–54 and 57–59.

Computer Test Bank You can use Chapter Tests and Extra Unit Questions to create your own tests for both testing and retesting.

Alternative Assessment

Chapter Resources Binder See the Alternative Assessment booklet in the *Social Studies Educator's Handbook* series.

Portfolio You might meet with students to choose appropriate work from the chapter for inclusion in their portfolios.

Author Note

Gary Paulsen A well-known and prolific author of children's books, Gary Paulsen has won three Newbery Awards. His works of fiction and nonfiction deal with such diverse subjects as the Vietnam War, tracking and hunting, and dogsled racing. In addition to giving public readings and performances, Paulsen is involved in a variety of activities and is active in civic causes.

Vocabulary

The vocabulary in this selection is not particularly difficult. Some students, however, might be unfamiliar with the use of dialect. Have them point out words or phrases that are examples of dialect.

Prereading Focus

You might have students reread pages 393–394 in Chapter 13 to review what they have learned about slave codes making it a crime for a slave to learn how to read or write.

Motivation/Prior Knowledge

Ask whether students are familiar with the phrase "Knowledge is power." Have a volunteer explain what it means. Then ask students whether or not they agree with the idea expressed in that phrase.

Purpose-Setting Question

Ask: Imagine that you are a slave who has been forbidden to learn to read or write. How would you respond if someone offered to teach you?

Discussion Questions

1. When Sarny used a stick to write "100 lbs." in the dirt, how did her mother react? Why? (She hit her in the head almost knocking her to the ground. She was fearful of what the owners would do if they saw Sarny writing anything; she knew the punishment could be severe.)

History Through LITERATURE

Nightjohn
Gary Paulsen

Introduction *Nightjohn*, set in the 1850s, is told by Sarny, a 12-year-old slave on a southern plantation. When John comes to live there, Sarny's life is changed forever. John had escaped to the North. Yet, he came back—to teach others to read. As this excerpt begins, Sarny is talking to John late at night in the slave quarters. She is deciding whether to let John teach her some letters.

I knew about reading. It was something that the people in the white house did from paper. They could read words on paper. But we weren't allowed to be reading. We weren't allowed to understand or read nothing but once I saw some funny lines on the side of a feed sack. It said:

100 lbs.

I wrote them down in the dirt with a stick and mammy gave me a smack on the back of the head that like to drove me into the ground.

"Don't you take to that, take to writing," she said.

"I wasn't doing it. I was just copying something I saw on a feed sack."

"Don't. They catch you doing that and they'll think you're learning to read. You learn to read and they'll whip you. . . . Or cut your thumb off. Stay away from writing and reading."

So I did. But I remembered how it had looked, the drawings on the sack and in the dirt, and it still puzzled me. . . .

[Remembering this incident, Sarny speaks to John.]

"You saying you can read?"

He nodded.

"I give you something to read, you can read it? Just like that?"

"I can." . . .

"Way it works," he said, "is you got to learn all the letters and numbers before you can learn to read. You got to learn the alphabet."

"Alphabet?"

He nodded. "There be lots of letters, and each one means something different. You got to learn each one."

. . . Then he made a drawing with his thumb.

A

"Tonight we just do *A*." He sat back on his heels and pointed. "There it be.". . .

"What does it mean?"

"It means *A*—just like I said. It's the first letter in the alphabet. And when you see it you make a sound like this: *ayyy*, or *ahhhh*."

2. (a) Why did John laugh when Sarny said reading was not "hard at all"? (Because all she had learned was the very first letter, but she thought she knew all about reading.)

3. Why do you think Sarny was not able to sleep? (Possible Answer: She had been introduced to a whole new world. She was excited about what reading could mean for her.)

Historical Sidelight

In his autobiography, the African American abolitionist Frederick Douglass recalled an experience he had as a young child. A woman in whose home Douglass was a slave, had begun to teach him to read. When her husband found out, he forbade the lessons. The man's reaction profoundly affected Douglass. He began to understand that knowledge is power. As long as slave-owners kept knowledge away from their slaves, they kept those slaves under their control.

As a result of that experience, Frederick Douglass became determined to learn to read and write. Knowledge offered him a path to power—and to freedom!

Late Night Lesson *By the mid-1800s, many southern states had made it illegal for slaves to learn to read and write. Yet, as this illustration shows, some slaves took risks to learn anyway.* **Daily Life** *One enslaved African American recalled, "My father and other boys used to crawl under the house an' lie on the ground to hear massa read the newspaper to missus." Why might slaves have considered education so valuable?*

"That's reading? To make that sound?"

He nodded. "When you see that letter on paper or a sack or in the dirt you make one of those sounds. That's reading."

"Well that ain't hard at all."

He laughed. That same low roll. Made me think of thunder long ways off, moving in a summer sky. "There's more to it. Other letters. But that's it."

"Why they be cutting our thumbs off if we learn to read—if that's all it is?"

"'Cause to know things, for us to know things, is bad for them. We get to wanting and when we get to wanting it's bad for them. They thinks we want what they got. . . . That's why they don't want us reading." He sighed. "I got to rest now. They run me ten miles in a day and worked me into the ground. I need some sleep."

He moved back to the corner and settled down and I curled up to mammy in amongst the young ones again.

A, I thought, *Ayyy, ahhhh.* There it is. I be reading.

"Hey there in the corner," I whispered.

"What?"

"What's your name?"

"I be John."

"I be Sarny."

"Go to sleep, Sarny."

But I didn't. I snuggled into mammy and pulled a couple of the young ones in for heat and kept my eyes open so I wouldn't sleep and thought:

A.

THINKING ABOUT LITERATURE

1. Why did Sarny's mother tell her to stay away from reading and writing?
2. According to John, why did the slave owners want to keep the slaves from learning to read and write?
3. **CRITICAL THINKING Analyzing Information** Based on this excerpt, what are some of John's qualities? How can you tell?

ACTIVITY List five ways that your life would be different if you could not read or write. Write a story or act out a skit about what your life would be like.

Unit 5
The Nation Torn Apart

Unit Focus

Have students examine the sculpture by Augustus Saint-Gaudens on these pages and read the caption that describes it. Ask: How does this scene make you feel? What might the soldiers' thoughts have been as they marched along? As students think about the Civil War era, have them read the three chapter summaries. You might use questions such as the following to stimulate discussion.

1. Does the sculpture make you feel excited about the possibility of going off to war? Explain.
2. (a) What do you know about slavery? (b) Why was slave labor more important to the South than to the North?
3. Most of you have heard of the Gettysburg Address. Who gave that speech, and how is it connected with the Civil War?
4. The caption on page 425 describes the Civil War as "long and bloody." Why do you think the rebuilding of the South took such a long time?
5. Notice the title of Unit 5 — The Nation Torn Apart. (a) Based on the information in the three chapter summaries, what attitudes caused this division? (b) Do you think that those attitudes disappeared just because the war ended? Explain.

Connections With Art
Background

Augustus Saint-Gaudens (1848–1907) was born in Ireland but brought to the United States as an infant. He became the leading American sculptor of his day. Saint-Gaudens was a teenager during the Civil War, and at the age of 13 he was apprenticed to a cameo cutter in New York City. In 1876, he was commissioned to create a statue of Admiral David Farragut. His success established his reputation. Saint-Gaudens did much of his work in bronze, and he sculpted many monuments in the United States.

The 54th Massachusetts, depicted in the *Shaw Memorial*

The Nation Torn Apart

CHAPTER 15
The Road to Civil War
(1820–1861)

After many attempts at compromise over the issue of slavery, the North and South went to war.

....

CHAPTER 16
Torn by War
(1861–1865)

The Civil War between the North and South tested the strength of the Union.

....

CHAPTER 17
Rebuilding the Nation
(1864–1877)

During Reconstruction, the South slowly rebuilt, African Americans gained new rights, and the United States became united once more.

(1897), was the first African American volunteer infantry regiment in the Civil War. It was led by Colonel Robert Gould Shaw. Shaw and half his troops died in battle at Charleston in July 1863, but the heroism of the regiment changed many people's views about African American soldiers. (The history of this regiment was re-created in the 1989 film *Glory;* Saint-Gaudens's monument is shown during the film's credits.) Today, the monument stands in Boston Common.

Connections With Art
Activity

Ask questions such as the following to stimulate discussion about the sculpture.
1. (a) Who is seated on the horse? (b) Why is everyone else walking?
2. This monument does not glorify war, but the figures in it do seem noble. When Saint-Gaudens was planning this work, what do you think he found noble about his subject matter?
3. How does this monument illustrate the deep divisions among the people of the United States?

Bulletin Board Suggestion

Have students create a bulletin board display of the key figures in the nation during the period 1820–1877. Among those whom they may wish to include are Abraham Lincoln, Ulysses S. Grant, Jefferson Davis, Daniel Webster, Henry Clay, Clara Barton, Sojourner Truth, and John C. Calhoun. Each figure should be represented by a picture and an index card briefly describing his or her importance.

Art Gallery Posters

Frederick Douglass Series, No. 31, by Jacob Lawrence, is appropriate for Unit 5. Lesson suggestions for the poster appear in the *Art Gallery: Our Common Heritage Posters* Teacher's Guide. The art also appears in Chapter 17, page 498, of the student book.

CD-ROM

Time Tour Access The Nation Torn Apart section of the Time Tour on the American Heritage® *History of the United States* CD-ROM to accompany Unit 5. (Enrichment/Average)

Differences between the North and South, especially over slavery, triggered a long and bloody civil war. This monument honors the 54th Massachusetts, an African American regiment in the war.

Unit 5 • 425

Connections With the World
Activity

Have students review the discussion of serfs on pages 62–63. Tell students that Russian serfs of the late 1800s lived much as they had during the Middle Ages — they were permanently attached to the land, and they could be sold along with the land. Furthermore, runaway serfs could be punished severely. Ask: How were serfs in Russia similar to slaves in the United States? Why do you think movements to end slavery appeared in different parts of the world during the 1800s? Encourage volunteers to find out more about the freeing of Russian serfs and then to report on their findings to the class.

Linking Past and Present
Activity

Have students examine the figures in the monument and comment on their uniforms and equipment. Ask: What kinds of weapons are they carrying? Do you think that carrying so much equipment on their backs would hinder them in battle? If any students have seen a reenactment of a Civil War battle, ask them to share their memories. Then ask: How are the weapons of soldiers and armies different today? Is warfare today any more efficient, or any less destructive, than the warfare of the mid-1800s?

Lessons	Teaching Resources
1 Slavery or Freedom in the West **Objectives** 1. Explain why the issue of slavery flared up in 1819. 2. Identify the Missouri Compromise. 3. Identify the goal of the Free Soil party.	**Lesson Planner** Cooperative Learning, p. 90 **Student Study Guide** Section 1 Study Guide, p. 120 **Chapter Resources Binder, Unit 5** *Geography in History* Slavery, Politics, and Farming in Illinois, pp. 5–6 **Interdisciplinary Connections:** The Debate Over Slavery ꞏ ■ *Arts* A Story That Moved the World, p. 86 　■ *Sciences* Components of a Compromise, p. 87 　■ *World* Abolitionists Abroad, p. 88 　■ *Economics* Two Systems of Labor Organization, p. 89 　■ *Civics* The Free Soil Party, p. 90
2 Saving the Union **Objectives** 1. Explain why the slavery question arose again in 1850. 2. Describe how the North and South reached another compromise. 3. Describe how the issue of fugitive slaves divided the North and South.	**Lesson Planner** Cooperative Learning, p. 91 **Student Study Guide** Section 2 Study Guide, p. 121 **Our Multicultural Heritage** *Milestone* Challenging the Fugitive Slave Law, p. 45 **Chapter Resources Binder, Unit 5** *Critical Thinking* Drawing Conclusions, p. 3
3 Bloodshed in Kansas **Objectives** 1. Identify the events that made the issue of slavery emerge again in 1854. 2. Explain why proslavery and antislavery forces moved into Kansas. 3. Describe how the Dred Scott decision divided the nation.	**Lesson Planner** Cooperative Learning, p. 92 **Student Study Guide** Section 3 Study Guide, p. 122 **Chapter Resources Binder, Unit 5** *History Through Literature* My Bondage and My Freedom, p. 4
4 Republicans Challenge Slavery **Objectives** 1. Explain why a new political party took shape in the mid-1850s. 2. Describe how Abraham Lincoln viewed slavery. 3. Describe how the raid on Harpers Ferry deepened differences between the North and South.	**Lesson Planner** Cooperative Learning, p. 93 **Student Study Guide** Section 4 Study Guide, p. 123 **Our Multicultural Heritage** *Biography* Carl Schurz, Man of Conscience, p. 43
5 The South Breaks Away **Objectives** 1. Describe how the South reacted to Lincoln's victory in 1860. 2. Identify the Confederate States of America. 3. Identify the events that led to the outbreak of the Civil War.	**Lesson Planner** Cooperative Learning, p. 94 **Student Study Guide** Section 5 Study Guide, p. 124 **Chapter Resources Binder, Unit 5** *Skill Application* Reading an Election Map, p. 2 **Our Multicultural Heritage** *Biography* Mary Boykin Chesnut, Civil War Diarist, p. 44

Multimedia Resources	Additional Resources	Chapter-Level Resources
Transparencies *Interdisciplinary Connections* Missouri Compromise, p. B-61 **CD-ROM** *Presidents* Zachary Taylor **Videotapes/Videodiscs** *United States History Video Collection* Liberty and the Constitution, Vol. 8, Ch. 25	**Voices of Freedom** A Question of Slavery in the West, p. 112 **Historical Outline Map Book** The Missouri Compromise, 1820, p. 45	**Lesson Planner** Activity Based, pp. 95–96 **Student Study Guide** Chapter 15 Study Guide, pp. 125–126 **Chapter Resources Binder** **Unit 5** Vocabulary Building, p. 1 Chapter Test A, pp. 7–9 Chapter Test B, pp. 10–12 Illustration Master, p. 13 Extra Unit Questions, pp. 43–45 **English Guided Reading** Guided Reading, pp. 29-30 **Spanish Resources** **Computer Test Bank** Chapter Tests A and B Extra Unit Questions **Guided Reading Audiotapes** Side 6 **CD-ROM** *Time Tour* The Road to Civil War (1820-1861) in The Nation Torn Apart
CD-ROM *Presidents* Millard Fillmore *Face the Issues* Fugitive Slave Law *History Makers* Harriet Beecher Stowe **Videotapes/Videodiscs** *United States History Video Collection* Slavery and the Western Territories, Vol. 8, Ch. 28	**Voices of Freedom** How Can the Union Be Saved?, pp. 113–114 A Plea to Preserve the Union, pp. 114–115 The Suffering of Uncle Tom, pp. 115–116 **Historical Outline Map Book** The Compromise of 1850, p. 46 **Customized Reader** Description of a Southern Slave Catcher, article IVB-4	
Transparencies *Geography and History* North Central States, p. I-73 **CD-ROM** *Presidents* Franklin Pierce **Videotapes/Videodiscs** *United States History Video Collection* Dred Scott vs. John F.A. Sandford, Vol. 8, Ch. 31	**Customized Reader** The Destruction of Lawrence, Kansas, article IVB-17 Editorials About Brooks' Beating of Sumner, article IVB-16 **Voices of Freedom** The Dred Scott Decision: A Black View, p. 117 **Historical Outline Map Book** Kansas-Nebraska Act, 1854, p. 47	
CD-ROM *Presidents* James Buchanan *Presidents* Abraham Lincoln	**Voices of Freedom** Singing the Praises of John Brown, pp. 117–118	
Videotapes/Videodiscs *United States History Video Collection* A House Divided, Vol. 8, Ch. 34; 1861 Crisis at Sumter, Vol. 9, Ch. 7		

Lesson Planner

For a fully developed **Activity-Based** lesson plan for Chapter 15, see the *Lesson Planner*, pages 95–96.

Chapter Resources

Vocabulary Building The Vocabulary Building worksheet for Chapter 15 from Unit 5, page 1, of the *Chapter Resources* binder can be used as a prereading activity or as a review of chapter vocabulary. (Reteaching/Easy)

 Student Study Guide

Chapter 15 Study Guide Refer students to pages 125–126 of the *Student Study Guide* for the Chapter 15 Study Guide. The study guide can be used for chapter review as well as for reteaching. (Reteaching/Average)

Guided Reading Audiotapes

Students can use *Guided Reading Audiotapes,* Chapter 15, side 6, to listen to section previews, summaries, and review questions. The tapes will benefit students who are auditory learners, students who have trouble reading, or students acquiring English. (Reteaching/Easy)

CHAPTER 15

The Road to Civil War

(1820–1861)

CHAPTER OUTLINE

1 Slavery or Freedom in the West

2 Saving the Union

3 Bloodshed in Kansas

4 Republicans Challenge Slavery

5 The South Breaks Away

1820 *The Missouri Compromise extended slavery to some territories west of the Mississippi River. Here, slaves pick cotton on a plantation.*

1852 *Harriet Beecher Stowe published* Uncle Tom's Cabin. *The novel helped stir antislavery feeling in the North.*

1850 *The Fugitive Slave Law enraged northerners. The law required that all citizens help catch runaway slaves.*

| 1820 | 1848 | 1850 | 1852 | 1854 |

 WORLD EVENT 1833 Slavery abolished in British Empire

WORLD EVENT 1848 France abolishes slavery in West Indian colonies

Chapter Time Line
Understanding Chronology

To check students' understanding of the sequence of events on this time line, divide the class into groups of three or four students each. Give each group an identical list of the events mentioned on the time line, with the items in the list out of order. See which group is the first to assign the correct dates to the items and then to sequence the events correctly.

Students Acquiring English
Activity

Students who are learning English as a second language often have difficulty with irregular verb tenses in English. When reading, these students will sometimes fail to make the connection between an irregular past tense verb and the present tense verb form. In writing, students will often use the present tense or attempt to form the past tense in the regular way by adding -ed; for example, they might write *growed* instead of *grew*. You may wish to call attention to the following irregular verbs from the chapter: *speak, become, choose, do, lose, draw, arise, win, fight, see, think, give, rise, come, read, tell, take, catch, write, buy,* and *feel.* Have students enter these verbs and their past tense in a writing journal for use later on.

Chapter Setting

On June 16, 1858, a lawyer named Abraham Lincoln spoke before a crowded convention hall in Springfield, Illinois:

“‘A house divided against itself cannot stand.’ I believe this government cannot endure permanently half slave and half free. I do not expect the Union to be dissolved—I do not expect the house to fall—but I do expect it will cease to be divided. It will become all one thing, or all the other. Either the opponents of slavery will arrest the further spread of it . . . or its [supporters] will push it forward till it shall become. . .lawful in all the states, old as well as new, North as well as South.”

Lincoln had just been chosen to run as the Republican candidate for the Senate. Few people outside Illinois had heard of him. His speech, however, became famous. Soon many northerners were repeating the phrase, "A house divided against itself cannot stand." They agreed that the nation could not go on half slave and half free.

By the 1850s, more and more northerners had turned against slavery. They strongly opposed southern attempts to open the new territories of the West to slavery. Time after time, North and South clashed over this issue.

By 1861, when Abraham Lincoln became President, Americans were worried. Could the Union that had existed for nearly a century remain whole?

ACTIVITY Read the lines from Lincoln's "house divided" speech out loud. Then draw a political cartoon that expresses the main idea of Lincoln's speech.

1854 *The Kansas-Nebraska Act led to violence in the Kansas Territory. Proslavery bands, like this one, clashed with antislavery forces there.*

1858 Illinois Senate candidates Abraham Lincoln and Stephen Douglas debated the issue of slavery. The debates earned Lincoln nationwide fame.

1860 South Carolina became the first state to secede from the Union. South Carolinians wore palmetto leaf ribbons as a symbol of defiance.

1854	1856	1858	1860	1862

WORLD EVENT
1861 Russian ruler frees serfs

Chapter 15 • **427**

Linking Past and Present
Activity

Discuss with students the definition of the word *compromise*. Bring out the concept that compromise is a settlement of differences in which each side agrees to give up some of what it wants. Have students provide examples of compromise from their own lives. Review the importance of compromise as a recurring theme in American history, especially at the Constitutional Convention. Then have students give examples of compromise in the operation of the federal government today. Make sure students understand that the lawmaking process requires that the House and the Senate, as well as the executive and legislative branches, reach compromises. Students might record examples of important compromises in American history on a time line.

Section 1
pp. 428–431

Bell Ringer

Ask students to list some reasons why slavery was a difficult issue on which to reach a compromise.

Lesson Plan

1. Focus The balance of free states and slave states in the westward-expanding nation was a divisive issue in the early 1800s. In this section, students focus on the growing conflict between the North and the South.

2. Instruct Have students present a dramatization in which senators in the 1840s debate the issue of slavery in the territories. Make sure the northern abolitionists, southern slave owners, and the two moderate positions mentioned in the text are represented. In a follow-up discussion, ask students to compare the arguments used.

3. Close To close the lesson, have students answer *Who, What, When, Where, Why,* and *How* questions about the debate over extending slavery into the Mexican Cession.

1
Slavery or Freedom in the West

FIND OUT
- Why did the issue of slavery flare up in 1819?
- What was the Missouri Compromise?
- What was the goal of the Free Soil party?

VOCABULARY sectionalism, popular sovereignty

In 1820, Thomas Jefferson was in his late seventies. The former President had vowed "never to write, talk, or even think of politics." Still, he voiced alarm when he heard about a fierce debate going on in Congress:

❝In the gloomiest moment of the revolutionary war, I never had any [fears] equal to what I feel from this source. . . . We have a wolf by the ears, and we can neither hold him nor safely let him go.❞

The "wolf" was the issue of slavery. Jefferson feared that the bitter quarrel would tear the country apart.

The Missouri Question

Louisiana was the first state carved out of the Louisiana Purchase, joining the Union as a slave state in 1812. Because slavery was well established there, few people protested. But when Missouri asked to join the Union as a slave state six years later, there was an uproar.

The admission of Missouri would upset the balance of power in the Senate. In 1819, there were 11 free states and 11 slave states. Each state had two senators. If Missouri became a slave state, the South would have a majority in the Senate. Determined not to lose power, northerners fought against letting Missouri enter as a slave state.

The argument over Missouri lasted many months. Finally, Senator Henry Clay proposed a compromise. During the long debate, Maine

A Slave Market *As Americans debated the issue of slavery, slave auctions like the one at left went on. The numbered tags were used by owners to identify slaves they rented out.* **Citizenship** *How did the entry of new states into the Union affect the debate over slavery?*

Cooperative Learning
Synthesizing Information

Divide the class into groups and ask students to imagine that they are part of a production team for a national news program, like *Nightline* or *The MacNeil/Lehrer Report*, on which major issues of the day are discussed in depth. Have students use the information in Section 1 to plan a program that would be informative to the public in the mid-1800s on the many issues surrounding the debate over slavery. Students must decide whom they would ask to be guests on the show and what they would ask each guest. They would also need to write a summary of the different political, economic, and moral positions toward slavery in order to provide the anchor with information he or she might need for the broadcast. Encourage each group to present its news program.

Connections With Language Arts
Background

During the debate over the Missouri Compromise, most congressmen wanted to have their stand on the issue entered into the record in the form of a speech. Many of the speeches were so boring that when North Carolina congressman Felix Walker asked to speak, the House refused to listen. Walker insisted that he be allowed to speak for his district, to "make a speech for Buncombe [County]." The phrase "speaking for Buncombe" became popular; it was also shortened to "bunkum" and then "bunk."

had also applied for statehood. Clay suggested admitting Missouri as a slave state and Maine as a free state. His plan, called the *Missouri Compromise,* kept the number of slave and free states equal.

As part of the Missouri Compromise, Congress drew an imaginary line across the southern border of Missouri at latitude 36° 30'N. Slavery was permitted in the part of the Louisiana Purchase south of that line. It was banned north of the line. The only exception was Missouri. (See the map on page 430.)

Slavery in the Mexican Cession

The Missouri Compromise applied only to the Louisiana Purchase. In 1848, the Mexican War added a vast stretch of western land to the United States. Once again, the question of slavery in the territories arose.

An antislavery plan. As you have read in Chapter 12, many northerners opposed the Mexican War. They feared that the South would extend slavery into the West. David Wilmot, a member of Congress from Pennsylvania, called for a law to ban slavery in any lands won from Mexico. Southern leaders angrily opposed the *Wilmot Proviso.* They said that Congress had no right to ban slavery in the territories.

In 1846, the House passed the Wilmot Proviso, but the Senate defeated it. As a result, Americans continued to argue about slavery in the West even while their army fought in Mexico.

Americans take sides. The Mexican War strengthened feelings of sectionalism in the North and South. Sectionalism is loyalty to a state or section, rather than to the country as a whole. Many southerners were united by their support for slavery. They saw the North as a growing threat to their way of life. Many northerners saw the South as a foreign country, where American rights and liberties did not exist.

As the debate over slavery heated up, people found it hard not to take sides. Northern abolitionists demanded that slavery be banned throughout the country. They insisted that slavery was morally wrong. By the late 1840s, a growing number of northerners agreed.

Southern slaveholders thought that slavery should be allowed in any territory. They also demanded that slaves who escaped to the North be returned to them. Even white southerners who did not own slaves agreed with these ideas.

Moderate views. Between these two extreme views were more moderate positions. Some moderates argued that the Missouri Compromise line should be extended across the Mexican Cession to the Pacific Ocean. Any new state north of the line would be a free state. Any new state south of the line could allow slavery.

Other moderates supported the idea of popular sovereignty. **Popular sovereignty** means control by the people. In other words, voters in a new territory would decide for themselves whether or not to allow slavery in the territory. Slaves, of course, could not vote.

A new political party. The debate over slavery led to the birth of a new political party. By 1848, many northerners in both the Democratic party and the Whig party opposed the spread of slavery. But the leaders of both parties refused to take a stand on the question. They did not want to give up their chance of winning votes in the South. Some also feared that the slavery issue would split the nation.

In 1848, antislavery members of both parties met in Buffalo, New York. There, they founded the *Free Soil party.* Their slogan was "Free soil, free speech, free labor, and free men." The main goal of the Free Soil party was to keep slavery out of the western territories. Only a few Free Soilers were abolitionists who wanted to end slavery in the South.

Chapter 15 • **429**

 Lesson Planner

For a developed **Cooperative Learning** lesson plan, see the *Lesson Planner,* page 90.

 Historical Outline Map Book

Historical Outline Map Use the map, The Missouri Compromise, 1820, on page 45 of the *American History Historical Outline Map Book.* Lesson ideas for this map can be found on page T15. (Reteaching/Average)

 Voices of Freedom

Primary Source You might assign selection 17-1, A Question of Slavery in the West, on page 112 of *Voices of Freedom.* The selection is from the Wilmot Proviso. (Enrichment/Average)

 Videotapes/ Videodiscs

United States History Video Collection Use the video segment "Liberty and the Constitution," from Volume 8, *Causes of the Civil War,* to enhance students' understanding of the issue of slavery in the territories. Approx. running time 1:50 min. (Enrichment/Average) Vol. 8, Ch. 25

 Chapter 25   Play

Connections With Civics
Background

Late in his long, illustrious political career, Senator Rufus King made the following comment about Missouri statehood: "Freedom and slavery are the parties which stand this day before the Senate; and upon its decision the empire of the one or the other will be established in the new state. . . . We are now about to pass our original boundary; if this can be done without affecting the principles of our free government, it can be accomplished only by the most vigilant attention to plant, cherish, and sustain the principles of liberty in the new states. . . . But if, instead of freedom, slavery is to prevail and spread as we extend our dominion, can any reflecting man fail to see the necessity of giving to the general government greater powers; to enable it to afford the protection that will be demanded of it; powers that will be difficult to control and which may prove fatal to the public liberties?"

Connections With Civics
Activity

The Wilmot Proviso was the first important rider to a routine congressional bill. Have students define the term *rider* as it applies to congressional legislation and have them find out the importance of riders in our congressional process. Ask students to research and report any pertinent information they can find out about an important or controversial rider to a recent congressional bill.

CONNECTIONS

For worksheets establishing connections between the Chapter 15 main idea, The Debate Over Slavery, and five other disciplines, see the *Interdisciplinary Connections* booklet. (Enrichment)

- **Arts** A Story That Moved the World, page 86 (Challenging)
- **Sciences** Components of a Compromise, page 87 (Average)
- **World** Abolitionists Abroad, page 88 (Average)
- **Economics** Two Systems of Labor Organization, page 89 (Easy)
- **Civics** The Free Soil Party, page 90 (Average)

Answer to Connections

It continued the line of the Ohio River west, and it formed the southern boundary of Missouri.

 Transparencies

Interdisciplinary Connections Use the transparency Missouri Compromise on page B-61 of *American History Transparencies*. Teaching suggestions can be found on page B-17. (Enrichment/Average)

ACTIVITY

Guided Instruction You may want to refer students to the map on page 437. As students conclude that Kansas and Nebraska would be admitted as free states, explain that in Section 2 they will see how this issue increased tensions later on.

| ARTS | SCIENCES | GEOGRAPHY | WORLD | ECONOMICS | CIVICS |

The Missouri Compromise—Why 36°30'?

In the Northwest Ordinance of 1787, Congress banned slavery north of the Ohio River. The ordinance applied to the newly acquired lands of the Northwest Territory. To antislavery forces, however, the Ohio River became a border between free and slave states. Before long, their decision to maintain that border was put to the test.

In 1818, Missouri applied for admission to the United States as a slave state, which caused turmoil. Antislavery forces pointed to the ban on slavery in the Northwest Ordinance. If the Ohio River line were carried westward, they pointed out, most of Missouri would lie north of it. To allow Missouri to enter as a slave state would break that line.

Debate dragged on through two sessions of Congress. When Maine applied for admission as a free state, some members of Congress saw a chance to resolve the issue.

They would allow Missouri to come in as a slave state. Then they would achieve a balance by admitting Maine as a free state. This proposal, however, failed to win enough support to be passed.

Hoping to break the deadlock, Senator Jesse B. Thomas of Illinois suggested an amendment. By the terms of Thomas's amendment, Congress would set the line 36°30'N as a permanent boundary between free and slave states west of the Mississippi River. Missouri, which already permitted slavery, would be the only exception. Thomas proposed 36°30' because it formed the southern boundary of Missouri. At the same time, it was only slightly south of 37°N, where the Ohio River ends.

Thomas's amendment turned the tide. In 1820, Congress passed the Maine-Missouri Bill. Maine entered the Union as a free state later that year. Missouri entered as a slave state in 1821.

■ Why did Congress choose the line 36°30' as the boundary between free states and slave states west of the Mississippi River?

Missouri Compromise

| | Free states and territories closed to slavery | | Slave states and territories open to slavery |

0   150   300 Miles
0   150   300 Kilometers

ACTIVITY On an outline map of the United States, locate and label Missouri, Kansas Territory, and Nebraska Territory. Then draw the Missouri Compromise line—36°30'N. Based on this line, would Kansas and Nebraska come in as free states or as slave states? Explain.

Team-Teaching Suggestion
Art

You might want to work with an art teacher to help students create murals and/or dioramas depicting what life was like for people living west of the Mississippi in 1820. You might advise students about how to research the information they need to know; the art teacher might advise them about how to better communicate the information visually.

A Three-Way Race *Slavery was an important issue in the 1848 presidential election. In this cartoon, the candidates race for the finish line—Zachary Taylor on a bloodhound, Martin Van Buren on a buffalo, and Lewis Cass on a bicycle.* **Citizenship** *What was each candidate's position on slavery?*

The Free Soil Challenge

While Americans debated the slavery question, the 1848 campaign for President took place. Free Soilers named former President Martin Van Buren as their candidate. Democrats chose Lewis Cass of Michigan. Whigs selected Zachary Taylor, a hero of the Mexican War.

For the first time, slavery was an important election issue. Van Buren called for a ban on slavery in the Mexican Cession. Cass supported popular sovereignty. Because Taylor was a slave owner from Louisiana, many southern voters assumed that he supported slavery.

In the end, Zachary Taylor won the election. Still, Van Buren took 10 percent of the popular vote. Thirteen other Free Soil candidates won seats in Congress. Only three months old, the Free Soil party had made a strong showing in the election. Their success showed that slavery had become a national issue.

SECTION 1 REVIEW

1. **Locate:** (a) Missouri, (b) Maine, (c) Missouri Compromise line.
2. **Identify:** (a) Missouri Compromise, (b) Wilmot Proviso, (c) Free Soil party, (d) Martin Van Buren, (e) Lewis Cass, (f) Zachary Taylor.
3. **Define:** (a) sectionalism, (b) popular sovereignty.
4. Why did Missouri's request to join the Union cause an uproar?
5. How did the Mexican War revive the issue of slavery?
6. **CRITICAL THINKING Analyzing Ideas** The slogan of the Free Soil party was "Free soil, free speech, free labor, and free men." Why might this slogan have appealed to voters in the North?

 Writing to Learn

Imagine that you are an African American living in the North in 1820. Write a letter to a newspaper to express your opinion of the Missouri Compromise.

Chapter 15 • **431**

Answer to Caption

Taylor—proslavery; Cass—popular sovereignty; Van Buren—no slavery in the western territories

 Chapter Resources

Geography in History Duplicate and distribute the worksheet, Slavery, Politics, and Farming in Illinois, from Unit 5, pages 5–6, of the *Chapter Resources* binder. (Enrichment/Challenging)

 CD-ROM

Presidents Access the biography of Zachary Taylor on the American Heritage® *History of the United States* CD-ROM. (Enrichment/Average)

Student Study Guide

Section 1 Study Guide Have students use the Section 1 Study Guide on page 120 of the *Student Study Guide* to review and reinforce the content of this section. (Reteaching/Average)

ACTIVITY

Guided Instruction Have students think about the early life experiences of the individuals they are pretending to be. For example, were they ever slaves? Are they free now, or are they fugitive slaves? Did they always live in the North? How did they learn to read and write? Challenge students to consider how these imaginary life experiences might motivate the letter writers.

Historical Sidelight

Background

Zachary Taylor was scheduled to be sworn in as President at noon on March 4, 1849—a Sunday. Not wanting to take an oath on the Sabbath, Taylor postponed his inauguration by one day. Thus, President Polk was succeeded by David Rice Atchison, the President Pro Tempore of the Senate. Atchison's 24-hour term of office was uneventful. In fact, Atchison spent most of the day asleep in bed. Taylor took over the presidency the next day, as rescheduled.

Answers to Section 1 Review

1. See the map on p. 430.
2. (a) Missouri Compromise, p. 429, (b) Wilmot Proviso, p. 429, (c) Free Soil party, p. 429, (d) Martin Van Buren, p. 431, (e) Lewis Cass, p. 431, (f) Zachary Taylor, p. 431
3. (a) sectionalism, p. 429, (b) popular sovereignty, p. 429
4. Missouri asked to join the Union as a slave state. Northerners protested admission because it would give the South a majority in the Senate, thus upsetting the balance of power between slave states and free states.
5. Americans had to decide whether to allow slavery in the Mexican Cession, which was not covered by the Missouri Compromise.
6. Possible Answer: Northern voters might be attracted by the word *free*; furthermore, the slogan made clear the party's antislavery stand, and a ban against slavery in the territories would give the North more power in Congress.

431

Section 2
pp. 432–435

Bell Ringer

Ask students to list as many states as they can that were in the Union by 1850. Have students mark each state as a free or a slave state. As they read on, students can revise or add to their lists.

Lesson Plan

1. Focus The issue of slavery flared up again when California applied for admission to the Union as a free state. In this section, students learn how three events fanned sectionalism: the Compromise of 1850, the Fugitive Slave Law, and the publication of *Uncle Tom's Cabin.*

2. Instruct Divide the class into several small groups. Ask students to imagine they are editors of newspapers. Some groups represent proslavery papers in the South; others, antislavery papers in the North. Have groups write editorials commenting on the Compromise of 1850. Students should describe the parts of the compromise, give their opinions of it, and predict how local people will react to it.

3. Close To close the lesson, have students answer the Find Out questions.

2
Saving the Union

FIND OUT

■ Why did the slavery question arise again in 1850?

■ How did the North and South reach another compromise?

■ How did the issue of fugitive slaves divide the North and South?

VOCABULARY fugitive, civil war

The issue of slavery in the West soon flared up again. In 1850, California asked to join the Union as a free state. Tempers raged as members of Congress tried to reach another compromise.

Senator Thomas Hart Benton of Missouri supported California's request. Most of California lay north of the Missouri Compromise line. Though a slave owner himself, Benton felt that the compromise had to be upheld. He denounced Senator Henry Foote of Mississippi for helping to block California's admission.

Foote rose angrily from his seat. Drawing a pistol, he pointed it at Benton's chest. As other senators watched in horror, Benton roared, "Let him fire! Stand out of the way and let the assassin fire!"

No blood was shed in the Senate that day. However, many Americans began to fear that a peaceful solution to the slavery issue was impossible.

Seeking a Compromise

For a time after the Missouri Compromise, both slave and free states had entered the Union peacefully. Between 1821 and 1848, Michigan, Iowa, and Wisconsin entered as free states. Arkansas, Florida, and

Texas came in as slave states. (See the graph below.)

When California requested admission as a free state, once again the balance of power in the Senate was threatened. Southerners did not want to give the North a majority in the Senate. They also feared that more free states might be carved out of the huge Mexican Cession. Some southerners even talked about seceding from the Union.

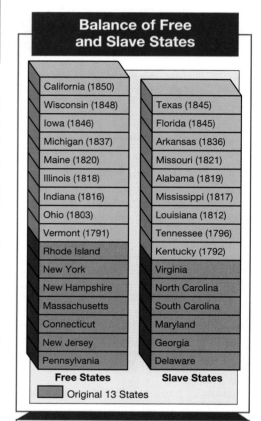

Balance of Free and Slave States

Free States	Slave States
California (1850)	
Wisconsin (1848)	Texas (1845)
Iowa (1846)	Florida (1845)
Michigan (1837)	Arkansas (1836)
Maine (1820)	Missouri (1821)
Illinois (1818)	Alabama (1819)
Indiana (1816)	Mississippi (1817)
Ohio (1803)	Louisiana (1812)
Vermont (1791)	Tennessee (1796)
Rhode Island	Kentucky (1792)
New York	Virginia
New Hampshire	North Carolina
Massachusetts	South Carolina
Connecticut	Maryland
New Jersey	Georgia
Pennsylvania	Delaware

▨ Original 13 States

GRAPH SKILLS *Both the North and the South were determined to maintain the delicate balance in the Senate between slave and free states.* ● *How did the admission of California affect this balance?*

A Great Debate *The Senate debated Henry Clay's proposed Compromise of 1850 for six months. Here, Clay appeals to his fellow senators to support his plan.* **Citizenship** *What was Clay's main goal in proposing the Compromise of 1850?*

Clay pleads for compromise. To resolve the crisis, Congress turned to Senator Henry Clay. Clay had won the nickname "the Great Compromiser" for working out the Missouri Compromise. Now, nearly 30 years later, the 73-year-old Clay was frail and ill. Still, he pleaded for the North and South to reach an agreement. If they failed to do so, Clay warned, the nation could break apart.

Calhoun replies. Senator John C. Calhoun of South Carolina prepared the South's reply to Clay. Calhoun was dying of tuberculosis and could not speak loudly enough to address the Senate. Wrapped in a heavy cloak, he glared at his northern foes while another senator read his speech.

Calhoun refused to compromise. He insisted that slavery be allowed in the western territories. Calhoun also demanded that **fugitive**, or runaway, slaves be returned to their owners in the South. Fugitives actually were few in number and not the real issue. Calhoun really wanted northerners to admit that southern slaveholders had the right to reclaim their "property."

If the North would not agree to the South's demands, Calhoun told the Senate, "let the states . . . agree to part in peace. If you are unwilling that we should part in peace, tell us so, and we shall know what to do." Everyone knew what Calhoun meant. If

an agreement could not be reached, the South would secede from the Union.

Webster calls for unity. Daniel Webster of Massachusetts spoke next. Webster had been Clay's rival for decades. Now he supported Clay's plea to save the Union. Webster stated his position clearly:

❝I speak today not as a Massachusetts man, nor as a northern man, but as an American. . . . I speak today for the preservation of the Union. . . . There can be no such thing as a peaceable secession. Peaceable secession is an utter impossibility.❞

Webster feared that the states could not separate without a civil war. A **civil war** is a war between people of the same country.

Like many northerners, Webster viewed slavery as evil. Disunion, however, he believed was worse. To save the Union, Webster was willing to compromise with the South. He would support the South's demand that northerners be required to return fugitive slaves.

A Compromise at Last

In 1850, while the debate raged, Calhoun died. His last words reportedly were "The South! The South! God knows what will become of her!" President Taylor also

Lesson Planner

For a developed **Cooperative Learning** lesson plan, see the *Lesson Planner,* page 91.

Answer to Caption

He wanted to preserve the Union.

 Voices of Freedom

Primary Source You might assign selection 17-2, How Can the Union Be Saved?, on pages 113–114 of *Voices of Freedom.* The selection is from Calhoun's speech in reply to Clay's proposal of compromise. (Enrichment/Average)
Primary Source You might assign selection 17-3, A Plea to Preserve the Union, on pages 114–115 of *Voices of Freedom.* The selection is from Daniel Webster's speech, in which he pleads to save the Union. (Enrichment/Average)

 Videotapes/ Videodiscs

United States History Video Collection Use the video segment "Slavery and the Western Territories" from Volume 8, *Causes of the Civil War,* to enhance students' understanding of attempts to solve the issue of the spread of slavery. Approx. running time 3:00 min. (Enrichment/Average) Vol. 8, Ch. 28

Chapter 28   Play

Critical Thinking
Asking Questions

Ask students to imagine that they are reporters preparing to interview Henry Clay, John C. Calhoun, and Daniel Webster about the Compromise of 1850. Have them prepare a list of questions that they would like to ask these leaders. Make sure students indicate whether the question is for one particular person or for all three.

Connections With Literature
Background

John Greenleaf Whittier, a noted New England poet and abolitionist, wrote about Daniel Webster in the poem "Ichabod": "All else is gone; from those great eyes / The soul has fled; / When faith is lost, when honor dies / The man is dead." Like many abolitionists, Whittier was disappointed by the Massachusetts senator's willingness to compromise.

died in 1850. Taylor had opposed Clay's compromise plan. The new President, Millard Fillmore, supported it. An agreement finally seemed possible.

Henry Clay gave more than 70 speeches in favor of a compromise. At last, however, he became too sick to continue. Stephen Douglas, a young and energetic senator from Illinois, took up the fight for him. Douglas tirelessly guided each part of Clay's plan, called the ***Compromise of 1850,*** through Congress.

The Compromise of 1850 had four parts. First, California was allowed to enter the Union as a free state. Second, the rest of the Mexican Cession was divided into the territories of New Mexico and Utah. In each territory, voters would decide the slavery question according to popular sovereignty. Third, the slave trade was ended in Washington, D.C., the nation's capital. Congress, however, declared that it had no power to ban the slave trade between slave states. Fourth, a strict new fugitive slave law was passed.

The North and South had reached a compromise. But neither side got all that it wanted. The new Fugitive Slave Law was especially hard for northerners to accept.

The Fugitive Slave Law of 1850

Most northerners had ignored the Fugitive Slave Law of 1793. As a result, fugitive slaves often lived as free citizens in northern cities. The ***Fugitive Slave Law of 1850*** was harder to ignore. It required all citizens to help catch runaway slaves. People who let fugitives escape could be fined $1,000 and jailed for six months.

The new law set up special courts to handle the cases of runaways. Judges received $10 for sending an accused runaway to the South. They received only $5 for setting someone free. Lured by the extra money, some judges sent African Americans to the South whether or not they were runaways. Fearful that they would be kidnapped and enslaved under the new law, thousands of free African Americans fled to Canada.

The Fugitive Slave Law enraged northerners. By forcing them to catch runaways, the law made northerners feel they were

Denouncing the Fugitive Slave Law *Many northerners viewed the Fugitive Slave Law as an "outrage to humanity." This engraving from a Boston newspaper shows abolitionist Wendell Phillips urging a crowd to disobey the hated law.* **Citizenship** *What does this picture suggest about the opponents of the Fugitive Slave Law?*

434 • Chapter 15

Connections With Literature
Background

The term *Uncle Tom* has meant different things at different times. Abolitionists in the mid-1800s used it to refer to a patient, suffering slave. To proslavery forces, *Uncle Tomism* meant "a love of blacks." The modern meaning, "a black who is submissive to whites," came into use in the 1940s.

Harriet Beecher Stowe, the author of *Uncle Tom's Cabin* (see page 435), wrote in the style of most women novelists of the day. For example, she depicted sentimental scenes such as the dramatic dying child-heroine, Little Eva, in *Uncle Tom's Cabin.* However, in the same book she also broke an important rule of "female" fiction by discussing politics.

part of the slave system. In several northern cities, crowds tried to rescue fugitive slaves from their captors. Martin R. Delany, an African American newspaper editor, spoke for many northerners, black and white:

66My house is my castle. . . . If any man approaches that house in search of a slave—I care not who he may be, whether constable or sheriff, magistrate or even judge of the Supreme Court . . . if he crosses the threshold of my door, and I do not lay him a lifeless corpse at my feet, I hope the grave may refuse my body a resting place.99

Calhoun had hoped that the Fugitive Slave Law would force northerners to admit that the slave owners did indeed have rights. Instead, each time the law was enforced, it convinced more northerners that slavery was evil.

An Antislavery Bestseller

An event in 1852 added to the growing antislavery mood of the North. That year, Harriet Beecher Stowe published a novel called *Uncle Tom's Cabin*. Stowe wrote the novel to show the evils of slavery and the injustice of the Fugitive Slave Law.

Stowe told the story of Uncle Tom, an enslaved African American noted for his kindness and his devotion to his religion. Tom is bought by Simon Legree, a cruel

Our Common Heritage
Elizabeth Cady Stanton praised Harriet Beecher Stowe for her work as a writer. Stowe, however, did not support Stanton's work for women's rights. In fact, she later wrote a book poking fun at Stanton and Victoria Woodhull, the first woman to run for President.

planter who treats his slaves brutally. In the end, Legree whips Uncle Tom until he dies.

The book had wide appeal in the North. In its first year, Stowe's novel sold 300,000 copies. It was also published in many different languages. Soon, a play based on the novel appeared in cities not only in the North but around the world.

Southerners claimed that *Uncle Tom's Cabin* did not give a true picture of slave life. Indeed, Stowe had seen little of slavery firsthand. Yet the book helped to change the way northerners felt about slavery. No longer could they ignore slavery as a political problem for Congress to settle. They now saw slavery as a moral problem facing every American. For this reason, *Uncle Tom's Cabin* was one of the most important books in American history.

SECTION 2 REVIEW

1. **Locate:** (a) California, (b) New Mexico Territory, (c) Utah Territory.
2. **Identify:** (a) Henry Clay, (b) John C. Calhoun, (c) Daniel Webster, (d) Stephen Douglas, (e) Compromise of 1850, (f) Fugitive Slave Law of 1850, (g) Harriet Beecher Stowe, (h) *Uncle Tom's Cabin.*
3. **Define:** (a) fugitive, (b) civil war.
4. Why did California's request for statehood raise the slavery issue again?
5. Why did many northerners and southerners support the Compromise of 1850?
6. What did northerners dislike about the Fugitive Slave Law of 1850?
7. **CRITICAL THINKING Forecasting** Do you think the Compromise of 1850 offered a lasting solution to the slavery question? Explain.

ACTIVITY **Writing to Learn**
Write a short skit showing how the Fugitive Slave Law of 1850 stirred northern feelings against slavery.

Our Multicultural Heritage

Milestone Have students read Challenging the Fugitive Slave Law, on page 45 of the *Our Multicultural Heritage* booklet. (Enrichment/Easy)

Chapter Resources

Critical Thinking Duplicate and distribute the worksheet, Drawing Conclusions, from Unit 5, page 3, of the *Chapter Resources* binder. This exposé of slavery is by Theodore Weld. (Enrichment/Average)

CD-ROM

History Makers Access the biography of Harriet Beecher Stowe on the American Heritage® *History of the United States* CD-ROM. (Enrichment/Average)

Student Study Guide

Section 2 Study Guide Have students use the Section 2 Study Guide on page 121 of the *Student Study Guide* to review and reinforce the content of this section. (Reteaching/Average)

ACTIVITY

Guided Instruction Encourage students to jot down the names of the characters and a little information about each one. As they write, encourage them to draw on the information they have jotted down. Students can perform their skits live or on video.

Answers to Section 2 Review

1. See the map on p. 437.
2. (a) Henry Clay, p. 433, (b) John C. Calhoun, p. 433, (c) Daniel Webster, p. 433, (d) Stephen Douglas, p. 434, (e) Compromise of 1850, p. 434, (f) Fugitive Slave Law of 1850, p. 434, (g) Harriet Beecher Stowe, p. 435, (h) *Uncle Tom's Cabin*, p. 435
3. (a) fugitive, p. 433, (b) civil war, p. 433
4. California's request threatened the balance between free and slave states in the Senate; southerners feared that more free

states might be carved out of the Mexican Cession.
5. Northerners supported it because California was admitted as a free state and the slave trade in Washington, D.C., was ended; southerners supported it because they won a new Fugitive Slave Law and gained popular sovereignty in western territories.
6. The law forced northerners to help capture runaway slaves, paid judges more money for sending African Americans to the South than

for setting them free, and made northerners feel like part of the slave system.
7. Possible Answer: Because the Compromise of 1850 left western territories open to popular sovereignty, it seemed likely that a crisis might erupt each time a new state entered the Union; also, the new Fugitive Slave Law angered those who opposed slavery on moral grounds.

Section 3
pp. 436–440

Bell Ringer

Challenge students to freewrite a response to this question: Would you help a fugitive slave escape to freedom even if it were against the law to do so? Why or why not?

Lesson Plan

1. Focus In this section, students explore how the Kansas-Nebraska Act of 1854 enraged northerners, who felt that it undid the Missouri Compromise. Students see how passions reached an explosive level in Kansas and how the crisis worsened with the Dred Scott decision.

2. Instruct Have students work in groups to plan the front pages of newspapers that might have appeared in Charleston and in Boston announcing news of the Kansas-Nebraska Act, violence in Kansas, or the Dred Scott decision. In addition to headlines, news accounts, and interviews, students should include editorials and drawings. Have each group share its front page with the class.

3. Close To close the lesson, play a Jeopardy!-like game with students. List key facts from the section on the chalkboard; then divide the class into two teams and see which team can form the correct question to the answers more quickly.

3
Bloodshed in Kansas

FIND OUT

- What events made the issue of slavery emerge again in 1854?
- Why did proslavery and antislavery forces move into Kansas?
- How did the Dred Scott decision divide the nation?

In the mid-1850s, proslavery and antislavery forces battled for control of the territory of Kansas. An observer described election day in one Kansas district in 1855:

❝On the morning of the election, before the polls were opened, some 300 or 400 Missourians and others were collected in the yard...where the election was to be held, armed with bowie-knives, revolvers, and clubs. They said they came to vote, and whip the...Yankees, and would vote without being sworn. Some said they came to have a fight, and wanted one.❞

Hearing of events in Kansas, Abraham Lincoln, then a young lawyer in Illinois, predicted that "the contest will come to blows, and bloodshed." Once again, the issue of slavery in the territories divided the nation.

Kansas-Nebraska Act

Americans had hoped that the Compromise of 1850 would end debate over slavery in the West. In 1854, however, the issue of slavery in the territories surfaced yet again.

In January 1854, Senator Stephen Douglas of Illinois introduced a bill to set up a government for the Nebraska Territory. The

Nebraska Territory stretched from Texas north to Canada, and from Missouri west to the Rocky Mountains.

Douglas knew that white southerners did not want to add another free state to the Union. He proposed dividing the Nebraska Territory into two territories, Kansas and Nebraska. (See the map at right.) In each territory, settlers would decide the issue of slavery by popular sovereignty. Douglas's bill was known as the ***Kansas-Nebraska Act.***

Undoing the Missouri Compromise. The Kansas-Nebraska Act seemed fair to many people. After all, the Compromise of 1850 had applied popular sovereignty in New Mexico and Utah. Others felt that Kansas and Nebraska were different. The Missouri Compromise had already banned slavery in those areas, they insisted. The Kansas-Nebraska Act would, in effect, undo the Missouri Compromise.

Southern leaders supported the Kansas-Nebraska Act. They were sure that slave owners from Missouri would move across the border into Kansas. In time, they hoped, Kansas would become a slave state. President Franklin Pierce, a Democrat elected in 1852, also supported the bill. With the President's help, Douglas pushed the Kansas-Nebraska Act through Congress.

Northern outrage. Northern reaction to the Kansas-Nebraska Act was swift and angry. Opponents of slavery called the act a "criminal betrayal of precious rights." Slavery could now spread to areas that had been free for more than 30 years.

Northerners protested by challenging the Fugitive Slave Law. Two days after Congress passed the Kansas-Nebraska Act, slave catchers in Boston seized Anthony Burns, a fugitive. Citizens of Boston poured into the streets to keep Burns from being sent to the South. It took two companies of soldiers to stop the crowd from freeing Burns. Such incidents showed that antislavery feeling was rising in the North.

Critical Thinking
Asking Questions

Senator Stephen Douglas represented a free state, Illinois, yet he pushed the Kansas-Nebraska Act through Congress. It is said that he cared more about territorial expansion than about slavery. In fact, he once said, "I do not care whether slavery is voted up or voted down." Have students imagine that they are political reporters for Illinois newspapers. Have them brainstorm questions that they would ask Douglas about the Kansas-Nebraska Act and his support of it.

Our Multicultural Heritage
Activity

Anthony Burns: The Defeat and Triumph of a Fugitive Slave by Virginia Hamilton tells the story of the last slave seized in Massachusetts under the Fugitive Slave Law. Burns was put on trial in Boston. Before he was returned to Richmond in 1854, the federal government had spent $100,000 for his capture. Encourage interested students to read and report on this biography.

The issue of whether or not to allow slavery in the territories created tension between the North and South.
1. Which territories were opened to slavery under the Compromise of 1850?
2. Which territories were opened to slavery in 1854?
3. **Analyzing Information** Locate the Missouri Compromise line. What happened to the Missouri Compromise after 1854?

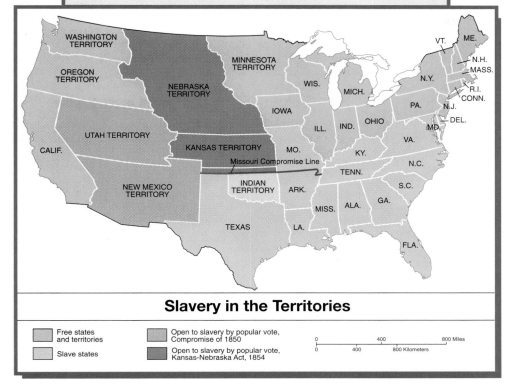

Slavery in the Territories

Free states and territories	Open to slavery by popular vote, Compromise of 1850	
Slave states	Open to slavery by popular vote, Kansas-Nebraska Act, 1854	

0   400   800 Miles
0   400   800 Kilometers

Kansas Explodes

Kansas now became a testing ground for popular sovereignty. Stephen Douglas hoped that settlers would decide the slavery issue peacefully on election day. Instead, proslavery and antislavery forces sent settlers to Kansas to fight for control of the territory.

Rushing to Kansas. Most of the new arrivals were farmers from neighboring states. Their main interest in moving to Kansas was cheap land. Few of these settlers owned slaves. At the same time, abolitionists brought in more than 1,000 settlers from New England.

Proslavery settlers moved into Kansas as well. They wanted to make sure that antislavery forces did not overrun the territory. Proslavery bands from Missouri often rode across the border. These ***Border Ruffians*** battled the antislavery forces in Kansas.

Chapter 15 • **437**

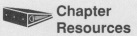
Divided Kansas. In 1855, Kansas held elections to choose lawmakers. Hundreds of Border Ruffians crossed into Kansas and voted illegally. They helped to elect a proslavery legislature.

The new legislature quickly passed laws to support slavery. One law said that people could be put to death for helping slaves escape. Another made speaking out against slavery a crime punishable by two years of hard labor.

Antislavery settlers refused to accept these laws. They elected their own governor and legislature. With two rival governments, Kansas was in chaos.

The first shots. In 1856, a band of proslavery men raided the town of Lawrence, an antislavery stronghold. The attackers destroyed homes and smashed the press of a Free Soil newspaper.

John Brown, an abolitionist, decided to strike back. Brown had moved to Kansas to help make it a free state. He claimed that God had sent him to punish supporters of slavery.

Brown rode with his four sons and two other men to the town of Pottawatomie (paht uh WAHT uh mee) Creek. In the middle of the night, they dragged five proslavery settlers from their beds and murdered them.

The killings at Pottawatomie Creek sparked more violence. Both sides fought fiercely. By late 1856, more than 200 people had been killed. Newspapers called the territory *Bleeding Kansas.*

Bloodshed in the Senate

Even before Brown's attack, the battle over Kansas spilled into the Senate. Charles Sumner of Massachusetts was the leading abolitionist senator. In one speech, Sumner denounced the proslavery legislature in Kansas. He then attacked his southern foes, singling out Andrew Butler, an elderly senator from South Carolina.

Bleeding Kansas *The struggle between proslavery and antislavery forces for control of Kansas erupted into violence. This eyewitness sketch shows a battle between proslavery and antislavery settlers.* **Citizenship** *How was the violence in Kansas related to the Kansas-Nebraska Act?*

438 • Chapter 15

Butler was not in the Senate on the day Sumner spoke. A few days later, however, Butler's nephew, Congressman Preston Brooks, marched into the Senate chamber. Using a heavy cane, Brooks beat Sumner until he fell, bloody and unconscious, to the floor.

Many southerners felt that Sumner got what was coming to him. Hundreds of people sent canes to Brooks to show their support. To northerners, however, the brutal act was just more evidence that slavery led to violence.

The Dred Scott Decision

With Congress in an uproar, many Americans looked to the Supreme Court to settle the slavery issue and restore peace. In 1857, the Court ruled on a case involving a slave named Dred Scott. But instead of bringing harmony, the Court's decision further divided North and South.

Dred Scott had lived for many years in Missouri. Later, he moved with his owner to Illinois and then to Wisconsin Territory, where slavery was not allowed. After they returned to Missouri, Scott's owner died. Antislavery lawyers helped Scott to file a lawsuit. They argued that since Scott had lived in a free territory, he was a free man.

A sweeping decision. In time, the case reached the Supreme Court. The Court's decision startled Americans. First, it ruled that Scott could not file a lawsuit because, as a

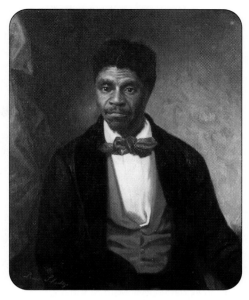

BIOGRAPHY Dred Scott *When his owner died, Dred Scott filed a lawsuit for his freedom. He argued that since he had lived in a free territory, he should be a free man. In a ruling that caused an uproar, the Supreme Court disagreed. After the Court's ruling, Scott was sold. His new owner then gave him his freedom.* **Citizenship** *How did the Dred Scott decision overturn the Missouri Compromise?*

black, he was not a citizen. The Justices also agreed that slaves were property.

The Court did not stop there. Instead, the Justices went on to make a sweeping decision about the larger issue of slavery in the territories. According to the Court, Congress did not have the power to outlaw slavery in *any* territory. The Court's ruling meant that the Missouri Compromise was unconstitutional.

The nation reacts. White southerners rejoiced at the **Dred Scott decision.** It meant that slavery was legal in all the territories—just what they had been demanding for years.

Our Common Heritage

As the dispute over slavery heated up, violence erupted a number of times in Congress. On one occasion, more than 20 members were brawling when someone grabbed someone else's hair. The hair turned out to be a wig! Fighting stopped as the members broke into laughter.

Chapter 15 • **439**

Answer to Caption

The Missouri Compromise had outlawed slavery in territories north of the Missouri Compromise line. In *Dred Scott,* the Supreme Court ruled that Congress did not have the power to outlaw slavery in any territory.

Customized Reader

Primary Source Order article IVB-16, Editorials About Brooks' Beating of Sumner, from the *American History Customized Reader.* (Enrichment/Average)

Voices of Freedom

Primary Source You might assign selection 17-5, The Dred Scott Decision: A Black View, on page 117 of *Voices of Freedom.* (Enrichment/Average)

Videotapes/ Videodiscs

United States History Video Collection Use the video segment "Dred Scott vs. John F.A. Sandford" from Volume 8, *Causes of the Civil War,* to enhance students' understanding of the significance of the Dred Scott decision. Approx. running time 3:45 min. (Enrichment/Average) Vol. 8, Ch. 31

Chapter 31

Play

Historical Sidelight
Background

The morning after the attack on Senator Sumner, Henry Wilson, the other senator from Massachusetts, addressed his colleagues: ". . . to assail a member of the Senate . . . 'for words spoken in debate,' is a grave offense not only against the rights of the senator but the constitutional privileges of this house; but, . . . to come into this chamber and assault a member in his seat until he falls exhausted and senseless on this floor, is an offense requiring the prompt and decisive action of the Senate." The Senate concluded that the

House of Representatives would have to punish Brooks. His expulsion was recommended by the House investigating committee but failed to get a two-thirds majority vote. Brooks resigned anyway—but was quickly reelected and returned to Washington.

The *Richmond Whig* commented on the incident by saying, "The only regret we feel is, that Mr. Brooks did not employ a horsewhip or cowhide upon [Sumner's] slanderous back, instead of a cane."

Our Multicultural Heritage
Background

While his case was tried before the state courts, Dred Scott remained under the authority of the sheriff in St. Louis, Missouri. The sheriff hired him out at the rate of five dollars a month. During the federal trials, Scott remained in St. Louis with no regular employment. After the Supreme Court decision, Scott was sold, and his new owner freed him. Scott then worked as a porter at Barnum's Hotel in St. Louis. He died from tuberculosis in 1858.

439

African Americans responded angrily to the Dred Scott decision. In the North, many held public meetings to condemn the ruling. At a meeting in Philadelphia, a speaker hoped that the Dred Scott decision would lead more whites to "join with us in our efforts to recover the long lost boon of freedom."

White northerners were also shocked by the ruling. Many had hoped that slavery would die out if it were restricted to the South. Now, however, slavery could spread throughout the West. Even northerners who disliked abolitionists felt that the Dred Scott ruling was wrong. A Cincinnati newspaper declared, "We are now one great. . . slave-holding community."

SECTION 3 REVIEW

1. **Locate:** (a) Kansas Territory, (b) Nebraska Territory.
2. **Identify:** (a) Kansas-Nebraska Act, (b) Franklin Pierce, (c) Border Ruffians, (d) John Brown, (e) Bleeding Kansas, (f) Charles Sumner, (g) Dred Scott decision.
3. How did the Kansas-Nebraska Act undo the Missouri Compromise?
4. Why did popular sovereignty lead to fighting in Kansas?
5. Explain how each of the following reacted to the Dred Scott decision: (a) white southerners, (b) African Americans, (c) white northerners.
6. **CRITICAL THINKING Analyzing a Quotation** After the Kansas-Nebraska Act was passed, Stephen Douglas stated that "the struggle for freedom was forever banished from the halls of Congress to the western plains." What did Douglas mean?

AC**TIVITY Writing to Learn**

Write two sets of headlines for the events in Section 3. One set should be for a northern newspaper, the other for a southern newspaper.

4
Republicans Challenge Slavery

FIND OUT
- Why did a new political party take shape in the mid-1850s?
- How did Abraham Lincoln view slavery?
- How did the raid on Harpers Ferry deepen differences between the North and South?

VOCABULARY arsenal

In the mid-1850s, people who opposed slavery in the territories were looking for a new political voice. Neither the Whig party nor the Democratic party would take a strong stand against slavery. "We have submitted to slavery long enough," an Ohio Democrat declared.

Free Soilers, northern Democrats, and antislavery Whigs met in towns and cities across the North. In 1854, a group gathered in Michigan to form the **Republican party.** The new party grew quickly. By 1856, it was ready to challenge the older parties for power.

The Republican Party

The main goal of the Republican party was to keep slavery out of the western territories. A few Republicans were abolitionists and hoped to end slavery in the South as well. Most Republicans, however, wanted only to stop the spread of slavery.

In 1856, Republicans selected John C. Frémont to run for President. Frémont was a frontiersman who had fought for California's independence. (See page 366.) He had little political experience, but he opposed the spread of slavery. In northern cities, Republicans marched through the streets singing Frémont's campaign song:

> 66 Arise, arise ye brave!
> And let our war-cry be,
> Free speech, free press, free soil,
>   free men,
> Frémont and victory! 99

The Whig party was very weak. Frémont's main opponent was Democrat James Buchanan. Buchanan was from Pennsylvania, but he sympathized with the southern position on slavery.

Supported by the large majority of southerners and many northerners, Buchanan won the election. Still, the Republicans made a strong showing. Without the support of a single southern state, Frémont won one third of the popular vote. Southerners worried that their influence in the national government was fading.

Abe Lincoln of Illinois

The next test for the Republican party came in 1858 in Illinois. Abraham Lincoln, a Republican, challenged Democrat Stephen Douglas for his seat in the Senate. The election captured the attention of the whole nation. Most Americans thought that Douglas would run for President in 1860.

A self-starter from Kentucky. Abraham Lincoln was born in the backcountry of Kentucky. Like many frontier people, his parents moved often to find better land. The family lived in Indiana and later in Illinois. As a child, Lincoln spent only a year in school. But he taught himself to read and spent hours reading by firelight.

After Lincoln left home, he opened a store in Illinois. There, he studied law on his own and launched a career in politics. After spending eight years in the state legislature, Lincoln served one term in Congress. Bitterly opposed to the Kansas-Nebraska Act, he decided to run for the Senate in 1858.

"Honest Abe" *Abraham Lincoln often poked fun at his own plain style and appearance. "The Lord prefers common-looking people," he said. "That is why He makes so many of them."* **American Traditions** *Why was Lincoln popular?*

"Just folks." When the race began, Lincoln was not a national figure. Still, people in Illinois knew him well and liked him. To them, he was "just folks"—someone who enjoyed picnics, wrestling contests, and all their other favorite pastimes.

People also admired his honesty and wit. His plainspoken manner made him a good speaker. Even so, a listener once complained that he could not understand one of Lincoln's speeches. "There are always some fleas a dog can't reach" was Lincoln's reply.

The Lincoln-Douglas Campaign Trail

One sunny day in August 1858, a train sped across the Illinois prairie. Inside his private railroad car sat Senator Stephen Douglas. Banners draped outside the car proudly announced the "Little Giant," as Douglas—

Lesson Plan

1. Focus Opponents of slavery in the western territories banded together in the 1850s to form the Republican party. In this section, students learn how Republican Abraham Lincoln first achieved national fame and how John Brown's raid heightened tensions between the North and the South.
2. Instruct Have students review the excerpt from Lincoln's speech on page 443 and restate Lincoln's remarks in their own words. Ask how they think Lincoln's words would have been received by a southern rather than a northern audience. Make sure that students support their answers with facts.
3. Close To close the lesson, have students answer a series of *Who, What, When, Where, Why,* and *How* questions on important facts in the section.

 Lesson Planner

For a developed **Cooperative Learning** lesson plan, see the *Lesson Planner*, page 93.

Answer to Caption

Possible Answer: Lincoln was considered to be an average, homey person. People admired his honesty and plainspoken ways.

 CD-ROM

Presidents Access the biography of James Buchanan on the American Heritage® *History of the United States* CD-ROM. (Enrichment/Average)

Historical Sidelight
Background

Stephen Douglas was a flamboyant, aggressive campaigner. He once boasted: "I live with my constituents, drink with them, pray with them, laugh, hunt, dance, and work with them. I eat their corn dodgers and fried bacon and sleep two in a bed with them."

Douglas called Abraham Lincoln "[t]he strong man of his party—full of wit, facts, dates—and the best stump speaker in the West . . . if I beat him, my victory will be hard won."

In the second debate, Lincoln forced Douglas to take a stand on the Dred Scott decision. Douglas upheld popular sovereignty and declared, "It matters not what way the Supreme Court may hereafter decide." These words won Douglas Illinois but lost him support in the South.

Our Multicultural Heritage

Biography Have students read the biography, Carl Schurz, Man of Conscience, on page 43 of the *Our Multicultural Heritage* booklet. (Enrichment/Average)

LINKING PAST AND PRESENT

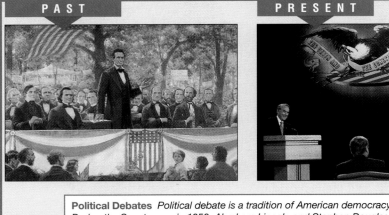

PAST

PRESENT

Political Debates *Political debate is a tradition of American democracy. During the Senate race in 1858, Abraham Lincoln and Stephen Douglas debated seven times. The painting at left shows one of the Lincoln-Douglas debates. Today, televised debates are part of presidential elections. At right, candidates Bob Dole and Bill Clinton respond to questions during the 1996 campaign.* ● *How has television changed political debate?*

only five feet tall—was called. Behind the senator's car was a flatcar mounted with a brass cannon. Whenever the train approached a station, two young men in uniform fired the cannon. Senator Douglas was coming to town!

Abraham Lincoln was traveling on the same train. Lincoln sat in a public car with other passengers. Lincoln knew that on his own he could never draw big crowds as Senator Douglas did. To remedy this, Lincoln followed his opponent around the state, answering him speech for speech.

A series of debates. To get more attention, Lincoln challenged Douglas to a series of debates. Although not really eager, Douglas agreed. During the campaign, the two men debated seven times.

The first debate took place in Ottawa, Illinois. It was a broiling-hot day. Dust clouds rose as farmers drove their wagons to town. Others floated down the Illinois

River in flatboats. Nobody minded the heat because this Senate election was especially important. Besides, politics was a favorite entertainment for Americans.

Douglas speaks. Standing before a crowd of 10,000, Douglas began his attack. Lincoln, he declared in a booming voice, was a hot-headed abolitionist who wanted blacks and whites to be complete equals—even to socialize with one another! Even worse, Douglas warned, Lincoln's call for an end to slavery would lead to war between the North and South.

Douglas then reminded the audience of his own views. Popular sovereignty, he urged, was the best way to solve the slavery crisis. Even though he personally disliked slavery, he did not care whether people in the territories voted "down or up" for it.

Lincoln replies. Lincoln rose to reply. He seemed unsure what to do with his long arms and big hands. But Lincoln's voice car-

Connections With Civics
Background

In one debate, Lincoln compared Douglas to a steamboat: "When I was a boy, I spent considerable time along the Sangamon River. An old steamboat plied on the river, the boiler of which was so small that when they blew the whistle, there wasn't enough steam to turn the paddle wheel. When the paddle wheel went around, they couldn't blow the whistle. My friend Douglas reminds me of that old steamboat, for it is evident that when he talks he can't think, and when he thinks he can't talk."

On another occasion, Douglas noted that he first met Lincoln in a general store, where Lincoln had sold him a drink of whiskey. Lincoln replied, "But now there's a difference between us: I've left my side of the counter, but he sticks to his as tenaciously as ever!"

When he was asked how he felt about losing the election, Lincoln replied, "Like the boy who stubbed his toe, I am too big to cry, and too badly hurt to laugh."

Connections With the World
Background

In 1859, slave owners formed the Southern Commercial Convention and demanded the right to reopen slave trade with Cuba, Brazil, and Africa. Southerners had been secretly smuggling in slaves from these areas for decades despite the constitutional ban against slave trade.

ried clearly to the edge of the crowd. If slavery was wrong, he said, Douglas and other Americans could not ignore it. They could not treat it as an unimportant question to be voted "down or up." On the contrary, if slavery was evil, it should be kept out of the territories.

Like nearly all whites of his day, Lincoln did not believe in "perfect equality" between blacks and whites. He did, however, believe that slavery was wrong. He declared:

❝There is no reason in the world why the [African American] is not entitled to all the natural rights [listed] in the Declaration of Independence, the right to life, liberty and the pursuit of happiness. I hold that he is as much entitled to these as the white man. . . . In the right to eat the bread . . . which his own hand earns, he is my equal and the equal of Judge Douglas, and the equal of every living man.❞

The debate went on for three hours. When it was over, Douglas's supporters marched away with their hero. A crowd of Republicans carried Lincoln on their shoulders, his long legs dangling nearly to the ground.

A leader emerges. Week after week, both men spoke nearly every day to large crowds. Newspapers reprinted their speeches. The more northerners read Lincoln's speeches, the more they thought about the injustice of slavery. Many could no longer agree with Douglas that slavery was simply a political issue. Like Lincoln, they believed that "if slavery is not wrong, nothing is wrong."

Douglas won the election by a slim margin. Still, Lincoln was a winner, too. He was now known throughout the country. Two years later, the two rivals would again meet face to face—both seeking the office of President. ■

John Brown's Raid

In the meantime, more bloodshed pushed the North and South farther apart. In 1859, John Brown carried his antislavery campaign from Kansas to the East. He led a group of followers, including five African Americans, to Harpers Ferry, Virginia. There, they raided a federal arsenal, or gun warehouse. Brown thought that enslaved African Americans would flock to the arsenal. He planned to give them weapons and lead them in a revolt.

Seizing the arsenal. Brown quickly gained control of the arsenal. No slave uprising took place, however. Instead, troops led by Robert E. Lee killed 10 of the raiders and captured Brown.

John Brown's Farewell *John Brown was captured at Harpers Ferry and tried for murder and treason. This painting shows Brown being led to his execution, as northerners imagined the scene.* **Culture** *How do you think southerners responded to this painting?*

 Voices of Freedom

Primary Source You might assign selection 17-6, Singing the Praises of John Brown, on pages 117–118 of *Voices of Freedom*. The selection is from a Union song about John Brown's attempt to start a slave revolt. "John Brown's Body" was sung by many Union troops early in the war. (Enrichment/Average)

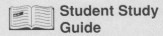

Student Study Guide

Section 4 Study Guide Have students use the Section 4 Study Guide on page 123 of the *Student Study Guide* to review and reinforce the content of this section. (Reteaching/Average)

Guided Instruction Tell students to label two columns on a sheet of paper Arguments Based on Reason and Arguments Based on Emotion. Have them list arguments for the defense or the prosecution in both categories. Have students decide which order for their arguments would be most effective. Invite volunteers to present their speeches.

Section 5
pp. 444–447

Bell Ringer

Write the term *civil war* on the chalkboard. Ask: In what ways is a civil war different from other wars? Why do you think that a civil war is considered by many to be the most tragic kind of war?

Lesson Plan

1. Focus After the election of Lincoln in 1860, seven states seceded from the Union to form the Confederate States of America. In this section, students examine these secessions and learn why the firing on Fort Sumter forced President Lincoln to take a stand against the Confederacy.

Most people, in both the North and the South, thought that Brown's plan to lead a slave revolt was insane. After all, there were not many enslaved African Americans in Harpers Ferry. At his trial, however, Brown seemed perfectly sane. He sat quietly as the court found him guilty of murder and treason and sentenced him to death.

Trial and death. Because he showed great dignity during his trial, Brown became a hero to many northerners. On the morning he was hanged, church bells rang solemnly throughout the North. In years to come, New Englanders would sing a popular song: "John Brown's body lies a mold'ring in the grave, but his soul is marching on."

To white southerners, the northern response to John Brown's death was outrageous. People were actually singing the praises of a man who had tried to lead a slave revolt! Many southerners became convinced that the North wanted to destroy slavery—and the South along with it. The nation was poised for a violent clash.

SECTION 4 REVIEW

1. **Identify:** (a) Republican party, (b) John C. Frémont, (c) James Buchanan, (d) Abraham Lincoln, (e) John Brown.
2. **Define:** arsenal.
3. What was the main goal of the Republican party?
4. Why did Americans pay special attention to the 1858 Senate race in Illinois?
5. Why did John Brown raid an arsenal at Harpers Ferry?
6. **CRITICAL THINKING Comparing** Compare Lincoln's and Douglas's views on slavery.

ACTIVITY Writing to Learn
Imagine that you are a lawyer at the trial of John Brown. Write a speech in which you call on the jury to reach a verdict of either guilty or not guilty.

5
The South Breaks Away

FIND OUT
- How did the South react to Lincoln's victory in 1860?
- What were the Confederate States of America?
- What events led to the outbreak of the Civil War?

In May 1860, thousands of people swarmed into Chicago for the Republican convention. They filled the city's 42 hotels. When beds ran out, they slept on billiard tables. All were there to find out one thing. Who would win the Republican nomination for President—William Seward of New York or Abraham Lincoln of Illinois?

On the third day of the convention, a delegate rushed to the roof of the hall. There, a man stood waiting next to a cannon. "Fire the salute," ordered the delegate. "Old Abe is nominated!"

As the cannon fired, crowds surrounding the hall burst into cheers. Amid the celebration, a delegate from Kentucky struck a somber note. "Gentlemen, we are on the brink of a great civil war."

The Election of 1860

The Democrats held their convention in Charleston, South Carolina. Southerners wanted the party to support slavery in the territories. But Northern Democrats refused to do so. In the end, the party split in two. Northern Democrats chose Stephen Douglas to run for President. Southern Democrats picked John Breckinridge of Kentucky.

Some Americans tried to heal the split between North and South by forming a new

---

Answers to Section 4 Review

1. (a) Republican party, p. 440, (b) John C. Frémont, p. 440, (c) James Buchanan, p. 441, (d) Abraham Lincoln, p. 441, (e) John Brown, p. 443
2. arsenal, p. 443
3. to outlaw slavery in the western territories
4. Democrat Stephen Douglas, the incumbent senator, was expected to run for President in 1860, and he debated the critical national issue of slavery with his opponent, Republican Abraham Lincoln.
5. to capture the arsenal and arm slaves
6. Possible Answer: Lincoln felt that slavery was morally wrong and should not be extended to the territories. Douglas personally disliked slavery, but he felt that people in the territories should decide the issue for themselves.

444

party. The Constitutional Union party chose John Bell of Tennessee, a Whig, to run for President. Bell was a moderate who wanted to keep the Union together. He got support only in a few southern states that were still seeking a compromise.

When the votes were counted, Lincoln had carried the North and won the election. Southern votes did not affect the outcome at all. Lincoln's name was not even on the ballot in 10 southern states. Northerners outnumbered southerners and outvoted them.

The Union Is Broken

Lincoln's election brought strong reaction in the South. A South Carolina woman described how the news was received:

66 The excitement was very great. Everybody was talking at the same time. One, . . . more moved than the others, stood up—saying . . . 'The die is cast—No more vain regrets—Sad forebodings are useless. The stake is life or death—'. . . No doubt of it. 99

To many southerners, Lincoln's election meant that the South no longer had a voice in national government. They believed that the President and Congress were now set against their interests—especially slavery. Even before the election, the governor of South Carolina had written to other southern governors. If Lincoln won, he wrote, it would be their duty to leave the Union.

Secession. Senator John Crittenden of Kentucky made a last effort to save the Union. In December 1860, he introduced a bill to extend the Missouri Compromise line to the Pacific. However, slavery in the West was no longer the issue. Many southerners believed that the North had put an abolitionist in the White House. They felt that secession was their only choice.

The first state to secede was South Carolina. On December 20, 1860, delegates to a convention in Charleston voted for seces-

sion. By February 1, 1861, Alabama, Florida, Georgia, Louisiana, Mississippi, and Texas had seceded. (See the map on page 453.)

A new nation. The seven states that had seceded held a convention in Montgomery, Alabama, in early 1861. They formed a new nation and named it the ***Confederate States of America.*** Jefferson Davis of Mississippi was named president of the Confederacy.

Most southerners believed that they had every right to secede. After all, the Declaration of Independence said that "it is the right of the people to alter or to abolish" a government that denies the rights of its citizens. Lincoln, they believed, would deny white southerners their right to own slaves.

Few southerners thought that the North would fight to keep the South in the Union. Should war come, however, they expected to win quickly.

War Comes

When Lincoln took the oath of office on March 4, 1861, he faced a dangerous situation. Lincoln warned that "no state . . . can lawfully get out of the Union." He pledged, however, that there would be no war unless the South started it.

Inauguration of Jefferson Davis *Southerners chose Jefferson Davis as president of the Confederate States of America. Here, a crowd watches as Davis takes the oath of office.* **Citizenship** *How was this moment a turning point for the South?*

2. Instruct Have students write diary entries from one of these perspectives: the son or daughter of a South Carolina planter, a northern abolitionist, a slave who had secretly learned how to read and write. Entries should discuss the election of Lincoln, the secession of South Carolina, the formation of the Confederacy, and/or the attack on Fort Sumter.
3. Close To close the lesson, have students write a cause and an effect for each event leading to the secession of the South.

 Lesson Planner

For a developed **Cooperative Learning** lesson plan, see the *Lesson Planner,* page 94.

Answer to Caption

The South had made a definitive break with the North.

 CD-ROM

Presidents Access the biography of Abraham Lincoln on the American Heritage® *History of the United States* CD-ROM. (Enrichment/Average)

 Videotapes/ Videodiscs

United States History Video Collection Use the video segment "A House Divided" from Volume 8, *Causes of the Civil War.* Approx. running time 2:10 min. (Enrichment/Average) Vol. 8, Ch. 34

Chapter 34   Play

Connections With Geography
Background

The census of 1860 showed that since 1850, the center of the nation's population had moved northwest, from near Parkersburg, West Virginia, to Chillicothe, Ohio.

News of Lincoln's nomination traveled westward to California faster than ever before because a month before the Republican Convention, the pony express started service between St. Joseph, Missouri, and Sacramento, California.

Critical Thinking
Comparing

Have students compare the reasons the southern states seceded from the Union with the reasons the American colonies declared independence from Great Britain in 1776. Ask students to write an essay or present an oral report identifying the similarities and differences between the causes of these two rebellions.

Connections With Technology
Activity

Jefferson Davis took the oath of office as President of the Confederate States of America in Montgomery, Alabama. Although his plantation was only 285 miles from Montgomery, Davis had to travel 600 miles by rail to get there. Ask: What did this say about the South's ability to move troops and supplies in the event of war?

Chapter Resources

Skill Application For additional practice, duplicate and distribute the worksheet, Reading an Election Map, from Unit 5, page 2, of the *Chapter Resources* binder. (Reteaching/Average)

Answers to Skill Lesson

1. (a) the election of 1860, (b) the four candidates in the election of 1860, (c) percentage of the popular vote and percentage of the electoral vote
2. (a) Republican, (b) Southern Democrat, (c) 39.5 percent, (d) 59 percent, (e) John Bell, (f) Kentucky, Virginia, and Tennessee
3. (a) People voted on the basis of sectional loyalty. (b) Possible Answer: The South had lost its voice in national government.

ACTIVITY

Guided Instruction Election maps and graphs analyzing the results of the last presidential election can be found in newspapers and in news magazines for the date of or the week following the last presidential election. Suggest that students consult the school library or a local public library for these back issues.

MAP, GRAPH, AND CHART SKILLS
Reading an Election Map

Maps can show different kinds of information. The election map below shows the results of the 1860 presidential election.

Presidential election maps are useful because they show which states each candidate won. Most presidential election maps are accompanied by circle graphs to show the percentage of the popular vote and the electoral vote that each candidate won.

1. Decide what is shown on the map and graphs. (a) What is the subject of the map? (b) What do the four colors stand for? (c) What do the graphs at bottom right show?

2. Practice using information from the map and graphs. (a) Which party won nearly all the northern states? (b) Which party won nearly all the southern states? (c) What percentage of the popular vote did the Republican party receive? (d) What percentage of the electoral vote did the Republican party receive? (e) Who was the candidate of the Constitutional Union party? (f) Which states did he win?

3. Draw conclusions about the election. Based on the map and graphs, draw conclusions about the election of 1860. (a) How does the map show that sectionalism was important in the election? (b) What did the election show about the political voice of voters in the South?

ACTIVITY
Locate the results for the most recent presidential election. Make an election map and two circle graphs for the electoral and the popular votes. Based on the map, do you think sectionalism played an important role in the results?

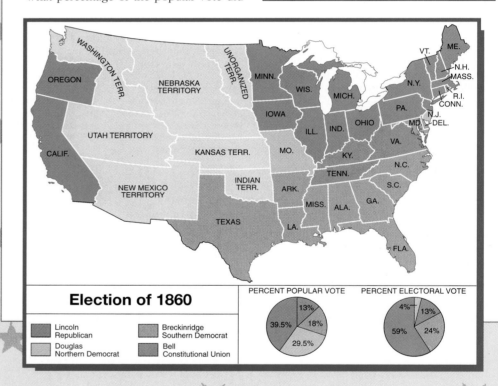

Students Acquiring English Activity

To provide SAE students with practice pronouncing difficult state names and structuring questions and answers correctly, have students ask each other questions about the presidential election maps that they have made. For example: Which southern states voted Republican and which voted Democratic? Which New England state voted for a different candidate from its neighboring states? You may wish to pronounce the state names for SAE students as they answer their classmates' questions.

Flags Over Fort Sumter *On April 13, 1861, Confederate troops shot down the Union flag, at right, that flew over Fort Sumter. They then raised the flag of the Confederacy over the fort, as shown in the painting.* **Geography** *Why was the location of Fort Sumter important to the Confederacy?*

Federal forts in the South. The Confederacy had already started seizing federal forts in the South. It felt that the forts were a threat because the United States was now a "foreign" power.

President Lincoln faced a difficult decision. Should he let the Confederates take over federal property? If he did, he would seem to be admitting that states had the right to leave the Union. But if he sent troops to hold the forts, he might start a war. He might also lose the support of the eight slave states that had not seceded.

In April, the Confederacy forced Lincoln to make up his mind. By then, Confederate troops controlled nearly all forts, post offices, and other federal buildings in the South. The Union held only three forts off Florida and one fort in South Carolina.

Opening shots. The fort in South Carolina, **Fort Sumter,** was important because it guarded Charleston Harbor. The Confederacy could not leave it in Union hands. On April 12, 1861, the Confederates asked for the fort's surrender.

Major Robert Anderson, the Union commander, refused to give in. Confederate guns then opened fire. Anderson and his troops quickly ran out of ammunition. On April 13, Anderson surrendered the fort. Amazingly, no one was injured.

As Confederate troops shelled Fort Sumter, people in Charleston gathered on their rooftops to watch. To many, it was like a huge fireworks display. No one knew that the fireworks marked the beginning of a terrible war that would last four years.

SECTION 5 REVIEW

1. **Identify:** (a) John Breckinridge, (b) John Bell, (c) John Crittenden, (d) Confederate States of America, (e) Jefferson Davis, (f) Fort Sumter.
2. Why did the Democratic party split in 1860?
3. What did Lincoln's victory in the 1860 election mean to the South?
4. What difficult decisions did Lincoln face when he became President?
5. Why was Fort Sumter important to the Confederacy?
6. **CRITICAL THINKING Solving Problems** Could the country have avoided war if the North and the South had reached an agreement about slavery in the territories? Explain.

ACTIVITY Writing to Learn
Write a campaign slogan for each of the four candidates in the presidential election of 1860.

Answers to Section 5 Review

1. (a) John Breckinridge, p. 444, (b) John Bell, p. 445, (c) John Crittenden, p. 445, (d) Confederate States of America, p. 445, (e) Jefferson Davis, p. 445, (f) Fort Sumter, p. 447
2. Southern Democrats wanted the party to support slavery in the territories; Northern Democrats refused to do so.
3. To southerners, Lincoln's election meant that the South no longer had a voice in national government; they believed that the President, the Senate, and the House were now set against their interests, especially slavery.
4. whether he should let the South secede; whether he should take action when Confederate troops seized Fort Sumter
5. Fort Sumter guarded Charleston Harbor and therefore was a threat to the Confederacy if it remained under Union control.
6. Possible Answer: No; by 1860, most southerners deeply distrusted northerners; many people in the North hoped that slavery would gradually die out everywhere—even in the South; the moral debate would not have died, even if a compromise on the western territories had been reached.

CHAPTER 15 REVIEW

Answers to Reviewing the Main Ideas

1. Moderates proposed extending the Missouri Compromise line across the Mexican Cession to the Pacific or applying popular sovereignty to the territories.

2. California was admitted as a free state; popular sovereignty applied to the rest of the Mexican Cession; the slave trade was banned in Washington, D.C.; a new Fugitive Slave Law was passed.

3. Northerners began to see slavery as a moral problem that no American could ignore.

4. (a) The Supreme Court ruled that slaves were property and that Congress did not have the power to outlaw slavery in a territory. (b) Southerners supported the decision; northerners opposed it.

5. (a) Douglas favored popular sovereignty. (b) Lincoln saw slavery as a moral evil.

6. Because of the dignity that Brown showed during his trial, he became a hero to northerners—an outcome that shocked southerners.

7. (a) The forts threatened southern nationhood. (b) He worried that the action might start a civil war or force other slave states to secede.

Answers to Thinking Critically

1. (a) Possible Answer: Slavery was a hotly debated issue with no clear-cut solutions. (b) Possible Answer: budget cuts, federal support of social programs, defense spending, trade agreements, health care

2. Students who agree might point out that expansion forced Americans to confront the slave issue. Students who disagree might argue that the conflict over slavery was inevitable, given growing economic differences between North and South.

3. Possible Answer: Many northerners might see secession as an act of rebellion rather than an exercise of states' rights.

Summary

- As settlers pushed west, the issue of slavery in the territories caused a growing division between the North and the South.
- The Fugitive Slave Law increased northern opposition to slavery.
- Proslavery and antislavery forces battled for control of Kansas Territory.
- The Republican party opposed expansion of slavery into the western territories.
- After Lincoln was elected President, seven southern states seceded from the Union.

Reviewing the Main Ideas

1. Discuss two moderate solutions to the slavery issue in the Mexican Cession.

2. List the four main parts of the Compromise of 1850.

3. How did *Uncle Tom's Cabin* affect people's view of slavery?

4. (a) What was the Dred Scott decision? (b) How did northerners and southerners view the decision?

5. (a) What plan did Stephen Douglas favor to settle the issue of slavery? (b) Why did Abraham Lincoln disagree with Douglas?

6. How did John Brown's death further divide the North and the South?

7. (a) Why did the Confederacy seize federal forts in the South? (b) Why did Lincoln hesitate to send troops to hold the forts?

Thinking Critically

1. Linking Past and Present (a) Why do you think it took months for Congress to pass both the Missouri Compromise and the Compromise of 1850? (b) What issues are difficult for Congress to agree on today?

2. Defending a Position If the United States had not expanded to the Pacific Ocean, a civil war would not have occurred. Do you agree with this statement? Explain.

3. Forecasting Lincoln said that "no state . . . can lawfully get out of the Union." Why do you think the North would be unwilling to let the South secede peacefully?

Applying Your Skills

1. Analyzing a Quotation Review Lincoln's response to Stephen Douglas on page 443. (a) According to Lincoln, what rights were slaves denied? (b) What does Lincoln mean by "the right to eat the bread . . . which his own hand earns"?

2. Reading an Election Map Look at the map on page 446. (a) Did Lincoln get electoral votes from states south of the Missouri Compromise line? (b) Did states on the West Coast vote the same way as the North or the South? (c) What evidence is there that border states between the North and South had a unique political outlook?

Thinking About Geography

Match the letters on the map with the following places: **1.** Missouri, **2.** Maine, **3.** California, **4.** Kansas Territory, **5.** Nebraska Territory, **6.** New Mexico Territory, **7.** Utah Territory. **Region** Which area listed above was admitted to the Union as a free state in 1850?

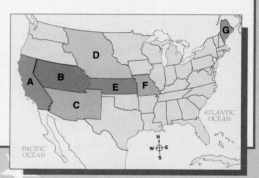

Answers to Applying Your Skills

1. (a) rights to life, liberty, the pursuit of happiness, and earnings, (b) Slaves were entitled to be paid for their labor.

2. (a) no, (b) California and Oregon voted the same as the North. (c) Border states such as Missouri, Kentucky, Tennessee, and Virginia voted for compromise and for pro-Union candidates Bell and Douglas.

Answers to Thinking About Geography

1. F **2.** G **3.** A **4.** E **5.** D
6. C **7.** B
Region: California

Debating Slavery in the Western Territories

Form into groups to explore the issue of slavery in the western territories. Follow the suggestions below to write, draw, or act to show what you have learned about the attempts to keep the nation together. You may use the textbook, encyclopedias, atlases, or other materials in your classroom library to complete the tasks. Be able to name your sources of information when you have finished the activity.

CARTOGRAPHERS On a large sheet of paper, create a map of the United States after the admission of California in 1850.
- Label the free states in one color.
- Label the slave states in another color.
- Add the date on which each state was admitted to the Union.

WRITERS Form into groups to write textbook entries for a younger child in which you explain each of the following: Missouri Compromise, Compromise of 1850, Fugitive Slave Law of 1850, Kansas-Nebraska Act, Dred Scott decision. Illustrate your entries with maps, graphs, charts, and pictures.

ARTISTS Divide into two groups: northern artists and southern artists. Have each group of artists create a political cartoon from the point of view of their group about one of the following: Missouri Compromise, Compromise of 1850, Bleeding Kansas, Dred Scott decision.

HISTORIANS List the important events and the attempts at compromise that led up to the Civil War, starting with the Missouri Compromise in 1820. Then use your list to make a time line of events leading to the Civil War. Be prepared to explain the significance of each event.

REPORTERS Create a "debate page" for an 1850s newspaper. Summarize background information, conduct and record "people in the street" interviews, draw cartoons, and write opposing editorials about one of the following: Missouri Compromise, Kansas-Nebraska Act, Compromise of 1850.

 Display each group's activity on a Debating Slavery in the Western Territories bulletin board.

Notice of meeting to protest Fugitive Slave Law

Handcuffs and shackles

Border Ruffians voting in Kansas

Lessons	Teaching Resources
1 Preparing for War **Objectives** 1. Describe how the states chose sides. 2. Identify the resources for war that each side had. 3. Identify the leaders of each side.	**Lesson Planner** Cooperative Learning, p. 97 **Student Study Guide** Section 1 Study Guide, p. 127 **Chapter Resources Binder, Unit 5** *Geography in History* One Virginia Becomes Two, pp. 19–20 *Skill Application* Reading a Table, p. 16
2 The Struggle Begins **Objectives** 1. Identify the military aims of each side. 2. Identify who won the early battles of the war. 3. Describe how the Union achieved two of its three war aims.	**Lesson Planner** Cooperative Learning, p. 98 **Student Study Guide** Section 2 Study Guide, p. 128 **Chapter Resources Binder, Unit 5** *History Through Literature* The Drummer Boy of Shiloh, p. 18
3 Freedom **Objectives** 1. Explain why Lincoln issued the Emancipation Proclamation. 2. Describe how Union war goals changed. 3. Describe how African Americans contributed to the Union war effort.	**Lesson Planner** Cooperative Learning, p. 99 **Student Study Guide** Section 3 Study Guide, p. 129 **Our Multicultural Heritage** *Biography* William H. Carney, Civil War Hero, p. 46 *Milestone* Native Americans in the Civil War, p. 48
4 Hardships of War **Objectives** 1. Describe what life was like in the Union and Confederate armies. 2. Identify problems that each side faced during the war.	**Lesson Planner** Cooperative Learning, p. 100 **Student Study Guide** Section 4 Study Guide, p. 130 **Our Multicultural Heritage** *Biography* Clara Barton, Angel of the Battlefield, p. 47 **Interdisciplinary Connections:** The War Up Close ■ *Arts* The Brady Style, p. 92 ▨ *Sciences* Anesthetics on the Battlefield, p. 93 ■ *Geography* A View of Vicksburg, p. 94 ■ *Economics* Mary Chesnut and the Blockade, p. 95 ■ *Civics* A Militant Hymn, p. 96
5 Victory at Appomattox **Objectives** 1. Identify the ideals that Lincoln expressed in the Gettysburg Address. 2. Identify the strategies that Grant used to defeat the Confederacy. 3. Describe how the war ended.	**Lesson Planner** Cooperative Learning, p. 101 **Student Study Guide** Section 5 Study Guide, p. 131 **Chapter Resources Binder, Unit 5** *Critical Thinking* Understanding Causes and Effects, p. 17

Multimedia Resources	Additional Resources	Chapter-Level Resources
Transparencies *Geography and History* Slavery and the Civil War, p. I-31 *Cause and Effect* The Civil War, p. F-21 **CD-ROM** *History Makers* Robert E. Lee **Videotapes/Videodiscs** *United States History Video Collection* Rush to Arms, Vol. 9, Ch. 10	**Voices of Freedom** The Bonnie Blue Flag, pp. 119–120 Encouraging Union Soldiers, pp. 120–121	**Lesson Planner** Activity Based, pp. 102–103 **Student Study Guide** Chapter 16 Study Guide, pp. 132–133 **Chapter Resources Binder** **Unit 5** Vocabulary Building, p. 15 Chapter Test A, pp. 21–23 Chapter Test B, pp. 24–26 Illustration Master, p. 27 Extra Unit Questions, pp. 43–45 **English Guided Reading** Guided Reading, pp. 31–32 **Spanish Resources** **Computer Test Bank** Chapter Tests A and B Extra Unit Questions **Guided Reading Audiotapes** Side 6 **CD-ROM** *Time Tour* Torn by War (1861–1865) in The Nation Torn Apart
Transparencies *Exploring Technology* Ironclad Ship, p. H-43 **Videotapes/Videodiscs** *United States History Video Collection* The Harsh Face of War, Vol. 9, Ch. 13; Western Front, Vol. 9, Ch. 28	**Voices of Freedom** The Battle of Antietam, pp. 122–123 **Historical Outline Map Book** Major Battles of the Civil War, p. 50 The Civil War in the East, p. 51 Union Advances, p. 52 **Customized Reader** Letter from a Union Soldier at Vicksburg, article VB-5	
Videotapes/Videodiscs *United States History Video Collection* Oh, Freedom!, Vol. 9, Ch. 16		
Transparencies *Fine Art* Rainy Day in Camp, p. D-41 *Interdisciplinary Connections* Civil War Medical Treatment, p. B-63 **CD-ROM** *History Makers* Clara Barton **Videotapes/Videodiscs** *United States History Video Collection* 1863 At Home, Vol. 9, Ch. 19; Angels of the Battlefield, Vol. 9, Ch. 22 **Listening to Literature Audiocassettes** *The American Experience* Willie Has Gone to War, side 5	**Voices of Freedom** A Southern Woman Takes Over at Home, p. 124 **Customized Reader** Journal of a Union Soldier in Andersonville, article VB-8	
Transparencies *Cause and Effect* The Civil War, p. F-21 **Videotapes/Videodiscs** *United States History Video Collection* Gettysburg, Vol. 9, Ch. 25; Toward Union Victory, Vol. 9, Ch. 31 **Listening to Literature Audiocassettes** *The American Experience* The Gettysburg Address, side 5	**Voices of Freedom** Lee Takes Pity on a Union Soldier, pp. 121–122 Lee and Grant Meet at Appomattox, p. 125 **Historical Outline Map Book** Union Advances, p. 52	

Lesson Planner

For a fully developed **Activity-Based** lesson plan for Chapter 16, see the *Lesson Planner,* pages 102–103.

 Chapter Resources

Vocabulary Building The Vocabulary Building worksheet for Chapter 16 from Unit 5, page 15, of the *Chapter Resources* binder can be used as a prereading activity or as a review of chapter vocabulary. (Reteaching/Easy)

 Student Study Guide

Chapter 16 Study Guide Refer students to pages 132–133 of the *Student Study Guide* for the Chapter 16 Study Guide. The study guide can be used for chapter review as well as for reteaching. (Reteaching/Average)

 Guided Reading Audiotapes

Students can use *Guided Reading Audiotapes,* Chapter 16, side 6, to listen to section previews, summaries, and review questions. The tapes might benefit students who are auditory learners, students who have trouble reading, or students acquiring English. (Reteaching/Easy)

C H A P T E R **16**

Torn by War

(1861–1865)

CHAPTER OUTLINE

1 Preparing for War
2 The Struggle Begins
3 Freedom
4 Hardships of War
5 Victory at Appomattox

1862 *Union and Confederate soldiers met in the Battle of Antietam. With over 23,000 casualties, Antietam was one of the bloodiest battles of the Civil War.*

1861 *The Civil War began when the Confederates seized Fort Sumter. The South soon adopted the "Stars and Bars" as its flag.*

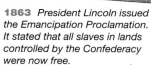

1863 *President Lincoln issued the Emancipation Proclamation. It stated that all slaves in lands controlled by the Confederacy were now free.*

1861   **1862**   **1863**

 WORLD EVENT
1861 Russian ruler frees serfs

 WORLD EVENT
1862 Britain denies recognition to Confederacy

450 • Chapter 16

Chapter Time Line
Critical Thinking

As students discuss the time line illustrations, captions, and World Event notes, have them analyze each one by asking *Who, What, Where, When, Why,* and *How* questions about it. Students can answer many of the questions with information from these two pages; for questions that they cannot answer, you might have them speculate about the answer. Whether they do so or just leave the question unanswered for now, encour-age them to save their responses and check them against the information in the chapter as they work through it.

Alternatively, have students examine the two predominant points of view presented here—those of the Union and those of the Confederacy. As you discuss each time line note, have students suggest and explain how each side's government and/or citizens might have reviewed the event mentioned.

Chapter Setting

> "I have just...heard a sermon...to the graduating class [of West Point]....There is a certain hymn that is always sung...the last Sunday that graduates attend church here. It commences 'When shall we meet again?'...And everyone felt the truth of the concluding words, 'Never, no more,' for in all probability in another year, the half of them may be in their graves...."

Tully McCrea, a young cadet, included this moving account in a letter to his sweetheart, Belle. President Lincoln had recently issued a call for troops to put down what he considered a revolt in the South. Now, the graduating class at West Point, the academy where army officers were trained, was preparing to take up arms.

The young men who had studied together would soon become enemies. Some would fight for the Union. Others would join the Confederacy.

Tully McCrea's own family was divided in its loyalties. Orphaned at a young age, Tully and a brother grew up with relatives in Ohio. Another brother and a sister grew up on a southern plantation. "My sister and aunt would rather see me dead in my grave than see me remain in the North," wrote Tully. "We are destined to have a long and bloody civil war, in which brother will be fighting against brother," he predicted.

McCrea was correct. The Civil War lasted four years. More Americans died than in any other war the nation has fought.

 ACTIVITY Role-play a conversation that might have taken place between Tully and his southern brother if they had met during the Civil War.

1865 The Civil War ended with the surrender of the Confederates at Appomattox Courthouse. Here, defeated southern troops tearfully roll up their flag.

1864 *News of Union victories helped Lincoln win reelection. Lincoln supporters carried lanterns like this one during nighttime parades.*

1863	1864	1865

▲

 WORLD EVENT
1864 First Red Cross societies established in Europe

Chapter 16 • **451**

Chapter Resources

English Guided Reading Duplicate and distribute to SAE students the Chapter 16 Guided Reading worksheet on pages 31–32 in the English Guided Reading section of the *Chapter Resources* binder. Students who have difficulty reading also might benefit from using this worksheet. Have students complete the worksheet before they begin reading. You might pair a more fluent student or a student who is a stronger reader with each SAE student to review. (Reteaching/Easy)

Spanish Resources See the Spanish Resources section of the *Chapter Resources* binder.

CD-ROM

Time Tour Access the Torn by War (1861–1865) section in The Nation Torn Apart on the American Heritage® *History of the United States* CD-ROM. (Enrichment/Average)

ACTIVITY

Guided Instruction You might begin by pairing students and having them brainstorm for similarities and differences between life in the North and life in the South. The responses might be factors in the brothers' beliefs and opinions. Invite pairs of volunteers to present their conversations to the class. Remind them to use facial expressions, vocal inflections, and physical gestures to help convey emotions. You might videotape the presentations to show other classes.

Students Acquiring English
Activity

Use the following strategy to improve communications with SAE students who are reluctant to speak up in class. Provide a notebook and explain that it is a student-teacher journal; in it, you and the student will write to one another about the social studies material. Try to write clearly (in some cases, you may need to print). Include one or two questions for the student to answer when he or she responds in the journal. If possible, exchange the journal every other day so the student is continually communicating with you. This strategy has several advantages for SAE students: It offers them a chance to respond to text material personally, to practice their writing, and to have a closer relationship with their teacher. The writing journal provides you with a good tool for assessing a student's progress and comprehension.

Linking Past and Present
Activity

Explain that for many the question of states' rights and the role of the federal government were the pivotal issues in determining which side to support in the Civil War. This debate has continued in one form or another to the present. Have students research and discuss in class recent national issues that raise questions about the relationship between state governments and federal authority.

Section 1
pp. 452–456

Bell Ringer

Write the following on the chalkboard: "WAR BETWEEN THE STATES: North and South Take Up Arms Against Each Other." Tell students to imagine that this is the headline in the morning newspaper. Have them freewrite about their thoughts and feelings.

Lesson Plan

1. Focus The outbreak of the Civil War pitted American against American. The South possessed superior military leadership and the advantage of fighting a defensive war. The North, however, had a larger population, a superior navy, and a strong industrial base. In this section, students compare the advantages and disadvantages of each side as the war began.

2. Instruct Divide the class into small groups. Have half the groups represent the Union, and the other half the Confederacy. Assign the groups the task of writing letters to legislatures in the border states, inviting them to join their cause. Remind groups that neither North nor South at this time claimed slavery to be the main issue in the war. The South argued for states' rights; the North argued for the preservation of the Union. Ask volunteers to read their letters aloud.

1
Preparing for War

FIND OUT
- How did the states choose sides?
- What resources for war did each side have?
- Who were the leaders of each side?

A few days after Fort Sumter fell, President Lincoln called for 75,000 volunteers to serve as soldiers for 90 days in a campaign against the South. The response was overwhelming. Throughout the North, crowds cheered the Stars and Stripes and booed the southern "traitors." Said a New Englander, "The whole population, men, women, and children, seem to be in the streets. . . . The people have gone stark mad!"

In the South, the scene was much the same. Southerners rallied to the Stars and Bars, as they called the new Confederate flag. Volunteers flooded into the Confederate army.

With flags held high, both sides marched off to war. Most felt certain that a single, gallant battle would resolve the issue. Few suspected that the North and South were entering on a long civil war—the most destructive war in the nation's history.

A Nation Divided

As the war began, each side was convinced of the justice of its cause. Southerners believed that they had the right to leave the Union. In fact, they called the conflict the War for Southern Independence. Northerners believed just as firmly that they had to fight to save the Union.

Choosing sides was most difficult in the eight slave states that were still in the Union

in April 1861. (See the map at right.) Four of these states—Virginia,* North Carolina, Tennessee, and Arkansas—quickly joined the Confederacy. But in the remaining states—Delaware, Kentucky, Missouri, and Maryland—many citizens favored the Union. These states were known as the border states. From the start, Delaware supported the Union. The other border states wavered between the North and the South. In time, all three decided to remain in the Union.

The Two Sides

In 1861, neither the North nor the South was prepared to fight a war. As the two sides rushed to build their armies, each had advantages and disadvantages. (See the chart on page 454.)

The South. The South had the key advantage of fighting a defensive war. It was up to the North to attack and defeat the South. If it did not, the Confederacy would become a separate country.

Defending their homeland gave southerners a strong reason to fight. "Our men must prevail in combat," one Confederate said, "or they will lose their property, country, freedom—in short, everything."

Southerners had skills that made them good soldiers. Hunting was an important part of southern life. From an early age, boys learned to ride horses and use guns. Wealthy young men often went to military school. Before the Civil War, many of the best officers in the United States Army were from the South.

The South, however, also had serious weaknesses. It had few factories to produce weapons, railroad tracks, and other vital supplies. Before the war, southerners bought most manufactured goods from the

---

*In the western part of Virginia, many people supported the Union. When Virginia seceded, the westerners formed their own government. They joined the Union as West Virginia in 1863.

Team-Teaching Activity
Language Arts

You might work with a language arts teacher to present a lesson about denotation and connotation in language when introducing this section. On the chalkboard, list these additional names applied to the war: The American Civil War; The War Between the States; The War of the Rebellion; The War of the Northern Aggression; The Second American Revolution. Discuss with the class the attitude toward the war suggested by each descriptor.

Connections With Geography
Background

The border state of Maryland was especially important to the Union because it borders on Washington, D.C. If Maryland seceded, the Union capital would have been surrounded by Confederate territory. In April 1861, a pro-southern mob attacked Union troops in Baltimore. Lincoln quickly declared martial law and sent troops there to restore order. Most Confederate supporters were imprisoned, and the state legislature decided to stay in the Union.

In April 1861, eight slave states were still in the Union. As war began, these states had to choose sides in the struggle.
1. Which states eventually seceded?
2. Which states stayed in the Union?
3. **Forecasting** How do you think that the decision of some slave states to remain in the Union might have affected Union goals in the war? Explain.

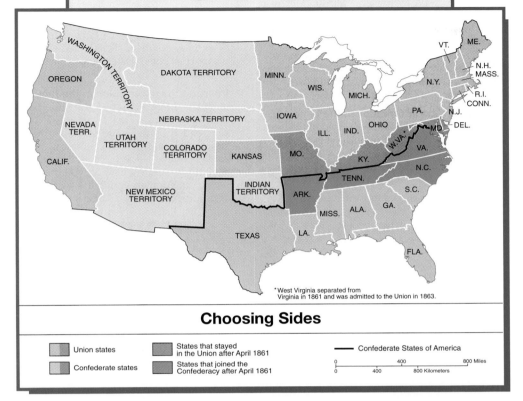

Choosing Sides

Union states

Confederate states

States that stayed in the Union after April 1861

States that joined the Confederacy after April 1861

—— Confederate States of America

*West Virginia separated from Virginia in 1861 and was admitted to the Union in 1863.

0   400   800 Miles
0   400   800 Kilometers

North or from Europe. The South also had few railroads to move troops and supplies. The railroads that it did have often did not connect to one another.

Finally, the South had a small population. Only about 9 million people lived in the Confederacy, compared with 22 million in the Union. More than one third of the population was enslaved. As a result, the South had fewer people eligible to become soldiers or able to support the war effort.

The North. The North had almost four times as many free citizens as the South. Thus, it had a large source of volunteers. It also had many people to grow food and to work in factories making supplies.

Industry was the North's greatest resource. Northern factories made 90 percent of the nation's manufactured goods. These factories quickly began making supplies for the Union army. The North also had more than 70 percent of the nation's rail lines.

Chapter 16 • **453**

3. **Close** To close the lesson, have students turn the subsection headings into questions and then answer them.

Lesson Planner

For a developed **Cooperative Learning** lesson plan, see the *Lesson Planner,* page 97.

Answers to Map Study

1. Virginia, North Carolina, Arkansas, Tennessee **2.** Delaware, Maryland, Missouri, Kentucky, West Virginia **3.** Possible Answer: It might have made the primary goal of the war the preservation of the Union rather than the abolition of slavery.

Chapter Resources

Geography in History Duplicate and distribute the worksheet, One Virginia Becomes Two, from Unit 5, pages 19–20, of the *Chapter Resources* binder. (Enrichment/Challenging)

Videotapes/ Videodiscs

United States History Video Collection Use "Rush to Arms" from Volume 9, *The Civil War,* to show the northern and southern response to the outbreak of war. Approx. running time 3:25 min. (Enrichment/Average) Vol. 9, Ch. 10

Chapter 10   Play

Cooperative Learning Activity

Divide the class into three groups and have each group prepare short dialogues among members living in a border state. Explain that one son plans to join the Union army while another son has volunteered to fight for the Confederacy. The dialogues might focus on the reasons each has for his choice of sides and the reaction of other family members.

Critical Thinking Applying Information

Divide the class into groups of three or four students. Have each group review the strengths and weaknesses of the North and South as the war began. Ask each group to imagine that it has been asked to lead a recruiting drive for the Union or the Confederate forces. Each group should select either the North or the South and write a speech to encourage young men to enlist. In writing speeches, groups should consider the audience, the reasons each side entered the conflict, the strengths of their side, the consequences of losing the war, and "patriotic" reasons why young men might join the war effort.

After groups have completed their speeches, collect all papers and invite several volunteers to read the speeches to the class. Tell students to listen critically to each speech and then decide which speeches are most persuasive, citing reasons for their opinions.

Chapter Resources

Skill Application For additional practice, duplicate and distribute the worksheet, Reading a Table, from Unit 5, page 16, of the *Chapter Resources* binder. (Reteaching/Average)

Answers to Skill Lesson

1. (a) Resources of the North and South, 1861 (b) by acres (c) by miles
2. (a) 20,600 (b) 15 percent (c) 71 percent
3. (a) the North (b) North—105,835 acres; South—56,832 acres (c) population
4. (a) the North (b) They might have kept northern troops better fed and supplied. (c) Answers will vary. One possibility is railroad track, because without it even available supplies might not reach the front.

ACTIVITY

Guided Instruction After students have completed their charts, encourage them to draw a comparison that makes a relevant statement about the outcome of the war. Have several volunteers read their comparisons aloud and use these as the basis for class discussion.

MAP, GRAPH, AND CHART SKILLS
Reading a Table

A table is used to present information in a way that is quick and easy to understand. Tables often present numbers or statistics. The numbers are set up in columns and rows.

The table below compares the resources of the North and South in 1861. Studying the table can help you to understand why the North won the Civil War.

1. Identify the information in the table. Note that the resources are measured in different ways. For example, population is measured in thousands of people. (a) What is the title of the table? (b) How is farmland measured? (c) How is railroad track measured?

2. Read the information in the table. Note that the table has five columns. The first column shows what each resource is. The second and third columns give the amount and percentage of each resource that the North had. The fourth and fifth columns give the same information for the South. (a) How many factories did the South have? (b) What percentage of the national total of factories did the South have?

(c) What percentage of the nation's railroad track did the North have?

3. Compare the information in the table. Use the chart to compare the resources of the North and South. (a) Which side had more workers in industry? (b) How many acres of farmland did each side have? (c) In which resource did the South come closest to equaling the North?

4. Interpret the information in the table. Interpret the information in the table based on your reading of the chapter. (a) Which side had the advantage in all of the resources shown? (b) How might these advantages have helped that side during the war? (c) Which resource do you think was the most important during the war? Explain your answer.

ACTIVITY
Make a chart with two columns, labeled Battles Won by the North and Battles Won by the South. Include the date and location of each battle. Then make a statement that compares the two sides of the chart.

Resources of the North and South, 1861

Resources	North		South	
	Number	Percent of Total	Number	Percent of Total
Farmland	105,835 acres	65%	56,832 acres	35%
Railroad Track	21,847 miles	71%	8,947 miles	29%
Value of Manufactured Goods	$1,794,417,000	92%	$155,552,000	8%
Factories	119,500	85%	20,600	15%
Workers in Industry	1,198,000	92%	111,000	8%
Population	22,340,000	63%	9,103,000 (3,954,000 slaves)	37%

Source: *Historical Statistics of the United States*

Students Acquiring English
Activity

SAE students might benefit by being paired with more advanced students to work on the Skill Lesson and its Activity. Partners might help the SAE students locate strategic battle sites on a map and assist in classifying regions of the country such as the Southeast, the Middle Atlantic States, and so on, which may not be specifically identified in this chapter.

The North also had a strong navy and a large fleet of private trading ships. With few warships and only a small commercial fleet, the South could do little to hurt the Union at sea.

Despite these advantages, the North faced a difficult military challenge. To bring the South back into the Union, northern soldiers had to conquer a huge area. Instead of defending their homes, they were invading unfamiliar land.

Wartime Leaders

The outcome of the war also depended on leadership. Presidents Abraham Lincoln in the North and Jefferson Davis in the South, as well as military leaders on both sides, played key roles in determining who won the war.

President Davis. Many people thought Davis was a stronger leader than Lincoln. Davis had attended West Point and served as an officer in the Mexican War. Later, he served as Secretary of War under President Franklin Pierce. Davis was widely respected for his honesty and courage.

Davis, however, did not like to turn over to others the details of day-to-day military planning. When Davis made a decision, he "could not understand any other man coming to a different conclusion," in the words of his wife. As a result, Davis wasted time arguing with his advisers.

President Lincoln. At first, some northerners had doubts about Abraham Lincoln's ability to lead. He had little experience in national politics or military matters. In time, however, Lincoln proved to be a patient but strong leader and a fine war planner.

Marching Off to War *Patriotic feeling was strong on both sides as the Civil War began. Here, the 7th New York Regiment marches proudly off to war.* **Citizenship** *Name two advantages the North had as war began.*

Lee and His Generals *Strong military leadership was one of the South's chief advantages in the Civil War. Here, Confederate generals meet on a hillside. Robert E. Lee is at right, on a white horse.* **Citizenship** *Why did Lee refuse when Lincoln asked him to command the Union army?*

Day by day, Lincoln gained the respect of those around him. Many especially liked his sense of humor. They noted that Lincoln even accepted criticism with a smile. When Secretary of War Edwin Stanton called Lincoln a fool, Lincoln commented, "Did Stanton say I was a fool? Then I must be one, for Stanton is generally right and he always says what he means."

Linking Past and Present

A Union official, Simon Cameron, decided to get even with Lee for siding with the Confederacy. He ordered Lee's plantation home in Arlington, Virginia, to be used as a burial ground for Union soldiers. Later, the government declared Arlington a national cemetery, and thousands of veterans of foreign wars are honored by burial there.

456 • Chapter 16

Choosing sides. After Fort Sumter fell, army officers in the South had to make a choice. They could stay in the Union army and fight against their home states. Or they could join the Confederate forces.

Robert E. Lee faced this kind of decision when his home state of Virginia seceded. President Lincoln asked Lee to command the Union army. Although he disliked slavery and had opposed secession, Lee refused. He explained in a letter to a friend:

❝I cannot raise my hand against my birthplace, my home, my children. I should like, above all things, that our difficulties might be peaceably arranged. . . . What ever may be the result of the contest, I foresee that the country will have to pass through a terrible ordeal.❞

Lee later became commander of the Confederate army.

SECTION 1 REVIEW

1. **Locate:** (a) Virginia, (b) Delaware, (c) Kentucky, (d) Missouri, (e) Maryland.
2. **Identify:** (a) Jefferson Davis, (b) Edwin Stanton, (c) Robert E. Lee.
3. (a) Name the eight slave states that were still in the Union in April 1861. (b) Which of these states remained in the Union?
4. Name two strengths and two weaknesses that each of the following had as a leader: (a) Jefferson Davis, (b) Abraham Lincoln.
5. **CRITICAL THINKING Comparing** (a) Compare the advantages and disadvantages of the North and South at the beginning of the war. (b) Which side do you think was better equipped to fight a long war? Explain.

ACTIVITY Writing to Learn

Imagine that you are Robert E. Lee at the beginning of the Civil War. Write a diary entry exploring your feelings about the war.

2
The Struggle Begins

FIND OUT

- What were the military aims of each side?
- Who won the early battles?
- How did the Union achieve two of its three war aims?

In the summer of 1861, the armies of both the North and the South marched off to war with flags flying and drums rolling. Each side expected to win and to win quickly. The reality of war soon shattered this dream. Abner Small, a volunteer from Maine, described a scene that would be repeated again and again:

> 66I can see today, as I saw then, the dead and hurt men lying limp on the ground. . . . From somewhere across the field a battery pounded us. . . . We wavered, and rallied, and fired blindly; and men fell writhing.99

It soon became clear that there would be no quick, easy end to the war. Leaders on both sides began to plan for a long, difficult struggle.

Strategies for Victory

Fighting during the Civil War took place in three major areas: the East, the West, and at sea. Union war plans involved all three areas.

Union plans. First, the Union planned to blockade southern ports. They wanted to cut off the South's supply of manufactured goods by halting its trade with Europe. Second, in the West, the Union planned to seize control of the Mississippi River. This would keep the South from using the river to sup-

ply its troops. It would also separate Arkansas, Texas, and Louisiana from the rest of the Confederacy. Finally, in the East, Union generals wanted to seize Richmond, Virginia, and capture the Confederate government headquartered there.

Confederate plans. The South's strategy was simpler: The Confederate army would stay at home and fight a defensive war. Northerners, they believed, would quickly tire of fighting. If the war became unpopular in the North, President Lincoln would have to give up the effort to bring the South back into the Union.

Southerners counted on European money and supplies to help fight the war. Southern cotton was important to the textile mills of England and other countries. Confederates were confident that Europeans would quickly recognize the South as an independent nation and continue to buy southern cotton for their factories.

Forward to Richmond!

"Forward to Richmond! Forward to Richmond!" Every day for more than a month, the influential *New York Tribune* blazed this "Nation's War-Cry" across its front page. Throughout the North, people were impatient. Sure of a quick victory, they called for an attack on Richmond, the Confederate capital.

A clash of untrained troops. Responding to popular pressure, President Lincoln ordered the attack. In July 1861, Union soldiers set out from Washington, D.C., for Richmond, about 100 miles (160 km) away. They had barely left Washington, however, when they clashed with the Confederates. The battle took place near a small stream called Bull Run, in Virginia. (See the map on page 459.)

July 21, 1861, was a lovely summer day. Hundreds of Washingtonians rode out to watch the battle, many of them carrying picnic baskets. In a holiday mood, they spread

Bell Ringer

Display a U.S. map that highlights the path of the Mississippi River. Have the class brainstorm for predictions of the ways in which the river might prove strategically important to both sides in the war.

Lesson Plan

1. Focus The Civil War was fought in the East, in the West, and at sea. The North tried to blockade southern ports, take control of the Mississippi River, and capture Richmond, Virginia. The South planned instead to fight a defensive war, supported by European money and supplies. In this section, students examine the early battles of the war and learn how the Union was able to split the Confederacy in half.

2. Instruct Divide the class into several small groups and assign each group one of the battles discussed in this section. Have each group prepare an account of its assigned battle from the viewpoint of a Union soldier, a Confederate soldier, or a reporter. After groups present their accounts, have students summarize the importance of each battle.

3. Close To close the lesson, ask students a series of rapid-fire *Who, What, Where, When, Why,* and *How* questions about the early battles of the Civil War.

Critical Thinking
Analyzing Information

In May 1861, the Confederacy moved its capital from Montgomery, Alabama, to Richmond, Virginia—only 100 miles from Washington, D.C. Ask: What were the advantages and disadvantages of this move?

Connections With Economics
Background

Confederate plans included the conservation of scarce resources. One observer noted: "Iron was now the precious metal. . . . Plantation bells [were] cast into cannon. . . . Society ladies began collecting all the broken pots and pans, and kettles in the Confederacy. . . . All idle nails were laid away for future use."

The Confederacy also encouraged landowners to grow food rather than cotton and tobacco. Southern harvests during the war years were reasonably abundant. However, inadequate rail lines and the northern blockade of shipping prevented the transportation of food supplies to areas where it was needed.

Lesson Planner

For a developed **Cooperative Learning** lesson plan, see the *Lesson Planner*, page 98.

Answer to Caption

as a battle for independence

Historical Outline Map Book

Historical Outline Maps Use the maps, Major Battles of the Civil War and The Civil War in the East, on pages 50 and 51 of the *American History Historical Outline Map Book.* Lesson ideas for these maps can be found on page T16. (Reteaching/Average)

Videotapes/ Videodiscs

United States History Video Collection Use the video segment "The Harsh Face of War" from Volume 9, *The Civil War,* to enhance students' understanding of early battles in the Civil War. Approx. running time 2:20 min. (Enrichment/Average) Vol. 9, Ch. 13

Chapter 13   Play

THE EAGLE'S NEST.
"THE UNION:IT MUST AND SHALL BE PRESERVED"

Guarding the Nest *Northerners viewed the Civil War as a fight to protect the Union from southern "traitors." In this 1861 cartoon, the American eagle reacts swiftly as dragons, serpents, and other "traitors" emerge from Confederate "eggs."* **Culture** *How did southerners view the Civil War?*

out on a grassy hilltop overlooking Bull Run. They were eager to see Union troops crush the Confederates.

The spectators, however, were disappointed. Southern troops did not turn and run as expected. Inspired by the example of General Thomas Jackson, they held their ground. A Confederate officer remarked that Jackson was standing "like a stone wall." From then on, the general was known as "Stonewall" Jackson.

A Union retreat. In the end, it was Union troops that retreated. One observer reported:

> 66 Off they went. . . across fields, toward the woods, anywhere, everywhere, to escape. . . . To enable them better to run, they threw away their blankets, knapsacks, canteens, and finally muskets, cartridge-boxes, and everything else. 99

The Confederates did not pursue the fleeing Union army. Had they done so, they might even have captured Washington, D.C. Instead, they remained behind to gather the gear thrown away by the panicked Union troops.

The **Battle of Bull Run** showed both sides that their soldiers needed training. It also showed that the war would be long and bloody.

"All quiet along the Potomac." After the disaster at Bull Run, President Lincoln appointed General George McClellan as commander of the Union armies. McClellan was a superb organizer. In six months, he transformed a mob of raw recruits into an army of trained soldiers.

McClellan, however, was very cautious. He delayed leading his troops into battle. Newspapers reported "all quiet along the Potomac" so often that the phrase became a national joke. Finally, President Lincoln lost patience. "If McClellan is not using the army," the President snapped, "I should like to borrow it."

A cautious move on Richmond. In March 1862, McClellan was at last ready to move. He and most of the Union army left Washington by steamboat and sailed down the Potomac River for Richmond. (See the map on page 459.) The rest of the army stayed in Washington.

Landing south of Richmond, McClellan began inching slowly toward the Confeder-

458 • Chapter 16

Historical Sidelight
Background

s a child, Jackson faced the double obstacle of being poor and being an orphan. Even as a child, though, he took for himself the motto "You may be whatever you resolve to be"— and he stuck to it. He managed to get an appointment to West Point, but he began at the very bottom of his class. Nevertheless, when he graduated in 1846 (in the same class as George McClellan, who ranked second in the class), he was in the top third of the class.

There is some question as to the real meaning of General Barnard Bee's reference to Jackson as a "stone wall." Was he inspiring the troops by pointing to a brave leader, or was he complaining about Jackson's inactivity (standing there like a stone wall)? The answer may never be known, for Bee died shortly afterward. In any case, the name "Stonewall" was taken as a badge of honor, and Jackson's troops became known as the Stonewall Brigade.

Connections With Art
Background

One problem at the Battle of Bull Run was that the design of the Confederate flag with "stars and bars" resembled the design of the United States flag. The Confederacy later redesigned the battle flag by changing the design to a simple red flag with a blue cross.

ate capital. Learning of the Union approach, General Robert E. Lee launched a series of brilliant counterattacks. Lee also sent General Stonewall Jackson north to threaten Washington. Lincoln was thus prevented from sending the rest of the Union army to help McClellan.

Cautious as usual, McClellan decided to abandon the attack and retreated. Once again, there was a lull in the war in the East.

Naval Action

Early in the war, Union ships blockaded southern ports. At first, enterprising southerners slipped through the blockade in small, fast ships. These "blockade runners" brought everything from matches to guns into the Confederacy.

In time, however, the blockade became more effective. Trade through southern ports dropped by more than 90 percent. The South desperately needed a way to break the Union blockade. One method it tried was the ironclad ship. (See Exploring Technology, on pages 460 and 461.)

At the start of the war, the Union abandoned a warship named the **Merrimack** near Portsmouth, Virginia. Confederates covered the ship with iron plates 4 inches thick and sent it into battle against the Union navy. On March 8, 1862, the *Merrimack* sank one Union ship, drove another aground, and forced a third to surrender. Their cannonballs bounced harmlessly off the *Merrimack*'s metal skin.

The Union countered with its own ironclads. One of these, the **Monitor,** struck back at the *Merrimack* in the waters off Hampton Roads, Virginia. The Confederate ship had more firepower, but the *Monitor* maneuvered more easily. In the end, neither ship seriously damaged the other, and both withdrew.

Ironclad ships changed naval warfare. Both sides rushed to build more of them. However, the South never mounted a seri-

MAP STUDY

Early in the war, General Lee led the Confederate army to one victory after another in the East.
1. *What victories did Lee win in the East in 1862?*
2. *Who claimed victory at Antietam?*
3. **Applying Information** *Based on the subsection Naval Action, locate Hampton Roads, Virginia, on the map.*

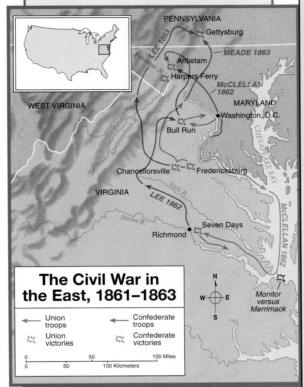

The Civil War in the East, 1861–1863

→ Union troops
← Confederate troops
☆ Union victories
☆ Confederate victories

0   50   100 Miles
0   50   100 Kilometers

ous attack against the Union navy. The Union blockade held throughout the war.

Antietam

In September 1862, General Lee took the offensive and marched his troops north into Maryland. He believed that a southern

Answers to Map Study

1. Seven Days and Bull Run 2. the Union 3. It is in approximately the same location as the site of the battle between the *Monitor* and the *Merrimack.*

Voices of Freedom

Primary Source You might assign selection 18-4, The Battle of Antietam, on pages 122–123 of *Voices of Freedom*. The selection is an account of the battle written by George Washburn Smalley, war correspondent for the *New York Tribune*. (Enrichment/Average)

Connections With Technology
Background

John Ericsson, the designer of the *Monitor,* was a naval engineer born in Sweden. He immigrated to the United States in 1839 and began designing iron ships—an idea that would revolutionize naval warfare. Ericsson secured more than 100 separate patents for inventions that went into the construction of the *Monitor*. Always looking to the future, Ericsson spent the years following the Civil War researching torpedoes and solar-powered engines.

Connections With Technology
Background

In taking possession of and refitting the *Merrimack,* the Confederacy also renamed the warship—from the U.S.S. *Merrimack* to the C.S.S. *Virginia*. Although the Union did not acknowledge the new name, it was the *Virginia* that battled with the *Monitor*.

The *Virginia* certainly was difficult to maneuver—a 180-degree turn took about 30 minutes. Furthermore, its engines were weak, and it was so heavy that it could not operate in shallow water and so unseaworthy that it could not venture into the open sea.

Answer to Exploring Technology

iron plating as protection from enemy fire and from ramming; special protection for the pilot house

Transparencies

Exploring Technology Use the transparency Ironclad Ship on page H-43 of *American History Transparencies*. Teaching suggestions can be found on page H-12. (Enrichment/Average)

Iron plates protected the *Monitor* from enemy fire and from ramming by enemy ships.

The 11-inch guns were large compared with the *Merrimack*'s.

Revolving gun turret

Boiler room

Boilers

Turret gears and machinery

Main engine

Engine room

Rudder

Propeller

Ironclad Ship *The* Monitor, *the first Union ironclad ship, looked like a "tin can on a raft." Its most unusual feature was the revolving gun turret, which made it possible to fire at the enemy from any angle. Before this, a captain might have had to turn his entire ship around in order to reach his target. In the picture at right, the* Monitor *is shown engaging the* Merrimack, *a Confederate ironclad.* **Technology** *What other advantages did ironclads offer?*

victory on northern soil would be a great blow to northern morale. Luck was not on Lee's side, however. A Confederate messenger lost Lee's battle plans. Two Union soldiers found them and turned them over to McClellan.

Even with Lee's battle plan before him, McClellan was slow to act. After waiting a few days, he finally attacked Lee's main force at Antietam (an TEET uhm) on September 17. In the daylong battle that followed, more than 23,000 Union and Confederate soldiers were killed or wounded.

On the night of September 18, Lee ordered his troops to slip back into Virginia. The Confederates breathed a sigh of relief when they saw that McClellan was not pursuing them.

Neither side won a clear victory at the **Battle of Antietam.** Because Lee had or-

Historical Sidelight
Background

Among both Union and Confederate troops, the fighting at Antietam was among the fiercest of the war. Speaking of the Confederate soldiers, one Union officer wrote at the time, "It is beyond all wonder how such men as the rebel troops can fight on as they do; that, filthy, sick, hungry, and miserable, they should prove such heroes in fight, is past explanation."

Rufus Dawes, a Union soldier, admits that there was a general lack of enthusiasm at first: "The truth is, when bullets are whacking against tree-trunks and solid shot are cracking skulls like egg-shells, the consuming passion in the breast of the average man is to get out of the way." Still, when his regiment was ordered to advance, "In a second the air was full of the hiss of bullets and the hurtle of grape-shot. The mental strain was so great that I saw at that moment . . . the whole landscape turned slightly red." Dawes was referring to a kind of fighting frenzy that made (and sometimes still makes) soldiers fight like reckless killing machines.

Connections With Mathematics
Activity

The army was organized as follows: 10 companies equaled 1 regiment; 4 regiments equaled 1 brigade; 4 brigades equaled 1 division; 2 or 3 divisions equaled 1 army corps. On paper, 1 regiment had about 1,000 troops and officers. Ask: Approximately how many soldiers were in 1 company? (100) In 1 brigade? (4,000) In 1 division? (16,000) In 1 army corps of 2 divisions? (32,000)

Air vent

Anchor

The captain, pilot, and helmsman directed the ship from the armor-plated pilot house.

Officers' quarters

Crew's quarters

Ammunition room

dered his forces to withdraw, however, the North claimed victory.

Winning the Mississippi

While McClellan hesitated in the East, Union forces gained ground in the West. As you have read, the Union war plan called for the North to gain control of the Mississippi River. General Ulysses S. Grant began moving toward that goal. (See the map on page 474.) In February 1862, Grant attacked and captured Fort Henry and Fort Donelson in Tennessee. These Confederate forts guarded two important tributaries of the Mississippi.

Shiloh. Grant now pushed south to Shiloh, a small village located on the Tennessee River. At Shiloh, on April 6, he was surprised by Confederate forces. Only after reinforcements arrived was Grant able to beat back the enemy.

The ***Battle of Shiloh*** was one of the bloodiest battles of the Civil War. More Americans were killed or wounded at Shiloh than in the American Revolution, the War of 1812, and the Mexican War combined.

The fall of Vicksburg. While Grant was fighting at Shiloh, the Union navy moved to gain control of the Mississippi River. In April 1862, Union gunboats captured the city of New Orleans. Other ships seized Memphis,

Chapter 16 • **461**

Cooperative Learning
Activity

Divide the class into groups of three or four. Have each group collaborate to write essays comparing the war goals of the North and the South in the early years of the war. Have them answer the following questions: How successful was each side in achieving its goals? What advantages did the North have that helped account for its success? What might either side have done to bring about a quicker end to the war? You might have groups concentrate on the third question. Select one member from each group to read the team's conclusions. Use these presentations as a springboard for class discussion.

The Siege of Vicksburg *Here, Grant first attacks Vicksburg. Six weeks later, the city surrendered. Defeat was made more bitter by the date of surrender—July 4. Vicksburg did not celebrate Independence Day again until 1945.* **Geography** *Why did the Union want to control Vicksburg?*

Tennessee. The Union now controlled both ends of the river. The South could no longer use the Mississippi as a supply line.

However, the North could not safely use the river, either. Confederates still held Vicksburg, Mississippi. **Vicksburg** sat on a cliff high above the river. Cannons there could shell boats traveling between New Orleans and Memphis.

Early in 1863, Grant's forces tried again and again to seize Vicksburg. The Confederates held out bravely. At last, Grant devised a brilliant plan. Marching his troops inland, he launched a surprise attack on Jackson, Mississippi. Then, he turned and attacked Vicksburg from the rear. After a six-week siege, Vicksburg finally surrendered on July 4, 1863.

The Union had achieved two of its military goals. First, its naval blockade had cut off the South's trade with Europe. Second, by taking control of the Mississippi River, the Union had split the Confederacy into two parts.

462 • Chapter 16

SECTION 2 REVIEW

1. **Locate:** (a) Richmond, (b) Washington, D.C., (c) Potomac River, (d) Fort Henry, (e) Fort Donelson, (f) New Orleans, (g) Memphis, (h) Vicksburg.
2. **Identify:** (a) Stonewall Jackson, (b) Battle of Bull Run, (c) George McClellan, (d) *Merrimack,* (e) *Monitor,* (f) Battle of Antietam, (g) Ulysses S. Grant, (h) Battle of Shiloh.
3. Describe the North's three-part plan for defeating the South.
4. What did both sides learn from the Battle of Bull Run?
5. **CRITICAL THINKING Analyzing Ideas** "The South could win the war by not losing, but the North could win only by winning." What does this statement mean?

ACTIVITY Writing to Learn

Study the drawing of the *Monitor* on page 460. Write two sentences describing features of the ship that would make it effective in naval battles.

Freedom

FIND OUT
- Why did Lincoln issue the Emancipation Proclamation?
- How did Union war goals change?
- How did African Americans contribute to the Union war effort?

VOCABULARY emancipate

At first, the Civil War was not a war against slavery. Yet wherever Union troops went, enslaved African Americans rushed to them, expecting to be freed. Most were sorely disappointed. Union officers often held these runaways prisoner until their masters arrived to take them back to slavery.

Some northerners began to raise new questions. Would the North support slavery by sending runaways back to their owners? Was slavery not the root of the conflict between North and South? Had tens of thousands of men died to bring a slaveholding South back into the Union? As a result of questions such as these, the mood of the North began to change.

"Forever Free"

The Civil War began as a war to restore the Union, not to end slavery. President Lincoln made this clear in the following statement:

> ❝If I could save the Union without freeing any slave, I would do it; and if I could save it by freeing all the slaves, I would do it; and if I could do it by freeing some and leaving others alone, I would also do that.❞

Lincoln had a reason for handling the slavery issue cautiously. As you have read, four slave states remained in the Union. The President did not want to do anything that might cause these states to shift their loyalty to the Confederacy. The resources of these border states might allow the South to turn the tide of the war.

Addressing the issue of slavery. By mid-1862, however, Lincoln came to believe that he could save the Union only by broadening the goals of the war. He decided to free enslaved African Americans living in the Confederacy. In the four loyal slave states, however, slaves would not be freed. Nor would slaves be freed in Confederate lands that had already been captured by the Union, such as New Orleans.

Abraham Lincoln and Son Tad *President Lincoln believed that his most important job was to save the Union, not to end slavery. He felt deeply, however, that slavery was "a moral, social, and political wrong."* **Citizenship** *Why did Lincoln handle the slavery issue cautiously?*

Connections With Music
Background

One northerner who saw the Civil War as a crusade against slavery was Julia Ward Howe. She wrote *Battle Hymn of the Republic,* the most famous Union marching song. It compared the mission of the Union to that of Jesus: "As He died to make men holy, let us die to make men free."

Connections With the World
Background

After the Emancipation Proclamation was issued, English workers refused to build ships for the Confederacy and the czar of Russia sent warships to New York and San Francisco to show support for the Union.

Answer to Caption
He did not want to risk having the four slave states that were still in the Union go over to the Confederacy.

Section 3
pp. 463–465

 Bell Ringer

Write the term *Presidential Proclamation* on the chalkboard. Ask students to explain what they think this term means.

Lesson Plan

1. Focus As the Civil War dragged on, Lincoln came to believe that he could save the Union only by broadening the goals of the war. After a badly needed Union victory at Antietam, he issued the Emancipation Proclamation. In this section, students learn how the Proclamation changed the character of the war and encouraged more African Americans to fight.

2. Instruct Review the provisions of the Emancipation Proclamation with the class. (If possible, obtain a copy of the document and read parts of it aloud.) Then ask students to assess how each of the following people might have reacted to news of the Proclamation: (a) a slave in Georgia, (b) a slave in Maryland, (c) a slave owner in each of those states, (d) a free African American in Pennsylvania, (e) an abolitionist in Boston, (f) a Union soldier, (g) a Confederate soldier.

Lesson Planner

For a developed **Cooperative Learning** lesson plan, see the *Lesson Planner,* page 99.

Answer to Caption

slaves living in Confederate lands at war with the Union at the time of the Proclamation; slaves in the four loyal slave states and in lands already captured by the Union

 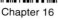 **Videotapes/ Videodiscs**

United States History Video Collection Use the video segment "Oh, Freedom!" from Volume 9, *The Civil War*, to enhance students' understanding of the significance of the Emancipation Proclamation. Approx. running time 5:00 min. (Enrichment/Average) Vol. 9, Ch. 16

Chapter 16   Play

Lincoln had practical reasons for this approach. He wanted to weaken the Confederacy without angering slave owners in the Union. Also, Lincoln was not sure whether most northerners would support freedom for enslaved African Americans. He hoped to introduce the idea slowly, by limiting it to territory controlled by the Confederacy.

The President had another motive, too. As you have read in Chapter 15, Lincoln believed that slavery was wrong. When he felt that he could act to free slaves without threatening the Union, he did so.

Lincoln was concerned about the timing of his announcement. He did not want Americans to think he was freeing slaves as a last, desperate effort to save a losing cause. He waited for a Union victory to announce his plan. The Battle of Antietam gave Lincoln his chance.

Issuing the Proclamation. On September 22, 1862, Lincoln issued a preliminary proclamation. It warned that on January 1, 1863, anyone held as a slave in a state still in rebellion against the United States would be emancipated. To **emancipate** means to set free.

Then, on January 1, 1863, Lincoln issued the formal ***Emancipation Proclamation.*** The Emancipation Proclamation declared:

“On the 1st day of January, in the year of our Lord 1863, all persons held as slaves within any state or. . . part of a state [whose] people. . . shall then be in rebellion against the United States, shall be then, thenceforward, and forever free.”

Since the rebelling states were not under Union control, no slaves actually gained freedom on January 1, 1863. Still, the Emancipation Proclamation changed the character of the war. Now, Union troops were fighting to end slavery as well as to save the Union.

Many Europeans applauded the Proclamation. As a result, it became less likely that Britain or any other European country would come to the aid of the South. The

Waiting for the Hour The Emancipation Proclamation went into effect at midnight, January 1, 1863. This painting shows a gathering of enslaved African Americans waiting for the hour to strike. **Citizenship** *Which slaves were affected by the Emancipation Proclamation? Which were not affected?*

Our Multicultural Heritage
Background

General Stand Watie, a Cherokee, led the last Confederate unit to surrender to Union forces. General Ely S. Parker, a Seneca, prepared the copies of the surrender papers that Lee and Grant signed at Appomattox.

Our Multicultural Heritage

The experiences of African Americans in the Civil War are described in two excellent books of historical fiction for young people. *Which Way Freedom?* by Joyce Hansen tells the story of a runaway slave called Obi, who fights with a black regiment of Union soldiers. *Corey* by Jane Miner is the story of a house slave whose freedom comes when General Sherman's troops destroy the North Carolina plantation where she lives.

Activity

Have students read these books. Then you might select two volunteers to act the parts of Obi and Corey. The actors should describe briefly to the class their lives during the Civil War. Once the actors have given their portrayals, other students can add experiences that Obi and Corey encountered and discuss the expectations and fears that these two young people had about freedom and their new lives.

Proclamation also prompted a wave of support for the Union from free African Americans.

African Americans in the War

When the war began, thousands of free blacks volunteered to fight for the Union. At first, federal law forbade African Americans to serve as soldiers. When Congress repealed that law in 1862, however, both free African Americans and escaped slaves enlisted in the Union army.

The army assigned these volunteers to all-black units, commanded by white officers. At first, the black troops earned only half the pay of white soldiers. Even so, about 200,000 African Americans fought for the Union. Nearly 40,000 lost their lives.

The 54th Massachusetts Regiment. Massachusetts was one of the first states to organize all-black regiments. One of them, the 54th, attacked Fort Wagner near Charleston in the summer of 1863. Under heavy fire, nearly 100 soldiers forced their way into the fort and engaged the Confederate troops in hand-to-hand combat. The commander, most of the officers, and almost half the regiment were killed.

The courage of the 54th Massachusetts and other regiments helped to win respect for African American soldiers. In a letter to President Lincoln, Secretary of War Stanton wrote that African Americans "have proved themselves among the bravest of the brave, performing deeds of daring and shedding their blood with a heroism unsurpassed by soldiers of any race."

Behind Confederate lines. As news of emancipation filtered into the South, enslaved African Americans found it hard to hide their joy. One woman heard the news just before she was to serve her master's dinner. She asked to be excused so that she could fetch water from a nearby spring. When she reached the quiet of the spring, she shouted: "Glory, glory hallelujah to Jesus! I'm free! I'm free!"

Despite the Proclamation, the war still raged and enslaved African Americans still had to work on plantations. Many slowed down their work, however. This was one way to undermine the South's war effort. They knew that when Union troops arrived in their area, they would be free.

Our Common Heritage

Sergeant William Carney of the 54th Massachusetts Regiment won the Congressional Medal of Honor for acts of bravery. He was the first of 16 African Americans to be honored in that way during the Civil War.

SECTION 3 REVIEW

1. **Identify:** (a) Emancipation Proclamation, (b) 54th Massachusetts Regiment.
2. **Define:** emancipate.
3. Why was Lincoln cautious about making abolition a war goal?
4. (a) Which areas of the nation were affected by the Emancipation Proclamation? (b) Were slaves actually freed when the Proclamation was issued? Explain.
5. (a) How did African Americans help the Union? (b) How did enslaved African Americans help to undermine the Confederacy?
6. **CRITICAL THINKING Drawing Conclusions** What did the treatment of blacks in the Union army reveal about northern attitudes toward African Americans?

 Writing to Learn Write the words to a song that an enslaved African American might have created after learning of the Emancipation Proclamation.

Answer to Caption

Possible Answer: Soldiers of both eras lack privacy and face the rigors of training and military discipline. The conditions are different in that Civil War camp conditions were cruder. For example, soldiers' diets probably had little variety. Furthermore, many Civil War soldiers had been drafted, whereas there is no draft in the armed forces at present.

Transparencies

Fine Art Use the transparency Rainy Day in Camp on page D-41 of *American History Transparencies*. Teaching suggestions can be found on page D-11. (Enrichment/Average)

Section 4
pp. 466–471

Bell Ringer

Create two columns on the chalkboard, with the headings Life in Combat and Life at Home. Have students list possible details about daily life in each environment during the Civil War.

Lesson Plan

1. Focus As the death toll climbed, support for the war waned. Northern industry prospered, but opposition to the war forced Lincoln to take stiff measures. Meanwhile, the southern economy declined. In this section, students look at life on the home front and at women's contributions to the war effort.

4
Hardships of War

FIND OUT
- What was life like in the Union and Confederate armies?
- What problems did each side face during the war?
- How did women help in the war effort?

VOCABULARY civilian, bounty, draft, habeas corpus, inflation, profiteer, tax-in-kind

In 1863, a Virginia woman wrote a letter to President Davis. In it, she pleaded with the Confederate president to send her son home from the war. "If you don't send [my son] home, I am bound to lose my crop and come to suffer," she wrote. "I am eighty-one years of age."

As this letter shows, the Civil War caused hardships not only for soldiers but for people at home as well. Southerners, especially, suffered from the war, because most of the fighting took place in the South.

On both sides, **civilians,** or people who were not in the army, worked on farms and labored in factories to support the war ef-

fort. They used their mules to move troops and supplies. They tended the wounded. As their hardships increased, so did opposition to the war.

The Blue and the Gray

Soldiers on each side came up with nicknames for the enemy. Union troops wore blue uniforms. They were called blues or Billy Yanks, short for Yankees. Confederate troops wore gray uniforms. They were called grays or Johnny Rebs, which was short for rebels.

The test of battle. Soldiers on both sides were young—most were under age 21. However, war quickly turned gentle boys into tough men.

Soldiers put in long hours drilling and marching. They slept on the ground even in rain and snow. Yet nothing hardened "fresh fish," as new recruits were called, like combat. Boys of 18 learned to stand firm while cannon blasts shook the earth and bullets whizzed past their ears.

Deadly weapons. New technology added to the horror of Civil War battles. Cone-shaped bullets, which made rifles twice as accurate, replaced round musket balls. New cannons could hit targets several miles away. As a result of these new, deadly weapons, one fourth or more of the soldiers in most battles became casualties. A casual-

A Rainy Day in Camp *On average, soldiers spent as many as 50 days in camp for each day in battle. This painting by Winslow Homer shows a rainy day in camp.* **Linking Past and Present** *How do you think life in the armed forces today is similar to army life during the Civil War? How is it different?*

Connections With Fashion
Background

Civil War soldiers often wore beards, partly as protection against the elements and partly because shaving at the front was inconvenient. "Let your beard grow so as to protect your throat and lungs," advised one Confederate manual. Union General Ambrose Burnside started a fashion trend by wearing whiskers that reached from the ear to the moustache—a style called "burnsides" and later "sideburns."

Critical Thinking
Making Decisions

Remind students that many soldiers on both sides during the Civil War were teenagers. Ask: How would you feel if you were asked to fight in a war right now? How do you think your family and friends would react? Under what conditions would you be willing to volunteer?

Johnny Rebs *Most of the soldiers in both armies were between the ages of 18 and 21. Some were even younger. The flag bearer in this picture of a Confederate artillery unit was not yet 16 years old.* **Linking Past and Present** *Could a 16-year-old serve in the armed forces today? Explain.*

ty is a soldier who is killed or seriously wounded.

In one battle, Union troops knew that they were greatly outnumbered. Each soldier wrote his name on a slip of paper and pinned it to his uniform. The soldiers wanted to make sure that their bodies could be identified when the battle was over.

Crude medical care. Soldiers who were sick, wounded, or captured faced other horrors. Medical care on the battlefield was crude. Surgeons routinely cut off the injured arms and legs of wounded men.

Many minor wounds became infected. With no medicines to fight infection, half the wounded died. Diseases like pneumonia and malaria swept through the camps, killing more men than guns or cannons did.

Prison camps. On both sides, prisoners of war faced appalling conditions. At Andersonville, a prison camp in Georgia, more than one Union prisoner out of three died of starvation or disease. One prisoner wrote:

66There is no such thing as delicacy here. . . . In the middle of last night I was awakened by being kicked by a dying man. He was soon dead. I got up and moved the body off a few feet, and again went to sleep to dream of the hideous sights.99

Discord in the North

Not everyone in the North supported the war. Some northerners thought the South should be allowed to leave the Union. Others favored calling a peace conference to work out a compromise with the South. Supporters of the war called these people *Copperheads,* after the poisonous snake.

Other northerners wanted to save the Union but opposed the way Lincoln was conducting the war. In the border states, many slave owners openly supported the South.

Filling the ranks. By 1863, with no end in sight, northerners became discouraged. Soon, there were not enough volunteers to fill the ranks of the Union army. The Union had been giving $100 **bounties,** or payments, to men who enlisted. Now, it raised the bounty to more than $300. Still, there were not enough volunteers. The government decided to take new measures.

In 1863, Congress passed a draft law. The **draft** required all able-bodied males between the ages of 20 and 45 to serve in the military if they were called. A man could avoid the draft by paying the government $300 or by hiring someone to serve in his place. This angered many people who could not afford the $300. They began to

467

---

2. Instruct Review Lincoln's reactions to draft riots in the North, as described on page 468. Then have the class debate the following resolution: that Lincoln's suspension of protesters' civil liberties was in the best interests of the Union. After the debate, have students use their notes to discuss what, if any, limits should be placed on civilian protest during time of war.

3. Close To close the lesson, name each woman mentioned in this section. Have students identify the contributions that each made during the Civil War.

 Lesson Planner

For a developed **Cooperative Learning** lesson plan, see the *Lesson Planner,* page 100.

Answer to Caption

No; the minimum age is 18.

 Audiocassettes

Listening to Literature Audiocassettes To give students a sense of the strong emotions expressed in ballads during the Civil War, play the selection, Willie Has Gone to War (side 5, 3:57), from *Listening to Literature Audiocassettes, The American Experience.* (Enrichment/Average)

Connections With Technology
Background

In 1862, American engineer Richard Jordan Gatling patented the "Gatling gun." This rapid-fire machine gun was able to fire hundreds of rounds of ammunition per minute. Casualties might have been even higher if this gun had been used, but the War Department opposed funding the production of the weapon.

Linking Past and Present
Activity

Explain that for every Union soldier killed in battle, two died from diseases (93,400 compared to 210,000). A similar ratio held for Confederate soldiers. Ask: How has medical care improved since the Civil War? (Possible answers include the use of anesthesia, vaccines, antibiotics and other medicines, the invention of X-ray and other diagnostic machines, and advanced surgical techniques such as laser and microsurgery.)

see the Civil War as "a rich man's war and a poor man's fight."

Riots in the cities. The draft law went into effect just a few months after President Lincoln signed the Emancipation Proclamation. As a result, some northerners believed that they were being forced to fight to end slavery. Riots broke out in several cities.

The worst riot took place in New York City during July 1863. For four days, white workers attacked free blacks. Rioters also attacked rich New Yorkers who had paid to avoid serving in the army. At least 74 people were killed during the riot.

Lincoln moved to stop the draft riots and other "disloyal practices." Several times, he suspended **habeas corpus** (HAY bee uhs KOR puhs), the right to have a hearing before being jailed. When people protested his action, Lincoln referred them to the Constitution. It gave him the power, he said, to deny people their rights "when in the cases of rebellion or invasion, the public safety may require it."

Trouble in the Confederacy

The Confederacy had its share of problems, too. In some areas of the South, such as eastern Tennessee, thousands of citizens opposed the war.

Jefferson Davis faced problems in creating a strong federal government in the South. Many southerners believed strongly in the idea of states' rights. They resisted paying taxes to a central government. They also did not give full cooperation on military or other matters. At one point, Georgia threatened to secede from the Confederacy!

Like the North, the South faced a shortage of soldiers. As early as 1862, the South passed a draft law. Under the law, men who owned or supervised more than 20 slaves

Lottery Wheel *Desperate for troops, the Union passed a draft law in 1863. In Wilmington, Delaware, this glass-sided lottery wheel was used to select the names of those who would serve.* **Citizenship** *Why did the draft law lead to rioting in some cities?*

did not have to serve in the army. This caused much resentment among the South's small farmers. Most of them owned no slaves, or only a few slaves. They felt it was unfair that they had to fight to preserve slavery and slave owners did not.

Toward the end of the war, the South was unable to replace soldiers killed or wounded in battle—or the thousands who deserted. There simply were not enough white men to fill the ranks. Robert E. Lee urged the Confederacy to let enslaved African Americans serve as soldiers. The Confederate congress finally agreed to Lee's plan. However, the war ended before any enslaved people put on gray uniforms.

War Boosts the Northern Economy

The Civil War cost far more than any earlier war. Both sides needed to find ways to pay for it.

Raising money in the North. In 1861, Congress passed the nation's first income tax law. It required all workers to pay a small part of their wages to the federal government.

The North also raised money by taxing luxuries like carriages, jewelry, and billiard tables. In addition, the Union issued bonds worth millions of dollars to help finance the war. People who bought bonds were in effect lending money to the Union.

Rising prices. Even with new taxes and bonds, however, the Union did not have enough money to pay for the war. To get the funds it needed, the North printed more than $400 million in paper money. People called these dollars "greenbacks" because of their color.

Historical Sidelight
Background

Most of the war was fought between a clearly defined North and South, but the fighting was quite different in the West. Missouri, Kansas, and Arkansas were torn by partisan fighting—guerrilla forces employing terrorist tactics. Sometimes, Confederate generals would hire bands of such fighters to conduct raids against Union troops. Quite often, however, these bands acted on their own. They struck under the direction of leaders with various motives, many of which had origins in the earlier conflicts of "Bleeding Kansas."

Perhaps the most infamous of these guerrilla leaders was William C. Quantrill of Missouri. He and his raiders murdered civilians as well as soldiers. When five of the raiders' relatives died while in Union custody in 1863, Quantrill gathered a force of 450 men. He led them to Lawrence, Kansas, where they slaughtered 182 innocent people. Among Quantrill's raiders were future outlaws Frank and Jesse James and Cole Younger.

The flood of greenbacks soon led to inflation, a rise in prices caused by an increase in the amount of money in circulation. As the money supply increased, each dollar was worth less. To make up for this, merchants charged more for their goods. During the war, prices for goods nearly doubled in the North.

An economic boost. In some ways, the war helped the North's economy. Because many farmers went off to fight, there was a greater need for machines to plant and harvest crops. Northern farmers bought 165,000 reapers during the war, compared to a few thousand the year before the war began. Farm production actually went up during the war.

Wartime demand for clothing, shoes, guns, and other goods brought a boom to many northern industries. Some northern manufacturers made fortunes by profiteering. Profiteers overcharged the government for goods desperately needed for the war.

Hard Times in the South

The South had great trouble raising money for the war. The Confederate congress passed an income tax as well as a tax-in-kind. The tax-in-kind required farmers to turn over one tenth of their crops to the government. The government decided to take crops because it knew that southern farmers had little cash to spare.

The economy suffers. Like the North, the South also printed

paper money. It printed so much, in fact, that wild inflation set in. By 1865, one Confederate dollar was worth only two cents in gold.

The war damaged the southern economy, especially the cotton trade. Cotton was the South's main source of income. Early in the war, Jefferson Davis halted cotton shipments to Britain. He was sure that Britain would side with the South in order to get cotton. The tactic backfired, however. Britain simply bought more cotton from Egypt and India. Davis succeeded only in cutting the South's income.

Effects of the blockade. The Union blockade hurt the South badly. It created severe shortages for both soldiers and civilians. By 1865, famine stalked the Confederacy. Even the wealthy went hungry. "I had a little piece of bread and a little molasses today for my dinner," wrote South Carolina plantation mistress Mary Boykin Chesnut in her diary.

The South spent precious dollars buying weapons in Europe. However, the blockade kept most from being delivered. When the southern troops won a battle, they had to scour the field for guns and unused bullets. Southerners hurried to build weapons factories, but the shortages continued.

Even when supplies were available, the South had trouble getting them to their troops. Union armies ripped up railroad tracks, and the South had few parts to make repairs. Soldiers sometimes waited weeks for food and clothing.

Supporting the War Effort *In both the North and South, women formed aid societies to support the war effort. Women in Chicago made and sold the antislavery potholders at left. In Richmond, women crafted the Confederate flag at right out of paper roses.* **Citizenship** *Why was the support of people on the home front so important to both sides?*

" " Voices of Freedom

Primary Source You might assign selection 18-6, A Southern Woman Takes Over at Home, on page 124 of *Voices of Freedom*. The selection is from an account of the difficult war years by Victoria Clayton, the wife of a wealthy Alabama planter and lawyer. (Enrichment/Average)

Connections With the World
Background

Although Great Britain did not officially support the Confederacy, some Britons became successful blockade runners for the South. (In fact, some officers resigned from the British navy to follow this promising source of wealth.) By 1864, the Confederacy was paying captains about $5,000 in gold for each successful round trip. Other officers and crew members earned lesser amounts—but everyone received something. Furthermore, British citizens who were caught were released for diplomatic reasons.

Connections With Economics
Background

How effective was the blockade? From one point of view, it was not very effective. Over the course of the war, an average of five out of every six blockade runners got through. On the other hand, shortages, such as those mentioned by Mary Chesnut, were a fact of life. Not only were more supplies needed because of the war, but even the amount of attempted shipping fell to approximately 40 percent of its prewar level.

Cooperative Learning
Activity

Review with students the steps in writing an outline. Then divide the class into six groups. Ask the members of each group to outline one of the six subsections of Section 4. Have students use their outlines to summarize the main points in each subsection. Call on a volunteer from each group to read its outline aloud. Help the class evaluate each summary for thoroughness and accuracy.

Our Multicultural Heritage

Biography Have students read the biography, Clara Barton, Angel of the Battlefield, on page 47 of the *Our Multicultural Heritage* booklet. (Enrichment/Average)

 CD-ROM

History Makers Access the biography of Clara Barton on the American Heritage® *History of the United States* CD-ROM. (Enrichment/Average)

 Videotapes/ Videodiscs

United States History Video Collection Use the video segment "Angels of the Battlefield" from Volume 9, *The Civil War*. Approx. running time 2:45 min. (Enrichment/Average) Vol. 9, Ch. 22

| Chapter 22 | Play |

 Student Study Guide

Section 4 Study Guide Have students use the Section 4 Study Guide on page 130 of the *Student Study Guide* to review and reinforce the content of this section. (Reteaching/Average)

ACTIVITY

Guided Instruction Have students keep in mind Chesnut's knowledge of events when phrasing questions.

Women at War

In both the North and South, women took over jobs as men left for the battlefields. "Women were in the field everywhere," wrote a northern traveler in 1863. They were "driving the reapers. . . and loading grain. . . a very unusual sight [before the war]." As the northern economy geared up for war production, women also took jobs in factories.

Soldiers and spies. There were some women who helped the war effort more directly. In April 1861, Susan Lear wrote to the governor of Virginia:

❝Send me a good Musket, Rifle, or double barrel Shot Gun. I think I would prefer the latter as I am acquainted with its use. I believe, Sir, if a Regiment of Yankees were to come we [women] would drive them away.❞

A few women disguised themselves as soldiers and fought in battle. Others served as spies.

Nursing the wounded. Women on both sides volunteered to work as nurses. Untrained women had served as nurses during the Revolution and in the Mexican War. During the Civil War, doctors were unwilling at first to permit even trained nurses to work in military hospitals. When wounded men began to swamp army hospitals, however, this attitude changed.

History and You
In 1863, women in Chicago collected 30,000 boxes of supplies for the Union troops. When the government did not have enough money to ship the supplies to the front, the women raised $100,000—far more than needed— by selling home-made items at a giant fair. Have you ever organized a fair or similar project to raise money for a cause?

Dorothea Dix, famous for her work reforming prisons and mental hospitals, became superintendent of nurses for the Union army. She set such strict rules for her nurses that they called her Dragon Dix. Dix, however, was just as hard on herself, toiling alongside the women she enlisted.

Clara Barton earned fame as a Civil War nurse and founder of the American Red Cross. Barton kept records on hundreds of wounded soldiers. She helped many families trace sons and husbands who were missing in action. Sojourner Truth, the antislavery leader, worked in Union hospitals and in camps for freed slaves.

In the South, Sally Louisa Tompkins opened a hospital in Richmond, Virginia. Of the 1,333 patients treated in Tompkins's hospital, only 73 died—an excellent record for the time.

SECTION 4 REVIEW

1. **Identify:** (a) Copperhead, (b) Dorothea Dix, (c) Clara Barton, (d) Sojourner Truth, (e) Sally Louisa Tompkins.
2. **Define:** (a) civilian, (b) bounty, (c) draft, (d) habeas corpus, (e) inflation, (f) profiteer, (g) tax-in-kind.
3. How did technology make Civil War battles deadlier than battles of earlier wars?
4. (a) Why did many northerners see the Civil War as "a rich man's war and a poor man's fight"? (b) Why did many southerners oppose the draft?
5. How did the Union blockade affect the South?
6. **CRITICAL THINKING Applying Information** Why were northerners who opposed the war called Copperheads?

ACTIVITY Writing to Learn
Mary Boykin Chesnut, whom you read about on page 469, kept a detailed diary throughout the Civil War. List five questions that you would ask Chesnut about her experiences during the war.

Answers to Section 4 Review

1. (a) Copperhead, p. 467, (b) Dorothea Dix, p. 470, (c) Clara Barton, p. 470, (d) Sojourner Truth, p. 470, (e) Sally Louisa Tompkins, p. 470
2. (a) civilian, p. 466, (b) bounty, p. 467, (c) draft, p. 467, (d) habeas corpus, p. 468, (e) inflation, p. 469, (f) profiteer, p. 469, (g) tax-in-kind, p. 469
3. Weapons were more accurate and could be fired faster and at greater distances, resulting in higher casualties.
4. (a) A man could avoid the draft by paying $300 or by hiring someone to serve in his place. (b) Southern men who owned more than 20 slaves did not have to serve in the army. Many small farmers who owned no slaves thought that it was unfair to fight to save slavery when slave owners were not required to go to war.
5. The blockade strangled the southern economy, causing shortages of all kinds.
6. Possible Answer: Copperheads are poisonous snakes; the name suggested that opponents of the war were poisonous to the country.

CONNECTIONS

| ARTS | SCIENCES | GEOGRAPHY | WORLD | ECONOMICS | CIVICS |

Nurses in the Civil War

When the Civil War began, the United States was not prepared to care for the wounded. There were no ambulances to take the wounded from the battleground. There were no field hospitals to receive them, no medical corps to treat their injuries, no professional nursing staff to speed their recovery. Even a minor injury might result in death.

At first, volunteers rushed to fill the need for nurses. A few, such as the nuns from Catholic nursing orders, were trained providers of medical care. Others had been trained by Protestant nurses from the Kaiserwerth School in Germany. On the whole, however, volunteers knew little about caring for the sick or wounded.

Dorothea Dix, who was known for reforming the treatment of the mentally ill, became head of army nurses for the Union. Dix brought to the job knowledge that she had gained in Europe. Among the places she had visited was the British military hospital in Scutari, Turkey. There, she saw firsthand how famed British nurse Florence Nightingale had reformed nursing.

Inspired by Nightingale's work abroad, Dix and others attacked the

Nursing the wounded

greatest obstacle to effective nursing: unsanitary conditions. They ordered hospitals cleaned, kitchens established, and bath houses constructed. They provided medicines and bandages. They also fought against the dread disease of scurvy by making sure that soldiers received green vegetables to eat.

The lack of trained nurses during the Civil War dramatized the need for change. Following the war, interest in nursing education was high, and three schools of nursing opened in the United States in 1873. At first, these schools closely followed the model that Nightingale had established in Europe. In time, however, they developed a slightly different plan to meet the special needs of nursing in the United States.

■ How was American nursing influenced by European methods?

Susie King Taylor, Union nurse

ACTIVITY

Design a series of postage stamps celebrating the achievements of nurses during the Civil War.

Section 5
pp. 472–477

Bell Ringer

Ask students to explain what they think is meant by the phrase "government of the people, by the people, for the people."

Lesson Plan

1. Focus Lee scored stunning victories at Fredericksburg and Chancellorsville but then lost at Gettysburg. Soon after, Lincoln turned control of the Union armies over to Ulysses S. Grant. Under Grant's direction, the Union broke the Confederacy's will to fight. In this section, students examine the drive to capture Richmond and Lee's surrender.

2. Instruct With the class, create a chart of major battles of the Civil War. Label the columns Battle, Date, Location, Outcome, and Importance. Have students skim Section 2 for additional battles to be included in the chart. Suggest that students keep copies of the chart for future reference and review.

3. Close To close the lesson, have students list causes for the Confederate defeat in the Civil War.

Lesson Planner

For a developed **Cooperative Learning** lesson plan, see the *Lesson Planner,* page 101.

5
Victory at Appomattox

FIND OUT

- What ideals did Lincoln express in the Gettysburg Address?
- What strategies did Grant use to defeat the Confederacy?
- How did the war end?

As you have read, the Union claimed victory at Antietam in September 1862. In the next few months, however, the Confederate army won several dazzling victories. "There never were such men in an army before," said General Lee. "They will go anywhere and do anything if properly led."

These were gloomy days in the North. Few people realized that the tide of war would soon turn and the Union would win.

Confederate Victories

The two stunning victories that gave Lee hope came in late 1862 and 1863. (See the map on page 459.) Lee won by outsmarting the Union generals who fought against him.

Fredericksburg. In December 1862, Union forces set out once again on a drive toward Richmond. This time, they were led by General Ambrose Burnside. Meeting Robert E. Lee's army outside Fredericksburg, Virginia, Burnside ordered his troops to attack.

After the two sides traded fire, Lee had his soldiers fall back, leaving the town to Burnside. The Confederates dug in at the crest of a treeless hill above Fredericksburg. There, they waited for the Yanks.

As the Union soldiers advanced, Confederate guns mowed them down by the thousands. Six times Burnside ordered his men to charge. Six times the rebels drove them back. Southerners could hardly believe the bravery of the doomed Union troops. "We forgot they were fighting us," one southerner wrote, "and cheer after cheer at their fearlessness went up along our lines." The battle was one of the Union's worst defeats.

Chancellorsville. The following May, Lee, aided by Stonewall Jackson, again outwitted the Union army. This time, the battle was fought on thickly wooded ground near Chancellorsville, Virginia. Lee and Jackson defeated the Union troops in three days.

Although the South won the battle, it suffered a severe loss. At dusk, nervous Confederate sentries fired at what they thought was a Union soldier riding toward them. The "Union soldier," it turned out, was Stonewall Jackson. Jackson died as a result of his injuries several days later. Lee said sadly, "I have lost my right arm."

Cooperative Learning
Activity

As you enter this final section of the chapter, brainstorm with the class to compile a list of important figures from the Civil War. Then divide the class into teams of three or four students each to prepare a Who's Who in the Civil War for class reference. Randomly divide the list equally among the teams, and ask members to begin profiles based on information in this chapter. If possible, work with the school librarian to allow additional research during a class period. After the teams have completed their profiles, have them alphabetize their entries in book form. Make copies of the completed works and distribute one to each student.

Critical Thinking
Analyzing Information

Doctors amputated Jackson's left arm to try to stop the advance of blood poisoning. When Lee heard the news, he said, "He has lost his left arm, but I have lost my right." Ask: What do you think Lee meant by this remark?

Many historians believe that Jackson was perhaps the only officer who fully understood how to carry out Lee's military strategies. Ask: How might Jackson's loss have affected subsequent battles? Explain.

Still, Lee decided to keep the Union off balance by moving north into Pennsylvania. He hoped to take the Yankees by surprise in their own backyard. If he was successful in Pennsylvania, Lee planned to swing south and capture Washington, D.C.

Lee at Gettysburg

By chance, on June 30, some of Lee's men came upon Union soldiers at the small town of Gettysburg, Pennsylvania. The two opposing sides scrambled to bring in additional troops. In the battle that followed the next day, Confederates drove the Union forces out of town. The Yankees took up strong positions on Cemetery Ridge, overlooking Gettysburg.

Cemetery Ridge. The next morning, July 2, General James Longstreet trained his field glasses on Cemetery Ridge. Longstreet, one of Lee's best generals, studied the tents, campfires, and lines of soldiers that dotted the ridge. He did not like what he saw. The Union position looked too strong to risk a battle.

Lee disagreed. "The enemy is there," Lee said, pointing to the distant hill, "and I am going to attack him there."

"If he is there," Longstreet replied, "it will be because he is anxious that we should attack him; a good reason, in my judgment, for not doing so." Longstreet urged Lee to march south, drawing the Union army after him. Then, Lee could choose more favorable ground for battle.

Lee's plan. Lee's mind was made up. His soldiers wanted to fight, not retreat. Lee hoped to destroy the Union army once and for all.

Lee ordered an attack on both ends of the long Union line. Southern troops fought hard and suffered heavy casualties. When the sun set after a day of savage fighting, however, the Union line had not broken.

Next morning, Longstreet again argued that Lee should move south. Lee, however, was convinced that a direct assault could overwhelm the troops on Cemetery Ridge. He sent 15,000 men under General George Pickett to charge the center of the Union line on Cemetery Ridge. To reach the Yankees, the men would have to cross an open field and then run up a steep slope.

Pickett's Charge. Pickett's men waited in a shady grove as Confederate cannons tried to soften up the Union line. At 3 P.M., an unhappy Longstreet gave Pickett the signal to proceed. "My heart was heavy," Longstreet recalled. "I could see the desperate and hopeless nature of the charge and the hopeless slaughter it would cause."

Pickett gave the order to charge. As the men rushed forward, Union rifles opened fire. Row after row of Confederates dropped to the ground, bleeding. Still, the wave of

The Armies Clash at Gettysburg *The Battle of Gettysburg was a major turning point in the war. This painting shows almost the entire Gettysburg battlefield on the final day. The view is from the center of the Union line.* **Geography** *What was General Longstreet's opinion of the Union position? What was General Lee's opinion?*

Historical Sidelight
Background

As he first looked over the battle site, Lee told Isaac Tremble, one of his division commanders, "I shall throw an overwhelming force on their advance, crush it, follow up the success, drive one corps back on another, and by successive repulses and surprises . . . create a panic and virtually destroy the army." He went on to say with confidence that then "the war will be over and we shall achieve the recognition of our independence."

Historical Sidelight
Background

In the West Point graduating class in which George McClellan had placed second and "Stonewall" Jackson had been in the top third, George Pickett had placed last. Up to this point in the war, Pickett had had few chances to show leadership ability; at Gettysburg, he hoped to distinguish himself. Indeed, Pickett romanticized warfare, which was evident in his personal appearance. According to historian James M. McPherson, "With his long hair worn in ringlets and his face adorned by a drooping mustache and goatee, Pickett looked like a cross between a Cavalier dandy and a riverboat gambler."

men in gray surged forward. But the bullets and shells kept all but a few from reaching the top of Cemetery Ridge. A Union soldier described the terrible scene at the crest:

66Men fire into each other's faces not five feet apart. There are bayonet thrusts, saber strokes, pistol shots, men going down on their hands and knees, spinning round like tops, throwing out their arms, gulping blood, falling, legless, armless, headless. There are ghastly heaps of dead men.99

In the end, *Pickett's Charge* failed. As the surviving rebel troops limped back, Lee rode among them. "It's all my fault," he admitted humbly. Lee had no choice but to retreat. The Confederates would never again invade the North. The war had reached its turning point. ∎

Honoring the Dead at Gettysburg

The Battle of Gettysburg left more than 40,000 dead or wounded. When the soldiers who died there were buried, their graves stretched as far as the eye could see. On

MAP STUDY

Union forces in the West enjoyed success early in the war. From the West, Union troops under General Sherman pushed into Georgia and the Carolinas.
1. *What coastal city did Sherman capture after marching from Atlanta?*
2. *In what bodies of water did the Union set up a naval blockade?*
3. **Drawing Conclusions** *Based on the map, why would the South be hurt more than the North—no matter who won the war?*

Union Advances

← Union troops   ← Confederate troops
✕ Union victories   Union naval blockade

0   150   300 Miles
0   150   300 Kilometers

Linking Past and Present
Background

The casualties at Gettysburg included about 23,000 out of 88,000 Union troops and more than 20,000 out of 75,000 Confederate troops. The site of the Battle of Gettysburg is today one of ten designated national military parks in the United States. Visitors can tour the battlefield and see where various events occurred, as well as the site of Lincoln's address. Other such parks include Shiloh and Vicksburg.

Connections With Language Arts
Background

According to legend, Lincoln hurriedly scribbled the words of the Gettysburg Address on the back of an envelope while riding on a train. Scholars dismiss this, noting that it is a brilliantly crafted speech that uses the structure and rhetorical elements of classical oratory first developed by the ancient Greeks. Lincoln actually began writing the speech in Washington and revised it after his arrival in Gettysburg. (A quote from it appears on page 475.) The first to recognize its greatness was the main speaker, Edward Everett. The day after the dedication, he wrote to the President, "I should be glad if I could flatter myself that I came as near to the central idea of the occasion in two hours as you did in two minutes."

November 19, 1863, northerners held a ceremony to dedicate this cemetery.

President Lincoln attended, but he was not the main speaker. At the time, his popularity was quite low. Lincoln sat with his hands folded as another speaker talked for two hours. Then, the President rose and spoke for about three minutes.

In his *Gettysburg Address,* Lincoln said that the Civil War was a test of whether or not a democratic nation could survive. He reminded Americans that their nation was founded on the belief that "all men are created equal." Looking out at the thousands of graves, Lincoln told the audience:

> ❝We here highly resolve that these dead shall not have died in vain— that this nation, under God, shall have a new birth of freedom—and that government of the people, by the people, for the people, shall not perish from the earth.❞

Few listened to Lincoln. Newspapers gave his speech little attention. "It is a flat failure," Lincoln said. "The people are disappointed." Later generations, however, have honored Lincoln's brief address as a profound statement of American ideals.

Total War

For three years, Lincoln had searched for a general who could lead the Union to victory. More and more, he thought of Ulysses S. Grant, who continued to win battles in the West. In 1864, after Grant's victory at Vicksburg, Lincoln appointed him commander of the Union forces.

Sheridan in the Shenandoah. Grant had a plan for ending the war. He wanted to destroy the South's ability to fight. Grant sent General Philip Sheridan and his cavalry into the rich farmland of Virginia's Shenandoah Valley. He instructed Sheridan:

> ❝Leave nothing to invite the enemy to return. Destroy whatever cannot

BIOGRAPHY Ulysses S. Grant *Many northerners questioned President Lincoln's choice of Ulysses S. Grant to lead the Union troops. Grant's stubbly beard and casual clothing gave him a scruffy, nonmilitary look. Lincoln, however, believed in Grant's ability to win. "I can't spare this man," he said. "He fights."* **Citizenship** *How did Grant wage total war against the South?*

be consumed. Let the valley be left so that crows flying over it will have to carry their rations along with them.❞

Sheridan obeyed. In the summer and fall of 1864, he marched through the valley, destroying farms and livestock.

Marching through Georgia. Grant also sent General William Tecumseh Sherman to capture Atlanta, Georgia, and then march to the Atlantic coast. Like Sheridan, Sherman had orders to destroy everything useful to the South. Sherman's troops captured Atlanta in September 1864. They burned the

Chapter 16 • **475**

Connections With Technology
Background

The photographs of Mathew Brady, a portrait photographer who had lost much of his eyesight, and the photographic teams who worked under his direction are one of the most valuable primary sources about the Civil War available to historians. Brady's teams photographed almost every aspect of the war. Theirs was the pioneer work in modern photojournalism. However, the cost of his endeavor ruined Brady financially. As a result, most of the original glass negatives were sold and used as greenhouse windows. Tragically, over time, the effects of sunlight and weather destroyed these priceless works.

476

Answers to Map Study

1. Petersburg 2. Spotsylvania; the direction of the arrow showing Lee's movements indicates the order of events. 3. Grant knew that the Union could replace both men and supplies but that the Confederacy could not.

Voices of Freedom

Primary Source You might assign selection 18-7, Lee and Grant Meet at Appomattox, on page 125 of *Voices of Freedom*. (Enrichment/Average)

Videotapes/ Videodiscs

United States History Video Collection Use the video segment "Toward Union Victory" from Volume 9, *The Civil War*, to enhance students' understanding of the final battles of the Civil War. Approx. running time 2:30 min. (Enrichment/Average) Vol. 9, Ch. 31

| Chapter 31 | Play |

United States History Video Collection Use the video segment "1865 Conclusion at Appomattox" from Volume 9, *The Civil War*, to enhance students' understanding of the end of the war. Approx. running time 1:45 min. (Enrichment/Average) Vol. 9, Ch. 34

| Chapter 34 | Play |

city in November when Sherman began his "march to the sea."

Sherman's troops ripped up railroad tracks, built bonfires from the ties, then heated and twisted the rails. They burned barns, homes, and factories.

MAP STUDY

The last battles of the war pitted Grant against Lee in Virginia. Grant attacked again and again. Finally, on April 9, 1865, Lee surrendered at Appomattox Courthouse.

1. *Where did Grant hold Lee under siege for nine months?*
2. *Which battle took place first: Cold Harbor or Spotsylvania? Explain.*
3. **Solving Problems** *Why did Grant press his attacks despite huge Union losses in men and supplies?*

The Final Battles

| Union troops | Confederate troops |
| Union victories | Confederate victories |

0   50   100 Miles
0   50   100 Kilometers

A new type of combat. Grant, Sherman, and Sheridan had created a new type of combat called total war. In the past, only soldiers were involved in wars. In total war, however, everyone was affected as the army destroyed food and equipment that might be useful to the enemy. As a result of the Union decision to wage total war, civilians in the South suffered the same hardships as soldiers.

Lincoln Is Reelected

In 1864, Lincoln ran for reelection. At first, his defeat seemed, in his own words, "extremely probable." Before the capture of Atlanta, Union chances for victory looked bleak. Lincoln knew that many northerners were unhappy with his handling of the war.

The Democrats nominated General George McClellan to oppose Lincoln. Although he had commanded the Union army, McClellan was more willing than Lincoln to compromise with the South. If peace could be achieved, he was ready to restore slavery.

When Sherman took Atlanta in September, the North rallied around Lincoln. Sheridan's smashing victories in the Shenandoah Valley in October further increased Lincoln's popular support. In the election in November, the vote was close, but Lincoln remained President.

The War Ends

Grant had begun a drive to capture Richmond in May 1864. Throughout the spring and summer, he and Lee fought a series of costly battles. Northerners read with horror that Grant had lost 60,000 dead and wounded in a single month at the battles of the Wilderness, Spotsylvania, and Cold Harbor. (See the map at left.) Still, Grant pressed on. He knew that the Union could replace men and supplies. The South could not.

Connections With Civics
Background

As might be expected, McClellan was eager to see Lincoln defeated. The Democratic party, therefore, condemned Lincoln for his leadership and called the entire Union campaign a failure. The party also called for an immediate end to the war, with a negotiated settlement. The Republicans called for an unconditional surrender of the Confederacy. As his running mate, Lincoln chose Andrew Johnson, in part because Johnson was a southern Democrat who had stayed with the Union.

McClellan was the clear frontrunner at first. In September, however, General Sherman captured Atlanta. With that victory and others, a defeat of the Confederacy seemed much more likely. The Democratic call for an armistice now looked foolish, so McClellan turned his back on his party's platform, calling for the preservation of the Union. Republicans jumped on this political blunder, telling voters, "Don't swap horses in the middle of the stream."

Richmond falls. As Grant knew, Lee's army was shrinking. To prevent further losses, Lee dug in at Petersburg, near Richmond. Here, Grant kept Lee under siege for nine months. At last, with a fresh supply of troops, Grant took Petersburg on April 2, 1865. The same day, Richmond fell.

CAUSES

- South fears that it will lose power in the national government
- Issue of slavery in the territories divides the North and South
- Northerners hate the Fugitive Slave Law
- Southern states secede after Lincoln's election
- Confederates bombard Fort Sumter

THE CIVIL WAR

EFFECTS

- Lincoln issues the Emancipation Proclamation
- Northern economy booms
- South loses its cotton trade with Britain
- Blockade creates southern shortages
- Total war destroys the South
- Hundreds of thousands of Americans killed
- Lee surrenders at Appomattox

CHART SKILLS *The Civil War pitted the North against the South for four long years.* • *What effect did the war have on the northern economy? List two ways in which the war affected life in the South.*

Lee surrenders. Lee and his army withdrew from Petersburg to a small Virginia town called Appomattox Courthouse. There, a week later, they were trapped by Union troops. Lee knew that his men would be slaughtered if he kept fighting. On April 9, 1865, Lee surrendered.

At Appomattox Courthouse, Grant offered the defeated Confederate army generous terms of surrender. Soldiers were required to turn over their rifles, but officers were allowed to keep their pistols. Soldiers who had horses could keep them. Grant knew that southerners would need the animals for spring plowing.

As the Confederates surrendered, Union soldiers began to cheer. Grant ordered them to be silent. "The war is over," he said. "The rebels are our countrymen again."

SECTION 5 REVIEW

1. **Locate:** (a) Fredericksburg, (b) Chancellorsville, (c) Gettysburg, (d) Atlanta, (e) Appomattox Courthouse.
2. **Identify:** (a) Pickett's Charge, (b) Gettysburg Address, (c) Ulysses S. Grant, (d) Philip Sheridan, (e) William Tecumseh Sherman.
3. (a) What victories in late 1862 and early 1863 encouraged the Confederates? (b) What battle marked the turning point of the war?
4. What was Grant's plan for ending the war?
5. Why was Grant better able than Lee to withstand tremendous losses?
6. **CRITICAL THINKING Making Decisions** How might Lee's brilliant successes at Fredericksburg and Chancellorsville have contributed to his defeat at Gettysburg?

 Writing to Learn
Use the maps on pages 474 and 476 and your text to describe the troop movements of one Union general.

Answer to Chart Skills

The northern economy boomed; effects on life in the South included the loss of the cotton trade with Britain, shortages as the result of blockades, and destruction of land, property, and lives.

 Chapter Resources

Critical Thinking Duplicate and distribute the worksheet, Understanding Causes and Effects, from Unit 5, page 17, of the *Chapter Resources* binder. The worksheet reinforces students' understanding of causal relationships while reviewing key facts and concepts from the chapter. (Enrichment/Average)

 Transparencies

Cause and Effect Use the transparency The Civil War on page F-21 of *American History Transparencies.* Teaching suggestions can be found on page F-6. (Enrichment/Average)

Student Study Guide

Section 5 Study Guide Have students use the Section 5 Study Guide on page 131 of the *Student Study Guide* to review and reinforce the content of this section. (Reteaching/Average)

ACTIVITY

Guided Instruction Remind students not to describe the war as a whole. Encourage them to have classmates check the sense of their drafts before submitting final copy.

Learning Styles
Kinesthetic Learners

You might have students perform a skit depicting Lee's surrender to Grant at Appomattox. Have students research the original surrender terms, the setting, and the ceremony before writing a scene in which the opposing generals meet. Include the following characters: Grant, Sherman, Sheridan, Lee, and others at the students' discretion. Female actors may play the parts of male officers. You might videotape the skits.

Answers to Section 5 Review

1. See the maps on pp. 459, 474, and 476.
2. (a) Pickett's Charge, p. 473, (b) Gettysburg Address, p. 475, (c) Ulysses S. Grant, p. 475, (d) Philip Sheridan, p. 475, (e) William Tecumseh Sherman, p. 475
3. (a) Fredericksburg, Chancellorsville, (b) Gettysburg
4. Grant pursued a total war to break the South's ability to fight.
5. The North had more troops and supplies than the South.
6. Possible Answer: Lee might have thought that the victories undermined northern confidence and that a full assault by Confederates would break Union resolve.

CHAPTER 16 REVIEW

Answers to Reviewing the Main Ideas

1. (a) Southern advantages included the fighting of a defensive war and possession of skilled officers and soldiers; northern advantages included a larger population, well-developed industries, an extensive railroad network, and a larger navy. (b) Southern weaknesses included a lack of factories, few railroads, and a smaller population; northern weaknesses included the need to wage an offensive war on unfamiliar land.

2. (a) Fort Henry, Fort Donelson, Shiloh, Jackson, and Vicksburg (b) blockade of the South and control of the Mississippi River

3. (a) freedom to slaves in rebelling states or in parts of states not already captured (b) It made abolition of slavery in the rebelling states a war goal.

4. Reasons included the desire to end human destruction, willingness to let the slave-holding South leave peacefully, rejection of the idea of abolition, and opposition to the draft.

5. (a) The South levied a tax-in-kind and issued paper money; the North imposed income and luxury taxes, sold bonds, and issued paper money. (b) Both sides experienced inflation, but it was far worse in the South. The war helped northern industries to boom and gave the federal government the power to tax incomes; the war wrecked the southern economy.

6. Women took over farm and factory jobs on the home front; in the war, they served as nurses, spies, and, in a few cases, soldiers.

7. Northern forces not only battled Confederate troops but also destroyed property and burned the land through which they passed. They wanted to leave nothing that might be of value to the Confederacy.

Answers to Thinking Critically

1. (a) cone-shaped bullets, more accurate rifles (b) Possible Answer: Technological advances (such as aircraft, missiles, nuclear warheads) have made war far more deadly.

2. Answers will vary. Students who agree might argue that total war left innocent civilians without even the means to feed themselves. Students who disagree might argue that the tactic ended the war more quickly, thus reducing bloodshed and suffering.

Summary

- Neither the Union nor the Confederacy was prepared for war, but the Union possessed important material advantages.
- The North had three war goals: to blockade the southern ports, to control the Mississippi, and to capture Richmond. The South planned to fight a defensive war.
- Lincoln broadened Union war goals by issuing the Emancipation Proclamation.
- Both sides experienced divisions over the war, resentments concerning the draft, and inflation.
- The tide of war turned at Gettysburg in 1863, and in 1865 Lee surrendered at Appomattox Courthouse.

Reviewing the Main Ideas

1. (a) What advantages did each side have as war began? (b) What weaknesses?

2. (a) Which battles did Grant win in the West? (b) Which war goals had the North achieved by 1863?

3. (a) What did the Emancipation Proclamation provide? (b) How did it change the nature of the war?

4. Why did some northerners oppose the war?

5. (a) How did each side raise money to fight the war? (b) How did the war affect the economy of each side?

6. How did women contribute to the war effort?

7. How did the Union wage total war on the South in 1864 and 1865?

Thinking Critically

1. Linking Past and Present (a) What advances in technology made Civil War battles deadly? (b) How would a war today be even more deadly?

2. Making Decisions Some people believe that Grant's decision to wage total war on the South was wrong because it hurt civilians as much as it hurt Confederate soldiers. Do you agree or disagree? Explain.

Applying Your Skills

1. Analyzing a Quotation In 1861, antislavery leader Frederick Douglass said: "This is no time to fight with one hand when both are needed. This is no time to fight with only your white hand, and allow your black hand to remain tied!" (a) What did Douglass mean by this statement? (b) What evidence from the chapter shows that the government came to agree with Douglass?

2. Making a Generalization General Robert E. Lee said of his soldiers: "There never were such men in an army before. They will go anywhere and do anything if properly led." List two facts to show that his generalization might also apply to Union forces.

Thinking About Geography

Match the letters on the map with the following places: **1.** Atlanta, **2.** Bull Run, **3.** Vicksburg, **4.** Gettysburg, **5.** Appomattox, **6.** Confederate states, **7.** Union states. **Location** Which battles shown on the map were fought in the Confederate states?

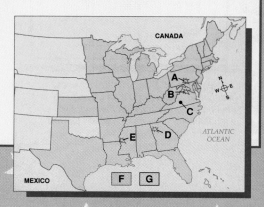

---

clear warheads) have made war far more deadly.

2. Answers will vary. Students who agree might argue that total war left innocent civilians without even the means to feed themselves. Students who disagree might argue that the tactic ended the war more quickly, thus reducing bloodshed and suffering.

Answers to Applying Your Skills

1. (a) Possible Answer: He opposed the law forbidding African Americans to serve in the army. (b) In 1862, Congress allowed African Americans to enlist in the Union army.

2. Possible Answer: Under Grant's direction, Union troops fought long and well to take Vicksburg; African American soldiers were called "among the bravest of the brave."

Answers to Thinking About Geography

1. D **2.** B **3.** E **4.** A **5.** C **6.** G **7.** F

Location: Bull Run, Atlanta, and Vicksburg

Fighting With the Blue and the Gray

Form into groups to review battlefield scenes during the Civil War. Follow the suggestions below to write, draw maps, plot graphs, or organize an exhibit to show what you have learned. You may use the textbook, encyclopedias, atlases, or other materials in your classroom library to complete the tasks. Be able to name your sources of information when you have finished the activity.

GEOGRAPHERS Imagine that you have been ordered to make a report for General Lee before the Battle of Gettysburg. Find out more about the geography of Gettysburg. Then draw a map showing main roads, bodies of water, hills, valleys, and major towns in the area. Include a scale and a directional arrow. Write a short report explaining the key points on your map and giving suggestions for winning the coming battle.

Drum of a Union regiment

SCIENTISTS Prepare fact sheets on medical care for soldiers during the Civil War. Include information on battle-field hospitals; diseases such as malaria, dysentery, and ty-phoid; and people who nursed the wounded, such as Clara Barton, Sojourner Truth, Sally Louisa Tompkins, and Dorothea Dix.

Confederate battle surgeon's field kit

WRITERS Imagine that you are an African American soldier fighting in the Union army. Write a series of diary entries describing your experiences and your feelings about the war.

MATHEMATICIANS Choose five major battles of the Civil War. Find out the casualties suffered by the North and South in each battle. Then use the information to make bar graphs showing northern and southern casualties.

ARTISTS Organize an exhibit of Civil War photographs and paintings. Prepare a catalog for your exhibit. Include information about each photograph and painting, and explain how it adds to your understanding of the war.

Family visit in a Union camp

 Set up a Fighting With the Blue and the Gray corner in your classroom. Display each group's finished activity or a description of it.

Learning Styles

The following chart indicates the activities appropriate for different learning styles.

Visual Learners
Geographers
Scientists
Writers
Mathematicians
Artists

Auditory Learners
Any or all of the suggested activities will appeal to these learners if you allow students to present oral reports and/or discuss their projects with the class.

Kinesthetic Learners
Geographers
Mathematicians
Artists

Evaluation

Geographers Maps must include all information requested and be completed to scale. Reports should show a working knowl-edge of basic military strategy and follow a logical course through the region.

Scientists Fact sheets should in-clude explanations of symptoms and effects of each disease men-tioned, and should highlight the important contributions of each individual in improving medical care.

Writers Diary entries should re-flect the emotions an African American soldier might have had in this situation as well as com-ments about the routine of daily military life.

Mathematicians Graphs must provide accurate statistics; the information presented should be easy to comprehend.

Artists Exhibits should be well organized and interesting. Cata-logs should highlight important information about each work pre-sented; explanations can reflect personal opinions about the scenes of war.

Assessment

Chapter Resources Binder For a more comprehensive evalua-tion of student understanding of this chapter, assign Chapter Tests A and B and/or Extra Unit Questions from Unit 5, pages 21–26 and 43–45.

Computer Test Bank You can use Chapter Tests and Extra Unit Questions to create your own tests for both testing and retest-ing.

Alternative Assessment

Chapter Resources Binder See the Alternative Assessment book-let in the *Social Studies Educa-tor's Handbook* series.

Portfolio You might meet with students to choose appropriate work from the chapter for inclu-sion in their portfolios.

Lessons	Teaching Resources
1 **First Steps Toward Reunion** **Objectives** 1. Identify the hardships that the South faced after the Civil War. 2. Identify President Lincoln's plan for reunion. 3. Explain why Congress opposed President Johnson's Reconstruction plan.	**Lesson Planner** Cooperative Learning, p. 104 **Student Study Guide** Section 1 Study Guide, p. 134 **Chapter Resources Binder, Unit 5** *Critical Thinking* Solving Problems, p. 31 *History Through Literature* O Captain! My Captain!, p. 32 **Our Multicultural Heritage** *Biography* Josephine White Griffing, Friend of the Freedmen, p. 49
2 **Congress Takes Charge** **Objectives** 1. Describe how white southerners tried to limit the rights of African Americans. 2. Identify the goals of Radical Republicans. 3. Explain why Congress tried to remove President Johnson from office. 4. Identify the Fourteenth and Fifteenth amendments.	**Lesson Planner** Cooperative Learning, p. 105 **Student Study Guide** Section 2 Study Guide, p. 135 **Our Multicultural Heritage** *Milestone* Fighting for the Franchise: Women and the Fourteenth Amendment, p. 51 **Interdisciplinary Connections:** Reconstruction ■ *Arts* The School That Music Built, p. 98 ▨ *Sciences* The Mathematics of Sharecropping, p. 99 ■ *Geography* Readmitting the Confederacy, p. 100 ▨ *World* Emancipation in Russia, p. 101 ■ *Economics* Getting Out of Debt, p. 102
3 **The Reconstruction South** **Objectives** 1. Identify the groups that dominated southern politics during Reconstruction. 2. Describe how some white southerners used terror to regain control of the South. 3. Identify what Reconstruction governments did to rebuild the South. 4. Describe what life was like for freedmen and poor whites during Reconstruction.	**Lesson Planner** Cooperative Learning, p. 106 **Student Study Guide** Section 3 Study Guide, p. 136 **Our Multicultural Heritage** *Biography* Blanche K. Bruce, Advocate of Justice for All, p. 50 **Chapter Resources Binder, Unit 5** *Skill Application* Finding Information in the Library, p. 30 *Geography in History* Birmingham: Steel Capital of the South, pp. 33–34
4 **End of an Era** **Objectives** 1. Explain why northerners lost interest in Reconstruction. 2. Identify what happened in the election of 1876. 3. Describe how white Conservatives tightened their control over the South. 4. Identify what the Supreme Court ruled in *Plessy* v. *Ferguson*.	**Lesson Planner** Cooperative Learning, p. 107 **Student Study Guide** Section 4 Study Guide, p. 137 **Posters** *Frederick Douglass Series, No. 31, by Jacob Lawrence*

Multimedia Resources	Additional Resources	Chapter-Level Resources

CD-ROM
Presidents Andrew Johnson
Videotapes/Videodiscs
United States History Video Collection
  Presidential Reconstruction, Vol. 10, Ch. 7
	Voices of Freedom
	A Planter Faces the Future, pp. 126–127
		Lesson Planner
		Activity Based,
		  pp. 108–109
		
		Student Study Guide
		Chapter 17 Study Guide,
		  pp. 138–139
		
		Chapter Resources
		  Binder
		Unit 5
		Vocabulary Building, p. 29
		Chapter Test A, pp. 35–37
		Chapter Test B, pp. 38–40
		Illustration Master, p. 41
		Extra Unit Questions,
		  pp. 43–45
		English Guided Reading
		Guided Reading,
		  pp. 33–34
		Spanish Resources
		
		Computer Test Bank
		Chapter Tests A and B
		Extra Unit Questions
		
		Guided Reading
		  Audiotapes
		Side 6
		
		CD-ROM
		Time Tour Rebuilding the
		  Nation (1864–1877) in
		  The Nation Torn Apart

Transparencies
Political Cartoons Andrew Johnson Mends
  the Union, p. G-19
Interdisciplinary Connections Dr. George
  Washington Carver, p. B-65
CD-ROM
Presidents Ulysses S. Grant
Videotapes/Videodiscs
United States History Video Collection
  Radical Reconstruction, Vol. 10, Ch. 10
	Voices of Freedom
	From the Black Codes, pp. 127–128
	Customized Reader
	Resolutions of the Illinois Convention of
	  Colored Men, article VA-14	

CD-ROM
History Makers Hiram Revels
Videotapes/Videodiscs
United States History Video Collection The
  White Redeemers, Vol. 10, Ch. 22; The
  Fate of the Freedmen, Vol. 10, Ch. 16;
  Economic Reconstruction, Vol. 10, Ch. 31
	Voices of Freedom
	A Former Slave on Reconstruction,
	  pp. 128–129	

CD-ROM
Presidents Rutherford B. Hayes
Videotapes/Videodiscs
United States History Video Collection The
  Persistence of Racism in the North, Vol. 10,
  Ch. 25; The End of an Era, Vol. 10, Ch. 28
	Voices of Freedom
	Winning and Losing the Right to Vote,
	  p. 129
	Historical Outline Map Book
	Election of 1876, p. 54	

Lesson Planner

For a fully developed **Activity-Based** lesson plan for Chapter 17, see the *Lesson Planner*, pages 108–109.

 Chapter Resources

Vocabulary Building The Vocabulary Building worksheet for Chapter 17 from Unit 5, page 29, of the *Chapter Resources* binder can be used as a prereading activity or as a review of chapter vocabulary. (Reteaching/Easy)

 Student Study Guide

Chapter 17 Study Guide Refer students to pages 138–139 of the *Student Study Guide* for the Chapter 17 Study Guide. The study guide can be used for chapter review as well as for reteaching. (Reteaching/Average)

 Guided Reading Audiotapes

Students can use *Guided Reading Audiotapes*, Chapter 17, side 6, to listen to section previews, summaries, and review questions. The tapes might benefit students who are auditory learners, students who have trouble reading, or students acquiring English. (Reteaching/Easy)

CHAPTER **17**

Rebuilding the Nation

(1864–1877)

CHAPTER OUTLINE

1 First Steps Toward Reunion

2 Congress Takes Charge

3 The Reconstruction South

4 End of an Era

1865 *Abraham Lincoln was assassinated. Across the nation, stunned Americans mourned the President's death.*

1867 *Congress passed the first Reconstruction Act. Under this law, southern states had to allow African American men to vote.*

1868 *Andrew Johnson was impeached. The trial created a furor, and spectators needed tickets to get in. In the end, the President was acquitted.*

| 1864 | 1866 | 1868 | 1870 |

WORLD EVENT
1867 Britain establishes the Dominion of Canada

Chapter Time Line
Activity

Divide students into four groups. Assign each group one event from page 480 and another from page 481 (for example, "1865" and "World Event/1870"). Have each group create two posters, one related to each event. Students may choose a single visual that clearly relates to the event (for example, Lincoln's funeral procession or a Klansman's white hood), they may create a collage (for example, assorted images that suggest the federal government's Reconstruction policies), or they may work with a combination of art and text (such as a quotation from someone associated with the event or a poem about it). You might use the eight finished posters to create a class time line, using construction paper for the time line itself.

Chapter Setting

" **W**ith malice toward none; with charity for all; with firmness in the right, as God gives us to see the right, let us strive on to finish the work we are in; to bind up the nation's wounds; to care for him who shall have borne the battle and for his widow, and his orphan—to do all which may achieve and cherish a just and lasting peace among ourselves, and with all nations. "

President Abraham Lincoln spoke these words on March 4, 1865, as part of his second inaugural address. In the South, cannons still roared and soldiers still died on the battlefield. Yet Americans knew that the Civil War was nearly over. Soon, it would be time to rebuild and reunite the nation.

Lincoln wanted all Americans to work together at this huge task. In his speech, he urged northerners to forgive the South. He called on northerners and southerners to build a "union of the hearts."

Not all northerners shared Lincoln's forgiving spirit. The South had caused the Civil War, they said, and the South should be punished for it. Some wanted Confederate leaders to stand trial for treason. Others wanted to seize southern plantations, break them up, and give the land to newly freed slaves.

Americans faced hard decisions in the years following the Civil War. The fighting ended in 1865, but the North and the South still had many problems to resolve before they could truly be reunited.

ACTIVITY List possible goals for rebuilding the South. Then choose one goal and brainstorm ways that this goal could best be achieved.

1870 *Congress outlawed the use of force to keep people from voting. They hoped to stop groups that used acts of terror to keep African Americans from the polls.*

1872 *President Ulysses S. Grant was reelected. Widespread corruption in Grant's government helped weaken support for Reconstruction policies.*

1877 *Rutherford B. Hayes became President after a disputed election. His decision to remove remaining federal troops from the South ended Reconstruction.*

| 1870 | 1872 | 1874 | 1876 |

▲ **WORLD EVENT 1870** Italy unified

▲ **WORLD EVENT 1871** Germany unified

Chapter 17 • **481**

Bell Ringer

Ask students to restate in their own words the meaning of the following from President Lincoln's second inaugural address: "With malice toward none; with charity for all."

Lesson Plan

1. Focus Even before the South surrendered, President Lincoln began planning the difficult task of rebuilding. However, when an assassin's bullet ended Lincoln's life, the program fell to Andrew Johnson. Johnson, like Lincoln, proposed a lenient policy toward the South; however, he faced opposition from Republicans in Congress. In this section, students examine the growing conflict between the President and Congress.

2. Instruct Draw a three-column chart on the chalkboard and have students make a replica in their notebooks. Tell students to use the chart to compare the Reconstruction plans favored by Lincoln, the Republicans in Congress, and Andrew Johnson. Ask: What requirements did southerners have to fulfill to regain voting rights under each plan? In order to hold office?

3. Close To close the lesson, play a Jeopardy!-like game with students. Provide key information from the section as answers, and have students create appropriate questions.

1
First Steps Toward Reunion

FIND OUT
- What hardships did the South face after the Civil War?
- What was President Lincoln's plan for reunion?
- Why did Congress oppose President Johnson's Reconstruction plan?

VOCABULARY freedman

The North lost more soldiers in the Civil War than the South did. Still, northern farms and cities were hardly touched by the war. As one returning Union soldier remarked, "It seemed . . . as if I had been away only a day or two, and had just taken up . . . where I had left off."

Confederate soldiers, however, had little chance of taking up where they had left off. The South faced staggering problems after the war. Southern cities and farmlands lay in ruins, and a whole way of life had ended. All southerners—rich and poor, black and white—faced a long, uphill struggle to rebuild their lives.

The Defeated South

Shortly after the Civil War ended, an Englishman visited the South. He was horrified by the destruction he saw:

66 [The land consists of] plantations in a state of semi-ruin, and plantations of which the ruin is for the present total and complete. . . . The trail of war is visible . . . in burnt-up [cotton gins], ruined bridges, mills, and factories . . . and in large tracts of

once cultivated land stripped of every vestige of fencing. The roads, long neglected, are in disorder, and . . . in many places . . . impassable. 99

Except for the battles of Gettysburg and Antietam, all the fighting of the war took place in the South. In some areas, every house, barn, and bridge had been destroyed. Two thirds of the South's railroad tracks had been turned into twisted heaps of scrap. The cities of Charleston, Richmond, Savannah, and Atlanta had been leveled. A quarter of a million Confederate soldiers died in the war. Thousands more were disabled by their wounds.

The war wrecked the South's financial system. After the war, Confederate money was worthless. People who lent money to the Confederacy were never repaid. Many southern banks closed, and depositors lost their savings.

Southern society was changed forever by the war. No longer were there white owners and black slaves. Nearly 4 million **freedmen**—men and women who had been slaves—now lived in the South. Most had no land, no jobs, and no education. Under slavery, they had been forbidden to own property and to learn to read and write. What would become of them?

Rival Plans for the South

Even before the war ended, President Lincoln worried about rebuilding the South. He wanted to make it reasonably easy for southerners to rejoin the Union. The sooner the nation was reunited, Lincoln believed, the faster the South would be able to rebuild.

As early as 1863, Lincoln outlined a plan for **Reconstruction.** Reconstruction refers to the period when the South was rebuilt, as well as to the federal government's program to rebuild it. Under Lincoln's **Ten Percent Plan,** as it was called, a southern state

---

Historical Sidelight
Background

While about 200,000 soldiers were killed in action or died of wounds in the Civil War, twice as many died from diseases such as typhoid, dysentery, and tuberculosis. Hundreds of thousands more were wounded, many severely. In 1866, one fifth of state revenues in Mississippi went to pay for artificial limbs for veterans.

Connections With Economics
Background

Much of the devastation wrought in Richmond was the work of retreating Confederate forces, who left timed explosives in key military and supply outposts. Destruction across the South was horrendous, and the cost of rebuilding was staggering. After the war, the debt of the former Confederate states increased by more than $100 million. Financial aid to the South was used primarily to finance the rebuilding of railroads and the establishment of public schools.

Lincoln Visits Richmond *In the final days of the Civil War, President Lincoln visited the captured Confederate capital of Richmond, Virginia. Many war-weary residents of the city, as well as African Americans eager for freedom, welcomed the Union President.* **Daily Life** *How does the painting show the damage that Richmond suffered during the war?*

could form a new government after 10 percent of its voters swore an oath of loyalty to the United States. Once it was formed, the new government had to abolish slavery. Voters could then elect members of Congress and take part in the national government once again.

Many Republicans in Congress thought Lincoln's plan was too generous toward the South. In 1864, they passed a rival plan for Reconstruction. The **Wade-Davis Bill** required a majority of white men in each southern state to swear loyalty to the Union. It also denied the right to vote or hold office to anyone who had volunteered to fight for the Confederacy.

Help for Freedmen

Lincoln refused to sign the Wade-Davis Bill because he felt it was too harsh. Congress and the President did agree on one proposal, however. A month before Lee surrendered, Congress passed a bill creating the **Freedmen's Bureau.** Lincoln quickly signed it.

Providing food and clothing. The Freedmen's Bureau provided food and clothing to former slaves. It also tried to find jobs for freedmen. The bureau helped poor whites as well. It provided medical care for more than a million people. One former Confederate was amazed to see "a Government which was lately fighting us with fire, and sword, and shell, now generously feeding our poor and distressed."

Setting up schools. One of the bureau's most important tasks was to set up schools for freed slaves in the South. By 1869, about 300,000 African Americans attended bureau schools. Most of the teachers were volunteers—often women—from the North.

Both old and young students were eager to learn. Grandmothers and granddaughters sat side by side in the classroom. One bureau agent in South Carolina observed that

For a developed **Cooperative Learning** lesson plan, see the *Lesson Planner,* page 104.

Answer to Caption

The painting shows that many of Richmond's buildings had been destroyed in the war and that its citizens had suffered economically.

 Voices of Freedom

Primary Source You might assign selection 19-1, A Planter Faces the Future, on pages 126–127 of *Voices of Freedom.* The selection is Susan Dabney Smede's account of how her father coped with life after the Civil War. (Enrichment/Average)

 Our Multicultural Heritage

Biography Have students read the biography, Josephine White Griffing, Friend of the Freedmen, on page 49 of the *Our Multicultural Heritage* booklet. (Enrichment/Challenging)

Historical Sidelight
Background

When President Lincoln pocket-vetoed the Wade-Davis Bill, the authors of the legislation—Ohio senator Ben Wade and Maryland representative Henry Davis—wrote a fiery letter to Lincoln, condemning him as a dictator. For Ben Wade at least, such challenges to authority were nothing new. In December 1859, when tempers at the Capitol were hot, Wade openly carried a sawed-off shotgun to his desk. During the Civil War, he marched to the White House, first to demand that President Lincoln fire General McClellan, and later to demand that he fire General Grant. In the latter case, when Lincoln declined, Wade exploded: "You are the father of every military blunder that has been made during this war. This government is on the road to hell, sir, by reason of your obstinacy, and you are not a mile from there this minute!" Lincoln replied, "Senator, that is just about the distance from here to the Capitol, is it not?"

Answer to Caption

It set up schools and provided teachers for freedmen throughout the South. It also created colleges and universities for African American students.

Chapter Resources

Critical Thinking Duplicate and distribute the worksheet, Solving Problems, from Unit 5, page 31, of the *Chapter Resources* binder. This worksheet encourages students to use a graphic organizer as they consider possible solutions to the problem of providing former slaves with an education. (Enrichment/Average)

freedmen "will starve themselves, and go without clothes, in order to send their children to school."

The Freedmen's Bureau laid the foundation for the South's public school system. It set up more than 4,300 grade schools. It also created colleges and universities for African American students, including Howard, Morehouse, Fisk, and Hampton Institute. Many graduates of these schools became teachers themselves. By the 1870s, African Americans were teaching in grade schools throughout the South.

Charlotte Forten and African American Education

For former slaves, attending school was one of freedom's most precious gifts. Even before the Freedmen's Bureau began setting up schools, newly freed African Americans built schools on their masters' abandoned lands. Many teachers from the North came to help in these schools. Among these teachers was a young woman named Charlotte Forten.

Forten volunteers. Charlotte Forten came from a wealthy African American family in Philadelphia. As a young girl, she was educated by private tutors. Later, she attended a teacher-training school. A strong abolitionist, Forten devoted her life to helping African Americans improve the quality of their lives through education.

During the Civil War, Forten was eager to serve. She got her chance early in the war, after Union troops captured the Sea Islands, off the coast of South Carolina. Plantation owners fled, but their slaves refused to go with them. Instead, they planted crops, built a church, and established a school. In 1862, when she was 25 years old, Charlotte Forten joined a group of northern teachers who came to help the Sea Islanders with their school.

Forten faced a stiff challenge. She was to teach reading, writing, spelling, history, and arithmetic. Yet there were few books or other supplies. Classes were large and included students of all ages. Still, Forten was excited by the willingness and enthusiasm of her students. She wrote:

❝I never before saw children so eager to learn. . . . They come here as other children go to play. The older ones . . . work in the fields . . . and then come to school, after their hard toil in the hot sun, as bright and as anxious to learn as ever. . . . It is wonderful how a people who have been so long crushed to the earth . . . can have so great a desire for knowl-

Learning to Read *"My Lord, Ma'am, what a great thing learning is!" a South Carolina freedman told a northern teacher. This painting shows a Virginia family using their new skills to read the Bible.* **Citizenship** *How did the Freedmen's Bureau help African Americans get an education?*

Our Multicultural Heritage
Background

Women, black and white, formed the backbone of the Freedmen's Bureau. In praising their work, W.E.B. DuBois later wrote: "Behind the mists of ruin . . . waved the calico dresses of women who dared, and after the hoarse mouthings of the field guns rang the rhythm of the alphabet."

African American poet Frances E. W. Harper described Reconstruction in a book of poems called *Sketches of Southern Life* (1872). The following lines described the Freedmen's Bureau: "Very soon the Yankee teachers / Came down and set up school; / But oh! how them Rebs did hate it, / It was agin' their rule."

edge, and such a capacity for attaining it. ❞

Forten loved her work as a teacher, and her students made good progress. She assisted the tiny community in other ways, too. She cared for sick babies, and from time to time even tended a local store.

Recruiting for the Freedmen's Bureau. After two years, poor health forced Charlotte Forten to return to the North. There, after the Civil War, she helped to recruit teachers for the Freedmen's Bureau schools that were opening throughout the South. The diary she kept of her experiences on the Sea Islands was later published as a book. ■

Lincoln Is Assassinated

President Lincoln hoped to convince Congress to accept his Reconstruction plan. Whether he would have succeeded will never be known.

On April 14, 1865, just five days after Lee's surrender, the President attended a play at Ford's Theater in Washington, D.C. As Lincoln watched the play, John Wilkes Booth, an actor, crept into the President's box. Booth, a southerner, blamed Lincoln for the South's crushing defeat. Now, taking careful aim, he shot Lincoln in the head. Within a few hours, the President was dead.

The relief felt at the end of the war suddenly turned to shock. Millions mourned Lincoln's death. Booth, meanwhile, fled Washington. He was later caught and killed in a barn outside the city.

Linking Past and Present
Today, Ford's Theater is a national monument. It houses a collection of items related to Lincoln's life and death. The theater has also been restored, and since 1968 has reopened for dramatic performances.

A New President, A New Plan

Vice President Andrew Johnson became President when Lincoln died. Johnson had served as governor of Tennessee and had represented that state in Congress. When Tennessee seceded in 1861, Johnson had remained loyal to the Union.

At first, many Republicans in Congress were pleased when Johnson became President. They believed that he would support a strict Reconstruction plan. After all, Johnson had stated that "traitors must be punished." As it turned out, Johnson's plan for Reconstruction was almost as mild as Lincoln's.

Johnson called for a majority of voters in each southern state to pledge loyalty to the United States. He also demanded that each state ratify the **Thirteenth Amendment,** which banned slavery throughout the nation. Congress had passed the Thirteenth Amendment in January 1865.

Rebellion in Congress

The southern states did what Johnson asked. In late 1865, the President approved their new state governments. Southern voters then elected new members of Congress. Many of those elected had held high office in the Confederacy. Alexander Stephens, the former vice president of the Confederacy, was elected senator from Georgia.

Republicans in Congress were outraged. The men who had led the South out of the Union were now being elected to the House and Senate. Also, nowhere in the South had African Americans been allowed to vote.

When Congress met in December 1865, many Republicans refused to let southern representatives take their seats. Instead, Republicans set up a Joint Committee on Reconstruction to draw up a new plan for the South. The stage was set for a showdown between Congress and the President.

Chapter 17 • **485**

 Chapter Resources

History Through Literature To provide students with one writer's eulogy of the slain Abraham Lincoln, duplicate and distribute the worksheet, O Captain! My Captain!, from Unit 5, page 32, of the *Chapter Resources* binder. (Enrichment/Average)

 CD-ROM

Presidents Access the biography of Andrew Johnson from the American Heritage® *History of the United States* CD-ROM. (Enrichment/Average)

 Videotapes/ Videodiscs

United States History Video Collection Use the video segment "Presidential Reconstruction" from Volume 10, *Reconstruction and Segregation (1865–1910),* to enhance students' understanding of Lincoln's and Johnson's plans for Reconstruction. Approx. running time 5:50 min. (Enrichment/Average) Vol. 10, Ch. 7

Chapter 7   Play

Student Study Guide

Section 1 Study Guide Have students use the Section 1 Study Guide on page 134 of the *Student Study Guide* to review and reinforce the content of this section. (Reteaching/Average)

Historical Sidelight
Background

John Wilkes Booth, a member of a famous southern acting family, had been with the Virginia militia group that captured John Brown in 1859. In 1864, Booth organized an attempt to kidnap Lincoln, hoping that this deed would end the war. When the plan failed, he began plotting the assassination.

Booth's crime did not diminish his family's popularity. His brother Edwin even built a theater in New York City in 1869.

Connections With Language Arts
Background

In jumping from the President's box to the stage, Booth broke a bone in his leg. As he fled, he stopped at the home of Dr. Samuel Alexander Mudd. Dr. Mudd set the bone, not knowing Booth's identity. The doctor was later arrested and sent to prison for conspiracy in the murder of Lincoln. He was pardoned in 1869, but people continued to treat his name with disrespect. Even today, we say to a person with a terrible reputation, "Your name is mud [Mudd]."

Team-Teaching Suggestion
Literature

You might work with a literature teacher to present a lesson about the elegy, the poetic form that mourns the death of an individual. Include in the discussion "O Captain! My Captain!," written by Walt Whitman on the occasion of Lincoln's death. (See Unit 5, page 32, of the *Chapter Resources* binder for the text.) You might also use a more difficult elegy for Lincoln, Whitman's "When Lilacs Last in the Dooryard Bloom'd."

485

Guided Instruction Before students begin writing their headlines, have them review the section headings and list the events that each heading brings to mind. Then have students select the event that had the most striking effect on them to use as the basis for creating headlines.

Section 2
pp. 486–491

 Bell Ringer

Ask students to define the word *radical* in their own words. Have them share with the class names and/or images that they associate with the term.

Lesson Plan

1. Focus In 1866, Radical Republicans won a majority in Congress. They pushed through a new Reconstruction policy and brought impeachment charges against President Johnson. In this section, students focus on the policy of Radical Reconstruction and its impact on the South.

2. Instruct Divide the class into three groups. Have students conduct a debate on this resolution: "Resolved—that President Andrew Johnson should be impeached." Have each group assume one of the following roles: (a) Radical Republican sen-

---

SECTION 1 REVIEW

1. **Identify:** (a) Reconstruction, (b) Ten Percent Plan, (c) Wade-Davis Bill, (d) Freedmen's Bureau, (e) Charlotte Forten, (f) Andrew Johnson, (g) Thirteenth Amendment.
2. **Define:** freedman.
3. Name two problems the South faced after the Civil War.
4. What did the Freedmen's Bureau do?
5. Why did Republicans in Congress refuse to seat the South's representatives?
6. **CRITICAL THINKING Analyzing Information** Could Charlotte Forten have taught African Americans in the South to read and write before the Civil War? Explain.

ACTIVITY Writing to Learn
Write newspaper headlines for three events discussed in Section 1.

2
Congress Takes Charge

FIND OUT

■ How did white southerners try to limit the rights of freedmen?

■ What were the goals of Radical Republicans?

■ Why did Congress try to remove President Johnson from office?

■ What were the Fourteenth and Fifteenth amendments?

VOCABULARY black codes

In the spring of 1866, disturbing reports trickled in to Congress. In some southern cities, peddlers openly sold Confederate flags. A New Orleans restaurant featured

---

"Stonewall Jackson soup" and "Confederate hash." Throughout the South, people sang a new song. "I'm a good old rebel," it declared, "and I don't want no pardon for anything I done."

These reports confirmed what many Republicans had suspected. Under President Johnson's plan, there was "evidence of an intense hostility to the federal union and an equally intense love of the late Confederacy." "The rebellion has not ended," declared one angry Republican. "It has only changed its weapons!"

A New Kind of Bondage in the South

Most southern states had ratified the Thirteenth Amendment, which banned slavery. However, most white southerners did not want to give African Americans real freedom. Southern legislatures passed **black codes,** laws that severely limited the rights of freedmen.

Black codes forbade African Americans to vote, own guns, or serve on juries. In some states, African Americans were permitted to work only as servants or farm laborers. In others, the codes required freedmen to sign contracts agreeing to work for a year at a time. Those without contracts could be arrested and sentenced to work on a plantation.

Black codes, however, gave African Americans some rights they did not have before the Civil War. For example, African Americans could legally marry and own some kinds of property. Still, the codes were clearly meant to keep freedmen from gaining political or economic power. As one African American veteran wrote, "If you call this Freedom, what do you call Slavery?"

The North Reacts

Republicans were angered by the black codes and the election of former Confederate leaders to Congress. The Joint Commit-

---

Cooperative Learning Activity

Work with students to compile a class list of problems that the South faced after the Civil War. After students have listed as many problems as they can, divide the class into groups of four students each. Have each group brainstorm solutions not mentioned in the text for the problems on the list. Select a member from each group to present the group's Reconstruction Plan in a brief oral report.

Answers to Section 1 Review

1. (a) Reconstruction, p. 482, (b) Ten Percent Plan, p. 482, (c) Wade-Davis Bill, p. 483, (d) Freedmen's Bureau, p. 483, (e) Charlotte Forten, p. 484, (f) Andrew Johnson, p. 485, (g) Thirteenth Amendment, p. 485
2. freedman, p. 482
3. Possible Answers: destruction of homes, barns, bridges, cities, and two thirds of the South's railroad track; end of an economy based on slave labor; wrecked financial system; death of a quarter-million men

4. It tried to provide food, clothing, education, jobs, and medical care for more than a million newly freed African Americans and poor white southerners.
5. Southerners had deprived African Americans of the right to vote and elected many former Confederate officials to office.
6. No; slave codes in the South made it a crime for slaves to read and write.

Starting a New Life *Left without homes or work, newly freed slaves had to find ways to support themselves. In this painting by Thomas P. Anshutz, a family tends their small cabbage patch.* **Citizenship** *How did southern legislatures limit the rights of African Americans after the Civil War?*

tee on Reconstruction sent President Johnson a report condemning southern practices. "There is yet among the southern people," the report said, "a desire to preserve slavery in its original form as much and as long as possible." When Johnson ignored the report, members of Congress vowed to take Reconstruction out of the President's hands.

Radicals. Those who led the opposition to President Johnson were called ***Radical Republicans,*** often shortened to Radicals.*

---

*A radical is a person who wants to make drastic changes in society.

Thaddeus Stevens of Pennsylvania led the Radicals in the House. Charles Sumner of Massachusetts was the chief Radical Republican voice in the Senate.

Radical Republicans had two main goals. First, they wanted to break the power of the rich planters who had ruled the South for years. These "aristocrats," Radicals believed, had caused the Civil War. Second, Radicals wanted to ensure that freedmen received the right to vote.

Moderates. Radical Republicans did not control Congress. To accomplish their goals, the Radicals needed the help of moderate Republicans, who made up the largest group in Congress.

Moderates and Radicals did not agree on all issues. However, they shared a strong political motive for favoring a strict policy toward the South. Most southerners were Democrats. With southerners barred from Congress, Republicans easily controlled both the House and the Senate. If southern Democrats were seated, Republicans might lose their power.

The President and Congress Clash

The conflict between President Johnson and Congress came to a head in 1866. In April, Congress passed the Civil Rights Act. The act gave citizenship to African Americans. By passing it, Congress hoped to combat the black codes and secure for African Americans the rights denied them by southern states. President Johnson vetoed the bill. But Republicans in Congress overrode the veto.

Citizenship for African Americans. Some Republicans worried that the Supreme Court might declare the Civil Rights Act unconstitutional. They remembered that in the Dred Scott decision in 1857, the Court had ruled that African Americans were not citizens. Hoping to avoid a similar legal challenge, Republicans now proposed the Fourteenth Amendment to the Constitution.

Chapter 17 • **487**

ators in favor of the resolution; (b) moderate Republican senators opposed to it; (c) moderators. Allow the debating groups time to prepare. Then have them present their arguments. The moderators may ask questions and should then decide which side presented the more convincing arguments.

3. Close To close the lesson, ask students a series of rapid-fire *Who, What, Where, When, Why,* and *How* questions about Radical Reconstruction.

 Lesson Planner

For a developed **Cooperative Learning** lesson plan, see the *Lesson Planner,* page 105.

Answer to Caption

Black codes kept them from voting, owning guns, or serving on juries. Some states also limited what kind of work blacks could do.

 Voices of Freedom

Primary Source You might assign selection 19-2, From the Black Codes, on pages 127–128 of *Voices of Freedom.* The selection contains several articles from the black codes. (Enrichment/Average)

 Transparencies

Political Cartoons Use the transparency Andrew Johnson Mends the Union on page G-19 of *American History Transparencies.* Teaching suggestions can be found on page G-5. (Enrichment/Average)

Connections With Civics
Background

After the Civil War, so many previously enslaved African American couples wanted to be legally married that mass wedding ceremonies were often held. Some involved as many as 70 couples at one time.

Historical Sidelight
Background

Thaddeus Stevens's dislike for Andrew Johnson was almost legendary. When someone described the President as "a self-made man," Stevens replied, "I never thought of it that way, but it does relieve God Almighty of a heavy responsibility!"

When Johnson labeled the Radical Republicans as traitorous as the Confederate rebels had been, the House of Representa-

tives braced itself for a reply from Stevens. To the representatives' surprise, Stevens rose and announced how he respected the President for his "integrity, patriotism, courage, and good intentions." As Stevens continued, however, it became clear that he was being sarcastic. Thus, each successive word of praise resulted in another round of congressional laughter.

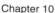
The *Fourteenth Amendment* granted citizenship to all persons born in the United States. This included nearly all African Americans. It also guaranteed all citizens "equal protection of the laws" and declared that no state could "deprive any person of life, liberty, or property without due process of law." This provision made it illegal for states to discriminate against an individual on unreasonable grounds such as the color of a person's skin.

Political rights for African Americans. In addition, the Fourteenth Amendment provided that any state that denied African Americans the right to vote would have its representation in Congress reduced. Republicans believed that freedmen would be able to defend their rights if they could vote.

With the Fourteenth Amendment, Republicans tried to secure basic political rights for African Americans in the South. In fact, the nation had far to go before all Americans achieved equality. Over the next 100 years, citizens would seek to obtain their rights by asking the courts to enforce the Fourteenth Amendment.

Election of 1866. President Johnson was furious. He violently opposed the Fourteenth Amendment and urged the former Confederate states to reject it. In time, all did so except Tennessee.

Johnson decided to make the Fourteenth Amendment an issue in the November 1866 congressional elections. Traveling through the North, the President called on voters to reject the Radical Republicans and endorse his plan for Reconstruction.

In many towns, audiences heckled the President. Losing his temper, Johnson yelled back. One heckler shouted that Johnson should hang Jefferson Davis. "Why not hang Thad Stevens?" the President replied. Many northerners criticized Johnson for acting in an undignified manner.

In July, white mobs rioted in New Orleans, Louisiana, killing 34 African Americans. This convinced many northerners that Johnson's policies were not succeeding. They felt that stronger measures were needed to protect freedmen.

The election results were a disaster for Johnson. Republicans won majorities in both houses of Congress. They also won every northern governorship and majorities in every northern state legislature.

The Radical Program

Republicans in Congress now prepared to take charge of Reconstruction. With overwhelming majorities in both the House and Senate, they could override Johnson's vetoes. The President, one Republican commented, was the "dead dog in the White House." The period that followed is often called *Radical Reconstruction.*

Radical Reconstruction begins. Congress passed the first *Reconstruction Act* over Johnson's veto in March 1867. The Reconstruction Act threw out the southern state governments that had refused to ratify the Fourteenth Amendment—all the former Confederate states except Tennessee. The act also divided the South into five military districts. Each district was commanded by an army general. Said one Radical senator, "This bill sets out by laying its hand on the rebel governments and taking the very life out of them."

The Reconstruction Act required the former Confederate states to write new constitutions. Congress also required the new state governments to ratify the Fourteenth Amendment before rejoining the Union. Most important, the act stated that African Americans must be allowed to vote in all southern states.

Elections in the South. Once the new constitutions were in place, the reconstructed states held elections to set up new state governments. To show their disgust with Radical Reconstruction policies, many white

Linking Past and Present
Background

The Fourteenth Amendment was the first clause of the Constitution to define citizenship. It also stipulated that states could not deny any citizen the rights of citizenship, and it guaranteed all citizens "equal protection of the laws." This right to equal protection is the legal basis for much of the civil rights legislation passed in the second half of this century.

Critical Thinking
Evaluating Information

Explain that during one election campaign for the Senate, Andrew Johnson told voters in Tennessee he wished that "every head of family in the United States had one slave to take the drudgery and menial service off his family." Have students use this comment as the basis for evaluating his attitude toward each of the following: enactment of the black codes; rise of Thaddeus Stevens and the Radical Republicans; ratification of the Fourteenth Amendment. Then, as a follow-up, ask: How would you expect Johnson to react to each of these events? Did Johnson's actions match your expectations? Why or why not?

CONNECTIONS

ARTS   SCIENCES   GEOGRAPHY   WORLD   ECONOMICS   CIVICS

Letter to a Former Owner

During Reconstruction, some freedmen stayed in the South with their former owners. They worked the land for a share of the crops they raised. Others left for the North and the dream of a better life. The following letter was written from Ohio in 1865. In it, freedman Jourdon Anderson responds to his former owner's request that he return to the South.

❝SIR: I got your letter, and was glad to find that you had not forgotten Jourdon, and that you wanted me to come back and live with you again. . . .

I am doing tolerably well here. I get twenty-five dollars a month, with [food] and clothing; have a comfortable home for Mandy—the folks call her Mrs. Anderson—and the children . . . go to school and are learning well. . . .

Mandy says she would be afraid to go back without some proof that you were disposed to treat us justly and kindly, and we have concluded to test your sincerity by asking you to send us our wages for the time we served you. . . . I served you faithfully for thirty-two years, and Mandy for twenty years . . . . If you fail to pay us for our

Form to help freedmen keep family records

A schoolroom during Reconstruction

faithful labors in the past, we can have little faith in your promises in the future. . . . We trust the good Maker has opened your eyes to the wrongs which you and your fathers have done to me and my fathers, in making us toil for you for generations without [pay]. . . .

In answering this letter, please state . . . if there has been any schools opened for the colored children in your neighborhood. The great desire of my life now is to give my children an education.

From your old servant,
—JOURDON ANDERSON❞

■ What rights did the Anderson family gain by their move?

 ACTIVITY Imagine that you are Jourdon Anderson. Describe what freedom means to you in terms of your five senses: Freedom looks like —, sounds like —, feels like —, smells likes —, tastes like —.

---

southerners stayed away from the polls. Freedmen, on the other hand, proudly turned out to exercise their new right to vote. As a result, Republicans gained control of the new southern state governments.

Congress passed several more Reconstruction acts, each time over Johnson's veto. It was Johnson's duty, as President, to enforce these laws. However, many Republicans feared he would not do so. Republicans in Congress decided to remove the President from office.

Showdown

On February 24, 1868, the House of Representatives voted to impeach President Johnson. As you have read, to impeach means to bring formal charges of wrongdoing against an elected official. According to the Constitution, the House can impeach the President only for "high crimes and misdemeanors." The case is tried in the Senate. The President is removed from office only if found guilty by two thirds of the senators.

During the trial, it became clear that the President was not guilty of high crimes and misdemeanors. Even Charles Sumner, Johnson's bitter foe, admitted that the charges were "political in character."

In the end, the Senate vote was 35 to 19. This was just one vote short of the two-thirds majority needed to remove Johnson from office. Despite intense pressure, seven Republican senators had refused to vote for conviction. They knew that Johnson was not guilty of any crime. The Constitution, they believed, did not intend for a President to be removed from office simply because he disagreed with Congress. Johnson served out the few months that were left in his term.

Grant Becomes President

In 1868, Republicans nominated General Ulysses S. Grant as their candidate for President. Grant was the Union's greatest hero in the Civil War.

By election day in November 1868, most of the southern states had rejoined the Union. As Congress demanded, the new southern governments allowed African Americans to vote. About 700,000 blacks went to the polls in the 1868 election. Nearly all cast their votes for Grant. He easily defeated his opponent, Democrat Horatio Seymour of New York.

The Fifteenth Amendment

In 1869, Republicans in Congress proposed another amendment to the Constitution. The *Fifteenth Amendment* forbade any

Lining Up to Vote *Throughout the South, African Americans exercised their newly won right to vote. In this picture, a federal soldier supervises an election in Richmond, Virginia.* **Citizenship** *Why do you think a soldier was present at this election?*

---

state from denying African Americans the right to vote because of their race.

Some Republicans supported the Fifteenth Amendment for political reasons. African American votes had brought Republicans victory in the South. If African Americans could also vote in the North, Republicans realized, they would help Republicans to win elections there, too.

Many Republicans had other reasons for supporting the Fifteenth Amendment. They remembered the great sacrifices that were made by African American soldiers in the Civil War. They felt it was wrong to let African Americans vote in the South but not in the North.

The Fifteenth Amendment was ratified in 1870. At last, all African American men over age 21 had the right to vote.

SECTION 2 REVIEW

1. **Identify:** (a) Radical Republicans, (b) Thaddeus Stevens, (c) Charles Sumner, (d) Fourteenth Amendment, (e) Radical Reconstruction, (f) Reconstruction Act, (g) Fifteenth Amendment.
2. **Define:** black codes.
3. How did southern legislatures limit the rights of freedmen?
4. Describe the Reconstruction plan adopted by Congress in 1867.
5. (a) Why did Republicans impeach Johnson? (b) What was the result?
6. **CRITICAL THINKING Analyzing Ideas**
   A senator who voted against the removal of President Johnson later said that he did not vote in favor of Johnson but in favor of the presidency. What do you think the senator meant?

ACTIVITY Writing to Learn
Take the position of either a radical or a moderate in the conflict over Reconstruction. Write a speech presenting your point of view.

3
The Reconstruction South

FIND OUT
- What groups dominated southern politics during Reconstruction?
- How did some white southerners use terror to regain control of the South?
- What did Reconstruction governments do to rebuild the South?
- What was life like for freedmen and poor whites during Reconstruction?

VOCABULARY scalawag, carpetbagger, sharecropper

By 1867, life in the South had changed dramatically. Gone forever were slave auctions and the hated slave patrols. African Americans were free—free to work for themselves, to vote, and to run for office. In Alabama, a group of freedmen drew up this ringing declaration:

66 We claim exactly *the same rights, privileges and immunities as are enjoyed by white men.* . . . The law no longer knows white nor black, but simply men, and consequently we are entitled to . . . hold office, sit on juries and do everything else which we have in the past been prevented from doing solely on the ground of color. 99

Before the Civil War, a small group of rich planters controlled southern politics. During Reconstruction, however, new groups dominated state governments. They tried to reshape the politics of the South.

 Student Study Guide

Section 2 Study Guide Have students use the Section 2 Study Guide on page 135 of the *Student Study Guide* to review and reinforce the content of this section. (Reteaching/Average)

ACTIVITY

Guided Instruction Before students begin writing their speeches, have them create a chart that lists the major issues facing Congress during Reconstruction and compares the positions taken by radicals and moderates. After students have chosen a position, they should organize their arguments in order of importance. Remind them to include a topic sentence at the beginning and a conclusion that restates or summarizes the point of view taken.

Section 3
pp. 491–496

 Bell Ringer

Tell students to imagine waking up in the middle of the night to find a large object on fire on their lawn and masked figures standing in the shadows. Ask: What would your thoughts and feelings be?

Lesson Plan

1. **Focus** Conservative Democrats in the South resented the influence exercised in state governments by scalawags, carpetbaggers, and freedmen.

Answers to Section 2 Review

1. (a) Radical Republicans, p. 487, (b) Thaddeus Stevens, p. 487, (c) Charles Sumner, p. 487, (d) Fourteenth Amendment, p. 488, (e) Radical Reconstruction, p. 488, (f) Reconstruction Act, p. 488, (g) Fifteenth Amendment, p. 490
2. black codes, p. 486
3. They passed black codes that forbade African Americans to vote, to own guns, or to serve on juries; restricted African American employment to working as servants or menial farm laborers; and forced freedmen to sign contracts binding them to service for a year.
4. It divided the South into five military districts and required southern states to ratify the Fourteenth Amendment and extend suffrage to African Americans.
5. (a) They feared that the President would not enforce Radical Reconstruction. (b) The Senate vote was one short of the number needed to remove Johnson from office.
6. Possible Answer: The grounds for Johnson's impeachment were political rather than "high crimes and misdemeanors." A vote in favor of his impeachment would have weakened the system of checks and balances established by the Constitution.

Groups such as the Ku Klux Klan struck back at African Americans and their supporters. At the same time, sharecroppers and small landowners faced a bleak future. In this section, students examine the problems faced by southerners during Reconstruction.

2. **Instruct** Have students use the headings and subheadings within this section to outline key facts and ideas. Have the class as a whole construct a final outline on the chalkboard.

3. **Close** Have the class turn the headings of the subsections into questions and answer them.

 Lesson Planner

For a fully developed **Cooperative Learning** lesson plan, see the *Lesson Planner,* page 106.

Answer to Caption

Possible Answer: intelligence, patience to deal with criticism and/or antagonism, and the courage of his convictions

 Our Multicultural Heritage

Biography Have students read the biography, Blanche K. Bruce, Advocate of Justice for All, on page 50 of the *Our Multicultural Heritage* booklet. (Enrichment/ Challenging)

 CD-ROM

History Makers Access the biography of Hiram Revels on the American Heritage® *History of the United States* CD-ROM. (Enrichment/Average)

Forces in Southern Politics

The state governments created during Radical Reconstruction were different from any the South had known before. The old leaders had lost much of their influence. Three groups stepped in to take their place. These were white southerners who supported the Republicans, northerners who moved south after the war, and freedmen.

Scalawags and carpetbaggers. Some white southerners supported the new Republican governments. Many were business people who had opposed secession in 1860. Now, they wanted to forget the war and get on with rebuilding the South. Many whites felt that any southerner who helped the Republicans was a traitor. They called white southern Republicans **scalawags,** a word used for small, scruffy horses.

Northerners who moved south after the war were another important force. White southerners called them **carpetbaggers.** They said that carpetbaggers had left in a hurry to get rich in the South. They had time only to fling a few clothes into cheap cloth suitcases, called carpetbags.

In fact, northerners went south for a number of reasons. A few were fortune hunters who hoped to profit as the South was being rebuilt. Many more were Union soldiers who had grown to love the South's rich land. Others, including many African Americans, were reformers who wanted to help the freedmen.

African Americans in public life. Freedmen were the third major group in southern politics during Reconstruction. Under slavery, African Americans had no voice in government. Now, they not only voted in large numbers, but they also ran for and were elected to public office.

African Americans became sheriffs, mayors, and legislators in the South's new local

BIOGRAPHY Blanche K. Bruce *The first African American to serve a full term in the Senate was Blanche K. Bruce. As senator from Mississippi, Bruce worked to improve conditions not only for African Americans but for Asians and Native Americans as well.* **Citizenship** *What personal traits do you think Bruce needed to succeed?*

and state governments. Between 1869 and 1880, 16 African Americans were elected to Congress. Hiram Revels and Blanche K. Bruce, both from Mississippi, won seats in the United States Senate.

White Southerners Fight Back

From the start, most southerners who had held power before the Civil War resisted Reconstruction. Nearly all were Democrats. These white southerners, known as **Conservatives,** wanted the South to change as little as possible. They were only willing to let African Americans vote and hold a few offices as long as real power remained in the hands of whites.

Spreading terror. Other white southerners took a harsher view. Some were wealthy planters who wanted to force African Americans back to work on plantations. Others were small farmers and laborers who felt threatened by the millions of freedmen who now competed with them for land and power. These whites declared war on anyone who worked with the Republican party. As Senator Ben Tillman of South Carolina recalled:

66 We reorganized the Democratic party with one plank, and only one plank, namely, that 'this is a white man's country, and white men must govern it.' Under that banner we went to battle. 99

Our Multicultural Heritage Background

While a United States senator, Blanche K. Bruce was one of the few members of Congress to defend the rights of Native Americans against unfair federal laws and to speak out against policies that excluded Chinese immigrants. He once received six votes for a vice presidential nomination. Bruce was appointed Registrar of the Treasury, and his signature appeared on United States dollars printed at the time.

Learning Styles Kinesthetic Learners

Have students work in small groups to plan a film biography of Blanche K. Bruce or Hiram Revels. Ask them to research their subject and find incidents from the subject's life that would make dramatic scenes in a movie. Each group should prepare an extended outline, detailing each scene, before they write their scripts. You might consider videotaping each group's production.

Linking Past and Present Background

In 1966, Edward W. Brooke of Massachusetts became the first African American to be elected to the United States Senate since Reconstruction. In 1960, nearly 7,000 African Americans held elected offices at the local, state, and national levels. In 1992, Carol Moseley Braun of Illinois became the first African American woman elected to the United States Senate.

RESEARCH SKILLS
Finding Information in the Library

You can find information in the library in many sources—such as books, encyclopedias, and magazines. In Skill Lesson 14 (page 407), you learned how to use the card catalog to find books in the library. Most libraries have several encyclopedias. Encyclopedias present useful overviews of many subjects. **Periodicals,** or magazines and newspapers, offer up-to-date articles on many subjects.

1. **Find information in an encyclopedia.** Encyclopedia articles are arranged in alphabetical order. At the end of each article are **cross-references** that tell you which other articles in the encyclopedia have information about the subject you are researching.

   Using an encyclopedia in your classroom or library, look up Andrew Johnson. (a) Are there any cross-references at the end of the article? (b) To what articles do the cross-references refer you?

2. **Practice using the Readers' Guide.** The *Readers' Guide to Periodical Literature* is an index, or list, of articles that appear in popular magazines. The *Readers' Guide* lists every article at least twice—once by the author's last name and again by the subject. Look at the sample from the *Readers' Guide* below. (a) What subject entries are shown? (b) Which article appears under an author entry? (c) What was the author's name?

3. **Look for information in the Readers' Guide.** Each subject entry in the *Readers' Guide* tells you the title of the article, the name of the author (for signed articles), and the title of the magazine. The entry lists the volume number of the magazine, the first page number of the article, and the date of the magazine. The date is in abbreviated form. At the front of the *Readers' Guide* is a list that tells you what the abbreviation stands for.

   Look at the sample from the *Readers' Guide.* (a) In which volume of *Ebony* did the article "The 100 most influential black Americans" appear? (b) On what page did the article begin? (c) In what magazine did the article "Five blacks seeking S. C. Congress seat" appear? (d) What was the date of the magazine in which the article appeared? (e) What date do you think is indicated by the abbreviation S '92?

 ACTIVITY In January 1996, the *Journal of American Ethnic History* printed an article on pages 79–85 entitled "A Glorious Age for African-American Religion," by Clarence Taylor. It appeared in volume 15. Write a Reader's Guide subject entry and author entry for this article.

	BLACK POLITICAL CANDIDATES Five blacks seeking S. C. Congress seat. il *Jet* 82:7 Ag 17 '92
Volume: page number	
	BLACKMON, DOUGLAS A. The resegregation of a southern school. *Harper's* 285:14-16+ S 17 '92
Magazine title	
	BLACKS The 100 most influential black Americans. il *Ebony* 47:62+ My '92
Abbreviated date (May 1992)	

Answer to Caption

to keep African Americans and white Republicans out of public office and to stop African Americans from voting

Videotapes/ Videodiscs

United States History Video Collection Use the video segment "The White Redeemers" from Volume 10, *Reconstruction and Segregation (1865–1910),* to enhance students' understanding of the tactics used by such terrorist organizations as the Ku Klux Klan. Approx. running time 1:15 min. (Enrichment/Average) Vol. 10, Ch. 22

Chapter 22   Play

Chapter Resources

Geography in History Duplicate and distribute the worksheet, Birmingham: Steel Capital of the South, from Unit 5, pages 33–34, of the *Chapter Resources* binder. The worksheet focuses on Birmingham's location and other factors that led to its success as an industrial center. (Enrichment/Challenging)

White southerners formed secret societies to help them regain power. The most dangerous was the **Ku Klux Klan,** or KKK. The Klan worked to keep blacks and white Republicans out of office.

Dressed in white robes and hoods to hide their identity, Klansmen rode at night to the homes of African American voters, shouting threats and burning wooden crosses. When threats did not work, the Klan used violence. Klan members murdered hundreds of African Americans and their white allies.

Congress responds. Many moderate southerners condemned the violence of the Klan. Yet they could do little to stop the Klan's reign of terror. Freedmen turned to the federal government for help. In Kentucky, African American voters sent a letter to Congress. They wrote:

66We believe you are not familiar with the Ku Klux Klan's riding nightly over the country spreading terror wherever they go by robbing, whipping, and killing our people without provocation.99

Congress acted to stop the Klan's violence. In 1870, Congress made it a crime to use force to keep people from voting. As a result, Klan activities decreased, but the threat of violence lingered. Some African

Our Common Heritage
When Hiram Revels won election as the first African American senator, he took over the seat that had been held by Jefferson Davis. Davis had resigned the seat in 1861 to become president of the Confederacy.

Spreading Terror *The Ku Klux Klan used acts of terror against blacks and their supporters. Sometimes they left miniature coffins, like the one at right, on the doorsteps of their enemies. Hoods, like the one at left, gave Klansmen a frightening appearance.* **Citizenship** *What was the goal of groups like the Ku Klux Klan?*

Americans continued to vote and hold office despite the risk. Many others, however, stayed away from the ballot box.

The Difficult Task of Rebuilding

Despite political problems, Reconstruction governments tried to rebuild the South. They built public schools for both black and white children. Many states gave women the right to own property. In addition, Reconstruction governments rebuilt railroads, telegraph lines, bridges, and roads. Between 1865 and 1879, the South laid 7,000 miles (11,200 km) of railroad track.

Rebuilding the economy. Cotton production, long the basis of the South's economy, recovered slowly. However, by 1880 planters were growing as much cotton as they had in 1860.

Industry also grew during Reconstruction. Birmingham, Alabama, became an important iron and steel center. It was often called the "Pittsburgh of the South." Still, the South lagged behind the rest of the nation in industry. By the end of the century, the South was actually producing a smaller part of the nation's manufactured goods than it had in 1860.

Problems of taxes and corruption. Rebuilding cost money. Before the war, south-

Linking Past and Present
Background

In 1915, the Ku Klux Klan, as an organized force, resurfaced to oppose Catholics, Jews, and immigrants as well as African Americans. Its membership began to grow. Violence committed in its name during the 1920s aroused public outcry, and its power shrank. During the 1950s and 1960s, the Ku Klux Klan became active again in response to the civil rights movement, and it is still a presence in American society today.

Connections With Science
Background

With the Civil War over, the United States made great industrial strides. In 1872, a company began making celluloid, marking the start of the synthetics industry. Most early industries in the South focused on processing the region's agricultural products. In addition to mills, the South built refineries to process sugar cane. The tobacco industry also grew rapidly during this period.

erners had paid very low taxes. Reconstruction governments raised taxes sharply. Higher taxes created discontent among many southern whites.

Southerners were further angered by widespread corruption in the Reconstruction governments. One state legislature, for example, voted $1,000 to cover a member's bet on a horse race. Other items billed to the state included hams, perfume, clothing, champagne, and a coffin.

Corruption was not limited to the South. After the Civil War, dishonesty plagued northern governments, too. In fact, most southern officeholders served their states well and honestly.

A Cycle of Poverty

In the first months after the war, freedmen left the plantations on which they had lived and worked. For many, moving away was a sign of freedom. As one woman said, "I must go. If I stay here, I'll never know I am free." Freedmen found few opportunities, however.

"Nothing but freedom." Some Radical Republicans talked about giving each freedman "40 acres and a mule." Thaddeus Stevens suggested breaking up big plantations and distributing the land. Most Americans opposed the plan, however. In the end, former slaves received—in the words of a freedman—"nothing but freedom."

Through hard work or good luck, some freedmen did become landowners. Most, however, had little choice but to return to where they had lived in slavery. Lizzie Atkins, a former slave from Texas, explained, "We was almost forced to stay on there with [Master], because no other white man would hire us or give us a place to stay."

Sharecropping. Some large planters had held onto their land and wealth through the war. Now, they had huge amounts of land but no slaves to work it. In the hard times of Reconstruction, many freedmen and poor whites went to work for the large

Back to the Plantation *For many African Americans, life changed little after the Civil War. Here, freedmen on a South Carolina plantation haul in the day's harvest of cotton, just as they had done as slaves.* **Daily Life** *Why did many freedmen go to work on plantations?*

 Videotapes/ Videodiscs

United States History Video Collection Use the video segment "The Fate of the Freedmen" from Volume 10, *Reconstruction and Segregation (1865–1910)*, to enhance students' understanding of the life of freed slaves. Approx. running time 4:30 min. (Enrichment/Average) Vol. 10, Ch. 16

Chapter 16   Play

United States History Video Collection Use the video segment "Economic Reconstruction" from Volume 10, *Reconstruction and Segregation (1865–1910)*, to enhance students' understanding of the system of sharecropping. Approx. running time 2:30 min. (Enrichment/Average) Vol. 10, Ch. 31

Chapter 31   Play

 Voices of Freedom

Primary Source You might assign selection 19-3, A Former Slave on Reconstruction, on pages 128–129 of *Voices of Freedom.* This selection is an account of the first years after the Civil War by an ex-slave, Katie Rowe. (Enrichment/Average)

Connections With Literature
Activity

Explain that during the late 1800s people interviewed former slaves to record their recollections of slave life. This technique is called oral history. Have students research some of these accounts for oral presentations before the class. One source of information is *Eyewitness: The Negro in American History* by William Loren Katz. You might also suggest that several students discover more about the experiences of African American women during Reconstruction and share their findings. Sources include passages from *Labor of Love, Labor of Sorrow* by Jacqueline Jones or *The Trouble They Seen: Black People Tell the Story of Reconstruction,* edited by Dorothy Sterling.

Connections With Civics
Background

Thaddeus Stevens declared, "Strip a proud nobility of their bloated estates, send them forth to labor . . . and you will thus humble the proud traitors."

Stevens believed that his plan would cost approximately $40 million—equal to what the Union forces spent during the course of three weeks of the war.

ACTIVITY

Guided Instruction Before students create their cartoons, review the elements and techniques of political cartooning. Give several examples from local newspapers, and allow students to model their cartoons on one of these if they wish.

Section 4
pp. 496–499

 Bell Ringer

Write the following clause from Article 1, Section 2, of the Constitution on the chalkboard: "Electors in each state shall have the qualifications requisite for Electors of the most numerous Branch of the State Legislature." Ask: How would you feel if you had to explain that clause before you were allowed to go to lunch today?

Lesson Plan

1. Focus Reconstruction ended in 1877 when President Hayes removed the last federal troops from the South. In this section, students learn about the closing years of Reconstruction.

---

planters. They farmed the planters' land, using seed, fertilizer, and tools that the planters provided. In return, they gave the landowners a share of the crop at harvest time. For this reason, these landless farmers were called **sharecroppers.**

Sharecroppers hoped to own their own land one day. In the meantime, most faced a day-to-day struggle just to survive. They did well if they had enough food for themselves and their families. For many, sharecropping was another form of slavery.

Even farmers who owned land faced hard times. Each spring, farmers received supplies on credit from a store owner. In the fall, they had to repay what they had borrowed. Often, the harvest did not cover the whole debt. As they sank deeper into debt, many farmers lost their land and became sharecroppers themselves. Much of the South became locked into a cycle of poverty.

SECTION 3 REVIEW

1. **Identify:** (a) Blanche K. Bruce, (b) Hiram Revels, (c) Conservatives, (d) Ku Klux Klan.
2. **Define:** (a) scalawag, (b) carpetbagger, (c) sharecropper.
3. What role did African Americans play in Reconstruction governments?
4. (a) What were two accomplishments of Reconstruction governments? (b) What were two problems?
5. Why did many African Americans and poor whites in the South become sharecroppers?
6. **CRITICAL THINKING Drawing Conclusions** Why do you think groups like the Ku Klux Klan did not exist before the Civil War?

ACTIVITY **Writing to Learn**

Draw a political cartoon about scalawags, carpetbaggers, the Ku Klux Klan, or another aspect of Reconstruction.

4
End of an Era

FIND OUT
- Why did northerners lose interest in Reconstruction?
- What happened in the election of 1876?
- How did white Conservatives tighten their control over the South?
- What did the Supreme Court rule in *Plessy* v. *Ferguson*?

VOCABULARY poll tax, literacy test, grandfather clause, segregation

In 1876, millions of Americans traveled to a great Centennial Exposition in Philadelphia. The fair celebrated the first hundred years of the United States. Visitors gazed at the latest wonders of modern industry—such as the telephone, the elevator, and a giant steam engine four stories high.

As Americans looked to the future, they lost interest in Reconstruction. By the late 1870s, conservative whites had regained control of the South.

Radicals in Decline

By the 1870s, Radical Republicans were losing power in Congress. Many northerners grew weary of trying to change the South. It was time to forget the Civil War, they believed, and let southerners run their own governments—even if that meant African Americans might lose the rights they had so recently gained.

Republicans were also hurt by widespread corruption in the government of President Grant. The President had appointed many friends to office. Some used their

---

Answers to Section 3 Review

1. (a) Blanche K. Bruce, p. 492, (b) Hiram Revels, p. 492, (c) Conservatives, p. 492, (d) Ku Klux Klan, p. 494
2. (a) scalawag, p. 492, (b) carpetbagger, p. 492, (c) sharecropper, p. 496
3. African Americans became sheriffs, mayors, and legislators at the local and state levels. A few won election to Congress.
4. (a) Possible Answer: Public schools were built; women were granted the right to own property; care for people who were physical-

ly and mentally ill was improved; and railroads, telegraph lines, bridges, and roads were rebuilt. (b) Possible Answer: Taxes soared and corruption was widespread.
5. Many African Americans and poor whites had no land, money, or credit, so they worked for large landowners as sharecroppers.
6. Possible Answer: The Ku Klux Klan was directed largely against black voters. Before the Civil War, blacks were not allowed to vote.

jobs to steal money. Grant won reelection in 1872, but many northerners had lost faith in Republican leaders and their policies.

In 1872, Congress passed a law pardoning former Confederate officials. As a result, nearly all white southerners could vote again. They voted solidly Democratic. At the same time, southern whites terrorized African Americans who tried to vote. One by one, the Republican governments in the South fell. By 1876, only three southern states were still under Republican control: South Carolina, Florida, and Louisiana.

The End of Reconstruction

The end of Reconstruction came with the election of 1876. Democrats nominated Samuel Tilden, governor of New York, for President. Tilden was known for fighting corruption. The Republican candidate was Rutherford B. Hayes, governor of Ohio. Like Tilden, Hayes vowed to fight dishonesty in government.

When the votes were tallied, Tilden had 250,000 more popular votes than Hayes. But Tilden had only 184 electoral votes—one

---

MAP STUDY

In the election of 1876, Samuel Tilden won the popular vote. However, Rutherford B. Hayes became President when a congressional commission awarded him the disputed electoral votes of three southern states.
1. In which three southern states were election results disputed?
2. Which candidate won in the other southern states?
3. **Analyzing Information** Based on the map, do you think that the end of the Civil War brought an end to sectionalism? Explain.

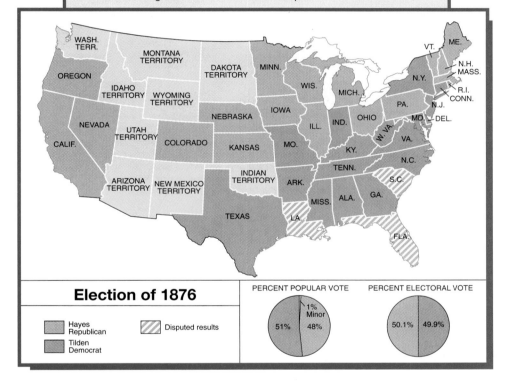

Election of 1876

- Hayes Republican
- Tilden Democrat
- Disputed results

PERCENT POPULAR VOTE: 51%, 48%, 1% Minor

PERCENT ELECTORAL VOTE: 50.1%, 49.9%

---

2. Instruct Divide the class into four groups of "Supreme Court justices." Assign one of the following to each group: Jim Crow laws, poll taxes, literacy tests, and grandfather clauses. Have students determine the constitutionality of the items on the basis of the Fourteenth Amendment. Call on "justices" to present majority and dissenting opinions.
3. Close Have students give at least one cause for each of the following effects: loss of African American voting rights, return of power to Democrats in the South, legal racial segregation.

 Lesson Planner

For a developed **Cooperative Learning** lesson plan, see the *Lesson Planner,* page 107.

Answers to Map Study

1. Louisiana, Florida, South Carolina 2. Tilden 3. No; the map shows that the vote is divided between North and South.

 Historical Outline Map Book

Historical Outline Map Use the map, Election of 1876, on page 54 of the *American History Historical Outline Map Book.* Lesson ideas can be found on page T17. (Reteaching/Average)

CD-ROM

Presidents Access the biography of Rutherford B. Hayes from the American Heritage® *History of the United States* CD-ROM. (Enrichment/Average)

Connections With Economics
Background

Grant's personal integrity is above dispute, but he was too trusting of others. One scandal particularly outraged voters. Jay Gould and Jim Fisk—two of the richest people in the country—used Grant's brother-in-law to persuade Grant to prevent the Treasury from selling gold on the New York market. Meanwhile, Gould and Fisk bought large amounts of gold to drive up its price. Their scheme failed when Grant ordered the Treasury to sell gold in order to end the shortage.

Connections With Civics
Background

In Tilden, the Democrats had a candidate who was popular and respected and who spoke about relevant issues. In 1876, however, they made a mistake that can be said to have cost them the election. In that year, the Democratic-majority House of Representatives pushed for Colorado statehood. They believed that Colorado's three electoral votes would go to Tilden. Instead, the new state's votes went to Hayes. If that had not been the case, Tilden almost certainly would have become the next President.

Art Gallery Posters

Frederick Douglass Series, No. 31, by Jacob Lawrence, appears in poster form in the *Art Gallery: Our Common Heritage Posters*. Lesson Suggestions for the poster are available in the Teacher's Guide.

Answer to Art Gallery: Our Common Heritage

Possible Answer: Although slavery had ended, the black codes still restricted the freedom of African Americans. Also, with the South in ruins, there was little work or economic opportunity in the South.

 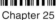

Videotapes/ Videodiscs

United States History Video Collection Use the video segment "The Persistence of Racism in the North" from Volume 10, *Reconstruction and Segregation (1865–1910)*, to enhance students' understanding of the existence of racial discrimination in the North. Approx. running time 1:15 min. (Enrichment/Average) Vol. 10, Ch. 25

| Chapter 25 | Play |

ART GALLERY: OUR COMMON HERITAGE

JACOB LAWRENCE
Frederick Douglass Series, No. 31 , 1938–1939

After the Civil War, thousands of freedmen moved to the North and West, seeking a better life. In this painting, African American artist Jacob Lawrence captured the spirit of this "black exodus." The bold colors and geometric shapes reflect the influence of African and Caribbean art on Lawrence's work. **Multicultural Heritage** *Why do you think many African Americans chose to leave the South even though slavery had been abolished?*

vote short of the number needed to win the election. Twenty other votes were in dispute. The outcome of the election hung on these votes. All but one of the disputed votes came from Florida, Louisiana, and South Carolina—the three southern states still controlled by Republicans.

As inauguration day drew near, the nation still had no one to swear in as President. Congress set up a special commission to settle the crisis. A majority of the commission members were Republicans. The commission decided to give all the disputed electoral votes to Hayes.

Critical Thinking
Evaluating Information

Show students two pictures: one of a dilapidated building, the other of a beautiful building. Ask: How would you feel if you could enter only the dilapidated building? Then show pictures of two approximately identical, beautiful buildings. Ask: How would you feel if you could enter only the building on the left? Does your reaction to the second example differ from your reaction to the first? Do you think that "separate" can be "equal"? Explain.

Linking Past and Present
Activity

Poll taxes were used against African Americans until 1964, when the Twenty-fourth Amendment outlawed them. Have students research other civil rights legislation since the 1960s that was designed to make discriminatory practices unlawful.

Connections With Language Arts
Background

The term *Jim Crow* does not refer to a historical person. It is derived from a stereotypically negative characterization of African Americans often found in pre-Civil War minstrel shows.

Southern Democrats could have fought the election of Hayes. But Hayes had privately agreed to end Reconstruction. Once in office, he removed all remaining federal troops from South Carolina, Florida, and Louisiana. Reconstruction was over.

Separate but Not Equal

With the North out of southern affairs, white Conservatives tightened their grip on southern governments. Some whites continued to use violence to keep African Americans from voting. Southern states also found other ways to keep African Americans from exercising their rights.

Voting restrictions. By the late 1880s, many southern states had passed poll taxes. Poll taxes required voters to pay a fee each time they voted. Because of the poll taxes, poor freedmen could rarely afford to vote.

Literacy tests required voters to read and explain a difficult part of the Constitution. Since freedmen had little education, such tests kept them away from the polls. Many southern whites were poor and illiterate, too. Some were not allowed to vote. Others were allowed to vote anyway by friendly white officials.

To allow more whites to vote, states passed grandfather clauses. If a voter's father or grandfather had been eligible to vote on January 1, 1867, the voter did not have to take a literacy test. Since no African Americans in the South could vote before 1868, grandfather clauses were a way to ensure that only white men could vote.

History and You
Lucy Hayes, who became First Lady in 1877, set an example for women of her time. She was the first First Lady to have attended college. She was also a strong supporter of temperance. Does the First Lady today set an example that Americans want to follow?

Jim Crow. At the same time that African Americans were losing the right to vote, segregation became the law of the South. Segregation means separating people of different races. Southern states passed laws that separated blacks and whites in schools, restaurants, theaters, trains, streetcars, playgrounds, hospitals, and even cemeteries. The laws were called *Jim Crow laws.*

African Americans brought lawsuits to challenge segregation. In 1896, the Supreme Court upheld segregation in *Plessy v. Ferguson.* The Court ruled that segregation was legal so long as facilities for blacks and whites were equal. In fact, facilities were rarely equal. For example, southern states spent much less on schools for blacks than they did on schools for whites.

Reconstruction was a time of both success and failure. Southerners, especially African Americans, faced hard times. But at last, all African Americans were citizens. Laws passed during Reconstruction, such as the Fourteenth Amendment, became the basis of the civil rights movement almost 100 years later.

SECTION 4 REVIEW

1. **Identify:** (a) Samuel Tilden, (b) Rutherford B. Hayes, (c) Jim Crow laws, (d) *Plessy* v. *Ferguson.*
2. **Define:** (a) poll tax, (b) literacy test, (c) grandfather clause, (d) segregation.
3. Why did Republicans lose support in the North?
4. How did Hayes gain southern support in the election of 1876?
5. **CRITICAL THINKING Evaluating Information** Do you think African Americans in the South benefited from Reconstruction?

ACTIVITY Writing to Learn
Imagine that you are an African American teenager in the South in the late 1880s. Describe five ways that Jim Crow laws might affect your life.

 Voices of Freedom

Primary Source You might assign selection 19-4, Winning and Losing the Right to Vote, on page 129 of *Voices of Freedom.* (Enrichment/Average)

 Videotapes/ Videodiscs

United States History Video Collection Use the video segment "The End of an Era" from Volume 10, *Reconstruction and Segregation (1865–1910),* to enhance students' understanding of the many forms of discrimination and segregation that kept African Americans unequal. Approx. running time 1:50 min. (Enrichment/Average) Vol. 10, Ch. 28

Chapter 28   Play

Student Study Guide

Section 4 Study Guide Have students use the Section 4 Study Guide on page 137 of the *Student Study Guide* to review and reinforce the content of this section. (Reteaching/Average)

ACTIVITY

Guided Instruction You might have students begin this activity by listing their typical daily activities. Tell them to check off each activity that might have been affected by Jim Crow laws and make a few notes about each choice.

Answers to Section 4 Review

1. (a) Samuel Tilden, p. 497, (b) Rutherford B. Hayes, p. 497, (c) Jim Crow laws, p. 499, (d) *Plessy* v. *Ferguson,* p. 499

2. (a) poll tax, p. 499, (b) literacy test, p. 499, (c) grandfather clause, p. 499, (d) segregation, p. 499

3. Northerners grew weary of trying to change the South. They wanted to forget the Civil War. Also, corruption within Grant's administration cast doubts on the Republican party.

4. Hayes privately agreed to end Reconstruction.

5. Possible Answer: African Americans benefited in some ways. Enslaved African Americans won their freedom, gained the rights of citizenship, and attended schools set up by the Freedmen's Bureau. On the other hand, African Americans found it difficult to earn a living because they had no education and/or money to buy land. Furthermore, southern whites deprived African Americans of their right to vote and passed Jim Crow laws.

CHAPTER 17 REVIEW

Answers to Reviewing the Main Ideas

1. (a) Lincoln's plan called for 10 percent of the voters in each southern state to swear an oath of loyalty to the United States and to abolish slavery. (b) They considered it too lenient toward the South.

2. They wanted to break the power of ex-Confederates and ensure the right of African Americans to vote.

3. It divided the South into five military districts, required southern states to ratify the Fourteenth Amendment, and guaranteed suffrage to African Americans.

4. freedmen, white southerners who supported the Republicans (scalawags), and northerners who moved south after the Civil War (carpetbaggers)

5. lack of money, land, or supplies; terrorism by secret societies such as the KKK; limits on voting, such as poll taxes, literacy tests, and grandfather clauses; and legal segregation as a result of Jim Crow laws

6. Some freedmen had little choice but to return to work for former masters; others became sharecroppers because they had no money to buy land or the education to find other jobs. Some landowners were forced to borrow money for supplies that they could not repay because of poor harvests, and as a result, they lost their land.

7. Hayes received the disputed electoral college votes necessary to win, in exchange for a promise to end Reconstruction.

Answers to Thinking Critically

1. Possible Answer: Because Lincoln guided the Union through the Civil War and had greater political skills than Johnson, he might have been able to push more lenient policies through the Republican Congress.

2. (a) Possible Answer: Voters generally oppose high tax hikes, but they will often accept increases for social programs such as social security. (b) Possible Answer: yes; education, environmental protection, national defense, and/or aid to Americans

Summary

- President Lincoln and President Johnson urged generous treatment for the South, but Congress rejected their proposals.
- Under Radical Reconstruction, Congress tried to break the power of rich planters and ensure that freedmen received the right to vote.
- Reconstruction governments made slow progress in rebuilding the South, and many southerners became caught in a cycle of poverty.
- Reconstruction ended in 1877, and African Americans lost many of their new-found freedoms.

Reviewing the Main Ideas

1. (a) What was Lincoln's plan for Reconstruction? (b) Why did some Republicans oppose it?

2. What did Radical Republicans want to achieve during Reconstruction?

3. What did the Reconstruction Act provide?

4. What three groups dominated southern governments during Reconstruction?

5. What problems did freedmen face?

6. Why did many southerners sink into a cycle of poverty during Reconstruction?

7. How did Hayes win the election of 1876 even though he received fewer popular votes than Tilden did?

Thinking Critically

1. **Forecasting** How might the history of Reconstruction have been different if Lincoln had not been assassinated?

2. **Linking Past and Present** Many white southerners were angered by high taxes imposed by Reconstruction governments. (a) How do voters today feel about paying high taxes for services? (b) Are there services that should be provided even if they require high taxes? Explain.

3. **Understanding Causes and Effects** Read the three statements that follow. Decide which one is an effect and which two are causes. Explain how the causes and the effect are connected. (a) Southern states passed black codes. (b) Southern states elected former Confederates to Congress. (c) Republicans opposed Johnson's plan to readmit southern states.

Applying Your Skills

1. **Making a Generalization** Reread the discussion of conditions in the South after the Civil War, on page 482. (a) List three facts about the South after the war. (b) Based on your list, make a generalization about the South after the war.

2. **Making a Review Chart** Make a chart with three columns. Label the columns Lincoln, Johnson, Radical Republicans. Then list the major points of the Reconstruction plan that each proposed. (a) Which plan was strictest? (b) Which plan was least strict? (c) Based on what you have read, how would you explain the differences?

Thinking About Geography

Match the letters on the map with the following places: **1.** South Carolina, **2.** Florida, **3.** Louisiana, **4.** Ohio, **5.** New York. **Region** Which southern states were under Republican control in 1876?

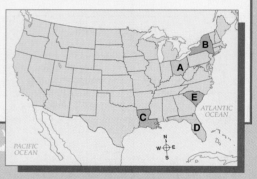

with disabilities

3. (a) cause, (b) cause, (c) effect; The events described in (a) and (b) led Radicals to believe that Johnson's moderate Reconstruction plan threatened to overturn the results of the Civil War, which resulted in their opposition to his plan.

Answers to Applying Your Skills

1. (a) Possible Answer: In some areas, every building had been destroyed; railroad tracks had been torn up; major cities were virtually leveled; and nearly 4 million freedmen had no land, jobs, or money. (b) Possible Answer: The South faced serious economic, political, and social problems after the war.

2. Check students' charts for accuracy. (a) Radical Republicans, (b) Lincoln's and Johnson's, (c) Possible Answer: Lincoln's primary goal was reunion, but the Radicals' primary goal was punishment. Johnson's southern roots might have softened his attitude toward the South.

Answers to Thinking About Geography

1. E **2.** D **3.** C **4.** A **5.** B
Region: Louisiana, South Carolina, and Florida

Looking Back at Reconstruction

Form into groups to review Reconstruction after the Civil War. Follow the suggestions below to write, draw, or act to show what you have learned about this period. You may use the textbook, encyclopedias, atlases, or other materials in your classroom library to complete the tasks. Be able to name your sources of information when you have finished the activity.

President
Andrew Johnson

LANGUAGE EXPERTS AND ARTISTS List the Reconstruction terms and words you have learned. Then organize them into a Reconstruction Glossary. Use original drawings or pictures cut from magazines to illustrate your glossary.

ARTISTS Review the goals of the Freedmen's Bureau. Then create a poster advertising the Bureau's work and encouraging people to participate.

ACTORS Find out more about the events and issues leading up to the trial of President Andrew Johnson. Then prepare a skit in which you act out Johnson's trial in the United States Senate.

A carpetbag

CITIZENS Study the text of the Thirteenth, Fourteenth, and Fifteenth amendments printed in the Reference Section. Then divide into groups to create a concept map for each amendment. Include the main ideas of each amendment and show how it affects the daily lives of Americans today. Illustrate your concept map with original drawings or pictures cut from magazines.

HISTORIANS Design a trivia game based on what you have learned about Reconstruction in Chapter 17. Include individuals, places, and events.

★ Organize a Looking Back at Reconstruction bulletin board. Include an example or summary of each group's work.

Celebrating the
Fifteenth Amendment

Assessment

Chapter Resources Binder For a more comprehensive evaluation of student understanding of this chapter, assign Chapter Tests A and B and/or Extra Unit Questions from Unit 5, pages 35–40 and 43–45.

Computer Test Bank You can use Chapter Tests and Extra Unit Questions to create your own tests for both testing and retesting.

Alternative Assessment

Chapter Resources Binder See the Alternative Assessment booklet in the *Social Studies Educator's Handbook* series.

Portfolio You might meet with students to choose appropriate work from the chapter for inclusion in their portfolios.

Stephen Crane Often called the first modern American writer, Stephen Crane (1871–1900) was a newspaper reporter, novelist, poet, and short-story writer. His works are known for their naturalism—for their objective and realistic presentation of characters and situations (including unfortunate or depressing ones). *The Red Badge of Courage* (1895) is Crane's most popular novel.

Vocabulary

Have students look up and discuss the words *doggedly, shirking, monotonous, province, pickets, philosophical, reflectively, reproached, infantile,* and *assurance* before they read the passage. Ask: To what aspects of military life might you apply words such as *doggedly* and *monotonous*? Why do you think that a story about war has so many words related to thought (such as *philosophical, reflectively,* and *assurance*)?

Prereading Focus

You might have students reread pages 466–467 in Chapter 16 to review what they learned about life in the military during the Civil War.

Motivation/Prior Knowledge

Have students list several military leaders of the Civil War and tell what they remember about each one. Then ask: How would you feel if you were a soldier but rarely saw your leaders in action?

Purpose-Setting Question

If students have understood Unit 5, they realize the destructiveness of war. Ask: If war can be so terrible, why do soldiers like Henry Fleming volunteer to fight?

History Through LITERATURE

The Red Badge of Courage
Stephen Crane

Introduction *The Red Badge of Courage* tells the story of Henry Fleming, a young volunteer for the Union army during the Civil War. The following passage is from an early chapter in the novel. It describes Henry's departure from home and his early days in the army.

Vocabulary Before you read the selection, find the meaning of these words in a dictionary: **doggedly, shirking, monotonous, province, pickets, philosophical, reflectively, reproached, infantile, assurance**

When [Henry] had stood in the doorway with his soldier's clothes on his back, and with the light of excitement and expectancy in his eyes almost defeating the glow of regret for the home bonds, he had seen two tears leaving their trails on his mother's scarred cheeks.

Still, she had disappointed him by saying nothing whatever about returning with his shield or on it. He had privately primed himself for a beautiful scene. He had prepared certain sentences which he thought could be used with touching effect. But her words destroyed his plans. She had doggedly peeled potatoes and addressed him as follows: "You watch out, Henry, an' take good care of yerself in this here fighting business—you watch out, an' take good care of yerself. Don't go a-thinkin' you can lick the hull rebel army at the start, because yeh can't. Yer jest one little feller amongst a hull lot of others, and yeh've got to keep quiet an' do what they tell yeh. I know how you are, Henry.

"I've knet yeh eight pair of socks, Henry, and I've put in all yer best shirts, because I want my boy to be jest as warm and comf'able as anybody in the army. Whenever they get holes in 'em, I want yeh to send 'em rightaway back to me, so's I kin dern 'em.

"An' allus be careful an' choose yer comp'ny. There's lots of bad men in the army, Henry. The army makes 'em wild, and they like nothing better than the job of leading off a young feller like you, as ain't never been away from home much and has allus had a mother, an' a-learning 'em to drink and swear. Keep clear of them folks, Henry....

"I don't know what else to tell yeh, Henry, excepting that yeh must never do no shirking, child, on my account. If so be a time comes when yeh have to be kilt or do a mean thing, why, Henry, don't think of anything 'cept what's right, because there's many a woman has to bear up 'ginst sech things these times, and the Lord'll take keer of us all.

"Don't forget about the socks and the shirts, child; and I've put a cup of blackberry jam with yer bundle, because I know

Discussion Questions

1. What did Henry's mother say about the possibility of Henry's death? (that he shouldn't avoid it simply out of fear of causing her grief; that she and other women must bear such loss as best they can)
2. Why was Henry embarrassed at his mother's farewell speech? (He had romanticized his departure and had wanted her to talk about the glory of war. Instead, she gave him instructions and practical advice.)
3. What does the narrator mean by saying that Henry soon saw himself "merely as a part of a vast blue demonstration"? (Possible Answer: Henry had lost his individuality and possibly his chance for gaining glory in battle.)

Historical Sidelight

The monotony that Henry experienced in camp was not unusual. Soldiers often spent weeks waiting to go into battle. All that free time helped popularize the game of baseball.

When baseball was invented in the early 1800s, it was largely a New York pastime. During the Civil War, New Yorkers taught the game to Union soldiers. Soon it was played in both Union and Confederate camps. By the end of the war, people from around the country played baseball.

Prisoners From the Front *The Civil War was long and bloody. More Americans died in it than in any other war. In Prisoners From the Front, Winslow Homer shows some of the sadness of the war.* **American Traditions** *Why do you think soldiers on both sides would have mixed feelings about the war?*

yeh like it above all things. Good-by, Henry. Watch out, and be a good boy."

He had, of course, been impatient under the ordeal of this speech. It had not been quite what he expected, and he had borne it with an air of irritation. He departed feeling vague relief.

Still, when he had looked back from the gate, he had seen his mother kneeling among the potato parings. Her brown face, upraised, was stained with tears, and her spare form was quivering. He bowed his head and went on, feeling suddenly ashamed of his purposes. . . .

After complicated journeyings with many pauses, there had come months of monotonous life in a camp. He had had the belief that real war was a series of death struggles with small time in between for sleep and meals; but since his regiment had come to the field the army had done little but sit still and try to keep warm. . . .

He had grown to regard himself merely as a part of a vast blue demonstration. His province was to look out, as far as he could, for his personal comfort. For recreation he could twiddle his thumbs and speculate on the thoughts which must agitate the minds of the generals. Also, he was drilled and drilled and reviewed, and drilled and drilled and reviewed.

The only foes he had seen were some pickets along the river bank. They were a sun-tanned, philosophical lot, who sometimes shot reflectively at the blue pickets. When reproached for this afterward, they usually expressed sorrow, and swore by their gods that the guns had exploded without their permission. The youth, on guard duty one night, conversed across the stream with one of them. He was a slightly ragged man, who spat skillfully between his shoes and possessed a great fund of bland and infantile assurance. The youth liked him personally.

"Yank," the other had informed him, "yer a right dum good feller." This sentiment, floating to him upon the still air, had made him temporarily regret war.

THINKING ABOUT LITERATURE

1. What advice did Henry's mother give him?
2. How was a soldier's life different from what Henry expected?
3. **CRITICAL THINKING Analyzing Information** What does Henry's experience with the enemy picket reveal about the special problems of fighting a civil war?

ACTIVITY Imagine that you are a recruitment officer for the Union army. Create a poster that will convince people to join the Union cause.

Unit 6
Reshaping the Nation

Unit Focus

Direct students' attention first to the painting on these pages— *The Bowery at Night,* by William Louis Sonntag, Jr. Ask them to imagine how they would feel if they were a part of the scene. As students consider the United States during that era, call on volunteers to read aloud the three chapter summaries. Ask questions such as the following to stimulate discussion.

1. What does the painting suggest about an American way of life at this time? How does that way of life differ from the ones that you have studied so far?

2. What do you know about the attitude of many white people toward Native Americans at this time? Explain.

3. (a) What are some technological devices you use every day? (b) Which of those devices do you think existed a century ago?

4. (a) What hopes did immigrants have about their new lives in the United States? (b) If you were an immigrant from a small village in Eastern Europe, how might you feel about seeing for the first time the scene depicted here?

5. Unit 6 is entitled Reshaping the Nation. Based on the information in the chapter summaries, how do you think the nation was reshaped by westward settlement, by the growth of industry, and by the arrival of greater numbers of immigrants?

Connections With Art
Background

William Louis Sonntag, Jr. (1869 – 1898) was the son of a well-known landscape artist. Unlike his father, he used landscapes not as subjects but as backgrounds for moving subjects, especially ships and trains. His works, in fact, contain careful attention to both architecture and mechanical detail.

During his short career, Sonntag worked as an illustrator for magazines such as *Harpers' Illustrated,* as well as books. Besides *The Bowery at Night,* his paintings include *South Street Seaport* and *Fifth Avenue at 59th Street.*

Reshaping the Nation

> **CHAPTER 18**
> **The Frontier West**
> (1865–1914)
>
> As settlers moved west, Native Americans lost their lands and saw their way of life threatened.
>
> ....
>
> **CHAPTER 19**
> **The Rise of Industry**
> (1865–1914)
>
> New inventions and ways of doing business spurred economic growth and transformed people's lives.
>
> ....
>
> **CHAPTER 20**
> **A Diverse Nation**
> (1865–1914)
>
> Immigrants contributed to the growth of cities and enriched American society.

504 • Unit 6

Connections With Art
Activity

Ask questions such as the following to stimulate discussion about *The Bowery at Night.*

1. Would you consider the people in this picture to be average Americans? Why or why not?

2. What technological advances allowed these people to be so busy after dark?

3. Do you think that the grandparents of these people lived in large cities, too? Explain.

4. This painting is classified as "Romantic"— that is, idealized— in style. In reality, what disadvantages might this way of life have?

A fter the Civil War, much of the nation changed from a rural, farm society to an urban, industrial one. By 1890, a third of Americans lived in cities. This painting shows a New York City street at night.

Unit 6 • **505**

Connections With the World
Activity

Several of your students may have ancestors who came to the United States during this era. Ask those students to bring in an artifact—for example, an old photograph or an heirloom that they have permission to borrow—and tell the class about where their ancestors came from and when they came to the United States. You might also want to extend the invitation to students who are first- or second-generation Americans; if so, have the groups compare their families' reasons for immigrating.

Linking Past and Present
Activity

Have students examine the painting and comment on the modes of public transportation (horse-drawn carriages, electric streetcars, steam-powered elevated trains). Ask: Are streetcars widely used today? What forms of mass transportation have taken their place? In what cities can elevated trains—run by electricity—be found? Invite students who have used any of these modes of transportation to recall the experience. Then ask: What forms of transportation that we use today would have been unfamiliar to the people in this painting?

Chapter 18 The Frontier West (1865–1914), pp. 506–533

Lessons	Teaching Resources
1 The Mining Frontier **Objectives** 1. Describe how mining changed the West. 2. Identify the builders of the first cross-country railroad. 3. Describe how railroads helped open the West.	**Lesson Planner** Cooperative Learning, p. 110 **Student Study Guide** Section 1 Study Guide, p. 140 **Our Multicultural Heritage** *Milestone* Next Steps for Immigrant Miners, p. 54
2 The Plains Indians **Objectives** 1. Identify the peoples who lived on the Great Plains. 2. Explain why the buffalo was important in the lives of the Plains Indians. 3. Identify the traditions that the Plains Indians followed.	**Lesson Planner** Cooperative Learning, p. 111 **Student Study Guide** Section 2 Study Guide, p. 141 **Chapter Resources Binder, Unit 6** *History Through Literature* These Were the Sioux, p. 4
3 Broken Promises **Objectives** 1. Explain why Native Americans and settlers came into conflict. 2. Describe how the destruction of the buffalo herds affected the Plains Indians' way of life. 3. Identify what happened at Wounded Knee.	**Lesson Planner** Cooperative Learning, p. 112 **Student Study Guide** Section 3 Study Guide, p. 142 **Chapter Resources Binder, Unit 6** *Geography in History* Indian Removal Continues, pp. 5–6 **Our Multicultural Heritage** *Biography* Susette La Flesche, Voice of the Displaced Indians, p. 52 **Interdisciplinary Connections:** The Twilight of Indian Power ■ *Sciences* Gatling's Deadly Invention, p. 104 ■ *Geography* Migration of the Cheyennes, p. 105 ■ *World* The Anglo-Zulu War, p. 106 ■ *Economics* The Importance of the Buffalo, p. 107 ■ *Civics* The Treatment of a Treaty, p. 108
4 Ranching and Farming **Objectives** 1. Identify the Cattle Kingdom. 2. Explain why the cattle boom ended. 3. Identify the Exodusters. 4. Identify the hardships that farmers faced on the Plains.	**Lesson Planner** Cooperative Learning, p. 113 **Student Study Guide** Section 4 Study Guide, p. 143 **Chapter Resources Binder, Unit 6** *Skill Application* A Painting as a Primary Source, p. 2 **Our Multicultural Heritage** *Biography* Nat Love, American Cowboy, p. 53 **Posters** *Vaquero,* by Luis Jimenez
5 Revolt of the Farmers **Objectives** 1. Identify problems that farmers faced in the late 1800s. 2. Identify the goals of the National Grange and the Farmers' Alliance. 3. Identify what the Populists demanded.	**Lesson Planner** Cooperative Learning, p. 114 **Student Study Guide** Section 5 Study Guide, p. 144 **Chapter Resources Binder, Unit 6** *Critical Thinking* Understanding Causes and Effects, p. 3

Chapter Manager

Multimedia Resources	Additional Resources	Chapter-Level Resources
Transparencies *Geography and History* Rocky Mountain States, p. I-77 **Videotapes/Videodiscs** *United States History Video Collection* The Railroads, Vol. 11, Ch. 7	**Voices of Freedom** Lizzie Miles of Superior, Montana, pp. 134–135 Building the Union Pacific, pp. 135–136 **Historical Outline Map Book** Opening the West, p. 56	**Lesson Planner** Activity Based, pp. 115–116 **Student Study Guide** Chapter 18 Study Guide, pp. 145–146 **Chapter Resources Binder** **Unit 6** Vocabulary Building, p. 1 Chapter Test A, pp. 7–9 Chapter Test B, pp. 10–12 Illustration Master, p. 13 Extra Unit Questions, pp. 43–45 **English Guided Reading** Guided Reading, pp. 35–36 **Spanish Resources** **Guided Reading Audiotapes** Side 7 **CD-ROM** *Time Tour* The Frontier West (1865–1914) in Reshaping the Nation
CD-ROM *History Makers* George Catlin	**Voices of Freedom** Family Life Among the Sioux, pp. 132–134	
Listening to Literature Audiocassettes *The American Experience* I Will Fight No More Forever, side 5 **Transparencies** *Geography and History* Land Lost by Indians, p. I-39 *Interdisciplinary Connections* Native American Life, p. B-67 **Videotapes/Videodiscs** *United States History Video Collection* The Battle for the West, Vol. 15, Ch. 7; A Lost Way of Life, Vol. 15, Ch. 10 **CD-ROM** *History Makers* Chief Joseph	**Voices of Freedom** Chief Joseph's Appeal, pp. 137–138 **Customized Reader** The Story of a Sioux Warrior, article VA-12 A Pomo Indian Speaks of the Importance of Family, article VIIIA-11 Flathead Indian Chief's Comment on Taxation, article VA-3	
Transparencies *Fine Art* Cowboy Singing, p. D-45 *Exploring Technology* A Sod House, p. H-45 *Fine Art* The Prairie Is My Garden, p. D-47 **Videotapes/Videodiscs** *United States History Video Collection* The Cattle Frontier, Vol. 11, Ch. 19; The Agricultural Revolution, Vol. 11, Ch. 22	**Voices of Freedom** The Old Chisholm Trail, pp. 138–139 Deadwood Dick, pp. 139–140 The Winter of '86–'87, pp. 140–141 Starting a New Life in Kansas, pp. 141–142 The Homestead Act, p. 142 **Customized Reader** The Oklahoma Land Rush of 1893, article VB-18	
	Voices of Freedom Bryan and the Cross of Gold, pp. 159–160	

CHAPTER 18

The Frontier West

(1865–1914)

CHAPTER OUTLINE

1 The Mining Frontier

2 The Plains Indians

3 Broken Promises

4 Ranching and Farming

5 Revolt of the Farmers

1870s *Western ranchers built a Cattle Kingdom. This saddle was part of the equipment used by vaqueros—Mexican American cowhands—on cattle drives.*

1869 *The nation's first transcontinental railroad was completed. This poster announced the "great event."*

1881 *Helen Hunt Jackson published* A Century of Dishonor. *The book detailed the long history of broken treaties between the United States government and Native Americans.*

| 1865 | 1870 | 1875 | 1880 | 1885 | 1890 |

WORLD EVENT
1879 British and Zulus go to war in southern Africa

WORLD EVENT
1885 Transcontinental railroad completed in Canada

Chapter Time Line
Understanding Chronology

Have students use notebook paper to create a set of eight time cards, labeling them as follows: 1869, 1870s, 1881, 1891, 1900, World Event/1879, World Event/1885, World Event/1890s. Check students' understanding of chapter chronology by reading statements such as the following and having students raise the time card that places it correctly:

- "Today at work I was approached about joining that new Populist party." (1891)
- "Now we have a transcontinental railroad, just like the United States." (World Event/1885)
- "What a shock it was to read some of the information in *A Century of Dishonor*!" (1881)

Invite students to create additional examples.

Chapter Setting

In 1909, Elinore Pruitt Stewart wrote to a friend from her farm in Burnt Fork, Wyoming:

❝This has been for me the busiest, happiest summer I can remember. I have worked very hard, but it has been work that I really enjoy. . . .

"I have done most of my cooking at night, have milked seven cows every day, and have done all the hay-cutting. . . . But I have found time to put up thirty pints of jelly and the same amount of jam for myself. . . . I wish I could get some of it to you, I am sure you would like it.❞

Stewart had traveled west from Arkansas to settle in Wyoming. She had worked hard and bought some land to start a farm of her own. Like thousands of Americans, she dreamed of building a new life in the frontier West.

For the new arrivals, the frontier was not one but many places. Some saw it as a place to raise sheep. Others came in search of riches from mining or to raise cattle on the open plains. Wherever they came from and whatever they came for, however, they disrupted the life of the Native Americans who had lived on the land for centuries. By the time the frontier closed, they had transformed the West in many ways.

> ### ACTIVITY
> Brainstorm to define "frontier." Then, on an outline map of the United States, use colored markers to show how the frontier of white settlement from the East moved between the 1600s and the time of this chapter.

1891 *The Populist party was formed. The party was a patchwork of different groups, including farmers and labor unions.*

1900 *The Great Plains had become home to more than half a million farmers. Plains farmers had to overcome many hardships.*

| 1890 | 1895 | 1900 | 1905 | 1910 | 1915 |

 WORLD EVENT
1890s Gold discoveries spark rush to western Australia

Chapter 18 • 507

Chapter Resources

English Guided Reading Duplicate and distribute to SAE students the Chapter 18 Guided Reading worksheet on pages 35-36 in the English Guided Reading section of the *Chapter Resources* binder. Students who have difficulty reading also might benefit from using this worksheet. Have students complete the worksheet before they begin reading. You might pair a more fluent student or a student who is a stronger reader with each SAE student to review. (Reteaching/Easy)

Spanish Resources See the Spanish Resources section of the *Chapter Resources* binder.

CD-ROM

Time Tour Access the time tour The Frontier West (1865-1914) in Reshaping the Nation from the American Heritage® *History of the United States* CD-ROM. (Enrichment/Average)

ACTIVITY

Guided Instruction Work with students to compile a list of possible meanings of "frontier"; then have students vote on the definition that seems most accurate. You might determine a standard set of dates for each frontier—for example, 1620, 1753, 1783, 1812, 1853, 1861, and 1890. Have students check each other's maps for accuracy. Then use the maps as a springboard for class discussion about the challenges of moving to "the frontier West."

Students Acquiring English Activity

Students learning English often have trouble with writing as well as with reading, and it may help to know why they make certain errors. For example, the blend /st/ never appears in the final position in Spanish words; in many Asian languages, it does not exist at all. As a result, SAE students may misspell /st/ words. You might encourage them to be on the lookout for words such as *first, last, east, west, ghost town, cost,* and *past* as they read this chapter.

Linking Past and Present Activity

In the Gold Rush days, people from all over the world flocked to California. This rich multicultural diversity continues today. Have students make graphs or charts comparing the numbers of California's multicultural population in 1850 with its present diversity. Then, based on their results, ask them to speculate about its population in the year 2050.

Section 1
pp. 508–511

Bell Ringer

Have students imagine that they have just arrived on the western frontier to search for gold. They enter a restaurant and are astonished to find that dinner costs $10. Ask: How could prices back then possibly be as high as they are today, almost a century and a half later?

Lesson Plan

1. Focus Because of the gold rush, by the mid-nineteenth century the frontier had reached the Pacific. In this section, students examine the causes of boom towns and ghost towns and study the creation and importance of the transcontinental railroad.

2. Instruct Explain to the class that late-nineteenth-century Americans lived through some of the most exciting times in the history of the United States. As students read this section, have them make a list of events that they feel qualify as "exciting."

3. Close To close the lesson, ask students to use the list they made while reading and identify one cause and/or one effect for each event.

Lesson Planner

For a developed **Cooperative Learning** lesson plan, see the *Lesson Planner,* page 110.

1
The Mining Frontier

FIND OUT
- How did mining change the West?
- Who built the first cross-country railroad?
- How did railroads help open the West?

VOCABULARY transcontinental railroad

Many Americans were lured to the West by the chance to strike it rich mining gold and silver. "What a clover-field is to a steer, the sky to the lark, a mudhole to a hog, such are new diggings to a miner," wrote one observer in 1862.

The western mining boom had begun with the California Gold Rush of 1849. From California, miners fanned out in search of new strikes. The merest rumor sent them racing east to seek their fortunes—in the Sierra Nevada and Rockies or in the Black Hills of the Dakotas. In this way, miners reversed the traditional pioneer movement from east to west. For them, the cry was not "Westward ho!" but "Eastward ho!"

Gold and Silver Strikes

In 1859, two young prospectors struck gold in the Sierra Nevada. Suddenly, another miner, Henry Comstock, appeared. "The land is mine," he cried, and demanded that they make him a partner. From then on, Comstock boasted about "his" mine. The strike became known as the **Comstock Lode.** A lode is a rich vein of gold or silver.

The Comstock Lode. It was clear from the start that the Comstock Lode was rich in gold. Unknown to its owners, however, it was even richer in another precious metal.

508 • Chapter 18

"Danged blue stuff." Comstock and his partners often complained about the heavy blue sand that was mixed in with the gold. It clogged the devices used for separating the gold and made the gold hard to reach.

Some Mexican miners became curious. They gathered a sack of the "danged blue stuff" and carried it to an expert in California. Tests showed that the sand was loaded with silver. Comstock had stumbled onto one of the richest silver mines in the world.

From mining camp to boom town. The Comstock Lode attracted thousands of prospectors. Miners came from across the United States, as well as from France, Germany, Ireland, Mexico, and China. By the 1860s, nearly one miner in three was Chinese.

A tent city formed at the edge of the desert, near the diggings. Later, wood-frame rooming houses, hotels, restaurants, and stores replaced the tents. The mining camp grew into the boom town of Virginia City, Nevada.

Other strikes. Heading eastward, miners moved into other areas. Some found valuable ore in Montana and Idaho. Others struck gold in Colorado. The cities of Denver and Colorado Springs grew up near rich gold mines. In the 1870s, miners also made major gold strikes in the Black Hills of South Dakota.

Effects of the Boom

Thousands of people came west to supply the miners' needs. Traders brought mule teams loaded with tools, food, and clothing. Merchants hauled in wagonloads of supplies and set up stores.

Most settlers on the mining frontier were men. However, enterprising women also profited in the area. Some women ran boarding houses and laundries. Others opened restaurants, where miners gladly paid high prices for a home-cooked meal. One woman baked pies for a living. In a single year, she earned $18,000.

Connections With the World
Background

California set the pattern for other gold rushes throughout the West (and for those in other countries). For example, the city of Denver got its start when gold was discovered at Pikes Peak, Colorado, in 1859. Gold rushes also brought people to Alaska, Arizona, New Mexico, Idaho, South Dakota, Montana, Utah, and Wyoming. Soon after the American gold strikes, gold was discovered in Australia in 1851, in New Zealand in 1861, in South Africa in 1886, and in the Yukon Territory of Canada between 1897 and 1898. In each case, the populations of nearby cities doubled or tripled within a few years.

508

PAST

PRESENT

Blue Jeans *In 1873, Levi Strauss and Jacob Davis received a patent for blue denim pants with copper rivets. Within two years, workers throughout the West, such as the miners at left, were wearing these sturdy "blue jeans." Today, men, women, and children all over the world wear blue jeans—for work and for play. At right, American teenagers wear jeans while they wash a car.*
● *Why do you think jeans have remained popular for more than a century?*

Boom towns and ghost towns. Towns grew up near all the major mining sites. Many lasted only a few years. When the ore was gone, boom towns often turned into ghost towns.

Other settlements lasted and grew. Some miners stayed on even when they found no gold. They opened stores, restaurants, and hotels.

Problems. The surge of miners into Colorado, Nevada, and the Dakotas created problems. Mines and towns polluted clear mountain streams. Miners cut down forests to get wood for buildings. As you will read, they also forced Native Americans from the land.

Foreign miners were often ill-treated. In many camps, mobs drove Mexicans from their claims. Chinese miners were heavily taxed or forced to work claims abandoned by others.

A few miners got rich quick. Most did not. Much of the gold and silver lay deep underground. It could be reached only with rock-crushing machinery and drills. Individual prospectors could not afford such costly equipment. Eventually, most mining in the West was taken over by large companies.

Spanning the Country by Rail

The people on the mining frontier needed food and clothing. Stagecoaches and mule teams could not carry enough supplies to fill the need. Railroad companies raced to lay track to the mines.

The federal government encouraged railroad building in the West. During the Civil War, Congress loaned money to railroad companies. It also gave them land. For every mile of track, a company received 1 square mile of land next to the track. Both

Chapter 18 • **509**

Answer to Linking Past and Present

Possible Answer: Jeans have remained useful to workers because the pants are sturdy. In the past few decades, they also have become accepted outside of the working world, possibly because of their comfort.

 Transparencies

Geography and History Use the transparency set, Rocky Mountain States, on page I-77 of *American History Transparencies.* The base map and overlay 1 offer information on the geography, topography, and state boundaries of the Rocky Mountain region. Teaching suggestions can be found on page I-13. (Enrichment/Average)

 Voices of Freedom

Primary Source You might assign selection 1-2, Lizzie Miles of Superior, Montana, on pages 134–135 of *Voices of Freedom.* The selection gives a woman's view of a Montana gold rush town. (Enrichment/Average)

 Our Multicultural Heritage

Milestone Have students read Working on the Railroads, on page 54 of the *Our Multicultural Heritage* booklet. (Enrichment/Easy)

Connections With Literature
Activity

Two well-known short stories in American literature are set in the world of mining camps and frontier boom towns: Bret Harte's "The Luck of Roaring Camp" and Mark Twain's "The Notorious Jumping Frog of Calaveras County." Invite interested students to read one of these stories and report to the class on the information that the story provides about the lives of prospectors.

Historical Sidelight
Background

Not all successful western miners made their fortunes in gold or silver. A few grew rich from borax, a crystalline compound used in the manufacture of detergents, porcelain, glassware, leather, and paper.

In 1880, Aaron and Rosie Winters heard that there was a fortune to be made in the California desert, where borax crystals littered Death Valley. The rumors were true, but laboring in the desert heat was a terrible hardship. Even worse, the nearest railroad junction was 165 miles away, and there was

no way to transport much borax to that site. Therefore, when William Coleman offered them $20,000 for their claim, the Winters sold out and moved on.

Under Coleman's supervision, a new type of wagon was designed. It could haul 36.5 tons—enough for a large load of borax, plus food and water for the crew and a team of 20 mules over a 10-day journey. The concept was such a success that Coleman's product became known as "20-Mule-Team Borax."

Congress and the railroad companies ignored the rights of Native Americans living on this land.

The race. In 1863, two companies began a race to build the first transcontinental railroad. A **transcontinental railroad** is one that stretches across a continent from coast to coast. The Union Pacific started building a rail line from Omaha, Nebraska, westward. The Central Pacific began in Sacramento, California, and built eastward. The Sacramento *Union* of January 8, 1863, reported:

❝The skies smiled yesterday upon a ceremony of vast significance. . . . With rites appropriate to the occasion . . . ground was formally broken at noon for the commencement of the Central Pacific Railroad—the California link of the continental chain that is to unite American communities now divided by thousands of miles of trackless wilderness.❞

Immigrant workers. Both companies had trouble getting workers. Labor was scarce during the Civil War. Also, the work was backbreaking and dangerous, and the pay was low.

The railroad companies hired immigrant workers, who accepted low wages. The Central Pacific brought in thousands of workers from China. The Union Pacific hired newcomers from Ireland. African Americans and Mexican Americans also worked for each line.

Railroad workers faced an enormous task. The Central Pacific first had to cross scorching deserts in California and then carve a path through the Sierra Nevada. The Union Pacific had to cut through the towering Rocky Mountains. Snowstorms and avalanches in the mountains killed workers and slowed progress. At times, crews advanced only a few inches a day.

The two lines meet. The Central Pacific and Union Pacific met at **Promontory Point,** north of the Great Salt Lake in Utah,

Working on the Railroad *Chinese and European immigrants worked side by side to complete the transcontinental railroad. These workers are posing in front of a locomotive stopped on a trestle they have built.* **Daily Life** *What dangers and hardships did railroad workers face?*

on May 10, 1869. Leland Stanford, president of the Central Pacific, hammered a golden spike into the rail that joined the two tracks.

People all over the country celebrated. With the Civil War still fresh in their minds, Americans applauded the sentiment engraved on the golden spike:

Linking Past and Present
After the ceremony at Promontory Point, Leland Stanford removed the golden spike because he feared it would be stolen. Today, it can be seen at the Stanford University Museum in California.

Our Multicultural Heritage
Activity

Historians estimate that about 9,000 of the 10,000 laborers who built the Central Pacific Railroad were Chinese. During the 1850s, more than 41,000 Chinese came to the United States. Many came after the California Gold Rush of 1849. Belief in the riches of the United States led the Chinese to call America Gum Shan, "Mountain of Gold." Railroad companies were eager to hire Chinese workers during the building of the transcontinental railroads, but when the railroads were completed in 1869, attitudes toward Chinese immigrants began to change.

If your class has students of Chinese descent, volunteers might be asked to tell the class when and why their families came to the United States. Students might also create a time line tracing the history of Chinese immigration to the United States. Refer students to the index in their textbooks for other information about this topic.

"May God continue the unity of our Country as the Railroad unites the two great Oceans of the world."

Railroads Bring Rapid Growth

Before long, other major rail lines linked the West and the East. The railroads brought growth and new settlement all across the West. They enabled people, supplies, and mail to move quickly and cheaply across the plains and mountains. Wherever rail lines went, towns and cities sprang up along the tracks.

Because of their rapid growth, western territories began to apply for statehood. Nevada became a state in 1864, Colorado in 1876, North Dakota, South Dakota, Montana, and Washington in 1889. Idaho and Wyoming entered the Union in 1890.

SECTION 1 REVIEW

1. **Locate:** (a) Virginia City, (b) Promontory Point.
2. **Identify:** (a) Comstock Lode, (b) Union Pacific Railroad, (c) Central Pacific Railroad.
3. **Define:** transcontinental railroad.
4. How did miners help to open the West?
5. (a) Why did railroad companies hire immigrants to build the transcontinental railroad? (b) How did the transcontinental railroad help bring more states into the Union?
6. **CRITICAL THINKING Linking Past and Present** Are railroads as important today as they were in the late 1800s? Explain.

ACTIVITY Writing to Learn
Review the words engraved on the golden spike linking the two parts of the transcontinental railroad, above. Then write a statement that you would have made to celebrate completion of the railroad.

2
The Plains Indians

FIND OUT
- What peoples lived on the Great Plains?
- Why was the buffalo important in the lives of Plains Indians?
- What traditions did Plains Indians follow?

VOCABULARY corral, jerky

Standing Bear, a Lakota, or Sioux* Indian, recalled the buffalo-rib sled his father made for him when he was a boy living on the Plains:

"After all the meat had been cleaned from the bones, my father took six of the ribs and placed them together. He then split a piece of cherry wood and put the ends of the bones between the pieces of wood. The whole affair was then laced together with rawhide rope.... This was my rib sleigh. After sliding down in the snow a few times, the bones would become smoother than most of the steel runners on the sleds of today."

A rib sled was only one of the many uses that Plains Indians had for the buffalo that roamed the land where they lived. Indians had been living on the Great Plains for centuries. As you will read, they had developed ways of life that were well suited to the harsh climate and rough terrain of the Great Plains region.

---

*Sioux was the French name for these Indians. In fact, the Sioux included many different groups who had their own names for themselves, including Lakota, Dakota, and Nakota.

Student Study Guide

Section 1 Study Guide Have students use the Section 1 Study Guide on page 140 of the *Student Study Guide* to review and reinforce the content of this section. (Reteaching/Average)

ACTIVITY

Guided Instruction Before students write their statements, you might have them review the goals of such a railroad. Also remind them that many railroad workers died during this construction project. Encourage students to share their statements. You also might have students prepare an artistic rendering of their statements for classroom display.

Section 2 pp. 511–514

Bell Ringer

Have students list ideas that come to mind when they think of the Plains Indians. Ask: Where did these ideas come from — television? movies? reading? As students read the section, encourage them to revise their lists, noting which items are probably true and which may have been "invented" to make a story more interesting.

Answers to Section 1 Review

1. See the map on p. 524.
2. (a) Comstock Lode, p. 508, (b) Union Pacific Railroad, p. 510, (c) Central Pacific Railroad, p. 510
3. transcontinental railroad, p. 510
4. The mining boom resulted in the development of the West and the building of the transcontinental railroad.
5. (a) Immigrants accepted lower wages than other workers. (b) Towns that were built in the path of the railroad had access to supplies and to distant markets, making them attractive to settlers. As the towns grew, the territories began to prepare for statehood.
6. Possible Answer: The country's freight routes are as important as they once were, since products such as coal are cheaper and easier to send by rail than by other means. Passenger routes, however, have shrunk since the invention of the airplane.

Nations of the Plains

Many different Native American nations lived on the Great Plains. (See the map on page 517.) Some nations, such as the Arikaras, had lived on the Plains for hundreds of years. Others, such as the Lakotas, moved to the Plains from surrounding areas in the 1700s.

Rich and varied cultures. Plains Indians had rich and varied cultures. They had well-organized religions, made fine handicrafts, and created much poetry.

Each nation had its own language. People from different nations used sign language to talk to each other. Little Raven, an Arapaho chief, explained:

> ❝I have met Comanches, Kiowas, Apaches, Caddos, Gros Ventres, Snakes, Crows, Pawnees, Osages... and other tribes whose vocal languages... we did not understand, but we communicated freely in sign language.❞

Taming the horse. At one time, most Plains Indians were farmers who lived in semipermanent villages. They sent out hunting parties that pursued buffalo and other animals on foot. Agriculture, however, was their main source of food.

During the 1600s, as you have read in Chapter 2, the Plains Indians' way of life changed. The Indians captured and tamed wild horses descended from animal herds the Spanish had brought to the Americas. On horseback, the Indians could travel farther and faster.

By the 1700s, hunting replaced farming as the basis of life for many Plains people. These Indians moved often, following the huge herds of buffalo that roamed the Plains. They began to live in tepees made of poles and buffalo skins. The tepees could easily be carried on a travois, along with other belongings.

Way of Life

The routine of the Plains Indians closely mirrored the movement of the buffalo. In winter, small groups of buffalo moved off the Plains to protected valleys and forests. In summer, when grass grew high on the Plains, buffalo gathered there in huge herds of as many as 4 million head. Plains Indians followed the same pattern. They spent the winter in small bands and gathered in large groups during the summer.

Working together. Small bands of about 100 people often lived together like a large family during the winter. Sometimes, a band included Native Americans from several nations, such as Cheyennes, Lakotas, and Blackfeet. People in each group shared chores and owned many things in common.

Moving Camp *During buffalo hunts, Plains women took care of the group's possessions. Here, women have loaded everything on a travois and are heading to a new location, where they will set up camp.* **Geography** *Why did the Plains Indians move from place to place during buffalo-hunting season?*

Our Multicultural Heritage
Background

Plains Indian nations often shared large territories with one another. They usually lived in peace. However, if a vital issue such as water rights was disputed, they would go to war.

War gave young Indian men a chance to win high rank among their people. One custom practiced by several nations was the skill of *counting coup.* This practice was considered even more courageous than killing an enemy. To count coup, a warrior had to ride close enough to an armed enemy to touch him with the hand or a coup stick and escape unharmed. Only warriors who had counted coup could wear eagle feathers in their hair. Eagle feathers were notched or dotted with paint to show how the coup had been achieved. Counting coup often was a rite of passage to adulthood. Sometimes a young man could not receive permission to marry until he had counted coup.

Buffalo Chase *This painting by George Catlin shows Plains Indians hunting buffalo. Indians used the buffalo to make a wide variety of products, such as the war shield at right.* **Daily Life** *What other uses did the Plains Indians make of the buffalo?*

Native Americans also gathered for buffalo drives. During a drive, the Indians built a **corral**, or enclosure, at the bottom of a steep hill. Then, shouting and waving colored robes, hunters drove a herd of buffalo into the corral. There, they killed the trapped buffalo. Women cut up the buffalo meat and dried it into **jerky.**

The buffalo. Plains Indians depended on the buffalo for food, clothing, and shelter. Buffalo meat, rich in protein, was a main item in the Indians' diet.

> **History and You**
> *Plains Indians rubbed buffalo fat on their skin to protect themselves from the weather and from insects. They also used paints made from clay, charred wood, and copper ore to decorate their faces. What materials do you use to decorate and protect your skin?*

Plains Indian women tanned buffalo hides to make leather. They also wove buffalo fur into a coarse, warm cloth. Buffalo horns and bones were carved into tools and toys, such as the rib sled you read about earlier. The sinews of the buffalo could be used as thread or bowstrings.

Role of women. Women oversaw life in the village and in the home. The home was the center of family life. There, children learned from their elders the customs and traditions of their people. Lakota Chief Standing Bear explained that, in the home, children "learned duty to parents, to lodge, to tribe, and to self."

Women were skilled in many crafts. They made clothing, tepees, tools—everything but weapons. In some tribes, women hunted with the men. A Blackfoot woman, Running Eagle, led many hunting parties herself. In other bands, a woman respected for her wisdom made the final decisions about important matters.

Chapter 18 • **513**

Student Study Guide

Section 2 Study Guide Have students use the Section 2 Study Guide on page 141 of the *Student Study Guide* to review and reinforce the content of this section. (Reteaching/Average)

ACTIVITY

Guided Instruction Before students write their descriptions, allow some time for class discussion of the painting. Suggest that students consider the following questions as they write:
- Who am I?
- Where am I — and why?
- What object am I using?
- What is the purpose or the importance of my actions?

Invite students to share their writing with partners or in small groups.

Section 3
pp. 514–521

 Bell Ringer

Have students imagine that a group of people they don't know have gained entrance to every house in their neighborhood. The people quickly pile each family's personal belongings on the sidewalk and order them to leave. Their last words to the residents are "Go away. This property belongs to us now. The police will arrest anyone who tries to return." Ask: How would you feel if this had happened to you? What would you do?

Traditions

In summer, many groups met on the Plains. They hunted together, played games, and staged foot and horse races.

Summer get-togethers were also the time for councils. At the councils, leaders consulted with elders about problems that affected the whole nation. Indian doctors treated the sick.

The Sun Dance. The most important event was a religious ceremony known as the Sun Dance. A person sponsored a Sun Dance to give thanks to the Great Spirit for help in times of trouble. Sponsoring the Sun Dance required sacrifice in terms of effort, wealth, and comfort. Thousands of people attended the ceremony, which lasted four days.

The Sun Dance took place in a lodge made of tree branches. A sacred tree stood in the middle, and people hung their offerings from it. Dancers circled the tree and asked the Great Spirit to give them good fortune during the coming year. When the camp broke up, the Sun Dance lodge was left standing just as it was until the Great Spirit destroyed it.

SECTION 2 REVIEW

1. **Define:** (a) corral, (b) jerky.
2. Name four Indian nations that lived on the Great Plains.
3. How did the horse change the Plains Indians' way of life?
4. What did the Plains Indians do at their summer get-togethers?
5. **CRITICAL THINKING Analyzing Information** How do you think the shift from agriculture to hunting affected the role of Plains Indians women?

ACTIVITY Writing to Learn

Imagine that you are one of the people in the painting on page 513. Write a paragraph describing what you are doing.

3
Broken Promises

FIND OUT
- Why did Native Americans and settlers come into conflict?
- How did destruction of the buffalo herds affect the Plains Indians' way of life?
- What happened at Wounded Knee?

VOCABULARY reservation

In 1876, Sitting Bull, a Lakota chief, wrote the following note to the commander of United States Army troops, who had been sent to force him off his land:

    ❝I want to know what you are doing on this road. You scare all the buffalo away. I want to hunt in this place. I want you to turn back from here. If you don't, I will fight you. . . . I want you to leave what you have got here and turn back from here. I am your friend.❞

After the Civil War, many Americans moved west, as you have read. They settled on the Great Plains east of the Rocky Mountains. At first, the United States government promised to protect Indian hunting grounds. But as settlers pushed westward, the government broke promise after promise. When Indians resisted this invasion, wars spread across the Great Plains.

Settlers and Indians Clash

Explorers who visited the Great Plains in the early 1800s sent back reports of a barren landscape, with few trees and little rain. Pioneers called the area the "Great American Desert," and they were content to leave it to the Indians.

Answers to Section 2 Review

1. (a) corral, p. 513, (b) jerky, p. 513
2. Students should choose from among the Apaches, Blackfeet, Caddos, Cheyennes, Comanches, Crows, Dakota Sioux, Gros Ventres, Kiowas, Lakota Sioux, Nakota Sioux, Osages, and Snakes.
3. The horse made it possible for Indian hunters to keep up with the herds of buffalo and kill them more easily than before. Horses pulling travois allowed the women to carry heavier loads than they could have when they used dogs.

4. During the summer, Indians from many nations met on the Plains to hunt, hold council meetings, and play games. They held a Sun Dance ceremony to offer thanks and to ask the Great Spirit for good fortune during the coming year.
5. Possible Answer: The women were freed from most of the daily farming chores. Thus they had more time to make clothing, tepees, baskets, clay pots, and ceremonial articles as well as to care for their children.

By the 1850s, however, Americans felt differently about the Plains. People who crossed the region on their way to California and Oregon told of land that was good for farming and ranching. Slowly, settlers began to move onto the Plains.

A new policy toward Indians. In 1851, federal government officials met with Indian nations near Fort Laramie in Wyoming. The officials asked each nation to keep to a limited area. In return, they promised money, domestic animals, agricultural tools, and other goods. Officials told the Native Americans that the lands they received would be theirs forever, "as long as waters run and the grass shall grow."

Native American leaders agreed to the government's terms in the *Fort Laramie Treaty.* Yet settlers continued to trespass on Indian lands. Then in 1858, miners struck gold at Pikes Peak in Colorado. The gold strike brought miners onto land that the government had promised to the Cheyennes and Arapahos.

"A trail of blood." In the 1860s, federal officials forced Indian leaders to sign a new treaty giving up the land around Pikes Peak. Some Native Americans refused to accept the agreement. They attacked trains, burned homes, and killed miners and soldiers.

The army struck back. In 1864, Colonel John Chivington led his soldiers against a Cheyenne village. These Cheyennes were not at war. In fact, the government had promised to protect them.

When Chivington attacked, the Indians raised a white flag to show that they surrendered. Chivington ignored the flag. He ordered his men to destroy the village and take no prisoners. "I have come to kill Indians," he said. In the *Chivington Massacre,* the soldiers slaughtered about 150 men, women, and children.

The Chivington Massacre outraged Native Americans. "When the white man comes in my country he leaves a trail of blood behind him," said Lakota War Chief

End of a Way of Life *The arrival of white settlers brought an end to the Plains Indians' way of life. Here, a Plains Indian stares in despair at what has happened to the lands that once belonged to his people.* **Daily Life** *What features in the painting represent changes brought by white settlers?*

Red Cloud. Across the Plains, soldiers and Indians went to war.

Efforts at Peace

In an effort to stop the conflict, federal officials set up a peace commission in 1867. The commission wanted to end the wars on the Plains so that railroad builders and miners would be safe.

"Walk the white man's road." The commission also wanted to force the Indians to "walk the white man's road." It urged Native Americans to settle down and live as white farmers did. Indians should also send their children to white schools to learn American ways.

Chapter 18 • **515**

Videotapes/ Videodiscs

United States History Video Collection Use the video segment "The Battle for the West" from Volume 15, *U.S. and the World,* to enhance students' understanding of the causes of the Indian Wars. Approx. running time 3:50 min. (Enrichment/Average) Vol. 15, Ch. 7

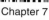

Chapter 7	Play

One group of Lakota children were taken from their homes and sent to a Quaker school in Indiana. When the children arrived there, they were horrified to hear that the Quakers planned to cut their long hair. Among the Lakotas, only cowards wore their hair short.

One Lakota girl, called Red Bird, hid from the teachers. But they found her and tied her to a chair.

66 I cried aloud, shaking my head all the while I felt the cold blades of the scissors against my neck, and heard them gnaw off one of my thick braids. Then I lost my spirit. **99**

A new treaty. In 1867, the southern Plains Indians—including the Kiowas, Comanches, and Arapahos—signed a new agreement with the government. These nations promised to move to the Indian Territory in present-day Oklahoma. The Indians were unhappy with the new treaty but knew they had no choice. The soil in Oklahoma was poor. Also, most Plains Indians were hunters, not farmers.

Indians of the northern Plains—the Lakotas and northern Arapahos—also signed a treaty. They agreed to live on reservations that included all of present-day South Dakota west of the Missouri River. A **reservation** is a limited area that is set aside for Native Americans.

Sioux War of 1876

Even on reservations, the Indians were not left in peace. In 1874, prospectors found gold in the Black Hills region of the Lakota reservation. Thousands of miners rushed to land that the government had given to the Lakotas. Led by Sitting Bull and Crazy Horse, another Lakota chief, the Indians fought back in what became known as the Sioux War of 1876.

The army attacks. In June 1876, Colonel George A. Custer led a column of soldiers into the Little Bighorn Valley. He had orders to drive the Indians to the reservation. Indian scouts warned Custer that Lakotas and Cheyennes were camped ahead. Although outnumbered, Custer did not wait for more soldiers. Instead, he attacked with only 225 men.

Before Custer's attack, Sitting Bull had a vision of a great victory. Inspired by this vision, Crazy Horse led his warriors against Custer.

During the battle, Custer and his men were trapped. One by one, the soldiers were killed. At the end, only Custer remained standing. He stood, said Sitting Bull, "like a sheaf of corn with all the ears fallen around him." Then he fell, too.

A hollow victory. The **Battle of Little Bighorn** was a victory for the Indians. The "triumph was hollow," however, pointed out

Little Bighorn *American newspapers presented the Battle of Little Bighorn as a heroic, doomed fight—"Custer's Last Stand." To the Lakotas, however, it was a brief moment of triumph. A Lakota artist painted this picture of the battle.* **Technology** *Based on the picture, what kinds of weapons did the Lakotas use in the battle?*

Connections With Art
Background

One of the customs of Plains Indian nations such as the Crow and Blackfeet was to make buffalo-hide robes to wear during the winter. Some of the robes, however, did double service as "calendars" of events.

The buffalo-hide calendars were known as winter counts. On the skin side of the robe, the artist painted one picture or symbol to represent each important event that had occurred during the year. Often the symbols began in the middle of the robe and spiraled outward. Some winter counts included pictures and symbols from more than one year. Such robes became tribal histories as well as wearable works of art.

Connections With Language Arts
Activity

Many Plains peoples named their children after events that occurred close to the time of their birth. A child born during a storm, for example, might have been named *Shappa,* which means "red thunder," or *Lokni,* which means "rain coming through a small hole in the roof." Invite students to find out some of the events that occurred on the day that they were born. Then have them use the information to create an appropriate name, following the Plains Indians' custom.

MAP STUDY

In the 1800s, Native Americans in the West steadily lost their land to settlers from the United States. Fighting between Native Americans and the United States government went on for years. In the end, most Indians were forced onto reservations.

1. In which areas of the country did the Indians still retain much of their land in 1870?
2. Which Indian nations were divided and sent to separate reservations?
3. **Analyzing Information** (a) Which battle took place on a reservation in Montana? (b) Based on your reading, why did that occur?

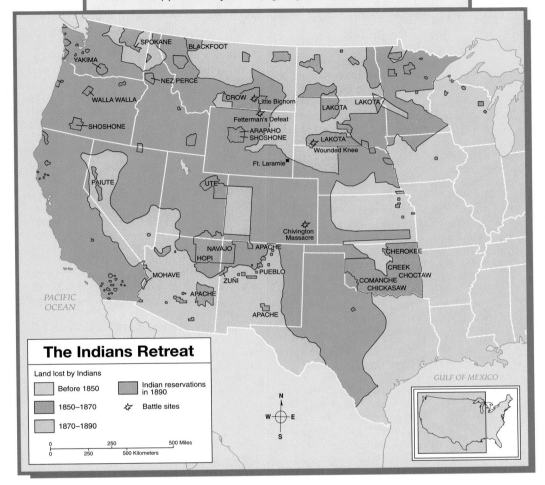

The Indians Retreat

Land lost by Indians

- Before 1850
- 1850–1870
- 1870–1890
- Indian reservations in 1890
- ☆ Battle sites

0   250   500 Miles
0   250   500 Kilometers

Customized Reader

Primary Source For firsthand insights into the thoughts and values of the Sioux as they prepared for war, order article VA-12, The Story of a Sioux Warrior, from the *American History Customized Reader*. In an interview with Charles Eastman, Rain-in-the-Face (a Sioux warrior) describes the days when his people fought to keep their land. He openly discusses the Battle of Little Bighorn, in which he took part. (Enrichment/Average)

Transparencies

Geography and History Use the transparency set Land Lost by Indians on page I-39 of *American History Transparencies*. This transparency set complements the Map Study feature on this page. Teaching suggestions can be found on page I-5. (Enrichment/Average)

Answers to Map Study

1. in parts of the desert in the Southwest and in the northern Great Plains 2. the Lakota, the Shoshones, and the Apaches 3. (a) the Battle of Little Bighorn (b) The Lakota reservation became valuable to prospectors when gold was discovered in the Black Hills. When miners tried to claim the land, the Lakotas fought back.

Team-Teaching Suggestion
Science

You might work with a science teacher to present a lesson on how Native Americans used natural materials to cure sickness and injury. For example, early Indian peoples discovered that willow bark could relieve pain. Today, we know that willow bark contains salicin, which is related to the salicylates, the major ingredient in aspirin. Furthermore, early settlers were amazed when they found Indian medicine men packing bleeding wounds with handfuls of cobweb. Today we know that cobweb helps blood to clot.

A good book on the subject to share with students is *North American Indian Medicine People* by Karen Liptak (1992).

Chapter Resources

Geography in History Duplicate and distribute the worksheet, Indian Removal Continues, from Unit 6, pages 5–6, of the *Chapter Resources* binder. The worksheet reviews government policies regarding the Plains Indians, with particular emphasis on the loss of Indian land in Oklahoma. (Enrichment/Challenging)

Customized Reader

Primary Source For a speech describing the changing ways of the Pomo people, order article VIIIA-11, A Pomo Indian Speaks of the Importance of Family, from the *American History Customized Reader.* The unnamed Pomo speaker questions the values of whites and laments the fact that many Pomos are adopting white ways. (Enrichment/Challenging)

Videotapes/ Videodiscs

United States History Video Collection Use the video segment "A Lost Way of Life" from Volume 15, *U.S. and the World,* to enhance students' understanding of the government's attempts to assimilate Native Americans into American society. Approx. running time 4:10 min. (Enrichment/Average) Vol. 15, Ch. 10

Chapter 10	Play

---

a Lakota warrior who fought there. As he explained,

> 66 A winter or so later, more soldiers came to round us up on reservations. There were too many of them to fight now. We were split up into bands and no longer felt strong. 99

The Lakotas and Cheyennes were forced onto reservations. A few Lakota leaders, including Sitting Bull, fled to Canada.

End of the Buffalo

The Plains Indians suffered from lost battles and broken treaties. Even worse for them, the buffalo were being destroyed.

The first threat to the buffalo arrived with the railroads in the 1860s. Hired hunters killed thousands of animals to provide food for crews laying tracks across the prairie. Later, buffalo hunting became a fashionable sport. Trainloads of easterners shot at the animals from the comfort of railroad cars.

The final blow came in the 1870s, when buffalo hide blankets became popular in the East. Commercial hunters shot as many as 100 animals an hour. With 2 to 3 million hides being taken every year, the number of buffalo on the Plains dropped from 13 million in 1860 to a few hundred in 1900.

With the buffalo gone, the Plains Indians faced starvation. The Indians struggled for survival. In the end, however, the army forced them to settle on reservations.

The Ghost Dance

Many Indians longed for their lost way of life. On the reservations, the Lakotas turned to a religious ceremony called the Ghost Dance. It celebrated the time when Native Americans lived freely on the Plains.

518 • Chapter 18

Wovoka's vision. The news began to spread in the summer of 1889. Far away, in the southern Plains, a prophet—Wovoka—had appeared. The Great Spirit had taken pity on his people, said Wovoka, and he would make them a new world.

A great flood would come, Wovoka promised, and the earth would roll itself up like a giant carpet. Underneath, sweet grass would grow. The buffalo would come back. The dead ancestors would be returned to life. All whites would disappear, and Indians would live in peace in a land of plenty.

All the Indians needed to do to bring about this new world was to dance the Ghost Dance. "All Indians must dance," said Wovoka. "Everywhere, keep dancing."

Wovoka's teachings spread across the Plains. In many places, Indians began performing the Ghost Dance and preparing for the new world.

The ceremony. Black Elk joined the Ghost Dance in the spring of 1890. He painted his face red and put on the sacred Ghost Dance shirt. The shirt was decorated with stars and birds and fringed in red. Ghost Dancers believed that the shirt protected the wearer from all harm, even from the bullets of soldiers' guns.

Black Elk joined hands with the other dancers, forming a large circle. Slowly, they began moving around and around. As the circle spun faster, the dancers wailed and cried and laughed.

Spinning with his eyes closed, Black Elk suddenly felt as if he were floating through the air. A "growing happiness" filled him, and he saw a glowing vision of a new and perfect world.

> 66 Many, many people were camping in a great circle. I could see that they were happy and had plenty. Everywhere there were drying racks full of meat. The air was clear and beautiful with a living light that was everywhere. 99

Critical Thinking
Analyzing Ideas

Looking back on the buffalo hunts, one white hunter later bragged: "If it had not been for the accomplishment of the buffalo hunters, the wild bison would still graze where Amarillo now is, and the red men would still reign supreme over the pampas of the Panhandle." Share this comment with students. Then ask: Why is this hunter proud? How does he feel about Native Americans? You also might incorporate this quotation into the Cooperative Learning Activity on this page.

Cooperative Learning
Activity

Write the following quotation from U.S. Army general Philip Sheridan on the chalkboard: "Let them kill, skin, sell until the buffalo is exterminated . . . it is the only way to bring lasting peace and allow civilization to advance." Explain that General Sheridan made these remarks when asked how he felt about the destruction of the buffalo herds of the Great Plains by white hunters.

Divide students into five groups. Assign each group one of the following people discussed in this section: Sitting Bull, Crazy Horse, Chief Joseph, Susette La Flesche, Helen Hunt Jackson. Ask each group to write a letter in which the person to whom they have been assigned responds to Sheridan's remarks. Before writing their responses, have students research the life and views of the person to whom they have been assigned. Have representatives from each group share the finished letters and invite the class to comment on the similarities and/or differences in the writers' views.

Settlers' reaction. As the Ghost Dance spread, settlers expressed alarm. The Indians, they said, were preparing for war. Settlers convinced the government to outlaw the Ghost Dance.

In December 1890, police officers entered the Standing Rock Reservation. They intended to arrest Sitting Bull, who had returned from Canada and was living on the reservation. They claimed that he was responsible for spreading the Ghost Dance among the Lakotas. In the struggle that followed, Sitting Bull was accidentally shot and killed. ■

Wounded Knee

Badly upset by Sitting Bull's death, groups of Lakotas fled the reservations. Army troops pursued them and brought them to Wounded Knee Creek, in present-day South Dakota. On December 29, the Indians agreed to surrender. Under the watchful eye of the nervous troops, they began to give up their guns.

Suddenly, a shot rang out. The army opened fire with rifles and machine guns. By the time the shooting stopped, nearly 300 Native American men, women, and children lay dead. About 30 soldiers also died.

The fighting at Wounded Knee marked the end of the Indian wars and the end of the Ghost Dance religion. Years later, Black Elk said of the events at Wounded Knee:

> ❝I did not know then how much was ended. When I look back now from this high hill of my old age, I can still see the. . . women and children lying [on the ground there]. . . . And I can see that something else died there. . . . A people's dream died there.❞

"I Will Fight No More Forever"

In the Far West, Native Americans also struggled to save their way of life. One of these groups was the Nez Percés.

The Ghost Dance *In this photograph, an Indian man and woman take part in the Ghost Dance. Dancers wore sacred shirts, like the one at right. The crows symbolized the belief that the Great Spirit would help dancers fly away from danger.* **Culture** *What was the purpose of the Ghost Dance?*

The Nez Percés lived in the beautiful Snake River valley, where Oregon, Washington, and Idaho meet. In the 1860s, gold strikes brought miners onto Nez Percé land. The government ordered the Nez Percés to move to a reservation in Idaho.

Chief Joseph, a leader of the Nez Percés, refused to leave their land. In 1877, he and his people fled north toward Canada. Army troops followed close behind.

Soldiers finally caught up with the Nez Percés a short distance from the Canadian border. They forced Chief Joseph to surrender. As he lay down his weapons, he said:

> ❝It is cold, and we have no blankets. The little children are freezing to death. . . . Hear me, my chiefs! I am tired. My heart is sick and sad. From where the sun now stands, I will fight no more forever.❞

Answer to Caption

It was meant to bring about a world of peace and plenty, in which no white people would live.

Audiocassettes

Listening to Literature Audiocassettes To provide students with the entire text of Chief Joseph's classic speech, play the selection, I Will Fight No More Forever (side 5, 1:40), from *Listening to Literature Audiocassettes, The American Experience.* (Enrichment/Easy)

❝❞ Voices of Freedom

Primary Source You might assign selection 1-4, Chief Joseph's Appeal, on pages 137–138 of *Voices of Freedom.* Because of this plea, the Nez Percés were allowed to return to their Northwest homes. (Enrichment/Average)

CD-ROM

History Makers Access the biography of Chief Joseph on the American Heritage® *History of the United States* CD-ROM. (Enrichment/Average)

❝❞ Customized Reader

Primary Source For a copy of a speech delivered by a Native American chief in an appeal to his people, order article VA-3, Flathead Indian Chief's Comment on Taxation, from the *American History Customized Reader.* (Enrichment/Challenging)

Connections With Geography
Background

Native American warriors followed a practice that suited the geography of the Plains. After a few encounters, the settlers began to copy their classic attacks—a strike at a surprising place or time; a strike at dawn; the killing or capture of as many men, women, and children as possible. An early French missionary once described Indian warfare as follows: "They approach like foxes, fight like lions, and disappear like birds."

Historical Sidelight
Background

After his 1881 arrest and imprisonment for his part in the Battle of Little Bighorn, Sitting Bull continued to campaign against the seizure of Sioux lands. In 1885, however, he left Standing Rock Reservation to spend one season touring with "Buffalo" Bill's Wild West Show. He returned to the reservation with a performing horse from the show. A few years later, when the Ghost Dance spread, Sitting Bull became one of its followers.

In the struggle that accompanied Sitting Bull's 1890 arrest by Sioux police officers, Sitting Bull and 14 other people were killed. The gunshots and fighting alerted Sitting Bull's horse. As if on cue, the horse went into its old show routine. Many of the survivors of the struggle believed that Sitting Bull's spirit had entered the horse for one last Ghost Dance.

CONNECTIONS

| ARTS | SCIENCES | GEOGRAPHY | WORLD | ECONOMICS | CIVICS |

Chief Joseph's Eloquent Plea

During the summer of 1877, Chief Joseph and a band of Nez Percés fled toward Canada. Troops of the United States Army chased after them. Their orders were to force the Indians onto a reservation. At last, after a trek of more than 1,000 miles, Chief Joseph surrendered.

Chief Joseph was giving up the fight against the United States government. He was not, however, giving up his right to speak out. No one has ever made a more stirring case against forcing Native Americans to live on reservations:

❝You might as well expect the rivers to run backward as that any man who was born a free man should be contented when penned up and denied liberty to go where he pleases. . . .

Chief Joseph

I have asked some great white chiefs where they get their authority to say to the Indian that he shall stay in one place, while he sees white men going where they please. They cannot tell me.

Let me be a free man—free to travel, free to stop, free to work, free to trade where I choose, free to choose my own teachers, free to follow the religion of my fathers, free to think and talk and act for myself— and I will obey every law, or submit to the penalty.❞

Despite these moving words, the army forced Chief Joseph and his followers to move far from their homeland. They were sent first to a barren plain in Indian Territory— now Oklahoma. Later, they were exiled to the Colville Reservation in Washington. There, in 1904, the great chief died. According to the reservation physician, Chief Joseph died "of a broken heart."

■ What arguments did Chief Joseph use to oppose the government's removal of the Nez Percés to a reservation?

ACTIVITY Find out more about the Nez Percés' long trek toward Canada. Draw a map showing their route. Illustrate the map with drawings of important events that happened along the way.

Team-Teaching Suggestion
Science

You might work with a science teacher to present a lesson on the environmental problems caused by the way the settlers changed the Plains. The first step might be a comparison using a chart or Venn Diagram to show how both Indians and settlers treated the land. Later, point out the problems that the settlers' actions created, and challenge students to come up with ways to repair the damage.

Team-Teaching Suggestion
Literature

You might work with a literature teacher to present a lesson on Native American literature. Examples might be taken from myths and legends, speeches, historical documents, and stories handed down by the various Indian nations. Some class time might also be set aside for student readings of selections that they have chosen.

Failed Reforms

The Native Americans were no longer able to resist the government. During the late 1800s, the army forced more Indians onto reservations every year.

Reformers speak out. Many people—Indian and white—spoke out against the tragedy taking place on the Great Plains. Susette La Flesche, daughter of an Omaha chief, wrote and lectured about the destruction of the Native American way of life. Her work led others to speak out and work for Indian causes.

One reformer influenced by La Flesche was Helen Hunt Jackson. In 1881, Jackson published *A Century of Dishonor.* The book vividly recounted the long history of broken treaties between the United States and the Native Americans.

Alice Fletcher also worked on behalf of the Indians. She became an agent of the Indian Bureau, the government department that handled Indian affairs.

The Dawes Act. Calls for reform led Congress to pass the Dawes Act in 1887. The act encouraged Native Americans to become farmers. It provided for some Native American lands to be divided up and given to individual families.

The Dawes Act did not work well, however. The Plains Indians' ideas about the land were different from those of the

Our Common Heritage

The Nez Percés traveled some 1,700 miles over extremely rugged terrain while they were fleeing toward Canada. The route was so difficult that one army officer wrote, "I have seen men become so exhausted that they were actually insane. I saw men who were very plucky sit down and cry like children because they could not hold out."

whites. To the Native Americans, the land was an open place to ride and hunt—not something to divide into small parcels. As a result, Indians often sold their parcels to whites for low prices.

Life on the reservations changed Native American culture. The federal government took away the power of Indian leaders. In their place, it appointed government agents to make most decisions. These agents believed that Native Americans should give up their old ways, including their language, religion, and customs.

Because Native Americans could no longer hunt buffalo, many had to depend on food and supplies guaranteed by treaties. Few Indians were content with life on the reservations.

SECTION 3 REVIEW

1. **Locate:** (a) Idaho, (b) South Dakota, (c) Oklahoma Territory, (d) Wounded Knee.
2. **Identify:** (a) Fort Laramie Treaty, (b) Chivington Massacre, (c) Battle of Little Bighorn, (d) Ghost Dance, (e) Chief Joseph, (f) Susette La Flesche, (g) Helen Hunt Jackson, (h) Dawes Act.
3. **Define:** reservation.
4. Why did treaties between Native Americans and the United States government fail to bring peace to the Plains?
5. (a) Why did the buffalo herds dwindle in the late 1800s? (b) What effect did this have on the Plains Indians?
6. Describe events at Wounded Knee.
7. **CRITICAL THINKING Analyzing Information** Why do you think the Ghost Dance attracted Native Americans?

ACTIVITY Writing to Learn
Review Section 3. Then write new heads and subheads for the section.

Answers to Section 3 Review

1. See the maps on p. 517 and p. 524.
2. (a) Fort Laramie Treaty, p. 515, (b) Chivington Massacre, p. 515, (c) Battle of Little Bighorn, p. 516, (d) Ghost Dance, p. 518, (e) Chief Joseph, p. 519, (f) Susette La Flesche, p. 521, (g) Helen Hunt Jackson, p. 521, (h) Dawes Act, p. 521
3. reservation, p. 516
4. The treaties were unsuccessful because every time the U.S. government promised a certain piece of land to the Indians, it was soon overrun by settlers.
5. (a) The herds dwindled because settlers and white hunters were killing off the buffalo herds. (b) The Plains Indians faced starvation because of the wholesale destruction of the buffalo.
6. In 1890, an uneasy peace had been declared between the Lakota nation and the U.S. Army. As the Lakota were surrendering their weapons, a shot rang out, and the army responded by killing more than 300 Native American men, women, and children. This confrontation was the last battle of the Indian wars.
7. Possible Answer: The Ghost Dance offered Native Americans some hope that their past glory could be restored.

Bell Ringer

Write the word *cowhand* in the middle of a large empty chalkboard space. Work with students to create an informal concept map by having them name objects and ideas that they associate with the word. You might have students copy the concept map and review it at the end of the section.

Lesson Plan

1. Focus After the Civil War, cattle ranching became big business as Texas ranchers began rounding up wild cattle and driving them north to the new rail lines. The passage of the Homestead Act brought many new farmers to the Plains, who vied with ranchers for the land. In this section, students find out what life was like for homesteaders and cowhands in the West.

2. Instruct Have students compare the lives of cowhands and sodbusters on the Plains. Ask: How were their homes, work, and family lives similar? How were they different? Then ask: Which of the two ways of life would you prefer if you had lived on the Plains? Have students explain their responses.

3. Close To close the lesson, review students' responses to the Bell Ringer activity. Discuss which ideas they might want to change now that they know more about life on the Plains.

4
Ranching and Farming

FIND OUT
- What was the Cattle Kingdom?
- Why did the cattle boom end?
- Who were the Exodusters?
- What hardships did farmers face on the Plains?

VOCABULARY longhorn, vaquero, sodbuster

"**W**ell, come along, boys, and listen to my tale;
I'll tell you of my troubles on the old Chisholm Trail.
With a ten dollar horse and a forty dollar saddle,
I started in herding these Texas cattle.**"**

In the 1860s, a new group of Americans began arriving on the Plains. These riders on horseback came from the South, leading dusty lines of bellowing cattle. They sang songs such as the "Old Chisholm Trail" to pass the time on the long ride from Texas.

The cattle herders were soon joined by hopeful farmers from the East, eager to carve a living from the soil. Along with the miners, these newcomers created a new way of life on the Great Plains.

Driving Cattle to Market

Before the arrival of settlers from the United States, the Spanish and then the Mexicans set up cattle ranches in the Southwest. Over the years, strays from these ranches grew into large herds of wild cattle, known as **longhorns.** They roamed freely across the grassy plains of Texas.

Increased demand for beef. At first, no one rounded up the longhorns because there was no way to get them to market. With the coming of the railroads in the 1860s, all that changed.

After the Civil War, the demand for beef increased. Growing cities in the East needed more meat. Miners, railroad crews, and soldiers in the West added to the demand. They no longer could depend on buffalo for food.

Cattles drives. Texas ranchers began rounding up herds of longhorns in the 1860s. They then drove the herds hundreds of miles north to rail lines in Kansas and Missouri. The long trips were called cattle drives.

Spring was the best time for a drive. Streams were full, and grass was plentiful. The slow-moving herds fattened up on their way to market.

One of the best-known cattle trails was cut by the wagon wheels of a trader, Jesse Chisholm. Chisholm was half Scotsman and half Cherokee Indian. In the late 1860s, he began hauling goods between Texas and the railroad. The Chisholm Trail crossed rivers at the best places and passed by water holes. (See the map on page 524.)

The Cowhand's Life

Cattle drives would not have been possible without cowhands. These hard workers rode alongside the huge herds in good and bad weather. They kept the cattle moving and rounded up strays.

Spanish heritage. American cowhands learned to ride, rope, and brand from the Spanish **vaqueros** (vah KEHR ohs). Vaquero comes from the Spanish word for cow. Vaqueros were skilled riders who tended cattle on ranches in Mexico, California, and the Southwest. Many cowhands on the cattle drives were Mexican Americans. Others were African Americans or Native Americans.

Connections With Health
Activity

It is no secret that the cowhand diet on cattle drives was nutritionally imbalanced. It consisted of three staple foods — baked beans, bacon, and biscuits. Have each student plan meals for two or three days. Each meal should be nutritious, nonperishable, easily portable, and simple to cook over a campfire. Canned goods may be included, since a process using glass (Mason) jars had been in use as early as 1858. Invite students to share their menus with the class.

Historical Sidelight
Background

Most cattle drives took longhorns from Texas directly north to Kansas or Missouri. As students will see on the map on page 524, however, one trail went westward into New Mexico and then north to Colorado.

In the spring of 1866, Charlie Goodnight, a former Texas ranger, stocked a supply wagon and prepared for his first cattle drive. He met and joined forces with Oliver Loving. Together with 18 cowhands, the partners started out for Denver with 2,000 longhorns. Along

the way, they reasoned, they would have good grazing to themselves. They might also be able to sell some of the herd to people who had profited from mining silver.

On this first journey, Goodnight and Loving drove the herd too hard, and several hundred animals died along the way. The partners made a profit, however, and learned from their mistakes. Later drives along the Goodnight-Loving Trail were completed without the loss of a single animal.

Much of the cowhand's gear was borrowed from the vaquero. Cowhands used the lariat—a leather rope—to lasso runaway cattle. Lariat comes from the Spanish word for rope. Cowhands wore a wide-brimmed hat like the Spanish sombrero. It protected them from both sun and rain. Leather leggings, called chaps, came from Spanish chaparreras (chap ah RAY rahs). Chaps kept a rider's legs safe from the chaparral (chap uh RAL), a thorny shrub of the Southwest.

On the trail. Cowhands did not have easy lives. A cattle drive was usually hot, dirty, tiring work. Cowhands learned to live with discomfort and danger.

Stampedes were one hazard faced by cowhands. A clap of thunder or a gunshot could set thousands of longhorns off at a run. Cowhands rode into the crush of hoofs and horns. They slowed down the stampeding herd by making the cattle turn in a wide circle.

Crossing rivers posed another danger. Cattle often panicked while wading in a swift current. Cowhands had to struggle to get the frightened animals to solid ground. Cowhands also fought grass fires and pulled cattle from swamps. They faced attacks from cattle thieves who roamed the countryside in the days after the Civil War.

The end of the trail. After long weeks on the trail, cowhands were happy to reach one of the cow towns along the railroads. (See the map on page 524.) For example, the Chisholm Trail ended in Abilene, Kansas. There, ranchers built pens for cattle. They shipped cattle from Abilene to markets in the East on the Kansas Pacific Railroad.

Cow towns such as Abilene and Dodge City boomed. After months on the trail, cowhands were ready for a bath, a good meal, and a soft bed. Dance halls, saloons, hotels, and restaurants catered to cowhands. Town sheriffs had a hard time keeping the peace. Some cowhands spent wild nights drinking, dancing, and gambling.

ART GALLERY
OUR COMMON HERITAGE

Luis Jimenez
Vaquero, 1980

The Mexican vaquero was a colorful figure. Sitting tall in the saddle, wide-brimmed sombrero on his head, chaparreras wrapped around his legs for protection, he herded cows along the open trail. Later, American cowboys took up the ways of the vaquero. Even the word vaquero became part of cowboy lore, becoming the American buckaroo. In this painting, Mexican American artist Luis Jimenez celebrates the courage and expert horsemanship of the vaquero. **Multicultural Heritage** Which items shown in the painting were adopted by the cowboy?

Chapter 18 • **523**

Lesson Planner

For a developed **Cooperative Learning** lesson plan, see the *Lesson Planner,* page 113.

Art Gallery Posters

Vaquero, by Luis Jimenez, appears in poster form in the *Art Gallery: Our Common Heritage Posters.* Lesson Suggestions for the poster are available in the Teacher's Guide.

Answer to Art Gallery: Our Common Heritage

lariat, wide-brimmed hat, chaps

Voices of Freedom

Primary Source You might assign selection 1-5, The Old Chisholm Trail, on pages 138–139 of *Voices of Freedom.* (Enrichment/Easy)

Transparencies

Fine Art Use the transparency of Thomas Eakins' painting Cowboy Singing on page D-45 of *American History Transparencies.* Teaching suggestions can be found on page D-13. (Enrichment/Easy)

Historical Sidelight
Background

Stampedes were the constant dread of cowhands on the annual long drive. Especially during the first days of the drive, every hand was on the alert. A cowhand would sleep on the ground with one end of a rope tied to his wrist and the other end tied to his horse, which remained saddled and bridled at all times.

For all his hard work, a cowhand was lucky to earn one dollar a day—which was low pay even in the 1870s.

Cooperative Learning
Activity

Remind students that because railroad lines were built through Kansas, the state became famous for its cow towns. Divide students into five groups and have each group choose a cow town from the following list: Abilene, Newton, Wichita, Dodge City, Ellsworth. Have each group create the front page of the town newspaper for any late-nineteenth-century date that its members choose. Content may be invented as long as the details remain true to the town and the era. Each student must have a personal assignment to complete, without which the page cannot be published.

Encourage students to add artwork for interest and to use nineteenth-century typography for the name of the paper and for headlines. Work with students to create a classroom display of all the front pages.

Our Multicultural Heritage

Biography Have students read the biography, Nat Love, American Cowboy, on page 53 of the *Our Multicultural Heritage* booklet. (Enrichment/Challenging)

Voices of Freedom

Primary Source You might assign selection 1-6, Deadwood Dick, on pages 139–140 of *Voices of Freedom.* Nat Love, a former slave, wrote about his adventures as a cowboy in the West. In this selection, Love tells how he became known as "Deadwood Dick." (Enrichment/Average)

Videotapes/ Videodiscs

United States History Video Collection Use the video segment "The Cattle Frontier" from Volume 11, *Industrialization and Urbanization,* to enhance students' understanding of life on the cattle frontier. Approx. running time 2:15 min. (Enrichment/Average) Vol. 11, Ch. 19

Chapter 19 | Play

M A P   S T U D Y

Miners, ranchers, and railroad builders all played a role in opening the West.
1. *Which states contained major mining centers?*
2. *In which state did cattle trails begin?*
3. **Drawing Conclusions** *Which cities were probably major centers for shipping cattle east by rail? Explain.*

Opening the West

- Railroads
- Cattle trails
- Mining centers

0   250   500 Miles
0   100   500 Kilometers

The Cattle Boom

A **Cattle Kingdom** grew up in the West during the 1870s. Ranching spread north from Texas across the Plains. Soon cattle grazed on the grassy plains from Kansas to present-day Montana.

The open range. The Plains were vast. Ranchers let their cattle run wild on the open range. Twice a year, they rounded up the animals and branded newborn calves. A brand was a symbol that cowhands burned into the cattle's hide. Each ranch had its own brand to identify its cattle.

Connections With Art
Activity

Emphasize the importance of branding as a way of distinguishing cattle that often grazed together on the open range. Explain that brands used letters, numbers, and symbols, as in these examples:

 Spur   Flying Heart

 Crazy R   ◎ Double Circle

 Rocking 7   ⴵ Bow and Arrow

You might mention that some ranchers showed a sense of humor in their brands. A rancher named Barwise, for example, used this brand: $\overline{YY}$.

Invite students to create their own brands. Have them share the results with a partner or with the entire class, explaining the meaning of the brand that they have created.

Connections With Language Arts
Background

Sam Maverick was one Texas rancher who had not branded his herd. Some people thought that this was a plan to claim all the cattle that Maverick's neighbors had not yet branded. In any case, cattle without brands came to be known as *mavericks*—as did people who, like Sam Maverick, were independent thinkers.

CRITICAL THINKING SKILLS
A Painting as a Primary Source

Primary sources, you recall, are materials that give firsthand descriptions of events and people in the past. Paintings are one important type of primary source. They show important details about a historical period. Often, they provide us with useful evidence about aspects of daily life such as food, clothes, games, and homes.

The picture below is called *California Vaqueros.* It was painted in the 1870s by James Walker, an American artist. Walker spent many years in the Southwest painting scenes he saw there.

Use the following steps to learn how to use a painting as a primary source.

1. **Identify the subject of the painting.** (a) Who are the people in the painting? (b) What animals are shown?

2. **Decide what the painting tells about the life of the people.** Study the painting. (a) What are the people wearing? (b) What are they doing? (c) Describe what you can about the landscape and the weather. (d) From this painting, what conclusions can you draw about the life of a vaquero?

3. **Decide if the painting is a reliable source.** A painting does not always tell the full story. The artist may have created the painting for a special reason or may have left out some details. You need to decide whether a painting is a reliable source of information. (a) Could the artist have seen actual vaqueros at work? How do you know? (b) Do you think the artist showed everything exactly as it was? Explain. (c) Does the painting give you a complete idea of the daily life of vaqueros? Explain.

ACTIVITY Find another painting in your textbook or in your classroom library that interests you. Follow the guidelines in this lesson to use the painting as a primary source.

 Chapter Resources

Skill Application For additional practice, duplicate and distribute the worksheet, A Painting as a Primary Source, from Unit 6, page 2, of the *Chapter Resources* binder. (Reteaching/Average)

Answers to Skill Lesson

1. (a) vaqueros, (b) longhorn cattle, horses
2. (a) fancy outfits with chaps and wide-brimmed hats, (b) Some are roping cattle with lariats; they are all riding horses. (c) The landscape is flat and the weather is hot. (d) Possible Answers: The work was dusty; if the sun was out, it would be very hot, with no shade in sight.
3. (a) Possible Answer: Yes; Walker painted the scene at the time of the Cattle Kingdom, and he lived in the Southwest for many years. (b) Possible Answer: Probably not; most likely it was even dustier than the painting shows, and the vaqueros would not have looked so neat and clean; most of the action, though, probably was true to life. (c) Possible Answer: No; Walker captures only one moment in time, not the vaqueros' entire daily routine.

ACTIVITY

Guided Instruction You might suggest that students select a painting by an artist or from an era with which they are familiar so that they can apply the lesson guidelines with some degree of knowledge.

Students Acquiring English
Activity

SAE students may have difficulty expressing in English the details of the painting as well as the conclusions they draw about it. You might encourage students to draft their responses in their native language and then work with an English-fluent student to complete the English version.

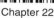
From time to time, cattle ranchers came into conflict with other people on the range. Water was scarce, and ranchers fought over water holes and streams.

When sheep ranchers moved onto the Plains, trouble increased. Sheep nibbled the grass so low that cattle could not eat it. As a result, cattle ranchers sometimes fought with sheep ranchers.

An era ends. In the 1870s, farmers began moving onto the range. By 1900, half a million farmers had arrived. They fenced in their fields with barbed wire. Sharp barbs kept cattle and sheep from pushing over fences and trampling plowed fields. As more farmers strung barbed wire, the open range began to disappear.

Bad weather speeded the end of the Cattle Kingdom. The winter of 1885 was harsh. The following summer was blistering hot and dry. The bitter cold of the next winter killed millions of head of cattle. By the spring of 1887, nine out of ten head of cattle on the northern Plains had frozen to death.

The days of the Cattle Kingdom were over. Cattle ranchers began to buy land and fence it in. Soon, farmers and ranchers had divided the open range into a patchwork of large fenced plots.

Farmers on the Plains

In 1862, Congress passed the *Homestead Act.* Under the act, the government gave 160 acres of land to anyone who farmed it for five years. The government wanted to encourage farmers to settle the West. It also wanted to give poor people in the East a chance to own their own farms.

Homesteaders. Many easterners rushed to accept the offer of free land. These homesteaders planted their 160 acres with wheat and corn. By 1900, half a million farmers had settled on the Great Plains under the Homestead Act.

The Homestead Act had its problems. Only about 20 percent of the homestead

land went directly to small farmers. Big land-owning companies took large areas of land illegally. They divided the land and resold it to farmers at a high price. Even when the land was free, few poor city folk had the money to move west and start a farm.

Exodusters. African Americans joined the rush for homestead land. The largest group moved west at the end of Reconstruction. At this time, southern blacks saw many of their hard-won freedoms slip away.

In 1879, a group of African Americans decided to move to Kansas. They called themselves Exodusters. They took the name from Exodus, the book of the Bible that tells about the Jews escaping slavery in Egypt.

White southerners did not want to lose the cheap labor supplied by African Americans. To prevent their leaving, whites stopped the boats carrying Exodusters up the Mississippi. An army general wrote to President Hayes, "Every river landing is blockaded by white enemies of the colored exodus; some of whom are armed and mounted." Despite the danger, between 40,000 and 70,000 African Americans moved to Kansas by 1881.

GEOGRAPHY AND HISTORY
Adapting to the Plains

The farmers who had settled on the Great Plains in the 1860s and 1870s were better off than later arrivals. The first farmers claimed sites near trees and water. Later settlers had to move onto the open Plains. There, even the most skilled farmers faced a life of constant struggle.

Houses of sod. Finding shelter was the first problem settlers faced. Because wood was scarce on the Plains, many farmers built houses of sod—soil held together by the prairie grass roots. Settlers cut the sod into long, flat bricks. They usually used at least two rows of sod bricks for the walls of their homes. Thick walls kept the homes cool in summer and warm in winter.

On the Homestead *For African Americans, the West offered the hope of freedom and opportunity. Here, the Shores family poses in front of their Nebraska sod house.* **Economics** *Why did some white southerners try to prevent African Americans from moving west?*

Rain was a serious problem for people living in "soddies," however. One pioneer woman complained that her sod roof "leaked two days before a rain and for three days after." Another pioneer woman recalled frying pancakes while someone held an umbrella over her and her stove.

New farm tools. The soil of the Plains was rich and fertile. However, early settlers had a hard time breaking through the thick layer of matted sod that covered the soil. The sod would break their wood or iron plows.

James Oliver of Indiana designed a special sodbusting plow that reached the market by 1877. The lightweight plow was made of strong steel. It helped **sodbusters,** as Plains farmers were called, to cut through the sod to the soil below.

Another help was the seed drill, which planted seeds deep in the earth. There, the seeds got the moisture they needed to grow. Farmers used new reapers, threshing machines, and binders to harvest their crops.

On the Plains, water often lay hundreds of feet below the surface. To tap a deep water source, farmers built windmills. Windmills used the strong winds that whipped across the open Plains to pump water to the surface.

Threats from nature. The farther west the sodbusters settled, the drier the climate was. When too little rain fell, crops shriveled and died. Dry weather also brought the threat of fire. Even the boldest pioneers feared grass fires. In a strong wind, a grass fire traveled "as fast as a horse could run."

Summers often brought swarms of grasshoppers that darkened the sky like a storm. "When they came down," one settler recalled, "they struck the ground so hard it sounded almost like hail." Grasshoppers ate everything in their path—crops, food, tree bark, even clothing.

However, pioneers dreaded winter most. The Plains had few trees or hills to block the wind. As a result, icy gusts built huge snowdrifts around barns and houses. Snow

Chapter 18 • 527

Connections With Science
Background

Many farmers on the Great Plains who grew corn and wheat met with near devastation due to droughts, scorching summer heat, and insects. Then, in the 1870s, the Mennonites, a religious group with Russian roots, arrived in Kansas. With them they carried the seeds of a new strain of wheat that could be grown even in the harsh climate of the Russian steppes. The new variety of wheat was called Turkey Red. It was winter wheat, which is planted in the fall.

The Mennonites shared their grain with the Kansas farmers, who planted it that very fall. Because winter wheat remains in the ground during the coldest months and is harvested in late spring, it escapes the heat, drought, and insects of summer. Because of Turkey Red, Kansas grew so much wheat that the state eventually became known as "the breadbasket of America."

buried farm animals and trapped families inside their homes. Wise sodbusters kept enough food on hand to help them survive during a long blizzard.

Hard times on the Plains discouraged many farmers. Some packed their belongings and fled back to the East. Others headed for the milder climates of the West Coast. Empty sod houses reminded settlers that no one was sure of success. ■

Women on the Plains

People had to be strong to survive the hardships of life on the Great Plains. With few stores, women made clothing, quilts, soap, candles, and other goods by hand. They also had to cook and preserve all the food needed through the long winter.

Women had many other duties. They educated the children. With no doctors nearby, they treated the sick and injured. Women also helped with the planting and harvesting. When needed, they helped build sod houses.

Families on the Plains usually lived miles apart. They greatly enjoyed any chance to get together with other families. "Don't think that all of our time and thoughts were taken up with the problems of living," one woman wrote. "We were a social people." She explained that pioneer families relaxed by visiting with neighbors and gathering for church services. Picnics, dances, and weddings were special events.

End of the Frontier

As farmers spread across the Plains, fewer areas remained to be settled. The last major land rush took place in Oklahoma in 1889.

At the time, Oklahoma was home to Native Americans. Some eastern Indians had been forced to move there in the 1830s. (See pages 338–341.) Later, the government had moved Plains Indians to the area. In 1885, however, the government bought back the land from the Indians.

Late in April 1889, as many as 100,000 land seekers lined up at the Oklahoma border. The government had announced that farmers could claim free homesteads in Oklahoma. Claims, however, could not be staked until noon on April 22. A homesteader described the scene:

Prairie Family
Families worked hard to survive on the Great Plains. Harvey Dunn, born on a South Dakota homestead, captured both the beauty and isolation of prairie life in this painting. **Daily Life** *What qualities of pioneer women does Dunn portray here?*

"Suddenly the air was pierced with the blast of a bugle. . . . The quivering limbs of saddled steeds. . . bounded forward into the 'beautiful land' of Oklahoma; and wagons and carriages and buggies and prairie schooners. . . joined in this. . . race, where every starter was bound to win a prize."

As the "boomers" charged into Oklahoma, they found to their surprise that others were already there. "Sooners" had sneaked into Oklahoma and staked out much of the best land.

The 1890 census reported that the United States no longer had a frontier. For 100 years, the frontier had absorbed immigrants, adventurers, and city folks. Now, the frontier was closed.

SECTION 4 REVIEW

1. **Locate:** (a) Kansas, (b) Montana, (c) Chisholm Trail, (d) Abilene, (e) Oklahoma.
2. **Identify:** (a) Cattle Kingdom, (b) Homestead Act, (c) Exoduster, (d) Sooner.
3. **Define:** (a) longhorn, (b) vaquero, (c) sodbuster.
4. (a) Why was the area from Kansas to Montana called the Cattle Kingdom? (b) Name two causes for the end of the Cattle Kingdom.
5. Why did the Exodusters move to the Plains?
6. How did farmers adapt to life on the Plains?
7. **CRITICAL THINKING Comparing** Compare the life of the cowhand with the life of the sodbuster. Which was more difficult?

ACTIVITY Writing to Learn
List five words that describe the people and the setting shown in the picture on page 528. Use the words to write a song suggested by the picture.

5
Revolt of the Farmers

FIND OUT
- What problems did farmers face in the late 1800s?
- What were the goals of the National Grange and the Farmers' Alliance?
- What did the Populists demand?

VOCABULARY cooperative, wholesale

"We were told two years ago to go to work and raise a big crop, that was all we needed. We went to work and plowed and planted. The rains fell, the sun shone, nature smiled, and we raised the big crop they told us to; and what came of it? Eight-cent corn, ten-cent oats, two-cent beef and no price at all for butter and eggs—that's what came of it. Then the politicians told us we suffered from overproduction."

These bitter words were uttered by Mary Elizabeth Lease, a fiery Kansas reformer. She was speaking of a dilemma facing many farmers on the Great Plains in the 1890s.

Farmers Unite

Despite hardships, farmers learned to survive and even thrive on the Plains. Soon, they were selling huge amounts of wheat and corn in the nation's growing cities and even in Europe.

Growing harvests, falling prices. The farmers, however, faced a strange problem. The more they harvested, the less they earned. In 1881, a bushel of wheat sold for $1.19. By 1894, the price had dropped by more than half. One Kansas farmer said that

Guided Instruction Before students begin to write, encourage them to experience the atmosphere of the picture as well as to understand its factual detail. They might start by identifying the emotion suggested by the picture and then making a list of words that express it. Suggest that students focus on one main point that they want their song to make. Students who write words to fit a familiar melody might make copies of the finished lyrics to use in a class sing-along.

Section 5 pp. 529–531

Bell Ringer

Have students imagine themselves as farmers who have bred a new strain of corn or wheat that grows fast in almost any climate and is resistant to disease. Explain that in the first year, their crops have brought in a great deal of money. The next year, however—though they have increased the acreage and grown more grain—they have earned only a percentage of the first year's profits. Have students speculate on what happened.

Answers to Section 4 Review

1. See the map on p. 524.
2. (a) Cattle Kingdom, p. 524, (b) Homestead Act, p. 526, (c) Exoduster, p. 526, (d) Sooner, p. 529
3. (a) longhorn, p. 522, (b) vaquero, p. 522, (c) sodbuster, p. 527
4. (a) Ranchers allowed their cattle to roam freely across the territory and cattle raising became a big industry there. (b) The open range disappeared as farmers moved in and fenced in their fields. Harsh weather led to the death of millions of cattle.

5. The Exodusters saw the possibility of a good life on the Plains, free from the constraints of the South and the low-paying industries of the North.
6. Farmers had the determination to deal with the hazards of Plains life—droughts, extreme weather, insects, the tough sod, and the general hard work. The inventions of sodbusting plows, seed drills, and mechanized reapers and threshers helped them to earn a profit.

7. Possible Answer: Cowhands and sodbusters worked very hard. In the long run, however, the settlers were better off than the cowhands were. Settlers owned the land they worked, and there was a chance that they could become prosperous. The cowhand's work, on the other hand, had little room for advancement.

1. Focus In the late 1800s, low grain prices caused problems. Farmers began to form organizations to help one another. In this section, students examine some of these organizations and study the rise of the Populist party.

2. Instruct Divide the class into an even number of groups. Have half of the groups prepare editorials for a southern or western newspaper supporting Bryan for President in 1896. Have the other half prepare editorials for an eastern newspaper supporting McKinley for President. The editorials should draw on information given throughout this section.

3. Close To close the lesson, have students explain why McKinley was elected President and why the Populist party broke up at about the same time.

Lesson Planner

For a developed **Cooperative Learning** lesson plan, see the *Lesson Planner,* page 114.

Answer to Caption

Falling prices meant smaller incomes—and less money to repay debts for the land and machinery that they had bought.

BIOGRAPHY Mary Elizabeth Lease *Born in Pennsylvania, Mary Elizabeth Lease moved to Kansas. Trained as a lawyer, she became one of the most stirring, dynamic speakers for the rights of farmers. The way to fight falling grain prices, she told Kansans, was to "raise less corn and more hell." Her sharp tongue earned her the nickname the "Kansas Python."* **Economics** *How did falling grain prices hurt farmers?*

even "with hundreds of hogs, scores of good horses and . . . 16,000 bushels of golden corn, we are poorer by many dollars than we were years ago."

Western farmers were hurt most by low grain prices. They had borrowed money during good times to buy more land and machinery. When wheat prices fell, they could not repay their debts. In the South, cotton farmers faced the same problem. Falling cotton prices saddled sharecroppers and small farmers with heavy debts.

The Grange. As early as the 1860s, farmers began to work together to improve conditions. In 1867, they formed the **National Grange.** Grangers worked to boost farm profits. They also worked to make railroads lower the rates that they charged small farmers to ship grain.

Grangers helped farmers set up cooperatives. In a **cooperative**, a group of farmers pooled their money to buy seeds and tools wholesale. **Wholesale** refers to the buying or selling of something in large quantities and at lower prices. Grangers built cooperative grain warehouses so that farmers could store grain cheaply while waiting for better selling prices.

Political action. The leaders of the Grange encouraged farmers to use their vote. In 1873, Grange members in the Plains states and the South agreed to vote only for candidates who supported their aims. They elected some officials who understood their problems. Several states passed laws that put a limit on prices for grain shipment and storage.

In spite of the efforts of Grangers, crop prices continued to drop. Farmers sank deeper and deeper in debt.

Farmers' Alliance. Another group, the *Farmers' Alliance,* joined the struggle in the 1870s. Like the Grange, the Alliance set up cooperatives and warehouses. The Farmers' Alliance spread from Texas through the South and into the Plains states. In the South, the Alliance brought black and white farmers together. Alliance leaders also tried to join with factory workers who were angry about their treatment by employers.

A New Political Party

In 1891, farmers and labor unions joined together to form the *Populist party.* At their first national convention, the Populists demanded government help with falling farm prices and regulation of railroad rates. They also called for an income tax, an eight-hour workday, and limits on immigration.

Free silver. Another demand made by the Populists was for free silver. That means that they wanted all silver mined in the West to be coined, or made into money. Populists believed that farm prices were dropping because too little money was in circulation.

An activist from Pennsylvania, Mary Elizabeth Lease moved to Kansas and joined the Farmers' Alliance movement. She sympathized with the farmers, who were barely making a profit, while bank and railroad monopolies were making millions.

Because the Populist party favored the government ownership of railroads (a plan that would end monopolies), Lease traveled through Kansas, encouraging farmers to join. Between 1891 and 1895, the Populists had so

many members that they could nominate a candidate for President.

In 1896, Lease left the Populists, but she did not stop fighting for reform. Instead, she worked for women's rights and other causes she believed in. Amid all her work and travel, she also found the time to write a book on politics and reform entitled *The Problem of Civilization Solved.*

Even today, groups of people continue to unite to buy supplies wholesale, thereby lowering prices for each person in the group. Have students list the names of any cooperatives or members-only stores that they have visited or know about through advertising or from others. Encourage students who have visited or shopped at such wholesale stores to describe them and to discuss their advantages and disadvantages.

Free silver would increase the supply of money. This would make it easier for farmers to repay their debts, argued Populists.

Eastern bankers and factory owners opposed free silver. They argued that increasing the money supply would cause inflation. (See page 469.) Business people feared that inflation would wreck the economy.

Popular support. Many Americans supported Populist ideas. The Populist candidate for President in 1892 won one million votes. The following year a severe depression brought the Populists new support. In, 1894, they elected six senators and seven representatives to Congress. Populists looked forward to bigger victories in the election of 1896.

The "Great Commoner"

The Populists entered the election of 1896 with high hopes. Their program had been endorsed by one of the great orators of the age—William Jennings Bryan.

Candidate Bryan. Bryan was a young Democratic congressman from Nebraska. Known as the "Great Commoner," he had championed the cause of common people all his life.

Bryan agreed with the Populists on several issues. He believed that the nation needed to increase the supply of money. A gifted speaker, he made many speeches on the benefits of free silver. He also spoke out on behalf of the farmer.

At the Democratic convention in 1896, Bryan made a powerful speech. With his booming voice, he held the audience spellbound. Delegates cheered wildly as he thundered against the rich and powerful and for free silver.

The next day, the Democrats nominated Bryan for President. After heated debate, the Populist party also supported him.

President McKinley. Bryan campaigned all around the country. Millions of people heard his electrifying speeches. Meanwhile, the Republican candidate, William McKinley, stayed at his Ohio home. McKinley knew that bankers and business people supported him. They were afraid that Bryan would ruin the economy.

In the election, Bryan carried the South and the West. McKinley won the heavily populated states of the East. In the end, Bryan narrowly lost.

Populist Party Fades

The Populist party broke up after 1896. One reason was that the Democratic party took up a number of Populist demands. Also, when prosperity returned in the late 1890s, people worried less about railroad rates and free silver.

Even though the Populist party died out, many of its ideas lived on. In the years ahead, the eight-hour workday became standard for American workers. In 1913, the states ratified an amendment authorizing an income tax.

SECTION **5** REVIEW

1. **Identify:** (a) National Grange, (b) Farmers' Alliance, (c) Populist party, (d) William Jennings Bryan.
2. **Define:** (a) cooperative, (b) wholesale.
3. Why did increased grain harvests create problems for farmers?
4. Explain how each group tried to help farmers: (a) National Grange, (b) Farmers' Alliance.
5. Name three demands of the Populists.
6. **CRITICAL THINKING Solving Problems** What methods did farmers use to solve their problems in the late 1800s? Suggest one other action they could have tried to reach their goals.

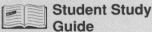 **Writing to Learn**

Write a series of newspaper headlines that summarize the events discussed in Section 5.

Voices of Freedom

Primary Source You might assign selection 3-6, Bryan and the Cross of Gold, on pages 159–160 of *Voices of Freedom*. The selection is from William Jennings Bryan's dramatic speech—a speech that led to his nomination for President. (Enrichment/Challenging)

Chapter Resources

Critical Thinking Duplicate and distribute the worksheet, Understanding Causes and Effects, from Unit 6, page 3, of the *Chapter Resources* binder. The worksheet encourages students to distinguish between causes and effects as it reviews several key facts relating to the settlement of the western frontier. (Enrichment/Average)

Student Study Guide

Section 5 Study Guide Have students use the Section 5 Study Guide on page 144 of the *Student Study Guide* to review and reinforce the content of this section. (Reteaching/Average)

ACTIVITY

Guided Instruction Remind students that headlines express key facts in a concise but memorable way. You might have the class vote on the events to be featured, but then have students work individually to complete the activity.

Answers to Section 5 Review

1. (a) National Grange, p. 530, (b) Farmers' Alliance, p. 530, (c) Populist party, p. 530, (d) William Jennings Bryan, p. 531
2. (a) cooperative, p. 530, (b) wholesale, p. 530
3. The abundant wheat and corn crops caused prices to fall. Many farmers were left unable to pay their debts.
4. (a) Grangers demanded that railroads lower shipping prices for small farmers; they formed cooperatives so farmers could buy supplies at wholesale prices; and they supported political parties that favored the farmers. (b) The Alliance set up cooperatives; it brought black and white farmers together; and it tried to unite with the factory workers who were demanding better treatment.
5. Possible Answer: an eight-hour workday, an income tax, limits on immigration, regulation of railroad rates, and free silver
6. Possible Answer: Farmers joined organizations, formed cooperatives, voted for people who agreed with them, and formed a new political party. Other actions might include boycotts, public protests, and a refusal to sell crops for less than they were worth.

CHAPTER 18 REVIEW

Answers to Reviewing the Main Ideas

1. It brought thousands of people who then built towns and cities near mining centers.

2. Builders had to lay tracks across deserts and mountains. They had to find people who would work for low pay in blowing sand and freezing cold.

3. Buffalo provided food, materials for clothing, blankets, tools, tepees, and even sinews for sewing the hides together.

4. (a) The Dawes Act encouraged Native Americans to become farmers, and to do this, it provided them with land. It also provided money to build schools to teach Indian children to live like white people. (b) Native Americans resisted change and were unhappy on reservations.

5. (a) to encourage farmers to settle in the West and to give poor people a chance to own their own farms (b) In most cases, the Homestead Act did not achieve its goals, since only 20 percent of the land went to individual owners. Many city people could not afford the transportation to western lands. Also, large landowning companies took over much of the land illegally and sold it at high prices.

6. (a) They saw the frontier as a place of opportunity, where they could begin a new life. (b) Southern whites did not want to lose their source of cheap labor.

7. (a) The Populists believed that coined silver would increase the money supply and make it easier for farmers to repay their debts. (b) The Democrats began to press for the same demands that the Populists called for, so there was no reason for the party to exist. Also, because the country enjoyed a new prosperity after 1896, people lost interest in railroad rates and free silver.

Answers to Thinking Critically

1. (a) Possible Answer: space, the sea, or frontiers of medical or scientific knowledge (b) Answers will depend on the type of frontier mentioned. Space frontiers, for example, are farther away than the western frontier

Summary

- Discovery of gold and silver hurried the settlement of the West and led to the building of the transcontinental railroad.
- Many Indian nations depended on the buffalo for survival.
- By the late 1880s, destruction of the buffalo and action by the United States government had forced most Plains Indians off their lands and onto reservations.
- After a cattle boom, farming became the major way of life on the Plains.
- Falling grain prices led farmers to join with labor unions to form the Populist party.

Reviewing the Main Ideas

1. How did the mining boom lead to the growth of western towns and cities?

2. What problems had to be overcome in building the transcontinental railroad?

3. What role did the buffalo play in the lives of the Plains Indians?

4. (a) What were the goals of the Dawes Act? (b) What were the results?

5. (a) Why did Congress pass the Homestead Act? (b) Did the Homestead Act achieve its goals? Explain.

6. (a) Why did African Americans leave the South after Reconstruction? (b) Why did southern whites try to stop them?

7. (a) Why did Populists support free silver? (b) Why did the Populist party decline after 1896?

Thinking Critically

1. Linking Past and Present The frontier was an important part of American life until 1890. (a) What frontier exists today? (b) How does that frontier compare with the frontier of the nation's earlier history?

2. Analyzing Information (a) Is the picture of the cowhands' life in today's TV programs and movies an accurate one? (b) Why have modern Americans created this romantic image of life on the cattle frontier?

Applying Your Skills

1. Reading a Map Study the map on page 517. (a) Name three sites of battles between the United States Army and Native Americans. (b) Which Indian nations were divided and sent to separate reservations? (c) How do you think the United States government justified moving Native Americans onto reservations?

2. Concept Mapping Review the information on pages 524–526 about the Cattle Kingdom. Then make a concept map showing the main ideas and supporting details.

3. Constructing a Time Line Make a time line showing at least four important events in the farmers' fight to improve their lives in the late 1800s. (a) Add the discovery of the Comstock Lode to your time line. (b) How is this discovery of silver related to the farmers' problems?

Thinking About Geography

Match the letters on the map with the following places: **1.** Texas, **2.** Colorado, **3.** Nevada, **4.** Promontory Point, **5.** Omaha, **6.** San Francisco. **Interaction** How did the transcontinental railroad change life in the West?

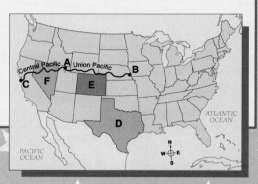

---

was, and possible space settlers will need much more information about it before anyone sets out. However, both the western frontier and the frontiers of space attract people willing to take risks.

2. (a) Possible Answer: The TV cowboy is a romantic figure. Most of a cowhand's work was exhausting, boring, dirty, and dangerous. (b) Possible Answer: Modern Americans have created this image because they like to look back on frontier work as exciting and heroic.

Answers to Applying Your Skills

1. (a) Little Bighorn, Fetterman's Defeat, Wounded Knee, Chivington Massacre (b) the Lakota, the Shoshones, and the Apaches (c) Possible Answer: The Native Americans were troublemakers; settlers deserved the land more.

2. Students' concept maps may include information about cattle drives, the cattle boom, the work of cowhands, and the end of the Cattle Kingdom.

3. Time line dates should include 1867, when farmers united; 1873, when Grange members agreed to vote for candidates who supported their aims; the 1870s, when the Farmers' Alliance joined the fight to help farmers; 1891, when the Populist party was formed; 1894, when Populists elected some representatives and senators; and 1896, when Bryan ran for President. (a) Discovery of Comstock Lode, 1859 (b) The Comstock Lode gave the farmers hope that if its silver were

INTERDISCIPLINARY ACTIVITY

Farming on the Plains

Form into groups to explore farming on the Great Plains. Follow the suggestions below to write, draw, or perform to show what you know. You may use the textbook, encyclopedias, atlases, or other materials in your classroom library to complete the tasks. Be able to name your sources of information when you have finished the activity.

SCIENTISTS Make a diagram or model of one of the important inventions that helped farmers on the Plains, such as the windmill, barbed wire, or steel plow. Be prepared to explain how the invention worked and why it was important to Plains farmers.

WRITERS Imagine that you are a woman living in a sod house on the Plains in the late 1800s. Write a diary entry describing a typical day.

ACTORS Choose two or more people from the picture on page 527. Prepare a skit in which those people are the main characters.

REPORTERS Form into two groups to prepare an interview of a group of Exodusters. One group should design interview questions. The other group should be prepared to answer the questions. When you have completed your preparations, videotape the interview for presentation to the class.

GOVERNMENT LEADERS AND ECONOMISTS Review the economic problems that Plains farmers faced at the end of the 1800s. Then organize a convention to discuss those problems and suggest solutions. Prepare charts, graphs, and other exhibits to use during the discussion.

★ Set up a Farming on the Plains bulletin board display. Include an example or summary of each group's completed activity.

Poster advertising free land

Model of a windmill

Homesteaders in front of their sod house

---

coined, the money supply would increase, making for easier repayment of farmers' debts.

Answers to Thinking About Geography

1. D **2.** E **3.** F **4.** A **5.** B **6.** C

Interaction: The railroad made it possible to develop the West's riches. Territories and towns grew. Thriving territories became states.

Assessment

Chapter Resources Binder For a more comprehensive evaluation of student understanding of this chapter, assign Chapter Tests A and B and/or Extra Unit Questions from Unit 6, pages 7–12 and 43–45.

Computer Test Bank You can use Chapter Tests and Extra Unit Questions to create your own tests for both testing and retesting.

Alternative Assessment

Chapter Resources Binder See the Alternative Assessment booklet in the *Social Studies Educator's Handbook* series.

Portfolio You might meet with students to choose appropriate work from the chapter for inclusion in their portfolios.

Interdisciplinary ACTIVITY

Learning Styles

The following chart indicates the activities appropriate for different learning styles.

Visual Learners
Scientists
Actors
Reporters
Government leaders and economists

Auditory Learners
Scientists
Actors
Reporters
Government leaders and economists

Kinesthetic Learners
Writers
Actors
Reporters
Government leaders and economists

Evaluation

Scientists Diagrams or models should be large enough for people to see the parts connected and understand how they function. Explanations should be clear and factually correct.

Writers Diary entries should seem true to life and should reflect the conditions of life on the Plains, as discussed in Section 4.

Actors Skits should reflect the goals and hopes of the Exodusters. Dialogue should be conversational, and it may reveal some sort of conflict, such as a difference of opinion.

Reporters Interviewers' questions should explore the Exodusters' past and their dreams for the future. Responses should be true to the group's pioneering spirit. Production quality need not be a criterion for the videotapes, but generally they should be easy to watch and hear.

Government leaders and economists Each attendee should speak on only one topic. Topics, as well as audiovisual aids, should be prepared well before each convention begins.

Chapter 19 The Rise of Industry (1865–1914), pp. 534–559

Lessons	Teaching Resources
1 Railroads: Key to Industrial Growth **Objectives** 1. Describe how railroads became more efficient after the Civil War. 2. Identify some abuses of the railroads. 3. Describe how railroads fueled the growth of industry.	**Lesson Planner** Cooperative Learning, p. 117 **Student Study Guide** Section 1 Study Guide, p. 147 **Chapter Resources Binder, Unit 6** *History Through Literature* John Henry, p. 18
2 Big Business **Objectives** 1. Identify what made steel an important industry. 2. Describe how the growth of railroads changed the way Americans did business. 3. Identify some of the great business leaders of the late 1800s. 4. Identify the arguments for and against big business.	**Lesson Planner** Cooperative Learning, p. 118 **Student Study Guide** Section 2 Study Guide, p. 148 **Chapter Resources Binder, Unit 6** *Geography in History* Pittsburgh: A Steelmaking Capital, pp. 19–20 **Interdisciplinary Connections:** New Industries and New Inventions ■ *Arts* Capturing Words and Music, p. 110 ▨ *Sciences* An Experiment That Went Wrong, p. 111 ■ *Geography* Bridging the Big River, p. 112 ■ *World* Chicago's Amazing World's Fair, p. 113 ■ *Civics* Roads for the Future, p. 114
3 An Age of Invention **Objectives** 1. Identify the inventions that improved communication in the 1800s. 2. Explain why Menlo Park was called an "invention factory." 3. Describe how Henry Ford revolutionized the automobile industry.	**Lesson Planner** Cooperative Learning, p. 119 **Student Study Guide** Section 3 Study Guide, p. 149 **Our Multicultural Heritage** *Milestone* Inventions—By Accident, p. 57
4 Workers and Unions **Objectives** 1. Identify what working conditions were like in factories of the late 1800s. 2. Explain why workers formed unions. 3. Describe the labor movement's treatment of immigrants and African Americans. 4. Explain why labor unions faced opposition.	**Lesson Planner** Cooperative Learning, p. 120 **Student Study Guide** Section 4 Study Guide, p. 150 **Our Multicultural Heritage** *Biography* Alice Hamilton, Medical Investigator, p. 55 *Biography* Mary Jones, Labor Reformer, p. 56 **Chapter Resources Binder, Unit 6** *Skill Application* Evaluating Information, p. 16 *Critical Thinking* Defending a Position, p. 17

Multimedia Resources	Additional Resources	Chapter-Level Resources
Videotapes/Videodiscs *United States History Video Collection* The Rise of Heavy Industry, Vol. 11, Ch. 10	**Customized Reader** The Pleasure of Overland Travel on the Pacific Railroad, article VB-10 The First Chinese Texans, article VA-2 The Early Days of Moran, Michigan, article VA-10	**Lesson Planner** Activity Based, pp. 121–122 **Student Study Guide** Chapter 19 Study Guide, pp. 151–152 **Chapter Resources Binder** **Unit 6** Vocabulary Building, p. 15 Chapter Test A, pp. 21–23 Chapter Test B, pp. 24–26 Illustration Master, p. 27 Extra Unit Questions, pp. 43–45 **English Guided Reading** Guided Reading, pp. 37–38 **Spanish Resources** **Guided Reading Audiotapes** Side 7 **CD-ROM** *Time Tour* The Rise of Industry (1865–1914) in Reshaping the Nation
Transparencies *Exploring Technology* The Brooklyn Bridge, p. H-49 *Interdisciplinary Connections* The Art of Advertising, p. B-69 *Political Cartoons* A Cartoonist's View of Standard Oil Company, p. G-21 **CD-ROM** *History Makers* Andrew Carnegie **Videotapes/Videodiscs** *United States History Video Collection* The Modern Corporation, Vol. 11, Ch. 13	**Voices of Freedom** The Talent for Wealth, pp. 146–147 Founding Standard Oil, pp. 148–149 **Customized Reader** How Oil Was Discovered at Spindletop, article VIB-4	
Transparencies *Exploring Technology* The Telegraph, p. H-41 *Exploring Technology* The Phonograph, p. H-51 *Exploring Technology* The Ford Assembly Line, p. H-57 **CD-ROM** *History Makers* Thomas Edison *History Makers* Henry Ford *History Makers* Orville and Wilbur Wright	**Voices of Freedom** A Cable Across the Atlantic, pp. 143–144 The Remarkable Mr. Woods, pp. 144–146 **Customized Reader** Motoring Through California in 1910, article VIB-15	
Transparencies *Cause and Effect* The Rise of Industry in the United States, p. F-23 **CD-ROM** *Face the Issues* Child Labor *History Makers* Samuel Gompers	**Voices of Freedom** A Bombing at Haymarket Square, pp. 151–152 **Customized Reader** Looking for Work in Chicago, article VIA-3	

Lesson Planner

For a fully developed **Activity-Based** lesson plan for Chapter 19, see the *Lesson Planner,* pages 121–122.

 Chapter Resources

Vocabulary Building The Vocabulary Building worksheet for Chapter 19 from Unit 6, page 15, of the *Chapter Resources* binder can be used as a prereading activity or as a review of chapter vocabulary. (Reteaching/Easy)

 Student Study Guide

Chapter 19 Study Guide Refer students to pages 151–152 of the *Student Study Guide* for the Chapter 19 Study Guide. The study guide can be used for chapter review as well as for reteaching. (Reteaching/Average)

 Guided Reading Audiotapes

Students can use *Guided Reading Audiotapes,* Chapter 19, side 7, to listen to section previews, summaries, and review questions. The tapes might benefit students who are auditory learners, students who have trouble reading, or students acquiring English. (Reteaching/Easy)

CHAPTER 19

The Rise of Industry

(1865–1914)

CHAPTER OUTLINE

1 Railroads: Key to Industrial Growth

2 Big Business

3 An Age of Invention

4 Workers and Unions

1882 John D. Rockefeller formed the Standard Oil trust to control the oil industry. This cartoon shows Rockefeller dressed in an oil barrel and an oil-lamp hat.

1876 Alexander Graham Bell perfected the telephone. Bell's invention, shown here, transformed the way Americans communicated.

1886 The American Federation of Labor was founded. The AFL adopted this seal during its battle for an eight-hour workday.

| 1865 | 1870 | 1875 | 1880 | 1885 | 1890 |

 WORLD EVENT
1871 England makes labor unions legal

 WORLD EVENT
1890 First electric underground rail line opens in England

534 • Chapter 19

Chapter Time Line
Critical Thinking

After students have discussed the inventions and innovations noted on the time line, divide the class into groups of three or four students each. Have each group choose one time line note that relates to technology and write an advertisement for it. Ask them to consider questions such as these: How would you drum up business for the telephone? How would you get people to switch from horses to "horseless carriages"? Invite groups to share their finished advertisements with the class.

Students Acquiring English
Activity

The use of discussion is important in unlocking meaning for SAE students. Include among your techniques in working with SAE students the use of gestures and facial expressions, frequent modeling, visual aids, and simplified speech. To review the material in the chapter, assign each SAE student to a peer partner with strong language skills. Instruct student pairs to discuss the main points, stopping for amplification when necessary. These pairs might also work together as homework partners.

Chapter Setting

Thomas A. Watson, Alexander Graham Bell's assistant, gave this exciting account of an early experiment with the telephone:

66 On the afternoon of June 2, 1875, we were hard at work on the same old job, testing some [minor changes] of the instruments. . . . One of the transmitter springs I was attending to stopped vibrating, and I plucked it to start it again.

It didn't start, and I kept on plucking it, when suddenly I heard a shout from Bell in the next room, and then out he came with a rush, demanding, 'What did you do then? Don't change anything. Let me see!' I showed him. 99

Bell was elated. He had transmitted sound over wire. His invention could work! One year later, in March 1876, Bell transmitted a complete sentence to Watson, who was standing in another room. At that moment, the telephone was born.

The telephone was just one of an enormous number of amazing new American inventions in the late 1800s. These inventions, along with rich resources and enterprising leadership, sparked an era of industry in the United States.

The growth of industry made the United States rich. It also created problems. Factory workers endured unsafe conditions and low pay. Workers banded together to improve conditions and gain a larger share of the profits. A new force was emerging in American society. That force was organized labor.

ACTIVITY Choose an invention from the list on page 549. Imagine that you live in the late 1800s. Role-play your reaction when you see the invention for the first time.

1913 Ford introduced the assembly line for the manufacture of automobiles. Soon, thousands of Americans were driving "horseless carriages."

1894 Workers at the Pullman railroad car factory went on strike to protest a wage cut. Here, federal troops escort a train.

1890	1895	1900	1905	1910	1915

 WORLD EVENT
1901 First transatlantic wireless message sent

 WORLD EVENT
1909 French aviator makes first plane flight across English Channel

Chapter 19 • **535**

Bell Ringer

Have students discuss this question: Are railroads as important today as they were in the 1800s? Why or why not?

Lesson Plan

1. Focus The rapid growth of railroads after the Civil War led to major changes in American life. In this section, students focus on the ways in which railroad owners lessened competition while enlarging the network of railroads that crisscrossed the nation.

2. Instruct Explain that to some people the railroad builders were "robber barons," but to others they were "industrial statesmen" or "captains of industry." Divide the class into several groups. Appoint some groups to be publicists for the railroads. Have them write speeches in praise of the railroad builders. Appoint other groups to be reformers who want the government to regulate the railroads. Have them write speeches condemning the railroad builders. Conclude by having representatives from the groups read their speeches.

3. Close To close the lesson, have students identify the most important fact or concept to remember from each subsection within Section 1.

1
Railroads: Key to Industrial Growth

FIND OUT
■ How did railroads become more efficient after the Civil War?

■ What were some abuses of the railroads?

■ How did railroads fuel the growth of industry?

VOCABULARY network, consolidate, rebate, pool

In 1876, the United States celebrated its one-hundredth birthday with a giant exhibition showing off its industrial progress. A German visitor to the Philadelphia Exhibition marveled at the nation's rapid growth. "In a short time, American industry has risen to a height of which those in Europe had no real idea," he said.

Visitors had good reason to marvel. As recently as 1860, industrial growth in the United States had lagged far behind that of European nations. By 1900, however, American industry would produce more goods than any other nation in the world. This industrial growth was spurred by a variety of factors. Perhaps none was more important than the railroad.

Creating a Railroad Network

The importance of railroads became clear during the Civil War. Railroads carried troops and supplies to the battlefronts. They also moved raw materials to factories. After the war, railroad companies began to build new lines all around the country.

Connecting lines. Early railroads had served local communities. Many lines ran for no more than 50 miles (80 km). Some-

times the rail lines were not connected to one another. When passengers and freight reached the end of one line, they had to move to a train on a different line to continue their journey.

Even if the lines had been connected, however, the problem would not have been solved. Different lines used rails of different gauges, or widths. Thus, trains from one line could not run on tracks of another line.

In 1886, railroads in the South decided to adopt the northern gauge. Some 13,000 miles (20,800 km) of railroad track had to be changed.

On May 30, 1886, southern railroads stopped running so that work could begin. One company hired 8,000 workers. Using crowbars and sledgehammers, they worked from dawn to dusk to move the rails a few inches farther apart. By the end of the day, all 2,000 miles of the company's track had been adjusted!

Once the gauge of the track was standardized, the railroads formed a **network**, or system of connected lines. All over the country, new rails knit the sprawling nation together. By 1900, there were more miles of tracks in the United States than in Europe and Russia combined!

Other improvements. Railroad travel was fast. Going to San Francisco from New York City took only six days. Before the railroads, the trip took months.

> ***Linking Past and Present***
> *To simplify train schedules, the railroad companies set up a system of time zones in 1883. Before that, each town kept its own time, based on the position of the sun. Illinois, for example, had 27 different local times! The new system divided the country into four time zones: Eastern, Central, Mountain, and Pacific. Every place within that time zone observed the same time.*

Connections With Technology
Background

The fact that different rail lines used different gauges was not an accident. Indeed, early railroad builders had laid tracks of different widths on purpose so that competitors could not run engines on their lines. The standard gauge, established in 1886, set rails 4 feet 8½ inches apart.

Connections With Geography
Activity

Have students imagine that they have won an all-expenses-paid trip by rail to anywhere in the United States. Have them develop a three-week itinerary for their trip, listing localities they would like to visit, places of interest they would like to see along the way, and sites they would like to see at major stopovers. Students should write at least one sentence describing the significance of each place listed on their itineraries. Have classmates check the itineraries against railroad maps to make sure that train lines to the places listed are available and also against train schedules to make sure that the projected travel times are practical.

A Nation Linked by Rail
By the late 1800s, a complex system of railroads connected the nation. This 1874 advertisement for the Erie Railway shows trains steaming into a station. **Technology** *How were the nation's local rail lines transformed into a network?*

Lesson Planner

For a developed **Cooperative Learning** lesson plan, see the *Lesson Planner,* page 117.

Answer to Caption

Southern rail lines were converted to the northern gauge, making it possible for rail lines to be connected.

Chapter Resources

History Through Literature To introduce students to a legend connected with the railroad boom, duplicate and distribute the worksheet, John Henry, from Unit 6, page 18, of the *Chapter Resources* binder. (Enrichment/Average)

Customized Reader

Primary Source For a copy of a guidebook written to entice easterners to try train travel to the West, order article VB-10, The Pleasure of Overland Travel on the Pacific Railroad, from the *American History Customized Reader.* (Enrichment/Average)

Primary Source For a description of the experiences of Chinese immigrants in Texas, order article VA-2, The First Chinese Texans, from the *American History Customized Reader.* This selection describes the contributions that the Chinese made to railroad construction, the hardships that they endured, and the discrimination that they faced. (Enrichment/Average)

Long-distance rail travel could be quite comfortable. Companies improved service by adding sleeping and dining cars to trains. A national magazine described train service in 1872:

66From Chicago to Omaha your train will carry a dining car. . . . You sit at little tables which comfortably accommodate four persons; you order your breakfast, dinner, or supper from a bill of fare which contains a surprising number of dishes; you eat from snow-white linen . . . admirably cooked food, and pay a modest price. 99

Consolidation

As railroads grew, they looked for other ways to become more efficient. Many companies began to **consolidate,** or combine. Larger companies bought up smaller ones or forced them out of business. The Pennsylvania Railroad, for example, consolidated 73 companies into its system.

Tough-minded business people known as railroad barons headed the drive for consolidation. The most powerful railroad baron was Cornelius Vanderbilt. The son of a poor farmer, Vanderbilt first earned his fortune in steamship lines. He then turned his attention to railroads and was soon buying up lines in New York State.

Sometimes Vanderbilt's tactics were ruthless. In the early 1860s, he decided to buy the New York Central Railroad. The owners, however, refused to sell. Suddenly, Vanderbilt announced that the New York Central passengers could not transfer to his trains. With its passengers stranded and business dropping sharply, the New York Central owners were forced to give in.

Vanderbilt then bought up most of the lines between Chicago and Buffalo. By the time of his death in 1877, he controlled 4,500 miles (7,200 km) of track connecting New York City and the Great Lakes region.

Building New Lines

Railroad builders raced to create thousands of miles of new tracks. In the years after Leland Stanford drove the golden spike in 1869, Americans built three more transcontinental railroads. James Hill, a Canadian, finished the last major cross-country line in 1893. (See the map on page 524.) His Great Northern wound from Duluth, Minnesota, to Everett, Washington.

Chapter 19 • **537**

Historical Sidelight
Background

George Pullman's newly developed sleeping car spared no luxuries. Drapes hung on the windows, Brussels carpeting spread across the floor, and chandeliers hung from the ceiling. Pullman's first model, called the Pioneer, was so large that it would not fit under many railroad bridges or next to station platforms. Railroads soon began to widen the clearances, especially after a Pioneer was used in President Lincoln's funeral train.

Connections With the World
Background

The expansion of railroads brought about the need for standardizing time within local areas. Time zones were established in the United States in 1883. In 1884, delegates from 27 nations met in Washington, D.C., and divided the entire world into the 24 time zones that are still in use today. The delegates also agreed to measure standard time from the Prime Meridian, which runs through Greenwich, England.

Connections With Local History
Activity

Have students research the history of your state and/or community to determine the importance of railroads to the area's early history and development. As part of this study, students might find out how early your town was connected to one or more major cities by rail.

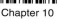
Railway Giant *Someone once told Cornelius Vanderbilt that some of his methods were illegal. Vanderbilt replied, "What do I care about the law? Hain't I got the power?" This 1879 cartoon shows Vanderbilt towering over his railroad empire.* **Economics** *Who do you think the other men in the cartoon are? Explain.*

Unlike other rail lines, the Great Northern was built without aid from Congress. As a result, Hill had to be sure that the railroad made a profit from the start.

Hill encouraged ranchers and farmers to move to the Northwest and settle near his railroad. He gave seed to farmers and helped them buy equipment. He even im-

ported a special breed of bulls to help ranchers raise hardy cattle. Hill once said, "We consider ourselves and the people along our line as co-partners in the prosperity of the country we both occupy." Not only was Hill's policy generous, it made good business sense.

Abuses

Soon, there were too many rail lines in some parts of the country. Between Atlanta and St. Louis, for example, 20 different lines competed for business. There was not nearly enough rail traffic to keep all these lines busy.

Cutthroat competition. In the West, especially, there were too few people for the railroads to make a profit. Competition was fierce. Rate wars broke out as rival railroads slashed their fares to win customers. Usually, all the companies lost money as a result.

To win or keep business, big railroads secretly offered **rebates,** or discounts, to their largest customers. Large railroads used rebates to capture much of the grain traffic in the West and the South. This in turn forced many small companies out of business. It also hurt small shippers, such as farmers, who used rail lines.

Railroad barons soon realized that cutthroat competition was hurting even their large railroad lines. They looked for ways to end the competition. One method was pooling. In a **pool,** several railroad companies agreed to divide up business in an area and then fix their prices at a high level.

Farmers react. The railroad barons' use of rebates and pools angered small farmers in the South and the West. Both practices kept shipping prices high for small farmers.

As you have read in Chapter 18, many farmers joined the Populist party. Populists called for government regulation of railroad rates. Congress and several states passed laws regulating the railroad companies. However, the laws did not end the abuses.

538 • Chapter 19

Connections With Economics
Background

The competition in the railroad business was so ruthless that although railroads formed pools, they often fell apart. Companies in the pool usually could not resist cutting prices to win customers, thus breaching the pool agreement.

Cornelius Vanderbilt was called "Commodore" not because he was a naval officer but because he had made his original fortune in shipping. He used some of the profits

from his railroad ventures to start a streetcar service in New York City, and later to order the construction of Grand Central Terminal, which is still a busy site for commuters in Manhattan today. When he died, Vanderbilt left a fortune worth more than $105 million, the largest estate in United States history up to that time. Vanderbilt University, in Nashville, Tennessee, was one of his main beneficiaries.

Railroad barons paid large bribes to officials to keep the laws from being enforced.

Railroads and Industry

Railroads had many problems. Still, more than any other development, it was the American railroad that made possible the rapid growth of industry after 1865.

Steelworkers turned millions of tons of iron into steel for tracks and engines. Lumberjacks cut down whole forests to supply wood for railroad ties. Miners sweated in dusty mine shafts digging coal to fuel railroad engines. The railroad companies themselves employed thousands of workers to build the network. They laid tracks, built trestles across rivers, and carved tunnels through mountains.

Railroads opened up every corner of the country to settlement and growth. They brought people together, especially in the West. New businesses sprang up, and new towns grew where rail lines crossed. With rail lines in place, the United States was ready to grow into the greatest industrial nation the world had ever seen.

SECTION 1 REVIEW

1. **Define:** (a) network, (b) consolidate, (c) rebate, (d) pool.
2. How did a railroad network develop after the Civil War?
3. How did competition affect the railroad industry?
4. List five ways that railroads fueled the growth of industry.
5. **CRITICAL THINKING Analyzing Information** Do you think that consolidation is a good business practice? Explain.

ACTIVITY Writing to Learn
List the vocabulary words in this section. Then write a definition for each that could be understood by a younger student.

2
Big Business

FIND OUT

- What made steel an important industry?
- How did the growth of railroads change the way Americans did business?
- Who were some of the great business leaders of the late 1800s?
- What were the arguments for and against big business?

VOCABULARY vertical integration, capital, corporation, stock, dividend, trust, monopoly, free enterprise system

On a chilly February day in 1865, an unusual auction took place in an Ohio oil refinery. The two owners of the refinery stood toe to toe—the only people in the room. They were each bidding to buy the other's share in the company.

The bidding opened at $500. It soon shot up to $72,500. "I'll go no higher, John," said one of the men. "The business is yours."

The men shook hands, and the bargain was struck. John would pay $72,500 to become sole owner of the company. It turned out to be a smart purchase. When he died more than 70 years later, John D. Rockefeller and his Standard Oil Company dominated the oil industry.

Rockefeller was one of a new breed of American business leaders that grew up in the late 1800s. They had imagination and vision. They could also be ruthless. Together, these leaders shaped the nation's emerging businesses and industries.

Chapter 19 • **539**

 Student Study Guide

Section 1 Study Guide Have students use the Section 1 Study Guide on page 147 of the *Student Study Guide* to review and reinforce the content of this section. (Reteaching/Average)

ACTIVITY

Guided Instruction Encourage students to define each word apart from its industrial context. You might also have students write a sentence that uses the word. Invite students to check their definitions by reading them to a younger student and see if he or she understands the definition.

Section 2
pp. 539–545

Bell Ringer

Ask students to name an industry or business that is as important today as the steel industry was in the late 1800s. Have students suggest problems that might arise if one company controlled the entire industry or business.

Lesson Plan

1. Focus The late 1800s were a time of great prosperity for a few. In this section, students learn about the tactics used by business leaders such as Andrew Carnegie, J. Pierpont Morgan, and John D. Rockefeller.

Answers to Section 1 Review

1. (a) network, p. 536, (b) consolidate, p. 537, (c) rebate, p. 538, (d) pool, p. 538
2. Track was standardized, thousands of miles of new track were laid, and sleeping and dining cars were added to trains.
3. Competition caused rate wars and led to such abuses as rebates and pooling.
4. Possible Answer: Railroads opened up every corner of the country to trade, providing new markets for industry; the steel industry provided steel for tracks and engines; the lumber industry provided wood for railroad ties; the coal mining industry provided coal to fuel trains; railroads employed thousands of workers; new towns and businesses sprang up where rail lines crossed.
5. Possible Answers: yes, because consolidation increases efficiency; no, because consolidation decreases competition, thereby giving control of vital industries to too few companies

2. Instruct Divide the class into groups. As you work through this section, ask each group: (a) What is the difference between a *stock* and a *dividend*? (b) How does incorporation help a business to expand? (c) How does a *trust* limit competition? (d) What is the difference between a *trust* and a *monopoly*? (e) What made Carnegie Steel a *vertically integrated* company? (f) Is there competition in a *free enterprise system*? Compare group answers.
3. Close To close the lesson, pair students and assign each pair one subsection in Section 2. Have them identify the most important fact or idea from the subsection.

Lesson Planner

For a developed **Cooperative Learning** lesson plan, see the *Lesson Planner,* page 118.

Answer to Caption

Possible Answers: heat, injuries such as burns, poor ventilation

Chapter Resources

Geography in History Duplicate and distribute the worksheet, Pittsburgh: A Steelmaking Capital, from Unit 6, pages 19–20, of the *Chapter Resources* binder. The worksheet explores the physical location of Pittsburgh as key to its growth as an industrial center. (Enrichment/Challenging)

The Steel Industry

The growth of railroads after the Civil War fueled the growth of the steel industry. Early trains ran on iron rails that wore out quickly. Some people referred to iron rails as "parallel lines of rust heading to the horizon." Railroad owners knew that steel rails were much stronger and not as likely to rust as iron. Steel, however, was costly and difficult to make.

A new way to make steel. In the 1850s, William Kelly in the United States and Henry Bessemer in England both discovered a new way to make steel. The ***Bessemer process,*** as it came to be called, enabled steelmakers to produce strong steel at a lower cost. As a result, railroads began to lay steel rails.

Other industries also found uses for the cheaper steel. New "skyscrapers," for example, used steel girders to support their great weight. Many everyday items, including nails, screws, needles, and pins, also began to be made of steel.

Steel mills spring up. Steel mills sprang up in cities throughout the Midwest. Pittsburgh became the steelmaking capital of the nation. Nearby coal mines and good transportation helped Pittsburgh's steel mills to thrive.

The steel mills brought jobs and prosperity to Pittsburgh and other steel towns. They also caused new problems. The mills belched thick black smoke that turned the air gray. Soot blanketed houses, trees, and streets. Waste polluted local rivers.

King of Steel

Many Americans made fortunes in the steel industry. None became richer or more powerful, however, than a Scottish immigrant named Andrew Carnegie.

Carnegie's career is like a history of American industry. As a young boy, he went to work in a textile mill. Later, as telegraph wires were strung from city to city, Carnegie became a telegraph operator. When the railroad boom started, he secured a job as secretary to an official of the Pennsylvania Railroad. He soon rose to the position of division manager.

Traveling in England in the 1870s, Carnegie became familiar with the Bessemer process. When he returned home, he built a steel mill at Homestead, Pennsylvania, close to Pittsburgh. Using the Bessemer process, he began producing steel. Because Carnegie was friendly with railroad owners, they agreed to buy steel from him.

A Steel Mill *Before the Bessemer process was introduced, American steel mills produced fewer than 2,000 tons of steel a year. By 1900, production was up to 7 million tons a year. Here, steelworkers strain to forge a cannon barrel.* **Daily Life** *Based on this painting, what were some dangers of working in a steel mill?*

Connections With Technology
Background

The first open-hearth steel furnace in the United States went into operation in 1862. The furnace produced quality steel by melting pig iron and scrap steel at high temperatures, largely by recirculating gases through the furnace. The quality was based on the amount of carbon in the steel, for it is the amount of carbon that determines the hardness and smoothness of steel.

Connections With Mathematics
Activity

Provide students with the following statistics:

Tons of Steel Ingots and Castings Produced

1870	68,750	1890	4,277,071
1875	389,799	1895	6,114,834
1880	1,247,335	1900	12,188,329
1885	1,711,920		

Source: *Historical Statistics of the United States*

Ask students: (a) How many tons of steel ingots and castings were produced in 1880? (b) How did the production of steel change between 1870 and 1875? (c) How many more tons of steel were produced in 1900 than in 1895? Have students make generalizations about steel production between 1870 and 1900.

Huge profits. Within a short time, Carnegie was earning huge profits from his steel mill. He used his profits to buy out rivals. He also bought iron mines, railroad and steamship lines, and warehouses.

Soon, Carnegie controlled all phases of the steel industry—from mining iron ore to shipping finished steel. Having control of all the steps required to change raw materials into finished products is known as **vertical integration.** Through vertical integration, Carnegie gained an advantage over other steel companies. In 1892, Carnegie combined all of his businesses into the Carnegie Steel Company. By 1900, it was turning out more steel than all of Great Britain!

A duty to society. Carnegie believed that the rich had a duty to improve society. He gave $60 million to build public libraries in towns all over the country. He gave millions more to charities. In 1901, he sold Carnegie Steel and retired. From then on, he spent his time and money helping people. "I started life as a poor man," he once said, "and I wish to end it that way."

New Ways of Doing Business

Before the railroad boom, nearly every American town had its own small factories. They produced goods such as soap, clothing, and shoes for people in the area. By the late 1800s, however, big factories were producing goods cheaper than small factories could. As railroads distributed these cheaper goods, the demand for local goods fell. As a result, many small factories closed.

Shopping by mail. When local plants closed, big factories increased their output. Business owners looked for ways to sell products to the whole country.

Companies such as Montgomery Ward and Sears, Roebuck—both based in Chicago—sold goods to western farmers by mail order. In its first four years, Ward's catalog grew from a single sheet of paper to a 150-page illustrated book.

BIOGRAPHY **Andrew Carnegie** *Steel tycoon Andrew Carnegie believed that the rich had a right to make money—and a duty to spend it for the public good. About those who held on to their wealth, Carnegie said, "The man who dies thus rich, dies disgraced."* **Economics** *How did Carnegie spend his money for the public good?*

Investment in business. As factories expanded, they needed capital, or money. Factory owners used the capital to buy raw materials, pay workers, and cover shipping and advertising costs. To raise capital, Americans adopted new ways of organizing their businesses.

In the 1800s, many American businesses that wanted to expand became corporations. A **corporation** is a business owned by investors. The corporation sells **stock,** or shares in the business, to investors, who are known as stockholders. The corporation can use the money invested by stockholders to build a new factory or buy new machines.

In return for their investment in the business, stockholders hope to receive dividends. A **dividend** is a share of a corporation's profit. To protect their investment, stockholders choose a board of directors to run the corporation.

Chapter 19 • **541**

CONNECTIONS

ARTS　SCIENCES　GEOGRAPHY　WORLD　**ECONOMICS**　CIVICS

Prices Then and Now

Thanks to advances in manufacturing and transportation, Americans had a vast choice of goods at the turn of the century. In cities, new department stores attracted middle-class shoppers. Chain stores offered goods for lower prices. Mail-order catalogs allowed farm families to purchase thousands of products without even leaving their homes.

As you can see from the chart below, the prices of goods in 1900 seem very low compared with today's prices. Were they really low, however?

Because of inflation, the prices of goods and services usually rise over a prolonged period of time. Wages, however, also tend to rise over time. If wages and prices rise at the same rate, the effect for consumers is the same as if they had not risen at all.

Economists have developed several measures to compare the prices of goods at different times. These measures allow us to make true comparisons because they allow for inflation. The most frequently used measure is the Consumer Price Index (CPI).

The CPI makes it possible to compare 1900 prices with today's prices. According to the CPI, a dollar in 1900 had a value of 9, compared to a value of 143 for today's

Early department store

The New Spring Styles in Suits and Skirts

Ad from *McClure's Magazine,* 1892

dollar. In other words, it would take $143 today to buy what $9 bought in 1900.

If a woman's tailored suit sold for $10 in 1900, how much would it cost in today's dollars? We can use the formula below, where x = today's price, to find out.

Step 1 $\dfrac{9}{143} = \dfrac{1900\ \text{price}}{x}$ — *Write the formula using x as the unknown.*

Step 2 $\dfrac{9}{143} = \dfrac{\$10}{x}$ — *Substitute the value.*

Step 3 $9x = 143$ times $\$10$ — *Cross-multiply.*

Step 4 $x = \dfrac{\$1{,}430}{9} = \$158.89$ — *Divide by 9.*

Step 5 $x = \$159$ — *Simplify.*

Answer: A woman's suit that cost $10 in 1900 would cost $159 today.

	1900 Prices	Today's Prices
Man's suit	$ 9.00	$ 143.00
Top-of-the-line bicycle	$ 48.50	$ _____
Board game	$ 0.85	$ 13.50
1 dozen oranges	$ 0.20	$ 3.17
1 pound butter	$ 0.18	$ _____

- What is the purpose of the Consumer Price Index?

ACTIVITY
Follow the model above to complete the chart comparing 1900 prices with prices today.

542 • Chapter 19

The rise of corporations helped American industry to grow. Thousands of people bought stock in corporations. Stockholders faced fewer risks than owners of private businesses. If a private business goes bankrupt, the owner has to pay all the debts. If a corporation goes bankrupt, however, stockholders cannot be forced to pay the corporation's debts.

The role of banks. After the Civil War, corporations attracted large amounts of capital from American investors. Corporations also borrowed millions of dollars from banks. These bank loans helped American industry grow at a rapid pace. At the same time, the loans made profits for the banks. In fact, bankers became leaders of business.

The most powerful banker of the late 1800s was J. Pierpont Morgan. Morgan's influence was not limited to banking, however. By using his banking profits to gain control of major corporations, he became a dominant figure in American industry.

During economic hard times in the 1890s, Morgan and his friends invested large amounts of money in the stock of troubled corporations. As large stockholders, they won seats on the boards of directors. They then directed the companies in ways that avoided competition and made big profits. "I like a little competition, but I like combination more," Morgan used to say.

Between 1894 and 1898, Morgan gained control of most of the nation's major rail lines. He then began to buy up steel companies and merge them into a single large corporation. By 1901, Morgan had become head of United States Steel Company. It included Carnegie Steel and was the first business in the United States worth more than $1 billion.

Plentiful Resources

Industry could not have expanded so quickly in the United States without the nation's rich supply of natural resources. Iron ore was plentiful, especially in the Mesabi Range of Minnesota. Large deposits of coal fueled the nation's steel mills. Coal sat beneath the soil of Pennsylvania, West Virginia, and the Rocky Mountain states. Minerals such as gold, silver, and copper were also located in the Rockies. Vast forests provided lumber for building.

Oil boom. In 1859, Americans discovered a valuable natural resource. That year, the nation's first oil strike was made near

Oil Boom *Oil derricks sprouted on the hills of western Pennsylvania during the oil boom of the 1860s. Such wells soon made the United States a major producer of oil.* **Linking Past and Present** *Is oil an important resource today? Explain.*

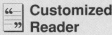
Connections With Economics
Activity

To help students understand the concept of vertical integration, ask them to imagine that they own an automobile company. Have them make a list of other companies that they would need to control in order to ensure a steady supply of raw materials and parts, dependable transportation, and market outlets. Students will need to consider all the steps required to turn raw materials into a finished and salable product.

Connections With Local Geography
Activity

Distribute to students, or have students create, an outline map of your region of the United States. Have students do research on the region's natural resources. Then instruct them to color the map to indicate any major deposits of coal and iron ore and any large forests in the region. As you discuss the completed maps, have students consider some of the markets to which these resources might go.

Titusville, Pennsylvania. Drillers stood dripping with oil as the Titusville gusher spurted skyward.

When news of the strike spread, an oil boom took place. Eager prospectors rushed to the western Pennsylvania countryside ready to drill wells in search of a "gusher." **Rockefeller and Standard Oil.** John D. Rockefeller did not rush into the oil-drilling business. He knew that oil had little value until it was refined, or purified. At the time, most oil was refined to make a fuel called kerosene.

Rockefeller came from a humble background. Born the son of a peddler in upstate New York, he moved with his family to Cleveland, Ohio, when he was 14. At age 23, Rockefeller invested in his first oil refinery.

Rockefeller believed that competition was wasteful. He used the profits from his refinery to buy up other refineries. He then combined the companies into a single corporation, the ***Standard Oil Company*** of Ohio.

Rockefeller was a shrewd businessman. He was always trying to improve the quality of his oil. He also did whatever he could to get rid of competition. Standard Oil slashed its prices to drive rivals out of business. It pressured its customers not to deal with other oil companies. Rockefeller even persuaded railroad companies eager for his business to grant rebates to Standard Oil. Lower shipping costs gave Rockefeller an important edge over his competitors.

> ***Our Common Heritage***
> *Native Americans in western Pennsylvania had taught white farmers that the annoying "black glue" in local streams could be used as a medicine. Farmers bottled the liquid and sold it as a cure for everything from cancer to fallen arches. Later, they discovered that the oil was also a good fuel.*

544 • Chapter 19

The Standard Oil trust. To tighten his control over the oil industry, Rockefeller formed the Standard Oil trust in 1882. A **trust** is a group of corporations run by a single board of directors.

Stockholders in smaller oil companies turned over their stock to Standard Oil. In return, they got stock in the new trust. The stock paid high dividends, but the stockholders gave up their right to choose the board of directors. The board of Standard Oil then managed the business of all the companies, which before had been rivals.

The Standard Oil trust ended competition in the oil industry. It created a monopoly. A **monopoly** is a company that controls all or nearly all the business of an industry. Through the Standard Oil trust, Rockefeller controlled 95 percent of all oil refining in the United States.

Other businesses followed Rockefeller's lead. They set up trusts and tried to build monopolies. By the late 1890s, monopolies and trusts controlled some of the nation's most important industries.

Big Business: Good or Bad?

In the late 1800s, some Americans argued that leaders of giant corporations were abusing the free enterprise system. In a **free enterprise system,** businesses are owned by private citizens. Owners decide what products to make, how much to produce, where to sell products, and what prices to charge. Companies compete to win customers by making the best product at the lowest price.

Arguments for competition. Trusts and monopolies often put an end to competition. Without competition, there was no reason for companies to keep their prices low or to improve their products. It was also hard for new companies to start up and compete against powerful trusts. Workers, moreover, often felt that they were treated badly by large corporations.

The Monster Monopoly *This cartoon criticizes monopolies by showing Standard Oil as a huge octopus.* **Economics** *What does the Standard Oil "octopus" have in its grip?*

Critics worried about the political influence of trusts as well as their economic power. Carnegie, Morgan, and Rockefeller were richer than Americans had ever been before. People worried that millionaires were using their vast wealth to buy favors from elected officials. The Chicago *Tribune* warned that "liberty and monopoly cannot live together." John Reagan, a member of Congress from Texas, put it this way:

❝The time was when none were poor and none rich. There were no beggars till Vanderbilts and . . . Rockefellers and . . . Morgans . . . shaped the actions of Congress and moulded the purposes of government. Then the few became fabulously rich, the many wretchedly poor.❞

Arguments for trusts. Naturally, business leaders defended trusts. Andrew Carnegie published articles arguing that competition ruined businesses and put people out of work. Supporters of trusts asserted that large corporations made goods cheaply and so helped the consumer.

Government reaction. For the time being, government did little to control these giant corporations. Some state governments passed laws to regulate business, but the corporations usually sidestepped them. Under pressure from voters, Congress approved the **Sherman Antitrust Act** in 1890. The act banned the formation of trusts and monopolies, but it was too weak to be very effective.

SECTION 2 REVIEW

1. **Identify:** (a) Bessemer process, (b) Andrew Carnegie, (c) J. Pierpont Morgan, (d) John D. Rockefeller, (e) Standard Oil Company, (f) Sherman Antitrust Act.
2. **Define:** (a) vertical integration, (b) capital, (c) corporation, (d) stock, (e) dividend, (f) trust, (g) monopoly, (h) free enterprise system.
3. How did railroads help bring about the decline of small factories?
4. How did J. Pierpont Morgan extend his influence over American business?
5. Why did some Americans think that big business threatened the free enterprise system?
6. **CRITICAL THINKING Understanding Causes and Effects** (a) What were two causes for the growth of the steel industry? (b) What were two effects?

ACTIVITY **Writing to Learn**

Imagine that you are president of United States Steel. Write an advertising brochure to attract investors to your corporation.

Answers to Section 2 Review

1. (a) Bessemer process, p. 540, (b) Andrew Carnegie, p. 540, (c) J. Pierpont Morgan, p. 543, (d) John D. Rockefeller, p. 544, (e) Standard Oil Company, p. 544, (f) Sherman Antitrust Act, p. 545
2. (a) vertical integration, p. 541, (b) capital, p. 541, (c) corporation, p. 541, (d) stock, p. 541, (e) dividend, p. 541, (f) trust, p. 544, (g) monopoly, p. 544, (h) free enterprise system, p. 544
3. When railroads brought in cheaper goods from large factories, the demand for local goods fell; as a result, many small, local factories closed.
4. J. Pierpont Morgan was the most powerful banker of the late 1800s, and he used his banking profits to buy troubled corporations. He gained control of major rail lines and steel companies, thus avoiding competition and making huge profits.
5. Big business tended to end competition. It was hard for companies to start up or to compete with big business. Workers often felt that they were treated badly by large companies. Furthermore, people feared that the wealthy and powerful would corrupt government officials to the advantage of big businesses and to the disadvantage of workers, small businesses, and consumers.
6. (a) Possible Answer: growth of the railroads, development of the Bessemer process, and the ingenuity of Andrew Carnegie (b) Possible Answer: increased pollution, greatly increased wealth and power for a few people like Carnegie, development of new business methods such as vertical integration

Section 3
pp. 546–550

Bell Ringer

Write the following names on the chalkboard: Alexander Graham Bell, Samuel F. B. Morse, Thomas Edison, Gustavus Swift, Jan Matzeliger. Ask students to guess what these people have in common. Then have students skim the section to find out what each man invented.

Lesson Plan

1. Focus In the late 1800s, inventions helped industry grow, changed the way in which businesses were run, and made daily life easier. In this section, students examine several inventions that started new industries and created new ways of doing business.
2. Instruct On separate index cards, write the name of each invention discussed in this section. Distribute the cards to each student or to pairs of students. On the back of the card, have them describe the importance of the invention. Then divide the class into teams and have them use their descriptions on the back of the cards to rank the inventions in order of importance. Have students justify their rankings.
3. Close To close the lesson, play a Jeopardy!-like game with students. Provide a list of key facts from the section, and challenge students to create a question for each fact.

3
An Age of Invention

FIND OUT
- What inventions improved communication in the 1800s?
- Why was Menlo Park called an "invention factory"?
- How did Henry Ford revolutionize the automobile industry?

VOCABULARY assembly line, mass production

In 1894, Representative George H. Murray, a freedman, rose to speak in the House of Representatives. In his hand was a list of 92 patents issued to African Americans since Reconstruction. Among them were Elijah McCoy's device for oiling machinery, Jan Matzeliger's shoemaking machine, and Granville T. Woods's automatic air brake for trains. In short, there were "inventions and improvements in...almost every department of labor."

These African American inventors were part of a wave of invention that swept the United States in the late 1800s. By the 1890s, Americans were patenting 21,000 new inventions a year. These new inventions helped industry to grow and become more efficient. They also made daily life easier for many Americans.

Advances in Communication

The telegraph, invented by Samuel F.B. Morse and in use since 1844, helped people around the nation stay in touch with each other. It also helped people do business. If steelmakers in Pittsburgh needed more iron ore from Minnesota, they could order it almost instantly.

546 • Chapter 19

Transatlantic cable. Morse's telegraph speeded communication within the United States. It still took weeks, however, for news from Europe to arrive by boat.

In 1858, Cyrus Field completed the laying of an underwater telegraph cable across the Atlantic Ocean. The cable carried a few messages and then snapped. Field tried again—with an improved cable—in 1866. This time, he succeeded. Field observed:

66Never was greater energy put into any enterprise.... In five months... the cable had been manufactured, shipped..., stretched across the Atlantic, and was sending messages... swift as lightning from continent to continent.99

Field's transatlantic cable brought Europe and the United States closer together.

The telephone. While Morse and Field were sending dots and dashes over telegraph wires, several inventors were trying to transmit voices. As you have read, Alexander Graham Bell, a teacher of the deaf, was one of those inventors. In March 1876, Bell was at last ready to test his telephone.

Before the test, Bell accidentally spilled battery acid on himself. His assistant, Thomas Watson, was in another room. Bell spoke into the machine, "Watson, come here, I want you!" Watson rushed to Bell's side. "Mr. Bell," he cried, "I heard every word you said, distinctly!" The telephone worked.

Bell's telephone did not arouse much interest at first. Scientists praised the invention. Most people, however, looked on it as a toy. Bell offered to sell the telephone to the Western Union Telegraph Company for $100,000. The company refused. In the end, the telephone earned Bell millions.

Bell formed the Bell Telephone Company in 1877. By 1885, he had sold more than 300,000 phones—mostly to businesses. The telephone speeded up the pace of business even more. People no longer had to go to a

---

Our Multicultural Heritage
Activity

Interested students can prepare a bulletin board display of African American inventors. In addition to the inventors named in this section, students can research the creative contributions made by Henry Blair (corn harvester), Frederick McKinley Jones (first refrigerated trucks), Lewis Latimer (incandescent light bulb with carbon filament), Granville T. Woods (mentioned in this section, but who also invented the third rail, which freed electric-powered trains from overhead cables), and Garrett Morgan (traffic light).

A useful reference for this activity is *The Negro Almanac: A Reference Work on the African-American,* edited by Harry Ploski, or *The Encyclopedia of Black Americans,* edited by W. A. Low and Virgil Clift.

546

telegraph office to send messages. Businesses could find out about prices or supplies simply by talking on the telephone.

Thomas Edison and the "Invention Factory"

In an age of invention, Thomas Edison was right at home. In 1876, he opened a research laboratory in Menlo Park, New Jersey. There, he and 15 co-workers set out to create "minor" inventions every 10 days and "a big thing every 6 months or so."

A new approach to invention. The key to Edison's success lay in his new approach. He turned inventing into a system. Teams of experts refined Edison's ideas and helped to make them real. Menlo Park became an "invention factory."

The results were amazing. Edison became known as the "Wizard of Menlo Park" for inventing the light bulb, the phonograph, the motion picture projector, the storage battery, and hundreds of other devices.

The electric power plant. One of Edison's most important creations was the electric power plant. Edison built the first power plant in New York City in 1882. He wired the business district first in hopes of attracting investors. With the flip of a switch, he set the district ablaze in light. It looked "like writing by daylight," said one reporter.

Within a year, Edison's power plant was supplying electricity to homes as well as to businesses. Soon, more power plants were built. Factories replaced steam-powered engines with safer, quieter electric engines. Electric energy powered streetcars in cities. The modern age of electricity had begun.

Marvels of Technology

Almost every day, it seemed, new American inventions made business more efficient and life more pleasant. The United States soon became known as the land of invention.

The Wizard of Menlo Park *On October 21, 1879, visitors watched in awe as Thomas Edison switched on the first electric light bulb.* **American Traditions** *Edison once said, "Genius is one percent inspiration and ninety-nine percent perspiration." What do you think he meant?*

African American inventors. As you have read, African Americans contributed to the flood of inventions. In 1872, Elijah McCoy created a special device that oiled engines automatically. The device was widely used on railroad engines and in factories.

Granville T. Woods found a way to send telegraph messages between moving railroad trains. Jan Matzeliger invented a machine that could perform almost all the steps in shoemaking that had been done before by hand. Patented in 1883, Matzeliger's machine was eventually used in shoe factories everywhere.

Chapter 19 • **547**

 Lesson Planner

For a developed **Cooperative Learning** lesson plan, see the *Lesson Planner,* page 119.

Answer to Caption

Possible Answer: Success depends on hard work, not just on getting a good idea.

 Voices of Freedom

Primary Source You might assign selection 2-1, A Cable Across the Atlantic, on pages 143–144 of *Voices of Freedom.* The selection describes the financial and technical difficulties he faced while laying a cable across the Atlantic. (Enrichment/Average)

CD-ROM

History Makers Access the biography of Thomas Edison on the American Heritage® *History of the United States* CD-ROM. (Enrichment/Average)

Transparencies

Exploring Technology Use the transparency The Telegraph on page H-41 of *American History Transparencies.* Teaching suggestions can be found on page H-11. (Enrichment/Average)

Exploring Technology Use the transparency The Phonograph on page H-51 of *American History Transparencies.* Teaching suggestions can be found on page H-16. (Enrichment/Average)

Historical Sidelight
Background

Alexander Graham Bell was more than a brilliant inventor. Indeed, he always referred to himself as a "teacher of the deaf." Both his father and grandfather were speech teachers, and Bell began his career teaching students with hearing impairment. His idea for the telephone developed out of his experiments with sending several telegraph messages over one wire at the same time and with creating a device that would help people with hearing impairment to speak. In the meantime, he continued to tutor deaf students on his own. In 1885, Bell counseled the parents of young Helen Keller to acquire a teacher from Boston's Perkins Institute for the Blind. It was thus partly due to his efforts that Helen Keller met Anne Sullivan, the teacher who helped her become instrumental in changing the world's view of people with disabilities.

Shoemaking Genius *Jan Matzeliger's shoemaking machine sparked tremendous growth in the shoe industry. Yet Matzeliger, like many other inventors, sold the rights to his machine for very little money.* **Science and Technology** *Describe two other inventions of the late 1800s.*

Because of racial prejudice, many African American inventors had trouble getting patents. Some never got credit for their inventions. Even so, in 1900, Henry E. Baker, an assistant in the patent office, compiled a list of patents issued to African American inventors. The list, together with drawings and plans of all the inventions, filled four huge volumes.

Inventions for everyday use. Christopher Sholes perfected the typewriter in 1868. This invention changed office work. With the typewriter, business people could produce letters, contracts, and reports much faster and more clearly.

Some inventions, such as the camera, affected individuals more than businesses. George Eastman introduced the lightweight Kodak camera in 1888. No longer did making photographs require the bulky equipment and chemicals used earlier. An advertisement for the new camera read:

❝The Kodak . . . is the smallest, lightest and simplest. . . . For the ten operations necessary with most cameras to make one exposure, we have only three simple movements. No focusing. No finder required. Size 3½ by 3¾ by 6½ ins. Makes 100 Exposures. Weight 35 oz.❞

The cost was only $25, including the first roll of film. After 100 snaps of the shutter, the owner returned the camera. The company developed the pictures and sent them back, along with a reloaded camera. Taking pictures became part of American life.

Refrigeration. One invention changed the American diet. In the 1880s, Gustavus Swift introduced refrigeration to the meat industry.

Swift set up a plant in Chicago, a railroad hub midway between the cattle ranches of the West and the cities of the East. Cattle were shipped by train to the Chicago plant. There, the animals were slaughtered and cut into sides of beef. The beef was loaded onto refrigerated railroad cars and carried to market. Even in summer, Swift sent fresh meat from Chicago to eastern cities. As a result, Americans ate more meat.

> ### History and You
> *Inventions of the 1800s transformed the way people lived and worked. In what ways do you think your life is better or worse because of these inventions? What inventions would you make to improve the world?*

Connections With Technology
Background

Many people tried to create a typing machine before Sholes came up with a machine that could produce words faster than it took to write them by hand. Even Sholes tried nearly 50 models before he was successful. Sholes sold his patent to E. Remington & Sons in 1873.

Over the years, many improvements were made. For example, Sholes's keyboard originally presented letters in alphabetical order, resulting in frequent jamming of the keys. Sholes rearranged the keyboard so that the most popular letters were scattered. The original carriage return was operated by a foot treadle; an attached carriage return was added later. Furthermore, the original keys produced only capital letters; lowercase letters were a later refinement.

Connections With Technology
Background

Among the inventors who changed American industry was Gail Borden, who had been a land surveyor in Stephen Austin's settlement in Texas. Borden devised dozens of inventions, including a dining table whose center revolved to bring food to diners. After experimenting with a condensed meat biscuit, Borden developed a method for condensing milk so that it did not need to be refrigerated.

A Time of Invention

Inventor	Date	Invention
Elisha Otis	1852	passenger elevator brake
Henry Bessemer	1856	perfected Bessemer process
Gordon McKay	1860	machine for sewing shoe soles onto uppers
George Pullman	1864	sleeping car
Thaddeus Lowe	1865	compression ice machine
George Westinghouse	1868	air brake
Elijah McCoy	1872	automatic engine-oiling machine
Andrew S. Hallidie	1873	cable streetcar
Stephen Dudley Field	1874	electric streetcar
Alexander Graham Bell	1876	telephone
Thomas Alva Edison	1877	phonograph
Anna Baldwin	1878	milking machine
Thomas Alva Edison	1879	first practical incandescent light bulb
James Ritty	1879	cash register
Jan E. Matzeliger	1883	shoemaking machine
Lewis E. Waterman	1884	fountain pen
Granville T. Woods	1887	automatic air brake
Charles and J. Frank Duryea	1893	gasoline-powered car
King C. Gillette	1895	safety razor with throwaway blades
John Thurman	1899	motor-driven vacuum cleaner
Leo H. Baekeland	1909	plastic

CHART SKILLS *Major inventions, such as the Bessemer process, had a dramatic effect on American industry. Lesser inventions also helped the economy grow.*
• *Which of these inventions might be found in a home today?*

The Automobile

No single person invented the automobile. Europeans produced motorized vehicles as early as the 1860s. By 1890, France led the world in auto making. Americans began building cars in the 1890s. However, only the wealthy could afford them.

Henry Ford. Henry Ford revolutionized auto making. He wanted to build "a motor car for the multitudes"—one that almost anybody could afford.

In 1913, Ford introduced the assembly line. On the **assembly line,** the car frames edged along a moving belt. Workers added parts as the cars passed by. This method cut the time needed to build a car. Soon other industries adopted it.

Ford's assembly line allowed mass production of cars. **Mass production** means making large quantities of a product quickly and cheaply. Because of mass production, Ford could sell his cars at a lower price than other auto makers could.

Chapter 19 • **549**

The Family Car At first, automobiles were expensive toys for the very wealthy. Prices soon dropped, however, and thousands of ordinary Americans, such as the family shown here, could afford to buy a car. **Science and Technology** Why did the price of cars drop?

Cars become popular. At first, most people laughed at automobiles. Some thought the "horseless carriage" was dangerous. A backfiring auto engine could scare a horse right off the road. Towns and villages across the nation posted signs: "No horseless carriages allowed." In Tennessee, a person planning to drive a car had to advertise the fact a week ahead of time! This warning gave others time to prepare for the danger.

Slowly, attitudes changed. No other means of travel offered such freedom. As prices dropped, more people bought cars. In 1900, only 8,000 Americans owned cars. By 1917, more than 4.5 million autos were chugging along American roads.

The Airplane

Meanwhile, two Ohio bicycle mechanics, Orville and Wilbur Wright, were experimenting with another new method of trans-

portation—flying. During the 1890s, the Wright brothers had read about European experiments with powered flight. Caught up by the dream of flying, they tried some experiments of their own.

The Wright brothers tested hundreds of designs. Finally, on December 17, 1903, they were ready to test their first "flying machine." At Kitty Hawk, North Carolina, Orville took off. The plane, powered by a small gasoline engine, stayed in the air for 12 seconds and flew a distance of 120 feet (37m).

The Wrights' flight did not attract much attention. Indeed, most people at the time saw little use for flying machines. Slowly, however, air pioneers built better planes and made longer flights. In time, the airplane, like the automobile, changed not only the United States but the world.

SECTION 3 REVIEW

1. **Identify:** (a) Cyrus Field, (b) Alexander Graham Bell, (c) Thomas Edison, (d) Elijah McCoy, (e) Granville T. Woods, (f) Jan Matzeliger, (g) Henry Ford, (h) Orville and Wilbur Wright.
2. **Define:** (a) assembly line, (b) mass production.
3. Describe two inventions that transformed communication in the late 1800s.
4. (a) What was Edison's approach to invention? (b) Why was his electric power plant important?
5. How did the assembly line change auto making?
6. **CRITICAL THINKING Drawing Conclusions** Why might inventors be more creative working in an "invention factory" than working on their own?

ACTIVITY Writing to Learn

Jot down ideas about how the invention of the telephone changed people's lives in the late 1890s.

4
Workers and Unions

FIND OUT
- What were working conditions like in factories of the late 1800s?
- Why did workers form unions?
- How were immigrants and African Americans treated by the labor movement?
- Why did labor unions face opposition?

VOCABULARY injunction

In 1896, Frederick Taylor observed workers in the Bethlehem Steel Plant. He counted the number of times a worker picked up a shovel and noted the exact motions he used to swing it. Taylor then redesigned the shovels and work pattern to make the workers more productive.

Many factory owners adopted Taylor's system of "scientific management." Workers, however, were upset. "The men are looked upon as nothing more than parts of the machinery they work," said one.

The nation needed workers. Workers built the factories and ran the machines. By the late 1800s, workers faced harsh new conditions that led them to organize.

A New Kind of Workplace

The factories of the late 1800s drew workers from many different backgrounds. Most workers were native-born white men. Many had left farms to take jobs in Chicago, Pittsburgh, and other large cities. Some northern factory workers were African Americans who had migrated from the South.

Millions of immigrants coming to the United States from Europe and Asia in the late 1800s also found jobs in factories. After 1900, many Mexicans entered the United States in search of factory jobs. More and more women and children worked in factories, too. African Americans, immigrants, women, and children were paid less than native-born white men.

Changed relations with employers. Workers had to adjust to life in the new kinds of factories of the late 1800s. Before the Civil War, most factories were small, family-run businesses. As one observer wrote, the boss of a workplace knew "every man in his shop; he called his men by name and inquired after their wives and babies."

During the 1870s and 1880s, the friendly relationship between worker and boss declined. In giant factories, workers did not chat with their employer. More likely, they stood all day tending a machine in a large, crowded, noisy room.

Dangerous conditions. Factories were filled with hazards. Owners spent little to improve the safety and comfort of workers. Some workers were killed or severely injured on the job. Others had their health destroyed.

Textile workers inhaled lung-damaging dust and fibers that filled the air in the mills. In coal mines, cave-ins buried miners alive. Others were killed by gas in mine shafts or by the coal dust they inhaled all day. Steelworkers risked injuries working close to red-hot vats of melted steel. In one year, 195 workers died in the steel mills of Pittsburgh alone.

Children in industry. The 1900 census reported nearly 2 million children under age 15 at work throughout the country. Many Americans believed that it was wrong for children to toil in factories. However, as long as factory owners could hire children at low pay, many of them did so.

Children worked in many industries—often doing hazardous jobs. In coal mines, they picked stones out of the coal for 12 hours a day, 6 days a week. Other children

Chapter 19 • **551**

Section 4
pp. 551–557

Bell Ringer

Ask students to imagine that at the age of 8 or 10, they had to work in a factory. Have them jot down how they think their lives and their futures would be different.

Lesson Plan

1. Focus In the late 1800s, working conditions in industry worsened. Workers stepped up their efforts to form unions and improve conditions. In this section, students learn about the formation and tactics of labor organizations and individual reformers in their struggle for fairer treatment.

2. Instruct Write the following quotation on the chalkboard: "They never go on strike for higher wages, have no labor unions, never get intoxicated or disorderly, never absent themselves from work without good cause, obey orders without growling, and are very reliable." A manufacturer in the 1800s was comparing his guard dogs to his workers. Ask: What attitudes does he reveal toward his workers? How might a union leader have responded?

3. Close To close the lesson, have students turn each of the subsection headings into questions and then answer them.

Historical Sidelight
Background

Frederick Taylor was an early efficiency expert. As industry became an ever-larger employer of labor, more and more factories sought the advice of efficiency experts.

One of the most famous efficiency experts was Lillian Gilbreth (1878–1972). She and her husband, Frank, were business partners who constantly looked for more efficient ways to use time and labor. They turned their own home into a laboratory for experiments in efficiency, setting up a "Family Council" to manage such day-to-day business as assigning household chores. Jobs such as painting or repairing went to whichever of the 12 Gilbreth children submitted the lowest bid. Two of the children later described their unusual home in the book *Cheaper by the Dozen.*

When Frank died suddenly in 1924, Lillian Gilbreth continued to run their business on her own. She maintained her reputation as an expert in scientific management, serving as a management and training consultant to many business firms.

551

Child Labor *Children—many of them from immigrant families—labored in the nation's mines and factories. This cartoon shows child workers as slaves of greedy employers.* **Daily Life** *How do you think the lives of children were affected by having to go to work at an early age?*

labored in textile mills, tobacco factories, and garment workshops. Working children could not attend school. They had little chance, therefore, for a better life as an adult.

Workers Organize

Low wages, long hours, and unsafe and unhealthful conditions threatened a worker's well-being. Since the early 1800s, workers had tried to band together to win better conditions. Most early efforts to form unions failed, however.

Knights of Labor. In 1869, workers formed a labor union called the ***Knights of Labor.*** At first, the union was open to skilled workers only. Workers held secret meetings and greeted each other with special handshakes. Secrecy was needed because employers fired workers who joined unions.

In 1879, the Knights of Labor chose Terence Powderly as their president. Powderly worked to make the union stronger. He ended secret meetings and let in women, blacks, immigrants, and unskilled workers.

Powderly was an idealist. He wanted the Knights to work to make the world a better place for both workers and employers. He did not believe in strikes. Instead, he relied on rallies and meetings to win public support. The goals of the Knights included a shorter workday, an end to child labor, and equal pay for men and women.

In 1885, some Knights of Labor members launched a major strike to protest a pay cut at the Missouri Pacific Railroad. They forced the company to restore their wages. The Knights did not officially support the strike. Still, workers everywhere saw the strike as a victory for the union. Membership soared to 700,000, including 60,000 African Americans.

Trouble for the Knights. The following year, the Knights of Labor ran into serious trouble. In 1886, workers went on strike against the McCormick Harvester Company in Chicago. As with the Missouri Pacific, the Knights did not endorse this strike, either.

552 • Chapter 19

Historical Sidelight
Background

At first, the Knights of Labor was a secret society of tailors. Although it remained a secret society, it soon expanded to include other trades. Powderly, who joined in 1874, was a machinist who had been active in the Machinists' and Blacksmiths' Union and in the Industrial Brotherhood. He rose quickly through the ranks and served as the society's president (or, more officially, as its Grand Master Workman) during its public and most influential years.

Although the Knights of Labor accepted unskilled workers, women, and African Americans (in segregated local unions) as members, the society strongly opposed immigration. It wanted to protect its members against competition from immigrant workers, who often worked for low wages and who, therefore, were quickly hired. Even after the decline of the Knights of Labor, Powderly remained concerned about immigration. From 1897 to 1921 he served in several government positions relating to the issue.

Critical Thinking
Asking Questions

Ask students to imagine that they are newspaper reporters in the late 1800s and that they have been assigned to interview industrial leaders about their views on labor unions. Have students select one of the industrial leaders discussed in Chapter 19 and write a list of questions that they would ask him about his treatment of workers and his views on labor unions.

On May 3, workers clashed with strike-breakers outside the factory. Chicago police opened fire. Four workers were killed.

The next day, thousands of workers gathered in Haymarket Square to protest the killings. Just as the meeting was ending, a bomb exploded, killing a police officer. Police peppered the crowd with bullets. Ten more people died, and 50 were injured.

Eight men were arrested for their part in the ***Haymarket Riot,*** as the incident was called. No real evidence linked these men to the bombing, but four were tried, convicted, and hanged. A wave of anti-labor feeling swept across the nation. Membership in the Knights of Labor dropped sharply.

American Federation of Labor

The failure of the Knights of Labor did not end the labor movement. In 1886, the year of the Haymarket Riot, Samuel Gompers formed a new union in New York City. The ***American Federation of Labor,*** or AFL, was open to skilled workers only.

Workers did not join the AFL directly. Rather, they joined a trade union, a union of persons working at the same trade. For example, they might join the cigarmakers' or typesetters' union. The trade union then joined the AFL. In effect, the AFL was a union made up of other unions.

Limited goals. The AFL was more practical than the Knights of Labor. It did not think it could change the world. Instead, it set limited goals. As one leader said,

&6&Our organization does not consist of idealists. We are going on from day to day. We are fighting only for immediate objects—objects that can be realized in a few years.&9&

The AFL stressed higher wages, shorter hours, and improved working conditions for its members. Unlike the Knights, the AFL believed in the use of strikes to achieve its goals.

A powerful union. The AFL collected money from its member unions. Some of it went into a strike fund. When AFL members struck, they were paid from the fund so that they could still feed their families. This helped to make strikes an effective weapon for the AFL.

The AFL's practical approach worked. It soon became the most powerful union in the nation. In 1886, its first year, the AFL claimed 150,000 members. By 1904, one million skilled workers swelled its ranks. However, because African Americans, immigrants, and unskilled workers were barred from most trade unions, they could not join the AFL.

Strikes

Economic depressions brought hard times to workers. During depressions, workers lost their jobs or faced pay cuts. Often, they had no money to pay rent or buy food.

Strikers win little sympathy. During a severe depression in the 1870s, railroad workers were forced to take several cuts in pay. In July 1877, workers went on strike, shutting down rail lines across the country. Riots erupted in many cities as workers burned rail yards and ripped track from the ground. In Pittsburgh, railroad companies hired an army of strikebreakers. A battle between strikebreakers and strikers left more than 20 people dead.

Strikers won little sympathy at first. Most Americans were not in favor of strikes. Few

Our Common Heritage
Early unions often excluded African Americans from their ranks. Richard Davis, a tireless labor organizer, helped to change that situation. In 1895, Davis became the first African American on the executive board of the United Mine Workers Union.

Chapter 19 • **553**

Answers to Skill Lesson

1. (a) the attorney for the defendants (b) at the trial that followed the Haymarket Riot (c) Yes; the speaker is the legal representative of the men accused of starting the riot.

2. (a) to exercise the right of free speech and to discuss the situation of the workingmen (b) no (c) the police

3. (a) The day before the riot, four workers who were on strike had been killed by police outside a McCormick Harvester Company factory. (b) They were protesting the killings. (c) peaceful

4. (a) Possible Answer: Some parts are accurate, some slanted. (b) Possible Answer: It exaggerates the "peaceful" mood of the workers and the "devilish" intent of the police. (c) Possible Answer: to win sympathy for his clients; to create outrage toward the police (d) Possible Answer: No; the viewpoint is slanted in favor of the workers.

ACTIVITY

Guided Instruction Explain to students that it is quite acceptable when writing letters to the editor of a newspaper to present a strong argument for one side of a controversial issue. Still, any facts stated in the letter should be accurate.

CRITICAL THINKING SKILLS
Evaluating Information

Primary sources provide valuable information about events and people of the past. Although primary sources can add to our knowledge, they are not always completely accurate. For example, an author may have a reason for presenting only part of the information or for exaggerating. As a result, it is important to evaluate any source carefully before accepting it as reliable.

The excerpt below is from a speech given at the trial that followed the Haymarket Riot. The speaker is the attorney for the defendants, the men accused of causing the riot. Follow the steps below to evaluate the information in the attorney's speech.

1. **Identify the source of information.** (a) Whose words are presented in the excerpt? (b) When was the speech given? (c) Is the speaker qualified to speak on this subject? Explain.

2. **Describe the information.** (a) According to the excerpt, why did the men come to Haymarket Square? (b) Did the men intend to hurt anyone? (c) Who else was at the meeting besides the workers?

3. **Compare the information with what you have already learned.** (a) What additional information about the Haymarket Riot appears in your textbook? (b) According to your text, what was the mood of the workers at the protest meeting? (c) How does the attorney's speech describe their mood?

4. **Evaluate the information.** (a) Do you think the excerpt is accurate? (b) Do you think it exaggerates anything? If so, what? (c) What might be the speaker's reason for presenting the information the way he does? (d) Is the excerpt a reliable source of information about the Haymarket Riot? Why or why not?

ACTIVITY
Write a letter to the editor of your school or local newspaper about an event or incident you have witnessed. Before sending the letter, have a classmate review it using the steps above to evaluate whether or not it is a reliable source.

❝[The workers] assembled there, gentlemen, under the provision of our Constitution, to exercise the right of free speech, to discuss the eight-hour question, to discuss the situation of the workingmen. They assembled there incidentally to discuss what they deemed outrages at McCormick's [Harvester Company]. No man expected that a bomb would be thrown; no man expected that anyone would be injured at that meeting; but while some of these defendants were there and while this meeting was in peaceful progress, the police, with a devilish design, as we expect to prove, came down upon that body with their revolvers in their hand and pockets, ready for immediate use, intending to destroy the life of every man that stood upon that market square.❞

Students Acquiring English
Activity

To practice speaking English, have SAE students prepare a dramatization of the excerpt from the defense lawyer's speech and present it before a judge and jury of their peers. Assign each student a coach, and give students time to practice. The presenter and his or her coach can decide which words or phrases to emphasize, where to pause, and how to use gestures and facial expressions effectively.

On Strike! *Many workers believed that the strike was the most powerful weapon they had. Here, striking garment workers demand shorter hours and better working conditions.* **Multicultural Heritage** *How does this photograph reflect the multicultural nature of the labor movement?*

supported unions. Americans believed that individuals who worked hard would be rewarded. Many thought that unions were run by foreign-born radicals. Because unions were unpopular, owners felt free to crush them.

The Pullman strike. The federal government usually sided with factory owners during strikes. Several Presidents sent in troops to end strikes. Courts ruled against strikers, too.

In 1894, a Chicago court dealt a serious blow to unions. A year earlier, George Pullman had cut the pay of workers at his railroad car factory. However, he did not lower the rents that workers paid for company-owned houses. Workers walked off the job in protest.

A federal judge in Chicago issued an injunction against the strikers. An **injunction** is a court order to do or not to do something. The judge ordered the Pullman workers to stop their strike.

Leaders of the ***Pullman strike*** were jailed for violating the Sherman Antitrust Act. This act had been meant to keep trusts from limiting free trade. The courts, however, said that the strikers were limiting free trade. This was a major setback for unions.

Slow progress for labor. Union workers staged thousands of strikes during the late 1800s. Skilled workers in the AFL won better conditions and higher pay. Overall, wages for workers rose slightly between 1870 and 1900. But progress was slow. In 1910, only 1 worker in 20 belonged to a union. Thirty years would pass before large numbers of unskilled workers were able to join unions.

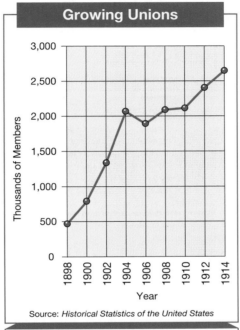

Growing Unions

Source: *Historical Statistics of the United States*

GRAPH SKILLS *A growing number of workers joined unions in the late 1800s and early 1900s. By 1904, the AFL alone had one million members.* ● *How much did union membership increase between 1898 and 1914?*

Connections With Art
Activity

Have students draw political cartoons on any one of these subjects: hazards on the job, the power of unions, the unpopularity of unions, or the Pullman strike. Students may wish to do additional research before drawing their cartoons. Display the finished cartoons in class and use them as a springboard to class discussion.

Learning Styles
Visual Learners

Tell students that the following statistics show how many thousands of workers were union members for each of the years listed. Have students use the statistics to create a line graph and then use the graph to make at least one generalization.

1898 — 467	1908 — 2,092
1900 — 791	1910 — 2,116
1902 — 1,335	1912 — 2,405
1904 — 2,067	1914 — 2,647
1906 — 1,892	

CAUSES

- Railroad boom spurs business
- Businesses become corporations
- Nation has rich supply of natural resources
- New inventions make business more efficient

THE RISE OF INDUSTRY IN THE UNITED STATES

EFFECTS

- Steel and oil become giant industries
- Monopolies and trusts dominate important industries
- Factory workers face harsh conditions
- Membership in labor unions grows

Understanding Causes and Effects
Industry boomed in the United States after the Civil War. The effects of industrial growth are still being felt today. • List two causes for the rise of industry. What effect did industrial growth have on factory workers?

Women in the Labor Movement

By 1890, one million American women had taken jobs in factories. In some industries, women formed the majority of workers. For instance, more women than men worked in the textile mills of New England and the tobacco factories of the South. In New York City, women outnumbered men in the garment, or clothing, industry.

During the 1800s, women formed their own unions to work for better conditions. A few, like the all-black Washerwomen's Association of Atlanta, struck for higher wages. None of these unions succeeded, however.

Mother Jones. Among the women who took part in the labor movement, perhaps the most famous was Mary Harris Jones, known as Mother Jones. Jones worked as a dressmaker in Chicago until the Chicago Fire of 1871 destroyed her shop. In 1877, she helped striking railroad workers in Pittsburgh. Later, she traveled around the country, organizing coal miners and campaigning for improved working conditions.

Mother Jones called attention to the hard lives of children working in textile mills. By pointing out such abuses, she paved the way for reform.

ILGWU. In 1900, men and women garment workers organized the International Ladies' Garment Workers Union, or ILGWU. In 1910, more than 20,000 women and men in the ILGWU walked off their jobs. After several weeks, employers met their demands for better pay and shorter hours. This was an important victory for the union. The ILGWU became a key member of the AFL.

Tragedy at the Triangle Shirtwaist Factory

 Despite the efforts of the ILGWU and other labor groups, most women with factory jobs did not join unions. They continued to work long hours for low pay. Many labored under unsafe conditions. Then, a tragic event focused attention on the dangers faced by women workers.

Fire breaks out. Just before quitting time on March 25, 1911, smoke drifted skyward from the 10-story Triangle Shirtwaist Factory in New York City. A fire had broken out in the lofts, where cloth was stored. Flames shot through the lint-filled air. Within minutes, the upper stories were ablaze.

The factory became a chamber of horrors as hundreds of workers raced for the exits. Some exit doors were locked. The company always locked the doors to keep

Deathtrap *Firefighters did their best to combat the blaze at the Triangle Shirtwaist Factory. Their hoses, however, did not have enough power and their ladders could reach only to the sixth floor of the 10-story building.* **Citizenship** *How have state and local governments tried to prevent tragedies such as the Triangle Fire from happening?*

workers at their jobs. Other doors opened only inward. Panicked workers ran headlong into the doors, blocking them with their bodies. Most of the elevators broke down. Fire escapes crumpled in the heat.

Death leaps. Fire trucks pulled up within minutes, but their ladders could not reach the upper floors. Screaming women with their hair on fire jumped from windows. Wrote one reporter:

> **"**As I looked up. . .there, at a window, a young man was helping girls to leap out. Suddenly one of them put her arms about him and kiss[ed] him. Then he held her into space and dropped her. He jumped next. Thud—dead, Thud—dead. . . I saw his face before they covered it.**"**

Cecilia Walker was luckier. The quick-witted 22-year-old pried open an elevator door, grabbed the cable, and lowered herself eight floors to safety. Pauline Grossman scrambled to the next building across a human chain of three male co-workers. When others tried to follow, the human chain snapped. The men tumbled to their deaths.

By eight o'clock that evening, the supply of coffins had run out. Still, the bodies came. All told, nearly 150 people died. Most were young women.

Shock results in reforms. A few days later, 80,000 New Yorkers marched up Fifth Avenue in a mournful parade. Another quarter of a million people looked on.

The **Triangle Fire** shocked the public. Because of the fire, New York and other states approved new safety laws to help protect factory workers. ∎

SECTION 4 REVIEW

1. **Identify:** (a) Knights of Labor, (b) Terence Powderly, (c) Haymarket Riot, (d) American Federation of Labor, (e) Pullman strike, (f) Mother Jones, (g) Triangle Fire.
2. **Define:** injunction.
3. How did factory work change in the late 1800s?
4. (a) What were the goals of the Knights of Labor? (b) What were the goals of the AFL?
5. How did the AFL keep out African Americans and immigrants?
6. Why did public opinion in the late 1800s usually support employers rather than workers?
7. **CRITICAL THINKING** **Analyzing Ideas** Why do you think that it often takes a tragedy to spur people to make reforms?

 Writing to Learn
Write a dialogue between Terence Powderly and Samuel Gompers about the goals and tactics of their unions.

Chapter 19 • **557**

CHAPTER 19 REVIEW

Answers to Reviewing the Main Ideas

1. (a) Track was standardized, thousands of miles of new track were laid, and sleeping and dining cars were added to trains. (b) rebates and pooling

2. The railroads opened up every part of the country to trade, providing markets for industry. The creation of a national network of rail lines also created many jobs.

3. The process enabled steel makers to make strong steel at a lower cost, so industry began using steel to make more and more products.

4. (a) by selling stock to investors (b) Stockholders could share in the corporation's profits by receiving dividends, but they were not forced to pay the corporation's debts if it went bankrupt.

5. (a) On an assembly line, the frame of a product moves on a belt, and workers on each side of the belt add parts to the frame. (b) It cut production time and made low-cost mass production possible.

6. Before the Civil War, most factories were small family-owned businesses. In the late 1800s, factories were larger, more crowded, and more noisy; relationships between workers and owners became more impersonal; and hazards increased.

7. (a) Factory owners hired strikebreakers when unions called for strikes. (b) Several presidents sent federal troops to end strikes, and courts ruled against striking workers.

Answers to Thinking Critically

1. (a) Possible Answer: Consolidated railroads could be more efficient. Passengers and freight could move faster because they would not need to transfer between different railroads. One schedule for rates, departures, and arrivals would replace schedules for each separate railroad. (b) Possible Answer: Consolidating small railroads into one large railway system could give railroad users fewer choices. Furthermore, if consolidation created a railroad monopoly in an area,

Summary

- After the Civil War, growth of the railroads fueled growth of many other industries.
- Business leaders such as Carnegie, Vanderbilt, and Rockefeller shaped the nation's industries in the late 1800s.
- A flood of inventions boosted industry and made life easier for many Americans.
- Faced with harsh conditions in the new factories of the 1800s, many workers joined unions to demand higher pay and better working conditions.

Reviewing the Main Ideas

1. (a) What improvements were made in the nation's railroads after the Civil War? (b) What methods did railroads use to limit competition?

2. How did the growth of the railroad spark the growth of industry?

3. How did the Bessemer process transform the steel industry?

4. (a) How did corporations raise capital? (b) What advantages did corporations offer investors?

5. (a) Describe an assembly line. (b) How did the assembly line transform production?

6. How were factories of the late 1800s different from factories before the Civil War?

7. Explain how each of the following tried to limit the power of the unions: (a) factory owners, (b) federal government.

Thinking Critically

1. Drawing Conclusions After the Civil War, railroads consolidated as large railroad companies took over smaller ones. (a) What were the advantages of consolidation? (b) What were its disadvantages?

2. Understanding Causes and Effects Which invention discussed in this chapter do you

think had the greatest impact on American life? Explain.

3. Linking Past and Present (a) What were the goals of the Knights of Labor? (b) How many of these goals have been achieved?

Applying Your Skills

1. Placing Events in Time Review Section 3 of this chapter. Then construct a time line of important inventors and their inventions. How did some inventions lead to the growth of other industries?

2. Making a Review Chart Make a chart with four columns and two rows. Title the columns Membership, Goals, Leaders, and Tactics. Title the rows Knights of Labor and AFL. Then fill in the chart. Which features of the AFL helped it succeed?

3. Analyzing a Quotation Jay Gould, a railroad baron, once said, "I can hire one half of the working class to kill the other half." (a) What do you think he meant? (b) Based on the statement, what do you think was Gould's opinion of unions? Explain.

Thinking About Geography

Match the letters on the map with the following places: **1.** Albany, New York, **2.** Buffalo, New York, **3.** Duluth, Minnesota, **4.** Seattle, Washington, **5.** Atlanta, Georgia, **6.** St. Louis, Missouri, **7.** Pittsburgh, Pennsylvania. **Place** Why did Pittsburgh become the steelmaking capital of the nation?

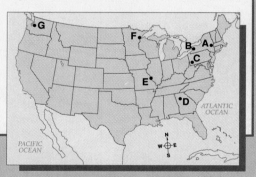

---

the company could raise its rates without fear of competition.
2. Possible Answer: the railroad, because it facilitated trade, growth, and national unity
3. (a) a shorter workday, equal pay for men and women, and an end to child labor, (b) Possible Answer: Today, workers have an eight-hour workday, and child labor is illegal. In most industries, men and women do not yet get equal pay for equal work.

Answers to Applying Your Skills

1. Time lines will vary, but cause-and-effect relationships should be clearly depicted.
2. Charts will vary. Students should note that practical goals and the use of strikes as a tactic helped the AFL succeed.
3. (a) Possible Answer: Because workers who strike can be re-

placed with other workers, strikers would be defeated or "killed" by strikebreakers of their own class. (b) Possible Answer: Gould disliked union and nonunion workers alike; he said that he could use them against one another to his own advantage.

Investigating Business and Industry

Ad for Chicago & Alton Railroad

Form into groups to review how industry changed the United States between 1865 and 1914. Follow the suggestions below to write, draw, or perform to show what you have learned. You may use the textbook, encyclopedias, atlases, or other materials in your classroom library to complete the tasks. Be able to name your sources of information when you have finished the activity.

ECONOMISTS Review the material on railroads and the growth of industry. Then make a concept map to show the industries that resulted from or were related to the growth of a railroad network in the United States.

WRITERS AND ARTISTS Create ads for a mail-order catalog selling the new inventions discussed in the chapter. Write text and use pictures to create your ads. Then organize your ads in a catalog.

ACTORS Prepare a humorous skit to show what it was like to ride in an early car, such as a Model T. Plan to present your skit to the class.

Ad for sewing machines

HISTORIANS Put together a "This Is Your Life" presentation for one of these business figures: Cornelius Vanderbilt, Andrew Carnegie, John D. Rockefeller, J. Pierpont Morgan, Elijah McCoy, Granville T. Woods, or Thomas Edison. Use your textbook, encyclopedias, and other library sources to gather information about the person you have chosen.

GEOGRAPHERS On an outline map of the United States, mark the location of important developments in the growth of industry in the late 1800s. Include such locations as the first oil well, Edison's invention factory, the route of the Great Northern Railroad, the steel capital of the nation, the home of the Montgomery Ward catalog, the site of the Haymarket Riot. Near each location, place a small illustration that shows why it is important.

Cash register

 Create an Investigating Business and Industry folder by assembling examples or descriptions of the activities from each group.

Alexander Graham Bell

Lessons	Teaching Resources
1 A Land of Promise **Objectives** 1. Explain why immigrants poured into the United States in the late 1800s. 2. Identify problems that the newcomers faced. 3. Explain why anti-immigrant feeling grew.	**Lesson Planner** Cooperative Learning, p. 123 **Student Study Guide** Section 1 Study Guide, p. 153 **Chapter Resources Binder, Unit 6** *Critical Thinking* Evaluating Information, p. 31 *Skill Application* Using a Special-Purpose Map, p. 30 *Geography in History* From the Old World to the New, pp. 33–34 **Our Multicultural Heritage** *Biography* Abiko Kyutaro, Champion of Japanese Immigrants, p. 58
2 Growth of Cities **Objectives** 1. Explain what caused cities to grow after the Civil War. 2. Identify problems that city dwellers faced. 3. Identify reforms that helped improve city life.	**Lesson Planner** Cooperative Learning, p. 124 **Student Study Guide** Section 2 Study Guide, p. 154
3 The Changing Face of Cities **Objectives** 1. Describe how cities changed in the late 1800s. 2. Describe how Americans spent their leisure time. 3. Explain how entertainment united Americans.	**Lesson Planner** Cooperative Learning, p. 125 **Student Study Guide** Section 3 Study Guide, p. 155 **Chapter Resources Binder, Unit 6** *History Through Literature* Casey at the Bat, p. 32 **Our Multicultural Heritage** *Milestone* The Baseball Barrier, p. 60 *Biography* Irving Berlin, American Songwriter, p. 59 **Interdisciplinary Connections:** The Lure of the City ▪ *Sciences* An Elevating Experience, p. 116 ▪ *Geography* Booming Birmingham, p. 117 ▪ *World* The Paris Plan, p. 118 ▪ *Economics* Marshall Field's Incredible Store, p. 119 ▪ *Civics* Helping Polish Immigrants, p. 120
4 A New American Culture **Objectives** 1. Describe how Americans improved education in the late 1800s. 2. Identify what Americans read in the late 1800s. 3. Identify American painters who won fame for their works.	**Lesson Planner** Cooperative Learning, p. 126 **Student Study Guide** Section 4 Study Guide, p. 156

Multimedia Resources	Additional Resources	
Listening to Literature Audiocassettes *The American Experience* Drill Ye Tarriers, side 5 **Transparencies** *Our Multicultural Heritage* Immigrants to the United States, 1840-1940, p. C-15 *Fine Art* Liberty Is Gold, p. D-43 **Videotapes/Videodiscs** *United States History Video Collection* The New Immigration, Vol. 12, Ch. 7; Family and Community, Vol. 12, Ch. 19; A Melting Pot? Vol. 12, Ch. 25; A Clash of Generations, Vol. 12, Ch. 28; Closing the Golden Door: China, Vol. 12, Ch. 31; Closing the Golden Door: Europeans, Vol. 12, Ch. 34	**Voices of Freedom** The Ethnic Map of New York, pp. 162–164 **Customized Reader** The Poetry of Chinese Immigrants at Angel Island, article VIA-16 **Interdisciplinary Explorations** A Nation of Immigrants	**Lesson Planner** Activity Based, pp. 127–128 **Student Study Guide** Chapter 20 Study Guide, pp. 157–158 **Chapter Resources Binder** **Unit 6** Vocabulary Building, p. 29 Chapter Test A, pp. 35–37 Chapter Test B, pp. 38–40 Illustration Master, p. 41 Extra Unit Questions, pp. 43–45 **English Guided Reading** Guided Reading, pp. 39–40 **Spanish Resources**
Transparencies *Geography and History* Growth of Population, p. I-45 **CD-ROM** *History Makers* Jane Addams **Videotapes/Videodiscs** *United States History Video Collection* The Rise of the Cities, Vol. 11, Ch. 25; Urban Pollution and Disease, Vol. 11, Ch. 31; The Squalor of the Cities, Vol. 12, Ch. 16	**Customized Reader** Going to Work at Hull House, article VA-11	**Computer Test Bank** Chapter Tests A and B Extra Unit Questions **Guided Reading Audiotapes** Side 7 **CD-ROM** *Time Tour* A Diverse Nation (1865–1914) in Reshaping the Nation
Transparencies *Exploring Technology* Skyscraper, p. H-47 *Interdisciplinary Connections* Ashcan School, p. B-71 **CD-ROM** *Arts & Entertainment* Ragtime **Videotapes/Videodiscs** *United States History Video Collection* Take Me Out to the Ballgame, Vol. 12, Ch. 43	**Voices of Freedom** A Bicycle Built for Two, p. 166 **Customized Reader** The Great Chicago Fire, article VB-12 Crossing the New Brooklyn Bridge, article VB-11	
Listening to Literature Audiocassettes *The American Experience* The Notorious Jumping Frog of Calaveras County, side 6 **Transparencies** *Fine Art* Young Mother Sewing, p. D-49 **CD-ROM** *Arts & Entertainment* Social Protest and Social Realism *History Makers* Mark Twain *History Makers* Winslow Homer **Videotapes/Videodiscs** *United States History Video Collection* Start Spreading the News, Vol. 12, Ch. 46		

Lesson Planner

For a fully developed **Activity-Based** lesson plan for Chapter 20, see the *Lesson Planner,* pages 127–128.

 Chapter Resources

Vocabulary Building The Vocabulary Building worksheet for Chapter 20 from Unit 6, page 29, of the *Chapter Resources* binder can be used as a prereading activity or as a review of chapter vocabulary. (Reteaching/Easy)

 Student Study Guide

Chapter 20 Study Guide Refer students to pages 157–158 of the *Student Study Guide* for the Chapter 20 Study Guide. The study guide can be used for chapter review as well as for reteaching. (Reteaching/Average)

 Guided Reading Audiotapes

Students can use *Guided Reading Audiotapes,* Chapter 20, side 7, to listen to section previews, summaries, and review questions. The tapes might benefit students who are auditory learners, students who have trouble reading, or students acquiring English. (Reteaching/Easy)

CHAPTER **20**

A Diverse Nation

(1865–1914)

CHAPTER OUTLINE

1 A Land of Promise

2 Growth of Cities

3 The Changing Face of Cities

4 A New American Culture

Mid-1800s *Immigrants from Northern Europe flocked to the United States. This pamphlet advertised a ship sailing from Sweden to Chicago.*

1882 *Congress passed the Chinese Exclusion Act. The new law banned Chinese immigrants, such as this family, for a period of 10 years.*

1886 *The Statue of Liberty, a gift from France, was unveiled in New York harbor. The statue welcomed millions of new immigrants from Eastern Europe.*

1865	1870	1875	1880	1885	1890

▲
WORLD EVENT
1881 Russia increases pogroms against Jews

Chapter Time Line
Critical Thinking

As students examine each illustration along the time line, have them consider what each image suggests. Invite them to create a generalization that relates to each image (for example, "The population of the United States became more of an ethnic mix" or "People began to expect a greater variety of goods and services"). List the generalizations on the chalkboard; use them as a springboard to discuss what life was like in the United States during this period.

Alternatively, have students compare the World Event information with the captions for the illustrations on page 560, looking for causes and effects.

Chapter Setting

With fear and hope, Rosa Cristoforo left her village in Italy in 1884 to join her husband in "l'America." She journeyed to the French port of Havre, where she boarded a steamship for the long voyage across the Atlantic Ocean. Rosa lived below deck "in a big dark room" with many other poor immigrants. After two weeks, she finally caught sight of land. She never forgot that moment.

"[I] stood and watched the hills and the land come nearer. Other poor people, dressed in their best clothes and loaded down with bundles, crowded around. America! The country where everyone could find work! Where wages were so high no one had to go hungry! Where all men were free and equal and where even the poor could own land! But now we were so near it seemed too much to believe. Everyone stood silent—like in prayer.**"**

Dreams of a better life brought millions of immigrants to the United States in the late 1800s. Life was hard for the newcomers. Yet over time, the people who came helped to build a strong and diverse nation, unlike any other.

> ## ACTIVITY
> Take a survey of class members to find out what national or ethnic backgrounds are represented. Then locate the nations or regions on a map.

Late 1890s *The invention of a new, safer bicycle led to a nationwide bicycle craze. As this painting shows, cycling was popular with both men and women.*

1902 *R. H. Macy's, one of the first department stores in the United States, opened in New York City. Shopping became a popular pastime.*

| 1890 | 1895 | 1900 | 1905 | 1910 | 1915 |

WORLD EVENT
1905 Chinese in Shanghai protest exclusion laws by boycotting American goods

WORLD EVENT
1910 Mexican Revolution begins

Chapter 20 • **561**

Play a recording of Neil Diamond's song "Coming to America," from the film *The Jazz Singer*. Have students discuss their thoughts and feelings about the song.

Lesson Plan

1. Focus In the years between the Civil War and 1914, millions of immigrants came to the United States. In this section, students learn why people left their homelands and the problems they faced in their adopted country.

2. Instruct Divide the class into teams. As you progress through the chapter, have each team select one group of immigrants who came to the United States between 1865 and 1914. Have each team use the text and outside research to describe that group's experiences, customs, distinctive foods, and clothing, as well as notable contributions by immigrants from that group. Schedule class presentations.

3. Close To close the lesson, ask students to list the factors that encouraged immigration in the late 1800s, places where immigrants settled, examples of how they adjusted to the new land, and reasons why native-born Americans reacted as they did to the immigrants.

1

A Land of Promise

FIND OUT

- Why did immigrants pour into the United States in the late 1800s?
- What problems did the newcomers face?
- Why did anti-immigrant feeling grow?

VOCABULARY push factor, pull factor, ethnic group, assimilation

---

Morris Horowitz was just 18 years old when he reached Chicago in 1870. The young man had learned no trade in his native Russia. Needing to earn a living in the United States, he became a peddler in the countryside. He walked from farm to farm, selling clothes and housewares. Some days, he trekked as many as 30 miles.

Horowitz dreamed of saving enough money to bring his family to the United States. As Jews in Russia, they faced persecution, possibly even death. Within five years, Morris's father, brothers, and sisters joined him in Chicago.

Like Morris Horowitz, millions of immigrants flooded into the United States after the Civil War. Their homelands at that time offered them little hope. The United States, they heard, was a land of opportunity. There they would find jobs, a better life, and a chance to contribute to the building of the young nation.

Hopes and Fears

Between 1866 and 1915, more than 25 million immigrants poured into the United States. Both push and pull factors played a part in this vast migration. **Push factors** are conditions that drive people to leave their homes. **Pull factors** are conditions that attract them to a new area.

Push factors. Many immigrants were small farmers or landless farm workers. As populations grew in other countries, land there became scarce. Small farms could barely support the families who worked the land. In some areas, the introduction of new farm machines caused farm workers to lose their jobs.

In Eastern Europe, political and religious persecution pushed many people to leave. In Russia and elsewhere, a person who criticized the government faced jail or exile. In the late 1800s, the Russian government supported pogroms (poh GRAHMZ), or organized massacres of Jews. "Every night," recalled a Jewish girl whose family fled Russia, "they were chasing after us, to kill everyone." After years of fear, her father said: "We're going to get out. . . . I want my family alive."

As you will read in Chapter 21, a revolution in Mexico acted as a push factor. As disorder and famine swept the country, thousands of Mexicans crossed the border into the American Southwest. For the Chinese, poverty and hardship in their native land acted as push factors, driving them to make new homes in the country they sometimes called "The Land of the Flowery Flag."

Pull factors. The promise of freedom and hopes for a better life attracted poor and oppressed people from Europe, Asia, and Latin America. Often, one bold family would set off for the United States. Before long, they sent home news of the riches of the new land.

These networks of families and friends helped pull neighbors from the "old country" to the United States. In the late 1800s, one out of every ten Greeks left their homes for the United States. Thousands of Italians, Poles, Hungarians, and Jews also sailed to the Americas.

Industry was another pull factor. American factories needed workers. Factory owners sent agents to Europe and Asia to hire

---

Connections With Local History
Activity

Invite a guest speaker to discuss push and pull factors that have influenced local migration patterns in the past and present. You might contact the sociology department of a local university, a regional planning board, the chamber of commerce, or an elected official. Brainstorm for appropriate questions the previous day. Tell students to take notes during the talk and ask follow-up questions. Afterward, help students create a past-and-present chart for classroom display.

Connections With Language Arts
Background

Emigrate means to leave the country in which you were born and to reside permanently in another. An individual who does this is called an *emigrant*. *Immigrate* means to enter a country in which you were not born in order to settle there permanently. A person who does this is called an *immigrant*. In the 1800s, large numbers of people *emigrated* from Russia and other European countries. Many of them *immigrated* to the United States.

workers at low wages. Steamship companies competed to offer low fares for the ocean crossing. Railroads posted notices in Europe advertising cheap land in the West.

The Unforgettable Voyage

Leaving home required great courage. Voyages across the Atlantic or Pacific were often miserable. Most immigrants could afford only the cheapest berths. Ship owners jammed up to 2,000 people in airless rooms below deck. On the return voyage, cattle and cargo filled those same spaces.

In such close quarters, diseases spread rapidly. A passenger recalled conditions aboard an immigrant ship.

“We left from Germany and we got water in the boat and all the children got measles. Some of them died and they threw them into the water like cattle. It was something I will never forget.”

A welcome symbol. For most European immigrants, the voyage ended in New York City. There, after 1886, they saw the ***Statue of Liberty*** as they entered the harbor. The

people of France had given the giant statue to the United States to honor the Declaration of Independence.

The Statue of Liberty became a symbol of the hope and freedom offered by the United States. Emma Lazarus wrote a poem, "The New Colossus," that was carved at the base of the statue. It welcomes all newcomers and ends with these lines:

“Give me your tired, your poor,
  Your huddled masses yearning
    to breathe free,
  The wretched refuse of your
    teeming shore.
  Send these, the homeless,
    tempest-tossed to me:
  I lift my lamp beside the golden
    door!”

A last hurdle. At the "golden door," immigrants faced one more hurdle. They had to pass an inspection before they could enter the United States.

After 1892, ships entering New York harbor stopped at ***Ellis Island.*** Newcomers waited for hours for the dreaded

Gateway to a New World *Millions of families like this one entered the United States through Ellis Island. They brought with them all their worldly belongings, including treasured items such as the embroidered vest below and the concertina shown above.* **Multicultural Heritage** *How do you think immigrants contributed to American culture?*

📖 **Lesson Planner**

For a developed **Cooperative Learning** lesson plan, see the *Lesson Planner,* page 123.

Answer to Caption

Answers will vary, but students should recognize that immigrants have contributed to cultural diversity by bringing their customs, foods, and arts to the United States.

🏛 **Transparencies**

Our Multicultural Heritage Use the transparency Immigration to the United States, 1840–1940 on page C-15 of *American History Transparencies.* Teaching suggestions can be found on page C-3. (Enrichment/Average)
Fine Art Use the transparency Liberty Is Gold on page D-43 of *American History Transparencies.* This work by Debbie Lee illustrates an immigrant's view of American life. Teaching suggestions can be found on page D-12. (Enrichment/Average)

Historical Sidelight
Background

Auguste Bartholdi, the French sculptor who created the Statue of Liberty, had been considering such a monument since 1865. The arm and torch of the statue were displayed in Philadelphia in 1876, as funds for the statue were being raised in France. Money for the pedestal was raised in the United States, largely through the efforts of immigrant publisher Joseph Pulitzer. On both sides of the Atlantic, schoolchildren were active fundraisers.

During the dedication ceremony for the statue (whose correct name is Liberty Enlightening the World), a boat pulled alongside the island. All of its passengers were members of the New York Suffrage Association. A spokesperson called out to those at the ceremony, "We praise the embodiment of liberty as a woman. But is it not despicable that if liberty had life, she could vote neither in the United States nor in France?"

Critical Thinking
Applying Information

Divide students into groups and have them use school library resources to learn about the Colossus at Rhodes. Have each group collaborate on written responses to these questions: Why did Emma Lazarus call the Statue of Liberty "The New Colossus"? Why is the New Colossus depicted as a woman? What modern adjective comes from the word *colossus,* and what does it mean?

Videotapes/ Videodiscs

United States History Video Collection Use the video segment "The New Immigration" from Volume 12, *Immigration and Cultural Change,* to enhance students' understanding of how immigration patterns began to change in the late 1800s. Approx. running time 3:15 min. (Enrichment/Average) Vol. 12, Ch. 7

| Chapter 7 | Play |

Chapter Resources

Critical Thinking Duplicate and distribute the worksheet, Evaluating Information, from Unit 6, page 31, of the *Chapter Resources* binder. The worksheet will give students an opportunity to evaluate the firsthand account of a young immigrant from Russia. (Enrichment/Average)

Customized Reader

Primary Source For a firsthand account of the experiences of three Chinese immigrants at Angel Island in 1910, order article VIA-16, The Poetry of Chinese Immigrants at Angel Island, from the *American History Customized Reader.* (Enrichment/Challenging)

examination. Doctors watched the men, women, and children climb a long flight of stairs. Anyone who appeared out of breath was stopped. The sick had to stay on Ellis Island until they got well. Those who failed to regain full health were sent back to Europe.

With hundreds of immigrants to process each day, immigration officials had just a few minutes to check each new arrival. To save time, they often changed names that they found difficult to spell. Krzeznewski became Kramer, for example, and Smargiasso ended up as Smarga. One Italian immigrant found that even his first name had been changed—from Bartolomeo to Bill.

A few lucky immigrants went directly from Ellis Island into the welcoming arms of friends and relatives. Most, however, stepped into a terrifying new land whose language and customs they did not know.

Asian immigrants. On the West Coast, immigrants from Asia faced harsher experiences than the Europeans in the East. By the early 1900s, many Asians were processed on *Angel Island* in San Francisco Bay. Because Americans wanted to discourage Asian immigration, new arrivals from Asia often faced long delays. As one immigrant looked across San Francisco Bay, he scratched these lines on the wall:

> **❝**Why do I have to languish in
> this jail?
> It is because my country is weak
> and my family poor.
> My parents wait in vain for
> news;
> My wife and child, wrapped in
> their quilt, sigh with
> loneliness. **❞**

Changing Patterns of Immigration

Earlier in the 1800s, most immigrants to the United States had come from Northern and Western Europe. English, Irish, German, and Scandinavian immigrants had helped to settle the frontier and build the cities. They

The New Immigrants

93%

Where They Came From 1840–1860

3%
2%
1.5%
.5%

Northern and Western Europe

Eastern and Southern Europe

Americas

Asia

All others

Where They Came From 1880–1900

33%
59%

6%
1%
1%

Source: *Historical Statistics of the United States*

GRAPH SKILLS *Patterns of immigration changed in the late 1800s. In 1840–1860, nearly all immigrants came from Northern and Western Europe.* ● *What percentage of immigrants came from Eastern and Southern Europe in 1840–1860? In 1880–1900?*

became known as "old immigrants." At first, old immigrants had faced some discrimination. But as the nation grew, they were drawn into American life.

In the late 1800s, the patterns of immigration changed. Large numbers of people arrived from Southern and Eastern Europe, Asia, and Latin America. Millions of Italians, Poles, Russians, Greeks, and Hungarians landed in the eastern United States. Chinese, Japanese, Koreans, Asian Indians, and Filipinos arrived on the West Coast.

Few of these later immigrants spoke English. Many of the Europeans were Catholic, Eastern Orthodox, or Jewish. Immigrants from Asia might be Buddhist or Daoist.

Connections With Science
Background

The medical inspection line was such a frightening part of the Ellis Island experience because the Immigration Service could turn away an immigrant for any number of reasons. A chalk-drawn letter on an immigrant's coat — *E* for suspected eye trouble and *X* for suspected mental illness, for example — meant that the immigrant would be detained for an exhaustive checkup, with no guarantee that permission to enter the United States would be granted. For example, to check for trachoma—a contagious eye infection that can result in blindness—a doctor would use a glove buttonhook to turn the immigrant's eyelids inside out for close inspection.

Their languages and religions set these "new" immigrants apart. As a result, new immigrants found it harder to adapt to life in the United States.

Adjusting to a New Land

Once in the United States, the new immigrants had to adjust their dreams to reality. Many had believed stories that the streets in the United States were paved with gold. One immigrant reported that he quickly learned three things:

> ❝First, the streets were not paved with gold. Second, the streets were not paved at all. Third, they expected me to pave them.❞

By the time the new immigrants arrived, much of the good farmland in the West had been taken. Also, few of them had enough money to buy land or the tools to farm it. In California, the law prohibited Asian immigrants from owning land.

Most immigrants stayed in the cities where they had landed. Some traveled to other cities to live with friends and relatives. The slums of lower Manhattan became home to thousands of poor immigrants. By 1900, this area of New York City was the most crowded place in the world.

Ethnic neighborhoods. Immigrants adjusted to their new lives by settling in neighborhoods with their own ethnic group. An *ethnic group* is a group of people who share a common culture. Across the United States, cities were patchworks of Italian, Irish, Polish, Hungarian, German, Jewish, and Chinese neighborhoods.

Within these ethnic neighborhoods, newcomers spoke their own language and celebrated special holidays with foods prepared as in the old country. Italians joined social groups such as the Sons of Italy. Hungarians bought and read Hungarian newspapers. Sharing laughter and tears with their own people eased the loneliness of life in a strange new land.

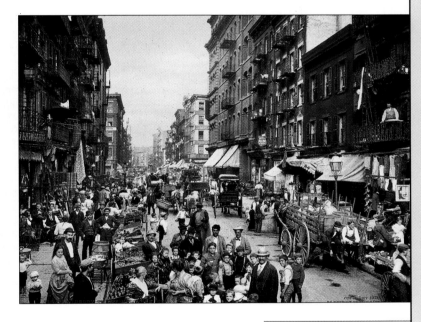

Street Scene *Immigrant neighborhoods often bustled with activity. This photograph shows a busy street in New York City.* **Daily Life** *What adjectives would you use to describe the scene in the picture?*

Chapter 20 • **565**

Our Multicultural Heritage
Activity

Bring the components of a tossed salad to class. Include ingredients of varied colors, shapes, and origins. Place all the chopped ingredients in a large bowl and mix. Discuss with students the fact that America has been called a "Salad Bowl" society. Ask: What do you think this means? Add a simple dressing (such as vinegar and oil); toss the salad. Explain that the dressing is like American culture (our shared hopes, experiences, and concerns). Ask: Does each ingredient retain its individuality? How does adding the dressing change the dish? Give each student a disposable plate and fork to sample the salad.

Chapter Resources

Skill Application For additional practice, duplicate and distribute the worksheet, Using a Special-Purpose Map, from Unit 6, page 30, of the *Chapter Resources* binder. (Reteaching/Average)

Answers to Skill Lesson

1. (a) E   (b) 4   (c) A
2. (a) Slavic, Jewish, and Italian (b) A3, B2, B3, C3, D3, D4, E3, E4
3. (a) A4, B2, C5, D3, D4 (b) Having a common language and common customs made the transition to American life easier.

ACTIVITY

Guided Instruction After adding grids to the map, students should label them, using a sequence of letters and numbers. Encourage original thinking in the questions. Answers should provide relevant information concerning the subject of the map.

MAP, GRAPH, AND CHART SKILLS
Using a Special-Purpose Map

Road maps and local maps often have grids, or networks of squares, to help people find towns and streets. You can locate a place easily if you know which square it is in.

The map below shows New York City in about 1900. Each color on the map marks a neighborhood in which people of one ethnic group lived. As you have learned, an ethnic group is a group of people who share a common culture. By 1900, 80 percent of the people in New York City were immigrants or the children of immigrants. Many ethnic groups other than the ones shown on the map lived in New York City.

Use the grid map at left to answer the following questions.

1. **Locate the squares on the grid.** The map has lines running from north to south and from east to west. The lines divide the map into squares. Across the top of the map are numbers. Each number marks one column of squares. Along the side of the map are letters. Each letter marks one row of squares. (a) Which letter marks the square where the Brooklyn Bridge is located? (b) Which number marks the same square? (c) Which letter marks the row of squares that is farthest to the north?

2. **Locate a place by identifying which square it is in.** To locate a place on the grid map, use the letter and the number of the square where the place appears. For example, the northern end of Broadway is in square A3. (a) What ethnic groups live in square D4? (b) What squares contain the largest Italian neighborhood?

3. **Draw conclusions using the grid map.** Use the grid map and your reading of this chapter to answer the following questions. (a) What square shows the widest variety of ethnic groups? (b) Why did people in the same ethnic group live in the same neighborhood?

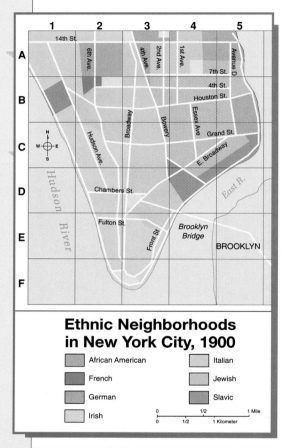

Ethnic Neighborhoods in New York City, 1900

- African American
- French
- German
- Irish
- Italian
- Jewish
- Slavic

0   1/2   1 Mile
0   1/2   1 Kilometer

ACTIVITY
Trace the map on page 571, Largest Cities in 1900. Then add to the map a grid with at least five rows and five columns. Write six questions based on the map and grid. Note the correct answers on a separate sheet of paper. Then trade maps with a classmate and answer each other's questions.

566 • Chapter 20

Students Acquiring English
Activity

Although mapreading skills are largely visual in nature, some students may have trouble interpreting information based on labels. SAE students might benefit by being paired with students who have demonstrated mapreading skills to work on the Skill Lesson and its Activity. Partners might check the SAE students' answers, offering help and encouragement.

Finding jobs. The newcomers soon set out to find work. European peasants living on the land had little need for money, but it took cash to survive in the United States. Through friends, relatives, and employment agencies, the new arrivals found jobs.

Becoming Americans. Often, newcomers were torn between their old traditions and the new American ways. Still, many struggled to learn English, an important step toward becoming a citizen. The process of becoming part of another culture is called assimilation.

Children assimilated more easily than their parents. They learned English in school and then helped their families learn to speak it. Because children wanted to be seen as Americans, they often gave up customs their parents honored. They played American games and dressed in American-style clothes. Immigrant parents felt both pride and pain as they saw their children change.

A Chinese Family and the Golden Mountain

Filled with ambition, 12-year-old Lowe Fat Yuen made the long trip across the Pacific Ocean to Golden Mountain, the Chinese name for the United States. He joined two older brothers who had opened a store in San Francisco's Chinatown. By the late 1800s, the three brothers were doing well. Lowe settled down to raise a family in his adopted land.

Years later, Lowe's eldest son, Pardee, wrote a book about his father's experiences. He called it *Father and Glorious Descendant*. In it, he recalls what it was like to grow up in a Chinese immigrant family.

American names. Like many immigrants, Lowe wanted his children to remember their heritage. At the same time, he wanted them to be "American." In *Father and Glorious Descendant,* Pardee describes a vexing problem his father faced as his children were born. It was a problem, says the author, that perplexed every Chinese father in California:

66 What names should he give us children born in this country? Father consulted his cronies. A Chinese name, it was realized, did not suffice. In order to establish beyond any doubt their American citizenship, Chinese children should be given Western names as well. 99

When Pardee was born, as first-born son he was given the Chinese name meaning "Glorious Descendant." He goes on to explain how his father chose his American name:

66 The problem of my American name . . . proved simple. Father was pleased to realize that my birthday . . . was also a holiday commemorating California's admission into the Union. At that time, the governor bore the name of Dr. George C. Pardee. 99

Family conflict. As Lowe's children grew up, they often clashed with their father. They became impatient with Lowe Fat Yuen's Chinese ways. In turn, their father became disappointed in them. As Pardee explains:

★★★

Linking Past and Present
Many Chinese immigrants had farmed in the Pearl River delta, a low-lying area of China that often flooded. In California, they used their skills to reclaim almost 5 million acres of flooded land in the Sacramento and San Joaquin valleys. Today, these acres are among the world's most valuable farmland.

Chapter Resources

Geography in History Duplicate and distribute the worksheet, From the Old World to the New, from Unit 6, pages 33–34, in the *Chapter Resources* binder. This worksheet shows how two ethnic groups settled in the United States. (Enrichment/Average)

Our Multicultural Heritage

Biography Have students read the biography, Abiko Kyutaro, Champion of Japanese Immigrants, on page 58 of the *Our Multicultural Heritage* booklet. (Enrichment/Average)

Interdisciplinary Explorations

A Nation of Immigrants Have students refer to the unit A Nation of Immigrants in the *Prentice Hall Interdisciplinary Explorations Series* to learn more about immigration to the United States. (Enrichment/Challenging)

Videotapes/ Videodiscs

United States History Video Collection Use the video segment "A Melting Pot?" from Volume 12, *Immigration and Cultural Change,* to enhance students' understanding of assimilation. Approx. running time 4:20 min. (Enrichment/Average) Vol. 12, Ch. 25

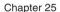

| Chapter 25 | Play |

Connections With Civics
Background

Naturalization is the granting of the rights of citizenship to an individual born in another country (an immigrant). Almost every country has a naturalization process. The U.S. Constitution authorized Congress to establish a "uniform Rule of Naturalization" for the United States. Congress delegated that power to the courts. There are several general requirements for becoming a naturalized American citizen: Applicants must have resided in the U.S. for at least five years; they must not have committed any serious crimes during that period of residency; they must affirm their belief in the principles of the Constitution and declare that they do not have hostile feelings toward the U.S. and its institutions; and finally, they must be able to read, write, and speak English and demonstrate a basic understanding of the Constitution and the processes of government.

Answer to Art Gallery: Our Common Heritage

Possible Answer: Chinese immigrants would have crossed the Pacific Ocean, and San Francisco was a busy West Coast seaport.

Videotapes/ Videodiscs

United States History Video Collection Use the video segment "A Clash of Generations" from Volume 12, *Immigration and Cultural Change*, to enhance students' understanding of the conflicts that often developed between immigrant parents and their assimilated children. Approx. running time 1:05 min. (Enrichment/Average) Vol. 12, Ch. 28

Chapter 28	Play

United States History Video Collection Use the video segment "Closing the Golden Door: China" from Volume 12, *Immigration and Cultural Change,* to enhance students' understanding of nativist efforts to end immigration from Asian nations. Approx. running time 1:20 min. (Enrichment/Average) Vol. 12, Ch. 31

Chapter 31	Play

ART GALLERY
OUR COMMON HERITAGE

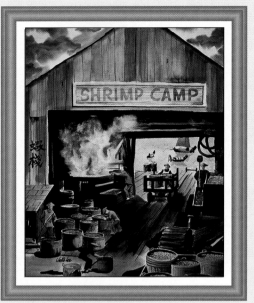

JAKE LEE
Shrimping Industry in San Francisco Bay, 1958

Chinese immigrants found work in many industries on the Pacific coast. Thousands entered the fishing trade in San Francisco, processing dried shrimp to ship back to China. Jake Lee, a modern Chinese American artist, has produced a series of paintings honoring the spirit and contribution of Chinese immigrants. Here, he depicts Chinese Americans hard at work in the shrimping industry. **Geography** Why did many Chinese immigrants settle in San Francisco?

❝According to Father's ideas, we children were to have an American education, but we were to follow

at home the ancestral ways. . . . At home our lives were a round of polite [greetings] and formal bowings and scrapings. For the most part, all this bored us, and we longed to escape from it and do as our American school friends did.❞

"He's my son." Pardee Lowe finished high school and worked his way through Stanford University. Later, his father helped him continue his education at Harvard.

Lowe Fat Yuen did not believe in praising his children for their accomplishments. He took it for granted that they would excel. It was not until he was a grown man that Pardee Lowe discovered that his father was proud of him.

In 1939, San Francisco was host to a World's Fair. Pardee was technical adviser for one of the exhibits, and he lectured about it twice a day. One day, by chance, Lowe Fat Yuen wandered in. He watched with interest as a group of 300 people hung on his son's words. After that, Lowe returned again and again. But he never said a word—either to praise or to criticize his son.

A friend, however, overheard an exchange between Lowe Fat Yuen and a visitor to the exhibit. He reported it to Pardee Lowe. As Pardee relates it:

❝'Do you know who the speaker is?' the visitor inquired of Father.
Father modestly replied, 'Yes.'
The visitor further questioned: 'Do you know him?'
'Of course,' said Father with a beaming smile. 'He's my son.'❞ ∎

Anti-Immigrant Feeling Grows

Many Americans felt overwhelmed by the flood of new immigrants. They feared that the newcomers would never assimilate because their languages, religions, and customs were too different.

Our Multicultural Heritage
Background

The friction between Lowe Fat Yuen and Pardee Lowe illustrates the fear of many Chinese-born fathers—that his child would be a *jook-sing*. The term originally referred to the hollow part of a piece of bamboo, but it was used to refer to Chinese Americans who were "empty" of Chinese traditions and culture.

Linking Past and Present
Activity

If there are students in your class who were born outside the United States, invite them to compare their experiences with those of Pardee Lowe. Ask: Which traditions of your homeland are you encouraged to continue? Which aspects of "becoming American" do you find most difficult?

As you have read, nativist feeling had exploded even before the Civil War. (See Chapter 13.) In the late 1800s, however, anti-immigrant feeling grew stronger.

Many workers resented the new immigrants because they took jobs for low pay. An editorial in one newspaper complained:

66The Poles, Slavs, Huns, and Italians come over without any ambition to live as Americans live and... accept work at any wages at all, thereby lowering the tone of American labor as a whole.99

Nativist pressure was especially strong on the West Coast. There, nativists worked to end immigration from China.

In the 1860s, railroad builders brought over thousands of Chinese workers. After the railroads were completed, the Chinese looked for other jobs. They found many doors closed to them. Some Chinese opened restaurants and laundries. Others worked as shoemakers, cigarmakers, tailors, and farmers. Sometimes, they became strikebreakers, which angered other workers. Most lived in cities in tight-knit communities called "Chinatowns."

Most Americans did not understand Chinese customs. Also, some Chinese did not try to learn American ways. Like many immigrants, they came to the United States to make money and then return home rich and respected. When that dream faded, many Chinese settled here permanently.

Barring Chinese immigration. The Chinese helped build the economy of the West. But as their numbers grew, so did the prejudice and violence against them. During economic hard times, especially, gangs attacked and even killed Chinese people.

Congress responded to this anti-Chinese feeling by passing the ***Chinese Exclusion Act*** in 1882. The act barred the immigration of Chinese laborers for 10 years. The Chinese Exclusion Act was the first limit on immigration into the United States. Congress renewed the law several times. It was finally repealed in 1943.

Other limits on immigration. In 1887, nativists formed the American Protective Association. It soon had one million members. The group campaigned for laws to restrict immigration. Congress responded by passing a bill that denied entry to people who could not read their own language.

President Cleveland vetoed the bill. It was wrong, he said, to keep out peasants just because they had never gone to school. Congress passed the bill again and again. Three more Presidents vetoed it. In 1917, Congress overrode President Wilson's veto, and the bill became law.

SECTION 1 REVIEW

1. **Locate:** (a) Italy, (b) Russia, (c) Greece, (d) China.
2. **Identify:** (a) Statue of Liberty, (b) Emma Lazarus, (c) Ellis Island, (d) Angel Island, (e) Chinese Exclusion Act.
3. **Define:** (a) push factor, (b) pull factor, (c) ethnic group, (d) assimilation.
4. What conditions in their home countries led many people to come to the United States?
5. (a) Where did "old" immigrants come from? (b) Where did "new" immigrants come from?
6. (a) Describe two problems faced by immigrants. (b) How did they adapt to the United States?
7. **CRITICAL THINKING Recognizing Points of View** What do you think was the main cause of conflict between Pardee Lowe and his father?

ACTIVITY Writing to Learn
Imagine that you are a 13-year-old immigrant in the late 1800s. Jot down 10 words that describe your feelings about coming to the United States.

Videotapes/ Videodiscs

United States History Video Collection Use the video segment "Closing the Golden Door: Europeans" from Volume 12, *Immigration and Cultural Change,* to enhance students' understanding of restrictions placed on European immigration. Approx. running time 2:00 min. (Enrichment/Average) Vol. 12, Ch. 34

Chapter 34

Play

Student Study Guide

Section 1 Study Guide Have students use the Section 1 Study Guide on page 153 of the *Student Study Guide* to review and reinforce the content of this section. (Reteaching/Average)

ACTIVITY

Guided Instruction Before students begin jotting down feelings, you might suggest that they list the various phases of the journey (for example, leaving their homeland, the sea voyage, their first view of the United States, or disembarking). When students have completed their lists, you might invite them to write a paragraph that describes the young immigrant's experiences and that incorporates at least five of their listed words. Encourage volunteers to share their work with the class.

Answers to Section 1 Review

1. See the World Map in the Reference Section.
2. (a) Statue of Liberty, p. 563, (b) Emma Lazarus, p. 563, (c) Ellis Island, p. 563, (d) Angel Island, p. 564, (e) Chinese Exclusion Act, p. 569
3. (a) push factor, p. 562, (b) pull factor, p. 562, (c) ethnic group, p. 565, (d) assimilation, p. 567
4. a shortage of farmland and, in Eastern Europe, political and religious persecution
5. (a) Most came from Northern and Western Europe. (b) Most came from Southern and Eastern Europe, Asia, and Latin America.
6. (a) Immigrants had difficulty reaching the U.S., passing through immigration, obtaining land, assimilating, and finding decent jobs and housing. (b) They formed ethnic neighborhoods; preserved ethnic traditions; and found jobs through friends, relatives, and employment agencies.
7. Possible Answer: The boy adapted more easily to American ways and yearned to follow them. The father, however, retained Chinese traditions and could not easily express pride in his son's accomplishments.

Bell Ringer

Write the expression *city life* on the chalkboard. Give students three minutes to freewrite about positive and negative images and feelings that this expression brings to mind.

Lesson Plan

1. Focus Immigration and rapid industrial expansion after the Civil War caused a population explosion in the cities. With this growth came urban problems. In this section, students learn about city life at various economic levels.

2. Instruct Have students imagine that they will stage a public meeting to discuss city problems in the late 1800s. Assign one group of students to play the role of city planners. This group should prepare an agenda and run the meeting. Assign other groups roles as tenement dwellers, members of the middle class, the wealthy, and social workers. These groups should prepare lists of topics they want to discuss. Afterward, have students list problems and proposed solutions in chart form. Ask: Which of these problems do cities still face? What new problems do cities face?

3. Close To close the lesson, have students write statements summarizing the main idea in each subsection and providing at least two supporting details.

2
Growth of Cities

FIND OUT

- What caused cities to grow after the Civil War?
- What problems did city dwellers face?
- What reforms helped to improve city life?

VOCABULARY tenement, settlement house

Bells pealed. Cannons thundered. Fireworks crackled in the afternoon sky. New Yorkers were celebrating the opening of the Brooklyn Bridge. In 1883, its soaring arches were a triumph of modern engineering. Linking Manhattan Island and Brooklyn, it was soon carrying 33 million people each year across New York City's East River.

New York, like other cities, was experiencing a population explosion. For new and old Americans alike, the golden door of opportunity opened onto the city.

City Populations Boom

As the United States industrialized after the Civil War, city populations boomed. In 1860, only one American in six lived in a city. By 1890, one out of every three Americans was a city dweller. By 1920, more than half of all Americans lived in cities. "We cannot all live in cities," said the newspaper publisher Horace Greeley, "yet nearly all seem determined to do so."

Causes. The flood of immigrants from Europe, Asia, and Latin America was one reason cities grew so fast. Also, by the 1890s, most of the land in the West had been divided into farms and ranches. As a result, fewer pioneers went there to home-

stead. In fact, many Americans left farms to move to cities. A young man in a story by Hamlin Garland summed up the feelings of many farmers:

> **❝**I'm sick of farm life . . . it's nothing but fret, fret, and work the whole time, never going any place, never seeing anybody.**❞**

In Chapter 18, you read about the hardships faced by small farmers. Like the new immigrants, farmers hoped to find a better life in the cities.

African Americans move north. African Americans, too, moved to cities to improve their lives. Most lived in the rural South. But when hard times hit or white prejudice led to violence, some African Americans headed north. By the 1890s, the south side of Chicago had a thriving African American community. As with immigrants from overseas, migration usually began with one family member moving north. Later, relatives and friends joined the bold pioneer.

The lure of jobs. Above all, jobs drew people to cities. As industries grew, they needed workers. New city dwellers took jobs in steel mills, meatpacking plants, and garment factories. They worked as salesclerks, waiters, barbers, bank tellers, and secretaries.

The bright lights and bustle of the city attracted people, too. Actors, singers, writers, dancers, and musicians found cities exciting places to live.

City Life

Cities grew outward from their old downtown sections. Before long, many took on a similar shape.

Poor families crowded into the city's center, the oldest section. Middle-class people lived farther out in neat row houses or new apartment buildings. Beyond them, the rich built fine homes with green lawns and plenty of trees.

Connections With Civics
Background

In his writings, George Washington cautioned Americans about "the tumultuous populace of large cities" and the violence of urban life. Thomas Jefferson had also been appalled by what he saw as the evils of European cities. Both envisioned the United States as a nation of independent farmers. Neither foresaw the urbanized, industrial giant that began to emerge in the late 1800s.

Connections With the World
Background

The rapid growth of American cities amazed many European travelers. An Italian poet marveled at this scene in Chicago: "The day of my arrival, I saw rubbish—still smoking—from a house burned the night before. The day of my departure (and I stayed but a single week), I saw on this same site, the iron framework of a new building, already erected to the height of a third story. . . ."

By 1900, six American cities had populations over 500,000.
1. In addition to New York, what other cities had over 500,000 people in 1900?
2. What was the westernmost city to have a population over 100,000?
3. **Drawing Conclusions** Which cities on the map do you think were probably most affected by the wave of new immigrants from Europe?

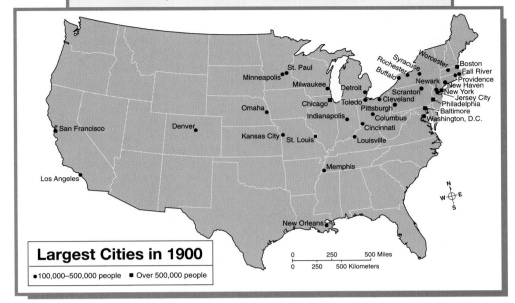

Largest Cities in 1900

● 100,000–500,000 people   ■ Over 500,000 people

0   250   500 Miles
0   250   500 Kilometers

 Lesson Planner

For a developed **Cooperative Learning** lesson plan, see the *Lesson Planner,* page 124.

Answers to Map Study

1. Boston, Philadelphia, Baltimore, Chicago, and St. Louis **2.** San Francisco **3.** Students might list port cities on the East Coast, such as New York, Philadelphia, and Boston.

 Transparencies

Geography and History Use the transparency set Growth of Population on page I-45 of *American History Transparencies.* The base map and overlays 1 and 2 offer students the opportunity to use maps for information other than political boundaries. Teaching suggestions can be found on page I-6. (Enrichment/Challenging)

 Videotapes/ Videodiscs

United States History Video Collection Use the video segment "The Rise of the Cities" from Volume 11, *Industrialization and Urbanization,* to enhance students' understanding of factors that led to the rapid growth of cities. Approx. running time 3:55 min. (Enrichment/Average) Vol. 11, Ch. 25

Tenement-house slums. Poor families struggled to survive in crowded slums. Streets were jammed with people, horses, pushcarts, and garbage.

Because space was so limited, builders devised a new kind of house that could hold more people. They put up buildings six or seven stories high. They divided the buildings into small apartments, called tenements. Many tenements had no windows, heat, or indoor bathrooms. Often, 10 people shared a single room in a tenement house. One magazine in 1888 described the crowded tenements as "great prison-like structures of brick."

Typhoid and cholera raged through the tenements. Babies, especially, fell victim to disease. In one Chicago slum, more than half of all babies died before they were 1 year old. Despite the terrible conditions, people poured into city slums.

Factory owners took advantage of low rents and cheap labor. They turned buildings into factories, further reducing people's living spaces.

"Striving upward." Beyond the slums stood the homes of the new middle class, including doctors, lawyers, office workers, business managers, and skilled machinists. Rows of neat houses lined tree-shaded streets. Here, disease rarely broke out.

Middle-class people joined singing societies and bowling leagues. They did charity work and belonged to religious organizations. Such activities gave them a sense of community. As one writer said, the clubs "bring together many people who are striving upward, trying to uplift themselves."

Chapter 20 • **571**

Chapter 25   Play

Connections With Literature
Activity

Find Carl Sandburg's poem "Chicago" and distribute copies to the class. Begin by having several volunteers read the poem aloud. Then draw two columns on the chalkboard. On one side, have students list negative points the poem makes about Chicago. On the other side, have students list positive points. Ask: Using this poem as evidence, why do you think that many people were attracted to Chicago in the late 1800s?

Learning Styles
Kinesthetic Learners

Have pairs of students prepare and present dialogues about life in an American city in the late 1800s. One student in each pair should play a poor immigrant living in a tenement. The other should play a millionaire living in a mansion on the outskirts of the city. Dialogue should focus on the different lifestyles of the rich and the poor and how these two groups probably felt about each other.

Life among the rich. On "the cool green rim of the city" lay the walled mansions of the rich. In Chicago, 200 millionaires lived along the exclusive lake front by the 1880s. In New York, huge homes dotted Fifth Avenue, still on the city's outskirts.

The rich traveled to Europe, buying priceless art. They threw lavish parties. At one banquet, the host handed out cigarettes rolled in hundred dollar bills.

Cleaning Up the Cities

As more and more people crowded into cities, problems grew. Tenement buildings were death traps if fires broke out. Garbage rotted in the streets. Factories polluted the air. Crime flourished. Thieves and pickpockets haunted alleys, especially at night.

By the 1880s, reformers were demanding change. They forced city governments to pass building codes. New buildings had

Amusements of the Rich *For the wealthy, city life offered a wide variety of recreations. The women in this advertisement prepare to go for a ride in an elegant automobile.* **Geography** *In a typical city, where did the richest people generally live?*

to have fire escapes and decent plumbing. Cities hired workers to collect garbage and sweep the streets. To reduce pollution, zoning laws kept factories out of neighborhoods where people lived.

Safety improved when cities set up professional fire companies and trained police forces. Gas—and later electric—lights made streets less dangerous at night. As you will read, many cities built new systems of public transportation as well.

Pushed by reformers, city governments hired engineers and architects. These experts designed new water systems. New York City, for example, dug underground tunnels to the Catskill Mountains—100 miles to the north. The tunnels brought clean water to the city every day.

Help for the Poor

Some groups looked for ways to help the poor. The Catholic Church ministered to the needs of Irish, Polish, and Italian immigrants. An Italian nun, Mother Cabrini, helped found more than 70 hospitals in North and South America. These hospitals treated poor people who could not afford a doctor.

Food and shelter. Protestant groups also set up programs for the poor. In 1865, a Methodist minister created the *Salvation Army* in London. By 1880, the Salvation Army had expanded to the United States. It offered food and shelter to the poor.

Other groups—like the YMCA (Young Men's Christian Association) and YWCA (Young Women's Christian Association)—taught classes, organized team sports, and held dances. Such activities offered young people a brief escape from slum life.

The settlement house movement. By the late 1800s, individuals began to organize settlement houses. A settlement house is a community center that offers services to the poor. The best known of these was *Hull House,* set up by Jane Addams.

A Friend to the Poor *Jane Addams devoted her life to improving conditions among the poor in Chicago's slums. The photograph shows the neighborhood where Addams founded Hull House.* **Citizenship** *What services did settlement houses offer?*

Addams came from a well-to-do family, but she felt strong sympathy for the poor. After college, she moved into one of the poorest slums in Chicago. There, in an old mansion, she founded Hull House in 1889.

Other idealistic young women soon joined Addams at Hull House. They provided day nurseries for children whose mothers worked outside the home. They organized sports and a theater for young people. They taught English to immigrants and gave classes in health care.

The energetic women at Hull House urged the government to help the poor. Alice Hamilton, a Hull House doctor, campaigned for better health laws. Florence Kelley worked to ban child labor.

Over the years, the settlement house movement spread. By 1900, about 100 such centers had opened in American cities.

SECTION **2** REVIEW

1. **Identify:** (a) Mother Cabrini, (b) Salvation Army, (c) Hull House.
2. **Define:** (a) tenement, (b) settlement house.
3. Why did cities grow in the late 1800s?
4. Describe three problems slum dwellers faced.
5. How did reformers try to improve city life?
6. **CRITICAL THINKING Comparing** Compare and contrast the lives of the rich, the middle class, and the poor in American cities in the late 1800s.

ACTIVITY **Writing to Learn**

Imagine that you are one of the people in the photograph above. Write a short story about how you live.

Chapter 20 • **573**

Answer to Caption

day nurseries for working mothers, activities for young people, classes in English and health care

 CD-ROM

History Makers Access the biography of Jane Addams on the American Heritage® *History of the United States* CD-ROM. (Enrichment/Average)

 Student Study Guide

Section 2 Study Guide Have students use the Section 2 Study Guide on page 154 of the *Student Study Guide* to review and reinforce the content of this section. (Reteaching/Average)

ACTIVITY

Guided Instruction Before students begin writing their short stories, review with them the elements of fiction: setting, characters, plot, theme, and point of view. Suggest that during the prewriting stage, they create a chart with these five elements as column heads and list writing ideas in the appropriate columns. Remind them that the child/narrator is also a character—one whose point of view is limited to what that character sees, hears, and knows. Encourage the use of dialogue rather than explanation to carry the action forward. In the revising stage, have partners check for consistency in the use of first-person narration.

Answers to Section 2 Review

1. (a) Mother Cabrini, p. 572, (b) Salvation Army, p. 572, (c) Hull House, p. 572
2. (a) tenement, p. 571, (b) settlement house, p. 572
3. A flood of immigrants came from Europe, and Americans moved from farms to cities.
4. Because there were no fire codes, tenement houses were potential deathtraps. Rotting garbage and factory pollution fouled the environment. Crime flourished on dark streets.
5. Reformers forced municipal governments to pass building codes and zoning laws. They also pushed for sanitation measures, such as the installation of new water systems.
6. Possible Answer: The rich lived on the outskirts of the cities, traveled to Europe to buy expensive art, and entertained lavishly. The middle class lived outside the slums in neat houses on shaded streets. They joined music, literary, and religious organizations and did charity work. The poor lived in crowded slum tenements with inferior ventilation and plumbing. They struggled to survive in a disease-ridden environment.

Bell Ringer

Tell students to imagine that they live in a world without movies, television, or radio. Have them brainstorm to name things that they would do for entertainment and ways in which they might spend leisure time.

Lesson Plan

1. Focus Population growth in cities led to a boom in the transportation and building industries. In this section, students learn how innovations such as trolley cars, skyscrapers, and department stores transformed city life. They also examine some of the athletic, musical, and literary interests of the era.

2. Instruct Divide the class into small groups. Ask each group to imagine that they are farmers who have come to New York or Chicago in 1895 for the first time. Have students write a letter home describing their first impressions of city life. Tell them to be sure to include technological advancements, shopping, sports, and recreational activities.

3. Close To close the lesson, ask students to identify at least five attractions they would have enjoyed and five things they would have done in cities in the late 1800s.

3
The Changing Face of Cities

FIND OUT
- How did cities change in the late 1800s?
- How did Americans spend their leisure time?
- How did entertainment unite Americans?

VOCABULARY vaudeville, ragtime

A small fire started in the barn behind the O'Leary cottage. Within hours, dry winds whipped the blaze into an inferno that raged across Chicago. Panicked residents fled their homes. A survivor described the scene:

> 66Everybody was running north. People were carrying all kinds of crazy things. A woman was carrying a pot of soup, which was spilling all over her dress. People were carrying cats, dogs, and goats. In the great excitement, people saved worthless things and left behind good things.99

The Chicago fire of 1871 killed nearly 300 people, left almost 100,000 homeless, and destroyed the entire downtown. Yet from the ashes, a new city rose with many tall, graceful buildings. By the 1890s, the city's population topped one million. Like other American cities, Chicago was undergoing vast changes.

Cities Take On a New Look

A building boom changed the face of American cities in the late 1800s. Cities like Chicago and New York ran out of space in their downtown areas. Resourceful city planners and architects decided to build up instead of out.

Going up! After fire leveled downtown Chicago, planners tried out many new building ideas. Using new technology, they designed tall buildings with many floors. These high-rise buildings had frames of lightweight steel to hold the weight of the structure. Newly invented electric elevators carried workers to upper floors. Elevators moved so quickly, said one rider, that "the passenger seems to feel his stomach pass into his shoes."

The first high-rise building was constructed in Chicago in 1885. It was 10 stories tall. As their methods improved, builders put up taller "skyscrapers"—buildings whose tops seemed to touch the sky.

Public transportation. As skyscrapers crowded more people into smaller spaces, cities faced a new problem: the traffic jam. In crowded downtown areas, streets were choked with horse-drawn buses, carriages, and carts.

Electricity offered one solution. In 1887, Frank Sprague, an engineer from Richmond, Virginia, designed the first electric streetcar system. Streetcars, or trolleys, were fast, clean, and quiet. Many cities built trolley lines running out from the center of town to the outlying countryside.

In 1897, Boston led the way in building the first American subway, or underground electric railway. In 1904, New York opened

Linking Past and Present
Today, speeding cars often pose a threat to people trying to cross city streets. In the 1870s and 1880s, city dwellers had to worry about runaway horses. According to the National Safety Council, horses killed nearly 10 times more pedestrians in the late 1800s than cars do today.

574 • Chapter 20

Connections With Technology
Background

The Chicago fire destroyed more than 3 square miles of the city. The inhabitants quickly set about rebuilding with imagination and vigor. The transformation was so great that in 1893, a renewed, larger, and more vibrant Chicago hosted a World's Fair. Visitors to the fair were dazzled by marvels such as hydraulic lifts, refrigerators, and the world's fastest locomotive (New York Central's No. 999). For a fee, one could view the fair from what *Scientific American* (July 1893) called "the wonderful 'merry-go-round' designed by Engineer George Ferris. . . . It carries thirty-six pendulum cars, each seating forty passengers; thus one revolution of the wheel carries 1,440 to a height of 250 feet in the air." This device—the Ferris wheel—remains a popular amusement today.

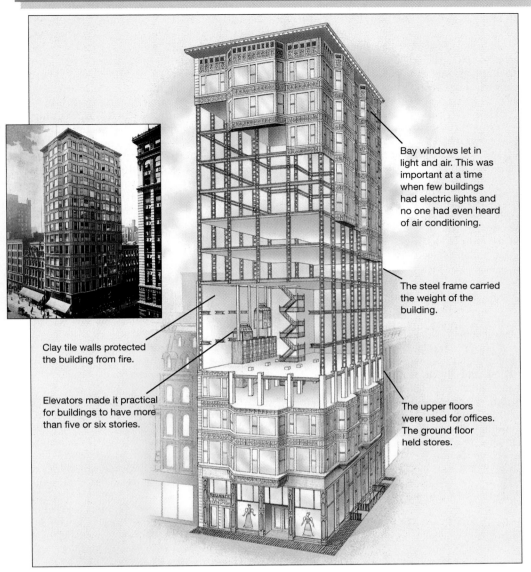

Bay windows let in light and air. This was important at a time when few buildings had electric lights and no one had even heard of air conditioning.

The steel frame carried the weight of the building.

Clay tile walls protected the building from fire.

Elevators made it practical for buildings to have more than five or six stories.

The upper floors were used for offices. The ground floor held stores.

Skyscraper *As people crowded into American cities, architects began building up instead of out. Today, the Reliance Building in Chicago, shown here, does not look very tall. When it was first built in the 1890s, however, its 16 stories made it a "skyscraper."* **Science and Technology** *Based on this drawing, what new building technology made skyscrapers possible?*

Chapter 20 • **575**

Lesson Planner

For a developed **Cooperative Learning** lesson plan, see the *Lesson Planner,* page 125.

Answer to Exploring Technology

elevators; the use of steel for a building framework

Transparencies

Exploring Technology Use the transparency Skyscraper on page H-47 of *American History Transparencies.* Teaching suggestions can be found on page H-14. (Enrichment/Average)

Customized Reader

Primary Source For an eyewitness account of Chicago's 1871 disaster, order article VB-12, The Great Chicago Fire, from the *American History Customized Reader.* Martin Stamm, the author, gives a riveting description both of the fire and the panic of those who tried to escape from it. (Enrichment/Average)

Customized Reader

Primary Source For a copy of a newspaper article describing the opening day of the Brooklyn Bridge, order article VB-11, Crossing the New Brooklyn Bridge, from the *American History Customized Reader.* (Enrichment/Average)

Cooperative Learning
Activity

Divide the students into groups of three or four. Have each group create a two-column chart labeled Cities Then and Cities Now. Have students review Sections 2 and 3 and list in the first column the distinctive features of American cities in the late 1800s. Group lists might include skyscrapers, department stores, traffic congestion, electric trains, and popular leisure-time activities. Have groups complete their lists by noting the distinctive features of city life today. Groups can begin by deciding which items in the first column remain a part of city life. Then have them add items that are more characteristic of life today. When charts are complete, have groups compare the two columns and write a paragraph comparing cities in the late 1800s with cities today.

Voices of Freedom

Primary Source You might assign selection 4-4, A Bicycle Built for Two, on page 166 of *Voices of Freedom*. The song "Daisy Bell" and the accompanying picture demonstrate the popular craze of bicycling during the 1890s. (Enrichment/Easy)

Our Multicultural Heritage

Milestone Have students read The Baseball Barrier on page 60 of the *Our Multicultural Heritage* booklet. (Enrichment/Easy)

Chapter Resources

History Through Literature To introduce students to a humorous poem that captures the flavor of the era, duplicate and distribute the worksheet, Casey at the Bat, from Unit 6, page 32, of the *Chapter Resources* binder. (Enrichment/Average)

Videotapes/ Videodiscs

United States History Video Collection Use the video segment "Take Me Out to the Ballgame" from Volume 12, *Immigration and Cultural Change,* to enhance students' understanding of sports that were popular in the late 1800s. Approx. running time 1:45 min. (Enrichment/Average) Vol. 12, Ch. 43

Chapter 43

Play

---

the first section of its subway system. These trains carried workers rapidly to and from their jobs.

Earlier, New York had built an elevated train, called the El. Steam engines pulled passenger cars along overhead tracks. An immigrant described her first trip on the El:

❝I was looking out the train window, and seeing what was going on. People had their windows open, and the train was going by. . . . I thought the train was going to go right through their rooms!**❞**

Open spaces. While cities grew up and out, some planners wanted to preserve open spaces. In the 1850s, Frederick Law Olmsted planned Central Park in New York City. Other cities followed this model. They set aside land for zoos and gardens so that city people could enjoy green grass and trees during their leisure time.

A New World for Shoppers

Shopping areas also got a new look. In the late 1800s, department stores sprang up. They sold all kinds of goods in one building. Earlier, people had bought shoes in one store, socks in another, and dishes in a third.

In 1902, R. H. Macy opened a nine-story building at Herald Square in New York City. It had 33 elevators and a motto that soon became famous: "We sell goods cheaper than any house in the world."

Before long, other cities boasted department stores like Macy's. They led to a new pastime—shopping. In their free time, people browsed each floor, looking at clothes, furniture, jewelry, and gifts.

A Passion for Sports

City dwellers also looked for fun outdoors. In sports, Americans found a great escape from the walls of factories, stores, and offices.

---

576 • Chapter 20

Take me out to the ball game. "What has 18 feet and catches flies?" Americans knew the answer to that riddle: a baseball team. By the late 1800s, baseball was becoming the nation's favorite sport.

Baseball was first played in New York in the 1840s. During the Civil War, New York soldiers showed other Union troops how to play the game. By the 1870s, the country had several professional teams and its first league.

At first, African Americans played professional baseball, too. In the 1880s, however, they were barred from major league baseball. In 1885, Frank Thompson organized a group of waiters into the first black professional team, the Cuban Giants of Long Island.

Early baseball was different from the game Americans know today. Pitchers threw the ball underhand. Catchers caught the ball after one bounce. Fielders did not wear gloves, so catching a hard-hit ball could be painful. As a result, high scores were common. One championship game ended with a score of 103 to 8.

Rough and tumble football. Another popular sport was football. It grew out of soccer, which Americans had played since colonial times.

Early football called for lots of muscle and little skill. On every play, the two teams crashed together like fighting rams. The quarterback ran or jumped over the tangle of bodies. To a European visitor, football involved "a heap of 22 bodies tumbling on top of one another, like a knot of serpents with human heads."

Players did not wear helmets and were often hurt. In one brutal season, 44 college players died from injuries. Some colleges banned the sport in response. Others drew up stricter rules of play.

An indoor sport. James Naismith taught physical education at a YMCA in Springfield, Massachusetts. He wanted to find a sport that could be played indoors in winter. In 1891, he invented basketball.

Linking Past and Present
Activity

Have students choose one sport discussed in this section, research its history from the late 1800s to the present, and write a brief report summarizing how this sport has changed over the years. You might also suggest that several students research the sport of boxing.

Our Multicultural Heritage
Background

Vaudeville provided opportunities for many people from minority backgrounds who found the traditional routes to fame and fortune blocked by discrimination. African Americans such as Bert Williams, Jewish Americans such as Eddie Cantor, and Native Americans such as Will Rogers were idolized as performers. A proud descendant of Cherokees, Rogers was once described as the most beloved man in America. Wearing a cowboy hat and twirling a rope, he would make humorous comments about American life and politics. Rogers used gentle wit to make serious comments about American ideals and injustices. When he died in a plane crash in 1935, admirers around the world mourned for him.

At first, Naismith planned to use square boxes, not round hoops, as goals in his new game. But the janitor at the YMCA nailed two bushel baskets on the gym walls. The players were to try to throw a soccer ball into the baskets. The game caught on. It spread to other YMCAs and then to schools and colleges around the country.

Other Entertainment

By the late 1800s, American cities supported a wide variety of cultural activities. Talented Italian, German, Jewish, and other immigrants contributed to a brilliant new world of music. Many large cities organized symphony orchestras and opera companies.

Generally, only the wealthy attended the symphony or the opera. For most city-dwelling Americans, leisure meant a visit to the vaudeville show or a trip to a music hall to hear ragtime. **Vaudeville** (VAWD vihl) was a variety show that included comedians, song-and-dance routines, and acrobats. (See Connections on page 578.) **Ragtime** was a new kind of music with a lively, rhythmic sound. Scott Joplin, an African American composer, helped make ragtime popular. His "Maple Leaf Rag" was a nationwide hit.

Popular songs. Songwriters produced many popular tunes, such as "Shine On, Harvest Moon." The new songs, heard in music halls and on vaudeville stages, quickly swept the country. Later, as Thomas Edison's phonograph caught on, a new industry grew up to record popular songs. By 1900, millions of phonograph records had been sold.

Towns and cities had marching bands that played the military music of John Philip Sousa. Sousa wrote more than 100 marches, including "The Stars and Stripes Forever." His marches became favorites at Fourth of July celebrations.

Shared experiences. Music and other kinds of entertainment brought Americans together. People from different cultures sang

Play Ball! *With more leisure time, city dwellers turned to sports for entertainment. This painting by Thomas Eakins shows baseball players practicing before a game.* ***Daily Life*** *What other sports were popular in the late 1800s?*

the same songs and saw the same shows. As the railroad system grew, acting companies, circuses, and "Wild West" shows toured the country. These traveling groups helped spread American culture beyond the cities to small towns everywhere.

SECTION 3 REVIEW

1. **Identify:** (a) Frank Sprague, (b) Frederick Law Olmsted, (c) Frank Thompson, (d) James Naismith, (e) Scott Joplin, (f) John Philip Sousa.
2. **Define:** (a) vaudeville, (b) ragtime.
3. How did technology influence American cities?
4. Describe two ways cities improved transportation.
5. What sports were popular in the late 1800s?
6. **CRITICAL THINKING Evaluating Information** What role do you think music played in helping immigrants assimilate?

 Writing to Learn
Imagine that you are an advertising writer for a department store in the late 1800s. Write an ad to attract shoppers to your store.

Interdisciplinary CONNECTIONS

For worksheets establishing connections between the Chapter 20 main idea, The Lure of the City, and five other disciplines, see the *Interdisciplinary Connections* booklet. (Enrichment)

- **Sciences** An Elevating Experience, page 116 (Average)
- **Geography** Booming Birmingham, page 117 (Easy)
- **World** The Paris Plan, page 118 (Average)
- **Economics** Marshall Field's Incredible Store, page 119 (Average)
- **Civics** Helping Polish Immigrants, page 120 (Challenging)

Answer to Connections

A variety-show format with 8 to 20 short acts, including music, dance, comedy, circus-style performances, and novelty acts.

ACTIVITY

Guided Instruction Explain that the opening act in a vaudeville show was often comedy. Also tell students that slow and fast acts should alternate. Program notes should be short and descriptive. If students express interest, you might have them create and stage a class vaudeville show.

| ARTS | SCIENCES | GEOGRAPHY | WORLD | ECONOMICS | CIVICS |

Vaudeville: Entertaining Americans

The Three Keatons

❝Did you send for the doctor when the baby swallowed the collar button?
You bet I did. It was the only one I had.❞

Comedians told jokes like this during vaudeville shows that entertained millions of Americans. For 25 cents, working people could enjoy anything from the silliest comedy to serious drama.

Vaudeville thrived from the 1890s to the late 1920s. In the heyday of vaudeville, touring companies played in more than 2,000 playhouses. Small companies had "one-night stands" in stuffy, dark halls in rural towns. Acts that made it to the "big time" performed in fancy theaters like the Palace in New York City.

Wherever the show went on, the curtain rose on 8 to 20 short acts. Audiences applauded or booed comedians, singers, dancers, acrobats, musicians, magicians, sword swallowers, animal acts, or pantomimists as the show built to a grand finale.

Many acts were family affairs. The Three Keatons were father, mother, and son Buster, who went on to stardom in the movies. George M. Cohan, who later wrote "Yankee Doodle Dandy," toured with his parents and his sister on the vaudeville circuit. Fred Astaire danced with his sister Adele. The Marx Brothers started in vaudeville and ended up in Hollywood.

Becoming a vaudeville star was a long shot at best. For African Americans, the odds were even greater. Some performers, however, like comedian Bert Williams, made it to the top despite discrimination. On more than one occasion, a white performer refused to appear on the same program with Williams. Sometimes, a hotel manager allowed him to stay in a white hotel but banned him from the main elevators. Williams once confided to Eddie Cantor, a famous white comedian: "It wouldn't be so bad, Eddie, if I didn't still hear the applause ringing in my ears."

Vaudeville poster

■ What kinds of entertainment did vaudeville offer?

Vaudeville poster

ACTIVITY
Create a list of acts for a vaudeville show. Then design a program to announce the entertainers.

Team-Teaching Suggestion
Art

You might work with an art teacher to present a lesson about stage design and setting. Include discussion of stage backdrops and placards used in vaudeville. Students might design backdrops and placards to accompany the lineup of attractions they created in the suggested activity.

Team-Teaching Suggestion
Music

You might work with a music teacher to present a lesson about the music of this era and its lasting influence on American composers and artists. Discuss such topics as the use of patriotic themes by many vaudevillians, the influence of Scott Joplin, and "Tin Pan Alley" composers such as Irving Berlin.

4 A New American Culture

FIND OUT

- How did Americans improve education in the late 1800s?
- What did Americans read in the late 1800s?
- What American painters won fame for their works?

VOCABULARY *yellow journalism, dime novel, realist*

The writer Mark Twain felt sure that the new mechanical typesetter would revolutionize publishing. After all, the machine could do the work of four people. He invested $5,000, a huge sum in 1880, in it. "Very much the best investment I have ever made," he concluded.

In fact, Twain did not make any money from his investment. The company that he backed was a failure.

The mechanical typesetter, however, did change publishing. The new machine made printing easier and cheaper. Mass-produced, affordable books and newspapers helped spread American culture.

Growth of Education

Before 1870, fewer than half of American children went to school. Many who did attended one-room schoolhouses. Often, several students shared a single book.

Public schools improve. As industry grew after the Civil War, the nation needed an educated work force. As a result, states improved public schools. In the North, most states passed laws that required children to attend school, usually through sixth grade. In the South, the Freedmen's Bureau built grade schools for both African American and white students.

In cities such as Boston and New York, public schools taught English to young immigrants. Native-born and immigrant children also learned the duties and rights of citizens.

Schools stressed discipline and obedience. A 13-year-old boy complained about the hardship of school life:

66 They hits ye if yer don't learn and they hits ye if ye whisper, and they hits ye if ye have string in yer pocket, and they hits ye if yer seat squeaks, and they hits ye if ye don't stan' up in time, and they hits ye if yer late, and they hits ye if ye ferget the page. 99

Many students disliked school so much they escaped into factory jobs.

High schools and colleges. Many cities and towns built public high schools after 1870. By 1900, the United States had 6,000 high schools.

Higher education also expanded. New private colleges for both women and men opened. Many states built universities that offered free or low-cost education to young women and men. However, African Americans and other nonwhites, like the Chinese, had fewer opportunities to get a college education.

Public libraries. Wealthy individuals, like Andrew Carnegie, gave money to towns and cities to build public libraries. Libraries were more than places to find books and magazines. Often, speakers gave talks on

History and You

In the late 1800s, communication was much slower than it is today. Newspapers often reported news that was several days—or even weeks—old. How does the instant communication of TV affect the way Americans today react to events?

Section 4
pp. 579–583

🔔 Bell Ringer

Guide the students in formulating a working definition of the word *realism* as it applies to literature and any variety of art forms. Have the class brainstorm for examples of realistic works they have read or seen.

Lesson Plan

1. Focus American culture thrived in the late 1800s. Schools improved, magazines and newspapers flourished, and authors and artists portrayed the American scene in a new realistic style. In this section, students read about the growth of American culture during this period.

2. Instruct Write the following statement on the chalkboard: "In the late 1800s, Americans became better read and better informed than ever before." Divide the class into small groups. Have each group write one or two paragraphs using this statement as a guide and providing factual evidence to support it. Select a volunteer from each group to present the brief essay to the class.

3. Close To close the lesson, play a Jeopardy!-like game with students. Provide facts that identify important people, places, and events; have students compose questions to which your prompts are the correct answers.

Critical Thinking
Applying Information

The ability to set type mechanically instead of by hand caused book publishers to look at their business and marketing methods in new ways. Ask: What development in your lifetime has created a similar revolution in publishing? Follow up with a brief discussion of the uses and advantages of personal computers in publishing, especially in the area of desktop publishing.

Connections With Science
Background

In the late 1800s, standard methods of teaching did not meet the needs of all children. Professor John Dewey of the University of Chicago urged schools to take a more scientific approach. He wrote, "I believe that the school must represent present life—life as real and vital to the child as that which he carries on in the home, in the neighborhood, or on the playground." Dewey's ideas were part of a broad movement called progressive education.

topics such as archaeology and medicine. Through schools and libraries, Americans learned to embrace new ideas.

Headlines and Scandals

"Read all about it!" cried newsboys, and Americans eagerly bought newspapers. As education spread, people read more, especially newspapers. The number of newspapers grew dramatically after 1880. By 1900, half the newspapers in the world were printed in the United States.

Staying informed. The large number of newspapers was linked to the growth of cities. In towns and villages, friends and neighbors shared news when they met. In the city, however, people had thousands of "neighbors." There was so much news every day that people needed newspapers to be informed.

Newspapers reported on important events of the day. Most featured short, colorful stories about local government, business, fashion, and sports. Many immigrants learned English by spelling their way through a daily paper. At the same time, they learned about life in the United States.

Americans, in turn, learned about immigrants through the papers. Stories about the Greek, Slavic, Polish, and Italian communities helped the established Americans understand their immigrant neighbors. In this way, newspapers made it possible for people to overcome cultural differences. They also gave city dwellers a sense of being New Yorkers, Chicagoans, or Bostonians.

Two newspaper giants. Joseph Pulitzer created the first modern, mass-circulation newspaper. Pulitzer was a Hungarian immigrant. In 1883, he bought the New York *World.* He set out to make it lively and "truly democratic."

To win readers, Pulitzer slashed the price to 2 cents and added sports pages and comic strips. He introduced pictures and bold headlines to make stories more exciting. The *World* splashed crimes and political scandals across its front page. Pulitzer sent a woman reporter, Nellie Bly, around the world. He then ran a contest so that readers could guess the exact day, hour, and minute of her return. Under Pulitzer's guidance, circulation of the *World* soared from 20,000 to one million.

William Randolph Hearst, who came to New York City from San Francisco, soon challenged Pulitzer. Hearst bought the New York *Journal* and began to print more scandals, crime stories, and gossip than the *World* did. Critics coined the term **yellow journalism** for the sensational reporting style of the *World* and the *Journal.* They complained that the papers offered less news and more scandal every day.

Women journalists. Newspapers competed for women readers. They added special sections on fashion, social events, health, homemaking, and family matters.

The Funny Papers *In 1894, the New York* World *published the first full-color comic strip. "The funnies" quickly became a favorite feature in most newspapers. One of the most popular comic strips was "Mutt and Jeff," which ran for almost 70 years.* **Linking Past and Present** *What comic strips are popular today?*

Linking Past and Present
Background

Joseph Pulitzer died in 1911. The School of Journalism at Columbia University in New York City, for which he had provided the funding, opened the next year. In his will, Pulitzer established a series of awards, known as the Pulitzer Prizes, to be administered by Columbia. These awards are still given each year for outstanding achievements in the fields of fiction, nonfiction, drama, music, and journalism.

Connections With Language Arts
Background

Although *yellow journalism* was an apt description of some of the popular reporting of this time, the term was not entirely new. Yellow had been used to refer to sensational writing as early as 1846. At that time, several sensational magazines and books were printed with inexpensive yellow covers. The term yellow stuck, even when there was nothing literally yellow about the publication.

The Morning News *Big-city newspapers of the late 1800s and early 1900s attracted readers with stories of crime, sports, and gossip. Here, New Yorkers crowded into a trolley eagerly read the morning news.* **Linking Past and Present** *How do people keep informed about the news today?*

Papers rarely pushed for women's rights, however. Most were afraid to take bold positions that might anger some readers.

A few women, like Nellie Bly, worked as reporters. Once, Bly pretended to be insane in order to find out about treatment of the mentally ill. Her articles about cruelty in mental hospitals led to reforms in the care of the mentally ill. Another pioneer woman reporter, Lorena Hickok, covered politics, kidnappings, and crime. She once spent a night in prison to interview a woman convicted of murder.

New Reading Habits

In the late 1800s, Americans read not only newspapers but also magazines and books. New printing methods lowered the cost of magazines. Magazines also added eye-catching pictures to attract readers.

Each magazine had its special audience. The *Ladies' Home Journal* appealed to middle-class women. It featured articles about famous people and stories by well-known authors. By 1900, it had one million readers. Other magazines, such as *Harper's Monthly* and the *Nation,* specialized in articles about politics and current events.

The paperback revolution. In the late 1800s, paperback books became popular. Bestsellers were often **dime novels.** These low-priced paperbacks offered thrilling adventure stories. Many told about the "Wild West." Young people read dime novels eagerly—even though parents often disapproved of the stories. One critic complained:

> ❝Stories for children used to begin, 'Once upon a time there lived—.' Now they begin, 'Vengeance, blood, death,' shouted Rattlesnake Jim.'❞

Tales of rags to riches. Horatio Alger, a popular writer, produced more than 100 books for children. Most told the story of a poor boy who became rich and respected through hard work and honesty. Americans snapped up these rags-to-riches stories. They offered the hope that even the poorest person could become rich and successful in the United States.

The realists. In the 1880s, a new crop of writers appeared. For the first time, Americans read more books by American authors than by British authors. Many writers had worked as newspaper reporters. They had seen the poverty created by the Industrial Revolution. They were **realists.** Realists wanted to show life just as it was.

Stephen Crane wrote one novel about a girl who is born and dies in a filthy slum. He is best known today for *The Red Badge of Courage,* a short novel about the Civil War.

Popular Reading *Americans loved to read "rags-to-riches" and adventure stories like these. The young hero might find success by saving a millionaire's life, by exposing a corrupt villain, or just by hard work.* **The Arts** *Why do you think stories like these were popular?*

Another author, Hamlin Garland, described the hard lives of farmers in the 1890s. Jack London, born in California, wrote about the hardships faced by miners and sailors on the West Coast.

Kate Chopin found an audience for her short stories about New Orleans life in women's magazines like *Vogue.* In her stories, she showed women breaking out of traditional roles.

Paul Laurence Dunbar. Paul Laurence Dunbar was the first African American to make a living as a writer. He wrote poems, such as "We Wear the Mask," in a serious, elegant style. In other poems, he used everyday language to express the feelings of African Americans of the time. Dunbar also wrote short stories and several novels.

Mark Twain

The most famous author of this period was Samuel Clemens, better known by his pen name, Mark Twain. Clemens was born in Missouri. As a young man, he worked on a Mississippi steamboat. There, he heard the boatman's cry "Mark Twain," meaning that the river was two "marks," or 12 feet, deep. He took it as his name when he sent out his first story.

Local color. Twain had an eye and an ear for "local color." That is, he described the special features of a region and captured the way people spoke in different parts of the nation.

Twain disliked snobs. He used homespun, no-nonsense characters to poke fun at people who acted important. Twain's stories became so well known that people would quote them to win an argument.

Huckleberry Finn. Twain's best-known works were *Tom Sawyer* and *The Adventures of Huckleberry Finn. Huckleberry Finn* takes place along the Mississippi River before the Civil War. Huck is a country boy who ends up helping an escaped slave named Jim. The two become good friends as they raft down the river together.

Twain wanted people to enjoy the novel, but he was also making a serious point. Friendship is more important to Huck than the unjust laws that made Jim a slave.

Although *Huckleberry Finn* became a classic, some schools and libraries refused to buy the book. They claimed that Huck was a crude character who would have a bad influence on "our pure-minded lads and lasses."

Realism in Art

Artists, too, sought to capture local color and the harsh, gritty side of modern life. In the late 1800s, leading artists painted everyday scenes rather than great events.

Winslow Homer. As a young man during the Civil War, Winslow Homer drew scenes of brutal battles for magazines. Later, he painted realistic scenes of New England. In 1883, he moved to Maine. There, he

---

Team-Teaching Suggestion
Literature

You might work with a literature teacher to present a lesson about the use of irony in Mark Twain's *The Adventures of Huckleberry Finn.* Discuss Huck's decision (Chapter 3) to help Jim, despite his belief that this would be "wickedness." Examine the apparent meaning of the words and Twain's real message. Then have students compare Huck's actions with such historical events as the

Boston Tea Party, Jefferson's writings of the first part of the Declaration of Independence, the activities of the Underground Railroad, and the civil rights sit-ins of the 1960s. Ask: Are Huck's actions in keeping with mainstream American beliefs? Whose actions today remind you of Huck's? What kinds of civil disobedience are appropriate? Inappropriate?

Connections With Fine Art
Background

Thomas Eakins often portrayed athletes. One of his most famous paintings, *The Gross Clinic,* shocked people because it realistically showed a surgeon performing an operation.

Whistler's most famous painting, popularly known as Whistler's Mother, found no buyer in the United States. The French government bought it.

Mary Cassatt is one of the most highly regarded American artists. She was also a champion of women's rights and world peace.

painted the ocean and the hardy fishing people of the coast.

Thomas Eakins and Henry Tanner. Another realist, Thomas Eakins, studied in Europe, but his style was uniquely American. He paid great attention to detail. He learned anatomy and dissected dead bodies to be able to paint the human form accurately. His paintings of surgical operations were as precise as photographs.

One student of Eakins was the African American painter Henry Tanner. Tanner won fame for pictures of black sharecroppers. Later, he moved to Paris to escape prejudice in the United States.

Americans abroad. Other American artists preferred to work in Europe, too. James Whistler left Massachusetts for Paris and London. His work influenced young European artists. John Singer Sargent also lived abroad. He made money painting portraits of wealthy Europeans.

The painter Mary Cassatt (kuh SAT) was born in Pennsylvania but settled in Paris. She carved out a place for herself in the French art world. Cassatt painted bright, colorful scenes of people in everyday situations. Her best-known works are paintings of mothers with their children.

The Banjo Lesson *Henry Tanner was the first African American artist to gain international fame. He is best known for his realistic studies of African American life, such as* The Banjo Lesson, *shown here.* **The Arts** *How does this painting stress the importance of family in African American life?*

SECTION 4 REVIEW

1. **Identify:** (a) Joseph Pulitzer, (b) William Randolph Hearst, (c) Nellie Bly, (d) Stephen Crane, (e) Paul Laurence Dunbar, (f) Mark Twain, (g) Winslow Homer, (h) Henry Tanner, (i) Mary Cassatt.
2. **Define:** (a) yellow journalism, (b) dime novel, (c) realist.
3. How did education change after the Civil War?
4. (a) What were newspapers like in the late 1800s? (b) What kinds of books did Americans enjoy?
5. (a) What was Mark Twain's message in *The Adventures of Huckleberry Finn*? (b) Why did some schools and libraries refuse to buy the book?
6. Describe the works of three American artists.
7. **CRITICAL THINKING Analyzing Information** Why do you think American writers and painters turned to realism in the late 1800s?

 Writing to Learn
Write a short story in the style of a Horatio Alger rags-to-riches novel.

Picturing the Past

Art Note

Visual History Written records of the past are extremely valuable, but visuals are no less important. In this feature, students take a close look at visuals that depict the lives and some of the interests of young people in the nineteenth century. They will see events and trends depicted through fine art, photography, engraving, and advertising art. Point out that any one of these visuals "shows" more about its subject than one could "tell" in the same amount of space.

Previewing Focus

Have students brainstorm for a list of key events of the nineteenth century. Ask: If you could have lived at any time in that century, which part would you choose? Do you think that you would have much in common with someone your age who actually did live during that time? What would be the best thing about living at that time? What would be the worst?

Linking Past and Present
Activity

Conditions in factories were often downright dangerous, especially for children. Over the years, child labor in the United States was first reformed and then ended. That does not mean, however, that "sweatshops" cease to exist. Challenge students to find out how factory labor in other countries (especially in developing nations) resembles the scene depicted at the top of the page—and how immigrant labor is used in illegal "sweatshops" in this country.

Working in Factories *Many children helped their families by going out to work in the 1830s. In this spinning mill, a young boy is working under the machine at left.*

Learning a Trade *Training for a trade began at an early age. Here, a young workman learns how to sharpen a scythe.*

A Game of Lacrosse *Traditional activities continued to play an important role in the lives of young Native Americans. Here, youths enjoy a game of lacrosse.*

Teenage Soldier *Boys as young as 14 or 15 fought in the Civil War. In this painting, Winslow Homer captures the innocence of a young Union soldier.*

584 • Chapter 20

Cooperative Learning
Activity

Have small groups of students research other aspects of "popular culture" in the mid- to late 1800s. For example, one group could find out which songs were popular; they might come up with a Top 10 list and even perform a few numbers for the class. Another group might learn more about the tastes of the magazine-reading public. Encourage students to display artwork (covers of magazines and sheet music, for example) wherever possible.

A Wild West Show *Americans of all ages flocked to see Buffalo Bill Cody's rollicking Wild West Show.*

Discussion Questions

1. Which would you rather do, be an apprentice and learn a trade or work in a factory? Why?
2. What kind of equipment is needed for a game of lacrosse?
3. (a) Why would someone your age want to go to war? (b) What kind of work could someone your age do to help your regiment?
4. Based on the poster, why do you think people would want to attend Buffalo Bill's Wild West show?

Answer to Picturing the Past

Possible Answers: baseball, following the adventures of high-profile journalists (in print or on television), lacrosse (usually as a school sport), training for a trade (as in school vocational programs)

A Board Game *Manufactured toys and games became popular in the late 1800s. This board game was inspired by the adventures of newspaper reporter Nellie Bly.*

Baseball *By the 1890s, baseball had become the nation's favorite sport. Americans followed the progress of professional baseball players such as the one shown here.*

Picturing the Past

Young Americans in the 1800s

As the nation expanded in the 1800s, so did the world of young Americans. Home and family were still the center of life. However, more young people began to find amusement and employment in the outside world. The Industrial Revolution, the Civil War, and the growth of cities all brought major changes in the lives of the nation's young people. ■ Which activities shown here are still part of the lives of young Americans today?

Chapter 20 • **585**

Historical Sidelight
Background

William Frederick Cody (Buffalo Bill) (1846–1917) was a wagon train guide, a pony express rider, and a scout for the Union during the Civil War—to name a few of his occupations. He was also a buffalo hunter, supplying meat for railroad workers in Kansas; there he earned his famous nickname. Cody later served as a scout for military forces fighting Native Americans in the West; in so doing, he became a popular hero.

Cody began his show-business career in 1872, acting in plays that sometimes featured his own adventures. In 1883, he organized "Buffalo Bill's Wild West." Cody took his troop of cowhands (North American cattle herders and South American *vaqueros*), Indians, and buffalo on tours across the United States and parts of Europe. The show, which featured displays of sharpshooting skill and a mock Indian battle, traveled for about 10 years, but "Buffalo Bill" performed until just before his death.

CHAPTER 20 REVIEW

Answers to Reviewing the Main Ideas

1. (a) Farmland became scarce in Europe, and machines displaced workers. Furthermore, some groups were subjected to political and religious persecution in their homelands. (b) The promise of freedom and hopes for a better life attracted people to the United States.

2. Children assimilated more easily. They learned English in school and adopted American customs and pastimes.

3. (a) The language, clothing, and customs of the Chinese—and their frequent unwillingness to change—set them apart. Also, Chinese people sometimes took jobs that made them strikebreakers. (b) In 1882, Congress passed the Chinese Exclusion Act, which barred immigration from China for 10 years. Congress renewed that law several times.

4. (a) inadequate water supply, garbage in the streets, fires, and crime (b) City governments hired planners, engineers, and architects to design new water systems. They passed building codes, hired workers to collect garbage and sweep streets, organized fire companies, trained police, improved public transportation, and installed street lights.

5. The movement established community centers that provided day-care services, athletic and cultural activities, and classes in English and health care.

6. (a) In the South, more grade schools were built. Northern states passed laws requiring children to attend school. Many towns and cities built public high schools. (b) New private colleges opened. Many states built universities that offered a free or low-cost college education. The number of private schools for women also increased.

7. (a) Stephen Crane, Hamlin Garland, and Jack London (b) Crane wrote about a young girl who lived in a slum and about the Civil War. Garland wrote about the hardships faced by farmers. London wrote about the hard lives of miners and mariners.

586

Summary

- Millions of immigrants from Southern and Eastern Europe, Asia, and Latin America poured into the United States after the Civil War.
- Cities grew rapidly in the late 1800s, and many poor people lived in crowded, dirty slums.
- Under pressure from reformers, cities passed building codes and built new systems of transportation.
- In the late 1800s, education improved in the United States, and Americans developed new reading habits.

Reviewing the Main Ideas

1. (a) What push factors caused immigrants to come to the United States? (b) What pull factors influenced immigration?

2. How did immigrant children help their families adjust to life in the United States?

3. (a) Why did Chinese immigrants face special prejudice? (b) How did Congress respond to anti-Chinese feeling?

4. (a) What problems did cities face as their populations grew? (b) What steps did cities take to improve conditions?

5. How did the settlement house movement help the poor?

6. (a) How did public schools improve after the Civil War? (b) In what ways did higher education expand?

7. (a) What realist writers were popular in the late 1800s? (b) What did they write about?

Thinking Critically

1. Defending a Position Was the United States a "golden door" for immigrants? Support your position.

2. Solving Problems Could immigrants preserve their native language and heritage

586 • Chapter 20

and still assimilate into American culture? Explain.

3. Linking Past and Present (a) What did city dwellers in the 1800s do to escape the pressures of city life? (b) How do people in cities today relax?

Applying Your Skills

1. Analyzing a Quotation "Immigrants work for almost nothing and seem to be able to live on wind." (a) Is this statement factual? Why or why not? (b) Who would most likely have made a statement like this? Explain your answer.

2. Exploring Local History (a) Are there branches of the Salvation Army, the YMCA, or the YWCA in your community? (b) What other similar groups exist in your area? (c) What have they done to help people?

3. Using Visual Evidence Study the painting on page 583. How does the painting reflect the realist style?

Thinking About Geography

Match the letters on the map with the following places: **1.** Northern and Western Europe, **2.** Eastern and Southern Europe, **3.** Americas, **4.** Asia, **5.** United States. **Region** (a) Name two countries in Northern and Western Europe. (b) In Eastern and Southern Europe.

Answers to Thinking Critically

1. Answers will vary. Many immigrants encountered discrimination, persecution, and poverty; on the other hand, social reforms, the availability of public education, and the growth of American industry provided opportunities for immigrants and their descendants that would not have been available in their native countries.

2. Answers will vary. Families might preserve customs and tra-

ditions through neighborhood activities and celebrations, but they also assimilate through educational and employment avenues.

3. Possible Answers: (a) In the 1800s, they read newspapers and books, shopped, participated in or watched athletic events, and attended theater and musical performances. (b) Today they relax by following many of the same pursuits, as well as by watching TV and movies and by playing computer games.

Answers to Applying Your Skills

1. Possible Answers: (a) Yes; many immigrants accepted low wages and lived simply, by American standards. (b) an individual who was prejudiced or a worker trying to obtain a pay raise or on strike

2. (a) Most towns have a branch of at least one of these organizations. (b) Answers will vary. (c) Answers will vary but may include services such as day care, litera-

INTERDISCIPLINARY **ACTIVITY**

Living in the City

Form into groups to review city life in the late 1800s and early 1900s. Follow the suggestions below to write, draw, or act to show what you have learned about life in American cities at this time. You may use the textbook, encyclopedias, atlases, or other materials in your classroom library to complete the tasks. Be able to name your sources of information when you have finished the activity.

ARCHITECTS Find out more about the layout and buildings of cities in the late 1800s. Then create a model of a city of the period. Include skyscrapers, tenements, stores, theaters, parks, and so on in your model.

POETS AND DANCERS Review the description of life in cities. Then form into groups to create a poem and dance showing what city life was like in the late 1800s and early 1900s. Poets can read their poems aloud while dancers perform for the class.

MATHEMATICIANS Locate statistics for the populations of American cities in the late 1800s and early 1900s. Use the statistics to create two graphs:
- A line graph showing the total population of American cities between 1880 and 1910.
- A bar graph showing the populations of the five largest American cities in 1900.

ARTISTS Find out more about the migration of African Americans to northern cities during the late 1800s and early 1900s. Create a mural depicting this migration. Be sure to include scenes of the life African Americans left behind in the South as well as of the life they found once they arrived in the North.

GOVERNMENT OFFICIALS Find out more about the problems of cities in the late 1800s and early 1900s. Form into groups to plan a reform campaign for each problem. Then present your campaign strategy in a series of posters or TV programs.

 Make a Living in the City collage. Include examples, photographs, or summaries of each group's activity.

Chicago World's Fair poster

Tenement life

Street scene

Chapter 20 • **587**

---

cy programs, employment guidance, and food and shelter for the homeless.
3. Possible Answer: *The Banjo Lesson* captures the distinctions of its location. In the painting, Henry Tanner depicts an unglamorized, everyday scene.

Answers to Thinking About Geography

1. C **2.** D **3.** B **4.** E **5.** A
Region: (a) Possible Answers: Sweden, Norway, the Netherlands, Great Britain (b) Possible Answers: Italy, Greece, Bulgaria, Romania

Assessment

Chapter Resources Binder For a more comprehensive evaluation of student understanding of this chapter, assign Chapter Tests A and B and/or Extra Unit Questions from Unit 6, pages 35–40 and 43–45.
Computer Test Bank You can use Chapter Tests and Extra Unit Questions to create your own tests for both testing and retesting.

Alternative Assessment

Chapter Resources Binder See the Alternative Assessment booklet in the *Social Studies Educator's Handbook* series.
Portfolio You might meet with students to choose appropriate work from the chapter for inclusion in their portfolios.

Interdisciplinary ACTIVITY

Learning Styles

The following chart indicates the activities appropriate for different learning styles.

Visual Learners
Architects
Poets and dancers
Mathematicians
Artists
Government officials

Auditory Learners
Poets and dancers
Government officials

Kinesthetic Learners
Architects
Poets and dancers
Mathematicians
Artists
Government officials

Evaluation

Architects Buildings should be representative of architectural styles up to and including the late 1800s. Individual buildings need not be drawn to scale, but overall design should be in perspective. City layouts should reflect the design plans of the era for the particular cities selected.
Poets and dancers Poems need not rhyme but should at least contain a natural rise and fall of syllables. Dancing ability need not be a criterion, but dances should creatively convey the facts about city life, as suggested in the poems.
Mathematicians Graphs should be easy to follow, with pertinent information labeled correctly; statistics must be accurate.
Artists Artistic ability need not be a criterion, but murals should illustrate various aspects of the African American experience before, during, and after this migration.
Government officials Suggest that each group first select no more than two problems and then concentrate on reform strategies for each. When campaign strategies are presented, problems should be clearly defined; solutions should be logical.

587

History Through Literature

Author Note

Anzia Yezierska wrote from the 1920s to the 1960s about the experiences of Eastern European Jews who came to America. Her many short stories and novels vividly depict the lives of Jews who settled on New York's Lower East Side. *How I Found America* combines two collections of Yezierska's fiction, *Hungry Hearts* and *Children of Loneliness,* that were published in her lifetime.

Vocabulary

Have students look up and discuss the words *rapture, oppressed, ghetto, fragrant,* and *dingy* before they read the passage. You might wish to place particular emphasis on the meaning of *ghetto,* since the understanding of this word is so central to the reading. Have students share their knowledge and understanding of ghettos with the class. Emphasize the difference between what we call ghettos in the United States and those that existed at the time in Europe.

Prereading Focus

You might have students reread pages 562–567 in Chapter 20 to review what they learned about the immigrant experience of the late 1800s.

Motivation/Prior Knowledge

Review the discussion of the push factors in immigration (page 562). Ask: How would you feel about leaving a place where you had been persecuted? What hopes would you have about your new home?

Purpose-Setting Question

Does America live up to the narrator's expectations? Why or why not?

History Through LITERATURE

How I Found America

Anzia Yezierska

Introduction   Life for most Jews in Russia in the late 1800s was harsh and cruel. As a result, hundreds of thousands of Jews fled to the United States. Anzia Yezierska made the journey in 1901. The following excerpt is from her short story "How I Found America." In it, she shows how the dream often conflicted with the reality of life in the United States.

Vocabulary   Before you read the selection, find the meaning of these words in a dictionary: **rapture, oppressed, ghetto, fragrant, dingy.**

Steerage—dirty bundles—foul odors—seasick humanity—but I saw and heard nothing of the foulness and ugliness around me. I floated in showers of sunshine; visions upon visions of the new world opened before me.

From lips to lips flowed the golden legend of the golden country:

"In America you can say what you feel—you can voice your thoughts in the open streets without fear of a Cossack."*. . .

"Everybody is with everybody alike, in America. Christians and Jews are brothers together."

"An end to the worry for bread. An end to the fear of the bosses over you. Everybody can do what he wants with his life in America."

"There are no high or low in America. Even the President holds hands with Gedalyeh Mindel."†

_____
*Russian soldier

†A man from the family's village in Russia who had already come to the United States

"Plenty for all. Learning flows free like milk and honey."

"Learning flows free."

The words painted pictures in my mind. I saw before me free schools, free colleges, free libraries, where I could learn and learn and keep on learning.

In our village was a school, but only for Christian children. In the schools of America I'd lift up my head and laugh and dance—a child with other children. Like a bird in the air, from sky to sky, from star to star, I'd soar and soar.

"Land! Land!" came the joyous shout.

"America! We're in America!" cried my mother, almost smothering us in her rapture. . . .

Age-old visions sang themselves in me—songs of freedom of an oppressed people.

America!—America!

Between buildings that loomed like mountains, we struggled with our bundles, spreading around us the smell of the steerage. Up Broadway, under the bridge, and through the swarming streets of the ghetto, we followed Gedalyeh Mindel.

I looked about the narrow streets of squeezed-in stores and houses, ragged clothes, dirty bedding oozing out of the

Discussion Questions

1. What hardships of immigrants' lives in Europe are mentioned in "the golden legend of the golden country"? (Students might mention fear of Cossacks, not being able to own land, being persecuted for being a Jew, hunger, fear of the bosses.)

2. When she speaks of school, why does the narrator compare herself to a bird? (She believes that she will be free to soar intellectually.)

Historical Sidelight

German Jews already living in the United States were moved by the plight of the desperately poor Eastern European Jews who were beginning to settle on New York's Lower East Side. Among those who offered help was Lillian Wald, who established the Henry Street Settlement in 1893. At first intended to provide medical care, the settlement was soon a center of recreation and education. With the assistance of people like Louise Wald, the new immigrants rapidly adjusted to the demands of life in America.

Life in the "Golden Country" *Immigrant neighborhoods were often close-knit communities where people met to shop, play, or gossip. In this painting, George Benjamin Luks captures a lively New York street scene.* **Daily Life** *Compare this view with the one in the story.*

windows, ash-cans and garbage-cans cluttering the side-walks. A vague sadness pressed down my heart—the first doubt of America.

"Where are the green fields and open spaces in America?" cried my heart. "Where is the golden country of my dreams?"

A loneliness for the fragrant silence of the woods that lay beyond our mud hut welled up in my heart, a longing for the soft, responsive earth of our village streets. All about me was the hardness of brick and stone, the stinking smells of crowded poverty.

"Here's your house with separate rooms like in a palace." Gedalyeh Mindel flung open the door of a dingy, airless flat.

"Oi weh!" my mother cried in dismay. "Where's the sunshine in America?"

She went to the window and looked out at the blank wall of the next house. "Gottuniu! Like in a grave so dark . . ."

"It ain't so dark, it's only a little shady." Gedalyeh Mindel lighted the gas. . . .

Again the shadow fell over me, again the doubt of America!

In America were rooms without sunshine, rooms to sleep in, to eat in, to cook in, but without sunshine. And Gedalyeh Mindel was happy. Could I be satisfied with just a place to sleep and eat in, and a door to shut people out—to take the place of sunlight? Or would I always need the sunlight to be happy?

And where was there a place in America for me to play? I looked out into the alley below and saw pale-faced children scrambling in the gutter. "Where is America?" cried my heart.

Source: Anzia Yezierska, from *How I Found America* (Persea Books, New York, 1991).

THINKING ABOUT LITERATURE

1. What do the narrator and her family dream of finding in the United States?
2. What causes the narrator to doubt her dream of the "golden country"?
3. **CRITICAL THINKING** **Evaluating Information** (a) Which of the narrator's dreams about life in the United States were based on fact? (b) Which were false? Explain.

ACTIVITY

Create a two-panel cartoon contrasting the dream and the reality of immigrant life in the United States in the late 1800s. The first panel should show how immigrants imagined life in the "golden country." The second panel should show the hardships many immigrants experienced in their adopted land.

Unit 7
A New Role in the World

Unit Focus

Have students examine the painting on these pages — *Flags, Tremont Street, Boston,* by Dodge MacKnight—and read its caption. As students consider the feelings of patriotism and nationalism that the painting depicts, read aloud the three chapter summaries. Ask questions such as the following to stimulate discussion.

1. (a) What does the painting suggest about the way that many Americans felt about themselves? (b) When are those same kinds of feelings shown today?

2. People usually benefit from advances in technology. What kinds of problems might advances in technology cause?

3. Do you think that the reasons for the United States expansion overseas were the same as the reasons for expansion across the North American continent had been? Explain.

4. (a) Why might the United States become involved in a war that was taking place across the ocean? (b) With which European nations did the United States ally itself?

5. A New Role in the World is the title of this unit. Based on the information in the three chapter summaries, how do you think the United States in 1919 differed from the United States in 1876?

Connections With Art
Background

Dodge MacKnight (1860–1950) was born in Rhode Island. As a teenager, he was apprenticed to a theatrical set designer. In 1883, he went to Paris to study with Fernand Cormon, the artist who taught such masters as Henri Matisse, Henri de Toulouse-Lautrec, and Vincent van Gogh. Although Europe — especially Paris — became his home for the next several years, MacKnight began to exhibit his work in Boston in 1888. He returned to the United States in 1897, settling on Cape Cod.

UNIT 7

A New Role in the World

> **CHAPTER 21**
> **Progressives and Reformers**
> (1876–1914)
>
> A reform movement swept the country as Americans struggled with problems created by an industrial age.
>
> ....
>
> **CHAPTER 22**
> **Expanding Overseas**
> (1865–1916)
>
> After years of expanding across the continent, Americans sought to extend their territory and power overseas.
>
> ....
>
> **CHAPTER 23**
> **World War I**
> (1914–1919)
>
> Although it tried to remain neutral, the United States finally entered World War I on the side of the Allies.

At first, most critics did not like MacKnight's work; they thought his colors were too bold, even savage. In time, however, Mac-Knight became so popular that the paintings exhibited in his annual shows sold out within an hour. *Flags, Tremont Street, Boston,* which he completed in 1918, today is part of the collection of the Museum of Fine Arts, Boston.

Connections With Art
Activity

Ask questions such as the following to stimulate discussion about the painting.

1. (a) Which detail in the painting catches your eye first? (b) Why might Dodge MacKnight have made the flags so big and the people so small?

2. (a) How do you think the people in the crowd felt that day? (b) What might the soldiers have been thinking?

3. The painting is impressionistic in style: There are no fine details, only shapes and colors that suggest details. What might Mac-Knight have been saying by using that style?

As Americans looked beyond their shores, the United States began to assume a new role in world affairs. Here, the city of Boston celebrates the return of victorious American troops from World War I.

Connections With the World
Activity

Have students preview the world events on the chapter time lines (pages 592–593, 620–621, and 646–647). Call on volunteers to use the world map on pages 890–891 to locate each nation or area mentioned. Then ask the class: What was going on in the United States at the same time as each world event? Which of the world events suggest that the United States might want to take "a new role in the world"? Explain.

Linking Past and Present
Activity

In this unit, students will see how the United States gradually took on a more complex role as a world power — namely, that of "international police officer." Have students create a preliminary definition of that term. Then ask: Did the United States pull back from the role of "international police officer" after World War I? How do you know? Has the United States exercised that role anywhere in the world in your lifetime or in the lifetime of your parents? Explain.

Lessons	Teaching Resources
1 Early Reforms **Objectives** 1. Explain why reformers wanted to end the spoils system. 2. Identify what the Civil Service Commission did. 3. Describe how Congress tried to regulate big business.	**Lesson Planner** Cooperative Learning, p. 129 **Student Study Guide** Section 1 Study Guide, p. 159
2 The Progressive Movement **Objectives** 1. Describe how bosses controlled city governments. 2. Describe how muckrakers influenced public opinion. 3. Identify the goals of the Progressives.	**Lesson Planner** Cooperative Learning, p. 130 **Student Study Guide** Section 2 Study Guide, p. 160 **Chapter Resources Binder, Unit 7** *Critical Thinking* Concept Mapping, p. 3 **Interdisciplinary Connections:** The Progressive Spirit ■ *Arts* Muckrakers With Cameras, p. 122 ■ *Sciences* A Scientific View of Education, p. 123 ■ *Geography* National Parks, p. 124 ■ *World* An Astonishing Anti-Imperialist, p. 125 ■ *Economics* Progressive Publishing, p. 126
3 Presidents Back Progressive Goals **Objectives** 1. Identify the Progressive reforms that Theodore Roosevelt supported. 2. Identify Woodrow Wilson's New Freedom program. 3. Describe how big business was regulated during the Progressive Era.	**Lesson Planner** Cooperative Learning, p. 131 **Student Study Guide** Section 3 Study Guide, p. 161 **Chapter Resources Binder, Unit 7** *Geography in History* Preserving the Public's Land, pp. 5–6
4 Women in the Progressive Era **Objectives** 1. Identify the goals that women pursued in the Progressive Era. 2. Identify the methods that women used to achieve their goals. 3. Identify the successes that women enjoyed in the Progressive Era.	**Lesson Planner** Cooperative Learning, p. 132 **Student Study Guide** Section 4 Study Guide, p. 162 **Chapter Resources Binder, Unit 7** *History Through Literature* The Story of an Hour, p. 4 *Skill Application* Reading a Political Cartoon, p. 2 **Our Multicultural Heritage** *Biography* Belva Ann Bennett Lockwood, Lawyer and Candidate, p. 61
5 Minorities Seek Equality and Justice **Objectives** 1. Identify problems that African Americans faced in the Progressive Era. 2. Describe how African American leaders tried to fight discrimination. 3. Identify what life was like for Asian Americans, Mexican Americans, and Native Americans during the Progressive Era.	**Lesson Planner** Cooperative Learning, p. 133 **Student Study Guide** Section 5 Study Guide, p. 163 **Our Multicultural Heritage** *Biography* Mary Church Terrell, Voice of Justice, p. 62 *Milestone* Working for Mexican American Rights, p. 63

Multimedia Resources	Additional Resources	Chapter-Level Resources
CD–ROM *Presidents* James A. Garfield; Chester A. Arthur; Grover Cleveland; Benjamin Harrison		**Lesson Planner** Activity Based, pp. 134–135 **Student Study Guide** Chapter 21 Study Guide, pp. 164–165 **Chapter Resources Binder** **Unit 7** Vocabulary Building, p. 1 Chapter Test A, pp. 7–9 Chapter Test B, pp. 10–12 Illustration Master, p. 13 Extra Unit Questions, pp. 43–45 **English Guided Reading** Guided Reading, pp. 41–42 **Spanish Resources**
Transparencies *Interdisciplinary Connections* Government Reform, p. B-73 **CD-ROM** *History Makers* Ida M. Tarbell **Videotapes/Videodiscs** *United States History Video Collection* Muckrakers and Bosses, Vol. 14, Ch. 13	**Voices of Freedom** Steffens Calls on the Boss of Philadelphia, pp. 176–177 La Follette Uses Scientific Methods, pp. 180–181 **Customized Reader** Campaign to Improve Sanitary Conditions in Idaho, article VIB-2	
CD-ROM *Presidents* William McKinley; Theodore Roosevelt; William Howard Taft; Woodrow Wilson **Videotapes/Videodiscs** *United States History Video Collection* Roosevelt and Wilson, Vol. 14, Ch. 19; Pollution and the Destruction of Nature, Vol. 11, Ch. 28	**Voices of Freedom** A Candid View of Theodore Roosevelt, p. 182 Why Taft Had Trouble, pp. 184–185 Ringside at the Republican Convention, pp. 185–186 A Contemporary Looks at Wilson, pp. 186–187	**Computer Test Bank** Chapter Tests A and B Extra Unit Questions **Guided Reading Audiotapes** Side 8 **CD-ROM** *Time Tour* Progressives and Reformers (1876–1914) in A New Role in the World
CD-ROM *Face the Issues* Women's Suffrage **Videotapes/Videodiscs** *United States History Video Collection* Women Take the Lead, Vol. 14, Ch. 7; Women Suffragists, Vol. 14, Ch. 25	**Voices of Freedom** Suffragists on a Hunger Strike, pp. 189–190	
CD-ROM *History Makers* W.E.B. DuBois **Videotapes/Videodiscs** *United States History Video Collection* Freedom? Whose Freedom?, Vol. 14, Ch. 22	**Voices of Freedom** The Need for Practical Skills, pp. 155–156 Du Bois Emphasizes Self-Respect, p. 157 Launching the NAACP, pp. 178–179	

CHAPTER **21**

Progressives and Reformers

(1876–1914)

CHAPTER OUTLINE

1 Early Reforms

2 The Progressive Movement

3 Presidents Back Progressive Goals

4 Women in the Progressive Era

5 Minorities Seek Equality and Justice

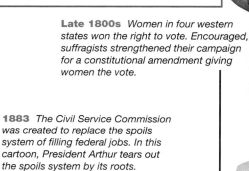

Late 1800s *Women in four western states won the right to vote. Encouraged, suffragists strengthened their campaign for a constitutional amendment giving women the vote.*

1883 *The Civil Service Commission was created to replace the spoils system of filling federal jobs. In this cartoon, President Arthur tears out the spoils system by its roots.*

1875	1880	1885	1890	1895

 WORLD EVENT
1875 Japan reforms its law courts

 WORLD EVENT
1893 New Zealand gives vote to women

592 • Chapter 21

Chapter Time Line
Critical Thinking

The time line illustrations, captions, and World Event notes relate to three broad areas of reform in the United States and abroad. During a class discussion of the time line, have students identify which pieces of information relate to reforms in government, which relate to reforms in women's rights, and which

relate to reforms in the treatment of consumers. When students identify several pieces of information that relate to one area of reform, encourage them to look for and comment on possible cause-and-effect relationships among them.

Students Acquiring English
Activity

Students who are acquiring English can benefit from understanding word relationships. Encourage students to use each form of the following words in a sentence: *politics/politician/political, reform/reformer, corrupt/corruption, crusade/crusader, labor/laborer, industry/industrial, economy/economic, competition/competitor, conserve/conservation.*

Chapter Setting

Publisher Samuel McClure handed Lincoln Steffens, a reforming journalist from New York, a railroad ticket. "Get out of here," he told the eager young reporter. "Travel, go—somewhere."

Steffens went to St. Louis. From there, he sent back shocking stories. The St. Louis city government was for sale. Corrupt politicians had even set prices for different favors, Steffens told readers of *McClure's Magazine:*

66There was a price for a grain elevator. . . a street improvement cost so much. . . . As there was a scale for favorable legislation, so there was one for defeating bills. It made a difference in the price if there was opposition, and it made a difference whether the privilege asked was [legal] or not.99

Steffens found similar corruption in other cities. Everywhere, politicians were taking bribes and payoffs. In 1904, Steffens published *The Shame of the Cities.* The book became a bestseller, and its revelations spurred a nationwide reform movement.

The rapid growth of cities and industry had created serious problems. By the late 1800s, reformers were demanding change— from better government to laws protecting children. As the new century dawned, new reforms helped to reshape government, the economy, and society.

ACTIVITY List reforms the United States should focus on as it enters the 2000s. Then create a poster to enlist support for one of the reforms.

Chapter Resources

English Guided Reading Duplicate and distribute to SAE students the Chapter 21 Guided Reading worksheet on pages 41–42 in the English Guided Reading section of the *Chapter Resources* binder. Students who have difficulty reading also might benefit from using this worksheet. Have students complete the worksheet before they begin reading. You might pair a more fluent student or a student who is a stronger reader with each SAE student to review. (Reteaching/Easy)

Spanish Resources See the Spanish Resources section of the *Chapter Resources* binder.

ACTIVITY

Guided Instruction Before students create their lists, have the class brainstorm for areas of social policy in which they believe reform is needed (for example, education, health care, job training, or environmental protection). Then ask individual students to identify specific reforms needed in one or more areas and the governmental level (local, state, or national) at which reform would be most effective. Before students create posters, suggest they choose slogans that capture the meaning and spirit of the reform message that they wish to convey. Encourage students to create artwork as appropriate.

ROOSEVELT'S GUIDING SPIRIT

1901 *After President McKinley was assassinated, Theodore Roosevelt became President. Here, the spirit of the dead President guides the young Roosevelt.*

1906 *Congress passed the Pure Food and Drug Act. The law was meant to protect the public from false advertising and from dangerous and useless medicines.*

1913 *Woodrow Wilson was inaugurated as President. In his program—the New Freedom—Wilson pledged to control the unfair practices of big businesses.*

1900	1905	1910	1915	1920

WORLD EVENT
1909 German universities admit women

WORLD EVENT
1919 Great Britain gives vote to women

Chapter 21 • **593**

Linking Past and Present
Activity

Explain that Lincoln Steffens was a pioneer reporter in the field that has become known as investigative journalism. Investigative journalists combine research and traditional reporting techniques with a specific point of view. Their purpose is usually to expose corruption, injustice, and abuse in society.

Have each student find two examples of current investigative reporting. One should be drawn from newspapers or magazines. The other can be from radio or television. (In the latter case, especially, students should be careful to distinguish between sensational stories and true investigative reporting.) Students should summarize the facts, explain the conclusions, and indicate whether the reporter gave a fair assessment.

Bell Ringer

Ask students to discuss ways in which individuals obtain various jobs in local, state, and federal government.

Lesson Plan

1. **Focus** In this section, students learn about efforts to curb corruption in government and business during the late 1800s.
2. **Instruct** Ask students to imagine that they are reformers living in the late 1800s. Have half the class work in small groups to write speeches in favor of setting up a civil service. Have the other half write speeches in favor of regulating big business.
3. **Close** To close the lesson, have students turn the headings for the subsections into questions and then answer them.

Lesson Planner

For a developed **Cooperative Learning** lesson plan, see the *Lesson Planner,* page 129.

CD-ROM

Presidents Access the biography of James A. Garfield from the American Heritage® *History of the United States* CD-ROM.

1
Early Reforms

FIND OUT

- Why did reformers want to end the spoils system?
- What did the Civil Service Commission do?
- How did Congress try to regulate big business?

VOCABULARY patronage, civil service

President James Garfield stood in the train station talking to his Secretary of State. It was early July, and Garfield was leaving Washington for a vacation. All of a sudden, Charles Guiteau, a disappointed office seeker, leaped from the shadows. He pulled out a pistol and fired at Garfield. A bullet lodged in the President's spine.

Garfield clung to life through the summer. Then on September 19, 1881, he died. The murder outraged Americans. It also focused attention on the spoils system, a practice that reformers wanted to end.

Taming the Spoils System

Since the days of Andrew Jackson, the spoils system had grown. When a new President took office, thousands of job seekers swarmed into Washington. They sought government jobs as rewards for their political support.

Giving jobs to loyal supporters is called **patronage.** Patronage existed at the national, state, and local levels. By handing out jobs, politicians cemented ties with their supporters and increased their control of government.

Patronage often led to corruption. Some officeholders helped themselves to public money. Many people appointed to government jobs had no skills for those jobs. One man who got a job as a court reporter in New York could not read or write.

Efforts at reform. Calls for reform in the spoils system slowly brought change. In 1877, Rutherford B. Hayes was elected President. Hayes took steps toward ending the spoils system. For example, he refused to appoint his own supporters to office unless they were qualified for the job.

James Garfield, a Republican like Hayes, entered the White House in 1881. He, too, tried to limit the spoils system. Garfield called for reform of the civil service. The **civil service** includes all federal jobs except elected positions and the armed forces.

Garfield thought that people should get government jobs on the basis of merit, or ability, rather than as rewards for political support. Garfield was shot by an angry office seeker before he could put his reform into practice. His death led to new efforts to reform the spoils system.

Exams for federal jobs. Upon Garfield's death, Vice President Chester Arthur became President. As a New York politician, Arthur had used the spoils system. But as President, he worked with Congress to tame it.

In 1883, Congress set up the *Civil Service Commission.* The commission was responsible for filling jobs in the federal government. It was made up of both Democrats and Republicans. The commission set up exams for federal jobs. Those who scored highest got the positions.

At first, the Civil Service Commission controlled only a few federal jobs. Under pressure from reformers, however, later Presidents added more jobs to the civil service list. By 1900, the commission controlled about 40 percent of all federal jobs.

Regulating Big Business

In 1877, Collis Huntington, builder of the Central Pacific Railroad, had a problem.

Historical Sidelight
Background

In the two-and-a-half months that President Garfield lingered, a team of surgeons performed three operations to drain the wound and clean out bone fragments. They also frequently examined the wound with bare fingers and unsterilized instruments. As a result, blood poisoning set in. This blood poisoning was the immediate cause of Garfield's death.

Charles Guiteau, the assassin, felt that his actions would do more than just compensate for his disappointment. He chose a .44 British Bulldog—an expensive pistol—for the job because he felt that it would look good in a museum. On the day of the assassination, Guiteau wrote, "The President's tragic death was a sad necessity, but it will . . . save the Republic." Later, on the day of Garfield's death, Guiteau wrote to Chester A. Arthur, "Never think of Garfield's removal as murder. It was an act of God, resulting from a political necessity for which he was responsible."

Linking Past and Present
Activity

Approximately 100 years after the reforms of the late 1800s, American presidents began calling for reforms of the federal government and civil service regulations and practices, based on a popular perception of waste and inefficiency in government. Have students research government reform issues of the 1980s and 1990s and compare them with those of a century before. Use their findings as a basis for class discussion.

Competing for Jobs *Civil service exams were meant to ensure that government jobs were awarded to those best qualified to do them. The women in this 1909 photograph are taking the test to become stenographers.* **Linking Past and Present** *What skills might government workers need today?*

 CD-ROM

A competitor had placed a bill before Congress. The bill was aimed at breaking Huntington's control of rail routes to southern California. To Huntington, the solution was simple: Bribe some members of Congress and kill the bill. "It costs money to fix things," he explained. Many other business leaders of the era agreed.

The behavior of men like Huntington convinced many Americans that big businesses controlled the government. Public outcry against railroads and other monopolies grew in the late 1800s.

Interstate Commerce Act. The government responded by taking steps to regulate railroads and other large businesses. In 1887, President Grover Cleveland signed the Interstate Commerce Act. The new law forbade unfair practices such as pools and rebates. (See page 538.)

The act also set up the **Interstate Commerce Commission,** or ICC, to oversee the railroad industry. At first, the ICC was weak.

⭐ *Our Common Heritage*
In the late 1800s, Americans adopted a Japanese term, "taikun," meaning great lord. They began to refer to powerful business leaders as tycoons.

In court challenges, most judges ruled in favor of the railroads.

To railroad owners, the ICC was not much of a threat. Richard Olney, an attorney for one of the owners, explained:

&& The Commission...satisfies the popular clamor for a government supervision of the railroads, at the same time that that supervision is almost entirely [ineffective]. . . . It thus

Industry Buys Power *In this cartoon, a railroad tycoon casts his giant shadow over Congress. He says, "The idea!—thinking of restraining me when I practically own this place."* **Citizenship** *In the cartoon, what weapons does the government have to cut the tycoon down to size? What weapons does the industrialist have?*

Connections With Civics
Background

At the time that Huntington made his statement, senators were still chosen by state legislatures. (They would not be chosen by direct popular election until 1913, with the ratification of the Seventeenth Amendment.) In 1877, it was not unusual for state legislatures to "sell" Senate seats to the highest bidder.

Linking Past and Present
Background

The act that established the ICC affected interstate railroad operations but not railroad operations within states. When this act first went into effect, the number of members of the commission was set at five; later, it was changed to seven, then nine, and then—in 1920—eleven. In 1983, the number of members was reduced back to five.

The power of the ICC has grown to include regulation of trucks and buses (1935), barges (1940) and freight forwarders (1942). It also regulated telephone, telegraph, and cable communication from 1910 to 1934 (after which time the Federal Communications Commission took over).

President Ronald Reagan felt that deregulation had made the ICC unnecessary, and several times during his term he tried to abolish the commission. Each time, however, Congress blocked his proposal.

Student Study Guide

Section 1 Study Guide Have students use the Section 1 Study Guide on page 159 of the *Student Study Guide* to review and reinforce the content of this section. (Reteaching/Average)

ACTIVITY

Guided Instruction Before students draft their news reports, have them answer *Who, What, Where, When, Why,* and *How* questions about the Civil Service Commission. Because the activity specifies television news, encourage students to think visually as they choose details. You might have students combine their results for a classroom television news program.

Section 2
pp. 596–601

Bell Ringer

Write the word *Progressive* on the chalkboard. Ask students to explain in their own words what they think it means.

Lesson Plan

1. Focus By the early 1900s, muckrakers were spurring many efforts at reform. Many of these efforts, aimed at corrupt local governments and unethical businesses, led to the Progressive Era. In this section, students examine some changes implemented in government and business during this period.

---

becomes a sort of barrier between railroad corporations and the people and a sort of protection against hasty and crude legislation hostile to railroad interests. **99**

Still, even though the Commission was weak at first, at least Congress had showed that it was ready to regulate big business. Later, it passed laws to make the ICC more effective.

Sherman Antitrust Act. In 1888, President Cleveland lost his bid for reelection. Benjamin Harrison became President. In 1890, Harrison signed the ***Sherman Antitrust Act.*** The act prohibited trusts or other businesses from limiting competition.

The Sherman Antitrust Act sounded uncompromising, but enforcing it proved difficult. Trusts used the courts to block enforcement. There, judges interpreted the act in favor of business. Instead of regulating trusts, the Sherman Antitrust Act was used to stop labor unions. (See page 545.) As the reform spirit spread, however, courts began to use the Sherman Act against monopolies.

SECTION 1 REVIEW

1. **Identify:** (a) Civil Service Commission, (b) Interstate Commerce Commission, (c) Sherman Antitrust Act.
2. **Define:** (a) patronage, (b) civil service.
3. (a) Why did reformers oppose the spoils system? (b) What did they want in its place?
4. (a) Why did Congress create the ICC? (b) Was the ICC effective? Explain.
5. **CRITICAL THINKING Synthesizing Information** Why do you think early efforts to regulate big business had little success?

ACTIVITY Writing to Learn
Write a television news report about the law that set up the Civil Service Commission.

---

596 • Chapter 21

2
The Progressive Movement

FIND OUT
- How did bosses control city governments?
- How did muckrakers influence public opinion?
- What were the goals of the Progressives?

VOCABULARY muckraker, public interest, primary, initiative, referendum, recall

Joseph Folk, newly elected city prosecutor of St. Louis, was furious. Folk had won office with the help of local politicians. After the election, they ordered him to hire men he felt were dishonest.

"I and my office, the criminal law, was to be run by—criminals!" he complained to reporter Lincoln Steffens. Folk fought back, leading a crusade against dishonest politicians and businessmen. Elsewhere, other reformers fought to oust corrupt politicians and to give voters greater power.

Reforming City Governments

How had city governments become so corrupt? Growing cities needed many improvements, such as new sewers, better garbage collection, and more roads. In many cities, politicians traded these jobs for money. In some places, bribes and corruption became a way of life.

Boss rule. Powerful politicians, known as "bosses," came to rule many cities. They controlled all work done in the city and demanded payoffs from businesses. Often, bosses did not hold office. Instead, they worked behind the scenes to influence officeholders.

Connections With Economics
Background

Senator John Sherman, for whom the Sherman Antitrust Act is named, was a financier and the younger brother of Union General William Tecumseh Sherman. For many years, he served on the Senate Committee on Finance and played a major role in formulating fiscal policy during the Civil War and Reconstruction. Sherman also served as Secretary of the Treasury under Hayes, but he returned to the Senate at the end of that President's term.

Answers to Section 1 Review

1. (a) Civil Service Commission, p. 594, (b) Interstate Commerce Commission, p. 595, (c) Sherman Antitrust Act, p. 596
2. (a) patronage, p. 594, (b) civil service, p. 594
3. (a) Reformers thought that the spoils system led to corruption and to incompetent people holding office. (b) a civil service system based on merit

4. (a) to oversee railroads and enforce the Interstate Commerce Act (b) Possible Answer: No; the courts favored big business over the ICC.
5. Possible Answer: The courts sided with big business in opposing government regulation of business. Furthermore, the power and wealth of big business opened the door to corruption of government officials.

City bosses were popular with the poor, especially with immigrants. Because the poor always needed help, it was easy for bosses to win them over. Bosses provided jobs. They made loans to the needy and gave them extra coal in winter. They handed out turkeys at Thanksgiving and organized dances in the parks. In exchange, the poor voted for the boss or his candidate on election day.

The Tweed ring. In New York City, Boss William Tweed carried corruption to new heights. During the 1860s and 1870s, Tweed cheated New York out of more than $100 million. Reformers tried to have him jailed. Journalists exposed his wrongdoings. In his cartoons in *Harper's Weekly,* Thomas Nast showed Tweed as a vulture destroying the city.

Tweed hated Nast's cartoons. Tweed's supporters might be unable to read, but they could understand pictures. Tweed offered Nast $500,000 to go to Europe and "study art." Nast turned down the bribe and kept up his attacks.

Faced with prison, Tweed fled to Spain. There, local police arrested him when they recognized him from a Nast cartoon. When Tweed died in jail in 1878, thousands of poor New Yorkers mourned his passing.

Good government leagues. Reformers targeted bosses like William Tweed in their campaigns. They formed good government leagues. Their goal was to replace corrupt officials with honest leaders.

Reformers met with some success. The good government league in Minneapolis sent a corrupt mayor and his henchmen to jail. In Cleveland, reformers elected Tom Johnson as mayor. Johnson improved garbage collection and sewage systems in the city. He also set up services to help the poor.

Rousing Public Opinion

To bring about change, reformers had to ignite public anger. A major weapon was the press.

Muckrakers. Newspaper reporters went to the slums. They described burned-out tenements and exposed the corruption that had led to inadequate fire protection. They talked to mothers whose babies were dying of tuberculosis. Photographers such as Jacob Riis provided vivid views of the horrors of slum life.

These crusading journalists became known as **muckrakers.** People said they raked the dirt, or muck, and exposed it to public view.

Lincoln Steffens, the reporter you read about at the beginning of the chapter, was a muckraker. His stories about corrupt city governments showed the need for change. Ida Tarbell, another muckraker, targeted big business. In a series of articles, she revealed unfair practices used by the Standard Oil

Child in the Slums *The wistful eyes of this child emphasized the need for change to many who saw the photograph. He probably lived in a dirty, overcrowded tenement building.* **Daily Life** *How do you think photographs like this one encouraged reform?*

A Muckraking Magazine *Some of the best muckraking journalists wrote for McClure's Magazine. Among them was Ida M. Tarbell, at left, who exposed the unfair practices used by John D. Rockefeller's Standard Oil Company.* **Linking Past and Present** *How do present-day "muckrakers" expose conditions that need reform?*

Company. Her stories led to demands for tighter controls on trusts.

The Jungle. Even more shocking was a novel by Upton Sinclair called **The Jungle.** The novel revealed gruesome details about the meatpacking industry in Chicago. Although the book was fiction, it was based on things Sinclair had seen himself. In one passage, he described the rats in the meatpacking houses:

> 66 These rats were nuisances, and the packers would put poisoned bread out for them: they would die, and then rats, bread, and meat would go into the hoppers together. This is no fairy story and no joke. . . there were things that went into the sausage in comparison with which a poisoned rat was a tidbit. 99

Citizens demand reform. Sinclair wrote *The Jungle* to show the misery of workers in the meatpacking houses. Readers, however, were much more upset about what went into their breakfast sausages. "I aimed at the public's heart and by accident I hit it in the stomach," Sinclair declared. The outcry led Congress to pass laws to improve meat inspection. (See page 604.)

Muckrakers helped change public opinion. For years, middle-class people had ignored corruption and the need for reform. When they saw how corrupt politicians and businesses menaced the nation, they joined with muckrakers to demand change.

Progressives in Action

By 1900, reformers were calling themselves Progressives. By that, they meant they were forward-thinking people who wanted to improve American life. They won many changes in the period from 1898 to 1917. This period is often called the **Progressive Era.**

Progressive beliefs. Progressives were never a single group with a single aim. They backed many different causes. What united them was their faith that the problems of society could be solved.

Progressives believed that the **public interest,** or the good of the people, should guide government actions. The public interest, they said, must not be sacrificed to the greed of a few trusts and city bosses.

Many women played leading roles in the Progressive Era. A new view of women had emerged in the mid-1800s. Many Americans came to believe that women were morally superior to men. In a world full of corruption, they felt that women had the moral force to bring about change. This view encouraged millions of women to work for reform.

"Battling Bob" and the Wisconsin Idea. Among the leading Progressives was Robert La Follette. In 1900, he was elected governor of Wisconsin. Nicknamed "Battling

CONNECTIONS

ARTS | SCIENCES | GEOGRAPHY | WORLD | ECONOMICS | CIVICS

"Golden Rule" Jones: Crusading Mayor of Toledo, Ohio

Samuel M. Jones's ideas about business and government seem ordinary today. In the late 1800s, however, they were revolutionary.

Jones was the owner of a successful factory in Toledo, Ohio. In 1895, he shocked his business friends by announcing that from then on he would run his factory "upon the basis of the Golden Rule." That is, he would follow the religious teaching, "Do unto others as you would have them do unto you."

Jones began by cutting the workday from ten to eight hours. He raised the minimum wage from $1.25 to $2.00 per day. He promised paid vacations and Christmas bonuses and gave his employees shares of stock in the company. He opened an employee restaurant and even created a park where workers could spend their lunch hours.

In time, "Golden Rule" Jones, as he was now known, decided to extend his reform efforts to government. In 1897, he ran for mayor of Toledo. Campaigning for "good government" and lower streetcar fares, Jones won a narrow victory.

As mayor, Jones set out to end corruption and greed in city government. He targeted the huge profits earned by public utilities such as the gas and electric companies and the street railway. He called for stronger regulation and public ownership of these vital services. He also raised taxes to provide improved police and fire protection.

Jones's policies angered Toledo's business leaders. At best, they showed he was not practical, they said. Some thought his attempts to apply the Golden Rule to politics proved he was a madman.

THE **RULE** THAT *GOVERNS THIS FACTORY.* "Therefore Whatsoever, Ye Would That Men Should Do Unto You Do Ye Even So Unto Them."

The Golden Rule

By the next election, Jones's enemies had united against him. Even his own party would not nominate him. Refusing to give up, Jones ran as an independent candidate.

On election day, Jones won by a landslide. As one newspaper put it, Jones's ideas appealed to "a class of voters who had nothing to lose and everything to gain." Jones explained it this way: "The people kept their minds on one great question: Shall we have the Golden Rule of all the people or the rule of cash by a few people?"

■ How did "Golden Rule" Jones reflect the Progressive spirit?

ACTIVITY

Create two political cartoons about "Golden Rule" Jones from opposing points of view. One cartoon should support his policies. The other cartoon should be critical of them.

Golden Rule Park

Answer to Caption

A graduated income tax required the wealthy to pay taxes at a higher rate than the poor or the middle class.

Voices of Freedom

Primary Source You might assign selection 6-4, La Follette Uses Scientific Methods, on pages 180–181 of *Voices of Freedom*. In this selection, La Follette describes how the Railroad Rate Commission carried out its job and reports on the results of its work. (Enrichment/Average)

Transparencies

Interdisciplinary Connections Use the transparency Government Reform on page B-73 of *American History Transparencies*. Teaching suggestions can be found on page B-23. (Enrichment/Average)

Bob," La Follette could stir up a crowd. "The will of the people shall be the law of the land," was his motto.

La Follette introduced a program of Progressive reforms in Wisconsin. For example, he lowered railroad rates. The result was increased rail traffic, which helped both railroad owners and customers.

Progressives from other states visited Wisconsin to study La Follette's system. Before long, voters in California, Indiana, Arkansas, Oregon, and New York were talking about the **Wisconsin Idea.** They, too, elected Progressive governors who introduced far-reaching changes.

The will of the people. Progressives believed that the people would make the right decisions if given the chance. As a result, they pressed for reforms to give voters more power. Among them were the primary, initiative, referendum, and recall.

Since Andrew Jackson's time, political parties had held conventions to pick a candidate for President. But party leaders still picked candidates for local and state offices. Progressives urged parties to hold primaries before a general election. In a **primary,** voters choose their party's candidate from among several people. Wisconsin was the first state to adopt the primary, in 1903. By 1917, all but four states had done so.

Until the early 1900s, only members of a state legislature could introduce bills. Progressives urged states to adopt the initiative. The **initiative** gave voters the right to put a bill directly before the state legislature. All they had to do was get enough people to sign a petition in favor of the bill.

The **referendum** went a step further. It gave voters the power to make a bill become law. If enough voters signed a referendum petition, the people of the state voted on the bill at the next election. With voter approval, the bill became state law.

Another Progressive measure was the recall. The **recall** allowed voters to remove an elected official from office. This gave ordinary people a chance to get rid of corrupt officials.

Other Progressive Reforms

Progressives fought for other changes, too. They favored lowering tariffs on imported goods. If American industry had to compete against foreign imports, they argued, consumers would benefit from lower prices.

Most Progressives also supported a graduated income tax. The tax would make up for money the government lost by lowering the tariff. A graduated tax meant that the wealthy would have to pay taxes at a higher rate than the poor or the middle class.

In 1895, the Supreme Court ruled that an income tax was unconstitutional. In response, Progressives campaigned to amend

---

Paying the Tax Collector *After the Sixteenth Amendment was ratified, Congress passed an income tax law. People who made more than $3,000 a year had to pay a tax of 1 percent. This cartoon shows a smooth ride for the amendment after years of debate.* **Economics** *Why did Progressives favor a graduated income tax?*

Connections With Art
Activity

Use a magazine or newspaper drawing to show students the Republican elephant and the Democratic donkey as they are traditionally depicted. Divide the class into three groups. Assign students in each group one of the following: (a) muckrakers, (b) Progressives, (c) political bosses. Have individuals choose an animal that symbolizes the assigned subject. Then have them draw a cartoon that illustrates the historical subjects' characteristics through emphasis or exaggeration of particular physical features. Ask volunteers to share their drawings with the class and explain the symbolism. Combine the individual projects into a booklet or display them on a bulletin board.

Connections With Local Civics
Activity

If your state has the initiative, the referendum, and/or the recall, have students research a recent case where voters used one of these powers. Ask them to present oral reports explaining what happened, when, and why. If your state does not have any of the three, ask students to research a recent issue in which voters might have used one of them if it had been available, and to explain why.

the Constitution. In 1909, Congress passed the *Sixteenth Amendment.* It gave Congress the power to impose an income tax. By 1913, three fourths of the states had ratified the amendment.

Progressives worked for another amendment. Since 1789, senators had been elected by state legislatures. Business leaders or others with special interests sometimes bribed lawmakers to vote for certain candidates. Progressives wanted to end such abuses by having voters elect senators directly. In 1912, Congress approved the *Seventeenth Amendment,* allowing for the direct election of senators. A year later, it was ratified.

SECTION 2 REVIEW

1. **Identify:** (a) William Tweed, (b) *The Jungle,* (c) Progressive Era, (d) Wisconsin Idea, (e) Sixteenth Amendment, (f) Seventeenth Amendment.
2. **Define:** (a) muckraker, (b) public interest, (c) primary, (d) initiative, (e) referendum, (f) recall.
3. (a) Why were city governments corrupt? (b) What was the goal of the good government leagues?
4. How did muckrakers help change public attitudes toward corruption?
5. (a) Why was Robert La Follette a hero of the Progressives? (b) How did he influence reformers in other parts of the country?
6. **CRITICAL THINKING Defending a Position** Do you agree with the Progressives that voters will make the right decision if given the chance? Why or why not?

 Writing to Learn
Write a dialogue between a poor person who supported Boss Tweed and a muckraker who wanted to expose Tweed's corrupt practices. Have a dramatic reading of your dialogue in class.

 3

Presidents Back Progressive Goals

FIND OUT

- What Progressive reforms did Theodore Roosevelt support?
- What was Woodrow Wilson's New Freedom program?
- How was big business regulated during the Progressive Era?

VOCABULARY trustbuster, conservation

The Republicans needed a reform-minded Vice President to run with William McKinley in 1900. They offered the job to Theodore Roosevelt. Roosevelt did not want the job. "I will not accept under any circumstances," he wrote.

In the end, Roosevelt accepted the nomination. "I do not expect to go any further in politics," he noted. A year later, McKinley was shot and Roosevelt became President.

By 1901, Progressives were having success in reforming local and state politics. With Theodore Roosevelt in the White House, they hoped to make headway in national reforms.

A Reforming President

In 1896, voters elected Republican William McKinley as President. In his first term, McKinley's popularity soared as business boomed. The terrible depression that had plagued the nation since 1893 had finally ended. As business expanded, unemployment fell.

By 1900, McKinley realized that the Progressives were gaining strength. With this in

---

 Chapter Resources

Critical Thinking Duplicate and distribute the worksheet, Concept Mapping, from Unit 7, page 3, of the *Chapter Resources* binder. The worksheet encourages students to support ideas with relevant details while reviewing key reforms discussed in this section. (Enrichment/Average)

Student Study Guide

Section 2 Study Guide Have students use the Section 2 Study Guide on page 160 of the *Student Study Guide* to review and reinforce the content of this section. (Reteaching/Average)

ACTIVITY

Guided Instruction Students might prepare for this activity by tape-recording unrehearsed interviews with each other "in character." Encourage several dramatic readings in class, and follow them up with a class review of the rise and fall of the Tweed ring.

Section 3 pp. 601–607

Bell Ringer

Have students spend three to five minutes freewriting about the term *big business.* Have students save their responses and see if they change after the class has read Section 3.

Answers to Section 2 Review

1. (a) William Tweed, p. 597, (b) *The Jungle,* p. 598, (c) Progressive Era, p. 598, (d) Wisconsin Idea, p. 600, (e) Sixteenth Amendment, p. 601, (f) Seventeenth Amendment, p. 601
2. (a) muckraker, p. 597, (b) public interest, p. 598, (c) primary, p. 600, (d) initiative, p. 600, (e) referendum, p. 600, (f) recall, p. 600
3. (a) There were many jobs to be done, and many politicians who would accept bribes in order to give out the jobs. (b) to replace corrupt officials with honest ones

4. Muckrakers wrote articles exposing corruption that middle-class readers could not ignore.
5. (a) La Follette introduced reforms in Wisconsin that Progressives favored. (b) Reformers borrowed ideas from Wisconsin to use in their own states.
6. Possible Answer: Yes; voters are well-intentioned people who deserve the right to express their will. Only when voters are poorly informed or prejudiced will they be unlikely to make the right decision.

1. Focus In the early 1900s, three Progressives gained the presidency of the United States. In this section, students study the presidencies of Theodore Roosevelt and William Howard Taft, and examine Woodrow Wilson's first term in office.

2. Instruct Draw a blank chart on the chalkboard with four columns. Label the columns Legislation, When Passed, President, and Purpose. In the first column, list the following: Elkins Act, Hepburn Act, Meat Inspection Act, Pure Food and Drug Act, Clayton Antitrust Act, Federal Reserve Act. Have students copy the chart in a notebook and complete it by adding the correct information in each of the other columns.

3. Close To close the lesson, play a Jeopardy!-like game with students. Have pairs of students provide key facts from the section. Then have the class provide an appropriate question for each fact.

 Lesson Planner

For a fully developed **Cooperative Learning** lesson plan, see the *Lesson Planner,* page 131.

 CD-ROM

Presidents Access the biography of William McKinley from the American Heritage® *History of the United States* CD-ROM.

---

mind, he chose Roosevelt as his running mate. The young New York politician was known as a reformer.

"TR." Teddy Roosevelt—or "TR," as he was called—came from an old, wealthy New York family. As a child, he suffered from asthma and was often sick. But he refused to accept weakness. To build his strength, he lifted weights, ran, and boxed.

Roosevelt could have lived a life of ease and privilege. Instead, he entered politics after college. Roosevelt supported many Progressive goals. He hated corruption and believed that the government should protect the public interest.

Rough and tumble politics. Roosevelt's friends mocked his political ambitions. Roosevelt later recalled:

> **66** They assured me that the men I met would be rough and brutal and unpleasant to deal with. I answered that I certainly would not quit until I . . . found out whether I was really too weak to hold my own in the rough and tumble. **99**

By age 26, Roosevelt was serving in the New York State legislature. Then personal tragedy almost ended his political career. In 1884, his mother and his young wife died on the same day. Overcome by grief, Roosevelt quit the legislature. He headed west to work on a cattle ranch in present-day North Dakota.

After two years, Roosevelt returned to the East and to politics. He served on the Civil Service Commission. Later, he held posts as head of the New York City police department and as assistant secretary of the navy.

When the United States went to war against Spain in 1898, Roosevelt signed up to fight. He fought well and returned home to a hero's welcome. In 1898, he was elected governor of New York.

Reform governor. Since his days in the legislature, Roosevelt had pushed for re-

form. Other legislators called him "a goo goo," a mocking name for someone who wanted good government. As governor, Roosevelt continued to work for reform. New York Republican bosses breathed a sigh of relief when Roosevelt ran with McKinley and won in November 1900.

In September 1901, an assassin shot President William McKinley. At age 42, Theodore Roosevelt became the nation's youngest President.

TR Takes on the Trusts

Many business people worried about the new President's Progressive ideas. Roosevelt reassured them. He said he would continue McKinley's pro-business policies. Roosevelt favored some changes, business leaders concluded, but not too many.

Good and bad trusts. Roosevelt believed that giant corporations were here to stay. He thought, however, that there were good trusts and bad trusts. Good trusts were efficient and fair. The government should leave them alone, TR said. On the other hand, bad trusts cheated the public and took advantage of their workers. The government should either control them or break them up.

The Northern Securities case. Roosevelt carefully chose the target for the government's test case against the trusts. In 1902, he ordered the Attorney General* to bring a lawsuit against the Northern Securities Company. This giant trust had been put together by J. Pierpont Morgan, and it had many enemies. Roosevelt argued that Northern Securities used unfair business practices in violation of the Sherman Act.

The case disturbed many business leaders. They feared that it would hurt their businesses, too. All trusts operated like Northern Securities. If its practices were illegal, so were theirs.

---

*The Attorney General is the chief lawyer for the United States government.

Critical Thinking
Recognizing Points of View

Tell students that Mark Hanna, an Ohio business tycoon and a dominant figure in the Republican party, opposed Roosevelt's nomination, saying, "Don't you realize there is but one heartbeat between the White House and this madman?" When McKinley was assassinated, Hanna fumed, "Now, look, that cowboy is President of the United States."

Discuss Hanna's comments with the class. Ask: What did Hanna mean by the question he asked? Why might a business leader consider Roosevelt a "madman"? What negative characteristics would an Ohio business leader associate with the term "cowboy"?

Connections With Sports
Background

Theodore Roosevelt has often been referred to as the most energetic of all Presidents. When he was visited by Jean-Jules Jusserand, the ambassador from France, Roosevelt engaged him in two sets of tennis, took him jogging, and worked out with him with the medicine ball. Roosevelt then asked, "What would you like to do now?" Jusserand replied, "If it's just the same to you, Mr. President, I'd like to lie down and die."

Stung by the lawsuit, J. Pierpont Morgan rushed to Washington. He asked the President if he meant to attack other trusts. "Certainly not," replied Roosevelt, "unless we find out that. . . they have done something we regard as wrong."

Stock prices on Wall Street fell at news of the lawsuit. One newspaper editor noted:

❝Wall Street is paralyzed at the thought that a President of the United States would sink so low as to try to enforce the [Sherman Antitrust] law.❞

While business leaders worried, ordinary people supported the President.

A victory for Roosevelt. The Northern Securities case reached the Supreme Court in 1904. The Court found that Northern Securities had violated the Sherman Antitrust Act by limiting trade. It ordered the trust to be broken up. The decision showed the effects of the Progressive Movement. In the 1890s, the Sherman Antitrust Act had been used to break up unions, not trusts.

President Roosevelt hailed the case as a victory. He then ordered the Attorney General to file suit against other trusts that had broken the law. The government accused Standard Oil and the American Tobacco Company of blocking free trade. The courts later ordered both trusts to be broken up.

Some business leaders called Roosevelt a **trustbuster** who wanted to destroy all trusts. Roosevelt responded that he preferred to control trusts, not "bust" them. Only companies that fought government regulation were brought to court, he said.

Trouble in the coal fields. Roosevelt also clashed with the nation's mine owners. In 1902, coal miners in Pennsylvania went on strike. They wanted better pay and a shorter workday. Mine owners refused even to talk to the miners' union.

As winter approached, schools and hospitals around the country ran out of coal.

Cracking the Whip As President *Theodore Roosevelt set out to control "bad trusts." Here, Roosevelt is shown taming the beef trust, the steel trust, and other powerful trusts.* **Economics** *Which of Roosevelt's actions might have inspired this cartoon?*

Roosevelt was furious at the stubbornness of the mine owners. Finally, he threatened to send in troops to run the mines. In response, owners sat down with the union and reached an agreement.

Working people around the country cheered Roosevelt's action. Earlier Presidents had used federal troops to break strikes. Roosevelt was the first to side with labor against mine owners. He forced them to work with the union.

The Promise of a Square Deal

In 1904, Roosevelt ran for President in his own right. During the campaign, he

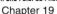
Historical Sidelight
Background

Theodore Roosevelt was a devoted family man. He doted on his six children and often joined in their frolics. When the Roosevelts moved into the White House, they brought their childish antics and wild energy with them. They played baseball on the White House lawn and tag in the hallways. They wrestled and had pillow fights. Their collection of pets included dogs, cats, rabbits, guinea pigs, snakes, lizards, flying squirrels, a badger, and a small black bear. Chief Usher "Ike"

Hoover called it "the wildest scramble in the history of the White House."

In that "scramble," the oldest child was Alice, a teenager. Once during a meeting with a friend, Roosevelt was interrupted by Alice time and time again. Finally, the friend complained, "Theodore, isn't there anything you can do to control Alice?" Roosevelt replied, "I can be President of the United States or I can control Alice. I cannot possibly do both."

Connections With Literature
Background

Upton Sinclair, author of *The Jungle,* later investigated a lengthy coal miners' strike in Colorado. His investigation led to the writing of a novel entitled *King Coal* (1917), which focused public attention on this industry. In the novel, a wealthy college student hides his identity and goes to work in a coal mine. He becomes a leader in the campaign for better working conditions and unionization. Along the way, Sinclair shows how the coal industry dominated many aspects of life in Colorado.

promised Americans a *Square Deal.* By this, he meant that many different groups—farmers and consumers, workers and owners—should have an equal opportunity to succeed. The promise of a Square Deal helped Roosevelt win a landslide victory in the election.

Regulating railroads. Railroads were a key target of Roosevelt's Square Deal. The President had seen that the Interstate Commerce Act of 1887 had done little to end rebates and other abuses. He urged Congress to pass the Elkins Act in 1903. It outlawed rebates. In 1906, Congress passed the Hepburn Act. It gave the ICC greater power, including the right to set railroad rates.

Protecting consumers. Roosevelt had read Upton Sinclair's shocking novel, *The Jungle.* In response, he sent more government inspectors to meatpacking houses.

The owners refused to let the inspectors in. Roosevelt then gave the newspapers copies of a government report that supported Sinclair's picture of the meatpacking industry. As public rage mounted, Congress passed the Meat Inspection Act of 1906. It forced packers to open their doors to more inspectors.

Roosevelt called for other reforms to protect consumers. Muckrakers had revealed that the food industry was adding dangerous chemicals to canned foods. They found, too, that drug companies made false claims about their medicines. In 1906, Congress passed the *Pure Food and Drug Act.* The new law required food and drug makers to list all ingredients on their packages. It also tried to end false advertising and ban the use of impure ingredients.

Protecting natural resources. Roosevelt loved the outdoors. As President, he grew alarmed about the destruction of the wilderness. To fuel the nation's industrial growth, lumber companies were cutting down whole forests. Miners were taking iron and coal from the earth at a frantic pace and leaving gaping holes.

Roosevelt objected to this destruction of the land. He believed in the protection of natural resources, or **conservation.** "The

Making Sausages *Photographs such as this view of a Chicago packinghouse caused consumers to worry about the quality of the food they were buying.* **Economics** *How did the Pure Food and Drug Act protect consumers?*

> ### Linking Past and Present
> *Even before Theodore Roosevelt, conservationists had worked to preserve the wilderness. In 1872, Yellowstone became the first national park. Sequoia and Yosemite national parks were set up in 1890. Today, millions of people visit these parks each year.*

PAST | PRESENT

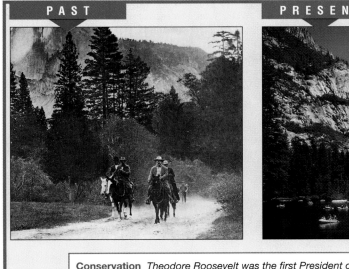

Conservation *Theodore Roosevelt was the first President committed to conservation. At left, Roosevelt rides through Yosemite Valley in California with fellow conservationist John Muir. Today, thanks to the work begun by Muir and Roosevelt, Yosemite and other wilderness areas have been preserved. At right, rafters enjoy the natural beauties of Yosemite National Park.* • *What natural resources do you think Americans need to conserve?*

 Voices of Freedom

Primary Source You might assign selection 7-1, Why Taft Had Trouble, on pages 184–185 of *Voices of Freedom.* The selection, written by Archibald Butt, is a letter about a trip Taft had made to the West, in which Butt contrasts the different personalities of Taft and Roosevelt. (Enrichment/Average)

 CD-ROM

Presidents Access the biography of William Howard Taft from the American Heritage® *History of the United States* CD-ROM.

---

rights of the public to natural resources," he said, "outweigh private rights, and must be given first consideration."

Roosevelt thought that natural resources could serve both the public interest and private companies. Some forest and mountain areas, he said, should be left as wilderness. Others could supply wood for lumber. He wanted lumber companies to replant trees in the forests they were clearing. Mining, too, should be controlled.

Taft and the Reformers

In 1908, Roosevelt threw his support behind William Howard Taft to succeed him as President. In the election, Taft easily defeated his Democratic rival. A confident Teddy Roosevelt said:

66 Taft will carry on the work . . . as I have. His policies, principles, purposes, and ideals are the same as mine. The Roosevelt policies will not go out with Roosevelt. 99

Roosevelt then set off for Africa to hunt big game for a year.

Taft versus TR. Taft was very different from Roosevelt. Unlike the hard-driving, energetic Roosevelt, Taft was quiet and cautious. Roosevelt loved power. Taft feared it.

Like Roosevelt, Taft supported many Progressive causes. He pushed ahead with

Chapter 21 • **605**

Linking Past and Present
Activity

Explain that conservationist John Muir founded and became the first president of the Sierra Club in 1892. Have students do research into the activities of the Sierra Club today. For example, students might learn about its program for wilderness preservation or about its publications. Encourage interested students to write directly to the Sierra Club at 730 Polk Street, San Francisco, California 94109.

Historical Sidelight
Background

A popular true story about Roosevelt and Taft tells of a dinner party at the White House in January 1908. After dinner, Roosevelt pretended to go into a trance. "I am the seventh son of a seventh daughter," he announced. "I have clairvoyant powers. I see a man standing before me weighing 350 pounds. There is something hanging over his head. . . . At one time it looks like the Presidency — then again it looks like the Chief Justiceship." Mrs. Taft cried out, "Make it the Presidency!" Mr. Taft cried out, "Make it the Chief Justiceship!" (Both turned out to be true, for Taft became Chief Justice after he served as President.)

The political tie between Taft and Roosevelt was so strong at the time that a common joke said that TAFT stood for "Take Advice From Teddy."

trustbusting even more vigorously than TR had done. However, Taft lost Progressive support when he signed a high tariff bill that Progressives had opposed. Progressives also attacked him for blocking conservation policies they favored.

Roosevelt returned from Africa only to learn that reformers felt Taft had betrayed them. Taft was "a flub-dub with a streak of the second-rate," declared Roosevelt. He decided to run against Taft for the Republican nomination in 1912.

"Strong as a bull moose." Many Republican business people distrusted Roosevelt. As a result, they chose Taft as their candidate. Progressive Republicans were furious and marched out of the convention. They

President Wilson *Woodrow Wilson's honesty and firm leadership inspired Progressives. Some Wilson supporters compared him with the nation's first President, George Washington, as can be seen from the song sheet at left.* **Economics** *What was the goal of Wilson's antitrust policy?*

I THINK WE'VE GOT ANOTHER WASHINGTON AND WILSON IS HIS NAME

set up a new party, the Progressive party. They chose Roosevelt to run for President.

Roosevelt gladly accepted the challenge. He entered the race with typical energy. "I feel as strong as a bull moose," he exclaimed. He and his supporters became known as the **Bull Moose party.**

A Democratic victory. Democrats chose Woodrow Wilson, a Progressive, as their candidate. Wilson had been born in the South. He had served as president of Princeton University and as governor of New Jersey. He was known as a brilliant scholar and a cautious reformer.

Wilson won the election of 1912. Together, Taft and Roosevelt gained more votes than Wilson. By splitting the Republicans, however, they had helped Wilson into the White House.

President Woodrow Wilson

On inauguration day, Wilson asked honest, forward-looking Americans to stand at his side. "God helping me," he pledged, "I will not fail them."

The New Freedom. At first, Wilson wanted to break up trusts into smaller companies. By doing so, he hoped to restore the competition that had once existed in the American economy. "If America is not to have free enterprise, then she can have freedom of no sort whatever," he said. Wilson called his program the **New Freedom.**

Wilson worked with Congress for laws to spur competition. He pushed first for a lower tariff to create more competition from foreign goods. After a long struggle, Congress lowered the tariff. It also imposed a graduated income tax to make up for lower tariffs. To regulate banking, Congress passed the **Federal Reserve Act** in 1913.

Controlling big business. Before long, Wilson realized he could not break up large corporations. Instead, like Roosevelt, he decided to control big business, not destroy it.

In 1914, he convinced Congress to create the **Federal Trade Commission.** This commission had power to investigate companies and order them to stop using unfair business practices.

That same year, Wilson signed the Clayton Antitrust Act. The law was weaker than he wanted. However, it did ban some business practices that limited competition. It also barred antitrust laws from being used against unions—a major victory for labor.

Despite Wilson's successes, the Progressive Movement slowed after 1914. By then, the Progressives had achieved many of their goals. In addition, the outbreak of war in Europe captured public attention. Americans watched in horror as the major European powers fought a deadly struggle.

SECTION 3 REVIEW

1. **Identify:** (a) Square Deal, (b) Pure Food and Drug Act, (c) William Howard Taft, (d) Bull Moose party, (e) New Freedom, (f) Federal Reserve Act, (g) Federal Trade Commission.
2. **Define:** (a) trustbuster, (b) conservation.
3. Explain the actions of Theodore Roosevelt in each of the following areas: (a) trusts, (b) railroads, (c) food industry, (d) conservation.
4. How did the Supreme Court's decision in the Northern Securities case show the influence of Progressives?
5. (a) What successes did Wilson have? (b) What setbacks did he experience?
6. **CRITICAL THINKING Understanding Causes and Effects** "I'm glad to be going," said Taft as he left the White House in 1913. "This is the lonesomest place in the world." Why might Taft have felt so lonely?

ACTIVITY Writing to Learn

In two or three paragraphs, evaluate whether the Progressives had achieved their goals by 1914.

4
Women in the Progressive Era

FIND OUT

- What goals did women pursue in the Progressive Era?
- What methods did women use to achieve their goals?
- What successes did women have in the Progressive Era?

VOCABULARY suffragist

---

 nez Milholland rose to speak. A leading spokesperson for suffrage, the young woman soon had the audience's attention.

> **❝**We want the vote, not for the sake of the vote itself, but as a means to an end. That end is the care and preservation and upbuilding of the lives of men and women and children. . . . Women are the mothers of the race, and as such are admittedly more concerned than any one else with all that goes to protect life. . . . **❞**

Inez Milholland was one of many women who worked for reforms during the Progressive Era. Women spoke out against trusts and in favor of pure food laws. They called for an end to child labor and a ban on the sale of alcohol. They also continued their long battle for the right to vote.

Votes for Women

The struggle for women's suffrage went back many years. As you have read in Chapter 14, the Seneca Falls Convention in 1848 called for women's suffrage. After the

Chapter 21 • **607**

Answers to Section 3 Review

1. (a) Square Deal, p. 604, (b) Pure Food and Drug Act, p. 604, (c) William Howard Taft, p. 605, (d) Bull Moose party, p. 606, (e) New Freedom, p. 606, (f) Federal Reserve Act, p. 606, (g) Federal Trade Commission, p. 607
2. (a) trustbuster, p. 603, (b) conservation, p. 604
3. (a) Roosevelt sought to do away with bad trusts, such as Northern Securities, but to leave good ones alone. (b) He worked to make regulation of railroads more effective through the Elkins Act. (c) He supported the Meat Inspection Act and Pure Food and Drug Act, resulting in increased protection for consumers. (d) He called for conservation of national resources, limits on lumbering, and the protection of wilderness areas.
4. It showed that the Supreme Court was responsive to the Progressive goal of regulating huge trusts.
5. (a) Wilson won a lower tariff and regulated banks. He set up the FTC to investigate and regulate large businesses. (b) Although he signed the Clayton Antitrust Act, it was not as strong as he wanted.
6. Possible Answer: By the time Taft was leaving office, many reformers no longer believed that he supported Progressive goals. He probably felt isolated from the people who had originally supported him.

1. Focus As women moved to the forefront during the Progressive Era, they began to demand more political and social rights. In this section, students learn how women won the right to vote, gained entry to higher education and various professions, and spurred social change.

2. Instruct Divide the class into two groups—members of the National American Woman Suffrage Association working for passage of the Nineteenth Amendment and members of the Women's Christian Temperance Union working for passage of the Eighteenth Amendment. Have each group stage a rally in favor of its cause.

3. Close To close the lesson, name each woman mentioned in this section. Have students identify the contributions each made to the cause of reform.

 Lesson Planner

For a developed **Cooperative Learning** lesson plan, see the *Lesson Planner,* page 132.

Answer to Caption

She gave stirring speeches and devised a detailed nationwide plan for winning the vote.

 Voices of Freedom

Primary Source You might assign selection 7-5, Suffragists on a Hunger Strike, on pages 189–190 of *Voices of Freedom.* (Enrichment/Average)

Civil War, Elizabeth Cady Stanton and Susan B. Anthony led a renewed drive to win the vote. In 1869, they formed the National Woman Suffrage Association. This group worked to amend the Constitution to give women the vote.

"We will come in with our women." Most politicians opposed women's suffrage. Still, in the late 1800s, women gained the right to vote in four western states: Wyoming, Utah, Colorado, and Idaho. Pioneer women had worked alongside men to build the farms and cities of the West. By giving women the vote, these states recognized women's contributions.

When Wyoming applied for statehood in 1890, many members of Congress wanted the state to change its voting law. During

---

BIOGRAPHY **Carrie Chapman Catt** *The only woman in the 1880 graduating class at Iowa State College, Carrie Chapman Catt was used to fighting against odds. Catt fought for suffrage. "Ours is not a true democracy," she declared, as long as women were denied the vote.* **American Traditions** *How did Catt contribute to the suffrage campaign?*

---

the debate, Wyoming lawmakers wired Congress: "We may stay out of the Union for 100 years, but we will come in with our women." Wyoming barely won admission.

Suffragists. In the early 1900s, the women's suffrage movement gained strength. More than 5 million women were earning wages outside the home. Although women were paid less than men, wages gave women a sense of power. Many demanded a say in making the laws that governed them.

Carrie Chapman Catt spoke powerfully in favor of the cause. Catt had worked as a school principal and a reporter. Later, she became head of the National American Woman Suffrage Association. Catt was an inspired speaker and a brilliant organizer. She devised a detailed battle plan for fighting the war for suffrage. Around the country, **suffragists,** or people who campaigned for women's right to vote, followed her lead.

The efforts of Catt and other suffragists slowly succeeded. Year by year, more states in the West and Midwest gave women the vote. For the most part, they were allowed to vote only in state elections. In time, more and more women called for an amendment to the Constitution to give them a voice in national elections. Some suffragists took strong measures to achieve their goal.

Protest at the White House

 All day, the protesters stood silently outside the White House. Next day, they came back again. Day after day, regardless of the weather, they reappeared. Some onlookers shouted insults. Others spoke words of support. President Wilson drove by and tipped his hat. The protesters remained silent.

Their banners spoke for them. One read: "Mr. President, What Will You Do For Woman Suffrage?" Another quoted the words of Inez Milholland: "Mr. President, how long must women wait for liberty?"

Connections With Civics
Background

Carrie Chapman Catt was a fiery campaigner from the northern plains, a woman with grit and determination. "To see her is like looking at sheer marble, flame-lit," wrote an awed reporter after one of her speeches.

One element of Catt's strategy was conspicuous patriotism. Despite the pacifism of many suffragists and her own hatred of war, Catt helped persuade the National American Woman Suffrage Association (NAWSA) to give strong support to the American effort in World War I. She even spoke out against

more radical suffragists who demonstrated against the war: "We stand on the threshold of final victory, and the only contribution these women make to it is to confuse the public mind." By impressing men with their patriotism, Catt and other NAWSA leaders advanced the suffrage cause. Catt also called for lobbying efforts at the state and national levels. In her outspoken way, she declared, "The United States has no right to talk about making the world safe for democracy as long as it believes in drawing the sex line."

Suffragists in Washington, D.C. *Alice Paul's protest was not the first time suffragists had marched on the capital. Here, women in 1913 take part in a "Votes for Women Pilgrimage" to Washington, D.C.* **Linking Past and Present** *For what causes have people organized protests in recent times?*

Alice Paul. Leading the protesters outside the White House was Alice Paul. She was a determined woman. When someone asked why she joined the suffrage movement, she spoke of her Quaker upbringing. "One of [the Quaker] principles. . . is equality of the sexes," she explained. "I never had any other idea."

In 1907, Paul had gone to England. There, she had marched with suffragists in London. She had been jailed and gone on hunger strikes—all to help British women win the vote. Later, Paul returned home to support the cause of suffrage for American women.

Paul and other suffragists had met with President Wilson soon after he took office in 1913. Wilson supported women's suffrage. He did not, however, support a constitutional amendment. Paul told the President what women wanted:

66 We said we're going to try and get [a constitutional amendment] through Congress, that we would like to have his help and needed his support very much. And then we sent him another delegation and another and another and another and another and another and another— every type of women's group we could get.99

Prison. In time, Paul grew weary of sending delegations to the President. In January 1917, she began the White House protests. After several months of these silent demonstrations, police began arresting the protesters. They were charged with obstructing sidewalks. Paul received a seven-month jail sentence. To protest their arrest, Paul and others went on a hunger strike.

When Paul refused to end her hunger strike, prison officials decided she was insane. They called in a doctor to examine her. He declared: "This is a spirit like Joan of Arc, and it is useless to try to change it. She will die, but she will never give up."

The jailing of the protesters brought added attention to the suffrage campaign. Upon release, Paul and the other women resumed their protests.

Victory at last. By early 1918, the tide began to turn in favor of the suffrage cause. The tireless work of Carrie Chapman Catt, Alice Paul, and others began to pay off. President Wilson agreed to support the suffrage amendment that Congress had finally begun to debate.

Finally, in 1919, Congress passed the amendment giving women the right to vote. By August 1920, the ***Nineteenth Amendment*** had won approval by three fourths of the states. The amendment doubled the number of eligible voters in the United States. ∎

Chapter 21 • **609**

Answers to Map Study

1. Wyoming **2.** New Mexico **3.** Possible Answer: Western states were the first to grant women full suffrage. Most states that granted no suffrage to women were in the East, especially the Southeast.

 Chapter Resources

History Through Literature To offer students a look at the lives of late-nineteenth-century women by a woman writer of the period, duplicate and distribute the worksheet, *The Story of an Hour*, from Unit 7, page 4, of the *Chapter Resources* binder. (Enrichment/Average)

 Videotapes/Videodiscs

United States History Video Collection Use the video segment "Women Suffragists" from Volume 14, *The Progressive Movement,* to enhance students' understanding of how women campaigned for and finally won the right to vote. Approx. running time 2:50 min. (Enrichment/Average) Vol. 14, Ch. 25

Chapter 25   Play

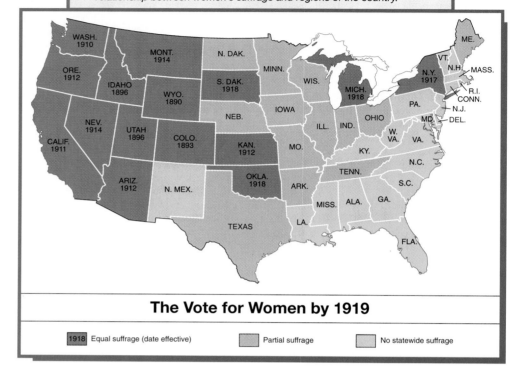

M A P   S T U D Y

By 1919, women in most states had won the right to vote in state and local elections.
1. *Which state was the first to grant women full suffrage?*
2. *What was the westernmost state in which women had no statewide suffrage by 1919?*
3. **Making Generalizations** *From this map, make a generalization about the relationship between women's suffrage and regions of the country.*

The Vote for Women by 1919

1918 Equal suffrage (date effective)   Partial suffrage   No statewide suffrage

Women Win New Opportunities

For years, women struggled to open doors to jobs and education. Most states refused to grant women licenses to practice in professions such as law, medicine, or college teaching. Myra Bradwell taught herself law, just as Abraham Lincoln had done. Still, Illinois denied her a license in 1869 because she was a woman. In 1890, Illinois at last let Bradwell practice law. Later, she argued cases before the Supreme Court.

Higher education. Despite obstacles, a few women managed to get the higher education needed to enter the professions. In 1877, Boston University granted the first Ph.D. to a woman. In the next decades, women made important advances. By 1900, 1,000 women lawyers and about 7,000 women doctors were in practice.

Connections With Local History
Activity

In the last quarter of the nineteenth century, many colleges for women were founded. Have students find out if any colleges for women were established in your state during this era and, if possible, the names of the first women to earn advanced degrees in your state. Interested students might also find out some of the later accomplishments of these graduates.

Critical Thinking
Comparing

Lead the class in a discussion comparing restrictions imposed on women in the early 1900s with their role in society today. Have the class brainstorm and list on the chalkboard opportunities available today that were not available then. Ask them to identify obstacles and adverse attitudes women may still encounter.

Women entered the sciences, too. Mary Engle Pennington earned a degree in chemistry. She became the nation's top expert on preserving foods.

Commitment to reform. Women in the Progressive Movement were committed to reform. Some entered the new profession of social work. Others joined the women's clubs that had sprung up in the late 1800s.

At first, clubwomen read books, went to plays, and sought other ways to improve their minds. By the early 1900s, they were caught up in the reform spirit. Clubwomen raised money for libraries, schools, and parks. They fought for laws to protect women and children, for pure food and drug laws, and for the right to vote.

Faced with racial barriers, African American women formed their own clubs. These clubwomen crusaded against lynching and racial separation, as well as for suffrage and other causes.

The Temperance Crusade

Many women united behind the temperance movement. In fact, women reformers were the major force in the crusade against alcohol. Many wives and mothers saw alcohol as a threat to their families.

In 1874, a group of women founded the Women's Christian Temperance Union, or WCTU. Frances Willard, who was a leader of the WCTU, worked to educate people about the evils of alcohol. She urged states to pass laws banning the sale of liquor.

Our Common Heritage
The 1893 Chicago Exposition had a Women's Building that displayed women's accomplishments. One exhibit, organized by J. Imogen Howard, showed the work of African American artists, doctors, musicians, inventors, and teachers.

Carry Nation. Another temperance crusader was Carry Nation. After her husband died from heavy drinking, Nation dedicated her life to fighting "demon rum."

Nation took her fight against alcohol into the saloons. Swinging a hatchet, she stormed into taverns where she smashed beer kegs and liquor bottles. Nation also went on lecture tours across the United States and Europe.

The Eighteenth Amendment. Temperance crusaders wanted to amend the Constitution to prohibit the sale of liquor. After 1917, support for such an amendment grew. In that year the United States entered World War I. Temperance forces argued that grain used to make liquor should go to feed American soldiers instead.

Congress passed the ***Eighteenth Amendment*** in 1917. By 1919, three fourths of the states had ratified the amendment. The amendment made it illegal to sell alcoholic drinks anywhere in the United States.

SECTION 4 REVIEW

1. **Identify:** (a) Carrie Chapman Catt, (b) Nineteenth Amendment, (c) Frances Willard, (d) Carry Nation, (e) Eighteenth Amendment.
2. **Define:** suffragist.
3. (a) What political goal did women seek in the Progressive Era? (b) How did they work to achieve it?
4. Describe two opportunities women gained in the late 1800s and early 1900s.
5. **CRITICAL THINKING Defending a Position** Do you think Alice Paul's actions to win suffrage for women were the best tactics? Explain your position.

ACTIVITY **Writing to Learn**
Imagine that you had worked for passage of the Eighteenth or Nineteenth Amendment. Write a letter to a friend describing your feelings on the day the amendment was ratified.

Our Multicultural Heritage

Biography Have students read the biography, Belva Ann Bennett Lockwood, Lawyer and Candidate, on page 61 of the *Our Multicultural Heritage* booklet. (Enrichment/Average)

Student Study Guide

Section 4 Study Guide Have students use the Section 4 Study Guide on page 162 of the *Student Study Guide* to review and reinforce the content of this section. (Reteaching/Average)

ACTIVITY

Guided Instruction Before students write their letters, have them list some of the actions taken by campaigners for these amendments. Ask: What do these actions suggest about the campaigners' devotion to their cause? Have students read their letters to the class, or make the letters part of a classroom display about these efforts at reform.

Historical Sidelight
Background

To meet its goals, the WCTU had several avenues of approach. An 1881 resolution read, in part: ". . . wisdom dictates the do-everything policy — constitutional amendment, where the way is open for it; Home Protection [championed especially by Frances Willard], when Home Protection is the strongest rallying cry; equal franchise, where the vote of women joined to that of men can alone give stability to Temperance legislation."

Answers to Section 4 Review

1. (a) Carrie Chapman Catt, p. 608, (b) Nineteenth Amendment, p. 609, (c) Frances Willard, p. 611, (d) Carry Nation, p. 611, (e) Eighteenth Amendment, p. 611
2. suffragist, p. 608
3. (a) suffrage (b) by campaigning for the Nineteenth Amendment
4. Women gained more access to higher education, and they gained entrance into the legal and medical professions.

5. Possible Answer: Paul's demonstrations and hunger strikes were necessary because women had worked for a long time for suffrage with only limited success. Still, perhaps other tactics might have been more effective.

Chapter Resources

Answers to Skill Lesson

1. (a) in a saloon; the scene is dominated by a bar (b) smashed glasses, bottles, and a beer keg (c) alcohol (d) Carry Nation; she has a hatchet in her hand and she is famous for this type of activity (e) George Washington

2. (a) She has smashed up the saloon because she believes that liquor is evil. (b) overweight, unattractive, old-fashioned, and unhappy or angry and stern (c) Possible Answer: to make her behavior seem childlike, because Washington was a child when he supposedly said these words; or to make her behavior seem noble, because Washington is admired for his honesty

3. (a) Possible Answer: that she was an extremist and a bit crazy; the cartoonist shows that she resorted to violence and destruction to achieve her goals. (b) Possible Answer: The attitude in the paragraphs is more objective than that in the cartoon.

ACTIVITY

Guided Instruction You might have students brainstorm for a list of local issues. Remind students of the techniques of political cartooning (such as humor, symbolism, and caricature) before they sketch their cartoons.

CRITICAL THINKING SKILLS
Reading a Political Cartoon

Political cartoons are drawings that comment on important political or social issues of the day. Often, they poke fun at the subject. Political cartoons usually appear in newspapers and news magazines. They provide a valuable source of information because they tell us about the issues that concern Americans.

Cartoonists try to get across their point of view using as few words as possible. Instead, they rely mainly on pictures. Political cartoons often exaggerate the facts to make a point. For example, a cartoonist might draw J. Pierpont Morgan with a head that looks like a sack of money. This might make the point that the tycoon thought only about money.

The cartoon below appeared in a newspaper in Wichita, Kansas, in 1901. Carry Nation had recently taken her hatchet to several saloons there.

1. Identify the symbols used in the cartoon. Cartoons use symbols to express a point of view. A symbol is something that stands for something else. For example, a lion is a symbol for courage, while a dove often stands for peace. To understand a cartoon, you must know what its symbols mean. (a)

Where does this cartoon take place? How can you tell? (b) What items lie on the floor? (c) What do these items stand for? (d) Who is the woman in the cartoon? How do you know? (e) What famous American is usually associated with the words spoken by the woman in the cartoon?

2. Analyze the meaning of the words and pictures. (a) What has the woman in the cartoon done? Why has she done this? (b) Based on the cartoonist's drawing of the woman, how would you describe her? (c) Why do you think the cartoonist has the woman say these words?

3. Interpret the cartoon. Draw conclusions about the cartoonist's point of view. (a) What do you think the cartoonist thought of Carry Nation? How can you tell? (b) Read the paragraphs about Nation on page 611. Do the paragraphs express an attitude toward Nation different from that of the cartoon? Explain.

ACTIVITY
Identify an important issue in your community or region. Draw a political cartoon expressing a point of view about the issue.

"I CANNOT TELL A LIE--I DID IT WITH MY LITTLE HATCHET!"

Students Acquiring English Activity

The cartoon is visual enough to be understood easily by SAE students. However, they may have some trouble understanding the questions. You might discuss the questions with the entire class to ensure understanding. For the activity, partners might assist SAE students in choosing visual images that convey, in the American idiom, the abstract ideas that SAE students wish to express.

Minorities Seek Equality and Justice

FIND OUT

■ What problems did African Americans face in the Progressive Era?

■ How did African American leaders try to fight discrimination?

■ What was life like for Asian Americans, Mexican Americans, and Native Americans during the Progressive Era?

VOCABULARY barrio

The Thirteenth Amendment abolished slavery in 1865. Yet 50 years later, life for many African Americans had not changed for the better. One African American woman declared:

❝Whether in the cook kitchen, at the washtub, over the sewing machine, behind the baby carriage, or at the ironing board, we are but little more than pack horses, beasts of burden, slaves!❞

In general, white Progressives had little concern for the needs of nonwhites. It was up to African Americans, Asian Americans, Mexican Americans, and Native Americans to form their own groups to fight for equality and help their communities.

African Americans Fight Discrimination

After the end of Reconstruction, African Americans in the South came under attack. As you have read, the courts, state laws, and racist groups denied blacks their political rights. Jim Crow laws led to segregation in schools, trains, and other public places. (See page 499.)

Northern blacks also faced prejudice. Landlords in white neighborhoods refused to rent homes to African Americans. Hotels and restaurants often would not serve blacks. In the North and the South, African Americans were hired for only the lowest-paying jobs.

Violence against African Americans. In the 1890s, life grew worse for African Americans. The depression of 1893 threw many people out of work. In some areas, mainly in the South, unemployed whites took out their anger on blacks. In the 1890s, lynch mobs murdered more than 1,000 blacks.

Such violence outraged the African American journalist Ida B. Wells. In 1892, she investigated the lynching of three African American businessmen in Memphis, Tennessee, where she lived. In her newspaper, *Free Speech,* she urged African Americans to protest the killings. She called on them to stop riding the streetcars or shopping in white stores. Wells continued to stand up for African American rights despite threats to her life.

A self-made man. Booker T. Washington offered another answer to the question of how to fight discrimination and violence. In his autobiography, *Up From Slavery,* Washington told how he had succeeded. Born into slavery, he taught himself to read. In 1881, he founded Tuskegee Institute in Alabama. It became a center for black higher education. Tuskegee continues today as a leading black college.

Washington stressed living in harmony with whites. He urged African Americans to work patiently and move slowly upward. First learn trades and earn money, said Washington. Only then would African Americans have the power to insist on political and social equality.

Section 5
pp. 613–617

Bell Ringer

Write the phrase *separate but equal* on the chalkboard. Ask students what they think it means. As necessary, guide them toward an understanding of this legal doctrine as it was applied to civil rights.

Lesson Plan

1. Focus In the 1890s and early 1900s, minority groups continued to face problems. In this section, students learn about the efforts of African American leaders to overcome discrimination, as well as the problems encountered by other minorities during this period.

2. Instruct Have students list causes and effects of discrimination against African Americans, Asian Americans, Mexican Americans, and Native Americans in the early 1900s. Ask: How was discrimination against each of these groups similar? What differences can you see?

3. Close To close the lesson, play a Jeopardy!-like game with students. Give key facts from the section as answers and challenge students to provide appropriate questions.

Lesson Planner

For a developed **Cooperative Learning** lesson plan, see the *Lesson Planner,* page 133.

Our Multicultural Heritage
Background

Ida B. Wells was a teacher in Memphis. She turned to journalism after her refusal to give up her seat in a "whites only" railroad car led to her dismissal. In 1891, she became co-owner and editor of *Free Speech,* a weekly newspaper.

As a result of Wells's investigative reports of the lynching (in which she named the people responsible), a mob of whites destroyed her office and her printing press. Wells moved to New York City. From there, she began an anti-lynching campaign that gave her many opportunities to speak for African Americans. Lecture tours took her across the United States and to England. In her speeches and articles, Wells pointed out that during the 1880s and 1890s, about 100 blacks were killed by mobs each year—yet in all that time, only three people were punished for the killings.

Later, in 1901, Wells carefully recorded and classified the reasons given for 504 lynchings of African Americans between 1896 and 1900. The reasons included "giving evidence," "insult," "unpopularity," "violating contract," and "frightening child by shooting at rabbits." Interestingly, Wells wore two guns strapped to her waist to protect herself.

Voices of Freedom

Primary Source You might assign selection 13-3, The Need for Practical Skills, on pages 155–156 of *Voices of Freedom*. The selection is from a speech Booker T. Washington made in 1895. (Enrichment/Average)

Our Multicultural Heritage

Biography Have students read the biography, Mary Church Terrell, Voice of Justice, on page 62 of the *Our Multicultural Heritage* booklet. (Enrichment/Average)

CD-ROM

History Makers Access the biography of W.E.B. DuBois on the American Heritage® *History of the United States* CD-ROM.

In the meantime, Washington seemed to accept segregation. "In all things that are purely social," he said, "we can be as separate as the fingers, yet one as the hand in all things essential to mutual progress."

Booker T. Washington was a spokesman for many African Americans. Business tycoons such as Andrew Carnegie and John D. Rockefeller gave him money to build trade schools for African Americans. Several Presidents of the United States sought his advice on racial issues.

A different view. Other African Americans disagreed with Washington, however. How could blacks move ahead, they asked, when whites denied them advanced education and jobs? Racial harmony was impossible when whites were lynching blacks and denying them the right to vote.

W.E.B. Du Bois (doo BOIS) was one leader who took this view. Du Bois was a professor, author, and public speaker. He was the first African American to earn a Ph.D. from Harvard University in 1895.

Du Bois agreed that "thrift, patience, and industrial training" were important. However, he urged blacks to fight discrimination. "So far as Mr. Washington apologizes for injustice," Du Bois said, "we must firmly oppose him."

Struggle for civil rights. In 1909, Du Bois joined with Jane Addams, Lincoln Steffens, and other reformers to form the ***National Association for the Advancement of Colored People,*** or NAACP. Blacks and whites in the NAACP worked together to gain equal rights for African Americans.

Most Progressives, however, thought little about the problems of African Americans. When some black soldiers were accused of rioting in Brownsville, Texas, President Roosevelt ordered their whole regiment to be dishonorably discharged. Later, President Wilson ordered the segregation of black and white government workers. Black leaders met with Wilson to protest this move. Wilson replied that "segregation is not humiliating, but a benefit." His action

Crusader for Equal Rights *W.E.B. Du Bois, seen here in his NAACP office, refused to accept discrimination. "The way for people to gain their reasonable rights," he said, "is not by voluntarily throwing them away." Du Bois edited the NAACP journal,* The Crisis, *for more than 20 years.*
Multicultural Heritage *How did the views of Du Bois differ from those of Booker T. Washington?*

Connections With Economics
Background

The first woman to become a bank president in the United States was Maggie Lena Walker, an African American. Walker worked at the Order of St. Luke, a fraternal organization that guaranteed its members medical care when they were sick and a decent burial when they died. By 1899, she reached the top position at the organization. As part of her work there, she established local chapters of St. Luke in African American churches and started a newspaper that featured stories about successful African Americans.

In 1903, Walker founded the St. Luke Penny Savings Bank. She made the bank such a success that the all-white, all-male Richmond government kept the city's tax monies there. Walker used the bank to assist African American homeowners and college students. She also founded the Richmond Council of Colored Women, which raised money to fund a home for delinquent girls, a tuberculosis sanatorium, and a community center.

Linking Past and Present
Activity

Encourage students to learn more about and report to the class on the history of the NAACP. Some students might want to research some of the organization's methods (court cases, voting, or use of the media, for example). Others might study some of the organization's leaders (such as Benjamin Hooks, Juanita Jackson, James Weldon Johnson, Vernon Jordan, Clarence Mitchell, Roy Wilkins, or Margaret Wilson). Alternatively, invite a local representative of the NAACP to address the class about the organization's history and goals.

The Search for Knowledge *In this photograph, a senior class at Tuskegee Institute in Alabama studies American history.* **American Traditions** *How did higher education fit into the goals of both W.E.B. Du Bois and Booker T. Washington?*

led restaurants, hotels, and stores in Washington to enforce racial segregation.

Racial pride. Some African Americans succeeded despite huge obstacles. Sarah Walker, better known as Madame C. J. Walker, was the first American woman—black or white—to earn over $1 million. Orphaned at age 6, Walker later became a laundry worker. In 1905, she created a line of hair care products for African American women. At first, she sold her products door to door. They were so popular that Walker's business became a major company.

George Washington Carver, too, contributed to black pride. Carver, a scientist, taught at Tuskegee Institute. Beginning in the 1890s, he discovered hundreds of new uses for crops grown in the South. For example, his experiments with peanuts led him to create peanut butter—a popular American food. In addition, Carver's writings about crop rotation changed southern farming practices.

Ordinary African Americans felt a sense of pride in their communities. Churches like the African Methodist Episcopal Church offered a strong foundation for religious and family life. They were also training grounds for African American leaders. Black colleges and universities trained young people to enter the professions. Black-owned banks, insurance companies, and businesses served community needs.

A New Generation of Native Americans

Native Americans struggled to survive in the face of poverty and discrimination. The Dawes Act had granted Native Americans 160-acre plots on reservation lands. With these lands, Indians were supposed to become farmers and enter the mainstream of American life. Instead, Indians were swindled out of millions of acres of land.

ART GALLERY: OUR COMMON HERITAGE

● **JAUNE QUICK-TO-SEE SMITH** *Buffalo, 1992* ●

Unlike their parents and grandparents, most young Native Americans of the early 1900s grew up on reservations. For them, it required a determined effort to recapture and preserve their heritage before it disappeared. Today, Flathead artist Jaune Quick-to-See Smith continues this effort. In works like Buffalo, Smith blends oil paint with a variety of printed materials. This collage creates a striking view of the Indians' past and present. **The Arts** *Why do you think Smith chose this subject for a painting?*

In the early 1900s, a new generation of Native American leaders emerged. One group set up the Society of American Indians. It included artists, writers, Christian ministers, lawyers, and doctors from many Native American groups. They worked for social justice and tried to educate other Americans about Native American life.

Our Multicultural Heritage
Activity

Ask a volunteer to explain the following statement: "Most white Progressives accepted the belief that white people were somehow superior to nonwhites, including Asians, Latinos, and Native Americans as well as African Americans." Divide the class into groups of three or four. Assign each group one of the minorities cited and ask each group to list issues that they would like to see reformers consider. For each issue listed, have members note the obstacles to change or reform in this area. Conclude by asking students why they think progress in the struggle for justice for minorities moved more slowly than reforms aimed at political corruption and unfair business practices. Use the lists to compile a Minority Group Progressive Agenda.

Asian American Experience

As you have read, anti-Chinese feelings led Congress to pass the Chinese Exclusion Act of 1882. With new immigration cut off, the Chinese population slowly declined.

Americans on the West Coast then turned to other Asian lands for cheap labor. They hired Filipino and Japanese workers, mostly young men. More than 100,000 Japanese entered the United States in the early 1900s.

Many Japanese were farmers. They settled on dry, barren land that other western farmers thought was useless. Through hard work and careful management, the Japanese made their farms profitable. Other Japanese immigrants worked in lumber mills, canneries, and mines.

American farmers and factory workers resented the newcomers. They called for limits on Japanese immigration. In response, President Roosevelt reached a *Gentlemen's Agreement* with Japan in 1907. Japan agreed to limit the number of workers coming to the United States. In exchange, the United States allowed the wives of Japanese men already here to join them.

Mexican Americans Defend Their Rights

In 1910, revolution and famine spread across Mexico. To escape the disorder, thousands of Mexicans crossed the border into the American Southwest. Although many later returned to Mexico, some remained.

Our Common Heritage
The young Native American Jim Thorpe became a superstar as an All-American college halfback and a gold medal winner at the 1912 Olympics. There, he won the decathlon and pentathlon.

Many Mexican immigrants worked in the fields, harvesting crops. They built highways and dug irrigation ditches. Some lived in shacks alongside the railroads they had helped to construct. Others moved to cities.

Like other immigrant groups, Mexicans created their own neighborhoods, called **barrios.** There, they preserved much of their culture, including their language.

Some Americans responded with violence to the flood of immigrants from Mexico. They attacked newcomers as well as Mexican Americans whose families had lived in the United States for generations. In 1912, the Mexican government protested the violence. In defense, Mexican Americans formed mutualistas, or mutual aid groups. Members pooled money to buy insurance and pay for legal advice.

SECTION 5 REVIEW

1. **Identify:** (a) Ida B. Wells, (b) Booker T. Washington, (c) W.E.B. Du Bois, (d) NAACP, (e) Gentlemen's Agreement.
2. **Define:** barrio.
3. Why did life for African Americans become more difficult in the 1890s?
4. What individuals and groups helped African Americans build racial pride?
5. How did the Chinese Exclusion Act affect Japanese immigration to the United States?
6. (a) What was the Society of American Indians? (b) Why did Mexican Americans form mutualistas?
7. **CRITICAL THINKING Comparing** How were the situations of African Americans and Mexican Americans similar in the Progressive Era?

ACTIVITY **Writing to Learn**
Write a dialogue between Booker T. Washington and W.E.B. Du Bois about the following question: What should African Americans do to fight discrimination and get ahead?

Chapter 21 • **617**

Our Multicultural Heritage

Milestone Have students read Working for Mexican American Rights, on page 63 of the *Our Multicultural Heritage* booklet. (Enrichment/Easy)

Student Study Guide

Section 5 Study Guide Have students use the Section 5 Study Guide on page 163 of the *Student Study Guide* to review and reinforce the content of this section. (Reteaching/Average)

ACTIVITY

Guided Instruction The two leaders shared some important goals but also had some important differences. The dialogues that students create will probably feature both similarities and differences. Therefore, you might have students create a comparison-and-contrast chart about the views of Washington and Du Bois before they begin to write. Invite several volunteers to share their finished dialogues. Follow up with class commentary and discussion.

Answers to Section 5 Review

1. (a) Ida B. Wells, p. 613, (b) Booker T. Washington, p. 613, (c) W.E.B. Du Bois, p. 614, (d) NAACP, p. 614, (e) Gentlemen's Agreement, p. 617
2. barrio, p. 617
3. Jim Crow laws and prejudice still governed the ways in which many whites treated African Americans. Furthermore, an economic depression increased racial tensions.
4. Individuals such as Sarah Walker and George Washington Carver and groups such

as the NAACP boosted African Americans' pride. Leaders such as Booker T. Washington and W.E.B. Du Bois spoke and wrote to encourage African Americans.
5. When the Chinese were excluded, their numbers declined, and some Americans turned to the Japanese as a cheap labor pool. As a result, more Japanese came to the United States to work.
6. (a) a group started in the early 1900s to work for social justice for Native Americans

and to teach others about Native American life (b) to defend themselves from violence by pooling money to buy insurance and pay for legal advice
7. Possible Answer: Both groups faced discrimination and violence; both settled in ethnic neighborhoods; both formed organizations to fight injustices.

Answers to Reviewing the Main Ideas

1. It required office seekers to pass examinations.

2. The ICC, which forbade pooling and rebates, was created to regulate railroads; the Sherman Antitrust Act, which forbade trusts from acting "in restraint of trade," was enacted.

3. Possible Answer: the Seventeenth Amendment; the creation of the primary, initiative, referendum, and recall

4. (a) Roosevelt felt that good trusts should be left alone and that bad trusts should be broken up. (b) He targeted Northern Securities as a bad trust and had the Attorney General bring a suit against it.

5. (a) The Elkins Act outlawed rebates. (b) The Hepburn Act increased the power of the ICC, permitting it to set railroad rates. (c) The Meat Inspection Act protected consumers by sending more inspectors into meatpacking plants.

6. More women were working outside the home, and they demanded more political power.

7. Minority groups—African Americans, Asian Americans, Mexican Americans, and Native Americans—continued to face poverty, violence, and prejudice.

8. (a) Washington stressed that learning a trade and earning money would give African Americans power to insist on political and social equality. (b) Du Bois urged African Americans to fight peacefully against discrimination; he was also a co-founder of the NAACP. (c) Carver became an inspiration for African Americans through his scientific achievements.

9. This organization worked for social justice and attempted to teach other Americans about Native American culture.

Answers to Thinking Critically

1. (a) Possible Answer: Tweed helped poor people get jobs and gave them food and other necessities. (b) Possible Answer: If people were loyal to Tweed and his henchmen, they might resist changes brought about by re-

Summary

- In the late 1800s, pressure from reformers led Congress to take steps to end the spoils system and stop unfair business practices.
- In the early 1900s, Progressives pushed for reforms, including limits on trusts, reform of city governments, laws to empower voters, and greater protection for consumers.
- Three Presidents—Theodore Roosevelt, William Howard Taft, and Woodrow Wilson—won new laws and backed amendments to achieve Progressive goals.
- Women took active roles in the Progressive Movement as they sought suffrage and campaigned for other reforms.
- Minorities such as African Americans, Asian Americans, Mexican Americans, and Native Americans worked for justice and equality in the face of prejudice and violence.

Reviewing the Main Ideas

1. How did the Civil Service Commission try to limit the spoils system?
2. How did Congress try to regulate railroads and big business in the late 1800s?
3. Describe three ways voters gained more power during the Progressive Era.
4. (a) What was Theodore Roosevelt's attitude toward trusts? (b) What did he do in the Northern Securities case?
5. Explain the effect of each of the following laws: (a) Elkins Act, (b) Hepburn Act, (c) Meat Inspection Act.
6. Why did the women's suffrage movement gain strength in the early 1900s?
7. What groups did not share in the advances made during the Progressive Era?
8. Explain how the following people worked to help the community: (a) Booker T. Washington, (b) W.E.B. Du Bois, (c) George Washington Carver.
9. What were the goals of the Society of American Indians?

Thinking Critically

1. **Analyzing Ideas** After Boss Tweed died, a reporter noted, "The bulk of the poorer voters of this city today [honor] his memory, and look on him as the victim of the rich man's malice; as, in short, a friend of the needy." (a) Why did the poor see Tweed as a friend? (b) How might this have made reform of city government more difficult?
2. **Linking Past and Present** Congress passed the Pure Food and Drug Act in 1906. (a) What does the law provide? (b) How does the government protect consumers today?

Applying Your Skills

1. **Outlining** Review the outlining skill on page 28. Then prepare an outline of Section 3, Presidents Back Progressive Goals. Using your outline, write a summary of the achievements of one of the Presidents.
2. **Making a Generalization** Make a generalization about minorities who tried to overcome injustice in the Progressive Era.

Thinking About Geography

Match the letters on the map with the following places: **1.** Washington, D.C., **2.** New York City, **3.** Chicago, Illinois, **4.** Wisconsin, **5.** Wyoming, **6.** Illinois, **7.** Pennsylvania, **8.** Alabama. **Region** Why did Wyoming and other western states give women the vote?

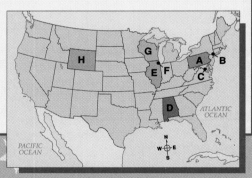

formers against Tweed. They would vote for the candidates that Tweed supported, who opposed reform.

2. (a) It requires food and drug manufacturers to list ingredients on packages, to stop false advertising, and to stop using impure ingredients. (b) Possible Answer: through stricter and more far-reaching laws controlling the labeling of products and the approval of new ones

Answers to Applying Your Skills

1. Check students' outlines and summaries for accuracy.
2. Possible Answer: Members of minority groups joined together to try to overcome injustice.

Answers to Thinking About Geography

1. C 2. B 3. F 4. G 5. H
6. E 7. A 8. D

Region: Women in the West had worked alongside men to build farms and cities.

Supporting the Suffragists

Form into groups to review the women's suffrage movement in the United States. Follow the suggestions below to write, draw, sing, or act to show what you have learned about this movement. You may use the textbook, encyclopedias, atlases, or other materials in your classroom library to complete the tasks. Be able to name your sources of information when you have finished the activity.

HISTORIANS Review the events in the suffrage movement, beginning with the Seneca Falls Convention and ending with passage of the Nineteenth Amendment. Then create an illustrated time line showing these events in chronological order.

GOVERNMENT OFFICIALS Review the steps necessary to pass an amendment to the Constitution. Then make a flowchart showing how the Nineteenth Amendment was passed.

REPORTERS Imagine that you are covering a suffragist march for a newspaper of the early 1900s. Write an article about the event.

MUSICIANS Make a list of the arguments in favor of suffrage used by women in the early 1900s. Then write a song for the suffragists. Perform your song for the class.

WRITERS AND ACTORS Find out about one of the leading women suffragists of the late 1800s or early 1900s. Writers can prepare a script for an oral biography of the person. Actors can "become" the person and present the oral biography.

★ Hold a Supporting the Suffragists Day. Have each group share its activity either on videotape or in a live presentation.

Celebrating the Nineteenth Amendment

Suffragist banner

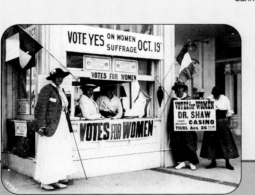

Seeking support

Assessment

Chapter Resources Binder For a more comprehensive evaluation of student understanding of this chapter, assign Chapter Tests A and B and/or Extra Unit Questions from Unit 7, pages 7–12 and 43–45.

Computer Test Bank You can use Chapter Tests and Extra Unit Questions to create your own tests for both testing and retesting.

Alternative Assessment

Chapter Resources Binder See the Alternative Assessment booklet in the *Social Studies Educator's Handbook* series.

Portfolio You might meet with students to choose appropriate work from the chapter for inclusion in their portfolios.

Lessons	Teaching Resources
1 **Americans Look Abroad** **Objectives** 1. Identify the early foreign policy of the United States. 2. Explain why American ships visited Japan in the 1850s. 3. Describe how the United States gained Alaska.	**Lesson Planner** Cooperative Learning, p. 136 **Student Study Guide** Section 1 Study Guide, p. 166 **Chapter Resources Binder, Unit 7** *History Through Literature* The Call of the Wild, p. 18 *Geography in History* Alaska: Icebox or Treasure Chest?, pp. 19–20
2 **Across the Pacific** **Objectives** 1. Explain why some Americans favored overseas expansion in the late 1800s. 2. Describe how Americans gained control of Hawaii. 3. Identify the policies that the United States followed in China.	**Lesson Planner** Cooperative Learning, p. 137 **Student Study Guide** Section 2 Study Guide, p. 167 **Our Multicultural Heritage** *Biography* Prince Kuhio, Royal Congressman, p. 64 *Milestone* History in Dance: The Hula, p. 66 **Interdisciplinary Connections:** American Imperialism ■ *Arts* Battle Scenes and Sentiments, p. 128 ▨ *Sciences* New Ships for a New Era, p. 129 ■ *World* Imperialism in Egypt, p. 130 ■ *Economics* The Promise of Imperialism, p. 131 ■ *Civics* Monarchy in Hawaii, p. 132
3 **War With Spain** **Objectives** 1. Identify the events that led to the Spanish-American War. 2. Identify the lands that the United States gained as a result of the war. 3. Explain why Americans fought in the Philippines after 1898.	**Lesson Planner** Cooperative Learning, p. 138 **Student Study Guide** Section 3 Study Guide, p. 168 **Chapter Resources Binder, Unit 7** *Skill Application* Using Note Cards, p. 16 **Our Multicultural Heritage** *Biography* Lola Rodríguez de Tió, Poet and Patriot, p. 65
4 **The Big Stick in Latin America** **Objectives** 1. Explain why the United States built the Panama Canal. 2. Identify the policies that Americans adopted toward Latin America. 3. Explain why the United States invaded Mexico in 1916.	**Lesson Planner** Cooperative Learning, p. 139 **Student Study Guide** Section 4 Study Guide, p. 169 **Chapter Resources Binder, Unit 7** *Critical Thinking* Comparing, p. 17

Multimedia Resources	Additional Resources	Chapter-Level Resources
Transparencies *Time Lines* The United States and the World, 1860–1900, p. E-21		**Lesson Planner** Activity Based, pp. 140–141 **Student Study Guide** Chapter 22 Study Guide, pp. 170–171 **Chapter Resources Binder** **Unit 7** Vocabulary Building, p. 15 Chapter Test A, pp. 21–23 Chapter Test B, pp. 24–26 Illustration Master, p. 27 Extra Unit Questions, pp. 43–45 **English Guided Reading** Guided Reading, pp. 43–44 **Spanish Resources** **Computer Test Bank** Chapter Tests A and B Extra Unit Questions
Transparencies *Cause and Effect* Overseas Expansion, p. F-25 *Geography and History* Alaska and Hawaii, p. I-85 *Interdisciplinary Connections* Asia and the Pacific, 1890s p. B-75 **CD-ROM** *History Makers* Alfred Thayer Mahan **Videotapes/Videodiscs** *United States History Video Collection* From Isolation to Empire, Vol. 15, Ch. 13	**Voices of Freedom** Looking Outward, pp. 170–171 Under Attack in China, pp. 174–175	
Transparencies *Fine Art* Charge of the Rough Riders at San Juan Hill, p. D-15 **Videotapes/Videodiscs** *United States History Video Collection* The Spanish-American War, Vol. 15, Ch. 16; The American Empire, Vol. 15, Ch. 19	**Voices of Freedom** Yellow Journalism Demands Action, p. 171 Remember the *Maine,* p. 172 Admiral Dewey at Manila Bay, pp. 173–174 **Historical Outline Map Book** The United States in the Caribbean, 1898–1917, p. 58 **Customized Reader** African American Troops in Florida in 1898, article VA-8	**Guided Reading Audiotapes** Side 8 **CD-ROM** *Time Tour* Expanding Overseas (1865–1916) in A New Role in the World
Transparencies *Political Cartoons* An Expanding Nation, p. G-23 *Cause and Effect* Overseas Expansion, p. F-25 **Videotapes/Videodiscs** *United States History Video Collection* The Panama Canal, Vol. 15, Ch. 25; The United States and Latin America, Vol. 15, Ch. 28	**Voices of Freedom** The Fight Against Yellow Fever, pp. 192–193 The Roosevelt Corollary, p. 191	

Lesson Planner

For a fully developed **Activity-Based** lesson plan for Chapter 22, see the *Lesson Planner,* pages 140–141.

Chapter Resources

Vocabulary Building The Vocabulary Building worksheet for Chapter 22 from Unit 7, page 15, of the *Chapter Resources* binder can be used as a prereading activity or as a review of chapter vocabulary. (Reteaching/Easy)

Student Study Guide

Chapter 22 Study Guide Refer students to pages 170–171 of the *Student Study Guide* for the Chapter 22 Study Guide. The study guide can be used for chapter review as well as for reteaching. (Reteaching/Average)

Guided Reading Audiotapes

Students can use *Guided Reading Audiotapes,* Chapter 22, side 8, to hear section previews, summaries, and review questions. The tapes might benefit students who are auditory learners, students who have trouble reading, or students acquiring English. Tapes are also available in Spanish. (Reteaching/Easy)

CHAPTER **22**

Expanding Overseas

(1865–1916)

CHAPTER OUTLINE

1 Americans Look Abroad

2 Across the Pacific

3 War With Spain

4 The Big Stick in Latin America

1898 *The United States defeated Spain in the Spanish-American War. This magazine cover celebrates the nation's swift victory.*

1867 *Secretary of State William Seward bought Alaska from Russia. This cigar case was given to Seward in honor of the purchase.*

1890s *The United States built up its navy in order to protect its growing overseas trade.*

| 1865 | 1890 | 1895 | 1900 |

WORLD EVENT
1870s Age of Imperialism begins

WORLD EVENT
1895 Cuba rebels against Spain

620 • Chapter 22

Chapter Time Line
Understanding Chronology

After you have discussed time-line captions, illustrations, and World Event notes with students, you might challenge their recall of geographical as well as chronological information. Prepare an outline map ahead of time of each of the following places:

Hawaii	Spain	Panama
Mexico	Cuba	Latin America
China	Alaska	

Have students identify each place. (You might ask them to verify their answers by comparing the outline maps to maps in their texts.) Then have them work with partners to identify the time line event associated with each place. On the basis of their responses, they should make a list of the places in "chronological" order. (The correct order is Alaska, Cuba, Spain, China and Hawaii [same date], Latin America, Mexico, and Panama.) Discuss the sequence in class, clearing up any misunderstandings.

Chapter Setting

The tattered envelope had come all the way from Cuba. Inside, J. M. McCurdy found a brief letter from his son, Allen. Allen wrote about how the Americans were faring in the war against Spain. With a rush of excitement, he described how he had taken part in a skirmish against Spanish troops:

66After firing from the woods for an hour, we charged up the hill and the Spaniards retreated to another fortified hill. . . . [W]e charged the next hill, and the Spaniards again retreated. This continued all day and was very hard work, several boys being sunstruck and exhausted by the heat. Our loss was heavy. 99

Like all soldiers, McCurdy complained about the food—especially stale bread fried in bacon grease. He told his father not to worry about him and said he would be home "in time to eat Christmas dinner with you at the farm." He also asked his father to mail him a new pair of shoes because his others had been worn out trudging through the Cuban underbrush.

Allen McCurdy was one of the Rough Riders, a group of young Americans who volunteered to fight against Spain in 1898. The war marked a new era in American history. The United States had expanded across the North American continent. Now, Americans were looking to expand their power overseas.

ACTIVITY

On a map of the world, locate the following places that became important in American history in the late 1800s: Japan, Alaska, Hawaii, China, Cuba, the Philippines, and Panama. How does the location of these places support the idea that Americans were expanding their power overseas?

Chapter Resources

English Guided Reading Duplicate and distribute the Chapter 22 Guided Reading worksheets on pages 43–44 in the English Guided Reading section of the *Chapter Resources* binder. Students who have difficulty reading might also benefit from using these worksheets. Have students complete the worksheets before they begin reading. You might pair a more fluent student or a student who is a strong reader with each SAE student to review. (Reteaching/Easy)

Spanish Resources See the Spanish Resources section of the *Chapter Resources* binder.

ACTIVITY

Guided Instruction Refer students to a classroom map of the world, or have them use the World Map on pages 890–891 of this text. You might have students measure the distance from the United States (say, from Washington, D.C.) to each place named, to help them better grasp the scope of the expansion. Discuss the question with the class as a whole, and have them come to a class interpretation of the information.

1900 *Hawaii became a United States territory. This coat of arms belonged to the Hawaiian royal family, who were swept from power when the Americans gained control.*

1904 *President Roosevelt declared that the United States had a right to intervene in Latin America. Here, Roosevelt, the "global policeman," stands guard over the world.*

1914 *The Panama Canal opened, creating a shorter sea route between the Atlantic and Pacific oceans. This postage stamp celebrated the twenty-fifth anniversary of the canal.*

| 1900 | 1905 | 1910 | 1915 |

WORLD EVENT
1900 Boxer Rebellion takes place in China

WORLD EVENT
1910 Mexican Revolution begins

Chapter 22 • **621**

Students Acquiring English
Activity

This chapter offers a good opportunity to build on the knowledge of students whose first language is Spanish. On the board, make a list of Spanish words and names from the chapter, such as the following: José Martí, Cuba, Puerto Rico, *Patria Libre* (newspaper), Lola Rodríguez de Tió, Filipinos, Balboa, Guantanamo, San Francisco, Colombia, Florida, Porfirio Díaz, Panama, Juan Finlay, mosquito, Havana, Venezuela, Nicaragua, Mexico, Honduras, Colón, Veracruz, and Francisco "Pancho" Villa. Ask students with some fluency in Spanish to pronounce and define or discuss each word for the class. Then, as they come across the words in their reading, have Spanish-speaking students discuss the meaning or background of each one in terms of the chapter.

Linking Past and Present
Activity

Ironically, the desire for new territory during the late 1800s also gave the United States its first experience in a role that it still holds—the role of world police officer. Have students work individually or in pairs to make cause-and-effect charts showing this change. Charts should reflect the growing concern and increased involvement of the United States in the affairs of other nations. Later, have students share their work, comparing the ideas and examples.

Bell Ringer

Have students imagine that they are business people who need new markets for their goods. Ask: How would you persuade the government to abandon its policy of isolation and begin seeking trade overseas? What arguments would you use? What advantages—for your own companies as well as for the nation—might result from overseas ventures?

Lesson Plan

1. Focus During the late 1800s, America annexed Alaska and Hawaii and opened trade with Japan and China. In this section, students learn how the United States moved away from its long-standing tradition of isolationism.

2. Instruct Have students make two columns on a piece of paper, labeling one Japan and the other Alaska. As they work through the section, have students note any facts that they consider important under each heading.

3. Close To close the lesson, pose a series of rapid-fire *Who, What, Where, When, Why,* and *How* questions about United States involvement in Japan and Alaska. Encourage students to use their notes to respond to any questions that they cannot answer immediately.

1
Americans Look Abroad

FIND OUT
- What was the early foreign policy of the United States?
- Why did American ships visit Japan in the 1850s?
- How did the United States gain Alaska?

VOCABULARY isolation

In 1880, the ruler of the Turkish empire thought of a way to save his country money. He planned to shut down his nation's embassies in "minor" countries. One of these minor countries was the United States. As everyone knew, the United States played only a small role in world affairs.

Turkey's plan was badly timed. By 1880, the United States was taking steps to increase its diplomatic contacts with other parts of the world.

A Tradition of Isolation

For its first 75 years, the United States had little to do with the rest of the world. In his Farewell Address, as you recall, George Washington had advised the nation to "steer clear of permanent alliances" with other countries. Later Presidents continued this policy of isolation, or having little to do with foreign nations. They had no wish to be pulled into Europe's frequent wars.

Isolation suited most Americans in the early 1800s. After all, they were busy building railroads and setting up new farms and factories. Few cared about other countries. One New York newspaper even suggested closing the Department of State, which handled foreign affairs. It had "outgrown its usefulness," the editors wrote.

Unlocking Japan

Despite a policy of isolation from the political affairs of other countries, Americans conducted a lively foreign trade. From the early 1700s, sailing ships loaded with American goods sailed to Europe. Other American trading ships traveled to Asia, including China and the Philippines. The Asian nation of Japan, however, refused to trade with the Americans.

A closed door. Japan was a small island nation. Fearing the influence of outsiders, in the 1600s it imposed complete isolation on itself. It expelled all Westerners* and ended trade with foreigners. Only one ship a year from the Dutch East India Company was allowed to trade at the port of Nagasaki.

Perry's mission. American merchants wanted to open Japan to trade. They also wanted the Japanese to help shipwrecked sailors who washed up on their shores. To achieve these goals, President Millard Fillmore sent Commodore Matthew Perry to Japan in the early 1850s.

Perry's four warships steamed into Tokyo Bay in July 1853. The Japanese had never seen steam-powered ships. They denounced Perry and his squadron as "barbarians in floating volcanoes" and ordered them to leave.

Before sailing away, Perry presented Japanese officials with a letter from President Fillmore. In it, the President asked the Japanese to open up trade with the United States. Perry said he would come back the following year for an answer.

A new treaty. Perry returned with seven warships in February 1854. The Japanese were impressed with this show of strength. The following month, the Japanese emperor signed the *Treaty of Kanagawa.* In it, he agreed to American demands to help shipwrecked sailors. He also opened two Japanese ports to trade.

---

*To the Japanese, Westerners were white people from Europe and North America.

Connections With the World
Background

The peoples who originally populated Japan probably traveled over narrow land bridges from the mainland. The first inhabitants were most likely Caucasians from Siberia. In later centuries, settlers arrived by sea from Korea and China. Others came from as far away as Polynesia and Indonesia. From this varied background came the modern Japanese people.

Team-Teaching Suggestion
Art

You might work with an art teacher to present a lesson on Japanese art. You may be able to borrow slides from a library or make your own slides/transparencies using such beautiful art books as Henri Stierlin's *Great Civilizations: The Cultural History of Japan.* Suggested artwork includes:
- Primitive clay figures of prehistoric Japan (through the third century A.D.)
- Clay, wood, and bronze statues of Buddha (sixth through eleventh centuries)

- Korean-inspired pottery and porcelain (seventeenth and eighteenth centuries)
- Murals and screen paintings (sixteenth and seventeenth centuries)
- Lacquerware and tiny netsuke statues (sixteenth through eighteenth centuries)
- Prints and paintings (eighteenth and nineteenth centuries)

Perry's visit had important effects. It launched trade between Japan and the West. It also made Japan realize the power of the industrial nations of the West. Japan soon set out to become a modern, industrial nation, taking the United States as one of its models.

GEOGRAPHY AND HISTORY
William Seward and American Expansion

American interest in Asia continued in the 1860s. When Abraham Lincoln became President in 1861, he made William Seward Secretary of State. Seward wanted the United States to dominate trade in the Pacific. Seward saw Alaska as the stepping stone toward that domination. Alaska, however, was a Russian colony.

Buying Alaska. One night in 1867, Seward was playing cards in Washington, D.C. He was interrupted by a message from the Russian ambassador. The czar of Russia, said the ambassador, was willing to sell Alaska to the United States for $7.2 million. Seward did not hesitate. He agreed to buy the land then and there.

"But your Department is closed," said the ambassador. "Never mind that," Seward replied. "Before midnight you will find me at the Department, which will be open and ready for business."

Next morning, Seward completed the deal. The cost came to 2 cents an acre. The purchase of Alaska increased the area of the United States by almost one fifth.

History and You
In the 1850s, Japan did not want to import goods from the United States. Today, some Americans are concerned that the United States imports too many products from Japan. What Japanese products do you use?

Meeting of Two Worlds *Commodore Perry's mission to Japan in 1853 ended more than 200 years of Japanese isolation. In this painting, a modern Japanese artist portrays Perry's historic meeting with Japan's leaders.* **United States and the World** *Why did the American government send Perry to Japan?*

"Seward's Folly." Seward's purchase of Alaska seemed foolish to many Americans. To them, Alaska was a barren land of icy mountains. They called the purchase Seward's Folly.

In fact, the lowlands of southern Alaska are well suited to farming. Alaska is also rich in natural resources such as copper and timber.

In 1896, prospectors found gold in Alaska. Thousands of Americans flocked to the Alaska gold rush. In 1968, drillers hit "black gold"—oil—in Alaska. As Americans discovered, Seward's Folly was far more valuable than they had thought in 1867.*

---
*Alaska remained a territory until 1959. That year, it was admitted as the forty-ninth state.

 Lesson Planner

For a developed **Cooperative Learning** lesson plan, see the *Lesson Planner,* page 136.

Answer to Caption

to open Japan up to American trade and to persuade Japan to help shipwrecked American sailors

 Transparencies

Time Lines Use the transparency, The United States and the World, 1860–1900, on page E-21 of *American History Transparencies.* This time line, which spans the last half of the nineteenth century, will help students see the relationships between events taking place in the United States and events occurring elsewhere in the world. (Enrichment/Average)

Chapter Resources

History Through Literature To show students how Alaska captured the imagination of some Americans, duplicate and distribute the worksheet, The Call of the Wild, from Unit 7, page 18, of the *Chapter Resources* binder. (Enrichment/Average)

Geography in History Duplicate and distribute the worksheet, Alaska: Icebox or Treasure Chest?, from Unit 7, pages 19–20, of the *Chapter Resources* binder. The worksheet explores the travels of prospectors after gold was discovered in "Seward's Folly." (Enrichment/Challenging)

Our Multicultural Heritage
Background

Four Native American groups inhabit Alaska. The Tlingits (TLIHNG gihts) live on the coastal lands of the southeast. Centuries ago, they developed a highly civilized culture. Today, they are still known for their decorative handiwork.

The Haidas (HĪ dahz), always voyagers and traders, also live in southeast Alaska. Many historians credit them with the idea of making totem poles to display tribal and family origins.

The Tsimshian (SIHM shee an) people once lived in British Columbia. Long before Europeans arrived, they discovered rich fishing areas off Alaska's Pacific coast. Eventually they settled on Annette Island near Ketchikan. Tsimshian artwork includes ceremonial masks and wood carvings, including totem poles.

The Athapascans (ath uh PAS kuhnz) are one of the few groups to live in Alaska's interior. They are best known for their leatherwork and multicolored beadwork.

Linking Past and Present
Background

The Alaskan Gold Rush of 1897 lives again (in a way) in the boom town of Skagway, Alaska. In fact, the entire area is part of Klondike Gold Rush National Historical Park. Downtown Skagway has been called a living artifact of one of the most colorful gold rushes. The stores and saloons on Broadway, for example, are near perfect re-creations of their 1897 counterparts. The only noticeable difference is that the dusty (or muddy) streets have since been paved.

Student Study Guide

Section 1 Study Guide Have students use the Section 1 Study Guide on page 166 of the *Student Study Guide* to review and reinforce the content of this section. (Reteaching/Average)

ACTIVITY

Guided Instruction Since the writing activity is so short, have students concentrate on the quality of their words. (This is the perfect opportunity to have them use a thesaurus or book of synonyms.) Encourage students to share their completed telegrams and decide which ones offer the most convincing reasons.

Section 2
pp. 624–630

Bell Ringer

Remind students that from the fifteenth through the seventeenth centuries, European nations founded colonies in North America. Ask: How was American imperialism similar to the early colonization of North America? How was it different?

Other schemes for expansion. Seward had other schemes for expanding the territory of the United States. In 1867, he convinced Congress to annex Midway Island, in the middle of the Pacific Ocean. He then urged the United States to take control of Hawaii. He also wanted to build a canal across Central America to link the Atlantic and Pacific oceans.

Congress, however, rejected most of Seward's proposals. A Philadelphia newspaper summed up the doubts of most Americans about overseas expansion:

66 The true interests of the American people will be better served . . . by a thorough and complete development of the immense resources of our existing territory than by rash attempts to increase it. 99

That mood would soon change. ■

SECTION 1 REVIEW

1. **Locate:** (a) Japan, (b) Alaska, (c) Midway Island.
2. **Identify:** (a) Matthew Perry, (b) Treaty of Kanagawa, (c) William Seward.
3. **Define:** isolation.
4. Why did a policy of isolation suit most Americans in the early 1800s?
5. What were two effects of Commodore Perry's visits to Japan?
6. How did the United States acquire the territory of Alaska?
7. **CRITICAL THINKING Understanding Causes and Effects** Do you think that the presence of Perry's warships affected Japan's decision to sign a trade treaty with the United States? Explain.

ACTIVITY Writing to Learn

Imagine that you are Secretary of State Seward. Write a telegram of 25 words or less explaining to President Lincoln why you bought Alaska.

2
Across the Pacific

FIND OUT
- Why did some Americans favor overseas expansion in the late 1800s?
- How did Americans gain control of Hawaii?
- What policies did the United States follow in China?

VOCABULARY imperialism, sphere of influence

In 1890, an American reporter, Nellie Bly, circled the globe on an assignment for the New York *World*. Signs of the mighty British empire were everywhere. "No matter where I went, I saw English soldiers stationed," she reported. Americans—soldiers or civilians—were rare.

Bly's articles hit home. By 1890, European countries were expanding their trade and seizing colonies around the world. Many Americans wanted to enter the race for resources and new markets.

Age of Imperialism

The period between 1870 and 1914 has often been called the Age of Imperialism. Imperialism is the policy of powerful countries that seek to control the economic and political affairs of weaker countries or regions. Between 1870 and 1914, Europeans seized control of almost the entire continent of Africa and much of Southeast Asia.

One reason for the growth of imperialism in the 1800s was economic. The industrial nations of Europe wanted raw materials from Africa and Asia. They also wanted the

---

Answers to Section 1 Review

1. See the map on p. 630.
2. (a) Matthew Perry, p. 622, (b) Treaty of Kanagawa, p. 622, (c) William Seward, p. 623
3. isolation, p. 622
4. Americans were busy developing their new nation, building railroads, and setting up new farms and factories. Few cared about what was happening in other countries.
5. His visits launched trade between Japan and the West. They also made Japan realize the power of the industrial nations of the

West. Japan soon set out to modernize, using the United States as its model.
6. Secretary of State Seward purchased it from Russia for $7.2 million.
7. Possible Answer: Perry meant the warships as a show of strength to persuade the Japanese to do what the United States wanted. The Japanese might have concluded that if they did not submit to the wishes of the United States, the country might use military force against them.

people of these regions to buy goods made in European factories.

Imperialism had other causes. Many Europeans believed that they had a duty to spread their religion and culture to people they considered "backward." British writer Rudyard Kipling called this "the white man's burden." Such thinking ignored the fact that Africans and Asians already had rich cultures of their own.

A third cause was competition. When a European country colonized an area, it often closed the area's markets to other countries. A European nation might take over an area just to keep a rival nation from gaining control of it.

The American Urge to Expand

Americans could not ignore Europe's race for colonies. By the 1890s, the United States was a world leader in both industry and agriculture. American factories turned out huge amounts of steel and other goods. American farms grew bumper crops of corn, wheat, and cotton. If these products were not sold abroad, many people believed, the American economy would go into a deep slump.

Arguments for expansion. Most Americans wanted to increase trade. Many, however, disliked imperialism. After all, the United States had once been a colony of Britain. Americans had fought a war to win their own independence. How could they now colonize other lands?

Expansionists argued that Americans shared the duty to extend their culture to others. The United States had a special mission, one minister said, to spread democracy and Christianity "down upon Mexico, down upon Central and South America, out

American Foreign Trade, 1865–1915

Value in Billions of Dollars vs Year

Source: *Historical Statistics of the United States*

CHART SKILLS *As American industry grew in the years after the Civil War, foreign trade expanded. Expansionists called for a large navy to defend the nation's trade.* ● *What was the value of American foreign trade in 1865? In 1900? In 1915?*

Chapter 22 • **625**

Lesson Plan

1. Focus Having had a taste of imperialism, the United States quickly moved to colonize. In this section, students examine problems that arose in the annexation of Hawaii, as well as the role of the United States in obtaining an "open door" policy for trade with China.
2. Instruct Have students work in small groups to prepare a TV news program about the annexation of Hawaii. Possible topics include the role of American planters in Hawaii, Queen Liliuokalani's attitude toward annexation, advantages gained by the United States in annexing Hawaii, the attitude of President Grover Cleveland toward annexation, and problems that the United States had to face in its new relationship with Hawaii.
3. Close To close the lesson, ask students to contrast United States policy in Hawaii with United States policy in China at the turn of the century.

 Lesson Planner

For a developed **Cooperative Learning** lesson plan, see the *Lesson Planner,* page 137.

Answer to Chart Skills

$0.5 billion; $2.5 billion; $4.75 billion

Historical Sidelight
Background

The comment about spreading democracy and Christianity came from Josiah Strong, whose influential book *Our Country, Its Possible Future and Its Present Crisis* (1885) described his vision of an American empire. In Strong's interpretation of the theory of "survival of the fittest," the "fittest" was the Anglo-Saxon (English) race: "Is it [clear] that the Anglo-Saxon holds in his hands the destinies of mankind . . . ? Is it evident that the United States is to be the home of this race, the principal seat of his power, the great center of his influence? . . . We stretch our hand into the future with power to mold the destinies of unborn millions."

Strong's next book, *The New Era* (1893), expressed the minister's belief that God would bless Christians who were active in social work. His philosophy of "Christian Socialism" was met with great resistance from tradition-al churches, so in 1898, Strong formed the League for Social Service (renamed the American Institute for Social Service in 1902). As part of this organization, Strong continued to write and lecture. Some of his social programs were put into use in Great Britain and South America as well as in the United States.

Answer to Caption

Many felt that a large navy would need bases around the world.

Transparencies

Cause and Effect Use the transparency, Overseas Expansion, on page F-25 of *American History Transparencies*. This chart highlights some of the major causes leading to American expansion overseas as well as some of its effects. Teaching suggestions can be found on page F-8. (Enrichment/Average)

Geography and History Use the transparency, Alaska and Hawaii, on page I-85 of *American History Transparencies*. This map offers basic information about Hawaii, but you also might use it to review the purchase of Alaska. Teaching suggestions can be found on page I-15.

Voices of Freedom

Primary Source You might assign selection 5-1, Looking Outward, on pages 170–171 of *Voices of Freedom*. In the selection, Alfred Mahan discusses the need for a more powerful American fleet. (Enrichment/Easy)

CD-ROM

History Makers Access the biography of Alfred Thayer Mahan on the American Heritage® *History of the United States* CD-ROM.

---

upon the islands of the sea, over Africa and beyond."

Other expansionists stressed the need to offset the vanishing frontier. For 100 years, the economy had boomed as Americans settled the western frontier. The 1890 census said that the frontier was gone. People in crowded eastern cities had no new land to settle.

The solution was to take new land overseas. "We must turn our eyes abroad," said one official, "or they will soon look inward upon discontent."

Sea power. Captain Alfred Mahan of the United States Navy added to the debate. Mahan argued that the future prosperity of the United States depended on foreign trade. In turn, increased trade required a bigger navy to protect American merchant ships. "When a question arises of control over distant regions," Mahan wrote, "it must ultimately be decided by naval power."

In Mahan's view, expanding the navy would force the United States to take territory overseas. The navy would need bases throughout the world. Mahan was especially interested in acquiring harbors in the Caribbean and the Pacific as links to Latin America and Asia.

Even before Mahan's appeal, Congress had begun to enlarge and modernize the navy. New steam-powered warships with steel hulls were already being built. By the late 1890s, the United States had a large and powerful navy. Its ships were called the **Great White Fleet** because they were all painted white.

Annexing Hawaii

One territory that Alfred Mahan wrote about was Hawaii. The Hawaiian Islands lay between the United States and Japan. Controlling Hawaii, Mahan said, would give the United States a commercial and military outpost in the Pacific Ocean.

626 • Chapter 22

Foreign Travels As the United States expanded its navy, American sailors visited foreign ports all around the world. One sailor created this textile painting as a reminder of his overseas travels. **United States and the World** How was the development of a large, modern navy related to overseas expansion?

Rich soils, warm climate. Europeans and Americans first learned about Hawaii in 1778. That year, a British sea captain, James Cook, stopped at the islands to load up with fresh water on his way to China. In Hawaii, Cook found a tropical paradise.

Hawaii is a chain of eight large islands and more than 100 smaller islands. They are located in the Pacific Ocean, about 2,400 miles (3,800 km) southwest of California. The islands have rich soil, a warm climate,

---

Historical Sidelight
Background

Alfred Mahan came close to never having the chance to voice his theories about naval power. As a midshipman in 1859, Mahan requested transfer to a ship named the *Levant*. Superiors denied the request—much to Mahan's later relief. After the *Levant* sailed off into the Pacific, it disappeared mysteriously, leaving no clue as to its ultimate fate.

Only a land formed from volcanoes can have the natural distinctions of the Hawaiian Islands. For example, though most of the beaches boast dazzling white sand, the "big island" of Hawaii has several beaches of deep black sand. The sand is powdered lava, burnt black by incredible heat. A few beaches on the same island even have rare "green sands"—also volcanic in origin, but with a different mix of elements and less heat.

Connections With Science
Background

An unusual phenomenon on the island of Kauai is the "spouting horn." It is a permanent waterspout of sorts, caused by the escape of harmless volcanic gases from deep inside the Earth. The gases have found a vent, or opening, on a section of rocky beach. When they spurt from the vent, they are still hot enough to turn cool ocean waters into rising steam!

and plenty of rain. These conditions make it possible to grow crops all year.

About 2,000 years ago, Hawaii was settled by people from Polynesia—islands in the Central and South Pacific. In the early 1800s, American ships bound for China stopped at Hawaii. In 1820, the first American missionaries arrived to convert the Hawaiians to Christianity.

Missionaries and planters. Missionaries and other Americans advised the rulers of Hawaii from the 1830s on. Americans also helped write Hawaii's first constitution in 1839.

By the mid-1800s, Americans had set up many large sugar plantations in Hawaii. The planters wanted cheap labor. They brought in thousands of workers from China, Korea, the Philippines, and Japan. By 1900, one fourth of the people of Hawaii had been born in Japan.

As the sugar industry in Hawaii grew, so did the power of American sugar planters. In 1887, they forced the Hawaiian king, Kalakaua, to accept a new constitution. It reduced the king's power while increasing the planters' influence.

Planters stage a revolt. In 1891, Kalakaua died. His sister Liliuokalani (lih lee oo oh kah LAH nee) came to the throne. As queen, she rejected the new constitution and tried to restore the kingdom's independence.

American planters opposed the queen's attempt to limit their power. In early 1893, they rebelled against Queen Liliuokalani. The American ambassador called for marines to land on Hawaii. He said that the marines were needed to protect American lives. In fact, they helped the American rebels.

Faced with American guns, the queen gave up her throne. She wrote a stinging protest to the United States:

> ❝I, Liliuokalani, . . . do hereby solemnly protest against any and all acts done against myself and the constitutional Government of the Hawaiian Kingdom. . . .
>
> I yield to the superior force of the United States of America, whose [ambassador]. . . has caused United States troops to be landed [on Hawaii]. . . .
>
> Now, to avoid any collision of armed forces and perhaps the loss of life, I do this under protest, and impelled by said force, yield my authority.❞

A United States territory. The planters quickly set up a republic and asked the United States to annex Hawaii. A debate raged in Congress for months. President Grover Cleveland blocked moves to take over the islands. "Our interference in the Hawaiian Revolution of 1893 was disgraceful," he said later. "I am ashamed of the whole affair."

Congress finally annexed Hawaii in 1898, after Cleveland left office. Two years later, Hawaii became a United States territory. In 1959, Hawaii became the fiftieth state.

BIOGRAPHY Liliuokalani
In her youth, Liliuokalani was educated by an American missionary. She also toured Europe and the United States. As queen of Hawaii, however, she worked to reduce foreign influence.
United States and the World
How did Liliuokalani oppose American influence in Hawaii?

Connections With Geography
Activity

The island of Kauai has a mountain said to be the wettest place on Earth. Because of the trade winds blowing across its slopes, Mount Waialeale (wī ah lay AHL ay) has an average rainfall of 460 inches a year. In fact, the air at the top of the mountain is so heavy with moisture that it forms a permanent fog into which people can almost disappear from sight!

Students might enjoy comparing the amount of moisture on Mount Waialeale with the average annual rainfall in other parts of the world. Have them research rainy areas and graph the results. Encourage them to present their studies in a variety of ways—pie charts, line charts, and pictograms, as well as horizontal and vertical bar graphs.

Answer to Caption

Possible Answer: It showed that the United States had enough power to influence the policies of other nations. Japan and the European powers did not like the Open Door Policy, but they agreed to accept it.

Voices of Freedom

Primary Source You might assign selection 5-5, Under Attack in China, on pages 174–175 of *Voices of Freedom*. The selection is from the diary of Katharine Lowry, the wife of an embassy employee, in which she describes the Boxers' siege of the mission in which she lived. (Enrichment/Average)

Transparencies

Interdisciplinary Connections Use the transparency Asia and the Pacific, 1890s on page B-75 of *American History Transparencies*. Teaching suggestions can be found on page B-24. (Enrichment/Average)

Rivalry in China

Hawaii gave Americans a foothold in the Pacific. However, the United States was a latecomer in the race for Pacific territory. Other nations, including Britain and Germany, were already rivals for colonies there.

In the late 1800s, the three nations almost clashed over Samoa, a chain of islands in the South Pacific. In the end, the United States and Germany took joint control of the islands. Great Britain took other territory in the Pacific. (See the Connections feature at right.)

Carving up China. Rivalry among industrial nations was especially fierce in China. China had once been the most advanced empire in the world. The early European explorer Marco Polo, as you recall, was awed by the wealth of China in the 1200s.

China, however, did not industrialize in the 1800s, as European nations did. As a result, it was not able to fight off Western nations attracted by its vast resources.

In the late 1800s, Britain, France, Germany, Russia, and Japan carved spheres of influence in China. A **sphere of influence** was an area, usually around a seaport, where a nation had special trading privileges. Each nation made laws for its own citizens in its own sphere.

An open door. American leaders feared that the Europeans and Japanese would try to keep them from trading in China. In 1899, Secretary of State John Hay sent a letter to all the nations that had spheres of in-

---

★★
Linking Past and Present
The portion of Samoa that Germany controlled is now the independent nation of Western Samoa. The other portion of Samoa is still a territory of the United States. Called American Samoa, it is administered by the Department of the Interior.

An Open Door in China *The Open Door Policy guaranteed the United States a share in the rich trade with China. In this cartoon, a towering Uncle Sam holds the key to the open doors of China. Around him, other nations wait to get in.* **United States and the World** *How did the Open Door Policy show that the United States had become a world power?*

---

fluence in China. He urged them to follow an **Open Door Policy** in China. Under the policy, any nation could trade in any other nation's sphere of influence. The nations reluctantly accepted the Open Door Policy.

The Boxers. Many Chinese resented the foreigners who were dividing up their country. In 1899, some Chinese set up a secret society called the Righteous Fists of Harmony, or Boxers. The Boxers wanted to rid China of "foreign devils."

In 1900, the Boxers rebelled. They attacked foreigners all over China, killing more than 200. The Boxers trapped hundreds of foreigners in Beijing, the Chinese capital.

Foreign governments quickly organized an international army that included 2,500 Americans. Armed with modern weapons, the army freed the trapped foreigners and crushed the rebellion.

Several nations saw the **Boxer Rebellion** as an excuse for them to take more land in China. Once again, Secretary of State Hay stepped in. He sent a second Open Door

---

Connections With the World
Background

The custom of footbinding in China began during the Sung dynasty (960–1279) when one of the court ladies was admired for her exceptionally tiny feet. Ever since, to keep them small, girls from the age of five had their feet tightly bound with bandages. "No one will marry a girl with big feet," they were told.

Centuries later, in 1899, a western visitor to a Chinese home was allowed to see her host-

ess's bound feet. This was her reaction: "Oh, what a horrid-looking thing a bound foot is! It is awful to think of slowly crushing and changing the shape of a human foot until there is no more resemblance to a foot than to a block of wood. . . . Oh, what a shapeless thing it is! The process of binding is so slow but yet persistent that the agony must be awful."

Linking Past and Present
Activity

Have students research the various types of dwellings in which modern Chinese live. Examples might include apartment houses in the cities and suburbs, farmhouses in the countryside, yurts of the Kazak nomads, and adobe homes of Uighur farmers. Encourage students to accompany their reports with visual aids, photos, and perhaps even their own artwork.

CONNECTIONS

ARTS   SCIENCES   **GEOGRAPHY**   WORLD   ECONOMICS   CIVICS

The Typhoon That Changed History

On the morning of March 15, 1889, seven warships—three American, three German, and one British—stood on alert in the harbor of Apia in Samoa. The three nations had long been rivals for control of Samoa. German ships had even shelled Samoan villages that were friendly to Americans. Now, tempers were high. The sailors were spoiling for a fight.

Suddenly, a terrible typhoon roared into the harbor. All thoughts of conflict vanished as the frightened seamen sought to escape the storm—one of the worst in Samoa's history.

Fighting the waves and winds, the captain of the U.S.S. *Nipsic* was able to steer his ship and all but six of his crew to safety. The U.S.S. *Vandalia* was not so lucky. High winds sent the *Vandalia* crashing against a reef. The ship sank, and its entire crew drowned. Shortly after, the U.S.S. *Trenton* was tossed onto the sunken *Vandalia*. Its hull split and half full of water, the *Trenton* drifted to shore. All the crew were saved.

Apia harbor, Samoa

For the German ships, disaster was complete. The storm sank all three. Only the British ship escaped totally unharmed. With more powerful engines, it fought its way through the typhoon winds to safety.

The typhoon was a terrible disaster. In the end, however, it had some positive results. Because of the storm, American, British, and German leaders directed their full attention to the South Pacific. They became alarmed when they realized just how close to war they had come. The three nations agreed to meet at the negotiating table and resolve their rivalry in a less destructive way.

■ How did a typhoon affect the course of history in Samoa?

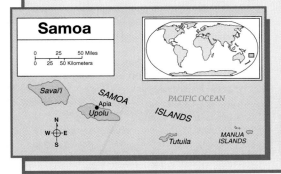

Samoa

0   25   50 Miles
0   25   50 Kilometers

Savai'i

SAMOA
Apia
Upolu

N
W–E
S

PACIFIC OCEAN

ISLANDS

Tutuila

MANUA
ISLANDS

ACTIVITY

Think of an important event in your life that was influenced by weather. Then prepare a newscast describing what happened.

Interdisciplinary CONNECTIONS

For worksheets establishing connections between the Chapter 22 main idea, American Imperialism, and five other disciplines, see the *Interdisciplinary Connections* booklet. (Enrichment)

- **Arts** Battle Scenes and Sentiments, page 128 (Easy)
- **Sciences** New Ships for a New Era, page 129 (Average)
- **World** Imperialism in Egypt, page 130 (Average)
- **Economics** The Promise of Imperialism, page 131 (Challenging)
- **Civics** Monarchy in Hawaii, page 132 (Average)

Answer to Connections

The destruction caused by the typhoon sobered the combatants and made them think about causing even more loss of life and property.

ACTIVITY

Guided Instruction You might have students spend a few minutes freewriting before they choose the event on which to report. Point out that although the form of the activity is relatively formal and objective, the content will be personal and thus informal and subjective. Before having volunteers share their finished newscasts with the class, allow students to review one another's drafts. As they review, they might offer constructive criticism about striking a balance between the form and the content of the newscast.

Team-Teaching Suggestion
Science

You might work with a science teacher to present a lesson about typhoons. In the presentation, explain how typhoons form and how they are similar to the hurricanes of the Atlantic Ocean. Mention, as well, the power of the storm surges that are created as typhoons move onto land. You might also discuss how these storms are tracked and the precautions taken to decrease the damage they cause.

Team-Teaching Suggestion
Mathematics

You might work with a mathematics teacher to present a lesson on money in the South Pacific and/or countries studied in this chapter—Japan, China, the Philippines, Cuba, Panama, Colombia, and Mexico. Students might be shown how exchange rates work by figuring how many yen, for example, they would receive for 10 American dollars. Then challenge them to work out problems exchanging their yen for pesos, and so on.

Answers to Map Study

1. Midway Island **2.** the Philippine Islands **3.** Alaska, Hawaii, Guam, and American Samoa

Student Study Guide

Section 2 Study Guide Have students use the Section 2 Study Guide on page 167 of the *Student Study Guide* to review and reinforce the content of this section. (Reteaching/Average)

ACTIVITY

Guided Instruction Remind students not only to make their paragraphs persuasive but also to take into consideration the audience. Point out that they will need arguments, or reasons, that will be persuasive to a particular group—in this case, the United States government.

As students write, remind them also to use a style of writing that seems similar to that which the queen used. In this way, their paragraphs will not seem so much like separate documents but rather like a continuation of the queen's letter.

MAP STUDY

In the late 1800s, the United States gained islands across the Pacific. American trading ships stopped at these islands to take on fuel and food on the way to China and Japan.

1. Which Pacific territory did the United States annex first?
2. Which territory was farthest from the United States mainland?
3. **Synthesizing Information** Compare this map to the chart on page 896. Which territories shown on this map are still part of the United States?

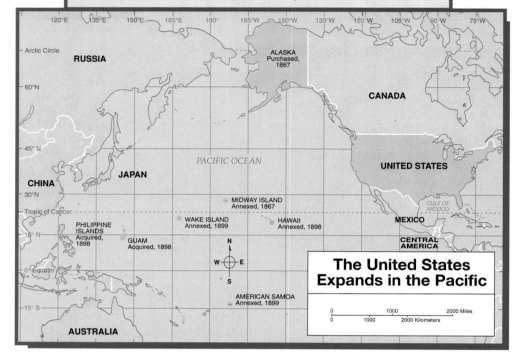

The United States Expands in the Pacific

letter urging all nations to respect China's independence. Hay's Open Door letters showed that the United States was playing a new role in world affairs.

SECTION 2 REVIEW

1. **Locate:** (a) Hawaii, (b) Samoa, (c) China.
2. **Identify:** (a) Alfred Mahan, (b) Great White Fleet, (c) Liliuokalani, (d) John Hay, (e) Open Door Policy, (f) Boxer Rebellion.
3. **Define:** (a) imperialism, (b) sphere of influence.
4. List three arguments Americans gave for expansion in the late 1800s.
5. (a) Why did planters stage a revolt in Hawaii? (b) How did the United States respond?
6. **CRITICAL THINKING Analyzing Ideas** How do you think the Open Door Policy helped the United States?

ACTIVITY Writing to Learn

Reread Queen Liliuokalani's letter on page 627. Continue the letter by writing a paragraph urging the United States not to support the planters.

Answers to Section 2 Review

1. See the map on p. 630.

2. (a) Alfred Mahan, p. 626, (b) Great White Fleet, p. 626, (c) Liliuokalani, p. 627, (d) John Hay, p. 628, (e) Open Door Policy, p. 628, (f) Boxer Rebellion, p. 628

3. (a) imperialism, p. 624, (b) sphere of influence, p. 628

4. Arguments include the belief that Americans had a special mission to spread democracy and Christianity; the economic need to offset the vanishing frontier; and the need for a strong navy to protect trade, which required territory for bases.

5. (a) They were responding to Queen Liliuokalani's attempt to limit their power. (b) The American ambassador called in the marines, who helped the rebels. The queen gave up her throne, and the planters set up a republic. In 1898, the United States annexed Hawaii.

6. Possible Answer: Other nations had already carved up China, and the United States had been left out. By calling for the Open Door Policy, the United States created a way to get a share of the China trade.

3 War With Spain

FIND OUT
- What events led to the Spanish-American War?
- What lands did the United States gain as a result of the war?
- Why did Americans fight in the Philippines after 1898?

For many years, Americans had looked longingly at Cuba, a lush island just 90 miles off the Florida coast. In 1823, Secretary of State John Quincy Adams compared Cuba to a ripe apple. A storm, he said, might tear that apple "from its native tree"—the Spanish empire—and drop it into American hands.

By the 1890s, Spain's once-vast empire in the Western Hemisphere had shrunk to two islands, Cuba and Puerto Rico. In 1895, Cuban rebels created the storm that Adams had hoped for.

A Hemispheric Giant

In the late 1800s, the United States grew richer and more powerful. Many Latin Americans worried that their northern neighbor wanted to dominate the Western Hemisphere.

A conference to improve relations. Concerned about growing anti-American feeling in Latin America, Secretary of State James G. Blaine set out to improve relations. In 1889, he invited Latin American nations to a conference in Washington, D.C. He hoped to increase cooperation among the nations of the Western Hemisphere. Blaine also wanted to remove barriers to trade between the United States and Latin America.

All but one Latin American nation sent delegates to the conference. The conference set up a group to work together to solve the problems of the hemisphere. In 1910, this group became known as the *Pan-American Union.*

Fears remain. Latin Americans were still suspicious of the United States. At the conference, they refused to open their borders to trade with the United States. They feared that a flood of American imports would ruin their own industries. Cuban patriot and writer José Martí warned that the goal of the conference was not good relations with Latin America but the "achievement of an era of United States dominion over the nations of America."

Revolt in Cuba

The United States became even more involved with Latin America in the 1890s. This involvement brought the nation to the brink of war with Spain. At the center of the dispute were the Spanish colonies of Cuba and Puerto Rico.

The Ever-Faithful Isle. Spain had once called Cuba its Ever-Faithful Isle. Unlike other Spanish colonies, Cuba did not rebel against Spanish rule in the early 1800s. In 1868, however, a violent revolution broke out in Cuba. It was finally crushed after 10 years of fighting.

Some of the Cuban revolutionaries fled to New York. There, patriots such as Lola Rodríguez de Tió and José Martí kept up the battle for freedom. Born in Puerto Rico, Rodríguez de Tió wrote patriotic poems in support of independence. Martí told of the Cuban struggle for freedom in his newspaper, *Patria.*

A new revolt. In 1895, Martí returned to Cuba. With cries of *Cuba Libre!*—Free Cuba!—rebels launched a new fight against Spain. Martí died in the first year of fighting, but the rebels won control of more than half the island.

Chapter 22 • **631**

Section 3
pp. 631–638

Bell Ringer

Have students imagine that each of them owns a small house. One day, strangers arrive and proceed to take over and occupy some of the rooms. Ask: What would you do as one of the unlucky homeowners? How is this situation similar to what the Americans did in their desire for more and more territory?

Lesson Plan

1. Focus During the late 1800s, the United States became increasingly involved in the affairs of Latin America. European influence in Latin America worried many Americans, and the United States took steps to protect its interests. In this section, students focus on events in the Caribbean, with special emphasis on the Spanish-American War.

2. Instruct Have students form five groups. Each group will prepare a 10-minute report on one of these events: the rebellion in Cuba; the explosion of the *Maine*; Commodore Dewey's victory in Manila; the Battle of San Juan Hill; and the end of the Spanish-American War. Reports could include news bulletins, eyewitness interviews, and discussions with leaders such as General Weyler, President McKinley, and Theodore Roosevelt.

3. Close To close the lesson, have students turn each subsection heading into a question and then answer it.

Historical Sidelight
Background

James G. Blaine was a newspaper editor who began a career in politics after election to the Maine state legislature in 1858. He served as Secretary of State under Presidents Garfield, Arthur, and Benjamin Harrison.

Blaine was a long-time advocate of closer relations with other nations of the Western Hemisphere. At the First Pan-American Conference (1889–1890), he had some success working out some tariff agreements with Latin American nations. More important, his efforts set up the framework that resulted in the Pan-American Union (the forerunner of today's Organization of American States).

Connections With Literature
Activity

In addition to being a political activist and journalist, José Martí was a creative literary writer. Indeed, he was one of the leaders of the Modernist movement in Latin American literature. Encourage interested students to find some of the poems that Martí wrote, perhaps in his collections *Ismaelillo* (1882) or *Simple Verses* (1891). Invite students to share the poems with the class, commenting on what each one suggests about the Cuban patriot.

BIOGRAPHY Lola Rodríguez de Tió *"Freedom comes if you want it, /Be you called a man or woman,"* wrote Lola Rodríguez de Tió. From her youth, Rodríguez de Tió worked for Puerto Rican independence. Her patriotic poems so angered the Spanish that she had to flee—first to Cuba, then to New York. **The Arts** Why might Cuba's Spanish rulers have feared Rodríguez de Tió's poems?

In response, Spain sent a new governor to Cuba, General Valeriano Weyler (WAY ee lair). General Weyler used brutal tactics to crush the revolt. His men herded half a million Cubans into detention camps. At least 100,000 died.

Americans react. In the United States, people watched the revolt in Cuba with growing concern. Cuba lay only 90 miles (144 km) south of Florida. American trade with the island was worth about $100 million a year.

Opinion split over whether the United States should intervene in Cuba. Many business leaders opposed American involvement. They thought that it might hurt trade. Other Americans sympathized with the Cuban desire for freedom and wanted the government to act.

War Fever

The press stirred up American feelings for Cuba. Two New York newspapers—Joseph Pulitzer's *World* and William Randolph Hearst's *Journal*—competed to print the most grisly stories about Spanish cruelty. The publishers knew that war with Spain would boost sales of their newspapers. "You supply the pictures," Pulitzer told a photographer bound for Cuba. "I'll supply the war."

"Blood, blood, blood!" Hearst and Pulitzer used yellow journalism, or sensational stories, to play on the emotions of readers. "Blood on the roadsides," one story cried, "blood in the fields, blood on the doorsteps, blood, blood, blood!" The press called the Spanish governor "Butcher" Weyler and portrayed him as a cruel villain.

President Cleveland wanted to avoid war with Spain. He called the war fever in the United States an "epidemic of insanity." When William McKinley became President in 1897, he also tried to keep the country neutral.

Remember the *Maine*! In 1898, fighting broke out in Havana, Cuba. President McKinley sent the battleship *Maine* to Havana to protect American citizens and property there.

On the night of February 15, the *Maine* lay at anchor. Just after the bugler played taps, a huge explosion ripped through the ship. The explosion killed at least 260 of the 350 sailors and officers on board.

"DESTRUCTION OF THE WARSHIP *MAINE* WAS THE WORK OF AN ENEMY," screamed one New York newspaper. "THE WARSHIP *MAINE* SPLIT IN TWO BY AN ENEMY'S SECRET INFERNAL MACHINE?" asked another.

The real cause of the explosion has never been determined. Most historians believe it was an accident. But Americans, led by Pulitzer and Hearst, clamored for war with Spain. "Remember the *Maine*!" was their rallying cry.

632 • Chapter 22

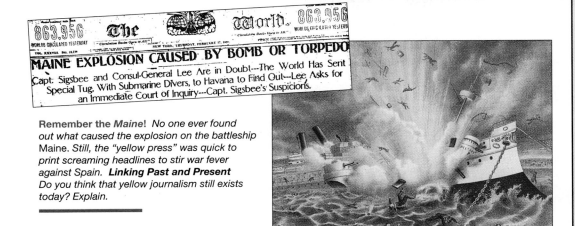

863,956 The World. 863,956
MAINE EXPLOSION CAUSED BY BOMB OR TORPEDO
Capt. Sigsbee and Consul-General Lee Are in Doubt---The World Has Sent
Special Tug, With Submarine Divers, to Havana to Find Out---Lee Asks for
an Immediate Court of Inquiry---Capt. Sigsbee's Suspicions.

Remember the *Maine*! *No one ever found out what caused the explosion on the battleship Maine. Still, the "yellow press" was quick to print screaming headlines to stir war fever against Spain.* **Linking Past and Present** *Do you think that yellow journalism still exists today? Explain.*

Still hoping to avoid war, McKinley tried to get Spain to talk with the Cuban rebels. In the end, he gave in to war fever. On April 25, 1898, Congress declared war on Spain.

The Spanish-American War

The *Spanish-American War* lasted only four months. The battlefront stretched from the nearby Caribbean to the distant Philippine Islands.

Dewey takes the Philippines. The Philippine Islands had been a Spanish colony for more than 300 years. Two months before the United States and Spain went to war, an alert young official in the Department of the Navy, Theodore Roosevelt, wired secret orders to the commander of the Pacific fleet, Commodore George Dewey. Prepare to attack the Philippines, Roosevelt said. When war broke out, Dewey sailed his fleet swiftly to Manila, the main city of the Philippines.

On April 30, Dewey's ships slipped into Manila harbor under cover of darkness. At dawn, Dewey told his flagship commander, Charles Gridley, "You may fire when you are ready, Gridley." The Americans bombarded the surprised Spanish ships. By noon, the Spanish fleet had been destroyed.

When news of Dewey's swift victory reached the United States, Americans rejoiced. In July, American troops landed in the Philippines. As in Cuba, local people had been fighting for independence from Spain for years. With the help of the rebels, led by Emilio Aguinaldo (ah gwee NAHL doh), the Americans captured Manila.

Fighting in Cuba. Meanwhile, American troops had also landed in Cuba. The expedition was badly organized. Soldiers wore heavy woolen uniforms in the tropical heat, and they often had to eat spoiled food. Yet most were eager for battle.

None was more eager than Theodore Roosevelt. When the war began, Roosevelt gave up his job as Assistant Secretary of the Navy. He then organized the First Volunteer Cavalry Regiment, later called the *Rough Riders.* The Rough Riders were a mixed crew—ranging from cowboys to college students and adventurers.

Battle for Santiago. During the battle for the key Cuban city of Santiago, Roosevelt led the Rough Riders on a charge up San Juan Hill and nearby Kettle Hill. They were joined by black soldiers of the 9th and 10th cavalries. Major John J. Pershing, commander of the 10th Cavalry, described how the troops united in battle:

Chapter 22 • **633**

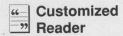
Historical Sidelight
Background

While awaiting orders to sail to the Philippines, George Dewey learned that the Spanish forces had mined the entrance to Manila Bay. He also learned that they had placed guns and cannons on the hills above the bay. Dewey's own fleet consisted of six small battleships. Outnumbered, he decided to gamble—to win or lose—all in one head-on attack.

When news of Dewey's victory reached the United States, people were overjoyed. One poet wrote this pun-based poem for him:

O Dewey was the morning
Upon the first of May
And Dewey was the Admiral
Down in Manila Bay:
And Dewey were the Regent's* eyes.
Them orbs of Royal Blue!
And Dewey feel discouraged?
I Dew not think we Dew.

*a reference to Maria Cristina of Austria, the mother of the next king of Spain, Alfonso XIII

Historical Sidelight
Background

The First Volunteer Cavalry went through several popular nicknames from the press before "Rough Riders" stuck. Among the names by which Roosevelt's brigade is *not* remembered are "Teddy's Terrors," "Roosevelt's Rough 'Uns," and "Teddy's Texas Tarantulas."

Leonard Wood, not Theodore Roosevelt, commanded this brigade. Still, his leadership qualities gained Roosevelt a promotion to colonel. Roosevelt later said, "I would rather have . . . earned my colonelcy than served three terms in the United States Senate."

Answers to Map Study

1. Hong Kong **2.** Cuba and Puerto Rico **3.** Possible Answer: Manila Bay has only one outlet to the ocean. By controlling the mouth of the bay, Dewey could prevent the Spanish ships from escaping.

 Transparencies

Fine Art Use the transparency, Charge of the Rough Riders at San Juan Hill, on page D-51 of *American History Transparencies.* This transparency shows Frederic Remington's interpretation of the Rough Riders, one of the few to portray the charge correctly. Teaching suggestions can be found on page D-16. (Enrichment/Easy)

  Videotapes/ Videodiscs

United States History Video Collection Use the video segment "The Spanish-American War" from Volume 15, *United States and the World,* to enhance students' understanding of the causes and effects of this important conflict. Approx. running time 2:55 min.(Enrichment/Average) Vol. 15, Ch. 16

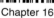

| Chapter 16 | Play |

MAP STUDY

During the Spanish-American War, American forces won victories in the Pacific and the Caribbean.
1. *From what port did Dewey sail to reach the Philippines?*
2. *On what islands in the Caribbean did United States forces land?*
3. **Drawing Conclusions** *Why do you think Dewey was able to trap the Spanish fleet in Manila Bay?*

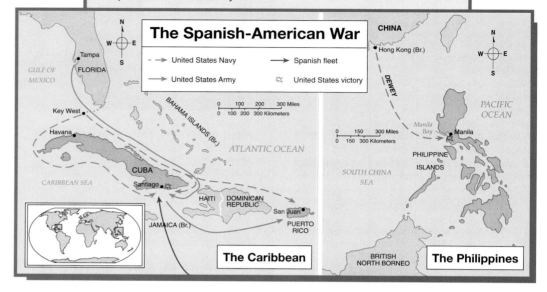

The Spanish-American War

"White regiments, black regiments, regulars and Rough Riders, representing the young manhood of the North and South, fought shoulder to shoulder. . .mindful of their common duty as Americans."

Under withering fire, American troops took the hill.

The ***Battle of San Juan Hill*** did not end the war. However, when the Americans destroyed the Spanish fleet in Santiago Bay two days later, the Spanish army in Cuba surrendered. American troops then landed on Puerto Rico and claimed the island.

Spain and the United States agreed to stop fighting on August 12. American loss-es in battle were not heavy—379 killed. However, five thousand more Americans died of other causes, such as yellow fever and malaria.

John Hay, who was soon to become Secretary of State, summed up American enthusiasm for the war. "It's been a splendid little war," he wrote. A malaria-ridden veteran of the war had a different view: "I was lucky—I survived."

The Fruits of Victory

In a peace treaty signed in Paris in December 1898, Spain agreed to grant Cuba its freedom. Spain also gave the United States two islands: Puerto Rico in the Caribbean

---

Historical Sidelight
Background

Teddy Roosevelt's famous assault on San Juan Hill with the Rough Riders did not happen quite the way in which it was reported. On July 1, 1898, the Rough Riders and other forces were encamped at the foot of San Juan Hill. When the signal to advance was given, Roosevelt turned and urged his forces in an unexpected charge up Kettle Hill, next to San Juan Hill. Surging on foot to the top, the Rough Riders easily seized the small Spanish outpost there.

Then Roosevelt looked across the valley between the two hills. Without hesitation, he gave a war whoop and charged headlong across the valley and up the other side of San Juan Hill, followed by his surprised men. Roosevelt's rush up Kettle Hill and his capture of the outpost so unnerved the Spanish defenders that by the end of the day, San Juan Hill also fell to the Americans.

Connections With Science
Background

Of the 5,462 Americans who died in the war, only 379 — about 6 percent — died as a result of battle wounds. Most of the others died of disease, especially yellow fever and malaria. Some people may also have died from food poisoning because canned meat that the Armour Company sold to the army was tainted.

RESEARCH SKILLS
Using Note Cards

Some time this year, you may be writing a research report. You will need to choose a topic, research it, take notes, and write your report.

To begin your research, write down several questions about the topic. Use the card catalog, encyclopedias, newspapers, and magazines to find information. Then write notes on note cards.

1. **Set up a note-taking system.** Fill out one note card for each question and for each source that you use. In the upper right corner, write your question. In the upper left corner, write the source. For books, include the title and author. For magazine articles, include the title and date. (a) What question does Card A answer? (b) What is the source for Card A?

2. **Record page numbers and indicate direct quotations.** Always include the number of the page on which you find information. Write the information in your own words unless you want to note a direct quotation. Put quotation marks around a direct quotation. (a) Which card has information that is a direct quotation? (b) In which book and on what page can this be found?

3. **Organize your note cards.** When you are ready to write your report, put all cards that cover the same questions together. (a) Which of the cards below belong together? (b) What question do they answer?

> **ACTIVITY** Jot down two questions about a topic discussed in the chapter. Then use the textbook to write notes answering the questions.

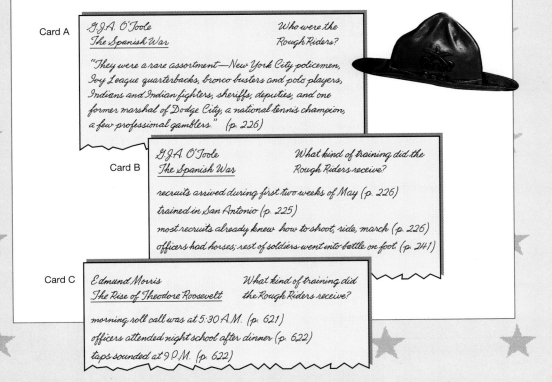

Card A

G.J.A. O'Toole
The Spanish War

Who were the Rough Riders?

"They were a rare assortment—New York City policemen, Ivy League quarterbacks, bronco busters and polo players, Indians and Indian fighters, sheriffs, deputies, and one former marshal of Dodge City, a national tennis champion, a few professional gamblers." (p. 226)

Card B

G.J.A. O'Toole
The Spanish War

What kind of training did the Rough Riders receive?

recruits arrived during first two weeks of May (p. 226)
trained in San Antonio (p. 225)
most recruits already knew how to shoot, ride, march (p. 226)
officers had horses; rest of soldiers went into battle on foot (p. 241)

Card C

Edmund Morris
The Rise of Theodore Roosevelt

What kind of training did the Rough Riders receive?

morning roll call was at 5:30 A.M. (p. 621)
officers attended night school after dinner (p. 622)
taps sounded at 9 P.M. (p. 622)

Charge! *Theodore Roosevelt's Rough Riders earned the nickname "Teddy's Terrors" from their fierce style of fighting. This painting by Frederic Remington shows the Rough Riders in their charge up San Juan Hill in Cuba. Commanders used bugles like the one at right to urge the men forward.* **Geography** *In which two main areas was the Spanish-American War fought?*

and Guam in the Pacific. Finally, in return for $20 million, Spain handed over the Philippines to the United States.

Before the Senate approved the peace treaty, a great debate took place. Many Americans objected to the treaty. They said it made the United States into a colonial power. The popular author Mark Twain commented:

"I have read carefully the treaty of Paris and I have seen that we do not intend to free, but to subjugate the people of the Philippines. We have gone there to conquer, not to redeem.**"**

Expansionists favored the treaty. They said that the navy needed bases in the Caribbean and the Pacific. They pointed out that the Philippines and Puerto Rico offered new territory for American businesses. Also, many Americans agreed with President McKinley, who said that the United States would "uplift and civilize and Christianize [the Filipinos]." In fact, most Filipinos already were Christians.

Urged on by McKinley, the Senate narrowly approved the treaty in early 1899. The dreams of expansionists had come true at last: The United States had an empire.

Ruling Cuba and Puerto Rico

Americans now had to decide how to rule their new territories. When the war with Spain began, the United States had pledged to "leave the government and control of [Cuba] to its people." The promise of liberty had given Cubans and Americans an idealistic cause to fight for.

636 • Chapter 22

Connections With Music
Background

Music has always been an important part of Puerto Rican culture, and the island's development and history have given its music many traditions. The earliest settlers developed a range of percussion instruments from native materials, such as dried gourds, woods, shoots, and beans. Later, under Spanish rule, came the *danza.* This music required a full string orchestra, woodwinds, and traditional dance movements.

During the nineteenth century, Puerto Ricans developed the *asalto,* which is a community festival featuring special holiday music, food, and dancing. Of all their traditional music, however, the *decima* may be the most lively form. It is played on various native strings and a few rhythm instruments. Its most common trademark is the verbal improvisation of two singers who try to outdo each other musically in alternating stanzas.

Liberty for Cuba? In practice, that promise was not kept. After the war, American soldiers stayed in Cuba while Congress debated. Many in Congress believed that Cubans were not ready to run their own government. American business leaders also opposed full independence. They wanted to protect their investments in Cuba.

In the end, the United States let the Cubans write their own constitution. However, the Americans forced Cuba to accept the *Platt Amendment.* The amendment limited Cuba's right to make treaties and borrow money. It allowed the United States to intervene in Cuba. It also gave the United States control of the naval base at Guantanamo Bay. The amendment meant that Cuba was not truly independent.

Limited freedom for Puerto Rico. The United States set up a new government for Puerto Rico under the *Foraker Act* of 1900. The act gave Puerto Ricans a limited say in their own affairs. In 1917, Puerto Ricans were made citizens of the United States. Americans set up schools, improved health care, and built roads on the island. Even so, many Puerto Ricans wanted to be free of foreign rule.

War in the Philippines

Filipino nationalists had begun fighting for independence long before the Spanish-American War. When the United States took over their land after the war, Filipinos felt betrayed. Led by Emilio Aguinaldo, they renewed their fight for independence.

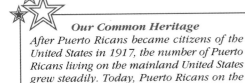

Our Common Heritage
After Puerto Ricans became citizens of the United States in 1917, the number of Puerto Ricans living on the mainland United States grew steadily. Today, Puerto Ricans on the mainland number more than 3 million.

BIOGRAPHY Emilio Aguinaldo *"Filipino citizens! Now is the occasion for shedding our blood for the last time, that we may achieve our beloved freedom." With these words, Emilio Aguinaldo urged Filipinos to throw off Spanish rule. Later, he led an unsuccessful revolt against United States control. Aguinaldo finally saw Filipino independence in 1946, when he was 77 years old.* **United States and the World** *Why did some Americans oppose United States control of the Philippines?*

As you recall, Aguinaldo had fought beside the Americans against Spain. Now, he fought against the Americans. Aguinaldo accused Americans of forgetting their own beginnings:

> 66 Let our Government not be charged with the ruin and disorder now existing; President McKinley and his party are responsible. . . . [They are attempting] to suppress the legitimate aspirations of a people, which is now struggling only for the same rights that the American people proclaimed more than a century ago. 99

■A■C■T■I■V■I■T■Y■

Guided Instruction Remind students that newspapers like the New York *World* tried to boost their sales by engaging in yellow journalism, or sensationalism, during the late 1800s. Therefore, this activity calls for headlines and lead paragraphs to be written in as dramatic a style as possible. Encourage students to think especially about vivid action verbs and colorful adjectives. You might want to use the finished articles as the focal point of a bulletin board display about the Spanish-American War.

Section 4
pp. 638–643

 Bell Ringer

To check students' prior knowledge, write the words *Panama Canal* in the middle of a large empty chalkboard space and have students name ideas, objects (for example, mosquitoes, swamps), and the names of people and countries that they may have heard associated with the building of the canal. Connect students' responses to the center word with radiating lines to group the related ideas. Finally, ask one student to make a written copy of the word web with which to compare students' ideas at the end of the section.

The war in the Philippines dragged on for years. At one point, more than 70,000 American troops were fighting there. The war finally came to an end when Aguinaldo was captured in 1901.

More than 4,000 Americans died in the Philippines. Filipino losses were much higher. Nearly 20,000 Filipino soldiers were killed. Another 200,000 civilians died from shelling, famine, and disease.

In 1902, the United States set up a government in the Philippines similar to the one in Puerto Rico. Filipinos, however, were not made American citizens because the United States planned to give them independence. It was not until 1946, however, that Filipinos were allowed to govern themselves.

SECTION 3 REVIEW

1. **Locate:** (a) Cuba, (b) Philippine Islands, (c) Puerto Rico, (d) Guam.
2. **Identify:** (a) Pan-American Union, (b) Lola Rodríguez de Tió, (c) Spanish-American War, (d) Emilio Aguinaldo, (e) Rough Riders, (f) Battle of San Juan Hill, (g) Platt Amendment, (h) Foraker Act.
3. What role did the press play in provoking war with Spain?
4. How did Americans react to the treaty ending the Spanish-American War?
5. Why did the Filipinos fight against the Americans after 1898?
6. **CRITICAL THINKING Analyzing Information** Secretary of State John Hay said that the Spanish-American War was a "splendid little war." (a) What do you think he meant by that statement? (b) What group of Americans would have agreed with him? (c) Who would have disagreed? Explain.

■A■C■T■I■V■I■T■Y■ Writing to Learn
Write a headline and first paragraph for an article about the rebellion in Cuba that might have appeared in the New York *World* or *Journal.*

638 • Chapter 22

4
The Big Stick in Latin America

FIND OUT
- Why did the United States build the Panama Canal?
- What policies did Americans adopt toward Latin America?
- Why did the United States invade Mexico in 1916?

VOCABULARY dollar diplomacy

Early one day in 1898, the battleship *Oregon* slipped through the Golden Gate, a strait near San Francisco. It was on its way to the Spanish-American War in Cuba.

The *Oregon* steamed down the Pacific coast toward the tip of South America. Then it circled Cape Horn and headed north. At last, two months and nearly 13,000 miles (20,900 km) after it had set out, the *Oregon* arrived off the coast of Florida, ready for battle. If it had taken much longer, the war would have been over.

By the late 1800s, the United States had built an empire that stretched from the Atlantic Ocean to the Pacific Ocean. Incidents such as the slow journey of the *Oregon* made it clear that the nation needed a shorter, quicker route between the two oceans.

"I Took the Canal Zone"

People had dreamed of connecting the Atlantic and Pacific oceans almost from the day Balboa first crossed the Isthmus of Panama in 1513. The isthmus is only about 50 miles (80 km) wide. A canal through the isthmus would cut the journey from San Francisco to New York City by nearly 8,000 miles (12,800 km). (See the map on page 640.)

Answers to Section 3 Review

1. See the maps on pp. 630 and 634.
2. (a) Pan-American Union, p. 631, (b) Lola Rodríguez de Tió, p. 631, (c) Spanish-American War, p. 633, (d) Emilio Aguinaldo, p. 633, (e) Rough Riders, p. 633, (f) Battle of San Juan Hill, p. 634, (g) Platt Amendment, p. 637, (h) Foraker Act, p. 637
3. The press stirred up feelings against Spain and created war fever.
4. Many Americans objected, saying that the treaty made the United States a colonial power. Expansionists, however, favored the treaty.

5. Filipino nationalists felt betrayed when the United States took over their land after the war instead of giving them independence.
6. Possible Answers: (a) It was a short war, and the United States won with relatively few casualties. It seemed very exciting as it was reported to the press. Furthermore, the United States won a great deal of territory as a result of the war. (b) Expansionists would have agreed with him. (c) Americans who believed that expansion was wrong would have disagreed with him.

638

Turned down by Colombia. When Theodore Roosevelt became President in 1901, he was eager to build a canal in Panama. At the time, Panama was part of Colombia.

Roosevelt asked Secretary of State John Hay to approach Colombia about building a canal. Hay offered Colombia $10 million cash plus $250,000 a year to rent a strip of land across Panama. Colombian officials turned down the offer.

President Roosevelt was furious at the delay. He knew that many Panamanians wanted the canal because it would make Panama a crossroads for world trade. Roosevelt also knew that some Panamanians wanted to break away from Colombia.

Roosevelt favored direct action. He often quoted an African proverb: "Speak softly and carry a big stick, and you will go far." He meant that words should be backed up with power. Roosevelt made it clear to the rebels in Panama that the United States would support them.

Revolution in Panama. On November 2, 1903, the *Nashville,* an American warship, dropped anchor in the port of Colón, Panama. The next day, the people of Panama rebelled against Colombia. American forces stopped Colombian troops from crushing the revolt. On November 3, Panama declared itself an independent republic.

The United States recognized the new nation at once. In turn, Panama quickly agreed to let the United States build a canal on terms similar to those it had offered to Colombia.

Linking Past and Present
The original agreement with Panama gave the United States control of the Panama Canal forever. In 1977, however, the United States signed two new treaties with Panama. Under these treaties, the United States will turn over control of the Panama Canal to Panama by the year 2000.

Roosevelt's high-handed action in Panama angered many Latin Americans. It also upset some members of the United States Congress. The President, however, was proud of his action. "I took the Canal Zone," he said later, "and let Congress debate."

Defeating a Tiny Enemy

Building the Panama Canal turned out to be more difficult than winning the right to build it. The canal builders faced great hazards. Not the least was a tiny enemy that could have ended the project before it even started.

Fighting Disease in Panama *Most of the labor on the Panama Canal was done by black workers from the West Indies. Here, a worker sprays insecticide on mosquito breeding grounds. Only after the mosquitoes were wiped out did construction of the canal begin.* **Geography** *Why did the United States want to build a canal across Panama?*

1. three 2. southeast 3. (a) Possible Answer: It is an area cutting through the middle of Panama, containing the canal and the land for about 5 miles on either side of it, as well as all of Gatán Lake. (b) Possible Answer: Many Panamanians probably resented a foreign country having control of a territory that cut their own country into two parts.

Voices of Freedom

Primary Source You might assign selection 8-2, The Fight Against Yellow Fever, on pages 192–193 of *Voices of Freedom*. The selection gives students an idea of the exasperating fight that army doctors faced in the Canal Zone. The source emphasizes how difficult it was for Dr. William Gorgas to deal with local conditions as well as the incompetence of his superiors. (Enrichment/Average)

Primary Source You might assign selection 8-1, The Roosevelt Corollary, on page 191 of *Voices of Freedom*. The selection is from Theodore Roosevelt's message to Congress in December 1904, in which he outlined a policy that eventually became known as the Roosevelt Corollary. (Enrichment/Challenging)

Deadly diseases. When William Gorgas first landed in Panama in 1904, he quickly noted the region's features: tropical heat, lots of rain, plenty of swamps. Panama was

MAP STUDY

The Panama Canal took about 43,000 workers almost 10 years to finish. A series of locks raise and lower the water level so that ships can move through the canal.

1. According to the map, how many locks do ships pass through on their way through the canal?
2. In which direction do ships travel from Colón to Balboa?
3. **Recognizing Points of View** The Canal Zone was under control of the United States. (a) Using the map, describe the location of the Canal Zone. (b) How do you think Panamanians felt about United States control of the zone?

The Panama Canal

- Canal Zone
- ⟶⟵ Locks
- .... The canal

0   5   10 Miles
0   5   10 Kilometers

CARIBBEAN SEA

Colón

PANAMA

Gatún Lake

Gaillard Cut

Balboa • Panama City

PANAMA

N W E S

PACIFIC OCEAN

UNITED STATES
ATLANTIC OCEAN
GULF OF MEXICO
CENTRAL AMERICA
CARIBBEAN SEA
PACIFIC OCEAN
Panama Canal

a paradise, Gorgas declared—a "mosquito paradise."

For engineers working on the Panama Canal, the biggest challenge was cutting through miles of rock. For Gorgas, a medical officer, the biggest problem was the tiny mosquito. Mosquitoes, Gorgas knew, carried two of the worst tropical diseases: malaria and yellow fever.

Yellow Jack. Gorgas had seen a co-worker die of yellow fever, or "Yellow Jack." The man shivered and burned with fever. His skin and eyes turned yellow, and he spat up dark blood. Toward the end, his fits grew so violent that two nurses had to hold him down.

Yellow fever caused fewer deaths than malaria did. However, the horrible way in which its victims died made those who saw the end never forget it. One poem warned:

❝You are going to have the fever,
    Yellow eyes!
In about ten days from now
Iron bands will clamp your
    brow. . . .
Your mouth will taste of untold
    things,
With claws and horns and fins
    and wings;
Your head will weigh a ton or
    more,
And forty gales within it roar!❞

A breakthrough. Gorgas had been fighting yellow fever since the Spanish-American War. A Cuban doctor, Juan Finlay, had discovered that mosquitoes carried the disease. In 1901, Gorgas led a campaign against the mosquito. In less than a year, the Cuban capital of Havana was free of Yellow Jack.

In Panama, the job was harder. Workers had to find every pool of water, where mosquitoes laid their eggs. Day after day, the workers drained swamps and paved muddy roads. A small army sprayed tons of insecticide and spread oil on still water to kill mosquito eggs.

Connections With Science
Activity

Without the work of dedicated doctors and researchers, yellow fever might never have been controlled in the Panama Canal Zone. Walter Reed proved that yellow fever was carried by a mosquito. William Gorgas learned to control the mosquitoes by filling in the ponds of water where they bred. Max Theiler developed an effective vaccine.

Have students research how vaccines are developed. Students will find that although some steps will vary, the making of most vaccines requires many common steps.

Connections With Mathematics
Activity

Make up your own math problems about the Panama Canal using the models that follow these statistics:

- receives 160 inches of rainfall per year
- is 40.27 miles long from coast to coast
- is 500 feet across at its narrowest point
- needed more than 40,000 workers per year
- saves 8,000 miles from San Francisco to New York by sea
- saves 2,000 miles from Europe to Australia
- guides 37 ships per day through its locks
- charges oceangoing ships $25,000 per trip

1. If it rains every day in the Canal Zone and if the same amount falls each day, how much rain falls per day? (0.44 inches)
2. If a ship sails from Southampton, England, to Sydney, Australia, and back seven times, how many miles are saved using the canal? (28,000 miles)

By 1906, Gorgas had won his battle. Yellow fever had disappeared from Panama. Malaria cases dropped dramatically. Work on the Panama Canal could proceed. ■

Digging the Big Ditch

Meanwhile, more than 40,000 workers struggled to dig the canal. Most were blacks from the West Indies. They blasted a path through mountains and carved out the largest man-made lake in the world. Then they built gigantic locks. Finally, in 1914, the first ocean-going steamship traveled through the Panama Canal.

The new waterway helped the trade of many nations. American merchants and manufacturers, who could now ship goods cheaply to South America and Asia, benefited most of all. Many Latin American nations, however, remained bitter about the way in which the United States had gained control of the canal.

Policing Latin America

The Panama Canal involved the United States more than ever in Latin America. Americans had to "police the surrounding premises," said one official.

Expanding the Monroe Doctrine. In 1902, several European countries sent warships to force Venezuela to repay its debts. The United States did not want Europeans to use force in Latin America. "If we intend to say hands off to the powers of Europe, then sooner or later we must keep order ourselves," President Roosevelt declared.

In 1904, Roosevelt announced an addition to the Monroe Doctrine. In the ***Roosevelt Corollary,*** he claimed the right of the United States to intervene in Latin America to preserve law and order. By using this "international police power," the United States could force Latin Americans to pay their debts to foreign nations. It would also keep those nations from meddling in Latin American affairs.

CAUSES

- Western frontier closes
- Businesses seek raw materials and new markets
- European nations compete for resources and markets

OVERSEAS EXPANSION

EFFECTS

- United States develops a strong navy
- Open Door Policy protects trade with China
- United States rules lands in the Caribbean and Pacific
- United States builds the Panama Canal
- United States sends troops to Latin American nations to protect its interests

Understanding Causes and Effects
In the late 1800s, the United States slowly changed its foreign policy from isolation to overseas expansion. • *Why was the closing of the frontier a cause of overseas expansion? List three effects of expansion in Latin America.*

The President had an opportunity to use his policy in 1905. When the Dominican Republic could not pay its debts, the United States took control of the country's finances and paid its debts. Over the next 20 years, several Presidents used this police power. Most Latin Americans strongly resented this interference in their affairs.

Chapter 22 • **641**

Answer to Understanding Causes and Effects

Restless Americans needed new opportunities to move on and to start again. The United States rules lands in the Caribbean and Pacific; Panama Canal helps defense and trade; troops invade Latin American nations to protect American interests.

 Transparencies

Political Cartoons Use the transparency An Expanding Nation on page G-23 of *American History Transparencies.* Teaching suggestions can be found on page G-7. (Enrichment/Average)
Cause and Effect Use the transparency Overseas Expansion on page F-25 of *American History Transparencies.* Teaching suggestions can be found on page F-8. (Enrichment/Average)

Videotapes/ Videodiscs

United States History Video Collection Use the video segment "The Panama Canal" from Volume 15, *United States and the World,* to enhance students' understanding of how the canal was built. Approx. running time 1:20 min. (Enrichment/Average) Vol. 15, Ch. 25

Chapter 25   Play

Linking Past and Present
Background

The Canal Zone, a strip of land on either side of the canal, had belonged to the United States since Panama sold it in 1903. In 1978, however, President Jimmy Carter signed a treaty in which the United States agreed to return the land to Panama by the year 2000. At the same time, though, he insisted on another treaty that gives the United States the right to defend the canal's neutrality.

Team-Teaching Suggestion
Foreign Language

You might work with a Spanish teacher (and perhaps a few of the students' parents or relatives from Latin America) to present a lesson on the languages and cultures of Latin America. (You and a student committee might meet first to decide who should be invited to participate and what the subjects will be.)

The lesson might emphasize cultural similarities and differences among the Latin American nations of Cuba, Nicaragua, Mexico, Puerto Rico, Colombia, and Panama. On the other hand, it might simply be an "international presentation" of crafts, photos, costumes, food, music, and dance.

MAP STUDY

In the early 1900s, the United States gained influence in the area along the Caribbean Sea.
1. *Which areas in the region did the United States control outright?*
2. *In which other areas did the United States exert influence?*
3. Applying Information *Review the discussion of the Roosevelt Corollary on page 641. In which areas shown on the map was the Roosevelt Corollary used to justify United States "police power"?*

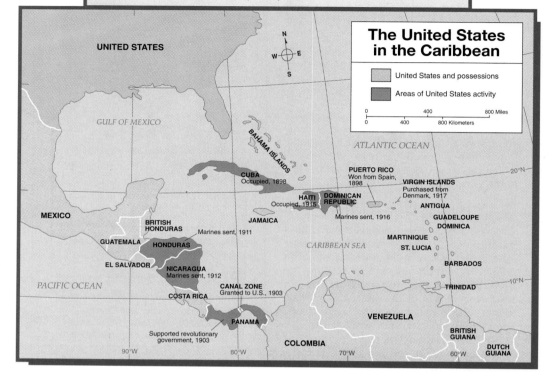

The United States in the Caribbean

☐ United States and possessions
■ Areas of United States activity

0   400   800 Miles
0   400   800 Kilometers

UNITED STATES

GULF OF MEXICO

ATLANTIC OCEAN

BAHAMA ISLANDS

CUBA
Occupied, 1898

PUERTO RICO
Won from Spain, 1898

VIRGIN ISLANDS
Purchased from Denmark, 1917

20°N

HAITI
Occupied, 1915

DOMINICAN REPUBLIC
Marines sent, 1916

ANTIGUA

MEXICO

JAMAICA

GUADELOUPE
DOMINICA

BRITISH HONDURAS
Marines sent, 1911

MARTINIQUE
ST. LUCIA

GUATEMALA   HONDURAS

CARIBBEAN SEA

EL SALVADOR

BARBADOS

PACIFIC OCEAN

NICARAGUA
Marines sent, 1912

CANAL ZONE
Granted to U.S., 1903

TRINIDAD

10°N

COSTA RICA

VENEZUELA

PANAMA
Supported revolutionary government, 1903

BRITISH GUIANA

COLOMBIA

DUTCH GUIANA

90°W   80°W   70°W   60°W

Dollars for bullets. Roosevelt's successor, William Howard Taft, also favored a strong American role in Latin America. Taft, however, wanted to "substitute dollars for bullets." He urged American bankers and business leaders to invest in Latin America. It was better to use trade than warships to expand American influence in Latin America, he said. This policy became known as **dollar diplomacy.**

American investors responded eagerly. They helped build roads, railroads, and harbors in Latin America. These improvements increased trade, helping both Americans and local governments. The new railroads, for example, brought minerals and other resources to Latin American ports. From there, they were shipped all over the world.

Dollar diplomacy created problems, too. American businesses, such as the United

642 • Chapter 22

Connections With Geography
Background

Like the United States, Mexico has several geographical regions. The Pacific Northwest, for example, is very dry. Along the mainland coast, however, irrigation provides some of Mexico's richest farmland.

The Plateau of Mexico, just south of Texas, is a varied area. Some places get enough rain to grow corn, beans, wheat, and barley. Many hills, however, are so dry that nothing will grow. The richest silver mines in Mexico are here. The mountains at the plateau's

edge are home to Mexico's volcanoes, of which the most famous are probably Popocatépetl (poh poh kah TEH peht 'l) and Ixtacihuatl (ees tah SEE waht 'l).

The gulf coastal plain and southern plateau are also dry regions; but up in the Chiapas highlands, descendants of the Mayas still grow coffee, fruit, and vegetables. The Yucatán Peninsula, where the Mayas once farmed and worshiped, is covered with tropical foliage.

Cooperative Learning
Activity

Divide students into groups of four or five students each and explain that together they will present an overview of Mexican history. Have students report on topics such as these: prehistoric Mexico; the Mayan and Zapotec civilizations; the Toltec and Aztec civilizations; the arrival of European explorers; and revolts against the Spaniards from the early 1800s to independence in 1821. Be sure that each student in each group has a task, and emphasize that all of its members will receive the same grade. Encourage groups to provide audiovisual materials to enliven their presentations.

Fruit Company, often meddled in the political affairs of host countries. Sometimes, the United States used military force to keep order. When a revolution erupted in Nicaragua, where Americans had invested in land and businesses, the United States sent in marines. Later, American troops occupied the Dominican Republic, Haiti, and Honduras. The United States claimed that its troops were protecting American lives and property. Many Latin Americans denounced these invasions.

Troubles in Mexico

Events in Mexico showed the problems caused by dollar diplomacy. Porfirio Díaz, Mexico's ruler from 1877 to 1911, welcomed American investment. By 1912, Americans had invested about $1 billion there. The money was used to develop mines, oil wells, railroads, and ranches.

Despite these investments, most Mexicans were poor. They worked the land of a few wealthy families and received little for their labor. In 1910, Mexicans rebelled against Díaz. The fighting lasted until 1917, as different groups battled for power.

On the Trail of "Pancho" Villa *Although they continued to chase him, Americans never captured Pancho Villa. One frustrated general reported, "According to all reliable data, Francisco Villa is currently everywhere and nowhere."* **United States and the World** *How did the pursuit of Villa damage United States relations with Mexico?*

Wilson's policy. In spite of the large American investments in Mexico, President Woodrow Wilson at first stayed neutral. He hoped that Mexico would develop a democratic government. However, he did not intend to invade Mexico to bring it about.

Wilson had trouble sticking to his policy. In 1914, Mexico arrested several American sailors. Furious, Wilson ordered the United States Navy to occupy Veracruz, a Mexican port. In 1916, General Francisco "Pancho" Villa, a rebel leader, raided the town of Columbus, New Mexico, killing 17 Americans. Wilson then sent General John J. Pershing across the border in a vain attempt to capture Villa.

Pershing's raid. Instead of taking a small force, Pershing led an army of 6,000 soldiers. Mexico protested the American invasion. In the end, Wilson withdrew the American troops. Still, the episode poisoned relations with Mexico for years.

SECTION 4 REVIEW

1. **Locate:** (a) Colombia, (b) Panama, (c) Panama Canal, (d) Dominican Republic, (e) Mexico.
2. **Identify:** (a) Roosevelt Corollary, (b) Francisco "Pancho" Villa, (c) John J. Pershing.
3. **Define:** dollar diplomacy.
4. How did the United States win the right to build the Panama Canal?
5. How did the Roosevelt Corollary expand American power in the Western Hemisphere?
6. **CRITICAL THINKING Understanding Causes and Effects** How did draining swamps and paving roads reduce the risk of yellow fever in Panama?

ACTIVITY **Writing to Learn**
Write three questions you would ask President Roosevelt about his policy of policing Latin American countries.

Chapter 22 • **643**

CHAPTER 22 REVIEW

Answers to Reviewing the Main Ideas

1. In the 1800s, with the frontier gone, American business leaders wanted new sources of raw materials as well as markets for manufactured goods.

2. (a) Perry opened trade with Japan. (b) Seward bought Alaska and persuaded Congress to annex Midway Island. (c) Mahan encouraged the growth of the navy and the acquisition of bases throughout the world. (d) Dewey accomplished a quick victory in the Philippines during the Spanish-American War; the United States gained possession of the Philippines when the war ended.

3. In 1893, American sugar planters aided by United States Marines staged a revolt against Queen Liliuokalani and set up a republic. They then asked to be annexed by the United States.

4. Their acceptance of the policy would guarantee American trading interests in China.

5. (a) The Cubans wanted independence from Spain. (b) Many Americans believed that the *Maine* had been sunk on purpose by the Spanish. They used this event to pressure President McKinley to declare war on Spain.

6. Puerto Rico, Guam, and the Philippines

7. (a) It was understood that an independent Panama would agree to let the United States build the canal. (b) The United States felt that it had to protect the trade that passed through the Panama Canal. Therefore, as soon as the canal was in operation, the United States automatically became more involved in the area.

8. (a) Most land was owned by a few wealthy families who paid poor Mexicans low wages for their labor. In 1910, the Mexicans rebelled against the government. The fighting lasted until 1917. (b) At first Wilson stayed neutral, hoping that Mexico would develop a democratic government. After "Pancho" Villa, a Mexican rebel leader, crossed the border and raided New Mexico, however, Wilson sent troops into Mexico to pursue Villa.

644

Summary

● In early moves toward a policy of expansion, the United States opened trade with Japan in 1854 and bought Alaska from Russia in 1867.

● Seeking to expand its influence in the Pacific, the United States annexed Hawaii and called for an Open Door Policy in China.

● Victory in the Spanish-American War made the United States a world power, with lands in the Caribbean and the Pacific.

● After building the Panama Canal, the United States became involved in the affairs of Latin American nations.

Reviewing the Main Ideas

1. Why did the United States shift from a policy of isolation to a policy of expansion in the late 1800s?

2. Explain how each of the following helped the United States expand: (a) Matthew Perry, (b) William Seward, (c) Alfred Mahan, (d) George Dewey.

3. How did the United States acquire the Hawaiian Islands?

4. Why did the United States want other nations to accept the Open Door Policy in China?

5. (a) Why did Cubans revolt in 1895? (b) What role did the battleship *Maine* play in the Spanish-American War?

6. What lands did the United States acquire as a result of the Spanish-American War?

7. (a) Why did the United States quickly recognize the independence of Panama? (b) How did the Panama Canal involve the United States more deeply in Latin American affairs?

8. (a) Why did Mexicans rebel against their government? (b) What policies did President Wilson follow toward Mexico during the Mexican Revolution?

644 • Chapter 22

Thinking Critically

1. Analyzing Information How do you think the rapid growth of the economy in the late 1800s influenced American interest in overseas expansion?

2. Comparing How was the Open Door Policy similar to the Monroe Doctrine?

3. Linking Past and Present What projects today present challenges as great as those posed by building the Panama Canal?

Applying Your Skills

1. Ranking List the events leading to the outbreak of the Spanish-American War. Then rank the events according to how big a role each played in causing the war.

2. Analyzing a Quotation Reread Emilio Aguinaldo's statement on page 637. What argument does Aguinaldo use to condemn American policy in the Philippines?

3. Making a Generalization List three actions that the United States took under the Roosevelt Corollary. Then write a generalization about United States policy in Latin America in the early 1900s.

Thinking About Geography

Match the letters on the map with the following places: **1.** United States, **2.** Puerto Rico, **3.** Panama Canal, **4.** Cuba, **5.** Nicaragua, **6.** Dominican Republic. **Place** Why was the Isthmus of Panama a good place to build the canal?

Answers to Thinking Critically

1. As businesses grew, American business leaders needed new markets to sell their products. They also needed new sources of raw materials.

2. Both policies claimed to be idealistic. The United States claimed that the purpose of the Monroe Doctrine was to protect the other nations of the Western Hemisphere. The Open Door Policy claimed to seek fair treatment for China. However, both policies furthered the interests of the United States.

3. Possible Answer: cleaning up the environment, disposing of nuclear waste, and dealing with global warming

Answers to Applying Your Skills

1. Events leading to war: Cuba revolts against Spain; Spain sends Weyler as governor of Cuba; American newspapers print sensational stories about Cuba; McKinley sends the *Maine* to Havana to protect Americans there; the *Maine* explodes, killing at least 260 people; Congress declares war on Spain. (b) Students' rankings will vary, but students should note that sensational press coverage and the explosion of the *Maine* were the main reasons that the United States declared war on Spain.

2. Aguinaldo says that the United States is fighting to prevent the Filipinos from gaining the rights and freedoms that Americans themselves fought for during the Revolution.

INTERDISCIPLINARY ACTIVITY

Investigating Overseas Expansion

Form into groups to review American overseas expansion before 1914. Follow the suggestions below to write, draw, or debate to show what you have learned about American expansion. You may use the textbook, encyclopedias, atlases, or other materials in your classroom library to complete the tasks. Be able to name your sources of information when you have finished the activity.

The eagle of American imperialism spreads its wings

HISTORIANS Review the American shift from isolation to expansion in the late 1800s. Then make a concept map summarizing the causes and effects of expansion.

REPORTERS Find out more about arguments for and against American expansion in the late 1800s. Then prepare a television debate among representatives of opposing points of view. You might videotape the debate for later presentation to the class.

ARTISTS List the events and dates related to overseas expansion, including territories gained. Then form into groups to create a combined time line and mural of American overseas expansion. First plot the time line. Then have each group illustrate an event in the proper place along the time line.

CARTOGRAPHERS On a large sheet of paper, draw a map of the world. On the map:
- Use a colored pencil or marker to fill in the territory of the United States in 1865.
- Label the territory gained by the United States between 1865 and 1914.
- Include a map key showing the country that each territory had belonged to and how that territory was acquired.

 Arrange an Investigating Overseas Expansion Day. Invite members of other classes to view your completed activities.

9th and 10th cavalries at San Juan Hill

Learning Styles

The following chart indicates the activities appropriate for different learning styles.

Visual Learners
Historians
Artists
Cartographers

Auditory Learners
Reporters

Kinesthetic Learners
Historians
Reporters
Artists
Cartographers

Evaluation

Historians Concept maps should clearly distinguish between causes and effects. The causes and effects presented should be logical as well as factually accurate.
Reporters Debates need not be very formal, but they should be orderly and should allow both viewpoints to be heard. If videotapes are made, they should be of reasonably good quality.
Artists Artistic quality need not be a criterion, but illustrations should clearly represent the events charted on the time line. The events themselves should be in correct sequence.
Cartographers Maps should accurately depict the regions most directly involved, with color choices and the map key making a clear distinction between the two dates.

---

3. Possible Answer: The United States took control of the finances of the Dominican Republic in 1905. United States Marines were sent into Nicaragua to put down a revolution there. American troops occupied the Dominican Republic, Haiti, and Honduras, claiming to protect American lives and property there. Generalization: The United States interfered in the affairs of many Latin American nations in the early 1900s.

Answers to Thinking About Geography

1. F 2. C 3. A 4. D 5. E
6. B
Place: It was only 50 miles wide.

Assessment

Chapter Resources Binder See the Alternative Assessment booklet in the *Social Studies Educator's Handbook* series.
Computer Test Bank You can use Chapter Tests and Extra Unit Questions to create your own tests for both testing and retesting.

Alternative Assessment

Chapter Resources Binder See the Assessing Student Understanding section of the *Chapter Resources* binder for opportunities.
Portfolio You might meet with students to choose appropriate work from the chapter for inclusion in their portfolios.

Lessons	Teaching Resources
1 Europe Explodes Into War **Objectives** 1. Explain why tensions were high in Europe in 1914. 2. Identify the immediate cause of the outbreak of war. 3. Describe how Americans responded to the war in Europe.	**Lesson Planner** Cooperative Learning, p. 142 **Student Study Guide** Section 1 Study Guide, p. 172
2 The Road to War **Objectives** 1. Explain why the United States went to war in 1917. 2. Describe how the government organized the war effort. 3. Describe the treatment of critics of the war.	**Lesson Planner** Cooperative Learning, p. 143 **Student Study Guide** Section 2 Study Guide, p. 173 **Chapter Resources Binder, Unit 7** *Critical Thinking* Synthesizing Information, p. 31 **Interdisciplinary Connections:** Being "Over There" ■ *Arts* Songs of the Soldiers, p. 134 ▨ *Sciences* Fighting the Flu, p. 135 ■ *Geography* The "Lost Battalion," p. 136 ■ *World* Revolution in Russia, p. 137 ■ *Economics* Funding the Fight, p. 138
3 "Over There" **Objectives** 1. Explain why the Allies welcomed American troops in 1917. 2. Describe how Americans helped end the war. 3. Identify the human costs of the war.	**Lesson Planner** Cooperative Learning, p. 144 **Student Study Guide** Section 3 Study Guide, p. 174 **Chapter Resources Binder, Unit 7** *History Through Literature* Three Soldiers, p. 32 *Geography in History* Battling Through a Forest, pp. 33–34 **Our Multicultural Heritage** *Biography* Sergeant York, Reluctant Hero, p. 67 *Milestone* A Turning Point for Native Americans, p. 69 **Posters** *War Knows No Color Line,* by E. Sims Campbell
4 Wilson and the Peace **Objectives** 1. Identify Wilson's Fourteen Points. 2. Describe how Wilson and the other Allies differed over plans for peace. 3. Explain why the Senate rejected the Versailles Treaty.	**Lesson Planner** Cooperative Learning, p. 145 **Student Study Guide** Section 4 Study Guide, p. 175 **Chapter Resources Binder, Unit 7** *Skill Application* Recognizing Propaganda, p. 30 **Our Multicultural Heritage** *Biography* Edith Wilson, the President's Partner, p. 68

Multimedia Resources	Additional Resources	Chapter-Level Resources
Transparencies *Exploring Technology* World War I Tank, p. H-53; Trench Warfare, p. H-55 **Videotapes/Videodiscs** *United States History Video Collection* The New Deadly Toys, Vol. 16, Ch. 7; Neutrality, Vol. 16, Ch. 10	**Voices of Freedom** The Coming of the "Grand Smash," pp. 196–197 **Historical Outline Map Book** Europe in World War I, p. 60	**Lesson Planner** Activity Based, pp. 146–147 **Student Study Guide** Chapter 23 Study Guide, pp. 176–177 **Chapter Resources Binder** **Unit 7** Vocabulary Building, p. 29 Chapter Test A, pp. 35–37 Chapter Test B, pp. 38–40 Illustration Master, p. 41 Extra Unit Questions, pp. 43–45 **English Guided Reading** Guided Reading, pp. 45–46 **Spanish Resources**
Transparencies *Critical Thinking* Cause and Effect: American Entry Into World War I, p. F-27 *Interdisciplinary Connections* Going Against the Tide, p. B-77 **CD-ROM** *History Makers* Jeannette Rankin **Videotapes/Videodiscs** *United States History Video Collection* The Road to War, Vol. 16, Ch. 13; The Dough Boys, Vol. 16, Ch. 16; America at War, Vol. 16, Ch. 19; Women at Work, Vol. 16, Ch. 25; Mind Mobilization, Vol. 16, Ch. 28	**Voices of Freedom** The Home Front: Changes and Traditions, pp. 199–200 **Customized Reader** Anti-German Intolerance During World War I, article VIB-1	**Computer Test Bank** Chapter Tests A and B Extra Unit Questions
Videotapes/Videodiscs *United States History Video Collection* Over There, Vol. 16, Ch. 34	**Voices of Freedom** How the Americans Helped, pp. 201–202 A Black Perspective on Black Soldiers, pp. 202–203 **Customized Reader** Sergeant York in the Argonne Forest, article VIB-14	**Guided Reading Audiotapes** Side 9 **CD-ROM** *Time Tour* World War I (1914–1919) in A New Role in the World
Videotapes/Videodiscs *United States History Video Collection* Wilson and the Peace, Vol. 16, Ch. 37; Post-War World, Vol. 16, Ch. 40; The Impact of the Great War on America, Vol. 16, Ch. 46	**Voices of Freedom** Versailles: An Insider's View, pp. 203–204 Versailles: A Novelist's View, pp. 204–205 Opposing the League of Nations, p. 206	

Lesson Planner

For a fully developed **Activity-Based** lesson plan for Chapter 23, see the *Lesson Planner,* pages 146–147.

Chapter Resources

Vocabulary Building The Vocabulary Building worksheet for Chapter 23 from Unit 7, page 29, of the *Chapter Resources* binder can be used as a prereading activity or as a review of chapter vocabulary. (Reteaching/Easy)

Student Study Guide

Chapter 23 Study Guide Refer students to pages 176–177 of the *Student Study Guide* for the Chapter 23 Study Guide. The study guide can be used for chapter review as well as for reteaching. (Reteaching/Average)

Guided Reading Audiotapes

Students can use *Guided Reading Audiotapes,* Chapter 23, side 9, to listen to section previews, summaries, and review questions. The tapes will benefit students who are auditory learners, students who have trouble reading, or students acquiring English. Tapes are also available in Spanish. (Enrichment/ Easy)

CHAPTER 23

World War I
(1914–1919)

CHAPTER OUTLINE
1 Europe Explodes Into War
2 The Road to War
3 "Over There"
4 Wilson and the Peace

The New York Times. EXTRA

LUSITANIA SUNK BY A SUBMARINE, PROBABLY 1,260 DEAD; TWICE TORPEDOED OFF IRISH COAST; SINKS IN 15 MINUTES; CAPT. TURNER SAVED, FROHMAN AND VANDERBILT MISSING; WASHINGTON BELIEVES THAT A GRAVE CRISIS IS AT HAND

1915 *German submarines sank the British liner* Lusitania. *The attack, which killed 128 Americans, drew cries of outrage from the United States.*

PRESIDENT
WILSON
Peace
Prosperity
GOVERNOR
DUNNE
⊗ DEMOCRATIC

1916 *Woodrow Wilson was reelected President. Wilson, who had so far kept the United States out of the European war, campaigned as the candidate of peace.*

1914	1915	1916	1917

 WORLD EVENT
1914 War begins in Europe

 WORLD EVENT
1917 Germany resumes submarine warfare

646 • Chapter 23

Chapter Time Line
Activity

Divide the class into groups of three or four students each. Have each group choose one of the illustrations or World Event entries. (You can avoid duplication by assigning a number to each illustration or event and then having a representative from each group pull numbered slips of paper from a container.) When each group has an event to consider, give the groups time to discuss:
■ when and where the event took place
■ why the event occurred
■ what the results of the event were
Student responses can be based on what they have learned thus far. Have the groups record their responses.

At the end of this chapter, have the groups reconvene, discuss the questions again, and compare their responses with their original replies.

Chapter Setting

The British passenger ship steamed through the inky Atlantic night. In the lounge, Floyd Gibbons, an American reporter, chatted with other passengers. They discussed the war that had been raging in Europe since 1914.

"What do you think are our chances of being torpedoed?" Gibbons asked. No one could cross the Atlantic in early 1917 without asking that question. German submarine attacks were a real danger.

"About 4,000 to 1," replied one passenger. "Nonsense," a British diplomat scoffed.

66 'Considering the zone that we are in and the class of the ship, I should put the chances down at 250 to 1 that we don't meet a sub.' At that minute the torpedo hit us. 99

For a time, all was smoke and confusion. Suddenly, five whistle blasts told passengers to abandon ship. Gibbons scrambled into a lifeboat and was lowered into the sea. Moments later, a second torpedo struck the *Laconia,* sending it to a watery grave. Gibbons survived a fearful night at sea and was rescued the next day.

The United States had tried to stay out of the struggle in Europe. Still, Americans could not avoid its effects, including German attacks on American ships.

In April 1917, President Woodrow Wilson reluctantly led the country into war. In his war message, he spoke of protecting "the freedom of the seas." More important, he pictured the war as a great crusade. "The world," he declared, "must be made safe for democracy."

ACTIVITY

Brainstorm the images that the word "crusade" brings to mind. Then create a poster illustrating Wilson's idea that the United States had to make the world "safe for democracy."

Chapter Resources

English Guided Reading Duplicate and distribute the Chapter 23 Guided Reading worksheets on pages 45–46 in the English Guided Reading section of the *Chapter Resources* binder. Students who have difficulty reading might also benefit from using this worksheet. Have students complete the worksheet before they begin reading. You might pair a more fluent student or a student who is a strong reader with each SAE student to review. (Reteaching/Easy)
Spanish Resources See the Spanish Resources section of the *Chapter Resources* binder.

ACTIVITY

Guided Instruction To help students brainstorm, encourage them to identify the wrongs that Americans were fighting against as well as the ideals that they were fighting for.

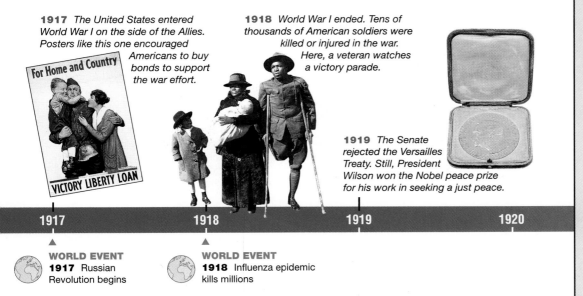

1917 The United States entered World War I on the side of the Allies. Posters like this one encouraged Americans to buy bonds to support the war effort.

For Home and Country
VICTORY LIBERTY LOAN

1918 World War I ended. Tens of thousands of American soldiers were killed or injured in the war. Here, a veteran watches a victory parade.

1919 The Senate rejected the Versailles Treaty. Still, President Wilson won the Nobel peace prize for his work in seeking a just peace.

| 1917 | 1918 | 1919 | 1920 |

▲ **WORLD EVENT**
1917 Russian Revolution begins

▲ **WORLD EVENT**
1918 Influenza epidemic kills millions

Chapter 23 • **647**

Students Acquiring English
Activity

Students learning English need to develop skills in writing as well as in reading. In teaching SAE students, it is helpful to know why they make certain errors. For example, in English, adjectives generally precede the nouns they modify, except in the case of predicate adjectives after the verb *be.* In languages such as Spanish, however, modifiers usually follow the nouns. As a result, some SAE students tend to misplace adjectives when they write in English. Thus, a student writing about the Belgian defense against the Germans in 1914 might discuss "the defense brave by Belgium neutral." Use student writing relevant to the chapter to teach a mini-lesson on this point.

Linking Past and Present
Activity

Ask students to find out if there are any war monuments in their community honoring World War I soldiers. If there are, have students find out as much information as they can about each monument. When was it built? How was it paid for? Who maintains it? Do names of soldiers appear on it? Are there any well-known names? Does any other writing (such as a quotation or poem) appear on it? Have students offer their own interpretations of the significance of any inscription.

Bell Ringer

Ask students to write their interpretation of this quotation: "Peace remains at the mercy of an accident." Tell students that a German diplomat said it in 1914.

Lesson Plan

1. Focus Archduke Franz Ferdinand of Austria-Hungary was assassinated in June 1914. Political alliances drew the nations of Europe into a conflict that lasted four years. In this section, students examine the events that led to World War I and learn how the United States became involved.

2. Instruct Draw two columns on the chalkboard. Label one Causes of World War I and the other Causes of United States Involvement. Work with students to fill in the two columns. Then ask: Which were long-term causes and which were short-term causes? Could World War I have been avoided? How? Which was the most important cause that brought the United States into the war? How might the United States have avoided involvement?

3. Close To close the lesson, have students turn the headings for the subsections into questions and then answer them.

---

1 Europe Explodes Into War

FIND OUT

- Why were tensions high in Europe in 1914?
- What was the immediate cause of the outbreak of war?
- How did Americans respond to the war in Europe?

VOCABULARY militarism, mobilize, kaiser, stalemate, trench warfare, propaganda

---

President Woodrow Wilson's friend and adviser Colonel Edward House visited Europe in May 1914. He quickly saw that the stories he had heard were true. Tensions among nations were threatening the peace of Europe.

"The situation is extraordinary," House noted. A kind of madness was gripping Europe. "There is too much hatred, too many jealousies." Not long after House returned home, Europe exploded into war.

Tensions in Europe

The fact that war erupted in August 1914 did not surprise many Europeans. For years, rivalries had caused tensions and divisions in Europe.

Nationalism. Nationalism fueled much of the tension. In the 1800s, nationalists called for freedom and self-government. People with a common language and culture sought to throw off foreign rule and form their own countries.

Although nationalism encouraged unity, it also set nation against nation. It created mistrust and even hatred. Bitter rivalry between France and Germany, for example, had led to war in 1870. As a result of that war, France had to give up Alsace-Lorraine, an area rich in iron ore, to Germany.

In Eastern Europe, nationalism deepened hostility between Austria-Hungary and Russia. Russia encouraged Serbs and other minorities in Austria-Hungary to rise up against their rulers.

Imperialism. Imperialism was another source of tension. Between 1870 and 1914, Britain, France, Germany, Italy, and Russia scrambled for colonies in Africa, Asia, and the Pacific. Each nation sought new markets and raw materials. Often, several nations competed for power in the same region. This competition led to wars in places far from Europe.

Militarism. Militarism was a third source of tension. **Militarism** is the policy of building up strong armed forces to prepare for war.

European nations expanded their armies and navies. The military buildup led to new tensions. When Germany expanded its navy, Britain felt that its own naval power was threatened. In response, Britain built more ships. This naval race strained relations between the two nations.

Rival alliances. To protect itself and isolate France, Germany organized the *Triple Alliance.* Besides Germany, members included Austria-Hungary and Italy. France responded by forming the *Triple Entente* (ahn TAHNT). The Triple Entente linked France to Russia and Britain.

The alliance system posed a new danger. Allies agreed to support one another in case of attack. Thus, a crisis involving one member also affected that nation's allies. This meant that a minor incident could spark a major war.

The Balkans in Crisis

For years, nationalism had caused turmoil in the Balkan peninsula in southeastern Europe. The rival nations of Albania, Bulgaria, Greece, Montenegro, Romania,

---

Historical Sidelight
Background

Woodrow Wilson ultimately played a major role in World War I. But in 1912 he was elected as a Progressive who had many ideas for domestic reforms. He stressed domestic policy in his inaugural address: "We have been proud of our industrial achievements, but we have not hitherto stopped thoughtfully enough to count the human cost, the cost of lives snuffed out, of energies overtaxed and broken, the fearful physical and spiritual cost to the men and women and children upon whom the dead weight and burden of it all . . . has fallen pitilessly the years through. The great Government we loved has too often been made use of for private and selfish purposes, and those who used it had forgotten the people. . . ." Perhaps he saw the war clouds building early on. Soon after taking office, Wilson wrote, "It would be the irony of fate if my administration had to deal chiefly with foreign affairs."

Linking Past and Present
Activity

Have students review the discussion of alliances above. Ask: What were the advantages of the alliance system? What were the dangers? Have interested students research one of the present-day alliances of the United States (such as NATO). Students can present their findings in oral reports. Encourage the class to compare and contrast what they know about current alliances to the alliances in Europe before World War I.

and Serbia battled for territory. Various nationalist groups also sought freedom from Austria-Hungary.

The fatal shots. A new crisis made headlines on June 28, 1914. That day, Archduke Franz Ferdinand, heir to the Austrian throne, visited Sarajevo. The city was the capital of Bosnia, a part of Austria-Hungary.

The archduke rode through the city in an open car. Along the route were several determined young Serbian nationalists. They were members of a terrorist group called the Black Hand. They wanted Bosnia to break free of Austria-Hungary and join with Serbia.

As the archduke passed, a man hurled a bomb into the car. Responding quickly, the archduke flung the bomb out of the car before it exploded. The archduke's driver sped away.

Suddenly, the car stopped. The driver had gone the wrong way. As the driver prepared to turn the car around, Gavrilo Princip stepped from the curb and fatally shot both the archduke and his wife.

Alliances lead to war. Austria-Hungary accused the Serbian government of hatching the murder plot. It threatened to go to war against Serbia. Russia moved to protect Serbia. Diplomats scurried to ease the crisis, but they met with no success. Then the system of alliances came into play.

On July 28, Austria-Hungary declared war on Serbia. The next day, Russia ordered its forces to **mobilize**, or prepare for war. Germany called on Russia to cancel the order to mobilize. When Russia did not reply, Germany declared war on Russia on August 1. On Sunday, August 2, the American ambassador to Britain, Walter Page, wrote his thoughts:

> 66 The Grand Smash is come. . . . I walked out in the night a while ago. The stars are bright, the night is silent, the country quiet—as quiet as peace itself. Millions of men are in camp and on warships. Will they all have to fight and many of them die—to untangle this network of treaties and alliances. . . so that the world may start again? 99

The answer came the next day. Germany declared war on Russia's ally France. When German armies marched through neutral Belgium on their way to France, Britain declared war on Germany. Long before, Britain had promised to defend Belgium if it were attacked.

Thus, what had begun as a local crisis in Bosnia exploded into a major war. For years, Europeans had expected war. When it came, many welcomed the chance to show their power and strength. Others, however, feared what war might bring.

Before the Bullets Struck *Austrian Archduke Franz Ferdinand and his wife, Sophie, arrive in Sarajevo. A few hours after this picture was taken, both of them were dead—struck down by an assassin.* **United States and the World** *Why was Franz Ferdinand assassinated?*

 Lesson Planner

For a developed **Cooperative Learning** lesson plan, see the *Lesson Planner*, page 142.

Answer to Caption

Franz Ferdinand was heir to the Austrian throne. The assassins were Serbian nationalists who wanted Bosnia to break free from Austria-Hungary.

 Voices of Freedom

Primary Source You might assign selection 9-1, The Coming of the "Grand Smash," on pages 196–197 of *Voices of Freedom*. The selection, which expands on the excerpt in the student text, is from Walter Page's memorandum, which he wrote as war broke out. (Enrichment/Average)

Historical Sidelight
Background

F. Cunliffe-Owen, an American journalist, was an expert on foreign affairs. However, he erred badly when it came to the assassination in Sarajevo. The morning after the shooting, his column in the New York *Sun* carried the banner "DEATH OF FRANCIS FERDINAND MAKES FOR PEACE OF EUROPE."

Cunliffe-Owen pointed out that the archduke had aggravated tensions in Europe by supporting aggressive policies: "It is impossible to deny that his disappearance from the scene is calculated to diminish the tenseness of the situation and to make for peace both within and without [Austria-Hungary]."

Critical Thinking
Forecasting

Ask students to imagine that they are news commentators in the summer of 1914. Have them write a brief commentary in which they suggest answers to these questions:
- Which other European countries may soon enter into the war, and why?
- Will the United States become involved—and, if so, why?

Use commentaries from volunteers to check students' understanding of events thus far and to preview upcoming material.

Videotapes/ Videodiscs

United States History Video Collection Use the video segment "The New Deadly Toys" from Volume 16, *The Great War,* to enhance students' understanding of the role played by new technology in World War I. Approx. running time 1:20 min. (Enrichment/Average) Vol. 16, Ch. 7

Chapter 7

Play

The "Great War" Begins

"You will be home before the leaves have fallen from the trees," the **kaiser,** or German emperor, told his troops as they marched off to war. In August 1914, most Europeans thought the war would end soon. They were mistaken, however. The war dragged on for four blood-soaked years. At the time, it was called the Great War. Later, it became known as World War I.

The war pitted the **Central Powers**—Germany, Austria-Hungary, and the Ottoman Empire—against the **Allied Powers**—France, Britain, and Russia. In time, 21 other nations, including Italy, joined the Allies.

The Germans advance. German generals had long before drawn up a plan for fighting both France and Russia. It called for a quick attack to defeat France in the west. Then they would fight the slow-moving Russian giant in the east.

MAP STUDY

The war in Europe was fought on several fronts. The Allies clashed with the Central Powers in France, Belgium, Russia, Italy, and the Ottoman Empire.

1. *In what country was Sarajevo located?*
2. *Which of the Central Powers bordered Russia?*
3. **Analyzing Information** *Judging from the map, why was the alliance between France and Russia a threat to Germany?*

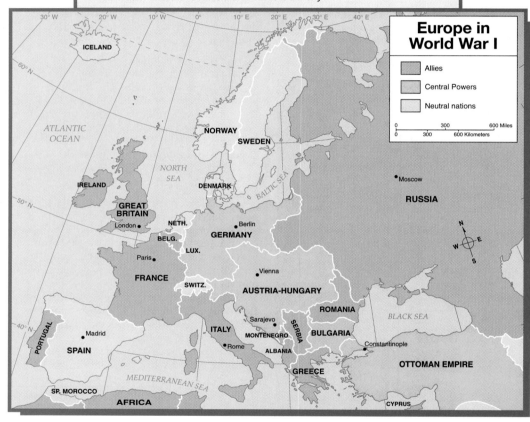

Europe in World War I

Connections With Language Arts
Activity

Explain that the word *kaiser,* like the Russian word *czar,* is derived from the word *caesar,* the title of the Roman emperor in ancient times. Ask students what they know about any of the caesars and what that information suggests about the rule of a kaiser. You might extend this activity by having students brainstorm and create a class list of other titles for a country's leader. Ask: Are any of these words an appropriate substitute for *kaiser?*

Connections With Geography
Activity

Challenge students to create, exchange, and solve additional questions about the map on page 650. You might use the following questions to get them started; then have them continue on their own.

■ About how far is Paris from Moscow? Berlin from Moscow?

■ Which countries bordered Serbia?

■ Which countries bordered Italy? Based on that information, why do you think Italy sided with the Allies?

The German plan mapped out a route to France that passed through Belgium. In August, German troops poured into Brussels, the Belgian capital. The tiny Belgian army fought bravely, but they were soon crushed.

German armies then thundered into France. By September, German guns were heard in Paris. At the Marne River, however, French and British troops slowed the German advance. The **Battle of the Marne** ended German hopes for a speedy victory in the West.

Trench warfare. By November 1914, fighting had produced a deadly stalemate. In a stalemate, neither side is strong enough to defeat the other. In the next three years, armies fought huge battles. No one, however, gained much territory.

Both sides dug in, creating a maze of trenches protected by mines and barbed wire. (See Exploring Technology on page 652.) In the trenches, soldiers lived in miserable discomfort. They spent weeks at a time in muddy, rat-infested ditches. One soldier later recalled: "The men slept in mud, washed in mud, ate mud, and dreamed mud."

Some trenches were shallow ditches. Others were elaborate tunnels that served as headquarters and first-aid stations. Between the front-line trenches of each side lay "no man's land." This area was a wasteland of barbed wire and deadly land mines.

In trench warfare, soldiers spent day after day shelling the enemy. Then, officers would order troops "over the top." Soldiers crawled out of the trenches to race across "no man's land" and attack the enemy. Most offensives resulted in many deaths but gained little new territory. The **Battle of Verdun** in 1916 lasted 10 months. The Germans lost some 400,000 men trying to overrun French lines. The French lost even more defending their positions.

Losses on the Eastern Front. Stalemate and trench warfare brought mounting tolls on the Eastern Front as well. The vast armies of Germany and Austria-Hungary faced off against those of Russia and Serbia. By mid-1916, the Russians had lost over one million soldiers. Yet neither side could win a decisive victory.

American Neutrality

In 1914, Americans were determined to avoid being dragged into the European war. President Woodrow Wilson had called on Americans to "be neutral in fact as well as in name."

Divided opinion. Officially, the United States was neutral. Public opinion, however, was divided. Most Americans favored the Allies. After all, the country had longstanding ties to Britain. The two peoples spoke the same language and shared many traditions. Also, the United States and France had been allies in the American Revolution.

On the other hand, about 8 million Americans were of German or Austrian descent. They felt ties to the Central Powers. Millions of Irish Americans also sympathized with the Central Powers. They hated Britain, which had ruled Ireland for centuries. Many American Jews also favored Germany against Russia. Some of them had fled persecution in Russia.

Impact of the war. The war had several immediate effects on the United States. First,

Linking Past and Present
Among those who opposed United States involvement were veterans of the Civil War. "I had my soul rent with indescribable agony," said Isaac Sherwood, "as I stood in the presence of comrades who were maimed, mangled, and dying on 42 battlefields of this Republic. . . . I feel it is my sacred duty to keep the. . . young men of today out of a barbarous war 3,500 miles away."

Historical Outline Map Book

Historical Outline Map Use the map, Europe in World War I, on page 60 of the *American History Historical Outline Map Book*. Lesson ideas for this map can be found on page T19. (Enrichment/Average)

Videotapes/ Videodiscs

United States History Video Collection Use the video segment "Neutrality" from Volume 16, *The Great War,* to enhance students' understanding of the reasons the United States tried to stay out of the war in Europe. Approx. running time 2:00 min. (Enrichment/Average) Vol. 16, Ch. 10

Chapter 10   Play

Historical Sidelight
Background

President Wilson not only held a personal conviction about the rightness of neutrality; he also advocated a wide-ranging campaign on the matter. He presented this view to the United States Senate in 1914: "The spirit of the nation in this critical matter will be determined largely by what individuals and society and those gathered in public meetings do and say, upon what newspapers and magazines contain, upon what ministers utter in their pulpits and men proclaim as their opinions on the street."

Historical Sidelight
Background

As President Wilson was campaigning for neutrality, a group of women called for an end to the war altogether. On August 29, 1914, about 1,500 women advocates for peace in Europe marched down Fifth Avenue in New York City. Many of them were dressed in black mourning clothes. Others were dressed in white but wore black armbands. Several of the marchers carried a white flag embroidered with the symbol of a dove and the word *peace* in gold letters.

Answer to Exploring Technology

Possible Answer: Trench warfare probably depleted local resources and left the land barren.

 Transparencies

Exploring Technology Use the transparency World War I Tank on page H-53 of *American History Transparencies*. This transparency examines how a new weapon, the armored tank, helped revolutionize ground warfare. Teaching suggestions can be found on page H-17. (Enrichment/Average)

Exploring Technology Use the transparency Trench Warfare on page H-55 of *American History Transparencies*. This transparency gives students additional information on trench warfare. Teaching suggestions can be found on page H-18. (Enrichment/Average)

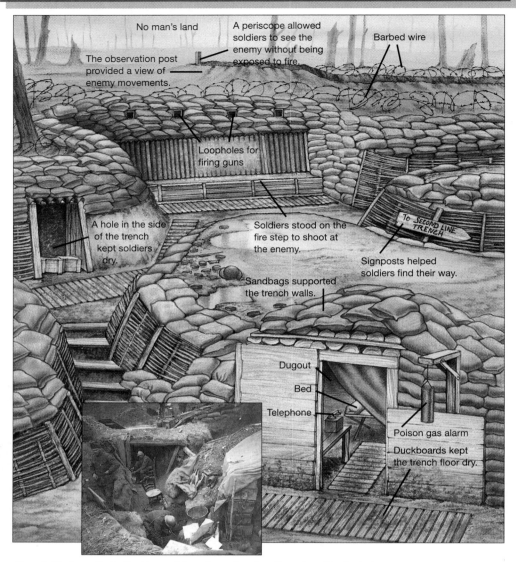

Trench Warfare *On both sides, soldiers dug networks of trenches. The typical trench was about 6 to 8 feet (1.8 to 2.4 m) deep and just wide enough for two men to pass. "No man's land," a stretch of ground protected by barbed wire and land mines, lay between enemy lines.* **Geography** *How do you think trench warfare affected the land and resources of the area where it took place?*

652 • Chapter 23

Connections With Language Arts
Background

The term *no man's land* had been used earlier to describe the strip of land ceded to the United States by Texas when it entered the Union. This area had no government until it became part of Oklahoma in 1890.

From life in the trenches came these terms:
trench coat — a coat worn by British officers in the trenches
trench fever — a severely infectious fever transmitted through lice

trench foot — a foot infection caused by standing in water in the trenches
trench mortar — a special cannon, effective only at a short range, used in the trenches
Foxhole is another term for trench, although originally it referred to a small trench, suitable for only a few soldiers. *Foxhole* was a British term, as were its synonyms *pit* and *Belgium pit*—but *foxhole* was the term that American soldiers later chose for it.

Connections With Language Arts
Activity

Based on the illustration and the information on page 651, ask students to imagine that they are soldiers. Have them write a letter to their families at home to describe their lives in the trenches. Encourage them to describe the sanitary conditions, the elaborate network of trenches, and the view of "no man's land" and possible sightings of the enemy. You might divide the class into small groups and have each group choose one letter from among those written by its members to feature in a bulletin board display.

the economy boomed. Both the Allies and the Central Powers needed food, weapons, oil, steel, and other goods. American farmers and manufacturers rushed to fill orders. By 1917, trade with the Allies had grown seven times in value and by a smaller amount with the Central Powers. This trade imbalance meant that the United States was not strictly neutral.

Both sides conducted a propaganda war in the United States. **Propaganda** is the spreading of ideas or beliefs that help a particular cause and hurt an opposing cause. Each side pictured the other as savage beasts who killed innocent civilians.

Freedom of the Seas

Allied propaganda did less to change American opinion than the issue of freedom of the seas. The United States argued that as a neutral nation it had the right to trade with either side. Britain, however, blockaded German ports, hoping to starve Germany into surrender. Germany responded by setting up a blockade around Britain.

Submarine warfare. Germany used a powerful new weapon in this sea war—its fleet of submarines. These U-boats, or undersea boats, as Germans called them, attacked any ship that entered or left British ports.

U-boat attacks on neutral shipping raised a storm of protest. Under international law, a country at war could stop and search a neutral ship suspected of carrying war goods. But submarines were slow. Also, their hulls were made of thin metal. If they surfaced to search a ship, they could easily be rammed or shelled. To prevent this, submarines simply torpedoed enemy and neutral ships, causing great loss of life.

Germany warned the United States and other neutral nations to keep their ships out of the blockade zone. President Wilson rejected this limit on neutral shipping. He vowed to hold Germany responsible if its submarines caused Americans to die or lose property.

Sinking of the *Lusitania*. Germany ignored Wilson's threat. On May 7, 1915, a German submarine torpedoed the *Lusitania,*

***Lusitania* Victims** *Nearly 1,200 people were killed when a German U-boat torpedoed the* Lusitania. *Many of the victims were buried in mass graves, such as the one shown here.* **Science and Technology** *Why did U-boat captains often torpedo neutral ships rather than search them for war goods?*

Chapter 23 • **653**

Section 2
pp. 654–660

Bell Ringer

Have students make a list of actions that the United States government would need to take in order to prepare to enter a war.

Lesson Plan

1. Focus Wilson tried to keep the United States out of the war in Europe. However, events in 1917 led to the end of neutrality. In this section, students trace the steps that brought the United States into the war.

2. Instruct Divide the class into teams. Ask them to imagine that they have been sent by Wilson to rally support for the war effort in 1917. Have each team give a speech on one of the following themes: (a) Why We Are Fighting (b) Join Up Now! (c) Buy Liberty Bonds! (d) Women—Do Your Part! After the presentations, ask: Why did most Americans support the war effort?

3. Close To close, ask students a series of *Who, What, Where, When, Why,* and *How* questions about the home front.

---

a British passenger ship, off the coast of Ireland. Nearly 1,200 people died, including 128 Americans.

An outraged Wilson called the sinking of the *Lusitania* "murder on the high seas." He threatened to break off diplomatic relations if Germany did not stop sinking passenger ships. Germany did not want to risk war with the United States. It later apologized for sinking another ship with Americans on board and agreed to stop attacking neutral ships without warning.

SECTION 1 REVIEW

1. **Locate:** (a) Great Britain, (b) France, (c) Germany, (d) Italy, (e) Russia, (f) Austria-Hungary, (g) Serbia, (h) Sarajevo.
2. **Identify:** (a) Triple Alliance, (b) Triple Entente, (c) Franz Ferdinand, (d) Gavrilo Princip, (e) Central Powers, (f) Allied Powers, (g) Battle of the Marne, (h) Battle of Verdun.
3. **Define:** (a) militarism, (b) mobilize, (c) kaiser, (d) stalemate, (e) trench warfare, (f) propaganda.
4. Give three reasons for tensions in Europe in 1914.
5. What event triggered the outbreak of war in 1914?
6. (a) What position did the United States take on the European war in 1914? (b) How did the United States benefit from the war?
7. How did the Central Powers and the Allies try to influence American public opinion?
8. **CRITICAL THINKING Analyzing Information** Could war in Europe have been avoided in 1914? Explain your answer.

ACTIVITY **Writing to Learn**
Imagine that you are President Wilson in 1915. Write a letter to the German ambassador about the sinking of the *Lusitania.*

2
The Road to War

FIND OUT
- Why did the United States go to war in 1917?
- How did the government organize the war effort?
- How were critics of the war treated?

VOCABULARY pacifist

The outbreak of war in Europe horrified Henry Ford. The automaker hated war. In December 1915, he sailed on a "peace mission" to end the fighting. "We're going to have the boys out of the trenches by Christmas," he announced as he left.

Ford invited about 100 well-known men and women to join him as "peace commissioners." They hoped to bring the warring powers together for peace talks. Christmas passed, yet "the boys" remained in the trenches. Although Ford's mission failed, it showed that many Americans believed peace could be won through negotiation.

"He Kept Us Out of War"

President Wilson, too, tried to bring both sides to peace talks. Like Ford, he failed. Despite his devotion to peace, Wilson saw the need to be prepared in case war could not be avoided. He called for a stronger army and navy.

In 1916, Wilson ran for reelection against Republican Charles Evans Hughes, a Supreme Court Justice and former governor of New York. Like Wilson, Hughes supported neutrality. As the race narrowed, however, Democrats portrayed Hughes as a warmonger. They boosted Wilson's image with the slogan: "He kept us out of war!"

Answers to Section 1 Review

1. See the map on p. 650.
2. (a) Triple Alliance, p. 648, (b) Triple Entente, p. 648, (c) Franz Ferdinand, p. 649, (d) Gavrilo Princip, p. 649, (e) Central Powers, p. 650, (f) Allied Powers, p. 650, (g) Battle of the Marne, p. 651, (h) Battle of Verdun, p. 651
3. (a) militarism, p. 648, (b) mobilize, p. 649, (c) kaiser, p. 650, (d) stalemate, p. 651, (e) trench warfare, p. 651, (f) propaganda, p. 653
4. Nationalism contributed to tensions between nations by encouraging hatred and

mistrust. Imperialism led to competition for colonies and even provoked small wars overseas. Militarism resulted in a naval arms race between Germany and Britain, further adding to tensions. The alliance system divided rival nations and made it possible for a minor crisis to start a general war.
5. the assassination of Archduke Franz Ferdinand, heir to the Austrian throne
6. (a) neutrality (b) By supplying the Allies with arms, steel, and other goods, American trade flourished.

7. Each side used propaganda to present its cause as just and its enemy as savage.
8. Possible Answer: War was unavoidable because of the growing tensions and an alliance system that brought other nations into the conflict once it began. Furthermore, attempts at negotiation failed.

On election night, Hughes went to bed believing he had won. Just after midnight, the telephone rang. "The President cannot be disturbed," a friend told the caller. "Well, when he wakes up," replied the caller, "just tell him he isn't President." Late returns showed that Wilson had won in California. Those votes gave him the election.

After the election, Wilson again pressed for peace. In January 1917, he called on the warring powers to accept "peace without victory." His call went unanswered.

Moving Toward War

Even as Wilson made his plea, Germany warned neutral nations that after February 1 it would sink any ship nearing Britain. Germany's decision to renew submarine warfare was a desperate effort to break the Allied blockade.

German leaders knew that U-boat attacks would probably bring the United States into the war. They gambled that they would defeat the Allies before American troops could reach Europe. To protest Germany's action, Wilson cut diplomatic relations. Even as he did so, however, he still hoped for peace.

A secret note. A few weeks later, a startling discovery moved the United States closer to war. In February, Wilson learned of a secret note from Germany's foreign secretary, Arthur Zimmermann, to the German minister in Mexico.

The ***Zimmermann telegram*** gave instructions to the German minister. It told him to urge Mexico to attack the United States if the United States declared war on Germany. In return, Germany would help Mexico win back its "lost provinces" in the American Southwest.* When Americans heard about the Zimmermann telegram, anti-German feeling soared.

---

*As you have read in Chapter 12, the United States gained this land after the Mexican War.

Zimmermann Telegram *Anti-German feeling soared when Americans learned that the German foreign minister had tried to enlist Mexico's support against the United States. In this cartoon, the German kaiser promises land in Arizona, New Mexico, and Texas to Mexico.* **United States and the World** *Why do you think the Germans believed that Mexico might fight against the United States?*

Revolution in Russia. Two events in early 1917 pushed the country still closer to war. First, German submarines sank several American merchant ships. Second, a revolution in Russia drove Czar Nicholas II from power.

For hundreds of years, czars, or Russian emperors, had ruled with absolute power. Several times in the 1800s and early 1900s, Russians had revolted against czarist rule. Their efforts all ended in failure.

When the war in Europe began in 1914, Russians united behind the czar. However, as conditions at home and on the front grew worse, discontent resurfaced. In March 1917, riots protesting the shortage of food turned into a revolution. The czar was forced to step down. Revolutionaries then set up the Provisional Government and called for democratic reforms.

Chapter 23 • **655**

 Lesson Planner

For a developed **Cooperative Learning** lesson plan, see the *Lesson Planner,* page 143.

 Chapter Resources

Critical Thinking Duplicate and distribute the worksheet, Synthesizing Information, from Unit 7, page 31, of the *Chapter Resources* binder. The worksheet asks students to analyze a political cartoon relating to President Wilson's desire for neutrality. (Enrichment/Average)

  Videotapes/ Videodiscs

United States History Video Collection Use the video segment "The Road to War" from Volume 16, *The Great War,* to enhance students' understanding of why the United States moved from neutrality to a declaration of war. Approx. running time 3:30 min. (Enrichment/Average) Vol. 16, Ch. 13

Chapter 13	Play

Answer to Caption

Possible Answer: If Mexico sided with Germany, and Germany won the war, Mexico might regain the lands it had lost to the United States.

Historical Sidelight
Background

Although the war in Europe dominated the presidential race in 1916, each party addressed domestic issues as well. Both parties, for example, supported suffrage and a ban on child labor.

Former President Theodore Roosevelt, who was still very popular, wanted to see the United States enter the war. He described people who favored neutrality as "flubdubs, mollycoddles, and flapdoodle pacifists." Roosevelt endorsed Hughes rather than Wilson. Catholics generally supported Hughes because of Wilson's dealings with Mexico, a largely Catholic country. The vote was close,

with Wilson receiving 49 percent of the popular vote to Hughes's 46 percent and 277 electoral votes to Hughes's 254.

In his inaugural address, even as he pleaded for "peace without victory," Wilson seemed to predict that his wishes would not be granted. He admitted: "We are provincials no longer. The tragic events of the thirty months of vital turmoil through which we have just passed have made us citizens of the world. There can be no turning back. Our own fortunes as a nation are involved whether we would have it so or not."

Connections With Technology
Background

Arthur Zimmermann's telegram was sent from Washington to Mexico by Western Union. Along the way, British intelligence intercepted the message and broke its code. When the British told Wilson about the Zimmermann telegram, however, they claimed that one of their agents had stolen it from Germans in Mexico. In the furor that followed, the authenticity of the message was questioned. Only when Western Union released its copy of the telegram did Zimmermann admit to sending it.

Answer to Caption

Answers will vary. Encourage students to offer factual support for their opinions.

Transparencies

Critical Thinking Use the transparency, Cause and Effect: American Entry Into World War I, on page F-27 of *American History Transparencies,* to highlight the main focus of this section. Teaching suggestions can be found on page F-9. (Enrichment/Average)

Interdisciplinary Connections Use the transparency Going Against the Tide on page B-77 of *American History Transparencies.* Teaching suggestions can be found on page B-25. (Enrichment/Average)

Videotapes/ Videodiscs

United States History Video Collection Use the video segment "The Dough Boys" from Volume 16, *The Great War,* to enhance students' understanding of American mobilization for the war. Approx. running time 2:15 min. (Enrichment/Average) Vol. 16, Ch. 16

Chapter 16	Play

President Wilson welcomed the Russian Revolution. He was a firm believer in democracy. It was against his principles to be an ally of the czar. With the new government in power, Wilson believed the Allied cause would be stronger.

Wilson's war message. On April 2, the President stood before Congress to ask for a declaration of war. His war message spelled out the nation's reasons for entering the struggle. He concluded:

> ❝It is a fearful thing to lead this great peaceful people into war, into the most terrible and disastrous of all wars, civilization itself seeming to be in the balance. But the right is more precious than peace, and we shall fight for the thing which we have always carried nearest our hearts—for democracy.❞

Congress voted for war 455 to 56. Among those who voted against war was Jeannette Rankin, the first woman elected to Congress. Like many Progressives, Rankin rejected the idea of war. "I want to stand by my country, but I cannot vote for war. I vote no!" she said.

On April 6, the President signed the declaration of war. It thrust Americans into the deadliest war the world had yet seen.

Calling Up the Troops

The day after Congress declared war, George M. Cohan wrote a new song, "Over There." The patriotic tune soon swept the nation. Its opening lines expressed American confidence:

> ❝Over there, over there,
> Send the word, send the word,
> over there,
> That the Yanks are coming . . . ❞

Its closing message promised: "We'll be over, we're coming over, And we won't come back till it's over over there."

Americans had to do more than sing patriotic tunes, however. They had to prepare to fight—and quickly. The Allies were desperate for everything from food to arms. Britain had only a few weeks' supply of food. In France, war-weary troops were on the verge of collapse. On the Eastern Front, Russian soldiers were deserting to join the revolution.

A chance to serve. To fight, the United States needed an army. On May 18, Congress passed the ***Selective Service Act.*** It required all young men from age 21 to 30 to register for the military draft.

In the next 18 months, 4 million men and women joined the armed forces. While

---

Raising an Army *The Selective Service Act required young men between the ages of 21 and 30 to register for the draft. In this photograph, Secretary of War Newton Baker selects the numbers of the men to be drafted.* **Citizenship** *Do you think that the draft is a fair way to raise an army? Explain.*

656 • Chapter 23

Connections With Music
Activity

Distribute copies to the class or write on the chalkboard the following lyrics from two American songs:

"I didn't raise my boy to be a soldier,
I brought him up to be my pride and joy.
Who dares to place a musket on his shoulder,
To shoot some other mother's darling boy?"

"America, I raised a boy for you,
America, You'll find him staunch and true,
Place a gun upon his shoulder,
He is ready to die or do."

Tell the class that the first lyrics are from a song that was popular in 1915 and the second lyrics are from a song that was popular in 1917. Ask: What different attitudes are expressed in the two songs? What events took place between 1915 and 1917 that might explain the differences?

Historical Sidelight
Background

President Wilson dreaded taking the United States into a major war because he felt it would change the character of Americans. "To fight you must be brutal and ruthless," he remarked, "and the spirit of ruthless brutality will enter into the very spirit of our national life, infecting Congress, the courts, the policeman on the beat, the man on the street."

Wilson's request for a declaration of war received a standing ovation. He said to an aide, "My message today was a message of death for your young men. How strange it seems to applaud that."

656

CONNECTIONS

ARTS | SCIENCES | GEOGRAPHY | WORLD | ECONOMICS | **CIVICS**

A Vote Against War

In 1916, Jeannette Rankin of Montana became the first woman elected to Congress. In her campaign, she supported women's suffrage, a ban on alcohol, and other reforms. She also promised to keep American soldiers out of the war in Europe.

Rankin did not have to wait long to test her campaign pledges. She arrived in the House of Representatives on April 2, 1917. That same day, President Wilson asked Congress to declare war against Germany.

Suddenly, Americans stopped worrying about what color dress the first congresswoman would wear or whether her hat would be decorated with birds or with flowers. Instead, they wondered how she would vote on the issue of war.

Rankin's supporters were torn. Many firmly believed that the United States should not go to war. At the same time, they worried that if Rankin voted against going to war, people would wonder if women were tough enough to hold public office.

Rankin, however, was a dedicated pacifist. To her, there was never any question. When her turn came to vote, she spoke up in

a clear voice: "I want to stand by my country, but I cannot vote for war. I vote no!" She explained later, "I felt at the time, that the first time the first woman had the chance to say no to war she should say it."

Rankin's pacifist stand turned some people away from her. She lost her

Jeannette Rankin

seat in Congress in the next election. She did not lose her spirit, however. She continued to work for peace across the United States and abroad. When world events once more threatened to draw the United States into war in 1940, Rankin ran for Congress again—and won. "The women elected me because they remembered that I'd been against our entering World War I," she said.

Once again, Rankin remained true to her beliefs. On December 8, 1941, she voted against American entry into World War II. She was the only member of Congress to do so. "You can no more win a war than you can win an earthquake," she said.

■ Why did Jeannette Rankin's supporters worry about her voting against United States entry into World War I?

ACTIVITY
Design an election campaign button for Jeannette Rankin. Make your button large enough to include reasons people should vote for her.

Antiwar demonstration

Voices of Freedom

Primary Source You might assign selection 9-3, The Home Front: Changes and Traditions, on pages 199–200 of *Voices of Freedom.* The selection is from historian David Kennedy's evaluation of how American history and traditions influenced the way the government mobilized the nation to support the war. (Enrichment/Average)

Videotapes/ Videodiscs

United States History Video Collection Use the video segment "America at War" from Volume 16, *The Great War,* to enhance students' understanding of the American home front during World War I. Approx. running time 2:40 min. (Enrichment/Average) Vol. 16, Ch. 19

| Chapter 19 | Play |

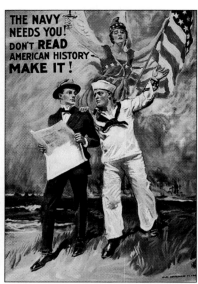

Call to Arms *Recruiting posters, like the one at left, urged Americans to help the war effort by joining the armed forces. Felix Sanchez of New Mexico, far left, was one of the many Americans who served.* **Citizenship** *What action did the government take to build up the armed forces quickly?*

men drilled for combat, women served as radio operators, clerks, and stenographers. At training camps, young men found there were not enough weapons for everyone. They trained using broomsticks for guns. Despite long hours of drill, soldiers got caught up in the war spirit. A young recruit wrote: "We don't know where we are going, but the band plays 'Over There' every day, and they can't send us any too soon."

To many, the war seemed like a great adventure. "Here was our one great chance for excitement and risk," wrote a volunteer. "We could not afford to pass it up."

"Fighting for democracy." People from every ethnic group enlisted. About 20,000 Puerto Ricans served in the armed forces. Many Filipinos also served. Scores of soldiers were immigrants who had recently arrived in the United States.

Because Native Americans could not be citizens, they also could not be drafted. Large numbers of Native Americans enlisted anyway. From one family of Winnebago In-

dians came 35 volunteers. They served together in the same unit.

At first, the armed forces did not allow African Americans in combat. When the government changed the rules, more than 2 million African Americans registered for the draft. Nearly 400,000 were accepted for duty. They were forced into segregated "black-only" units commanded mostly by white officers.

African Americans rallied behind the war. Blacks like W.E.B. Du Bois believed in the war's goals:

66 Let us, while the war lasts, forget our special grievances and close ranks . . . with our fellow citizens and the allied nations that are fighting for democracy. 99

Organizing the War Effort

The United States reorganized its economy to produce food, arms, and other goods needed to fight the war. President Wilson

658 • Chapter 23

Connections With Music
Activity

Have interested students research "Over There" or other patriotic songs such as "Keep the Home Fires Burning" or "It's a Long Way to Tipperary," and perform the songs or play recordings of them for the class. Discuss how the songs reflected the mood of the country at the time they were written, and have students describe what effect they think the songs had on the public. The words to "Over There" and other World War I songs can be found in *Legion Airs: Songs of the Armed Forces,* edited by Lee O. Smith.

Connections With Art
Background

The famous recruiting poster showing Uncle Sam pointing outward over the words "I WANT YOU" was first used during World War I. It was designed by noted illustrator James Montgomery Flagg, who used his own face as the model for Uncle Sam.

Our Multicultural Heritage
Background

Although black units were commanded by white officers, about 1,400 African Americans became captains and lieutenants after a special training camp for black officers was set up in Des Moines, Iowa.

set up government agencies to oversee the effort.

Food for victory. Wilson chose Herbert Hoover to head the Food Administration. Hoover's job was to boost food production. The nation had to feed its troops and help the Allies. "Food Will Win the War," proclaimed a Food Administration poster.

Farmers grew more crops, and families planted "victory gardens." People went without wheat on "wheatless Mondays." They did not eat meat on "meatless Tuesdays." The food they saved helped the men in the trenches. A magazine urged:

66 Do not permit your child to take a bite or two from an apple and throw the rest away; nowadays even children must be taught to be patriotic to the core. 99

Factories and labor. A new government agency, the War Industries Board, told factories what they had to produce. It also divided up limited resources. The War Labor Board settled disputes over working hours and wages and tried to prevent strikes. With workers in short supply, unions were able to win better pay and working conditions.

Winning public support. Millions of Americans supported the war effort with their savings. Movie stars, such as Charlie Chaplin and Mary Pickford, helped sell **Liberty Bonds.** By buying bonds, American citizens were lending money to the government to pay for the war. The government raised $21 billion through the sale of Liberty Bonds.

To rally public support for the war, the government sent out "Four-Minute Men." Their name recalled the Minutemen of 1776. It also referred to the four-minute speeches the men gave at public events and even at movies and theaters. The speakers urged Americans to make sacrifices for the goals of freedom and democracy.

Women at work. As men joined the armed forces, women stepped in to do their jobs. Women received better pay in war industries than they did in other jobs they had held. In factories, women assembled weapons and airplane parts. Some women drove trolley cars and delivered the mail. Others served as police officers. By performing well in jobs once thought to be for men only, women changed the view that they were fit for only certain kinds of work.

Women Help to Win the War
As the war took male workers away from home industries, women rushed in to do their jobs. These shipyard workers are holding the tongs and buckets they used to work with red-hot steel rivets. **Citizenship** *How do you think their wartime work helped women win the right to vote after the war?*

Our Multicultural Heritage
Activity

The start of World War I had unexpected consequences for many minority groups in the United States. For example, when the war began, Herbert Hoover headed the U.S. Food Administration. Hoover asked the Department of Labor to ease restrictions that limited Mexican migrants to farm work. As a result, many Mexicans were able to enter skilled professions. Mexican Americans took jobs such as machinists, mechanics, and upholsterers. During the war years, large numbers of Mexican Americans moved to cities in the Midwest, finding employment in Detroit automobile factories; in Gary, Indiana, meatpacking plants; and in Ohio and Pennsylvania steel mills.

As war industries in the North grew, so did the attraction for African Americans from the South who were looking for work. Fearful of losing their work force, some southern cities and towns began a campaign to keep African Americans in the South. Some used threats; others required migrant agents to pay a fee for doing business.

Tensions and Protests

The war encouraged a sense of common purpose, but racial and other tensions remained. During the war, almost a half million African Americans left the South and moved to cities in the North. They sought to escape poverty and discrimination. In northern cities, many found better paying jobs in war industries.

Violence against African Americans. In the North, too, African Americans ran into prejudice and racial violence. Competition for housing and jobs led to race riots. In 1917, 39 African Americans were killed during a riot in East St. Louis, Illinois. A New York parade protested the deaths. Marchers' signs demanded: "Mr. President, Why Not Make AMERICA Safe for Democracy?"

Immigrants from Mexico. In the Southwest, ranchers pressed the government to let more Mexicans cross the border. Almost 100,000 Mexicans entered the United States to work on farms. Some moved on to Chicago, Omaha, and St. Louis to work in factories. These workers made an important contribution to the war effort. Yet after the war, the United States tried to force them to return to Mexico.

Attacks on German Americans. German Americans were subjected to suspicion and intolerance during the war. Newspapers questioned their loyalty. Mobs attacked them. In 1918, a mob lynched Robert Prager, whose only crime was that he had been born in Germany. A jury later refused to convict the mob leaders.

Jailing critics. Some Progressives, such as Jane Addams and Carrie Chapman Catt, opposed the war. Antiwar feeling also ran high among socialists* and radical labor

---
*Socialists believed that the means of producing goods—such as banks and factories—should be publicly owned. They thought all people should share in the work and in the goods produced.

groups. They believed that the war benefited wealthy owners but not workers. Other critics included **pacifists**, people who refuse to fight in any war.

To encourage unity, Congress passed laws making it a crime to criticize the government or to interfere with the war. Nearly 1,600 men and women were arrested for breaking these laws. One woman went to prison for writing these words: "I am for the people, and the government is for the profiteers." Eugene V. Debs, Socialist candidate for President five times, was jailed for protesting the draft. So, too, was William "Big Bill" Haywood, head of the Industrial Workers of the World.

A few people questioned these laws. To them, silencing critics violated the Constitution's guarantee of freedom of speech. Most Americans, however, felt that the laws were necessary in wartime.

SECTION 2 REVIEW

1. **Identify:** (a) Zimmermann telegram, (b) Selective Service Act, (c) Liberty Bonds.
2. **Define:** pacifist.
3. Describe three events that brought the United States into the war.
4. (a) List three government agencies that were set up to organize the war effort. (b) What did each agency do?
5. How did women help the war effort?
6. **CRITICAL THINKING Concept Mapping** Review the subsection entitled Tensions and Protests, at left. Make a concept map for the information presented in the subsection.

ACTIVITY Writing to Learn
Imagine that you are the lawyer for someone who was jailed for speaking against the war. Outline the arguments you would make in your client's defense.

Answers to Section 2 Review

1. (a) Zimmermann telegram, p. 655, (b) Selective Service Act, p. 656, (c) Liberty Bonds, p. 659
2. pacifist, p. 660
3. Germany's decision to resume U-boat attacks on neutral ships traveling to Britain outraged the United States. The Zimmermann telegram revealed that Germany was plotting with Mexico against the United States. The Russian Revolution that overthrew the czar made Wilson feel more comfortable about fighting on the Allied side.

4. (a) Food Administration, War Industries Board, War Labor Board (b) The Food Administration boosted food production; the War Industries Board managed factory production and divided up resources; the War Labor Board settled labor disputes and tried to prevent strikes.
5. Women took jobs formerly held by men, such as making war materials and driving trolleys. Some women carried out clerical and communications tasks for the army.

6. Student concept maps should show main ideas: Reaction toward minority groups (subtopics: violence against African Americans and German Americans; Mexican workers encouraged to immigrate); Critics of the war (subtopics: socialists, Progressives, some labor unions, and pacifists oppose the war; ban on criticism of government and the war).

3
"Over There"

FIND OUT
- Why did the Allies welcome American troops in 1917?
- How did Americans help end the war?
- What were the human costs of the war?

VOCABULARY armistice

Soon after war was declared, a War Department official asked the Senate for $3 billion for arms and other supplies. "And we may have to have an army in France," he added. "Good grief!" sputtered one senator. "You're not going to send soldiers over there, are you?"

In fact, the United States would send more than 2 million soldiers to France. The buildup took time. First, troops had to be trained and armed. By March 1918, fewer than 300,000 American troops had reached France. Then they poured in. Fresh and eager to fight, they gave the Allies a much-needed boost.

Hard Times for the Allies

The first American troops reached France in June 1917. They saw for themselves the desperate situation of the Allies. The Allies had lost millions of soldiers. Troops in the trenches were exhausted and ill. Many civilians in Britain and France were near starvation.

A second Russian revolution. To make matters worse, Russia withdrew from the war. In November 1917, the **Bolsheviks** seized power from the Provisional Government. Led by V. I. Lenin, the Bolsheviks

wanted to bring a communist revolution to Russia.

Lenin had embraced the ideas of Karl Marx, a German thinker of the 1800s. Marx had predicted that workers around the world would unite to overthrow the ruling class. After the workers revolted, they would end private property and set up a classless society, Marx said. Lenin was determined to lead such a revolution in Russia.

Once in power, Lenin opened talks with Germany. He had opposed the war, arguing that it benefited only the ruling class. In March 1918, Russia and Germany signed the **Treaty of Brest-Litovsk.** Although Russia

---

Revolution in Russia *In November 1917, Bolsheviks led by V. I. Lenin, shown here, overthrew the Provisional Government in Russia. Once in power, they negotiated a peace treaty with Germany.* **Economics** *Why did Lenin want to end the war with Germany?*

Chapter 23 • **661**

Answer to Caption
Lenin felt that only the ruling class would benefit from the war's continuation.

Section 3
pp. 661–666

Bell Ringer

Ask students to write a paragraph explaining why during World War I people might have referred to the conflict as "the war to end all wars."

Lesson Plan

1. Focus When American troops arrived in Europe, the situation looked bleak. The Allies were suffering terrible losses, Russia had dropped out of the war, and Germany had launched a massive offensive. In this section, students focus on the role that American soldiers played in the winning of the war.

2. Instruct Divide the class into three groups and have the groups choose to represent American troops, French or British troops, or German troops in World War I. Have group members discuss each of the following events: (a) January 1918 — the arrival of American troops in France (b) June 25, 1918 — the Battle of Belleau Wood (c) November 11, 1918—World War I ends. Encourage students to describe the events and their feelings about them.

Historical Sidelight
Background

Theodore Roosevelt played the "Rough Rider" to the end of his life. When the United States entered World War I, Roosevelt proposed that he be made commanding general of a division of "horse riflemen," whom he would recruit from among his friends, just as he had done in the Spanish-American War. General Hugh Scott, army chief of staff, flatly vetoed the proposal. Scott argued that trench warfare made the use of cavalry obsolete and that Roosevelt, almost 60, was too old for a field command.

Connections With Technology
Background

One of the most deadly weapons of the war was mustard gas—first used by the Germans against British troops in 1917. Mustard gas was a compound of carbon, hydrogen, sulfur, and chlorine that caused the skin to blister. If inhaled, it could damage the lungs and cause death.

3. Close
To close the lesson, have students summarize the role that American troops played in World War I.

 Lesson Planner

For a developed **Cooperative Learning** lesson plan, see the *Lesson Planner,* page 144.

Answers to Map Study

1. France **2.** Marne, Somme, Meuse, and Aisne **3.** Possible Answer: American troops gave the Allies new strength. From 1914 to 1918, the Allies battled German troops over a very small area. In 1918, the Allies were able to mount an offensive that pushed the Germans eastward.

 Voices of Freedom

Primary Source You might assign selection 9-4, How the Americans Helped, on pages 201–202 of *Voices of Freedom.* The selection is from newspaper journalist and soldier Alden Brook's analysis of the part played by America during the war. (Enrichment/Average)

MAP STUDY

During World War I, opposing armies battled back and forth across the Western Front. Tens of thousands of soldiers fell in costly attacks on enemy positions. In 1918, fresh American troops gave the Allies new strength.

1. *In which country did most of the fighting take place?*
2. *Name three rivers that were near major battle sites.*
3. **Understanding Causes and Effects** *How does this map show the effect of the arrival of American troops in 1918?*

The Western Front

— Farthest German advance, 1914
- - - Armistice line, 1918
← Allied offensive, 1918
�֍ Major battles

0   50   100 Miles
0 50 100 Kilometers

---

had to give up land to Germany, Lenin welcomed peace. With war ended, he could focus on the communist revolution.

The Allies saw the treaty as a betrayal. It gave Germany coal mines and other resources in Russia. More important, peace with Russia meant that Germany could move its armies from the Russian front into France. In early 1918, Germany used these troops in an all-out attack on the Allies.

A new German push. By March 21, German forces had massed near the French town of Amiens. (See the map at left.) They talked of a "peace offensive." They hoped that a final push would end the war. Late at night, 6,000 German cannons began pounding the British troops camped at Amiens. Despite heavy fire, the British held on. The battle lasted for two weeks. At last, on April 4, the Germans gave up their attack.

The Germans continued their offensive elsewhere. By late May, they had smashed through Allied lines along the Aisne (EHN) River. On May 30, they reached the Marne River, just east of Château-Thierry (SHA toh tee ER ee). Paris lay only 50 miles (80 km) away. At this point, American troops entered the war in force.

Americans in France

By June 1918, Americans were reaching France in record numbers. Commanding the American Expeditionary Force (AEF) was General John J. Pershing. Pershing was well known at home for leading American troops into Mexico to hunt for Francisco "Pancho" Villa. (See page 643.)

Allied generals wanted the fresh troops to reinforce their own war-weary soldiers. Pershing refused. He insisted that his troops operate as independent units.

The United States wanted to have a major role in shaping the peace. Only by playing "a definite and distinct part" in the war would it have power at the peace table.

Historical Sidelight
Background

Early in his career, General John J. Pershing earned the nickname "Black Jack" because he commanded an all-black unit. He had led the famous black 10th Cavalry in the Battle of San Juan Hill during the Spanish-American War.

After World War I, Congress honored Pershing by re-creating for him the title General of the Armies, previously held only by George Washington.

Connections With Language Arts
Background

An American soldier at this time might refer to a British soldier as a *Tommy* (short for "Tommy Atkins," the British equivalent of "John Doe") or a *Limey* (referring to the fact that British sailors used to eat limes to prevent scurvy). A British soldier might call an American soldier a *Yank* (short for "Yankee") or a *Sammy* (from "Uncle Sam"). The most wide-

ly used word for an American soldier, however (even among Americans), was *doughboy.* Several logical origins for *doughboy* have been given. The term probably refers to the fact that the brass buttons on the soldiers' uniforms resembled a fried cornmeal cake, also called a "doughboy," that members of the military had eaten since the 1770s.

In the end, Pershing agreed to let some Americans fight with the British and French. At the same time, he set up an American operation to defend part of the Western Front.

Harlem Hell Fighters in Action

By the spring of 1918, the 369th United States Infantry had taken up its position on the front lines. Nicknamed the Harlem Hell Fighters, the unit was an African American force attached to the French army.

The United States allowed few African Americans to train for combat. Most served in support roles—as laborers, cargo handlers, and waiters. The French, however, respected the bravery of African American soldiers and were glad to fight side by side with them. In the end, the Harlem Hell Fighters spent more time under fire than any other American unit.

A hint of danger. Privates Henry Johnson and Needham Roberts faced their first trial by fire on the night of May 13. They were guarding a tiny outpost near Montplaisir. German raiders were reported to be in the area. So far, Johnson and Roberts had seen no one. Then Roberts heard a faint clicking sound. He asked Johnson to listen.

The two men stood silently, straining to hear through the darkness. At last, Johnson heard the clicking noise, too. He recognized the sound at once—wire clippers. German soldiers were cutting through the barbed wire. At any moment, they would attack.

Sounding the alarm. Johnson and Roberts quickly fired a flare. They wanted to light up the field where they suspected the Germans were hiding. Suddenly, the dugout that the Americans were guarding exploded. Grenades tossed by the Germans wounded both men. Farther down the line, reinforcements were pinned down by enemy fire.

ART GALLERY
OUR COMMON HERITAGE

E. SIMS CAMPBELL
War Knows No Color Line, 1976

Until the late 1940s, the United States armed forces rigidly separated black and white troops. During World War I, African American combat troops served in segregated "black-only" units. In his painting War Knows No Color Line, *modern African American artist E. Sims Campbell pays tribute to the courage and sacrifice of black soldiers in World War I.* **Multicultural Heritage** *What do you think is the meaning of the title of Campbell's painting?*

Art Gallery Posters

War Knows No Color Line, by E. Sims Campbell, appears in poster form in the *Art Gallery: Our Common Heritage Posters.* Teaching suggestions for the poster are available in the Teacher's Guide.

Answer to Art Gallery: Our Common Heritage

Possible Answer: The need for heroism can be fulfilled by a soldier of any race; all races involved in a war can expect to face death during the fighting.

Voices of Freedom

Primary Source You might assign selection 9-5, A Black Perspective on Black Soldiers, on pages 202–203 of *Voices of Freedom.* The selection describes what Dr. Robert Moton, principal of Tuskegee Institute, said to African American and white American troops he visited in France at the end of the war. (Enrichment/Average)

Our Multicultural Heritage
Background

The all-black 369th Regiment held two distinctions: It was the first of all Allied regiments to reach the Rhine River; and of all American units in the war, it remained in continuous combat the longest.

The 371st and 372nd Regiments, two other all-black units, were commanded by the French division commander General Goybet. Of these troops he said, " . . . the most formidable defense, the nests of machine guns, the best organized positions, the artillery barrages most crushing, could not stop them."

Most African Americans who served in the war were assigned to service rather than combat units. Some of these units worked as stevedores at French ports for the American Expeditionary Force. The only African Americans to serve in the navy during the war were some 10,000 messmates. Only 1 out of every 2,600 African Americans in the service became an officer, and no African American officer was promoted above the rank of colonel.

Chapter Resources

History Through Literature To provide students with an author's firsthand account of life in a World War I hospital, duplicate and distribute the worksheet, Three Soldiers, from Unit 7, page 32, of the *Chapter Resources* binder. (Enrichment/Average)

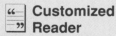

Customized Reader

Primary Source For Sergeant York's personal account of how he single-handedly captured 132 German soldiers during the battle for the Argonne Forest, order article VIB-14, Sergeant York in the Argonne Forest, from the *American History Customized Reader*. (Enrichment/Average)

Our Multicultural Heritage

Biography Have students read the biography, Sergeant York, Reluctant Hero, on page 67 of the *Our Multicultural Heritage* booklet. (Enrichment/Average)
Milestone Have students read A Turning Point for Native Americans, on page 69 of the *Our Multicultural Heritage* booklet. (Enrichment/Average)

Johnson and Roberts had to face at least two dozen Germans alone.

Hand-to-hand combat. Roberts was too badly hurt to get up, but he began tossing grenades at the enemy. As enemy soldiers poured into the trench, Johnson fired three rounds. He downed several attackers, but others kept coming. "There was no time for reloading," an American officer later reported. "Johnson swung his rifle round his head, and brought it down . . . upon the head of the German. The German went down. . . . "

Johnson turned to find out how Roberts was doing and saw two Germans carting him away. Johnson would not let them take Roberts prisoner. He sprang on the Germans, stabbing them with his knife.

Johnson glanced around again. The German he had clubbed earlier was up and shooting at him. Johnson felt a sharp pain. He fell to his knees. As the German closed in, Johnson stabbed his attacker. This time, the man did not get up.

The remaining attackers fled, hauling away their dead and wounded. Despite his wounds, Johnson followed, pelting them with grenades. When help finally arrived, Johnson was near collapse.

A hero's welcome. For their bravery, Johnson and Roberts were awarded the Croix de Guerre, a French medal of honor. Later, their unit won other decorations.

When the 369th Regiment had left for Europe, no one had given it a going-away parade. Only white units received such honors. After the war, however, the 369th marched in a huge welcome-home parade down Fifth Avenue in New York City. Flowers and ticker tape showered the heroes, Henry Johnson and Needham Roberts. A million New Yorkers greeted them. "God bless you, boys!" they cheered. The unit commander felt a rush of joy:

❞They [New Yorkers] did not give us their welcome because ours was a regiment of colored soldiers. . . . They greeted us that day from hearts filled with gratitude and pride and with love, because ours was a regiment of men, who had done the work of men.❞ ■

Final Battles

In the meantime, the Germans continued their "peace offensive." As they rolled across the Aisne River, the French prepared to evacuate Paris.

The marines will hold. In June 1918, American troops plunged into their first major battle in Belleau (BEH loh) Wood, outside Paris. A French general sent General James Harbord of the United States a message: "Have your men prepare entrenchments some hundreds of yards to the rear in case of need." Harbord replied: "We dig no trenches to fall back on. The marines will hold where they stand."

The **Battle of Belleau Wood** raged for three weeks. At last, on June 25, General Harbord passed along the good news: "Wood now exclusively U.S. Marine Corps."

Turning the tide. In mid-July, the Germans launched another drive to take Paris. They pushed the Allies back until they came up against American troops. In three days, the Allies "turned the tide of the war." Even the Germans knew they had lost as their troops were forced to retreat.

The Allies took the offensive. Marshal Ferdinand Foch (FOHSH), a Frenchman, commanded the Allied forces. He ordered attacks along a line from Verdun to the North Sea. American forces stormed the area between the Meuse (MYOOZ) River and the Argonne Forest. (See the map on page 662.) The land was a crazy quilt of hills and ravines—perfect for the Germans to defend.

Into the Argonne Forest. On September 26, more than a million Americans pushed into the Argonne Forest. Years of war had

Team-Teaching Suggestion
Language Arts

You might work with a language arts teacher to present a lesson about *All Quiet on the Western Front* or to guide students in reading excerpts from it or even the entire work. This 1929 novel by Erich Maria Remarque gives an account of World War I from a German soldier's point of view. As the lesson or series of lessons are presented, encourage students to comment on what the novel suggests about the horror and pointlessness of war.

Historical Sidelight
Background

During the Battle of Belleau Wood, American Captain Lloyd Williams received orders to retreat. With determination he replied, "Retreat, hell! We just got here!"

In this battle, the 4th Marine Brigade attacked so fiercely that the Germans called them *Teufelhunden*—"devil dogs." "Devil dogs" has been a nickname for the United States Marine Corps ever since.

Americans on the Move *Troops from the United States played a key role in the battles of 1918. Here, American troops move equipment up to the front.* **United States and the World** *What effect did the arrival of American troops have on the war?*

left the land scarred with trenches and shell holes. The air still smelled of poison gas from earlier battles.

At first, the Americans advanced despite heavy German fire. Then, rains and the thick woods slowed their movement. Small units drove forward to capture deadly German positions. Finally, after 47 days, the Americans broke through the German defense. They had won the ***Battle of the Argonne Forest.*** The cost was high, however. The Americans and Germans each suffered more than 100,000 casualties.

British, French, and Belgian forces also smashed through the German lines in their areas. By November, German forces on the Western Front were in retreat. The "war to end all wars" was nearing its end.

Peace at Last

On October 4, Prince Max of Baden, head of the German cabinet, secretly cabled President Wilson:

66 To avoid further bloodshed, the German government requests the President to arrange the immediate conclusion of an armistice on land, by sea, and in the air. 99

An **armistice** is an agreement to stop fighting. Wilson set two conditions for an armistice. Germany must accept his plan for peace, and the German emperor must give up power.

Germany in turmoil. While German leaders debated a response, unrest surfaced.

Answer to Caption
They boosted the strength of the Allied forces and probably forced the Germans to retreat.

 Chapter Resources

Geography in History Duplicate and distribute the worksheet, Battling Through a Forest, from Unit 7, pages 33–34, of the *Chapter Resources* binder. The worksheet focuses on the physical features of the Argonne Forest. (Enrichment/Challenging)

 Videotapes/ Videodiscs

United States History Video Collection Use the video segment "Over There" from Volume 16, *The Great War,* to enhance students' understanding of the contribution of American troops to the Allied victory in World War I. Approx. running time 2:20 min. (Enrichment/Average) Vol. 16, Ch. 34

Chapter 34

Play

Connections With Technology
Background

In addition to U-boats and tanks, airplanes were used in battle for the first time in World War I. Both sides armed airplanes with machine guns, and fighter pilots engaged in fierce battles called dogfights. Famous pilots of this war include Eddie Rickenbacker, the American who downed the largest number of enemy airplanes; Eugene Bullard, the most prominent African American pilot; and Manfred von Richthofen of Germany, nicknamed the "Red Baron."

Linking Past and Present
Background

President Wilson proclaimed the first Armistice Day. Every November 11 after that, Armistice Day was celebrated as a holiday. In 1954, Congress changed the name of the holiday to Veterans Day to honor all United States war veterans. Veterans Day, as depicted on page 667, is still observed on November 11.

Costs of the War for the Allies

	Money Spent	Casualties
British Empire	$ $ $ $	🧍 🧍 🧍 ǀ
France	$ $ $	🧍 🧍 🧍 🧍 🧍 🧍 ǀ
Russia	$ $ ǀ	🧍 🧍 🧍 🧍 🧍 🧍 🧍 🧍 🧍 ǀ
United States	$ $	🧍 (365,000)

$ 10 billion dollars 🧍 1 million casualties

Source: V. J. Esposito, *A Concise History of World War I*

GRAPH SKILLS *During World War I, there were millions of casualties, that is, people dead or wounded. In addition, the war effort cost each side billions of dollars.* ● *Which Allied nation had the greatest number of casualties? How much did the United States spend on the war?*

German sailors rebelled. Revolutions simmered in several German cities. On the battlefront, German armies lost ground daily.

On November 9, the German emperor was forced to resign. He and his son fled to Holland. Germany became a republic. The new German leaders agreed to the armistice terms. At 11 A.M. on November 11, 1918—the eleventh hour of the eleventh day of the eleventh month—World War I ended.

The costs of war. The human costs of the war were staggering. Between 10 million and 13 million people died in battle. Germany, alone, lost about 2 million men. More than 4 million Russian, French, and British soldiers were killed. The United States lost over 50,000 men. Many more died of diseases. More than 20 million soldiers on both sides were wounded.

Much of northern France was destroyed. Millions of Germans were near starvation. In 1918, a new disaster struck. A terrible influenza epidemic spread around the world. Between 1918 and 1919, more than 500,000 Americans died in the epidemic. The death toll in other countries reached the millions.

SECTION 3 REVIEW

1. **Locate:** (a) Amiens, (b) Marne River, (c) Château-Thierry, (d) Paris, (e) Meuse River.
2. **Identify:** (a) Bolsheviks, (b) V. I. Lenin, (c) Treaty of Brest-Litovsk, (d) John J. Pershing, (e) Harlem Hell Fighters, (f) Ferdinand Foch, (g) Battle of Belleau Wood, (h) Battle of the Argonne Forest.
3. **Define:** armistice.
4. Describe the situation of the Allies in 1917.
5. What helped turn the tide of the war in 1918?
6. What conditions did Europeans face at the end of the war?
7. **CRITICAL THINKING Drawing Conclusions** Why do you think that African American soldiers, like Henry Johnson, were often treated better in Europe than at home?

*AC**TIVITY*** **Writing to Learn**
Write a radio news report about one battle in which Americans took part.

4
Wilson and the Peace

FIND OUT

■ What were Wilson's Fourteen Points?

■ How did Wilson and the Allies differ over plans for peace?

■ Why did the Senate reject the Versailles Treaty?

VOCABULARY self-determination, reparations

Huge crowds cheered Woodrow Wilson when he reached France in December 1918. Some people cried with joy to see the American leader. After years of suffering, people turned to Wilson as a symbol of hope. He was the man who had promised to make the world "safe for democracy."

Wilson went to France determined to achieve a just and lasting peace. His goals, however, were often at odds with those of the other Allies.

Wilson's Plan for Peace

In Europe, Wilson visited London, Milan, and Rome as well as Paris. Everywhere, cheering crowds welcomed him. Wilson felt sure these people supported his goals for peace. He was wrong. The people who greeted Wilson so warmly hated Germany deeply. They and their leaders were determined to punish the Germans for the war.

The Fourteen Points. In January 1918, even before the war ended, Wilson outlined his goals for peace. His plan, known as the *Fourteen Points,* was meant to prevent international problems from causing another war.

Wilson's first point called for an end to secret agreements. Secrecy, Wilson felt, had created the rival alliances that had helped lead to war. Next, he called for freedom of the seas, free trade, and a limit on arms. He urged peaceful settlement of disputes over colonies.

Celebrating the Armistice *In every Allied country, citizens cheered the signing of the armistice. This painting by George Benjamin Luks shows the celebration in New York City.* **Linking Past and Present** *Armistice Day, November 11, is now known as Veterans Day. How do many Americans celebrate it?*

Section 4
pp. 667–671

🔔 Bell Ringer

Write the expression *peace without victory* on the chalkboard. Remind students that this was one of President Wilson's goals. Ask students to write what they think Wilson meant. Have them save their interpretations and later see how well they matched the actual resolution to the war.

Lesson Plan

1. Focus Wilson's dream for "peace without victory" was never fully realized. The Allies wanted revenge on Germany. Wilson also faced strong opposition to the peace treaty in Congress. In this section, students examine the peace conference and its aftermath.

2. Instruct Tell students to imagine that they are reporters preparing to interview Wilson after he left office. Have students write questions that they would ask about World War I and his peace efforts. Have students write the replies that they think Wilson would have given.

3. Close To close the lesson, have students identify the most important fact or concept from each subsection in Section 4.

Critical Thinking
Synthesizing Information

Tell students that a 1983 poll of historians rated Woodrow Wilson sixth among the country's greatest Presidents, with Abraham Lincoln first, Franklin Roosevelt second, and George Washington third. Remind students that a fellow Virginian said that George Washington was "first in war, first in peace, and first in the hearts of his countrymen."

Divide students into groups for the purpose of writing a eulogy for Woodrow Wilson. The eulogy should describe Wilson's actions as a wartime President, his efforts to make peace, and where he stood "in the hearts of his countrymen." In the process, groups might discuss why historians rate Wilson's presidency so high despite his failure to convince the Senate to accept the Treaty of Versailles or the League of Nations. Encourage groups to present their eulogies to the class and discuss points on which the eulogies agree and disagree.

Key goals. A key part of Wilson's plan was national **self-determination.** National groups, he said, had the right to their own territory and forms of government.

Wilson's most important goal was his fourteenth point. It called for a "general association of nations," or ***League of Nations.*** Its job would be to protect the independence of all countries—large or small. As Wilson noted:

> ❝An evident principle runs through the whole programme I have outlined. It is the principle of justice to all peoples and nationalities, and their right to live on equal terms of liberty and safety with one another, whether weak or strong. ❞

Weaknesses of the plan. Wilson persuaded the Allies to accept the Fourteen Points as the basis for making peace. But although many Europeans welcomed Wilson's ideas, the peace plan soon ran into trouble. Some goals were too vague. Others conflicted with reality. In Paris, therefore, Wilson faced a constant battle to save his Fourteen Points.

The Paris Peace Conference

Diplomats from more than 30 nations met in Paris and Versailles (vuhr sī), hoping to make a lasting peace. Key issues were decided by the Big Four—Woodrow Wilson of the United States, David Lloyd George of Britain, Georges Clemenceau (kleh mahn soH) of France, and Vittorio Orlando of Italy.

Differing aims. Each leader had his own aims. Wilson had called for "peace without victory." He opposed punishing the defeated powers.

The other Allies, however, ached for revenge. Germany must pay, they said. They insisted on **reparations,** or payments for the losses they had suffered during the war. Further, they wanted Germany to accept responsibility for the war. They also tried to protect themselves against future German attacks.

An unsatisfactory treaty. During the months of haggling, Wilson had to compromise on his Fourteen Points in order to save his key goals. By June 1919, the ***Versailles Treaty*** was ready. No one was satisfied with it. Germany had not even been allowed to send delegates to the peace talks. It was horrified by the terms of the treaty. Still, it had no choice but to sign.

Under the treaty, Germany had to take full blame for the war. It had to disarm completely and pay the Allies huge reparations. It was stripped of its colonies, which were put under the control of other nations.

Wilson's successes. Wilson won a few victories, however. In Eastern Europe, several new nations were created based on the goal of self-determination. They included Poland, Czechoslovakia, and Yugoslavia. They were created out of lands once ruled by Germany, Russia, and Austria-Hungary. (See the map on page 669.) Still, national groups were mixed together within these new nations so that many people remained dissatisfied. Many Germans, for example, had settled in Poland and Czechoslovakia. In time, Germany would seek to regain control of German-speaking peoples in Eastern Europe.

For Wilson, his greatest success was including the League of Nations in the peace treaty. "A living thing is born," he declared. "It [the League] is definitely a guarantee of peace."

> ***Our Common Heritage***
> *W.E.B. Du Bois organized a Pan-African Congress in Paris in 1919. Delegates from the United States, the West Indies, and Africa protested the Paris peace talks that were deciding the fate of German colonies in Africa without consulting Africans.*

Connections With Civics
Background

President Wilson stirred up antagonism from his opponents well before he arrived in France. In 1918, he tried to make the congressional elections into a vote on his policies. He urged Americans to elect Democrats who would support him. It was the Republicans, however, who gained control of both the House and the Senate. Republican leaders announced that their victory meant that the voters rejected Wilson's foreign policy.

The President further angered his opponents by naming only one Republican to the negotiating team in Paris. As a result, Republicans viewed the treaty as a Democratic treaty and thus were not inclined to favor it.

In addition, critics were enraged when Wilson decided to lead the delegation to Paris himself. Never before had a President met foreign leaders on foreign soil. Many people felt that he should stay home and deal with the problems of adjusting to peace. Wilson ignored them all when he sailed for Europe in December 1918.

Connections With the World
Background

Although criticized at home, Woodrow Wilson was regarded as a savior in the Allied countries of Europe. One French woman wrote to him, "You have saved our fiancés; love blooms again."

In 1920, Wilson became the second United States President to receive the Nobel peace prize. He was honored for his efforts to create the League of Nations.

MAP STUDY

The treaties that ended World War I created several new nations. At the urging of President Wilson, the Allies recognized the right of these nations to self-determination.
1. Which new nations in Eastern Europe bordered Russia?
2. In which new nation was the city of Sarajevo located?
3. **Synthesizing Information** Compare this map with the map on page 650. Which nations had to give up land as a result of World War I?

Europe After World War I

New nations

Answers to Map Study

1. Finland, Estonia, Latvia, and Poland 2. Yugoslavia 3. Germany, Austria-Hungary, Russia, and Bulgaria

Voices of Freedom

Primary Source You might assign selection 9-8, Opposing the League of Nations, on page 206 of *Voices of Freedom*. The selection is a cartoon that comments on the debate in Congress over the League. (Enrichment/Average)

Videotapes/Videodiscs

United States History Video Collection Use the video segment "Post-War World" from Volume 16, *The Great War*, to enhance students' understanding of the results of World War I. Approx. running time 1:35 min. (Enrichment/Average) Vol. 16, Ch. 40

Chapter 40   Play

United States History Video Collection Use the video segment "The Impact of the Great War on America" from Volume 16, *The Great War*, to enhance students' understanding of how the war affected life in the United States. Approx. running time 1:25 min.(Enrichment/Average) Vol. 16, Ch. 46

Chapter 46   Play

The Senate and the Treaty

When the President returned home, he faced a new battle. He had to convince the Senate to approve the Versailles Treaty.

Many Americans opposed the peace treaty. Some said that it was too soft on the defeated powers. Many German Americans felt that it was too harsh. Isolationists—or people who wanted the United States to stay out of world affairs—opposed the League of Nations.

Henry Cabot Lodge. Critics of the treaty found a leader in Senator Henry Cabot

Historical Sidelight
Background

As discussed on pages 669 and 671, Senator Lodge led the move to amend the Versailles Treaty—specifically to add a set of reservations to it. European diplomats and Wilson's own advisers tried to get the President to see the need to accept at least some of the Lodge reservations. Even Lodge, however, noted: "Never under any set of circumstances in this world could [Wilson] be induced to accept a treaty with Lodge reservations appended to it." As he explained, Wilson's dislike for him was "as strong as any cable with its strands wired and twisted together." Indeed, Wilson once exclaimed, "Accept the Treaty with the Lodge reservations! Never! Never! I shall never consent to adopt any policy with which that impossible name is so prominently identified." As he told his wife, Edith, "Better to go down fighting than to dip your colors to dishonorable compromise." Many critics at the time and present-day historians believe that the antagonism that Wilson and Lodge held for each other played as great a part as any other in keeping the United States out of the League of Nations.

Cooperative Learning
Activity

Organize a debate around this statement: "The United States should have agreed to the Versailles Treaty and joined the League of Nations." Have one team of students prepare a list of reasons supporting the statement and another team prepare a list of reasons opposing it. You may wish to have a third group prepare a list of questions to ask the speakers. After the teams have argued their points, take a class vote on whether the United States should have joined the League of Nations.

Chapter Resources

Skill Application For additional practice, duplicate and distribute the worksheet, Recognizing Propaganda, from Unit 7, page 30, of the *Chapter Resources* binder. (Reteaching/Average)

Answers to Skill Lesson

1. (a) to commit the United States to fight in future wars (b) to achieve a lasting peace, allow for national self-determination — and punish Germany (c) The textbook account is fact because it can be proven to be true. (d) that joining the League will increase the chances of war, negate the Monroe Doctrine and Washington's warning, and put American forces under League control
2. (a) that League membership commits the United States to participation in foreign affairs (b) Examples include "War-Breeding Covenant" and "Evil Thing With a Holy Name." (c) It identifies with George Washington. (d) It represents the other side as making the United States surrender an important policy.
3. (a) Possible Answer: It is effective because it uses emphasis and simple words. (b) Possible Answer: It might have caused people to question the wisdom of League membership.
4. Possible Answer: Its use might help convince members of Congress to vote a certain way.

A C T I V I T Y

Guided Instruction Encourage students to look through a variety of magazines; they are likely to find propaganda in every ad.

CRITICAL THINKING SKILLS
Recognizing Propaganda

Propaganda is a deliberate attempt to spread ideas that help a certain cause or hurt an opposing cause. It is used to shape public opinion. Propaganda has been used throughout history. It is important to be able to recognize propaganda in order to understand historical events.

During World War I, newspapers and governments on both sides used propaganda to win public support for the war effort. For example, both Britain and Germany used propaganda to convince Americans to enter the war on their side. After the war, propaganda, such as the advertisement below, was used to keep the United States from joining the League of Nations. Propaganda can be visual, such as a drawing or poster. It can be written, such as an advertisement, pamphlet, or book. Sometimes it is both.

1. Identify the facts. Remember that facts are statements that can be proved. Opinions, on the other hand, are the beliefs or ideas of a person or group. Opinions are not necessarily true. Compare the advertisement below about the Treaty of Versailles with what you have read in your textbook. (a) According to the advertisement, what was the goal of the treaty? (b) What does your textbook say is the purpose of the treaty? (c) Which is fact? How do you know? (d) What opinions does the advertisement express?

2. Identify the propaganda technique. Propaganda can shape public opinion in several ways. Some propaganda presents half-truths. For example, a picture, newspaper article, or chart can show facts that are correct, but show only some of the facts.

A second propaganda technique is name-calling. One side might call the other side barbarians. A third technique is identifying a cause with a famous person or a noble idea. A fourth is using symbols or words that show the other side in the worst possible light.

Look closely again at the advertisement below. (a) What half-truths are contained in the advertisement? (b) Find an example of name-calling. (c) Does the advertisement identify its cause with a famous person or a noble idea? Explain. (d) How does the advertisement show the other side in the worst possible light?

3. Draw conclusions based on the evidence. (a) Do you think this advertisement is an effective piece of propaganda? Why? (b) How do you think this advertisement affected public opinion in the United States at the time it was printed?

4. Make a generalization. Why do you think propaganda is used when important laws or treaties are before Congress?

AMERICANS, AWAKE!

Shall We Bind Ourselves to the War-Breeding Covenant?

It surrenders the Monroe Doctrine!
Flouts George Washington's Warning!
Entangles Us in European And Asiatic Intrigues!
Sends Our Boys to Fight Throughout the World by Order of a League!
The Evil Thing With a Holy Name!

A C T I V I T Y
Look through current magazines and newspapers to locate two advertisements that contain propaganda. Identify the propaganda technique used in the advertisements. Are the advertisements effective? Why or why not?

Students Acquiring English
Activity

To practice speaking English, have SAE students discuss advertising that is directed specifically to their own ethnic groups, comparing it to advertising that is directed to a more general audience. Students can identify similarities and differences in the kinds of products that are advertised, the celebrities that are chosen to endorse the products, and the images that are used to encourage or discourage the use of a product.

Lodge of Massachusetts. Lodge, a Republican, was chairman of the Senate Foreign Relations Committee. Although he accepted the idea of the League of Nations, he wanted changes in the treaty.

Lodge objected to Article 10. It called for the League to protect any member whose independence or territory was threatened. Lodge argued that Article 10 could involve the United States in future European wars. He wanted changes in the treaty that would ensure that the United States remained independent of the League. He also wanted Congress to have the power to decide whether the United States would follow League policy.

No compromise. Wilson was sure that Lodge's changes would weaken the League. When advisers urged the President to compromise, he replied, "Let Lodge compromise." He refused to make any changes.

As the battle grew hotter, the President took his case to the people. In early September 1919, Wilson set out across the country to defend the League. He made 37 speeches in 29 cities. He urged people to tell their senators that they supported the treaty.

On September 25, the weary President complained of a headache. His doctors canceled the rest of the trip. Wilson returned to Washington. A week later, his wife found him unconscious. He had suffered a stroke that left him bedridden for weeks.

The treaty is dead. In November 1919, the Senate rejected the Versailles Treaty. "It is dead," Wilson mourned, "[and] every morning I put flowers on its grave." Gone, too, was Wilson's cherished goal—American membership in the League of Nations.

The United States did not sign a peace treaty with Germany until 1921. By then, many nations had joined the League of Nations. Without the United States, however, the League had limited power and influence. In the years ahead, the League would be unable to live up to its goals of protecting members against aggression.

A Witches' Brew *For President Wilson, the League of Nations represented the hope of world peace. For many Americans, however, it seemed like a bubbling brew of trouble.* **United States and the World** *Why were many Americans against the League?*

SECTION 4 REVIEW

1. **Identify:** (a) Fourteen Points, (b) League of Nations, (c) Versailles Treaty, (d) Henry Cabot Lodge.
2. **Define:** (a) self-determination, (b) reparations.
3. (a) Who were the Big Four? (b) What country did each represent?
4. Why did Wilson have to compromise on his Fourteen Points?
5. Why did some Americans dislike the idea of the League of Nations?
6. **CRITICAL THINKING Evaluating Information** Many historians blame Wilson for the defeat of the Versailles Treaty in Congress. Do you agree or disagree? Explain.

ACTIVITY Writing to Learn
Write a speech that President Wilson might have given to promote the League of Nations.

Historical Sidelight
Background

During President Wilson's illness, his wife, Edith, unofficially took on many of his duties. She handled all of his communications, and it was reported that she even guided his hand as he signed documents. Some have called her "the first woman President."

Answers to Section 4 Review

1. (a) Fourteen Points, p. 667, (b) League of Nations, p. 668, (c) Versailles Treaty, p. 668, (d) Henry Cabot Lodge, p. 669
2. (a) self-determination, p. 668, (b) reparations, p. 668
3. (a and b) Woodrow Wilson—United States; David Lloyd George—Great Britain; Georges Clemenceau—France; Vittorio Orlando—Italy.
4. The other Allies had different goals for the peace than did Wilson. He decided to give in on some issues in exchange for the Allies' acceptance of others.
5. They felt the League of Nations might drag the United States into future wars fought in Europe.
6. Possible Answer: Wilson's refusal to compromise with Lodge and others who opposed the treaty led to its defeat. Had Wilson been willing to compromise with Lodge, the treaty might have been approved.

Answers to Reviewing the Main Ideas

1. (a) Nationalism set countries with different languages and cultures against each other. (b) Imperialism bred competition among European nations for colonies in Africa and Asia. (c) Militarism led European nations to expand their armies and navies, which increased fears of war.

2. Trench warfare involved heavy bombardment of soldiers in underground trenches, followed by attacks "over the top"—in which troops left the trenches and raced across "no man's land" under fire. Thousands of men were thrown into such attacks and were mowed down with little land gained by either side.

3. (a) neutrality (b) Public opinion was divided: some Americans supported the Allies; others—including German Americans, Irish immigrants, and some Jewish immigrants from Russia—favored the Central Powers. Also, trade with the Allies increased at a much greater rate than trade with the Central Powers did.

4. Reasons include attacks by German U-boats on neutral ships; Allied propaganda; sympathy for Britain and France; and German interference in relations between Mexico and the United States, as revealed in the Zimmermann telegram. Indirectly, however, President Wilson also hoped that the outcome of the war would provide for making the world safe for democracy.

5. By 1917 the Allies were exhausted by the long and costly war; they lacked food and weapons.

6. (a) an end to secret diplomacy, freedom of the seas, free trade, arms reductions, support for self-determination, and a League of Nations to protect the peace (b) Wilson had to compromise on many goals, but he did help set up Poland, Czechoslovakia, and Yugoslavia, which were based partly on self-determination. The League of Nations was established in the peace treaty, even though the United States Senate rejected the treaty and the League.

7. The Senate rejected the treaty in part because Wilson would not

Summary

- Years of tensions in Europe exploded in 1914 into war between the Allied and Central powers.
- President Wilson tried to keep the United States neutral, but the nation was drawn into World War I in 1917.
- American troops helped stop the final German offensive and turned the tide in favor of the Allies.
- The Senate rejected the Versailles Treaty and refused to let the United States join the League of Nations.

Reviewing the Main Ideas

1. Explain how each of the following contributed to the outbreak of war in Europe in 1914: (a) nationalism, (b) imperialism, (c) militarism.

2. What was trench warfare like during World War I?

3. (a) What policy did the United States proclaim at the outbreak of war in Europe? (b) Why was it difficult for the government to maintain that policy?

4. Why did the United States declare war on Germany?

5. Why did the Allies welcome American help in 1917?

6. (a) What were Wilson's goals for the peace? (b) Did he achieve them? Explain.

7. Why did the Senate reject the Versailles Treaty?

Thinking Critically

1. **Analyzing Ideas** (a) How did the United States government regulate the free enterprise system during the war? (b) Why do you think Americans accepted government interference in the economy?

2. **Analyzing Information** The government tried to stop people from criticizing the war. Do you agree with the government's view that protesters were dangerous to the war effort? Explain.

3. **Linking Past and Present** Before and after World War I, many Americans were isolationists. (a) When did the tradition of isolation begin? (b) How did this position change in the late 1800s? (c) What position does the United States take today?

Applying Your Skills

1. **Understanding Causes and Effects** Identify each of the following as a cause or an effect of the murder of Franz Ferdinand: (a) growth of nationalism among the Slavs, (b) Austro-Hungarian declaration of war on Serbia, (c) German invasion of Belgium.

2. **Reading a Map** Study the map on page 669. (a) Name three new nations created after World War I. (b) In what part of Europe were most of these nations located? (c) What new nation was located north of Austria?

Thinking About Geography

Match the letters on the map with the following places: **1.** Allied Powers, **2.** Central Powers, **3.** Sarajevo, **4.** Great Britain, **5.** France, **6.** Russia, **7.** Germany, **8.** Austria-Hungary. **Movement** Why did European nations seek colonies in Africa and Asia?

make any changes in Article 10. Opponents in particular feared that Article 10 would force the United States to become involved in foreign wars.

Answers to Thinking Critically

1. (a) The government set up agencies to oversee and manage food and factory production. (b) Possible Answer: Americans who supported the war effort probably saw the need for such controls during wartime to make

sure that enough food, weapons, and other war goods were produced and sent overseas.

2. Answers will vary. Students might consider the balance between the rights guaranteed in the Constitution—especially the right to freedom of speech—and the special laws passed by Congress during wartime.

3. (a) Isolationism dates back to the first American Presidents and specifically to George Washington's warning in his Farewell Address. (b) In the late 1800s, the United States gained territory

overseas and became more involved in world affairs. (c) The United States today is a superpower involved in every part of the world.

Answers to Applying Your Skills

1. (a) cause (b) effect (c) effect
2. (a) Poland, Yugoslavia, Czechoslovakia, Austria, Hungary, Lithuania, Latvia, Estonia, and Finland (b) Eastern Europe (c) Czechoslovakia

Fighting World War I on the Home Front

Form into groups to explore life on the home front during World War I. Follow the suggestions below to write, draw, or perform to show what you have learned about the war effort at home. You may use the textbook, encyclopedias, atlases, or other materials in your classroom library to complete the tasks. Be able to name your sources of information when you have finished the activity.

ARTISTS Imagine that you have been hired by the government to help win support at home for World War I. Brainstorm a list of images that express the reasons the United States is fighting the war. Then create a poster to convince Americans to support the war effort.

ACTORS Review the information about Four-Minute Men in the chapter. Then prepare and deliver a speech that might have been given by a "Four-Minute Man" to convince Americans on the home front to make sacrifices for the goals of freedom and democracy. Ask classmates to evaluate how well the speech would have persuaded an audience during the war.

MUSICIANS Learn a song about the war by George M. Cohan, or write one of your own. Perform your song for the class.

WRITERS Find out more about how World War I affected people on the home front. Then write a short story from the point of view of a person of your age who lived during that time. The story should reflect the effects of the war on your life.

ECONOMISTS Find out more about the effects that the war had on the nation's economy. Then make a concept map showing these effects.

Sheet music

Girl Scouts working for the war effort

 Set up a Fighting World War I on the Home Front corner in your classroom. Include an example or description of the completed activity from each group.

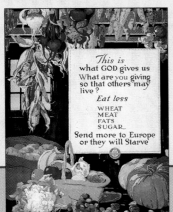

Food poster

Chapter 23 • **673**

Answers to Thinking About Geography

1. G **2.** H **3.** F **4.** A **5.** B
6. E **7.** C **8.** D
Movement: They wanted to profit from new markets and raw materials.

Assessment

Chapter Resources Binder For a more comprehensive evaluation of student understanding of this chapter, assign Chapter Tests A and B and/or Extra Unit Questions from Unit 7, pages 35–40 and 43–45.
Computer Test Bank You can use Chapter Tests and Extra Unit Questions to create your own tests for both testing and retesting.

Alternative Assessment

Chapter Resources Binder See the Alternative Assessment booklet in the *Social Studies Educator's Handbook* series.
Portfolio You might meet with students to choose appropriate work from the chapter for inclusion in their portfolios.

Learning Styles

The following chart indicates the activities appropriate for different learning styles.

Visual Learners
Artists
Actors
Musicians
Economists

Auditory Learners
Actors
Musicians
Writers (if stories are presented orally)

Kinesthetic Learners
Actors
Musicians

Evaluation

Artists Artistic ability need not be a criterion, but posters should be attractive and emotionally powerful. They should reflect an understanding of simple persuasive techniques and some of the important issues of World War I.
Actors Speeches should last four minutes and should reflect some understanding of persuasive techniques and the demands that a government makes of its people for a successful war effort. The delivery of the speech is as important as the content and should receive equal value.
Musicians Singing ability need not be a criterion, but students may perform the songs with partners or in small groups if they choose. Original song lyrics should fit the melody of the tune composed or selected to go with them.
Writers Stories should be based on plausible events and conflicts during the time of World War I. The details of plot, setting, and characterization should be historically accurate. Also, the point of view from which the story is told must be consistent throughout.
Economists Information on the concept maps must be accurate, complete, concise, and organized to show the relationship between the war and the nation's economy.

History Through
LITERATURE

Author Note

Ernest Hemingway A novelist and short story writer, Ernest Hemingway (1899–1961) had an originality of thought and style that earned him a lasting place in American literature. Many of his characters—such as Frederick Henry, the narrator in *A Farewell to Arms* (1929)—try to prove themselves by seeking danger. The same could be said of Hemingway, who frequently worked overseas as a war correspondent and enjoyed dangerous sports. Hemingway received the Nobel prize for literature in 1954.

A Farewell to Arms is one of the best-known novels about the horrors of World War I. It is also considered one of Hemingway's finest works.

Vocabulary

Have students look up and discuss the words *bombardment* and *concentrated* before they read the passage. Ask: What value might a *bombardment* have besides just causing damage? Why might one side want to conduct a concentrated bombardment of the other? You might also make sure that students recognize the meanings of *counter-attack, line, post, stretcher, shell, brigade, corps, cut off, division,* and *evacuate* in this context.

Prereading Focus

Review Chapter 23, sections 1 and 3 (especially pages 650–651 and 662–665). Discuss the tremendous destruction of life and property caused by the war.

Motivation/Prior Knowledge

Review some of the methods of enlisting support for the war. Then ask: Do you think that Americans clearly understood the combat conditions "over there"?

A Farewell to Arms
Ernest Hemingway

Introduction   During the final years of World War I, Ernest Hemingway worked as an ambulance driver for the Red Cross in Italy. At the time, he was 19 years old. This excerpt from his novel *A Farewell to Arms* provides a glimpse of what the war was like in Italy. The Italians were fighting the Austrians, Croatians, and Germans.

Vocabulary Before you read the selection, find the meaning of these words in a dictionary: **bombardment, concentrated**

The wind rose in the night and at three o'clock in the morning with the rain coming in sheets there was a bombardment and the Croatians came over across the mountain meadows and through patches of woods and into the front line. They fought in the dark in the rain and a counter-attack of scared men from the second line drove them back. There was much shelling and rifle fire all along the line. They did not come again and it was quieter and between the gusts and wind and rain we could hear the sound of a great bombardment far to the north.

The wounded were coming into the post, some were carried on stretchers, some walking and some were brought on the backs of men that came across the field. They were wet to the skin and all were scared. We filled two cars with stretcher cases as they came up from the cellar of the post and as I shut the door of the second car and fastened it I felt the rain on my face turn to snow. The flakes were coming heavy and fast in the rain.

When daylight came the storm was still blowing but the snow had stopped. It had melted as it fell on the wet ground and now it was raining again. There was another attack just after daylight but it was unsuccessful. We expected an attack all day but it did not come until the sun was going down. The bombardment started to the south below the long wooded ridge where the Austrian guns were concentrated. We expected a bombardment but it did not come. It was getting dark. Guns were firing from the field behind the village and the shells, going away, had a comfortable sound.

We heard that the attack to the south had been unsuccessful. They did not attack that night but we heard that they had broken through to the north. In the night word came that we were to prepare to retreat. The captain at the post told me this. He had it from the Brigade. A little while later he came from the telephone and said it was a lie. The Brigade had received orders that the line of the Bainsizza should be held no matter what happened. I asked about the break through and he said that he had heard at the Brigade that the Austrians had broken through the twenty-seventh army corps up toward Caporetto.

Purpose-Setting Question

Read aloud the introduction to the excerpt. Ask: Would an ambulance driver be safer on a battlefield than a soldier would be? Explain.

Discussion Questions

1. Why does the narrator say that the shells have "a comfortable sound"? (The shells are aimed at the enemy, so he feels safer when he hears them.)
2. Which has the higher rank—the Brigade or the Division? How can you tell? (The Division is higher; the Brigade gets its information and its order to hold the line from the Division.)
3. Whom does the narrator fear most—the Austrians, the Croatians, or the Germans? Explain. (Possible Answer: He fears the Germans most. He mentions a Croatian attack but says that the Allies pushed the Croatians back. He names the Austrians only briefly. However, when the Germans are named, the narrator declares that he and others felt fear.)

The Walking Wounded *This group of wounded Americans and captured Germans was painted by combat artist Harvey Dunn. The soldiers' weary expressions reveal how enthusiasm for battle was quickly worn away by the horrors of trench warfare.* **Culture** *What important contribution do combat artists and photographers make?*

There had been a great battle in the north all day. . . .

"It's Germans that are attacking," one of the medical officers said. The word Germans was something to be frightened of. We did not want to have anything to do with the Germans.

"There are fifteen divisions of Germans," the medical officer said. "They have broken through and we will be cut off."

"At the Brigade, they say this line is to be held. They say they have not broken through badly and that we will hold a line across the mountains from Monte Maggiore."

"Where do they hear this?"

"From the Division."

"The word that we were to retreat came from the Division."

"We work under the Army Corps," I said. "But here I work under you. Naturally when you tell me to go I will go. But get the orders straight."

"The orders are that we stay here. You clear the wounded from here to the clearing station."

"Sometimes we clear from the clearing station to the field hospitals too," I said. "Tell me, I have never seen a retreat—if there is a retreat how are all the wounded evacuated?"

"They are not. They take as many as they can and leave the rest."

"What will I take in the cars?"

"Hospital equipment."

"All right," I said.

THINKING ABOUT LITERATURE

1. What kinds of weapons are used in the battles the narrator describes?
2. Why is the narrator concerned about the orders from the Brigade?
3. **CRITICAL THINKING Drawing Conclusions** Why do the ambulances take hospital equipment instead of wounded soldiers during a retreat?

ACTIVITY Based on the excerpt and what you have read in Chapter 23 about battlefield conditions, write a continuation of this excerpt. Describe what happens next to the narrator and his feelings and thoughts about his experiences.

Answers to Thinking About Literature

1. rifles, machine guns, and artillery
2. The narrator realizes that conflicting orders have been received. One set of orders tells them to retreat; the other demands that they hold the line at all costs.
3. Possible Answer: The army believes that more good can be done for more soldiers if the medical equipment can be saved, or it believes that any wounded soldiers left behind will receive medical treatment from the Germans.

Unit 8
Prosperity, Depression, and War

Unit Focus

Discuss with students the painting on these pages — *Waiting Room*, by Raphael Soyer — and its caption. Ask them to imagine why the people seem unhappy. Explain the difference between an emotional depression and an economic depression, and encourage students to keep this information in mind as they read the chapter summaries. You might ask questions such as the following to stimulate discussion.
1. Which word—*prosperity, depression,* or *war*—best fits the painting? Explain.
2. The Jazz Age has also been called the Roaring Twenties. What kinds of words and images come to mind when you hear that expression?
3. (a) Based on the information in the summary for Chapter 25, what do you think the New Deal was? (b) What kinds of people might have needed the help that the New Deal offered?
4. (a) Which nations belonged to the Axis powers? (b) Which of their leaders can you name?
5. Notice the title of Unit 8 — Prosperity, Depression, and War. Based on the information in the chapter summaries, how do you think these experiences changed the United States and its people?

Connections With Art
Background

Raphael Soyer (1899 – 1987) and his family came to the United States in 1912 when they were exiled from Russia for being Jewish. Encouraged by their father, Soyer, his twin brother Moses, and his younger brother Isaac all became painters. Raphael Soyer took a variety of art classes in New York City but did not exhibit his work until 1926. After a successful one-person show in 1929, he was able to paint full-time, and he exhibited regularly for more than 30 years afterward.

UNIT 8
Prosperity, Depression, and War

CHAPTER **24**
The Jazz Age
(1919–1929)

The 1920s was a period of economic boom and rapid social and cultural change.

....

CHAPTER **25**
Depression and the New Deal
(1929–1941)

The New Deal sought to provide relief and recovery from the worst economic depression in the nation's history.

....

CHAPTER **26**
World War II
(1939–1945)

The United States used all its resources to help defeat the Axis powers during World War II.

As one of the American Scene painters, Soyer specialized in depicting average, working-class people with sympathy and occasional sadness. *Waiting Room* shows the interior of the 125th Street Station of the New York Central Railroad. Today, the painting is part of the collection of the Corcoran Gallery of Art in Washington, D.C.

Connections With Art
Activity

Ask questions such as the following to stimulate discussion about *Waiting Room*.
1. What are these people doing?
2. (a) What questions would you ask these people about their lives? (b) What answers might you get?
3. Which detail in the painting impresses you the most? Why?

4. Raphael Soyer is considered a Social Realist—an artist who makes a political or social comment by showing everyday subjects in a true-to-life fashion. Why is *Waiting Room* a good example of Social Realism?

After World War I, the United States moved from prosperity to depression and back to war again. This painting from the 1930s captures the despair people felt during the Great Depression.

Bulletin Board Suggestion

Have the class create a bulletin board display dedicated to the 1920s. Assign individuals or groups to prepare illustrations or to collect photographs of the fashions, fads, products, sports, music, dances, and popular literature of the period. Topics should include the Harlem Renaissance, the emergence of the "flapper," the effects of Prohibition, and important figures of the Jazz Age. If students would like to incorporate in the design a depiction of the conditions that led to the Great Depression, encourage them to do so.

 ## Art Gallery Posters

La Reunión, by Tony Ortega, is appropriate for Unit 8. Lesson suggestions for the poster appear in the *Art Gallery: Our Common Heritage Posters* Teacher's Guide. The art also appears in Chapter 25, page 728, of the student book.

 ## CD-ROM

Time Tour Access the time tour Prosperity, Depression, and War from the American Heritage® *History of the United States* CD-ROM to accompany Unit 8.

Connections With the World
Activity

Explain that the Great Depression was felt not only in the United States; it resulted in economic problems for other parts of the world, especially for Europe. Ask: Do you think that a depression would have spread so quickly a century earlier? What does your answer tell you about the growing role of the United States in the world economy? Invite students to suggest other ways in which one nation's economy can affect another's.

Linking Past and Present
Activity

Several of your students may have family members or neighbors who can recall their own experiences in the United States during the years 1919–1945. Ask students to interview these people and bring in one anecdote from each one. Give students large (4" x 6") lined index cards. Have students write out the anecdotes and supply an appropriate credit line. Then categorize the cards as "Jazz Age," "Great Depression," or "World War II," and bind them as a memory book for your classroom library.

Lessons	Teaching Resources
1 Republicans in the White House **Objectives** 1. Identify what President Harding promised the nation. 2. Identify the Teapot Dome Scandal. 3. Identify the role that the United States played in world affairs.	**Lesson Planner** Cooperative Learning, p. 148 **Student Study Guide** Section 1 Study Guide, p. 178
2 Business Fever **Objectives** 1. Describe how World War I affected the American economy. 2. Describe how the auto industry fueled the growth of the economy in the 1920s. 3. Explain why consumer spending increased during the 1920s.	**Lesson Planner** Cooperative Learning, p. 149 **Student Study Guide** Section 2 Study Guide, p. 179 **Chapter Resources Binder, Unit 8** *Geography in History* Black Migration After World War I, pp. 5–6 *Critical Thinking* Linking Past and Present, p. 3 **Our Multicultural Heritage** *Biography* Lillian Gilbreth, Pioneer of Scientific Management, p. 70
3 New Ways of Life **Objectives** 1. Explain why a national ban on alcohol failed. 2. Describe how life changed for women in the 1920s. 3. Describe how Americans amused themselves during the 1920s.	**Lesson Planner** Cooperative Learning, p. 150 **Student Study Guide** Section 3 Study Guide, p. 180 **Chapter Resources Binder, Unit 8** *Skill Application* Using the Computerized Card Catalog, p. 2
4 The Roaring Twenties **Objectives** 1. Explain why Harlem was a center of culture during the 1920s. 2. Identify the popular heroes of the 1920s. 3. Identify the aspects of American life that writers criticized.	**Lesson Planner** Cooperative Learning, p. 151 **Student Study Guide** Section 4 Study Guide, p. 181 **Chapter Resources Binder, Unit 8** *History Through Literature* The Negro Speaks of Rivers, p. 4 **Interdisciplinary Connections: The 1920s** 　▨ *Sciences* An Age of Amazing—and Odd—Achievements, p. 140 　▨ *Geography* An Increasingly Urban Population, p. 141 　▨ *World* American Writers in Paris, p. 142 　■ *Economics* One Stockbroker's Story, p. 143 　■ *Civics* Battling the Bootleggers, p. 144 **Our Multicultural Heritage** *Biography* Zora Neale Hurston, Leader of the Harlem Renaissance, p. 71 *Milestone* The "Uptown Met": Harlem's Apollo Theater, p. 72
5 Signs of Trouble **Objectives** 1. Identify the Americans who did not share in the economic boom of the 1920s. 2. Explain why the United States moved to limit immigration. 3. Describe the treatment of African Americans after World War I.	**Lesson Planner** Cooperative Learning, p. 152 **Student Study Guide** Section 5 Study Guide, p. 182

Multimedia Resources	Additional Resources	Chapter-Level Resources
Transparencies *Time Lines* The United States and the World, 1900–1933, p. E-23 **CD-ROM** *Presidents* Warren G. Harding; Calvin Coolidge	**Voices of Freedom** Harding Creates an Image, pp. 211–213	**Lesson Planner** Activity Based, pp. 153–154 **Student Study Guide** Chapter 24 Study Guide, pp. 183–184 **Chapter Resources Binder** **Unit 8** Vocabulary Building, p. 1 Chapter Test A, pp. 7–9 Chapter Test B, pp. 10–12 Illustration Master, p. 13 Extra Unit Questions, pp. 43–45 **English Guided Reading** Guided Reading, pp. 47–48 **Spanish Resources** **Computer Test Bank** Chapter Tests A and B Extra Unit Questions **Guided Reading Audiotapes** Side 9 **CD-ROM** *Time Tour* The Jazz Age (1919–1929) in Prosperity, Depression, and War
Transparencies *Exploring Technology* The Ford Assembly Line, p. H-57 **Videotapes/Videodiscs** *United States History Video Collection* The Third Industrial Revolution, Vol. 17, Ch. 7	**Voices of Freedom** Will Rogers Gives His Opinions, pp. 213–214 A New Car, p. 216	
Videotapes/Videodiscs *United States History Video Collection* Prohibition, Vol. 17, Ch. 37; The Revolution in Manners and Morals, Vol. 17, Ch. 16; The Silver Screen, Vol. 17, Ch. 28	**Customized Reader** "Public Service Is My Motto," article VIB-3 Al "Wallpaper" Wolff Talks About the Untouchables, article VIB-11 One Woman's Experience Working in a Department Store in the 1920s, article VIA-6	
Listening to Literature Audiocassettes *The American Experience* Take the A Train, side 7; Any Human to Another, side 8; The Negro Speaks of Rivers, side 8 **Transparencies** *Fine Art* Battle of the Big Horns, p. D-57 *Interdisciplinary Connections* A Work by Aaron Douglas, p. B-79 **CD-ROM** *History Makers* Louis Armstrong; Langston Hughes; Babe Ruth; Charles Lindbergh **Videotapes/Videodiscs** *United States History Video Collection* The Jazz Age, Vol. 17, Ch. 31	**Voices of Freedom** Two Poems of the Harlem Renaissance, pp. 216–218 Lindbergh Conquers the Atlantic, pp. 218–220	
Transparencies *Fine Art* The Migration of the Negro, p. D-53 **CD-ROM** *Presidents* Herbert Hoover **Videotapes/Videodiscs** *United States History Video Collection* The Red Scare, Vol. 16, Ch. 43; Nativists and Fundamentalists, Vol. 17, Ch. 40	**Voices of Freedom** The Red Scare, pp. 207–208 Vanzetti Addresses the Court, pp. 208–209 Getting Ready to Head North, pp. 210–211 **Customized Reader** The Ku Klux Klan in Pekin, Illinois, article VIB-10	

Lesson Planner

For a fully developed **Activity-Based** lesson plan for Chapter 24, see the *Lesson Planner*, pages 153–154.

 Chapter Resources

Vocabulary Building The Vocabulary Building worksheet for Chapter 24 from Unit 8, page 1, of the *Chapter Resources* binder can be used as a prereading activity or as a review of chapter vocabulary. (Reteaching/Easy)

 Student Study Guide

Chapter 24 Study Guide Refer students to pages 183–184 of the *Student Study Guide* for the Chapter 24 Study Guide. The study guide can be used for chapter review as well as for reteaching. (Reteaching/Average)

 Guided Reading Audiotapes

Students can use *Guided Reading Audiotapes*, Chapter 24, side 9, to hear section previews, summaries, and review questions. The tapes might benefit students who are auditory learners, students who have trouble reading, or students acquiring English. Tapes are also available in Spanish. (Enrichment/Easy)

CHAPTER 24

The Jazz Age

(1919–1929)

CHAPTER OUTLINE

1 Republicans in the White House

2 Business Fever

3 New Ways of Life

4 The Roaring Twenties

5 Signs of Trouble

1919 *The Eighteenth Amendment banned the sale and manufacture of alcoholic beverages. The new law launched the 14-year period known as Prohibition.*

1920 *The American Professional Football Association was formed. Star athlete Jim Thorpe, shown here, was president of the new league, which later became the NFL.*

1923 *The Teapot Dome Scandal erupted. A member of President Harding's Cabinet was eventually sent to jail for taking bribes from oil companies.*

1918	1920	1922	1924

 WORLD EVENT
1919 German women gain the vote

WORLD EVENT
1922 Union of Soviet Socialist Republics formed

678 • Chapter 24

Chapter Time Line
Understanding Chronology

After briefly discussing the time line illustrations, captions, and World Event entries, help students to reinforce their grasp of the sequence of time line events. Point out that two of the events took place in 1919 and two in 1926. When students have determined which four events are associated with those dates, they can fill in the rest—first with the four events that occurred after 1919 (but before 1926) and then with the two events that occurred after 1926 (but before 1930).

Students Acquiring English
Activity

In their reading of the chapter and in the chapter activities, SAE students will encounter many slang terms and topics that were used almost exclusively in this colorful era. To make it easier for them to assimilate this information, have SAE students work in small collaborative groups or with partners who are fluent in English.

Have SAE students interview their group members or partners about chapter content whenever anything is unclear to them. This strategy gives second-language learners an opportunity to increase comprehension through oral as well as written language. As chapter content becomes more familiar to them, you may want to encourage SAE students to switch roles with their groups or partners and become the interviewees.

Chapter Setting

"'FORGET about the war,' seems to be the slogan of the American people just at present. Spend; travel; dine; jazz; dash off to Florida, to California, to Europe, anywhere, everywhere; buy expensive automobiles, luxurious houses, costly jewelry; throw money right and left, but—forget about the war.**"**

This is how *Life* magazine summed up the mood of Americans in January 1920. The "war to end all wars" was over. Millions had died to make the world "safe for democracy," as President Woodrow Wilson had put it. Now, Americans were tired of crusades. They wanted to settle down to the business of having fun.

New inventions—radios, movies, and automobiles—helped Americans amuse themselves in the 1920s. They also helped the economy grow. As people spent money on exciting new consumer goods, the economy boomed as never before.

New attitudes also grew in the 1920s. Young people listened to an exciting new music called jazz. They shocked their parents by doing wild dances, using strange new words, and wearing unusual clothes.

Many Americans worried about the way the country was changing. To them, it seemed that older American values were dying out. However, whether they welcomed the changes or feared them, Americans could not ignore the upheaval that came with the decade known as the Jazz Age.

ACTIVITY Imagine that you lived during the 1920s. Role-play your reaction to seeing each of the following for the first time: radio, movies, automobiles, electric refrigerators, vacuum cleaners.

1924 *The cost of a Model T dropped to $290. By making cars more affordable, Henry Ford encouraged a steady growth in sales.*

Car Sales, 1920–1929

Year: 1920, 1921, 1922, 1923, 1924, 1925, 1926, 1927, 1928, 1929

Millions of Cars: 0 1 2 3 4 5

= 1 million cars

Source: Historical Statistics of the United States

1926 *Langston Hughes published his first volume of poetry. Hughes was part of a flowering of African American culture known as the Harlem Renaissance.*

1929 *More than 10 million American homes had radios. Families gathered around receivers like this one to listen to music, news, comedies, and sports.*

1924   1926   1928   1930

▲ **WORLD EVENT**
1926 Revolution in Nicaragua

▲ **WORLD EVENT**
1928 Kellogg-Briand Pact outlaws war

Chapter 24 • **679**

Chapter Resources

English Guided Reading Duplicate and distribute the Chapter 24 Guided Reading worksheet on pages 47–48 in the English Guided Reading section of the *Chapter Resources* binder. Students who have difficulty reading might also benefit from using this worksheet. Have students complete the worksheet before they begin reading. You might pair a more fluent student or a student who is a strong reader with each SAE student to review. (Reteaching/Easy)

Spanish Resources See the Spanish Resources section of the *Chapter Resources* binder.

ACTIVITY

Guided Instruction Students might prepare for their role-playing by remembering their first experience with a personal computer or video game. Alternatively, discuss how people met the needs that the new inventions fulfilled *before* the inventions came along.

Allow students to present dramatic monologues or to role-play in small groups. Scenarios might include a sales person promoting the invention to potential customers or members of a family discussing a neighbor's purchase of the invention.

Linking Past and Present
Activity

If one era changed American society more than any other, it was probably the 1920s. As students work through the chapter, have them note changes in ideas, individual behavior, and external influences on life that are still present today.

For example, students may point out that the dress and behavior of flappers may have influenced some of today's wilder fashions or contributed to the raised consciousness of women as they have campaigned for recognition of their equality with men. Others may note that jazz had deep and direct influences on modern music, and that the artists and writers of the Harlem Renaissance may have encouraged African Americans today in their artistic pursuits.

Encourage students to remain aware of these links between past and present as they read the chapter. Set aside some time at the end of the reading to allow students to share their notes and realizations.

Section 1
pp. 680–682

Bell Ringer

Ask students to imagine that they are soldiers returning home from Europe at the end of World War I. Ask them to talk about some of the hardships that they have experienced overseas and how they hope their lives will become "normal" again.

Lesson Plan

1. Focus After World War I, Americans voted for a return to "normalcy" by electing Warren G. Harding as President. After a troubled presidency, Harding died in office and was succeeded by Vice President Calvin Coolidge. In this section, students examine the foreign and domestic policies of these two Presidents.

2. Instruct Have students list at least five ways in which American life was disrupted by World War I. Then divide the class into groups of four or five students each. Have each group prepare a campaign speech for Warren G. Harding in the election of 1920. Students should consider what Harding's pledge to "return to normalcy" meant and why it appealed to many Americans. Have volunteers from the groups read their speeches aloud. Afterward, ask students to vote on the most persuasive speech.

1
Republicans in the White House

FIND OUT
- What did Harding promise the nation?
- What was the Teapot Dome Scandal?
- What role did the United States play in world affairs?

VOCABULARY disarmament

The word on the page was plain as day: "normality." But Warren G. Harding, who was running for President, got it wrong. What the country needs is "normalcy," he declared. No such word existed, but the crowd knew what Harding meant.

In 1920, Americans longed for calm after years of reform and war. In Harding, a Republican from Ohio, they found what they wanted. Harding's slip of the tongue soon became his slogan: "Back to Normalcy." By this, he meant a return to life as it had been before World War I.

Harding's "Best Minds"

In the 1920 election, Harding swamped the Democratic candidate, James Cox. Republicans led the country for the next 12 years.

Harding chose the "best minds" of his party for top Cabinet jobs. These men followed strongly pro-business policies. For Secretary of the Treasury, he chose Andrew Mellon, the millionaire aluminum king of Pittsburgh. Mellon balanced the budget and lowered taxes.

Herbert Hoover became Secretary of Commerce. Hoover was a mining engineer

who had spent many years abroad. During World War I, Hoover earned the world's respect by supplying food to millions of starving Belgians. As Commerce Secretary, he used his knowledge of other countries to help American businesses expand overseas.

The Ohio Gang. President Harding was honest and hardworking. Still, he once told a friend, "I knew that this job would be too much for me." To help with the burdens of office, Harding brought in many political friends from Ohio. They became known as the Ohio Gang.

The Ohio Gang soon caused problems. Harding had made Charles Forbes head of the Veterans Bureau. In 1923, Forbes was convicted of stealing millions of dollars from the bureau.

Harding looked on Forbes's crime as a betrayal. When rumors of new scandals sur-

---

Washday in Washington *Political scandals in Harding's government rocked the nation. In this cartoon, both the Democratic donkey and the Republican elephant are shamed by the public display of their "dirty linen."* **Economics** *What was the "oil scandal" referred to in the cartoon?*

Connections With Language Arts
Background

Harding enjoyed giving grand, lofty speeches—an activity he called "bloviating." Some of his critics complained that Harding's love for ornate language and invented usages obscured his ideas. Others, such as Democratic leader William G. McAdoo, took the criticism one step further: "His speeches leave the impression of an army of pompous phrases moving over the landscape in search of an idea."

Journalist and critic H. L. Mencken felt that "Gamalielese" (after Gamaliel, Harding's middle name) was the worst English that he had ever heard. He said, "It reminds me of a string of wet sponges; it reminds me . . . of stale bean soup, of college yells, of dogs barking idiotically through endless nights. It . . . crawls to the topmost pinnacle of posh."

A perfect example of Harding's style can be seen in the 1920 speech from which *normal-*

cy came: "America's present need is not heroics but healing, not nostrums but normalcy, not revolution but restoration, not agitation but adjustment, not surgery but serenity, not the dramatic but the dispassionate, not experiment but equipoise, not submergence in internationality but sustainment in triumphant nationality."

faced, he was even more distressed. "I can take care of my enemies all right," Harding said, "but my friends . . . keep me walking the floors nights!"

In August 1923, Harding had a heart attack and died. Many believed that the scandals involving his friends caused his death.

New scandals. After Harding died, new scandals were revealed. The ***Teapot Dome Scandal*** was the most serious.

The Teapot Dome Scandal involved Secretary of the Interior Albert Fall. Fall had secretly leased government land in California and at Teapot Dome, Wyoming, to oil companies. In exchange, Fall accepted large bribes. Tried and found guilty, he became the first Cabinet official ever sent to prison.

President Coolidge

The day Harding died, Vice President Calvin Coolidge was visiting his father on his farm in Vermont. Coolidge recalled, "I was awakened by my father. . . . I noticed that his voice trembled." Coolidge's father, a justice of the peace, swore his son in as President. The simple ceremony reassured Americans.

Coolidge was very different from the outgoing Harding. He came from an old New England family and was tight with both money and words. A woman reportedly told Coolidge she had bet that she could get the President to say more than three words. "You lose," replied Coolidge.

"Silent Cal," as he was known, forced the officials involved in scandals to resign. In the 1924 election, Coolidge ran against Democrat John Davis and Progressive Robert La Follette. Voters chose to "Keep Cool With Coolidge" and returned the cautious New Englander to office.

Like Harding, Coolidge believed that prosperity for all Americans depended on business prosperity. He cut government regulations and named business leaders to government agencies.

"Keep Cool With Coolidge" *With his air of quiet honesty, Calvin Coolidge helped restore people's faith in government. Wisconsin—the home of Progressive candidate Robert La Follette—was one of the few states that Coolidge did not carry in the 1924 election.* **Citizenship** *What were Coolidge's views on the role of business?*

Foreign Affairs

After World War I, many Americans wanted to stay out of European affairs. The war, however, had weakened the nations of Europe. The United States was now the world's leading economic and political power. Europeans expected the United States to take a leading role in world affairs.

Presidents Harding and Coolidge had much more limited goals. They wanted to keep the hard-won peace in Europe. However, they did not want to commit the United States to the job of keeping world peace. Most Americans supported this isolationist policy.

In 1921, Harding signed separate peace treaties with Germany, Austria, and Hungary—the powers defeated in World War I. The United States sent observers to the League of Nations but would not join. One American diplomat condemned this isolationist mood:

66 Our attitude is that we do not need friends. We feel that we can stand outside all international organizations and that our prosperity is such that it cannot be touched by

3. Close To close the lesson, lead a class discussion on why Harding won by such a landslide.

 Lesson Planner

For a developed **Cooperative Learning** lesson plan, see the *Lesson Planner,* page 148.

Answer to Caption

He supported pro-business policies. He cut government regulations and put business leaders in charge of government agencies.

 Voices of Freedom

Primary Source You might assign selection 10-4, Harding Creates an Image, on pages 211–213 of *Voices of Freedom.* This selection by Evelyn Walsh MacLean, one of Harding's friends, shows how Harding modified his image to fit the views of voters. (Enrichment/Average)

 CD-ROM

Presidents Access the biography of Warren G. Harding from the American Heritage® *History of the United States* CD-ROM.
Presidents Access the biography of Calvin Coolidge from the American Heritage® *History of the United States* CD-ROM.

Linking Past and Present
Activity

Invite students to research similarities between what are sometimes referred to as the "Harding Scandals" (of which Teapot Dome was one) and Watergate, the scandal that caused President Richard Nixon to resign in 1974. You might begin by pointing out that both scandals touched Republican Presidents who put a lot of power into the hands of unsupervised advisers. Encourage students to go on from there. Students may wish to present their results in chart form or in a group oral presentation.

Connections With Language Arts
Background

In the slogan "Keep Cool With Coolidge," *cool* had nothing to do with being fashionable; rather, it referred to calm restfulness. Coolidge was a great fan of this philosophy. He once said, "Four-fifths of all our troubles in this life would disappear if we would only sit down and keep still." Coolidge also was a prodigious sleeper, averaging 11–12 hours a night. His overall lack of energy once prompted journalist Walter Lippmann to say, "Inactivity is a political philosophy and a party program with Mr. Coolidge."

Historical Sidelight
Background

Few Presidents have been the subject of as many anecdotes—both true and fictitious—as Calvin Coolidge. According to one of the most famous anecdotes, Coolidge went to church alone one Sunday because his wife was unable to go. When he returned, she asked him what the minister's sermon had been about. "Sin" was Coolidge's reply, and he did not elaborate. Mrs. Coolidge, frustrated, asked, "But what did he *say*?" The President responded, "He was against it."

external events. We are profoundly mistaken. **"**

The Soviet Union. Meanwhile, V. I. Lenin was creating the world's first communist state in the Soviet Union.* The United States refused to recognize Lenin's government. Most Americans disliked communism. It shocked them when the Soviet Union did away with private property.

Despite these feelings, when famine threatened Russia in 1921, Congress voted $20 million in aid. American aid may have saved as many as 10 million Russians from starvation. Although Americans disapproved of the Soviet government, they were still willing to help the Russian people.

Latin America. During World War I, Latin America had been cut off from Europe. As a result, American trade and investment in the region had increased. This trend continued after the war.

At times, the United States intervened to protect its interests in Latin America. In 1926, a revolution broke out in Nicaragua, where Americans owned plantations and railroads. United States Marines were sent in to oversee new elections.

In Mexico, the United States chose to negotiate rather than invade. In 1927, Mexico announced plans to take over foreign-owned oil and mining companies. American investors called on President Coolidge to send in troops. Instead, Coolidge sent a diplomat, Dwight Morrow, to Mexico. After much hard bargaining, Morrow was able to

---

* After the communist revolution, Russia was officially renamed the Union of Soviet Socialist Republics (USSR), or Soviet Union.

Linking Past and Present
In recent years, the United States and Mexico have cooperated closely. The United States buys large quantities of Mexican oil.

work out a compromise with the Mexican government.

Declaring Peace

Many people believed that an arms race in Europe had helped cause World War I. For this reason, the United States worked for disarmament in the 1920s. **Disarmament** means reducing a nation's armed forces and weapons of war.

At the Washington Conference of 1921, the United States, Britain, and Japan agreed to limit the size of their navies. In 1928, the United States joined 61 other nations in the ***Kellogg-Briand Pact.*** This treaty outlawed war. Secretary of State Frank Kellogg signed the treaty with a foot-long pen made of gold. "Peace is proclaimed," he said.

The treaty had a fatal flaw. It did not set up any means for keeping the peace. One nation could still use force against another without fear of punishment.

SECTION 1 REVIEW

1. **Identify:** (a) Warren G. Harding, (b) Teapot Dome Scandal, (c) Calvin Coolidge, (d) Dwight Morrow, (e) Kellogg-Briand Pact.
2. **Define:** disarmament.
3. How did Harding try to restore "normalcy"?
4. Why did Harding feel betrayed by the Ohio Gang?
5. Describe American relations with Latin America in the 1920s.
6. **CRITICAL THINKING Recognizing Points of View** Reread the diplomat's comment condemning isolationism, on pages 681–682. Then state an opposing argument that isolationists might have used.

ACTIVITY **Writing to Learn**
Write a newspaper article, including a headline, about the signing of the Kellogg-Briand Pact.

Answers to Section 1 Review

1. (a) Warren G. Harding, p. 680, (b) Teapot Dome Scandal, p. 681, (c) Calvin Coolidge, p. 681, (d) Dwight Morrow, p. 682, (e) Kellogg-Briand Pact, p. 682
2. disarmament, p. 682
3. Harding promoted business programs at home and refused to commit the United States to involvement as an international peacekeeper. He did, however, send observers to the League of Nations and approved aid for the victims of famine in Russia.
4. He had given them positions of responsibility, but some of them used their new power for personal gain. Charles Forbes, for example, stole millions from the Veterans Bureau, and other scandals involving the Ohio Gang were revealed.
5. The United States traded with and invested in the region but also took a political interest in Latin America. Marines were sent into Nicaragua to oversee elections. In Mexico, armed intervention was avoided through negotiation.
6. Possible Answer: We have just been through the worst war that the world has seen. We have secured peace for Europe. Now it is up to Europe to keep that peace.

2
Business Fever

FIND OUT
- How did World War I affect the American economy?
- How did the auto industry fuel the growth of the economy in the 1920s?
- Why did consumer spending increase in the 1920s?

VOCABULARY installment buying, bull market, on margin

Soon after his election, President Calvin Coolidge gave a speech to a group of newspaper editors. In simple words, he stated his philosophy. "The business of America is business," he said. "The man who builds a factory builds a temple. The man who works there worships there."

In the 1920s, factories poured out a growing stream of new-fangled goods. For the first time, many Americans had refrigerators and other electric appliances in their kitchens. Even some factory workers could afford to buy new, low-priced cars. As output and consumer spending rose, the economy boomed.

A Booming Economy

Many Americans enjoyed economic good times in the 1920s. People called it the Coolidge prosperity. The quantity of goods made by industry almost doubled in the decade. More important to most Americans, their incomes rose. As a result, people bought more goods. This in turn fueled further growth.

World War I had helped the economy. When war broke out, Europeans ordered vast amounts of supplies from American fac-

tories. After the United States entered the war in 1917, the government spent millions of dollars on equipment for American soldiers. To meet the demand for military supplies, American factories expanded and became more efficient.

During the war, millions of Americans moved from rural areas to cities. There, they took jobs in booming factories. By 1920, more Americans lived in cities than in rural areas. Over half a million African Americans moved from the South to look for work in northern cities.

A New Stove *In the 1920s, like today, Americans were eager to buy new devices that made life easier. This advertisement promises that an up-to-date stove will free homemakers from drudgery.* **Linking Past and Present** *What labor-saving devices do Americans buy today?*

You will always be glad you bought a Glenwood

Gold Medal **Glenwood** *Pearl Gray*
Makes Cooking Easy

Chapter 24 • **683**

Section 2
pp. 683–686

 Bell Ringer
Write on the chalkboard the statement "The business of America is business." Ask: Do you think that Americans today would agree with Coolidge? Why or why not?

Lesson Plan

1. Focus The 1920s saw a boom in new industries, consumer goods, and time-saving methods of production. Students focus on the pro-business policies and the prosperity of the Coolidge administration.

2. Instruct Divide the class into groups of four or five students each. Assign each group one of the subsections of Section 2, and have each group write a statement that summarizes the main idea of its subsection. Then write each group's statement on the chalkboard and have the rest of the class find facts that support the statement.

3. Close To close the lesson, have students contrast the business boom in the 1920s with the state of business today.

 Lesson Planner
For a developed **Cooperative Learning** lesson plan, see the *Lesson Planner*, page 149.

Connections With Economics
Activity

Share with students this comment from writer Edward Purinton about the national attitude toward business in the 1920s: "Among the nations of the earth today America stands for one idea: Business. . . . The finest game is business. The rewards are for everybody, and all can win. There are no favorites. And in

this game there is no 'luck.' The speed and size of your winnings are for you alone to decide." Ask: Does Purinton's statement apply to all Americans in the 1920s? Who might have been left out? Have students record their responses and review them when they reach Section 5 (pages 698–703).

Connections With Technology
Background

Some of the new items that advertisers used to attract consumers were cigarette lighters, wristwatches, dry ice, and Pyrex glass cookware. Furthermore, the development of synthetics such as rayon and cellophane revolutionized whole industries. New sources for established products were also considered: George Washington Carver made shaving lotion and axle grease from peanuts and shoe polish from sweet potatoes.

When the war ended, more than 2 million soldiers came home and began to look for jobs. At the same time, factories stopped turning out war materials. The result was a sharp recession. After 1921, however, factories switched to producing consumer goods. From 1923 to 1929, the economy grew rapidly.

The Auto Industry Fuels Growth

The auto industry was the engine of the American economy in the 1920s. Car sales grew rapidly during the decade. The auto boom spurred growth in related fields such as steel and rubber.

Affordable cars. One reason for the auto boom was a drop in prices. By 1924, the cost of a Model T had decreased from $850 to $290. As a result, ordinary Americans—not just the rich—could afford to buy a car.

Car prices fell because factories became more efficient. As you have read, Henry Ford introduced the assembly line in his factory in 1913. (See page 549.) The goal, Ford said, was to make the cars identical, "just like one pin is like another pin." Before the assembly line, it took 14 hours to put together a Model T. In Ford's new factory, workers could assemble a Model T in 93 minutes!

Other companies copied Ford's methods. In 1927, General Motors passed Ford as the top auto maker. Unlike Ford, General Motors sold cars in a variety of models and colors. Henry Ford had once boasted that people could have his cars in "any color so long as it's black." Faced with the success of General Motors, he changed his tune. His next car, the Model A, came in different colors.

A ripple effect. Car sales spurred growth in other parts of the economy. By 1929, some 4 million Americans owed their

> ★★★ *History and You*
> The number of people owning cars and radios jumped sharply in the 1920s, changing the way many Americans lived and worked. Can you think of a technological innovation of the past five years that has changed your life?

EXPLORING TECHNOLOGY

Wheels   Tires

The doors and seats are mounted on the body.

Gas tanks

The gas tank and engine are mounted on the frame.

Frame

Historical Sidelight
Background

Henry Ford knew that jokes about his cars were good advertising, and he offered $100 for any story about a Ford that made him laugh. Some jokes were aimed at the construction of the Model T: "A lady sent all her tomato cans to Detroit and got back a Model T"; "Model T's are being shipped in asbestos crates because they come off the line hot and smoking." Other jokes were based on the car's affordability: "Cheap, cheap, cheap, the chicken chirped, having been knocked across the road by a rampaging Ford."

Ford was also good at making up his own jokes. He told one joke about a man who wanted to be buried with his Ford because the car "had gotten him out of every hole he had ever gotten into and he thought it might get him out of this one." Ford also had one-line jokes painted on the outside of his cars. Some of the jokes were funny names for the cars, such as "Tin Lizzie" and "Bone Crusher." Others were comments such as "I'm from Texas. You can't steer me" and "Don't laugh—I'm paid for."

jobs to cars, directly or indirectly. Tens of thousands of people worked in steel mills, producing metal parts for cars. Others made tires, paint, and glass for cars. Some drilled for oil in the Southwest or worked in refineries that produced gasoline.

The car boom had other effects. States and towns paved more roads and built new

highways. To serve the millions who traveled by car, gas stations, tourist cabins, and restaurants sprang up across the country. As you will read in Section 3, cars also changed the way Americans, especially young Americans, behaved.

The Ford Assembly Line *Henry Ford transformed manufacturing with the automobile assembly line. Workers stood at their stations while unfinished cars moved past them on a conveyor belt. Each worker performed one task on each car as it passed by.* **Science and Technology** *What disadvantages might there be to working on an assembly line?*

Tires are mounted on the wheels and lowered down the wheel chute.

The roof frame and roof are mounted on the body.

The assembled body is lowered onto the frame.

The radiator, wheels, fenders, and lamps are attached to the frame.

The car is driven off the assembly line.

Radiator bridge

Chapter 24 • **685**

Answer to Exploring Technology

Possible Answer: Assembly-line work seems monotonous, offering little challenge or room for advancement.

Transparencies

Exploring Technology Use the transparency The Ford Assembly Line on page H-57 of *American History Transparencies*. This transparency gives students further opportunities to explore the workings of an automobile assembly line. Teaching suggestions can be found on page H-19. (Enrichment/Average)

Videotapes/ Videodiscs

United States History Video Collection Use the video segment "The Third Industrial Revolution" from Volume 17, *The Roaring Twenties,* to enhance students' understanding of the impact of the automobile on American society. Approx. running time 3:35 min. (Enrichment/Average) Vol. 17, Ch. 7

Chapter 7   Play

Critical Thinking
Understanding Causes and Effects

Many of the inventions and innovations that students will read about in this chapter, such as the automobile, have led to far-reaching cultural and social changes in American life. New industries, leisure-time activities, factory production techniques, and shifts in trade patterns are just a few of the long-term effects that could result from a single invention. Labor-saving devices, such as the carpet sweeper and the sewing machine, freed women from many time-consuming house-

hold chores and enabled them to take on new roles in American society.

Have each student choose one of the inventions or innovations, such as factory production techniques. Using only prior knowledge and critical thinking skills, have them list the effects of the invention or innovation on life today. You may want to create a model list for them, using the invention of refrigeration to guide their thinking.

Connections With Technology
Background

In 1920, highways were merely rough dirt roads. Driving could be dangerous. In 1921, Congress passed the Federal Highway Act to encourage road building. State governments taxed gasoline to raise money for highway construction. The Bronx River Parkway, which opened in New York City in 1927, was the first of many limited-access highways that ran through parklike settings.

New Goods for Sale

The automobile was just one of many new products in the 1920s. Electric refrigerators, radios, phonographs, vacuum cleaners, and many other appliances took their place in American homes. Also, more people got telephones.

Buy now, pay later. With so many new products, Americans often wanted to buy things they could not afford. In response, businesses allowed **installment buying,** or buying on credit. For example, buyers could take home a new refrigerator just by paying down a few dollars. Each month, they paid an installment until they had paid the full price plus interest.

The new policy of "buy now, pay later" helped Americans buy things they could not pay for all at once. Installment buying increased the demand for goods. At the same time, however, consumer debt also jumped. By the end of the decade, consumers owed more than the amount of the federal budget. The comedian Will Rogers joked:

> ❝If we want anything, all we have to do is go and buy it on credit. So that leaves us without any economic problems whatsoever, except perhaps some day to have to pay for them.❞

Advertising. In the 1920s, businesses used advertising to boost sales. Advertisements showed a world of happy young couples surrounded by new products. They encouraged people to think that they would be happy if they bought the products.

Stocks Surge

The economic boom of the 1920s gave the stock market a big boost. As you have read in Chapter 19, corporations sold stocks, or shares of ownership, to investors.

During the 1920s, more people invested in the stock market than ever before. Toward the end of the decade, stock prices rose so fast that some people became rich almost overnight by buying and selling stocks. Stories of ordinary people making a fortune drew others into the stock market. Soon millions of Americans were investing in the **bull market,** as the soaring market was called.

People bought stocks **on margin,** a practice similar to installment buying. A person could buy a stock for just a 10-percent down payment. The buyer held the stock until the price rose and then sold it at a profit. The system worked as long as stock prices kept going up.

In 1928 and 1929, however, the prices of many stocks rose faster than the value of the companies themselves. That was an unhealthy sign. A few experts warned that the "Great Bull Market" would end. "Something has to give," said some. Most investors, however, ignored the warnings. They wanted to believe that the bull market would last forever.

SECTION 2 REVIEW

1. **Identify:** Henry Ford.
2. **Define:** (a) installment buying, (b) bull market, (c) on margin.
3. How did World War I help the American economy?
4. (a) How did new business methods encourage consumer spending in the 1920s? (b) Why did consumer debt grow?
5. Why did some experts worry that the bull market would end?
6. **CRITICAL THINKING Understanding Causes and Effects** Explain how the boom in car sales spurred growth in other industries.

ACTIVITY Writing to Learn

Imagine that you are an advertiser. Write a short radio commercial urging people to take advantage of installment buying to purchase an electric refrigerator.

3 New Ways of Life

FIND OUT

■ Why did a national ban on alcohol fail?

■ How did life change for women in the 1920s?

■ How did Americans amuse themselves in the 1920s?

VOCABULARY bootlegger, speakeasy

In the 1920s, a new kind of American woman was emerging. She wore short skirts, bobbed her hair, and drove fast cars. "Is 'the old-fashioned girl,' with all that she stands for in sweetness, modesty, and innocence, in danger of becoming extinct?" wondered one magazine in 1921.

Many people welcomed the new ways. Others, however, worried that American so-ciety was changing too fast. They wanted to hold on to the ways of thinking and behaving that they knew in the past.

The Noble Experiment

At the stroke of midnight on January 15, 1920, church bells rang all across the United States. What some people called the "noble experiment" had begun. The experiment was *Prohibition,* a ban on making and selling alcohol anywhere in the United States. The ban became law when the Eighteenth Amendment was ratified. (See page 611.)

Then, as today, alcohol abuse was a serious problem. Many Americans hoped the ban on liquor would improve American life. "Now for an era of clear thinking and clean living!" declared the Anti-Saloon League. In fact, alcoholism and liver diseases caused by liquor did decline during Prohibition. In the end, however, the ban did not work.

Getting around the law. One reason why Prohibition failed was that people found ways to get around the law. Some people made their own alcohol. Others,

Enforcing the Law *The government struggled to stop the illegal flow of liquor during Prohibition. At right, federal agents destroy cases of beer found during a raid in Philadelphia. The two men in disguise at left, "Izzy" Einstein and "Moe" Smith, were among the most effective Prohibition agents. Working undercover, the partners made more than 4,000 arrests.* **Daily Life** *Why did many Americans support Prohibition?*

Section 3
pp. 687–692

🔔 Bell Ringer

Most students already dream of the day when they will be able to drive and be able to vote. Invite volunteers to share their thoughts on the matter. Then ask students to imagine an entire population feeling that way.

Lesson Plan

1. Focus With the end of World War I came many changes in American society. Women now enjoyed the right to vote as well as the right to accept expanded opportunities. The spreading popularity of movies, radio, and automobiles also changed the ways in which Americans spent their leisure time. In this section, students look at some of the changes in American life during the 1920s.

2. Instruct Ask students to make at least five generalizations about ways in which American life changed during the twenties. Then have them name and discuss as many supporting facts as possible for each generalization.

Cooperative Learning
Activity

Write this example of 1920s slang on the chalkboard or on a transparency:

Last night my sheik took me to a ritzy speakeasy. Everyone in the place was a hepcat, and the music was the bee's knees. The band leader was so hep he sounded like Benny Goodman on the licorice stick. The canary sang some swell songs, and we danced until our dogs hurt. That evening was the cat's meow.

Have pairs or small groups of students research and define these expressions:

■ moonshine
■ bump off
■ canary
■ hepcat
■ jake
■ gams
■ dogs

■ big cheese
■ bee's knees
■ cat's meow
■ fall guy
■ flapper
■ heebie-jeebies
■ licorice stick

■ speakeasy
■ bootlegger
■ hep
■ sheik
■ sheba
■ Kilroy
■ ritzy

Then have students collaboratively rewrite the paragraph, using standard English "translations," or have them write a second paragraph using the slang words they "translated."

Connections With Civics
Activity

Before Prohibition, average Americans were by and large honest and observant of the nation's laws. During Prohibition, however, many "good" citizens brazenly disobeyed the law. In fact, it actually became the fashionable thing to do. (Even President Harding had a liquor cabinet.) Discuss with students this flagrant disregard for the law and the ways in which Prohibition might have unwittingly affected people's attitudes to future laws.

3. Close To close the lesson, have students identify changes begun during the 1920s that are still in effect today. Allow the class to speculate on how their lives today would be different if these changes had not taken place.

Lesson Planner

For a developed **Cooperative Learning** lesson plan, see the *Lesson Planner,* page 150.

Customized Reader

Primary Source For a copy of an interview with gangster Al Capone, order article VIB-3, "Public Service Is My Motto," from the *American History Customized Reader.* (Enrichment/ Easy)

Primary Source For a copy of an interview with Al Wolff, in which he discusses his work with Eliot Ness, order article VIB-11, Al "Wallpaper" Wolff Talks About the Untouchables, from the *American History Customized Reader.* (Enrichment/Easy)

Videotapes/ Videodiscs

United States History Video Collection Use the video segment "Prohibition" from Volume 17, *The Roaring Twenties,* to enhance students' understanding of the causes and effects of the ban on alcohol. Approx. running time 1:10 min. (Enrichment/Average) Vol. 17, Ch. 37

Chapter 37   Play

---

known as **bootleggers,** smuggled in millions of gallons of liquor from Canada and the Caribbean.

Speakeasies, or illegal bars, opened in nearly every city and town. A visitor to Pittsburgh reported that it took him only 11 minutes to find one. In some ways, speakeasies made drinking liquor even more popular. Before Prohibition, it was not considered proper for a woman to go into a bar. Speakeasies, however, welcomed women as well as men.

Gangsters. Prohibition gave a big boost to organized crime. Every speakeasy needed liquor, and gangsters took over the job of supplying it. Bootleggers earned big profits, and crime became a big business. "Ours is a business nation," said one official. "Our criminals apply business methods."

Gangsters divided up cities and forced speakeasy owners to buy from them. Sometimes they gunned down rivals in battles over turf. More often, gangsters worked together. They used some of their profits to bribe policemen, public officials, and judges.

Repeal. Prohibition reduced drinking but never stopped it. Every day millions of Americans broke the law to buy liquor in speakeasies. By the mid-1920s, almost half of all federal arrests were for Prohibition crimes.

Most Americans agreed that Prohibition was undermining respect for the law. In 1933, the Eighteenth Amendment was repealed. The noble experiment had ended.

The New Woman

Another constitutional amendment also changed American life, but in a very different way. The Nineteenth Amendment, ratified in 1920, gave women the right to vote.

The vote. Women went to the polls for the first time in November 1920. Their votes helped elect Warren Harding as President. Women did not vote as a group, however,

as some people had feared. Like men, some women voted for Republicans, some for Democrats. Some did not vote at all.

In 1920, Carrie Chapman Catt, head of the National Woman Suffrage Association, set up the League of Women Voters. The league worked to educate voters, as it still does today.

As women in the United States voted for the first time, women in Puerto Rico asked if the new law applied to them. As you have read, Puerto Ricans were made citizens of the United States in 1917. They were told that it did not. Led by Ana Roqué de Dupvey, an educator and writer, Puerto Rican women crusaded for the vote. In 1929, their crusade finally succeeded.

Fighting for equal rights. Leaders in the suffrage movement also worked for other goals. Alice Paul, who had been a leading suffragist, called for an equal rights amendment (ERA) in 1923. The ERA stated that "equality of rights under the law shall not be denied or abridged by the United States or by any State on account of sex." Many people feared that the ERA went too far. They said it would lead to women being drafted and sent to war. Paul worked vigorously for the ERA until her death in 1977. The amendment, however, was never passed.

New freedoms. Women's lives changed in other ways in the 1920s. During World War I, thousands of women had worked outside the home for the first time. They filled the jobs of men who had gone off to war. When the troops came home, many

> *Our Common Heritage*
> *The League of Women Voters today plays an important role in presidential elections by sponsoring televised debates between the major candidates.*

Historical Sidelight
Background

Many of the best-known speakeasies were in New York City. Some, like the Artists' and Writers' Club, were patronized by newspaper editors and radio personalities. Others were elite clubs where membership was a prerequisite. The most unusual speakeasy, however, was named the Bridge Whist Club, which was open at all hours and provided excellent food and drink. What made it so unusual? It was owned and operated by the

Prohibition Bureau of the United States government!

The reason for this fantastic venture was supposedly to trap bootleggers. Its hidden microphones were meant to gather evidence on both buyers and sellers. In general, though, the Bridge Whist Club did little to curb bootlegging, and in fact it continued to be a popular after-hours spot.

Linking Past and Present
Background

Today, the League of Women Voters continues to educate voters. In addition to conducting campaigns to register and inform voters on local issues, its members volunteer in campaigns and at voting booths in local, state, and federal elections. The League also plays a prominent role in presidential elections by sponsoring debates among the candidates of the Republican, Democratic, and independent parties.

RESEARCH SKILLS
Using the Computerized Card Catalog

Most libraries have computerized card catalogs in addition to or in place of standard card catalogs. Although computerized card catalogs may vary, all use menus and screens to help you locate information. Follow the steps below to use a computerized card catalog to research women's rights.

1. **Use the main menu to start your search.** When you begin, the computer will present you with a list of options. These options make up the Main Menu. Look at Screen 1 below. To find information on the subject of women's rights in the twentieth century, you would type the number 3. (a) What number would you type to find a book by Ana Roqué de Duprey? (b) What number would you type to find out if the library owns the book *Century of Struggle?*

2. **Narrow your search.** Follow the instructions on the screens that follow the Main Menu to locate the books you need. On Screen 2, type the words Women's Rights to see a list of books on the subject. (a) How many books does this library have on women's rights? (b) What number would you select on Screen 3 to locate books on women's rights in the twentieth century?

3. **Scan the list and select the books you need.** On the next screen that appears, scan the list of books available on your topic. Write down the call numbers, titles, and authors of the books that will help in your research. Study Screen 4. Imagine that you are writing a report on voting rights for women. (a) Which book title is closest to what you are researching? (b) What is its call number? (c) For which title or titles might you ask for more details? Why?

ACTIVITY Identify a topic in this chapter that you would like to learn more about. Then go to your school or local library and use the computerized card catalog to locate two books on your topic.

Screen 1

MAIN MENU

Select one of the options below:

1. Author
2. Title
3. Subject

Enter your selection (1–3) and press <RETURN>: 3___

Screen 2

Enter SUBJECT and press <RETURN>:

Subject: Women's Rights ___

Screen 3

YOUR SEARCH: Women's Rights 61

1. Women's Rights--History--20th century 27
2. Women's Rights--Canada--History 7
3. Women's Rights--China 3

Enter line number 1___

Screen 4

YOUR SEARCH: Women's Rights--History--20th century

AUTHOR/TITLE /CALL NUMBER
1. Flexner, Eleanor--Century of Struggle--305.42 FLE
2. Smith, Betsy--Women Win the Vote--324.6 SMI
Enter a title number for more detail: ____

Chapter Resources

Skill Application For additional practice, duplicate and distribute the worksheet, Using the Computerized Card Catalog, from Unit 8, page 2, of the *Chapter Resources* binder. (Reteaching/Average)

Answers to Skill Lesson

1. (a) 1 (b) 2
2. (a) 61 (b) 1
3. (a) *Women Win the Vote* (b) 324.6 SMI (c) *Century of Struggle;* to see how much detail it provides about voting rights for women

ACTIVITY

Guided Instruction If your school library has a computerized book file, ask the librarian to help you teach its operation to students. Otherwise, you might take a field trip to the public library, arranging beforehand to have one of the librarians explain its system. After students have completed their research, have them share the titles they found and comment on the electronic search.

Students Acquiring English Activity

Students for whom English is a second language may understand the operation of the electronic card catalog but have difficulty reading what comes up on the screen. If at all possible, have a bilingual student or the librarian interpret the data during each step of the scanning process. Later, have SAE students work with partners to review the process and discuss the information located in each step. Pair these students again whenever such research skills are needed.

women were forced to give up their jobs. Still, some remained in the work force.

For some women, working outside the home was nothing new. Poor women and working-class women had been cooks, servants, and seamstresses for many years. In the 1920s, they were joined by middle-class women, who worked as typists, secretaries, and store clerks. A few women even managed to become doctors and lawyers, despite discrimination.

Life at home also changed for women. Electric appliances such as refrigerators,

The "It Girl" *Clara Bow became a popular movie star by playing restless, fun-seeking young women. Her nickname was the "It Girl." This poster advertises Bow in* Wings, *a World War I drama that won the first Academy Award for Best Picture.* **Science and Technology** *How did new technology change movies in the 1920s?*

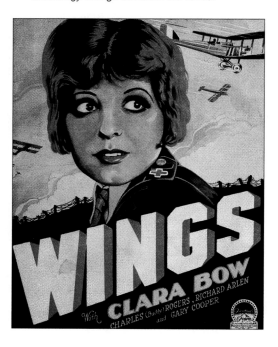

washers, irons, and vacuum cleaners made housework easier. Even so, women who worked outside the home found they had to do a second shift after work. Most husbands expected their wives to cook, clean, and care for children even if they held full-time jobs.

The Movies

Leisure gained a new meaning in the 1920s. Rising wages and labor-saving appliances gave families more money and more time in which to spend it. They looked for new ways to have fun.

In the late 1800s, Thomas Edison and George Eastman had helped to develop the first moving picture cameras. In the 1920s, the movie industry came of age. Southern California's warm, sunny climate allowed filming all year round. Soon, Hollywood became the movie capital of the world.

In the 1920s, millions of Americans went to the movies at least once a week. They thrilled to westerns, romances, adventures, and comedies. In small towns, theaters were bare rooms with hard chairs. In cities, they were huge palaces with red velvet seats.

The first movies had no sound. Audiences followed the plot by reading "title cards" that appeared on the screen. A pianist played music that went with the action. Sometimes the audience also provided sound effects. As one movie-house musician recalled:

66To provide sound for Western or battle scenes, the older [children] would fire cap pistols. The younger ones, identifying with the hero as he was being stalked, would blurt hysterical warnings: 'Look out! He's behind the door!' There were always children reading aloud to their immigrant parents....They supplied . . . translations into Italian, Yiddish, or German. 99

Fans adored the Hollywood movie stars. The most popular actor of the time was Rudolph Valentino. In *The Sheik,* the dashing Valentino galloped across the desert on a white horse. To millions of women, he was the hero of their dreams. When Valentino died at the age of 31 in 1926, more than 100,000 people lined up outside the funeral home to mourn the passing of their favorite star.

In 1927, Hollywood produced *The Jazz Singer,* causing a sensation. It was a "talkie"—a movie with a sound track. Soon, all movies were talkies.

A Mass Society

Movies helped create a new, national culture in the United States. When a new Charlie Chaplin comedy opened, for example, Americans from Maine to Oregon rushed to see it. Newcomers from Italy and native-born Americans laughed till they cried. Movies, said a Hollywood executive, reached "audiences speaking twenty different languages but understanding in common the universal language of pictures."

Radio. Like movies, radio became very popular in the 1920s. The country's first radio station started broadcasting in Pitts-

Families With Radios 1922–1929

Source: *Historical Statistics of the United States*

GRAPH SKILLS *The 1920s could be called the age of radio. Millions of American families bought radios and listened to popular programs.* ● *About how many families bought radios in 1924? In 1928?*

burgh in 1920. By 1929, more than 10 million families owned radios.

A new lifestyle emerged. Each night, families gathered around the radio to tune in to shows such as "Roxy and His Gang" and "Jack Frost's Melody Moments." Radio listeners enjoyed comedies, westerns, and mysteries, as well as classical music and jazz.

A car culture. "Why on earth do you need to study what's changing this country?" one man asked the experts. "I can tell you what's happening in just four letters: A-U-T-O."

Chapter 24 • **691**

Student Study Guide

Section 3 Study Guide Have students use the Section 3 Study Guide on page 180 of the *Student Study Guide* to review and reinforce the content of this section. (Reteaching/Average)

 ACTIVITY

Guided Instruction If you can find a silent movie in a library or a video store, show part of it to students to demonstrate what the titles should be like.

Section 4
pp. 692–697

🔔 **Bell Ringer**

To check students' prior knowledge of the 1920s, begin a concept map entitled *The Roaring Twenties* and have students list ideas and images that they associate with this era.

Lesson Plan

1. Focus In the 1920s, African American artists, writers, and musicians created what became known as the Harlem Renaissance. Other Americans also gained fame through writings, movies, radio, and sports. In this section, students focus on American culture during the Jazz Age.
2. Instruct Have volunteers find and read aloud Claude McKay's "If We Must Die" Ask: How does this poem express pride? How does it express anger?

In the 1920s, Americans traveled to more places and moved more quickly than ever before—all because of the automobile. By making it easier to travel, cars let Americans learn more about each other.

Cars shaped life in the city and the country. Many city dwellers wanted to escape crowded conditions. They moved to nearby towns in the country, which soon grew into suburbs.

With cars, suburban families could drive to the city even though it was many miles away. They could also drive to stores, schools, or work. No longer did people have to live where they could walk or take a trolley to work.

In the country, cars brought towns, shops, and the movies closer. In the past, such trips took several hours by horse and buggy. One farm woman bought a car before she got indoor plumbing. "You can't go to town in a bathtub," she explained.

SECTION 3 REVIEW

1. **Identify:** (a) Prohibition, (b) Carrie Chapman Catt, (c) Ana Roqué de Duprey, (d) Alice Paul, (e) Rudolph Valentino.
2. **Define:** (a) bootlegger, (b) speakeasy.
3. (a) What was one good effect of Prohibition? (b) What was a bad effect?
4. How did the Nineteenth Amendment change women's lives?
5. Give two reasons for the new interest in leisure activities in the 1920s.
6. Describe how cars changed the way Americans lived.
7. **CRITICAL THINKING Linking Past and Present** Do cars play as important a role in American society today as they did in the 1920s?

ACTIVITY **Writing to Learn**

Think of a scene from a recent movie. Then imagine that the movie was silent and write "titles" to explain the action.

---

4 The Roaring Twenties

FIND OUT
- Why was Harlem a center of culture in the 1920s?
- Who were the popular heroes of the 1920s?
- What aspects of American life did writers criticize?

VOCABULARY fad, flapper

When asked about her favorite pastime, a young woman instantly replied, "I adore dancing. Who doesn't?" The Charleston, the Lindy, and other dance crazes forever marked the 1920s as the "Jazz Age" and the "Roaring Twenties."

During the 1920s, new dances, new music, new games, and other new ways to have fun swept the country. For all the serious business of the 1920s, the decade also roared with laughter and defiance.

Fads and Fashions

"Ev'ry morning, ev'ry evening, ain't we got fun?" went a hit song of 1921. During the Era of Wonderful Nonsense—yet another nickname for the 1920s—fun came in many forms.

Fads caught on, then quickly disappeared. A **fad** is a style or an activity that is popular for a short time. Flagpole sitting was one fad. Another was the dance marathon. Mah-jongg, a Chinese game, also was a fad of the 1920s.

Perhaps no one pursued the latest fads more intensely than the flappers. **Flappers** were young women who rebelled against traditional ways of thinking and acting. Flappers wore their hair bobbed, or cut short. They wore their dresses short, too—

Answers to Section 3 Review

1. (a) Prohibition, p. 687, (b) Carrie Chapman Catt, p. 688, (c) Ana Roqué de Duprey, p. 688, (d) Alice Paul, p. 688, (e) Rudolph Valentino, p. 691
2. (a) bootlegger, p. 688, (b) speakeasy, p. 688
3. (a) Alcoholism and alcohol-related liver diseases declined. (b) Many people disliked the law and found ways around it; organized crime grew.
4. It gave women the right to vote.
5. Higher wages and new labor-saving devices gave Americans more money and free time; new forms of entertainment, such as

motion pictures, became available or became more popular.
6. People traveled more. By making it easier to travel, Americans learned more about each other. Suburbs grew as city dwellers moved out of town. With cars, suburban families could drive to the city many miles away. People no longer needed to live where they could walk or take a trolley to work. In the country, a car increased accessibility to towns, shops, and the movies.
7. Possible Answer: Americans still depend very heavily on cars; in fact, cars may play an even greater role today than in the 1920s.

ART GALLERY: OUR COMMON HERITAGE

PHOEBE BEASLEY *Dance Band, 1986*

The decade of the 1920s became famous for its lively dances and driving rhythms. In Dance Band, *Phoebe Beasley uses a blend of oil paint and tissue paper to capture the excitement of the Roaring Twenties. Beasley is best known for her collages that celebrate African American life.* **The Arts** *What types of instruments does Beasley show? What does this suggest about the dance music of the 1920s?*

shorter than Americans had ever seen before. Flappers shocked their parents by wearing bright-red lipstick.

The way flappers behaved was even more shocking than how they looked. Flappers smoked cigarettes in public and drank alcohol in speakeasies. A song from a 1925 musical became an informal flapper anthem:

> ❝Flappers are we
> Flappers are we
> Flappers and fly and free.

3. Close To close the lesson, lead a class discussion comparing the fads and fashions of the 1920s with those of the 1990s.

 Lesson Planner

For a developed **Cooperative Learning** lesson plan, see the *Lesson Planner,* page 151.

Answer to Art Gallery: Our Common Heritage

jazz instruments, such as piano, trumpet, clarinet, trombone, drums, bass; It suggests that dance music was a jazz-oriented, big-band sound.

 Transparencies

Fine Art Use the transparency Battle of the Big Horns on page D-57 of *American History Transparencies.* Teaching suggestions can be found on page D-19. (Enrichment/Average)

 Videotapes/ Videodiscs

United States History Video Collection Use the video segment "The Jazz Age" from Volume 17, *The Roaring Twenties,* to enhance students' understanding of how jazz came to symbolize the 1920s. Approx. running time 4:55 min. (Enrichment/Average) Vol. 17, Ch. 31

| Chapter 31 | Play |

Historical Sidelight
Background

The fad of flagpole sitting (mentioned on page 692) originated with and was mastered by Alvin "Shipwreck" Kelly. It began in 1924, when Kelly topped a Los Angeles flagpole for 13 hours. "I just went up for a breath of fresh air," he explained. Kelly set the world record in 1930, when he spent 49 days atop a flagpole in Atlantic City.

Kelly had many imitators, though no one of that era broke his record. LeRoy Haines spent 12 days atop a Denver flagpole; Bennie Fox had an 18-hour "sit" in Chicago. Bobby Mack, a woman, sat for 21 days in Los Angeles; and Avon Freeman, a 15-year-old from Baltimore, amazed his friends with a juvenile record of 10 days.

Connections With Language Arts
Background

A *flapper* was a new kind of woman, but the word *flapper* has a long history. At the time of the American Revolution, a *flapper* was a duck that was not yet old enough to fly. By the late 1800s, it had come to refer to a girl who was too young to wear her hair "up." By the eve of World War I, *flapper* was the term for any independent young woman who supported women's rights. It was a short step from that meaning to the meaning that became popular in the 1920s.

Audiocassettes

Listening to Literature Audiocassettes To give students a sense of the music of the Jazz Age, play Take the A Train (side 7, 4:40) from *Listening to Literature Audiocassettes, The American Experience.* The song is one of the best-known works by Duke Ellington (1899–1974), African American jazz composer. (Enrichment/Easy)

CD-ROM

History Makers Access the biography of Louis Armstrong on the American Heritage® *History of the United States* CD-ROM.

Transparencies

Interdisciplinary Connections Use the transparency A Work by Aaron Douglas on page B-79 of *American History Transparencies.* Teaching suggestions can be found on page B-26. (Enrichment/Average)

Voices of Freedom

Primary Source You might assign selection 11-3, Two Poems of the Harlem Renaissance, on pages 216–218 of *Voices of Freedom.* The selection includes the poem "Common Dust" by Georgia Douglas Johnson and "O Black and Unknown Bards" by James Weldon Johnson. (Enrichment/Challenging)

Never too slow
All on the go. . . .
Dizzy with dangerous glee. **"**

Only a few young women were flappers. Still, they set a style for others. Slowly, older women began to cut their hair and wear makeup and shorter skirts. For many, the fashions pioneered by the flappers symbolized a new freedom.

New Music

Another contribution of the 1920s was jazz. Jazz was a new kind of music that combined African rhythms and European harmonies. Black musicians in New Orleans and Chicago created jazz from ragtime and blues. The new music swept the United States and then quickly spread around the world.

Louis Armstrong was one of the brilliant young musicians who helped create jazz. Armstrong learned to play the trumpet in the New Orleans orphanage where he grew up. Too young to play in clubs, Armstrong made his debut at a picnic. One musician remembers, "Everyone in the park went wild over this boy in knee trousers who could play so great."

With jazz came new styles of dancing. Dance floors shook to the bouncy steps of the Charleston, shimmy, and other dances.

Many older Americans worried that jazz and the new dances were a bad influence on the nation's young people. Despite their complaints, jazz continued to grow more popular. Today, jazz is recognized as a uniquely American art form created by African Americans. It is considered one of the most important cultural achievements of the United States.

Literature

A new generation of American writers earned worldwide fame in the 1920s. Many criticized American society for caring too much about money and fun. Some became so unhappy with life in the United States that they moved to Europe. Black writers celebrated their African American heritage while protesting prejudice and racism.

Young writers. Ernest Hemingway was one of the most popular writers of the 1920s. Still a teenager at the outbreak of World War I, he traveled to Europe to drive an ambulance on the Italian front. Hemingway drew on his war experiences in *A Farewell to Arms,* a novel about a young man's growing disgust with the war. Hemingway's simple but powerful style influenced many other writers.

Sinclair Lewis grew up in a small town in Minnesota and later moved to New York. In novels such as *Babbitt* and *Main Street,* he presented small-town Americans as dull and narrow-minded. Lewis reflected the attitude of many city dwellers toward rural Americans.

The young writer who best captured the mood of the Roaring Twenties, however, was F. Scott Fitzgerald. In *The Great Gatsby* and other novels, Fitzgerald told about wealthy people who attended endless parties but could not find happiness. He became a hero to college students and flappers, among others.

Edna St. Vincent Millay, a poet, was enormously popular. She expressed the frantic pace of the 1920s in her verse:

"My candle burns at both ends;
It will not last the night;
But ah, my foes, and oh, my friends—
It gives a lovely light. **"**

Harlem Renaissance

In the 1920s, large numbers of African American musicians, artists, and writers settled in Harlem, in New York City. "Harlem was like a great magnet for the Negro intellectual," said one black writer. This gathering of black artists and musicians led to the

---

Connections With Music
Activity

Students may enjoy listening to some of the jazz that gave the "Roaring Twenties" its "roar." Since many of the old recordings have been remastered, the local library may have a collection from which students can borrow. An excellent twenties starter album is *Stars of the Apollo Theatre* on the Columbia label.

Have a group of students listen to several albums and discuss:

- Which selections best mirror the innovative spirit of the 1920s

- How each selection is similar to and/or different from the others
- Which selection is each individual artist's best or most famous

Have the group prepare a report for the class that summarizes their discussion and provides examples with brief excerpts from the music. Encourage the class to comment on the group's conclusions.

Learning Styles
Auditory/Kinesthetic Learners

Invite students to read portions of works by Ernest Hemingway, Sinclair Lewis, F. Scott Fitzgerald, or Edna St. Vincent Millay (or other works of the era that you approve). Then have each reader explain to the class what his or her selection reveals about life in America during the 1920s. Other students might dramatize parts of Lewis's *Main Street* or Fitzgerald's *The Great Gatsby* for the class.

CONNECTIONS

ARTS | SCIENCES | GEOGRAPHY | WORLD | ECONOMICS | CIVICS

Aaron Douglas: Creating a Bridge Between Peoples

Like many other African American artists, Aaron Douglas was drawn to New York City in the 1920s. A painter and illustrator, he arrived from the Midwest ready to take part in the creative explosion known as the Harlem Renaissance.

By creating works with African themes, Douglas hoped to reunite American blacks with their African heritage. He enhanced his paintings with the flat, somewhat angular shapes and stylized figures seen in African sculpture. The power of his images quickly attracted the attention of writers such as Countee Cullen and Langston Hughes, who asked him to illustrate their works.

Encouraged by his success, Douglas sought a bigger canvas for his talent. He soon became one of the nation's leading muralists. In his murals, Douglas celebrated both the African heritage and the African American experience—from slavery to the present.

Douglas believed that art was at the heart of life and that it could serve as a bridge between peoples. He spent three decades of his life teaching this philosophy to students at the primarily African American Fisk University in Tennessee.

■ How did Aaron Douglas contribute to the Harlem Renaissance?

> **ACTIVITY** Read the excerpt from the Langston Hughes poem on page 696. Using original drawings, shapes cut from colored paper, pictures from magazines, and any other images, create an illustration for the Hughes poem that reflects the African American heritage.

From Slavery Through Reconstruction

Chapter 24 • **695**

Interdisciplinary CONNECTIONS

For worksheets establishing connections between the Chapter 24 main idea, The 1920s, and five other disciplines, see the *Interdisciplinary Connections* booklet. (Enrichment)

■ **Sciences** An Age of Amazing—and Odd—Achievements, page 140 (Average)
■ **Geography** An Increasingly Urban Population, page 141 (Average)
■ **World** American Writers in Paris, page 142 (Easy)
■ **Economics** One Stockbroker's Story, page 143 (Challenging)
■ **Civics** Battling the Bootleggers, page 144 (Average)

Answer to Connections

Douglas attempted to give African Americans new self-awareness and new self-esteem by creating art with African stylistic elements and powerful African themes.

> **ACTIVITY**

Guided Instruction After students have read "My People" two or three times, have students brainstorm the ideas and images that the poem brings to mind. Have students settle on a single idea for their illustrations; then allow a wide variety of interpretations. Arrange a display of students' work. Share it with other grades and classes if possible.

Team-Teaching Suggestion
Humanities

Arrange with a literature or drama teacher to pull together a variety of elements of the Jazz Age. This might involve showing a feature-length film (approved by whoever is the responsible party), listening to a variety of period music, or even taking a field trip to see a live performance of a play from the 1920s. The point of this activity is to show new styles in clothing, music, art, philosophy, and literature in the context of people's lives, as opposed to showing each element in isolation. After the activity, both teachers might lead a discussion on the way in which the film, music, or drama depicted the era.

Team-Teaching Suggestion
Civics

You might work with a specialist in African American studies or a local representative of the NAACP to present a lesson about the state of civil rights in the 1920s. Discuss not only advances that were made during this decade but also areas of disappointment. You might also discuss how the Harlem Renaissance was viewed by African Americans in other parts of the United States.

BIOGRAPHY Zora Neale Hurston *Writer Zora Neale Hurston was dismayed to discover that African American folklore was disappearing. For two years, she traveled across the South to talk to sharecroppers, preachers, and blues singers. Her book* Mules and Men *became one of the most important records of black American culture.* **Multicultural Heritage** *Why is it important to preserve the heritage of all Americans?*

Harlem Renaissance, a rebirth of African American culture. For the first time, white Americans took notice of the achievements of black artists.

Black writers such as Countee Cullen and Claude McKay wrote of the experiences of African Americans. A graduate of New York University and Harvard, Cullen taught in a Harlem high school. In the 1920s, he won prizes for his books of poetry. McKay came to the United States from Jamaica. In his poem "If We Must Die," he condemned the lynchings and other mob violence that black Americans suffered after World War I.

Langston Hughes. Langston Hughes became a leading poet of the Harlem Renaissance. He published his first poem, "The Negro Speaks of Rivers," soon after graduating from high school. Like McKay, he denounced violence against African Americans. In "My People" Hughes wrote proudly about being black:

❝The night is beautiful,
So the faces of my people.

The stars are beautiful,
So the eyes of my people.

Beautiful, also, is the sun.
Beautiful, also, are the souls of
my people. ❞

Zora Neale Hurston. Zora Neale Hurston, who grew up in Florida, wrote novels, essays, and short stories. Hurston drove an old car through the South and collected the folk tales, songs, and prayers of black southerners. She later published these in a collection titled *Mules and Men*.

Heroes and Heroines

Radio, movies, and newspapers created heroes and heroines known across the country. Americans followed the exploits of individuals whose achievements made them stand out from the crowd.

Athletes. Some of the best-loved heroes of the decade were athletes. Each sport had its stars. Bobby Jones won almost every golf championship. Bill Tilden and Helen Wills ruled the tennis courts. Nineteen-year-old Gertrude Ederle awed the world when she became the first woman to swim the English Channel.

College football also drew huge crowds. Many Americans who had never attended college rooted for college teams. Flappers and their dates paraded in the stands wearing the very latest fashion—thick, warm raccoon coats.

Our Common Heritage
Claude McKay's poem "If We Must Die" ends with these lines:

❝ *Like men we'll face the murderous,*
cowardly pack,
Pressed to the wall, dying, but fighting back!❞

Connections With Sports
Background

The 1927 Yankees are considered by many to be the greatest baseball team of all time. They won 110 games, 19 games ahead of the second-place team, and won the World Series in four straight games. In addition to Babe Ruth, the team included Lou Gehrig, Bob Meusel, and Tony Lazzeri.

Historical Sidelight
Background

"Lucky Lindy" Lindbergh (pictured on page 697) had a strategy that was different from those of the pilots who had come before him. When his plane, *The Spirit of St. Louis,* was being designed and built, Lindbergh decided to forgo a radio, preferring to have extra fuel instead. To save weight for fuel, Lindbergh didn't even have a parachute. If he were forced to bail out over the sea, he reasoned, he would take a rubber raft, and that was all.

He had sacrificed every bit of weight possible, even tearing out the blank pages of his logbook and cutting out the parts of the map that he wouldn't need!

By the time Lindbergh was ready to take off for Paris, *The Spirit of St. Louis* carried 450 gallons of gasoline, which made the total weight of the plane 5,250 pounds, 115 pounds more than it was designed to lift. Lindbergh had to be very lucky indeed!

Honoring "Lucky Lindy" *After his solo flight from New York to Paris, Charles Lindbergh became a hero on both sides of the Atlantic. In France, an artist wove this five-foot-long tapestry. In the United States, people honored Lindbergh in a variety of ways. Even a dance—the Lindy—was named after the aviator.* **American Traditions** *What qualities do you think people most admired in Lindbergh?*

The Babe. Americans loved football, but baseball was their real passion. The greatest player of the 1920s was Babe Ruth. Ruth had grown up in an orphanage and was often in trouble as a boy. Through hard work, he became the star of the New York Yankees. Fans flocked to games to see "the Babe" hit home runs. The 60 home runs he hit in one season set a record that lasted more than 30 years.

Lucky Lindy. The greatest hero of the decade, however, was not an athlete but an aviator. On a gray morning in May 1927, Charles A. Lindbergh took off from an airport in New York. He planned to fly to Paris, France—alone.

For 33½ hours, Lindbergh piloted his tiny plane, *The Spirit of St. Louis,* over the stormy Atlantic. At last, he landed in Paris. The crowd awaiting him lifted him on their shoulders and carried him across the field. "Lucky Lindy" returned to America as the hero of the decade.

SECTION 4 REVIEW

1. **Identify:** (a) Ernest Hemingway, (b) F. Scott Fitzgerald, (c) Edna St. Vincent Millay, (d) Harlem Renaissance, (e) Countee Cullen, (f) Langston Hughes, (g) Zora Neale Hurston, (h) Babe Ruth, (i) Charles A. Lindbergh.
2. **Define:** (a) fad, (b) flapper.
3. Why did flappers shock some Americans?
4. Why did some American writers move to Europe in the 1920s?
5. Describe three main contributors to the Harlem Renaissance and their accomplishments.
6. **CRITICAL THINKING Analyzing Ideas** How do you think Millay's line "My candle burns at both ends" reflects the spirit of the 1920s?

ACTIVITY Writing to Learn

Write a short poem that reflects the spirit of the 1920s.

Chapter 24 • **697**

Bell Ringer

Call on volunteers to name as many aspects of the "good times" of the 1920s as they can. Ask: Do you think that anyone was kept away from these "good times"? Do you think such "good times" can last forever?

Lesson Plan

1. Focus Despite the glamour and prosperity of the 1920s, significant problems lay below the surface. Farmers fell deeper into debt, labor unrest infected the nation, and anti-foreign feelings were strong. In this section, students examine the situation of Americans who did not share in the prosperity of the 1920s.

2. Instruct Have students work in small groups to prepare a television news program summarizing the issues and events covered in this section. Some groups should prepare reports on events such as the execution of Sacco and Vanzetti and the Scopes trial. Other groups should prepare interviews with prominent figures such as A. Mitchell Palmer or Marcus Garvey or with groups such as farmers, labor leaders, Ku Klux Klan members, and African Americans. Assign two or three students to act as anchors for the program.

3. Close To close, have students interpret the meaning of the section title, "Signs of Trouble," and support their statements with examples from the text.

5
Signs of Trouble

FIND OUT
- Which Americans did not share in the economic boom of the 1920s?
- Why did the United States move to limit immigration?
- How were African Americans treated after World War I?

VOCABULARY anarchist, quota system

Writing in his magazine *The Nation*, Oswald Garrison Villard warned Americans that the dream of the Roaring Twenties could not last. Under the surface of good times, millions "were steadily sinking... worse housed and fed than any peasants in Europe."

Villard was "crying in vain from the housetops." No one wanted to listen. "Nobody wanted anything but to be left alone to make money," he complained.

Villard was right, however. "Coolidge prosperity" had never included everyone. By the end of the decade, clouds on the horizon showed that the good times would soon end.

The Other Half

Many Americans did not share in the boom of the 1920s. Workers in the clothing industry, for example, were hurt by changes in women's fashions. Shorter skirts meant that less cloth was needed to make dresses. Coal miners also faced hard times as oil replaced coal as the major source of energy. Railroads cut employment as trucks and cars cut into their profits.

Farmers suffer. Farmers were hit the hardest. During World War I, Europeans had

bought American farm products, sending prices up. In response, farmers borrowed money to buy more land and tractors.

When the war ended, however, farmers in other countries were again able to produce for their own needs. The result was a sharp drop in farm prices. American farmers were unable to pay their debts. Farm prices dropped throughout the 1920s. By the end of the decade, the farmers' share of national income had shrunk by almost half.

Setbacks for labor. For labor unions, the 1920s were a disaster, too. During the war, unions had worked with the government to keep production high. Labor's cooperation helped the United States win the war. Union leaders expected the government to support labor in return.

After the war, workers demanded higher pay. Wages had not kept up with prices during the war. When employers refused, the unions launched a wave of strikes that rocked the country. The government did nothing to help labor, and management crushed the strikes. Many workers felt betrayed.

The wave of strikes turned the public against labor. One strike in particular angered Americans. In 1919, the city of Boston fired 19 police officers who had tried to join the AFL. Boston police struck in protest. The sight of police leaving their posts shocked the country.

The later 1920s saw even more setbacks for labor. In one court case after another, judges limited the rights of unions. At the same time, employers struck at labor by creating company unions. Company unions claimed to represent workers, but they were actually controlled by management. As a result, union membership dropped from 5 million in 1920 to 3.4 million by 1929.

Fear of Radicals

During the war, Americans had been on the alert for spies and sabotage. These wartime worries led to a growing fear of for-

---

Students Acquiring English
Activity

In this last section, students cannot help but contrast the lives of immigrants and African Americans with the Jazz Age styles of much of the rest of the country. This activity may help SAE students, in particular, to understand the examples in the text.

Write these passages from page 698 on the chalkboard or on a transparency:
- Under the surface of good times, millions "were steadily sinking. . . ."
- Villard was "crying in vain from the house-tops."

- By the end of the decade, clouds on the horizon showed that the good times would soon end.

Take each of the figures of speech separately, having students brainstorm associations with individual words and phrases. When several associations have been suggested, ask students to follow that line of reasoning to deduce what the authors meant. Additional examples can be found throughout the section.

Linking Past and Present
Activity

Have groups of students research the economic problems of farmers at the time of the Homestead Act in 1862 and again during the 1920s. Then have them compare the problems in these two eras with the difficulties that farmers face today. Encourage students to make charts and graphs that illustrate profits and losses or the number of acres farmed in the United States during each of these eras. Have groups present the results of their research to the class.

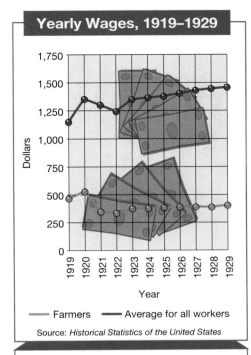

Yearly Wages, 1919–1929

Dollars (y-axis): 0, 250, 500, 750, 1,000, 1,250, 1,500, 1,750

Year (x-axis): 1919, 1920, 1921, 1922, 1923, 1924, 1925, 1926, 1927, 1928, 1929

Legend: —— Farmers —— Average for all workers

Source: *Historical Statistics of the United States*

GRAPH SKILLS *On average, farmers earned less than most other workers. As a result, they could not buy many of the new goods that became available in the 1920s.* • *How far below the average was the yearly wage of farmers in 1920? In 1929?*

eigners. The rise of communism in the Soviet Union fanned that fear. Lenin, the communist leader, called on workers everywhere to overthrow their governments. Many Americans saw strikes as the start of a communist revolution.

The actions of **anarchists,** or people opposed to organized government, added to the sense of danger. A group of anarchists plotted to kill well-known Americans, including John D. Rockefeller, the head of Standard Oil. Because many anarchists were foreign born, these attacks led to an outcry against all foreigners.

The government took harsh actions against both communists—Reds, as they were sometimes called—and anarchists. During the ***Red Scare,*** thousands of radicals were arrested and jailed. Many foreigners were deported. Officials failed to uncover a plot against the government, and the panic died down. Yet anger against foreigners led to a new move to limit immigration.

Closing the Golden Door

Efforts to limit immigration dated back to the 1800s. Antiforeign feeling again gained strength after World War I. As you recall, this antiforeign feeling was also known as nativism.

Sacco and Vanzetti. The trial of two Italian immigrants in Massachusetts came to symbolize the nativism of the 1920s. Nicola Sacco and Bartolomeo Vanzetti were arrested for robbery and murder in 1920. The two men admitted that they were anarchists but insisted they had committed no crime. A jury convicted them, however, and Sacco and Vanzetti were sentenced to death.

The ***Sacco and Vanzetti trial*** created a furor across the nation. The evidence against the two men was limited. The judge was openly prejudiced against the two immigrants. Many Americans thought that Sacco and Vanzetti were convicted because they were immigrants and radicals.

The two men waited in jail during a six-year fight to overturn their convictions. Their appeals were turned down. In 1927, they were executed. The issue of whether or not Sacco and Vanzetti received a fair trial has been debated ever since. In the meantime, many Americans felt the case proved that the United States had to keep out dangerous radicals.

Limiting immigration. After World War I, much of Europe lay in ruins. Millions of Europeans hoped to escape to the United States. American workers feared that a flood of newcomers would force wages down.

Chapter 24 • **699**

Connections With Civics
Background

The remarkably swift success of the Russian Revolution, in which the Bolsheviks took over the government, led American conservatives to overestimate the power of radicals at home. One senator advocated sending American citizens with radical views to a penal colony in Guam. In Indiana, a jury deliberated for only two minutes before acquitting a man who had shot and killed a radical for yelling, "To hell with the United States!"

Between 1919 and 1920, when Attorney General A. Mitchell Palmer was trying to curb the actions of radicals, he authorized raids on suspected "Reds" and other foreign-born citizens. About 4,000 men and women were arrested during this time, and many were held without the right to contact their lawyers. In some cases, even citizens who were not under suspicion were arrested for simply visiting those who were.

Sacco and Vanzetti *Millions of Americans mourned when Nicola Sacco and Bartolomeo Vanzetti were executed. They believed the immigrants were victims of prejudice. In this painting by Ben Shahn, the two men are shown handcuffed together as they await their fate.* **Citizenship** *How did the Sacco and Vanzetti case fuel anti-immigrant feeling?*

Middle-class Americans worried that communists and anarchists would invade the United States.

Congress responded by passing the Emergency Quota Act in 1921. The act set up a **quota system** that allowed only a certain number of people from each country to enter the United States. "America must be kept American," said Calvin Coolidge.

The quota system favored immigrants from Northern Europe, especially Britain. In 1924, Congress passed new laws that further cut immigration, especially from Eastern Europe. In addition, Japanese were added to the list of Asians denied entry to the United States.

Immigrants From Latin America

Latin Americans and Canadians were not included in the quota system. In 1917, the Jones Act made Puerto Ricans American citizens. Poverty on the island led to a great migration to the United States. In 1910, only 1,500 Puerto Ricans lived in the mainland United States. By 1930, there were 53,000.

Farms and factories in the Southwest depended on workers from Mexico. By 1930, a million or more Mexicans had crossed the border. Most came to work in the vegetable fields, orchards, and factories of the Southwest. The pay was low and the housing was poor. Still, the chance to earn more money was a very powerful lure. During the 1920s, more and more Mexicans began to settle in the large cities of the Midwest, too.

Solo in Chicago

Just before World War I, exciting news began filtering across the border into Mexico:

❝In the early days...one heard only of the states of Texas and California. The few Mexicans that left Mexico went there and wrote back from there. After a while we heard of New Mexico and Arizona, but beyond that there was no more United States to us. I remember distinctly with what great surprise we received a letter in our pueblo from a Mexican who had gone to Pennsylvania. 'Oh, where can that be! That must be very, very far away.'❞

As news about jobs in the United States spread, young Mexican men made their way to El Paso or Laredo, Texas. There, they

---

Connections With Art
Background

Many artists and writers actively protested the executions of Sacco and Vanzetti. Ben Shahn did a series of paintings on the topic; one of the paintings is shown on this page. Shahn once said, "I hate injustice." In his long career, he often used his artistic talent to promote the causes in which he believed.

Our Multicultural Heritage
Background

Members of Congress bypassed the group most entitled to call themselves "Americans"—Native Americans. When Congress passed the Dawes Act of 1887, the lawmakers had hoped that Native Americans would adopt the customs of white America. Under this act, however, Native Americans lost more than 60 percent of their land. A 1926 report on conditions among Native Americans declared that a majority were "extremely poor" and suffered from poor health and inadequate education.

caught trains heading north. They called themselves solos, meaning single men.

In 1916, a solo arrived in Chicago on a chilly November day. His name is not known, but he left a record of his experiences. We will call him Luis.

Finding a home. When he arrived in Chicago in 1916, Luis could not find an apartment. He lived with 16 other solos in a boxcar camp, a collection of old railroad cars with the wheels removed. The solos did their best to make the boxcars a home. Some planted gardens outside. Others kept a few chickens for food.

Finding work. The next step was to find a job. Luis joined other solos on Madison Street. "Compañero! Amigo!" shouted labor agents called enganchistas. The agents tried to enganchar, or "hook," solos into signing with them. "What kind of a job do you want? We can give you anything you want. Go upstairs and sign up," they cried.

Luis did not sign up. He wanted to look around for himself. After several days, he took a job at a restaurant that was owned by the railroads.

A new life. Luis slowly began to feel at home in Chicago. He found Mexican stores where he could get all the tortillas he wanted for a quarter. He also made Mexican friends.

Soon, Luis was ready to move out of the boxcar camp. He met a family of circus acrobats. They were one of the few Mexican families who had been in Chicago for many years. He rented a room in their apartment.

The next year, Luis sent money to his mother and sister back in Mexico. With the money, they bought train tickets to Chicago. Meanwhile, Luis bought a house and furniture, hired a cook, and started a boardinghouse.

Luis had made a new life in Chicago. Other Mexican newcomers did the same. "Some of my young boarders went south after they made some money, got their families, and returned to Chicago," Luis said.

Chicago *An immigrant arriving in a big city must have found it a lonely and frightening place. In his painting* Chicago, *Louis Lozowick captures the spirit of a city in an age of machines.* **Daily Life** *What kinds of jobs could an immigrant who spoke little English expect to get in a city like Chicago?*

From a few solos living in boxcars, a thriving Mexican community grew in Chicago. Most worked in steel mills, railroad yards, and meatpacking plants. ■

The Scopes Trial

In the 1920s, cities drew thousands of people from farms and small towns. Those who stayed in rural areas often saw cities as a threat. They felt that new ways of life in the city were ruining traditional values.

In 1925, the clash between old and new ways of life made headlines in the Scopes trial. John Scopes was a young biology teacher in the small town of Dayton, Tennessee. He taught his students Charles Darwin's theory of evolution—even though teaching the theory violated state law.

Chapter 24 • **701**

Videotapes/ Videodiscs

United States History Video Collection Use the video segment "Nativists and Fundamentalists" from Volume 17, *The Roaring Twenties,* to enhance students' understanding of the important role of conservative social forces in the United States during the 1920s. Approx. running time 3:25 min. (Enrichment/Average) Vol. 17, Ch. 40

Chapter 40   Play

Historical Sidelight
Background

According to the account left by "Luis," he was very wary of the enganchistas' promises. He had also learned from the other solos that these agents could not be trusted. He recorded this account: "I once signed up with an enganchista who spoke no Spanish and it cost me $8 for the job when I had already paid him $1. He told me to sign something, and I did."

Connections With Literature
Activity

The play *Inherit the Wind* by Jerome Lawrence and Robert E. Lee is a fictionalized account of the Scopes trial. Invite students who are interested in literature and drama to present a scene from the play. Later, have students discuss the arguments used on both sides.

Answer to Caption

Possible Answer: American traditions uphold the principles of equality and law. The Klan preached the superiority of white, native-born Protestants and used violence and terror.

Customized Reader

Primary Source For historian Carl Hallberg's discussion of the rise in popularity of the Ku Klux Klan, order article VIB-10, The Ku Klux Klan in Pekin, Illinois, from the *American History Customized Reader.* (Enrichment/Challenging)

Voices of Freedom

Primary Source You might assign selection 10-3, Getting Ready to Head North, on pages 210–211 of *Voices of Freedom.* The selection from Richard Wright's novel *Black Boy* includes his description of how he left home to seek a better future. (Enrichment/Average)

Transparencies

Fine Art Use the transparency, The Migration of the Negro, on page D-53 of *American History Transparencies.* The artist Jacob Lawrence painted this picture, which is part of a series of 60 panels called *The Black Migration.* Teaching suggestions can be found on page D-17. (Enrichment/Average)

Darwin's theory. Darwin claimed that all life had evolved, or developed, from simpler forms. Some churches condemned the theory, saying it denied the teachings of the Bible. By the mid-1920s, Tennessee, Mississippi, and Arkansas had passed laws that banned the teaching of Darwin's theory.

Two of the nation's best-known lawyers faced each other in Scopes's trial. William Jennings Bryan, who had run for President three times, argued the state's case against Scopes. Clarence Darrow, a Chicago lawyer who had helped unions and radicals, defended Scopes.

The nation watches. As the trial began, the nation's attention was riveted on Dayton. Reporters scribbled every word of the battle between Bryan and Darrow. "Scopes isn't on trial," Darrow thundered at one point, "civilization is on trial." Darrow even put Bryan on the witness stand to show how little he knew about science.

Despite Darrow's defense, Scopes was convicted and fined. The law against teaching about evolution stayed on the books. It was rarely enforced, however.

The New Klan

Fear of change gave new life to an old organization. In 1915, a group of white men trudged up Stone Mountain in Georgia. At its peak, they burned a huge cross and declared the rebirth of the Ku Klux Klan. The original Klan had used terror to keep African Americans from voting after the Civil War. (See page 494.) The new Klan had a broader aim: to preserve the United States for white native-born Protestants.

The new Klan's main targets were immigrants, especially Catholics and Jews. Klan members burned crosses outside people's homes. They used whippings and lynchings to terrorize immigrants and African Americans. The Klan strongly supported efforts to limit immigration.

Because of its large membership, the Klan gained political influence. In the mid-1920s, however, many Americans became alarmed at the Klan's growing power. At the same time, scandals surfaced that showed Klan leaders had stolen money from members. Klan membership dropped sharply.

Responding to Racism

Blacks had hoped that their sacrifices during World War I would lessen racism. However, black soldiers came home from Europe to find that the South was still a segregated society. Even in the North, racial prejudice was widespread.

African Americans in northern cities. Many African Americans moved north during and after the war. They took factory jobs in Chicago, Detroit, New York, Philadelphia,

The Ku Klux Klan *Many Americans were alarmed by the rebirth of the Ku Klux Klan. Journalist William Allen White warned, "To make a case against a birthplace, a religion, or a race is wickedly un-American and cowardly."* **American Traditions** *Why do you think White described the Klan as "un-American"?*

Connections With Civics Background

Renewed interest in the Ku Klux Klan during the 1920s was mainly a reaction against radicals and anarchy (although many joined the Klan at that time simply because of its pageantry).

The Klan was a powerful organization that could influence even national politics. At the 1924 Democratic convention, for example, Senator Oscar W. Underwood of Alabama publicly condemned the Klan, and he was not nominated. Some historians believe that this action alone might have cost Underwood the nomination as well as his Senate seat.

Our Multicultural Heritage Background

Marcus Garvey, founder of the Universal Negro Improvement Association, was born in Jamaica. He founded the association there in 1914 and brought it to the United States in 1916, hoping to influence African Americans who lived in the North. From his headquarters in New York City, Garvey gained about 2 million followers, most of whom were poor African Americans who saw in Garvey's ideas a new hope for equality with whites. Garvey's followers sent him thousands of dollars, which he used to set up African American businesses.

and other cities. The newcomers often found that only the lowest-paying jobs were open to them. In addition, whites in many neighborhoods refused to rent them apartments. At the same time, many newcomers wanted to live near one another. As a result, areas with large black populations grew in many northern cities.

Many white workers in the North felt threatened by the arrival of so many African Americans. Racial tension grew. In 1919, race riots broke out in several cities. The worst race riot took place in Chicago, leaving 38 dead.

Marcus Garvey. Shocked by the racism of white northerners, African Americans looked for new ways to cope. Marcus Garvey, a popular black leader, organized the Universal Negro Improvement Association. He hoped to promote unity and pride among African Americans. "I am the equal of any white man," Garvey said.

Garvey urged African Americans to seek their roots in Africa. Although few black Americans actually went to Africa, Garvey's "Back to Africa" movement built racial pride.

The Election of 1928

By 1928, Republicans had led the nation for eight years. They pointed to prosperity as their greatest achievement. Asked about the election, President Coolidge said tersely, "I do not choose to run." Herbert Hoover easily won the Republican nomination. The Democrats chose Alfred E. Smith, the former governor of New York.

Our Common Heritage
In 1928, voters in a Chicago district elected Oscar DePriest to Congress. He was the first African American member of Congress from the North—and the first black to serve in Congress since Reconstruction.

The 1928 election showed the tensions lurking below the surface of American life. The two candidates had widely different appeals. Hoover was a midwesterner and a self-made millionaire. He won strong support from rural Americans and big business. Smith, the son of Irish immigrants, was the first Catholic to run for President. City dwellers—many of whom were immigrants and Catholics—rallied around Smith.

Voters saw a clear choice between Smith and Hoover. Smith opposed Prohibition. His religion and New York roots made him a symbol of the urban United States. In the election, Smith won the country's 12 largest cities. Rural and small-town voters, however, supported Hoover. He won by a landslide.

Many voters hoped Hoover would keep the country prosperous. Less than a year after Hoover took office, however, these hopes would come crashing down.

SECTION 5 REVIEW

1. **Identify:** (a) Red Scare, (b) Sacco and Vanzetti trial, (c) John Scopes, (d) Marcus Garvey, (e) Herbert Hoover.
2. **Define:** (a) anarchist, (b) quota system.
3. Why did some Americans face hard times in the 1920s?
4. Why did the Red Scare lead to demands to limit immigration?
5. What conditions did African Americans find in northern cities?
6. **CRITICAL THINKING Comparing** How were the Mexicans who migrated to northern cities after World War I similar to the immigrants who came from Europe in the late 1800s?

ACTIVITY **Writing to Learn**
Imagine that you are an African American soldier returning home after fighting in Europe during World War I. Write a letter to a newspaper expressing your reaction to the renewed activity of the Ku Klux Klan.

 CD-ROM

Presidents Access the biography of Herbert Hoover from the *American Heritage® History of the United States* CD-ROM.

 Student Study Guide

Section 5 Study Guide Have students use the Section 5 Study Guide on page 182 of the *Student Study Guide* to review and reinforce the content of this section. (Reteaching/Average)

ACTIVITY

Guided Instruction Students' reaction to the Klan may be based largely on emotion. Their letters, however, need to be based on fact and logic in order to be effective. You might encourage students to have a partner evaluate their drafts and comment on the logic of the presentation. Invite volunteers to share their finished letters as a springboard for class discussion.

Answers to Section 5 Review

1. (a) Red Scare, p. 699, (b) Sacco and Vanzetti trial, p. 699, (c) John Scopes, p. 701, (d) Marcus Garvey, p. 703, (e) Herbert Hoover, p. 703
2. (a) anarchist, p. 699, (b) quota system, p. 700
3. Farmers suffered because they had borrowed money to buy land and tractors to keep up with demand during World War I. When farm prices dropped in the 1920s, farmers were deeply in debt, and their incomes had shrunk. Labor suffered because wages had not kept up with prices during World War I. When workers struck for higher wages, management struck back, and the government did nothing to help labor. Immigrants suffered because anti-foreign feelings rose. African Americans suffered despite their sacrifice in World War I; they were still victims of prejudice and discrimination in both North and South.
4. Because many anarchists were foreign-born, Americans demanded limits on immigration.
5. African Americans often found that only the lowest-paying jobs were open to them. Whites in many neighborhoods refused to rent apartments to them. In 1919, race riots broke out in several northern cities. The worst race riot took place in Chicago, leaving 38 dead.
6. Possible Answer: In both cases, individuals came, struggled, and made a life for themselves. Then they sent for the rest of their family.

CHAPTER 24 REVIEW

Answers to Reviewing the Main Ideas

1. In 1921, Harding signed peace treaties with Germany, Austria, and Hungary. The United States worked for disarmament in the 1920s. At the Washington Conference of 1921, the United States, Britain, and Japan agreed to limit the size of their navies. In 1928, the United States signed the Kellogg-Briand Pact, outlawing war.

2. (a) The growth of the auto industry spurred growth in other parts of the economy. (b) Development of many new products— such as electric refrigerators, vacuum cleaners, and other appliances—spurred consumer spending. (c) Installment buying allowed people to buy now and pay later, thus boosting the demand for consumer goods.

3. Prohibition encouraged contempt for the law and the growth of organized crime. It reduced drinking but never stopped it.

4. More middle-class women worked outside the home; housework was made easier by new labor-saving appliances.

5. Because most Americans heard the same radio programs and watched the same movie stars, a new national culture developed. By making travel easier, cars allowed Americans to learn more about each other.

6. (a) Hughes wrote proudly about being an African American. (b) Lewis wrote about small-town Americans, presenting them as dull and narrow-minded. (c) Fitzgerald wrote about wealthy people who attended endless parties but could not find happiness.

7. (a) farmers, labor, foreigners, and African Americans (b) Farmers saw farm prices fall sharply, leaving them deeply in debt; labor found that wages had not kept up with prices during World War I; foreigners faced hostility because many anarchists were foreign-born; African Americans returned from fighting in World War I to face the same—or worse—discrimination.

8. Congress passed the Emergency Quota Act in 1921. Under the act, only a certain number of people from each country were

Summary

- After years of reform and war, Americans elected Republicans who promised "normalcy" and prosperity in the 1920s.
- Sales of cars, radios, and other new products spurred an economic boom.
- Women gained new rights and Americans found new ways to spend their leisure time.
- Flappers, jazz musicians, and black and white writers challenged old ways of thinking and acting.
- American farmers and labor unions suffered setbacks, and immigrants and African Americans came under attack.

Reviewing the Main Ideas

1. How did the United States work for peace in the 1920s?

2. Explain how each of the following contributed to an economic boom in the 1920s: (a) auto industry, (b) new products, (c) installment buying.

3. Why did Prohibition fail?

4. Describe two ways in which women's lives changed in the 1920s.

5. Explain how movies, radio, and cars helped create a mass society.

6. Describe the writings of each of the following: (a) Langston Hughes, (b) Sinclair Lewis, (c) F. Scott Fitzgerald.

7. (a) Which groups did not share in the prosperity of the 1920s? (b) What problems did they face?

8. How did the United States limit immigration in the 1920s?

Thinking Critically

1. Forecasting During the 1920s, many Americans bought consumer goods and stocks on credit. What problems did this

cause them when the economy suddenly slowed down?

2. Linking Past and Present (a) Why did anti-immigration feelings grow in the 1920s? (b) Does anti-immigration sentiment exist in the United States today? (c) At what groups is it directed? (d) What might be some reasons for resentment of those groups?

3. Defending a Position "Groups such as the Ku Klux Klan have a right to exist under the Constitution." Do you agree or disagree with this statement? Defend your position.

Applying Your Skills

1. Using Visual Evidence Study the photograph on page 702. (a) What does the photograph show? (b) What symbols did the Ku Klux Klan use? (c) What impression do you think Klan members wanted to make?

2. Making a Concept Map List the main ideas and supporting details for Section 5, Signs of Trouble. Then use your list to make a concept map for the section.

Thinking About Geography

Match the letters on the map with the following places: **1.** Vermont, **2.** California, **3.** Minnesota, **4.** Massachusetts, **5.** Tennessee, **6.** New Orleans, Louisiana, **7.** Chicago, Illinois, **8.** New York City. **Region** What part of New York City was a center of African American culture during the 1920s?

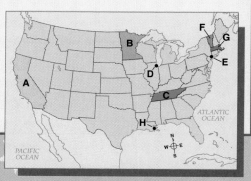

---

allowed to enter the United States. In 1924, Congress passed new laws that further cut immigration, especially from Eastern Europe. In addition, Japanese were added to the list of Asians denied entry to the United States.

Answers to Thinking Critically

1. Possible Answer: When the economy slowed down, people were not able to repay their debts.

2. (a) People were afraid of anarchists, many of whom were foreign-born. (b, c, and d) Answers will vary, but students should recognize that some Americans today fear immigrants as a source of economic competition.

3. Some students might argue that the First Amendment gives the right of freedom of speech to all groups. Others might argue that the use of violence by the Klan is not protected by the Constitution.

Answers to Applying Your Skills

1. (a) a meeting of the Ku Klux Klan (b) robes, white hoods, and crosses (c) Possible Answer: fear, even terror

2. Main idea: Prosperity and good times did not extend to all Americans. Supporting details: problems of farmers, workers, African Americans, foreigners. Main idea: Tensions between old and new ways. Supporting details: Scopes trial, rural people see city people as a threat

INTERDISCIPLINARY **ACTIVITY**

Roaring Into the Jazz Age

Form into groups to review the Roaring Twenties. Follow the suggestions below to write, dance, draw, or perform to show what you have learned about the 1920s. You may use the textbook, encyclopedias, atlases, or other materials in your classroom library to complete the tasks. Be able to name your sources of information when you have finished the activity.

LANGUAGE EXPERTS Find out the meaning of the following slang terms from the 1920s: applesauce, bee's knees, big cheese, bunk, cat's meow, cheaters, dogs, hepcat, hokum, horsefeathers, jake, main drag, ritzy, scram, sheik, spiffy, swanky. Then put together a Jazz Age glossary. Illustrate your glossary with original drawings or pictures from magazines.

Ruby Green, singer

DANCERS Learn the dance called the Charleston. Plan to perform it, then teach it to the rest of the class.

HISTORIANS Divide into small groups. Have each group research one of the key figures of the Harlem Renaissance. Organize your findings into short profiles and present them to the class. Be sure to include examples of each artist's or writer's work as part of your presentation.

POETS Locate works by poets of the Harlem Renaissance—such as Claude McKay, Langston Hughes, and Countee Cullen. Prepare a poetry reading for the class.

ARTISTS Brainstorm a list of images that represent the Jazz Age. Then use the images to create a Jazz Age collage.

Dancing the Charleston

 Organize a Roaring Into the Jazz Age festival. Invite other classes to see the presentations or completed activities of each group.

King Oliver's Creole Jazz Band

Chapter 24 • **705**

Answers to Thinking About Geography

1. F   **2.** A   **3.** B   **4.** G   **5.** C
6. H   **7.** D   **8.** E
Region: Harlem

Assessment

Chapter Resources Binder For a more comprehensive evaluation of student understanding, assign Chapter Tests A and B and/or Extra Unit Questions from Unit 8, pages 7–12 and 43–45.
Computer Test Bank You can use Chapter Tests and Extra Unit Questions to create your own tests for both testing and retesting.

Alternative Assessment

Chapter Resources Binder See the Alternative Assessment booklet in the *Social Studies Educator's Handbook* series.
Portfolio You might meet with students to choose appropriate work from the chapter for inclusion in their portfolios.

Interdisciplinary ACTIVITY

Learning Styles

The following chart indicates the activities appropriate for different learning styles.

Visual Learners
Language experts
Dancers
Historians
Artists

Auditory Learners
Historians
Poets

Kinesthetic Learners
Dancers
Poets

Evaluation

Language experts Glossary entries should appear in alphabetical order and have sensible definitions. You might want students to offer examples of each term in a sentence. Not every term needs to be illustrated, but any illustrations included should show effort.

Dancers Before they demonstrate the Charleston, students might learn and explain its history as well as its most important steps.

Historians Each group of students should follow the same format in researching and presenting its work. As a group, the presentations should give an accurate idea of the themes and varied forms of expression of the Harlem Renaissance.

Poets Several poets of the movement should be presented. Through tone, pitch, use of pauses, and facial expressions and gestures, readers should convey the attitudes and feelings present in each writer's work.

Artists In addition to symbols and images on the collage, students might also include artwork of several Jazz Age personalities. All images—alone and together—should suggest a main idea about the Jazz Age.

Lessons	Teaching Resources
1 **The Bubble Bursts** **Objectives** 1. Identify what caused the Great Depression. 2. Describe how Hoover tried to end the depression. 3. Identify the Bonus Army.	**Lesson Planner** Cooperative Learning, p. 155 **Student Study Guide** Section 1 Study Guide, p. 185 **Chapter Resources Binder, Unit 8** *Skill Application* Exploring Local History, p. 16
2 **FDR and the New Deal** **Objectives** 1. Explain why Americans elected Roosevelt in 1932. 2. Explain why FDR closed the banks for eight days. 3. Identify the main goals of FDR's New Deal programs.	**Lesson Planner** Cooperative Learning, p. 156 **Student Study Guide** Section 2 Study Guide, p. 186 **Our Multicultural Heritage** *Biography* Fiorello La Guardia, New York's Reforming Mayor, p. 74 *Milestone* African Americans Recall Their Past, p. 75
3 **Reaction to the New Deal** **Objectives** 1. Identify what critics disliked about the New Deal. 2. Explain why Roosevelt clashed with the Supreme Court. 3. Describe how New Deal programs affected workers and older Americans. 4. Explain why the New Deal was a turning point in American history.	**Lesson Planner** Cooperative Learning, p. 157 **Student Study Guide** Section 3 Study Guide, p. 187
4 **Surviving the Depression** **Objectives** 1. Identify what caused the Dust Bowl. 2. Describe how the Great Depression affected women. 3. Describe how New Deal programs affected minorities. 4. Identify the role that movies and radio played during the depression.	**Lesson Planner** Cooperative Learning, p. 158 **Student Study Guide** Section 4 Study Guide, p. 188 **Chapter Resources Binder, Unit 8** *Geography in History* Dust Bowlers on the Move, pp. 19–20 *History Through Literature* The People, Yes, p. 18 *Critical Thinking* Understanding Causes and Effects, p. 17 **Interdisciplinary Connections:** The Dust Bowl ■ *Arts* Woody Guthrie, A Voice for the Disadvantaged, p. 146 ■ *Geography* Fleeing the "Dust Bowl," p. 147 ■ *World* Africa's Dust Bowl, p. 148 ■ *Economics* The Falling Wages of Farm Workers, p. 149 ■ *Civics* Working for the CCC, p. 150 **Our Multicultural Heritage** *Biography* Carlos Bulosan, Immigrant Writer, p. 73 **Posters** *La Reunión,* by Tony Ortega

Multimedia Resources	Additional Resources	Chapter-Level Resources
Transparencies *Fine Art* Isaac Soyer, Unemployment Office, p. D-55 **Videotapes/Videodiscs** *United States History Video Collection* From Boom to Bust, Vol. 18, Ch. 7; The Great Crash and Mr. Hoover, Vol. 18, Ch. 10.	**Voices of Freedom** Pipe City, pp. 223–224 Going on Relief in Baltimore, pp. 224–225 Letters to the White House, pp. 225–226	**Lesson Planner** Activity Based, pp. 159–160 **Student Study Guide** Chapter 25 Study Guide, pp. 189–190 **Chapter Resources Binder** **Unit 8** Vocabulary Building, p. 15 Chapter Test A, pp. 21–23 Chapter Test B, pp. 24–26 Illustration Master, p. 27 Extra Unit Questions, pp. 43–45 **English Guided Reading** Guided Reading, pp. 49–50 **Spanish Resources** **Computer Test Bank** Chapter Tests A and B Extra Unit Questions **Guided Reading Audiotapes** Side 10 **CD-ROM** *Time Tour* Depression and the New Deal (1929–1941) in Prosperity, Depression, and War
Transparencies *Critical Thinking* The New Deal, p. F-29 **CD-ROM** *Presidents* Franklin D. Roosevelt **Videotapes/Videodiscs** *United States History Video Collection* The First New Deal, Vol. 18, Ch. 13	**Voices of Freedom** The First Inaugural Address, pp. 227–229 What Was the New Deal?, pp. 229–230 Millard Ketchum in the CCC, pp. 230–231	
Transparencies *Political Cartoons* The New Deal Ties Up Government Resources, p. G-25 **Videotapes/Videodiscs** *United States History Video Collection* The Second New Deal, Vol. 18, Ch. 28	**Voices of Freedom** Father Coughlin Presents His Principles, pp. 233–234 Evelyn Finn Organizes a Union, pp. 238–239 That Gentleman in the White House, pp. 242–243 **Customized Reader** The Great Sit-Down Strike, article VIIB-10 Older Americans Seek Help During the Depression, article VIIB-8	
Transparencies *Interdisciplinary Connections* Water Cycle, p. B-81 *Fine Art* Edward Hopper, Nighthawks, p. D-59 **CD-ROM** *History Makers* Eleanor Roosevelt **Videotapes/Videodiscs** *United States History Video Collection* African Americans and the Great Depression, Vol. 18, Ch. 19; The Legacy of the New Deal, Vol. 18, Ch. 34	**Voices of Freedom** Losing the Farm, pp. 239–241 **Customized Reader** A Reporter Describes the Dust Bowl, article VIIB-7 One of Arizona's First African American Lawyers, article VIIA-11 Mexican Americans and the Depression, article VIIA-6 **Interdisciplinary Explorations** Back to the Thirties	

Lesson Planner

For a fully developed **Activity-Based** lesson plan for Chapter 25, see the *Lesson Planner*, pages 159–160.

 Chapter Resources

Vocabulary Building The Vocabulary Building worksheet for Chapter 25 from Unit 8, page 15, of the *Chapter Resources* binder can be used as a prereading activity or as a review of chapter vocabulary. (Reteaching/Easy)

 Student Study Guide

Chapter 25 Study Guide Refer students to pages 189–190 of the *Student Study Guide* for the Chapter 25 Study Guide. The study guide can be used for chapter review as well as for reteaching. (Reteaching/Average)

 Guided Reading Audiotapes

Students can use *Guided Reading Audiotapes,* Chapter 25, side 10, to listen to section previews, summaries, and review questions. The tapes will benefit students who are auditory learners, students who have trouble reading, or students acquiring English. Tapes are also available in Spanish. (Enrichment/ Easy)

CHAPTER 25

Depression and the New Deal

(1929–1941)

CHAPTER OUTLINE

1 The Bubble Bursts

2 FDR and the New Deal

3 Reaction to the New Deal

4 Surviving the Depression

1929 *A plunge in stock prices marked the start of the Great Depression. This cartoon depicts the stock market before and after the crash.*

1932 *Franklin Delano Roosevelt was elected President. He promised voters that he would take bold action to end the depression.*

1933 *The Civilian Conservation Corps was created as part of Roosevelt's New Deal. The CCC put young men like these to work on conservation projects.*

| 1929 | 1931 | 1933 | 1935 |

 WORLD EVENT
1930 Worldwide economic depression begins

 WORLD EVENT
1933 Economic hard times lead to rise of dictator in Germany

706 • Chapter 25

Chapter Time Line
Critical Thinking

Write the following statement on the chalkboard: "In the 1930s, economic depression caused problems around the world." Invite students to support the statement by referring to the time line. Students can find evidence both in World Event information (for example, "Economic hard times lead to rise of dictator in Germany" [1933]) and in captions for the visuals (for example, "The Civilian Conservation Corps was created as part of Roosevelt's New Deal" [1933]). Alternatively, have students use time line information to support one of these other statements:
- "During the depression, as never before in American history, the government stepped in to create jobs for its citizens."
- "The varied needs of Americans during the depression were met in a variety of ways."

Encourage students to keep their responses and test their accuracy as the class works through the chapter.

Chapter Setting

As a boy, Louis Banks dreamed of becoming a chef. Then, in 1929, the economy slid into a severe depression. The disaster ended the boy's dreams. At age 14, he left home to look for a job. He spent 10 years "riding the rails" in search of work. Much later, he told an interviewer how he lived in encampments that grew up next to the railroad tracks:

66 Black and white, it didn't make no difference who you were, 'cause everybody was poor. . . . We used to take a big pot and cook food, cabbage, meat and beans all together. We all set together, we made a tent. Twenty-five or thirty would be out on the side of the rail, white and colored. They didn't have no mothers or sisters, they didn't have no home, they were dirty, they had overalls on, they didn't have no food, they didn't have anything. 99

As an African American, Banks had an especially hard time. Employers refused to hire him "because I didn't belong to the right kind of race." Even when he did get a job, he was paid less than white co-workers. In time, Banks found work and raised a family. Still, the memory of those hard times never left him.

Like Louis Banks, millions of Americans were jobless in the 1930s. Each day, they struggled just to survive. In 1932, Americans turned to a new President: Franklin Roosevelt. He held out the hope of better days. Despite the President's confident talk, recovery was slow in coming.

 Form into small groups to discuss what unemployment might mean to individuals and their families. Then write a song or a poem that expresses the thoughts of a jobless worker.

1935 *The government set up the Works Progress Administration. The WPA created jobs for people in the arts as well as for laborers.*

1939 The Wizard of Oz *opened. Like many movies of the 1930s, this musical fantasy offered a brief escape from the hardships of daily life.*

| 1935 | 1937 | 1939 | 1941 |

 WORLD EVENT
1939 World War II begins in Europe

Chapter Resources

English Guided Reading Duplicate and distribute the Chapter 25 Guided Reading worksheets on pages 49–50 in the English Guided Reading section of the *Chapter Resources* binder. Students who have difficulty reading might also benefit from using this worksheet. Have students complete the worksheet before they begin reading. You might pair a more fluent student or a student who is a strong reader with each SAE student to review. (Reteaching/Easy)

Spanish Resources See the Spanish Resources section of the *Chapter Resources* binder.

ACTIVITY

Guided Instruction You might allow students to spend 3–5 minutes freewriting to generate ideas for their songs or poems. Musically talented students may wish to write both lyrics and melodies; other students might write new lyrics for well-known melodies. Invite students to perform their songs or poems for the class in groups if they wish.

CD-ROM

Time Tour Access the Depression and the New Deal (1929–1941) in Prosperity, Depression, and War on the American Heritage® *History of the United States* CD-ROM. (Enrichment/Average)

Students Acquiring English
Activity

Making concept maps can be helpful in organizing essential information for SAE students. The following example is based on the information in section 1, pages 708–713. Write the heading "An Economy in Trouble" on the chalkboard and draw a circle around it. Then model the process of concept mapping by thinking out loud as you choose information for the surrounding circles on the map. For example, you might say, "Let's see . . . the first sign of trouble in the economy mentioned in this section is unstable farm prices.

I'll put that in one of these circles." Continue in this fashion, adding more circles to designate signs of economic trouble mentioned in this section (lowering demand for new homes and offices, falling sales in heavy machinery, declining consumer buying). This strategy gives SAE students a visual and simplified means of understanding basic information. After you have modeled the process several times, encourage students to try concept mapping on their own.

Linking Past and Present
Activity

Have interested students interview relatives or neighbors who lived through the Great Depression. Encourage students to ask questions such as the following:

- Were members of your family out of work? How did you cope with unemployment?
- What did your family think of FDR's New Deal?

Have students use the responses to compile an oral history of the period.

Bell Ringer

Write the words *Great Depression* on the chalkboard. Have students brainstorm for facts that they already know about this period of American history.

Lesson Plan

1. Focus The prosperity of the 1920s kept many Americans from seeing the growing economic problems of the nation. In this section, students learn about the signs of an economic slowdown, the presidential election of 1928, and the collapse of the stock market.

2. Instruct Have students imagine that they are newspaper reporters preparing for a press conference with Herbert Hoover in 1931. Have students prepare a list of questions about the causes of the depression, its immediate effects, and what Hoover was doing to solve the problems. List some of these questions on the chalkboard and ask students how Hoover might have answered them.

3. Close To close the lesson, have students decide which fact or concept in each subsection in Section 1 is most important to remember.

Lesson Planner

For a developed **Cooperative Learning** lesson plan, see the *Lesson Planner,* page 155.

1
The Bubble Bursts

FIND OUT
- What caused the Great Depression?
- How did Hoover try to end the depression?
- What was the Bonus Army?

VOCABULARY relief, public works program, bonus

Herbert Hoover campaigned for election confidently in 1928. He declared:

    66We in America are nearer to the final triumph over poverty than ever before in the history of any land. The poorhouse is vanishing from among us. 99

The following year, the stock market crashed. The United States began a plunge into the worst depression in its history. Everywhere, stunned people asked: How could this have happened?

An Economy in Trouble

When Hoover took office in 1929, he saw a growing economy. Along with most of the nation's leaders, he did not recognize the signs that warned of trouble.

Many Americans, as you have read, did not share in the prosperity of the 1920s. Farmers, especially, faced hard times. Once in office, President Hoover tried to help farmers. He persuaded Congress to create the Federal Farm Board. The Farm Board helped farmers to sell their products and worked to keep prices stable—neither rising too high nor dropping too low. Farmers,

however, did not reduce production. As a result, prices for farm products stayed low.

Besides low farm prices, other signs pointed to an economic slowdown. The demand for new homes and office buildings declined. The sale of heavy machinery fell. Consumers were buying less. However, the government kept few detailed records in the 1920s. Therefore, most Americans were not aware of the trouble.

The Stock Market Plunges

By August 1929, a few investors had begun selling their stocks. They felt the boom might end soon. In September, more people decided to sell. The rash of selling caused stock prices to fall.

A nervous market. The President reassured nervous investors. "The business of the country is on a sound and prosperous basis," he stated. Words were not enough, however. As the selling continued, prices tumbled.

Many investors had bought stock on margin. (See page 686.) Now, brokers asked investors to pay the money they still owed for the stock. Investors who could not pay had to sell their stock. This caused prices to drop even more. Between October 24 and October 29, desperate people tried to unload millions of shares of stock.

Stock market crash. On Tuesday, October 29, a stampede of selling hit the New York Stock Exchange. On Black Tuesday, as it was soon called, prices plummeted because there were no buyers for the stock. People who thought they owned valuable stocks were left with worthless paper. Overnight, millionaires lost their fortunes.

Business leaders and bankers tried to restore confidence in the economy. John D. Rockefeller told reporters, "My son and I have for some days been purchasing some common stocks." Replied comedian Eddie Cantor, "Sure, who else has any money left?"

Connections With Civics
Background

During World War I, Herbert Hoover had organized a massive relief effort in Europe that had fed millions of people. Later, as Secretary of Commerce, he had promoted American business. His Iowa background and his reputation for success influenced many voters.

Hoover was the first President born west of the Mississippi and the last President whose term ended on March 3. The Twentieth Amendment (ratified in 1933) changed the date to January 20 to shorten the lame duck period.

Connections With Economics
Background

When many people buy stocks, prices rise, which creates a "bull market." When many people sell stocks and there are fewer buyers, prices fall, creating a "bear market." The terms come from the way the two animals attack. A bull attacks by tossing its horns up in the air; a bear sweeps its paws downward.

Linking Past and Present
Background

On October 19, 1987, the Dow Jones Industrial Average fell 508 points. This was nearly twice the 1929 stock market crash. The crash of 1987, however, did not have the severe consequences of the crash of 1929.

Panic! *In October 1929, screaming headlines announced the stock market crash. Here, people gather on the street to read the alarming news.* **Economics** *What effect did panic have on stock prices?*

Sliding into depression. Following the stock market crash, the economy slid into a severe depression. The crash did not cause the depression, but it did shake confidence in the economy. Many people who had invested their savings in stocks suddenly had little or nothing left.

Causes of the Depression

The economic hard times that lasted from 1929 to 1941 are known as the ***Great Depression.*** Many Americans experienced the despair of joblessness. As the depression worsened, people tried to understand how the prosperity of the 1920s had turned into the nightmare of the 1930s.

Too many goods, too few buyers. Among the chief causes of the Great Depression was overproduction. American farms and factories produced vast amounts of goods in the 1920s. Wages did not rise as much as prices, however. As a result, workers could not afford to buy many goods. Farm families also had little money for cars and other expensive items.

Soon, factories and farms were producing more goods than people were buying. As orders slowed, factories closed or laid off workers.

Problems in the banking system. Another cause of the depression was weakness in the banking system. During the 1920s, banks made loans to people who invested in the stock market. When the stock market crashed, borrowers could not repay their loans. Without the money from the loans, the banks could not give depositors their money when they asked for it. Many banks were forced to close.

More than 5,000 banks closed between 1929 and 1932. When a bank closed, depositors lost the money they had in the bank. A family's savings could disappear overnight.

A cycle of disaster. After the stock market crash, the economy skidded downhill. One disaster triggered another. The stock market crash, for example, ruined many investors. Without money from investors, or capital, businesses could no longer grow and expand.

With the banks in trouble, businesses could not turn to them for capital, either. Businesses cut back on production. Production cutbacks led to wage cuts and employee layoffs. Unemployed workers, in turn, had little or no money to spend. As a result, they bought less. The demand for clothing, cars, and other goods fell. In the end, many businesses went bankrupt.

Answer to Caption
The panic caused stock prices to fall dramatically, shaking confidence in the national economy.

  Videotapes/ Videodiscs

United States History Video Collection Use the video segment "From Boom to Bust" from Volume 18, *The Great Depression and the New Deal,* to enhance students' understanding of the causes of the economic collapse in the late 1920s. Approx. running time 3:00 min.(Enrichment/Average) Vol. 18, Ch. 7

Chapter 7   Play

Connections With Economics
Activity

Between 1929 and 1933, the gross national product fell from $103 billion to $56 billion. Carmakers operated at only one-fifth capacity; steel production fell 75 percent.

Have interested students draw diagrams illustrating the chain reaction of economic disasters following the crash of the stock market in October 1929.

Connections With Economics
Background

Not only had factories overproduced in the 1920s, but many of the items that they had overproduced were *durable goods*—products designed to last for several years. These included automobiles, stoves, and tractors. By 1929, many people either already owned the durable goods they wanted or could not afford to buy more, even on credit. The demand for such goods, therefore, decreased, and the quantity of unsold goods climbed.

Answer to Graph Skills

1933; The rate of unemployment decreased continually from 1936 to 1937, rose between 1937 and 1938, and then decreased steadily between 1938 and 1941.

📖 Voices of Freedom

Primary Source You might assign selection 12-2, Pipe City, on pages 223–224 of *Voices of Freedom*. This excerpt describes a shantytown of "forgotten men" during the 1930s. (Enrichment/Average)

Primary Source You might assign selection 12-3, Going on Relief in Baltimore, on pages 224–225 of *Voices of Freedom*. This selection from Russell Baker's autobiography describes his family's efforts at survival during the depression. (Enrichment/Average)

Primary Source You might assign selection 12-4, Letters to the White House, on pages 225–226 of *Voices of Freedom*. According to this selection, many Americans refused to believe that economic conditions in the 1930s were as bad as they were. (Enrichment/Challenging)

🏛 Transparencies

Fine Art Use the transparency Isaac Soyer, Unemployment Office on page D-55 of *American History Transparencies*. This painting expresses the mood of thousands of people who were unemployed during the Great Depression. Teaching suggestions can be found on page D-18. (Enrichment/Average)

Worldwide depression. In the 1920s, the United States had made large loans to European nations. When American banks stopped making loans, European banks also began to fail. The Great Depression spread from one nation to another, leading to a worldwide economic collapse. You will read more about the effects of the depression on other countries in Chapter 26.

Hard Times

The United States had suffered other economic depressions. None, however, was as bad as the Great Depression. The Great Depression lasted longer than other depressions. Also, in earlier times, most Americans lived on farms and grew their own food. In the 1930s, millions of Americans lived in cities and worked in factories. When factories closed, the jobless had no money for food and no land on which to grow it.

Soaring unemployment. As the depression spread, the number of jobless people soared. By the early 1930s, one in every four workers was unemployed. Millions more worked shortened hours or had to take pay cuts. Many of the jobless lost their homes.

The chance of finding work was small. On an average day, one New York job agency had 5,000 people looking for work. Only about 300 found jobs. In another city, police had to keep order as 15,000 women pushed and shoved to apply for six jobs cleaning offices.

Some of the jobless sold apples from sidewalk stands. Others shined shoes on street corners. The man now looking for a handout, noted a reporter, "might be the same fellow who a few months . . . ago had cheerfully O.K.'d your loan at the bank."

Families in crisis. During the depression, families suffered. Marriage and birth rates dropped. Hungry parents and children searched through city dumps and restaurant

Unemployment, 1929–1941

Percent of Workers vs. Year

Source: *Historical Statistics of the United States*

GRAPH SKILLS *During the depression, millions of Americans were out of work.* ● *According to the graph, in which year was unemployment the highest? What happened to unemployment between 1936 and 1941?*

garbage cans. A teacher ordered a thin little girl to go home to eat. "I can't," said the girl. "This is my sister's day to eat."

The pressure of hard times led some families to split up. Fathers and even children as young as 13 or 14 left home to hunt for work. Their leaving meant the family had fewer people to feed.

The homeless. Homeless, jobless men and women drifted from town to town looking for work. Some "rode the rails." They lived in railroad cars and hitched rides on freight trains. In cities across the country, the homeless built shacks out of wooden crates and scrap metal.

The Great Depression lowered people's standard of living. It also shook their belief

Cooperative Learning
Activity

Milton Meltzer's book *Brother, Can You Spare a Dime?* is a history of the Great Depression written for young people. It uses songs and firsthand accounts of the period to tell the story of the depression and the New Deal. The following songs found in the Meltzer book will be used in this activity: "Brother, Can You Spare a Dime?," "I Don't Want Your Millions, Mister," "Pastures of Plenty," "Beans, Bacon, and Gravy," and "Soup Song." In addition, "Discrimination Blues" in *The Ballad of America* by John Scott can also be used.

Divide the students into five or six groups. Have each group choose a different song and make a mural about life during the depression based on the lyrics of the song. Students may illustrate each line or each verse of the song. Alternatively, the class as a whole can choose one song, allowing different groups to illustrate different verses.

Historical Sidelight
Background

As unemployment spread, millions of unemployed workers joined food lines to wait for handouts of bread. In some large cities, the bread lines extended for blocks. One New Yorker observed: "You'd see these men silent, shuffling along in lines. Shabby clothes, but you could see they had been pretty good clothes."

CRITICAL THINKING SKILLS
Exploring Local History

The Great Depression affected Americans across the nation. You can learn about its impact on people in your local area by studying primary sources of the 1930s.

Your library is one valuable resource. Besides books on local history, it may have county and city newspapers on microfilm. Other sources of information are local historical societies. They may be able to show you letters, diaries, and pictures. Senior citizens can tell you their experiences. Even the buildings, roads, and parks around you may yield information about your community's past.

The excerpt below is from *Making Do: How Women Survived the '30s*. In this excerpt, Kate Pemberton recalls trying to find work near her home in rural West Virginia during the depression.

1. **Determine basic information from the excerpt.** (a) What time period is Pemberton discussing? (b) How old was she? (c) Where did she live? (d) What are some of the jobs Pemberton took?

2. **Analyze the contents of the excerpt.** (a) Why did Pemberton look for work 10 miles from home? (b) Why did she "hitch" rides to town? (c) List words that describe the type of person Pemberton was.

3. **Draw conclusions about local effects of the depression.** (a) Do you think Pemberton's situation was unusual in her community? (b) Why might it have been especially hard for a teenage girl to get work? (c) What other sources might you consult to get a fuller picture of life in West Virginia during the depression?

ACTIVITY Explore local history in your community by trying to find the answers to these questions: When was the community founded? Why did people choose to live there? What was life like in the early days? Identify sources of information you could use to find the answers to the questions. Use at least one of those sources to see what you can learn about the early days of your community.

66There were no jobs for sixteen-year-old girls in Fairview. Nobody in that town had a steady job except the mailman, and he made thirty-two dollars a month. We all thought he was rich.

So I started doing odd jobs. . . anything I could find. I cleaned house and canned tomatoes. The very first job I had was washing jars because I only weighed ninety-five pounds and my tiny hand could get all the way into a jar.

I worked for a quarter here and thirty cents there.

Finally, people in Fairview didn't even have a quarter to pay me so I started hitching rides into Fairmont about ten miles away. . . . It cost fifty cents round trip on the streetcar, and that was out of the question. . . .

By 1938 I'd been out of school for six years without a steady job. When I heard they were moving a . . . lamp plant down from New Jersey to Fairmont, I was so excited I got sick. The day they started hiring I was in that line at 5 A.M.

Guess what the first requirement was? You had to be five feet six inches tall. That let me out. I was only five feet one inch. . . .

But they soon changed the rule since there weren't ten girls in Fairmont that tall. You know five feet four inches was tall for a woman then. . . .

Six months later I got the call and was hired by [the lamp factory]. Worked there for the next six years. They paid forty cents an hour to start.99

---

in themselves. When people lost their jobs, they felt ashamed. "No matter that others suffered the same fate, the inner voice whispered, 'I'm a failure,'" one man wrote.

Hoover Takes Action

When hard times hit, President Hoover saw the suffering of the jobless. He tried to restore confidence in the economy by predicting better times ahead. However, he did not think the government should get directly involved in helping businesses. He felt it was up to businesses to work together to end the downslide.

At first, the President also opposed government relief programs. **Relief** means giving help to the needy. Instead, Hoover urged business leaders to keep workers employed. He also called on private charities to help Americans in need.

Private relief. Private charities did what they could. Churches and groups such as the YMCA fed the hungry at soup kitchens. Leaders of ethnic communities organized their own relief programs. The Six Companies in San Francisco's Chinatown gave food and clothing to needy Chinese. In New York's Harlem, Father Divine, an African American religious leader, fed 3,000 hungry people a day. Mexican Americans and Puerto Ricans turned to their mutualistas, or aid societies, for help.

Government programs. The numbers of needy soon overwhelmed private charities. Hoover realized he had to take other steps. He set up **public works programs.** The government hired workers to construct schools and courthouses, build dams, and pave highways.

By providing jobs, these government programs helped people earn money. Workers could then spend their wages on goods. The increased demand for goods, it was hoped, would cause businesses to expand and lead to economic recovery.

Hoover also approved the ***Reconstruction Finance Corporation,*** or RFC. The RFC loaned money to railroads, banks, and insurance companies to help keep them in business. Saving these businesses, Hoover hoped, would keep workers on their jobs.

Failed efforts. Hoover did more to reverse the depression than any previous

Lining Up for a Meal
As the depression deepened, millions of Americans went hungry. Here, people in a rural area line up for a meal at a soup kitchen.
American Traditions
How did private citizens help provide relief during the depression?

President had done during an economic panic. Still, his efforts had little effect. The depression grew worse. "Men are sitting in the parks all day long and all night long, hundreds and thousands . . . out of work, seeking work," wrote a man in Detroit.

Many people blamed the President for doing too little. They called the shacks where the homeless lived *Hoovervilles.* The newspapers that the homeless covered themselves with to keep warm were called "Hoover blankets." An empty pocket turned inside out was a "Hoover flag." In food lines, people waited for a bowl of thin soup that they called "Hoover stew."

The Bonus Army

Protests erupted against the government. The unemployed mounted hunger marches. Veterans of World War I also took action. After the war, Congress had voted to give veterans a bonus, or sum of money, to be paid in 1945. In 1932, more than 20,000 jobless veterans marched to Washington to demand the bonus right away.

The Bonus Army assembles. The veterans traveled to the capital as cheaply as possible. One decorated soldier walked from New Jersey. "I done it all by my feet—shoe leather," he told members of Congress. "I come to show you people that we need our bonus." Some veterans brought their wives and children. For two months, the *Bonus Army,* as the veterans were called, camped in a tent city along the Potomac River.

In the end, the Senate rejected a bill to pay the bonus to the veterans immediately. Senators thought that the cost would destroy any hope for the country's recovery. Many veterans packed up and went home. Thousands remained, however, vowing to stay until 1945 if necessary.

A "pitiful spectacle." Local police tried to force the veterans to leave. Battles with police left four people dead. The President then ordered General Douglas MacArthur to clear out the veterans. Using cavalry, tanks, machine guns, and tear gas, MacArthur moved into the camp and burned it to the ground. The *Washington News* expressed the shock of many Americans at Hoover's action.

66 What a pitiful spectacle is that of the great American Government, mightiest in the world, chasing unarmed men, women, and children with Army tanks. . . . If the Army must be called out to make war on unarmed citizens, this is no longer America. 99

After the attack on the Bonus Army, the President lost what little support he still had. Americans turned to a new leader.

SECTION 1 REVIEW

1. **Identify:** (a) Herbert Hoover, (b) Great Depression, (c) Reconstruction Finance Corporation, (d) Hooverville, (e) Bonus Army.
2. **Define:** (a) relief, (b) public works program, (c) bonus.
3. What economic problems existed when Hoover took office?
4. What caused stock prices to plunge on October 29, 1929?
5. (a) What steps did Hoover take to ease the economic crisis? (b) What were the effects of his efforts?
6. **CRITICAL THINKING** **Understanding Causes and Effects** (a) Describe two causes of the Great Depression. (b) How did cutbacks in factory production make the depression worse?

ACTIVITY **Writing to Learn**
Imagine that you are a reporter interviewing a veteran in the Bonus Army. Write five questions you would ask him.

Student Study Guide

Section 1 Study Guide Have students use the Section 1 Study Guide on page 185 of the *Student Study Guide* to review and reinforce the content of this section. (Reteaching/Average)

ACTIVITY

Guided Instruction Encourage students to write questions that are structured to require an explanation rather than a simple *yes* or *no* answer. You might also suggest that they include follow-up questions that explore an issue in greater depth. You might have groups of students compile their questions, choose and answer 10 of them, record them as an interview, and play the recording for the class.

Answers to Section 1 Review

1. (a) Herbert Hoover, p. 708, (b) Great Depression, p. 709, (c) Reconstruction Finance Corporation, p. 712, (d) Hooverville, p. 713, (e) Bonus Army, p. 713
2. (a) relief, p. 712, (b) public works program, p. 712, (c) bonus, p. 713
3. Farmers were producing too much and earning little, consumers were buying less, demand for new homes and offices was declining, and sales of heavy machinery were falling.
4. People had lost faith in the boom of the 1920s and had decided to sell their stocks.

Furthermore, banks began calling loans on stocks purchased on margin. Too many people were trying to sell, and there were no buyers.
5. (a) Hoover set up public works programs to provide jobs so that workers would have money to buy products and in turn expand business and provide more jobs; he approved the Reconstruction Finance Corporation to lend money to railroads, banks, and insurance companies to save their businesses. (b) The effects were inconsequential; the depression grew worse.

6. (a) Possible Answers: overproduction, a weakness in the banking system that led to many bank failures and losses for depositors, a lack of capital after the stock market crash, layoffs resulting from cutbacks in production, and high unemployment (b) Cutbacks in production led to layoffs of workers; the layoffs in turn led to a decrease in spending because jobless workers had no money to buy goods.

Bell Ringer

Have students list groups that they think would be especially hard hit by an economic depression. Ask students to give their reasons for including each group on the list.

Lesson Plan

1. Focus In 1933, the new President, Franklin D. Roosevelt, began an ambitious program of government action to steer the nation toward economic recovery. In this section, students examine Roosevelt's goals—the New Deal—and learn how his goals were carried out.
2. Instruct The three goals of the New Deal were relief, recovery, and reform. Help students use the information in this section to classify the New Deal programs under these three headings. As you list the programs on the chalkboard, ask students which goal of the New Deal they think was most important and why.
3. Close To close the lesson, have students turn the headings of the subsections into questions and then answer them.

 Lesson Planner

For a developed **Cooperative Learning** lesson plan, see the *Lesson Planner,* page 156.

2
FDR and the New Deal

FIND OUT
- Why did Americans elect Roosevelt in 1932?
- Why did FDR close the banks for eight days?
- What were the main goals of FDR's New Deal programs?

VOCABULARY fireside chat

As the nation tumbled deeper into crisis, many people despaired. The government seemed as helpless as they were. In 1932, Democrats chose New York's governor, Franklin Delano Roosevelt, to run for President. Roosevelt seemed to respond to people's suffering. He told a friend:

“I have looked into the faces of thousands of Americans. They have the frightened look of lost children. . . . They are saying: 'We're caught in something we don't understand; perhaps this fellow can help us out.'”

A Powerful Partnership

Roosevelt came from a wealthy, well-connected family. Before starting law school, he married his cousin Eleanor Roosevelt, a niece of Theodore Roosevelt. Together, they forged a powerful partnership.

During World War I, FDR, as Roosevelt was called, served as Assistant Secretary of the Navy. Then, in the summer of 1921, he was struck with polio. The disease left his legs paralyzed.

With his wife's help, FDR struggled to rebuild his strength. The battle taught him patience and courage. After a person spends

two years just trying to wiggle his small toe, Roosevelt once joked, everything else seemed easy. In the end, he was able to walk only with the aid of heavy leg braces and crutches.

In time, Roosevelt returned to public life. In 1928, he was elected governor of New York. Then, in 1932, the Democrats nominated him to be their presidential candidate. Although they knew he would not win, the Republicans once again nominated Hoover.

Pledging a "New Deal"

Roosevelt set a new tone right from the start. He broke tradition by taking a plane to the Democratic convention to accept the nomination in person. Standing before the delegates, he declared: "I pledge myself to a new deal for the American people."

A hopeful note. FDR did not spell out what he meant by "a new deal." Still, he sounded a hopeful note. In campaign speeches, he promised to help the jobless, poor farmers, and the elderly.

Voters responded to FDR's confident manner and personal charm. On election day, Roosevelt defeated Hoover in a landslide victory. Democrats also gained seats in Congress.

Call to action. Roosevelt expressed optimism when he addressed the American people on inauguration day.

“This great nation will endure as it has endured, will revive and will prosper. So, first of all, let me assert my firm belief that the only thing we have to fear is fear itself—nameless, unreasoning, unjustified terror which paralyzes needed efforts to convert retreat into advance.”

FDR issued a call to action. "The nation asks for action and action now." Many Americans welcomed any change, especial-

---

Historical Sidelight
Background

Theodore Roosevelt was not the only President related to Franklin Delano Roosevelt. A genealogist once determined that FDR also was related to 10 other Presidents: George Washington, John Adams, James Madison, John Quincy Adams, Martin Van Buren, William Henry Harrison, Zachary Taylor, Ulysses S. Grant, Benjamin Harrison, and William Howard Taft.

Connections With Science
Background

Poliomyelitis — polio, for short — was also known as infantile paralysis, for it often struck infants and children. In 1916, a polio epidemic killed over 6,000 American children and paralyzed about 27,000 others. In 1937, at the peak of another polio epidemic, FDR announced the creation of the National Foundation for Infantile Paralysis for the research of polio. People were asked to send a dime to the White House; this became the March of Dimes. Not until the mid-1950s did Dr. Jonas Salk develop a vaccine to prevent polio.

Historical Sidelight
Background

Eleanor Roosevelt traveled widely. During her first year as First Lady, she traveled 38,000 miles; during her second year, she traveled 42,000 miles. When she gave speeches, she often took questions from the audience afterward. A listener once asked her pointedly, "Do you think your husband's illness has affected your husband's mentality?" Eleanor Roosevelt replied, "The answer is yes. Anyone who has gone through great suffering is bound to have a greater sympathy and understanding of the problems of mankind."

ly since Hoover's cautious approach had failed to end the crisis.

Expert advisers. During his campaign for the presidency, FDR had sought advice on how to fight the depression. He turned to a number of college professors who were experts on economic issues. These experts, nicknamed the ***Brain Trust,*** helped him plan new programs.

Once in office, President Roosevelt chose able advisers. Harold Ickes (IH keez), a Republican reformer from Chicago, became Secretary of the Interior. FDR named social worker Frances Perkins as Secretary of Labor. Perkins was the first woman to hold a Cabinet post.

The Hundred Days

The new President moved forward on many fronts. He urged his staff to "take a method and try it. If it fails, admit it and try another. But above all try something."

Restoring faith in banks. Roosevelt's first challenge was the nation's banking system. It was near collapse. Many banks had closed. Fearful depositors had withdrawn their savings from others. People hid their money under mattresses or buried it in their yards.

FDR knew that without sound banks, the economy could not recover. On his second day in office, he declared a "bank holiday." He closed every bank in the country for eight days. He then asked Congress to pass the Emergency Banking Relief Act. Under this act, only those banks with enough funds to meet depositors' demands could reopen. Others had to stay closed.

A week after taking office, President Roosevelt spoke to Americans by radio. He explained that under the new law "it is safer to keep your money in a reopened bank than under your mattress."

Fireside chats. The radio broadcast worked. FDR explained things so clearly,

First Woman Cabinet Member *As Secretary of Labor, Frances Perkins won the respect of labor unions with her firm support of workers' rights. Here, Perkins greets workers after touring the Carnegie Steel plant in Pittsburgh.* **Linking Past and Present** *Which current members of the President's Cabinet can you name? Are any of them women?*

said humorist Will Rogers, that even the bankers understood it. Depositors returned their money to banks, and the banking system grew stronger.

FDR gave 30 radio speeches while in office. He called them **fireside chats** because he spoke from a chair near a fireplace in the White House. Families gathered around their radios to listen. Many felt the President understood them and their problems.

A flood of legislation. The bank bill was the first of many bills FDR sent to Congress during his first three months in office. Between March 9 and June 16, 1933, Congress passed 15 major new laws. Even the President admitted he was "a bit shell-shocked"

Chapter 25 • **715**

Answer to Caption
Answers will vary; have students give names wherever possible.

 Voices of Freedom

Primary Source You might assign selection 13-1, The First Inaugural Address, on pages 227–229 of *Voices of Freedom.* In this selection, President Roosevelt lists some ways in which he felt the government could help restore the economy to health. (Enrichment/Challenging)

 Transparencies

Critical Thinking Use the transparency, The New Deal, on page F-29 of *American History Transparencies.* The cause-and-effect chart on this transparency shows the events in the depression that led to the New Deal. Teaching suggestions can be found on page F-10. (Enrichment/Average)

 CD-ROM

Presidents Access the biography of Franklin D. Roosevelt from the American Heritage® *History of the United States* CD-ROM.

Historical Sidelight
Background

Frances Perkins had begun her career as a social worker in Jane Addams's Hull House in Chicago. As head of the New York State Industrial Board, she won reduction of the work week for women in New York—from 54 to 48 hours.

At first, the AFL opposed Perkins's appointment because she had never been a union official. Her firm stand for workers' rights, however, won her the organization's respect.

Team-Teaching Suggestion
Language Arts

You might work with a language arts teacher to present a lesson about some of the literature related to Roosevelt's presidency. Some of the works from which you might read excerpts include *Eleanor and Franklin* by Joseph P. Lash; Dore Schary's play *Sunrise at Campobello,* which dramatizes Franklin D. Roosevelt's struggle against polio; and *This Is My Story* by Eleanor Roosevelt.

Connections With Mathematics
Activity

Give students the following statistics about the number of bank failures between 1928 and 1933 and have students convert them into a bar graph. Then ask them to write a paragraph stating the conclusions they can draw from the graph.

1928—499   1930—1,352   1932—1,146
1929—656   1931—2,294   1933—4,004

(Source: *Historical Statistics of the United States*)

Voices of Freedom

Primary Source You might assign selection 13-2, What Was the New Deal?, on pages 229–230 of *Voices of Freedom.* In this selection, Secretary of Labor Frances Perkins describes what the New Deal meant in the beginning. (Enrichment/Challenging)

Primary Source You might assign selection 13-3, Millard Ketchum in the CCC, on pages 230–231 of *Voices of Freedom.* This selection is from an interview with a young man in the Civilian Conservation Corps. (Enrichment/Average)

 Our Multicultural Heritage

Biography Have students read the biography, Fiorello La Guardia, New York's Reforming Mayor, on page 74 of the *Our Multicultural Heritage* booklet. (Enrichment/Average)

Milestone Have students read African Americans Recall Their Past, on page 75 of the *Our Multicultural Heritage* booklet. (Enrichment/Average)

by the ***Hundred Days,*** as this period was called.

The bills covered programs from job relief to planning for economic recovery. Together, they made up Roosevelt's ***New Deal.*** The New Deal had three main goals: relief for the unemployed, plans for recovery, and reforms to prevent another depression.

Relief for the Unemployed

In 1933, when Roosevelt took office, 13 million Americans were out of work. The President asked Congress for a variety of programs to help the jobless.

CCC. Among the earliest New Deal programs was the Civilian Conservation Corps (CCC). The CCC hired unemployed single men between the ages of 18 and 25. For $1 a day, they planted trees, built bridges, worked on flood control projects, and developed new parks. The CCC served a double purpose. It conserved natural resources, and it gave jobs to young people.

FERA. The Federal Emergency Relief Administration (FERA) gave federal money to state and local agencies. These agencies distributed the money to the unemployed.

WPA. In 1935, the Emergency Relief Appropriations Act set up the Works Progress Administration (WPA). The WPA put the jobless to work building hospitals, schools, parks, playgrounds, and airports.

The WPA also hired artists, photographers, actors, writers, and composers. Artists painted murals on public buildings. Writers collected information about American life, folklore, and traditions. WPA writers interviewed African Americans who had lived under slavery. Today, scholars still use these "slave narratives" to learn firsthand about slave life.

Critics accused the WPA of creating make-work projects that did little to benefit the nation in the long run. "People don't eat in the long run," replied a New Dealer. "They eat every day."

Programs to Promote Recovery

To bring about recovery, the President had to boost both industry and farming. He called for programs that greatly expanded the government's role in the economy.

Codes for industry. To help industry, New Dealers drew up plans to control production, stabilize prices, and keep workers on the job. A key new law was the National Industrial Recovery Act (NIRA). According to this law, each industry wrote codes, or a set of rules, for production, wages, prices, and working conditions. The NIRA tried to end price cutting and worker layoffs.

To enforce the new codes, Congress set up the National Recovery Administration (NRA). Companies that followed the NRA codes stamped a blue eagle on their products. The government encouraged people to do business only with companies displaying

NRA at Work *The blue eagle was the symbol of the National Recovery Administration. Here, Pomo Chief Little John and his great-great-grandson, Little Eagle Feather, "do their part" to support the NRA.* ***Economics*** *What was the purpose of the NRA?*

Our Multicultural Heritage
Background

During the 1930s, only about 200,000 African Americans served in the CCC. Because applications were selected by state and local relief agencies, some areas chose to omit African Americans from the program.

Many women protested the CCC and other New Deal programs because the jobs were available only to men. Married and single women felt that the government was overlooking their needs. Many married women were the sole support of their families and were as desperate for jobs as men. Single women argued that they had as much right to jobs as men did.

Connections With Local History
Activity

Workers for the WPA built hospitals, schools, parks, and airports. They also put in sidewalks and painted murals in public buildings. Like the WPA, the CCC worked on projects around the country. Have students do research to learn whether any projects in their area were completed by the WPA or CCC. Have students report on their findings, showing illustrations or photographs wherever possible.

New Deal Programs

Program	Initials	Begun	Purpose
Civilian Conservation Corps	CCC	1933	Provided jobs for young men to plant trees, build bridges and parks, and set up flood control projects
Tennessee Valley Authority	TVA	1933	Built dams to provide cheap electric power to seven southern states; set up schools and health centers
Federal Emergency Relief Administration	FERA	1933	Gave relief to unemployed and needy
Agricultural Adjustment Administration	AAA	1933	Paid farmers not to grow certain crops
National Recovery Administration	NRA	1933	Enforced codes that regulated wages, prices, and working conditions
Public Works Administration	PWA	1933	Built ports, schools, and aircraft carriers
Federal Deposit Insurance Corporation	FDIC	1933	Insured savings accounts in banks approved by the government
Rural Electrification Administration	REA	1935	Loaned money to extend electricity to rural areas
Works Progress Administration	WPA	1935	Employed men and women to build hospitals, schools, parks, and airports; employed artists, writers, and musicians
Social Security Act	SSA	1935	Set up a system of pensions for the elderly, unemployed, and people with disabilities

CHART SKILLS *Congress created dozens of new laws as part of FDR's New Deal. This chart lists 10 major programs.* • *Which programs provided work for the unemployed? Which provided financial aid?*

the NRA eagle. The NRA soon ran into trouble, however. Many companies ignored the codes. Also, small businesses felt that the codes favored the biggest firms.

Public Works Administration. The NIRA also set up the Public Works Administration (PWA). It promoted recovery by hiring workers for thousands of projects. PWA workers built the Grand Coulee Dam in Washington, public schools in Los Angeles, two aircraft carriers for the navy, and a deep-water port in Brownsville, Texas. Despite these efforts, the PWA did little to bring about recovery.

Programs for farmers. On farms, overproduction remained the main problem. Farm surpluses kept prices and farmers' incomes low.

To help farmers, the President asked Congress to pass the Agricultural Adjustment Act (AAA). Under the AAA, the government paid farmers not to grow certain crops. Roosevelt hoped that with smaller harvests, prices would rise.

The government also paid farmers to plow surplus crops under the soil and to dispose of surplus cows and pigs. Americans were outraged that crops and livestock were being destroyed when people in the cities were going hungry. Yet, the plan seemed necessary to help farmers.

Electricity for rural Americans. One New Deal program that transformed farm life was the Rural Electrification Administration (REA). The REA loaned government money to extend electric lines to rural areas.

Chapter 25 • **717**

Answers to Map Study

1. the Cumberland River   **2.** B-5
3. Possible Answer: The area had many rivers whose power could be harnessed to provide electricity.

 Student Study Guide

Section 2 Study Guide Have students use the Section 2 Study Guide on page 186 of the *Student Study Guide* to review and reinforce the content of this section. (Reteaching/Average)

The number of farms with electricity rose from 1 in 10 to 1 in 4. A farm woman recalled, "I just turned on the light and kept looking at Paw. It was the first time I'd ever seen him after dark."

Reforms for the Long Term

The third New Deal goal was to prevent another depression. During the Hundred Days, Roosevelt asked Congress to pass laws regulating the stock market and reforming the banking system. The Truth-in-Securities Act was designed to end the kind of wild speculation that led to the stock market crash.

The Banking Act of 1933 was used to set up the ***Federal Deposit Insurance Corpo-***

ration (FDIC). The FDIC insured savings accounts in banks approved by the government. If an FDIC-insured bank failed, the government would make sure depositors received their money.

Later New Deal laws strengthened government regulations. Laws regulated gas and electric companies. In 1938, a new law extended the Pure Food and Drug Act of 1906. It protected consumers by requiring manufacturers to list the ingredients of certain products. Medicines also had to undergo strict tests before they could be sold.

A Bold Experiment

Perhaps the most daring program of the Hundred Days was the ***Tennessee Valley***

MAP STUDY

The Tennessee Valley Authority helped millions of people.
1. *Besides the Tennessee River, what river was part of the TVA?*
2. *Give the letter and number of the square or squares where most of the TVA dams were located.*
3. **Understanding Causes and Effects** *Based on the map, why was the Tennessee Valley a good area in which to develop hydroelectric power?*

Tennessee Valley Authority

Major dam | Area served by TVA electric power

Cooperative Learning
Activity

Divide students into groups. Have each group choose a New Deal program and create a slogan, bumper sticker, or T-shirt emblem that could be used to show support for the program. Before beginning, show students some New Deal insignia, such as the NRA eagle depicted on page 716. Note that more than 200 songs were written about the NRA's blue eagle, with such titles as "The Blue Eagle's Flying High," "Hurray for the NRA," and "Good-bye Blue Eagle Blues." (Critics of the NRA claimed the initials stood for "National Run Around," "Nuts Running America," or "Never Roosevelt Again.")

After groups have presented their slogans or designs, discuss the functions of slogans and symbols in depression-era politics. Ask: Are slogans and symbols as important today in building support for government programs? Why or why not?

Authority (TVA). It set out to remake the Tennessee River valley. This vast region often suffered terrible floods. Because the farmland was so poor, more than half the families were on relief.

The TVA was a bold experiment in regional planning. It called for 40 dams in 7 states to control flooding. (See the map at left.) The dams also produced cheap electric power. In addition to building dams, the TVA deepened river channels for shipping. It planted new forests to conserve soil and developed fertilizers to improve farmland. It also set up schools and health centers.

The TVA sparked a furious debate. Critics argued that the government had no right to interfere in the economy of the region. Supporters replied that the TVA showed how the government could use its resources to help private enterprise.

SECTION 2 REVIEW

1. **Locate:** Tennessee River.
2. **Identify:** (a) Brain Trust, (b) Frances Perkins, (c) Hundred Days, (d) New Deal, (e) Federal Deposit Insurance Corporation, (f) Tennessee Valley Authority.
3. **Define:** fireside chat.
4. What steps did Roosevelt take to save the banks?
5. (a) What were the three main goals of the New Deal? (b) Describe one law aimed at fulfilling each goal.
6. **CRITICAL THINKING Defending a Position** FDR called for "bold, persistent experimentation." Do you think experimenting was the best way to battle the depression? Explain.

ACTIVITY **Writing to Learn**
Imagine that you are on FDR's campaign staff in 1932. Write a radio commercial telling Americans why they should support your candidate.

3
Reaction to the New Deal

FIND OUT
■ What did critics dislike about the New Deal?
■ Why did Roosevelt clash with the Supreme Court?
■ How did New Deal programs affect workers and older Americans?
■ Why was the New Deal a turning point in American history?

VOCABULARY collective bargaining, sitdown strike, deficit spending

---

The first hundred days of the New Deal encouraged a sense of hope among Americans. As noted political writer Walter Lippmann commented:

66At the end of February, we were a [group] of disorderly panic-stricken mobs and factions. In the hundred days from March to June, we became again an organized nation confident of our power to provide for our own security and control our own destiny.99

Still, the New Deal failed to end the depression. Soon, voices of protest against it could be heard across the land.

Angry Voices

From the beginning, some Americans opposed FDR and his policies. As the depression lingered, critics of the New Deal multiplied. Most wanted the government to do more. A few wanted it to do less.

Answers to Section 2 Review

1. See the map on p. 718.
2. (a) Brain Trust, p. 715, (b) Frances Perkins, p. 715, (c) Hundred Days, p. 716, (d) New Deal, p. 716, (e) Federal Deposit Insurance Corporation, p. 718, (f) Tennessee Valley Authority, p. 718
3. fireside chat, p. 715
4. Roosevelt asked Congress to pass the Emergency Banking Relief Act; he also closed all banks for eight days while the government decided which were healthy banks and should reopen and which should remain closed.
5. (a) relief for the unemployed, plans for economic recovery, and reforms to prevent another depression (b) Relief included jobs programs like the CCC, FERA, and WPA. Recovery programs included the NIRA to regulate industry, the PWA to hire workers for public works projects, and the AAA to help farmers. Reform programs included the Truth-in-Securities Act, created to end the kind of speculation that led to the stock market crash; and the Banking Act of 1933, which set up the FDIC.
6. Possible Answer: By 1932, many people were out of work, many banks and businesses had closed, and farmers were struggling. Hoover's measures had not succeeded in ending the depression, so people were ready for a change—even if it involved experimentation.

THE TATTOOED MAN

Tattooing Uncle Sam *Critics made fun of the many New Deal programs and their confusing initials. In this 1934 cartoon, Uncle Sam winces as a member of Roosevelt's Brain Trust tattoos yet another set of initials on his arm.* **Citizenship** *Identify three of the New Deal programs tattooed on Uncle Sam in this cartoon.*

Huey Long. Some critics—such as Senator Huey Long of Louisiana—had supported Roosevelt in 1932. Long soon turned on the President, however. Long, nicknamed the Kingfish, championed the poor. His motto was "Share Our Wealth." He called for heavy taxes on the rich. He promised to use that tax money to provide every family with a house, a car, and a decent annual income. Millions of people, especially the poor, cheered Long's idea. They chose to overlook his use of bribery and threats to win political power.

Francis Townsend. A California doctor, Francis Townsend, also had a plan. The sight of three elderly women picking through garbage cans had awakened his anger. The government, he said, had turned its back on older citizens.

Townsend wanted everyone over age 60 to get a pension of $200 a month. People receiving the pension would have to retire, thus freeing a job for someone else. They would also agree to spend the pension money at once to boost the economy.

Father Coughlin. Another critic of the New Deal was Charles Coughlin (KAWG lihn), a Catholic priest. Known as the radio priest, Father Coughlin spoke over the radio each week to almost 10 million listeners. He criticized Roosevelt for not taking strong action against bankers and rich investors.

Liberty League. A conservative group, the Liberty League, also attacked the New Deal. The League complained that the New Deal interfered too much with business and with people's lives. The government, they warned, was taking away basic American freedoms.

FDR and the Supreme Court

In 1935, the Supreme Court entered the debate. Roosevelt and his advisers defended the New Deal by comparing the depression to a national emergency. The government had to increase its powers, they said, just as it had during World War I. The Supreme Court disagreed.

Striking down New Deal laws. In 1935, the Supreme Court ruled that the National Industrial Recovery Act was unconstitutional. The NIRA, said the Court, gave too much power to the President and to the federal government.

A year later, the Court struck down the Agricultural Adjustment Act. Then it overturned nine other New Deal laws. To Roosevelt, the Supreme Court rulings threatened not only the New Deal but his ability to lead the nation.

FDR strikes back. Roosevelt waited until after the 1936 election to take action. He

---

had easily won reelection. He thought the results showed that Americans favored his programs.

Soon after his inauguration in January 1937, Roosevelt put forward a plan to reshape the federal courts. He called for raising the number of Justices on the Supreme Court from 9 to 15. The change would make it possible for him to appoint 6 new Justices who supported his programs.

Howls of protest. The President's move raised a loud outcry. Both supporters and critics of the New Deal accused him of trying to pack the Court with Justices who supported his views. They saw his move as a threat to the separation of powers so carefully set up by the Constitution.

For six months, the President fought for his plan. Even his allies in Congress deserted him, however. In the end, Roosevelt withdrew his proposal.

Changes on the Court. In the end, Roosevelt got the majority he wanted in a different way. One Justice who had voted against many New Deal laws changed his views. Another Justice opposed to the New Deal retired. FDR then chose a new Justice who was favorable to his programs. During his years in office, FDR had the chance to appoint nine new Justices—more than any President since George Washington.

Labor Reforms

During the New Deal, FDR pushed for programs to help workers. In 1935, Congress passed the National Labor Relations Act, or *Wagner Act.* Senator Robert Wagner, the act's sponsor, was a strong supporter of labor.

Growth of unions. The Wagner Act protected American workers from unfair management practices, such as firing a worker if he or she joined a union. It also guaranteed workers the right to collective bargaining. **Collective bargaining** is the process in which a union representing a group of workers negotiates with management for a contract. Workers had fought for this right since the late 1800s.

The Wagner Act helped union membership grow from 3 million to 9 million during the 1930s. Union membership got a further boost when John L. Lewis set up the Congress of Industrial Organizations (CIO). The CIO represented unions in whole industries, such as steel, automobiles, and textiles.

With more members, unions increased their bargaining power. They also became a powerful force in politics.

Labor struggles. Despite the Wagner Act, employers tried to stop workers from joining unions. Violence often erupted between workers and employers.

Workers then tried a new strategy. At the Goodyear Tire Factory in Akron, Ohio, workers staged a **sitdown strike.** They stopped all machines and refused to leave the factory until Goodyear recognized their union. The sitdown strike worked. Soon, workers at other factories adopted this method.

A minimum wage. Roosevelt persuaded Congress to help nonunion workers, too. The Fair Labor Standards Act of 1938 set a minimum wage of 40 cents an hour. The act also set maximum hours—44 a week—in a number of industries. At the same time, it banned children under the age of 16 from working in these industries.

History and You

Sitdown strikers in Akron took care to behave well. As one striker recalled, "We had guys patrol the plant. . . . If anybody got careless with company property . . . he was talked to. You couldn't paint a sign on the wall or anything like that." Why do you think strikers were so careful of company property?

Voices of Freedom

Primary Source You might assign selection 14-2, Evelyn Finn Organizes a Union, on pages 238–239 of *Voices of Freedom.* A seamstress recalls how she helped organize a union in her shop. (Enrichment/Challenging)

Videotapes/ Videodiscs

United States History Video Collection Use the video segment "The Second New Deal" from Volume 18, *The Great Depression and the New Deal,* to enhance students' understanding of Roosevelt's later goals and programs. Approx. running time 2:30 min.(Enrichment/Average) Vol. 18, Ch. 28

| Chapter 28 | Play |

Customized Reader

Primary Source For a description of the events of a 1936 strike against General Motors, order article VIIB-10, The Great Sit-Down Strike, from the *American History Customized Reader.* (Enrichment/Average)

Voices of Freedom

Primary Source You might assign selection 14-6, A Cotton Mill Worker Speaks, on page 244 of *Voices of Freedom.* In this selection, a 67-year-old worker tells how he feels about Roosevelt. (Enrichment/Challenging).

Connections With Civics
Background

The Supreme Court struck down 11 laws in a little more than a year. In its previous 140 years, the Court had declared only 60 laws unconstitutional.

When Roosevelt proposed changes to the federal courts, he also suggested that one new Justice be appointed for each one who was more than 70 years old.

Connections With Economics
Activity

Have students do research and create a line graph to show the date and amount of each subsequent raise in the minimum wage. Have the class examine the line graph and make some generalizations based on the statistics presented.

Linking Past and Present
Activity

Have students find out more about the Social Security system as it exists today. Encourage them to consider the following questions:

■ Have the goals of Social Security changed since 1935? How?

■ What groups of people are covered now who were not covered then?

■ What criticisms do people have of the Social Security system today?

■ When students are old enough to take advantage of Social Security, how well is it expected to provide for them?

Customized Reader

Primary Source For an insight into the desperation of the elderly during the depression, order article VIIB-8, Older Americans Seek Help During the Depression, from the *American History Customized Reader*. These letters to Eleanor Roosevelt reveal the elderly's need for government assistance. (Enrichment/Challenging)

Voices of Freedom

Primary Source You might assign selection 14-5, That Gentleman in the White House, on pages 242–243 of *Voices of Freedom*. In this selection, a businessman offers his solution to the economic problems of the time. (Enrichment/Challenging)

Student Study Guide

Section 3 Study Guide Have students use the Section 3 Study Guide on page 187 of the *Student Study Guide* to review and reinforce the content of this section. (Reteaching/Average)

ACTIVITY

Guided Instruction Encourage students to build their editorials around a specific main idea and to support their evaluations with factual details rather than further judgments about the New Deal government.

Social Security

On another front, the President sought to help the elderly. In the 1930s, the United States was the only major industrial nation that did not have a system of pensions for retired people. FDR and Secretary of Labor Frances Perkins pushed hard to gain an old age pension program.

In September 1935, Congress passed the ***Social Security Act.*** The new law had three parts. First, it set up a system of pensions for older people. Payments from employers and employees supported this system.

Second, the new act set up the nation's first system of unemployment insurance. People who lost their jobs received small payments until they found work again. The third part of the act gave states money to support dependent children and people with disabilities.

Critics condemned Social Security. Some argued that it did too little for the elderly and unemployed. Others pointed out that it did not include farm workers and the self-employed—many of them women, Mexican Americans, Asian Americans, and African Americans. Still other critics felt that Social Security was just another way for the government to meddle in people's lives.

Despite these attacks, the Social Security system survived. It has been expanded over the years. Today, it provides medical benefits to older Americans as well as pensions and unemployment insurance.

The New Deal: Good or Bad?

Before the 1930s, most Americans had little contact with the federal government. FDR's programs, however, touched almost every American. The federal government grew in size and power. It took on new jobs—from helping the needy to ensuring that the economy prospered.

Critics. Many people worried about the increased power of government. Others warned that the government spent more than it took in from taxes. This practice is called **deficit spending.** It meant a large increase in the national debt, or what the government owes.

Business leaders claimed that the New Deal was making labor unions too powerful. They also pointed out that it was not bringing economic recovery. In fact, full recovery did not come until 1941. By then, the United States was producing goods for nations fighting in World War II.

Supporters. New Deal supporters argued that the government must meet the needs of all citizens. Programs like Social Security, they said, were necessary for the public good. They believed that the government must regulate industries such as banking to prevent another depression.

In time, Americans slowly came to accept the expanded role of government. Their fears that regulation would destroy the free enterprise system faded.

SECTION 3 REVIEW

1. **Identify:** (a) Huey Long, (b) Francis Townsend, (c) Charles Coughlin, (d) Wagner Act, (e) John L. Lewis, (f) Social Security Act.
2. **Define:** (a) collective bargaining, (b) sitdown strike, (c) deficit spending.
3. Give three reasons why people criticized the New Deal.
4. (a) What Supreme Court rulings angered FDR? (b) How did the President respond to the Court's actions?
5. List three ways that the Wagner Act helped workers.
6. **CRITICAL THINKING Analyzing Information** How did the Social Security Act meet the goals of relief, recovery, and reform?

ACTIVITY Writing to Learn

Write an editorial about the way government's role changed under the New Deal. Explain whether you think the change was good or bad.

Answers to Section 3 Review

1. (a) Huey Long, p. 720, (b) Francis Townsend, p. 720, (c) Charles Coughlin, p. 720, (d) Wagner Act, p. 721, (e) John L. Lewis, p. 721, (f) Social Security Act, p. 722
2. (a) collective bargaining, p. 721, (b) sitdown strike, p. 721, (c) deficit spending, p. 722
3. Critics such as Huey Long said that the government was doing too little to help the poor; Francis Townsend felt that the government was overlooking the elderly; Father

Charles Coughlin wanted stronger action against wealthy people and banks.
4. (a) the Supreme Court rulings that the NIRA, the AAA, and nine other New Deal laws were unconstitutional (b) FDR planned to reform the Court by increasing the number of Justices from 9 to 15 and appointing 6 new Justices who supported his programs.
5. The Wagner Act protected a worker's right to join a union, protected the right to collective bargaining, and helped unions grow stronger.

6. Possible Answer: The Social Security Act brought relief to retired people, unemployed people, and dependent children. The act did not really address the goal of recovery, except in the sense that if people had money, they might spend it and help business recover. The act brought reform to a system that had no provision for retired or unemployed people.

4
Surviving the Depression

FIND OUT
- What caused the Dust Bowl?
- How did the Great Depression affect women?
- How did New Deal programs affect minorities?
- What role did movies and radio play during the depression?

VOCABULARY migrant worker

A cotton picker in Texas sat by the road as other pickers worked in nearby fields. "I picked all week and made 85 cents," the man said in a hopeless voice. "I can starve sitting down a lot easier than I can picking cotton."

Across the country, Americans struggled to survive. New Deal programs helped some. Others made ends meet as best they could.

Drought and Dust

Late in 1933, a dust storm howled through Beadle County, South Dakota. By noon, the sky was darker than night. "A wall of dirt," said a resident, "blew across the land." When the storm ended, "fences, machinery, and trees were gone, buried."

Blinding dust storms. During much of the 1930s, states from Texas to the Dakotas suffered a severe drought. The topsoil dried out. High winds carried the soil away in blinding dust storms. Much of the area of the Great Plains earned a new name—the **Dust Bowl.**

MAP STUDY

The Dust Bowl stretched across the Great Plains from Texas to North Dakota.
1. *Which states were affected by dust storms?*
2. *What was the average precipitation of the states affected by dust storms?*
3. **Evaluating Information** *Judging from this map, do you think that lack of precipitation was a cause of the Dust Bowl? Explain.*

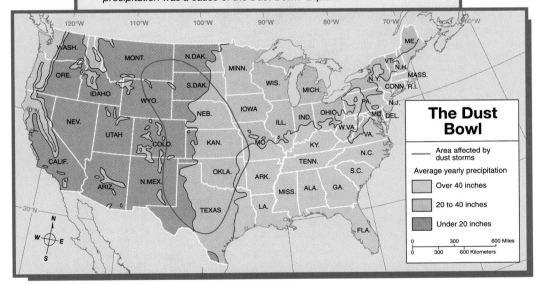

The Dust Bowl

— Area affected by dust storms

Average yearly precipitation

Over 40 inches

20 to 40 inches

Under 20 inches

0   300   600 Miles
0   300   600 Kilometers

Answers to Map Study

1. Montana, North Dakota, South Dakota, Wyoming, Nebraska, Colorado, Kansas, Iowa, Missouri, Arkansas, Oklahoma, New Mexico, Texas 2. from 20–40 inches per year to less than 20 inches per year 3. Possible Answer: Yes; lack of rain made the topsoil dry out and become light enough to be blown away.

Section 4
pp. 723–731

Bell Ringer

Write the term *black blizzard* on the chalkboard. Ask: What do you think would cause a black blizzard? How do you think it would feel to be in the middle of one?

Lesson Plan

1. **Focus** Burdened by problems, average Americans looked to the radio and movies for escape. Women and minority groups faced special problems during the depression. In this section, students focus on American society during the New Deal.
2. **Instruct** Have groups of students prepare television news programs about life during the depression. Some groups might prepare interviews with well-known people mentioned in this section; others might prepare segments about African Americans, Native Americans, Asian Americans, or Mexican Americans. The program might also include reviews of films, books, or a Federal Theater production.

Historical Sidelight
Background

In the fall of 1934, Rexford Tugwell, a member of Roosevelt's "Brain Trust," reported that the wheat crop in the area affected by the Dust Bowl was so bad that it resembled "the stubble on an old man's chin." That year, the Agricultural Adjustment Administration decided not to have excess wheat plowed back into the ground—because there was no excess wheat. Edward O'Neal of the Farm Bureau Federation predicted, "Unless something is done for the American farmer, we will have revolution in the countryside in less than 12 months."

Linking Past and Present
Activity

Parts of the Great Plains could be threatened again. The largest underground lake, called the Ogallala aquifer, which stretches from South Dakota to Texas, may be drying up. Have students research information about this vast underground lake. Have them report on what threatens this important water supply and whether scientists and government officials are doing anything to protect it.

For worksheets establishing connections between the Chapter 25 main idea, The Dust Bowl, and five other disciplines, see the *Interdisciplinary Connections* booklet. (Enrichment)

- **Arts** Woody Guthrie, A Voice for the Disadvantaged, page 146 (Average)
- **Geography** Fleeing the Dust Bowl, page 147 (Easy)
- **World** Africa's Dust Bowl, page 148 (Average)
- **Economics** The Falling Wages of Farm Workers, page 149 (Average)
- **Civics** Working for the CCC, page 150 (Challenging)

Answer to Connections

using new plows that cut deeper into the soil; planting crops that did not hold the soil in place well

ACTIVITY

Guided Instruction Encourage students to consider some of these ideas as they plan their posters: planting a "shelter belt" of trees for windbreaks, restoring soil nutrients, and contour farming.

Transparencies

Interdisciplinary Connections Use the transparency Water Cycle on page B-81 of *American History Transparencies* to understand the link between the water cycle and disasters like the Dust Bowl. Teaching suggestions, page B-27. (Enrichment/Average)

CONNECTIONS

| ARTS | SCIENCES | GEOGRAPHY | WORLD | ECONOMICS | CIVICS |

The Dust Bowl

Across the southern Plains, the storms kept coming. Day after day, the clouds of dirt rolled in. Everything in their path turned black. A vast area, from Texas to the Dakotas, earned a dreadful new nickname—the Dust Bowl.

Why did the Dust Bowl occur where and when it did? Scientists point to several possible causes.

For thousands of years, tall grasses covered the Plains. Their complex root systems held the soil in place.

Drought Stricken Area by Alexander Hogue

Then, in the early 1900s, farmers introduced a new technology on the Plains. New kinds of plows pulled by tractors cut deep into the soil and ripped out the root systems that had been in place for centuries. The wheat and other crops farmers planted did not hold the soil in place the same way the natural grasses did. By the 1930s, much of the soil had become dry and loose.

Sand-covered plow

At about the same time, the usually dry Plains became drier. Beginning in 1931, a severe drought struck the Plains. When strong winds whipped through the region, they blew the dry, loose soil away.

The winds blew off and on for 10 years. Between 1932 and 1939, an average of 50 storms a year howled across the Great Plains. The "black blizzards" lasted anywhere from an hour to three days. In 1935, one storm carried twice as much soil from the Plains as had been dug to make the Panama Canal. "This is the ultimate darkness," declared one Kansan. "So must come the end of the world."

The federal government sent aid to people in the Dust Bowl. The Soil Conservation Service taught farmers ways to conserve and protect the soil. It encouraged them to plant grasses and to prevent overgrazing of livestock. In addition, the government planted more than 18,500 miles (29,800 km) of trees to break the force of the winds. By 1936, restoring the Dust Bowl was underway.

■ What human activities helped to bring on the Dust Bowl?

ACTIVITY
Imagine that you work for the Soil Conservation Service. Make a poster urging Dust Bowl farmers to conserve and protect the soil.

Team-Teaching Suggestion
Science

You might work with a science teacher to present a lesson on ecosystems in grassland areas. Students can research plants and animals that live in grasslands and then prepare a visual presentation either for a bulletin board or in the form of a diorama. The presentation should illustrate the interdependence of plant and animal life in the grasslands.

Team-Teaching Suggestion
Art

You might work with an art teacher to present a lesson about the American Scene painters who were at the peak of their creativity during the 1930s. American Scene painters such as Thomas Hart Benton, John Stewart Curry, Edward Hopper, and Grant Wood found inspiration in views of rural and small-town life.

The dust storms, often called black blizzards, buried farmhouses and forced drivers to use headlights in daytime. People put shutters over doors and windows. Still, the dust blew in. Even food crunched when it was chewed.

Dust storms were widespread. One storm blew dust from Oklahoma to Albany, New York, and out into the Atlantic Ocean. A Kansas farmer sadly reported that he sat by his window counting the farms going by. When the dry winds came, a third of the Great Plains just blew away.

Causes of the disaster. Years of overgrazing by cattle and plowing by farmers destroyed the grasses that once held the soil in place. The drought of the 1930s and high winds did the rest. A newspaper reporter described his uncle's farm in South Dakota. "It was a farm until he plowed it. Then it blew away."

Okies and Arkies. The drought and dust storms hurt poor farmers in Oklahoma and Arkansas the hardest. Many Okies and Arkies, as they were called, packed their belongings into cars and trucks and headed west. They became **migrant workers**— people moving from one region to another in search of work. They hoped to find jobs in orchards and farms on the West Coast.

Once they reached California, Oregon, or Washington, the migrants faced a new disaster—they were not wanted. Sometimes, local citizens blocked the highways and sent the migrants away. Those who did find work were paid little. They lived in tents and cardboard shacks without any water or electricity.

Working Women

Working women faced special problems during the depression. If jobs were available, employers hired men before they would hire women. Even the federal government refused to hire a woman if her husband had a job.

Striking for Better Wages *Pecan shellers in San Antonio, Texas, made only $3 for a 54-hour work week. In 1938, they went on strike for higher wages and better working conditions. In this picture, strike leader Emma Tenayuca leads a rally.* **Daily Life** *What special problems did working women face during the depression?*

Still, millions of women earned wages in order to support themselves and their families. Educated women took jobs as secretaries, school teachers, and social workers. Other women earned a living as maids, factory workers, and seamstresses.

Some women workers struck for better pay. In San Antonio, Texas, for example, at least 80 percent of the pecan shellers were Mexican American women. When employers lowered their pay, a 22-year-old worker, Emma Tenayuca, organized the shellers and led them off the job. Tenayuca said later, "I had a basic faith in the American idea of freedom and fairness. I felt something had to be done."

An Active First Lady

Eleanor Roosevelt created a new role for herself as First Lady. Acting as the "eyes and ears" of the President, she toured the nation. She talked to the unemployed, visited coal

Chapter 25 • **725**

3. Close To close the lesson, play a Jeopardy!-like game with students. Provide key facts from the section as answers; then have students create appropriate questions.

 Lesson Planner

For a developed **Cooperative Learning** lesson plan, see the *Lesson Planner,* page 158.

Answer to Caption

Men usually were considered for a job before women; women were often expected to work for low pay.

 Customized Reader

Primary Source For a description of the Dust Bowl, order article VIIB-7, A Reporter Describes the Dust Bowl, from the *American History Customized Reader.* In this letter to Eleanor Roosevelt, reporter Lorena Hickok depicts the devastation and misery of the Dust Bowl. (Enrichment/Average)

Chapter Resources

Geography in History Duplicate and distribute the worksheet, Dust Bowlers on the Move, from Unit 8, pages 19–20, of the *Chapter Resources* binder. The worksheet traces the extent of the Dust Bowl and the routes taken by those who headed west to escape its devastation. (Enrichment/Challenging)

Critical Thinking
Drawing Conclusions

Explain that folk singer Woody Guthrie wrote many songs about what he heard and saw during the depression. Then share this stanza from "Pastures of Plenty," one of his best-known songs:

I've worked in your orchard of peaches and prunes,
Slept on the ground in the light of the moon;
On the edge of your city you've seen us and then,

We come with the dust and we go with the wind.

Based on the information in this stanza and on what they know from the text, have students discuss the following questions:
- Who is the speaker? What kind of a life has this speaker been living?
- To whom is this person speaking? Explain.
- Why have the speaker and those for whom he speaks "come with the dust"?

Historical Sidelight
Background

Eleanor Roosevelt led a sheltered, privileged childhood. As a teenager, she attended a finishing school in England; there she learned more about the world around her and grew in self-confidence. By the time of her engagement to FDR, she was teaching children at a settlement house in New York City. Her activities as her husband's "eyes and ears" began in earnest when FDR was governor of New York.

mines, and went into the homes of poor families. Back in Washington, she told the President what she had seen and heard.

Eleanor Roosevelt had her own career, as well. She wrote a newspaper column and had a radio program. As a reformer, she called on Americans to live up to the goal of equal justice for all. By speaking out on social issues, the First Lady angered some people. However, many other Americans admired her strong stands.

African Americans in the Great Depression

"The Negro was born in depression," said an African American commenting about the 1930s. "It only became official when it hit the white man." Hard times were nothing new to most African Americans, he explained grimly.

Racial prejudice. In the 1930s, black workers were the first to lose their jobs. Often, they were denied public works jobs because of their race. At relief centers, young African American men were threatened or beaten when they signed up for work. Some charities even refused to serve blacks at centers giving out food to the needy.

Eleanor Roosevelt and others close to the President tried to improve the situation of African Americans. Thousands of young black men learned a trade through the CCC, for example.

FDR's Black Cabinet. FDR reached out to African Americans. In doing so, he won their support for the Democratic party. The President invited black leaders to the White House to advise him. These unofficial advisers became known as the ***Black Cabinet.*** They included Robert C. Weaver, a Harvard-educated economist, and Mary McLeod Bethune, a well-known educator. Both held high-level jobs in the government.

Often, Roosevelt followed the advice of the Black Cabinet. However, when African American leaders pressed the President to

support an antilynching law, he refused. He feared that by doing so he would lose the support of southerners in Congress for his New Deal programs.

Demand for equal rights. Many black leaders believed that African Americans had to unite to achieve justice. They used their votes, won higher-level government jobs,

Marian Anderson at the Lincoln Memorial *In 1939, African American singer Marian Anderson was barred from performing in a private hall in Washington, D.C. Outraged, Eleanor Roosevelt arranged for Anderson to give a concert at the Lincoln Memorial. This painting shows some of the 75,000 people who gathered to hear Anderson sing.* **Citizenship** *Why do you think the First Lady set up a concert for Marian Anderson?*

and kept up pressure for equal treatment. Slowly, they made a few gains. The struggle for civil rights, however, would take many more years.

Mexican Americans Face Discrimination

By the 1930s, Mexican Americans lived and worked in cities around the country. A large number, however, were farm workers in the Southwest and West. There, they faced discrimination in education, jobs, and at the polls.

In good times, employers had encouraged Mexicans to move north and take jobs in factories or on farms. When the depression struck, many Americans wanted the government to force Mexicans out of the country. More than 400,000 Mexicans were rounded up and sent to Mexico. Some were citizens who had been born in the United States.

Mexican Americans who stayed in the United States tried to provide a good education for their children. Mexicans, however, had to attend poorly equipped "Mexican schools." Local school boards admitted that if Mexican American children were well educated, farmers would lose their supply of cheap labor.

"We Don't Serve Mexicans Here"

Many Mexican American children seldom attended school. They were too busy helping their families try to earn a living. Cesar Chavez was one such child.

From landowner to migrant worker. One day when he was six years old, Cesar helped his family pile their belongings onto a wagon. The Chavezes had lived in the North Gila Valley of Arizona for two generations. Cesar had grown up on the land his father inherited from *his* father. Now they were leaving.

From the hushed talk of his parents, Cesar learned that the bank had refused to approve loans for the Chavez family. Years later, Chavez explained: "It so happened that the president of the bank . . . wanted our land."

For two years, Cesar and his family lived in another, smaller house. Then they were forced to move again.

This time, they climbed into a secondhand car and headed west to California. There, they became migrant workers, moving from farm to farm to harvest crops. Cesar found "following the crops" a strange life. He missed his old home:

66 We had been poor, but we knew every night there was a bed *there,* and that *this* was our room. There was a kitchen. It was. . . a settled life, and we had chickens and hogs, eggs and all those things. But that all of a sudden changed. 99

Life on the road. As migrants, the family carried everything they owned in their car. They never stayed anywhere long. Once they lived under a bridge near a dry creek. In 8 years, Cesar attended 37 schools. Often, he had to miss school to work in the fields.

The growers paid low wages. Sometimes, the entire family brought in only $5 for an entire week's work. If Cesar's father went on strike for better pay, the growers forced the family to move on.

A painful encounter. Cesar suffered from the prejudice of white Americans. One day, the family stopped for coffee in a small California town. "White Trade Only," read a sign outside the restaurant. Cesar's father could read, but he did not understand the sign. He entered the restaurant. "We don't serve Mexicans here. Get out of here," snarled a young waitress.

"I'm sure for the rest of her life, she never thought of it again," Cesar later said. "But every time we thought of it, it hurt us."

Customized Reader

Primary Source For the story of an African American lawyer, order article VIIA-11, One of Arizona's First African American Lawyers, from the *American History Customized Reader.* In this selection, an African American judge in Phoenix tells of his early struggles. (Enrichment/Easy)

Our Multicultural Heritage

Biography Have students read the biography, Carlos Bulosan, Immigrant Writer, on page 73 of the *Our Multicultural Heritage* booklet. (Enrichment/Challenging)

Customized Reader

Primary Source For an interview with a Mexican American woman who survived the depression, order article VIIA-6, Mexican Americans and the Depression, from the *American History Customized Reader.* In this selection, Nico Rodriguez describes her struggles to find work and provide her children with an education. (Enrichment/Average)

Critical Thinking
Defending a Position

Remind students that the New Deal did not include any civil rights legislation. Have students respond to and defend their responses to questions such as the following:

- Should President Roosevelt have worked harder to bring civil rights legislation before Congress?
- Could he have gotten an anti-lynching law passed?
- Did he help African Americans through indirect methods?

Connections With Art
Activity

After students have read the Up Close feature about Cesar Chavez, invite them to respond to the narrative in an artistic form of their choice. Some students, for example, might want to interpret the expression "following the crops" in a poster. Others might create a painting of the restaurant that refused to serve the Chavezes. Still others may want to work on a collage or clay sculpture. Encourage students to present their finished work, or work with students to create a display.

ART GALLERY: OUR COMMON HERITAGE

TONY ORTEGA *La Reunión, 1993*

Many Mexican Americans labored as migrant workers. In this painting, Mexican American artist Tony Ortega shows a reunión—a "coming together"—of migrant workers. They are coming together not just as a work team, says Ortega, but also as a community. Ortega's use of color shows the influence of Mexican artistic styles. **United States and the World** *How did the depression affect many Mexicans living in the United States?*

As you will read in Chapter 28, Cesar Chavez went on to found a union, the United Farm Workers of America, to represent migrant workers. The union fought for higher wages and better working conditions. Chavez never forgot his early experiences:

66Some people put this out of their minds and forget it. I don't. I don't want to forget it. I don't want it to take the best of me, but...this is what happened. This is the truth, you know. History.99 ■

Linking Past and Present
Background

Chavez rose to national prominence in 1965, when workers in California voted to support striking Filipino farm workers in California vineyards. Ironically, the strike took place in the town of Delano.

Historical Sidelight
Background

In California and Texas, Mexican American farm workers of the 1930s tried to organize. Several strikes led to the creation of new unions of agricultural workers. One union boasted 10,000 members by 1934. In northern and western cities, Mexican Americans joined industrial unions, particularly in the clothing industry. Rosa Pesotta, a labor organizer for the International Ladies' Garment Workers' Union, predicted that Mexican seamstresses could become "the backbone of our union on the West Coast."

Asian Americans in the Depression

Like other minority groups, Asian Americans faced discrimination during the depression. They were often refused service at barber shops, restaurants, and other public places. White Americans resented Chinese, Japanese, and Filipino workers who competed with them for scarce jobs. Sometimes violence against Asians erupted.

The government sought to reduce the number of Asians in the United States. In the 1920s and 1930s, Congress had passed laws restricting the number of Asians who could enter the country. Then, in 1935, FDR signed the Repatriation Act. This law provided free transportation for Filipinos who agreed to return to the Philippines and not come back. Many took advantage of this offer.

Native Americans and the New Deal

In 1924, Congress had granted Indians citizenship. Still, Native Americans faced discrimination and lived in terrible poverty. FDR encouraged new policies toward Native Americans.

Reforms. In the 1930s, Congress passed a series of laws that have often been called the *Indian New Deal.* The laws gave Native American nations greater control over their own affairs.

The President chose John Collier, a long-time defender of Indian rights, to head the Bureau of Indian Affairs. He ended the government policy of breaking up Indian land holdings. In 1934, Congress passed the Indian Reorganization Act (IRA). It protected and even expanded land holdings of Indian reservations.

The government also ended its policy of destroying Native American religions. It supported the right of Indians to live according to their own traditions. Further, it strengthened Native American governments by letting reservations organize corporations and develop their own economic projects.

Jobs. To provide jobs during the depression, the government set up the Indian Emergency Conservation Work Group. It employed Native Americans in programs of soil erosion control, irrigation, and land development. In 1935, Congress launched the Indian Arts and Craft Board. By promoting the sale of Indian art, it encouraged Native Americans to create new works.

CAUSES

- Great Depression deepens
- Banking system nears collapse
- Millions of people are jobless
- Many businesses are bankrupt
- FDR becomes President

THE NEW DEAL

EFFECTS

- Congress approves programs for relief, recovery, and reform
- Supreme Court strikes down some programs
- Union membership and power increase
- Social Security and savings insurance continue to the present
- Role of government in the economy increases

Understanding Causes and Effects
President Roosevelt's New Deal included bold programs. ● *Do you think the effects of the New Deal have been mostly positive or mostly negative? Explain.*

Answer to Understanding Causes and Effects

Possible Answer: The effects are mostly positive, providing various kinds of aid; the effects that may be seen as negative relate to the power wielded by the federal government and by labor unions.

 Chapter Resources

History Through Literature To offer students one poet's inspirational view of Americans who were surviving the Great Depression, duplicate and distribute the worksheet, The People, Yes, from Unit 8, page 18, of the *Chapter Resources* binder. (Enrichment/Challenging)

 Videotapes/ Videodiscs

United States History Video Collection Use the video segment "The Legacy of the New Deal" from Volume 18, *The Great Depression and the New Deal,* to enhance students' understanding of the long-term effects of the New Deal. Approx. running time 1:40 min.(Enrichment/Average) Vol. 18, Ch. 34

Chapter 34   Play

Our Multicultural Heritage
Activity

Have students read novels that are set during the Great Depression. As they review the books for the class, encourage students to offer insights about the unique struggles that people from various cultures faced during those difficult times.

Three books by Yoshiko Uchida—*A Jar of Dreams, The Best Bad Thing,* and *Happi-*

est Endings—trace the life of Rinko, a Japanese American girl growing up in Berkeley, California, during the depression. Ask students who read these books to note the ways in which Rinko's experiences in the 1930s were similar to and different from other Americans' experiences at the same time.

Our Multicultural Heritage
Background

John Collier showed his understanding of Native American culture when he said, "The Indian by tradition was not concerned with possession, did not worry about titles or recordings, but regarded the land as a fisherman might regard the sea, as a gift of nature, to be loved and feared, to be fought and revered, and to be drawn on by all as an inexhaustible source of life and strength."

Voices of Freedom

Primary Source You might assign selection 14-3, Losing the Farm, on pages 239–241 of *Voices of Freedom*. In this selection from John Steinbeck's *Grapes of Wrath,* men representing landowners encourage poor farmers to trek west to California in search of work. (Enrichment/ Challenging)

Chapter Resources

Critical Thinking Duplicate and distribute the worksheet, Understanding Causes and Effects, from Unit 8, page 17, of the *Chapter Resources* binder. The worksheet encourages students to look for crucial relationships among key events discussed in this chapter. (Enrichment/Average)

Transparencies

Fine Art Use the transparency Edward Hopper, Nighthawks on page D-59 of *American History Transparencies*. The painting represents one great American artist's view of urban life. Teaching suggestions can be found on page D-20. (Enrichment/Challenging)

Radio and Movies Provide Escape

Americans found ways to escape the hard times of the 1930s. Among their favorite pastimes were listening to the radio and going to the movies.

"Furniture that talks." A 1930s comedian called radio "furniture that talks." Every night, millions of Americans tuned in to their favorite programs. Comedians such as George Burns and Gracie Allen made people forget their troubles for a time. Classical music programs were also popular. Radio let Americans enjoy music that they could not have heard otherwise.

With so many people out of work, daytime radio shows were popular. People listened to serials, or programs that told a story over weeks or months. These serials were called "soap operas" because they broadcast advertisements for soap companies.

Perhaps the most famous broadcast took place after dark on Halloween 1938. That night, actor Orson Welles gave a make-believe newscast based on a novel called *The War of the Worlds*. Welles grimly reported the landing of invaders from the planet Mars. People who tuned in late missed hearing that the newscast was not real. Thousands of terrified people ran into the streets and raced off in their cars, seeking ways to escape the Martian invasion.

The silver screen. In the 1930s, movie makers tried to restore people's faith in the United States. Movies told stories about happy families in comfortable neighborhoods. Child actors such as Shirley Temple and Mickey Rooney starred in hugely successful movies.

One of the most popular movies was Walt Disney's *Snow White and the Seven Dwarfs*. It was the first full-length animated film. In 1939, Judy Garland won American hearts with *The Wizard of Oz*. The movie told of a young girl's escape from a bleak life in depression Kansas to the colorful land of Oz.

730 • Chapter 25

The longest, most expensive, and most profitable movie of the 1930s was *Gone With the Wind*. It showed the Civil War in a romantic light. For more than three hours, many Americans could forget their worries as they watched the story of love and loss amid the battlefields of the South. The movie also encouraged many Americans. They had survived hard times before. They would do so again.

Images of Depression Life

Creative artists recorded images of depression life. Many writers depicted the hard times Americans faced across the country. In *The Grapes of Wrath,* John Steinbeck told the heartbreaking story of the Okies.

66Carloads, caravans, homeless and hungry. . . . They streamed over the mountains, hungry and restless— restless as ants, scurrying to find work to do . . . anything, any burden to bear, for food. 99

Black writers of the Harlem Renaissance continued to create new works. In *Uncle*

An American Classic The Grapes of Wrath *told the heartbreaking story of a family of Okies who headed west in search of a better life.* **Geography** *Why did so many farm families from Oklahoma and Arkansas head west in the 1930s?*

Portraits of Despair *During the depression, photographers captured the sufferings of the rural poor in powerful pictures. Dorothea Lange took the photographs shown here. The image at right has become a symbol of the Great Depression.* **The Arts** *Why do you think these photographs are such a powerful record of the times?*

Tom's Children, Richard Wright described racial violence against African Americans in the South.

Many painters turned to themes familiar to ordinary Americans. In huge murals, Thomas Hart Benton brought to life the history of the frontier. In *American Gothic,* a painting that has become a classic, Grant Wood portrayed an Iowa farmer and his daughter. The pair look determined enough to survive any hardship.

Photographers captured vivid images of hardship. The photographs of Dorothea Lange showed the suffering of Dust Bowl farm families. (See above.) Margaret Bourke-White photographed poor tenant farmers in the South. In their works, photographers left a lasting record of American life during the Great Depression.

Our Common Heritage
In 1931, the Rochester Philharmonic Orchestra performed Afro-American Symphony *by William Grant Still. This was the first time that a major orchestra performed a symphonic work written by an African American composer.*

SECTION 4 REVIEW

1. **Identify:** (a) Dust Bowl, (b) Eleanor Roosevelt, (c) Black Cabinet, (d) Mary McLeod Bethune, (e) Indian New Deal, (f) John Steinbeck, (g) Richard Wright, (h) Dorothea Lange.
2. **Define:** migrant worker.
3. (a) Give two causes of the dust storms of the 1930s. (b) What problems did people in the Dust Bowl face?
4. Explain how each of these people tried to improve life for others during the depression: (a) Emma Tenayuca, (b) Eleanor Roosevelt, (c) Robert C. Weaver, (d) John Collier.
5. How did Americans find an escape from the hardships of the depression?
6. **CRITICAL THINKING Understanding Causes and Effects** Why do you think Mexican Americans such as Cesar Chavez and his family suffered more discrimination during the depression than during good times?

 Writing to Learn
Imagine that you are a member of the family shown in the photograph above. Write a diary entry about what is happening in your life.

Answers to Reviewing the Main Ideas

1. The stock market crash caused people to lose confidence in the economy and helped trigger the banking crisis; furthermore, people who lost money in the crash had no capital to invest in business.

2. (a) The Bonus Army was a group of World War I veterans who went to Washington, D.C., hoping to get the promised veterans' bonus immediately, instead of in 1945. (b) No; the army moved into their camp and burned it to the ground.

3. (a) The New Deal helped the unemployed by providing relief and government jobs. (b) It helped farmers by paying them to limit production so that farm prices would rise. (c) It helped factory workers by protecting unions, setting up codes for industries, and establishing a minimum wage.

4. The TVA controlled flooding in the Tennessee Valley, and its dams produced cheap electricity for factories and homes. The TVA also deepened river channels, thereby improving shipping, and it tried to restore the environment.

5. (a) The Supreme Court ruled that some of the laws passed under the New Deal were unconstitutional. (b) Roosevelt had little support for changing the Court; both his critics and his supporters accused him of trying to pack the Court in his own favor.

6. FDR consulted with African Americans through his unofficial Black Cabinet; he supported reforms, known as the Indian New Deal, that sought to give Native Americans more control over their own affairs.

7. The government wanted to reduce the number of Asians in the United States. New laws restricted immigration from Asia, and the Repatriation Act encouraged Filipinos to leave the country.

8. (a) Radio and movies offered an escape from hard times. (b) Possible Answers: *Gone With the Wind, Snow White, The Wizard of Oz.*

Summary

● After the stock market crash of 1929, the nation sank into the longest, deepest economic depression in its history.

● Franklin D. Roosevelt's New Deal sought to provide relief for the unemployed, promote economic recovery, and enact reforms to prevent another depression.

● Some Americans criticized FDR and his policies.

● The depression brought especially hard times to drought-plagued farmers in the Dust Bowl, as well as to minority groups.

Reviewing the Main Ideas

1. How did the stock market crash help bring about the Great Depression?

2. (a) What was the Bonus Army? (b) Did they achieve their goal? Explain.

3. Describe how the New Deal helped each of the following groups: (a) the unemployed, (b) farmers, (c) factory workers.

4. How did the TVA improve conditions in the Tennessee River valley?

5. (a) Why did Roosevelt try to reshape the Supreme Court? (b) Why did he back down?

6. How did FDR try to reach out to African Americans and Native Americans?

7. How were Asian Americans treated by the government during the depression?

8. (a) Why were radio and movies so popular during the Great Depression? (b) Name two movies that enjoyed great success during the 1930s.

Thinking Critically

1. Analyzing Ideas (a) Why do you think farmers were unwilling to reduce production unless the government paid them to do so? (b) Why do you think other Americans were angry about government payments to farmers and curbs on production?

2. Linking Past and Present (a) Describe five ways in which the federal government directly affects your life today. (b) Do you think you are better off or worse off as a result? Explain.

Applying Your Skills

1. Analyzing a Quotation Review the excerpt from FDR's inauguration speech on page 714. (a) Explain what he meant. (b) Why might Americans have found his words comforting?

2. Exploring Local History Interview someone in your area who remembers the Great Depression. Prepare a list of questions before you conduct your interview. Take notes or use a tape recorder to get an oral history of life during the depression.

3. Reading a Graph Study the graph on page 710. (a) About how many Americans were unemployed in 1932? In 1934? In 1938? (b) Why do you think unemployment fell in the 1940s?

Thinking About Geography

Match the letters on the map with the following places: **1.** Tennessee Valley Authority, **2.** Dust Bowl, **3.** Oklahoma, **4.** Arkansas, **5.** California, **6.** Washington, D.C. **Interaction** How did the Tennessee Valley Authority solve the problem of flooding in the valley?

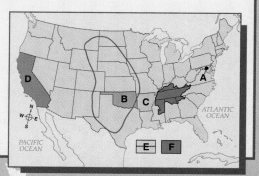

Answers to Thinking Critically

1. (a) Possible Answer: Farmers were probably afraid that if they cut back production, their earnings would drop even lower. (b) Possible Answer: They did not understand the problems of the farmers and felt it was a waste to pay farmers not to produce, especially when many people were going hungry.

2. (a) Possible Answers: The federal government collects taxes and Social Security contributions, provides national defense, guarantees college loans, sets standards for fuel consumption, makes rules about labeling on food packages, and delivers mail. (b) Answers will vary; students should explain their answers.

Answers to Applying Your Skills

1. (a) Possible Answer: FDR meant that part of the problem was in the people's state of mind. Fear was paralyzing the nation. If people could overcome their fears, the nation could move ahead to recovery. (b) Possible Answer: People were afraid. FDR's confidence and hope helped them to feel more confident and hopeful.

2. Questions for interviews will vary but should include some that explore the person's personal experience and some about general conditions or attitudes of the time.

3. (a) 24 percent; 22 percent; 19 percent (b) Possible Answer: The demand for goods increased after World War II began.

INTERDISCIPLINARY ACTIVITY

Understanding the New Deal

Form into groups to review Franklin Delano Roosevelt's New Deal. Follow the suggestions below to write, draw, or perform to show what you have learned about the New Deal. You may use the textbook, encyclopedias, atlases, or other materials in your classroom library to complete the tasks. Be able to name your sources of information when you have finished the activity.

ECONOMISTS Review the events leading to the near collapse of the banking system in the 1930s. Then find out more about the steps taken by FDR to resolve the banking crisis. Prepare a television program for third graders that explains the banking crisis and how FDR's actions ended it. Use charts and graphs to illustrate your program.

ACTORS Imagine that you are FDR. Prepare and present a series of fireside chats about the following issues: the banking crisis, unemployment, low farm prices, treatment of factory workers, treatment of minorities.

ARTISTS Learn about the work of mural artists such as Victor Arnautoff who were employed by the Works Progress Administration during the Great Depression. Then imagine that you are a WPA artist. Select a topic related to the depression, and create a mural to illustrate it.

GEOGRAPHERS Find out more about the Dust Bowl. Then write a report to submit to President Roosevelt explaining how to help the states in the Dust Bowl. Include information about how to prevent another Dust Bowl in the future.

MUSICIANS In songs such as "Roll On, Columbia," Woody Guthrie celebrated some of the achievements of the New Deal. Find out more about Woody Guthrie's songs. Then write a song of your own celebrating or criticizing a New Deal action.

★ Make an Understanding the New Deal folder and enclose an example or summary of each group's completed activity.

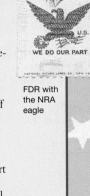

FDR with the NRA eagle

Poster for a WPA play

TVA dam builders

Chapter 25 • **733**

Answers to Thinking About Geography

1. F **2.** E **3.** B **4.** C **5.** D
6. A
Interaction: by building a string of dams along the Tennessee River

Assessment

Chapter Resources Binder For a more comprehensive evaluation of student understanding of this chapter, assign Chapter Tests A and B and/or Extra Unit Questions from Unit 8, pages 21–26 and 43–45.
Computer Test Bank You can use Chapter Tests and Extra Unit Questions to create your own tests for both testing and retesting.

Alternative Assessment

Chapter Resources Binder See the Alternative Assessment booklet in the *Social Studies Educator's Handbook* series.
Portfolio You might meet with students to choose appropriate work from the chapter for inclusion in their portfolios.

Interdisciplinary ACTIVITY

Learning Styles

The following chart indicates the activities appropriate for different learning styles.

Visual Learners
  Economists
  Artists

Auditory Learners
  Economists
  Actors
  Geographers (if reports are presented orally)
  Musicians

Kinesthetic Learners
  Economists
  Actors
  Artists

Evaluation

Economists Information on the charts and graphs must be accurate, simple, and concise, and they should be organized to show the causes and results of the banking crisis as well as FDR's reforms.
Actors Fireside chats should reflect an understanding of the issues and crises of the depression years. Delivery is as important as content and should receive equal attention. Speakers should demonstrate that they have a specific audience and purpose in mind.
Artists Murals should reflect an understanding of the era. Images should be organized around unifying themes, such as the harsh realities of unemployment, the Dust Bowl, or active movements for social reform.
Geographers Reports should contain information about the relationship between natural and human causes of the disaster. Generalizations, conclusions, and solutions for the future offered in the report should be based on accurate information and logical thinking.
Musicians Students can write both lyrics and melodies for their songs, or they can write lyrics to go with a well-known melody. Either way, the lyrics should fit the tune. If they wish, allow students to perform their songs with partners or in small groups.

733

Chapter 26   World War II (1935–1945), pp. 734–765

Lessons	Teaching Resources
1 **War Clouds Gather** **Objectives** 1. Identify the influences that shaped American foreign policy during the 1930s. 2. Describe how dictators threatened world peace. 3. Identify the causes of World War II.	**Lesson Planner** Cooperative Learning, p. 161 **Student Study Guide** Section 1 Study Guide, p. 191 **Chapter Resources Binder, Unit 8** *Skill Application* Writing a Research Paper, p. 30 *History Through Literature* The Diary of Anne Frank, p. 32
2 **The Axis Powers Advance** **Objectives** 1. Describe how the United States responded to the outbreak of World War II. 2. Identify the purpose of Lend-Lease. 3. Explain why the United States was drawn into the war.	**Lesson Planner** Cooperative Learning, p. 162 **Student Study Guide** Section 2 Study Guide, p. 192
3 **The Home Front** **Objectives** 1. Describe how Americans prepared for war. 2. Explain why women were vital to the war effort. 3. Describe how the war affected different ethnic groups in the United States.	**Lesson Planner** Cooperative Learning, p. 163 **Student Study Guide** Section 3 Study Guide, p. 193 **Our Multicultural Heritage** *Biography* Oveta Culp Hobby, Wartime Commander, p. 77 **Interdisciplinary Connections:** The Home Front ■ *Arts* Depicting the "Four Freedoms," p. 152 ▨ *Sciences* Synthetics Stake Their Claim, p. 153 ■ *Geography* Locating a Laboratory, p. 154 ▨ *World* Entertaining the Troops, p. 155 ■ *Civics* Scrap Drives and Victory Gardens, p. 156
4 **Winning the War** **Objectives** 1. Identify the problems that the Allies faced in 1942. 2. Describe how the Allies turned the tide of war. 3. Explain why the invasion of France was a turning point.	**Lesson Planner** Cooperative Learning, p. 164 **Student Study Guide** Section 4 Study Guide, p. 194 **Chapter Resources Binder, Unit 8** *Geography in History* Battle for a Pacific Island, pp. 33–34 **Our Multicultural Heritage** *Biography* Dr. Charles Drew, Blood Plasma Pioneer, p. 76
5 **Peace at Last** **Objectives** 1. Describe how the Allies planned to defeat Japan. 2. Explain why Truman dropped two atomic bombs on Japan. 3. Explain why World War II was the deadliest war in history.	**Lesson Planner** Cooperative Learning, p. 165 **Student Study Guide** Section 5 Study Guide, p. 195 **Chapter Resources Binder, Unit 8** *Critical Thinking* Recognizing Points of View, p. 31 **Our Multicultural Heritage** *Milestone* The Manhattan Project, p. 78

Chapter Manager

Multimedia Resources	Additional Resources	Chapter-Level Resources
Transparencies *Time Lines* The United States and the World, 1933–1945, p. E-25 **Videotapes/Videodiscs** *United States History Video Collection* The Coming of War, Vol. 19, Ch. 7	**Historical Outline Map Book** Aggression in Europe, p. 64	**Lesson Planner** Activity Based, pp. 43–44 **Student Study Guide** Chapter 26 Study Guide, pp. 196–197 **Chapter Resources** **Binder** **Unit 8** Vocabulary Building, p. 29 Chapter Test A, pp. 35–37 Chapter Test B, pp. 38–40 Illustration Master, p. 41 Extra Unit Questions, pp. 43–45 **English Guided Reading** Guided Reading, pp. 51–52 **Spanish Resources** **Computer Test Bank** Chapter Tests A and B Extra Unit Questions **Guided Reading** **Audiotapes** Side 10 **CD-ROM** *Time Tour* World War II (1935–1945) in Prosperity, Depression, and War
Videotapes/Videodiscs *United States History Video Collection* The War for Britain, Vol. 19, Ch. 10; From Neutrality to Lend Lease, Ch. 13; Pearl Harbor, Ch. 16	**Customized Reader** Hitler's Game in America, article VIIA-1 They Remember It Well: Memories of Pearl Harbor, article VIIB-11	
Transparencies *Interdisciplinary Connections* The Homefront, p. B-83 **Videotapes/Videodiscs** *United States History Video Collection* Americans on the Move, Ch. 25; The Internment of Japanese Americans, Ch. 31	**Voices of Freedom** Running a Norton OD Grinder, pp. 255–257 The Detention of Japanese Americans, pp. 257–259 **Customized Reader** In Basic Training for the Women's Army Corps, article VIIA-7 Childhood Memories of the Homefront in Michigan, article VIIB-6 The Heroism and Bravery of Japanese American Soldiers in World War II, article VIIIA-14 "I Don't Want to Go Back": A Japanese American's Feelings About the West Coast, article VIIA-15	
CD-ROM *Presidents* Harry S. Truman **Videotapes/Videodiscs** *United States History Video Collection* The Road to Victory, Vol. 19, Ch. 37	**Voices of Freedom** Life Aboard a United States Destroyer, pp. 259–260 Normandy on the Day After D-Day, pp. 261–262 **Customized Reader** War Hero Recounts a Battle in Germany, article VIIB-1	
Videotapes/Videodiscs *United States History Video Collection* The War in the Pacific, Vol. 19, Ch. 40; The Bomb, Ch. 43	**Voices of Freedom** A "Sheet of Sun" at Hiroshima, pp. 267–269 A Voice from the Holocaust, pp. 265–267 **Historical Outline Map Book** World War II in the Pacific, p. 66	

Lesson Planner

For a fully developed **Activity-Based** lesson plan for Chapter 26, see the *Lesson Planner*, pages 166–167.

 Chapter Resources

Vocabulary Building The Vocabulary Building worksheet for Chapter 26 from Unit 8, page 29, of the *Chapter Resources* binder can be used as a prereading activity or as a review of chapter vocabulary. (Reteaching/Easy)

 Student Study Guide

Chapter 26 Study Guide Refer students to pages 196–197 of the *Student Study Guide* for the Chapter 26 Study Guide. The study guide can be used for chapter review as well as for reteaching. (Reteaching/Average)

 Guided Reading Audiotapes

Students can use *Guided Reading Audiotapes,* Chapter 26, side 10, to hear section previews, summaries, and review questions. The tapes might benefit students who are auditory learners, students who have trouble reading, or students acquiring English. Tapes are also available in Spanish. (Enrichment/Easy)

CHAPTER **26**

World War II

(1935–1945)

CHAPTER OUTLINE
1 War Clouds Gather
2 The Axis Powers Advance
3 The Home Front
4 Winning the War
5 Peace at Last

1935 *Congress passed the first Neutrality Act. Isolationists hoped that laws such as this one would keep the nation out of war in Europe.*

1936 *President Roosevelt visited Argentina to strengthen ties with Latin America. A popular song, "Viva Roosevelt," celebrated FDR's Good Neighbor Policy.*

1940 *As World War II engulfed Europe, the United States set up a military draft. Here, the Secretary of the Navy draws draft lottery numbers.*

1934	1936	1938	1940

▲ **WORLD EVENT**
1937 Japan launches full-scale war against China

▲ **WORLD EVENT**
1939 World War II begins

734 • Chapter 26

Chapter Time Line
Activity

Most of the events on the time line focus on the United States, Germany, and Japan. Have each student choose one of the three countries and then create a concept map or a flowchart that depicts the sequence of time line events related to that country. As students work through the chapter, encourage them to add to their diagrams. At the end of the chapter, have students who have chosen the same country meet to compare and discuss their diagrams.

Students Acquiring English
Activity

Because this chapter has so many names of people, events, and battles, students learning English may benefit from the following strategy to keep them straight. List on the board the names of people, places, objects, and ideas that appear in the chapter. Have students copy the list in their journals or learning logs, leaving a few spaces blank after each item. As the names appear in their reading, instruct students to identify each one in writing under its respective name. Suggest that they use their completed lists to summarize and review chapter content.

Chapter Setting

The American reporter William Shirer visited Nuremberg, Germany, in September 1934. There, he watched a week-long rally organized by Adolf Hitler, the leader of Germany. Germans marched in endless parades. They chanted slogans praising Hitler and his Nazi party. One day, the army staged a mock battle. Shirer noted in his diary:

❝It is difficult to exaggerate the frenzy of the three hundred thousand German spectators when they saw their soldiers go into action, heard the thunder of the guns, and smelt the powder.❞

At Nuremberg, Hitler promised Germans, "We are strong and will get stronger." Shirer tried to alert Americans to the Nazi threat. Hitler meant to gobble up all of Europe, he warned. Few Americans listened.

In 1939, Hitler plunged the world into war. "We may be destroyed," he thundered, "but if we are, we shall drag the world with us—a world in flames." Only 20 years after the Paris Peace Conference ended World War I, fighting engulfed the world again. As before, Americans tried to stay out of the struggle. As before, they could not avoid becoming involved.

ACTIVITY

Imagine that you are an American during the Great Depression. Draw a cartoon showing your reaction to Shirer's warnings about trouble in Europe.

1941 On December 7, Japanese planes bombed the United States naval base at Pearl Harbor, Hawaii. The next day, Congress declared war on Japan.

1945 World War II ended with the surrender of Germany and later Japan. Americans, such as this young couple, joyfully celebrated the return of peace.

1944 On D-Day, June 6, Allied forces launched the invasion of Europe. General Dwight Eisenhower, shown here, commanded the attack against German forces.

1940	1942	1944	1946

WORLD EVENT
1940 France surrenders to the Axis powers

WORLD EVENT
1943 Soviets defeat Germans at Leningrad and Stalingrad

Chapter 26 • **735**

Bell Ringer

Have students imagine that they live in a country that used to be a world power but has lost power and is now suffering in many ways. Ask: How would you feel about a politician who promised to restore your country's former glory? What kinds of things would you expect such a person to say?

Lesson Plan

1. Focus During the 1930s, the rise of dictators in Europe led to new threats of war. Meanwhile, isolationists at home tried to keep the United States out of foreign conflicts. In this section, students focus on the conditions that enabled European dictators to gain power, the events that led to the war, and the position of the United States as war broke out.

2. Instruct Work with the class to develop a list of the causes of World War II. Then ask: Which event on the list do you think was the most important or was the immediate cause of the outbreak of war? Have students rank the remaining causes in order of importance. Lead a class discussion on what the United States, England, France, or the Soviet Union might have done to prevent the war.

3. Close To close the lesson, ask students to copy the list of causes from the chalkboard, placing them in order of importance as the class has identified them.

1
War Clouds Gather

FIND OUT
- What influences shaped American foreign policy in the 1930s?
- How did dictators threaten world peace?
- What were the causes of World War II?

VOCABULARY dictator, totalitarian state, collective farm, aggression, appeasement

After World War I, many Americans believed that the nation should never again become involved in a war. As one writer noted:

❝Humanity is not helpless. This is God's world! We can outlaw this war system just as we outlawed slavery and the saloon.❞

In the 1930s, however, war clouds again gathered. In Italy, Germany, and Japan, economic hard times helped topple democratic governments. Ambitious rulers gained power and set out to conquer neighboring lands. When other nations did not act to stop their expansion, the rulers became bolder.

Depression Diplomacy

In the United States in the 1930s, people had too many economic worries to care much about events overseas. As threats of war in Europe and Asia grew, a strong isolationist mood gripped the country.

Ensuring neutrality. Isolationists were determined to keep the United States out of any war. Isolationists in Congress pressed

for a series of **Neutrality Acts.** These laws banned arms sales or loans to countries at war. They also warned Americans not to travel on ships of countries at war. By limiting economic ties with warring nations, the United States hoped to stay out of any foreign conflict.

Cooperation with Latin America. Closer to home, the United States tried to improve relations with Latin American nations. In 1930, President Hoover rejected the Roosevelt Corollary to the Monroe Doctrine. The United States, he declared, no longer claimed the right to intervene in the affairs of Latin American nations.

When Franklin Roosevelt took office, he announced a **Good Neighbor Policy.** He withdrew American troops from Nicaragua and from Haiti. He also withdrew the Platt Amendment, which had limited the independence of Cuba. (See page 637.)

On a visit to Argentina in 1936, FDR urged close ties among the nations of the Western Hemisphere. As war clouds loomed in other parts of the world, the United States was eager to build friendly relations close to home. Roosevelt said,

❝[Outside nations seeking] to commit acts of aggression against us will find a hemisphere wholly prepared to consult together for our mutual safety and our mutual good.❞

Fascists in Italy

In Europe, the danger of war was growing. By the 1930s, dictators had won power in both Italy and Germany. A **dictator** is a ruler who has complete power over a country. These dictators exploited economic troubles and feelings of extreme nationalism to win support.

Mussolini. In 1922, Benito Mussolini seized power in Italy. Mussolini played on Italian anger about the Versailles Treaty end-

Learning Styles
Kinesthetic Learners

Kinesthetic learners may enjoy presenting a skit about President Roosevelt's visits to Latin America to promote his Good Neighbor Policy. Select a few students to write the skit based on their own research as well as that of the group. Select one student to direct the skit, and have students divide the acting and other duties among themselves on a voluntary basis. Note that this plan also lends itself to a readers theater performance.

Historical Sidelight
Background

Benito Mussolini was born in northeastern Italy in an area called the Romagna, a region famous for its independent—even revolutionary—spirit. Mussolini's mother, Rosa, was a schoolteacher and a devout Catholic. His father, Alessandro, was a blacksmith and an avowed socialist.

Benito, named after the Mexican revolutionary leader Benito Juarez, shared his father's fiery temper. By the time he was a teenager, Benito's violent behavior had landed him—as well as his father—in jail more

than once. At school, Benito was a class bully, known for his rebelliousness and his frequent, violent outbursts. However, his teachers recognized his intelligence and managed to overlook all but his most violent behavior. By the time he graduated, Benito had become an eccentric; a flamboyant figure who wore a long black scarf; an anarchist who delighted in calling attention to himself. The spirit of the Romagna had found itself a leader.

ing World War I. Many Italians felt cheated by the treaty because it did not grant Italy all the territory it wanted. Mussolini also used economic unrest and fears of a communist revolution to win support for his *Fascist party.*

Once in power, Mussolini outlawed all political parties except his own. He controlled the press and banned criticism of the government. In schools, children recited the motto "Mussolini is always right." They learned total obedience to "Il Duce" (ihl DOO chay)—the leader—as Mussolini was called.

Invading Ethiopia. In the 1930s, Mussolini used foreign conquest to distract Italians from the economic depression at home. Recalling the glory of ancient Rome, he promised to restore Italy to greatness.

As a first step to building a new Roman empire, Mussolini invaded Ethiopia in 1935. The Ethiopians fought bravely. However, their cavalry and old-fashioned rifles were no match for the tanks and airplanes of Mussolini's modern army.

Emperor Haile Selassie (HI lee suh LAS ee) of Ethiopia called on the League of Nations for help. The League responded weakly. The great powers, Britain and France, were concentrating on their own economic problems. Also, grim memories of World War I made the British and French unwilling to risk another war. Without help, Ethiopia fell to the invaders.

Rise of Nazi Germany

Like Mussolini in Italy, Adolf Hitler took advantage of German anger about the Versailles Treaty. Germans bitterly resented the treaty, which blamed their country for World War I. Hitler organized a political party—the National Socialist German Workers' Party, or *Nazis*—to help him win power.

A message of hatred. Hitler and the Nazis preached a message of racial and religious hatred. Hitler claimed that Germans be-

Two Dictators *Italy's Benito Mussolini, left, watches a parade with German leader Adolf Hitler. To further their dreams of conquest, the two dictators formed an alliance called the Rome-Berlin Axis.* **Citizenship** *What features made Mussolini's government a dictatorship?*

longed to a superior "Aryan" race. He blamed Jews for Germany's troubles. Germany had not lost the war, he said. Rather, Jews and other traitors had "stabbed Germany in the back" in 1918. The argument was false, but in troubled times, people clung to it.

Hitler was a powerful speaker and skillful leader. By the late 1920s, a growing number of Germans had accepted his ideas. When the depression struck, many Germans turned to Hitler as a strong leader with answers to their problems.

Chapter 26 • **737**

Have students draw small arrows next to the causes and list a specific effect of each one.

 Lesson Planner

For a developed **Cooperative Learning** lesson plan, see the *Lesson Planner,* page 161.

Answer to Caption

Possible Answer: In fascist Italy, there was only one political party, and all criticisms of the government were banned.

 Transparencies

Time Lines Use the transparency, The United States and the World, 1933–1945, on page E-25 of the *American History Transparencies.* This time line will help students understand the relationship between World War II and domestic issues in the United States. Teaching suggestions can be found on page E-8. (Enrichment/Average)

Critical Thinking
Analyzing Ideas

The following comments were made by Mussolini about his life and his involvement in World War II. Have students discuss the meaning of each one.

Students may participate in the activity independently or in pairs by writing their interpretations. If the comments are discussed in groups, have students designate one person to take down the group's opinion. Students with limited English proficiency might find it helpful to work in pairs with English-proficient students.

- "Invention is more useful than the truth."
- "You can usually get away with ninety-seven cents' worth of mere public clamor and three cents of solid achievement."
- "Italy will keep healthy only by fighting a war every twenty-five years."
- "If I'd been successful, not one person in Italy would have questioned my entering the war on Hitler's side. In politics there is no morality— only success or failure."

Chapter Resources

Skill Application For additional practice, duplicate and distribute the worksheet, Writing a Research Paper, from Unit 8, page 30 of the *Chapter Resources* binder. (Reteaching/Average)

Answers to Skill Lesson

1. (a) World War II (b) Pearl Harbor (c) one of the narrower topics, such as Pearl Harbor or War effort at home

2. (a) Economic troubles (b) Outlawed opposition parties; Controlled press (c) Invasion of Ethiopia; this major topic encompasses the two subtopics— League fails to help Ethiopia and Ethiopia defeated.

3. (a) introduction; it sets out the main ideas of the paper and suggests that more information is to come (b) Possible Answer: Mussolini's goal was to make Italy great again.

ACTIVITY

Guided Instruction Students will probably need several days to complete this Activity. You might have them work with partners to check their outlines in progress. Remind students that finished outlines should follow the capitalization and indentation style and the parallel phrasing illustrated in the sample.

RESEARCH SKILLS
Writing a Research Paper

In previous Skill Lessons, you learned how to collect information for a research paper. Before you begin writing, you must organize your notes and ideas.

1. **Select a topic.** Choose a topic that is narrow enough to be covered in your paper. Look at the sample topics below. (a) Which topic is the broadest? (b) Which topic is the narrowest? (c) Which topic or topics could you cover in a short paper?

2. **Prepare an outline.** An outline lets you organize information in a logical way. Study the sample outline below for a research paper on Benito Mussolini. The Roman numeral is the major topic. The letters are subtopics.

   Copy the outline into your notebook. Then complete the outline with the appropriate information. (a) What subtopic did you put under I.C? (b) What subtopics fit under II.A and II.B? (c) What major topic did you use for III? Why?

3. **Use the outline to write the paper.** Begin your paper with an introduction that sets out the main ideas of the paper. Then write the body of the paper. Be sure that each paragraph contains a topic sentence. Support topic sentences with facts. End the paper with a conclusion that summarizes the main points you have made. Read the writing sample below. (a) Is it an introduction or a conclusion? How can you tell? (b) What is the main idea of the paragraph?

ACTIVITY
Prepare an outline for a research paper on a topic related to World War II. Use your textbook and other reference materials in the classroom to help you choose your topic. Then organize your research by developing an outline.

Sample topics
Pearl Harbor
World War II
War effort at home
Benito Mussolini

Writing Sample
Benito Mussolini set out to restore Italy to greatness. With spellbinding speeches, he inspired Italians to feelings of extreme nationalism. Then he took steps to build a new Roman empire. Ethiopia was his first victim.

Sample outline
Paper topic: Benito Mussolini
  I. Conditions leading to his rise
     A. Resentment over Versailles Treaty
     B. Fear of communist revolution
     C. _____
 II. Mussolini in power
     A. _____
     B. _____
III. _____
     A. League fails to help Ethiopia
     B. _____

Controlled press
Ethiopia defeated
Economic troubles
Invasion of Ethiopia
Outlawed opposition parties

Students Acquiring English
Activity

Although SAE students will probably be able to distinguish between broad and narrow topics and between main ideas and supporting details, they will be challenged by many of the linguistic fine points related to outlining. For example, they need to understand the meaning of each topic. They must also create parallel phrasing for their outlines.

You might have students work through Skill Lesson 26 in small groups. Comments from several peers may help to clarify the thinking of SAE and English-proficient students alike.

Hitler comes to power. In 1933, Hitler became chancellor, or head, of the German government. Within two years, he ended democratic government. He crushed all rivals and created a totalitarian state. In a **totalitarian state,** a single party controls the government and every aspect of the lives of the people. Citizens must obey the government without question. Criticism of the government is not permitted.

In Nazi Germany, the government controlled the press, schools, and religion. The Nazis passed laws against Jews. Jews were deprived of their citizenship, forbidden to use public facilities, and driven out of almost every type of work.

As Nazi power grew, attacks on Jews increased. The government rounded up thousands of Jews and sent them to concentration, or prison, camps. In time, Hitler would unleash his plan to kill all the Jews in Europe. He called the plan the Final Solution. (See page 760.)

Under Hitler, Germany built up its armed forces, in violation of the Versailles Treaty. Hitler also claimed that Germany had the right to expand to the east.

The League of Nations condemned Hitler's actions. Hitler ignored the League and moved ahead with his plans. The rest of Europe will "never act," he boasted. "They'll just protest. And they will always be too late."

Our Common Heritage

In 1936, Germany hosted the Olympic Games. Hitler expected his athletes to win many medals and prove that the "Aryan" race was superior. African American track star Jesse Owens dashed Hitler's plans by winning four gold medals. When Owens returned to the United States, he was greeted as a national hero.

A Dictator in the Soviet Union

In the Soviet Union, Joseph Stalin took Hitler's boast seriously. He knew the Nazis hated communism and wanted to expand eastward. As you recall, communists under V. I. Lenin had staged a revolution in Russia in 1917. Later, they set up the Soviet Union.

Stalin had gained power after Lenin's death in 1924. To strengthen the Soviet economy, Stalin launched a series of five-year plans. His goal was to modernize Soviet industry and farming.

Like Hitler, Stalin used all the weapons of the totalitarian state. He urged the Soviet people to make superhuman efforts to produce more goods. Anyone who resisted the government faced prison or death.

In the 1930s, the government ordered peasants to hand over their land and farm animals and to join **collective farms,** or government-run farms. When farmers resisted, millions were executed or sent to labor camps.

Despite Stalin's harsh rule, the Soviet economy expanded. Steel and oil production rose. These materials, Stalin knew, would be needed to fight any German aggression. **Aggression** is any warlike act by one country against another without just cause.

Military Rulers in Japan

Japan's economy suffered severely in the Great Depression. Trade slowed as the depression spread around the world. Before long, many businesses failed. As the economic crisis worsened, many Japanese grew impatient with their democratic government.

In the early 1930s, military leaders took power in Japan. As a small island nation, Japan lacked many important resources, such as coal and oil. The new leaders believed that Japan, like Britain and France, had the right to win an overseas empire. They set out to expand into Asia.

Chapter 26 • **739**

Answers to Map Study

1. Albania 2. the Rhineland 3. Possible Answer: Yes; in 1938 and 1939, Germany had taken over Austria, then the Sudetenland, and then Czechoslovakia. Poland was the next country in line.

Attack on Manchuria. In 1931, Japanese forces seized Manchuria in northeastern China. The Japanese wanted Manchuria because it is rich in coal and iron. Japan set up a state there, which they called Manchukuo.

China called on the League of Nations for help. The League condemned Japanese aggression but did little else for the Chinese. The United States refused to recognize Manchukuo. However, it took no other action against Japan. In 1933, Japan left the League of Nations.

War against China. In 1937, Japan began an all-out war against China. Japanese

MAP STUDY

In the late 1930s, Hitler and Mussolini threatened the peace of Europe.
1. *Which European country did Italy seize in 1939?*
2. *What was the first territory taken over by Germany?*
3. **Drawing Conclusions** *Based on this map, do you think Hitler's invasion of Poland could have been predicted? Explain*

Aggression in Europe

Areas taken over by Germany by September 1, 1939	Areas taken over by Italy by September 1, 1939

0   300   600 Miles
0   300   600 Kilometers

Connections With Civics
Background

The United States protest over the invasion of Manchuria came from Secretary of State Henry L. Stimson. Stimson believed in military preparedness, but he also believed in arms limitation and in international law. His protest to the Japanese — the Stimson Doctrine — refused to acknowledge any territorial changes that resulted from conquest. The League of Nations adopted the Stimson Doctrine but did not take steps to enforce it.

Historical Sidelight
Background

As noted on page 741, by 1939 Hitler had already seized Austria and partitioned Czechoslovakia. The treaties that Hitler had signed with Britain and the Soviet Union had proved—or would soon prove—worthless. World War II was becoming inevitable — but the United States was not going to get involved. Instead, Americans were focused on New York City, where the 1939 World's Fair had opened with its trylon and perisphere, a huge three-sided needle and a globe. The fair featured a "town of tomorrow," a Japanese Shinto shrine with a replica of the Liberty Bell in diamonds and pearls, and a special show sponsored by General Motors. The prognosis for Europe was not good, but in 1939 Americans preferred to stay at home.

planes bombed Beijing, Shanghai, and other Chinese cities. Thousands of Chinese civilians were killed. On land, Japanese troops defeated Chinese armies and occupied northern and central China.

The Japanese advance into China alarmed American leaders. They felt it undermined the Open Door Policy. It also threatened the Philippines, which the United States controlled. Despite the Japanese threat, however, isolationist feeling kept the United States from taking a strong stand.

War in Europe

In the meantime, Hitler also pressed ahead with plans for conquest. In 1936, he moved troops into the Rhineland, near the border of France and Belgium. His action violated the terms of the Versailles Treaty. France and Britain protested, but they took no action. In 1938, Hitler annexed Austria, again violating the 1919 treaty.

Aggression in Czechoslovakia. Later that year, Hitler claimed the Sudetenland, the western part of Czechoslovakia. Britain and France had signed treaties to protect Czechoslovakia.

Hitler invited the leaders of Britain and France to meet with him in Munich, Germany, in September 1938. At the ***Munich Conference,*** Hitler assured the European leaders that he wanted no more territory.

Britain and France gave in to German claims in the Sudetenland. They hoped that the agreement would preserve peace in Europe. This practice of giving in to aggression in order to avoid further conflict is known as appeasement. Despite his promise not to occupy more territory, Hitler's troops gobbled up the rest of Czechoslovakia the following year.

Stalin and Hitler become allies. Britain and France realized that they must act to stop further Nazi aggression. Britain tried to form an alliance with the Soviet Union. Stalin had long opposed Hitler, but he thought Britain and France lacked the will to fight. Rejecting Britain's offer, he signed a treaty with Germany in August 1939.

In the ***Nazi-Soviet Pact,*** Hitler and Stalin agreed not to attack each other. Secretly, the two nations agreed to divide up Poland and other parts of Eastern Europe.

The agreement left Hitler free to attack Poland without fear of having to fight the Soviet Union at the same time. At dawn on September 1, 1939, German armies marched into Poland. Two days later, Britain and France declared war on Germany. "It's come at last," sighed President Roosevelt. "God help us all."

SECTION 1 REVIEW

1. **Locate:** (a) Italy, (b) Germany, (c) Soviet Union, (d) Japan, (e) Manchuria, (f) China, (g) Czechoslovakia, (h) Poland.
2. **Identify:** (a) Neutrality Acts, (b) Good Neighbor Policy, (c) Benito Mussolini, (d) Fascist party, (e) Adolf Hitler, (f) Nazis, (g) Joseph Stalin, (h) Munich Conference, (i) Nazi-Soviet Pact.
3. **Define:** (a) dictator, (b) totalitarian state, (c) collective farm, (d) aggression, (e) appeasement.
4. What were two goals of American diplomacy in the 1930s?
5. Describe one way in which each of the following countries threatened world peace in the 1930s: (a) Italy, (b) Japan, (c) Germany.
6. **CRITICAL THINKING Understanding Causes and Effects** (a) What was an immediate cause of the outbreak of war in Europe in 1939? (b) What were two long-term causes?

ACTIVITY Writing to Learn

Write a letter to the editor of an American newspaper in 1939. In it, express the reaction of an isolationist upon hearing that war had broken out in Europe.

Chapter 26 • **741**

Answers to Section 1 Review

1. See the maps on pp. 740 and 758.
2. (a) Neutrality Acts, p. 736, (b) Good Neighbor Policy, p. 736, (c) Benito Mussolini, p. 736, (d) Fascist party, p. 737, (e) Adolf Hitler, p. 737, (f) Nazis, p. 737, (g) Joseph Stalin, p. 739, (h) Munich Conference, p. 741, (i) Nazi-Soviet Pact, p. 741
3. (a) dictator, p. 736, (b) totalitarian state, p. 739, (c) collective farm, p. 739, (d) aggression, p. 739, (e) appeasement, p. 741
4. to stay out of European conflicts; to pursue a Good Neighbor Policy in Latin America
5. (a) Italy invaded and conquered Ethiopia. (b) Japan seized Manchuria and started a full-scale war against China. (c) Germany occupied the Rhineland and the Sudetenland.
6. (a) Hitler's invasion of Poland (b) Possible Answer: the economic depression; resentment over the Versailles Treaty

Bell Ringer

Have students imagine that they are British teenagers living in London in the spring of 1940. German forces are moving closer to England and there is no other country in Europe that can come to their aid. Have students freewrite for 3–5 minutes, focusing on their feelings as they consider the future.

Lesson Plan

1. Focus When World War II began in 1939, the United States remained neutral. However, after Japan bombed Pearl Harbor in 1941, the United States quickly entered the war on the side of the Allies. In this section, students learn about the early war years and the events that drew the United States into the war.

2. Instruct Divide the class into an even number of groups. Tell students to imagine that it is June 1941 and that they are advisers to President Roosevelt. Have half the groups list reasons why the United States should remain neutral and the other half list reasons why the United States should join the Allies and enter the war. Compile a master list for each position and discuss.

3. Close To close the lesson, ask: Do you think the United States would have entered the war eventually even if Japan had not bombed Pearl Harbor? Why or why not?

2
The Axis Powers Advance

FIND OUT

■ How did the United States respond to the outbreak of World War II?

■ What was the purpose of Lend-Lease?

■ Why was the United States drawn into the war?

VOCABULARY blitzkrieg

"**I** hate war," FDR had told an audience as he campaigned for the presidency in 1936. "I have passed unnumbered hours, I shall pass unnumbered hours, thinking and planning how war may be kept from this nation."

As German tanks rolled into Poland, Roosevelt sought to keep the nation out of the conflict. In the end, he had no choice. By 1941, the United States was once again at war.

A Global Battleground

Germany's invasion of Poland triggered World War II. In time, Italy, Japan, and six other nations would join Germany to form the *Axis* powers. Opposing the Axis powers were the *Allies.* Before the war was over, the Allies included Britain, France, the Soviet Union, the United States, China, and 45 other countries.

World War II was truly a global conflict. Armies fought in cities and villages around the world and on the great oceans. It was the most destructive war in human history. Many millions of people were killed. When it finally ended, cities across Europe and Asia lay in ruins.

Nazis Overrun Europe

In September 1939, German forces launched a swift, massive attack against Poland using planes and tanks. Poles resisted the German blitzkrieg, or lightning war, with old rifles and cavalry. Hopelessly outmatched, the Poles soon surrendered.

While Germany stormed in from the west, the Soviet Union seized eastern Poland. Stalin's forces also invaded Finland and later annexed Estonia, Lithuania, and Latvia. Stalin took these steps, he claimed, to strengthen Soviet defenses. He suspected that Hitler would eventually attack the Soviet Union, in spite of the Nazi-Soviet Pact.

France surrenders. In April 1940, Hitler's armies marched north and west. They smashed through Denmark and Norway. In May, they overran Holland and Belgium and pushed into France. Hitler's ally, Italy, attacked France from the south.

Britain sent troops to help France resist the assault. The British and French, however, were quickly overpowered. By May, the Germans had forced them to retreat to Dunkirk, a French port on the English Channel. There, they were trapped.

In a bold action, the British sent every available merchant ship, fishing boat, and pleasure craft across the channel to rescue the trapped soldiers. They carried 338,000 soldiers to safety in England.

Unhindered, German armies marched on to Paris, the French capital. On June 22, 1940, France surrendered.

Britain fights on alone. Britain then stood alone. The new British prime minister, Winston Churchill, warned people to prepare for what lay ahead. "I have nothing to offer," he warned, "but blood, toil, tears, and sweat." Still, he urged the British to stand firm. Even as France crumbled, he promised:

"We shall defend our island, whatever the cost may be, we shall fight

---

Connections With Language Arts
Background

The invasion of Norway in April 1940 threw the neutral country into confusion. Shortly after the invasion, Vidkun Quisling, a Norwegian Nazi, declared himself Prime Minister. He was in office for only a week, however, when the German government removed him. In 1942, the Nazis returned Quisling to office but refused to grant him any power to rule. Quisling's fellow Norwegians hated him, and after the war they tried and executed him for treason. Ever since, the word *quisling* has been a synonym for *traitor.*

Connections With Art
Activity

In the midst of World War II, some boys from Lascaux in southwestern France made a discovery in the fields one day. Finding a gap in the rocks, hidden for centuries by undergrowth, they climbed in and found a cave whose walls were covered with crude but brilliantly colored drawings!

Have interested students learn more about the drawings and prepare reports on their findings. The reports may be oral or written, drawn or painted—or made into murals, mobiles, or collages. The following information might be included:

■ the date of the discovery
■ the identity of the artist(s)
■ the date or age of the drawings
■ descriptions of the artwork, naming or showing colors and details
■ the current location of the cave pictures
■ what the pictures suggest about the kind of life the artist(s) lived

PAST

PRESENT

Christiane Amanpour
Vitez, Bosnia-Hercegovina

Reporting on War *Modern communications have made war real to people far from the field of battle. In 1940, Americans tuned in their radios to hear Edward R. Murrow, at left, report live from London during the Battle of Britain. In 1995, television reporters such as Christiane Amanpour, at right, brought the sights and sounds of the conflict in Bosnia-Herzegovina directly into American homes.* ● *How do you think modern reporting methods might affect people's attitudes toward war?*

on the beaches, we shall fight on the landing grounds, we shall fight in the fields and in the streets, we shall fight in the hills; we shall never surrender. 99

Linking Past and Present
Radar works because radio waves bounce off things that get in their way. When radio waves bounce off an airplane in the sky, a blip appears on a screen. During World War II, radar helped the British fight the Battle of Britain. Today, radar is used to guide ships, track storms, and direct air traffic.

German planes pounded London and other British cities during the **Battle of Britain.** British fighter pilots used radar, a new invention, to detect the approach of enemy planes. They then took to the air, gunning down nearly two thousand German planes. By late 1940, after months of bombing, Hitler gave up his planned invasion of Britain. Still, German armies occupied most of Europe.

American Neutrality

After Hitler invaded Poland, President Roosevelt announced that the United States would remain neutral. He realized that most Americans sympathized with the Allies but

Chapter 26 • **743**

did not want to be drawn into the fighting. In a fireside chat, he told Americans, "This nation will remain a neutral nation, but I cannot ask that every American remain neutral in thought as well."

Supplying arms to the Allies. Right after war broke out, the President tried to change the Neutrality Acts. He asked Congress to repeal the law that banned the sale of arms to warring nations. Isolationists blocked the move. In the end, FDR won a compromise. Under a "cash-and-carry" plan, the United States could sell arms to the Allies. The Allies had to pay cash for the goods and carry them away in their own ships.

By 1940, German submarines were sinking many British ships along with tons of supplies. Churchill asked the United States for ships. Roosevelt agreed to give Britain 50 old American destroyers. In exchange, Britain gave the United States 99-year leases on military bases in Newfoundland and the Caribbean.

Preparing for war. The United States took other steps to prepare for war. Congress approved greater spending for the army and navy. In September 1940, it passed a law that set up the first peacetime draft in American history.

Isolationists opposed these moves, especially aid for Britain. Many other Americans, however, felt that the United States had no choice. If Britain fell, Hitler might control the Atlantic Ocean.

A Third Term for FDR

The threat of war convinced FDR to run for a third term in 1940. His decision broke the precedent set by George Washington of serving only two terms as President.

Republicans nominated Wendell Willkie. Willkie and Roosevelt agreed on many issues. Like Roosevelt, Willkie favored sending aid to Britain. Both candidates also pledged not to send Americans into any for-

eign wars. Willkie, however, attacked Roosevelt for breaking the two-term tradition.

Even some Democrats thought that FDR should not run again. Roosevelt answered critics by quoting Abraham Lincoln's slogan in the 1864 presidential campaign: "Don't change horses in mid-stream."

Voters gave FDR a clear victory. "Safe on 3rd," declared one Roosevelt supporter on election night.

Arsenal of Democracy

By late 1940, Britain was running out of cash to buy arms. Roosevelt boldly suggested lending supplies to Britain. Isolationists were outraged. "Lending war equipment is . . . like lending chewing gum," said one senator. "You don't want it back."

Lending a "garden hose." Roosevelt answered with a different everyday comparison. Suppose your neighbor's house caught fire, he said, and you had a garden hose. You would not waste time talking about how much the hose cost, you would lend it. That reasoning helped convince many Americans to support the loans.

In March 1941, Congress passed the *Lend-Lease Act.* It allowed sales or loans of war materials to "any country whose defense the President deems vital to the defense of the United States."

To Roosevelt, the United States and Britain were defending democracy against totalitarian forces. "We must be the great arsenal of democracy," he declared. He also called on Americans to defend "Four Freedoms"—freedom of speech, freedom of worship, freedom from want, and freedom from fear.

Aid for Britain and the Soviets. Under Lend-Lease, the United States sent airplanes, tanks, guns, and ammunition to Britain. The goods were loaded onto British merchant ships. To safeguard the supplies, American warships accompanied the ships as far as Iceland.

744 • Chapter 26

Cooperative Learning
Activity

The multivolume documentary videotape series *The World at War* is available through many school media centers and video rental stores. Rent or borrow copies of several tapes in the series, and divide students into groups of four or five students each. Give each group a tape; after they view it, have group members find additional information about the events it records. Then have each group write a short introduction to its video and make a list of discussion questions. After "hosting" a video, have group members lead discussions using their questions.

Connections With the World
Background

On December 29, 1940, President Roosevelt broadcast a plea for aid to the countries that were fighting the Nazis. In what has come to be known as the "Arsenal of Democracy" speech, he warned: "If Great Britain goes down, the Axis Powers will . . . be in a position to bring enormous military and naval resources against this hemisphere. It is no exaggeration to say that all of us in the Americas would be living at the point of a gun. . . ." FDR went on to say that the danger would not go away by ignoring it. The recent history of Europe offered a sad lesson: "We know now that a nation can have peace with the Nazis only at the price of total surrender."

Making his plea for aid, FDR said, "The people of Europe who are defending themselves do not ask us to do their fighting. They ask us for the implements of war, the planes, the tanks, the guns, the freighters which will enable them to fight for their liberty and for our security. Emphatically we must get these weapons to them . . . in sufficient volume and quickly enough so that we and our children will be saved the agony and suffering of war which others have had to endure."

In June 1941, Hitler launched a surprise invasion of the Soviet Union. The German armies pushed deep into Russia. Although Roosevelt condemned Stalin's totalitarian rule, he decided to extend Lend-Lease aid to the Soviet Union. Roosevelt and Churchill agreed that defeating Hitler outweighed all else.

Goals for the postwar world. In August 1941, Roosevelt and Churchill issued the **Atlantic Charter.** It set up goals for the postwar world.

In the Atlantic Charter, the two leaders agreed to seek no territorial gain from the war. They pledged to support "the right of all peoples to choose the form of government under which they will live." The charter also called for a "permanent system of general security," such as an organization like the League of Nations.

Japan Expands in Asia

To Roosevelt, Japanese actions in Asia were as alarming as Germany's advance through Europe. After Germany defeated Holland and France in 1940, Japan prepared to seize their colonies in Southeast Asia.

(See the map on page 758.) At the same time, in September 1940, the Japanese signed an alliance with Germany and Italy.

The United States tried to stop Japanese aggression by refusing to sell oil and scrap metal to Japan. This move angered the Japanese because they badly needed these resources. "Sparks will fly before long," predicted an American diplomat.

Japanese and American officials held talks in November 1941. Japan asked the United States to lift the embargo on oil and scrap metal. The United States called on Japan to withdraw its armies from China and Southeast Asia. Neither side would compromise. As the talks limped along, Japan completed plans for a secret attack on the United States.

Disaster at Pearl Harbor

At 7:55 A.M. on Sunday, December 7, 1941, Japanese planes swept through the skies over Pearl Harbor, Hawaii. There, the American Pacific fleet rode peacefully at anchor. In less than two hours, Japanese bombs sank or seriously damaged 19 American ships, destroyed almost 200 American

Forging the Atlantic Charter
In August 1941, President Roosevelt, at left, met with Prime Minister Winston Churchill aboard a British ship off the coast of Newfoundland. The two leaders worked out the Atlantic Charter. **United States and the World** *Describe two goals set forth in the Atlantic Charter.*

Historical Sidelight
Background

From the earliest days of the war, both the Axis and the Allies used propaganda. They classified propaganda as *white, gray,* and *black.* Those using *white* propaganda made no effort to hide its source. If British planes dropped leaflets on Berlin urging people to surrender, everyone knew that the Allies had dropped them. It was obviously white propaganda. *Gray* propaganda revealed no source at all. For example, sometimes the Allies dropped small newspapers over Axis encampments. The soldiers guessed that the

Allies were the source, but because they were eager for any kind of news they usually read the newspapers anyway. *Black* propaganda was always the most creative, since it had to *seem* to come from the Axis. For example, a British broadcast to Germans might sound like a warning from the German army noting that some German planes were unsafe. Then, when the Germans denied the rumor, the news became that much more "real"—and that much more demoralizing.

Learning Styles
Visual Learners

The 1970 film *Tora! Tora! Tora!* (rated G) recounts the events leading up to the bombings at Pearl Harbor from both American and Japanese perspectives. It contains a highly acclaimed re-creation of the attack itself (in fact, the film won the Academy Award for best visual effects). You might show that segment of the film (available on videotape) to the class, allowing interested students to view and report on the film in its entirety.

Student Study Guide

Section 2 Study Guide Have students use the Section 2 Study Guide on page 192 of the *Student Study Guide* to review and reinforce the content of this section. (Reteaching/Average)

ACTIVITY

Guided Instruction Remind students that newspaper headlines condense a lot of information into a short and memorable announcement. Encourage students to use the finished headlines as a study guide for Section 2.

Pearl Harbor in Flames *The photograph at left was taken soon after the bombing of Pearl Harbor, December 7, 1941. Within hours, newspaper "extras" were on the street with the story of the Japanese sneak attack.* **United States and the World** *Why did Japan and the United States come into conflict?*

planes, and killed about 2,400 people. Fortunately for the United States, two aircraft carriers of its Pacific fleet were at sea at the time.

"A date which will live in infamy." A stunned nation sat by radios listening to the news from Pearl Harbor. The day after the bombing, a grim President Roosevelt asked Congress to declare war on Japan.

66 Yesterday, December 7, 1941—a date which will live in infamy—the United States of America was suddenly and deliberately attacked by naval and air forces of the Empire of Japan. . . . No matter how long it may take us to overcome this premeditated invasion, the American people, in their righteous might, will win through to absolute victory. 99

War is declared. Congress swiftly approved the war request. Only Representative Jeannette Rankin, who had also opposed American entry into World War I, voted against the measure. (See Connections on page 657.) Three days later, Germany and Italy declared war on the United States.

The Allies had been fighting for two years before the United States joined them in battle. Ahead lay the most difficult days of the war. In the United States, however, the shock of Pearl Harbor united people in the cause of freedom. Even isolationists backed the war effort.

SECTION 2 REVIEW

1. **Locate:** (a) Poland, (b) France, (c) Britain, (d) Dunkirk, (e) Pearl Harbor.
2. **Identify:** (a) Axis, (b) Allies, (c) Battle of Britain, (d) Lend-Lease Act, (e) Atlantic Charter.
3. **Define:** blitzkrieg.
4. What countries did Hitler conquer in 1939 and 1940?
5. How did the Lend-Lease Act help the Allies?
6. **CRITICAL THINKING Analyzing Ideas** Why do you think Roosevelt called December 7, 1941, "a date which will live in infamy"?

ACTIVITY Writing to Learn

Write a series of newspaper headlines summarizing the events in Section 2.

746 • Chapter 26

3
The Home Front

FIND OUT
- How did Americans prepare for war?
- Why were women vital to the war effort?
- How did the war affect different ethnic groups in the United States?

The bombing of Pearl Harbor plunged the United States into war. Isolationism died almost overnight as the nation mobilized all its resources to fight the enemy. As one woman recalled,

❝There was a great coming together of people, working as a team, being proud of what you were doing because you knew it was contributing something to the war effort. Everybody did their share, from the oldest gentleman on the street . . . to little children who saved things that were crucial at that time—paper, tin cans, scrap, anything that could be reused for the war.❞

Most Americans spent the war years far away from the battlefields. Yet their efforts to support and supply Allied forces were vital. Victory depended on successfully mobilizing the home front.

Mobilizing for Victory

After Pearl Harbor, millions of men and women volunteered to serve in the armed forces. Many others found work in key war industries. They produced guns, tanks, aircraft, and other supplies needed to win the war.

Training for combat. During World War II, 10 million men were drafted. Another 6 million men and women enlisted.

In 1941, the military's first task was to train forces for combat. The army, navy, and air force built bases across the country. There, recruits trained to fight in the jungles of the Pacific, the deserts of North Africa, and the towns and farmlands of Europe.

Women joined all the armed services. Women pilots logged 60 million air miles ferrying bombers from base to base, towing targets, and teaching men to fly. Although women were not allowed in combat, many served close to the front lines.

Organizing the economy. Even more than in World War I, the government controlled the economy during World War II. Government agencies set prices, negotiated with labor unions, and rationed scarce goods. The War Production Board, for example, helped factories shift from making consumer goods to making war goods. Auto makers switched from turning out cars to producing tanks and trucks.

The wartime demand for goods quickly ended the Great Depression. Unemployment fell as millions of jobs opened up in factories. Minority workers found jobs where they had been rejected in the past.

During the war, wages rose. Farmers prospered, too, when prices for farm goods doubled. Relief programs like the CCC and WPA were no longer needed, and they passed into history.

A miracle of production. A Nazi leader scoffed at early American efforts to increase production. "Americans can't build planes," he said, "only electric iceboxes and razor blades." He was wrong. During the war, Americans performed a miracle of production. FDR set staggering goals for 1942, including 60,000 planes and 8 million tons of shipping. American workers topped those goals.

Consumers suffered some shortages because industries were making war goods.

Chapter 26 • **747**

Section 3
pp. 747–752

🔔 Bell Ringer

Ask: During a time of war, what can civilians do to support the armed forces? Have the class brainstorm for suggestions. See which ones are mentioned as students read Section 3.

Lesson Plan

1. Focus Americans united behind the war effort. In this section, students examine the effects of World War II at home, as well as the contributions of women and various ethnic groups.
2. Instruct Write the following two statements on the chalkboard:
- World War II led to increased liberties and opportunities for many Americans.
- World War II led to decreased liberties and opportunities for many Americans.

Have students list facts in the text that support each generalization under the appropriate statements. Discuss the reasons some groups made advances during the war, while others faced discrimination. Ask: Why are civil liberties often restricted during wartime? Should such restrictions be allowed?
3. Close To close the lesson, play a Jeopardy!-like game with students. Divide the class into three teams and give each team an identical list of key facts from Section 3. Have the teams compete to create a complete set of appropriate, correct questions.

Team-Teaching Suggestion
History

Contact a recruiting officer or a representative from a veterans' organization to help you teach a lesson on women in the military during World War II. Ask the guest speaker to compile a composite picture of the accomplishments of the women who enlisted.

Have the speaker explain the terms *WACS, WAVES, WASPS,* and *SPAR,* acronyms used by the four branches of the military.

Invite the speaker to describe what life was like in boot camp and what the women learned to help them cope with wartime casualties and shortages. Encourage the speaker to use anecdotes to relay the fun times as well as the times of pain—and times when the work that women did meant life or death to Allied efforts. Be sure to allow 5 or 10 minutes at the end of class for questions.

After February 1942, no new cars were made. Tires were scarce because most new tires were used on military vehicles. If people asked for scarce items, they heard the reply, "Don't you know there's a war on?"

New Roles for Women

"If you can drive a car," the government told American women, "you can run a machine." Newspapers and magazines echoed this call to American women to work for victory. "Why do we need women workers?" asked a radio announcer. The answer: "You can't build ships, planes, and guns without them."

During World War II, women responded to the urgent need for their labor. More than 6 million women entered the work force. They replaced men who joined the armed services. Many women worked in offices. Millions more kept the nation's factories operating around the clock. Some welded, ran huge cranes, and tended blast furnaces. Others became bus drivers, police officers, and gas station attendants.

Better pay. Because women were needed in industry, they were able to win better pay and working conditions. The government agreed that women and men should get the same pay for the same job. Many employers, however, found ways to avoid equal pay.

The war changed fashions for women. Instead of wearing skirts, many women dressed in trousers. On the job, they wore overalls and tied scarves around their hair.

History and You
Under World War II gasoline rationing, the average person was entitled to 3 gallons a week. How many gallons of gas does your family use each week?

Growing confidence. More important, war work gave many women a new view of themselves. One woman noted how her confidence increased:

> I never could handle the simplest can openers, or drive a nail without getting hurt, and now I put in half my nights armed with hammers and wrenches handling the insides of giant machines.

African Americans Seek Social Change

When the war began, African Americans rallied to their nation's cause. The war helped end some of the worst discrimination against African Americans. Still, the struggle for equality was not easy.

Plans for a march. As industry geared up for war, factories replaced "No Help Wanted" signs with "Help Wanted, White" signs. Discrimination angered African Americans. In 1941, A. Philip Randolph, head of the Brotherhood of Sleeping Car Porters, called for a protest march on Washington. The government, he said, "will never give the Negro justice until they see masses—ten, twenty, fifty thousand Negroes on the White House lawn."

Government officials worried that such a march would feed Hitler's propaganda machine. "What will Berlin say?" they asked. After meeting with Randolph, FDR ordered employers doing business with the government to end discrimination in hiring. As a result, the employment of skilled black craftsworkers doubled during the war.

Segregation in the military. FDR refused, however, to end racial segregation in the military. Nearly a million African Americans enlisted or were drafted. They had to serve in all-black units commanded by white officers.

Despite such shabby treatment, blacks served heroically. One all-black air force

---

Connections With Economics
Background

On the home front, rationing—the distribution of scarce goods—made life difficult. Because the troops received supplies first, many goods were hard to get. To make sure that everyone had an equal share, families were issued ration books of coupons to buy such scarce items as gasoline, meat, sugar, and milk. When the coupons were gone, so was the chance of buying these goods until new ration books arrived the next month.

Cotton, wool, tea, rubber, and coffee were also scarce—even with ration books. Instead of sugar, people used honey, molasses, or corn syrup. Lard tinted with vegetable dye substituted for butter. Furthermore, canned goods nearly disappeared because the troops needed all the metal that was available.

Ration books became so much a part of life that even small children knew their value. The tale is told of a minister who read a kindergarten class the story of Noah. Later, he had the class draw a scene from the story, showing Noah taking only his most valuable goods onto the crowded ark. When their pictures were finished, every child had drawn Noah clutching a ration book in his hand!

Our Multicultural Heritage
Activity

Have groups of students research chosen African American units and the honors they acquired, either while still segregated or after the desegregation process (initiated in 1944). Each group member must contribute to the research, and all material must be worked into the final report. Encourage groups to make creative presentations—videotapes, for example, or dramatic readings or plays.

CONNECTIONS

ARTS SCIENCES GEOGRAPHY WORLD **ECONOMICS** CIVICS

Rosie the Riveter

"Do your part, free a man for service." Slogans like this one urged women to enter the labor force during World War II.

By 1945, six million American women had answered the call. Three and a half million women worked on assembly lines in war industries—mainly in munitions factories, shipyards, and aircraft assembly plants.

Building an airplane

Rosie the Riveter button

To symbolize this new American worker, a pair of songwriters wrote "Rosie the Riveter." "She's making history working for victory," went the refrain. Popular artist Norman Rockwell painted "Rosie" for a magazine cover. The picture showed a strong, independent woman who could do any job a man could do—and was proud of it.

Many of the women who joined the war effort had never worked outside the home before. Once on the job, however, they quickly learned to drive rivets, weld, and operate lathes. Before long, women were doing most any job that needed to be done.

Factory work had its drawbacks. Many male workers resented the presence of women, and they teased and even insulted them. Women workers often received less pay than men for the same work. It was also hard for women to be promoted. As one riveter reported, "Managers were determined that no woman would ever become an A-mechanic or an A-riveter."

Women with children faced a special problem—finding good child care. The federal government helped out by building and operating some 2,800 child-care centers. The centers, however, had space for only about 10 percent of eligible children.

Despite the problems, a 1944 study by the Department of Labor showed that 80 percent of female war workers wanted to keep their jobs after the war. Said one machinist: "For me, defense work was the beginning of my emancipation as a woman. For the first time in my life I found out that I could do something with my hands besides bake a pie."

■ How did women workers contribute to the war effort?

ACTIVITY Imagine that you are a woman factory worker during World War II. Design a T-shirt celebrating your contributions to the war effort.

Interdisciplinary CONNECTIONS

For worksheets establishing connections between the Chapter 26 main idea, The Home Front, and five other disciplines, see the *Interdisciplinary Connections* booklet. (Enrichment)
- **Arts** Depicting the "Four Freedoms," page 152 (Easy)
- **Sciences** Synthetics Stake Their Claim, page 153 (Challenging)
- **Geography** Locating a Laboratory, page 154 (Challenging)
- **World** Entertaining the Troops, page 155 (Average)
- **Civics** Scrap Drives and Victory Gardens, page 156 (Average)

Answer to Connections

Women moved from the home to the factory in astonishing numbers. In factories, women worked on assembly lines and operated machinery. Their work helped to achieve record production in munitions factories, shipyards, and aircraft assembly plants.

ACTIVITY

Guided Instruction Encourage students *not* to use the "Rosie the Riveter" design in their T-shirts but to capture the spirit of achievement and independence felt by women factory workers of the era. T-shirt designs need not include slogans but should be attractive and upbeat. Interested students may want to transfer their design to a T-shirt, using any of the variety of fabric paints available in craft stores.

Team-Teaching Suggestion
Language Arts

You might work with a language arts teacher to present a lesson about words and expressions that were popular with women workers and other Americans during World War II. You might distribute lists such as the following and discuss with students the meaning of each word: *bebop, blitz, carpool, crash-land, flak, freebie, gobbledygook, gremlin, jeep, on-the-job training, radar, walkie-talkie.*

Team-Teaching Suggestion
Music

You might work with a music teacher to present a lesson about the big band era, whose music was so much a part of both civilian and military life. Offer examples of the music of several of the swing bandleaders of the day, such as Tommy Dorsey, Duke Ellington, Benny Goodman, Harry James, Glenn Miller (who led the Glenn Miller Army Air Force Band and disappeared in a 1944 plane crash), and Artie Shaw. As students listen to the music, encourage them to comment on ways in which this music, now half a century old, may have influenced the development of the current music with which they are more familiar.

Winning Their Wings *In March 1942, the first class of African American pilots graduated from the U.S. Army Air Corps flying school. This picture shows members of the class with one of their instructors.* **Science and Technology** *Why were pilots very important during World War II?*

squadron came to be known as the Black Eagles because of their success. By the end of the war, the Eagles had destroyed or damaged about 400 enemy aircraft. The courage of black fighting units finally convinced President Truman to end segregation in the armed forces in 1948.

Racial tension. In many cities, racial tension grew during the war. Thousands of Americans—blacks and whites—moved to cities to work in industry. Competition for scarce housing led to angry incidents and even violence. In 1943, race riots broke out in Detroit, New York, and other American cities.

Other Ethnic Groups in the War

People from every ethnic and racial group in the nation contributed to the war effort. Many men and women in the armed

forces were recent immigrants or the children of immigrants.

Native Americans. Native Americans supplied the highest proportion of servicemen of any ethnic group. More than one out of three able-bodied Native American men were in uniform. Navajo soldiers in the Pacific made an unusual contribution. They used their own language as a code for sending vital messages. Although the Japanese intercepted the messages, they could not understand these Navajo "code-talkers."

Hispanics. Thousands of Puerto Ricans and Mexican Americans served in the armed forces during the war. They often fought in units made up of Hispanics, or Spanish-speaking Americans. Hispanics won many awards for bravery, including 17 Congressional Medals of Honor. A Marine Corps private, Guy Gabaldon, received a Silver Star for capturing 1,000 Japanese.

In spite of their contribution to the war effort, Mexican Americans still faced racial prejudice. During the war, young Mexican Americans in Los Angeles adopted a new fashion, known as "zoot" suits. In June 1943, white sailors on leave from their ships attacked a group of young men in zoot suits. Newspapers blamed the violence on the Mexican Americans. Eleanor Roosevelt disagreed. In her newspaper column, she noted that the riots were the result of "longstanding discrimination against the Mexicans in the Southwest."

Relocation of Japanese Americans

The war brought suffering to many Japanese Americans. Most Japanese Americans lived on the West Coast or in Hawaii. Many of those on the West Coast were successful farmers and business people. For years, they had faced prejudice, in part because of their success.

After Pearl Harbor, many people on the West Coast questioned the loyalty of Japanese Americans. Japanese Americans, they

Our Multicultural Heritage
Background

The concept of Navajo code-talkers came from the son of a Navajo missionary. He knew that not even the Japanese, who were expert code-breakers, could decipher Navajo.

For words that were not too complex, the code-talkers found Navajo words to associate with these military terms. For example, the word for *observation plane* became *ne-as-jah*, the Navajo word for "owl"; *submarine* became *besh-lo*, Navajo for "iron fish." For proper nouns that did not suggest specific words, the code-talkers made up a system based on the alphabet. For the name of the city Saipan, for example, they sent out the following:

dsibeh —	**S**heep
wol-la-chee —	**A**nt
tkin —	**I**ce
bi-sodih —	**P**ig
wol-la-chee —	**A**nt
nesh-chee —	**N**ut

"Were it not for the Navajo code talkers," said one marine, "we never would have taken Iwo Jima."

Historical Sidelight
Background

Fear of Japanese Americans caused a failure to make an important distinction among the generations. The *Issei* were Japanese Americans who had been born in Japan; the *Nisei* were their American-born children. (A third generation, the *Sansei*, was just beginning to appear at the war's start.)

said, might act as spies and help Japan invade the United States. No evidence of disloyalty existed. Yet the President agreed to move Japanese Americans to inland camps set up by the Wartime Relocation Agency (WRA). About 120,000 Japanese Americans were forced to sell their homes and businesses at great loss.

In WRA camps, Japanese Americans lived in crowded barracks behind barbed wire. Most were American citizens. They could not understand why they were singled out for such treatment. German Americans and Italian Americans were not sent to camps. Even Japanese Americans in Hawaii were not moved to camps.

In 1944, the Supreme Court ruled that the camps were a necessary wartime measure. Only after the Allies were certain of victory were Japanese Americans allowed to return to their homes.

Memories of a Bitter Time

"On the evening of December 7, 1941, my father was at a wedding. He was dressed in a tuxedo," recalled Peter Ota, a Japanese American. At the time, Ota was a boy of 15. His father owned a successful fruit and vegetable business in Los Angeles.

When the reception ended, FBI agents rounded up many of the guests, including Peter's father. The world suddenly changed for Peter and his family. After days of waiting, they heard that Mr. Ota was in jail.

❝When we found out, my mother, my sister, and myself went to [the] jail. I can still remember waiting in the lobby. When my father walked through the door, my mother was so [ashamed]. She didn't say anything. She cried. He was in prisoner's clothing, with a denim jacket and a number on the back.❞

Breakup of a family. Mr. Ota was sent to a WRA camp in Montana. It was one of 10 camps the government had set up for Japanese Americans. The shame tore into Mrs. Ota. She became ill and went to the hospital with tuberculosis. She died a short time afterward.

Peter and his 12-year-old sister were alone. Then, in April 1942, they were taken to a holding center at the Santa Anita racetrack in California.

❝At the time, we didn't know where we were going, how long we'd be gone. We didn't know what to take. A toothbrush, toilet supplies, some clothes. Only what you could carry. . . . My sister and I were fortunate enough to stay in a barracks. The people in the stables had to live with the stench. Everything was communal. We had absolutely no privacy.❞

In September, the children and their father were reunited. It was a happy yet sad moment. The children were glad to see their father. They were sad, however, because the outgoing, successful businessman they remembered had been replaced by a tired, resigned man.

Life in camp. The Otas were sent to a WRA camp in Colorado. For days, their train crawled eastward with its shades drawn. The new camp sat in a barren wasteland surrounded by barbed wire and watchtowers. Armed guards patrolled the area.

The family lived in a single room in a barracks building. The room contained a potbellied stove, three cots, and a few blankets. The children attended school. "One of our basic subjects was American history," said Peter. "They talked about freedom all the time."

Peter's sister lived in the camp until the war ended. His father was moved from camp to camp. Like more than 30,000 other young Japanese American men, Peter

---

Forced From Their Homes
"Herd 'em up, pack 'em off," recommended one newspaper columnist as the proper treatment for Japanese Americans. Here, troops move the Kitamoto family from their home in the state of Washington. **Citizenship** What reasons did the government give for forcing American citizens out of their homes and into camps?

eventually served in the armed forces. He spent his leaves visiting his father and sister in the camps.

Postwar years. After the war, the Otas returned to Los Angeles. Peter married and had a family. His daughter became a lawyer. Years later, she joined a group that worked to win a government apology for Japanese Americans.

Peter's father, however, never recovered from his years in the camps. Forced to sell his business, he lived the rest of his life in poverty and died a broken man. ■

Loyal Service and a Delayed Apology

Even though they and their families were treated unfairly, thousands of Japanese American men served in the armed forces. Most were put in segregated units and sent to fight in Europe. There, they won many honors for bravery. The 442nd Nisei Regimental Combat Team became the most highly decorated military unit in United States history.

Years later, Americans began to recognize the injustice that had been done to Japanese Americans. In 1988, Congress reviewed the government's wartime policy toward Japanese Americans. Lawmakers ad-

mitted that they could not right the wrong that had been done. They did, however, vote to apologize to Japanese Americans who had been driven from their homes in World War II. They also approved a payment of $20,000 to every survivor of the camps.

SECTION 3 REVIEW

1. List two ways that Americans prepared for war.
2. Describe three ways that the war changed women's lives.
3. (a) Why did A. Philip Randolph call for a march on Washington? (b) How did FDR deal with African American demands for equality?
4. Explain one way in which the war affected each of these groups: (a) Native Americans, (b) Hispanics.
5. **CRITICAL THINKING Drawing Conclusions** Why do you think Japanese Americans were the only Americans moved to WRA camps?

ACTIVITY Writing to Learn
List four ways that the outbreak of war affected the American economy.

4

Winning the War

FIND OUT

■ What problems did the Allies face in 1942?

■ How did the Allies turn the tide of war?

■ Why was the invasion of France a turning point?

When British Prime Minister Winston Churchill heard about the attack on Pearl Harbor, he rejoiced. "We have won the war," he remarked. Churchill felt sure that the United States would lead the Allies to victory.

Despite Churchill's optimism, Allied prospects seemed grim in December 1941. Hitler's armies occupied most of Europe and much of North Africa. Japan was advancing across Asia and the Pacific. As 1942 began, the outlook grew even more bleak.

A Time of Peril

The Allied leaders had to cooperate if they were to succeed against the Axis powers. Roosevelt, Churchill, and Stalin met twice during the war to discuss how to achieve their goals.

Even before Pearl Harbor, American and British planners agreed that the Allies must defeat Germany and Italy first. Then they would send their combined forces to fight Japan.

In early 1942, however, the Germans seemed unbeatable. They held lands from Norway to Greece. German armies were closing in on Moscow, Leningrad, and Stalingrad in the Soviet Union. If they were not stopped, they would gain control of Soviet oil fields and farmlands.

Soviet resistance. The Soviets resisted fiercely even as they retreated. They burned crops and destroyed farm equipment to keep them out of the hands of the advancing Germans. In Leningrad and elsewhere, people suffered terrible hardships. More than one million Russian men, women, and children died during the 900-day siege of Leningrad.

Japanese advances. At the same time, Japanese forces were on the move in the Pacific. After Pearl Harbor, they seized Guam, Wake Island, Hong Kong, and Singapore. (See the map on page 758.) General Douglas MacArthur, commander of United States forces in the Pacific, faced a difficult task. With few troops, he had to defend a huge area.

MacArthur led the defense of the Philippines. American and Filipino troops fought bravely against enormous odds. In the end, MacArthur was forced to withdraw. "I shall return," he vowed. A Filipino described the defeat in these words:

66Besieged on land and blockaded
    by sea,
We have done all that human
    endurance can bear. . . .
Our defeat is our victory.99

The Japanese pressed on. They captured Malaya, Burma, and the Dutch East Indies.

The Tide Turns

By mid-1942, the Allies had suffered through the worst days of the war. German submarines were sinking ships faster than the Allies could replace them. Yet despite the Axis successes, the Allies began to turn the tide.

Victories at sea. In June 1942, at the *Battle of Midway,* American planes sank four Japanese aircraft carriers. The battle severely hampered the Japanese offensive. It also kept Japan from attacking Hawaii again.

Bell Ringer

Ask students to imagine that they are Winston Churchill. Have students brainstorm and list on the chalkboard some of the things Churchill might now be able to accomplish with American help. Have one volunteer copy the list. At the end of the section, the class can compare the list with Allied progress made through the spring of 1945.

Lesson Plan

1. Focus After initial defeats, the Allies were able to turn the tide of the war. By 1944, they had launched a successful invasion of France and began pushing toward Germany. In this section, students learn about further efforts to defeat the Axis forces.

2. Instruct Inform students that radio and newspaper reporters landed in Normandy on D-Day along with the fighting forces. Have small groups of students prepare radio broadcasts for American listeners describing the invasion or other Allied campaigns discussed in this section. If possible, you might give groups time to do additional research.

3. Close To close the lesson, list the following battles on the board: (a) Midway and Guadalcanal (b) El Alamein and Tunisia (c) Stalingrad. Have students explain why each was a turning point in the war.

Connections With Geography
Background

The siege of Leningrad began in September 1941. At first, the Germans moved quickly. As winter neared, however, their attacks slowed. In fact, October snows heralded a winter such as even the Russians had seldom seen. One marine wrote that "the winter of 1941–1942 was one of the most bitter on record. The temperatures averaged nine degrees above zero in December, and four degrees below zero in January. Every day, icy winds howled

out of the north and swept the city. First the people burned up all their kerosene. Next the coal ran out. Then they burned furniture, park benches, porch steps, anything they could find. Finally there was nothing left to burn."

Many of the people of Leningrad survived that winter and two more. At Stalingrad, the story was the same—the Russian winter stopped the Nazis in their tracks.

Learning Styles
Visual/Auditory Learners

Have students find out more about resistance movements. Visually oriented students might research the underground movement in a single country and then present what they have learned in videotapes, skits, collages, or picture stories. Students who learn best in the auditory mode might listen to recorded novels and books of nonfiction about resistance movements. Have them make audiotapes of their own that include short passages from the tapes they have heard.

753

Midway *The Battle of Midway was a new kind of naval battle. American and Japanese ships never engaged each other in action. Instead, the battle was fought entirely from the air. In this painting, attacking Japanese planes are shot down by American anti-aircraft fire.* **Geography** *Why was victory at Midway important?*

In August, United States Marines landed on Guadalcanal, in the Solomon Islands. In a long, hard-fought battle, the marines won control of the island. It became a base from which to counterattack.

Victories in North Africa. British and American forces began to push back the Germans in North Africa. In October 1942, the British won an important victory at El Alamein in Egypt. German forces under General Erwin Rommel were driven west into Tunisia.

Meanwhile, American troops landed in North Africa. Under the command of General Dwight D. Eisenhower, they occupied Morocco and Algeria. The Allied armies trapped Rommel's forces in Tunisia. In May 1943, his army had to surrender.

Victories in Italy. From bases in North Africa, the Allies organized the invasion of Italy. They used paratroopers, or airborne troops, and soldiers brought by sea to capture Sicily. In early September 1943, the Allies crossed from Sicily to the mainland of Italy.

By then, the Italians had overthrown Mussolini. The new Italian government sided with the Allies. The Germans, however, still occupied much of the country. In a series of bloody battles, the Allies slowly fought their way up the Italian peninsula. On June 4, 1944, Allied troops marched into Rome. It was the first European capital to be freed from Nazi control.

Victories on the Russian front. Despite the massive German assault on the Soviet front, the Russians held their ground. In 1943, the Soviet army pushed the Germans back from Leningrad. At Stalingrad, after months of fierce house-to-house fighting, Soviet soldiers forced the German army to surrender. Slowly, the Soviet army pushed the Germans westward through Eastern Europe.

Opening a Second Front

Soon after Hitler had invaded the Soviet Union in 1941, Stalin called on the Allies to open a second front, or area of fighting. He wanted them to send armies across the Eng-

754 • Chapter 26

Connections With Art
Background

During the war, many Hollywood stars who had not enlisted or been drafted traveled overseas to perform for the troops and boost morale. Others traveled around the country to meet soldiers in training or on leave or to promote the sale of war bonds.

A variety of morale-boosting films came out during this era. Some directors assumed that people were tired of the war and wanted to be entertained. The "service comedies" made by the team of Bud Abbott and Lou

Costello—such as *Buck Privates, In the Navy,* and *Keep 'Em Flying*—remain classics today. Troops and civilians alike hailed the classic dramas *Mrs. Miniver, Thirty Seconds Over Tokyo,* and *Casablanca.* Furthermore, when filmmakers worked with the armed services, they produced acclaimed documentaries such as *The Battle of Midway* and *Fighting Lady,* a full-length film about life on an aircraft carrier.

Critical Thinking
Recognizing Points of View

If possible, have students view a film about World War II made during the 1940s, such as *A Walk in the Sun, Battleground,* or *Back to Bataan.* Students may also want to view some of the Warner Brothers cartoons made during the time—and still shown on TV—that referred to the war. Then have them write reviews of the ones they have seen, noting the portrayal of Allied troops and the attitude toward the enemy. Have students conclude by telling how American audiences in the 1940s might have felt after seeing each film.

lish Channel into France. Such an attack would ease pressure on the Soviet Union.

A cross-channel invasion would take much careful planning, however. Not until December 1943 did Churchill and Roosevelt finally agree to attempt it.

Planning the invasion. Years of planning went into **Operation Overlord,** the code name for the invasion of Europe. General Eisenhower was appointed commander of Allied forces in Europe. He would direct the invasion.

Eisenhower faced an enormous task. He had to organize a huge army, ferry it across the English Channel, and provide it with ammunition, food, and other supplies. By June 1944, almost 3 million troops were ready for the invasion.

The Germans knew an attack was coming. They did not know when or where. They had built a strong "Atlantic wall" against an Allied invasion. They had mined beaches and strung barbed wire. Machine guns and concrete antitank walls stood ready to stop an advance.

Landing at Normandy. On June 6, 1944, known as **D-Day,** a fleet of 4,000 Allied ships carried the invasion force to France. Allied troops scrambled ashore at Normandy. Despite intense German gunfire and heavy losses, they pushed on. Every day, more soldiers landed to reinforce the advance. On August 25, 1944, the Allies entered Paris. After four years under Nazi rule, French men, women, and children greeted their liberators with joy.

Linking Past and Present
African American surgeon Dr. Charles Drew organized blood bank programs and developed ways to send blood plasma overseas. His work helped save millions of lives. Today, blood banks in the United States collect over 11 million units of blood a year.

Advancing on Germany

By September, the Allies were moving east toward Germany. Then their advance slowed. The Allies suffered a shortage of gasoline fuel for their trucks. As a result, they had trouble supplying their advancing troops.

On December 16, 1944, German forces began a fierce counterattack. They pushed the Allies back, creating a bulge in the front lines. The **Battle of the Bulge,** as it was later called, slowed the Allies but did not stop them.

While Allied armies advanced on the ground, their planes bombed Germany. At night, British planes dropped tons of bombs on German cities. By day, American planes bombed factories and oil refineries. The bombing caused severe fuel shortages. However, it did not break German morale or slow war production.

Election of 1944

By mid-1944, the Allied advance shared headlines in American newspapers with the upcoming election. President Roosevelt ran for a fourth term against Governor Thomas E. Dewey of New York, who was nominated by the Republicans.

"All that is within me cries to go back to my home on the Hudson," FDR wrote in 1944. Roosevelt was tired and ill. Still, he and his running mate, Senator Harry S. Truman of Missouri, campaigned strongly. Their efforts paid off. Roosevelt won more than 54 percent of the vote.

Death of the President. In early April 1945, FDR was on vacation in Georgia. As he sat to have his portrait painted, he complained of a headache. Within two hours, he was dead.

Franklin D. Roosevelt was mourned by people all over the world. His death especially shocked Americans. Roosevelt had been President for 12 years. Many Americans

Chapter 26 • **755**

  Videotapes/ Videodiscs

United States History Video Collection Use the video segment "The Road to Victory" from Volume 19, *World War II,* to enhance students' understanding of the progress and end of the war in Europe. Approx. running time 2:35 min. (Enrichment/Average) Vol. 19, Ch. 37

Chapter 37   Play

Voices of Freedom

Primary Source You might assign selection 16-4, Life Aboard a United States Destroyer, on pages 259–260 of *Voices of Freedom.* In this selection, a navy officer describes shipboard life and tells how he felt during his first military action. (Enrichment/Average)

Primary Source You might assign selection 16-5, Normandy on the Day After D-Day, on pages 261–262 of *Voices of Freedom.* In this selection, war correspondent Ernie Pyle describes the scene on the beach the day after the invasion of Normandy. (Enrichment/Average)

Our Multicultural Heritage

Biography Have students read the biography, Dr. Charles Drew, Blood Plasma Pioneer, on page 76 of the *Our Multicultural Heritage* booklet. (Enrichment/Average)

Historical Sidelight
Background

The Battle of the Bulge was the biggest battle fought on the Western Front during the war—more than one million soldiers were involved. During this battle, German soldiers began to slip behind Allied lines wearing American uniforms. American soldiers devised passwords to guard against such tactics. "Who is [movie star] Betty Grable's husband?" a sentry might challenge. American soldiers would reply "Harry James"—a well-known trumpet player and bandleader. German soldiers never even understood the question, much less the answer, and were promptly captured.

Historical Sidelight
Background

On the afternoon of April 12, 1945, Eleanor Roosevelt was attending a charity benefit in Washington, D.C. When word came about FDR's death, aides brought the First Lady back to the White House and told her the news. She responded, "I am more sorry for the people of this country and of the world than I am for ourselves."

At the same time, Vice President Truman was visiting the office of Sam Rayburn, Speaker of the House of Representatives. A message arrived, asking Truman to call Steve Early, the White House press secretary, at

once. When Truman reached Early, he could hear tension in the press secretary's voice: "Please come right over as quickly and quietly as you can." Bewildered, Truman arrived at the White House and was taken in to see Eleanor Roosevelt. "Harry," she said quietly, "the President is dead." Truman was speechless, but he quickly recovered and asked her, "Is there anything I can do for you?" Perhaps remembering that Truman had been Vice President for only three months, she replied, "Is there anything *we* can do for *you?* For you are the one in trouble now."

756

Answers to Map Study

1. 1943; 1944; 1944   2. Tunis
3. Possible Answer: The map shows that El Alamein marked the beginning of the Allies' westward advance across North Africa. From North Africa, the Allies then invaded Italy.

Customized Reader

Primary Source For a firsthand account of an extraordinary act of heroism, order article VIIB-1, *War Hero Recounts a Battle in Germany*, from the *American History Customized Reader*. In this selection, Audie Murphy, the most decorated American soldier of World War II, describes the events that earned him the Congressional Medal of Honor. (Enrichment/Easy)

CD-ROM

Presidents Access the biography of Harry S. Truman from the *American Heritage® History of the United States* CD-ROM.

Student Study Guide

Section 4 Study Guide Have students use the Section 4 Study Guide on page 194 of the *Student Study Guide* to review and reinforce the content of this section. (Reteaching/Average)

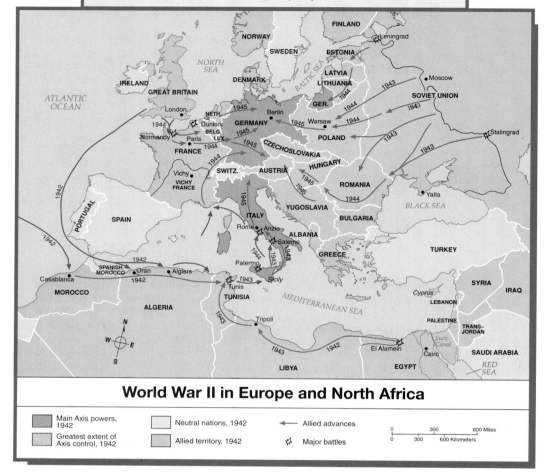

MAP STUDY

During the early years of the war, the Axis powers gained control of most of Western Europe and North Africa. In 1943, however, the tide turned.

1. **When did the Allies first invade Italy? France? Germany?**
2. **From which African port did the Allies launch the invasion of Sicily?**
3. **Analyzing Information** The battle of El Alamein has been called a turning point in the war. Based on this map, why do you think this was so?

World War II in Europe and North Africa

■ Main Axis powers, 1942	□ Neutral nations, 1942	← Allied advances
■ Greatest extent of Axis control, 1942	■ Allied territory, 1942	✫ Major battles

could hardly remember anyone else as their leader.

A new President takes over. Vice President Harry S. Truman had to take over a country in the midst of war. Truman described his reaction:

66[When] they told me yesterday what had happened, I felt like the moon, the stars, and all the planets had fallen on me. I've got the most terribly responsible job a man ever had.99

756 • Chapter 26

Historical Sidelight
Background

The "S" in "Harry S. Truman" is often written without the period — for "S" was the President's full middle name, not an initial. Truman's parents could not decide whether to make his middle name "Shippe," for his father's father, or "Solomon," for his mother's father. Using "S" as the middle name kept both sides of the family happy.

Cooperative Learning
Activity

Truman's comment on page 756 is an excerpt from his remarks at a press conference held the day after he became President. Have students work together to prepare and present a re-creation of that press conference. Some students might do research to find out more about what was actually said. Other students might prepare questions for the new President and Truman's likely responses. You might want to use the students' presentation to close the study of Section 4.

Victory in Europe

By April 1945, Truman knew that the war in Europe was almost over. Germany was collapsing. American troops were closing in on Berlin from the west. Soviet troops were advancing from the east. On April 25, American and Soviet troops met at Torgau, 60 miles (96 km) south of Berlin.

In Berlin, Hitler hid in his underground bunker as Allied air raids pounded the city. Unwilling to accept defeat, he committed suicide on April 30. A week later, on May 7, 1945, Germany surrendered to the Allies. On May 8, the Allies celebrated the long-awaited *V-E Day*—Victory in Europe!

SECTION 4 REVIEW

1. **Locate:** (a) Stalingrad, (b) Philippines, (c) Guadalcanal, (d) El Alamein, (e) Sicily, (f) English Channel, (g) Normandy.
2. **Identify:** (a) Battle of Midway, (b) Dwight D. Eisenhower, (c) Operation Overlord, (d) D-Day, (e) Battle of the Bulge, (f) Harry S. Truman, (g) V-E Day.
3. Why was 1942 a terrible time for the Allies?
4. Explain why each of these was important for Allied victory: (a) Battle of Guadalcanal, (b) Operation Overlord.
5. (a) Why did Stalin want a second front in Europe? (b) Why did it take so long to launch the invasion of France?
6. **CRITICAL THINKING Analyzing Ideas** Winston Churchill called the Battle of El Alamein "the turning point in British military fortunes." Why do you think this particular battle was so important to the Allies?

ACTIVITY Writing to Learn
Imagine that you are an American soldier with the troops about to invade France in June 1944. Write daily diary entries for the week leading up to D-Day.

5
Peace at Last

FIND OUT
- How did the Allies plan to defeat Japan?
- Why did Truman drop two atomic bombs on Japan?
- Why was World War II the deadliest war in history?

VOCABULARY island hopping

Soon after FDR's death, a reporter addressed Harry Truman. "Mr. President..." he began. "I wish you didn't have to call me that," Truman interrupted.

As Vice President, Truman had met with Roosevelt fewer than 10 times. He knew little about plans for ending the war or for the postwar peace. As President, Truman had to learn quickly. Just weeks after he took office, Germany surrendered. The Allies then turned their full attention to defeating Japan.

Island Hopping in the Pacific

Even while the war raged in Europe, the Allies kept up pressure on Japan. By mid-1942, the United States had two main goals in the Pacific war: to regain the Philippines and to invade Japan.

For its plan to work, the United States had to control the Pacific Ocean. It conducted an island-hopping campaign. **Island hopping** meant capturing some Japanese-held islands and going around others. Americans used the islands they won as stepping stones toward Japan.

A deadly routine. Island hopping became a deadly routine. First, American ships shelled a Japanese-held island. Next, troops waded ashore under heavy gunfire. Then, in

---

Guided Instruction To make their diaries sound authentic, suggest that students find a book, magazine, or newspaper that covers the weeks of preparation for D-Day and use that for their factual material. You might have them share finished diary entries by having students tape their week's worth of entries onto large sheets of colored construction paper. Together, the sheets will make a class display.

Section 5
pp. 757–761

Bell Ringer

Ask students to imagine that they are President Truman in July 1945. Have students write, as Truman might have done, the thoughts and questions that troubled him as he pondered whether to use the atomic bomb on Japan. Suggest that students save their papers and use them as prewriting notes for the end-of-section Activity on page 761.

Lesson Plan

1. **Focus** After their victory in Europe, the Allies turned their full attention to the Pacific. After two atomic bombs were dropped on Japan, the Japanese surrendered. In this section, students study the closing days of World War II.

Answers to Section 4 Review

1. See the maps on pp. 756 and 758.
2. (a) Battle of Midway, p. 753, (b) Dwight D. Eisenhower, p. 754, (c) Operation Overlord, p. 755, (d) D-Day, p. 755, (e) Battle of the Bulge, p. 755, (f) Harry S. Truman, p. 755, (g) V-E Day, p. 757
3. Japan had captured lands in the Pacific—Guam, Wake Island, Hong Kong, Singapore, the Philippines, the Dutch East Indies, Malaya, and Burma. German troops held most of Europe and threatened Moscow, Leningrad, and Stalingrad.
4. (a) After the Allies won the battle, Guadalcanal became a base from which to attack Japanese forces. (b) Operation Overlord was a turning point in the European war. After the invasion on D-Day, Allied forces were able to push forward toward defeating Germany.
5. (a) Stalin wanted to relieve some of the pressure felt by Soviet forces. (b) Many arrangements had to be made, including gathering forces, working out transportation and supply routes—and keeping the details a secret from the Germans.
6. Possible Answer: It was the first step in defeating Rommel's army and freeing North Africa from German troops.

2. Instruct Have students conduct a classroom debate about this statement: "President Truman was justified in using the atomic bomb against Japan." Assign one group of students to argue in favor of the statement and one group to argue against it. Have the rest of the class act as judges for the debate. Be sure that students use facts from the text to support their positions.

3. Close To close the lesson, have students make review charts of the major battles of World War II. Draw a blank chart on the chalkboard with columns labeled *Battle, Date,* and *Significance.* Ask volunteers to list battles in the first column, in chronological order. Then have the class work together to complete the other two columns.

Lesson Planner

For a developed **Cooperative Learning** lesson plan, see the *Lesson Planner,* page 165.

Historical Outline Map Book

Historical Outline Maps Duplicate and distribute the map, World War II in the Pacific, on page 66 of the *American History Historical Outline Map Book.* Lesson ideas for this map can be found on page T21. (Enrichment/Average)

Answers to Map Study

1. 1942; 1944; 1945 **2.** about 1,000 miles (about 1,600 km) **3.** island hopping

hand-to-hand fighting, Americans overcame fierce Japanese resistance.

In October 1944, American forces under General MacArthur finally returned to the Philippines. By February 1945, they had taken Manila, the capital. In hard-fought battles, the Americans then captured the islands of Iwo Jima (EE woh JEE muh) and Okinawa (oh kuh NAH wuh), just 350 miles (563 km) from the Japanese home islands.

Closing in on Japan. At Okinawa and elsewhere, the Japanese fought back with

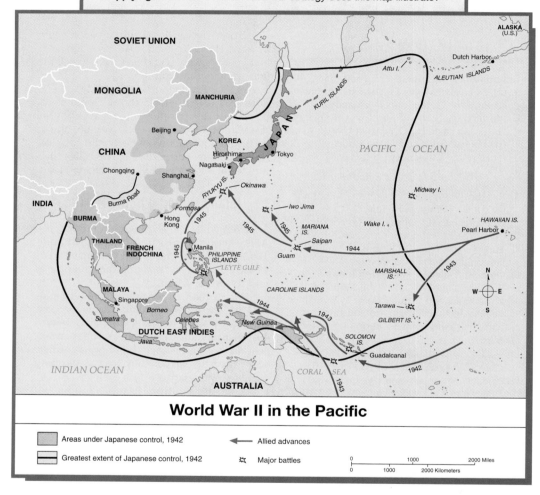

MAP STUDY

By 1942, Japan controlled much of China, Southeast Asia, and the Pacific. After the Battle of Midway, however, the United States took the offensive.
1. In what year did the Allies reach Guadalcanal? Guam? Okinawa?
2. About how far would an airplane have to fly from Okinawa to Tokyo?
3. **Applying Information** What Allied war strategy does this map illustrate?

World War II in the Pacific

Areas under Japanese control, 1942

Greatest extent of Japanese control, 1942

Allied advances

Major battles

Cooperative Learning
Activity

Students who are interested in tanks, trucks, airplanes, jeeps, landing craft, and other equipment used during the war may be encouraged to make a display of drawings, photos, or models. Working with partners or in small groups, students can compare and contrast the equipment of the Allied and Axis powers. For example, students who are interested in airplanes might compare and contrast the types that each side used, classifying the planes as fighters, bombers, paratrooper planes, supply and rescue craft, and planes for gathering intelligence. Other students might research tanks, trucks, and landing craft; make models; and classify them according to purpose. When the display is complete, have each pair or small group explain to the class the category of vehicle studied. If possible, you or a student may want to videotape the display and the presentations.

Learning Styles
Kinesthetic Learners

Encourage students to write and perform a skit based on one of the incidents in World War II. For example, one group might choose the plot of German officers to kill Hitler; another, the bravery of ordinary people to save the lives of Jews; and a third, one of the successful sabotage achievements of the underground, or resistance, in a particular country. Encourage students to practice thinking and reacting like the characters they play to make their portrayal as realistic as possible.

758

fanatic zeal. Japanese pilots carried out kamikaze (kah muh KAH zee) attacks. They loaded old planes with bombs. The pilots then deliberately crashed their planes into Allied ships.

By April 1945, American bombers were pounding Japanese factories and cities. American warships bombarded the coast and sank ships. The Japanese people were suffering terribly. Still, their leaders talked about winning a glorious victory over the Allies.

United States military leaders made plans to invade Japan in the autumn. They warned that the invasion might cost over a million casualties.

Defeat of Japan

In late July 1945, the Allied leaders—Truman, Churchill, and Stalin—met at Potsdam, Germany. While there, Truman received startling news from home. American scientists had successfully tested a secret new weapon—the atomic bomb. The new weapon was so powerful that a single bomb could destroy an entire city. Some scientists believed that it was too dangerous to use.

Using the atomic bomb. From Potsdam, the Allied leaders sent a message to Japan. In the **Potsdam Declaration,** they told Japan to surrender or face "prompt and utter destruction." Japanese military leaders did not know about the atomic bomb. They ignored the Allied message.

On August 6, 1945, the *Enola Gay,* an American bomber, dropped an atomic bomb on Hiroshima, Japan. The blast killed at least 70,000 people and injured an equal number. It destroyed at least 80 percent of the city.

Two days later, the Soviet Union declared war on Japan. Still, Japan did not surrender. On August 9, the United States dropped a second atomic bomb—this time on Nagasaki. About 40,000 residents died instantly. Later, many more people in both

Navajo Code-Talkers *These marines are among a group of Navajos who served as code-talkers in the Pacific. They baffled the Japanese by sending messages in their unique language.* **Multicultural Heritage** *How did the code-talkers contribute to the Allied effort in the Pacific?*

Nagasaki and Hiroshima died from the effects of atomic radiation released by the bombs.

Japan surrenders. After a furious debate in the Japanese cabinet, the emperor of Japan announced that the nation would surrender on August 14, 1945. It is known as *V-J Day* for Victory over Japan.

The formal surrender took place on September 2 aboard the U.S.S. *Missouri* in Tokyo Bay. The warship flew the same American flag that had waved over Washington on the day Japan bombed Pearl Harbor.

Counting the Costs

News of Japan's surrender sparked wild celebrations across the United States. Cars honked their horns. Soldiers and sailors danced in victory parades. Workers in tall office buildings showered confetti on people in the streets below.

The death toll. After the celebrations, people began to count the costs of the war—the deadliest in human history. The exact number of casualties will probably never be known. However, historians estimate that somewhere between 30 and 60 million people were killed in battle or behind the lines. The chart on page 765 shows one estimate of civilian and battle casualties on both sides.

World War II was different from World War I, which had been fought mainly in trenches. During World War II, planes bombed cities and towns. The bombing destroyed houses, roads, bridges, railroads, factories, and farms. The use of fire bombs and atomic bombs took a terrible toll of civilian dead and wounded. By 1945, millions more were homeless and had no way to earn a living.

Mistreatment of prisoners. During the war, stories trickled out about the mistreatment of prisoners. Afterward, Americans learned horrifying details about brutal events such as the ***Bataan Death March.*** After the Japanese captured the Philippines in 1942, they forced about 60,000 American and Filipino prisoners to march 100 miles

(160 km) with little food or water. About 10,000 people died or were killed.

The Holocaust

In the last months of the European war, the Allied forces uncovered other horrors. The Allies had heard about Nazi death camps. As they advanced into Germany and Eastern Europe, they discovered the full extent of the ***Holocaust***—Hitler's policy of killing Jews.

During the war, the Nazis imprisoned Jews from Germany, Poland, and other nations they conquered. In huge prison camps, they tortured, starved, and murdered more than 6 million Jews. At death camps such as Auschwitz, Maidanek, Dachau, and Treblinka, Allied troops saw the large gas chambers the Nazis had used to murder hundreds of thousands. Battle-hardened veterans wept to see the piles of dead and dying human beings.

Photographers such as Margaret Bourke-White made a record of the horrors. She worked "with a veil over my mind. . . . I hard-

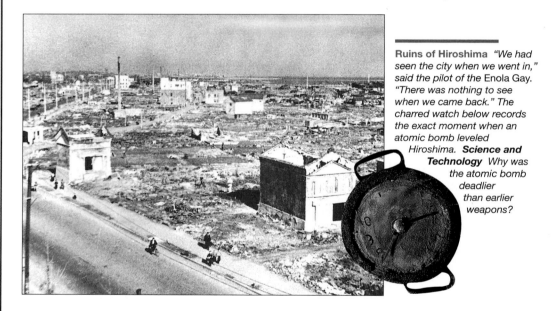

Ruins of Hiroshima *"We had seen the city when we went in,"* said the pilot of the Enola Gay. *"There was nothing to see when we came back."* The charred watch below records the exact moment when an atomic bomb leveled Hiroshima. **Science and Technology** *Why was the atomic bomb deadlier than earlier weapons?*

Holocaust Survivors *American troops were shocked when they entered Nazi concentration camps. One sergeant recalled, "I saw what should be considered human beings, that had been reduced to the point where they were just merely surviving."* **Daily Life** *What does this photograph reveal about conditions in the camps?*

ly knew what I had taken until I saw prints of my own photographs." After touring one death camp, General Omar Bradley wrote:

> ❝The smell of death overwhelmed us even before we passed through the stockade....More than 3,200 naked, emaciated bodies had been flung into shallow graves. Others lay in the streets where they had fallen.❞

The Nazis murdered other groups as well as Jews. Nearly 6 million Poles, Slavs, and Gypsies were also victims of the death camps. Nazis killed prisoners of war and people they considered unfit because of physical or mental disabilities.

War Crimes Trials

After the war, the Allies decided to put Axis leaders on trial. In 1945 and 1946, they conducted war crimes trials in Nuremberg, Germany. As a result of the **Nuremberg Trials,** 12 Nazi leaders were sentenced to death. Thousands of other Nazis were found guilty of war crimes and imprisoned. The Allies also tried and executed Japanese leaders accused of war crimes.

Our Common Heritage
A number of American cities have built Holocaust museums or memorials to remind Americans of the Nazi destruction of European Jews. The best known is the Holocaust Memorial Museum. It opened in Washington, D.C., in 1993.

SECTION 5 REVIEW

1. **Locate:** (a) Philippines, (b) Iwo Jima, (c) Okinawa, (d) Hiroshima, (e) Nagasaki.
2. **Identify:** (a) Potsdam Declaration, (b) V-J Day, (c) Bataan Death March, (d) Holocaust, (e) Nuremberg Trials.
3. **Define:** island hopping.
4. (a) What two goals did the United States set for the war in the Pacific? (b) What strategy did it adopt to achieve those goals?
5. (a) What secret weapon did the United States develop? (b) How was it used?
6. Why was World War II more deadly than World War I?
7. **CRITICAL THINKING** **Drawing Conclusions** Why do you think the Allies held war crimes trials?

 Writing to Learn

Write a diary entry in which President Truman discusses why he decided to use the atomic bomb instead of trying to invade Japan.

Picturing the Past

Art Note

Art and Values This feature illustrates some of the things that young Americans of the first half of the twentieth century considered important—going to school, attending to their personal appearance, entertaining themselves, and supporting their country. In that sense, the young people depicted in this feature are not so different from many young people today. As students discuss the feature, encourage them to imagine themselves in the situations depicted and to comment about how they might have felt in each of these situations.

Previewing Focus

With the exception of the first photograph, this feature focuses on young Americans' leisure time and/or extracurricular activities. Remind students that the introduction of labor-saving conveniences and changes in child labor laws resulted in more free time for teenagers. You might also review some of the forms of entertainment (such as radio and movies) that were available at the time. Ask: Would you trade places with a teenager from your grandparents' time? Why or why not?

Linking Past and Present
Activity

After students discuss the photograph taken in the Kentucky classroom, ask them to speculate about the school's probable dress code. Have them compare their responses to what they know about dress codes today. You might also invite their comments about some schools' decision not only to return to a dress code but to require a uniform. Ask: What school problems might the requirement of uniforms solve? How might you persuade your friends to wear a uniform?

In the Classroom *In the 1920s, schools often taught grooming along with math and history. Here, Kentucky students undergo a fingernail inspection.*

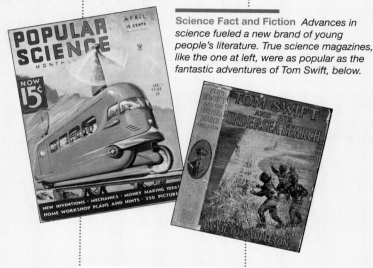

Science Fact and Fiction *Advances in science fueled a new brand of young people's literature. True science magazines, like the one at left, were as popular as the fantastic adventures of Tom Swift, below.*

Clubs *In the 1930s, social and athletic clubs gave city youngsters a chance to escape the harsh conditions of life during the Great Depression. These boys belonged to the Chicago Athletic Club.*

Connections With Literature
Background

The leading magazine of what has been called the "Golden Age of Science Fiction" was *Amazing Stories*. This was the magazine in which every aspiring science-fiction writer hoped to be published. One young writer's dreams came true in 1938 when *Amazing Stories* accepted a short story from an as-yet-unpublished 18-year-old named Isaac Asimov.

Connections With Art
Background

"Little Orphan Annie" was originally "Little Orphan Otto"—at least that was the name proposed by Harold Gray, the comic strip's creator. However, more than three dozen other comic strips starred boys at the time. When Gray presented his idea to Capt. J. M. Patterson, the founder of New York's *Daily News,* Patterson said, "Put skirts on the kid and call her Orphan Annie." Orphan Annie is the title character in James Whitcomb Riley's poem "Little Orphan Annie," which the paper sometimes reprinted. Gray went on to draw the comic strip for the next 44 years.

Little Orphan Annie *Both boys and girls followed the adventures of Little Orphan Annie on radio and in the comics.*

Sandlot Baseball *Baseball continued to be the favorite sport of Americans. Young boys like these could turn any vacant lot into a ballfield.*

Picturing the Past

Young Americans 1900–1945

Between 1900 and 1945, growing up in the United States became more complex. Technology provided new interests and new amusements. The Great Depression and two world wars touched young people's lives. Still, some things did not change. Going to school and having fun continued to be two major concerns of young Americans.

■ *Based on these pictures, make a list of questions you would like to ask someone who grew up between 1900 and 1945.*

Victory Garden *During World War II, young people grew "victory gardens" to relieve wartime food shortages. These blind children form a "V for Victory" around their garden.*

1. Why do you think the students in Kentucky are having a fingernail inspection? (Possible Answer: to make sure that their nails are clean and well cared for)
2. What kinds of articles might you have found in *Popular Science* in 1940? (Possible Answer: articles about new or improved technological products; instructions about how to build a device such as a simple radio; information about some of the technology in use in the war in Europe)

Answer to Picturing the Past

Questions will vary but may include inquiries into the young Americans' daily lives (school, home life, chores, and so on), their thoughts about the future (for example, the kinds of careers they might expect to have or the technology that they hope will be available), and their feelings about the historical events taking place at the time (such as the Depression or World War II).

Cooperative Learning Activity

Divide the class into six groups and have each group select one of the six topics depicted in this feature. Then have the members of each group work together to create a promotional brochure relating to the topic — for example, a pamphlet inviting teenage boys of the 1930s to join the Chicago Athletic Club or urging people to grow victory gardens during World War II. Encourage students to do additional research into the chosen topic and to spend time thinking about the purpose and audience for each brochure. Also encourage the use of artwork. Students may want to imitate a period style, or they may prefer to give the brochure a look for the 1990s. Have one or two representatives from each group present and explain the finished brochure.

CHAPTER 26 REVIEW

Answers to Reviewing the Main Ideas

1. (a and b) Both leaders played on their people's resentment about the outcome of World War I and the economic problems of their countries. Both seized power and then set up totalitarian states.

2. to gain needed raw materials such as coal and oil

3. (a) by selling arms to the Allies on a cash-and-carry basis and later by lending war materials to them (b) because of the surprise attack by the Japanese on Pearl Harbor

4. (a) Women took over jobs previously done by men; they served in the armed forces; they gained confidence because of their new positions. (b) Many African Americans fought in the armed forces; at home, many were able to get better jobs, but they still faced discrimination. (c) Japanese Americans were removed from their homes on the West Coast and forced to live in WRA camps. Later, Japanese American men were allowed to enter the armed forces to fight in Europe.

5. After the D-Day invasion, the Allies advanced on Germany while planes bombed German industries and cities. American troops advancing from the west met Soviet troops advancing from the east to march on Berlin.

6. The Allies devised an island-hopping plan, capturing some islands from the Japanese and going around others. By 1945, American planes were bombing Japan, and American ships were bombarding Japan's coast. In August 1945, the United States dropped atomic bombs on Hiroshima and Nagasaki, forcing Japan to surrender.

7. Hitler's policy of killing millions of Jews

Answers to Thinking Critically

1. (a) Washington wanted to be sure that Presidents did not assume too much power and become like kings. (b) FDR felt that the country needed to be united behind one person who was known and respected by the Allies.

2. Possible Answer: Protecting American lives and ending the war were Truman's first duties; on the other hand, it was wrong to kill tens of thousands of Japanese civilians.

3. (a) the surprise attack on Pearl Harbor, Hawaii, by the Japanese (b) Possible Answer: Millions of people died; cities and factories were destroyed; people found out that the atomic bomb could work.

Summary

- As war clouds gathered in the 1930s, the United States followed a policy of isolation.
- The Japanese bombing of Pearl Harbor brought the United States into the war.
- Americans from all ethnic groups supported the war effort.
- The war in Europe ended with the surrender of Germany in May 1945.
- After two atomic bombs were dropped on Japan, the Japanese surrendered in August 1945.

Reviewing the Main Ideas

1. Describe the steps each of the following took to increase his power: (a) Benito Mussolini, (b) Adolf Hitler.
2. Why did Japan want to expand into Asia?
3. (a) How did the United States help the Allies in the early years of World War II? (b) Why was the United States drawn into the war?
4. Explain how the war affected each of these groups: (a) women, (b) African Americans, (c) Japanese Americans.
5. How did the Allies win the war in Europe?
6. Describe how the Allies fought to defeat Japan.
7. What was the Holocaust?

Thinking Critically

1. **Linking Past and Present** (a) Why do you think George Washington chose to retire after two terms? (b) Why do you think FDR broke this precedent?
2. **Defending a Position** After the war, President Truman said he had agreed to the use of the atomic bomb "to shorten the agony of war [and] save the lives of thousands of young Americans." Do you think he made the right decision? Defend your position.

3. **Understanding Causes and Effects** (a) What was the immediate cause of the United States entry into World War II? (b) What was an immediate effect of the war?

Applying Your Skills

1. **Making a Time Line** Make a time line of World War II. Then write a statement about the cause-and-effect relationship between two events on your time line.
2. **Using a Photograph as a Primary Source** Study the photographs on pages 752, 760, and 761. (a) What is the subject of each photograph? (b) Based on the photographs, write two statements about the nature of World War II.
3. **Researching Local History** Interview someone in your area who served in the armed forces or worked in a war industry during World War II. Draw up a list of questions before you begin your interview. Write a script for a TV program about the person's experiences during the war.

Thinking About Geography

Match the letters on the map with the following places: **1.** Main Axis powers, 1942, **2.** Axis territory, 1942, **3.** Allied territory, 1942, **4.** Normandy, **5.** Sicily, **6.** Berlin. **Movement** (a) What body of water did the Allies cross to reach Normandy? (b) Sicily?

---

faced in World War II must never be allowed to happen again.

3. Scripts will vary but should reveal both factual information and personal feelings about the era.

Answers to Applying Your Skills

1. Time lines and statements will vary, but both should be accurate and logical.

2. (a) the internment of Japanese Americans; Hiroshima after the atomic bomb had been dropped; survivors of a Nazi concentration camp (b) Possible Answer: In wartime, some countries treat even their own citizens in inhumane ways; the indignities and horrors that many people

Answers to Thinking About Geography

1. D **2.** E **3.** F **4.** C **5.** B **6.** A

Movement: (a) English Channel (b) Mediterranean Sea

Fighting a Global War

Form into groups to review World War II. Follow the suggestions below to show what you have learned about the global nature of the war. You may use the textbook, encyclopedias, atlases, or other materials in your classroom library to complete the tasks. Be able to name your sources of information when you have finished the activity.

Invasion of Normandy

GEOGRAPHERS Create a gazetteer of the countries, cities, and bodies of water involved in World War II. List the places in alphabetical order, and provide a brief description of the role each played in the war.

CARTOGRAPHERS Imagine that you have been asked to supply information for the Allies. Find out more about the areas where World War II was fought. Then prepare a map showing the locations of major battles. On the map, list the special problems that troops might have faced in each area, such as terrain, climate, and so on.

WRITERS Imagine that you are a war correspondent assigned to one of the following: surrender of France, Battle of Britain, siege of Leningrad, invasion of Normandy, fall of the Philippines, recapture of the Philippines. Write and record a radio broadcast reporting the event.

Ribbon awarded to American soldiers who served overseas

SCIENTISTS Find out about the scientists from many lands who helped to develop the atomic bomb. Create a biographical dictionary listing their names, country of origin, and contribution to the project.

MATHEMATICIANS Use the chart below to create bar graphs showing the casualties suffered by each country in World War II. Make a pie graph showing the proportion of total casualties suffered by each nation.

 Create a Fighting a Global War mini-museum in your classroom. Include samples or summaries of each group's completed activity.

Casualties in World War II

	Military Dead	Military Wounded	Civilian Dead
Britain	389,000	475,000	65,000
France	211,000	400,000	108,000
Soviet Union	7,500,000	14,102,000	15,000,000
United States	292,000	671,000	*
Germany	2,850,000	7,250,000	5,000,000
Italy	77,500	120,000	100,000
Japan	1,576,000	500,000	300,000

All figures are estimates.
*Very small number of civilian dead.
Source: Henri Michel, *The Second World War*

Assessment

Chapter Resources Binder For a more comprehensive evaluation of student understanding of this chapter, assign Chapter Tests A and B and/or Extra Unit Questions from Unit 8, pages 35–40 and 43–45.

Computer Test Bank You can use Chapter Tests and Extra Unit Questions to create your own tests for both testing and retesting.

Alternative Assessment

Chapter Resources Binder See the Alternative Assessment booklet in the *Social Studies Educator's Handbook* series.

Portfolio You might meet with students to choose appropriate work from the chapter for inclusion in their portfolios.

Interdisciplinary ACTIVITY

The following chart indicates the activities appropriate for different learning styles.

Visual Learners
Geographers
Cartographers
Mathematicians

Auditory Learners
Writers
Scientists (if dictionaries are shared orally)

Kinesthetic Learners
Cartographers
Writers
Mathematicians

Evaluation

Geographers Gazetteers should be accurate. Places should be alphabetized and described correctly; comments about the role of each place should demonstrate logical (probably cause-and-effect) thinking.

Cartographers Maps should cover Europe, North Africa, Asia, and the South Pacific, with major battles labeled correctly. A variety of terrains and climates should be addressed, with the notes about each easy to find and read.

Writers Factual information must be accurate. Oral delivery is very important, too, and should be evaluated accordingly. Radio reports should also give the impression that the reporter is actually witnessing the events described.

Scientists Biographical dictionaries should be well researched and should show a variety of contributions to the team effort of developing the atomic bomb.

Mathematicians Graphs should be easy to read and accurate, with countries ranked from most to fewest casualties, as follows: Soviet Union, Germany, Japan, United States, Britain, France, Italy.

History Through Literature

Author Note

Jeanne Wakatsuki Houston was only seven years old at the time of her family's internment at the Manzanar War Relocation Center. She later went to college and married writer and professor James D. Houston (b. 1933). They coauthored *Farewell to Manzanar,* described by the *Los Angeles Times* as "a voice for a heretofore silent segment of society." *Farewell to Manzanar* became an award-winning TV movie in 1976. Jeanne Wakatsuki Houston was presented with the Wonder Woman Award from Warner Communications in 1984.

Vocabulary

Have students look up and discuss the words *Caucasians, evacuation, anguish, destination, barracks, expectantly, ominously, intact,* and *hysterical* before they read the passage. Ask: Which of these words might describe the federal government's decision to relocate Japanese Americans? Which words describe how you might feel if you were one of the people being relocated?

Prereading Focus

You might have students review Chapter 26, Section 3 (especially pages 750–752). Discuss how the relocation of Japanese Americans to WRA camps disrupted the lives of tens of thousands of families.

Motivation/Prior Knowledge

Explain that the first war relocation proclamation was issued in March 1942, that Manzanar was the first WRA camp to open, and that the Wakatsukis were relocated there in April 1942. Ask: Why was the government so eager to remove Japanese Americans from their homes on the West Coast?

History Through LITERATURE

Farewell to Manzanar

Jeanne Wakatsuki Houston and James D. Houston

Introduction   After the bombing of Pearl Harbor, more than 100,000 Japanese Americans were forced to relocate to camps set up by the Wartime Relocation Agency. Jeanne Wakatsuki Houston was a young girl when she and her family were relocated to Manzanar, a camp in eastern California. In the following excerpt from her book about her experiences, Houston describes the bus ride to Manzanar.

Vocabulary   Before you read the selection, find the meaning of these words in a dictionary: **Caucasians, evacuation, anguish, destination, barracks, expectantly, ominously, intact, hysterical**

The name Manzanar meant nothing to us when we left Boyle Heights. We didn't know where it was or what it was. We went because the government ordered us to. And, in the case of my older brothers and sisters, we went with a certain amount of relief. They had all heard stories of Japanese homes being attacked, of beatings in the streets of California towns. They were as frightened of the Caucasians as Caucasians were of us. Moving, under what appeared to be government protection, to an area less directly threatened by the war seemed not such a bad idea at all. For some it actually sounded like a fine adventure.

Our pickup point was a Buddhist church in Los Angeles. It was very early, and misty, when we got there with our luggage. Mama had bought heavy coats for all of us. She grew up in eastern Washington and knew that anywhere inland in early April would be cold. I was proud of my new coat, and I remember sitting on a duffel bag trying to be friendly with the [bus] driver. I smiled at him. He didn't smile back. He was befriending no one. Someone tied a numbered tag to my collar and to the duffel bag (each family was given a number, and that became our official designation until the camps were closed), someone else passed out box lunches for the trip, and we climbed aboard.

I had never been outside Los Angeles County, never traveled more than ten miles from the coast, had never even ridden on a bus. I was full of excitement, the way any kid would be, and wanted to look out the window. But for the first few hours the shades were drawn. Around me other people played cards, read magazines, dozed, waiting. I settled back, waiting too, and finally fell asleep. The bus felt very secure to me. Almost half its passengers were immediate relatives. Mama and my older brothers had succeeded in keeping most of us together, on the same bus, headed for the same camp. I didn't realize until much later what a job that was. The strategy had been, first, to have everyone living in the same district when the evacuation began, and then to get all of us included under

Purpose-Setting Question

Find Owens Valley, California—the site of Manzanar—on a map. Then ask: What might a family do to keep up their spirits in such an isolated place?

Discussion Questions

1. Why was the trip to Manzanar exciting for the narrator? (She had never been far from home, so she looked upon this trip out of Los Angeles County as an adventure.)
2. What had her family achieved that made them "lucky"? Explain. (Unlike many families they knew, the Wakatsukis had been able to keep their extended family together. They were relocated together and did not have to face the problem of finding family members who had been relocated elsewhere.)
3. What does the narrator's first view of Manzanar suggest about the camp and the people who prepared it? (Possible Answer: It was meant to be functional rather than pleasant; it was prepared with little thought for the comfort of those who would be living there.)

Arrival in Camp *Like thousands of other Japanese Americans, artist Henry Sugimoto and his family were interned during World War II. This self-portrait shows the Sugimoto family just after they arrived at a WRA camp.* **Citizenship** *Why might people be more likely in wartime to tolerate government decisions that deny citizens' rights?*

the same family number, even though names had been changed by marriage. Many families weren't as lucky as ours and suffered months of anguish while trying to arrange transfers from one camp to another.

We rode all day. By the time we reached our destination, the shades were up. It was late afternoon. The first thing I saw was a yellow swirl across a blurred, reddish setting sun. The bus was being pelted by what sounded like splattering rain. It wasn't rain. This was my first look at something I would soon know very well, a billowing flurry of dust and sand churned up by the wind through Owens Valley.

We drove past a barbed-wire fence, through a gate, and into an open space where trunks and sacks and packages had been dumped from the baggage trucks that drove out ahead of us. I could see a few tents set up, the first rows of black barracks, and beyond them, blurred by sand, rows of barracks that seemed to spread for miles across this plain. People were sitting on cartons or milling around, with their backs to the wind, waiting to see which friends or relatives might be on this bus. As we approached, they turned or stood up, and some moved toward us expectantly. But inside the bus no one stirred. No one waved or spoke. They just stared out the windows, ominously silent. I didn't understand this. Hadn't we finally arrived, our whole family intact? I opened a window, leaned out, and yelled happily. "Hey! This whole bus is full of Wakatsukis!"

Outside, the greeters smiled. Inside there was an explosion of laughter, hysterical, tension-breaking laughter that left my brothers choking and whacking each other across the shoulders.

THINKING ABOUT LITERATURE

1. Why did the narrator's older brothers and sisters feel relief at being relocated?
2. Why did the narrator feel secure on the bus?
3. **CRITICAL THINKING Analyzing Ideas** Why was it important for the Wakatsukis to keep their family together?

ACTIVITY Draw a political cartoon that comments on the relocation of Japanese Americans during World War II.

Unit Focus

Direct students' attention to the painting on these pages—*Liberty States,* by Tsing-fang Chen. Ask: What does this painting suggest about the United States today? Do you think the same answer will be true 50 or 100 years from now? As students consider the present and the future of the United States, call on volunteers to read aloud the four chapter summaries. Ask questions such as the following to stimulate discussion.

1. How do you think someone who admires what the painting suggests would feel about communism? Why?

2. (a) What do you know—from television, movies, records, or family members—about the 1950s and 1960s? (b) Does anyone know somebody who served in Vietnam?

3. (a) Which two Presidents held office for most of the 1980s? (b) How did the Cold War end?

4. (a) When you think of the expression "the twenty-first century," what images come to mind? (b) Which of those images might come true in your lifetime?

5. Unit 9 is entitled The Nation Today and Tomorrow. Based on the information in the four chapter summaries, what might be the greatest challenges for the United States now—and in the near future? Explain.

Connections With Art
Background

Born in Taiwan in 1936, Tsing-fang Chen came to the United States after years of study and work in Paris. While he was in Paris in the 1970s, he developed his distinctive approach to art. "I belong to a new generation in civilization," Chen said, ". . . which synthesizes a new society for everyone. I am neither Eastern nor Western—I belong to both at the same time, the whole." His approach, called neo-iconography, rejects the consistent use of a single style. Instead, it selects the subject matter first and then chooses the method of presentation from the styles of all artistic periods and all cultures.

Chen has had more than 70 one-person shows around the world. In 1983, he was awarded the Achievement Award in Arts and Humanities by the Taiwan-American Foundation. Today, Chen lives in the SoHo district of New York City. His works are on permanent display in galleries there and in Taiwan.

The Nation Today and Tomorrow

CHAPTER 27
The Fifties
(1945–1960)

The postwar period brought prosperity at home and the Cold War abroad.

CHAPTER 28
A Time of Turmoil
(1960–1980)

The nation faced years of turmoil as Americans pressed for equal rights and protested the Vietnam War.

CHAPTER 29
New Directions
(1980–Present)

A conservative revolution in the 1980s and 1990s took the nation in new directions. At the same time, the end of the Cold War signaled a new era in world affairs.

CHAPTER 30
Toward a New Century

Americans are eager to face the challenges of the future as the nation heads into the twenty-first century.

Connections With Art
Activity

Ask questions such as the following to stimulate discussion about *Liberty States.*

1. What do you notice first about the painting?

2. (a) What figure (in addition to the continental United States) appears in the painting? (b) Why do you think that Tsing-fang Chen chose that figure?

3. Compare the art in the nine Unit Openers. Does Chen's painting remind you of any of them or is it completely different? Explain.

4. How would you represent the United States as a "land of liberty" artistically?

Today, as in the past, the United States continues to change and to grow. Still, the ideals of freedom and liberty that have guided Americans from the start remain the cornerstone of the nation.

Unit 9 • **769**

Bulletin Board Suggestion

Have students use the bulletin board to create an illustrated time line that covers events of the past 12 months. Students can use magazines and newspapers to create a list of important recent events. Then they can cut out pictures or draw their own illustrations for the time line. The time line can provide a frame of reference for students to add notes and/or symbols to show how events since World War II continue to influence current events.

Art Gallery Posters

Day and Crepuscule, by Tsing-fang Chen, is appropriate for Unit 9. Lesson suggestions for the poster appear in the *Art Gallery: Our Common Heritage Posters* Teacher's Guide. The art also appears in Chapter 30, page 874, of the student book.

CD-ROM

Time Tour Access The Nation Today and Tomorrow section of the Time Tour on the American Heritage® *History of the United States* CD-ROM to accompany Unit 9.

Connections With the World
Activity

Distribute to small groups of students a few recent newspapers. Have each group choose and report on an international news item that has had an impact on the United States. Then ask: According to the news story, how did the event affect the United States? Lead a class discussion on how newspapers, radio, and television have brought different parts of the world together—and how those ties might become even stronger in the twenty-first century.

Linking Past and Present
Activity

As students examine the chapter headings, point out that their own lifetimes are now part of the history of the United States. (In fact, to students of the future, the 1990s may seem as distant as the American Revolution or the Great Depression seems to students today.) Ask: How do you think your children will view the end of the twentieth century? What events of the past few years might show up in the history books that your great-grandchildren will use? Explain.

769

Chapter 27   The Fifties (1945–1960), pp. 770–795

Lessons	Teaching Resources
1 The Nation Faces a Cold War **Objectives** 1. Describe how the Soviet Union expanded its power after World War II. 2. Describe how the Marshall Plan helped prevent the spread of communism. 3. Explain why the Cold War spread to Africa and Asia.	**Lesson Planner** Cooperative Learning, p. 168 **Student Study Guide** Section 1 Study Guide, p. 198 **Chapter Resources Binder, Unit 9** *Critical Thinking* Analyzing Ideas, p. 3
2 The Cold War Turns Hot **Objectives** 1. Identify the result of the civil war in China. 2. Explain why the United States became involved in the Korean War. 3. Describe how Senator Joseph McCarthy increased fears of communism. 4. Identify the result of the arms race between the United States and the Soviet Union.	**Lesson Planner** Cooperative Learning, p. 169 **Student Study Guide** Section 2 Study Guide, p. 199 **Our Multicultural Heritage** *Biography* Charles Bussey, American Officer in Korea, p. 79 *Milestone* Integrating the Armed Forces, p. 81 **Interdisciplinary Connections:** A Change in Lifestyles ■ *Arts* The Rockin' Fifties, p. 158 ■ *Sciences* Stopping a Killer, p. 159 ■ *Geography* Heading for the Suburbs, p. 160 ■ *Economics* The "Good Life," p. 161 ■ *Civics* Separate and Unequal, p. 162
3 The Changing Face of the Nation **Objectives** 1. Describe how the economy expanded after World War II. 2. Explain why the suburbs grew rapidly in the 1950s. 3. Describe how television affected American life.	**Lesson Planner** Cooperative Learning, p. 170 **Student Study Guide** Section 3 Study Guide, p. 200 **Chapter Resources Binder, Unit 9** *Geography in History* Boston: From City to Suburb, pp. 5–6 *Skill Application* Using Public Opinion Polls, p. 2 **Our Multicultural Heritage** *Biography* Billy Graham, Evangelist to All Nations, p. 80
4 Roots of the Civil Rights Movement **Objectives** 1. Identify the advances that were made in the fight against segregation. 2. Explain why African Americans boycotted the buses in Montgomery, Alabama. 3. Identify the methods that Martin Luther King, Jr., used to fight for equal rights.	**Lesson Planner** Cooperative Learning, p. 171 **Student Study Guide** Section 4 Study Guide, p. 201 **Chapter Resources Binder, Unit 9** *History Through Literature* For My Sister Molly Who in the Fifties, p. 4

Multimedia Resources	Additional Resources	Chapter-Level Resources
Transparencies *Time Lines* The United States and the World, 1945–1960, p. E-27 *Critical Thinking* The Cold War, p. F-31 **Videotapes/Videodiscs** *United States History Video Collection* The Cold War, Vol. 20, Ch. 16	**Voices of Freedom** The Hungarian Revolution Fails, pp. 278–280 **Historical Outline Map Book** Germany Divided, p. 67 Europe After World War II, p. 68 **Customized Reader** Why "Getting Tough" With the Soviet Union Is a Mistake, article VIIIB-11	**Lesson Planner** Activity Based, pp. 172–173 **Student Study Guide** Chapter 27 Study Guide, pp. 202–203 **Chapter Resources Binder** **Unit 9** Vocabulary Building, p. 1 Chapter Test A, pp. 7–9 Chapter Test B, pp. 10–12 Illustration Master, p. 13 Extra Unit Questions, pp. 57–59 **English Guided Reading** Guided Reading, pp. 53–54 **Spanish Resources** **Computer Test Bank** Chapter Tests A and B Extra Unit Questions **Guided Reading Audiotapes** Side 11 **CD-ROM** *Time Tour* The Fifties (1945–1960) in The Nation Today and Tomorrow
Transparencies *Political Cartoons* A Cartoonist's View of Cold War Hysteria, p. G-27 *Interdisciplinary Connections* Escape Velocity, p. B-85 **Videotapes/Videodiscs** *United States History Video Collection* The Cold War at Home, Vol. 20, Ch. 19; McCarthyism: The Second Red Scare, Ch. 22	**Voices of Freedom** A Marine's Korean War Journal, pp. 274–276 **Historical Outline Map Book** The Korean War, p. 69 **Customized Reader** *Sputnik* Startles the People of the United States, article VIIIB-8	
Transparencies *Geography and History* Growth of the Population, 1890–1990, p. I-45 **Listening to Literature Audiocassettes** *The American Experience* Rock Around the Clock, side 8 **CD-ROM** *Presidents* Dwight D. Eisenhower *Virtual Buildings* 1950s Suburban Home **Videotapes/Videodiscs** *United States History Video Collection* A Fair Deal for Americans, Vol. 20, Ch. 10; The Crabgrass Frontier, Ch. 13	**Voices of Freedom** Eisenhower Proposes a Middle Way, pp. 283–284 **Customized Reader** Coal Miners Out of Work, article VIIIB-12	
CD-ROM *Face the Issues* Brown *v.* Board of Education *History Makers* Thurgood Marshall **Videotapes/Videodiscs** *United States History Video Collection* The Civil Rights Movement, Vol. 20, Ch. 28	**Voices of Freedom** The Montgomery Boycott, pp. 286–288 **Customized Reader** African Americans Are Terrorized in a Chicago Housing Project, article VIIIA-6 Ending the Montgomery Bus Boycott, article VIIIA-1	

Lesson Planner

For a fully developed **Activity-Based** lesson plan for Chapter 27, see the *Lesson Planner,* pages 172–173.

 Chapter Resources

Vocabulary Building The Vocabulary Building worksheet for Chapter 27 from Unit 9, page 1, of the *Chapter Resources* binder can be used as a prereading activity or as a review of chapter vocabulary. (Reteaching/Easy)

 Student Study Guide

Chapter 27 Study Guide Refer students to pages 202–203 of the *Student Study Guide* for the Chapter 27 Study Guide. The study guide can be used for chapter review as well as for reteaching. (Reteaching/Average)

 Guided Reading Audiotapes

Students can use *Guided Reading Audiotapes,* Chapter 27, side 11, to listen to section previews, summaries, and review questions. The tapes will benefit students who are auditory learners, students who have trouble reading, or students acquiring English. Tapes are also available in Spanish. (Enrichment/Easy)

C H A P T E R 27

The Fifties

(1945–1960)

CHAPTER OUTLINE

1 The Nation Faces a Cold War

2 The Cold War Turns Hot

3 The Changing Face of the Nation

4 Roots of the Civil Rights Movement

1945 *The United Nations was founded. The UN flag shows the Earth surrounded by olive branches, a symbol of peace.*

1947 *George Marshall proposed an aid plan for war-torn Europe. The Marshall Plan helped Western European nations rebuild their economies.*

1950 *The Korean War began. These American soldiers were part of a UN force sent to help South Korea fight off a North Korean invasion.*

| 1945 | 1947 | 1949 | 1951 | 1953 |

 WORLD EVENT
1945 World War II ends

 WORLD EVENT
1949 Chinese communists set up People's Republic of China

Chapter Time Line
Understanding Chronology

Discuss the time line illustrations and captions, and give students time to learn which dates are linked to which events. Then check their understanding by having them complete statements such as the following:

- When the United Nations was founded, Chiang Kai-shek governed China. Communists won control of the country _____ years later. (four)
- Only _____ years after World War II ended, the Korean War began. (five)

- A period of _____ years separates the proposal of the Marshall Plan for Western Europe and the formation of the Warsaw Pact for Eastern Europe. (eight)
- Alaska and Hawaii achieved statehood _____ years after the Interstate Highway Act was passed and _____ years after school segregation was declared illegal. (three; five)

Invite students to suggest additional examples.

Chapter Setting

In Fulton, Missouri, on March 5, 1946, former British Prime Minister Winston Churchill gave a speech that made headlines across the United States. In it, he warned that the Soviet Union posed a grave threat to world peace:

66 From Stettin in the Baltic to Trieste in the Adriatic, an iron curtain has descended. . . . Behind that line lie all the capitals of. . . Central and Eastern Europe. Warsaw, Berlin, Prague, Vienna, Budapest, Belgrade, Bucharest, and Sofia,. . . all are subject. . . to a very high. . . measure of control from Moscow. 99

To Churchill, the iron curtain was an impassable barrier cutting off Eastern Europe from the rest of the world. Behind that barrier, the Soviet Union was setting up harsh governments. Citizens who protested were imprisoned or killed. Churchill pleaded for Americans to stand firm against the Soviet dictator, Stalin.

For the next 45 years, the United States and the Soviet Union faced each other as rival superpowers. Both sides armed themselves with powerful atomic weapons. In this struggle, the United States led the fight to protect democratic governments around the world.

ACTIVITY On an outline map of the world, fill in the places mentioned in Churchill's speech. Then draw a line representing the "iron curtain."

1954 *The Supreme Court ruled that school segregation was illegal. Here, a mother shares the news of the ruling with her daughter.*

1956 *Congress passed the Interstate Highway Act to link the nation by road. This painting captures the crush of traffic on the nation's highways.*

1959 *Alaska and Hawaii joined the Union as the forty-ninth and fiftieth states. Two stars were added to the American flag to represent the new states.*

| 1953 | 1955 | 1957 | 1959 | 1961 |

 WORLD EVENT
1950s Many African nations gain independence

 WORLD EVENT
1955 Soviet Union forms Warsaw Pact

Chapter 27 • **771**

Chapter Resources

English Guided Reading Duplicate and distribute the Chapter 27 Guided Reading worksheets on pages 53–54 in the English Guided Reading section of the *Chapter Resources* binder. Students who have difficulty reading might also benefit from using this worksheet. Have students complete the worksheet before they begin reading. You might pair a more fluent student or a student who is a stronger reader with each SAE student to review. (Reteaching/Easy)
Spanish Resources See the Spanish Resources section of the *Chapter Resources* binder.

ACTIVITY

Guided Instruction Have students locate on a map of Europe the cities and bodies of water that Churchill mentions. Then help students to trace the "iron curtain." Ask: Which of these countries had been under Nazi control during World War II? Which countries might have reason to feel threatened next by this "iron curtain"?

 CD-ROM

Time Tour Access The Fifties (1945–1960) section in The Nation Today and Tomorrow on the American Heritage® *History of the United States* CD-ROM. (Enrichment/Average)

Students Acquiring English
Activity

Many errors that SAE learners make in their writing are a result of differences in languages. For example, students who are native Spanish speakers will often pluralize words in English by adding *-es* because that is the way words are pluralized in Spanish. Thus, a word such as *nation* might become *nationes* when Spanish-speaking students write it. Use student writing relevant to the chapter to teach a mini-lesson on forming plurals in English.

Linking Past and Present
Activity

As students will learn in Section 3, the number of babies born between 1945 and 1965 in the United States was greater than ever before in American history. People born during those years became known as "baby boomers." Ask: How old are the baby boomers now? Have students predict five major effects they think this population explosion had on American life in the 20 years following World War II. Encourage them to supplement the text's information about baby boomers by researching other sources. Then discuss how closely their predictions matched the actual effects. Ask: How does the baby boom affect American life currently? How might baby boomers affect American life in the future?

Answer to Caption

Stalin broke his promise of allowing free elections in Eastern Europe and maintained communist control over the lands the Soviet Union had occupied.

Section 1
pp. 772–777

 Bell Ringer

Write the term *Cold War* on the chalkboard and ask students what they think it means. Have them describe the differences between a "cold" war and a "hot" war.

Lesson Plan

1. Focus In April 1945, the United Nations was created to foster world peace and to reduce hunger and disease. The United States and the Soviet Union were both members of the United Nations, yet they found themselves on opposite sides of a cold war. In this section, students learn how tensions between these countries developed after World War II.
2. Instruct Have a student read aloud the statement by President Truman on page 773. Help students analyze the quotation using these questions: What role did Truman think the United States had in world affairs? What did Truman think would happen if the United States did not exercise a leadership role? How did the attitude expressed by Truman lead to the Truman Doctrine and the Marshall Plan?

1
The Nation Faces a Cold War

FIND OUT
■ How did the Soviet Union expand its power after World War II?
■ How did the Marshall Plan help to prevent the spread of communism?
■ Why did the Cold War spread to Africa and Asia?

In 1945, much of Europe lay in ashes. Two atomic explosions had left Japan shaken and defeated. "A new era is upon us," General Douglas MacArthur observed. "The utter destructiveness of war now blots out this alternative. We have had our last chance."

Most Americans agreed with General MacArthur. Another world war had to be avoided at all costs. Yet in the new atomic age, the United States and the Soviet Union became caught up in a new kind of struggle. The ***Cold War,*** as it became known, was a state of tension between nations without actual fighting. It soon divided the world into opposing camps.

Roots of the Conflict

During World War II, the Allies had worked together to defeat the Axis powers. Yet the United States and Britain deeply distrusted the Soviet Union. The Soviets also distrusted the United States and Britain. When the war ended, this distrust grew.

Soviet expansion. In 1944 and 1945, Soviet troops drove the Germans out of Soviet territory and chased them west. By the end of the war, the Soviets occupied much of Eastern Europe.

772 • Chapter 27

At meetings during the war, Stalin had promised the other Allies that he would hold "free elections as soon as possible" in Poland and other Eastern European nations. After the war, however, he went back on his promise. "A freely elected government in any of the Eastern European countries would be anti-Soviet," he said, "and that we cannot allow."

In 1946, as you have read, the British statesman Winston Churchill warned of an "iron curtain" walling off Soviet-dominated nations from the rest of the world. (See page 771.) At first, some people thought Churchill exaggerated the danger of Soviet expansion. By 1948, however, the government of every Eastern European country was under communist control.

The Soviet Threat *Following World War II, fear of the Soviet Union grew among Western nations. This French poster shows the Soviet military threatening the peace of Europe. Stalin is the small figure in the center.* **Citizenship** *How did Stalin's actions in Eastern Europe help feed Western fears?*

SIBERIE

Connections With Language Arts
Background

The term *Cold War* probably originated with Walter Lippmann in 1947. Lippmann (1889–1974) was one of the leading political analysts of the twentieth century. His many books, magazine articles, and newspaper columns (which earned him the Pulitzer Prize in 1958 and again in 1962) discussed the contemporary world, with special emphasis on political and social problems in the United States. During the 1950s, he opposed the policy of containment (see the Linking Past and Present note on page 773) but favored the United States involvement in rebuilding Europe's economy.

Connections With Language Arts
Activity

A few years after the term *iron curtain* became part of Americans' vocabulary, a related term was added—*bamboo curtain.* Have students define *bamboo curtain,* drawing upon their understanding of *iron curtain* and their geographical knowledge of Southeast Asia. Save their definition and review it as students progress through Chapters 27 and 28.

Communist parties supported by the Soviet Union were also active in Western Europe. After the war, the Italian Communist party won 104 out of 556 seats in the Italian parliament. In Greece, communist rebels fought a civil war to overthrow the king. Neighboring Turkey felt Soviet pressure, too, when Stalin canceled a treaty of friendship between the two nations.

American response. President Truman grew more and more concerned about Soviet expansion. Like Churchill, he saw the danger of letting communist governments take power in other countries.

Truman decided that a show of strength was needed to stop Soviet expansion. In March 1947, he asked Congress for $400 million in military and economic aid for Greece and Turkey. In a statement to Congress, later called the **Truman Doctrine,** the President declared:

> ❝The free peoples of the world look to us for support in maintaining their freedoms. If we falter in our leadership, we may endanger the peace of the world—and we shall surely endanger the welfare of our own nation.❞

Under the Truman Doctrine, the United States pledged to help nations threatened by communist expansion. With American aid, both Greece and Turkey put down communist revolts.

Aid for Europe. Other European nations needed aid, too. The war had left homes, roads, and factories in ruins throughout Europe. Secretary of State George Marshall toured Europe. There, he saw thousands of refugees without homes. He saw others struggling just to find food to eat.

Marshall feared that hungry, homeless people might support communist revolutions. As a result, in June 1947, he proposed a large-scale plan to help Europe rebuild its economy. The President and Congress accepted the **Marshall Plan.**

Between 1948 and 1952, the Marshall Plan provided more than $12 billion in aid to Western European countries. By helping these nations recover, the Marshall Plan lessened the chance of communist revolutions in Western Europe.

Focus on Berlin

In 1948, a crisis developed. It focused around the former German capital, Berlin.

After the war, the Allies had divided Germany into four zones. American, British, French, and Soviet troops each occupied a zone. Berlin also was divided among the Allies. Berlin, however, was located deep inside the Soviet zone.

The United States, Britain, and France had meant the division of Germany to be temporary. By 1948, they were ready to allow Germans to reunite into a single nation. Stalin, on the other hand, opposed a unified Germany. He was determined to stop Germany from becoming a strong nation that might again threaten the Soviet Union. Also, he wanted to keep Soviet influence in the eastern part of Germany.

Soviet blockade. In June 1948, the United States, Britain, and France announced that they would join their zones into the German Federal Republic, or West Germany. In response, Stalin closed all the roads, railway lines, and river routes connecting Berlin with West Germany. The blockade cut off West Berlin from the rest of the world.

President Truman was in a difficult position. He did not want to let West Berlin fall into Soviet hands. Yet he also feared ordering American troops to open a path to West Berlin through the Soviet-occupied zone. Such an action might lead to a new war.

A huge airlift. Truman decided to set up a huge airlift. Day after day, planes flew in food, fuel, and other supplies to 2 million West Berliners. At the height of the Berlin Airlift, more than 5,000 tons of supplies arrived daily. A plane landed or took off every

3. Close To close the lesson, have students turn the headings for the subsections into questions and then answer them.

 Lesson Planner

For a developed **Cooperative Learning** lesson plan, see the *Lesson Planner,* page 168.

 Transparencies

Time Lines Use the transparency, The United States and the World, 1945–1960, on page E-27 of *American History Transparencies.* The transparency shows students what global events were occurring as the United States struggled with its postwar problems. Teaching suggestions can be found on page E-9. (Enrichment/Average)

 Chapter Resources

Critical Thinking Duplicate and distribute the worksheet, Analyzing Ideas, from Unit 9, page 3, of the *Chapter Resources* binder. The worksheet explores the reasoning behind and the effects of the Truman Doctrine. (Enrichment/Average)

Linking Past and Present
Activity

The political philosophy behind the Truman Doctrine was known as *containment.* According to this view, the United States should counter communism wherever it threatened to develop.

Have small groups of students research and present to the class examples of how the United States allowed the idea of containment — either of communism or of some other political ideology — to shape its foreign-policy decisions in the past 45 years. Use their information as a springboard for class discussion.

Connections With the World
Background

Despite its political overtones, the Marshall Plan was promoted as a goodwill gesture of social aid. At a commencement address at Harvard in 1947, Marshall explained, "Our policy is directed not against any country or doctrine but against hunger, poverty, desperation, and chaos."

One of the programs established through the Marshall Plan was the Displaced Persons Plan. Under this program, approximately 300,000 Europeans — many of whom were Jewish survivors of the Holocaust — gained American citizenship.

Connections With Economics
Background

Stalin pointed to "technical difficulties" as the reason for stopping traffic into Berlin. Actually, part of his reason may have been his frustration at having a secret plan of his discovered. His blockade came quickly after the Allies introduced a new currency into the Western zones — a currency made necessary by the fact that the Soviets had been flooding the area with counterfeit money in an attempt to undermine its economy.

Customized Reader

Primary Source For a dissenting view on United States Cold War policy, order article VIIIB-11, Why "Getting Tough" With the Soviet Union Is a Mistake, from the *American History Customized Reader*. In this speech, Henry A. Wallace, a member of Truman's Cabinet, argues against the arms race. (Enrichment/Challenging)

Historical Outline Map Book

Historical Outline Maps Duplicate and distribute the maps, Germany Divided, and Europe After World War II, on pages 67 and 68 of the *American History Historical Outline Map Book*. Lesson ideas for these maps can be found on page T21. (Reteaching/Average)

Airlift *The United States daily flew in tons of supplies to blockaded Berlin. Here, children wave to planes bringing in food.* **United States and the World** *Did the airlift achieve its purpose? Explain.*

three minutes. A *Life* magazine article described the scene:

> ❝By now the planes are passing overhead hundreds of times a day. In the crowded lunchroom at Tempelhof [Airfield] quiet, tired American pilots grab coffee and a sandwich. . . . Outside, on the edge of the field, a ragged German crowd gathers . . . and German boys squint through holes in the field fence with the open-mouthed fascination of American kids watching a ball game.❞

Germany remains divided. Stalin could see that the western powers were determined to keep Berlin open. In May 1949, nearly a year after he first imposed the blockade, he ended it.

Both Germany and Berlin remained divided, however. With aid from the United States, West Germany rebuilt its economy. The Soviet zone became the German Democratic Republic, or East Germany.

Keeping the Peace

Many of the disputes in the Cold War were debated in the new international peacekeeping organization known as the **United Nations** (UN). The UN came into being in October 1945, when 51 original members ratified its charter.

The United Nations. Every member of the UN had a seat in the General Assembly, where world problems could be discussed. For conflicts that threatened the peace, a smaller Security Council met. Under the United Nations charter, member nations agreed to bring disputes before the UN for peaceful settlement.

Over the years, the UN's greatest successes have been in fighting hunger and disease and improving education. United Nations health officers have vaccinated millions of children. UN relief programs have provided tons of food, clothing, and medicine to victims of disasters.

Preventing wars has proved more difficult. Sometimes, nations have refused to go along with United Nations decisions. In other cases, the UN has kept crises from becoming full-scale wars. As you will read, the UN played an active part in the Korean War.

Opposing alliances. As another way of keeping international order, the United States formed alliances with friendly nations. In 1949, it joined with Western European countries to form the **North Atlantic Treaty Organization,** or NATO. (See the map at right.) By joining NATO, the United States made it clear that it would help defend the nations of Western Europe against any Soviet aggression.

Our Common Heritage
Ralph Bunche, grandson of an enslaved African American, helped write the charter of the United Nations. "If the United Nations cannot insure peace," he declared, "there will be none." In 1950, Bunche became the first African American to win the Nobel peace prize.

Our Multicultural Heritage
Background

Ralph Bunche (discussed in the Our Common Heritage note in the text) was born in Detroit and raised by his grandmother after his parents died. He took his grandmother's advice about getting a good education: He graduated first in his class at Jefferson High School in Los Angeles and went on to Harvard, where he became the first African American to earn a Ph.D. in political science.

In a time of widespread discrimination, Bunche found that his education opened many doors. An expert on Africa and the Far East, he held a high-level job in the State Department. In 1948, Bunche joined the UN mission to the Middle East. In the face of constant death threats, he worked to make peace between Israel and its Arab neighbors. It was his success at negotiating an armistice that earned him the Nobel peace prize.

Bunche later helped to settle serious conflicts in the Congo and in Cyprus. "There are no warlike people," he insisted, "only warlike leaders."

Cooperative Learning
Activity

The United Nations is linked with numerous independent agencies. Have pairs or small groups of students research and report on any of the following:

■ Food and Agriculture Organization
■ International Atomic Energy Agency
■ International Labor Organization
■ International Monetary Fund
■ United Nations Children's Fund
■ United Nations Educational, Scientific, and Cultural Organization
■ World Health Organization

In 1955, the Soviet Union formed its own military alliance, called the **Warsaw Pact.** The Soviet Union demanded complete loyalty from its Warsaw Pact neighbors.

In Hungary, freedom fighters hoped to gain independence from Soviet control. Encouraged by the United States, they staged an uprising in 1956. The Soviet Union responded by sending in the army to crush the revolt. To many Americans, the invasion of Hungary showed how dangerous the Soviet Union was.

MAP STUDY

By 1955, the United States and 14 other nations, including 10 Western European nations, belonged to NATO. That year, the Soviet Union and seven Eastern European nations formed the Warsaw Pact.

1. Which nonaligned nation bordered the Soviet Union?
2. Which NATO nations bordered Warsaw Pact nations?
3. **Analyzing Information** Why do you think most European nations belonged either to NATO or to the Warsaw Pact?

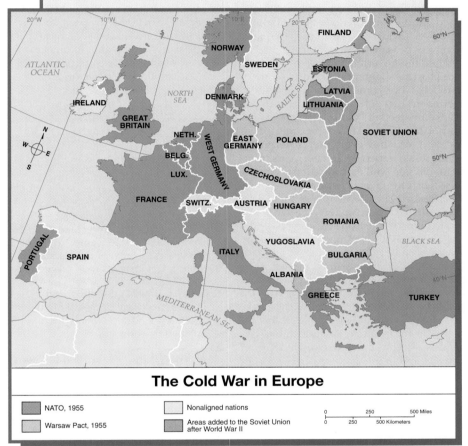

The Cold War in Europe

NATO, 1955
Warsaw Pact, 1955
Nonaligned nations
Areas added to the Soviet Union after World War II

0   250   500 Miles
0   250   500 Kilometers

Answers to Map Study

1. Finland   2. West Germany, Greece, and Turkey   3. Possible Answer: Most countries felt that they would be less vulnerable to attack if they belonged to a military alliance. The Soviet bloc nations may also have felt that they had no choice.

Voices of Freedom

Primary Source You might assign selection 17-5, The Hungarian Revolution Fails, on pages 278–280 of *Voices of Freedom.* This selection presents Hungary's plea and the world's general response. (Enrichment/Challenging)

Videotapes/ Videodiscs

United States History Video Collection Use the video segment "The Cold War" from Volume 20, *Post-War U.S.A.*, to enhance students' understanding of the roots of the conflict between the United States and the communist world. Approx. running time 5:10 min.(Enrichment/Average) Vol. 20, Ch. 16

Chapter 16   Play

Historical Sidelight
Background

In October 1956, discontent over the return to power of Matthias Rakosi — a communist dictator who had ruled Hungary from 1949 to 1953 — resulted in street fighting in Budapest, the capital, and quickly spread throughout the country. Imre Nagy, the more moderate premier who had replaced Rakosi from 1953 to 1955, declared Hungary a neutral country. His government, however, was put down after only a few days, with the arrival of Soviet troops. Nagy and his colleagues were convicted of treason and were executed in 1958.

During the revolution, about 200,000 Hungarians fled the country. Cardinal Joseph Mindszenty, the leader of the Roman Catholic Church in Hungary, had been a political prisoner since 1949 but was freed during the revolution. He sought asylum in the United States embassy in Budapest, where he lived until 1971, when he was finally allowed to leave Hungary.

Linking Past and Present
Background

The year 1989 brought several changes to Hungary. First, the 1958 trial of Imre Nagy and his colleagues was declared illegal, and the bodies of the executed leaders were reburied with honor. Even more important, Hungary's constitution was revised. Political freedoms were greatly expanded, and the one-party communist government was restructured as a multiparty, parliamentary democracy, led by a president. In 1990, Hungary had its first multiparty elections since 1949.

Emerging Nations

After World War II, peoples in Africa and Asia began to demand independence. For years, they had been governed as European colonies. In the postwar years, many new nations gained independence. (See the map at right.)

Philippines. In Asia, the United States gave independence to the Philippines. On July 4, 1946, crowds in Manila braved heavy rains to attend the independence ceremony. As the American flag was lowered and the Filipino flag hoisted high, a warship fired a 21-gun salute.

The transition to independence was not easy. A small number of wealthy Filipinos owned most of the land. Many Filipinos wanted to divide the land more equally among the peasant farmers.

When the government moved slowly to make changes, fighting broke out. Some of the rebels were communists. By 1954, the government had defeated the rebels. It also made some needed land reforms.

After Ferdinand Marcos became president in 1965, however, the government became less democratic. In later years, noncommunists as well as communists continued to push for greater reforms.

India. In 1947, the people of India won independence from Britain. The land was divided into two nations, however—India and Pakistan. Both the United States and the Soviet Union tried to win the support of these nations. India remained neutral. Pakistan became an ally of the United States.

Southeast Asia. In Southeast Asia, Indonesia won freedom from the Netherlands. Burma, Malaysia, and Singapore became independent from Britain. In Indochina,* nationalists fought for independence from France. Fighting in Indochina lasted for almost 30 years. Before it ended, it involved

*Indochina included the present-day countries of Laos, Cambodia, and Vietnam.

the United States in a long war, as you will read in Chapter 28.

Africa. Africans also worked for independence after the war. Libya, a former Italian colony, became fully independent in 1951. Not until 1956, however, did France give independence to Morocco and Tunisia. The people of Ghana gained independence from Britain in 1957. Over the next decade, more than 25 other new African nations were formed.

Cold War battlegrounds. As the Cold War continued, the nations of Africa and Asia became battlegrounds in the struggle between the communist and noncommunist world. Communist rebels often campaigned to overthrow European control of their countries. The United States and its allies tried to prevent the Soviet Union from expanding its power and influence. In this state of continued tension, it was not long before a shooting war broke out.

SECTION 1 REVIEW

1. **Locate:** (a) Greece, (b) Turkey, (c) Berlin, (d) Hungary, (e) India, (f) Ghana.
2. **Identify:** (a) Cold War, (b) Truman Doctrine, (c) Marshall Plan, (d) United Nations, (e) North Atlantic Treaty Organization, (f) Warsaw Pact.
3. (a) What was the "iron curtain"? (b) Why were Americans concerned about it?
4. What was the goal of the Marshall Plan?
5. What major changes took place in Asia and Africa after World War II?
6. **CRITICAL THINKING Synthesizing Information** Why do you think the wartime friendship among the Allies fell apart after World War II?

ACTIVITY **Writing to Learn**
Imagine that you live in Berlin in 1949. Write a letter to a cousin in the United States about the Berlin Airlift.

MAP STUDY

At the end of World War II, only four nations in Africa were free of colonial rule. Today, there are more than 50 independent African nations.

1. Which African nations were independent before 1945?
2. Which was the first nation to gain independence after World War II? In what year?
3. **Drawing Conclusions** Why do you think the newly independent nations became a battleground in the struggle between communist and noncommunist forces in the Cold War?

Nations of Africa

- Independent before 1945
- Independent 1945–1965
- Independent 1966–Present

Answers to Map Study

1. Egypt, Liberia, Ethiopia, and South Africa   2. Libya; 1951   3. Possible Answer: The leaders of a newly independent country might look to established governments for advice; communists were already at work in Africa, and the United States wanted to keep communism from spreading.

Chapter 27 • **777**

Connections With the World
Background

As students work through the Map Study feature, you might mention the following facts:

- After it became independent, Libya was a constitutional monarchy. It remained as such until 1969, when a junta led by Muammar al-Qaddafi seized power.
- Before its independence, Ghana was known as the Gold Coast. Côte d'Ivoire retained its colonial name — the Ivory Coast — until 1985.
- The nations of Rwanda and Burundi were once united as the UN trusteeship of Ruanda-Urundi, administered by Belgium.

- Tanzania became a nation in 1964, as the result of the joining of Tanganyika (the former British colony on the mainland that had gained its independence in 1961) and Zanzibar (the two islands off Tanganyika's coast that gained independence from Britain in 1963).
- Until 1980, Zimbabwe was known as Rhodesia. The older name was in honor of Cecil Rhodes, who had conquered the area for the British South Africa Company in the 1890s.

Critical Thinking
Understanding Causes and Effects

In the summer of 1960, many French colonies gained independence — Benin, Burkina Faso, Chad, Côte d'Ivoire, the Congo, Gabon, Madagascar, Niger, and Senegal. In a class discussion, ask: Why were so many colonies granted independence in such a short period? How might these events have changed the role of France in world affairs? How might they have changed other governments' thinking about Africa? Encourage students to do research to support their responses.

Section 2
pp. 778–783

Bell Ringer

Have students locate China on a world map. Ask: Why would American leaders of the late 1940s be alarmed at the possibility of China's coming under communist control?

Lesson Plan

1. Focus After World War II, several Asian countries gained independence and several others became embroiled in civil wars. In this section, students examine major developments in China and Korea that led the United States to dispatch troops to Asia.

2. Instruct Divide the class into six groups. Have each group present a television news report on events of the Korean War during one of the following months: June 1950, August 1950, September 1950, November 1950, April 1951, and July 1953. Post a large map of Korea and have students refer to the map during their reports. Reports should provide background information and may include interviews with soldiers and political leaders.

3. Close To close the lesson, have students create a class time line that presents the key events of the Korean War.

2
The Cold War Turns Hot

FIND OUT

- What was the result of the civil war in China?
- Why did the United States become involved in the Korean War?
- How did Senator Joseph McCarthy increase fears of communism?
- What was the result of the arms race between the United States and the Soviet Union?

"**F**or me, it was a typical Sunday night in Japan," recalled Sergeant First Class Bill Menninger. Menninger was part of the United States Army that was stationed in Japan after World War II. The time was June 1950.

&& It had rained all day. My wife was giving the kids a bath prior to putting them to bed, and I was reading a book... when the call came for me to report at once to headquarters! The wife wanted to know what the call was about. 'Something must be wrong with next week's training schedule,' I answered. 'I'll be back as soon as I can.' &&

As it turned out, Menninger did not return for 11 months. When he got to headquarters, he learned that communist North Korea had invaded South Korea. The Cold War had turned hot. American troops suddenly found themselves in the middle of a deadly shooting war.

Growing Interest in Asia

Few Americans in 1950 knew very much about Korea. Why did the United States send troops there to fight and die?

Events in Asia affected the United States in many ways. For more than 100 years, American ships had traded regularly with China and Japan. Between 1899 and 1946, the United States had governed territory in Asia—the Philippines. Also, the attack on Pearl Harbor in 1941 had proved that Americans could not ignore events halfway around the world.

The Cold War focused even more attention on Asia. Would communism spread to newly independent nations such as India and Indonesia? Rebels were fighting for independence in Vietnam and other Southeast Asian lands. Some of these rebels were communists.

People's Republic of China

In the late 1940s, Americans focused special attention on China. Chiang Kai-shek (chang kì SHEHK) was the ruler of China. For years, he had fought a war against the Chinese communists, led by Mao Zedong (mow dzuh DOONG). By 1945, Mao's forces occupied northern China. Chiang's armies held the south.

The United States gave Chiang Kai-shek millions of dollars in aid. Chiang's government was corrupt, however, and he lost the support of his people. In 1949, the battle for the Chinese mainland ended with a communist victory. Mao Zedong set up the People's Republic of China. Chiang Kai-shek and his forces retreated to Taiwan, an island about 100 miles (160 km) off the coast of China.

Mao Zedong's victory meant that the largest nation in Asia had become communist. The Chinese communists did not always agree with the Soviet Union. Yet between them, these two communist nations dominated almost one fourth of the Earth's surface. Many Americans worried that communist forces would soon take over all of Asia. As you will read, some Americans became obsessed with their fears of communism.

Connections With the World
Background

The struggle between Chiang Kai-shek and Mao Zedong dated back to the 1920s. However, when Japan invaded China in 1937, the two leaders agreed to set aside their differences in order to better fight their common enemy. Their alliance was always uneasy, and with the end of World War II, they again turned on each other. The United States attempted to mediate the dispute but withdrew in 1947.

Linking Past and Present
Activity

Explain that for the next 30 years the United States continued to recognize as the legitimate government of all China only the nationalists on Taiwan. This decision was reinforced through United States military protection of Taiwan. Challenge students to find out how and why that position changed. Encourage interested students to use visuals, historic reenactments, and so on to present their information.

Triumph of the Communists *In January 1949, Mao Zedong led his forces into Beijing, the capital of China. This wall poster was created to celebrate Mao's triumph.* **United States and the World** *Why was Mao's victory a blow to the United States?*

Fighting in Korea

Meanwhile, trouble was brewing in Korea. From 1910 to 1945, Korea had been a Japanese colony. After World War II, Korea was divided at the 38th parallel of latitude. North Korea was governed by communists supported by the Soviet Union. A noncommunist government in South Korea was backed by the United States.

In June 1950, North Korean soldiers swept across the 38th parallel into South Korea. President Truman acted quickly. He asked the United Nations to send armed forces to Korea to stop the invasion.

Setting up a UN force. The Security Council agreed to set up a UN force. Its commander would be a general chosen by President Truman. The President chose General Douglas MacArthur for the job. About 80 percent of the UN forces were Americans.

If the Soviet representative had been present, he probably would have vetoed the decision of the Security Council. At the time, however, the Soviets were boycotting Security Council meetings because the UN had denied membership to the People's Republic of China.

A daring counterattack. MacArthur's job was to push the North Koreans out of South Korea. At first, however, UN forces were outnumbered and poorly supplied. Armed with huge new Soviet tanks, the North Koreans rumbled south. By August 1950, communist troops controlled almost all of South Korea.

Then MacArthur launched a daring counterattack. He landed by sea at Inchon, behind North Korean lines. Caught by surprise, North Koreans were forced back across the 38th parallel. (See the map on page 780.)

Chinese invasion. MacArthur's original orders called for him to drive the North Koreans out of South Korea. Truman and his advisers, however, wanted to punish North Korea for its aggression. They also wanted to unite the two Koreas. To meet these goals, they won UN approval for MacArthur to cross into North Korea.

Linking Past and Present
American soldiers in Korea noticed that Koreans had a unique way of heating their houses. Heat circulated beneath stone floors, warming the rooms above. In recent years, American architects have adopted the same system as a way to conserve energy.

 Lesson Planner

For a developed **Cooperative Learning** lesson plan, see the *Lesson Planner,* page 169.

Answer to Caption

The American-supported government of Chiang Kai-shek fell, making the largest nation in Asia a communist state.

Historical Outline Map Book

Historical Outline Maps Duplicate and distribute the map, The Korean War, on page 69 of the *American History Historical Outline Map Book.* Lesson ideas for this map can be found on page T21. (Reteaching/Average)

 ### Videotapes/ Videodiscs

United States History Video Collection Use the video segment "The Cold War at Home" from Volume 20, *Post-War U.S.A.,* to enhance students' understanding of the impact of the Cold War within the United States. Approx. running time 1:40 min. (Enrichment/Average) Vol. 20, Ch. 19

Chapter 19   Play

Historical Sidelight
Background

General MacArthur's surprise attack at Inchon was a daring gamble that paid off. Many other military officers opposed a landing there because the troops would be required to land both at high tide and in daylight—a combination that occurred only a few days each month. Even worse, there were 30-foot tides, which fell so quickly that in 10 minutes, troops in landing boats could find themselves stranded on mud flats and at the mercy of enemy guns. But the Marine Corps successfully negotiated the landing and quickly moved on to recapture Seoul.

A career soldier, MacArthur had served in World War I. He had also been superintendent of West Point and chief of staff of the army. Retired in 1937, he was recalled in 1941 to lead United States forces in the Far East. During World War II, he was true to his promise to liberate the Philippines and was considered a hero on the islands.

Connections With Technology
Background

During World War II, helicopters had been used for observation and rescue work. In Korea, however, they were used for the first time in an extensive program of troop and supply transport. It also was during this war that the nicknames *chopper, egg beater,* and *whirlybird* came into use for *helicopter.*

Answers to Map Study

1. North Korea; South Korea; South Korea **2.** about 35 miles (50 km) **3.** Possible Answer: probably, because in September 1950 — just before the UN counterattack — North Korea controlled almost the entire peninsula

Voices of Freedom

Primary Source You might assign selection 17-3, A Marine's Korean War Journal, on pages 274–276 of *Voices of Freedom*. This excerpt, from a marine's diary, describes his feelings during one of his platoon's missions. (Enrichment/Average)

Our Multicultural Heritage

Biography Have students read the biography, Charles Bussey, American Officer in Korea, on page 79 of the *Our Multicultural Heritage* booklet. (Enrichment/Average)

Milestone Have students read Integrating the Armed Forces, on page 81 of the *Our Multicultural Heritage* booklet. (Enrichment/Easy)

Transparencies

Political Cartoons Use the transparency A Cartoonist's View of Cold War Hysteria on page G-27 of *American History Transparencies*. Students can use this lesson to explore viewpoints on the fear of communism. Teaching suggestions can be found on page G-9. (Enrichment/Challenging)

MAP STUDY

When North Korean forces drove deep into South Korea, a United Nations force came to the aid of the South.

1. Which side controlled Seoul in September 1950? In November 1950? At the end of the war?
2. How close to North Korea is Inchon?
3. **Drawing Conclusions** Based on the map, do you think communist forces would have won control of all of Korea if the UN had not sent troops?

The Korean War

——— Farthest North Korean advance, September 1950

——— Farthest UN advance, November 1950

- - - - Farthest North Korean-Chinese advance, January 1951

——— Armistice line, July 1953

Quickly, MacArthur pushed northward. Alarmed, the Chinese communists warned that they would not "sit back with folded hands" if the United States invaded North Korea. When UN forces neared the Chinese border, thousands of Chinese crossed the Yalu River into North Korea. They helped the North Koreans turn back the UN forces. Once again, MacArthur was forced to retreat deep into South Korea.

Ending the War

By March 1951, UN troops had regained control of the south. By then, General MacArthur was convinced that the UN could win in Korea only if it attacked China. President Truman, on the other hand, had become more cautious. An American attack on China, he believed, might start a new world war. He preferred to limit the war and restore the old boundary between North and South Korea.

Truman fires MacArthur. MacArthur complained publicly that politicians in Washington were holding him back. "We must win," he insisted. "There is no substitute for victory." Angry that MacArthur was defying orders, Truman fired the general.

Many Americans were furious. They gave MacArthur a hero's welcome when he returned to the United States. Truman, however, strongly defended his action. He felt that MacArthur's statements undermined attempts to reach a peace settlement. Under the Constitution, he pointed out, the President is commander in chief. As commander in chief, it was Truman—not the general—who had power to make the key decisions about war and peace.

Cease-fire. Peace talks began in July 1951. At first, there was little progress. Then, in 1952, the popular World War II General Dwight D. Eisenhower was elected President. To fulfill a campaign promise, he journeyed to Korea to get the stalled peace talks moving.

Historical Sidelight
Background

As the Korean peace talks began, Americans were shocked when 21 American prisoners of war chose to remain in China. It was commonly believed that these men had been brainwashed—that is, their loyalties had been turned as a result of physical and emotional torture and nonstop communist indoctrination. The Chinese used the term *hsi nao*—literally, "to wash the brain"—to refer to the technique, and the English translation *brainwash* stuck.

In 1952, Americans again had cause to suspect that communists used brainwashing. When North Korea was plagued by epidemics that spring, the communists blamed the United Nations. To support their claim, they produced 38 captured American pilots who confessed to dropping cholera-infested insects on North Korea. After the war, the UN proved that the claim was false, and all 38 pilots repudiated their confessions.

Cooperative Learning
Activity

Have groups of students organize a project to record oral histories from older relatives or neighbors who are veterans of the Korean War. Each group can develop a list of questions for an interview with veterans about their experiences in Korea. Have each group prepare and present a report about what its members have learned.

In July 1953, the two sides finally signed a cease-fire agreement ending the war. More than 54,000 Americans lost their lives in the Korean War. Nearly 2 million Koreans and Chinese also were killed in the fighting.

In one sense, the Korean War changed nothing. The cease-fire set the border between North and South Korea near the 38th parallel, where it had been before. Yet by fighting the Korean War, the UN had pushed back North Korea's invasion. The United States and its allies showed that they were ready to fight communist expansion into noncommunist nations.

Hunting Communists at Home

Cold War tensions fed fears of communism at home. In 1949, officials in the United States announced that they had detected radiation from a secret test of atomic weapons in the Soviet Union. Americans were shaken. The United States was no longer the only nation with the ability to build an atomic bomb.

Between 1946 and 1950, a number of people in the United States, Canada, and Great Britain were arrested as Soviet spies. In the United States, Ethel and Julius Rosenberg were accused of stealing secrets about nuclear weapons. A jury found the Rosenbergs guilty, and they were sentenced to die. Such a severe sentence for civilians convicted of espionage was unusual. Still, despite worldwide protests, the Rosenbergs were executed in 1953.

McCarthy's reckless claims. Were other Soviet agents secretly working against the United States government? Early in 1950, Senator Joseph McCarthy of Wisconsin announced that he had a list of 205 State Department employees who were Communist party members. McCarthy's claim was never proved. Yet his dramatic charges won him national attention.

During the next four years, McCarthy made many more accusations about communists in the government. Thousands of government employees had to undergo questioning. Little evidence of communist activity was found.

McCarthy's campaign spread fear and suspicion across the nation. Businesses, colleges, and even movie studios questioned

CAUSES

- Soviet Union takes control of Eastern European nations
- Communism gains in Western Europe, the Middle East, and Asia
- Western powers fear Soviet expansion

THE COLD WAR

EFFECTS

- United States gives economic aid to Greece, Turkey, and Western Europe
- Berlin Airlift ends a Soviet blockade
- Western powers and the Soviet Union form separate military alliances
- Korean War breaks out
- Americans fear communist influence at home
- Arms race develops between United States and the Soviet Union

Understanding Causes and Effects
After World War II, the Cold War broke out. The Soviet Union and its satellites were on one side, and the United States and its allies were on the other. • List two causes of the Cold War. Which effect of the Cold War involved Americans in actual fighting?

Connections With Civics
Background

The Rosenbergs may have been the least guilty of the alleged spies connected with the atomic center at Los Alamos, New Mexico; there was much stronger evidence against others in the group. The Rosenbergs claimed innocence, but they took the Fifth Amendment when questioned about their views on communism. Unlike the others on trial, the couple refused to help the prosecution—a decision that many political analysts feel led directly to their death sentence by the electric chair.

Historical Sidelight
Background

When Senator McCarthy investigated the film industry, a parade of movie stars—including future President Ronald Reagan, president of the Screen Actors Guild—testified about suspected communists in film. Others refused to "name names" of possible communists. Playwright Lillian Hellman refused to disclose the names of communists she had known: "I cannot and will not cut my conscience to fit this year's fashions."

Ten witnesses, known as the "Hollywood 10," were imprisoned for contempt, for refusing to give testimony against others. Many other talented people were barred from working in films because some film producers adopted a "blacklist" of suspected communists. The hearings destroyed the careers of scores of writers, producers, and performers, although, in the end, there was little evidence of communist influence in Hollywood.

employees. Scores of loyal citizens lost their jobs.

The senator's downfall. In 1954, the Senate held televised hearings to investigate McCarthy's charges that there were communists in the United States Army. Millions of Americans watched as the senator from Wisconsin made wild charges without having any proof. Under the glare of the television lights, McCarthy came across to the public as a bully, not a hero.

In December 1954, the Senate passed a resolution condemning McCarthy for "conduct unbecoming a member." As a result, McCarthy began to lose power and popularity. By the time of his death three years later, the worst of the red scare was over.

The Arms Race

As the Cold War continued, the United States and the Soviet Union entered an arms race. Each side built up its supply of missiles and atomic weapons.

In 1953, the Soviet Union tested a powerful hydrogen bomb—similar to one developed by the United States. In 1957, a Soviet rocket launched the world's first artificial satellite, called *Sputnik.* (See Connections, at right.) Americans were stunned. If the Soviets could launch a satellite into outer space, their atomic missiles could reach the United States as well.

The new leader of the Soviet Union, Nikita Khrushchev (KROO shawf), bragged that his nation would soon surpass the United States. Khrushchev boasted that new rockets were coming off Soviet factory lines "like sausages."

Many Americans worried that the United States faced a "missile gap." In fact, the United States remained well ahead of the Soviet Union in the arms race. Between 1958 and 1960, the number of atomic weapons stockpiled by the United States tripled— from 6,000 to 18,000.

To protect against possible atomic attacks, some families and communities built "fallout shelters." These underground hideaways were designed to protect against the radiation of an atomic blast. In school, students took part in air-raid drills that taught them what to do in case of an atomic missile attack.

In the arms race, both sides spent billions of dollars on weapons and missiles. Even though fighting never broke out between the United States and the Soviet Union, tensions remained high. Atomic weapons posed the threat of one final war that might end civilization on Earth.

SECTION 2 REVIEW

1. **Locate:** (a) China, (b) North Korea, (c) South Korea, (d) 38th parallel, (e) Yalu River.
2. **Identify:** (a) Chiang Kai-shek, (b) Mao Zedong, (c) General Douglas MacArthur, (d) Ethel and Julius Rosenberg, (e) Joseph McCarthy, (f) *Sputnik,* (g) Nikita Khrushchev.
3. (a) What two groups battled in China? (b) Which group won?
4. (a) What action led to the Korean War? (b) Why did the Chinese join the fighting? (c) How did the war end?
5. (a) How did Senator Joseph McCarthy come to national attention? (b) What events helped bring an end to McCarthy's influence?
6. Why did the United States and the Soviet Union enter an arms race?
7. **CRITICAL THINKING Analyzing Information** Why do you think the Constitution made the President the commander in chief of the military?

ACTIVITY Writing to Learn
Write a series of newspaper headlines summarizing the events of the Korean War.

CONNECTIONS

Reading, 'Riting, 'Rithmetic—and Science

On Saturday morning, October 5, 1957, Americans learned the shocking news. The Soviet Union had launched the world's first artificial satellite! It weighed a little over 184 pounds and hurtled around the Earth at 18,000 miles an hour. Called *Sputnik I,* or "fellow traveler" in Russian, the satellite orbited the Earth once every hour and 35 minutes.

To Americans, it was frightening that the Soviets were so far ahead in the space race. In the words of Washington Senator Henry Jackson, *Sputnik* was "a devastating blow to the prestige of the United States as the leader in the scientific and technical world."

Many Americans accused the schools of failing to train students in science and mathematics. It was time to return to the basics, they said. "The schools," commented an Illinois minister, "should cut out the three H's—hoopin', hollerin', and hullabalooin'—and drill the three R's."

Responding to the public outcry, Congress passed the National Defense Education Act (NDEA) in 1958. The law declared that "the security of the Nation requires the fullest development of the mental resources and technical skills of its young men and women."

Soviet Premier Khrushchev holding model of *Sputnik*

The $1 billion NDEA was meant to produce more scientists and more science teachers in the United States. It provided money for loans to students wishing to continue their science education—especially for those planning to teach science in elementary or secondary schools. It also provided funds for laboratories and scientific equipment for schools and colleges.

For the next few years, American schools committed themselves to a "pursuit of excellence." Student test scores rose in science and math. Meanwhile, the United States made progress in the "space race," launching its own satellite, *Explorer I,* into orbit early in 1958 and landing the first person on the moon in 1969. Despite early fears, the Soviets had not won the "space race."

■ How did the launching of *Sputnik* affect American education?

Diagram of *Sputnik*

ACTIVITY

Improving American education has once again become an important national goal. Create a poster presenting your ideas about how education should be improved.

Chapter 27 • **783**

Answer to Connections

It prompted a greater emphasis on science and mathematics education, including the use of government funds to provide student loans and to build and equip school science laboratories.

ACTIVITY

Guided Instruction You might begin by having the class brainstorm to generate ideas. Then have students work individually or in small groups to create the posters. Encourage various forms of artistic expression, but remind students to keep the focus of each poster simple. As time permits, you might expand this activity to involve students' parents and/or the local school board.

Team-Teaching Suggestion
Science

You might work with a science teacher to present a lesson about milestones in the development of satellite technology and about the use of satellites today. Consider involving students in the preparation of the lesson by having them report (possibly on a videotape) on a recent news item that demonstrated the usefulness of weather or communications satellites.

Team-Teaching Suggestion
Mathematics

You might work with a mathematics teacher to present a lesson that shows how math is used in planning orbital missions. Prepare and help students solve problems relating to escape velocity, thrust, fuel usage, orbital altitude and speed, and so on.

Section 3
pp. 784–789

Bell Ringer

Ask students what they think of when they hear the term *suburbs*. Give them 3 to 5 minutes to freewrite, jotting down words, thoughts, and images.

Lesson Plan

1. Focus A rapidly growing population in the late 1940s and the 1950s led to a building boom and the growth of the suburbs. A prosperous economy enabled more Americans to purchase luxury items. In this section, students examine the social and economic changes of the 1950s.

2. Instruct Ask students to make at least six generalizations about how American life changed in the 1950s. Write these on the chalkboard. Then have students list supporting facts for each generalization. Discuss how each fact supports the generalization.

3. Close To close the lesson, play a Jeopardy!-like game with students. Have pairs of students provide three facts from the section, exchange facts with those provided by another pair, and create appropriate questions for the facts received.

3
The Changing Face of the Nation

FIND OUT

■ How did the economy expand after World War II?

■ Why did suburbs grow rapidly in the 1950s?

■ How did television affect American life?

VOCABULARY closed shop, baby boom

Sylvia Porter, a newspaper columnist, had been reading United States census figures. She noticed that an astonishing number of babies were being born in the United States. What, she wondered, would be the effect of all these new Americans?

66Take the 3,548,000 babies born in 1950. Bundle them into a batch, bounce them all over the bountiful land that is America. What do you get? Boom. The biggest, boomiest boom ever known in history. Just imagine how much these extra people, these new markets, will absorb—in food, in clothing, in gadgets, in housing, in services. Our factories must expand just to keep pace.99

Porter was right. After World War II, the United States entered a long period of economic growth. These years were also a time of important social change.

A Peacetime Economy

When World War II ended in 1945, the nation faced the task of changing back to a peacetime economy. During the war, mil-

lions of Americans had been employed in making goods for the military. With the war over, where would defense workers and returning soldiers find jobs? Many experts feared that the unemployment of the Great Depression would return.

In 1944, even before the war ended, Congress passed what became known as the ***GI Bill of Rights.*** Under it, the government spent billions of dollars to help veterans set up farms and businesses. Many GIs received loans to go to college. The act also gave veterans unemployment insurance for a period of up to one year.

Inflation and strikes. A major economic problem after the war was inflation. During the war, the government had controlled the price of food and other goods as well as wages. When the war ended, the government removed wage and price controls. The price of food, clothing, and other goods soared.

Because of wage controls, workers had not received pay increases during the war. Now, they demanded more pay. When employers refused worker demands, unions went on strike. Steelworkers, meatpackers, auto workers, coal miners, and railroad workers walked off the job.

In 1947, Congress voted to pass the ***Taft-Hartley Act*** over President Truman's veto. The act was meant to prevent a new wave of strikes. It allowed the government to apply for a court order delaying for 80 days any strike that threatened public health or safety. Also, the act banned the closed shop. A closed shop is a business or factory that agrees to hire only union members.

The economy expands. As the economy expanded, the wave of strikes ended. Americans who had saved their money during the war now wanted to spend it. They wanted new houses, cars, and clothing.

---

*GI stands for "government issue." During World War II, a GI came to mean any member of the United States armed forces.

Connections With Civics
Background

The official name of the GI Bill of Rights was the Servicemen's Readjustment Act. In signing it, President Franklin D. Roosevelt stated, "It gives emphatic notice to the men and women in the armed forces that the American people do not intend to let them down." Under its terms, all veterans were offered money for up to four years schooling; veterans with special skills were funded for three years. By 1947, more than four million veterans were taking advantage of the various opportunities afforded by the GI Bill of Rights.

Linking Past and Present
Activity

Invite a representative from a local armed forces recruitment office to address the class about the benefits available to service personnel and veterans today. Have the speaker focus especially on those areas that the GI Bill of Rights addressed—education, housing, insurance, and employment. Allow a question-and-answer time afterward.

Connections With Civics
Background

As may well be imagined, organized labor had fiercely resisted the Taft-Harding Act. The AFL said that it had been "conceived in a spirit of vindictiveness"; the CIO said that it had been "conceived in sin." A group of 1,450 Californians went to Washington, D.C., to protest what they called the "slave labor bill." President Truman himself had received some 800,000 letters and 500,000 signatures against it—a fact that probably shaped his last-minute decision to veto the bill.

The postwar economy was also helped by government spending. As the Cold War continued, the government spent billions of dollars on new military weapons. The Korean War also created a demand for new arms. In addition, laws such as the GI Bill increased government spending for education and welfare.

Postwar Leaders

The strikes and soaring prices helped Republicans who were running for Congress in 1946. "Had enough?" one slogan read. "Vote Republican!" Many Americans did. For the first time in years, Republicans won a majority in both the House and the Senate.

Election of 1948. In 1948, Truman's popularity seemed at an all-time low. Republicans confidently nominated Governor Thomas Dewey of New York as their candidate for President. Truman fought back, crisscrossing the country by train. At every stop, he made hard-hitting speeches attacking the "do-nothing" Eightieth Congress. He warned that Republicans were "just a bunch of old mossbacks all set to do a hatchet job on the New Deal." Crowds warmed to his scrappy style.

Still, most people expected a Dewey victory on election night. They were in for a surprise. When all the votes were counted, Truman squeaked past Dewey to victory.

The Fair Deal. The tight race demonstrated the mood of the voters. Americans were not ready to give up the reforms of the New Deal, which Truman supported. Still, they were not willing to push those reforms much further.

After the election, Truman proposed a broad package of reforms known as the Fair Deal. Congress passed only some of the President's measures. It raised the minimum wage. It expanded Social Security to cover more people. But Congress rejected a bill that would have provided health insurance financed by the government.

Truman versus Dewey *The 1948 presidential election stirred heated debate across the country. In this painting by Norman Rockwell, a husband argues in favor of Thomas Dewey, while his wife sticks by President Harry Truman.* **Citizenship** *Why are political arguments an important part of American life?*

In 1952, Truman announced that he would not run for reelection. Democrats nominated Adlai Stevenson, the governor of Illinois. Republicans rallied behind General Dwight Eisenhower, whom they fondly called Ike. Campaigning with the slogan "I like Ike," Eisenhower won a landslide victory. After 20 years of Democratic Presidents, a Republican moved into the White House.

History and You
Wearing a button to state a political preference is an old American tradition. Design a button in support of a political cause or candidate. Think of a lively slogan to put on it.

 Lesson Planner

For a developed **Cooperative Learning** lesson plan, see the *Lesson Planner*, page 170.

Answer to Caption

Possible Answer: Political arguments are one form of a free, democratic exchange of ideas. Such debates also help citizens explore the issues faced by the nation.

Videotapes/ Videodiscs

United States History Video Collection Use the video segment "A Fair Deal for Americans" from Volume 20, *Post-War U.S.A.,* to enhance students' understanding of President Truman's domestic goals and accomplishments after World War II. Approx. running time 3:00 min.(Enrichment/Average) Vol. 20, Ch. 10

Chapter 10   Play

Customized Reader

Primary Source For a magazine article on the coal industry, order article VIIIB-12, Coal Miners Out of Work, from the *American History Customized Reader*. The article discusses the effects of a mine closing on a small community in Pennsylvania. (Enrichment/Average)

Connections With Civics
Background

The Twenty-second Amendment to the Constitution, passed by a Republican majority in Congress, went into effect in 1951. It limited a President to two full terms in office. The amendment did not apply to President Truman, who was already in office. It had the same effect, however. In 1952, Truman chose not to run for reelection.

Historical Sidelight
Background

Looking back on his White House years, Truman said in a 1959 interview, "Some of the Presidents were great and some of them weren't. I can say that because I wasn't one of the great Presidents; but I had a good time trying to be one." In 1960, Truman campaigned for presidential candidate John F. Kennedy. At Truman's death in 1972, President Richard M. Nixon — the Republican Truman had helped to defeat in 1960 — eulogized him graciously. Noting that Truman had been thrust into the presidency "at one of the most critical moments of our history," Nixon said that Truman "met that moment with courage and vision. His farsighted leadership. . . has helped ever since to preserve peace and freedom in the world."

Truman's successor was a more reluctant candidate. Eisenhower was pressured to run in 1948, but he refused, explaining, "I cannot conceive of any circumstance that could drag out of me permission to consider me for any political post from dogcatcher to Grand High Supreme King of the Universe."

Voices of Freedom

Primary Source You might assign selection 18-3, Eisenhower Proposes a Middle Way, on pages 283–284 of *Voices of Freedom*. The selection gives Eisenhower's views on government. (Enrichment/Average)

CD-ROM

Presidents Access the biography of Dwight D. Eisenhower from the American Heritage® *History of the United States* CD-ROM.

Virtual Buildings Access the 1950s Suburban Home on the American Heritage® *History of the United States* CD-ROM.

Transparencies

Geography and History Use the transparency, Growth of the Population, 1890–1990, on page I-45 of *American History Transparencies* to show growth in population density in the United States. Teaching suggestions are on page I-6. (Enrichment/Average)

Chapter Resources

Geography in History Duplicate and distribute the worksheet, Boston: From City to Suburb, from Unit 9, pages 5–6, of the *Chapter Resources* binder. It explores how and why the suburbs of Boston grew as they did. (Enrichment/Challenging)

The road down the middle. Like most Republicans, Eisenhower believed that the federal government should limit its control over the economy. Still, he kept some New Deal programs, such as Social Security. As you will read, Eisenhower also supported a large government program to build a system of superhighways. The President summed up his goals when he said, "The great problem of America today is to take that straight road down the middle."

The Eisenhower years were prosperous for many Americans. In 1956, Eisenhower won reelection easily. In 1957, however, the nation suffered an economic slowdown. As unemployment rose, some Democrats called for more New Deal-style programs. Eisenhower resisted. By 1959, the economy had improved. The President felt that his middle-of-the-road course had worked.

In 1959, the United States reached another landmark. That year, it grew to include 50 states when Alaska and Hawaii entered the Union.

Life in the 1950s

The United States was growing in more than one way. In the late 1940s and 1950s, the birthrate—or number of children being born—soared. Population experts talked about a **baby boom.** In the 1950s, the population grew by 29 million, compared to 19 million in the 1940s and 9 million in the 1930s.

Growing families. In part, American families were growing quickly to make up for lost time. During the hard times of the Great Depression, it was difficult to support a large family. Many couples who married during World War II waited until after the war to have children.

Improvements in health and medical care also contributed to the baby boom. Better care for pregnant women and new-born infants meant that more babies survived. Fewer children died from childhood diseases than in the past, too. In 1955, for example, Dr. Jonas Salk introduced a vaccine against polio, a virus that killed or crippled both adults and children.

The suburbs grow. Growing families led many Americans to look for new housing. During World War II, some families had moved in together to save money and use all the available space. Others lived in basements. In 1945, houses were so scarce that one newspaper jokingly advertised a large icebox that "could be fixed up to live in."

As Americans pursued the dream of owning a home of their own after the war, many looked to the suburbs. During the 1950s, suburbs grew 40 times faster than cities. The government encouraged the building of new houses by offering low-interest loans to veterans.

In the 1940s and 1950s, William Levitt pioneered a new way of building suburban houses. He bought large tracts of land and then subdivided them into small lots. On each lot, he built an identical house. Because these houses were mass produced, they cost less to build than custom-made houses.

Levitt began his first big project in 1947. On Long Island, outside New York City, he put up 17,000 homes. Each house had the same plan. Teams of carpenters, plumbers, and electricians moved from house to house. When they worked on schedule, a new house was finished every 16 minutes! Levitt called the project **Levittown.** He went on to build other Levittowns in New Jersey and Pennsylvania.

Cars and highways. As people moved to the suburbs, cars became more important to American life. Unlike most city dwellings, suburban houses were far from stores. Also, workers usually needed a car to commute to work. By 1960, 9 out of 10 families living in the suburbs owned a car.

Connections With Economics
Background

With the growth of postwar prosperity, the time allotted for leisure activities increased for many Americans. The 40-hour work week (compared with the 70-hour work week of 100 years earlier) left more time available for play. By 1959, Americans were spending $30 to $40 billion annually on recreation—20 times more per person than in 1900. In 1959, 33 million people went swimming at least once, 32 million went fishing, 32 million dancing, 18 million bowling, and 16 million hunting.

Critical Thinking
Understanding Causes and Effects

Tell students that one unexpected change in postwar family life was a rise in the divorce rate. Even in 1946—the first full year after the war's end—there were more divorces than ever before in American history. Ask: How might this information relate to the fact that many couples romanced and wed quickly before the men went off to war? How might being apart during the war years have changed the relationships of husbands and wives?

Connections With Art
Background

New styles transformed the visual arts in the 1950s, as many American artists moved from realistic painting to a form known as abstract impressionism. Viewers of the new art were often puzzled by what appeared to be paint splashed on canvas, but the abstract impressionists were serious painters. Some, such as Jackson Pollock, used swirling colors to absorb the viewer in emotion. Pollock often laid a canvas flat on the floor and poured or dripped paint onto it. "I can control the flow of paint," he said. "There is no accident."

MAP, GRAPH, AND CHART SKILLS
Using Public Opinion Polls

In a country with a democratic form of government, public opinion—or what people think about different issues—is important. Since the 1930s, Americans have been conducting public opinion polls. These polls measure the opinions, attitudes, or beliefs of large numbers of people.

Polls are conducted by newspapers, radio stations, and politicians, as well as by private groups whose main job is surveying public opinion. In 1958, *Scientific American* magazine polled 3,000 high school students across the United States to get their views on a variety of issues. Below are statements that teens were asked to respond to and their answers.

1. **Identify the subject of the poll.** (a) When was the poll taken? (b) What issues did the pollsters ask about?

2. **Practice reading the data.** (a) What percentage of students believed there should be more women in public office? (b) With which statement did the largest percentage of students agree? (c) Which statement dealt with the teenagers' views concerning authority?

3. **Evaluate the information.** (a) What did teenagers of the 1950s think about the importance of citizen involvement in government? How do you know? (b) What did teenagers of the 1950s think about politics? How do you know? (c) Why do you think communism was a major concern for teenagers in the 1950s? (d) After examining these poll results, list some words you would use to describe American teenagers of the 1950s.

ACTIVITY
Find out how the views of students today compare with those of students of the 1950s. Ask 10 students in your school to respond to the statements in the 1958 *Scientific American* poll. Record their answers and present your findings to the class. How are the views similar to the views of students in 1958? How are they different? What might account for any differences?

The most serious danger to democracy in the United States comes from communists and communist-dominated groups.

Agree	76%
Disagree	13%
Uncertain	11%

Obedience and respect for authority are the most important virtues that children should learn.

Agree	75%
Disagree	16%
Uncertain	9%

Sending letters and telegrams to members of Congress has little influence on legislators.

Agree	41%
Disagree	36%
Uncertain	23%

If a person is uncertain how to vote, it is better that he or she does not vote.

Agree	44%
Disagree	45%
Uncertain	11%

The average citizen is justified in remaining aloof from dirty politics that may exist in his or her community.

Agree	57%
Disagree	24%
Uncertain	19%

There should be more women in public office.

Agree	36%
Disagree	46%
Uncertain	18%

Chapter Resources

Skill Application For additional practice, duplicate and distribute the worksheet, Using Public Opinion Polls, from Unit 9, page 2, of the *Chapter Resources* binder. (Reteaching/Average)

Answers to Skill Lesson

1. (a) 1958 (b) communism, family relationships, and citizenship and civics issues

2. (a) 36% (b) the first statement, regarding the threat of communism (c) the second statement

3. (a) Possible Answer: They probably did not consider it very important because their responses show doubts about citizens' effectiveness in influencing legislators and the value of voting. (b) Possible Answer: The responses suggest that teenagers felt that politics was the arena of an elite group who were not necessarily trustworthy. (c) Of the students polled, 76 percent called communism the greatest threat to the United States. (d) Possible Answers: conservative, traditional, pessimistic

ACTIVITY

Guided Instruction You might encourage class members to tell the source of the questions (some of which may seem odd to teenagers of the 1990s) to the students they poll. As students try to explain the differences in their completed polls, urge them to consider how relationships with the former Soviet Union have changed and how teenagers today are encouraged to take a greater interest in politics.

Students Acquiring English
Activity

SAE students should have little trouble interpreting the percentages in the responses given or in computing the percentages for their own polls. It is vital, however, that they fully understand the six statements. As a whole-class activity, you might discuss the meaning of each statement, calling on volunteers to rephrase each one in their own words as many times as is necessary to ensure student understanding.

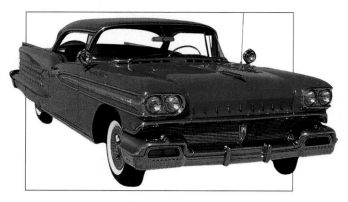

The Latest Model *Long bodies, bright colors, polished chrome, and sweeping tail fins were features of American cars in the 1950s. This 1958 Holiday Coupe sold for a list price of $3,262.* **Linking Past and Present** *List three ways in which this car differs from most cars today.*

Federal, state, and local governments encouraged the move to the suburbs by building thousands of miles of new highways. In 1956, Congress passed the **Interstate Highway Act.** It called for a network of high-speed roads linking the entire nation. To complete the system, federal, state, and local governments spent over $250 billion. It was the largest public works project in history.

As they grew in importance, automobiles also grew longer and more stylish. Auto makers competed with one another to design models with bigger engines, wider bodies, and sweeping tail fins. As one manufacturer commented, the new styles were "gasaroony!"

Shopping centers sprang up near suburban housing developments. In the 1950s, shopping centers were a brand-new sight. They had department stores, sparkling new supermarkets, and huge lots where parking was free.

Television

As the economy prospered, many Americans were able to buy goods that once were considered luxuries. Appliances such as refrigerators, electric toasters, and irons, as well as clothes washers and dryers, made life easier.

The product that probably had the greatest effect on American life was television. In 1946, only about 17,000 television sets existed in the entire country. In the 1950s, almost 7 million television sets were sold each year.

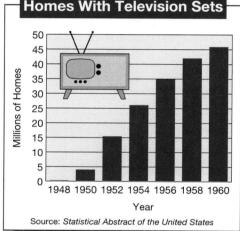

Homes With Television Sets

Source: *Statistical Abstract of the United States*

GRAPH SKILLS *Before 1950, television was a novelty. By the end of the decade, however, television sets were a common feature in American homes.● During which two-year period did the number of homes with television sets increase the most? How many homes had television sets by 1960?*

788 • Chapter 27

788

Television brought news, sports, and entertainment into people's homes every day. In 1952 and 1956, millions of Americans watched political conventions on TV for the first time. Television also created a new crop of celebrities. Every week, some 20 million teenagers tuned in to Dick Clark's *American Bandstand*. On the program, they saw and heard rock 'n' roll stars sing their latest hits.

The new shows offered something for everyone. Children enjoyed *Howdy Doody*, a puppet show that featured characters named Buffalo Bob, Clarabelle, and Phineas T. Bluster. Parents watched variety specials, quiz shows, and westerns. The husband and wife team of Desi Arnaz and Lucille Ball starred in the zany family comedy series *I Love Lucy*. As more and more families bought television sets, television—for better or for worse—became a major influence in American life.

SECTION 3 REVIEW

1. **Identify:** (a) GI Bill of Rights, (b) Taft-Hartley Act, (c) Dwight Eisenhower, (d) Jonas Salk, (e) Levittown, (f) Interstate Highway Act.
2. **Define:** (a) closed shop, (b) baby boom.
3. (a) Name two problems that the economy faced after World War II. (b) Name two things that helped the economy in the postwar years.
4. How did the growth of suburbs affect the nation?
5. Name two ways in which television changed American life.
6. **CRITICAL THINKING Understanding Causes and Effects** Describe three effects of the baby boom.

ACTIVITY Writing to Learn
Imagine that you are an advertising writer in the 1950s. Write an ad for a house in a suburb like Levittown.

4
Roots of the Civil Rights Movement

FIND OUT
- What advances were made in the fight against segregation?
- Why did African Americans boycott the buses in Montgomery, Alabama?
- What methods did Martin Luther King, Jr., use to fight for equal rights?

VOCABULARY civil disobedience

In 1957, William Myers, Jr., went looking for a house. He and his wife were expecting a baby, and they needed more living space. Myers, a World War II veteran, liked the look of Levittown, Pennsylvania, a new suburban community of about 60,000 people.

Myers and his family were African Americans. When they moved into their Levittown house, hostile white residents threw a rock through their picture window. Others made threatening telephone calls. It took a court order and a statement from Pennsylvania's governor to restore calm.

In both the North and the South, African Americans faced segregation in jobs, housing, and education. African American groups, such as the NAACP, stepped up the struggle for change.

Segregation in the North and South

African Americans throughout the country continued to face discrimination in the 1950s. In the North, many qualified African Americans could not get jobs that paid well.

Answers to Section 3 Review

1. (a) GI Bill of Rights, p. 784, (b) Taft-Hartley Act, p. 784, (c) Dwight Eisenhower, p. 785, (d) Jonas Salk, p. 786, (e) Levittown, p. 786, (f) Interstate Highway Act, p. 788
2. (a) closed shop, p. 784, (b) baby boom, p. 786
3. (a) Possible Answers: Wage and price controls imposed during the war were lifted and inflation resulted; unions went on strike for higher wages. (b) Possible Answers: The demand for products increased; people began

to spend the money they had saved during the war.
4. Many tract homes were built because they could be produced more quickly and inexpensively than custom-built homes; the car became more important to American life; shopping centers became popular.
5. Possible Answers: People were able to watch the news, political events, and sports competitions from their own homes; television created a new crop of celebrities.

6. Possible Answers: a booming economy to satisfy the increased demand for goods and services from a growing population; expansion from the cities into the suburbs as more growing families wanted to buy their own homes; increased importance of cars in American life because people in the suburbs had less access to public transportation; the growth of an interstate highway system to handle increased traffic; suburban shopping centers

2. Instruct Write the following excerpt from the Supreme Court's decision in *Brown* v. *Board of Education* on the chalkboard:

> To separate [black students] from others of similar age and qualifications solely because of their race generates a feeling of inferiority as to their status in the community that may affect their hearts and minds in a way unlikely ever to be undone.

Lead a discussion on how *Brown* v. *Board of Education* reversed *Plessy* v. *Ferguson.*

3. Close To close the lesson, have students answer a series of *Who, What, When, Where, Why,* and *How* questions about people and events in Section 4.

 Lesson Planner

For a developed **Cooperative Learning** lesson plan, see the *Lesson Planner,* page 171.

Answer to Caption

Possible Answer: Fans responded positively to this African American athlete, which meant that others would also probably be accepted.

 CD-ROM

Face the Issues Use the segment about *Brown* v. *Board of Education* from the American Heritage® *History of the United States* CD-ROM. (Enrichment/Challenging)

Black people were often forced to live in segregated neighborhoods. In the South, Jim Crow laws segregated the races. These laws kept blacks out of public places such as hotels, restaurants, libraries, movie theaters, and laundromats.

Those seeking an end to segregation won a small success in 1948. That year, President Truman ordered the armed forces to stop segregating blacks into separate units. During the Korean War, black and white soldiers fought together in integrated, or mixed, units.

In the area of voting rights, there was less progress. As part of the Fair Deal, Truman asked Congress for a law banning poll taxes. Poll taxes, you recall, were fees a person had to pay in order to vote. Poll taxes had often kept poor African Americans from voting. Congress, however, rejected the bill to ban poll taxes.

A Major Victory

Despite setbacks, African American leaders continued to work for equality. Their efforts became known as the **civil rights movement.** One of their first targets was segregated schools.

In 1896, the Supreme Court had decided in *Plessy* v. *Ferguson* that "separate but equal" facilities for blacks and whites were constitutional. (See page 499.) The NAACP had challenged this idea with some success in the 1940s. Yet, in the early 1950s, laws in

> ***Our Common Heritage***
> *In 1959, Lorraine Hansberry wrote a play about an African American family in Chicago that buys a house in an all-white suburban neighborhood. The play,* A Raisin in the Sun, *became the first play by a black woman to be produced on Broadway.*

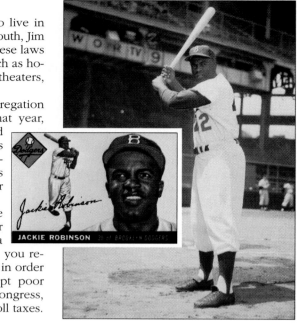

BIOGRAPHY Jackie Robinson *African American baseball players competed in a segregated league until 1947, when the Brooklyn Dodgers signed Jackie Robinson. Ignoring insults and threats, Robinson won over fans with his daring play. He later became the first black player elected to the Baseball Hall of Fame.* **Multicultural Heritage** *How might Robinson have paved the way for African Americans in other sports?*

---

21 states and the District of Columbia still allowed segregated public schools.

Challenging the law. Oliver Brown of Topeka, Kansas, decided to challenge the Kansas law. He asked the local school board to let his daughter, Linda, attend the all-white school near their home rather than the distant, segregated school where she had been assigned. The school board refused Brown's request.

With the help of the NAACP, Brown filed a suit against the school board. The case of ***Brown* v. *Board of Education of Topeka*** reached the Supreme Court.

Our Multicultural Heritage
Activity

Have students create a geographic history of the early civil rights movement in the United States. Post a large map of the United States on a classroom bulletin board. Then instruct students to put a symbol of their own design at each place on the map where a key event in the civil rights struggle took place. Among the places that students might note are Topeka, Kansas; Montgomery, Alabama; and Little Rock, Arkansas. Have students write a notecard to accompany each place marked on the map. The notecard should explain why the place has been recognized. As students read Section 4, they will be able to add other places to the map. Then have them mark on the map the route for a historical tour of the early civil rights movement.

Connections With Sports
Background

After Jackie Robinson's success, several major league teams actively recruited not only African Americans, but also Latin American players. At other levels, change came more slowly. Not until 1962 was an African American hired to coach a team. In that year, Buck O'Neil became coach of the Chicago Cubs. Four years later, Emmett Ashford became the first African American umpire in the major leagues. Finally, in 1974, Frank Robinson was hired by the Cleveland Indians as the first African American manager of a major league team.

Brown's lawyer, Thurgood Marshall,* argued that "separate" could never be "equal." Segregated schools, he said, could never provide equal education. By their very nature, segregated schools violated the Fourteenth Amendment, which gave "equal protection" to all citizens.

The Supreme Court ruled in Brown's favor in 1954. In writing the decision, Chief Justice Earl Warren noted that segregation affected the "hearts and minds" of black students "in a way unlikely ever to be undone." A year later, the Court ordered the schools to be desegregated "with all deliberate speed."

Integrated schools. In a few places, schools were integrated fairly smoothly. In others, problems arose.

In Little Rock, Arkansas, Governor Orval Faubus opposed integration. In 1957, he called out the National Guard to keep African American students from attending Central High School. President Eisenhower stepped in because the Arkansas governor was defying a federal law. Eisenhower sent troops to Little Rock. Under their protection, black students entered Central High.

The Voices of Montgomery

Meanwhile, African Americans began challenging other segregation laws. In some parts of the South, they took their case to the public through mass protests.

Rosa Parks is arrested. Rosa Parks was riding home from work on a crowded bus in Montgomery, Alabama, in December 1955. The driver ordered her to give up her seat so that a white man could sit down, as Alabama's Jim Crow laws required.

Parks was a quiet woman who rarely argued with anyone. On this afternoon, how-

---

*In 1967, Thurgood Marshall was appointed to the United States Supreme Court. He thus became the first African American Justice on the nation's highest court.

BIOGRAPHY Thurgood Marshall *As a lawyer and as the first African American Supreme Court Justice, Thurgood Marshall never stopped fighting for equal rights for all Americans. Perhaps his greatest triumph came when he won the case of* Brown v. Board of Education of Topeka. ***Citizenship*** *What was the result of that case?*

ever, she was very tired. Politely but firmly, she refused to leave her seat. She was arrested, fingerprinted, and sent to jail.

The news spread quickly among Parks's friends. They gathered the money needed to post bail to get her out of jail. Should they fight the case in court? they wondered. Parks, a member of the NAACP, was willing. She had to convince her family, however. "The white folks will kill you, Rosa," warned her husband. Parks decided to take the risk.

Organizing a boycott. A number of women from the NAACP met at midnight. They composed a letter to the black community of Montgomery:

66[A] Negro woman has been arrested and thrown into jail because she

---

Connections With Civics
Background

Even before 1957, President Eisenhower had tried to enforce school desegregation in Little Rock. As a result, Republicans actively campaigned in African American neighborhoods when Eisenhower was up for reelection in 1956. On election day, Eisenhower received 40 percent of the African American vote — a figure that no Republican candidate for President has matched since.

A key voice for Eisenhower's "Task Force '56" was a Democrat from the House of Representatives — Adam Clayton Powell, an African American minister from the community of Harlem in New York City. Powell, who had begun his Washington career in 1945, had himself done much to desegregate the halls of Congress. Ignoring the list of "Do's and Don'ts for Negro Congressmen" that he had received on his arrival, Powell had broken the color barrier in the House and Senate dining rooms and had become the first African American to use the congressional showers and barbershop. Furthermore, through Powell's efforts, black members of the Capitol police force received more equitable treatment and black reporters were admitted to the press gallery.

Historical Sidelight
Background

Melba Pattillo Beals, a black student who helped integrate Central High School in Little Rock, Arkansas, later recalled how she had been harassed: "We'd be showering in the gym and someone would turn your shower into scalding. You'd be walking out to the volleyball court and someone would break a bottle and trip you on the bottle. I have scars on my right knee from that."

Chapter Resources

Voices of Freedom

refused to get up out of her seat on the bus and give it to a white person. . . . The next time it may be you, or you, or you. This woman's case will come up Monday. We are, therefore, asking every Negro to stay off the buses on Monday in protest of the arrest and trial. **99**

Through the night, the women made hundreds of copies of the letter. Over the weekend, they distributed the copies around Montgomery. Then they waited. Would the boycott work?

Dr. King. At dawn on Monday, the Reverend Martin Luther King, Jr., one of the boycott's supporters, peered anxiously out his front window. Next to him stood his wife, Coretta. Suddenly, they spotted a bus coming down the street. It was empty!

Hopeful and excited, King hurried to his car and drove around town. Every bus he saw was empty or had only a handful of white riders.

That afternoon, Montgomery's black leaders met. They decided to extend the boycott. They chose King to head the organization they were forming to continue the boycott. It was called the Montgomery Improvement Association. As his first action, Dr. King called a public meeting for Monday evening at the Holt Street Baptist Church.

"Serious business." Well before time for the meeting, hundreds of people had already crowded into the pews. Thousands more stood outside. Upon his arrival, it took King 15 minutes to work his way through the crowd. Then Dr. King spoke—slowly and clearly. "We are here this evening—for serious business." "Yes, yes!" the crowd shouted. As King's words rolled out, the crowd cheered him on:

66 I want it to be known—that we're going to work with grim and bold determination—to gain justice on the buses in this city. And we are not wrong. . . . If we are wrong—the Supreme Court of this nation is wrong! . . . If we are wrong—justice is a lie. And we are determined here in Montgomery—to work and fight until justice runs down like water, and righteousness like a mighty stream! **99**

King was stunned by the roar from the crowd. His words had struck a spark. Martin Luther King, Jr., was only 26 years old. Yet

Rosa Parks and the Montgomery Bus Boycott *For refusing to give up her seat to a white man, Rosa Parks landed in jail. She also made history. Her simple "no" sparked the Montgomery bus boycott and boosted the civil rights movement.* **American Traditions** *Give other examples of how an individual's actions can change society.*

Historical Sidelight
Background

Our Multicultural Heritage
Background

Nonviolent Protest *Martin Luther King, Jr., talks to reporters after his arrest during the Montgomery bus boycott. King was inspired by Mohandas Gandhi of India, who had used civil disobedience to win independence from Britain.* **Economics** *Why are boycotts an effective method of nonviolent protest?*

Answer to Caption

Possible Answer: By cutting off a source of income, protesters show those being boycotted the seriousness of their complaint and their determination to bring about change.

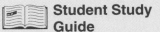 **Customized Reader**

Primary Source For a newspaper article on the end of the Montgomery bus boycott, order article VIIIA-1, Ending the Montgomery Bus Boycott, from the *American History Customized Reader.* The article reveals that the year-long boycott ended because of a Supreme Court decision. (Enrichment/Easy)

Student Study Guide

Section 4 Study Guide Have students use the Section 4 Study Guide on page 201 of the *Student Study Guide* to review and reinforce the content of this section. (Reteaching/Average)

ACTIVITY

Guided Instruction Students might brainstorm to generate personal, moral, and/or legal arguments for their letters. Invite students to compare their finished letters in small groups.

he was already becoming the nation's most powerful voice for civil rights.

A hard-won battle. The Montgomery Improvement Association did not win its battle easily. In the months that followed, King and others were arrested. King's house was bombed. Still, the boycott continued.

King insisted that his followers limit their actions to **civil disobedience,** or nonviolent protests against unjust laws. He said, "We must use the weapon of love. We must have compassion and understanding for those who hate us."

The boycott in Montgomery attracted national attention. In 1956, the Supreme Court ruled that segregation on buses was unconstitutional. The Montgomery bus company agreed to integrate the buses and also to hire black bus drivers.

Still, segregation remained widespread. The protests of the 1950s would grow into a much larger protest in cities and towns all across the United States. ∎

SECTION 4 REVIEW

1. **Identify:** (a) civil rights movement, (b) *Brown* v. *Board of Education of Topeka,* (c) Thurgood Marshall, (d) Rosa Parks, (e) Martin Luther King, Jr.
2. **Define:** civil disobedience.
3. (a) List three ways in which segregation affected African Americans. (b) What arguments did Thurgood Marshall use against segregated schools?
4. (a) What prompted the Montgomery bus boycott? (b) What was the outcome?
5. **CRITICAL THINKING Making Decisions** Do you think that civil disobedience is an effective method of protest? Explain.

ACTIVITY Writing to Learn

Imagine that you are Linda Brown. Write a letter to the Topeka Board of Education explaining why you should be allowed to attend the school of your choice.

Answers to Section 4 Review

1. (a) civil rights movement, p. 790, (b) *Brown* v. *Board of Education of Topeka,* p. 790, (c) Thurgood Marshall, p. 791, (d) Rosa Parks, p. 791, (e) Martin Luther King, Jr., p. 792
2. civil disobedience, p. 793
3. (a) Most African Americans lived in segregated neighborhoods; went to segregated and usually inferior schools; were prevented from getting many jobs; and, in the South, were kept out of certain public places. (b) Thurgood Marshall argued that segregated schools could never provide equal education and that segregated schools violated the Fourteenth Amendment, which gave "equal protection" to all citizens.

4. (a) Rosa Parks was arrested for refusing to give up her bus seat to a white man. (b) The Supreme Court ruled that segregation on buses was unconstitutional. The bus company agreed to integrate the buses and to hire black bus drivers. Furthermore, the strike brought Martin Luther King, Jr., national attention.

5. Possible Answers: Yes, because civil disobedience draws attention to injustice without intentionally harming anyone; no, because civil disobedience can be a slow process, because spectators can too easily ignore or forget civil demonstrations, and because real change results from stronger actions.

CHAPTER 27 REVIEW

Answers to Reviewing the Main Ideas

1. (a) The United States believed that communism took away people's freedom. It also believed that the Soviet Union would threaten world peace if it became too strong. (b) Under the Truman Doctrine, the United States sent aid to other countries so that their governments could restore order, put down revolts, and rebuild after the war.

2. President Truman ordered fuel, food, and other supplies to be airlifted into West Berlin.

3. The UN has fought hunger and disease, improved education, and saved many cultural treasures. UN health officers have vaccinated millions of children. UN relief programs have provided tons of food, clothing, and medicine to victims of wars and natural disasters.

4. After World War II, many nations in Asia and Africa sought independence. Both the United States and the Soviet Union tried to win the support of these emerging nations. The new nations became battlegrounds in the struggle between communism and democracy.

5. (a) In June 1950, North Korean soldiers invaded South Korea. (b) President Truman asked the UN to send in troops. American soldiers made up 80 percent of the UN force. (c) The border between North and South Korea was set at the 38th parallel; a demilitarized zone was created; the United States showed its willingness to fight communism actively.

6. McCarthy's campaign spread fear and caused many innocent people to lose their jobs.

7. (a) The baby boom created a demand for housing and an increased availability of goods and services. (b) More Americans owned their own homes and commuted to work; downtown districts of cities declined. (c) Television changed the way in which Americans viewed the world.

8. Most African Americans had little choice but to accept unskilled and low-paying jobs and inferior housing and schools. Many were barred from some public places

Summary

- After World War II, tensions between communist and noncommunist nations led to the Cold War.
- American soldiers fought in Korea against communist forces from North Korea. At the same time, fear of communism led to a red scare at home.
- The face of the nation changed as the population grew rapidly and many people moved to the suburbs.
- New African American leaders emerged to lead the civil rights movement and fight discrimination.

Reviewing the Main Ideas

1. (a) Why did the United States object to Soviet expansion? (b) How did the Truman Doctrine try to combat Soviet expansion?

2. How did the United States respond to the Berlin blockade?

3. What major successes has the UN had?

4. How did the new nations of Africa and Asia become involved in the Cold War?

5. (a) What was the immediate cause of the Korean War? (b) How did the United States get involved in the war? (c) Describe one result of the war.

6. How did Senator McCarthy's anticommunist campaign affect the nation?

7. Explain how the following affected American life in the 1950s: (a) the baby boom, (b) move to the suburbs, (c) television.

8. What kinds of discrimination did African Americans face in the 1950s?

Thinking Critically

1. Analyzing Information After World War I, the United States returned to an isolationist policy and refused to join the League of Nations. Why do you think the United

States did not return to isolationism after World War II?

2. Making Decisions Was President Truman right to fire General MacArthur? Explain.

3. Linking Past and Present In the 1950s, Americans watched political conventions on television for the first time. How does television affect political campaigns today?

Applying Your Skills

1. Reading a Map Study the map of the Korean War on page 780. (a) How many times did North Korea advance into South Korea? (b) In 1950, General MacArthur landed at Inchon. Was he in North Korea or South Korea? (c) Why might China have become alarmed at the American invasion?

2. Comparing Compare the Supreme Court decision in *Plessy* v. *Ferguson,* on page 499, to its decision in *Brown* v. *Board of Education of Topeka.* (a) What issue was brought up in both cases? (b) What was the Supreme Court decision in each case? (c) Why do you think the 1890 decision differed from the 1954 decision?

Thinking About Geography

Match the letters on the map with the following places: **1.** West Germany, **2.** East Germany, **3.** Philippines, **4.** India, **5.** Pakistan, **6.** China, **7.** North Korea, **8.** South Korea, **9.** Ghana. **Region** Which country listed above was behind the "iron curtain" described by Churchill?

Answers to Thinking Critically

1. Possible Answer: The United States recognized that its failure to join the League of Nations may have contributed to World War II; it realized that possession of the atomic bomb gave the United States new responsibilities in the world.

2. Possible Answer: Truman was

and those who could not pay poll taxes were barred from voting.

justified in doing so because as commander of the armed forces, Truman could not allow one of his officers to defy his authority.

3. Possible Answer: Television is probably the most important aspect of a political campaign today. Not only do people see candidates and hear their views, but they also see news events related to the campaign almost instantaneously. Furthermore, they hear political experts analyze the candidates, the campaign, and the related news events.

Answers to Applying Your Skills

1. (a) twice (b) South Korea (c) Possible Answer: because China borders North Korea on the north and U.S. troops would have been perceived as a threat to China's border

2. (a) the fairness of racial segregation (b) In *Plessy* v. *Ferguson,* the Supreme Court ruled that "separate but equal" facilities were constitutional. In *Brown* v. *Board of Education,* the Court

Revisiting the Cold War

Form into groups to review the Cold War. Follow the suggestions below to speak, write, or dance to show what you have learned. You may use the textbook, encyclopedias, atlases, or other materials in your classroom library to complete the tasks. Be able to name your sources of information when you have finished the activity.

GOVERNMENT LEADERS Divide each group into small delegations representing a member of the United Nations in 1948. Then find out more about the Berlin blockade. Hold a debate about the blockade and the action that you think the UN should take in response to it.

POETS Find out more about the revolt in Hungary in 1956. Then write a poem about what happened.

GEOGRAPHERS Learn about the geography of Korea. Among the topics you might research are its location in Asia and its landforms, climate, and vegetation. Then find out more about battle campaigns during the Korean War. Prepare a briefing explaining how Korea's geography affected the Korean War. Use maps and pictures to illustrate your briefing.

DANCERS Review what you have learned about the fear and suspicion fostered by Senator Joseph McCarthy during the early 1950s. Then portray through dance the atmosphere of the period.

REPORTERS Interview two people who lived during the 1950s. Ask them what they remember about the launching of *Sputnik* in 1957. Combine their recollections with information from other sources to prepare a magazine article about *Sputnik* and its impact on Americans.

★ Make a Revisiting the Cold War scrapbook. Use examples as well as summaries or pictures of completed activities to make your scrapbook informative.

Cartoon showing the Russian bear and the Western powers in Berlin

Eisenhower with American troops in Korea

Anticommunist crusader

ruled that separate schools were inherently unfair. (c) Possible Answer: African American leaders were actively calling for change, and the public in 1954 was more willing to support civil rights.

Answers to Thinking About Geography

1. A **2.** B **3.** F **4.** D **5.** E
6. C **7.** G **8.** H **9.** I
Region: East Germany

Chapter 28   A Time of Turmoil (1960–1980), pp. 796–823

Lessons	Teaching Resources
1 Years of Crisis and Change **Objectives** 1. Identify the goals that Presidents Kennedy and Johnson had for the nation. 2. Describe how the Vietnam War affected events at home. 3. Identify the Watergate Affair. 4. Identify the problems that the nation faced under Carter.	**Lesson Planner** Cooperative Learning, p. 174 **Student Study Guide** Section 1 Study Guide, p. 204 **Interdisciplinary Connections:** Working for Change ■ *Arts* Singing to Protest, p. 164 ■ *Sciences* Photos of a Threat, p. 165 ■ *Geography* The Harvest Route, p. 166 ■ *Economics* Outrage Over Income, p. 167 ■ *Civics* The People of VISTA, p. 168
2 Cold War Clashes **Objectives** 1. Identify the clashes that took place between the superpowers in the 1960s. 2. Describe how Nixon changed United States policy toward China. 3. Describe how the policy of détente eased tensions between the United States and the Soviet Union.	**Lesson Planner** Cooperative Learning, p. 175 **Student Study Guide** Section 2 Study Guide, p. 205
3 A Distant War Divides the Nation **Objectives** 1. Explain why the United States sent troops to Vietnam. 2. Explain why many Americans opposed United States involvement in the Vietnam War. 3. Describe how the fighting in Vietnam resulted in civil war in Cambodia.	**Lesson Planner** Cooperative Learning, p. 176 **Student Study Guide** Section 3 Study Guide, p. 206 **Chapter Resources Binder, Unit 9** *Geography in History* The Battles of Ia Drang, pp. 19–20 *Skill Application* Using a Song as Historical Evidence, p. 16 **Our Multicultural Heritage** *Milestone* Women in the Vietnam War, p. 84
4 Struggle for Civil Rights **Objectives** 1. Identify the civil rights laws that were passed in the 1960s. 2. Describe how civil rights groups brought about change. 3. Explain why violence broke out in American cities in the 1960s.	**Lesson Planner** Cooperative Learning, p. 177 **Student Study Guide** Section 4 Study Guide, p. 207 **Chapter Resources Binder, Unit 9** *Critical Thinking* Making Decisions, p. 17 **Our Multicultural Heritage** *Biography* Fannie Lou Hamer, Hero of the Civil Rights Movement, p. 82
5 The Spirit of Reform Spreads **Objectives** 1. Describe how Latinos worked for reforms. 2. Identify the steps that Native Americans took to achieve more rights. 3. Identify the goals of the women's rights movement.	**Lesson Planner** Cooperative Learning, p. 178 **Student Study Guide** Section 5 Study Guide, p. 208 **Chapter Resources Binder, Unit 9** *History Through Literature* A Vision Beyond Time and Place, p. 18 **Our Multicultural Heritage** *Biography* Humberto Medeiros, Bishop of the Migrant Workers, p. 83

Multimedia Resources	Additional Resources	Chapter-Level Resources
Transparencies *Time Lines* The United States and the World, 1960–1980, p. E-29 *Interdisciplinary Connections* The Peace Corps, p. B-87 *Political Cartoons* Lyndon Johnson's Relationship to Congress, p. G-29 **CD-ROM** *Presidents* John F. Kennedy; Lyndon B. Johnson; Richard M. Nixon; Gerald R. Ford; Jimmy Carter	**Voices of Freedom** LBJ in Action, pp. 292–293 The King and the Prosecutor, pp. 306–307 Ford vs. Carter From a Front-Row Seat, pp. 309–310 **Customized Reader** Lee Harvey Oswald's Mother Speaks Out, article IXB-10 The Resignation of President Nixon, article IXB-8	**Lesson Planner** Activity Based, pp. 179–180 **Student Study Guide** Chapter 28 Study Guide, pp. 209–210 **Chapter Resources Binder** **Unit 9** Vocabulary Building, p. 15 Chapter Test A, pp. 21–23 Chapter Test B, pp. 24–26 Illustration Master, p. 27 Extra Unit Questions, pp. 57–59 **English Guided Reading** Guided Reading, pp. 55–56 **Spanish Resources** **Computer Test Bank** Chapter Tests A and B Extra Unit Questions **Guided Reading Audiotapes** Side 11 **CD-ROM** *Time Tour* A Time for Turmoil (1960–1980) in The Nation Today and Tomorrow
	Customized Reader The Cuban Missile Crisis, article IXB-14	
CD-ROM *Face the Issues* The Vietnam War *History Makers* Maya Lin	**Voices of Freedom** The Death of a Village, pp. 300–301 **Customized Reader** A Woman Journalist in Vietnam, article IXA-5 The Student Occupation of Columbia University in 1968, article IXB-2 A Vietnamese Refugee's Experiences, article IXA-2	
CD-ROM *History Makers* Martin Luther King, Jr.	**Customized Reader** Malcolm X Explains Black Nationalism, article IXA-14	
Transparencies *Our Multicultural Heritage* Immigration to the United States, 1960–1990, p. C-23 **CD-ROM** *History Makers* Cesar Chavez	**Voices of Freedom** Organizing Farm Workers, pp. 296–297 Trial After a "Fish-In," pp. 297–299 A New Kind of Woman, pp. 299–300	

Lesson Planner

For a fully developed **Activity-Based** lesson plan for Chapter 28, see the *Lesson Planner,* pages 179–180.

 Chapter Resources

Vocabulary Building The Vocabulary Building worksheet for Chapter 28 from Unit 9, page 15, of the *Chapter Resources* binder can be used as a prereading activity or as a review of chapter vocabulary. (Reteaching/Easy)

 Student Study Guide

Chapter 28 Study Guide Refer students to pages 209–210 of the *Student Study Guide* for the Chapter 28 Study Guide. The study guide can be used for chapter review as well as for reteaching. (Reteaching/Average)

 Guided Reading Audiotapes

Students can use *Guided Reading Audiotapes,* Chapter 28, side 11, to hear section previews, summaries, and review questions. The tapes might benefit students who are auditory learners, students who have trouble reading, or students acquiring English. Tapes are also available in Spanish. (Reteaching/Easy)

CHAPTER 28

A Time of Turmoil

(1960–1980)

CHAPTER OUTLINE

1 Years of Crisis and Change
2 Cold War Clashes
3 A Distant War Divides the Nation
4 Struggle for Civil Rights
5 The Spirit of Reform Spreads

1960 *John F. Kennedy was elected President of the United States. Kennedy was the first Roman Catholic and, at 43, the youngest person to be elected President.*

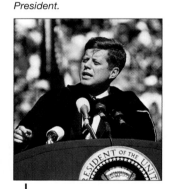

1965 *President Lyndon Johnson introduced the Great Society. The program included laws to help elderly and needy Americans pay for medical care.*

1968 *Civil rights leader Martin Luther King, Jr., was assassinated in Memphis, Tennessee. Here, thousands of mourners follow King's funeral procession.*

1960   1965   1970

 WORLD EVENT
1961 Berlin Wall is built

WORLD EVENT
1968 Soviet Union cracks down on new freedoms in Czechoslovakia

Chapter Time Line
Critical Thinking

Discuss the time line illustrations and captions with the class, or allow students to discuss them in small groups. Then have students suggest categories into which various events might be classified (for example, *Political Clashes, Economic Changes, Social Issues,* and so on). You might challenge students to come up with more than one category for each event.

Students Acquiring English
Activity

Limited English speakers may benefit from working in roundtable sessions with small groups of native speakers. Suggest to SAE students that they be prepared to interview the members of their roundtable in order to enhance their understanding of the chapter content. Explain to the other students that they should be prepared to explore and discuss the issues of the chapter at the roundtable. This strategy gives SAE students an opportunity to use oral language and to clarify meaning of the chapter material.

Chapter Setting

Friday, January 20, 1961, dawned bright but cold in Washington, D.C. Workers hurried to clear Pennsylvania Avenue for the inauguration parade. They used flame throwers to melt frozen snowdrifts around the reviewing stand in front of the Capitol.

A few minutes after noon, President-elect John F. Kennedy stepped out onto the platform. Hatless and coatless, he stood quietly as Chief Justice Earl Warren administered the oath of office.

Then, the new President spoke: "Let the word go forth from this time and place that the torch has been passed to a new generation of Americans." He went on:

66 Now the trumpet summons us again . . . as a call to bear the burden of a long twilight struggle . . . a struggle against the common enemies of man: tyranny, poverty, disease, and war itself. 99

He ended with these stirring words: "And so, my fellow Americans, ask not what your country can do for you—ask what you can do for your country."

At age 43, John F. Kennedy was the youngest person ever elected President of the United States. His youthful ideals were echoed by others during the 1960s. Yet ahead lay the tragic deaths of several American leaders and a war that tore the nation apart. Americans would face years of turmoil as they tried to fulfill the goals they had set for the nation.

ACTIVITY List the qualities you think a person needs to be a good President. Give examples—from history or from current events—of these presidential qualities in action.

1973 *The United States withdrew its troops from Vietnam. This statue honors the women who served in the Vietnam War.*

1975 *The Voting Rights Act provided for bilingual elections. The new law made it easier for Spanish-speaking Americans to vote.*

Late 1970s *Rising inflation damaged the nation's economy. The government tried to curb rising prices with little success.*

| 1970 | 1975 | 1980 |

 WORLD EVENT
1975 Vietnam War ends

 WORLD EVENT
1979 Soviet troops invade Afghanistan

Chapter 28 • **797**

Linking Past and Present
Activity

On the day that John Kennedy was inaugurated, a young man in Mississippi watched the ceremony on television. James Meredith, an African American Air Force veteran, had heard Kennedy say that the rights of man come not from the state but from God. The next day, Meredith wrote for an admissions application to the University of Mississippi, a segregated school. After the courts ruled that he had to be accepted, Kennedy had to order federal troops to disband protesters who prevented Meredith from enrolling.

Have students compare statistics on African American attendance at colleges and universities in 1960 and in the present. Then add statistics on African American professionals, technical workers, and managers (excluding sports and entertainment). Have students share their results with the class.

Bell Ringer

Have students read the title of the section and the section introduction. Ask them to use their prior knowledge to identify any of the events to which the title *Years of Crisis and Change* refers. If students are unaware of the events of the 1960s and 1970s, ask them to predict from the title and introduction what they will learn.

Lesson Plan

1. Focus Between 1961 and 1980, five Presidents faced many challenges. Each had both successes and failures. In this section, students examine the achievements and problems of Presidents Kennedy, Johnson, Nixon, Ford, and Carter.

2. Instruct Group the class into five teams. Have each team prepare and present a television press conference with one of the Presidents discussed in this section. One person in each group will play the President and the rest will play reporters. Groups should work together to prepare both questions and answers. After all the press conferences have been given, ask: Which President was most successful in meeting his goals?

3. Close To close the lesson, have students list the five Presidents in this section and explain why none of them served two complete terms.

1
Years of Crisis and Change

FIND OUT

■ What goals did Presidents Kennedy and Johnson have for the nation?

■ How did the Vietnam War affect events at home?

■ What was the Watergate Affair?

■ What problems did the nation face under Carter?

VOCABULARY poverty line

At Ford Motor Company, Robert McNamara was known as a "whiz kid." His memory for detail and his nonstop work habits astonished everyone around him. When John F. Kennedy became President, he appointed McNamara Secretary of Defense.

McNamara was only one of the many "whiz kids" that President Kennedy brought into his administration. Kennedy confidently believed that the nation's problems could be solved by gathering together the "best and the brightest" minds of his generation.

However, Kennedy and the Presidents that followed him faced challenges that stumped even the "best and the brightest." Racial discrimination persisted. A foreign war divided the nation. Inflation and oil shortages threatened the economy. For American Presidents—and for the nation as a whole—the 1960s and 1970s were years of turmoil.

The Kennedy Years

In 1960, the Republicans chose Vice President Richard Nixon to run for President. The Democrats chose Senator John F. Kennedy. Kennedy was a wealthy young Irish American from Massachusetts. During

World War II, he commanded a torpedo boat in the Pacific. After the war, he served in the House and the Senate.

Kennedy's youth and charm appealed to many Americans. He promised to lead the nation "to the edge of a new frontier." Nixon was more earnest, defending his record under Eisenhower. The two candidates faced off in the first televised debates ever held in a presidential election. In a remarkably close contest, Kennedy won.

Economic and social policies. Like Franklin Roosevelt, President Kennedy believed that the government should play an active role in keeping the economy prosperous. In 1962, inflation threatened when steel companies raised prices. Kennedy denounced the companies and pressured them to reduce their prices.

Kennedy wanted Congress to pass laws to help the 39 million Americans living in poverty. In his travels as a candidate, he had been shocked to find hungry families in the United States. Visiting a poor coal-mining area in West Virginia, Kennedy exclaimed, "Just imagine, kids who never drink milk!"

Congress did not support the President's poverty programs. It did, however, approve funds to explore the "new frontier" of space. It also funded the Peace Corps. (See Connections on page 800.)

Assassination. Kennedy proposed many other programs. Before these could be enacted, however, a tragic event shattered the nation. On November 22, 1963, Kennedy arrived in Dallas, Texas, on a political tour. As his open car rode past cheering crowds, shots rang out. The President lurched forward, then slumped back in his seat. The President's car raced to a nearby hospital, but it was too late. President Kennedy was dead. That afternoon, Vice President Lyndon Johnson was sworn in as President.

Dallas police arrested Lee Harvey Oswald for the murder. Two days later, as police escorted Oswald to a more secure jail, Jack Ruby shot and killed him. Millions of

---

Connections With Language Arts
Activity

While a senator from Massachusetts, John F. Kennedy wrote *Profiles in Courage,* a book about American leaders who faced difficult situations bravely. The 1956 book earned Kennedy a Pulitzer Prize. Have interested students read parts of the book and report to the class on what they have learned. Be sure to coordinate the chapters so that no student reports on a chapter already chosen by another student.

Historical Sidelight
Background

There were four Kennedy-Nixon debates. Most political analysts feel that the first—held on September 26 and drawing some 70 million viewers—was the most critical one. Kennedy proved in that debate that he understood the issues, but both candidates spoke well. Ironically, how the candidates looked seemed more important than what they said. Kennedy appeared fit, tan, and self-assured; Nixon—who had recently gotten out of the hospital and who refused to wear makeup for the television lights—seemed pale, drawn, even threatening.

Cooperative Learning
Activity

In May 1961, President Kennedy declared that the United States should make it a national goal to complete a successful manned lunar landing mission by the end of the decade. The first step toward that goal was the Mercury program, which began and concluded while Kennedy was in office. Have students prepare and present an overview of the Mercury program, covering such topics as the astronauts involved, the achievements of various missions, and the scientific knowledge that resulted. Encourage students to include visuals with their presentation.

horrified Americans viewed the murder, which took place during a live television broadcast.

The tragedy in Dallas raised many questions. Did Oswald act alone? How was Ruby able to get near him? Chief Justice Earl Warren led an investigation. The **Warren Commission** concluded that Oswald had acted alone. However, some questions about Kennedy's death still remain unanswered.

President Lyndon Johnson

As the nation mourned Kennedy's death, Lyndon Johnson took office. Sensing the sad mood of the country, the new President said simply, "I'll do my best. That's all I can do." Johnson assured Americans that he would continue Kennedy's programs.

In November 1964, voters chose to keep Johnson in the White House. He defeated Republican Senator Barry Goldwater of Arizona in a landslide victory.

Early years. Lyndon Johnson had grown up on a farm in southwestern Texas. He lived through the hard times of the 1920s and 1930s. "When I was young," Johnson recalled later, "poverty was so common that we didn't know it had a name."

The tall Texan was first elected to Congress in 1937. From the start, he strongly supported the New Deal. While in Congress, Johnson learned the art of persuading lawmakers to do what he thought was best. One senator recalled the "Johnson treatment" as being like "a great overpowering thunderstorm that consumed you as it closed in around you."

An ambitious goal. As President, Johnson developed a plan he called the **Great Society.** Its ambitious goal was to improve the standard of living of every American. Congress had been unwilling to pass such a plan under Kennedy. Johnson, however, made Congress act. During his first two years in office, he persuaded Congress to pass more than 50 new laws.

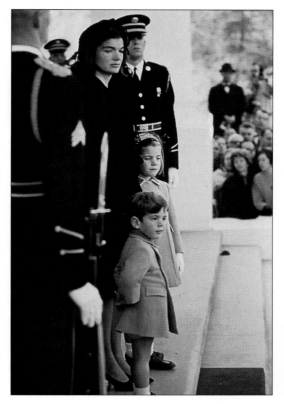

A Nation Mourns *The assassination of John F. Kennedy stunned the nation. Here, the President's wife, Jackie, and their two children prepare for the funeral procession.* **Citizenship** *Why was it important to swear in the new President immediately after Kennedy's death?*

An important Great Society program was **Medicare.** Under this plan, the government helped pay the hospital bills of citizens over age 65. Another program, **Medicaid,** gave states money to help poor people of all ages with their medical bills.

Fighting poverty. To achieve his Great Society, Johnson called on the nation to join him in a "war on poverty." He wanted to help Americans who lived below the

Chapter 28 • **799**

Lesson Planner

For a developed **Cooperative Learning** lesson plan, see the *Lesson Planner,* page 174.

Answer to Caption

Possible Answer: to ensure that the leadership of the country would continue without interruption

Transparencies

Time Lines Use the transparency, The United States and the World, 1960–1980, on page E-29 of *American History Transparencies.* This time line shows events that occurred in the United States and the world during the period. Teaching suggestions can be found on page E-10. (Enrichment/Average)

CD-ROM

Presidents Access the biography of John F. Kennedy from the American Heritage® *History of the United States* CD-ROM.
Presidents Access the biography of Lyndon B. Johnson from the American Heritage® *History of the United States* CD-ROM.

Customized Reader

Primary Source For an interview with Marguerite Oswald, order article IXB-10, Lee Harvey Oswald's Mother Speaks Out, from the *American History Customized Reader.* In this selection, Mrs. Oswald claims that her son was framed. (Enrichment/Average)

Linking Past and Present
Activity

More than 30 years after the event, many Americans remain fascinated by the Kennedy assassination. Invite interested students to take an opinion poll regarding assassination theories. (You may want to limit the poll to people who are old enough to remember the event.) As students share their responses, have them decide which theory or theories are most commonly held and why.

Historical Sidelight
Background

President Johnson spoke of his Great Society program in his inaugural address. In that speech, he said, "Our enemies have always made the same mistake. In my lifetime—in depression and in war—they have awaited our defeat. Each time, from the secret places of the American heart, came forth the faith they could not see or that they could not even imagine. . . . For this is what America is all about. It is the uncrossed desert and the unclimbed ridge. It is the star that is not reached and the harvest sleeping in the unplowed ground."

Learning Styles
Auditory Learners

To help auditory learners better understand the Medicare and Medicaid programs, ask them to interview one or both of the following:
- at least one relative or neighbor who has benefited from one of these programs
- a health-care professional who works with Medicare or Medicaid patients

Have students find out how these programs work by asking about specific cases. You may wish to have them reinforce their understanding by reporting to the class.

For worksheets establishing connections between the Chapter 28 main idea, Working for Change, and five other disciplines, see the *Interdisciplinary Connections* booklet. (Enrichment)

- **Arts** Singing to Protest, page 164 (Easy)
- **Sciences** Photos of a Threat, page 165 (Average)
- **Geography** The Harvest Route, page 166 (Average)
- **Economics** Outrage Over Income, page 167 (Challenging)
- **Civics** The People of VISTA, page 168 (Average)

Answer to Connections

to teach and to give technical advice to people in developing nations in Asia, Africa, Eastern Europe, and Latin America

ACTIVITY

Guided Instruction Have students work in groups to do further research about the Peace Corps and to write their brochures. Let each group appoint a leader who will evaluate each member's work and pull all the information together. One or more students in the group may be asked to design illustrations for their brochure. If possible, have students publish the brochures using desktop publishing software. Have group leaders work together to design a display showcasing their work.

CONNECTIONS

| ARTS | SCIENCES | GEOGRAPHY | **WORLD** | ECONOMICS | CIVICS |

A "Peace Army"

Late one night in 1960, presidential candidate John Kennedy was addressing some 10,000 students at the University of Michigan. How many of you, he asked, would like to join a "peace army" dedicated to helping the poor of the world? How many of you would give up two years of your life to make such a program work? Kennedy beamed as 10,000 voices lifted in a deafening roar of approval.

After he became President, Kennedy remembered the students' response. On March 1, 1961, Kennedy asked Congress to set up "a permanent Peace Corps, a pool of trained American men and women sent overseas. . .to help foreign countries meet their needs for skilled manpower." Under the program, volunteers would give technical advice or teach in developing countries in Asia, Africa, and Latin America.

Peace Corps volunteer in Kenya

Just five months later, the first 500 Peace Corps volunteers left the United States. Within five years, 15,000 volunteers—mostly in their twenties—were working overseas. They came to be called "Kennedy's Kids." Today, the Peace Corps is still active, with Eastern Europe added to the list of destinations in the 1990s.

Peace Corps volunteers serve a two-year tour of duty. They receive only a modest allowance for living expenses and a small payment at the end of the tour. They might set up a health clinic or build an irrigation system or start a new school. Many volunteers live in remote villages. All are expected to use the local language and live as the local people do.

Peace Corps members feel that they accomplish much more than building, doctoring, and teaching. Said one:

> 66By communications on a person-to-person level, the people of the world may some day eliminate the word [stranger]. . . . Communications, after all, can breed understanding. And understanding can breed peace. I like to think that is what the Peace Corps is all about. 99

■ What is the purpose of the Peace Corps?

ACTIVITY
Prepare a recruiting brochure for the Peace Corps. Describe the goals of the Peace Corps, the jobs that volunteers do, and the reasons for joining. Include illustrations of volunteers at work.

Team-Teaching Suggestion
Science

You might work with a science teacher to present a lesson on agricultural methods in developing countries. Include in the presentation a discussion of problems that Peace Corps volunteers may encounter, such as poor soil, drought, or lack of information or tools. Have the class brainstorm ways in which each problem might be overcome. If possible, have the science teacher bring in photos of places in which Peace Corps volunteers have worked, perhaps even showing the class "before" and "after" shots.

Team-Teaching Suggestion
Language Arts

You might work with a language arts teacher to present a lesson about President Kennedy's Peace Corps speech and the results it effected. Distribute a copy of the speech and work together to examine its most important points. Afterward, have students summarize President Kennedy's ideas, noting which ones have been achieved and how life has improved in places where the volunteers have worked.

Johnson "Plays" Congress *Few Presidents were as skillful in working with Congress as Lyndon Johnson. One observer noted that "bills were coming out of Congress like candy bars from a slot machine."* **Citizenship** *Why do Presidents need the help of Congress to achieve their goals?*

poverty line. The poverty line is the minimum income that people need to survive.

At Johnson's urging, Congress passed the *Economic Opportunity Act* in 1964. The act set up job-training programs for the poor. It also gave loans to poor farmers and to businesses in poor sections of cities.

The government also set up programs to build housing for low-income and middle-income families. To carry out these programs, Congress created the Department of Housing and Urban Development, or HUD. Robert Weaver was named to head the department. He became the first African American to serve in a Cabinet post.

1968: Year of Crisis

Johnson's political skills helped him pass most of his Great Society programs. In the area of foreign policy, however, he ran into trouble. His greatest problems arose when he increased United States involvement in a war in Vietnam, a country in Southeast Asia. You will read more about the Vietnam War later in this chapter.

Violent protests. Many Americans opposed the nation's involvement in the Vietnam War. On college campuses, students burned draft cards, refusing to serve in the military. Thousands of protesters marched on Washington, D.C. Hoping to bring calm to the nation, a weary and anguished Johnson announced that he would not seek re-election in 1968.

Several Democrats sought the party's nomination. One was New York senator Robert Kennedy, brother of the late President. While campaigning in Los Angeles, Kennedy was shot and killed by a Palestinian who opposed the senator's support for the country of Israel. (See page 844.)

Election. At their convention in Chicago, the Democrats selected Vice President Hubert Humphrey to be their candidate. Humphrey's chances for success were hurt, however, by events outside the convention hall. Police clashed with antiwar demonstrators in violent battles in the streets of the city.

The Republicans again nominated former Vice President Richard Nixon to run for President. He promised to bring "peace with honor" in Vietnam and "law and order" at home. Alabama governor George Wallace entered the race as a third-party candidate. Helped by this and by divisions in the Democratic party, Nixon narrowly won the election.

Richard Nixon as President

The new President saw himself as a leader of what he called the "silent majority." Nixon sided with Americans who were disturbed by the protests and unrest of the 1960s. As part of a "law-and-order" program, he used federal funds to help local

Answer to Caption
Congress has the power to approve or disapprove legislation prepared by the President.

 Transparencies

Interdisciplinary Connections Use the transparency The Peace Corps on page B-87 of *American History Transparencies*. Teaching suggestions can be found on page B-30. (Enrichment/Average)
Political Cartoons Use the transparency Lyndon Johnson's Relationship to Congress on page G-29 of *American History Transparencies*. Teaching suggestions can be found on page G-10. (Enrichment/Challenging)

 Voices of Freedom

Primary Source You might assign selection 19-3, LBJ in Action, on pages 292–293 of *Voices of Freedom*. In this selection, two people who worked closely with LBJ tell revealing anecdotes about the President. (Enrichment/Average)

Historical Sidelight
Background

President Johnson wanted to be remembered for his domestic programs: "I do not want to be the President who built empires, or sought grandeur, or extended dominion. I want to be the President who educated young children to the wonders of their world . . . who helped to feed the hungry and to prepare them to be taxpayers instead of tax-eaters . . . who helped the poor to find their own way and who protected the right of every citizen to vote in every election . . . who helped to end hatred among his fellow men and who promoted love among the peoples of all races and all religions and all parties . . . who helped to end war among the brothers of this earth."

Johnson left office unhappy that the Vietnam War had so distracted him from his goal. He told Harvard professor Doris Kearns, "I knew from the start that if I left the woman I really loved—the Great Society—in order to fight [that] war . . . then I would lose everything at home. All my hopes . . . my dreams."

Connections With Civics
Background

In the Chicago riots, some 700 demonstrators and 80 police officers were wounded. There were 650 arrests. Most of the clashes took place in full view of news cameras, causing the protesters to chant, "The whole world's watching!" Hysteria even invaded the convention hall—security guards scuffled with delegates and reporters.

A presidential panel later concluded that although the protesters had provoked the officers, the police had responded with "unrestrained and indiscriminate" violence.

police departments. He also named four Justices to the Supreme Court. The new Justices were more conservative than those who had retired.

Nixon opposed some programs of the Great Society. He thought they were too ambitious and costly and that they contributed to rapid inflation. As a result, Nixon backed off from the reforms of the Johnson years. He cut federal funds for job training, low-income housing, and education.

In 1972, President Nixon easily defeated the Democratic candidate for President, Senator George McGovern of South Dakota. McGovern was a leader of the movement against the Vietnam War.

A burglary. Nixon's triumph was cut short by news of a burglary that had taken place during the campaign. On June 17, 1972, police caught five men breaking into Democratic party headquarters in the Watergate apartment building in Washington, D.C. Evidence suggested that the burglars were linked to Nixon's reelection committee. The President assured the public that no one in the White House was involved in the *Watergate Affair.*

However, new evidence soon linked the burglars to the White House. In May 1973, a Senate committee began public hearings. The hearings revealed that Nixon had made secret tape recordings of all conversations in his office. These tapes showed that the President and several close advisers had been involved in trying to cover up the truth about the Watergate break-in.

Nixon's fall. In the midst of the Watergate Affair, another scandal erupted. Vice President Spiro Agnew was accused of taking bribes and was forced to resign. Under the Twenty-fifth Amendment, the President had to choose a new Vice President. Nixon selected Representative Gerald R. Ford of Michigan, who had served in Congress for 25 years. Congress quickly approved the appointment.

The Watergate crisis came to a head in 1974. In July, a committee of the House of Representatives passed three articles of impeachment against the President. These charges included obstructing, or blocking, justice. Nixon decided to spare himself and the nation the ordeal of an impeachment trial. In August 1974, Richard Nixon became the first President to resign from office.

A Time to Heal

"Our long national nightmare is over." With these words, Nixon's successor, Gerald Ford, tried to reassure the nation. The new President pledged to be open and honest.

Change of Presidents *"I shall resign the presidency effective at noon tomorrow,"* Richard Nixon announced on August 8, 1974. Here, a marine replaces Nixon's portrait with one of Gerald Ford. **Citizenship** Ford was the first person to become President without being elected either President or Vice President. How did this happen?

Soon after Ford took office, he granted Nixon a "full, free and absolute pardon." Some felt that Nixon should have been brought to trial. Ford, however, wanted to save the country from a long and bitter debate over Watergate.

In 1976, Ford won the Republican nomination for President. The Democrats chose Jimmy Carter, a former governor of Georgia. Carter had no experience in Washington. He remarked:

❝I have been accused of being an outsider. I plead guilty. Unfortunately, the vast majority of Americans . . . are also outsiders.**❞**

Carter promised a change from Washington politics and scandals. In the election, he narrowly defeated Ford.

The Carter White House

President Carter brought new people and new ideas to national government. As an outsider, however, he had trouble getting Congress to pass his programs. With inflation and recession at home and mounting tensions abroad, Carter faced a difficult task.

Problems at home. Carter's term began with hope for a fresh approach to the nation's problems. During his first year in office, the new President sent Congress almost a dozen major bills. They included reforms in Social Security and tax laws. One bill encouraged oil and coal companies to find new sources of energy. Carter, however,

Linking Past and Present
In the midst of troubled times, the nation took time out to celebrate its 200th birthday. On July 4, 1976, in New York City, 7 million people watched a flotilla of 212 ships from around the world sail up the Hudson River.

Inauguration Day *After taking the oath of office, President Jimmy Carter walked to the White House with his family. The last President to walk from his inauguration had been Thomas Jefferson in 1801.* **Citizenship** *What problems did Carter face as President?*

could not win the support of Congress for his legislation.

Another problem the President faced was "double-digit" inflation—inflation that was 10 percent or higher. The government tried to slow inflation, yet prices kept rising. Many families had a hard time paying for basic needs such as food, clothing, and rent.

Working with other nations. Carter took a firm stand on human rights. In 1975, the United States had signed the ***Helsinki Agreement.*** In it, 35 nations pledged to respect basic rights such as religious freedom

---

Answer to Caption

a national economy plagued by inflation and recession and several tense situations with other nations

 Voices of Freedom

Primary Source You might assign selection 20-3, The King and the Prosecutor, on pages 306–307 of *Voices of Freedom*. This selection is Art Buchwald's fablelike retelling of the Watergate story. (Enrichment/Average)

Primary Source You might assign selection 20-5, Ford vs. Carter From a Front-Row Seat, on pages 309–310 of *Voices of Freedom*. This excerpt from the journal of reporter Elizabeth Drew concerns the first televised debate between President Ford and challenger Jimmy Carter. (Enrichment/Average)

CD-ROM

Presidents Access the biography of Jimmy Carter from the American Heritage® *History of the United States* CD-ROM.

Connections With Civics
Background

The same month in which he pardoned Nixon, President Ford offered clemency to evaders of the Vietnam War draft and to deserters of the armed forces. Anyone who wanted to take advantage of the offer had to swear allegiance to the United States and serve for two years in public service or in the military. Veterans' groups were furious. Many evaders felt that to accept clemency would be to admit they had been wrong.

President Carter later pardoned all draft evaders (though not deserters), a move that many veterans' groups condemned.

Historical Sidelight
Background

President Carter had a well-known reputation for personal integrity. He used the title *Why Not the Best?* for his campaign book and also for a campaign motto. The expression dates back to a 1948 interview with Admiral Hyman Rickover. Carter, who was seeking admission to the nuclear submarine program, admitted to Rickover that he had not always done his best at school. Rickover challenged him: "Why not?" Carter got into the program but never forgot the question.

Connections With the World
Background

Despite his successes at Helsinki and with leaders in Egypt and Israel, President Carter faced problems abroad at the end of his term. In 1979, he took a hard stand against the Soviet Union when it invaded Afghanistan, and led an international boycott of the 1980 Olympic Games in Moscow. As students will read in Chapter 29, Carter's last months in office were also plagued by the continuing hostage crisis in Iran. Indeed, the hostages were not freed until the day that Carter left office.

Student Study Guide

Section 1 Study Guide Have students use the Section 1 Study Guide on page 204 of the *Student Study Guide* to review and reinforce the content of this section. (Reteaching/Average)

ACTIVITY

Guided Instruction Before writing their headlines, you might have the class compile a list of events to be covered. Remind them to use vivid, memorable words to capture the events in headline form. Encourage students who choose the same events to compare their completed headlines.

Section 2
pp. 804–808

 Bell Ringer

Have students locate Cuba on a map of the world. Ask: Geographically, why do you think the United States would be concerned about events in Cuba?

Lesson Plan

1. Focus From 1960 to 1980, rivalry between the United States and the Soviet Union dominated world affairs. Policy toward the Soviet Union changed from Cold War to détente, only to chill again during the late 1970s. In this section, students learn about shifting relations among the United States, the Soviet Union, and China.

---

and freedom of thought. Carter took this pledge seriously. The United States, he said, should not aid countries that violated human rights.

President Carter won praise for helping to bring about a peace treaty between Egypt and Israel, as you will read in Chapter 29.

End of an era. By 1980, the nation had gone through 20 years of reform, change, and unrest. Major reforms had expanded the government's role in fighting poverty and economic hardship. A war in Vietnam had divided Americans. One President had been assassinated and another forced to resign.

Many Americans looked for a return to calmer times. When President Carter ran for a second term in 1980, he was soundly beaten. The winner was Ronald Reagan, a Republican from California. Reagan's election marked the end of an unsettled political era.

SECTION 1 REVIEW

1. **Identify:** (a) Warren Commission, (b) Great Society, (c) Medicare, (d) Medicaid, (e) Economic Opportunity Act, (f) Watergate Affair, (g) Helsinki Agreement.
2. **Define:** poverty line.
3. (a) What did President Kennedy think should be the role of the government in the economy? (b) Describe two Great Society programs that became law.
4. How did the Vietnam War influence the 1968 election?
5. What stand did President Carter take on human rights?
6. **CRITICAL THINKING Analyzing Information** Referring to the Watergate Affair, President Ford said, "The Constitution works." What do you think he meant?

ACTIVITY Writing to Learn
Write 10 newspaper headlines summarizing key domestic events during the terms of Presidents Kennedy, Johnson, Nixon, Ford, and Carter.

2
Cold War Clashes

FIND OUT
■ What clashes took place between the superpowers in the 1960s?
■ How did Nixon change United States policy toward China?
■ How did the policy of détente ease tensions between the United States and the Soviet Union?

VOCABULARY superpower, exile, détente

In September 1959, Soviet premier Nikita Khrushchev arrived in New York. He had come to address the United Nations. At first Khrushchev spoke calmly, expressing hopes that the Cold War between the United States and the Soviet Union would end. Later on, however, Khrushchev's manner changed. Twice, he became so angry that he took off his shoe and pounded it on the table.

Khrushchev's visit, with its calm and storms, symbolized the ups and downs of the continuing Cold War. Although tensions between the United States and the Soviet Union sometimes eased, many basic differences remained.

Conflicts in Cuba

During the 1960s and 1970s, the United States and the Soviet Union faced each other as superpowers. A **superpower** is a nation with enough military, political, and economic strength to influence events in many areas of the globe. One place where the superpowers clashed was Cuba.

In 1959, Fidel Castro had led a revolution in Cuba. Soon after, Castro began to take over American-owned businesses in his

---

Critical Thinking
Comparing and Contrasting

Point out that the presidencies of Johnson, Nixon, Ford, and Carter were marked by serious political and social unrest. Have students find interesting ways of comparing and contrasting each President's style, economic and social concerns, political aims, and accomplishments in foreign relations. Suggest colorful charts and graphs for areas in which statistics are important and encourage students to come up with other compare/contrast strategies of their own.

Answers to Section 1 Review

1. (a) Warren Commission, p. 799, (b) Great Society, p. 799, (c) Medicare, p. 799, (d) Medicaid, p. 799, (e) Economic Opportunity Act, p. 801, (f) Watergate Affair, p. 802, (g) Helsinki Agreement, p. 803
2. poverty line, p. 801
3. (a) Kennedy believed that the federal government should be involved in the economy. (b) Medicare helped pay medical bills for older Americans; Medicaid gave money to states to be used to help poor people pay for medical care.
4. The civil unrest caused by the war led Johnson to withdraw from the race. It also

caused rioting at the Democratic convention in Chicago. As a result, Richard Nixon was able to win a close election.
5. Carter believed that the United States should not aid countries that violated people's basic rights.
6. Possible Answer: Even though the President may have done something wrong, the Constitution supplied a method for dealing with it—the possibility of impeachment for Nixon and a smooth passing of power to Ford.

804

country, where he set up a socialist state.* The Soviet Union supplied Cuba with large amounts of economic aid. Thousands of Cubans who opposed Castro, especially those from the middle and upper classes, fled to the United States. These Cuban exiles told how Castro had seized their property and taken away their freedoms. **Exiles** are people who are forced to leave their own country.

Castro's actions worried American leaders. After all, Cuba is located just 90 miles (145 km) off the coast of Florida. Also, Castro began to encourage revolutions in other Latin American countries.

A badly planned invasion. When President Kennedy took office in 1961, he approved a plan of the Central Intelligence Agency, or CIA, to overthrow Castro. Under the plan, the CIA trained a group of Cuban exiles as a secret invasion force. On April 17, 1961, about 1,200 exiles landed at the **Bay of Pigs** on the southern coast of Cuba. They thought other Cubans who opposed Castro would join them as they marched on the capital.

The invasion was badly planned. The United States did not use its military planes to provide air support. And no rebel forces joined the invaders. The mission collapsed. As it turned out, the invasion increased Castro's popularity in Cuba and embarrassed the United States.

The missiles of October. Alarmed by the Bay of Pigs invasion, the Soviet Union decided to give more weapons to Cuba. In October 1962, President Kennedy learned that the Soviets were secretly building missile bases on the island. If the bases were completed, atomic missiles could reach American cities within minutes of being launched.

For a week, Kennedy and his advisers debated in secret about how to respond.

*In a socialist state, the government owns all major industries.

Disaster at the Bay of Pigs *The Bay of Pigs invasion badly embarrassed the United States. It also caused Americans to question the use of secret military operations to make political changes in foreign countries.* **United States and the World** *What was the goal of the Bay of Pigs invasion? What were its effects?*

Then, in a dramatic television statement, the President told the American people about the missile sites. He announced that the navy would begin a "strict quarantine" of Cuba. American warships would turn back any Soviet ship with missiles on board.

Tension builds. A tense week followed as Soviet ships steamed toward Cuba. Would they turn back? Or would the **Cuban missile crisis** lead to a nuclear war between the two superpowers? Attorney General Robert Kennedy recalled the mood in the White House:

66 Was the world on the brink of a holocaust? Was it our error? A mistake? . . . [The President's] hand went up to his face and covered his mouth. He opened and closed his fist. His face seemed drawn, his eyes pained, almost gray. We stared at each other across the table. 99

Chapter 28 • **805**

2. **Instruct** Divide the class into groups of three students each. Have the groups create political cartoons for one of the following: the Cuban missile crisis, the building of the Berlin Wall, the Soviet invasion of Czechoslovakia, the arms race, the signing of the SALT agreement, or the Soviet invasion of Afghanistan. Display students' completed cartoons and schedule time for students to discuss their work.
3. **Close** To close the lesson, have students make time lines tracing relations between the United States and communist countries between 1960 and 1980. Ask: How did each event improve or worsen American relations with the communist world?

 Lesson Planner

For a developed **Cooperative Learning** lesson plan, see the *Lesson Planner,* page 175.

Answer to Caption

to overthrow the government of Fidel Castro; embarrassment to the United States and strengthening of Castro's support in Cuba

Historical Sidelight
Background

Before the Bay of Pigs invasion, General Shoup of the Marine Corps argued against the attack. He placed an outline of Cuba over a map of the United States. Cuba stretched from New York City to Chicago. Shoup then placed a tiny red dot over the outline of Cuba. "That, gentlemen, represents the size of the island of Tarawa," noted the general, who had fought at Tarawa in the Pacific during World War II, "and it took us three days and 18,000 Marines to take it." In spite of this graphic presentation, Shoup—as well as most of Kennedy's staff—lost the argument.

Connections With Language Arts
Activity

Have interested students imagine that they are teenagers or adults during the Cuban missile crisis of 1962. Instruct them to do some reading on the topic and then to write a week's worth of diary entries.

Remind writers to adopt their characters' points of view so the fear and anxiety that people felt then will seem real when read from the pages of their diaries. Entries from *Anne Frank: The Diary of a Young Girl* or *A Gathering of Days* may give students an idea of journal tone and style.

Note: This activity may be especially helpful for LEP students, who can model their diary entries on published models.

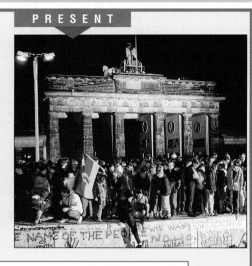

PAST   PRESENT

The Berlin Wall *For 28 years, the concrete and barbed wire Berlin Wall stood as a grim symbol of the Cold War. At left, a West Berlin woman perches on the wall with a friend to speak to her mother on the other side. In 1989, East Germany gave in to demands for democratic reform and opened its borders. At right, East and West Berliners celebrate their new freedom atop the wall.* • *How did the opening of the Berlin Wall mark a major change in the world?*

At the last minute, the Soviet ships turned back. "We're eyeball to eyeball," said Secretary of State Dean Rusk, "and I think the other fellow just blinked."

President Kennedy's stand led Khrushchev to compromise. The Soviet leader agreed to take the missiles out of Cuba. In turn, the United States agreed not to invade the island.

The Cold War in Europe

Tension also built in the city of Berlin in Germany. As you recall, Berlin was located in the middle of communist East Germany. In the early-morning hours of August 13, 1961, tanks and trucks rolled through the streets of East Berlin. As surprised West Berlin sentries looked on, East German sol-

diers unloaded barbed wire, fence posts, and concrete blocks. In a matter of days, a wall tightly sealed off East Berlin from West Berlin—and from the rest of the noncommunist world.

Since 1949, 3 million unhappy East Germans had fled to West Berlin. They then continued on to West Germany. The flight of so many people embarrassed East Germany and the Soviet Union. East Germany decided to build the wall to cut off East Berliners from freedom in the West. For decades, the ***Berlin Wall*** remained a symbol of the Cold War that divided Europe.

In 1968, the Soviet Union again moved to limit freedom—this time in Czechoslovakia. There, government leaders had introduced reforms that allowed citizens to express their opinions more freely. Alarmed at

806 • Chapter 28

---

this show of independence, the Soviets sent thousands of troops into Czechoslovakia in August 1968. They occupied Prague, the capital, and ended the new freedoms. The United States spoke out against the invasion of Czechoslovakia but took no direct action.

Recognizing China

When Richard Nixon became President in 1969, he looked for ways to ease world tensions. Soon, he moved to improve relations with the People's Republic of China.

In 1949, Mao Zedong had won control of the Chinese mainland. At that time, the United States refused to recognize Mao's communist government. In fact, throughout the 1950s, Nixon had spoken strongly against dealing with communist China.

By 1971, however, Nixon thought it was time for a change. In secret talks, he began exploring closer ties with China. To show that it was willing to be more flexible, China invited the United States ping pong team to a competition in Beijing.

To the surprise of many Americans, President Nixon himself visited the People's Republic of China in February 1972. Television cameras captured the President walking along the Great Wall of China and attending state dinners with Chinese leaders.

The visit was a triumph for Nixon and the start of a new era in relations with China. As tensions continued to ease, President Carter established formal diplomatic relations with China in 1979.

A Brief Thaw

President Nixon followed his visit to China with another historic trip. In May 1972, he became the first American President to visit the Soviet Union since the Cold War began. The trip was part of Nixon's effort to reduce tensions between the superpowers. This policy was known as **détente** (day TAHNT), or an easing of tensions.

Efforts at détente. Détente eased the Cold War by allowing more trade and other contacts between the United States and the Soviet Union. More important, the two nations signed a treaty agreeing to limit the number of nuclear warheads and missiles that they built. This treaty was known as the **SALT Agreement.** SALT stands for Strategic Arms Limitation Talks.

Détente continued under both Presidents Ford and Carter. Trade between the United States and the Soviet Union increased. The Soviets bought tons of American wheat. In 1975, Soviet and American astronauts conducted a joint space mission. In

Nixon in China *Americans were startled when Richard Nixon announced plans to visit communist China. Here, the President and First Lady Pat Nixon join Chinese leaders at a banquet in Shanghai.* **United States and the World** *Why was Nixon's visit a turning point in American-Chinese relations?*

Cooperative Learning
Activity

Have interested students form groups to dramatize one of the crises of the 1960s. Students may use simple formats such as readers theater or more complex ones such as a customized video version.

Suggested events may include the building of the Berlin Wall, the Bay of Pigs invasion, the Cuban missile crisis, the SALT talks, and the invasion of Czechoslovakia.

The writers are responsible for the accuracy of facts relating to the event as well as for making the dialogue appropriate and realistic. Actors are to portray their characters as accurately as possible, even if it involves some in-depth research of their own.

Groups may find it helpful to write from a narrator-character point of view to explain events that preceded and/or followed their own. If several dramatizations will be presented in a single day, groups may want to consider a narrator that "floats," uniting all the dramas.

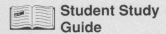

Student Study Guide

Section 2 Study Guide Have students use the Section 2 Study Guide on page 205 of the *Student Study Guide* to review and reinforce the content of this section. (Reteaching/Average)

Guided Instruction This activity will help students understand how both personal and official attitudes change over time. Have students review United States policy toward China in the 1950s and make a list of the attitudes and actions it suggests. Have them do the same for 1971. Then have students write their memos, reminding them to use the perspective of President Nixon.

Section 3
pp. 808–814

Bell Ringer

Through the media and perhaps through family stories, students may have some mental associations with the word *Vietnam.* Have students freewrite for 3 to 5 minutes using that word as a focus.

Lesson Plan

1. Focus American involvement in the war in Vietnam escalated as the United States first sent advisers and then troops to back Ngo Dinh Diem. Meanwhile, opposition to the war increased at home. In this section, students

---

June 1979, President Carter met with Soviet leader Leonid Brezhnev (BREHZH nehf). They worked out the details of a SALT II Treaty.

Détente ends. Before the Senate could ratify this new treaty, hopes for détente faded. In December, Soviet troops invaded Afghanistan. They seized major cities and gave military support to a pro-Soviet government. Afghan rebels fought back fiercely.

"The Soviet Union must pay a price for its aggression," President Carter declared. He withdrew the SALT II Treaty from the Senate and ended grain sales to the Soviet Union. He also announced that American athletes would not compete in the 1980 Olympic Games in Moscow.

In the long run, the war in Afghanistan became so costly for the Soviets that it contributed to the downfall of the Soviet Union. For the time being, however, détente ended.

SECTION 2 REVIEW

1. **Locate:** (a) Cuba, (b) Berlin, (c) Czechoslovakia, (d) China, (e) Afghanistan.
2. **Identify:** (a) Bay of Pigs, (b) Cuban missile crisis, (c) Berlin Wall, (d) SALT Agreement.
3. **Define:** (a) superpower, (b) exile, (c) détente.
4. Describe a Cold War clash that occurred in each of these places: (a) Cuba, (b) Berlin, (c) Czechoslovakia, (d) Afghanistan.
5. How did relations with China change in the 1970s?
6. Why did détente end?
7. **CRITICAL THINKING Making Decisions** (a) What were two actions President Carter took in response to the Soviet invasion of Afghanistan? (b) What was one possible effect of each action?

ACTIVITY Writing to Learn
Imagine that you are Richard Nixon. Write two memos expressing your attitude toward China. Date one memo 1950s. Date the other 1971.

3
A Distant War Divides the Nation

FIND OUT
- Why did the United States send troops to Vietnam?
- Why did many Americans oppose United States involvement in the Vietnam War?
- How did the fighting in Vietnam result in civil war in Cambodia?

VOCABULARY guerrilla, escalate

In 1961, reporter Stanley Karnow stopped by the White House to talk with Attorney General Robert Kennedy. Karnow had been reporting from Southeast Asia for several years. He wanted to warn Kennedy that the nation of Vietnam was becoming a serious trouble spot.

The President's brother was not convinced. "We've got 20 Vietnams a day to handle," said Kennedy. Karnow turned out to be right, though. During the 1960s, a small conflict in Asia grew steadily into the longest war in American history.

The Two Vietnams

For many years France had ruled Vietnam as a colony. After World War II, however, a Vietnamese communist named Ho Chi Minh (HOH CHEE MIHN) led a war for independence. In 1954, an international conference divided Vietnam into two nations. North Vietnam, led by Ho Chi Minh, received aid from the Soviet Union. South Vietnam, under Ngo Dinh Diem (NOH DIN dee EHM), was backed by the United States.

By the time President Kennedy took office in 1961, many South Vietnamese had

---

Answers to Section 2 Review

1. See the map on pp. 890–891.
2. (a) Bay of Pigs, p. 805, (b) Cuban missile crisis, p. 805, (c) Berlin Wall, p. 806, (d) SALT Agreement, p. 807
3. (a) superpower, p. 804, (b) exile, p. 805, (c) détente, p. 807
4. (a) A crisis occurred when the United States discovered that the Soviets were building missile bases in Cuba. A possible war was averted when the Soviets agreed to withdraw the missiles. (b) East Germany built a

wall to separate East and West Berlin, thus ending a flow of refugees from East Germany to the West. (c) To end reforms that offered more freedoms, Soviet troops invaded and occupied Czechoslovakia. (d) Soviet troops invaded Afghanistan to support its pro-Soviet government.
5. Relations became more cordial, leading up to formal diplomatic relations with China in 1979.

6. The Soviets invaded Afghanistan, causing the United States to withdraw the proposed SALT II Treaty.
7. (a) withdrawal of the SALT II Treaty and boycott of the 1980 Olympic Games, (b) Possible Answer: could lead to the manufacture of more weapons; could remove some of the prestige of the Olympic Games that year.

come to distrust Diem. They felt that he favored the nation's few wealthy landowners and ignored the problems of its peasants. To oppose Diem, many peasants joined the **Vietcong**—communist guerrillas supported by North Vietnam. **Guerrillas** (guh RIHL uhz) are fighters who use hit-and-run attacks. They do not wear uniforms or fight in large forces.

Growing American Involvement

The successes of the Vietcong worried American leaders. If South Vietnam fell to the communists, they reasoned, other countries in Southeast Asia would fall, too—like a row of falling dominoes. This idea became known as the **domino theory.**

Sending military advisers. President Kennedy believed in the domino theory. He thought that the United States should aid South Vietnam so that other nations in Southeast Asia would not become communist. In 1961, he sent military advisers to help Diem fight the Vietcong.

When President Johnson took office, he increased American aid to South Vietnam. The Vietcong, however, continued to gain influence.

Sending troops. Then, in August 1964, North Vietnamese torpedo boats attacked an American ship patrolling in the Gulf of Tonkin. (See the map at right.) A second attack was reported but never confirmed. North Vietnam claimed that the American ships were spying in North Vietnamese waters.

In response, President Johnson asked Congress to pass the **Gulf of Tonkin Resolution.** It allowed the President "to take all necessary measures to repel any armed attack or to prevent further aggression." Johnson used the resolution to order the bombing of North Vietnam. American planes also bombed targets in South Vietnam.

Soon, American soldiers became more than military advisers. They began fighting communist forces all across South Vietnam. By 1968, President Johnson had sent more than half a million troops to fight in the **Vietnam War.**

MAP STUDY

During the Vietnam War, North Vietnam supplied arms to communist guerrillas in South Vietnam. The system of supply routes from the north was known as the Ho Chi Minh Trail, after the leader of North Vietnam.
1. *What countries bordered Vietnam in the west?*
2. *Through which countries did the Ho Chi Minh Trail run?*
3. **Analyzing Information** *How did the Ho Chi Minh Trail help extend the conflict outside Vietnam?*

War in Southeast Asia

| 0 | 200 | 400 | 600 Miles |
| 0 | 200 | 400 | 600 Kilometers |

learn about the escalation and costs of the war in Vietnam.

2. Instruct Tell students to imagine that they are about to interview the following people: an American veteran of the Vietnam War; an antiwar protester; a supporter of American involvement in Vietnam; and a Vietnamese refugee. Have students work in small groups to list questions that they would ask each person about the Vietnam War. Then have students brainstorm answers each person might give.

3. Close To close the lesson, have students summarize the main events in the Vietnam War, using the section heads and subheads as guides.

Lesson Planner

For a developed **Cooperative Learning** lesson plan, see the *Lesson Planner,* page 176.

Answers to Map Study

1. Laos and Cambodia   2. North Vietnam, Laos, South Vietnam, and Cambodia   3. Possible Answer: Because it ran through Laos and Cambodia, it drew attacks beyond Vietnam's borders.

Customized Reader

Primary Source For a journalist's memoirs of Vietnam, order article IXA-5, A Woman Journalist in Vietnam, from the *American History Customized Reader.* In this article, journalist Anne Allen recalls the hardships and rewards of being a journalist in Vietnam. (Enrichment/Easy)

Historical Sidelight
Background

The ship attacked on August 2, 1964, was a navy destroyer, the *Maddox.* At the time, it was claimed that the *Maddox* was in international waters, but later evidence placed the ship within North Vietnam's territorial waters. Three North Vietnamese patrol boats confronted the *Maddox.* One of the boats was sunk and the other two were turned back by the *Maddox,* which was supplemented by jet fighters from the nearby aircraft carrier (or *birdfarm,* as such ships came to be called during the war) *Ticonderoga.*

Before calling for passage of the Gulf of Tonkin Resolution, President Johnson ordered an air strike against North Vietnam. During the raids, pilot Everett Alvarez, Jr., was shot down and captured. Alvarez became the first American POW of the war, and he was held by Hanoi until 1972.

The Gulf of Tonkin Resolution was passed by a unanimous vote in the House of Representatives and by a vote of 88 to 2 in the Senate. It was the closest that Congress ever came to a formal declaration of war.

Chapter Resources

Geography in History Duplicate and distribute the worksheet, The Battles of Ia Drang, from Unit 9, pages 19–20, of the *Chapter Resources* binder. The worksheet focuses on the first conflicts of the Vietnam War that involved large numbers of United States and North Vietnamese forces. (Enrichment/Challenging)

CD-ROM

Face the Issues Use the segment about the Vietnam War from the American Heritage® *History of the United States* CD-ROM. (Enrichment/Challenging)

As the fighting **escalated,** or increased, Johnson relied on the draft for raising troops. The draft hit American youths unequally. Middle-class and upper-class youths often found ways to avoid service. As a result, large numbers of poor people—especially African Americans and Latinos*—were sent into combat in Vietnam.

The Uncertain Enemy

American soldiers quickly discovered that the Vietnam War was different from other wars. Vietcong forces were hard to pin down. When Americans took territory, the Vietcong retreated into the jungle. When the Americans moved on, the Vietcong often returned and reclaimed the territory.

Infantryman Thomas Bird experienced some of the challenges of jungle warfare. On a chilly, rainy day in November 1965, he and his unit were patrolling the hilly countryside in central Vietnam. Their "search-and-destroy" mission seemed simple enough: Search for Vietcong strongholds. Destroy them. Move on. For nine hours, Bird's unit marched through forests and along steep banks of muddy red clay. Always, they watched for the enemy.

Ambush! Suddenly, Bird heard gunfire from the right. He took cover behind a tree, then began to advance toward the firing. The attack continued—this time from the left and rear. Ping, ping, ping—the sound of bullets filled the air. Now, mortar charges fell from the sky, exploding around him. Bird's unit was caught in an ambush!

The soldiers radioed for help. The low clouds made it hard for helicopters to reach them, though. By nightfall, most of the unit had run out of ammunition.

*Latinos are Spanish-speaking people from Latin America. See pages 817–819.

Capture—and rescue. After one final burst of fire and screaming shells, it was over. Bird was lucky—he survived. His captors turned out to be about 40 North Vietnamese soldiers.

66 Twelve of us were taken prisoner. We put our hands on top of our helmets. . . . Then everybody got twined by the wrist and we were led in a column back into the wood line where they came from. 99

For several days, Bird was forced to kneel in the North Vietnamese forest camp, his wrists tied to his ankles. Then suddenly, the enemy troops disappeared into the darkness of the forest. The next morning, Bird and his companions were found by an-

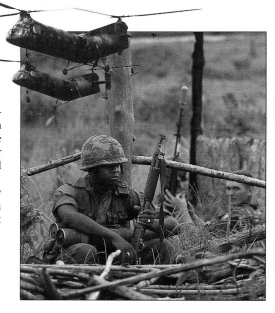

On the Lookout *The enemy in Vietnam could be anywhere. Here, American soldiers keep careful watch for signs of Vietcong activity. Helicopters, used both to transport troops and remove the wounded, were a major feature of the Vietnam War.* **Geography** *How did Vietnam's geography make fighting difficult for American troops?*

---

other American unit. Helicopters took the soldiers to a hospital to recover.

A grim routine. Within a week, Bird was back in action. He also was back to the same routine: Search and destroy, search and destroy—and always keep your eyes open.

In some ways, Bird was lucky: He knew the enemy he was fighting. Just as often, Americans could not tell which villagers were Vietcong. Was the old woman cooking rice outside her hut a friend or an enemy? What about the man walking down the village path to the market? As one American explained,

66The farmer you waved to from your jeep in the day . . . would be the guy with the gun out looking for you at night.99

If soldiers could not tell friend from enemy, how could they fight? In such an uncertain situation, it was difficult to win clear victories. ■

Protests at Home

As more and more troops were sent to Vietnam, many Americans called for an end to the war. Every night, Americans watched television news programs that showed in great detail the horrors of the war. They watched villages burn and saw wounded soldiers, children, and old people.

Protests against the war were especially strong on college campuses. Students staged sit-ins and marches. They charged that American lives and money were being wasted on an unjust war. The government of South Vietnam, they said, was no better than the Vietcong or the North Vietnamese.

Peace Without Victory

After President Nixon was elected in 1968, he promised to withdraw all American troops from Vietnam. Over the next five years, Nixon gradually brought the troops

Stop the War Now! *Antiwar protests grew as American involvement in Vietnam increased. Here, senior citizens join a demonstration in Washington, D.C. "Peace" signs, such as the one at right, became a symbol of the antiwar movement.* **Science and Technology** *What role did television play in the antiwar movement?*

home. Meanwhile, peace talks were held in Paris. In January 1973, Henry Kissinger, Nixon's national security adviser, reached a cease-fire agreement.

The United States continued to send billions of dollars in aid to South Vietnam. Still, the South Vietnamese were unable to stop the North Vietnamese advance. In April 1975, communist forces captured Saigon, the capital of South Vietnam. They renamed it Ho Chi Minh City. Soon after, Vietnam was reunited.

Civil War in Cambodia

Throughout the war, North Vietnamese soldiers carried supplies and arms into South Vietnam along trails in neighboring

---

Connections With Music
Activity

Have interested students find recordings of songs specifically about the Vietnam War, written and performed during the 1960s or early 1970s. Encourage students to locate songs that evince both positive and negative emotions (for example, "The Ballad of the Green Berets," "Billy, Don't Be a Hero," and perhaps Simon and Garfunkel's "Evening News/Silent Night"). Have students play several of the songs and ask the class to identify the feelings that each one expresses about the war.

Historical Sidelight
Background

The invasion of Cambodia sparked protests all over the country, especially on college campuses. President Nixon dubbed the antiwar protesters *bums.*

The reaction at Kent State University in Ohio was also strong. When a sit-in was staged in the faculty buildings, the Ohio National Guard was called in to offset the possibility of violence. On May 4, though the demonstration was peaceful, soldiers surrounded the campus. Suddenly, a group of

students surged forward, and in a panic the troops fired into the crowd. In all, four students were killed and eleven others wounded. A reporter who tried to interview the father of one dead girl described him as dazed and unbelieving. Unable to answer any questions, the man just looked sorrowfully into the television cameras and said, "My child was not a bum."

Chapter Resources

Skill Application For additional practice, duplicate and distribute the worksheet, Using a Song as Historical Evidence, from Unit 9, page 16 of the *Chapter Resources* binder. (Reteaching/Average)

Answers to Skill Lesson

1. (a) Possible Answer: war; racism; people's unwillingness to change (b) 1962 (c) Possible Answer: to call attention to or protest the fact that social change is so slow in coming
2. (a) Possible Answer: war, the arms race, racism (b) Possible Answer: indifference to problems, war (c) Possible Answer: racism (d) Possible Answer: at those who have the power to work for change but who fail to do so (e) Possible Answer: Solutions to these problems are difficult; they might be on the way or they might prove too elusive to grasp.
3. (a) the Vietnam War, racism (b) Possible Answer: yes, because the song offers specifics about life in the 1960s and it shows that some people cared about peace and social justice

ACTIVITY

Guided Instruction Suggest that students choose songs that are meaningful to them or that have a specific message. Be sure that students indicate the song's usefulness as a reflection of life today.

CRITICAL THINKING SKILLS
Using a Song as Historical Evidence

Sometimes songs can give useful historical evidence. A song can tell you how people in an earlier time lived. The words in a song can help you understand how those people thought about their world or the issues that concerned them.

The lines here are from a song written by folk singer Bob Dylan in 1962. The song, "Blowin' in the Wind," established 21-year-old Dylan as an important new songwriter of the 1960s. In a 1962 interview, Dylan said, "Some of the biggest criminals are those that turn their heads away when they see wrong and know it's wrong."

1. **Identify the subject of the song.** Read all three verses of the song. (a) What is the subject of the song? (b) When was it written? (c) Why do you think it was written?

2. **Study the content of the song.** (a) What specific issues does Dylan concern himself with in the first verse of the song? (b) In the second verse? (c) In the third verse? (d) At whom is Dylan aiming his criticism? (e) What do you think Dylan meant when he wrote, "The answer is blowin' in the wind"?

3. **Use the song as historical evidence.** Review the material in this chapter. (a) What issues or events did Americans protest

against in the 1960s? (b) Do you think this song is a good source of information about life in the 1960s? Why or why not?

Blowin' in the Wind

"How many roads must a man walk down
Before you call him a man?
Yes, 'n' how many seas must a white dove sail
Before she sleeps in the sand?
Yes, 'n' how many times must the cannon balls fly
Before they're forever banned?
The answer my friend, is blowin' in the wind,
The answer is blowin' in the wind.

How many times must a man look up
Before he can see the sky?
Yes, 'n' how many ears must one man have
Before he can hear people cry?
Yes, 'n' how many deaths will it take 'till he knows
That too many people have died?
The answer my friend, is blowin' in the wind,
The answer is blowin' in the wind.

How many years can a mountain exist
Before it is washed to the sea?
Yes, 'n' how many years can some people exist
Before they're allowed to be free?
Yes, 'n' how many times can a man turn his head
Pretending he just doesn't see?
The answer my friend, is blowin' in the wind,
The answer is blowin' in the wind."

ACTIVITY
Write down the words to a song that is popular among young people today. Then follow the steps above to use the song as historical evidence about life today.

Students Acquiring English
Activity

Because this lesson and its Activity depend so heavily on language skills, SAE students may need considerable guidance. Pair SAE students with English-fluent partners both to analyze "Blowin' in the Wind" and to write original lyrics — but also be prepared to step in and ask questions to check students' understanding, offering guidance when needed.

Boat People *Fleeing Vietnam in leaky, unsafe boats, "boat people" like these faced starvation, drowning, and attacks by pirates. After weeks at sea, some lucky survivors reached refugee camps in Thailand or Hong Kong. Others found a safe haven in the United States.* **United States and the World** *Why do you think many Vietnamese refugees wanted to come to the United States?*

Cambodia. They also used Cambodia as a place where they could escape American and South Vietnamese forces. In 1969, President Nixon secretly ordered the bombing of communist bases in Cambodia. American and South Vietnamese forces also made ground attacks on the bases in 1970.

As Cambodians took sides in the struggle, their nation was plunged into a civil war. It was won by the communist ***Khmer Rouge*** (kuh MER rooj) in 1975. They renamed the country Kampuchea (kam poo CHEE uh).

For the next few years, Cambodians suffered under a brutal reign of terror. The Khmer Rouge forced millions of people to work in the fields from dawn to dark. Over a million people were killed or starved to death. In 1979, Vietnam invaded Cambodia and set up a new communist government. It was less harsh, but it could not end the fighting in that war-torn country.

After 1975, hundreds of thousands of people fled Vietnam and Cambodia. Vietnamese escaped in small boats. Many of these "boat people" drowned or died of hunger and thirst. The United States took in many refugees. It also supported UN efforts to provide food and medical care.

Vietnam Balance Sheet

For all concerned, the Vietnam War was a bloody conflict. Between 1961 and 1973, more than 58,000 American soldiers lost their lives. For the Vietnamese, the statistics were even more grim. More than a million Vietnamese soldiers and perhaps half a million civilians died.

The Vietnam War era was one of the most painful periods in American history. The government spent vast amounts of money on the war. By 1967, the cost had reached $24 billion a year. Much money that might have been spent on Great Society programs went to pay for the war instead. The goals of helping the nation's poor were overshadowed by the Vietnam War.

Chapter 28 • **813**

Connections With Local History
Activity

Have interested students find out whether any Vietnamese or Cambodian refugees live in your area—and, if so, how they have adjusted to life in the United States. If possible, invite a refugee to school and ask him or her to address your class.

Connections With Architecture
Background

The Vietnam Veterans Memorial (shown on page 814) was designed by Maya Ying Lin, a Yale undergraduate student in architecture. In 1980, she had entered a design competition sponsored by the Veterans Memorial Fund. Months later, a jury of distinguished architects, sculptors, and design specialists chose her design from the more than 1,400 entries received. Many ideas had come from established architects all over the world, but Lin's design was praised for its simplicity and its goal of immortalizing all the Americans who had died in Vietnam. It won out over the protests of those who wanted a more "military" memorial. It was dedicated in November 1982 and remains one of the most popular sites in Washington, D.C.

Answer to Caption

Possible Answer: to pay respect to those who gave their lives; to remember acts of heroism or honor the ideal of freedom

ACTIVITY

Guided Instruction To help students write new titles and subtitles, have them identify the information referred to in the textbook titles and subtitles and then brainstorm for other titles and subtitles. Afterward, have students form groups. Have group members read their titles and evaluate each other's work.

Section 4
pp. 814–817

Bell Ringer

Point out when Martin Luther King Day was celebrated this year. Ask: Why is this day set aside? What ideals does it honor?

Lesson Plan

1. Focus During the 1960s and 1970s, African Americans used a variety of methods to work for social and political freedom. In this section, students examine some of these methods and the leaders who employed them.

2. Instruct Write the following statement on the chalkboard: "The civil rights movement of the 1950s and 1960s finished the struggle for racial equality in the United States." As students read, have them evaluate the statement.

Vietnam Memorial *The Vietnam Veterans Memorial in Washington, D.C., bears the names of the more than 58,000 Americans killed in the war.* **The Arts** *What is the purpose of war memorials such as this one?*

SECTION 3 REVIEW

1. **Locate:** (a) Vietnam, (b) Cambodia.
2. **Identify:** (a) Vietcong, (b) domino theory, (c) Gulf of Tonkin Resolution, (d) Vietnam War, (e) Khmer Rouge.
3. **Define:** (a) guerrilla, (b) escalate.
4. (a) Why did President Kennedy send advisers to Vietnam? (b) Why did President Johnson escalate the war?
5. What arguments did protesters use against the Vietnam War?
6. (a) Why did civil war break out in Cambodia? (b) What was the result of the war?
7. **CRITICAL THINKING** **Comparing** How was fighting in the Vietnam War different from fighting in other wars in which Americans had fought?

ACTIVITY **Writing to Learn**
Write a new title and subtitles for Section 3.

4
Struggle for Civil Rights

FIND OUT
- What civil rights laws were passed in the 1960s?
- How did civil rights groups bring about change?
- Why did violence break out in American cities in the 1960s?

VOCABULARY affirmative action

One day in 1960, four college students sat talking in their dorm room. The students, all African Americans, went to college in Greensboro, North Carolina. Downtown, the "whites only" lunch counters refused to serve blacks. The students were upset at the unjust laws that kept white and black Americans segregated.

The more they talked, the more the students felt that they ought to do something to change the situation. They went to a local department store and sat down at a segregated lunch counter. When the waitress would not serve them, they refused to leave.

News of the sit-in spread rapidly. The next day, 19 students came to protest. The day after, 85 arrived. In the months ahead, thousands of blacks and whites conducted sit-ins at public places across the South. The protests signaled a new determination to bring about equality for all Americans.

The Need for Change

Segregated lunch counters were only one example of the discrimination in the South in 1960. Segregation laws also kept whites and blacks separated in bus stations, restrooms, and other public places.

Civil rights groups. The Greensboro sit-ins inspired African American leaders to

---

Answers to Section 3 Review

1. See the map on p. 809.
2. (a) Vietcong, p. 809, (b) domino theory, p. 809, (c) Gulf of Tonkin Resolution, p. 809, (d) Vietnam War, p. 809, (e) Khmer Rouge, p. 813
3. (a) guerrilla, p. 809, (b) escalate, p. 810
4. (a) Kennedy believed in the domino theory, which emphasized the importance of stopping communism in one place to avoid its spreading to other places. (b) North Vietnam attacked two American ships in the Gulf of Tonkin.

5. They charged that American lives and money were being wasted on an unjust war. They said that the government of South Vietnam was no better than that of the Vietcong or the North Vietnamese.
6. (a) American and South Vietnamese forces attacked bases in Cambodia from which the North Vietnamese had been supplying communist forces in South Vietnam. As Cambodians took sides in this struggle, they began the civil war. (b) Under the Khmer Rouge's reign of terror, more than a million

Cambodians were killed or starved to death.
7. Possible Answer: In Vietnam, Americans were fighting guerrillas, who made quick attacks and then disappeared into the jungle. In other wars, Americans fought traditional armies, whose uniforms were easy to recognize.

press harder for change. Several civil rights organizations led the way. The oldest group, the NAACP, brought cases of discrimination before the courts. The Southern Christian Leadership Conference (SCLC) was a religious organization led by Martin Luther King, Jr. The Congress of Racial Equality (CORE) organized "Freedom Rides." *Freedom Riders* rode buses from town to town, trying to integrate bus terminals.

Civil rights groups held firmly to the tactics of peaceful civil disobedience. Doing so took courage. Police sometimes used attack dogs, water hoses, or electric cattle prods to break up protest marches. More than once, mobs bombed the houses and churches of black leaders. Many civil rights workers, black and white, were killed.

March on Washington. In 1963, more than 200,000 Americans marched on Washington, D.C. They wanted Congress to pass laws to end discrimination and help the poor. Among the speakers that day was Martin Luther King, Jr. In a now-famous speech, he proclaimed:

66 When we let freedom ring, when we let it ring from every village and every hamlet, from every state and every city, we will be able to speed up that day when all of God's children, black men and white men, Jews and Gentiles, Protestants and Catholics, will be able to join hands and sing in the words of the old Negro spiritual,

Our Common Heritage

A teenager who attended the March on Washington wrote, "I had a feeling of pride for my race and for the whites who thought enough to come. . . . All around, in the faces of everyone, there was this sense of hope for the future. . . . It could be heard in the voices of the people singing and seen in the way they walked. It poured out into smiles."

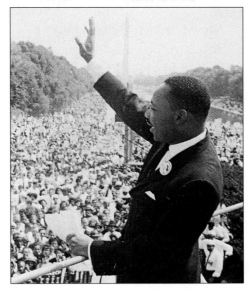

I Have a Dream *Martin Luther King, Jr., gave a stirring speech at the March on Washington. "I have a dream," he thundered, "that my four little children will one day live in a nation where they will not be judged by the color of their skin, but by the content of their character."* **Citizenship** *What was the purpose of the March on Washington?*

'Free at last! Free at last! Thank God Almighty, we are free at last!' 99

Civil rights laws. The protests spurred Presidents Kennedy and Johnson to push for strong civil rights laws. The *Civil Rights Act of 1964* protected the right of all citizens to vote. It outlawed discrimination in hiring and ended segregation in public places.

Other laws soon followed. In 1964, the Twenty-fourth Amendment was ratified. It banned poll taxes, which had been used to keep African Americans from voting. In 1965, the *Voting Rights Act* ended literacy tests. It also allowed federal officials to register voters in states where local officials practiced discrimination. These laws helped tens of thousands of African Americans to vote for the first time.

Chapter 28 • **815**

3. Close To close the lesson, have students discuss the Voting Rights Act of 1965, making a connection between the Voting Rights Act and the growing number of African Americans elected to political office.

 Lesson Planner

For a developed **Cooperative Learning** lesson plan, see the *Lesson Planner,* page 177.

Answer to Caption

to urge Congress to legislate an end to discrimination and increased aid to the poor

 CD-ROM

History Makers Access the biography of Martin Luther King, Jr., on the American Heritage® *History of the United States* CD-ROM.

Connections With Civics
Activity

Have interested students study the First Amendment to the Constitution and then describe forms of protest used in the civil rights movement. Ask them to decide which forms of protest would be protected under the First Amendment and which would be in violation of it. Then have students classify the various civil rights demonstrations and protests discussed in the text as *legal* or *illegal* according to the Constitution.

Team-Teaching Suggestion
Literature

You might work with a literature teacher to present a lesson about King's "I Have a Dream" speech (excerpted on this page). Perhaps using an overhead projector, study the brief speech, line by line, noting King's use of repetition, parallel structure, allusion, and other rhetorical devices that make the speech easy to follow—and remember. Students may also enjoy hearing a tape of the speech or seeing it on videotape.

Connections With Art
Background

For years, African Americans had been portrayed in movies as servants or comic figures. By the 1960s, however, protests against insulting stereotypes grew. African American actors began to appear in positive roles in such classic films as *To Sir With Love, A Raisin in the Sun, Lilies of the Field, Guess Who's Coming to Dinner?,* and *In the Heat of the Night.* Sidney Poitier was the first African American actor to appear on the list of top box-office stars.

Answer to Caption
continued racial discrimination, especially in housing and jobs

Our Multicultural Heritage

Biography Have students read the biography, Fannie Lou Hamer, Hero of the Civil Rights Movement, on page 82 of the *Our Multicultural Heritage* booklet. (Enrichment/Average)

Customized Reader

Primary Source For a press conference statement by Malcolm X, order article IXA-14, Malcolm X Explains Black Nationalism, from the *American History Customized Reader*. In this statement, Malcolm X calls for African American unity and a response to the violence inflicted on African Americans. (Enrichment/Easy)

Chapter Resources

Critical Thinking Duplicate and distribute the worksheet, Making Decisions, from Unit 9, page 17, of the *Chapter Resources* binder. The worksheet has students evaluate various methods advocated by civil rights leaders. (Enrichment/Challenging)

New Leaders, Differing Views

Despite new civil rights laws, discrimination remained a problem. Northern states had no formal system of segregation. Informally, though, housing in certain neighborhoods and employment in many jobs remained closed to African Americans. Millions of blacks lived in rundown areas of cities. Many were unemployed or could get only low-paying jobs.

Debate over goals and tactics. Black leaders disagreed over how to bring about change. Some, like the ***Black Muslims,*** believed that African Americans could succeed only if they separated from white society.

One Black Muslim minister, Malcolm X, won many followers in the early 1960s. An assassin's bullet ended his life in 1965. By that time, he had changed his views. Instead of racial separation, Malcolm X looked for "a society in which there could exist honest white-black brotherhood."

BIOGRAPHY Malcolm X *A fiery leader, Malcolm X called for the complete separation of the black and white races. Before his death, however, he rejected separatism and expressed hopes for "honest white-black brotherhood."* **Multicultural Heritage** *What conditions led leaders like Malcolm X to call for radical solutions?*

Other African Americans, such as Angela Davis and Stokely Carmichael, wanted to reduce the role of whites in the civil rights movement. They called for "black power." Radical groups, such as the ***Black Panthers,*** urged African Americans to arm themselves and fight for their rights when necessary.

Moderates accepted the idea of black power. However, they stressed nonviolence and urged blacks to start their own businesses. African Americans began studying their African heritage more seriously. In his bestseller *Roots,* Alex Haley traced his family back to Africa. A song by James Brown, a popular rhythm and blues singer, summed up what many blacks felt: "Say It Loud—'I'm Black and I'm Proud.'"

Urban riots. In crowded city neighborhoods, many young blacks were angry about poverty, the lack of jobs, and discrimination. In several cities, their anger exploded into violence. One of the most violent riots took place in Watts, a black neighborhood in Los Angeles. During six days in August 1965, rioters set fire to buildings and looted stores. Some 4,000 people were arrested, 34 were killed, and 1,000 were injured.

Death of Dr. King. During the years of riots, Martin Luther King, Jr., remained committed to nonviolence. In April 1968, he went to Memphis, Tennessee, to support black sanitation workers who were on strike. When he stepped outside his motel room, a white gunman shot and killed him.

King was buried in Atlanta, Georgia. His life has continued to inspire Americans to work for peaceful change. In 1986, his birthday was made a national holiday.

Some Progress Is Made

During the 1970s, the civil rights movement began to show results. African Americans won election to public office in small towns and large cities. Atlanta, Newark, Cleveland, Detroit, New Orleans, and Los Angeles all had black mayors by 1979.

Our Multicultural Heritage
Background

Black Muslim leader Malcolm X said: "It takes no one to stir up the sociological dynamite that stems from the unemployment, bad housing, and inferior education already in the ghettoes. This explosively criminal condition has existed for so long [that] it needs no fuse; it fuses itself."

Our Multicultural Heritage
Background

Martin Luther King, Jr., had been busy planning the Poor People's March on Washington during the first week of April 1968. However, he decided to go to Memphis, Tennessee, to help African American union members there in their strike against the city. Although he attracted great crowds wherever he went, he had seemed sad that week and spoke of his death only the night before his assassination. Noting that his life had been threatened once again, King encouraged his listeners to go on no matter what happened to him: "It really doesn't matter with me now, because I've been to the mountain top, and I don't mind. I just want to do God's will. And he's allowed me to go up to the mountain and I've seen the Promised Land. I may not get there with you. But I want you to know tonight that we as a people will get to the Promised Land."

African Americans made gains in the federal government as well. In 1966, Edward Brooke of Massachusetts became the first black senator since Reconstruction. A year later, President Johnson appointed Thurgood Marshall to the Supreme Court. Black support was crucial for both John F. Kennedy in 1960 and Jimmy Carter in 1976.

More businesses and universities also opened their doors to African Americans. Affirmative-action programs were set up to hire and promote minorities, women, and others who had faced discrimination. The purpose of **affirmative action** is to provide equal opportunities in areas such as jobs and college admissions for minorities and women. By the 1970s, more African Americans were entering professions such as medicine and law. Still, many blacks faced discrimination in receiving promotions and advancement in their jobs.

SECTION 4 REVIEW

1. **Identify:** (a) Freedom Rider, (b) Martin Luther King, Jr., (c) Civil Rights Act of 1964, (d) Voting Rights Act, (e) Black Muslims, (f) Malcolm X, (g) Black Panthers, (h) Alex Haley.
2. **Define:** affirmative action.
3. (a) How did African Americans use peaceful civil disobedience to win equal rights? (b) What dangers did they face?
4. Describe one law that helped African Americans win equal rights.
5. (a) How did the black power movement propose to bring about change? (b) How did moderate African American leaders respond to the idea of black power?
6. **CRITICAL THINKING Understanding Causes and Effects** Why did some cities erupt in violence in the 1960s?

ACTIVITY Writing to Learn
Jot down a list of civil rights leaders of the 1960s. Describe the main goals or views of each.

5
The Spirit of Reform Spreads

FIND OUT
■ How did Latinos work for reforms?
■ What steps did Native Americans take to achieve more rights?
■ What were the goals of the women's rights movement?

VOCABULARY bilingual, bracero, termination

essie Lopez de la Cruz had been a farm worker all her life. She grew up picking lettuce on her hands and knees and thinning row after row of beets under a hot sun. Then, in 1962, a knock on her door changed her life. She recalled,

66There were three men. One of them was Cesar Chavez. . . . The next thing I knew, they were sitting around our table talking about a union. . . . Cesar said, 'The women have to be involved.' So I sat up straight and said to myself, 'That's what I want!' 99

Lopez became active in the farm workers' union led by Cesar Chavez. Like many other Latinos, she began to demand better conditions for her people. As the spirit of reform spread during the 1960s, Latinos, Native Americans, and women struggled to win equal rights.

Spanish-speaking Americans

By the end of the 1970s, more than 10 million Latinos lived in the United States. Latinos are Spanish-speaking people from the countries of Latin America, including

Answers to Section 4 Review

1. (a) Freedom Rider, p. 815, (b) Martin Luther King, Jr., p. 815, (c) Civil Rights Act of 1964, p. 815, (d) Voting Rights Act, p. 815, (e) Black Muslims, p. 816, (f) Malcolm X, p. 816, (g) Black Panthers, p. 816, (h) Alex Haley, p. 816
2. affirmative action, p. 817
3. (a) Possible Answer: sit-ins, boycotts, marches, court cases (b) Possible Answers: being attacked by dogs, water hoses, or cattle prods; being shot or having property burned
4. Possible Answer: The Civil Rights Act of 1964 outlawed discrimination in hiring, voter registration, and the use of public places; the Voting Rights Act ended literacy tests; the Twenty-fourth Amendment ended poll taxes.
5. (a) by taking whites out of the civil rights movement and by using violence if necessary to achieve their goals (b) by stressing nonviolence and by encouraging African Americans to start their own businesses and learn more about their own heritage
6. Possible Answer: because their residents could no longer stand the unfair treatment they were receiving in housing, education, and jobs

chart. Ask: Which group had the most success in reaching its goals? Why?

3. Close To close the lesson, have students answer a series of rapid-fire *Who, What, Where, When, Why,* and *How* questions about section content.

Mexico, Central and South America, and many islands of the Caribbean.

Puerto Ricans. Most Latinos in the eastern United States trace their origins to Puerto Rico. As you recall, Puerto Ricans became American citizens in 1917. Since 1898, Puerto Rico had been governed by the United States. In 1952, the island became a self-governing commonwealth. This gave the people more say over their own affairs. Many Puerto Ricans were happy to remain a commonwealth under United States protection. Others called for full independence.

In the 1950s, thousands of people left Puerto Rico in search of work. Many took jobs in the garment factories of New York City, New Jersey, Connecticut, and Pennsylvania. Others settled in cities such as Boston, Chicago, and San Francisco.

Puerto Ricans did not have an easy time on the mainland. Many faced discrimination in housing and jobs. In response, Puerto Ricans formed groups to help their communities and to fight for equal treatment.

One result of these efforts was the ***Voting Rights Act of 1975.*** This law required areas with large numbers of non-English-speaking citizens to hold bilingual elections. **Bilingual** means in two languages. In a bilingual election, information is provided in more than one language. As a result, it was easier for Latinos to vote.

Other important laws were the Bilingual Education Acts of 1968 and 1973. These laws promoted bilingual programs in public schools with Spanish-speaking and Asian students.

Cuban Americans. Another major Latino group came from Cuba. After Fidel Castro set up a communist government in Cuba in 1959, more than 200,000 Cubans fled to the United States. (See page 805.) Most settled in southern Florida. Many were well educated and adapted quickly to their new home.

In 1980, a new wave of Cubans arrived when Castro allowed 125,000 people to leave the country. Again, many settled in southern Florida. The new refugees were unskilled workers who found it harder to make a living.

As their numbers grew, Cuban Americans became an important force in southern Florida. Miami—the city with the greatest

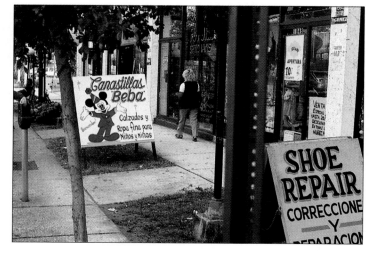

A Cuban Community in Florida *So many refugees from Cuba settled in a section of downtown Miami that it became known as Little Havana, after the Cuban capital.* **United States and the World** *Why did many Cuban immigrants come to the United States after 1959?*

818 • Chapter 28

Our Multicultural Heritage
Activity

Before World War II, only about 70,000 Puerto Ricans had moved to the mainland, most of whom had lived in and around New York City. By 1960, more than 600,000 had arrived. Have interested students research the present locations of Puerto Ricans in the United States. Have them break down the numbers by state and illustrate the totals for the top 10 states in colorful bar graphs or pie charts. Display their work on classroom bulletin boards.

Connections With Music
Activity

From the soundtrack of the musical *West Side Story,* play the song "America"—sung by Puerto Rican teenage immigrants about the good and bad things they find about life in the United States. Afterward, ask: What does this song tell you about problems that Puerto Ricans faced on the mainland? Why do the singers have mixed emotions?

number of Cuban immigrants—took on a new look. Shop windows displayed signs in Spanish. Cuban restaurants opened. Cubans published Spanish-language newspapers and operated radio and television stations.

Mexican Americans. Large numbers of Mexicans had been living in the Southwest when the United States annexed the region after the Mexican War. Mexicans continued to migrate to the area, especially after 1910.

From 1960 to 1980, the largest number of immigrants to the United States came from Mexico. By 1980, more than 8 million Mexicans had settled throughout the United States.

Mexican Americans Fight for Equality

Many Mexican Americans lived and worked in urban areas. Many others were migrant farm workers. They traveled from farm to farm, stopping wherever they were needed to plant or harvest crops. The pay was low, and working conditions were poor.

Problems of migrant workers. Migrants had little chance to get an education. Families moved often, and it was hard for children to attend school. Also, few schools offered programs for children whose first language was Spanish.

A government program that had begun in the 1940s resulted in special problems for Mexican American migrant workers. The program permitted employers to bring in temporary farm workers from Mexico. Braceros (bruh SER ohs), as these workers were called, worked for very low wages. As a result, they took away jobs from other migrant workers.

Forming a union. During the 1960s, many Mexican Americans worked for reform. For example, Cesar Chavez tried to help migrant farm workers by forming a union.

Chavez formed the National Farm Workers Association in 1962. He traveled 300,000 miles in six months to sign up members. When owners refused to talk to the union, Chavez used nonviolent tactics like those of Martin Luther King, Jr. He called for a nationwide boycott of grapes, lettuce, and other farm products. Slowly, the boycotts worked. Farm owners had to recognize the union, and workers won higher wages.

The struggle continues. Like blacks, Mexican Americans began to take increased pride in their history and culture. Some expressed this pride by calling themselves Chicanos, a name that comes from the Spanish word Mexicano.

Chicano groups actively supported the civil rights movement. They registered voters and made sure that voting laws were enforced. As a result, voters elected more Latino officials to represent their interests. With an increased role in government, Mexican Americans continued to press for better education and other reforms.

Native Americans

Native Americans also worked to achieve full rights under the law. In their case, they claimed rights not only as individuals but as members of tribal groups. Over the years, the federal government had recognized tribal governments by signing treaties with them. As you have read, tribal governments had also been given a greater voice in controlling their own affairs during the New Deal. (See page 729.)

A new policy. During the late 1940s and the 1950s, however, government attitudes changed. Federal agencies sought to break up tribal governments. Indians were encouraged to leave their reservations. Many Indians objected to this policy, which was known as termination. As a Blackfoot chief explained:

> 66 In our Indian language, the only translation for termination is to 'wipe out' or 'kill off.'. . . How can we plan

Our Multicultural Heritage

Biography Have students read the biography, Humberto Medeiros, Bishop of the Migrant Workers, on page 83 of the *Our Multicultural Heritage* booklet. (Enrichment/Average)

Voices of Freedom

Primary Source You might assign selection 19-5, Organizing Farm Workers, on pages 296–297 of *Voices of Freedom.* In this selection, Cesar Chavez tells how his labor movement started. (Enrichment/Average)

CD-ROM

History Makers Access the biography of Cesar Chavez on the American Heritage® *History of the United States* CD-ROM.

Our Multicultural Heritage
Background

Dr. Héctor Pérez García was another leader in the struggle for civil rights for Latinos. In 1946, he founded the GI Forum to help Latino veterans of World War II get proper medical treatment. The organization's goals soon expanded to campaign for better public schools and for government-funded nutrition programs serving poor and needy families.

By the 1960s, García was leading successful nonviolent protests, such as strikes and boycotts, against school segregation. In the legislature and in the courts, he fought for the repeal of unconstitutional laws that prevented Latinos from voting and serving on juries.

President Johnson appointed García to be the first Latino on the Commission on Civil Rights, as well as an ambassador to the United Nations. President Carter named García to a committee that selected federal judges. In 1984, President Reagan awarded García the Medal of Freedom, the nation's highest civilian award, in recognition of his fight for equality and justice.

Connections With the World
Background

American Indians were not the only native peoples to be challenged to assimilate. By the 1960s, the aborigines of Australia had for the most part been assimilated. Of the 80,000 aborigines in 1960, only about 7,500 were living in conditions similar to those of Native Americans. Today, aborigines have Australian citizenship and are eligible to vote.

Chapter Resources

History Through Literature To help students see one difference in the thinking of Native Americans and other Americans, duplicate and distribute the worksheet, A Vision Beyond Time and Place, from Unit 9, page 18, of the *Chapter Resources* binder. (Enrichment/Challenging)

" " Voices of Freedom

Primary Source You might assign selection 19-6, Trial After a "Fish-In," on pages 297–299 of *Voices of Freedom*. This selection describes a group of Native Americans who hold a "fish-in" to protest violation of their ancient fishing rights. (Enrichment/Average)

Primary Source You might assign selection 19-7, A New Kind of Woman, on pages 299–300 of *Voices of Freedom*. In this excerpt from *Born Female*, Caroline Bird discusses the characteristics and vision of the liberated woman of the 1970s. (Enrichment/Average)

our future when the [government] threatens to wipe us out as a race? "

Organizing for change. During the next 20 years, thousands of Indians moved to cities. By the late 1960s, more than half of all Indians lived off the reservations, mainly in urban areas. Over the years, city life weakened traditional tribal ties and customs.

Native Americans organized to counter the government's policies. The National Congress of American Indians, founded in 1944, regularly sent delegations to Washington to defend Indian rights. It also strongly opposed the policy of termination.

Another organization, the Native American Rights Fund, stressed legal action. Its members worked to regain title to lands or to mineral and fishing rights that had been given to them in earlier treaties. In some cases, courts awarded Native Americans money for lands that had been taken illegally. The Native American Youth Council also focused on regaining treaty rights.

Organized protests. In 1969, a group called Indians of All Tribes took over Alcatraz Island in San Francisco. They offered to buy Alcatraz for $24 "in glass beads and red cloth"—the price Peter Minuit paid for Man-

hattan in 1626. This protest called attention to the many treaties that had been broken by the government.

The ***American Indian Movement*** (AIM) also actively protested the treatment of Indians. In 1973, AIM members occupied Wounded Knee, South Dakota, for several weeks. As you have read, the United States Army had massacred nearly 300 Indians at Wounded Knee in 1890. AIM wanted to remind people of the government's failure to deal fairly with Native Americans.

Protests and court cases have won sympathy for Indian causes. Today, Native Americans continue to speak out forcefully to achieve their goals.

Rights for Women

Like other groups, women struggled to win equal rights. Women faced discrimination in jobs, pay, and education.

Job discrimination. Many employers refused to hire women for certain jobs even though the women were qualified. Even when women were hired, they were not treated the same as men. A female steelworker complained:

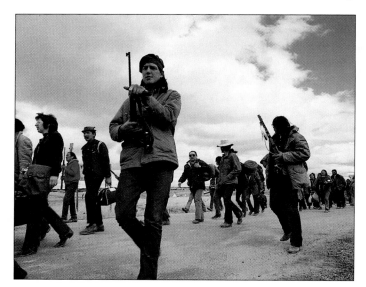

Protest at Wounded Knee *In 1973, members of the American Indian Movement took over the trading post at Wounded Knee. The protest focused national attention on the continuing struggle for rights.* **Linking Past and Present** *Why did AIM choose to hold its protest at Wounded Knee?*

Our Multicultural Heritage
Background

Annie Dodge Wauneka, the daughter of the first chairman of the Navajo nation, grew up on the Navajo homeland in Arizona. Even as a young girl, she was concerned about the poor living conditions of her people. After her father's death, Wauneka became the first woman to be elected to the Navajo council. In that position, she committed herself to improving health care among the Navajos, especially in the fight against tuberculosis. Through her efforts, clean water and modern

medicines became common on the reservation. Navajo children were vaccinated against dangerous diseases, which caused a sharp drop in the death rate on the reservation.

Many Navajos, including two of Wauneka's daughters, became health-care professionals. In 1963, Wauneka received the Presidential Medal of Freedom for her work. The Navajos also honored her fight against diseases by bestowing upon her the title "Warrior Who Scouts the Enemy."

Historical Sidelight
Background

During his first year in office, President Kennedy appointed a Commission on the Status of Women. The commission was headed by former First Lady Eleanor Roosevelt, who had campaigned for women's rights during the New Deal. The commission concluded that discrimination against women existed in almost every aspect of American life.

"One woman's husband was a weight lifter and she could also lift weights. She worked in the masonry department. She could carry two buckets when most of the men carried only one. She got fired because she was too short and they said it was unsafe for her."

When men and women held the same job, women were often paid less. Also, women were seldom promoted as fast as men. Many law schools and medical schools gave preference to male applicants.

Struggle for equality. In 1966, Betty Friedan helped to set up the *National Organization for Women* (NOW). It worked for equal rights for women in jobs, pay, and education. Since the 1960s, this struggle for equality has become known as the *women's rights movement.*

Women made some gains through new laws. The Equal Pay Act of 1963 required equal pay for equal work. The Civil Rights Act of 1964 outlawed discrimination in hiring based on gender as well as on race. Yet some employers continued to deny women equal opportunities. As a result, women brought many cases to the courts.

In 1972, Congress passed a proposal for an equal rights amendment to the Constitution. However, Americans were divided over whether the amendment was needed. After 10 years of campaigning, the amendment failed to be ratified in enough states. Even so, the decades of reform brought women more power and equality. The lead-

History and You
Does your school have a strong sports program for girls? If so, it is probably because of a law passed by Congress in 1972 as a result of the women's rights movement. The law forbids discrimination by sex at any school that receives federal aid.

The Women's Movement *Like other groups, the National Organization for Women gained influence by electing women to public office.* **Citizenship** *What were the goals of NOW?*

ers of the women's movement vowed to continue the fight for equal pay and equal opportunity.

SECTION 5 REVIEW

1. **Locate:** (a) Mexico, (b) Puerto Rico, (c) Cuba.
2. **Identify:** (a) Voting Rights Act of 1975, (b) Cesar Chavez, (c) American Indian Movement, (d) National Organization for Women, (e) women's rights movement.
3. **Define:** (a) bilingual, (b) bracero, (c) termination.
4. How did Cesar Chavez focus national attention on the problems of some Latinos?
5. What rights did Native American tribal groups try to gain?
6. **CRITICAL THINKING Comparing** Compare the goals of the women's rights movement of the 1960s with the goals of Native American organizations.

ACTIVITY **Writing to Learn**
Imagine that you are a leader in the Latino, Native American, or women's rights movement of the 1960s. Write a speech to inspire other Americans to support your cause.

Chapter 28 • **821**

Answer to Caption
equal rights for women in jobs, pay, and education

 Student Study Guide

Section 5 Study Guide Have students use the Section 5 Study Guide on page 208 of the *Student Study Guide* to review and reinforce the content of this section. (Reteaching/Average)

ACTIVITY
Guided Instruction If students have not already done so, you might at this point have them create a chart showing the goals of each movement. Encourage students to find a single, meaningful statement upon which to build their speeches. Invite volunteers to present their finished speeches in small groups or before the entire class.

Our Multicultural Heritage
Activity

Have students choose one of the groups highlighted in this chapter—African Americans, Native Americans, Latinos, or women—and design a poster supporting the group's struggle for equal rights. Suggest that students first make some sort of graphic organizer to focus their ideas and to identify what they consider to be the most important ones. Make a display of students' posters, perhaps arranged by groups, in a large area of the classroom.

Answers to Section 5 Review

1. See the map on pp. 890–891.
2. (a) Voting Rights Act of 1975, p. 818, (b) Cesar Chavez, p. 819, (c) American Indian Movement, p. 820, (d) National Organization for Women, p. 821, (e) women's rights movement, p. 821
3. (a) bilingual, p. 818, (b) bracero, p. 819, (c) termination, p. 819
4. Chavez organized a farm workers' union and a nationwide boycott of certain farm products on behalf of migrant farm workers.

5. recognition that the federal government had cheated Native Americans out of land and rights by ignoring treaties; end to the termination policy
6. Possible Answer: Both faced discrimination, but Native Americans were focused on trying to regain tribal rights, whereas women were working for individual rights in employment and education.

CHAPTER 28 REVIEW

Answers to Reviewing the Main Ideas

1. Possible Answers: civil rights laws, programs to help the poor
2. Nixon supported a "law-and-order" program. He appointed conservative Justices to the Supreme Court. Opposing some programs of the Great Society as too costly, he backed off from some reforms of the Johnson years. (b) the Watergate Affair
3. (a) Cuba, just 90 miles off the coast of the United States, became a Soviet ally and encouraged revolutions in other parts of Latin America. (b) an American plan to overthrow Castro
4. In 1972, Nixon visited Moscow, and the United States and Soviet Union signed the SALT Agreement; the United States sold wheat to the Soviets; in 1975, Soviet and American astronauts conducted a space mission together. The United States also established formal diplomatic relations with the People's Republic of China.
5. (a) President Kennedy sent American advisers to South Vietnam in 1961. By 1968, more than 500,000 Americans were fighting in Vietnam. (b) In 1969 and 1970, the United States began bombing communist bases in Cambodia and attacking these bases on the ground.
6. (a) King led the nonviolent civil rights movement. His life and death inspired people to work for peaceful change. (b) The Civil Rights Act of 1964 protected the right of all citizens to vote, outlawed discrimination in hiring, and ended segregation in public places. (c) The Voting Rights Act of 1965 helped many African Americans to vote for the first time.
7. (a) Puerto Ricans worked for passage of laws setting up bilingual education and bilingual elections; Mexican Americans formed a union and organized a boycott to improve pay and working conditions of migrant workers. (b) Native Americans worked through the courts and used direct action to gain recognition of treaty rights and of tribal governments. (c) Women worked for laws to provide equal pay for equal work and to end discrimination against women in education and hiring.

822

Summary

● Presidents in the 1960s and 1970s faced many challenges overseas and at home.
● Cold War crises erupted in Cuba, Berlin, and Czechoslovakia, although tensions eased for a time under détente.
● The Vietnam War, the longest war in the nation's history, divided the American people.
● The civil rights movement made important gains in the fight for equal rights.
● Latinos, Native Americans, and women worked for reforms.

Reviewing the Main Ideas

1. What social programs did Presidents Kennedy and Johnson support?
2. (a) What were the goals of Nixon's domestic program? (b) Why did he resign?
3. (a) Why did Castro's revolution in Cuba worry the United States? (b) What was the Bay of Pigs invasion?
4. What efforts at détente were made in the 1970s?
5. (a) How did the United States get involved in the Vietnam War? (b) How did the fighting spread to Cambodia?
6. Explain the importance of each of the following in the civil rights movement: (a) Martin Luther King, Jr., (b) Civil Rights Act of 1964, (c) Voting Rights Act of 1965.
7. Give an example of how each of the following groups tried to win greater rights in the 1960s and 1970s: (a) Latinos, (b) Native Americans, (c) women.

Thinking Critically

1. **Comparing** Compare the Great Society programs of the 1960s with the New Deal programs of the 1930s. (a) How were they similar? (b) How were they different?

2. **Making Decisions** Do you think that President Ford was right to pardon Richard Nixon? Explain.
3. **Linking Past and Present** Since the 1960s, the role of women in society has changed greatly. How do women's roles today differ from their roles in the early years after World War II?

Applying Your Skills

1. **Concept Mapping** Make a concept map about the Cold War in the 1960s and 1970s. Include at least three main ideas and supporting details for each.
2. **Making a Time Line** Make a time line showing the main events of United States involvement in the war in Vietnam. Then describe a cause-and-effect relationship between at least two events on your time line.
3. **Making a Generalization** Review the description of the women's rights movement on pages 820–821. Make a generalization about the movement. Then give two facts to support your generalization.

Thinking About Geography

Match the letters on the map with the following places: **1.** Soviet Union, **2.** Cuba, **3.** People's Republic of China, **4.** Afghanistan, **5.** Vietnam. **6.** Mexico. **Movement** Why did Cubans flee to the United States in the 1960s?

Answers to Thinking Critically

1. (a) Possible Answer: Both tried to help Americans by providing job training and employment opportunities. Both were based on the belief that the government should help the poor. (b) Possible Answer: The New Deal programs, which came during a terrible economic depression that affected almost all Americans, were focused mainly on economic goals. The Great Society focused more on social goals that would help the poor take part in the general prosperity and opportunity the rest of the nation enjoyed.
2. Possible Answer: Ford was right, because if Nixon had not been pardoned, the nation would have been so consumed with Nixon's wrongdoing that important national business would have been neglected. On the other hand, perhaps Nixon should have had to submit to the entire legal process and been punished for his wrongdoing.
3. Possible Answer: Many more women work outside the home and hold higher ranking jobs in business and government. Women also have much more freedom today in the way they dress and behave in public.

Answers to Applying Your Skills

1. Main ideas include: Confrontations in Cuba; Berlin Wall; Soviets enter Czechoslovakia. Concept maps should include appropriate supporting details.
2. Possible Events: 1954—Vietnam divided; 1961—Kennedy sends military advisers; 1964—American ships attacked in Gulf

Focusing on Civil Rights

Form into groups to review the civil rights movement. Follow the suggestions below to write, perform, or draw to show what you have learned. You may use the textbook, encyclopedias, atlases, or other materials in your classroom library to complete the tasks. Be able to name your sources of information when you have finished the activity.

CARTOGRAPHERS Find out more about places in the United States that are connected with the civil rights movement. Then create a civil rights landmarks map. On an outline map of the United States, locate and label the following places:

- Atlanta, Georgia
- Birmingham, Alabama
- Greensboro, North Carolina
- Watts (Los Angeles, California)
- Little Rock, Arkansas
- Memphis, Tennessee
- Montgomery, Alabama

Next to each place, write a sentence identifying its role in the civil rights struggle. Illustrate your map with original drawings or pictures cut from magazines.

Indian rights poster

HISTORIANS Divide into small groups to find out more about each of the following civil rights leaders of the 1960s: Stokely Carmichael, Martin Luther King, Jr., Malcolm X, Thurgood Marshall. Then stage a debate between the leaders about the goals and tactics of the civil rights movement.

MUSICIANS Learn some songs that were used in the civil rights movement. Perform these songs for the class. Then hold a discussion to explore how songs can play an important role in a reform movement.

ARTISTS Brainstorm events, people, treaties, laws, and speeches relating to the civil rights movement. Then design a cover for a book on this subject.

CITIZENS Review what you have learned about the advances in civil rights for Americans. Then make a civil rights time line showing these events. Be sure to include civil rights advances by African Americans, various Latino groups, Native Americans, and women.

Civil rights march in Alabama

 Conduct a Focusing on Civil Rights talk show. Have a representative from each group discuss the group's activity.

Lessons	Teaching Resources
1 **The Conservative Revolution** **Objectives** 1. Describe the conservative revolution. 2. Identify President Clinton's goals. 3. Identify the issues that concerned American voters in 1996.	**Lesson Planner** Cooperative Learning, p. 181 **Student Study Guide** Section 1 Study Guide, p. 211 **Our Multicultural Heritage** *Biography* Sarah Brady, Fighter for a Cause, p. 85
2 **An End to the Cold War** **Objectives** 1. Describe how democracy spread in Eastern Europe. 2. Identify the events that led to the breakup of the Soviet Union. 3. Explain why civil war broke out in Yugoslavia. 4. Describe United States policy toward Yugoslavia.	**Lesson Planner** Cooperative Learning, p. 182 **Student Study Guide** Section 2 Study Guide, p. 212 **Interdisciplinary Connections:** The Quest for Peace ■ *Arts* Remembering, p. 170 ▨ *Sciences* Dangerous Waste, p. 171 ■ *Geography* Our Uneasy World, p. 172 ■ *World* Keeping the Peace, p. 173 ■ *Economics* The NAFTA Debate, p. 174 **Chapter Resources Binder, Unit 9** *History Through Literature* Hallelujah!, p. 32
3 **The Search for a More Democratic World** **Objectives** 1. Identify the moves that South Africa made toward greater democracy. 2. Describe how people in Asia struggled for freedom in the 1970s and 1980s. 3. Identify United States policy toward Latin America during the 1980s.	**Lesson Planner** Cooperative Learning, p. 183 **Student Study Guide** Section 3 Study Guide, p. 213 **Our Multicultural Heritage** *Milestone* Visit of Nelson Mandela, p. 87 **Chapter Resources Binder, Unit 9** *Skill Application* Analyzing Newspaper Editorials, p. 30
4 **Crisis and Hope in the Middle East** **Objectives** 1. Describe how events in the Middle East affected the United States. 2. Identify major steps that were taken toward peace in the Middle East. 3. Identify the action taken by the United States when Iraq invaded Kuwait.	**Lesson Planner** Cooperative Learning, p. 184 **Student Study Guide** Section 4 Study Guide, p. 214 **Chapter Resources Binder, Unit 9** *Geography in History* Trading Black Gold, pp. 33–34 *Critical Thinking* Understanding Causes and Effects, p. 31 **Our Multicultural Heritage** *Biography* Colin Powell, Military Hero, p. 86

Multimedia Resources	Additional Resources	Chapter-Level Resources
Transparencies *Time Lines* The United States and the World, 1980–Present, p. E-31 **CD-ROM** *Presidents* Ronald Reagan *Presidents* George Bush *History Makers* Sandra Day O'Connor *Presidents* William J. Clinton	**Voices of Freedom** American Traditions in Today's World, pp. 314–316 **Customized Reader** The Reagan Campaign Visits Milwaukee, article XB-1	**Lesson Planner** Activity Based, pp. 185–186 **Student Study Guide** Chapter 29 Study Guide, pp. 215–216 **Chapter Resources Binder** **Unit 9** Vocabulary Building, p. 29 Chapter Test A, pp. 35–37 Chapter Test B, pp. 38–40 Illustration Master, p. 41 Extra Unit Questions, pp. 57–59 **English Guided Reading** Guided Reading, pp. 57–58 **Spanish Resources**
Transparencies *Interdisciplinary Connections* Eastern Europe, p. B-89 *Cause and Effect* End of the Cold War, p. F-33		**Computer Test Bank** Chapter Tests A and B Extra Unit Questions
	Historical Outline Map Book Central America and the Caribbean, p. 81	**Guided Reading Audiotapes** Side 12 **CD-ROM** *Time Tour* New Directions in The Nation Today and Tomorrow
	Voices of Freedom Tense Days at Camp David, pp. 311–312 The Meaning of the Hostage Crisis, pp. 312–314 **Customized Reader** Panic at the Pump, article IXB-9 Camp David: The President's Weekend Retreat, article XB-8	

Lesson Planner

For a fully developed **Activity-Based** lesson plan for Chapter 29, see the *Lesson Planner,* pages 185–186.

 Chapter Resources

Vocabulary Building The Vocabulary Building worksheet for Chapter 29 from Unit 9, page 29, of the *Chapter Resources* binder can be used as a prereading activity or as a review of chapter vocabulary. (Reteaching/Easy)

 Student Study Guide

Chapter 29 Study Guide Refer students to pages 215–216 of the *Student Study Guide* for the Chapter 29 Study Guide. The study guide can be used for chapter review as well as for reteaching. (Reteaching/Average)

 Guided Reading Audiotapes

Students can use *Guided Reading Audiotapes,* Chapter 29, side 12, to listen to section previews, summaries, and review questions. The tapes will benefit students who are auditory learners, students who have trouble reading, or students acquiring English. Tapes are also available in Spanish. (Reteaching/ Easy)

CHAPTER **29**

New Directions

(1980–Present)

CHAPTER OUTLINE

1 The Conservative Revolution

2 An End to the Cold War

3 The Search for a More Democratic World

4 Crisis and Hope in the Middle East

1980 Ronald Reagan was elected President. He and his Vice President, George Bush, promised "Peace Through Strength" by building up the military.

1984 The budget deficit reached nearly $200 billion. As this cartoon shows, the President could not keep his promise of a balanced budget.

1987 President Reagan and Soviet leader Mikhail Gorbachev signed the INF Treaty. In this pact, the superpowers agreed to do away with many nuclear missiles.

| 1980 | 1982 | 1984 | 1986 | 1988 |

 WORLD EVENT
1980 Iraq-Iran war begins

 WORLD EVENT
1987 Costa Rican President Arias arranges peace plan for Nicaragua

824 • Chapter 29

Chapter Time Line
Understanding Chronology

Although 11 events are noted on the time line, only 7 dates are involved. After students have discussed the time line illustrations, captions, and World Event entries, check their understanding by distributing a list of the 11 events. Then have students identify which events can be paired by date (1980, 1987, 1989, and 1991). Finally, have them sequence the events chronologically.

Students Acquiring English
Activity

To help SAE students access information in this chapter, have them work in small collaborative groups or with a partner who is fluent in English. Have SAE students interview their partners or group members about the chapter content. Suggest that students use the Find Out items and the Section Reviews as guidelines for the interviews. This peer-group strategy gives SAE students an opportunity to increase comprehension through oral language summaries. As the content becomes more familiar to them, they can switch roles with their classmates and become interviewees.

Chapter Setting

British statesman Winston Churchill would have been astonished if he could have visited the town of Fulton, Missouri, on the morning of May 6, 1992. There, 46 years earlier, Churchill had ushered in the Cold War with a warning that the Soviet Union had drawn an "iron curtain" across Europe. (See page 771.) Now, outside the gym where Churchill had spoken, another speaker addressed the crowd. He was Mikhail Gorbachev, former president of the Soviet Union. He was there to announce that the Cold War was over. Gorbachev proclaimed,

66 We live today in a watershed era. One epoch has ended and a second is commencing. No one yet knows [what it will be like]—no one. Having long been [dedicated] communists, we were sure that we knew. But life once again has [proved wrong] those who claim to be know-it-alls and messiahs. 99

Few people could have predicted how quickly the world would change during the 1980s and 1990s. When Ronald Reagan took office as President, the Soviet Union ranked as one of the world's two superpowers. Eleven years later, in 1992, it no longer even existed. As the Cold War came to an end, both the United States and the former Soviet Union scrambled to adjust to a quickly changing world.

ACTIVITY
Brainstorm to list five ways in which the Cold War affected everyday life in the United States. Then list five changes that might be brought by the end of the Cold War.

1989 Hundreds of banks failed. Notices like this announced that the government had taken over a bank and would repay its depositors.

1991 United Nations allies defeated Iraq in the Persian Gulf War. Women provided important support for American combat forces in the Gulf.

1996 Bill Clinton was reelected President. Here, the Democractic National Convention in Chicago launches his campaign.

1988	1990	1992	1994	Present

WORLD EVENT
1989 South Africa moves away from apartheid

WORLD EVENT
1991 Soviet Union breaks up

WORLD EVENT
1993 Israel and PLO sign peace agreement

Chapter 29 • **825**

Answer to Caption

With a dislike for "big government," Reagan cut back on government programs and reduced the number of government regulations.

Section 1
pp. 826–831

Bell Ringer

Ask students to volunteer words, phrases, and images that they associate with the term *conservative*. Tell them not to limit their associations to politics. Write the responses on the chalkboard and relate them to the class discussion that follows.

Lesson Plan

1. Focus In 1980, the public's discontent with high taxes and government spending helped Ronald Reagan win election as President. Reagan's programs led to a conservative "revolution." In 1989, Reagan was succeeded by his Vice President, George Bush. Bush continued on Reagan's conservative course. The election of Bill Clinton in 1992 seemed to mark a new direction, but the 1994 elections brought Republican majorities to both houses of Congress. In 1996 Clinton faced Republican Bob Dole in his bid for reelection. In this section, students examine the domestic policies of Presidents Reagan, Bush, and Clinton, as well as the 1996 presidential election.

1
The Conservative Revolution

FIND OUT

- What was the conservative revolution?
- What goals did President Clinton set for his presidency?
- What issues concerned voters in 1996?

VOCABULARY balanced budget, downsizing, recession

"**G**overnment is not the solution to our problem; government is the problem." Ronald Reagan spoke those words in 1981 after being sworn in as President of the United States. The new President called for a conservative revolution that would change the direction of the federal government.

Reagan's Program

Reagan's ideas contrasted sharply with the liberal goals of the 1960s and 1970s. Liberal Presidents like John F. Kennedy and Lyndon Johnson believed that the federal government should take an active part in managing the economy. They sponsored federal programs that tried to erase poverty or provide medical care to those who could not afford it.

Many Republicans also agreed that the federal government should protect the welfare of citizens. President Richard Nixon had created agencies to set safety standards for workers and to protect the environment.

To conservatives of the 1980s, however, "big government" created big problems. Ronald Reagan and others argued that federal social programs had become too costly. In their view, government regulations kept

826 • Chapter 29

businesses from growing. Conservatives preferred to let state and local governments decide what regulations were needed.

Conservatives such as Reagan also called for a return to traditional values. They praised family life, loyalty, and patriotism. In 1980, many Americans welcomed that message, after so many years of reform, protest, and change.

The Great Communicator. Ruggedly handsome, Ronald Reagan was a popular movie actor during the 1930s and 1940s. After entering politics, he was twice elected governor of California. His skill at presenting ideas earned him the title the Great Communicator.

Reagan easily won election as President in 1980. He was reelected by an even greater margin in 1984.

Economic policies. Once in office, Reagan quickly persuaded Congress to try to

---

A Popular President *With his relaxed and good-humored manner, Ronald Reagan was a popular President. Here, Reagan waves to the crowd at his 1981 inauguration.* **Citizenship** *How did Reagan change the direction of the federal government?*

Historical Sidelight
Background

In the 1930s and 1940s, Ronald Reagan was a Democrat and a union leader. He idolized Franklin D. Roosevelt, campaigned for Democratic candidates at the national level as late as 1950, and did not change his party affiliation to Republican until the early 1960s. Reagan gained nationwide attention as a conservative spokesperson when he gave a televised address supporting Barry Goldwater before the 1964 presidential election.

Connections With Economics
Background

During the 1980 campaign, Ronald Reagan declared that the United States was in an economic depression. President Carter responded that it was a recession, not a depression. Reagan then told reporters, "If the President wants a definition, I'll give him one. Recession is when your neighbor loses his job, depression is when you lose yours, and recovery will be when Jimmy Carter loses his."

Linking Past and Present
Activity

Have students compare Reagan's program to Franklin D. Roosevelt's program during the Great Depression. Ask: Did Reagan roll back the New Deal? In what ways? Why do you think Reagan, even after he became a conservative, considered FDR his political idol?

826

stimulate the economy by cutting taxes. The President hoped that taxpayers would use the extra money to buy more. That would benefit businesses selling goods and services. He also hoped that taxpayers would save more. That would help banks, which could use the increased money in savings accounts to invest in new projects.

With fewer taxes coming in, Reagan looked for ways to cut government spending. His proposals reduced social programs such as welfare and aid to education. Critics charged that spending cuts hurt the poor, the aged, minorities, and young children. Supporters responded that Reagan was just trimming programs that did not work.

The President also reduced the number of regulations issued by the government. Some regulations were meant to set limits on pollution or to protect workers. Others attempted to protect consumers from unsafe products or prevent banks from making rash investments.

Mixed results. At first, the President's program slowed the economy. Many people lost their jobs. By late 1982, however, the economy was expanding. It continued to grow through the end of the 1980s.

One of Reagan's goals—balancing the budget—proved more difficult to achieve. With a **balanced budget,** the government spends only as much as it takes in from taxes. Although Reagan worked to cut back social programs, he sharply increased military spending. He said that the nation needed

more strength to stand up to the Soviet Union.

With military spending rising and taxes being cut, the President could not balance the budget. In fact, the deficit soared. A deficit, you will recall, is the amount the government spends beyond its income. The deficit for 1986 was $240 billion—almost ten times higher than under any other president. Deficits remained high throughout the Reagan years.

Federal Budget Deficit 1980–1992

Source: *Statistical Abstract of the United States*

GRAPH SKILLS *The rapidly growing federal budget deficit worried many Americans in the 1980s and early 1990s. • What was the budget deficit in 1980? During which two-year period did the deficit decrease?*

History and You
Balancing the budget of a government is not the same as balancing a family budget. What would happen if you or your family spent more each year than you earned? How are government finances different from yours?

Chapter 29 • **827**

2. Instruct Begin by quickly reviewing the economic policies of Kennedy, Johnson, Nixon, Ford, and Carter. (See Chapter 28, Section 1.) Ask: Which Presidents made assistance to the poor a priority? Which Presidents made defense a priority? What did these Presidents do with social programs? Have students make several generalizations about the economic programs of Republicans and Democrats.
3. Close To close the lesson, play a Jeopardy!-like game with students based on the section.

 Lesson Planner

For a developed **Cooperative Learning** lesson plan, see the *Lesson Planner,* page 181.

Answer to Graph Skills

approximately $75 billion; 1986–1988

 Transparencies

Time Lines Use the time line, The United States and the World, 1980–Present, on page E-31 of *American History Transparencies.* This time line shows how issues are interconnected globally in a changing world. Teaching suggestions can be found on page E-11. (Enrichment/Average)

CD-ROM

Presidents Access the biography of Ronald Reagan on the American Heritage® *History of the United States* CD-ROM. (Enrichment/Average)

Connections With Economics
Background

Although the economy expanded after 1982, the benefits of that expansion were not distributed equally. Only 2 percent of the new jobs went to African Americans. Unemployment rates remained high for young African Americans and Latinos. Women most often found jobs in health, education, government, and social services, where pay was lower than in the private sector. By the mid-1980s, a growing percentage of the nation's poor were women.

Connections With Economics
Background

The proposed federal budget for the 1984 fiscal year was almost $850 billion—a figure so large that it meant little to the average person. So President Reagan, with the help of economists, devised examples to clarify it. If 850 billion one-dollar bills were laid end to end, Reagan said, they would extend more than 80 million miles—almost to the sun. Also, if $1 million had been spent every day for the past 2,000 years, $120 million of the $850 billion would still be left!

Critical Thinking
Summarizing Information

After students have read and discussed the subsection Reagan's Program, have them summarize the information by making a list of the key characteristics of the economic program known as "Reaganomics." Students can use their lists to compare Reagan's policies to those of Presidents Bush and Clinton.

George Bush Carries On

The policies of the Reagan years were continued under President George Bush, who took office in 1989. Bush, a Republican from Texas, had served as Vice President under Ronald Reagan. In a dramatic campaign speech, Bush promised to cut the deficit without raising taxes. "Read my lips," he proclaimed boldly. "No new taxes."

Financial crisis. It was a promise Bush was unable to keep. Democrats and Republicans could not agree on which government programs to cut in order to reduce the deficit. By 1990, Congress and the President were deadlocked. Finally Bush agreed to raise taxes in order to save some popular programs. Many of his supporters felt betrayed because he had broken his earlier promise.

President Bush also faced a banking crisis. Under Reagan, the government had done away with many regulations for savings banks. With fewer rules, some of these banks made risky or illegal loans. Sometimes these loans were not paid back and the banks lost their money. During the late 1980s, hundreds of banks went bankrupt.

Since the time of the New Deal, the federal government has insured bank accounts. If a bank went bankrupt, the government paid back most of the money people would have lost from their accounts. With so many savings banks failing, billions of dollars were needed to repay depositors. By 1992, Congress had set aside $87 billion to rescue bankrupt or weakened savings banks.

The economy weakens. The banking crisis contributed to a weaker economy. Banks became more cautious about loaning money. Many businesses that wanted to expand had their requests for loans turned down. Other businesses tried to cut costs by using fewer people to do the same work more efficiently. This practice is known as **downsizing.** While downsizing brought more profits to business, it also left more people out of work.

These conditions combined to push the nation into a recession. A **recession** is an economic slump that is milder than a depression. The recession continued for more than a year.

Changes on the Supreme Court

George Bush and Ronald Reagan both had a chance to extend their conservative revolution to the Supreme Court. Between them, Bush and Reagan appointed five Supreme Court Justices. One of President Reagan's choices was Sandra Day O'Connor, the first woman to serve as a Justice on the Court.

The new members of the Court showed their conservative bent in several major decisions. For example, the Court placed new limits on the rights of suspected criminals. It also limited the rights of prisoners to appeal their convictions to a higher court.

In the area of civil rights, the Court cut back on busing to achieve school integration. It also made it harder for workers to win job discrimination cases.

A Democrat in the White House

Running for reelection in 1992, President Bush faced a stiff challenge. Unemployment had risen to 7.8 percent—the highest level in eight years. The economy had not pulled itself out of the recession.

In addition, many voters were unhappy with their government. The President and Congress seemed unable to work together to solve the nation's problems. Many Americans felt that the government responded more to the needs of big companies and organizations than to the needs of average Americans.

A vote for change. The Democrats nominated Bill Clinton, governor of Arkansas, as their candidate for President. His running mate was Tennessee Senator Albert Gore. At ages 46 and 44, Clinton and Gore were the youngest ticket in American history. They campaigned vigorously, promising to involve the government more actively in areas that had been ignored by Reagan and Bush.

Texas billionaire Ross Perot emerged as a strong independent candidate for President. Perot attracted citizens who were annoyed with both the Republicans and the Democrats. He hurt his chances, however, when he suddenly withdrew from the race for several months. By the time he resumed his campaign, many of his supporters had deserted him.

On election day, voters sent a clear signal for change. Only 38 percent voted for Bush. Clinton received 43 percent and Perot, 19 percent. Winning 370 electoral votes, Clinton became President.

Clinton's moderate policies. The new President pursued a middle-of-the-road course. On the one hand, he convinced Congress to increase some taxes and reduce spending. This led to a drop in the federal deficit for three years in a row. It was the first such drop in over 40 years.

At the same time, Clinton also added programs to stimulate the economy and help rebuild the nation. Americorps was a national service program like the Peace Corps. In the program, over 20,000 young volunteers worked in communities across the nation in exchange for help with college tuition.

Health care. The President pushed hardest to reform the American health care system. In 1994, 37 million Americans had no health insurance. Even for those who did, the cost of medical care was rising sharply. Clinton appointed a team headed by his wife, Hillary Rodham Clinton, to draw up reforms.

The Clintons' plan called for a national system guaranteeing health insurance for almost all Americans. After heated debate, however, Congress defeated the President's proposals. Many Americans worried that the plan would prove too costly.

Conservatives at High Tide

The defeat of health care reform in the fall of 1994 left many Americans frustrated. A Democratic President and a Democratic Congress had not been able to pass one of its key programs. In many other areas as well, Congress seemed ineffective.

When voters went to the polls in November, they gave the Republicans a resounding victory. For the first time since the 1950s, the Republicans held a majority in both the Senate and the House of Representatives. Toby Roth, a Republican from Wisconsin, was overjoyed. "It was a revolution," he boasted.

The Republican Program. Representative Newt Gingrich of Georgia became the

New Speaker of the House In 1994, Republicans gained control of Congress. Representative Newt Gingrich, as Speaker of the House, worked to pass the Republicans' conservative program into law. **Citizenship** What is the role of the Speaker of the House in the lawmaking process?

Answer to Caption

Possible answer: The outcome shows that the electorate was more comfortable with Clinton's policies than with those proposed by Dole.

new Speaker of the House. He led the Republican charge.

The House quickly drew up legislation designed to cut back on social welfare programs, such as food stamps. Other bills eliminated environmental regulations, to allow businesses to expand more easily. Still other proposals targeted rising costs in certain health care programs. At the same time, Republicans proposed a $245 billion tax cut.

President Clinton attacked many of the proposals as unfair to poor and middle-class Americans. He vetoed the Republican budget. Angrily, Republicans cut off funds, forcing government agencies to close for several weeks. Gradually, public opinion turned against the new Congress.

In the end, Congress compromised with the President. In 1996, it enacted laws to fight crime and drugs, to reform welfare, and to promote education.

The 1996 Election. Running against President Clinton in 1996 was former Senator Bob Dole, Republican from Kansas. A veteran of World War II, Dole chose for his running mate Jack Kemp, former Congressman and Cabinet member. Ross Perot also became a candidate, on behalf of the new Reform Party.

Dole proposed a tax cut of 15 percent to all Americans. He said Congress could cut taxes and still balance the federal budget by 2002. President Clinton countered that the nation could not afford such a steep cut. He argued that the lives of most Americans had improved while he was in office.

Voters elected President Clinton to a second term. For the time being, it seemed most Americans wanted a smaller federal government. Yet they were not ready to accept all of Speaker Gingrich's "revolutionary" changes.

Clinton Victory *In 1996, Bill Clinton was reelected President over Republican Bob Dole. Here he celebrates his victory.* **Citizenship** *How did the election of 1996 reflect the nation's view of Clinton's presidency?*

830 • Chapter 29

Critical Thinking
Understanding Causes and Effects

Have students suggest one or two causes for each of the following: (1) President Reagan was unable to balance the budget. (2) The American economy weakened in the early 1990s. (3) Congress did not pass a health care reform bill. (4) In 1994, voters elected Republican majorities in each house.

Historical Sidelight
Background

In his inaugural address on January 20, 1993, President Clinton told his listeners, "There is nothing wrong with America that cannot be cured by what is right with America." He went on to say, "To renew America we must be bold. We must do what no generation has had to do before. We must invest more in our own people — in their jobs and in their future — and at the same time cut our massive debt. And we must do so in a world in which we must compete for every opportunity. It will not be easy. It will require sacrifice. But it can be done and done fairly. Not choosing sacrifice for its own sake, but for our own sake. . . . We must do what America does best: offer more opportunity to all and demand more responsibility from all." Ask students: By 1996, how far had the nation come in reaching Clinton's goal of renewing America?

SECTION 1 REVIEW

1. **Identify:** (a) Sandra Day O'Connor, (b) Bill Clinton, (c) Ross Perot, (d) Newt Gingrich, (e) Bob Dole.
2. **Define:** (a) balanced budget, (b) downsizing, (c) recession.
3. Describe Reagan's economic policies.
4. (a) Describe an important goal of Clinton's presidency. (b) What did the Republicans try to accomplish after 1994?
5. What issues concerned voters in 1996?
6. **CRITICAL THINKING Analyzing Information** (a) Why is naming Supreme Court Justices one of the President's most important powers? (b) How did Presidents Reagan and Bush use that power?

ACTIVITY Writing to Learn

Write campaign slogans for Ronald Reagan, George Bush, Bill Clinton, and Bob Dole.

2
An End to the Cold War

FIND OUT

■ How did democracy spread in Eastern Europe?

■ What events led to the breakup of the Soviet Union?

■ Why did civil war break out in Yugoslavia?

■ What policy did the United States take toward Yugoslavia?

VOCABULARY glasnost

It was one of the strangest celebrations Europe had ever seen. Far into the night, people cheered, sang songs, and set to work with pickaxes and sledgehammers. It was November 1989, and in the city of Berlin, the wall between East and West was coming down.

Nearly 30 years earlier, in 1961, communist East German troops had put up a wall dividing East and West Berlin. They had poured concrete and strung barbed wire to close the routes of escape to the West. Ever since, this wall had stood as a symbol of tensions between the communist world and the free world. (See page 806.)

By the late 1980s, however, the Soviet Union was dying. The Cold War that had lasted nearly 45 years was coming to an end. Berlin was only one of many places where citizens celebrated their new freedoms.

Reagan's Foreign Policy

When President Reagan took office in 1981, the communist governments in Europe still seemed powerful. Only two years earlier, the Soviet Union had invaded Afghanistan. At the same time, Soviet-style governments throughout Europe continued to outlaw independent political parties or open debate.

President Reagan wanted to deal with the Soviets from a position of strength. As you have read, he convinced Congress to sharply increase military spending. His defense program included research on weapons that he hoped would shoot down Soviet missiles from space. The system was nicknamed *Star Wars*.

Soviet reforms. Cracks in the Soviet empire began to appear in the mid-1980s. Growing economic problems plagued the Soviet Union. Soviet citizens spent hours waiting in lines for poorly made goods. The time was ripe for a new leader.

In 1985, Mikhail Gorbachev (mee kah EEL GOR buh chawf) became Soviet premier. Gorbachev believed that he must take bold steps to improve the failing Soviet economy.

Chapter 29 • **831**

 Student Study Guide

Section 1 Study Guide Have students use the Section 1 Study Guide on page 211 of the *Student Study Guide* to review and reinforce the content of this section. (Reteaching/Average)

ACTIVITY

Guided Instruction Before students plan their campaign slogans, discuss with the class some famous campaign slogans associated with earlier presidential candidates and the message that each conveyed. Examples might include "He Kept Us Out of War!" (Wilson), "A New Deal for the American People" (Franklin D. Roosevelt), and "I Like Ike" (Eisenhower). Suggest that students first identify a key issue and the chosen candidate's position on that issue. Have students then freewrite words and phrases they associate with that position and use these associations to develop a slogan. Invite volunteers to share their finished slogans.

Section 2
pp. 831–836

Bell Ringer

Ask students to imagine themselves as teenagers in an Eastern European country in the late 1980s. Have them write down their thoughts and feelings on learning about the breakup of the Soviet Union.

Answers to Section 1 Review

1. (a) Sandra Day O'Connor, p. 828, (b) Bill Clinton, p. 828, (c) Ross Perot, p. 829, (d) Newt Gingrich, p. 829, (e) Bob Dole, p. 830
2. (a) balanced budget, p. 827, (b) downsizing, p. 828, (c) recession, p. 828
3. (a) to cut taxes, reduce inflation, and balance the budget
4. (a) Possible answer: Clinton worked to bring about health care reform. He hoped to guarantee health care insurance for almost all Americans. (b) They tried to cut back on government spending and cut taxes.

5. They were concerned about government "gridlock" and the size of government.
6. (a) Possible Answer: The Supreme Court interprets the Constitution and may declare any law unconstitutional. Furthermore, because Supreme Court Justices are appointed for life, they will have influence long after a President has left office. (b) Between them, Presidents Reagan and Bush appointed five new Justices, giving the Court a decidedly conservative bent.

CONNECTIONS

| ARTS | SCIENCES | GEOGRAPHY | WORLD | ECONOMICS | CIVICS |

"How Can We Avoid War?"

In 1983, a fifth-grader in Manchester, Maine, grew increasingly fearful about the future. Tensions were building once again between the Soviet Union and the United States. "I was watching the news and nuclear war was on TV a lot," Samantha Smith explained. "It got so steady, I was worried."

Samantha pondered what she might be able to do about the problem. She decided to write to the newly named Soviet leader, Yuri V. Andropov, and confront him with her fears. "Are you going to vote to have a war or not?" she asked. "If you aren't, please tell me how you are going to help to [avoid war]?"

Soviet stamp honoring Smith

Smith in Moscow

A few months passed with no response. Then a letter came! Premier Andropov wrote Samantha that no one in his country wanted war. "We want peace for ourselves and for all peoples of the planet. For our children and for you, Samantha."

Andropov ended his letter with a stunning surprise for Samantha. Would she like to come to the Soviet Union to talk with the people there? Samantha was thrilled. Within days, she became a celebrity. She was interviewed on television and quoted in the press.

For two weeks the following summer, Samantha toured the Soviet Union. She never actually met Premier Andropov, but she did meet many ordinary citizens. She found them "more like me than I ever realized."

Sadly, Samantha died in an airplane crash just two years later. Samantha's letter may not have greatly affected relations between the United States and the Soviet Union. Still, she is remembered for expressing the feelings of millions of people worldwide about the quest for peace.

■ Why did Samantha Smith write to Premier Andropov?

ACTIVITY Choose a problem—international, national, state, or local—that concerns you. Write a letter to someone you think might be able to do something about it. Express your viewpoint about the problem and ask the person to take action to help resolve it.

832 • Chapter 29

He called for **glasnost,** a policy of speaking out honestly and openly. For the first time, Soviet newspapers could write about poor harvests, crime, and corruption. Gorbachev hoped that allowing public discussion of problems would help the nation find solutions to them.

Improved relations. Gorbachev also wanted to improve relations with the United States. He and President Reagan held three summit meetings. In 1987, they signed an arms control pact called the ***INF Treaty***. In the treaty, the superpowers agreed to get rid of short-range and medium-range missiles.

In 1989, Gorbachev withdrew Soviet troops from Afghanistan. This action removed another barrier to cooperation between the superpowers.

Democracy Spreads in Eastern Europe

The peoples of Communist Eastern Europe greeted news of Gorbachev's reforms with demands of their own. To their surprise, Gorbachev saw these protests as signs of needed change. As demands for reform grew, most Eastern European governments did not dare use military force to block change.

In 1989, Poland's communist government held the nation's first free elections in 50 years. Rejecting communism, the Poles voted into office all the candidates of a worker's trade union, called ***Solidarity***. For years, the Polish government had outlawed Solidarity. The Solidarity leader, Lech Walesa, became head of the government.

In Romania, demonstrators overthrew and executed a brutal dictator. Communist governments also fell in Hungary, Czechoslovakia, Bulgaria, and Albania.

In 1989, peaceful protests swept major cities in East Germany. That nation's communist government was forced out and replaced with reformers who promised demo-

cratic changes. It was then that East and West Berliners celebrated by taking down the wall that had divided their city since 1961. Within a year, East Germany and West Germany were reunited under a democratic government.

Breakup of the Soviet Union

The Soviet Union was made up of 15 republics. During the Cold War, Soviet rulers used a strong central government to hold the republics together. They allowed few freedoms. When the central government loosened its control in the late 1980s, the nation began to fall apart.

By 1990, unrest led to a flare-up of ancient rivalries among some of the nation's 120 ethnic groups. Some groups, including Lithuanians and Estonians, boldly demanded self-rule.

Democratic reforms. Amid the turmoil, Gorbachev announced new moves toward democracy. Under one reform, new political parties could form. This made it possible for groups to oppose the communists openly for the first time.

In August 1991, some desperate communist officials tried to overturn the new reforms. Holding Gorbachev captive, they sent military forces to surround the parliament building in Moscow. Thousands of Russians turned out to block the soldiers. Led by a politician named Boris Yeltsin, the reformers turned the tide. "Aggression will not go

History and You
After the fall of communist governments in Hungary and Poland, the United States opened Peace Corps programs in those two nations. Would you want to join the Peace Corps program in Hungary or Poland? Why or why not?

Interdisciplinary CONNECTIONS

For worksheets establishing connections between the Chapter 29 main idea, The Quest for Peace, and five other disciplines, see the *Interdisciplinary Connections* booklet. (Enrichment)
- ■ **Arts** Remembering, page 170 (Easy)
- ■ **Sciences** Dangerous Waste, page 171 (Average)
- ■ **Geography** Our Uneasy World, page 172 (Average)
- ■ **World** Keeping the Peace, page 173 (Average)
- ■ **Economics** The NAFTA Debate, page 174 (Challenging)

Answer to Connections

She was worried about the threat of nuclear war between the Soviet Union and the United States.

ACTIVITY

Guided Instruction Remind students that their letters should use appropriate forms of address and salutations; should remain respectful, even when expressing strong feelings; and use correct grammar, mechanics, and spelling. Encourage students to share their finished letters with partners or in small groups.

 Transparencies

Interdisciplinary Connections Use the transparency Eastern Europe on page B-89 of *American History Transparencies*. Teaching suggestions can be found on page B-31. (Enrichment/Challenging)

Connections With Technology
Background

After the breakup of the Soviet Union, several nations tried to hire Soviet nuclear scientists. However, the United States and other countries warned against the danger of spreading nuclear weapons technology. They set up and funded a research institute in Russia where these scientists could work on peaceful uses for nuclear energy. The Clinton administration also continued efforts begun earlier to reach agreement with Russia, Ukraine, Belarus, and Kazakhstan (the four republics in which nuclear missile sites were located) to begin dismantling both their missiles and the missiles of the United States.

Cooperative Learning
Activity

As the student text notes, the late 1980s saw the end of communist governments in Poland, Romania, Hungary, Czechoslovakia, Bulgaria, Albania, and East Germany. Divide the class into seven groups, assigning each group one of these countries. Have each group research and report to the class on how communist rule ended in its country and how that country has fared since.

forward!" shouted Yeltsin, standing on a tank which the crowd had surrounded. "Only democracy will win!"

In the months that followed, republic after republic declared its independence from the Union of Soviet Socialist Republics. In December 1991, Gorbachev resigned and the Soviet Union ceased to exist.

The move toward free markets. A new federation, the Commonwealth of Independent States, replaced the old Soviet Union. The Commonwealth was made up of 10 of the 15 former Soviet republics. Of these, Russia had the most influence. With Boris Yeltsin as its president, Russia began the difficult task of rebuilding its economy and introducing a free market system.

Along with Western European nations, the United States provided economic aid to Russia. In addition, American experts advised business leaders in the former republics and in Eastern Europe about the shift to a free market system. The United States hoped that the former communist states would in time become profitable trading partners.

The move toward a free market economy proved difficult for Russia. Its economy was hobbled by inflation. As the central government weakened, organized crime spread. Meanwhile, the once-mighty Russian army was unable to quell a rebellion in the small province of Chechnya.

In December 1995 the Communists made a strong comeback in the nation's Parliament, gaining nearly a majority of seats. The following summer, however, Russians voted to continue moving toward a free market economy. They reelected Boris Yeltsin to a second term as President over his Communist opponent. President Clinton expressed hope that the reelection of Yeltsin would help Russia move forward in its democratic and economic reforms. He said,

❝After centuries of imperial rule, and decades of communist oppression, [Russians] have asserted their right to have a voice in the decisions that affect their lives. . . . Today was a triumph for democracy in Russia.❞

Communism Falls *Americans cheered the collapse of communism in the Soviet Union and Eastern Europe. Here, Russians gather around a toppled statue of Lenin, the communist leader of the 1917 Russian Revolution.* **United States and the World** *Why was the fall of communism important to Americans?*

Linking Past and Present
Background

Still, Russians faced many challenges as they worked to bring stability and prosperity to their nation.

Civil War in Yugoslavia

As communism fell in Eastern Europe, Yugoslavia was torn apart by a bloody civil war. Yugoslavia was made up of several republics, including Serbia, Croatia, and Bosnia-Herzegovina.* After the fall of communism, several republics declared their independence, including Croatia and Bosnia.

In 1991 and 1992, Serbs in Croatia and Bosnia began fighting to prevent the new governments from splitting away from Yugoslavia. With powerful military forces, the Serbs soon took control of about 70 percent of Bosnia, as well as some of Croatia.

Horrors of war. The civil war was the latest episode in a long history of conflict among ethnic groups in Yugoslavia. As the war dragged on for four years, cities were destroyed and 2 million people were forced to flee their homes. Over 250,000 people died.

Zlata Filipovic, an 11-year-old native of Serbia, wrote in her diary about the war.

❝Today a shell fell on the park in front of my house, the park where I used to play and sit with my girlfriends. A lot of people were hurt. . . . AND NINA IS DEAD. . . . She was such a nice, sweet girl.❞

Beginning in 1992 Serbs forced tens of thousands of Bosnian Muslims into detention camps. They called this practice "ethnic cleansing." Other reports, however, claimed that the Serbs were carrying out mass executions. By the end of 1995, the War Crimes Tribunal, located in the Netherlands, had charged nearly 50 Serbs with crimes against

---

*The nation of Bosnia-Herzegovina, formed in 1992, is often referred to simply as Bosnia.

The sudden and rapid fall of communist governments transformed the map of Eastern Europe.
1. Which nations border Romania?
2. Compare this map to the map on page 775. Which nations shown here had been part of the Soviet Union?
3. **Analyzing Information** Review the information in this section. Name three events that changed the borders of Europe in the early 1990s.

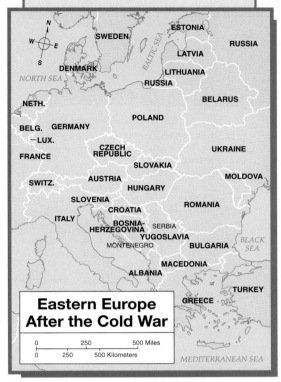

Eastern Europe After the Cold War

0   250   500 Miles
0   250   500 Kilometers

humanity. They included Radovan Karadzic, the leader of the Bosnian Serbs.

An uneasy peace. European leaders negotiated many cease-fires, but none lasted long. In 1992, the UN began providing food, medicine, and other aid to war-torn areas. However, Serbian forces often did not allow

Chapter 29 • **835**

Answer to Caption

She probably hoped that the troops would help bring safety for her child and a new chance for a better life.

ACTIVITY

Guided Instruction Begin by pointing out that the essence of the telegraphic style is identifying essential information and summarizing it accurately. You may want to set a realistic word limit (for example, 25 words). Remind students of the importance of correct spelling and sentence structure to avoid possible misinterpretation. You might use the completed telegrams as part of a student-created "War and Peace in Yugoslavia" time line.

Working With NATO *In 1995, President Clinton sent American troops to Bosnia to work with NATO and Russian forces as peacekeepers.* **Daily Life** *How might the mother at right have felt about the arrival of peacekeeping troops?*

the aid to get through. Both Presidents Bush and Clinton pressed for European nations to act more firmly to stop the fighting in the region. Still, neither President was willing to send American ground troops to combat Serbian aggression.

Serious peace talks began only after Bosnian and Croatian forces began to win back territory. In November 1995, the United States hosted peace talks at an air base in Dayton, Ohio. The Dayton Accord called for Bosnia to remain a single nation, but to be governed as two separate republics.

To help guarantee the peace, President Clinton sent some 17,000 American ground troops to Bosnia. There, they joined NATO and Russian forces in a peacekeeping mission. The civil war in Yugoslavia showed that even if the Cold War was over, regional conflicts continued to threaten the peace. As a leader in world affairs, the United States needed to find effective ways to prevent small wars from becoming big ones.

836 • Chapter 29

SECTION 2 REVIEW

1. **Locate:** (a) Soviet Union, (b) Poland, (c) Germany, (d) Russia, (e) Yugoslavia, (f) Serbia, (g) Bosnia-Herzegovina.
2. **Identify:** (a) Star Wars, (b) Solidarity, (c) INF Treaty, (d) Boris Yeltsin.
3. **Define:** glasnost.
4. Why did the Soviet Union cease to exist?
5. (a) What democratic changes took place in Poland? (b) In Germany?
6. (a) How did the United States respond to the breakup of the Soviet Union? (b) How did it respond to civil war in Yugoslavia?
7. **CRITICAL THINKING Analyzing Ideas** Why was the United States concerned about peace in Bosnia?

ACTIVITY Writing to Learn

Imagine you are a foreign correspondent for an American newspaper. Write telegrams to send to your home office reporting events in Yugoslavia.

Answers to Section 2 Review

1. See the maps on p. 775 and p. 835.
2. (a) Star Wars, p. 831, (b) Solidarity, p. 833, (c) INF Treaty, p. 833, (d) Boris Yeltsin, p. 833
3. glasnost, p. 833
4. Possible Answer: Corruption, inefficiency, and the rising cost of the arms race had weakened the Soviet economy; widespread opposition in Eastern Europe made suppression of demands for self-rule impractical; leaders born after the Russian Revolution were more receptive to popular cries for reform.
5. (a) Free elections were held, and the candidates of the once-banned trade union Solidarity gained power. (b) The Berlin Wall was torn down. The hard-line communist government of East Germany was replaced by reformers, leading to the reunification of East and West Germany.
6. (a) It offered economic aid, expertise, and trade opportunities to the newly formed republics and initiated negotiations to disarm or dismantle nuclear weapons. (b) It was horrified but did not commit American troops to end the war; in 1995, the United States sponsored peace talks that led to the Dayton Accord. It then sent troops to Bosnia to help NATO and Russian forces keep the peace.
7. It wanted to keep a small conflict from building into a larger war.

3
The Search for a More Democratic World

FIND OUT

- How did South Africa move toward greater democracy?
- How did people in Asia struggle for freedom in the 1970s and 1980s?
- What was United States policy toward Latin America in recent years?

VOCABULARY apartheid, economic sanctions

It was near dawn when Elsie Njokweni left her home to catch an early train. She and thousands of other South African blacks rode joyfully toward the city of Pretoria. In the aisles of the trains Mrs. Njokweni joined others in a toyi-toyi—a foot-stomping dance and song of celebration.

Mrs. Njokweni had good reason to celebrate. She and other South Africans were going to the inauguration of Nelson Mandela. On May 10, 1994, Mandela became the first black president in the history of South Africa. Mandela's election marked an astonishing change in South African society. In other areas of the world, too, there seemed to be opportunities for change. As the Cold War faded, the United States worked with many nations to create a world that was more democratic and more stable.

Change Comes to South Africa

For many years South Africa had been a nation divided. In 1948, its government began enforcing a policy of **apartheid** (uh PAHR tayt), or separation of the races. Non-whites—blacks, people of mixed races, and Asians—made up about 85 percent of South Africa's population by 1990. Yet they had been segregated and not allowed any voice in the government.

Economic pressure. Many Americans called for economic sanctions against South Africa. **Economic sanctions** are actions, such as boycotts, taken against a country in the hope of bringing about a change in its policy. Supporters of the sanctions hoped they would pressure South Africa into ending apartheid.

In 1986, Congress passed a law calling for economic sanctions against South Africa. The law forbade American companies to invest in South Africa or to import South African products. The United Nations and other international organizations also put pressure on South Africa to end apartheid.

Moving toward reform. In 1989, South Africa slowly began moving away from apartheid. Its new president, F. W. de Klerk, ended many segregation laws.

De Klerk's most dramatic act was to free Nelson Mandela. Mandela was a black opponent of apartheid who had been in prison 28 years for his antigovernment activities.

Mandela's Visit *Shortly after his release from a South African prison, Nelson Mandela toured the United States. His speeches drew huge crowds of cheering supporters.* **United States and the World** *Why did many Americans admire Nelson Mandela?*

🔔 **Bell Ringer**

Ask students to imagine the following headline in the morning newspaper: "ARMY CRUSHES REVOLT AT [YOUR SCHOOL]: Many Students Killed or Imprisoned." Have students write down their thoughts and feelings as if this had happened. Use their responses as the basis for a class discussion.

Lesson Plan

1. Focus In the last decades of the 1900s, calls for popular reform and political change sprang up all over the world. In this section, students examine efforts to end apartheid in South Africa; struggles for freedom in the Philippines, China, and other Asian countries; political clashes in Latin America.
2. Instruct Have students use the headings and subheadings within this section to outline key facts and ideas. With the class as a whole, construct a final outline on the chalkboard.
3. Close To close the lesson, have the class turn the headings of the subsections into questions and answer them.

Historical Sidelight
Background

When Nelson Mandela visited the United States in 1990, he was given a hero's welcome. His schedule (which proved to be exhausting to the 71-year-old South African) included a visit to New York City's famous Yankee Stadium. Donning a Yankee cap and jacket, Mandela proclaimed, "Now I know who I am. I am a Yankee!" One New York sportswriter, however, noted that Mandela was having a much better year than were the New York Yankees.

Under a new constitution, elections were held in 1994. For the first time in the history of South Africa, all races were permitted to vote.

The new National Assembly chose Nelson Mandela to be president. At his inauguration Mandela set out his vision for a peaceful future:

Protest in China *In 1989, pro-democracy demonstrators raised their own Statue of Liberty in Beijing's Tiananmen Square. Their hopes were short-lived, however. Government troops moved in, killing more than 5,000 people.* **Citizenship** *Compare this picture to the picture on page 834. How were the events shown in these photographs similar? How were they different?*

66 We enter into a covenant that we shall build the society in which all South Africans, both black and white, will be able to walk tall, without any fear in their hearts, assured of their inalienable right to human dignity—a rainbow nation at peace with itself and the world. **99**

Struggles for Freedom in Asia

People in several Asian nations also struggled to create more democratic governments in the 1980s. One of these nations was the Philippines.

Filipino "people power." Filipinos had reason to push for change. Their president, Ferdinand Marcos, had ruled as a dictator since 1972. In 1986, he had finally agreed to hold a new election. Marcos won, but only because his supporters cheated. Some stuffed ballot boxes with fake votes. Others threatened people who tried to vote against Marcos.

Thousands of Filipinos took to the streets of Manila, the capital, in protest. They proclaimed "people power" and refused to recognize Marcos as president. When the army came out on the side of the people, Marcos fled the country. The United States supported Corazon Aquino, the woman who had run against him.

In 1992, Filipinos elected Fidel Ramos to succeed Aquino. The United States continued to provide economic aid to support the democratic government there.

China's struggle. In China, the path to reform was uneven. During the 1980s, the government took some steps to move China toward a free economy. However, Chinese leaders refused to accept political reforms.

In 1989, students and workers launched a bold campaign to bring democracy to China. Hundreds of thousands gathered at Tiananmen Square in the nation's capital, Beijing.

838 • Chapter 29

CRITICAL THINKING SKILLS
Analyzing Newspaper Editorials

In a free society, newspapers and news magazines play an important role. They inform readers of the news. Most also print editorials. An *editorial* is an article that gives a newspaper's or magazine's opinion on an issue.

An editorial may have one of several purposes: to criticize, persuade, explain, or praise. Often, editorials criticize a decision or an action. Some try to persuade people to follow a certain course of action. Others explain an issue or an event. Still others praise a person or an organization for doing a good job. Sometimes, an editorial serves several purposes at the same time.

1. **Identify the subject of the editorial.** Read the editorial reprinted below. (a) What is the subject of the editorial? (b) Where did it appear? (c) When did it appear?

2. **Decide what opinion the editorial expresses.** Review Skill Lesson 8, Distinguishing Fact From Opinion, on page 256. (a) Identify one fact in the editorial. (b) What opinion does the editorial express about President Bush's recent actions? (c) What actions does the editorial favor?

3. **Analyze how editorials might influence public opinion.** Many news readers want to know what the editors of the newspaper or magazine think about an issue or an event. (a) Which of the four purposes described earlier do you think the editorial has? (b) How did the editorial help you understand the issue?

ACTIVITY Imagine that you are editor-in-chief of your school newspaper. Write an editorial expressing your point of view on a school-related issue. When you have finished your editorial, reread it to determine which editorial purpose it serves.

---

66 It's all over in China, at least on the surface. The guys with the guns won and now they are busy scrubbing off the bloodstains, tearing down the democracy posters—and rewriting the history of this most remarkable Chinese spring.

The United States, in its desire to maintain good relations with official China, must take care not to . . . slip into pretending that nothing really happened in Tiananmen Square, Beijing.

This nation will and should continue to deal with those who govern China, but it must do so now without . . . rose-colored glasses. . . . Never again can it be business as usual.

President Bush has sought and hit—for now—the 'proper, prudent balance' between supporting desire for democracy in China and promoting the desire for a working relationship with China in this country. He has been right in choosing limited . . . measures against China and in choosing his words. In his press conference Thursday, he stressed the fundamental importance to this country of the trade and political relationship that he helped develop with China. And he stressed the need for Beijing to 'recognize the validity of the students' [goals]' if normal relations are to be resumed.

Let us hope that official China was listening, and cares. 99

St. Paul Pioneer Press & Dispatch
June 10, 1989
St. Paul, Minnesota

Chapter Resources

Skill Application For additional practice, duplicate and distribute the worksheet, Analyzing Newspaper Editorials, from Unit 9, page 30, of the *Chapter Resources* binder. (Reteaching/Average)

Answers to Skill Lesson

1. (a) United States policy toward China after events in Tiananmen Square (b) the *St. Paul Pioneer Press & Dispatch* (c) June 10, 1989
2. (a) Possible Answer: "The guys with the guns won . . ." (b) The editorial agrees with President Bush's actions. (c) Possible Answer: limited measures against China; recognition of the importance of trade and political relationships, while encouraging Beijing to recognize the students' goals
3. (a) explain, praise, persuade (b) Possible Answer: It helped make clear President Bush's policies toward China after the massacre.

ACTIVITY

Guided Instruction Have students brainstorm for important issues. Remind students to determine the purpose(s) of their editorials and to revise any parts that do not support their opinions. You might make the finished editorials the focal point of a classroom display.

Connections With Art
Activity

Have students draw political cartoons either about the prodemocracy protests in China, the defeat of the movement, or the United States refusal to take strong action in response to the Tiananmen Square massacre. Encourage students to explain their finished cartoons to the class. You might also work with students to create a bulletin board display of the cartoons.

Students Acquiring English
Activity

SAE students might benefit by being paired with more advanced students to work on the Skill Lesson and its Activity. Partners might help the SAE students revise their editorials by checking for correct spelling and syntax, as well as by making suggestions concerning the use of idioms, if necessary.

However, this Chinese "people power" was not enough. The Chinese army crushed the demonstrations. Many people were killed or arrested. President Bush disapproved of the crackdown, but he did not take strong action against the government. Instead, he hoped to influence China by keeping communication open between the two countries. President Clinton followed a similar policy.

The question of democratic government also concerned Hong Kong, an island at the mouth of China's Canton River. In 1898, China agreed to lease Hong Kong to Great Britain, which ruled it as a colony. In 1997, that arrangement is due to end. China will then govern Hong Kong. In 1994, Hong Kong began to make democratic reforms, but China opposed them. Hong Kong's future remains uncertain.

Other Asian nations. Other nations in Asia have had mixed success with political reforms. During the 1970s, South Korea developed a booming economy. At the same time, it remained undemocratic politically. However, after fierce protests by Korean students and other citizens in 1987, the government allowed more democratic elections to take place.

In 1989, Cambodia gained its freedom from Vietnam after 10 years of Vietnamese rule. (See page 813.) Democracy did not come easily, however. After months of talks, the United Nations sponsored elections in 1993. Eager Cambodians flocked to the polls. As a result of the election, a new government was formed in Cambodia.

Linking Past and Present
According to Freedom House, a human rights group, more than half the countries in the world were democracies by 1991. Of the 1.7 billion people listed as "not free," two thirds of them lived in China.

Relations With Latin America

Closer to home, the United States has had ups and downs in its relations with the countries of Latin America. In the days when Teddy Roosevelt carried a "big stick," the United States frequently interfered in the internal affairs of Latin American nations. (See pages 641–643.) As a result, Latin Americans often resented the United States.

In the 1930s, Franklin Roosevelt's Good Neighbor Policy set a new direction. (See page 763.) FDR believed that the United States should intervene less in Latin America. Since then, the United States has often sent economic aid to Latin American nations. President Kennedy, for example, set up a program in 1961 called the ***Alliance for Progress***. The Alliance tried to help the people of Latin America build schools and hospitals, improve farming, and bring about economic and social reform.

During the Cold War, many Latin American communists worked to overthrow dictatorships in their countries. This threat of communism concerned many Americans. They debated how the nation should react. Many believed the United States should act to contain communism, even if it meant supporting dictators or military rulers. Others felt, however, that the United States should encourage the overthrow of dictators, even if the new governments were dominated by communists.

Nicaragua and El Salvador

During the 1980s, President Reagan gave aid to anticommunists in both Nicaragua and El Salvador. In El Salvador, Reagan sent arms and military advisers to help the government in a civil war that raged there. The United States supported the government even though it was often brutal and oppressive.

In Nicaragua, American aid went to rebels trying to overthrow the socialist government. The government was run by the

---

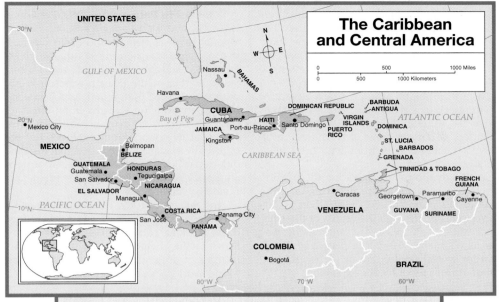

The Caribbean and Central America

0   500   1000 Miles

0   500   1000 Kilometers

UNITED STATES

GULF OF MEXICO

Nassau

BAHAMAS

Havana

CUBA

Bay of Pigs

Guantánamo

Mexico City

MEXICO

JAMAICA

Kingston

Belmopan

BELIZE

GUATEMALA

Guatemala

San Salvador

HONDURAS

Tegucigalpa

EL SALVADOR

NICARAGUA

Managua

PACIFIC OCEAN

COSTA RICA

San José

PANAMA

Panama City

DOMINICAN REPUBLIC

HAITI

Port-au-Prince

Santo Domingo

BARBUDA

ANTIGUA

VIRGIN

ISLANDS

PUERTO

RICO

DOMINICA

ST. LUCIA

BARBADOS

GRENADA

TRINIDAD & TOBAGO

ATLANTIC OCEAN

CARIBBEAN SEA

Caracas

VENEZUELA

Georgetown

GUYANA

Paramaribo

SURINAME

FRENCH

GUIANA

Cayenne

COLOMBIA

Bogotá

BRAZIL

MAP STUDY

Since the 1800s, the United States has taken a strong interest in Central America and the Caribbean.
1. Which two nations share an island in the Caribbean?
2. About how far is it from Puerto Rico to the United States mainland?
3. **Geography** Based on the map, why is the United States concerned about events in Central America and the Caribbean?

Answers to Map Study
1. Haiti and the Dominican Republic 2. approximately 1,100 miles (1,800 km) 3. Possible Answer: The nations in these areas are geographically close to the United States.

Sandinistas, a revolutionary group that had taken power in 1979 and won free elections in 1984. Its opponents were known as Contras, from the Spanish word meaning "against."

The Iran-Contra deal. Not all Americans supported President Reagan's policy of aiding the Contras. In fact, Congress passed a law banning military aid to them. To get around the ban, members of Reagan's staff decided to provide military aid secretly. These staff members had already sold military weapons to Iran, a country in the Middle East. They used the profits from the sale to send military aid to the Contras.

In 1986, news reporters discovered the details of the secret **Iran-Contra deal**. The news stirred a great deal of debate because officials working for the President had lied to Congress about their dealings. Representative Lee Hamilton of Indiana expressed the dismay of many Americans when he said,

66If . . . high officials do not provide complete and accurate answers to the Congress, what can we do? How can our system of government work if the Administration is not candid in its answers to the Congress?99

Chapter 29 • **841**

Connections With the World
Background

Many Americans were shocked by the Iran-Contra deal because President Reagan had vowed never to bargain with terrorists. "The United States gives terrorists no rewards and no guarantees," he said. "We make no deals."

In the late 1980s, another shocking development occurred. Stories began to emerge about massive fraud and other illegal activities involving a multinational bank, the Bank of

Commerce and Credit International (BCCI). Allegations charged that BCCI, which operated in 73 different countries, laundered money for drug dealers (including Manuel Noriega of Panama), did business with terrorist organizations, financed missile shipments as part of the Iran-Contra deal, and provided nuclear-weapons technology to several countries.

After an investigation, several members of the President's staff were put on trial. The President, however, said he did not know his staff had done anything to break the law.

A peace plan. In 1987, a year after the Iran-Contra scandal, President Oscar Arias of Costa Rica helped arrange a peace plan for Nicaragua. In elections in 1990, Nicaraguans rejected the Sandinistas and voted in new leaders. After the new government took over, Nicaragua's relations with the United States improved.

El Salvador. In El Salvador, the fighting between rebels and the government went on for 12 years and cost more than 50,000 lives. Finally, through the efforts of the United Nations, a cease-fire agreement was reached in early 1992. The people of El Salvador were hopeful that peace would last. One former rebel leader explained,

> 66 This is a new country. . . . It is good for the world to know there is at least one place where a peace process has been successful. 99

Democratic elections were held in El Salvador in 1994. Many hoped the elections would lead to greater democracy and stability in the country.

The "Big Stick" Again

Elsewhere in Latin America, the United States intervened more directly. Events in Grenada and Panama captured newspaper headlines.

Invasion of Grenada. In Grenada, the smallest nation in Latin America, extremists seized power with the help of Cuba. President Reagan feared that Americans living in Grenada were in danger. In October 1983, he ordered troops to land on the island and seize control. They stayed until the people of Grenada elected a new government friendly to the United States.

Clashes in Panama. In 1989, President Bush clashed with Panama's military ruler, Manuel Noriega. American officials claimed that Noriega was helping South American criminals smuggle drugs into the United States. Earlier, while Reagan was still President, the United States had imposed economic sanctions on Panama in an effort to force Noriega from power. American frustration grew when Noriega refused to recognize the results of an election that his candidate had lost. Later, Noriega's supporters attacked several United States soldiers stationed in Panama.

In December 1989, Bush sent troops to Panama to capture Noriega. After a few days, Noriega turned himself in. He was flown to the United States to stand trial on charges of drug smuggling. In 1992, a jury found Noriega guilty, and he was sent to prison.

In both Grenada and Panama, the United States had used its "big stick." Many Americans supported such military action as necessary to protect American interests. Critics, including many Latin Americans and Europeans, thought that the United States had unwisely intervened in the affairs of other countries.

International Interventions

President Bill Clinton also acted to promote stability in Latin America. He hoped to avoid using a "big stick" where possible. Instead, he tried to act in cooperation with other international agencies, such as the United Nations.

Democratic reforms in Haiti. Haitian citizens had elected Jean-Bertrand Aristide president in 1990. However, Haitian military leaders took control of the government. They forced Aristide to leave the country. The United Nations imposed economic sanctions in an attempt to force the Haitian military from power.

842 • Chapter 29

Return of President Aristide *Under pressure from the United States and other countries, Haiti's military leaders stepped down. When President Jean-Bertrand Aristide returned to Haiti, thousands of Haitians gathered to welcome him.* **Citizenship** *How did Aristide become president of Haiti?*

At first, the sanctions seemed to work. Haitian military leaders promised to let Aristide return. They soon broke their promise, however.

In response, President Clinton persuaded the United Nations to intervene. He then sent United States troops to Haiti as part of the UN mission. By the time the first American forces arrived, however, Haitian military leaders had agreed to step down. Over 20,000 American soldiers worked with other UN troops to restore order to Haiti. In the fall of 1994, President Aristide returned to his country. The following year, new elections were held. In February 1996, power passed peacefully from Aristide to his successor, René Préval.

Financial crisis in Mexico. American aid to Latin America was not always military. In 1995 the value of Mexico's currency fell sharply in international markets. International investors feared that the Mexican economy might fail, along with many of its banks.

President Clinton worried that the financial crisis might spread to other developing nations. He used his emergency authority to provide Mexico with a loan of $20 billion. Clinton also convinced other nations to loan billions of dollars. By the end of 1995, the Mexican economy had begun to recover.

SECTION 3 REVIEW

1. **Locate:** Locate: (a) South Africa, (b) Philippines, (c) China, (d) Hong Kong, (e) Cambodia, (f) Nicaragua, (g) El Salvador, (h) Grenada, (i) Panama, (j) Haiti, (k) Mexico.
2. **Identify:** (a) F.W. deKlerk, (b) Nelson Mandela, (c) Corazon Aquino, (d) Alliance for Progress, (e) Iran-Contra deal, (f) Jean-Bertrand Aristide.
3. **Define:** (a) apartheid, (b) economic sanctions.
4. (a) How did the United States and other nations try to influence South Africa to end apartheid? (b) What moves toward democracy did South Africa make?
5. Why is the future of Hong Kong uncertain?
6. (a) What was the United States policy toward Nicaragua? (b) Why did the Iran-Contra deal stir debate?
7. **CRITICAL THINKING Analyzing Information** Why was the election of René Préval in Haiti significant?

ACTIVITY **Writing to Learn**
Imagine you are a newscaster. Write a report on the election of 1994 in South Africa to be broadcast on nationwide television in the United States.

Bell Ringer

Write the word *oil* on the chalkboard. Have the class brainstorm for ways in which American society depends on oil.

___

Lesson Plan

1. Focus In the Middle East, conflicts between Israel and the Arab states continued to pose problems for the United States. Iraq's 1990 invasion of Kuwait further involved the United States in Middle Eastern affairs. Subsequent events kindled hopes that a lasting peace might one day be achieved in the region, but many obstacles remained. In this section, students focus on events in the Middle East during these turbulent years.

2. Instruct Have students list at least one cause and one effect for each of the following: (1) In the 1930s and 1940s, thousands of European Jews flocked to Palestine. (2) In 1973, several Arab countries cut off oil shipments to the United States. (3) President Carter invited Anwar el-Sadat and Menachem Begin to Camp David in 1978. (4) A revolution in 1979 brought the Ayatollah Khomeini to power in Iran. (5) In 1991, the United States and its UN allies launched air attacks against Iraq. (6) In 1993, Israel and the Palestine Liberation Organization signed a peace agreement.

4
Crisis and Hope in the Middle East

FIND OUT

- How did events in the Middle East affect the United States?
- What major steps were taken toward peace in the Middle East?
- What action did the United States take when Iraq invaded Kuwait?

In the fall of 1973, American motorists got a shock. "Sorry, No Gas Today," read hand-lettered signs in front of many service stations. Where stations did have gas, motorists waited in long lines for a chance to fill up their tanks.

Some station owners worked out rationing systems. Motorists with license plates ending in an odd number were served on Monday, Wednesday, and Friday. Those with even-numbered plates could buy gas on Tuesday, Thursday, or Saturday.

The gas lines of 1973 came about when nations in the Middle East decided to cut back on the amount of oil they exported.* Suddenly, Americans discovered how much their lives could be affected by events in faraway lands. In many different ways, conflicts in the Middle East have posed a challenge for American foreign policy.

A Crossroads of the World

The Middle East has long been one of the key "crossroads of the world." It links Europe, Africa, and Asia. It is also the focus

___

*Oil-producing nations of the Middle East belong to the Organization of Petroleum Exporting Countries (OPEC), founded in 1960. OPEC members also include nations in Africa and Latin America.

of world attention because it has large oil reserves.

The Middle East is the birthplace of three major religions: Judaism, Christianity, and Islam. Over the centuries, tensions among various religious groups have often led to violence.

In dealing with the Middle East, the United States has had to balance conflicting interests. It has strongly supported Israel, the Jewish state created in 1948. Yet it has also tried to maintain ties with the Arab states that have opposed Israel.

Tensions Build

Israel was set up in a land along the Mediterranean coast known as Palestine. Muslim and Christian Arabs had lived there for hundreds of years.

European Jews began to arrive in the late 1800s. They hoped to create a Jewish state in Palestine, the home of their people in ancient times. The number of Jewish settlers increased in the 1930s as European Jews fled Nazi persecution. (See page 739.) The Palestinian Arabs resented the growing number of Jews who were settling on land they claimed as their own.

Arab-Israeli wars. In 1948, Jewish residents of Palestine announced the creation of the state of Israel. The United Nations recognized the new state. So did the United States and other world powers.

The Arabs who lived in Palestine and the Arab nations bordering Israel refused to recognize Israel. To do so would have meant giving up Arab claims to the land. Determined to resist, they attacked the new state.

Israel won the 1948 war. It even added to its territory. After 1948, more than 500,000 Arabs fled Palestine. They gathered in refugee camps in Jordan, Lebanon, and Syria. (See the map on page 845.)

Israel and its Arab neighbors fought two more wars—in 1967 and in 1973. Both

___

Connections With the World
Activity

Divide the class into three groups, assigning each group one of the three major religions noted in the student text: Judaism, Islam, and Christianity. Have each group do research and prepare a presentation that explains the basis for each religion's claims in the Middle East and how those claims have in the past led to conflict—between the nations of the Middle East and other nations with an interest in the area.

Connections With Civics
Background

One Jewish settler in Palestine was Golda Meir, a Russian-born American schoolteacher. In 1969, at the age of 71, she became Israel's first woman prime minister.

In Israel, a prime minister is the single most important leader of the government. (The duties of the president are largely ceremonial.) The prime minister is the leader of the political party that holds the largest number of seats in the Knesset, Israel's parliament. He or she also heads the cabinet and has the final say in that body's decisions.

MAP STUDY

The Middle East has been the site of much fighting since the end of World War II. Oil wealth has played a key role in both war and politics in the region.
1. Where are most of the oil fields in the Middle East located?
2. Which nations are located on the Persian Gulf?
3. **Analyzing Information** Based on the map, why do you think the United States wants control of the Persian Gulf to remain in friendly hands?

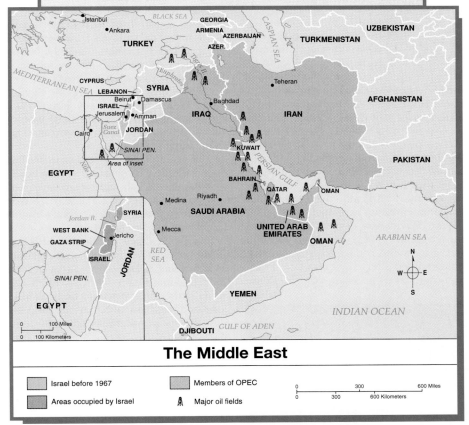

The Middle East

Israel before 1967	Members of OPEC
Areas occupied by Israel	Major oil fields

0   300   600 Miles
0   300   600 Kilometers

times, Israel won. During these wars, Israel seized lands from Egypt, Jordan, and Syria. The seized lands became known as the "occupied territories."

Oil as a weapon. The United States supported the Israelis with arms and supplies in the 1973 war. In response, the oil-producing Arab countries cut off oil shipments to the United States. They also slowed down oil production. This caused oil shortages and higher oil prices all over the world. The long gas lines at American service stations were only one sign of a larger international crisis.

Chapter 29 • **845**

3. **Close** To close the lesson, display a map of the Middle East. As you point to different countries, have volunteers state relevant facts about that country and its association with this section.

 Lesson Planner

For a developed **Cooperative Learning** lesson plan, see the *Lesson Planner,* page 184.

Answers to Map Study

1. along the Persian Gulf 2. Iraq, Saudi Arabia, Iran, Kuwait, Bahrain, Qatar, the United Arab Emirates, and Oman 3. Possible Answer: As long as the Persian Gulf is in friendly hands, the United States has access to the oil resources of the region.

Customized Reader

Primary Source For examples of what happened during the OPEC oil embargo, order article IXB-9, Panic at the Pump, from the *American History Customized Reader.* The article gives an overview of how different people reacted to the gasoline shortage. (Enrichment/Easy)

Learning Styles
Auditory Learners

To help students better understand the effects of the 1973 oil embargo, invite a member of the community who owned a service station at that time to talk to the class. Ask him or her to explain how the embargo affected the station's business and how he or she managed to keep the station's customers supplied with gasoline.

845

Voices of Freedom

Primary Source You might assign selection 21-1, Tense Days at Camp David, on pages 311–312 of *Voices of Freedom.* In this excerpt from his memoirs, President Carter describes what happened when it looked as though the Camp David talks might fail. (Enrichment/Average)

Customized Reader

Primary Source For a history of Camp David, order article XB-8, Camp David: The President's Weekend Retreat, from the *American History Customized Reader.* In this article, journalist Alex Heard shares a number of colorful anecdotes. (Enrichment/Average)

Chapter Resources

Geography in History Duplicate and distribute the worksheet, Trading Black Gold, from Unit 9, pages 33–34, of the *Chapter Resources* binder. The worksheet examines the world's oil resources and the oil needs of the United States. (Enrichment/Challenging)

The oil embargo showed that the Arab states were willing to use oil as an economic weapon. They wanted the United States to pressure Israel to return the occupied lands. Although this attempt failed, the Arab nations lifted the oil embargo in 1974.

A Meeting at Camp David

In 1977, an important step toward peace took place when President Anwar el-Sadat of Egypt visited Israel. He met with Israeli Prime Minister Menachem Begin (muh NAHK uhm BAY gihn). Sadat was the first Arab head of state ever to visit Israel. His visit led to a series of peace talks between the two nations.

When peace talks threatened to break down, President Carter stepped in. In a daring move, he invited both Sadat and Begin to meet together at Camp David, the President's retreat in Maryland. There they could try to hammer out an agreement.

Camp David was nestled on top of a small mountain. Shady paths led through the trees from one cottage to another, each building named after a different tree. President Carter stayed in Aspen cottage, Prime Minister Begin in Birch, and President Sadat in Dogwood. The small kitchen facilities were crowded because three different cooks prepared American, Egyptian, and Israeli foods.

The peaceful setting allowed Carter, Begin, and Sadat to concentrate on their goal. There were no distracting television cameras, no reporters to ask questions.

Even so, all three men knew that their mission was difficult. As Prime Minister Begin pointed out, there had not been an agreement between a Jewish nation and Egypt for more than 2,000 years.

In meeting after meeting, the Egyptians and Israelis discussed key issues. Would Egypt agree to recognize Israel? Would Israel withdraw its forces from occupied lands in the Sinai Peninsula?

President Sadat insisted that the Palestinian question be discussed. Sadat believed that Palestinians should receive the right to govern themselves in some way. However, Begin feared that self-rule for Palestinians might be too risky for Israel.

At times fierce arguments broke out. "Their faces were flushed," Carter noticed, as Begin and Sadat argued. Sadat "pounded the table" and Begin interrupted him. Occasionally the tension would be broken by a joke or shared laughter. On one long night, discussions continued until 3:30 in the morning.

Carter had hoped the meeting would take three days. It stretched to ten, with still no agreement in sight. On Day 11, Carter received an urgent visit from Secretary of State Cyrus Vance. Vance had just learned that Sadat had given up hope.

Peace Negotiatons *In 1977, President Sadat, President Carter, and Prime Minister Begin met at Camp David to try to hammer out an agreement between Israel and Egypt. Here, the three leaders take a walk around the grounds during a break.* **Geography** *Why was Camp David a good setting for the negotiations?*

"Vance burst into the room [at the President's cottage]. His face was white, and he announced, 'Sadat is leaving. He and his aides are already packed. He asked me to order him a helicopter!'"

Carter took a moment alone to pray. Then he went to Sadat's cottage. Using every argument he could find, he tried to persuade the Egyptian leader to stay another day or two. Sadat agreed.

Finally, on Day 13, Carter met with success. Sadat and Begin agreed to a timetable for Israel to return the Sinai Peninsula. Egypt agreed to recognize the state of Israel.

The **Camp David Accords** made possible a peace treaty between Egypt and Israel. Sadat and Begin signed the treaty in Washington, D.C., in 1979. The leaders had taken a huge risk for peace.

Their achievement seemed all the more impressive because it had nearly failed. ■

The Palestinians

Many stumbling blocks to peace remained. Although Israel had signed an agreement with Egypt, no other Arab nation recognized the Jewish state. At the same time, Israel still ruled the remaining occupied territories—the West Bank along the Jordan River and the Gaza Strip.

The Palestinian question also remained unresolved. Most Palestinians lived in the occupied territories or in refugee camps outside Israel. They had been driven out or had left their homes when Israel was created. Most wanted to live in their homeland under a Palestinian government. Many supported the **Palestine Liberation Organization**, or PLO. For years, the PLO waged a guerrilla war against Israel. Its goal was to destroy Israel.

In 1987, Palestinians in the occupied territories took to the streets to protest Israeli rule. They called their uprising the intifada, or "the shaking." The violent outbreaks called attention to the need for solutions to Arab-Israeli problems.

The Road Toward Peace

In 1991, the United States finally convinced Israel and its Arab neighbors to sit down together at the bargaining table. In the meetings that followed, it became clear that many obstacles to peace existed. Still, the talks continued, with encouragement from President Clinton.

A dramatic breakthrough. Then, in 1993, Israel and the PLO reached a peace agreement. The PLO agreed to recognize "the right of the State of Israel to exist in peace and security." It also promised to give up violence as a means of dealing with Israel. For its part, Israel agreed to negotiate with the PLO on the tough issues confronting the Palestinians and Israel.

A moving ceremony took place in Washington, D.C., hosted by President Clinton. Israel and the PLO signed a pact granting self-rule to Palestinians in the Gaza Strip and in Jericho on the West Bank. Clinton praised the two sides for making a "brave gamble that the future can be better than the past." He said,

"For too long the young of the Middle East have been caught in a web of hatred not of their own making. For too long they have been taught from the chronicles of war; now we can give them the chance to know the season of peace."

Progress and setbacks. As the peace process continued, it brought new achievements. In 1994, Israel signed a peace treaty with its neighbor Jordan. The two nations had been in a formal state of war for 46 years.

The following year, Israel granted Palestinians the right to set up a government in some areas of the West Bank that Israel had

Critical Thinking
Asking Questions

After students have read about both the 1979 and 1993 peace treaties, have them imagine that they are reporters at a press conference after either treaty was signed. Have them create a list of questions to ask about either historic event. In the case of the 1993 signing, some of the questions might draw parallels between the two events.

Historic Handshake *In 1993, Israel and the PLO stunned the world by signing a peace agreement. Here, President Clinton watches as Israeli Prime Minister Yitzhak Rabin, left, shakes hands with PLO leader Yasir Arafat, right.* **United States and the World** *How could the United States continue to aid the peace process?*

occupied for over 30 years. Yasir Arafat became the leader of the new ***Palestinian National Authority*** (PNA). Eager Palestinians elected a council to administer the area.

As peace drew nearer, radical groups on both sides tried to disrupt the progress. In 1994, a Jewish gunman killed 29 Arabs worshiping at a mosque. The following year a radical Jewish law student assassinated Yitzhak Rabin, the Israeli Prime Minister who had signed the peace accords with the Palestinians. Arab radicals launched a series of suicide bombings in urban areas of Israel.

The incidents showed that the road to peace would not be easy. Then, in 1996, Israel elected a new Prime Minister, Benjamin Netanyahu, who opposed giving up land to Israel's neighbors, in exchange for peace. Later that year, violence erupted between Palestinians and Israeli soldiers on the West Bank and more than 70 people were killed. The United States helped bring the parties back to the bargaining table. However, the chances for resolution of the conflict remained uncertain.

Changes in Iran

Israel and its neighbors were not the only hot spot in the Middle East. In 1979, a crisis flared in Iran.

Since World War II, the United States had supported Iran's ruler, Shah Muhammad Reza Pahlavi—in part because he was anticommunist. Many Iranians, however, opposed the shah. Devout Muslims were unhappy about his plans to make Iran more like Western countries. Others criticized the shah's undemocratic rule and his use of brutal secret police to silence opposition.

In 1979, a revolution forced the shah to flee. A Muslim religious leader, the Ayatollah Khomeini (i yuh TOH luh koh MAYN ee), took command. The new ruler forced Iranians to return to the strict traditions of Islam. Khomeini also led Iranians in a strong anti-American campaign.

In November 1979, President Carter let the exiled shah enter the United States for medical treatment. Angry Iranian revolutionaries responded by seizing the American embassy in Teheran, the Iranian capital. The revolutionaries took 53 American hostages. They did not free the hostages until January 1981.

Oil and War in the Middle East

Oil has continued to have a tremendous economic impact on the Middle East. The oil embargo of 1973 showed that the more oil a nation controlled, the more power it commanded. During the 1980s and 1990s,

---

Connections With Language Arts
Activity

Have students find and read newspaper editorials about the hostage crisis in Iran. Have them list several of the suggestions proposed at the time for ending the crisis. Ask: What finally won the release of the hostages?

Linking Past and Present
Background

During the Persian Gulf War, yellow ribbons became a symbol of support for American troops in the Middle East. Many Americans wore ribbons, while others displayed them in their homes, on their cars, or at their offices.

The tradition has a long history. During the Civil War, soldiers' wives would hang ribbons on trees to show that they were waiting for their husbands to come home. From 1979 to 1981, Americans used yellow ribbons to show their concern for the hostages in Iran.

Connections With Language Arts
Activity

Have interested students read selections from the book *Letters From the Sand: The Letters of Desert Storm and Other Wars*, compiled by the United States Postal Service. Have volunteers select appropriate letters and read the letters aloud to the class. Discuss what the letters reveal about the experiences of American troops during the Persian Gulf War.

Desert Victory *Allied troops used precision bombing to win a swift victory in the Persian Gulf War. Here, General Colin Powell explains the bombing strategy.* **Economics** *What role did oil play in the outbreak of the Persian Gulf War?*

Iraq attacked two of its oil-rich neighbors. Iraq's dictator, Saddam Hussein, hoped to increase his nation's power.

In 1980, Hussein began a war with Iran. After eight years of exhausting fighting, both sides agreed to a UN-sponsored cease-fire. Saddam Hussein had gained little.

In August 1990, however, Hussein struck again. This time, Iraq's army invaded neighboring Kuwait. Kuwait is one of the richest oil-producing nations in the Middle East. The sudden attack of 120,000 troops met with little resistance.

President Bush feared that Hussein's invasion was the beginning of a larger plan to gain control of the region's oil. To prevent further Iraqi aggression, he sent American forces to Saudi Arabia. He also convinced the United Nations to impose a trade boycott on Iraq. The United States and its allies set January 15, 1991, as the deadline for Iraq to withdraw from Kuwait.

The Persian Gulf War

The January 15 deadline came and went. Defiant, Iraq remained in Kuwait.

On January 16, 1991, the UN allies launched an air attack on Iraq. Troops from 28 nations—including Saudi Arabia, Syria, and Egypt—joined Americans in flying bombing missions against Baghdad.

Saddam Hussein swore to wage the "mother of all battles" against his foes. Iraq, however, could not counter the superior technology of UN forces. By the end of February, allied troops had driven the Iraqis out of Kuwait. The Persian Gulf War lasted only six weeks.

Iraq's military strength was weakened by the war, but Saddam Hussein maintained a firm grip on power. He continued to resist international efforts to limit his influence in the region.

SECTION 4 REVIEW

1. **Locate:** (a) Israel, (b) Sinai Peninsula, (c) West Bank, (d) Iran, (e) Persian Gulf, (f) Iraq, (g) Kuwait.
2. **Identify:** (a) Camp David Accords, (b) Palestine Liberation Organization, (c) Palestinian National Authority, (d) Persian Gulf War.
3. How did the 1973 Arab-Israeli war affect the United States?
4. Why did Israel and the Arab nations go to war?
5. How did Saddam Hussein threaten the peace and stability of the Middle East?
6. **CRITICAL THINKING Forecasting** What might have happened if the meetings at Camp David had failed?

 Writing to Learn

Imagine that you witnessed the signing of the historic pact between Israel and the PLO. Write a letter to a friend telling about the experience.

Chapter 29 • **849**

Answers to Section 4 Review

1. See the map on p. 845.
2. (a) Camp David Accords, p. 847, (b) Palestine Liberation Organization, p. 847, (c) Palestine National Authority, p. 848, (d) Persian Gulf War, p. 849
3. In retaliation for American support of Israel, Arab oil-producing countries cut off shipments and slowed production. This action resulted in oil shortages and higher oil prices in the United States.
4. They disputed claims to the land designated as the modern state of Israel.
5. In 1990, Hussein invaded Kuwait and threatened Saudi Arabia. This action led to the Persian Gulf War. After the war, Hussein continued to defy UN weapons inspectors.
6. Possible Answer: It might have taken much longer before there was peace in the Middle East; there might have been another war.

Picturing the Past

Art Note

Art and Trends This feature presents several pursuits that students may associate with their parents or even their grandparents. The topics depicted here underscore the fact that in "popular culture" tastes can change dramatically from one generation to the next. As students discuss the feature, you might point out that the characteristics of popular culture of their own teenage years may well seem outdated to teenagers in the future.

Previewing Focus

The "baby boomers" dominate this feature, so be sure to review the term. (See Chapter 27, Section 3.) Ask: As the "baby boomers" grow older, how do you see their tastes continuing to influence the culture of the United States?

Point out that the topics depicted in this feature show how teenagers became a new target market, with many goods and activities promoted only to the youth culture. Challenge students to look for evidence of that statement in the feature and ask them how they would support that same statement today.

Connections With Music
Background

The Beatles—John Lennon, Paul McCartney, George Harrison, and Ringo Starr—first came to the United States in February 1964, and their premiere appearance on *The Ed Sullivan Show* drew a record 73 million viewers. To a nation still mourning the murder of President Kennedy, the youth, vitality, and witty irreverence of the "Fab Four" were a breath of fresh air. Many parents complained about The Beatles' music and about "Beatlemania" (a term coined by the *Daily Mirror* of London) in general, but other adults rose to their defense, noting the lyrical skill of the Lennon-McCartney songwriting team and the growing sophistication of the band's music. Indeed, their 1967 *Sgt. Pepper's Lonely Hearts Club Band* remains a milestone not only in Beatles'

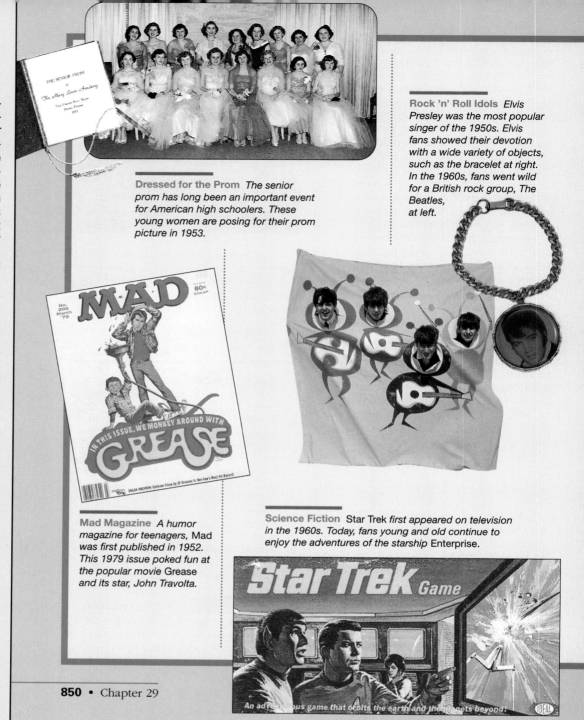

Dressed for the Prom *The senior prom has long been an important event for American high schoolers. These young women are posing for their prom picture in 1953.*

Rock 'n' Roll Idols *Elvis Presley was the most popular singer of the 1950s. Elvis fans showed their devotion with a wide variety of objects, such as the bracelet at right. In the 1960s, fans went wild for a British rock group, The Beatles, at left.*

Mad Magazine *A humor magazine for teenagers, Mad was first published in 1952. This 1979 issue poked fun at the popular movie Grease and its star, John Travolta.*

Science Fiction *Star Trek first appeared on television in the 1960s. Today, fans young and old continue to enjoy the adventures of the starship Enterprise.*

850 • Chapter 29

---

history but in the history of rock music.

The Beatles were the first of many bands to cross the Atlantic during the musical "British invasion." Of all the bands in that category, only the Rolling Stones and the Kinks have performed continuously since the mid-1960s.

Linking Past and Present
Activity

Probably several students in the class know Trekkies—devotees of *Star Trek*—or are Trekkies themselves. Ask such students to share with the class why *Star Trek* continues to be so popular. For example, ask: How did the original series blaze new territory in television? How does the updated series differ from the original? What is it about the ideals and values in the original show and the updated version that many people find appealing?

Sharing a Pizza *Young people's lives reflect the growing cultural diversity of the United States. Here, a group of students share a pizza.*

New Fads *By the 1980s, sneakers had changed from athletic footwear to items of everyday dress. That same decade, video games became the newest craze among young Americans.*

Roller Blades *In the early 1700s, a Dutch inventor created the first roller skates. In the 1990s, roller blades put an exciting new twist on the popular old pastime.*

Picturing the Past

Young Americans 1945–Present

The postwar "baby boomers" differed from earlier generations in many ways. Especially in the suburbs, young Americans had more money to spend. New forms of amusement, such as television and rock 'n' roll, helped create a "youth culture." Today, the baby boomers are parents, and their children follow even newer trends. Yet the same basic needs and concerns unite young people of all generations. ■ What pictures would you add to this photo essay to reflect what is most important in your life?

Chapter 29 • **851**

CHAPTER 29 REVIEW

Answers to Reviewing the Main Ideas

1. tax cuts, cuts in social spending, increased military spending

2. (a) The banking crisis weakened the economy; tight credit blocked business expansion; the real estate market slumped; unemployment rose; oil prices rose following the Iraqi invasion of Kuwait; the U.S. military reaction to the invasion was expensive. (b) Voters thought the government was gridlocked; debate centered on the role of the federal government.

3. (a) Reforms led to the creation of new political parties opposed to the communists and less central control over the individual republics; revived ethnic rivalries led to increased unrest; the failed coup of 1991 made reformers even bolder; republics began declaring their independence. (b) Several republics tried to break away from Yugoslavia; the Serbs in Bosnia and Croatia tried to prevent the secession. Longstanding ethnic hatred also contributed to the civil war.

4. President deKlerk began to end apartheid; first all-race elections were held in 1994, leading to the election of the first black African president, Nelson Mandela.

5. (a) They demonstrated in the streets of the capital, proclaiming "people power"; they refused to recognize Ferdinand Marcos as president. (b) Presidents Bush and Clinton condemned the crackdown but took no action that would interfere with relations between the two countries.

6. The United States sent troops as part of a UN mission to bring down Haitian military rulers; the troops stayed as peacekeepers.

7. President Carter brokered the Camp David Peace Agreement between Egypt and Israel; President Clinton hosted the signing of the peace agreement between Israel and the PLO; the United States has continued to support the peace process there.

8. The Iraqis were driven from Kuwait; Iraqi military power was weakened; Saddam Hussein remained in power and tried to rebuild Iraqi military strength in spite of UN sanctions.

Summary

- The conservative revolution that began under Reagan continued when Republicans won control of Congress in 1994. Results of the 1996 election reflected voters' view of the revolution.
- The Cold War ended and many countries in the former Soviet Union and Eastern Europe underwent democratic reforms. A bloody civil war broke out in Yugoslavia.
- The United States closely watched changes in South Africa, Asia, and Latin America.
- The Arab-Israeli conflict and the importance of oil have influenced United States policy toward the Middle East.

Reviewing the Main Ideas

1. What changes did Ronald Reagan hope to make as President?

2. (a) What problems did the economy face under President Bush? (b) What were the key issues in the election of 1996?

3. (a) Describe the events leading to the end of the Soviet Union. (b) What were the causes of the civil war in Yugoslavia?

4. How did South Africa become more democratic?

5. (a) How did the people in the Philippines bring greater democracy to their country? (b) How did the United States react to events in Tiananmen Square in China?

6. How did the United States promote democracy in Haiti?

7. How has the United States tried to bring about peace in the Middle East?

8. What were the results of the Persian Gulf War?

Thinking Critically

1. **Synthesizing Information** Speaker of the House Newt Gingrich called himself a

"genuine revolutionary." Do you think this is an accurate description? Explain.

2. **Linking Past and Present** Compare relations between the United States and Latin America in recent years with relations in the 1890s and early 1900s. (a) How were they similar? (b) How were they different?

3. **Solving Problems** (a) What actions did the United States and other nations take to try to end the civil war in Yugoslavia? (b) What other actions could countries have taken? (c) What actions could individuals have taken?

Applying Your Skills

1. **Reading a Map** Study the map of the Middle East on page 845. (a) Which countries border Israel? (b) Which two seas touch Israel? (c) Which Arab nations belong to OPEC? (d) How might its location make Israel feel threatened?

2. **Exploring Local History** Plan to interview two adults about the end of the Cold War. List five questions that you would ask to explore their reactions to the changes that have taken place.

Thinking About Geography

Match the letters on the map with the following places: **1.** El Salvador, **2.** Panama, **3.** Cuba, **4.** Grenada, **5.** Nicaragua. **Location** Why was the United States concerned about events in these countries?

Answers to Thinking Critically

1. Possible Answer: The description is accurate in that Gingrich tried to reverse liberal policies, cut social programs, and reduce the size of government; however, by 1996, he had failed to achieve many of his goals.

2. (a) In both eras, the United States frequently intervened in the internal affairs of Latin American countries. (b) In more recent years, the United States has sent economic aid in an attempt to bring about social and economic reform.

3. (a) European leaders tried to arrange cease-fires; the UN sent food and other aid to the people; the United States hosted the talks that led to the Dayton Accord; the United States, NATO, and Russia sent peacekeepers to the area. (b) Possible Answer: They could have sent troops sooner; they could have reacted strongly against "ethnic cleansing." (c) Possible Answer: They could have helped send food and clothing to the region; they could have written to government leaders urging action.

Answers to Applying Your Skills

1. (a) Lebanon, Jordan, Syria, and Egypt (b) the Mediterranean Sea and the Red Sea (c) Saudi Arabia, Iraq, Iran, Kuwait, Qatar, Bahrain, and the United Arab

Thinking About a Changing World

Form into groups to review the theme of a changing world. Follow the suggestions below to write, draw, or perform to show what you have learned concerning the rapid changes in the world. You may use the textbook, encyclopedias, atlases, or other materials in your classroom library to complete the tasks. Be able to name your sources of information when you have finished the activity.

HISTORIANS Recall what you have learned about the end of the Cold War. Then make a cause-and-effect chart about the Cold War. Illustrate the chart with original drawings or with pictures from magazines or newspapers.

CARTOGRAPHERS On a large sheet of poster paper, draw a map of Latin America. Then, on note cards, write brief captions describing important events in Latin American nations from 1980 to the present. Attach the captions to their correct locations on the map. Give a talk to the class explaining each event and showing where it took place.

American soldiers in Haiti

ARTISTS Think about what you have learned about events related to human rights in South Africa and China. Then draw a political cartoon about one of the events. Make sure the cartoon reflects a point of view.

REPORTERS Gather newspaper articles for a week or more about one country discussed in this chapter. Assemble the clippings in a scrapbook. Then write a paragraph summarizing the events and explaining how they relate to what you learned about the country in the chapter.

ACTORS Divide into small groups representing countries that have experienced major changes during the 1980s and 1990s. Have each group find out more about its country. Then organize a Teenagers' Convention where representatives from the different countries share information about what is happening in their land and how it affects their daily lives. You might bring in maps, graphs, pictures, or other articles to illustrate the discussion.

★ Create a Changing World bulletin board display. Include samples from each activity as well as current news articles about the world today.

Providing aid to war-torn Bosnia

American soldier in Kuwait

Emirates (d) Israel is encircled on land by Arab countries.
2. Answers will vary.

Answers to Thinking About Geography

1. B   2. D   3. A   4. E   5. C
Location: The United States was concerned about communist takeovers of the governments of certain Latin American countries.

Assessment

Chapter Resources Binder For a more comprehensive evaluation of student understanding of this chapter, assign Chapter Tests A and B and/or Extra Unit Questions from Unit 9, pages 35 – 40 and 57 – 59.
Computer Test Bank You can use Chapter Tests and Extra Unit Questions to create your own tests for both testing and retesting.

Alternative Assessment

Chapter Resources Binder See the Alternative Assessment booklet in the *Social Studies Educator's Handbook* series.
Portfolio You might meet with students to choose appropriate work from the chapter for inclusion in their portfolios.

Interdisciplinary ACTIVITY

Learning Styles
The following chart indicates the activities appropriate for different learning styles.

Visual Learners
Historians
Cartographers
Artists
Reporters
Actors

Auditory Learners
Cartographers
Actors

Kinesthetic Learners
Historians
Cartographers
Artists
Reporters
Actors

Evaluation

Historians All points on the charts must relate to the Cold War, with ideas presented clearly and concisely. Artwork selected should highlight the main ideas.
Cartographers Maps should project a reasonable image of Latin America. Boundaries should be accurate, and all countries must be included and properly identified. Oral presentations should be interesting and informative.
Artists Artistic ability need not be a criterion, but cartoons should reflect personal opinions about human rights issues in either of these countries.
Reporters Scrapbooks should be neat and well organized. Paragraphs should accurately summarize the articles selected and provide reasonable connections to the material presented in this chapter.
Actors Information should be accurate and be presented from the point of view of a teenager who is a resident of the particular country discussed. You might encourage comparisons of lifestyles among the various groups.

Lessons	Teaching Resources
1 Advances in Science and Technology **Objectives** 1. Describe how medical advances are improving our lives. 2. Identify the benefits and drawbacks of the widespread use of computers. 3. Identify some achievements of the space program.	**Lesson Planner** Cooperative Learning, p. 187 **Student Study Guide** Section 1 Study Guide, p. 217 **Chapter Resources Binder, Unit 9** *History Through Literature* Morning — "The Bird Perched for Flight," p. 46 **Our Multicultural Heritage** *Biography* Sally Ride, Astronaut and Astrophysicist, p. 88
2 Culture and Technology **Objectives** 1. Describe how technology has affected the entertainment industry. 2. Identify new methods that newspapers are using. 3. Describe how spectator sports have changed.	**Lesson Planner** Cooperative Learning, p. 188 **Student Study Guide** Section 2 Study Guide, p. 218
3 The United States in a World Economy **Objectives** 1. Explain why Americans are worried about the federal deficit. 2. Describe how the American economy has changed since the 1960s. 3. Explain why American businesses face stiff competition from abroad.	**Lesson Planner** Cooperative Learning, p. 189 **Student Study Guide** Section 3 Study Guide, p. 219
4 Concern for the Environment **Objectives** 1. Identify the goals of the environmental movement. 2. Describe how nations are working together to protect the environment. 3. Identify steps that Americans are taking to use energy wisely.	**Lesson Planner** Cooperative Learning, p. 190 **Student Study Guide** Section 4 Study Guide, p. 220 **Chapter Resources Binder, Unit 9** *Skill Application* Forecasting, p. 44 *Geography in History* Water for Los Angeles, pp. 47–48

5 A Diverse Society
Objectives
1. Describe how immigration patterns have been changing.
2. Identify ways in which the United States is a diverse society.
3. Identify issues that Americans face as they approach a new century.
	Lesson Planner
	Cooperative Learning, p. 191
	Student Study Guide
	Section 5 Study Guide, p. 221
	Chapter Resources Binder, Unit 9
	Critical Thinking Asking Questions, p. 45
	Our Multicultural Heritage
	Milestone Preserving the Heritage of Native Americans, p. 90
	Biography Maggie Kuhn, Founder of the Gray Panthers, p. 89
	Interdisciplinary Connections: People Face the Future
	  ■ *Sciences* The Technological Life, p. 176
	  ■ *Geography* Demographics, p. 177
	  ■ *World* Who Should Save the Earth?, p. 178
	  ■ *Economics* A Looming Crisis, p. 179
	  ■ *Civics* Everyone Is a Citizen, p. 180
	Posters
	Day and Crepuscule, by Tsing-fang Chen

Multimedia Resources	Additional Resources	Chapter-Level Resources

Transparencies
Fine Art Moonwalk, p. D-65
Exploring Technology Space Shuttle,
  p. H-61
	Voices of Freedom
	Are Computers Alive?, pp. 316–318
	Customized Reader
	The First People on the Moon, article IXB-6
	Interdisciplinary Explorations
	Mars: The Next Frontier
		Lesson Planner
		Activity Based,
		  pp. 192–193
		
		Student Study Guide
		Chapter 30 Study Guide,
		  pp. 222–223
		
		Chapter Resources
		  Binder
		Unit 9
		Vocabulary Building, p. 43
		Chapter Test A, pp. 49–51
		Chapter Test B, pp. 52–54
		Illustration Master, p. 55
		Extra Unit Questions,
		  pp. 57–59
		English Guided Reading
		Guided Reading,
		  pp. 59–60
		Spanish Resources
		
		Computer Test Bank
		Chapter Tests A and B
		Extra Unit Questions
		
		Guided Reading
		  Audiotapes
		Side 12
		
		CD-ROM
		Time Tour Toward a New
		  Century in The Nation
		  Today and Tomorrow

	Customized Reader Stevie Ray Vaughn: Playing a Blue Streak, article XB-2	
	Voices of Freedom A New Way to Look at the World, pp. 326–328 The Energy Dilemma, pp. 318–320 **Historical Outline Map Book** The Middle East, p. 78	
Transparencies *Our Multicultural Heritage* Immigration to the United States, 1960–1990, p. C-23; American Ancestors, p. C-31; Changing Ethnic Makeup of the United States, p. C-33; Latino Population of the United States, p. C-37; Languages Spoken in American Homes, p. C-35 *Political Cartoons* Education Then and Now, p. G-31 *Interdisciplinary Connections* Looking at the Future, p. B-91	**Customized Reader** The New Battle Over Indian Rights, article XA-6 Martha Collins: Kentucky's First Woman Governor, article XA-10 Helping the Handicapped at the New York Public Library, article XA-4 Why We Eat Dogs: Cultural Differences in America, article XA-5 A Hispanic Radio Personality, article XA-7 The Debate Over Multiculturalism in Schools, article XA-3	

CHAPTER **30**

Toward a New Century

CHAPTER OUTLINE

1 Advances in Science and Technology

2 Culture and Technology

3 The United States in a World Economy

4 Concern for the Environment

5 A Diverse Society

1969 *American astronauts became the first humans to land on the moon. This emblem celebrates the Apollo 11 moon mission.*

1970s *Americans celebrated the first Earth Day. This event was designed to make people aware of the need to protect the environment.*

1960s *The American economy began to shift from manufacturing to service industries. Service workers range from bankers and sales clerks to this architect and home builder.*

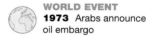

| 1960 | 1970 | 1980 |

▲
WORLD EVENT
1973 Arabs announce oil embargo

854 • Chapter 30

Chapter Time Line
Activity

Divide students into three groups. Assign each group one World Event and two other events from the time line (for example, "1969," "1990s," and "World Event/1980s"). Have each group create three commemorative postage stamps, one for each of its assigned events. Students may choose a single visual that symbolizes an event (for example, a gas pump with a "NO GAS" sign for the 1973 oil embargo), or they may prefer to try to depict an event as it happened (as did an actual United States stamp that showed Neil Armstrong setting foot on the moon in 1969). Encourage the use of color and detail, but remind students that some detail may become muddy or may be lost altogether when the stamp is reduced to actual size. Also, remind students to incorporate the initials *USA* and the price of the stamp in the design. Have the groups display their finished postage stamp designs.

Chapter Setting

In Stanford, California, 40-year-old Willem Van Buuren was dying. His heart was heavily damaged by disease.

Then one night, a 16-year-old boy was killed in an auto accident. The boy's heart was young and strong. Medical technicians rushed it to Stanford. There, doctors replaced Van Buuren's 40-year-old heart with the heart of the 16-year-old boy.

Van Buuren received his new heart in 1970. He went on to live another 22 years. Van Buuren was very lucky. Only a few years earlier, he would have been doomed. Instead, a remarkable advance in medical science gave Van Buuren a new chance at life.

Transplanting human organs is a very new field. To some observers, however, it ranks among the greatest achievements in medicine. One doctor predicts:

❝Surgeons in the twenty-first century will spend most of their time replacing parts rather than removing them, as they have in the last century.❞

Organ transplants are only one example of how technology is changing Americans' lives. Americans are pioneers in such areas as medical treatment, computers, and space exploration. Breakthroughs in these and other fields have changed the lives of people around the world.

> ### ACTIVITY
> Brainstorm a list of ways in which technology makes your life different from the lives of your parents when they were your age. Illustrate your list with original drawings or pictures from magazines.

1980s Immigration from Latin America and Asia increased sharply. Here, a group of immigrants take the oath to become United States citizens.

1990s Women took a greater role in government than ever before. Carol Moseley Braun, shown here, became the first African American woman elected to the Senate.

1990 Congress passed the Americans With Disabilities Act. The law prohibited discrimination against people with disabilities.

1980 ———————— **1990** ———————— **Present**

WORLD EVENT
1980s Concern grows about global warming and holes in ozone layer

WORLD EVENT
1992 Earth Summit meeting held in Brazil

Chapter 30 • **855**

1

Advances in Science and Technology

FIND OUT

- How are medical advances improving our lives?
- What are the benefits and drawbacks of the widespread use of computers?
- What are some achievements of the space program?

VOCABULARY vaccine, Internet

Maria needs a quick snack before sports practice, so she pops a frozen pizza into the microwave. John slips a disk into a CD player. Music sweeps over him, as if his favorite musicians were in the room. On the highway, a car swerves across the center line and strikes Lin's car head-on. An air bag inflates and saves Lin's life.

Much of the technology Americans use today was unknown 15 or 20 years ago. Now we take it for granted. What seemed like science fiction only yesterday has become a part of everyday life.

Medical Advances

New technology has led to many advances in medical science. One device, known as a CAT scanner, helps doctors diagnose illnesses. A CAT scanner takes three-dimensional X-ray pictures of parts of the body that once could be seen only during surgery. CAT scanning has been especially important in helping doctors diagnose cancer and diseases of the brain. Magnetic Resonance Imaging (MRI) is a way to help doctors see inside the body without radiation.

Other devices help or replace the body's own organs. Pacemakers help weak hearts to beat more regularly. Dialysis machines clean the blood of patients whose kidneys have failed. Artificial hearts keep people alive while they wait for a heart transplant.

In another area, researchers have improved old vaccines and developed new ones. **Vaccines** are substances that cause a mild form of a disease. As a result, they strengthen the body's defenses to fight off the full disease. In the 1950s, Dr. Jonas Salk discovered a vaccine against the crippling disease of polio. Today, almost no one gets polio. Smallpox, too, is no longer a problem. A worldwide vaccination campaign from 1967 to 1980 wiped out most cases of this deadly disease.

AIDS. Successes against some diseases have been offset by new challenges. The biggest challenge is **AIDS**, or acquired immune deficiency syndrome. AIDS is life-threatening because it prevents the body from fighting infections.

AIDS appeared suddenly around 1980. By 1995, over a quarter of a million Americans had died of the disease. As many as 4.5 million people around the world had developed AIDS and some 19 million others had HIV, the virus that causes AIDS. Almost all of them were expected to develop AIDS eventually. Researchers are working to find a cure.

Computers Change American Life

Computers have become a part of everyday life. They affect the way Americans do their jobs, the way they work at school, and the way they spend their leisure time.

Development of computers. The first electronic computers were built in the 1940s. They were huge. One early model, called ENIAC, was as big as a railroad boxcar. It had 18,000 vacuum tubes and weighed 30 tons. Despite its vast size, however, ENIAC was very slow and its computing power was limited.

Battle Against AIDS *This giant patchwork quilt is made up of tributes to people who have died of AIDS. Many Americans wear red ribbons like the one at right to promote awareness of this deadly disease.* **The Arts** *How might the AIDS quilt help in the fight against AIDS?*

In the 1960s, researchers developed integrated circuits, or "chips." Chips may be smaller than a fingernail. Yet one chip can contain millions of instructions to the computer. With chips, computer scientists could build much smaller and faster computers.

Computers can be linked with each other over telephone lines. The system that makes this network of computers possible is called the Internet. With the Internet, one computer user can get information from or send messages to users of other computers. At first, only military and scientific computers were linked by the Internet. Today, however, millions of Americans can go "on-line" to visit computer sites on the Internet's World Wide Web.

Effects on daily life. In the early years, most computers were owned by businesses or government offices. As costs came down in the 1970s and 1980s, however, computers were purchased for home and school use. By the mid-1990s, millions of Americans used personal computers.

As computers became more widespread, some people expressed concern. Computers keep records about almost everything we do. As a result, people using them could threaten our privacy. Also, "hackers" who learn how to tap into central computer networks could pose a threat to national security.

Tracking a Computer Spy

Clifford Stoll hated unsolved problems. Now, he discovered that someone had used a computer for a few seconds without paying for the time. Stoll was determined to find out who the culprit was.

Stoll worked as a computer systems manager at Lawrence Berkeley Laboratory, in California. Thousands of scientists and scholars used Lawrence's giant computers, paying $300 an hour for computer time. The bill for August 1986 was $2,387. Of the total, 75 cents (about nine seconds' worth) was unaccounted for. Who had "stolen" the computer time?

Stoll checked and rechecked. At last, he discovered that someone named Hunter had used the mysterious computer time. But

History and You
The first electronic computers got their instructions from punched cards. Workers had to feed in thousands of cards to run a program. Today's instructions, called "software," are simpler. How do you load software when you use a computer?

Chapter 30 • **857**

who was Hunter? No one by that name had a right to use the computers.

Trailing the thief. Hunter was getting into the computer system over the telephone lines. Stoll began to trail Hunter electronically. Whenever Hunter called the system, two beeps sounded. A printer recorded Hunter's every keystroke.

Stoll learned that Hunter was using Lawrence Lab as a way station to break into computers all over the world. He was tapping into computers at American military bases in Germany and Japan. He had even managed to get into Defense Department computers.

Stoll resolved to stop this "computer terrorism." He reasoned,

66 I'm not just an American; I'm also a member of an international community—one connected by computers and networks. And when somebody attacks your country or community . . . you're a citizen. You have a responsibility to your fellow citizens and electronic neighbors. 99

Stoll knew that he had to find Hunter without letting him know he had been discovered. Stoll called the FBI to ask for a phone trace. The local agent laughed. "You're calling us because you've lost 75 cents in computer time?" The FBI would not

Challenges of the Computer Age *Computers have made thousands of tasks easier—from solving mathematics problems in school to designing new spacecraft.* **Science and Technology** *Why do some people find computers a cause for concern?*

take action in any case involving less than $1 million, the agent told Stoll.

Finally, Stoll found a judge who granted him a search warrant, and telephone companies traced the calls. Stoll learned that Hunter was not in the United States. He was in West Germany. What's more, he was clearly after military secrets!

Catching the spy. At last, government spy trackers paid attention. With their help, Stoll set a trap, using a fake computer file for bait. In June 1987, when Hunter tried to get into the file, West German police arrested him. Stoll was a hero. He had helped break up a computer spy ring before any critical secrets were lost. ■

The Space Age

The space age dawned in October 1957 when the Soviet Union launched the first artificial satellite, *Sputnik.* (See page 783.) The next year, the United States sent its own satellite, *Explorer I,* into orbit. Within four years, both American and Soviet astronauts had rocketed into space.

Reaching for the moon. In 1961, President Kennedy had told Congress, "I believe we should go to the moon . . . before this decade is out." *The National Aeronautics and Space Administration*, or NASA, set to work. They built more powerful rockets and larger capsules.

In 1969, astronauts Neil Armstrong and Buzz Aldrin piloted a small landing craft onto the moon's surface. With millions of people around the world watching, Armstrong became the first person to step onto the moon. "That's one small step for a man, one giant leap for mankind," he radioed back to Earth. American astronauts visited the moon five more times.

Other missions in space. The United States pursued many other space goals. It sent unpiloted spacecraft past the moon, to the edges of the solar system. They explored planets they passed along the way.

Astronaut attaches
satellite to robot arm

Engines

TV cameras

Robot arm

Commander

Sleeping
bags

Cargo bay doors

Cargo bay

Astronaut controls robot
arm while viewing satellite
adjustment on TV screen

Flight deck

Astronauts pass through
airlock to walk in space

Middeck where astronauts
eat, sleep, and exercise

Space Shuttle *The United States has a fleet of space shuttles that are used for tasks ranging from medical tests to the launching of communications satellites. After each mission, they return to Earth, gliding down and landing on a gigantic runway.* **Science and Technology** *What are the advantages of reusable spacecraft?*

Chapter 30 • **859**

Answer to Exploring Technology

Possible Answer: A reusable spacecraft would be less expensive in the long run than a spacecraft that could be used only once.

 ## Our Multicultural Heritage

Biography Have students read the biography, Sally Ride, Astronaut and Astrophysicist, on page 88 of the *Our Multicultural Heritage* booklet. (Enrichment/Average)

 ## Transparencies

Exploring Technology Use the transparency Space Shuttle on page H-61 of *American History Transparencies*. Teaching suggestions can be found on page H-21. (Enrichment/Average)

Interdisciplinary Explorations

Mars Have students refer to the unit Mars: the Next Frontier from the *Prentice Hall Interdisciplinary Explorations* series to consider the future of space travel. (Enrichment/Challenging)

Connections With Technology
Background

Space shuttles are designed to take off like rockets and to fly like airplanes. Earlier space capsules were carried into space by rockets, but they could not fly back into Earth's atmosphere. Instead, they fell into the sea, where a ship picked them up. From this practice comes the term *splashdown.*

Connections With Technology
Activity

Remind students that the United States has been a leader in technology for a long time. Have students use information from this text and from other sources to make a list of inventions from the 1700s to the present that have changed the way Americans live (for example, the cotton gin, steel plow, railroad, and automobile). Ask: What recent inventions have affected the way you live? In what areas of technology is the United States still a world leader? In what areas of technology has it fallen behind?

Student Study Guide

Section 1 Study Guide Have students use the Section 1 Study Guide on page 217 of the *Student Study Guide* to review and reinforce the content of this section. (Reteaching/Average)

 ACTIVITY

Guided Instruction You might have students freewrite to generate ideas for their diary entries. Because of the personal nature of diaries, you might make the sharing of the entries an option rather than a requirement.

Section 2
pp. 860–862

🔔 **Bell Ringer**

Ask students to create one list of the music styles that they like and one list of the music styles that their parents enjoy. Then have them comment on the similarities, differences, and variety of both lists.

Lesson Plan

1. Focus New technologies and corporate mergers have greatly affected mass culture in the United States. In this section, students focus on new developments in entertainment, music, and publishing.

Meanwhile, NASA built a space shuttle for projects closer to Earth. A fleet of these spacecraft shuttled back and forth between Earth and space. Each shuttle could be used again and again.

Then, a tragic accident altered NASA's plans for monthly shuttle missions. In January 1986, seconds after liftoff, the shuttle *Challenger* exploded. All seven people aboard were killed. Investigators found a design problem in the shuttle rocket, which had caused the explosion. The problem was corrected, and shuttle flights resumed in 1988.

Future plans. As the year 2000 approached, the United States space program stood at a crossroads. What would be its mission during the century to come? One plan called for building a permanent space station that would orbit the Earth. Another favored sending astronauts to explore Mars. However, with the Cold War at an end and military goals less urgent, the space program had to compete with other national goals.

SECTION 1 REVIEW

1. **Identify:** (a) CAT scanner, (b) AIDS, (c) National Aeronautics and Space Administration, (d) Neil Armstrong, (e) Buzz Aldrin.
2. **Define:** (a) vaccine, (b) Internet.
3. Describe two advances in medical science made possible by technology.
4. How have computers changed people's daily lives?
5. Name two accomplishments of the American space program since 1969.
6. **CRITICAL THINKING Defending a Position** Do you think that computers are a threat to privacy? Explain.

ACTIVITY **Writing to Learn**
Imagine that you have been chosen for the first trip to Mars. Write a diary entry describing your thoughts and feelings on the day before you are to blast off.

FIND OUT
- How has technology affected the entertainment industry?
- What new methods are newspapers using?
- How have spectator sports changed?

High above the Earth's surface, satellites beam down a steady stream of television signals. Receiving dishes catch the signals in cities and small villages in India, Brazil, Nigeria—almost everywhere. All over the world, people watch 10-year-old American comedy programs or catch the latest news beamed live from the United States.

New technologies have helped spread American popular culture to all corners of the globe. They have also reshaped the daily lives and leisure activities of Americans.

The Entertainment Industry

The rise of television in the 1950s revolutionized the entertainment industry. Many Americans stopped going to movies. In the 1970s, however, the film industry made a comeback as movie houses added more screens and created "multitheaters." Video-cassette recorders, or VCRs, gave studios a new market for films.

Television. Television itself changed dramatically during the 1980s as cable systems spread throughout the country. In the past, viewers could choose among only a handful of broadcast networks. Now, cable companies offer dozens of channels. Soon, there may be hundreds of choices for entertainment and information.

Popular music. Popular music changed, too. During the 1950s, "rock 'n' roll" became

---

popular, especially among teenagers. In the 1960s and 1970s, rock musicians adopted more amplified guitars and other electronic sound effects. Performers dressed up their stage acts with eye-catching light and sound shows. They began to use music videos to reach a wider audience.

Today, American popular music is an exciting blend of ethnic and musical traditions. From the Caribbean come salsa and reggae. Urban streets provide the sounds and lyrics of rappers. Irish, English, continental, and other influences add to the richness of the blend.

Trend Toward Giant Companies

The entertainment industry has grown tremendously in recent years. Like many other American companies, entertainment companies have merged. By the early 1990s, for example, six giant companies accounted for 93 percent of all music sales.

At the same time, there has been a trend toward giant media companies. These companies do everything—from growing trees to making paper to printing books to turning books into movies to showing movies on their cable network channels.

Sports

During the twentieth century, sports have come to play an increasing role in American culture. Millions of spectators watch teams compete in baseball, basketball, and football. Millions of other Americans play sports in local teams and leagues.

Our Common Heritage
Salsa means "sauce," and salsa music is a saucy arrangement of fast rhythms. Salsa's roots are mainly Cuban. However, salsa also has roots in Africa, where many Cubans trace their ancestry.

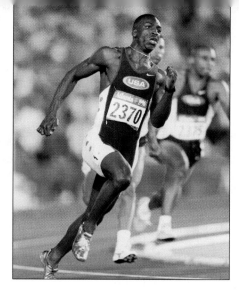

Running for the Gold *In 1996, athletes from around the world came to Atlanta, Georgia, to compete in the Olympic games. One of many Americans who took home gold medals was Michael Johnson of Dallas, Texas. Johnson became the first runner in Olympic history to win both the 200- and 400-meter races.* **United States and the World** *Do you think events like the Olympic Games help to bring the world closer together? Explain.*

As more and more Americans work at desk jobs, they look for new ways to exercise and keep their bodies fit. Many join health clubs, which offer exercise machines and swimming pools. Other Americans pursue a wide range of outdoor activities, such as skiing, riding bikes, paddling canoes, or climbing mountains.

Sports, too, are affected by new technology. Some cities have huge domed stadiums, such as New Orleans's Superdome and Houston's Astrodome. In these protected spaces, teams can play in any weather.

Millions of sports fans stay home and watch games on television. Some events—like the Olympic Games—attract billions of viewers in many countries. Sports figures such as the American gymnast Shannon

2. Instruct Bring in copies of *USA Today* and a local or metropolitan newspaper. Help students compare the two newspapers in terms of layout, subjects of stories, style of graphics, and audience. Ask: What are the advantages of a national newspaper like *USA Today*? What are the disadvantages?
3. Close To close the lesson, have students summarize the reasons for the development of a mass culture.

 Lesson Planner

For a developed **Cooperative Learning** lesson plan, see the *Lesson Planner,* page 188.

Answer to Caption

Possible Answer: Yes; they bring together athletes from many nations in a spirit of friendly competition. They also bring television viewers closer to the athletes from many nations.

Customized Reader

Primary Source For a magazine article about a blues guitarist, order article XB-2, Stevie Ray Vaughn: Playing a Blue Streak, from the *American History Customized Reader.* In this article, the author interviews Vaughn and explores the roots of his music. (Enrichment/Easy)

Connections With Technology
Background

The revolution in communication has all but eliminated distance. For example, when President Lincoln was shot in 1865, the news took five days to reach London, England. When President Ronald Reagan was shot in 1981, a man living one block away from the shooting first heard the news by telephone from someone who had seen it on television—in London.

Connections With Economics
Activity

The popularity of CDs is an example of supply and demand in the marketplace. When CDs first came out, they were very expensive. As companies began making more CDs, the price fell. Have students compare ads from the mid-1980s with current ads to find out the price difference for CDs.

Connections With Music
Background

In 1970, there were 658 opera companies and 1,441 symphony orchestras in the United States. By 1990, there were 1,285 opera companies and 1,666 symphony orchestras. Many of these groups have been funded by the government. Interest in the classical arts has been stimulated further by broadcasts on public television.

Student Study Guide

Section 2 Study Guide Have students use the Section 2 Study Guide on page 218 of the *Student Study Guide* to review and reinforce the content of this section. (Reteaching/Average)

 ACTIVITY

Guided Instruction Encourage students to consider both positive and negative changes and trends for each of the topics discussed in the section: television, music, newspapers, literature, sports, and entertainment. Have volunteers share and explain their responses. You also might encourage students to save their responses and see which of them come to pass.

Section 3
pp. 862–865

Bell Ringer

Ask students to name items they own or use that were made abroad and to identify the nations where the items were made.

Lesson Plan

1. Focus Because the world has "shrunk" since World War II, the economy of the United States has become more dependent on events in other parts of the world. In this section, students read about the soaring federal deficit, the growth of service industries, competition from abroad, and economic developments in other nations.

Miller and basketball's "Dream Team" have become known throughout the world.

Newspapers and Books

"SO LONG," the headlines read. "SAD FAREWELL." Across the nation, newspapers have been closing down. Most Americans do not seem to have time to read anymore. Instead, they catch the news on television. As a result, many cities that once had three or four newspapers now have just one.

Meanwhile, those newspapers that remain are adopting new technologies. One newspaper sends pages by satellite to printing plants around the country. Many papers spruce up the news with color and graphics. Some make their articles available to computer users over the Internet.

New technologies have affected literature and the arts, as well. Through giant bookstore chains, millions of copies of "blockbuster" books can be sold. At the same time, computers and desktop publishing software have opened new opportunities for small publishers.

SECTION 2 REVIEW

1. **Identify:** (a) Superdome, (b) "Dream Team."
2. How have the television and film industries changed since the 1950s?
3. (a) Why have many newspapers gone out of business? (b) What new technologies have newspapers adopted?
4. **CRITICAL THINKING Analyzing Information** (a) If a few big companies controlled entertainment and information, what advantages might be gained? (b) What problems might result?

ACTIVITY Writing to Learn
Jot down ideas about how popular culture might change in the next 10 years. What current trends do you think will last the longest? Explain.

3
The United States in a World Economy

FIND OUT
■ Why are Americans worried about the federal deficit?
■ How has the American economy changed since the 1960s?
■ Why do American businesses face stiff competition from abroad?

VOCABULARY gross domestic product, service industry, trade deficit

When George Washington was President, five clerks, a messenger, and an office keeper handled all the business of the Department of State. The War Department had three clerks. The army consisted of 840 men.

Today, the federal government employs more than 3 million people. In two minutes, it spends more than the government under George Washington spent in a year. Its actions reach into all areas of the nation's economy.

Some Americans worry that the government has grown too big. Others feel that the government should be handling even more projects. The question of the proper size and role of the government tops the list of economic issues facing the nation today.

A Bigger Government

The move toward a larger, more active government began in the 1890s, with the Progressive movement. Both federal and state governments expanded their power to regulate the abuses of large corporations and monopolies.

Connections With Local History
Activity

Ask students to find out how a newspaper from your area has coped with a declining readership and the challenges of new technology. For example, they might find out if any local newspapers have gone out of business in the past 10 years, how those that have survived try to be as timely as television news reports, and what the newspapers feel their role will be 10 years from now.

Answers to Section 2 Review

1. (a) Superdome, p. 861, (b) "Dream Team," p. 862
2. Cable systems have spread throughout the country, offering television viewers dozens of channels to choose from. Movie houses have created "multitheaters." Videocassette recorders, or VCRs, have provided a new market for feature films.
3. (a) Readership has dropped because people who cannot find the time to read newspapers have turned to television to get their news. (b) Newspapers are using color and graphics to attract readers and are exploring ways to supply news via home computers.
4. (a) Possible Answer: A limited number of large companies might provide greater quality control; with their financial reserves, they might afford to present entertainers who are not guaranteed money-makers. (b) Possible Answer: Those large companies could restrict the free flow of ideas and information; thus, they could influence what people think about important issues.

During the Great Depression, the federal government took on hundreds of new tasks. It offered to protect Americans with such programs as Social Security. In the 1960s, such social programs as Medicare and Medicaid made the government even bigger.

Soaring deficit. During the 1980s, federal spending mushroomed to record levels. One cause was a massive defense buildup that cost billions of dollars. Increased spending for social programs was another cause.

The government failed to raise enough money to pay for these programs. Year after year, it spent more than it took in. Between 1989 and 1993, the gap between spending and income averaged $250 billion a year. This gap, or deficit, was far higher than it had ever been before.

Finding a solution. Most Americans agree that something must be done to reduce the deficit. However, they do not always agree on a solution. Some people argue for higher taxes, especially for upper-income Americans. Others stress the need to cut government spending. For years, Presidents and Congress have tried to find a solution.

Even those who wish to cut spending cannot agree on what should be cut. Should military spending be reduced, now that the Cold War is over? Can social programs be cut without hurting middle-class and lower-class Americans?

In 1995 both President Clinton and Congress agreed to try to eliminate the budget deficit within seven years. That goal, however, would not be easy to reach.

A Shift to Service

The American economy has undergone tremendous changes over the last 30 years. These changes present a second economic challenge to the nation.

A key measure of an economy is the **gross domestic product** (GDP). The gross domestic product is the total value of goods

The National Debt Mounts *By the 1990s, the soaring federal deficit contributed to an enormous national debt. This electronic sign ticked off growth of the debt, second by second.* **Economics** *According to this sign, how fast was the debt increasing? How did the debt affect average Americans?*

and services produced each year within a country. Since 1960, the GDP in the United States has soared from $513 billion to more than $6 trillion.

Meanwhile, the nature of the economy was shifting, just as it did a century ago. Until 1865, the United States had been mainly a nation of farmers. Then, between 1865 and 1900, industries grew. "Smokestack industries"—industries that make products such as steel in large factories—became the backbone of the economy.

During the 1960s, the economy began to change again. Professions and service industries overtook manufacturing. A **service industry** is one in which workers perform

History and You
Service workers also include doctors, teachers, lawyers, hairdressers, and waiters. What service workers helped you today?

Lesson Planner

For a developed **Cooperative Learning** lesson plan, see the *Lesson Planner,* page 189.

Answer to Caption

The debt was increasing at a rate of $13,000 per second; according to the sign, every American family would have to pay a share of the debt.

Historical Sidelight
Background

Near the end of 1995, President Clinton and the Republican-controlled Congress clashed over the best way to reduce the federal deficit. President Clinton acknowledged the need to reduce government spending, but conservative Republicans felt his proposed cuts were not deep enough. For seven long months, they failed to agree on a budget. During this agonizing period, there were 12 temporary spending bills and two partial government shutdowns, one idling some 800,000 workers. In April 1996, a budget deal was finally reached. It reduced spending by $23 billion from 1995 levels and eliminated 200 federal programs. President Clinton supported the deal because it preserved money for education, environmental protection, and job-training programs.

Cooperative Learning
Activity

Challenge students to create a comprehensive list of service workers. Working with partners or in small groups, have students use the classified ads from a local newspaper and/or the local Yellow Pages to compile a list. Then have student groups exchange and compare lists. You might work with the entire class to compile a master list.

services rather than manufacture goods. Service workers include bankers, sales clerks, and teachers. The United States still manufactures billions of dollars worth of products each year. Most Americans, however, now work in service jobs.

Competition From Abroad

A third economic challenge comes from abroad. Today, American businesses sell their products in a world marketplace. The United States must compete with such economic powers as Germany and the nations of the Pacific Rim. (See the map below.)

This competition has posed some problems for the United States. First, many foreign products cost less than similar American products. Sometimes they are better, too. Second, American businesses return more of their profits to shareholders than foreign companies do. They also pay workers at a higher rate than workers are paid in most other countries. That means American firms have less to invest in new technology.

More imports than exports. Foreign competition has caused a trade deficit for the United States. A **trade deficit** occurs when a nation buys more goods and services from foreign countries than it sells to them.

How can the United States reduce its trade deficit? One way is for businesses to become more efficient. Many American firms have built more efficient factories. Another way is to produce superior products that will attract customers abroad. The gov-

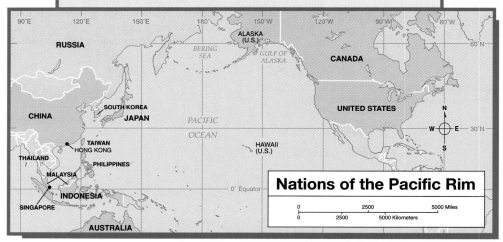

MAP STUDY

Industrial nations of the Pacific Rim play a vital role in the world economy. Japan and the four "Little Dragons"—South Korea, Taiwan, Hong Kong, and Singapore—are both trading partners and trading rivals of the United States.
1. *What is the distance between Hong Kong and Hawaii?*
2. *Which of the "Little Dragons" is farthest from the United States?*
3. Drawing Conclusions *Look at the map of the United States on pages 892–893. Which states do you think would be most concerned about trade issues within the Pacific Rim?*

Nations of the Pacific Rim

Linking Past and Present
Background

The economies of the Pacific Rim nations boomed in the 1980s, and these nations play a major role in the world economy. Not only have their exports penetrated global markets, but Japan is fast becoming one of the world's largest providers of foreign aid. In the future, Japan will give more than $1 billion in assistance to developing countries.

Because of its location on the eastern side of the Pacific Rim, the United States has always played a major role in the region. It has provided military support, technological know-how and equipment, essential natural resources and foodstuffs, and an immense market for Asian exports.

Today, ties between the United States and the Pacific Rim nations are close. Americans buy more goods from the Pacific Rim than from any other region. Nearly half of all foreign students in the United States are from Pacific Rim countries. Many American companies have moved their factories to Pacific Rim countries, and American service industries are greatly expanding in the region.

Connections With the World
Background

During the 1980s, foreign companies acquired many major American firms. In 1990, 1 out of every 10 Americans employed in manufacturing worked for a foreign-owned company. In 1990, foreigners had invested some $390 billion in American real property and stocks and bonds. The British owned the largest amount—$21 billion—which was more than the amount invested by Japanese businesses. The third and fourth highest investors were the Dutch and the Canadians.

Foreign Trade, 1978–1994

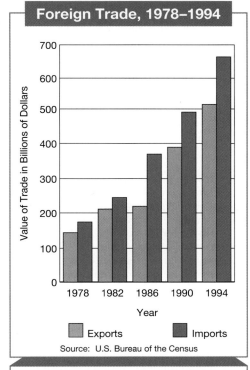

GRAPH SKILLS *A balanced foreign trade is important for a healthy economy. In recent years, many Americans worried because the United States imported more goods than it exported.* • *Can you learn from the graph when this trend began? Explain.*

ernment can also protect American industries by raising tariffs.

Trade agreement. After months of bitter debate, in 1993 Congress ratified the ***North American Free Trade Agreement*** (NAFTA). NAFTA will slowly do away with trade barriers between the United States, Canada, and Mexico.

Opponents of NAFTA worried that it would lead to a loss of American jobs. Companies, they said, would move their factories to Mexico, where they could pay workers lower wages. Supporters argued that NAFTA would increase United States exports and thus help reduce the nation's trade deficit.

Coming Together NAFTA joined the nations of Canada, Mexico, and the United States in a free trade agreement. **United States and the World** *What were the arguments for and against NAFTA?*

President Clinton strongly supported NAFTA, saying,

    66 At a time when many of our people are hurting from the strains of this tough global economy, we chose to compete, not retreat. **99**

By 1995, NAFTA had produced economic changes. Some American jobs were lost to Mexican workers. Others, though, were created as American companies exported more goods to Mexico. Many Americans invested in Mexican businesses. In the long run, those investments may lead to increased prosperity for both countries.

SECTION 3 REVIEW

1. **Identify:** (a) Pacific Rim, (b) North American Free Trade Agreement.
2. **Define:** (a) gross domestic product, (b) service industry, (c) trade deficit.
3. Give two reasons why the federal budget deficit grew sharply after 1980.
4. In what important ways has the economy changed since the 1960s?
5. How has foreign competition affected the United States economy?
6. **CRITICAL THINKING Understanding Cause and Effect** Why does the United States have a trade deficit?

 Writing to Learn
Write five questions that you would like to ask an expert about the United States economy.

Bell Ringer

To illustrate the problem of trash disposal, have students keep a record of all the items they throw out in a single day. Compile the lists and classify the kinds and amounts of garbage. Ask: Which items could have been reused?

Lesson Plan

1. Focus Concern for protecting the environment became a major issue affecting public-policy decisions beginning in the 1960s. In this section, students examine the debate over how the United States should deal with dangers to the environment.
2. Instruct Discuss the meaning of each of these goals: (a) reducing gasoline consumption, (b) reducing acid rain, (c) ending ocean dumping of wastes, (d) developing solar energy, (e) reducing the greenhouse effect. Have students imagine themselves as advisers to the President. Have them work in groups to decide which two items should be given top priority and to explain the reasons for their choices.
3. Close To close the lesson, have students summarize the concerns and goals of the environmental movement.

Lesson Planner

For a developed **Cooperative Learning** lesson plan, see the *Lesson Planner,* page 190.

4
Concern for the Environment

FIND OUT
- What are the goals of the environmental movement?
- How are nations working together to protect the environment?
- What steps are Americans taking to use energy wisely?

VOCABULARY environmentalist, ozone layer, global warming, solar energy, renewable resource

In a long house near Seattle, Washington, a Tulalip elder raises his arms. "O Great Spirit!" he chants. "Will you hear us?" The Tulalip people sing and dance around a fire. They are performing an ancient rite to welcome the first salmon of spring.

This year, the salmon in the Tulalip ceremony comes from Alaska. Human activities such as logging and building dams have harmed salmon-breeding grounds in Washington, and local salmon are scarce. Private groups and government agencies, however, are restocking the rivers with fish. One day, they hope, millions of salmon will live there again.

Since the 1960s, Americans have become increasingly aware of dangers to the environment. Today, concerned citizens are working to teach Americans how their everyday choices can help—or harm—the Earth on which we live.

The Environmental Movement

American science writer Rachel Carson helped focus attention on environmental dangers. In her 1962 book, *Silent Spring,* she charged that farm pesticides were poi-

soning the Earth. Carson imagined a bleak future for the world:

> ❝It was a spring without voices. On the mornings that had once throbbed with the dawn chorus of robins, catbirds, doves, jays, wrens, and scores of other bird voices there was now no sound; only silence lay over the fields and woods and marsh.❞

Growing awareness. Carson's warning struck a nerve. Americans noticed further problems. Chemical wastes turned rivers into sewers. Factory smokestacks belched foul-smelling fumes. Massive oil tankers that broke apart spilled oil into the sea. Careless people tossed litter along roads.

Reformers known as **environmentalists** formed groups to prod the nation into controlling pollution and protecting land, water, and air. In 1970, environmental groups declared the first ***Earth Day***. Millions of people took part in activities designed to educate people about environmental issues. Since then, people around the world celebrate Earth Day every spring.

New laws. Congress responded to environmental concerns with a flurry of new laws. It created the ***Environmental Protection Agency*** (EPA) to lead the attack on pollution. The Clean Air Act of 1970 forced auto makers to clean up car exhausts. The Clean Water Act of 1972 fought pollution in

Linking Past and Present
One of the earliest American environmentalists was John Muir, a Scottish immigrant. Muir took President Theodore Roosevelt camping in the western wilderness to win his support for national parks. He also founded the Sierra Club, one of today's major environmental groups.

Connections With Local History
Activity

An Environmental Impact Statement must be filed before work begins on any federally funded project. The study describes the probable consequences to the environment that the project will have. Have students find out where the nearest recent Environmental Impact Statements have been filed, by whom, and for what purposes.

Connections With Science
Background

One of the greatest concerns of environmentalists is acid rain — rain that has picked up pollutants from the air. The Industrial Revolution marked the first time that chemicals produced by humans polluted the air. By 1872, a British scientist coined the term *acid rain* to describe the characteristics of the rain that washed these chemicals back to Earth. Today, scientists suggest that acid rain changes the soil itself, depriving trees of nutrients. It kills plants, fish, and birds — and it may pose a health risk to humans. Acid rain also wears away most metals more rapidly

than regular rain, and it damages materials such as marble and limestone. As a result, about 35,000 historic buildings and 10,000 monuments are in danger in the northeastern United States alone. Acid rain is a problem in other countries, too. It has even been detected in Antarctica — Earth's last great wilderness area.

Experts believe that the harmful effects of acid rain can be stopped. To do so, however, countries must agree to reduce their power-plant emissions and car-exhaust fumes by 50 percent.

MAP, GRAPH, AND CHART SKILLS
Forecasting

No one can know what will happen in the future. However, people often make forecasts, or predictions, based on information that is available today. Long-term planners in business may make forecasts in order to predict what goods to produce. Government planners make forecasts in order to see what laws are needed. These planners make forecasts for 5, 10, 20, or even 50 years from now.

The graph and map below give information about the current garbage crisis in the United States. The graph shows the amount of garbage Americans generate. The map shows how many years it will take before the nation's landfills are used up. A landfill is a place where communities dump garbage that they do not recycle.

1. **Identify the problem.** (a) What does the graph show about the amount of garbage Americans generate? (b) What does the map show about landfill space? (c) When you put the information from the map and the graph together, what problem is made clear?

2. **Identify long-term solutions.** (a) How could Americans generate less garbage? (b) How could communities make their landfill space last longer? (c) What should communities be doing with their garbage today to prepare for the future?

3. **Forecast possible future developments.** (a) Describe what you think a typical family's responsibilities regarding their garbage will be in the future. (b) What do you think communities will do to dispose of their garbage?

ACTIVITY

Study the graph, Sources of Immigration to the United States, 1941–1990, on page 873. Based on the information shown in the graph, what possible developments can you forecast for the future?

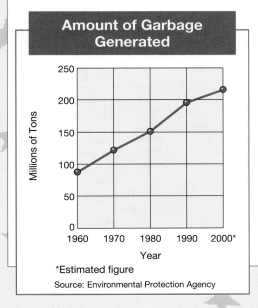

Amount of Garbage Generated

Millions of Tons (y-axis): 0, 50, 100, 150, 200, 250
Year (x-axis): 1960, 1970, 1980, 1990, 2000*

*Estimated figure

Source: Environmental Protection Agency

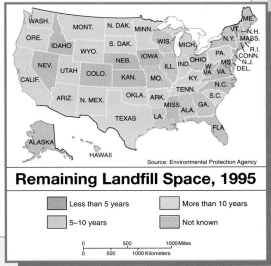

Remaining Landfill Space, 1995

Less than 5 years
5–10 years
More than 10 years
Not known

Source: Environmental Protection Agency

0   500   1000 Miles
0   500   1000 Kilometers

Chapter Resources

Geography in History Duplicate and distribute the worksheet, Water for Los Angeles, from Unit 9, pages 47–48, of the *Chapter Resources* binder. The worksheet examines how Los Angeles meets its inhabitants' needs for a reliable supply of fresh water. (Enrichment/Challenging)

Voices of Freedom

Primary Source You might assign selection 22-4, A New Way to Look at the World, on pages 326–328 of *Voices of Freedom*. This excerpt from Alvin Toffler's book *The Third Wave* discusses an increased need for global thinking. (Enrichment/Challenging)

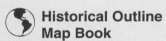

Historical Outline Map Book

Historical Outline Map Duplicate and distribute the map, The Middle East, on page 78 of the *American History Historical Outline Map Book.* Lesson ideas for this map can be found on page T24. (Reteaching/Average)

rivers and lakes. The Waste Cleanup Act of 1980 created a "superfund" to clean up chemical dumps.

Since the election of 1994, many Republicans in Congress have pushed to reduce the number of environmental regulations. Such laws led the government to "overregulate the economy," they argued. Congress proposed sharp cuts in money for the Environmental Protection Agency. Still, public sentiment for protecting the environment remained strong.

International Cooperation

Pollution does not stop at national boundaries. Leaders in nations around the world have joined hands to protect the environment. They have focused on a number of key problems.

Holes in the ozone layer. Miles above the Earth's surface is a layer of ozone. The ozone layer wraps around the Earth like a blanket. It blocks out harmful ultraviolet rays from the sun. These rays can cause skin cancer and other health problems.

During the 1980s, scientists found holes in the ozone layer. The holes were letting the harmful rays through.

Scientists concluded that gases used in homes and industries were escaping into the ozone layer and destroying it. The scientists pointed especially to gases used in aerosol cans and in refrigerators and air conditioners. Nations all over the world agreed to phase out the use of the dangerous gases.

Global warming. In the 1980s, a period of warmer-than-usual weather caused problems in many parts of the world. African countries suffered droughts. China received unusually heavy rains.

Some scientists thought that the Earth's atmosphere was warming up. They concluded that human activities, such as driving cars and operating factories, were adding carbon dioxide to the atmosphere. Carbon dioxide holds in heat that would otherwise escape into space. The scientists predicted a slow but steady rise in the world's average temperature. A warming trend might one day turn green fields into deserts!

Not all scientists agreed with the theory of global warming. Some said that the Earth might be having just a temporary "heat wave."

World leaders, however, took the threat of global warming seriously. They gathered at the *Earth Summit*, a meeting in Brazil in 1992. There, they pledged to reduce the amounts of carbon dioxide their countries released into the atmosphere.

The Energy Question

Americans make up only 5 percent of the total population of the world, yet they consume nearly one fourth of its energy supply. In recent years, Americans have begun to question this enormous use of energy. They have also started looking for new sources of energy to meet future needs.

A rude awakening. The Arab oil embargo of 1973 jarred Americans. (See page 845.) For the first time, the public realized that the United States depended a great deal on foreign energy sources to keep its cars and industries running. When the OPEC nations stopped shipping oil, American supplies quickly dwindled.

When oil shipments resumed in 1974, prices skyrocketed. Within 10 years, the fuel used by homes and industries cost four times as much as before the embargo. Businesses increased prices to cover the added costs of the fuel they used. As a result, consumers paid more for goods and services.

Conserving energy. Americans tried to use less energy. Under government pressure, auto companies made cars that used less gasoline. Homeowners added insulation to reduce the amount of fuel needed to cool or heat their homes. Environmentalists pointed out that conserving energy did

---

Connections With Science
Background

Seven of the Earth's warmest years since 1880 occurred between 1979 and 1990. In 1992, however, the average world temperature was actually lower than normal. This drop was caused by the eruption of Mt. Pinatubo, a volcano in the Philippines, the year before. Volcanic ash in the air helped to shield the Earth from the sun's rays.

Connections With the World
Background

In 1988, the United States joined 30 other nations in approving an international treaty to ban the use of chlorofluorocarbons. These industrial chemicals, used in refrigeration, insulating foam, and aerosol propellants, damage the ozone layer and thus contribute to the greenhouse effect. The nations signing the treaty agreed to roll back production by 50 percent by 1999. The United States was the first major producer and user of chlorofluorocarbons to ban their use.

Connections With the World
Background

In 1986, an explosion at the Chernobyl nuclear power plant in the Soviet Union spread radiation across much of northern and eastern Europe. Immediately after the accident, the Soviet government halted all farming within a 19-mile radius of Chernobyl. The ban was later extended to a 37-mile radius. Radioactive material from the Chernobyl accident was later detected in parts of Europe that were hundreds of miles away.

A Dangerous Position *The Arab oil embargo made Americans think about the need for a steady supply of energy. This cartoon calls attention to the dangers of relying on imported oil.* **Economics** *What steps have Americans taken to reduce their dependence on foreign oil?*

more than save money. It also helped cut down on pollution.

Other energy sources. Since the 1970s, Americans have sought to develop other sources of energy. Many factories have switched from oil to coal. The United States has nearly one fifth of the world's coal reserves. However, compared to oil, coal is a dirty fuel. Coal-burning plants have to use "scrubbers" and other devices to reduce the smoke and acids they emit into the air. That adds to the cost of using coal.

Nuclear power is another alternative to oil. Today, nuclear plants generate about one fifth of the nation's electric power. Still, nuclear power is costly, and it produces long-lasting radioactive wastes. An accident at a nuclear power plant could release

harmful radioactive gases into the air. Carried by the wind, these gases would endanger not only local residents but people living hundreds of miles away.

Scientists are working to harness **solar energy,** or power from the sun. Solar energy is appealing because it is renewable and clean. A **renewable resource** is one that can be quickly replaced by nature. However, for many uses solar energy remains expensive.

Wind and water are other renewable sources of energy. Rows of windmills in the California hills create electricity for thousands of homes. Huge dams such as the Hoover Dam in Nevada generate hydroelectric power. Hydroelectric power—electric power generated by water—accounts for more than 13 percent of all electricity produced in the United States.

SECTION 4 REVIEW

1. **Identify:** (a) Rachel Carson, (b) Earth Day, (c) Environmental Protection Agency, (d) Earth Summit.
2. **Define:** (a) environmentalist, (b) ozone layer, (c) global warming, (d) solar energy, (e) renewable resource.
3. What changes came about as a result of the environmental movement?
4. (a) List two environmental problems that affect the whole world. (b) What are nations doing about them?
5. (a) How did the Arab oil embargo change American attitudes toward oil? (b) What alternate fuels are Americans developing?
6. **CRITICAL THINKING** **Synthesizing Information** During the 1960s, American energy use increased by 52 percent. The increase slowed to 14 percent in the 1970s and 7 percent in the 1980s. Why might these changes have occurred?

 Writing to Learn

List five ways in which you might help protect the environment.

Bell Ringer

Have students locate your state on a map. Ask: What percentage of the state's population is Asian? What percentage is Latino? Do our communities and classrooms reflect the figures for the state?

Lesson Plan

1. Focus Changing social patterns have presented the United States with many challenges in the 1990s. In this section, students examine critical issues for African Americans, women, older Americans, Native Americans, immigrants, and the disabled.
2. Instruct Have students work in groups to research one group of new immigrants who came to the United States after 1965. Students can research distinctive foods, clothing, customs, contributions, and notable individuals of each immigrant group. Have each team present an oral report. You may also wish to include immigrant groups from the Caribbean and Central America not specifically mentioned in this chapter.

5
A Diverse Society

FIND OUT
- How have immigration patterns been changing?
- In what ways is the United States a diverse society?
- What issues face Americans as they approach a new century?

VOCABULARY mainstream

Historians used to describe the United States as a "melting pot." By this, they meant that people of different ethnic backgrounds came to the United States and blended into a single American culture.

Today, many Americans argue that the "melting pot" description is not accurate. They say that the United States is a multicultural society in which many distinct cultures exist side by side. In the words of Mayor Saul Ramirez of Laredo, Texas: "We're a salad. We're all different. All together, we make something good." Civil rights leader Jesse Jackson described the nation this way:

> ❝Our flag is red, white, and blue, but our nation is a rainbow—red, yellow, brown, black, and white. . . . America is not like a blanket—one piece of unbroken cloth, the same color, the same texture, the same size. America is more like a quilt—many patches, many pieces, many colors, many sizes, all woven and held together by a common thread. ❞

Native Americans

The nation's Native American population is now about 2,200,000. More than half live in urban areas. Some 700,000 live on

reservations, where they retain many of their customs and traditional ways of life.

Actions by Indians during the 1970s and 1980s brought numerous changes. New federal policies began to focus on the right of Native Americans to determine their own lives. At the same time, new laws opened up additional sources of jobs and income for Native Americans.

New policies. By 1970, the federal government had abandoned the policy of termination of Indian reservations. (See page 819.) Instead, Native Americans were encouraged to use their own organizations to govern their lives.

Educational policies also changed. The Indian Education Act of 1972 focused increased attention on the unique educational needs of American Indians. Community control of schools, parental involvement, and the need to include Native American culture and history in the curriculum were stressed.

In 1987, Congress passed the American Indian Religious Freedom Act. This law directed federal agencies not to interfere with Native American religious practices. For ex-

---

Native American Bank *Like other groups, Indians have moved to take greater control of their lives. Native American-owned businesses, such as this bank, are an important step toward economic independence.* **Economics** *Why might many Native Americans prefer to do business at an Indian-run bank?*

Our Multicultural Heritage
Background

Native Americans have differing views on promoting Indian interests. Traditionalists seek to maintain old values and lead a distinctively Native American way of life. Modernists, on the other hand, favor blending into the general American society. Many modernists have become doctors, engineers, or civil servants. Sometimes disputes arise when traditionalists and modernists compete for influence.

In some parts of the United States, disputes also pit Indians against their non-Indian neighbors. Some Native American groups have sued to recover land that had been taken from them. For example, the Taos Pueblo in New Mexico recovered Blue Lake, which was sacred to them but which had become part of a national park. Native Americans in Maine sued for the recovery of more than one third of the state. The courts awarded them $81 million with the provision that they be allowed to purchase 300,000 acres of land in Maine.

Critical Thinking
Analyzing Information

Tell students that the Navajo nation occupies the largest reservation in the United States — 16 million acres (6.5 million hectares) — covering parts of Utah, New Mexico, and Arizona. The Navajos have tried to encourage outside companies to set up operations on the reservation, hoping to improve the local economy. Ask: How would the presence of outside companies help the Navajo reservation and its people?

ample, the navy now allows Shoshone Indians to visit traditional healing springs on the China Lake Naval Weapons Center.

In 1988, Congress passed the Indian Gaming Regulatory Act. This law recognized that Indian nations had the right to make gambling legal within the boundaries of their reservations. Since the law's passage, more than 100 Native American groups in Florida, Washington, and other states have raised funds by running nightly bingo games or operating gambling casinos.

Control of cultural artifacts. Congress has also responded to Native American demands for control over artifacts from their past. A 1990 law requires museums to list the Indian objects in their collections. They must then give Native American groups a chance to reclaim such items as human remains and religious objects.

African Americans

African Americans are still struggling to gain full equality in American society. Despite the gains won by the civil rights movement, challenges such as racism and poverty remain.

Achievements on many fronts. The civil rights movement of the 1950s and 1960s toppled many of the barriers to African American advancement. New jobs opened up. Restrictions on voting were removed. Civil rights laws barred the most obvious forms of discrimination, such as segregated housing and public transportation.

African Americans began to make rapid advances in politics and government. In cities such as Chicago, Los Angeles, Atlanta, Seattle, and New York, voters elected black mayors. In 1989, Douglas Wilder of Virginia became the first of his race to be elected governor of a state. General Colin Powell was appointed the first African American chairman of the Joint Chiefs of Staff.

African Americans made notable advances in other areas, too. Reginald Lewis

BIOGRAPHY Toni Morrison *In novels such as* Song of Solomon *and* Jazz, *Toni Morrison creates vivid portraits of African American life. In 1993, Morrison became the first African American to win the Nobel prize for literature.* **Culture** *How does the title* Jazz *reflect the heritage of African Americans?*

became a Wall Street financier and one of the nation's richest men. Whitney Houston and Michael Jordan became superstars of the entertainment and sports worlds.

Jesse Jackson was an important African American spokesperson in the 1980s and 1990s. Jackson's Rainbow Coalition—made up of people of all colors working together for the good of all people—stressed the needs of the cities, nonwhites, farmers, and the unemployed.

Continuing problems. Despite such advances, many African Americans were still trapped by poverty in urban slums. Black and white leaders alike warned that an "underclass" of poorly educated, jobless blacks was growing.

Meanwhile, the wages of African Americans lagged behind those of whites. The unemployment rate for blacks was more

Chapter 30 • **871**

3. Close To close the lesson, have students decide on the most important fact or concept to remember for each subsection in Section 5.

 Lesson Planner

For a developed **Cooperative Learning** lesson plan, see the *Lesson Planner,* page 191.

Answer to Caption

Jazz as a form of music was created and developed by African Americans early in the twentieth century.

Our Multicultural Heritage

Milestone Have students read Preserving the Heritage of Native Americans, on page 90 of the *Our Multicultural Heritage* booklet. (Enrichment/Average)

Customized Reader

Primary Source For a magazine report on Native American issues, order article XA-6, The New Battle Over Indian Rights, from the *American History Customized Reader.* In this article, the author discusses contemporary treaty disputes. (Enrichment/Average)

Connections With Civics
Background

To provide greater educational and employment opportunities for African Americans and other minorities, the federal government has pursued a policy of *affirmative action* since the 1960s. Under this policy, special opportunities were provided for groups that had been discriminated against in the past. Critics argued that the policy encouraged reverse discrimination. If it was wrong to discriminate against a group in the past, they argued, it is just as wrong to favor the group now.

In 1978, the Supreme Court addressed affirmative action in *Regents of the University of California* v. *Bakke.* Allan Bakke, who is white, argued that he had been denied admission to the University of California medical school as a result of the school's racial quota system. The Court ruled in Bakke's favor. It said that a rigid quota system based on race was unconstitutional; but it also held that race could be considered in forming admissions policy.

Support for affirmative action has gradual-

ly weakened. Supreme Court rulings have limited the use of minority-preference plans. In 1996, the California Board of Regents voted to end all preferential admissions policies. President Clinton also issued a set of proposals to reduce minority preferences for federal contracts.

than twice that for whites. By 1993, more than 40 percent of African American children were living in poverty.

Civil rights leaders warned that the nation's commitment to equal rights seemed to be slipping. They urged renewed attention to the problems of inner-city poverty and racial discrimination.

In October 1995, hundreds of thousands of Americans, most of them African American men, gathered in Washington, D.C. They were participating in a "Million Man March" organized by the Nation of Islam and its leader, Louis Farrakhan. The rally urged black men to renew their efforts to build and strengthen their families and the black community.

Women Today

The women's rights movement has continued to press for equal treatment of women. It claims many successes.

New jobs. Prodded by affirmative action programs, businesses hired and promoted many talented women. For the first time, women held large numbers of managerial and professional jobs.

In government, women have taken increasingly prominent roles. In 1981, Sandra Day O'Connor became the first woman Justice of the United States Supreme Court. Twelve years later, a second woman, Ruth Bader Ginsburg, was appointed to the Court. Still, women held only a small percentage of all elective positions. In 1996, for example, women held only 7 of the 100 Senate seats.

Overall, women's incomes continued to rise. On average, however, women earned just 70 percent of what men earned. Some jobs were still seen as "women's work" and paid less than "men's work."

Changing role in the family. By the 1990s, almost 60 percent of American women worked outside the home. With many Americans struggling to make ends meet,

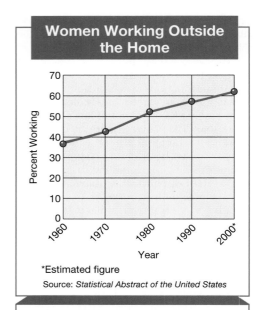

Women Working Outside the Home

Percent Working (y-axis: 0, 10, 20, 30, 40, 50, 60, 70)
Year (x-axis: 1960, 1970, 1980, 1990, 2000*)

*Estimated figure

Source: *Statistical Abstract of the United States*

GRAPH SKILLS *For most of the nation's history, the majority of American women did not work outside the home. By the 1980s, however, that situation changed dramatically.* • *During which period did the number of women working outside the home pass 50 percent?*

the two-job family had become typical of two-parent families.

At the same time, more and more households were headed by single women. Such households were likely to be poor. More than half the children in families headed by women lived below the poverty line. To address this problem, women's groups proposed reforms in child care and job training.

Americans With Disabilities

New laws have allowed people with disabilities to move into the mainstream of American life. Laws require ramped curbs, special parking spaces, and wheelchair lifts on buses.

872 • Chapter 30

Other laws have opened up new educational opportunities. For example, a 1975 law ensured access to public schools for children with disabilities. Some children with disabilities have been **mainstreamed,** or placed in regular classes. Others attend small classes with specialized help.

The Americans With Disabilities Act of 1990 has been called a "bill of rights" for people with disabilities. It outlaws discrimination against people with physical or mental disabilities.

New Immigrants

Since the 1970s, immigrants have been arriving in the United States at a faster rate than at any time since the start of the twentieth century. More than 7 million immigrants arrived in the 1980s. Even more will have come by the end of the 1990s. As in the past, the new arrivals are helping to reshape the nation.

From the 1920s to the 1960s, a quota system set limits on the number of people who could come from each nation. (See page 700.) The quota system favored immigrants from Europe. In 1965, Congress ended the quota system. New immigration laws made it easier for non-Europeans to enter the country. Today, most new Americans come from Asia, Latin America, and the Caribbean.

From Asia and the Pacific Islands. Wars and famines in Asia have pushed many people to seek new homes in other parts of the world. As you have read, "boat people" from Vietnam, Cambodia, and other Asian countries sought refuge in the United States. (See page 813.) Other immigrants came from such places as the Philippines, Bangladesh, and Thailand.

In the 1980s, the Asian American community doubled in size. Today, Asian Americans are the fastest-growing ethnic group. The United States has more than 7 million people of Asian heritage.

Author Amy Tan has written novels that portray the Chinese American experience. In *The Joy Luck Club*, the author has captured the mixed emotions that many immigrants feel. They are eager to adapt to American ways of life yet do not want to abandon the more familiar traditions of their homeland.

From Latin America and the Caribbean. Latinos have lived in what is now the United States since the days when Spain ruled Florida and the Southwest. In more recent years, new generations of Latinos have been arriving. Some of them fled civil wars

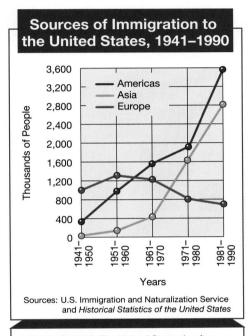

Sources of Immigration to the United States, 1941–1990

Thousands of People / Years

— Americas
— Asia
— Europe

Sources: U.S. Immigration and Naturalization Service and *Historical Statistics of the United States*

GRAPH SKILLS *The United States is often called a nation of immigrants. In recent years, the patterns of immigration have changed.*
● *Every 10 years, the government gathers information about the nation's population. In which 10-year period did people from the Americas become the largest group of immigrants?*

Chapter 30 • **873**

Answer to Graph Skills
1961–1970

 Transparencies

Our Multicultural Heritage Use the transparencies Immigration to the United States, 1960–1990, American Ancestors, Changing Ethnic Makeup of the United States, and Latino Population of the United States on pages C-23, C-31, C-33, and C-37 of *American History Transparencies.* Teaching suggestions can be found on pages C-4, C-6, C-7, and C-9. (Enrichment/Easy)

 Customized Reader

Primary Source For a Vietnamese cultural perspective, order article XA-5, Why We Eat Dogs: Cultural Differences in America, from the *American History Customized Reader.* In this article, journalist Andrew Lam discusses the idea that America is a collection of many disparate cultures. (Enrichment/Challenging)

Historical Sidelight
Background

Hearing-impaired students at Gallaudet College in Washington, D.C. used the protest tactics of the 1960s to bring about change. Gallaudet College was founded as a school for the hearing-impaired — but its presidents had always been people who could hear. In 1988, students rejected the choice of yet another school president who was not deaf. Their demonstrations attracted national attention. As a result, Gallaudet hired its first deaf president.

In 1987, actress Marlee Matlin (who is hearing-impaired) won an Academy Award for her performance in the movie *Children of a Lesser God.* At about the same time, organizations for hearing-impaired actors began to stage protests after learning that actors with hearing ability were cast as characters who could not hear.

Art Gallery Posters

Day and Crepuscule, by Tsing-fang Chen, appears in poster form in the *Art Gallery: Our Common Heritage Posters.* Lesson suggestions for the poster are available in the Teacher's Guide.

Answer to Art Gallery: Our Common Heritage

from Europe; from Asia, Latin America, and the Caribbean

" " Customized Reader

Primary Source For a magazine article about a popular Latino broadcasting figure, order article XA-7, A Hispanic Radio Personality, from the *American History Customized Reader.* Orlando Miranda, who has the longest running show in Chicago's Latino radio history, is described in this article. (Enrichment/Easy)

● **TSING-FANG CHEN** *Day and Crepuscule, 1986* ●

In 1986, Americans celebrated the one hundredth birthday of the Statue of Liberty. After a century of welcoming immigrants into New York harbor, the statue remains a symbol of hope and opportunity. As part of the birthday celebration, Taiwanese-born artist Tsing-fang Chen painted 100 studies of the statue. This one, Day and Crepuscule, *shows the statue at different times of day.* **American Traditions** *From what areas of the world did most immigrants come in 1886? In 1986?*

in Nicaragua, El Salvador, and Guatemala during the 1980s. Others fled harsh governments in such places as Cuba and Chile. Still others came to escape rural poverty in Mexico, Brazil, and other nations.

There are more than 22 million Latinos in the United States. They are the nation's second largest ethnic minority, after African Americans. The number of Latinos continues to grow. By the year 2000, Latinos are

874 • Chapter 30

Our Multicultural Heritage
Background

In 1980, there were only six people of Latino heritage in Congress. By 1990, there were twice as many. Since 1980, Hispanics have also served as mayors of several large cities. For example, Henry Cisneros became the first Mexican American mayor of San Antonio, Texas, since 1842. Cisneros went on to become Secretary of Housing and Urban Development in the Cabinet of President Clinton. The first Latinos to hold Cabinet positions were Laura R. Cavazos (Secretary of Education) and Manuel Lujan (Secretary of the Interior), who had been appointed by President Bush during the previous administration.

Connections With Language Arts
Activity

Interested students might like to learn more about the Immigration Reform and Control Act passed in 1986 (see page 875). After studying the act, have students write an editorial explaining why this act was passed, what its goals were, and how it has affected immigrants. Have students conclude their editorials with a statement about whether they think that passage of this legislation was a good idea. Students should give facts and examples to support their opinions.

expected to outnumber African Americans in the United States.

Hundreds of thousands of immigrants have also come from the islands of the Caribbean. They have come from such places as Jamaica, the Dominican Republic, and Haiti. The people are a rich mixture of African, Latino, and other backgrounds.

New immigration policy. People who want to immigrate to the United States must apply for admission. Those with relatives in the United States or with valuable job skills are usually accepted. Thousands of others, however, are turned down. In addition many people become illegal immigrants, entering the nation without permission.

In 1986, Congress tried to reduce illegal immigration by passing the *Immigration Reform and Control Act*. The act allowed people who had arrived illegally before 1982 to remain and apply for citizenship. To discourage further illegal immigration, the act imposed stiff fines on employers who hire illegal immigrants.

During the 1990s, states with large immigrant populations found it increasingly expensive to provide education, medical care, and other services to illegal immigrants. In 1994, California adopted a law that banned schooling and most health services for illegal immigrants. Two years later, Congress passed a new law aimed at further reducing illegal immigration. The law nearly doubled the number of officials who patrol the borders where immigrants try to enter illegally. It also allowed local police to arrest illegal immigrants who do manage to enter the country.

Trends and Issues of the Nineties

Rushing toward the twenty-first century, Americans face both opportunities and challenges. They are adjusting to a changing world. At the same time, they are grappling with new challenges.

An aging population. Birth rates have been declining. Also, thanks to better medical care, people are living longer. As a result, the average American is older now than in the past. About one person in every eight is over the age of 65.

Americans who are over age 65 have political strength. Many have joined organizations such as the Gray Panthers and the *American Association of Retired Persons* (AARP). Those groups pay special attention to issues related to Social Security, which provides pensions and medical care to senior citizens.

Educating the next generation. Americans believe that education is the key to a better life. The nation has made great strides in assuring an education for all its citizens. Since the 1960s, the federal government has supported a number of special programs. One program, Head Start, prepares needy preschoolers for elementary school. Today, about 85 percent of all Americans graduate from high school, compared with 60 percent in the early 1950s.

Despite these advances, critics say the schools are in trouble. Scores on standardized tests have dropped since the 1960s. In 1983, the Department of Education issued a report on the nation's schools, called "A Nation at Risk." The report concluded,

66If an unfriendly foreign power had attempted to impose on America the mediocre educational performance that exists today, we might well have viewed it as an act of war.99

The report called for tougher standards and longer school days and school years. It also recommended more homework and more attention to basic academic subjects. It proposed higher pay for teachers and better teacher training. "A Nation at Risk" touched off a flurry of educational reforms. In the 1990s, Congress debated a plan to establish a national system of standards and tests.

Transparencies

Our Multicultural Heritage Use the transparency, Languages Spoken in American Homes, on page C-35 of *American History Transparencies*. This transparency provides information on the cultural diversity of the United States. Teaching suggestions can be found on page C-8. (Enrichment/Average)

Customized Reader

Primary Source For a discussion of multiculturalism, order article XA-3, The Debate Over Multiculturalism in Schools, from the *American History Customized Reader*. The article summarizes the debate between those who advocate an Afrocentric approach to history and those who believe that the Afrocentric approach sometimes distorts historical facts. (Enrichment/Easy)

Our Multicultural Heritage

Biography Have students read the biography, Maggie Kuhn, Founder of the Gray Panthers, on page 89 of the *Our Multicultural Heritage* booklet. (Enrichment/Average)

Connections With Civics
Activity

Older Americans tend to use their political power more than younger Americans do. For example, in the presidential election of 1988, only 44.9 percent of Americans between the ages of 18 and 20 were registered, and of those, only 33.2 percent voted; but 78.4 percent of people over 65 were registered, and of those, 68.8 percent voted. Have students find comparable statistics for the most recent presidential election. Then have them discuss strategies for encouraging younger Americans to vote.

Cooperative Learning
Activity

Divide students into groups to conduct a poll on these two questions: (1) What are the four most serious problems that Americans face today? (2) What are the four most serious problems that Americans will face in the year 2015? Have each group poll a different age group and interview at least 10 people. Age groups might include 13 to 15, 16 to 19, 20 to 30, 31 to 40, 41 to 59, and those over 60.

Have groups compile their data and identify the top four responses. Each group can report its top four responses to each question along with a description of the age group it interviewed. Then, as a class, students can compare the responses from the different age groups and speculate about reasons for differences of opinion.

Combatting drug abuse. Around many urban schools are signs printed with the words "Drug-Free Zone." The signs point up one of the serious social problems of the 1990s—the use and abuse of illegal drugs. Schools are in the front lines in the war against drug abuse. They are trying to protect students from dangerous substances like cocaine and heroin.

Americans have been torn between two approaches to fighting drugs. Some favor treating the social problems that may lead to drug abuse. They emphasize treatment centers to help drug users end their addictions. Others see drug abuse as a criminal problem. They want stiffer penalties for drug dealers and users. Since 1980, the United States has spent billions of dollars pursuing drug smugglers and dealers. Yet drug abuse remains widespread.

Terrorism Since the 1960s, terrorist bombings, kidnappings, and hijackings became widespread in Europe, the Middle East, and elsewhere. Americans were sometimes the victims of such acts. However, not until the 1990s did terrorism within the United States seem a real threat. In 1993, a bomb rocked the World Trade Center in New York City. Two years later, a blast at a federal building in Oklahoma City killed 168 people, including 15 preschool children. In July 1996, an airliner exploded off the coast of New York, sparking new fears of terrorism.

In response, Americans debated ways to combat terrorism. Some wanted to increase security in public places and to give the government more freedom to tap the phones of suspected terrorists. Others feared that such measures would threaten the traditional freedom of American society.

Moving Into the Future

Americans face difficult problems in the coming years. Yet Americans have faced difficult challenges before. Indeed, in 1776, the challenges were so great that Americans were not even sure that their new nation would survive.

From the beginning, the motto of the United States has been *E pluribus unum*—"From out of many, one." This motto reflects the nation's varied regions, peoples, cultures, and traditions. This variety has always been a major source of the nation's strength. And so, the bold experiment continues. Under a single democratic government, the United States brings together many peoples. As we move toward the year 2000, Americans continue to celebrate freedom: the freedom to be ourselves, to respect one another, and to work together using each other's strengths to become a better nation.

SECTION 5 REVIEW

1. **Identify:** (a) Colin Powell, (b) Jesse Jackson, (c) Ruth Bader Ginsburg, (d) Americans With Disabilities Act of 1990, (e) Amy Tan, (f) Immigration Reform and Control Act, (g) American Association of Retired Persons.
2. **Define:** mainstream.
3. (a) Name the three main regions from which immigrants have come in recent years. (b) Why have these people left their homelands?
4. Explain how each of the following groups has made progress toward full equality and what problems each group still faces: (a) African Americans, (b) Native Americans, (c) women, (d) Americans with disabilities.
5. **CRITICAL THINKING Defending a Position** Would you be willing to give up some of your personal freedom in order to protect against terrorism? Why or why not?

ACTIVITY Writing to Learn
Create a slogan for a poster to be used in the war against drugs.

Answers to Section 5 Review

1. (a) Colin Powell, p. 871, (b) Jesse Jackson, p. 871, (c) Ruth Bader Ginsburg, p. 872, (d) Americans With Disabilities Act of 1990, p. 873, (e) Amy Tan, p. 873, (f) Immigration Reform and Control Act, p. 875, (g) American Association of Retired Persons, p. 875
2. mainstream, p. 873
3. (a) Asia, Latin America, and the Caribbean (b) Asians have come to escape poverty and war and to seek a better life; Latin Americans have come to escape war, political oppression, or poverty; people from the Caribbean have fled dictatorship and poverty.

4. (a) African Americans have found equality in voting; there are more African Americans in public office and more members of the middle class. (b) New federal policies enabled Native Americans to determine their own lives, and new laws have opened additional sources for jobs and income. They have gained autonomy of their education and religion, and have begun reclaiming artifacts of their past from museums. (c) Women have found more jobs and careers open to them, including political offices. (d) Congress has passed laws banning discrimination against people with disabilities. Each group still faces various forms of discrimination, including lower pay.
5. Possible Answer: Some students may feel that it is worth enduring longer luggage searches at airports or computer security checks for jobs or other reasons, in exchange for greater safety from terrorism. Others may feel that the loss of personal freedom is an intrusion by the government and, in the long run, will hurt Americans more than will terrorism.

CONNECTIONS

ARTS · SCIENCES · GEOGRAPHY · WORLD · ECONOMICS · CIVICS

"On the Pulse of Morning"

Maya Angelou

December 1, 1992, dawned as an ordinary day for poet Maya Angelou—that is, if any day can be ordinary in the life of a woman who has been a dancer, singer, song lyric writer, actor, director, and teacher. Then came a telephone call from President-elect Bill Clinton. He called to ask Angelou if she would write a poem for his inauguration and read it at the ceremony.

For the next few weeks, Angelou worked day and night to shape the poem she would call "On the Pulse of Morning." Below is an excerpt from the poem she created and read at President Clinton's inauguration on January 20, 1993.

❝Lift up your faces, you have a piercing
   need
For this bright morning dawning for you.
History, despite its wrenching pain,
Cannot be unlived, but if faced
With courage, need not be lived again.

Lift up your eyes upon
This day breaking for you.
Give birth again

To the dream.
Women, children, men
Take it into the palms of your hands,
Mold it into the shape of your most
Private need. Sculpt it into
The image of your most public self.

Lift up your hearts
Each new hour holds new chances
For a new beginning.
Do not be wedded forever
To fear, yoked eternally
To brutishness.

The horizon leans forward,
Offering you space to place new steps of
   change.
Here, on the pulse of this fine day
You may have the courage
To look up and out and upon me, the Rock,
   the River, the Tree, your country. . . .

Here, on the pulse of this new day
You may have the grace to look up and out
And into your sister's eyes, and into
Your brother's face, your country
And say simply
Very simply
With hope—
Good morning.❞

■ What is Maya Angelou asking Americans to do?

 ACTIVITY Prepare a dramatic reading of "On the Pulse of Morning" to present in class.

Interdisciplinary CONNECTIONS

For worksheets establishing connections between the Chapter 30 main idea, People Face the Future, and five other disciplines, see the *Interdisciplinary Connections* booklet. (Enrichment)
- **Sciences** The Technological Life, page 176 (Easy)
- **Geography** Demographics, page 177 (Average)
- **World** Who Should Save the Earth?, page 178 (Average)
- **Economics** A Looming Crisis, page 179 (Challenging)
- **Civics** Everyone Is a Citizen, page 180 (Average)

Answer to Connections

Possible Answer: To face the future with courage and hope; to shape the future so that all Americans have the possibility of fulfilling their dreams.

ACTIVITY

Guided Instruction Allow students to work together to prepare their readings of the poem. Partners can listen to each other and make suggestions for improving the readings. Some students may want to work in small groups, each member preparing a section of the poem.

Transparencies

Interdisciplinary Connections Use the transparency Looking at the Future on page B-91 of *American History Transparencies*. Teaching suggestions can be found on page B-32. (Enrichment/Challenging)

Team-Teaching Suggestion
Art

You might work with an art teacher to have students develop a series of images to illustrate Angelou's poem. Students might photograph images in the real world, create their own artwork, or put together a collage of images taken from news magazines and other publications. Students can transfer the images to slides and organize them as a slide presentation to accompany their dramatic readings of the poem.

Team-Teaching Suggestion
Literature

You might work with a literature teacher to present a lesson on other literary works by Maya Angelou. An excellent starting place is her autobiography, *I Know Why the Caged Bird Sings.* Students might then read one of Angelou's novels, essays, or several of her other poems and discuss with the class the major themes of her writing.

Answers to Reviewing the Main Ideas

1. (a) Possible Answer: technological breakthroughs such as CAT scans, new vaccines, organ transplants (b) Possible Answer: AIDS is a growing problem for which, as yet, there is no solution.

2. American astronauts were the first people to visit the moon; an unmanned spacecraft went to the edges of the solar system.

3. (a) Cable systems spread throughout the country. (b) Viewers had many more channels to choose from.

4. Economic challenges include reducing the national debt, reducing the trade deficit, and continuing to change from a manufacturing economy to a service economy.

5. (a) Possible Answer: air and water pollution, global warming, breakdown of the ozone layer (b) Possible Answer: antipollution and recycling laws at home, a search for cleaner sources of energy, and international agreements to reduce use of certain chemicals

6. Recent immigrants have come mainly from Asia, Latin America, and the Caribbean rather than from Europe.

7. In 1986, Congress passed a law imposing stiff penalties on employers who hire illegal immigrants. A 1996 law increased border patrols to limit the entrance of illegal immigrants.

8. rehabilitation in drug treatment centers and imposing stiffer criminal penalties for drug pushers and users

Answers to Thinking Critically

1. (a) Possible Answer: Nuclear energy is a clean alternative to oil or coal for producing electricity; however, it also produces toxic waste. Nuclear power plants have had accidents, which have resulted in the release of radioactivity into the air. (b) Possible Answer: We would be better off without nuclear energy because its destructive uses and the dangers of producing it outweigh its positive uses.

2. (a) Possible Answer: Both movements were based on a desire to better one's standard of

---

Summary

- Research has brought important advances in science and technology.
- New technology has changed the entertainment industry.
- Americans have been debating the proper size and role of government in a time of economic challenge from abroad.
- The United States has worked with nations around the world to protect and restore the environment.
- As patterns of immigration change, the United States has been enriched by the many new ethnic groups that help make up American society.

Reviewing the Main Ideas

1. (a) Describe one recent achievement of medical science. (b) Describe one challenge facing medical science.

2. What were two achievements of the American space program?

3. (a) How did television change in the 1980s? (b) How did this change affect viewers?

4. Describe three economic challenges the nation faces in the 1990s.

5. (a) What problems have environmentalists pointed out? (b) What steps have Americans taken to deal with those problems?

6. How do recent immigrants differ from past immigrants?

7. What steps has the nation taken to stop illegal immigration?

8. What two approaches do Americans favor to reduce drug abuse?

Thinking Critically

1. Drawing Conclusions We speak of technological "advances," but technology can create problems as well as solve them. (a) List the good and bad effects of one of the

technological developments mentioned in Chapter 30. (b) Would we be better off with this technological development or without it? Explain.

2. Linking Past and Present (a) How is the move to the Sunbelt today similar to the westward movement of early settlers? (b) How is it different?

3. Defending a Position Do you think that schools in the United States should establish tougher standards for students and have longer school days and school years? Why or why not?

Applying Your Skills

1. Making a Generalization Based on your study of history this year, make a generalization about a trend in American life since the 1600s. List two or three facts to support your generalization.

2. Ranking List four events or developments in science and technology that you have read about in this chapter. Rank them according to their importance. Explain your ranking.

Thinking About Geography

Match the letters on the map with the following places: **1.** Indonesia, **2.** South Korea, **3.** Japan, **4.** Hawaii, **5.** Taiwan, **6.** Philippines. **Region** Name two nations in North America that are part of the Pacific Rim.

---

iving. (b) Possible Answer: The move to the Sunbelt is easier and less time-consuming than the westward movement. Also, people are moving to the Sunbelt because of jobs, while most people moved West for cheap land.

3. Possible Answers: Yes, because Americans now have to compete in a global economy with students in other countries who are better educated because they study longer and harder; no, because doing so would only prolong the frustration of children who are not learning now; it is more important to improve the learning that goes on in American schools as they now exist.

Answers to Applying Your Skills

1. Possible Answer: Women and minority groups are gaining power and taking more leadership roles. These groups were at first denied voting rights, but they now have gained the vote; job opportunities were limited for women and minorities, but now laws forbid job discrimination.

2. Possible Answer: the dialysis machine, artificial heart, pacemaker, and air bag would rank near the top because they all save lives directly; the CAT scan has the potential to save lives; computers have probably affected the world in general more significantly than any other recent development; spacecraft allow scientists to advance scientific knowledge; cable TV affects masses of people, but it ranks at the bottom because its value is limited primarily to entertainment.

INTERDISCIPLINARY ACTIVITY

Looking Toward the Future

Form into groups to review what you have read about American life of today and tomorrow. Follow the suggestions below to write, draw, or record to show what you have learned. You may use the textbook, encyclopedias, atlases, or other materials in your classroom library to complete the tasks. Be able to name your sources of information when you have finished the activity.

Fiber optic cables

HISTORIANS Find out more about recent advances in medical science. Make a list of 15 medical breakthroughs during the past 30 years. Then create a time line showing these events. Below each event on the time line, write a sentence explaining why it is important.

ARTISTS Choose an environmental issue that you think is important. Then create a poster urging Americans to take action on this issue. Be sure to include information on your poster that describes the problem and why it needs to be resolved.

SCIENTISTS Find out more about alternative energy sources, such as solar energy, nuclear energy, wind power, and water power. Make a chart showing the advantages and disadvantages of each. Accompany your chart with diagrams that show how each energy source creates power. Include a recommendation about the alternative energy sources you think Americans should develop.

Hologram of blood vessels

MUSICIANS Using radio, tapes, and CDs, make an audiotape with examples of different types of popular music today. Write and record an introduction for each selection. Play your tape for the class.

ECONOMISTS Plan a TV talk show titled "Economy 2000." Divide into groups to find out more about the problems facing the American economy as we move toward the year 2000 and to suggest some solutions. Then present your findings in the talk show. Use charts and graphs to illustrate the discussion.

 Plan a Looking Toward the Future Day. Invite members of other classes to a show of your completed activities.

A space satellite

Answers to Thinking About Geography

1. D 2. E 3. A 4. B 5. F
6. C
Region: Possible Answers: Canada, United States, Mexico

Assessment

Chapter Resources Binder For a more comprehensive evaluation of student understanding of this chapter, assign Chapter Tests A and B and/or Extra Unit Questions from Unit 9, pages 49–54 and 57–59.
Computer Test Bank You can use Chapter Tests and Extra Unit Questions to create your own tests for both testing and retesting.

Alternative Assessment

Chapter Resources Binder See the Alternative Assessment booklet in the *Social Studies Educator's Handbook* series.
Portfolio You might meet with students to choose appropriate work from the chapter for inclusion in their portfolios.

Interdisciplinary ACTIVITY

Learning Styles

The following chart indicates the activities appropriate for different learning styles.

Visual Learners
Historians
Artists
Scientists
Economists

Auditory Learners
Musicians
Economists

Kinesthetic Learners
Historians
Artists
Scientists

Evaluation

Historians Information on time lines must be accurate and visually clear. Explanatory sentences should reflect any relationships that exist between one medical breakthrough and another.
Artists Posters should be attractive and persuasive. They should reflect an understanding of the causes of the environmental problem and the possible solutions.
Scientists Information on the charts must be accurate, concise, and organized into suitable categories. Recommendations should reflect an understanding of how the alternative energy sources create power and should integrate the advantages and disadvantages of each.
Musicians Selections included on audiotapes should demonstrate a familiarity and knowledge of popular music. Students' introductions should point out similarities and differences among the selections and might reflect the attitude of the student toward each selection.
Economists Presentations should be informative and lively. Panelists should demonstrate knowledge of different points of view about economic problems and solutions. Charts and graphs must be relevant to the discussion, visually clear, and accurate.

Author Note

Born in Jalcocotán, Mexico, Ernesto Galarza (1905–1984) spent the early part of his career working with the Pan-American Union and the National Farm Labor Union. He later acted as a consultant to several government committees and projects relating to immigration and Latino issues. Galarza's autobiographical *Barrio Boy* (1971) is considered a groundbreaking work in revealing the Chicano (Mexican American) experience. During the 1970s, Galarza also created the *Colección Mini-Libros,* the first major collection of books for young readers written by a Chicano author.

Vocabulary

Have students look up and discuss the words *withering, radiant, maneuvering, idiocies, anchorage, recitations, consultations,* and *phonetic* before they read the passage. Ask: Are *withering* and *radiant* fairly similar in meaning or are they almost opposites? From what you know or can imagine about ships, what might an *anchorage* be? Which of these words seem to relate to the study of language?

Prereading Focus

Have students review Chapter 30, Section 5 (especially pages 873–875). As they read the literature selection, encourage them to comment on how young Galarza's experience might have been similar to the experiences of other young Latino immigrants.

Motivation/Prior Knowledge

Encourage students to recall the kinds of things they would expect to learn in first grade. Ask: Which learning goals would become much more difficult for a student who did not speak English?

Purpose-Setting Question

Read aloud the Introduction to the excerpt. Then ask: What do you think would be the greatest

History Through
LITERATURE

Barrio Boy
Ernesto Galarza

Introduction   The United States continues to attract millions of immigrants. Like those who came earlier, they face the double challenge of adjusting to life in a new land while preserving their cultural identity. Ernesto Galarza came to the United States from Mexico. In this excerpt from his autobiography, *Barrio Boy,* Galarza recalls his early years at school in his adopted country.

Vocabulary   Before you read the selection, find the meaning of these words in a dictionary: withering, radiant, maneuvering, idiocies, anchorage, recitations, consultations, phonetic

Miss Ryan took me to a seat at the front of the room, into which I shrank—the better to survey her. She was, to skinny, somewhat runty me, of a withering height when she patrolled the class. And when I least expected it, there she was, crouching by my desk, her blond radiant face level with mine, her voice patiently maneuvering me over the awful idiocies of the English language.

During the next few weeks Miss Ryan overcame my fears of tall, energetic teachers as she bent over my desk to help me with a word in the pre-primer. Step by step, she loosened me and my classmates from the safe anchorage of the desks for recitations at the blackboard and consultations at her desk. Frequently she burst into happy announcements to the whole class. "Ito can read a sentence," and small Japanese Ito, squint-eyed and shy, slowly read aloud while the class listened in wonder: "Come, Skipper, come. Come and run."

The Korean, Portuguese, Italian, and Polish first graders had similar moments of glory, no less shining than mine the day I conquered "butterfly," which I had been persistently pronouncing in standard Spanish as boo-ter-flee. "Children," Miss Ryan called for attention. "Ernesto has learned how to pronounce *butterfly*!" And I proved it with a perfect imitation of Miss Ryan. From that celebrated success, I was soon able to match Ito's progress as a sentence reader with "Come, butterfly, come fly with me."

Like Ito and several other first graders who did not know English, I received private lessons from Miss Ryan in the closet, a narrow hall off the classroom with a door at each end. Next to one of these doors Miss Ryan placed a large chair for herself and a small one for me. Keeping an eye on the class through the open door she read with me about sheep in the meadow and a frightened chicken going to see the king, coaching me out of my phonetic ruts in words like *pasture, bow-wow-wow, hay,* and *pretty,* which to my Mexican ear and eye had so many unnecessary sounds and letters. . . . The main reason I was graduated with honors from the first

adjustment for a student in Galarza's position? Why?

Discussion Questions

1. Why does the narrator describe the English language as filled with "awful idiocies"? (Possible Answer: English is full of expressions that cannot be translated exactly; there are many exceptions to the rules regarding English grammar, usage, and mechanics.)

2. According to the narrator, why did he do so well in first grade? (He was inspired by Miss Ryan, a beloved teacher who helped and encouraged him.)
3. Miss Hopley, who is mentioned in the final paragraph of the excerpt, was the principal of Lincoln School. What does this information add to your understanding of the passage? (Possible Answer: It shows that the administration and the teachers

were interested in the children's progress and wanted them to take pleasure in their various cultural heritages.)

grade was that I had fallen in love with Miss Ryan. Her radiant, no-nonsense character made us either afraid not to love her or love her so we would not be afraid. I am not sure which. It was not only that we sensed she was with it, but also that she was with us.

Like the first grade, the rest of the Lincoln School was a sampling of the lower part of town where many races made their home. My pals in the second grade were Kazushi, whose parents spoke only Japanese; Matti, a skinny Italian boy; and Manuel, a fat Portuguese who would never get into a fight but wrestled you to the ground and just sat on you. Our assortment of nationalities included Koreans, Yugoslavs, Poles, Irish, and home-grown Americans.

At Lincoln, making us into Americans did not mean scrubbing away what made us originally foreign. The teachers called us as our parents did, or as close as they could pronounce our names in Spanish or Japanese. No one was ever scolded or punished for speaking in his native tongue on the playground. Matti told the class about his mother's down quilt, which she had made in Italy with the fine feathers of a thousand geese. Encarnación acted out how boys learned to fish in the Philippines. I astounded the third grade with the story of my travels on a stagecoach, which nobody else in the class had seen except in the museum at Sutter's Fort. After a visit to the Crocker Art Gallery and its collection of heroic paintings of the golden age of

California, someone showed a silk scroll with a Chinese painting. Miss Hopley herself had a way of expressing wonder over these matters before a class, her eyes wide open until they popped slightly. It was easy for me to feel that becoming a proud American, as she said we should, did not mean feeling ashamed of being a Mexican.

Thinking About Literature

1. Who attended the Lincoln School?
2. How did Miss Ryan encourage students to learn English?
3. **CRITICAL THINKING Analyzing Information** Galarza comments that, "At Lincoln, making us into Americans did not mean scrubbing away what made us originally foreign." (a) What does he mean? (b) Why is this an important idea?

ACTIVITY Make a list of the countries that Ernesto and his classmates came from. Then draw a map of the world, and locate the countries on it. Based on the map, make a generalization about immigrants to the United States.

Getting Involved

Issues for Today

You have just finished a year's study of American history. You have learned about the people and events that have shaped our nation. You have also tried to connect those past events with your life today.

At the beginning of your study, you were introduced to five major issues of American history: Multicultural Nation, Spirit of Democracy, Changing Economy, Environment, and Global Interdependence. These issues, as you recall, help tie the facts of American history together. Tracing these issues helped you to understand not just *what happened* in American history but *why* and *how* it happened.

On the following pages, you will have a chance to explore these issues of American history in a slightly different way. First, Milestones lists the major events and dates related to each issue. A Case Study tells how people your age turned ideas about each issue into action. Finally, a suggested activity related to the issue gives you a chance to *get involved*.

Multicultural Nation

CASE STUDY
Helping Immigrant Children

Every year, thousands of immigrants enter the United States from all over the world. The new arrivals have to learn a new language, find a place to live, get a job. Children have to make new friends and attend American schools, which may seem strange to them. For many, the first years in their new land can be lonely and confusing.

In New York City, members of the City Volunteer Corps (CVC) wondered if they could do something to help new immigrants. CVC is a youth service group that works to improve the quality of life in the city. CVC members come from many different cultural backgrounds, and many are recent immigrants themselves.

The CVC group volunteered in a Korean Youth Center that served some of New York City's large Korean population. The volunteers tutored children in the center's after-school program. They helped the children to read English, to complete their homework assignments, and to improve their conversational skills. They also organized games and activities.

The CVC members helped hundreds of Korean children adapt to their new lives in the United States. Their work had another effect, too. Their daily contacts with the Korean children gave the young CVC members a chance to know and appreciate people of another culture.

Getting Involved

Work with your classmates to find out if there are immigrants or other new residents in your community. What problems do these people face? Do they need help with language or customs? Do they need advice about finding homes, jobs, stores, or schools? Identify ways in which you can help. Then organize a program to help the newcomers feel more at home.

MILESTONES

70,000–50,000 years ago
First Americans arrive from Asia

1500s–1700s
Europeans found colonies

1619
Africans arrive in Virginia

1840s
Immigration from Northern Europe continues

1880s
Immigration from Southern and Eastern Europe begins

1980s
Immigration from Latin America, Asia, and Caribbean increases

Spirit of Democracy

CASE STUDY
Celebrating the First Amendment

In 1989, a group of students from Scottsdale, Arizona, visited the Lincoln Memorial in Washington, D.C. They recalled that Martin Luther King, Jr., had delivered a now-famous speech on the steps of the Memorial in 1963. Before a hushed crowd of 200,000 people, King spoke of his dream: a United States in which all people were truly equal.

Inspired by this memory, the students came up with the idea of setting up a museum in vacant exhibit space at the Lincoln Memorial. The exhibit would honor Dr. King's speech.

To promote their plan, the students created information packets and wrote letters to officials. They rounded up the support of local officials, civic groups, and the press. Finally, they made another trip to Washington to meet with the National Park Service and a subcommittee of the House of Representatives.

The group's hard work paid off. The plan was approved. A new exhibit, informally called the Legacy of Lincoln, opened at the Lincoln Memorial at the end of 1994.

The exhibit honors rights guaranteed by the First Amendment to the Constitution—freedom of speech, religion, press, assembly, and petition. It includes displays showing the many ways in which those rights have been expressed at the Lincoln Memorial. Among these are video excerpts of Dr. King's 1963 speech.

Getting Involved

Find out when your representative to Congress will be in your area. Then arrange a class visit to the representative's district office. Plan for the visit by researching several issues that Congress is currently debating. Make a list of questions to ask your representative about these issues.

884 • Getting Involved

Changing Economy

CASE STUDY
Volunteering in a Children's Center

Volunteers have always been a part of American life. By giving their time to hospitals, libraries, schools, and fire departments, they have enabled their communities to expand services without increasing costs. Today, volunteers are more important than ever. Their services form an important part of the economy.

One volunteer who made a difference in his community is 14-year-old Dennis Chisholm, Jr. Dennis lives in Winston-Salem, North Carolina. He volunteered to work at the Children's Center for the Physically Handicapped. He gave his time during summer vacations and after school.

Dennis performed a variety of tasks at the center. He helped feed the children and assisted them with physical therapy. He also helped adapt computer equipment and software for their use. He even started a weekly newsletter and encouraged the children to act as reporters.

For the children at the center, Dennis was a valuable friend and helper. For the people who run the center, he was an important resource. Like many of the nation's social agencies, Winston-Salem's Children's Center had suffered severe cutbacks in spending. Only with help from volunteers like Dennis can the center fulfill its goal of service.

Getting Involved

With your class, set up a service to run errands or do other chores for elderly or shut-in members of your community. Possible services can include mailing letters, shopping, light cleaning, or simply reading to people. Create and distribute a flyer advertising your service. Provide a telephone number where you can be reached. Take turns processing the calls and assigning volunteers to do the work.

MILESTONES

5,000 years ago
Farming in Americas

1600s
Farming and trade in colonies

1790
First factory

1800
Interchangeable parts

Early 1800s
Internal improvements

1869
Transcontinental railroad

Late 1800s
Rise of industry and big business

1890s
Overseas trade increases

1913
Assembly line

1930s
Government role increases

1970s
Computer Age

1980s
Shift from manufacturing to services

1993
NAFTA

Getting Involved • **885**

CASE STUDY
Setting Up a Recycling Center

The people of Sprague, Washington, had never paid much attention to all the talk about recycling. They simply saved up their trash and then took it to the local dump. Getting rid of garbage this way was easy—and cheap.

Then the dump closed. Sprague residents had to hire a company to collect their garbage. They were shocked at the cost. For the first time, garbage became an issue in the tiny farming town.

Chris Victor, a local teenager, decided to act. Chris belonged to a community service group called Camp Fire. He suggested that the group set up a recycling center in Sprague. He pointed out that they could reduce garbage collection bills *and* help the environment.

The teens set to work. First, they scouted possible places for the center. They decided that an unused portion of Sprague's senior citizen's center would be a good location. The group then presented their plan to the mayor, who gave his approval.

Next, the group set up bins for glass, aluminum, paper, and cardboard. They also made a video to educate the town about the program. When the program was underway, the group emptied the bins once a month. They hauled the contents to a nearby recycling plant.

From the start, the program was a great success. In the first month alone, the center collected 1,500 pounds of paper, 500 pounds of glass, 100 pounds of aluminum cans, and 1,000 pounds of cardboard!

Getting Involved

With your classmates, set up a recycling program for your school. First, decide what you will recycle and where. Then present your plan to the teacher for approval. Finally, create a poster explaining your program. Arrange to bring what you collect to a recycling plant.

Global Interdependence

CASE STUDY
Protecting the World's Children

Eighth graders in Readington, New Jersey, were studying about children in different parts of the world. As part of their studies, they read about the United Nations Convention on the Rights of the Child. This international treaty is designed to protect the basic rights of all children. These rights include the right to food, shelter, and health care. They also include freedom of speech and freedom from discrimination.

The Readington students were troubled to think that some children in the world were denied these basic rights. "We wanted to help them," they said. They set out to learn more about the UN treaty.

The students discovered that 102 nations had ratified the Convention on the Rights of the Child. The United States, however, was not one of them. The students decided to try to change that.

The class wrote a petition urging the United States to approve the treaty. They sent the petition to more than 40 schools, asking other students to support their campaign. More than 2,000 students signed the petition! They also wrote letters to government leaders and to local newspapers, calling for approval of the treaty.

By the end of the school year, the United States had still not ratified the treaty. The Readington students were encouraged, however. They had made people aware of the treaty to protect the rights of children around the world.

Getting Involved

Contact an international agency such as the UN or the Red Cross to find out what you might do to help children in troubled areas of the world. For example, you might collect and sort needed items such as clothing, food, medical supplies, books, and so on. Form into groups and assign members tasks needed to carry out the project.

MILESTONES

1492
Columbian Exchange begins

1823
Monroe Doctrine

1854
Trade opens with Japan

1914
Panama Canal

1933
Good Neighbor Policy

1945
United Nations

1948
Marshall Plan

1949
NATO

1961
Peace Corps

1961
Alliance for Progress

1975
Helsinki Agreement

1993
NAFTA

Getting Involved • **887**

Reference Section

EUROPE

0   250 Miles

0   250 Kilometers

Pacific Time Zone

Mountain Time Zone

Central Time Zone

CANADA

130°W 125°W 120°W 115°W 50°N 110°W 105°W 100°W

45°N

Seattle
Spokane
WASHINGTON 1889
Olympia

Great Falls

Minot

Grand Forks

NORTH DAKOTA 1889
Bismarck

Portland
Salem
Eugene

Helena ★ **MONTANA 1889**

Billings

OREGON 1859

IDAHO 1890
★ Boise

40°N

Pocatello

WYOMING 1890
Casper

SOUTH DAKOTA 1889
Rapid City Pierre ★
Sioux Falls

Reno
Carson City
NEVADA 1864

Ogden
Great Salt Lake
★ Salt Lake City

Cheyenne ★

NEBRASKA 1867

Sacramento ★
San Francisco
Oakland
San Jose

UTAH 1896

Denver ★
Colorado Springs

Lincoln ★

35°N

CALIFORNIA 1850

Las Vegas

COLORADO 1876

KANSAS 1861

Wichita

Los Angeles
Long Beach
Salton Sea
San Diego

★ Santa Fe
Albuquerque

OKLAHOMA 1907
Oklahoma City ★

ARIZONA 1912
Phoenix ★

NEW MEXICO 1912

PACIFIC OCEAN

30°N

Tucson

Las Cruces

Dallas
Ft. Worth

El Paso

TEXAS 1845

120°W 115°W 110°W

Austin ★

San Antonio

MEXICO

160°W 155°W
Hawaii–Aleutian Time Zone
Honolulu ★ **HAWAII 1959**

180° 170°W 160°W 150°W
RUSSIA Alaska Time Zone
Arctic Circle
140°W 130°W
PACIFIC OCEAN
20°N
Fairbanks
ALASKA 1959
CANADA
Pacific Time Zone

0 50 100 Miles
0 50 100 150 Kilometers

Anchorage
60°N

50°N 170°E
Hawaii–Aleutian Time Zone
PACIFIC OCEAN

BERING SEA
Gulf of Alaska
Juneau ★

25°N

0 200 400 Miles
0 200 400 600 Kilometers

100°W

892 • Reference Section

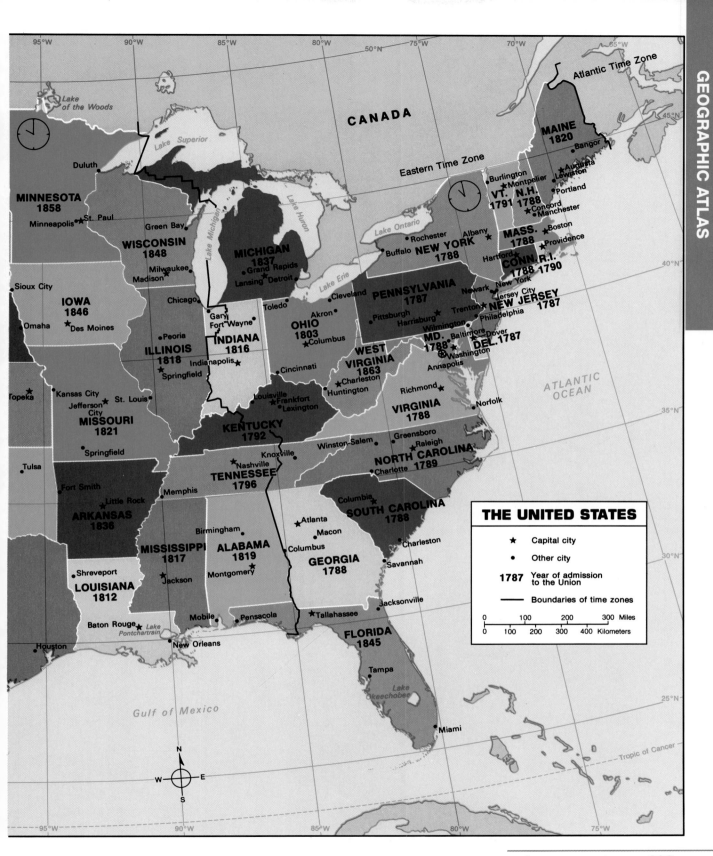

Atlantic Time Zone

CANADA

Eastern Time Zone

MAINE
1820
• Bangor

• Burlington
Montpelier ★ • Augusta
Lewiston
VT. N.H. • Portland
1791 1788
★ Concord ★
Manchester

MASS. • Boston
1788
• Rochester • Albany ★ ★ • Providence
NEW YORK Hartford **CONN. R.I.**
• Buffalo **1788** ★ **1788 1790**
Newark • • New York
PENNSYLVANIA Jersey City **NEW JERSEY**
1787 • **1787**
• Pittsburgh Harrisburg ★ • Trenton ★
• Philadelphia
Wilmington • ★ Dover
MD. Baltimore • **DEL. 1787**
1788 ★ • Washington
Annapolis

Lake Superior

• Duluth

MINNESOTA
1858
Minneapolis ★ • St. Paul

• Green Bay

WISCONSIN
1848
• Milwaukee
Madison ★

Lake Michigan

MICHIGAN
1837
• Grand Rapids
Lansing ★ • Detroit

Lake Huron

Lake Ontario

Lake Erie

• Cleveland

• Sioux City

IOWA
1846
• Omaha
★ Des Moines

• Chicago

• Toledo

• Akron

OHIO
1803
★ Columbus

Gary •
Fort Wayne •

INDIANA
1816

• Peoria

ILLINOIS
1818
Indianapolis ★
★ Springfield

• Cincinnati

WEST
VIRGINIA
1863
• Charleston
• Huntington

• Richmond ★

ATLANTIC
OCEAN

• Topeka

Kansas City • ★ St. Louis
Jefferson •
City
MISSOURI
1821
• Springfield

Louisville •
Frankfort ★
• Lexington

KENTUCKY
1792

VIRGINIA
1788

• Norfolk

Winston-Salem •

• Greensboro
• Raleigh ★

• Tulsa

• Knoxville
Nashville ★

TENNESSEE
1796

NORTH CAROLINA
Charlotte • **1789**

• Fort Smith

• Little Rock

• Memphis

ARKANSAS
1836

• Columbia ★

SOUTH CAROLINA
1788

• Atlanta ★
• Macon

• Charleston

• Birmingham

MISSISSIPPI
1817

ALABAMA
1819
• Columbus

GEORGIA
1788

• Savannah

• Shreveport
Jackson ★ Montgomery ★

LOUISIANA
1812

• Mobile • Pensacola

★ Tallahassee

• Jacksonville

• Baton Rouge ★ Lake
Pontchartrain

• Houston
• New Orleans

FLORIDA
1845

Gulf of Mexico

• Tampa

Lake
Okeechobee

• Miami

Tropic of Cancer

THE UNITED STATES

★ Capital city

• Other city

1787 Year of admission
to the Union

── Boundaries of time zones

0   100   200   300 Miles
0 100 200 300 400 Kilometers

N
W ✦ E
S

95°W 90°W 85°W 80°W 75°W 70°W 65°W
50°N 45°N 40°N 35°N 30°N 25°N

Reference Section • **893**

PHYSICAL FEATURES

Elevations

- Above 10,000 feet (3,000 meters)
- 7,000–10,000 feet (2,000–3,000 meters)
- 3,000–7,000 feet (1,000–2,000 meters)
- 700–3,000 feet (200–1,000 meters)
- 0–700 feet (0–200 meters)
- Below sea level

CAPE COD

Long Island

Chesapeake Bay

CAPE HATTERAS

ATLANTIC COASTAL PLAIN

APPALACHIAN MOUNTAINS

Lake Ontario

Lake Erie

Tennessee R.

Lake Huron

Lake Michigan

Lake Superior

PLAIN

COASTAL

GULF

INTERIOR

PLAINS

Mississippi R.

Missouri R.

OZARK
PLATEAU

OUACHITA
MTS.

Arkansas R.

Red R.

Platte R.

GREAT

PLAINS

LLANO
ESTACADO

BLACK
HILLS

Pikes Peak

Mt. Elbert

Rio Grande

ROCKY

MOUNTAINS

Colorado R.

Snake R.

Great
Salt
Lake

GRAND
CANYON

Missouri R.

Columbia R.

GREAT
BASIN

Mt. Rainier

CASCADE
RANGE

SIERRA NEVADA

Mt. Whitney

N E S W

0   250   500   500 Miles
0   250   500   750 Kilometers

BROOKS RANGE

Mt. McKinley

0   500 Miles
0   750 Kilometers

Kauai
Oahu
Molokai
Maui
Mauna
Kea
Hawaii

0   100 Miles
0   100 Kilometers

POPULATION DISTRIBUTION

Persons per square mile	Persons per square kilometer
Over 500	Over 200
100-499	40-199
50-99	20-39
5-49	2-19
0-4	0-1

N E S W

500 Miles
250   250
250   500
750 Kilometers

ALASKA

500 Miles
0   0
750 Kilometers

HAWAII

100 Miles
0   0
100 Kilometers

ECONOMIC ACTIVITIES

Agriculture

- Dairy cattle, hay
- Livestock, feed grains
- Wheat
- General farming
- Fruits and vegetables
- Grazing

Industry

- Iron and steel works
- Chemicals
- Petroleum and coal products
- Lumber
- Furniture
- Textiles

N E S W

250   500   750 Kilometers
250   500   500 Miles

750 Kilometers
500 Miles

100 Miles
100 Kilometers

NATURAL RESOURCES

	Aluminum		Copper		Magnesium		Natural gas		Sulphur
▲		●		+		◄		◔	
	Chromium		Gold		Manganese		Nickel		Tin
△		■		●		◆		■	
	Coal		Iron Ore		Mercury		Oil		Uranium
◖		▲		○		✚		◆	
	Cobalt		Lead		Molybdenum		Silver		Zinc
◆		◔		△		●		✚	

MAINE

N.H.

VT.

MASS.

CONN. R.I.

NEW YORK

N.J.

PENNSYLVANIA

MD. DEL.

OHIO

W. VA.

VIRGINIA

NORTH CAROLINA

SOUTH CAROLINA

MICHIGAN

INDIANA

KENTUCKY

TENNESSEE

GEORGIA

FLORIDA

ALABAMA

MISSISSIPPI

WISCONSIN

ILLINOIS

IOWA

MISSOURI

ARKANSAS

LOUISIANA

MINNESOTA

NORTH DAKOTA

SOUTH DAKOTA

NEBRASKA

KANSAS

OKLAHOMA

TEXAS

MONTANA

WYOMING

COLORADO

NEW MEXICO

IDAHO

UTAH

ARIZONA

WASHINGTON

OREGON

NEVADA

CALIFORNIA

N W E S

500 Miles
250
250
750 Kilometers
500
500

ALASKA

500 Miles
0
750 Kilometers
0

HAWAII

100 Miles
0
100 Kilometers
0

897

The Fifty States

State	Date of Entry to Union (Order of Entry)	Area in Square Miles	Population 1994 (In Thousands)	Number of Representatives in House	Capital	Largest City
Alabama	1819 (22)	51,705	4,219	7	Montgomery	Birmingham
Alaska	1959 (49)	591,004	606	1	Juneau	Anchorage
Arizona	1912 (48)	114,000	4,075	6	Phoenix	Phoenix
Arkansas	1836 (25)	53,187	2,453	4	Little Rock	Little Rock
California	1850 (31)	158,706	31,431	52	Sacramento	Los Angeles
Colorado	1876 (38)	104,091	3,656	6	Denver	Denver
Connecticut	1788 (5)	5,018	3,275	6	Hartford	Bridgeport
Delaware	1787 (1)	2,044	706	1	Dover	Wilmington
Florida	1845 (27)	58,664	13,953	23	Tallahassee	Jacksonville
Georgia	1788 (4)	58,910	7,055	11	Atlanta	Atlanta
Hawaii	1959 (50)	6,471	1,179	2	Honolulu	Honolulu
Idaho	1890 (43)	83,564	1,133	2	Boise	Boise
Illinois	1818 (21)	56,345	11,752	20	Springfield	Chicago
Indiana	1816 (19)	36,185	5,752	10	Indianapolis	Indianapolis
Iowa	1846 (29)	56,275	2,829	5	Des Moines	Des Moines
Kansas	1861 (34)	82,277	2,554	4	Topeka	Wichita
Kentucky	1792 (15)	40,409	3,827	6	Frankfort	Louisville
Louisiana	1812 (18)	47,751	4,315	7	Baton Rouge	New Orleans
Maine	1820 (23)	33,265	1,240	2	Augusta	Portland
Maryland	1788 (7)	10,460	5,006	8	Annapolis	Baltimore
Massachusetts	1788 (6)	8,284	6,041	10	Boston	Boston
Michigan	1837 (26)	58,527	9,496	16	Lansing	Detroit
Minnesota	1858 (32)	84,402	4,567	8	St. Paul	Minneapolis
Mississippi	1817 (20)	47,689	2,669	5	Jackson	Jackson
Missouri	1821 (24)	69,697	5,278	9	Jefferson City	Kansas City
Montana	1889 (41)	147,046	856	1	Helena	Billings
Nebraska	1867 (37)	77,355	1,623	3	Lincoln	Omaha
Nevada	1864 (36)	110,561	1,457	2	Carson City	Las Vegas
New Hampshire	1788 (9)	9,279	1,137	2	Concord	Manchester
New Jersey	1787 (3)	7,787	7,904	13	Trenton	Newark
New Mexico	1912 (47)	121,593	1,654	3	Santa Fe	Albuquerque
New York	1788 (11)	49,108	18,169	31	Albany	New York
North Carolina	1789 (12)	52,669	7,070	12	Raleigh	Charlotte
North Dakota	1889 (39)	70,703	638	1	Bismarck	Fargo
Ohio	1803 (17)	41,330	11,102	19	Columbus	Columbus
Oklahoma	1907 (46)	69,956	3,258	6	Oklahoma City	Oklahoma City
Oregon	1859 (33)	97,073	3,086	5	Salem	Portland
Pennsylvania	1787 (2)	45,308	12,052	21	Harrisburg	Philadelphia
Rhode Island	1790 (13)	1,212	997	2	Providence	Providence
South Carolina	1788 (8)	31,113	3,664	6	Columbia	Columbia
South Dakota	1889 (40)	77,116	721	1	Pierre	Sioux Falls
Tennessee	1796 (16)	42,144	5,175	9	Nashville	Memphis
Texas	1845 (28)	266,807	18,378	30	Austin	Houston
Utah	1896 (45)	84,899	1,908	3	Salt Lake City	Salt Lake City
Vermont	1791 (14)	9,614	580	1	Montpelier	Burlington
Virginia	1788 (10)	40,767	6,552	11	Richmond	Virginia Beach
Washington	1889 (42)	68,138	5,343	9	Olympia	Seattle
West Virginia	1863 (35)	24,231	1,822	3	Charleston	Charleston
Wisconsin	1848 (30)	56,153	5,082	9	Madison	Milwaukee
Wyoming	1890 (44)	97,809	476	1	Cheyenne	Cheyenne
District of Columbia		69	570	1 (nonvoting)		

Self-Governing Areas, Possessions, and Dependencies	Area in Square Miles	Population (in Thousands)	Capital
Puerto Rico	3,515	3,522	San Juan
Guam	209	133	Agana
U.S. Virgin Islands	132	102	Charlotte Amalie
American Samoa	77	52	Pago Pago

Gazetteer of American History

This gazetteer, or geographical dictionary, lists places that are important in American history. The approximate latitude and longitude are given for cities, towns, and other specific locations. See text page 4 for information about latitude and longitude. In the Gazetteer, after the description of each place, there are usually two numbers in parentheses. The first number refers to the text page where you can find out more about the place. The second appears in slanted, or *italic*, type and refers to a map *(m)* where the place is shown.

A

Abilene (39°N/97°W) Former cow town in Kansas. Grew in 1860s as the railhead at the end of the Chisholm Trail. (p. 523, *m524*)

Afghanistan Land-locked country in south-central Asia. Invaded by the Soviet Union in 1979. (p. 808, *m890–891*)

Africa Second largest continent in the world. (p. 65, *m66*)

Alabama 22nd state. Nicknamed the Heart of Dixie or the Cotton State. (p. 898, *m892–893*)

Alamo (29°N/99°W) Mission in San Antonio, Texas, where 183 rebels died during the Texas war for independence. (p. 358, *m357*)

Alaska 49th state. Largest in size but one of the least populated states. (p. 898, *m892–893*)

Albany (43°N/74°W) Capital of New York State. Called Fort Orange by the Dutch of New Netherland. (p. 171, *m170*)

Amiens (50°N/2°E) World War I battle site in northeastern France. (p. 662, *m662*)

Andes Rugged mountain chain in South America. (p. 52, *m51*)

Appalachian Mountains Heavily forested mountain chain that stretches from Georgia to Maine and Canada. A barrier to colonial expansion. (p. 18, *m19*)

Appomattox Courthouse (37°N/79°W) Small town in Virginia where Lee surrendered to Grant on April 9, 1865. (p. 477, *m476*)

Argentina Country in South America. Gained independence from Spain in 1816. (p. 317, *m315*)

Arizona 48th state. Nicknamed the Grand Canyon State. (p. 898, *m892–893*)

Arkansas 25th state. Nicknamed the Land of Opportunity. (p. 898, *m892–893*)

Asia Largest of the world's continents. (p. 62, *m11*)

Atlanta (34°N/84°W) Capital and largest city of Georgia. Burned by Sherman during the Civil War. (p. 475, *m474*)

Atlantic Ocean World's second largest ocean. (p. 15, *m11*)

Austria-Hungary One of the Central Powers in World War I. Divided into several countries after 1918. (p. 648, *m650*)

B

Baltimore (39°N/77°W) Port city in Maryland. (p. 289, *m288*)

Barbary States North African nations Morocco, Algiers, Tunis, and Tripoli. Americans paid a tribute to their rulers so they would not attack American ships. (p. 279, *m280*)

Bay of Pigs (22°N/81°W) Located in southern Cuba. Site of an unsuccessful invasion to overthrow Fidel Castro. (p. 805)

Beijing (40°N/116°E) Capital of China. (p. 628, *m890–891*)

Belgium Small country in northwestern Europe. (p. 651, *m650*)

Belleau Wood (49°N/3°E) World War I battle site in northeastern France. (p. 664, *m662*)

Bering Sea Narrow sea between Asia and North America. Scientists think a land bridge existed here during the last ice age. (p. 32, *m33*)

Berlin (53°N/13°E) City in Germany. Split into East Berlin and West Berlin after World War II; divided by the Berlin Wall from 1961 to 1989. (p. 773, *m890–891*)

Bosnia and Herzegovina Country in Eastern Europe. Broke away from Yugoslavia in 1991. Plagued by civil war and ethnic violence. (p. 835, *m835*)

Boston (42°N/71°W) Seaport and industrial city in Massachusetts. (p. 95, *m96*)

Brazil Largest country in South America. Gained independence from Portugal in 1822. (p. 317, *m315*)

Breed's Hill (42°N/71°W) Overlooks Boston harbor. Site of fighting during the Battle of Bunker Hill. (p. 162)

Buena Vista (26°N/101°W) Site of an American victory in the Mexican War. (p. 366, *m365*)

Buffalo (43°N/79°W) Industrial city in New York State on Lake Erie. Free Soil party was founded there in 1848. (p. 429, *m892–893*)

Bunker Hill (42°N/71°W) Overlooks Boston harbor. Site of first major battle of the Revolution. (p. 161)

C

Cahokia (39°N/90°W) Fur-trading post in southwestern Illinois in the 1700s. Captured by George Rogers Clark in 1778 during the Revolution. (p. 176, *m175*)

California 31st state. Nicknamed the Golden State. Ceded to the United States by Mexico in 1848. (p. 366, *m437*)

Cambodia Nation in Southeast Asia. (p. 811, *m809*)

Canada Northern neighbor of the United States. Second largest nation in the world. Made up of 10 provinces: Ontario, Quebec, Nova Scotia, New Brunswick, Alberta, British Columbia, Manitoba, Newfoundland and Labrador, Prince Edward Island, and Saskatchewan. (p. 133, *m890–891*)

Canadian Shield Lowland region that lies mostly in eastern Canada. Its low hills and plains are rich in minerals. (p. 19, *m19*)

GAZETTEER

Chancellorsville (38°N/78°W) Site of a Confederate victory in 1863. (p. 472, *m459*)

Charleston (33°N/80°W) City in South Carolina. Site of a British victory in the American Revolution. (p. 180, *m181*)

Château-Thierry (49°N/3°E) World War I battle site in northeastern France. (p. 662, *m662*)

Chesapeake Bay Large inlet of the Atlantic Ocean in Virginia and Maryland. (p. 289, *m288*)

Chicago (42°N/88°W) Third largest city in the United States. Developed as a railroad and meatpacking center in the late 1800s. (p. 18, *m892–893*)

China Country in East Asia. Now the world's most populous nation. (p. 562, *m890–891*)

Chisholm Trail Cattle trail from Texas to the railroad at Abilene, Kansas. Opened in 1865. (p. 523, *m524*)

Coastal Plains Region consisting of the Atlantic Plain on the east coast and the Gulf Plain which lies along the Gulf of Mexico. (p. 20, *m19*)

Colombia Country in South America. (p. 639, *m642*)

Colorado 38th state. Nicknamed the Centennial State. (p. 898, *m892–893*)

Columbia River Chief river of the Pacific Northwest. (p. 352, *m353*)

Concord (43°N/71°W) Village near Boston, Massachusetts. Site of the first fighting in the American Revolution on April 19, 1775. (p. 155, *m163*)

Connecticut One of the original 13 states. Nicknamed the Constitution State or the Nutmeg State. (p. 95, *m96*)

Cowpens (35°N/82°W) Located in South Carolina. Site of a decisive American victory in 1781 during the Revolution. (p. 181, *m181*)

Cuba (22°N/79°W) Island nation in the Caribbean. Gained independence from Spain in 1898. Strongly influenced by the United States until Fidel Castro established communist control in 1959. (p. 631, *m634*)

Cumberland Gap (37°N/84°W) Pass in the Appalachian Mountains near the border of Virginia, Kentucky, and Tennessee. (p. 304, *m306*)

Cuzco (14°S/72°W) Inca capital located high in the Andes Mountains of Peru. (p. 52, *m51*)

Czechoslovakia Country in Eastern Europe. Created after World War I. Under communist control from 1945 to 1989. Split into two separate republics in 1992. (p. 741, *m740*)

D

Delaware One of the original 13 states. Nicknamed the First State or the Diamond State. (p. 103, *m102*)

Delaware River Flows into the Atlantic Ocean through Delaware Bay. (p. 171, *m170*)

Detroit (42°N/83°W) Largest city in Michigan. (p. 287, *m288*)

District of Columbia Located on the Potomac River. Seat of the federal government of the United States. (p. 247, *m892–893*)

Dominican Republic Country in the Caribbean. Shares the island of Hispaniola with Haiti. Invaded by the United States in 1905, 1916, and 1965. (p. 641, *m642*)

Dunkirk (51°N/2°E) French port on the English Channel where British and French troops were trapped by the Germans during World War II. (p. 742, *m756*)

E

East Indies Islands in Southeast Asia that are now part of Indonesia. Source of spices in the 1500s and 1600s. (p. 65)

Egypt Country in the Middle East that borders Israel. Controls the Suez Canal. (p. 845, *m847*)

El Alamein (31°N/29°E) Located on the northern coast of Egypt. Site of a decisive British victory over the German army in World War II. (p. 754, *m756*)

El Salvador Country in Central America. Won independence from Spain in 1821. Torn by civil war in recent years. (p. 841, *m841*)

England Part of Great Britain. (p. 65, *m80*)

English Channel Narrow body of water separating Britain from the European mainland. Site of D-Day crossing of Allies into France during World War II. (p. 742, *m756*)

Equator Line of latitude labeled 0°. Separates the Northern Hemisphere and Southern Hemisphere. (p. 11, *m11*)

Erie Canal Linked the Hudson and Mohawk rivers with Buffalo and Lake Erie. Built between 1817 and 1825. (p. 308, *m308*)

Europe Smallest continent except for Australia. (p. 62, *m11*)

F

Florida 27th state. Nicknamed the Sunshine State. (p. 898, *m892–893*)

Fort Donelson (37°N/88°W) Located in Tennessee. Captured by Grant in 1862. (p. 461, *m474*)

Fort Henry (37°N/88°W) Located in Tennessee. Captured by Grant in 1862. (p. 461, *m474*)

Fort McHenry (39°N/77°W) Located in Baltimore harbor. British bombardment there in 1814 inspired Francis Scott Key to write "The Star-Spangled Banner." (p. 289)

Fort Necessity (40°N/79°W) Makeshift stockade built by the British near the Monongahela River during the French and Indian War. (p. 136, *m139*)

Fort Pitt (40°N/80°W) British name for Fort Duquesne after its capture from the French in 1758. (p. 140, *m175*)

Fort Sumter (33°N/80°W) Guarded the entrance to Charleston harbor in South Carolina. Confederates fired the first shots of the Civil War at the fort in 1861. (p. 447, *m474*)

Fort Ticonderoga (44°N/74°W) Originally French, then British fort at the south end of Lake Champlain. Captured by Ethan Allen in 1775. (p. 160, *m163*)

France Country in Western Europe. First ally of the United States. Scene of heavy fighting in both World Wars. (p. 65, *m890–891*)

Fredericksburg (38°N/78°W) Located in eastern Virginia. Site of a Confederate victory in 1862. (p. 472, *m459*)

G

Gadsden Purchase Land purchased from Mexico in 1853. Now part of Arizona and New Mexico. (p. 366, *m367*)

Gaza Strip (31°N/34°E) Narrow strip of land between Israel and the Mediterranean Sea. Palestinians were granted self-rule of the territory in 1993. (p. 845)

Georgia One of the original 13 states. Nicknamed the Peach State or the Empire State of the South. (p. 898, *m892–893*)

Germany Country in central Europe. Divided from the end of World War II until 1989 into East and West Germany. (p. 648, *m650*)

Gettysburg (40°N/77°W) Small town in southern Pennsylvania. Site of a Union victory in 1863 and Lincoln's Gettysburg Address. (p. 473, *m459*)

Ghana Country in Africa. Gained independence from Great Britain in 1957. (p. 776, *m777*)

Gonzales (29°N/97°W) City in Texas near San Antonio. Site of the first Texan victory over Mexico in 1835. (p. 357, *m357*)

Great Britain Island nation of Western Europe. Includes England, Scotland, Wales, and Northern Ireland. (p. 136, *m890–891*)

Great Lakes Group of five freshwater lakes in the heart of the United States. (p. 21, *m19*)

Great Plains Western part of the Interior Plains. Once grazed by large herds of buffalo. Now an important wheat-growing and ranching region. (p. 18, *m19*)

Great Wagon Road Early pioneer route across the Appalachians. (p. 105, *m102*)

Greece Country in southeastern Europe. Member of NATO since 1952. (p. 562, *m890–891*)

Grenada (12°N/61°W) Island nation in the Caribbean. Invaded by the United States in 1983 to end the threat of communist influence there. (p. 842, *m841*)

Guam (14°N/143°E) Island in the Pacific Ocean. Territory of the United States. Acquired from Spain in 1898. (p. 636, *m630*)

Guatemala Country in Central America. Gained independence from Spain in 1821. Mayas built an advanced civilization there over 3,000 years ago. (p. 48, *m890–891*)

Gulf of Mexico Body of water along the southern coast of the United States. (p. 133, *m133*)

Gulf of Tonkin (20°N/108°E) Located off the coast of North Vietnam. Attack on American destroyers there in 1964 led to a widening of the Vietnam War. (p. 809, *m809*)

H

Haiti Country in the West Indies. Won independence from France in the early 1800s. Occupied by United States troops from 1915 to 1934. (p. 272, *m890–891*)

Harpers Ferry (39°N/78°W) Town in West Virginia. Abolitionist John Brown raided the arsenal there in 1859. (p. 443, *m459*)

Hawaii Newest of the 50 states. Nicknamed the Aloha State. (p. 898, *m892–893*)

Hawaiian Islands Region composed of a group of eight large islands and many small islands. The islands are the tops of volcanoes that erupted through the floor of the Pacific Ocean. (p. 20, *m19*)

Hiroshima (34°N/133°E) City in southern Japan. Mostly destroyed by an atomic bomb dropped there on August 6, 1945. Largely rebuilt since 1950. (p. 759, *m758*)

Hudson Bay Large inlet of the Arctic Ocean. Named for the explorer Henry Hudson. (p. 78, *m80*)

Hudson River Largest river in New York State. Explored by Henry Hudson in 1609. (p. 78, *m87*)

Hungary Country in central Europe. Site of anti-Soviet uprising in 1956. (p. 775, *m775*)

I

Idaho 43rd state. Nicknamed the Gem State. Acquired by the United States as part of the Oregon Territory. (p. 898, *m892–893*)

Illinois 21st state. Nicknamed the Inland Empire. Settled as part of the Northwest Territory. (p. 898, *m892–893*)

Independence (37°N/96°W) City in Missouri. Starting point of the Oregon Trail. (p. 353, *m361*)

India Country in south Asia. World's second most populated country. Gained independence from Britain in 1947. (p. 776, *m890–891*)

Indiana 19th state. Nicknamed the Hoosier State. Settled as part of the Northwest Territory. (p. 898, *m892–893*)

Interior Plains Region of the central United States that stretches from the Rockies to the Appalachians. (p. 18, *m19*)

Intermountain Region Rugged and mostly dry region from the Rocky Mountains to the Sierra Nevada and coastal mountains of the western United States. (p. 18, *m19*)

Iowa 29th state. Nicknamed the Hawkeye State. Acquired by the United States as part of the Louisiana Purchase. (p. 898, *m892–893*)

Iran Oil-producing country in the Middle East. Commands sea routes through the Persian Gulf. (p. 846, *m847*)

Iraq Oil-producing country in the Middle East. Fought United Nations forces in Persian Gulf War of 1991. (p. 848, *m847*)

Israel Country in the Middle East. Set up as a Jewish homeland in 1948. (p. 844, *m847*)

Isthmus of Panama Narrow strip of land joining North and South America. (p. 638, *m640*)

Italy Country in southern Europe. Fought with the Allies in World War I and the Axis Powers in World War II. (p. 648, *m650*)

Iwo Jima (25°N/141°E) Small island in the Pacific Ocean. Site of a hard-won American victory in World War II. (p. 758, *m758*)

J

Jamestown (37°N/77°W) First successful English colony in North America. (p. 85, *m87*)

Japan Densely populated industrial nation in East Asia. Opened up to trade with the West by Commodore Matthew Perry. One of the Axis Powers in World War II. (p. 622, *m630*)

GAZETTEER

K

Kansas 34th state. Nicknamed the Sunflower State. Acquired by the United States as part of the Louisiana Purchase. (p. 898, *m892–893*)

Kaskaskia (38°N/90°W) Fur-trading post on an island in the Mississippi River. Captured by George Rogers Clark in 1778. First state capital of Illinois. (p. 176, *m175*)

Kentucky 15th state. Nicknamed the Bluegrass State. Was the first area west of the Appalachians to be settled by early pioneers. (p. 898, *m892–893*)

Kilwa (8°S/39°E) East African trading state in the 1400s. (p. 66, *m66*)

King's Mountain (35°N/81°W) Located in South Carolina. Site of an American victory in the Revolution. (p. 179, *m181*)

Kuwait Oil-rich country in the Middle East. Invaded by Iraq in 1990. (p. 848, *m847*)

L

Lancaster Turnpike Road built in the 1790s linking Philadelphia and Lancaster, Pennsylvania. (p. 305, *m306*)

Latin America Name for those parts of the Western Hemisphere where Latin languages such as Spanish, French, and Portuguese are spoken. Includes Mexico, Central and South America, and the West Indies. (p. 315, *m315*)

Lexington (42°N/71°W) Site of the first clash between minutemen and British troops in 1775. Now a suburb of Boston. (p. 155, *m163*)

Liberia Country in West Africa. Set up in 1822 as a colony for free African Americans. (p. 403, *m777*)

Little Bighorn Site of a Sioux and Cheyenne victory over Custer in 1876. (p. 516, *m517*)

Long Island Located in New York. Site of a British victory in the Revolution. (p. 169, *m170*)

Los Angeles (34°N/118°W) City in southern California. Second largest city in the United States. First settled by Spanish missionaries. (p. 816, *m892–893*)

Louisbourg (46°N/60°W) French fort in eastern Canada. Changed hands several times between France and Britain. (p. 139, *m139*)

Louisiana 18th state. Nicknamed the Pelican State. First state created out of the Louisiana Purchase. (p. 898, *m892–893*)

Louisiana Purchase Region between the Mississippi River and the Rocky Mountains that was purchased from France in 1803. (p. 273, *m273*)

M

Maine 23rd state. Nicknamed the Pine Tree State. Originally part of Massachusetts, Maine gained separate statehood in 1820 under the terms of the Missouri Compromise. (p. 898, *m892–893*)

Mali Kingdom in West Africa that reached its peak between 1200 and 1400. (p. 66, *m66*)

Manchuria (48°N/125°E) Industrialized region of northeastern China. Seized by Japan in the 1930s. Returned to China after World War II. (p. 740, *m758*)

Marne River (48°N/4°E) Located in France. Site of heavy fighting in World War I. (p. 651, *m662*)

Maryland One of the original 13 states. Nicknamed the Old Line State or the Free State. (p. 898, *m892–893*)

Mason-Dixon Line 244-mile boundary between Pennsylvania and Maryland surveyed and marked by Charles Mason and Jeremiah Dixon. (p. 106)

Massachusetts One of the original 13 states. Nicknamed the Bay State or the Old Colony. (p. 898, *m892–893*)

Memphis (35°N/90°W) City in Tennessee on the Mississippi River. Captured by Grant in 1862. (p. 461, *m474*)

Meuse River (51°N/5°E) Crosses France, Belgium, and the Netherlands. Battleground in World War I. (p. 664, *m662*)

Mexican Cession Lands acquired by the United States from Mexico under the Treaty of Guadalupe Hidalgo in 1848. (p. 366, *m367*)

Mexico Southern neighbor of the United States. Gained independence from Spain in 1821. (p. 315, *m315*)

Mexico City (19°N/99°W) Capital of Mexico. Was the capital of New Spain. Site of the ancient Aztec city of Tenochtitlán. (p. 366, *m365*)

Michigan 26th state. Nicknamed the Great Lake State or the Wolverine State. Settled as part of the Northwest Territory. (p. 898, *m892–893*)

Middle East Region at the eastern end of the Mediterranean Sea. Source of much of the world's oil. (p. 63, *m847*)

Midway Island (28°N/179°W) Annexed by the United States in 1867. American victory here was a turning point in World War II. (p. 624, *m630*)

Minnesota 32nd state. Nicknamed the Gopher State. Most of it was acquired by the United States as part of the Louisiana Purchase. (p. 898, *m892–893*)

Mississippi 20th state. Nicknamed the Magnolia State. (p. 898, *m892–893*)

Mississippi River Longest river in the United States. Links the Great Lakes with the Gulf of Mexico. (p. 20, *m19*)

Missouri 24th state. Nicknamed the Show Me State. Acquired by the United States as part of the Louisiana Purchase. (p. 898, *m892–893*)

Missouri Compromise line Line drawn across the Louisiana Purchase at latitude 36°/30'N to divide free states from slave states. (p. 429, *m430*)

Missouri River Second longest river in the United States. Rises in the northern Rocky Mountains and joins the Mississippi River near St. Louis. (p. 274, *m273*)

Mogadishu (2°N/45°E) East African trading state in the 1400s. (p. 66, *m66*)

Montana 41st state. Nicknamed the Treasure State. Acquired by the United States in part through the Louisiana Purchase. (p. 898, *m892–893*)

Montgomery (32°N/86°W) City in Alabama. Site of bus boycott that led, in part, to the start of the civil rights movement. (p. 791, *m892–893*)

GAZETTEER

Montreal (46°N/74°W) Major city in Canada. Located on the St. Lawrence River. Settled by the French. (p. 163, *m163*)

N

Nagasaki (33°N/130°E) Japanese port city. Largely destroyed by the atomic bomb dropped on August 9, 1945. (p. 759, *m758*)

National Road Early road to the West that began in Cumberland, Maryland. Now part of U.S. Highway 40. (p. 306, *m306*)

Nauvoo (41°N/91°W) Town founded by the Mormons in Illinois in the 1840s. (p. 369)

Nebraska 37th state. Nicknamed the Cornhusker State. Acquired by the United States as part of the Louisiana Purchase. (p. 898, *m892–893*)

Nevada 36th state. Nicknamed the Sagebrush State or the Battle Born State. Acquired by the United States at the end of the Mexican War. (p. 898, *m892–893*)

Newfoundland (48°N/57°W) Island at the mouth of the St. Lawrence River. Part of Canada. (p. 78, *m80*)

New France Colony established by France in North America. (p. 80, *m80*)

New Hampshire One of the original 13 states. Nicknamed the Granite State. (p. 898, *m892–893*)

New Jersey One of the original 13 states. Nicknamed the Garden State. (p. 898, *m892–893*)

New Mexico 47th state. Nicknamed the Land of Enchantment. Acquired by the United States at the end of the Mexican War. (p. 898, *m892–893*)

New Netherland Dutch colony on the Hudson River. Taken over by the English and renamed New York in 1664. (p. 82)

New Orleans (30°N/90°W) Port city in Louisiana near the mouth of the Mississippi River. Settled by the French in the 1600s. Site of a battle between the Americans and the British at the end of the War of 1812. (p. 272, *m273*)

New Spain Area ruled by Spain for 300 years. Included colonies in the West Indies, Central America, and North America. (p. 74, *m72*)

New York One of the original 13 states. Nicknamed the Empire State. (p. 898, *m892–893*)

New York City (41°N/74°W) Port city at the mouth of the Hudson River. Founded by the Dutch as New Amsterdam. First capital of the United States. (p. 169, *m170*)

Nicaragua Country in Central America. Won independence from Spain in 1821. Ruled by the Sandinistas from 1979 to 1990. (p. 841, *m841*)

Normandy Region in northwest France. The Allies landed there on D-Day in World War II. (p. 755, *m756*)

North America World's third largest continent. Separated from South America by the Isthmus of Panama. (p. 15, *m11*)

North Carolina One of the original 13 states. Nicknamed the Tar Heel State or the Old North State. (p. 898, *m892–893*)

North Dakota 39th state. Nicknamed the Sioux State or the Flickertail State. Acquired by the United States as part of the Louisiana Purchase. (p. 898, *m892–893*)

North Korea Country in east Asia created by the division of Korea after World War II. (p. 779, *m780*)

Northwest Territory Name for lands north of the Ohio River and east of the Mississippi River. Acquired by the United States by the Treaty of Paris in 1783. (p. 191, *m192*)

Nueces River Claimed by Mexico in the Mexican War as the southern border of Texas. (p. 364, *m365*)

O

Ohio 17th state. Nicknamed the Buckeye State. Settled as part of the Northwest Territory. (p. 898, *m892–893*)

Ohio River Important transportation route. Begins at Pittsburgh and joins the Mississippi River at Cairo, Illinois. (p. 133, *m133*)

Okinawa Small island in the Pacific Ocean, south of Japan. Captured by Americans at the end of World War II. (p. 758, *m758*)

Oklahoma 46th State. Nicknamed the Sooner State. Acquired by the United States as part of the Louisiana Purchase. (p. 898, *m892–893*)

Oregon 33rd state. Nicknamed the Beaver State. Acquired by the United States as part of the Oregon Territory. (p. 898, *m892–893*)

Oregon Country Area in the Pacific Northwest. Claimed by the United States, Britain, Spain, and Russia in the early 1800s. (p. 350, *m353*)

Oregon Trail Overland route from Independence, Missouri, on the Missouri River to the Columbia River valley. (p. 353, *m353*)

P

Pacific Coast Highest and most rugged region of the United States. Includes the Cascades and the Sierra Nevada. (p. 18, *m19*)

Pacific Ocean World's largest ocean. (p. 15, *m11*)

Pacific Rim Region consisting of countries and states that border on the Pacific Ocean. Area of increasingly important economic activity. (p. 864, *m864*)

Pakistan Country in south Asia. Gained independence from Britain in 1947. (p. 776, *m890–891*)

Panama Country on the isthmus separating North and South America. Gained independence from Colombia in 1903. (p. 638, *m642*)

Panama Canal Canal dug through the Isthmus of Panama to link the Atlantic and the Pacific oceans. (p. 639, *m640*)

Paris (49°N/2°E) Capital of France. (p. 651, *m650*)

Pearl Harbor (21°N/158°W) United States naval base in Hawaii. Site of Japanese surprise attack on December 7, 1941. (p. 745, *m758*)

Pennsylvania One of the original 13 states. Nicknamed the Keystone State. (p. 898, *m892–893*)

Persian Gulf (28°N/51°E) Major sea route for ships carrying oil exports of Middle Eastern countries. (p. 848, *m847*)

Peru Country in South America. Gained independence from Spain in 1821. (p. 74, *m890–891*)

GAZETTEER

Philadelphia (40°N/75°W) Major port and chief city in Pennsylvania. Second capital of the United States. (p. 103, *m102*)

Philippine Islands (14°N/125°E) Group of islands in the Pacific Ocean. Acquired by the United States in 1898. Gained independence in 1946. (p. 71, *m630*)

Pikes Peak (39°N/105°W) Mountain located in the Rocky Mountains of central Colorado. (p. 278, *m273*)

Plymouth (42°N/71°W) New England colony founded in 1620 by Pilgrims. Absorbed by the Massachusetts Bay Colony in 1691. (p. 89, *m87*)

Poland Country in Eastern Europe. First among Eastern European nations to overturn communist rule and hold free elections. (p. 741, *m740*)

Port Royal (45°N/65°W) Permanent colony founded by Champlain in Nova Scotia. (p. 80, *m139*)

Portugal Country in Western Europe. In the 1400s, sailors set out from there to explore the coast of Africa. (p. 65, *m66*)

Potomac River Forms part of the Maryland-Virginia border. Flows through Washington, D.C., and into Chesapeake Bay. (p. 458, *m459*)

Prime Meridian Line of longitude labeled 0°. (p. 11, *m11*)

Princeton (40°N/75°W) City in New Jersey. Site of an American victory during the Revolution. (p. 171, *m170*)

Promontory Point (42°N/112°W) Located just north of the Great Salt Lake. Place where the Central Pacific and the Union Pacific railroads were joined to form the first transcontinental railroad. (p. 510, *m524*)

Puerto Rico (18°N/67°W) Island in the Caribbean Sea. A self-governing commonwealth of the United States. (p. 71, *m634*)

Q

Quebec (47°N/71°W) City in eastern Canada on the St. Lawrence River. Founded in 1608 by the French explorer Samuel de Champlain. (p. 80, *m80*)

R

Rhode Island One of the original 13 states. Nicknamed Little Rhody or the Ocean State. (p. 898, *m892–893*)

Richmond (38°N/78°W) Located on the James River. Capital of Virginia. Capital of the Confederacy during the Civil War. (p. 458, *m459*)

Rio Grande River that forms the border between the United States and Mexico. (p. 364, *m365*)

Roanoke Island (36°N/76°W) Island off the coast of North Carolina. Site of the "lost colony" founded in 1587. (p. 84, *m87*)

Rocky Mountains Mountains extending through the western United States. Barrier to travel in pioneer days. (p. 18, *m19*)

Russia Largest country in the world, spanning Europe and Asia. A communist revolution took place there in 1917. Part of the Soviet Union until 1991. (p. 648, *m890–891*)

S

Sacramento (39°N/122°W) Capital of California. Developed as a gold rush boom town. (p. 369, *m892–893*)

St. Augustine (30°N/81°W) City in Florida. Founded by Spain in 1565. Oldest European settlement in the United States. (p. 75, *m75*)

St. Lawrence River Waterway leading from the Great Lakes to the Atlantic Ocean. Forms part of the border between the United States and Canada. (p. 78, *m80*)

St. Louis (38°N/90°W) City in Missouri on the Mississippi River. Lewis and Clark began their expedition there. (p. 274, *m273*)

Salt Lake City (41°N/112°W) Largest city in Utah. Founded in 1847 by Mormons. (p. 370, *m892–893*)

Samoa Chain of islands in the South Pacific. Joint control over the islands was established by the United States and Germany in 1889. (p. 628, *m629*)

San Antonio (29°N/99°W) City in southern Texas. Chief Texan settlement in Spanish and Mexican days. Site of the Alamo. (p. 357, *m357*)

San Diego (33°N/117°W) City in southern California. Founded as the first Spanish mission in California. (p. 362, *m361*)

San Francisco (38°N/122°W) City in northern California. Boom town of the California gold rush. (p. 370, *m892–893*)

Santa Fe (35°N/106°W) Capital of New Mexico. First settled by the Spanish. (p. 361, *m361*)

Santa Fe Trail Overland trail from Independence to Santa Fe. Opened in 1821. (p. 362, *m361*)

Sarajevo (44°N/18°E) Capital city of Bosnia and Herzegovina. Site of the shooting of the Archduke Ferdinand in 1914. (p. 649, *m650*)

Saratoga (43°N/75°W) City in eastern New York. The American victory there in 1777 was a turning point in the American Revolution. (p. 172, *m170*)

Savannah (32°N/81°W) Oldest city in Georgia. Founded in 1733. (p. 180, *m181*)

Serbia Balkan country in southeastern Europe. Involved in the beginning of World War I. (p. 649, *m650*)

Sicily Island in the Mediterranean that is part of Italy. Invaded by the Allies in World War II. (p. 754, *m756*)

Sierra Nevada Mountain range mostly in California. (p. 18, *m19*)

Songhai West African kingdom in the 1400s. (p. 66, *m66*)

South Africa Country at the southern tip of Africa. Government enforced policy of apartheid from 1948 until early 1990s. (p. 838, *m890–891*)

South America World's fourth largest continent. Part of the Western Hemisphere. (p. 15, *m11*)

South Carolina One of the original 13 states. Nicknamed the Palmetto State. (p. 898, *m892–893*)

South Dakota 40th state. Nicknamed the Coyote State or the Sunshine State. Acquired by the United States as part of the Louisiana Purchase. (p. 898, *m892–893*)

South Korea Country in East Asia created by division of Korea after World War II. (p. 779, *m780*)

Soviet Union Short name for the Union of Soviet Socialist Republics, or USSR. Broke up in 1991. (p. 741, *m740*)

904

Spain Country in southwestern Europe. Columbus sailed from Spain in 1492. (p. 65, *m890–891*)

Spanish borderlands Area that spanned the present-day United States from Florida to California. (p. 72, *m75*)

Spanish Florida Part of New Spain. Purchased by the United States in 1821. (p. 282, *m273*)

Stalingrad (49°N/45°E) City in the Soviet Union. Renamed Volgograd in 1961. Site of decisive Soviet victory over Germany in World War II. (p. 754, *m756*)

Strait of Magellan (53°S/69°W) Narrow water route at the tip of South America. (p. 15)

T

Tennessee 16th state. Nicknamed the Volunteer State. Gained statehood after North Carolina ceded its western lands to the United States. (p. 898, *m892–893*)

Tenochtitlán (19°N/99°W) Capital of the Aztec empire. Now part of Mexico City. (p. 50, *m51*)

Texas 28th state. Nicknamed the Lone Star State. Proclaimed independence from Mexico in 1836. Was a separate republic until 1845. (p. 898, *m892–893*)

Thirty-eighth parallel Line of latitude along which Korea was divided after World War II. (p. 779, *m780*)

Tikal (17°N/90°W) Ancient Mayan city. (p. 48, *m51*)

Timbuktu (17°N/3°W) City on the Niger River in Africa. Flourished as a center of trade and learning. (p. 66, *m66*)

Trenton (41°N/74°W) Capital of New Jersey. Site of an American victory in the Revolution. (p. 171, *m170*)

Turkey Country in the Middle East. Member of NATO since 1952. (p. 773, *m775*)

U

Utah 45th state. Nicknamed the Beehive State. Settled by Mormons. (p. 898, *m892–893*)

V

Valley Forge (40°N/76°W) Winter headquarters for the Continental Army in 1777–1778. Located near Philadelphia. (p. 172, *m170*)

Veracruz (19°N/96°W) Port city in Mexico on the Gulf of Mexico. (p. 366, *m365*)

Vermont 14th state. Nicknamed the Green Mountain State. First new state to join the Union after the American Revolution. (p. 898, *m892–893*)

Vicksburg (42°N/86°W) City on a high cliff overlooking the Mississippi River. Site of a Union victory in 1863. (p. 462, *m474*)

Vietnam Country in Southeast Asia. Divided into North and South Vietnam in 1954. Remained divided until North Vietnam defeated South Vietnam in a long war. (p. 808, *m809*)

Vincennes (39°N/88°W) City in Indiana. Settled by the French. British fort there was captured by George Rogers Clark in 1779. (p. 176, *m175*)

Vinland Viking settlement in present-day Newfoundland. (p. 54)

Virgin Islands (18°N/64°W) Territory of the United States. Purchased from Denmark in 1917. (p. 898, *m890–891*)

Virginia One of the original 13 states. Site of the first English settlements in the Americas. Nicknamed the Old Dominion. (p. 898, *m892–893*)

Virginia City (39°N/120°W) City in Nevada. Boom town in 1800s because of Comstock Lode mines. (p. 508, *m524*)

W

Washington 42nd state. Nicknamed the Evergreen State. Acquired by the United States as part of Oregon Territory. (p. 898, *m892–893*)

Washington, D.C. (39°N/77°W) Capital of the United States since 1800. Called Federal City until it was renamed for George Washington in 1799. (p. 289, *m288*)

Western Hemisphere Western half of the world. Includes North and South America. (p. 15, *m890–891*)

West Indies Islands in the Caribbean Sea. Explored by Columbus in 1492. (p. 67, *m72*)

West Virginia 35th state. Nicknamed the Mountain State. Separated from Virginia early in the Civil War. (p. 898, *m892–893*)

Willamette River Flows across fertile farmlands in northern Oregon to join the Columbia River. (p. 350, *m353*)

Wisconsin 30th state. Nicknamed the Badger State. Settled as part of the Northwest Territory. (p. 898, *m892–893*)

Wounded Knee (43°N/102°W) Site of a massacre of Indians in 1890. Located in what is now South Dakota. (p. 519, *m517*)

Wyoming 44th state. Nicknamed the Equality State. (p. 898, *m892–893*)

Y

Yalu River River along the border between North Korea and China. (p. 780, *m780*)

Yorktown (37°N/76°W) Town in Virginia near the York River. Site of the surrender of Cornwallis to the Americans in 1781. (p. 181, *m181*)

Yugoslavia Country in Eastern Europe. Torn by civil war after the fall of communism in the 1990s. (p. 835, *m835*)

Glossary

This glossary defines all vocabulary words and many important historical terms and phrases. These words and terms appear in blue or dark slanted type the first time that they are used in the text. The page number after each definition refers to the page on which the word or phrase is first discussed in the text. For other references, see the Index.

Pronunciation Key

When difficult names or terms first appear in the text, they are respelled to help you with pronunciation. A syllable printed in SMALL CAPITAL LETTERS receives the greatest stress. The pronunciation key below lists the letters and symbols that will help you pronounce the word. It also includes examples of words using each sound and showing how they would be pronounced.

Symbol	Example	Respelling
a	hat	(hat)
ay	pay, late	(pay), (layt)
ah	star, hot	(stahr), (haht)
ai	air, dare	(air), (dair)
aw	law, all	(law), (awl)
eh	met	(meht)
ee	bee, eat	(bee), (eet)
er	learn, sir, fur	(lern), (ser), (fer)
ih	fit	(fiht)
i	mile	(mīl)
ir	ear	(ir)
oh	no	(noh)
oi	soil, boy	(soil), (boi)
oo	root, rule	(root), (rool)
or	born, door	(born), (dor)
ow	plow, out	(plow), (owt)

Symbol	Example	Respelling
u	put, book	(put), (buk)
uh	fun	(fuhn)
yoo	few, use	(fyoo), (yooz)
ch	chill, reach	(chihl), (reech)
g	go, dig	(goh), (dihg)
j	jet, gently bridge	(jeht), (JEHNT lee), (brihj)
k	kite, cup	(kit), (kuhp)
ks	mix	(mihks)
kw	quick	(kwihk)
ng	bring	(brihng)
s	say, cent	(say), (sehnt)
sh	she, crash	(shee), (krash)
th	three	(three)
y	yet, onion	(yeht), (UHN yuhn)
z	zip, always	(zihp), (AWL wayz)
zh	treasure	(TREH zher)

A

abolitionist person who wanted to end slavery in the United States. (p. 404)

Act of Toleration (1649) law that gave religious freedom to all Christians in Maryland. (p. 107)

Adams-Onís Treaty agreement by which Spain gave Florida to the United States. (p. 319)

adobe sun-dried clay brick. (p. 36)

affirmative action action taken to provide equal opportunities in areas such as jobs and college admissions for minorities and women. (p. 817)

aggression any warlike act by one country against another without just cause. (p. 739)

AIDS (acquired immune deficiency syndrome) disease that prevents the body from fighting infections. (p. 856)

Albany Plan of Union Benjamin Franklin's plan for a Grand Council to make laws, raise taxes, and set up defense of the colonies. (p. 137)

alien foreigner. (p. 260)

Alien Act (1798) law that allowed the President to expel foreigners thought to be dangerous to the country. (p. 260)

Alliance for Progress organization set up in 1961 to bring about social and economic reforms in Latin America. Included the United States and Latin American nations. (p. 841)

Allied Powers nations that fought Germany and its allies in World War I. Included Britain, France, Russia, and the United States. (p. 650)

Allies nations that fought against the Axis powers in World War II. Included Britain, France, the Soviet Union, the United States, China, and 45 other countries. (p. 742)

altitude height above sea level. (p. 22)

amend change. (p. 207)

amendment formal written change. (p. 225)

American Colonization Society group founded in 1817 to set up a colony for free blacks in Africa. (p. 403)

American Indian Movement (AIM) organization that protested the treatment of Indians. (p. 820)

American System plan devised by Henry Clay providing for high tariffs and internal improvements to promote economic growth. (p. 313)

anarchist person opposed to organized government. (p. 699)

annex add on, such as territory. (p. 360)

Antifederalist person opposed to the Constitution during the ratification debate in 1787. (p. 205)

apartheid South African policy of separation of the races enforced by law. (p. 838)

appeal ask that a decision be reviewed by a higher court. (p. 234)

appeasement practice of giving in to an aggressor nation's demands in order to preserve the peace. (p. 741)

apprentice person who learns a trade or craft from a master craftsworker. (p. 121)

appropriate set aside money for a special purpose. (p. 230)

archaeology study of evidence left by early peoples. (p. 34)

armistice agreement to stop fighting. (p. 665)

arsenal gun warehouse. (p. 443)

Articles of Confederation first constitution of the United States. (p. 189)

artifact object made by humans and used by archaeologists to recreate a picture of the past. (p. 34)

assembly line method of production in which workers add parts to a product that moves along on a belt. Introduced by Henry Ford in 1913. (p. 549)

assimilation process of becoming part of another culture. (p. 567)

astrolabe instrument used by sailors to measure the positions of stars and figure out their latitude at sea. (p. 63)

Atlantic Charter (1941) agreement between the United States and Britain that set goals for the postwar world. (p. 745)

Axis nations that fought the Allies in World War II. Included Germany, Italy, Japan and six other nations. (p. 742)

B

baby boom increased birthrate in the United States during the late 1940s and 1950s. (p. 786)

backcountry area along the eastern slopes of the Appalachian Mountains. (p. 105)

Bacon's Rebellion uprising led by Nathaniel Bacon against Native American villages in 1676. (p. 107)

balanced budget spending plan in which the government cannot spend more than its income. (p. 827)

Bank of the United States national bank set up by Congress in 1791. (p. 248)

barrio neighborhood of Spanish-speaking people, such as Mexicans. (p. 617)

Bear Flag Republic country set up in 1845 by Americans in California. (p. 366)

Bessemer process way of making strong steel at a low cost. (p. 540)

bilingual in two languages. (p. 818)

bill proposed law. (pp. 203, 223)

bill of rights document that lists freedoms the government promises to protect. (p. 189)

Bill of Rights first 10 amendments to the Constitution. (p. 207)

Black Cabinet African Americans who became unofficial advisers to President Franklin Roosevelt. (p. 726)

black code laws that limited the rights of freedmen in the South after the Civil War. (p. 486)

Black Muslims group that believed that African Americans should separate from white society. (p. 816)

Black Panthers radical group that urged African Americans to use force, if necessary, to gain their rights. (p. 816)

Bleeding Kansas name given to the Kansas Territory by newspapers because of the violence there over slavery. (p. 438)

blitzkrieg German word meaning lightning war, which describes the swift attacks launched by the Germans in World War II. (p. 742)

blockade shutting off a port by ships to keep people or supplies from moving in or out. (p. 163)

bond certificate that promises to pay the holder the money loaned plus interest on a certain date. (p. 245)

bonus extra sum of money. (p. 713)

Bonus Army 20,000 jobless World War I veterans who marched to Washington, D.C., in 1932 to claim bonuses promised to them by the government. (p. 713)

bootlegger person who smuggled liquor into the United States during Prohibition. (p. 688)

Border Ruffians proslavery bands from Missouri who battled antislavery forces in Kansas. (p. 437)

Boston Massacre shooting of five Bostonians by British soldiers on March 5, 1770. (p. 149)

Boston Tea Party protest in which Bostonians dressed as Indians dumped British tea into the harbor. (p. 153)

bounty payment made to men who joined the Union army. (p. 467)

boycott to refuse to buy certain goods or services. (p. 144)

bracero Mexican farm worker brought to the United States to harvest crops. (p. 819)

Brain Trust experts who helped President Franklin Roosevelt plan programs to fight the depression. (p. 715)

Brown* v. *Board of Education of Topeka (1954) Supreme Court ruling that ordered schools to be desegregated. (p. 790)

bull market rising stock market. (p. 686)

Bull Moose party supporters of Theodore Roosevelt in the election of 1912. (p. 606)

burgess representative to the colonial assembly of Virginia. (p. 86)

C

Cabinet group of officials who head government departments and advise the President. (pp. 227, 245)

canal channel dug out and filled with water to allow ships to cross a stretch of land. (p. 307)

capital money raised for a business venture. (p. 541)

capitalist person who invests money in a business to make a profit. (p. 297)

caravel ship with a steering rudder and triangular sails. (p. 65)

carpetbagger name for a northerner who went to the South during Reconstruction. (p. 492)

cartographer mapmaker. (p. 8)

cash crop surplus of crops sold for money on the world market. (p. 104)

Cattle Kingdom region from Texas north across the Plains, where ranchers let their cattle roam freely during the 1870s. (p. 524)

caucus private meeting of political party leaders to choose a candidate. (p. 330)

cavalry troops on horseback. (p. 174)

cede give up, as land. (p. 366)

Central Powers European nations that fought the Allied Powers in World War I. Included Germany, Austria-Hungary, and the Ottoman Empire. (p. 650)

charter legal document giving certain rights to a person or company. (p. 85)

checks and balances system set up by the Constitution in which each branch of the federal government has the power to check, or control, the actions of the other branches. (p. 203)

Chinese Exclusion Act (1882) act barring the immigration of Chinese laborers for 10 years. (p. 569)

civil disobedience nonviolent protest against unjust laws. (p. 793)

civilian person not in the military. (p. 466)

civilization advanced culture. (p. 48)

Civil Rights Act of 1964 law protecting the right of all citizens to vote. (p. 815)

civil rights movement the efforts of African Americans and others who worked for equality. (p. 790)

civil service all government jobs except for elected positions or those in the armed forces. (p. 594)

civil war war between people of the same country. (p. 433)

climate average weather of a place over a period of 20 or 30 years. (p. 22)

clipper ship fast-sailing ship of the mid-1800s. (p. 379)

closed shop business or factory that agrees to hire only union members. (p. 784)

Cold War period after World War II of a state of tension between nations without actual fighting. (p. 772)

collective bargaining process whereby a union negotiates with management for a contract. (p. 721)

collective farm government-run farm in the Soviet Union. (p. 739)

colony group of people settled in a distant land who are ruled by the government of their native land. (p. 68)

committee of correspondence group of colonists who wrote letters and pamphlets to inform and unite colonists against British rule. (p. 147)

compromise settlement in which each side gives up some of its demands in order to reach an agreement. (p. 197)

Compromise of 1850 agreement over slavery that admitted California to the Union as a free state, allowed popular sovereignty in New Mexico and Utah, banned the slave trade in Washington, D.C., and passed a strict fugitive slave law. (p. 434)

Confederate States of America nation formed by the states that seceded from the Union in 1860 and 1861. (p. 445)

conquistador Spanish word for conqueror. (p. 70)

conservation protection of natural resources. (p. 604)

consolidate combine, such as businesses. (p. 537)

constituent person who elects a representative to office. (p. 232)

constitution document that sets out the laws and principles of a government. (p. 188)

Constitutional Convention meeting of delegates from 12 states who wrote a constitution for the United States in 1787. (p. 195)

Continental Army army set up by the Second Continental Congress to fight the British. (p. 161)

continental divide mountain ridge that separates river systems. (p. 276)

Convention of 1800 document in which Napoleon Bonaparte agreed to stop seizing American ships in the West Indies. (p. 260)

cooperative group of farmers who put their money together to buy seeds and tools at lower prices. (p. 530)

Copperhead northerner who thought the South should be allowed to leave the Union. (p. 467)

corduroy road log road. (p. 306)

corporation business owned by investors who buy shares of stock. (p. 541)

corral enclosure used for catching and holding large numbers of animals. (p. 513)

cotton gin invention of Eli Whitney's that speeded the cleaning of cotton fibers. (p. 296)

Cotton Kingdom in the 1850s, region where large plantations produced cotton. Stretched from South Carolina to Texas. (p. 388)

coureur de bois French phrase meaning runner of the woods. Trapper or trader in New France. (p. 81)

creole person born in the Americas to Spanish parents. (p. 76)

Cuban missile crisis (1962) tense situation caused by the Soviet effort to build missile bases in Cuba. (p. 805)

culture entire way of life of a people. (p. 34)

culture area region in which people share a similar way of life. (p. 37)

D

Daughters of Liberty group of colonial women who protested the Stamp Act. (p. 145)

Dawes Act (1887) act that encouraged Native Americans to become farmers and set up schools for Indian children. (p. 521)

D-Day (June 6, 1944) day that Allies began the invasion of Europe in World War II. (p. 755)

Declaration of Independence (1776) document that stated that the colonies had become a free and independent nation. (p. 166)

deficit spending government practice of spending more than it takes in from taxes. (p. 722)

democratic ensuring that all people have the same rights. (p. 268)

détente easing of tensions. (p. 807)

dictator ruler who has complete power. (p. 736)

dime novels low-priced paperback books offering adventure stories, which became popular in the late 1800s. (p. 581)

disarmament reduction of a nation's armed forces or weapons of war. (p. 682)

discrimination policy or attitude that denies equal rights to certain groups of people. (p. 386)

dividend payment to stockholders from a corporation's profits. (p. 541)

dollar diplomacy President Taft's policy of encouraging Americans to invest in Latin America. (p. 642)

domestic tranquillity peace at home. (p. 217)

domino theory belief that if South Vietnam became communist, other countries in Southeast Asia would become communist. (p. 809)

downsizing practice of trying to cut costs by using fewer people to do the same work. (p. 828)

draft law requiring men of a certain age to serve in the military. (p. 467)

Dred Scott decision Supreme Court decision in 1857 that stated slaves were property, not citizens. (p. 439)

drought long dry spell. (p. 36)

due process of law right of every citizen to the same fair rules in all cases brought to trial. (pp. 208, 236)

dumping selling goods in another country at very low prices. (p. 312)

E

Earth Day day set aside each year since 1970 to educate people about the environment. (p. 866)

economic depression period during which business activity slows, prices and wages fall, and unemployment rises. (p. 194)

economic sanctions actions taken against a country in the hope of bringing about a change in its policy. (p. 840)

electoral college group of electors from each state that meets every four years to vote for the President and Vice President. (p. 203)

elevation height above the surface of the Earth. (p. 16)

emancipate set free. (p. 464)

Emancipation Proclamation (1863) President Lincoln's declaration freeing slaves in the Confederacy. (p. 464)

embargo ban on trade with another country. (p. 281)

Embargo Act (1807) law forbidding Americans to export or import any goods. (p. 281)

encomienda right to demand taxes or labor from Native Americans in the Spanish colonies. (p. 76)

English Bill of Rights (1689) document that protected the rights of English citizens. (p. 116)

environmentalist person who works to control pollution and protect the land. (p. 866)

Environmental Protection Agency (EPA) government agency concerned with protecting the environment. (p. 866)

Equator imaginary line that lies at 0° latitude and divides the Earth into the Northern and Southern hemispheres. (p. 11)

escalate build up or increase. (p. 810)

ethnic group group of people who share a common culture. (p. 565)

execute carry out. (p. 189)

executive agreement informal agreement made by the President of the United States with other heads of state. (p. 232)

executive branch part of a government that carries out the laws. (p. 197)

exile person forced to leave his or her own country. (p. 805)

Exoduster African Americans who moved to Kansas in the late 1800s. (p. 526)

export trade goods sent to markets outside a country. (p. 113)

extended family close-knit family group that includes grandparents, parents, children, aunts, uncles, and cousins. (p. 394)

F

factory system method of producing goods that brings workers and machines together in one place. (p. 297)

fad style or fashion that becomes popular for a short time. (p. 692)

famine severe shortage of food. (p. 384)

federal national. (p. 221)

Federal Deposit Insurance Corporation (FDIC) corporation set up to insure savings accounts in banks approved by the government. (p. 718)

federalism division of power between the states and the national government. (p. 201)

Federalist supporter of the Constitution in the ratification debate in 1787. Favored a strong national government. (p. 205)

Federal Reserve Act (1913) laws passed by Congress to regulate banking. (p. 606)

feudalism system of rule by lords who owed loyalty to their king. (p. 62)

Fifteenth Amendment constitutional amendment that gave African Americans the right to vote in all states. (p. 490)

fireside chat radio speech given by President Franklin Roosevelt. (p. 715)

First Continental Congress meeting of delegates from 12 colonies in Philadelphia in September 1774. (p. 154)

flapper young woman in the 1920s who declared her independence from traditional rules. (p. 692)

forty-niner person who went to California during the Gold Rush in 1849. (p. 370)

Fourteen Points President Wilson's goals for peace after World War I. (p. 667)

Fourteenth Amendment constitutional amendment that granted citizenship to all persons born in the United States. (p. 488)

freedman freed slave. (p. 482)

Freedmen's Bureau agency that helped former slaves. (p. 483)

Freedom Rider civil rights worker who tried to integrate bus terminals. (p. 815)

free enterprise system economic system in which businesses are owned by private citizens, not by the government. (p. 544)

Free Soil party political party founded in 1848 by antislavery Whigs and Democrats. (p. 429)

French and Indian War conflict between the French and British in North America. Fought from 1754 to 1763. (p. 136)

fugitive runaway, such as an escaped slave in the 1800s. (p. 433)

Fugitive Slave Law of 1850 law that required all citizens to help catch runaway slaves. (p. 434)

G

General Court representative assembly in the Massachusetts Bay Colony. (p. 95)

general welfare well-being of all the people. (p. 218)

gentry highest social class in the 13 English colonies. (p. 118)

geography study of people, their environments, and their resources. (p. 4)

Gettysburg Address speech given by President Lincoln in 1863 after the battle of Gettysburg. (p. 475)

GI Bill of Rights act passed in 1944 to help returning veterans of World War II. (p. 784)

glacier thick sheet of ice. (p. 32)

glasnost Mikhail Gorbachev's policy of speaking out openly and honestly about problems in the Soviet Union. (p. 832)

global warming theory that the Earth's atmosphere is warming up. (p. 868)

Good Neighbor Policy President Franklin Roosevelt's policy intended to strengthen friendly relations with Latin America. (p. 736)

grandfather clause law passed by southern states after the Civil War. Excused a voter from a poll tax or literacy test if his father or grandfather had voted before 1867. Kept most African Americans from voting. (p. 499)

Great Awakening religious movement in the colonies in the 1730s and 1740s. (p. 120)

Great Compromise Roger Sherman's plan at the Constitutional Convention for a two-house legislature. Settled differences between large and small states. (p. 198)

Great Depression period of economic hard times from 1929 to 1941. (p. 709)

Great Society President Lyndon Johnson's plan to improve the standard of living of every American. (p. 799)

gross domestic product (GDP) total value of goods and services produced within a country in one year. (p. 863)

guerrilla fighter who uses hit-and-run attacks. (p. 809)

H

habeas corpus right to have charges filed or a hearing before being jailed. (p. 468)

Harlem Renaissance flowering of African American culture in the 1920s. (p. 696)

hemisphere half of the Earth. (p. 11)

hieroglyphics system of writing that uses pictures to represent words and ideas. (p. 49)

hill area of raised land. Lower, less steep, and more rounded than a mountain. (p. 16)

history account of what has happened in the lives of different peoples. (p. 4)

hogan Navajo house built of mud plaster over a framework of wooden poles. (p. 40)

Holocaust Hitler's policy of killing Jews. (p. 760)

Homestead Act (1862) law giving 160 acres of land in the West to anyone who farmed it for five years. (p. 526)

House of Burgesses representative assembly in colonial Virginia. (p. 86)

House of Representatives lower house of Congress. Each state is represented according to its population. (p. 228)

Hull House settlement house set up by Jane Addams in Chicago in 1889. (p. 573)

Hundred Days the first three months of Franklin Roosevelt's presidency. (p. 716)

I

igloo Inuit house made of snow and ice. (p. 38)

immigrant person who enters a country in order to settle there. (p. 384)

impeach bring formal charges against an official such as the President. (pp. 203, 231)

imperialism policy by which one country takes control of the economic and political affairs of another country or region. (p. 624)

import trade good brought into a country. (p. 113)

impressment act of seizing men from a ship or village and forcing them to serve in the navy. (p. 280)

indentured servant person who signed a contract to work for a certain length of time in exchange for passage to the colonies. (p. 118)

Indian Removal Act (1830) law that forced Native Americans to sign treaties agreeing to move west of the Mississippi. (p. 339)

Industrial Revolution process by which machines replaced hand tools, and new sources of power, such as steam and electricity, replaced human and animal power. (p. 296)

inflation economic cycle in which the value of money falls and the prices of goods rise. (p. 469)

initiative procedure that allows voters to introduce a bill by collecting signatures on a petition. (p. 600)

injunction court order to do or not to do something. (p. 555)

installment buying method of buying on credit. (p. 686)

interchangeable parts identical parts of a tool or instrument that are made by machine. (p. 301)

Internet system that links a network of computers with each other over telephone lines. (p. 857)

Intolerable Acts laws passed in 1774 to punish colonists for the Boston Tea Party. (p. 153)

irrigate bring water to an area. (p. 6)

island hopping strategy of Allies in World War II of capturing some Japanese held islands and going around others. (p. 757)

isolation policy of having little to do with foreign nations. (p. 622)

isthmus narrow strip of land. (p. 16)

J

Jay's Treaty (1795) agreement to stop British attacks on American merchant ships and settle other differences. (p. 252)

GLOSSARY

jerky dried meat. (p. 513)

Jim Crow law law passed by southerners that segregated public places. (p. 499)

joint committee group made up of members of both the House of Representatives and the Senate. (p. 230)

judicial branch part of a government that decides if laws are carried out fairly. (p. 197)

judicial review power of the Supreme Court to decide whether laws passed by Congress are constitutional. (pp. 228, 270)

Judiciary Act (1789) law that organized the federal court system into district and circuit courts. (p. 245)

jury panel of citizens. (p. 234)

justice fairness. (p. 216)

K

kachina masked dancer who represented the spirits in Pueblo religious ceremonies. (p. 40)

kaiser name for the German emperor. (p. 650)

Kansas-Nebraska Act (1854) law that divided Nebraska into two territories. Provided for the question of slavery in the territories to be decided by popular sovereignty. (p. 436)

kayak small boat made of animal skins. (p. 38)

Kentucky and Virginia resolutions (1798, 1799) declarations that states had the right to declare a law unconstitutional. (p. 260)

kitchen cabinet group of unofficial advisers to President Andrew Jackson. (p. 334)

kiva underground chamber where Pueblo men held religious ceremonies. (p. 40)

Know-Nothing party political party organized by nativists in the 1850s. (p. 385)

Ku Klux Klan secret group first set up in the South after the Civil War. Members terrorized African Americans and other minority groups. (p. 494)

L

laissez faire (lehs ay FAYR) French term meaning let alone. Referred to the idea that government should play as small a role as possible in economic affairs. (p. 269)

Land Ordinance of 1785 law that set up a system for settling the Northwest Territory. (p. 192)

latitude distance north or south from the Equator. (p. 4)

League of Nations association of nations proposed by Woodrow Wilson in his Fourteen Points. (p. 668)

League of the Iroquois alliance of the five Iroquois nations. Formed in 1570. (p. 46)

legislative branch part of a government that passes laws. (p. 197)

legislature group of people with power to make laws for a country or colony. (p. 115)

liberty freedom to live as you please as long as you obey the laws and respect the rights of others. (p. 218)

literacy test examination to see if a person can read and write. (p. 499)

longhorn wild cattle that once roamed free in Texas. (p. 522)

long house Iroquois dwelling. (p. 46)

longitude distance east or west from the Prime Meridian. (p. 4)

Louisiana Purchase large territory purchased from France in 1803. (p. 273)

Loyalist colonist who stayed loyal to Great Britain during the American Revolution. (p. 167)

M

Magna Carta document that guaranteed rights to English nobles in 1215. (p. 86)

magnetic compass device that shows which direction is north. (p. 63)

mainstream practice of placing students with disabilities in regular classes. (p. 873)

Manifest Destiny belief that the United States had the right to all the land between the Atlantic and Pacific oceans. (p. 363)

manor part of a lord's holding in the Middle Ages, including the castle, peasants' huts, and surrounding villages or fields. (p. 62)

map projection way of drawing the Earth on a flat surface. (p. 8)

Marbury* v. *Madison (1803) Supreme Court case that set the precedent of judicial review. (p. 270)

Marshall Plan American plan to help European nations rebuild their economies after World War II. (p. 773)

mass production making large quantities of a product quickly and cheaply. (p. 549)

Mayflower Compact (1620) agreement signed by Pilgrims before they landed at Plymouth. (p. 89)

Medicaid Great Society program to help poor people pay medical bills. (p. 799)

Medicare Great Society plan to help pay the hospital bills of citizens over age 65. (p. 799)

mercantilism economic theory that a nation's strength came from building up its gold supplies and expanding its trade. (p. 112)

mestizo person in the Spanish colonies of mixed Spanish and Indian background. (p. 76)

Middle Ages period from about 500 to 1350 in Europe. (p. 62)

Middle Colonies colonies of New York, New Jersey, Pennsylvania, and Delaware. (p. 100)

Middle Passage ocean trip from Africa to the Americas in which thousands of slaves died. (p. 111)

migrant worker person who moves from place to place in search of work. (p. 725)

militarism policy of building up strong military forces to prepare for war. (p. 648)

militia army of citizens who serve as soldiers during an emergency. (p. 154)

minuteman volunteer who trained to fight the British in 1775. (p. 154)

mission religious settlement. Run by Catholic priests and friars in the Spanish colonies. (p. 75)

Missouri Compromise (1820) plan proposed by Henry Clay to keep the number of slave and free states equal. (p. 429)

mobilize prepare for war. (p. 649)

monopoly company that completely controls the market of a certain industry. (p. 544)

GLOSSARY

Monroe Doctrine policy statement of President James Monroe in 1823. Warned European nations not to interfere in Latin America. (p. 319)

Mormon member of the Church of Jesus Christ of Latter-day Saints. (p. 369)

Mound Builders Native Americans who built thousands of huge earth mounds from eastern Oklahoma to the Atlantic. (p. 34)

mountain high, rugged land usually at least 1,000 feet (300 m) above the surrounding land. (p. 16)

Mountain Man trapper in the West in the early 1800s. (p. 351)

muckraker person who reported on corrupt politicians and other problems of the cities. (p. 597)

N

National Association for the Advancement of Colored People (NAACP) organization formed in 1909 to work to gain equal rights for African Americans. (p. 614)

national debt total sum of money a government owes. (p. 245)

National Grange group of farmers who worked together to improve conditions. Formed in 1867. (p. 530)

nationalism pride in or devotion to one's country. (p. 282)

National Organization for Women (NOW) organization set up in 1966 to work for equal rights for women. (p. 821)

Native American descendant of people who reached the Americas thousands of years ago. (p. 33)

nativist person who wanted to limit immigration and preserve the United States for native-born white Americans. (p. 385)

Navigation Acts laws that governed trade between England and its colonies. (p. 114)

Nazi member of the German National Socialist Workers party, organized by Adolf Hitler. (p. 737)

network system of connected railroad lines. (p. 536)

neutral choosing not to fight on either side in a war. (p. 174)

New Deal name for the programs of President Franklin Roosevelt. (p. 716)

New England Colonies colonies of Massachusetts, New Hampshire, Connecticut, and Rhode Island. (p. 94)

New Freedom President Woodrow Wilson's program to break up trusts into smaller companies to spur competition. (p. 606)

Nineteenth Amendment (1919) constitutional amendment that gave women the right to vote. (p. 609)

nominating convention meeting at which a political party selects a candidate for President. (p. 330)

nonimportation agreement promise of colonial merchants and planters to stop importing goods taxed by the Townshend Acts. (p. 145)

North American Free Trade Agreement (NAFTA) (1993) Agreement with Canada and Mexico that will slowly do away with trade barriers among the three nations. (p. 865)

North Atlantic Treaty Organization (NATO) alliance formed in 1949 by the United States and Western European nations to fight Soviet aggression. (p. 774)

Northwest Ordinance (1787) law that set up a government for the Northwest Territory. It also set up a way for new states to be admitted to the United States. (p. 192)

northwest passage waterway through or around North America. (p. 78)

nullification idea of declaring a federal law illegal. (p. 337)

nullify cancel. (p. 260)

O

on margin practice that allowed people to buy stock with a down payment of 10 percent of the full value. (p. 686)

Open Door Policy (1899) policy toward China that allowed a nation to trade in any other nation's sphere of influence. (p. 628)

override overrule. Congress can override a President's veto if two thirds of both houses vote to do so. (pp. 203, 223)

ozone layer layer of the atmosphere that protects the Earth from harmful rays. (p. 868)

P

pacifist person who refuses to fight in a war. (p. 660)

Patriot colonist who supported the American Revolution. (p. 167)

patronage practice of giving out government jobs as favors to loyal party workers. (p. 594)

patroon rich landowner in the Dutch colonies. (p. 101)

peninsulare person sent from Spain to rule the Spanish colonies. (p. 76)

pet bank state bank used by President Jackson and Roger Taney to deposit government money. (p. 336)

Pilgrims group of English settlers who sought religious freedom in the Americas. (p. 87)

plain broad area of fairly level land. (p. 16)

plantation large estate farmed by many workers. (p. 76)

plateau large raised area of flat or gently rolling land. (p. 18)

Platt Amendment amendment to Cuba's constitution that limited Cuba's freedom and allowed the United States to intervene in Cuban affairs. (p. 637)

Plessy v. Ferguson (1896) ruling by the Supreme Court that segregation was legal as long as facilities for blacks and whites were equal. (p. 499)

poll tax fee paid by a voter in order to vote. (p. 499)

pool method of ending competition used by railroads and other businesses in the late 1800s. Railroads divided up business in an area and fixed prices at a high level. (p. 538)

popular sovereignty control by the people; allowing each territory to decide for itself whether or not to allow slavery. (p. 429)

Populist party political party that was formed by farmers and union members in 1891. (p. 530)

potlatch ceremonial dinner among some Native Americans of the Northwest Coast. (p. 39)

poverty line minimum income the government says that people need in order to live. (p. 801)

preamble an opening statement. (p. 216)

GLOSSARY

precedent act or decision that sets an example for others to follow. (pp. 227, 244)

precipitation water that falls from the sky in the form of rain or snow. (p. 22)

presidio fort that housed soldiers in the Spanish colonies. (p. 74)

primary election held before a general election in which voters choose their party's candidate for office. (p. 600)

Proclamation of 1763 British law that forbade American colonists to settle west of a line that ran along the Appalachian Mountains. (p. 143)

profiteer person who takes advantage of an emergency to make money. (p. 469)

Progressive Era period from 1898 to 1917 when reformers won many changes to improve American life. (p. 598)

Prohibition period from 1920 to 1933 when the making and sale of liquor were illegal in the United States. (p. 687)

propaganda spreading of ideas or beliefs that help a particular cause and hurt an opposing cause. (p. 653)

proprietary colony English colony in which the king gave land to proprietors in exchange for a yearly payment. (p. 101)

protective tariff tax placed on imported goods to protect from foreign competition. (p. 248)

public interest the good of all the people. (p. 598)

public school school supported by taxes. (p. 121)

public works program government program that hires workers for projects such as building schools, courthouses, dams, and highways. (p. 712)

pueblo adobe dwelling of the Anasazis; Spanish word for village or town. (pp. 36, 74)

pull factor condition that attracts people to a new area. (p. 562)

Pure Food and Drug Act (1906) law requiring food and drug makers to list all ingredients on their packages. (p. 604)

Puritans group of English Protestants who settled in Massachusetts. (p. 94)

push factor condition that drives people to leave their homes for a new area. (p. 562)

Q

Quakers Protestant reformers who settled in Pennsylvania. (p. 102)

Quartering Act (1765) law that required English colonists to provide housing, candles, bedding, and beverages to British soldiers stationed in the colonies. (p. 147)

quota system limit on immigration that allowed only a certain number of people to immigrate to the United States from each country. (p. 700)

R

racism belief that one race is superior to another. (p. 111)

Radical Reconstruction period after the Civil War when Republicans controlled Congress and passed strict laws affecting the South. (p. 488)

Radical Republicans group of Republicans in Congress who wanted to protect the rights of freedmen in the South and keep rich southern planters out of power. (p. 487)

ragtime popular music in the late 1800s that had a lively, rhythmic sound. (p. 577)

ratify approve. (pp. 182, 220)

realist writer or artist who shows life as it really is. (p. 581)

rebate discount on services or merchandise. (p. 538)

recall special election that allows voters to remove an elected official from office. (p. 600)

recession mild depression in which business slows down and some workers lose their jobs. (p. 829)

Reconstruction period after the Civil War when the South was rebuilt; also, the federal program to rebuild it. (p. 482)

Red Scare period in the 1920s during which radicals were arrested and foreigners deported because of a fear of communism. (p. 699)

referendum process by which people can vote directly on a bill. (p. 600)

relief difference in height of land. (p. 16)

relief government program that gives help to the needy. (p. 712)

rendezvous yearly meeting where Mountain Men traded furs for supplies. (p. 351)

renewable resource natural resource that can be quickly replaced by nature. (p. 869)

reparations payments for losses that a nation has suffered during a war. (p. 668)

repeal cancel. (p. 145)

representative government system of government in which voters elect representatives to make laws for them. (pp. 86, 220)

republic nation in which voters elect representatives to govern them. (p. 199)

Republican party political party formed in 1854 by a group of Free Soilers, northern Democrats, and antislavery Whigs. (p. 440)

reservation limited area set aside for Native Americans by the government. (p. 516)

Roosevelt Corollary (1904) expansion of the Monroe Doctrine announced by President Theodore Roosevelt. Claimed the right of the United States to intervene in Latin America to preserve law and order. (p. 641)

Rough Riders volunteer cavalry regiment organized by Theodore Roosevelt for the Spanish-American War. (p. 633)

S

sachem tribal chief of the Iroquois. (p. 46)

scalawag white southerner who supported Radical Republicans. (p. 492)

secede withdraw. (p. 338)

Second Great Awakening religious movement that swept the nation in the early 1800s. (p. 402)

sectionalism loyalty to a state or section rather than to the whole country. (p. 429)

sedition stirring up rebellion against a government. (p. 260)

Sedition Act (1798) law that allowed citizens to be fined or jailed for criticizing public officials. (p. 260)

GLOSSARY

segregation separation of people of different races. (p. 499)

self-determination right of national groups to their own territory and forms of government. (p. 668)

Senate upper house of Congress. Each state is represented by two senators. (p. 230)

Seneca Falls Convention (1848) meeting at which leaders of the women's rights movement voted on a plan for achieving equality. (p. 411)

separation of powers system in which the power of a government is divided among separate branches. (p. 201)

serf peasant who was bound to the land for life. (p. 62)

service industry industry in which workers perform services rather than produce goods. (p. 863)

settlement house community center offering help to the poor. (p. 572)

sharecropper farmer who works land owned by another and gives the landowner part of the harvest. (p. 496)

Shays' Rebellion (1786) revolt of Massachusetts farmers against increased taxes. (p. 194)

Sherman Antitrust Act (1890) act prohibiting trusts or other businesses from limiting competition. (pp. 545, 596)

sitdown strike work stoppage in which workers shut down all machines and refuse to leave a factory until their demands are met. (p. 721)

skilled worker person with a trade, such as a carpenter, a printer, or a shoemaker. (p. 382)

slave code laws that controlled behavior of slaves and denied them basic rights. (p. 111)

Social Security Act (1935) law that provided for the elderly and unemployed. (p. 722)

sodbuster Plains farmer. (p. 527)

solar energy power from the sun. (p. 869)

Sons of Liberty group of colonial men who joined together to protest the Stamp Act and protect colonial liberties. (p. 145)

Southern Colonies colonies of Maryland, Virginia, North and South Carolina, and Georgia. (p. 106)

speakeasy illegal bar that served liquor during Prohibition. (p. 688)

speculator person who invests in a risky venture in the hope of making a large profit. (p. 247)

sphere of influence area in China where a foreign nation had special trading privileges and made laws for its own citizens. (p. 628)

spinning jenny machine that let a person spin several threads at once. (p. 296)

spoils system practice of rewarding supporters with government jobs. (p. 334)

Square Deal Theodore Roosevelt's promise that all groups should have an equal opportunity to succeed. (p. 604)

stalemate situation in which neither side is strong enough to defeat the other. (p. 651)

Stamp Act (1765) law passed by Parliament that taxed legal documents, newspapers, almanacs, playing cards, and dice. (p. 143)

standard time zone one of the 24 time divisions of the world as measured from the Prime Meridian. (p. 13)

standing committee permanent committee in the House of Representatives or the Senate. (p. 230)

states' rights idea that individual states have the right to limit the power of the federal government. (p. 337)

stock shares in a corporation run by a single board of directors. (p. 541)

strike refusal by union workers to do their jobs until their demands are met. (p. 384)

suffrage right to vote. (p. 330)

suffragist person who campaigned for women's right to vote. (p. 608)

superpower nation with enough political and economic strength to influence events in many areas of the world. (p. 804)

Supreme Court highest court in the United States. (p. 234)

T

Taft-Hartley Act (1947) law meant to prevent strikes by workers. (p. 784)

tariff tax on foreign goods brought into a country. (p. 248)

Tariff of Abominations name given by southerners to the Tariff of 1828. (p. 336)

tax-in-kind tax paid with goods rather than money. (p. 469)

Tea Act (1773) British law that let the British East India Company sell tea directly to colonists. (p. 150)

telegraph device that sends electrical signals along a wire. (p. 378)

temperance movement campaign against the sale or drinking of alcohol. (p. 415)

tenement apartment in a six- or seven-story building in a city. (p. 571)

Tennessee Valley Authority (TVA) New Deal program to control flooding and bring electric power to the Tennessee River valley. (p. 718)

tepee cone-shaped tent made of buffalo hides. (p. 41)

termination federal policy aimed at breaking up and ending tribal governments of Native Americans. (p. 819)

Thirteenth Amendment (1865) constitutional amendment that banned slavery in the United States. (p. 485)

Three-Fifths Compromise agreement of delegates to the Constitutional Convention that three fifths of the slaves in any state be counted in its population. (p. 198)

toleration willingness to let others practice their own beliefs. (p. 96)

totalitarian state country where a single party controls the government and every aspect of the lives of the people. (p. 739)

Townshend Acts (1767) British laws that taxed goods such as glass, paint, paper, silk, and tea. (p. 145)

trade deficit situation that occurs when a nation buys more goods and services from foreign countries than it sells to them. (p. 864)

trade union association of workers formed to win better wages and working conditions. (p. 384)

Trail of Tears forced march of Native Americans to lands west of the Mississippi. (p. 340)

traitor person who betrays his or her country. (p. 165)

transcontinental railroad railroad that stretches across a continent from coast to coast. (p. 510)

travois sled used by Plains people to haul gear. (p. 43)

Treaty of Ghent (1814) treaty that ended the War of 1812 between Britain and the United States. (p. 291)

Treaty of Greenville (1795) treaty between the United States and 12 Indian nations of the Northwest Territory. (p. 252)

Treaty of Paris (1763) treaty that ended the French and Indian War. (p. 141)

Treaty of Paris (1783) treaty that ended the American Revolution. (p. 182)

trench warfare type of fighting during World War I in which both sides dug trenches protected by mines and barbed wire. (p. 651)

triangular trade colonial trade route between New England, the West Indies, and Africa. (p. 114)

tributary branch of a river. (p. 20)

Truman Doctrine statement of President Truman that promised military and economic support to nations threatened by communism. (p. 773)

trust group of corporations run by a single board of directors. (p. 544)

trustbuster person who wanted to end all trusts. (p. 603)

turnpike road built by a private company. Charged tolls to those using it. (p. 306)

tyranny cruel and unjust government. (p. 220)

U

unconstitutional not permitted by the Constitution. (pp. 223, 255)

underground railroad secret network of people who helped runaway slaves to reach freedom in the North or Canada. (p. 405)

United Nations international organization formed in 1945 to help solve conflicts between nations. (p. 774)

unskilled worker person who does a job that requires little or no special training. (p. 384)

V

vaccine substance that causes a mild form of a disease. Injected into a healthy person to cause the body to build up the ability to fight off the disease. (p. 856)

vaquero Spanish cowboy. (p. 522)

vaudeville variety show that included comedians, song-and-dance routines, and acrobats. (p. 577)

V-E Day (May 8, 1945) Marked the end of World War II in Europe. Stands for Victory in Europe. (p. 757)

Versailles Treaty treaty that ended World War I. (p. 668)

vertical integration method of controlling an industry from raw materials to finished products. (p. 541)

veto reject. (pp. 203, 223)

viceroy official who rules an area in the name of a king or queen. (p. 96)

vigilante self-appointed law enforcer who deals out punishment without holding a trial. (p. 371)

V-J Day (August 14, 1945) Marked the end of World War II in the Pacific. Stands for Victory over Japan. (p. 759)

Voting Rights Act (1965) law that ended literacy tests for voting and allowed federal officials to register voters in states that practiced discrimination. (p. 815)

W

Wade-Davis Bill Reconstruction plan passed by Republicans in Congress in July 1864. Vetoed by President Lincoln. (p. 483)

Wagner Act (1935) law that protected workers from unfair management practices. (p.721)

War Hawks members of Congress who wanted war with Britain in 1812. (p. 282)

Watergate Affair political scandal that led to the resignation of President Nixon. (p. 802)

weather condition of the Earth's atmosphere at any given time and place. (p. 22)

Whiskey Rebellion (1794) revolt of farmers to protest the tax on whiskey. (p. 250)

wholesale refers to buying and selling of goods in large quantities and at a lower price. (p. 530)

Wisconsin Idea program of progressive reforms introduced by Robert La Follette in Wisconsin in the early 1900s. (p. 600)

women's rights movement the struggle of women for equality. (p. 821)

writ of assistance legal document that let a British customs officer inspect a ship's cargo without giving any reason for the search. (p. 145)

X

XYZ Affair (1797) incident in which French agents asked American ambassadors in Paris for a bribe. (p. 259)

Y

Yankee nickname given to merchants from New England. (p. 114)

yellow journalism sensational style of reporting used by some newspapers in the late 1800s. (p. 580)

Z

Zimmermann telegram secret message from Germany to Mexico urging Mexico to attack the United States if the United States declared war on Germany in World War I. (p. 655)

Connections With Literature

CONNECTIONS WITH LITERATURE

Topic	Author	Work/Genre	See Prentice Hall Literature*
UNIT 6 Reshaping the Nation			
Driving Cattle to Market, The Cowhand's Life, pages 522–523	J. Frank Dobie	Sancho (narrative essay)	Silver, page 431
Spanning the Country by Rail, pages 509–510	Adrien Stoutenburg	The Hammerman (folk tale)	Silver, page 643
Spanning the Country by Rail pages 509–510		John Henry (folk song)	Silver, page 650
Way of Life, pages, 512–513	Mari Sandoz	These Were the Sioux (essay)	Bronze, page 411
The Cowhand's Life pages 522–523	Harold W. Felton	Pecos Bill: The Cyclone (tall tale)	Silver, page 673
Realism in Art, pages 582–583	H. N. Levitt	Winslow Homer: America's Greatest Painter (essay)	Bronze, page 395
UNIT 7 A New Role in the World			
William Seward and American Expansion pages 623–624	Robert Service	The Cremation of Sam McGee (poetry)	Bronze, page 445
William Seward and American Expansion pages 623–624	Jack London	The King of Mazy May (short story)	Copper, page 25
Annexing Hawaii, pages 626–627	Vivian L. Thompson	The Riddling Youngster (folk tale)	Copper, page 585
Ruling Cuba and Puerto Rico, pages 636–637	Pura Belpre	The Legend of the Hummingbird (legend)	Bronze, page 621
UNIT 8 Prosperity, Depression, and War			
Harlem Renaissance, pages 694–696	Langston Hughes	Harlem Night Song, Winter Moon (poetry)	Silver, pages 558 and 578
Hard Times, pages 710–712	Russell Baker	No Gumption (autobiography)	Bronze, page 329
African Americans in the Great Depression, pages 726–727	Mildred Taylor	Song of the Trees (short story)	Bronze, page 111
The Holocaust, pages 760–761	Frances Goodrich and Albert Hackett	The Diary of Anne Frank (drama)	Silver, page 303
UNIT 9 The Nation Today and Tomorrow			
The Voices of Montgomery, pages 791–793	Raymond Richard Patterson	Martin Luther King, Jr. (poetry)	Bronze, page 523
The Uncertain Enemy, pages 810–811	Le Ly Hayslip	Fathers and Daughters (autobiography)	Silver, page 421
Native Americans, pages 870–871	Virginia Driving Hawk Sneve	The Medicine Bag (short story)	Silver, page 225
African Americans, pages 871–872	Richard Wesley	The House of Dies Drear (drama)	Silver, page 245

*The page references to Prentice Hall Literature are from the Paramount Edition.

CONNECTIONS WITH LITERATURE

Connections With Science

918 • Reference Section

Topic	See Prentice Hall Science

UNIT 5 The Nation Torn Apart

Naval Action, page 459
(water displacement and ironclad ships)

Matter: Building Block of the Universe, Volume and Density, pages N20–N25

The Blue and the Gray, pages 466–467
(infection and disease)

Human Biology and Health, Infectious Diseases, pages H203–H205

UNIT 6 Reshaping the Nation

Way of Life, pages 512–513
(Plains Indians)

Exploring Earth's Weather, Connections: A Pharmacy on the Prairie, page K105

Plentiful Resources, pages 543–544
(oil)

Ecology: Earth's Natural Resources, What Are Fossil Fuels? pages L12–L18

Advances in Communication, pages 546–547
(telephone)

Electricity and Magnetism, Transmitting Sound, pages P95–P98

Thomas Edison and the "Invention Factory,"
page 547 (electricity)

Electricity and Magnetism, Electric Charges and Currents, pages P10–P39; Electricity From Magnetism, pages P72–P80

UNIT 7 A New Role in the World

The Promise of a Square Deal, pages 603–605
(protecting natural resources)

Ecology: Earth's Living Resources, Wildlife Conservation, pages G99–G123

The Temperance Crusade, page 611
(alcohol)

Human Biology and Health, Alcohol, pages H219–H222

Annexing Hawaii, pages 626–627
(Hawaii)

Exploring Earth's Weather, Tropical Rain Forests, pages K99–K100

Dynamic Earth, Formation of a Volcano, pages J40-J46

UNIT 8 Prosperity, Depression, and War

The Auto Industry Fuels Growth, pages 684–685
(automobile)

Heat Energy, Internal-Combustion Engines, pages Q55–Q56

A Mass Society, pages 691–692
(radio)

Sound and Light, Radio Waves, pages R72–R75

Electricity and Magnetism, Transmitting Sound, pages P95–P98

Drought and Dust, pages 723–725
(Dust Bowl)

Exploring Earth's Weather, Problem Solving: What Causes a Drought? page K89

Defeat of Japan, page 759
(atomic bomb)

Chemistry of Matter, Nuclear Fission, pages O126–O127

UNIT 9 The Nation Today and Tomorrow

Television, pages 788–789
(television)

Electricity and Magnetism, Transmitting Pictures, pages P99–P101

Medical Advances, page 856
(AIDS)

Human Biology and Health, AIDS, pages H201–H202

Computers Change American Life, pages 856–857
(computers)

Electricity and Magnetism, Computers, pages P102–P107

The Space Age, pages 858–860
(space shuttle)

Exploring the Universe, The Space Age, pages M126–M131

The Energy Question, pages 868–869
(conservation of resources)

Ecology: Earth's Natural Resources, Conserving Earth's Resources, pages L95–L107

CONNECTIONS WITH SCIENCE

Reference Section • **919**

Connections With Fine Art

CONNECTIONS WITH FINE ART

* This is a partial list of the fine art found in *The American Nation*. For source information for all works, see the illustration credits on pages 970–974.

Reference Section • **921**

Presidents of the United States

1. **George Washington** (1732–1799)
   Years in office: 1789–1797
   No political party
   Elected from: Virginia
   Vice Pres.: John Adams

2. **John Adams** (1735–1826)
   Years in office: 1797–1801
   Federalist party
   Elected from: Massachusetts
   Vice Pres.: Thomas Jefferson

3. **Thomas Jefferson** (1743–1826)
   Years in office: 1801–1809
   Democratic Republican party
   Elected from: Virginia
   Vice Pres.: Aaron Burr, George Clinton

4. **James Madison** (1751–1836)
   Years in office: 1809–1817
   Democratic Republican party
   Elected from: Virginia
   Vice Pres.: George Clinton,
             Elbridge Gerry

5. **James Monroe** (1758–1831)
   Years in office: 1817–1825
   Democratic Republican party
   Elected from: Virginia
   Vice Pres.: Daniel Tompkins

6. **John Quincy Adams** (1767–1848)
   Years in office: 1825–1829
   National Republican party
   Elected from: Massachusetts
   Vice Pres.: John Calhoun

7. **Andrew Jackson** (1767–1845)
   Years in office: 1829–1837
   Democratic party
   Elected from: Tennessee
   Vice Pres.: John Calhoun,
             Martin Van Buren

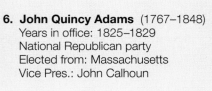

8. **Martin Van Buren** (1782–1862)
   Years in office: 1837–1841
   Democratic party
   Elected from: New York
   Vice Pres.: Richard Johnson

9

9. **William Henry Harrison*** (1773–1841)
   Years in office: 1841
   Whig party
   Elected from: Ohio
   Vice Pres.: John Tyler

10. **John Tyler** (1790–1862)
    Years in office: 1841–1845
    Whig party
    Elected from: Virginia
    Vice Pres.: none

10

11. **James K. Polk** (1795–1849)
    Years in office: 1845–1849
    Democratic party
    Elected from: Tennessee
    Vice Pres.: George Dallas

12. **Zachary Taylor*** (1784–1850)
    Years in office: 1849–1850
    Whig party
    Elected from: Louisiana
    Vice Pres.: Millard Fillmore

11

12

13. **Millard Fillmore** (1800–1874)
    Years in office: 1850–1853
    Whig party
    Elected from: New York
    Vice Pres.: none

14. **Franklin Pierce** (1804–1869)
    Years in office: 1853–1857
    Democratic party
    Elected from: New Hampshire
    Vice Pres.: William King

13

14

15. **James Buchanan** (1791–1868)
    Years in office: 1857–1861
    Democratic party
    Elected from: Pennsylvania
    Vice Pres.: John Breckinridge

16. **Abraham Lincoln**** (1809–1865)
    Years in office: 1861–1865
    Republican party
    Elected from: Illinois
    Vice Pres.: Hannibal Hamlin,
                Andrew Johnson

15

16

*Died in office   **Assassinated

PRESIDENTS OF THE UNITED STATES

17

19

21

23

25

17. **Andrew Johnson** (1808–1875)
    Years in office: 1865–1869
    Republican party
    Elected from: Tennessee
    Vice Pres.: none

18. **Ulysses S. Grant** (1822–1885)
    Years in office: 1869–1877
    Republican party
    Elected from: Illinois
    Vice Pres.: Schuyler Colfax,
       Henry Wilson

19. **Rutherford B. Hayes** (1822–1893)
    Years in office: 1877–1881
    Republican party
    Elected from: Ohio
    Vice Pres.: William Wheeler

20. **James A. Garfield**** (1831–1881)
    Years in office: 1881
    Republican party
    Elected from: Ohio
    Vice Pres.: Chester A. Arthur

21. **Chester A. Arthur** (1830–1886)
    Years in office: 1881–1885
    Republican party
    Elected from: New York
    Vice Pres.: none

22. **Grover Cleveland** (1837–1908)
    Years in office: 1885–1889
    Democratic party
    Elected from: New York
    Vice Pres.: Thomas Hendricks

23. **Benjamin Harrison** (1833–1901)
    Years in office: 1889–1893
    Republican party
    Elected from: Indiana
    Vice Pres.: Levi Morton

24. **Grover Cleveland** (1837–1908)
    Years in office: 1893–1897
    Democratic party
    Elected from: New York
    Vice Pres.: Adlai Stevenson

25. **William McKinley**** (1843–1901)
    Years in office: 1897–1901
    Republican party
    Elected from: Ohio
    Vice Pres.: Garret Hobart,
       Theodore Roosevelt

26. **Theodore Roosevelt** (1858–1919)
    Years in office: 1901–1909
    Republican party
    Elected from: New York
    Vice Pres.: Charles Fairbanks

18

20

22

24

26

924 • Reference Section

27

28

27. **William Howard Taft** (1857–1930)
Years in office: 1909–1913
Republican party
Elected from: Ohio
Vice Pres.: James Sherman

28. **Woodrow Wilson** (1856–1924)
Years in office: 1913–1921
Democratic party
Elected from: New Jersey
Vice Pres.: Thomas Marshall

29. **Warren G. Harding*** (1865–1923)
Years in office: 1921–1923
Republican party
Elected from: Ohio
Vice Pres.: Calvin Coolidge

30. **Calvin Coolidge** (1872–1933)
Years in office: 1923–1929
Republican party
Elected from: Massachusetts
Vice Pres.: Charles Dawes

31. **Herbert C. Hoover** (1874–1964)
Years in office: 1929–1933
Republican party
Elected from: California
Vice Pres.: Charles Curtis

32. **Franklin D. Roosevelt*** (1882–1945)
Years in office: 1933–1945
Democratic party
Elected from: New York
Vice Pres.: John Garner, Henry
　　　　　　 Wallace, Harry S. Truman

33. **Harry S. Truman** (1884–1972)
Years in office: 1945–1953
Democratic party
Elected from: Missouri
Vice Pres.: Alben Barkley

34. **Dwight D. Eisenhower** (1890–1969)
Years in office: 1953–1961
Republican party
Elected from: New York
Vice Pres.: Richard M. Nixon

35. **John F. Kennedy**** (1917–1963)
Years in office: 1961–1963
Democratic party
Elected from: Massachusetts
Vice Pres.: Lyndon B. Johnson

36. **Lyndon B. Johnson** (1908–1973)
Years in office: 1963–1969
Democratic party
Elected from: Texas
Vice Pres.: Hubert Humphrey

30

32

34

29

31

33

35

36

*Died in office　　**Assassinated

PRESIDENTS OF THE UNITED STATES

Reference Section • **925**

37

39

41

37. **Richard M. Nixon***** (1913–1994)
Years in office: 1969–1974
Republican party
Elected from: New York
Vice Pres.: Spiro Agnew,
              Gerald R. Ford

38. **Gerald R. Ford** (1913–)
Years in office: 1974–1977
Republican party
Elected from: Michigan
Vice Pres.: Nelson Rockefeller

39. **Jimmy Carter** (1924–)
Years in office: 1977–1981
Democratic party
Elected from: Georgia
Vice Pres.: Walter Mondale

40. **Ronald W. Reagan** (1911–)
Years in office: 1981–1989
Republican party
Elected from: California
Vice Pres.: George H.W. Bush

41. **George H.W. Bush** (1924–)
Years in office: 1989–1993
Republican party
Elected from: Texas
Vice Pres.: J. Danforth Quayle

42. **William J. Clinton** (1946–)
Years in office: 1993–
Democratic party
Elected from: Arkansas
Vice Pres.: Albert Gore, Jr.

38

40

42

***Resigned

★ All pictures in Presidents of the United States are official portraits.

The Declaration of Independence

On June 7, 1776, the Continental Congress approved the resolution that "these United Colonies are, and of right ought to be, free and independent States." Congress then appointed a committee to write a declaration of independence. The committee members were John Adams, Benjamin Franklin, Robert Livingston, Roger Sherman, and Thomas Jefferson.

Jefferson actually wrote the Declaration, but he got advice from the others. On July 2, Congress discussed the Declaration and made some changes. On July 4, 1776, it adopted the Declaration of Independence in its final form.

The Declaration is printed in black. The headings have been added to show the parts of the Declaration. They are not part of the original text. Annotations, or explanations, are on the tan side of the page. Page numbers in the annotations show where a subject is discussed in the text. Difficult words are defined.

When in the course of human events it becomes necessary for one people to dissolve the political bands which have connected them with another and to assume, among the powers of the earth, the separate and equal station to which the laws of nature and of nature's God entitle them, a decent respect to the opinions of mankind requires that they should declare the causes which impel them to the separation.

dissolve: break **powers of the earth:** other nations **station:** place **impel:** force

The colonists feel that they must explain to the world the reasons why they are breaking away from England.

The Purpose of Government Is to Protect Basic Rights

We hold these truths to be self-evident, that all men are created equal; that they are endowed by their Creator with certain unalienable rights; that among these are life, liberty, and the pursuit of happiness. That, to secure these rights, governments are instituted among men, deriving their just powers from the consent of the governed; that, whenever any form of government becomes destructive of these ends, it is the right of the people to alter or to abolish it, and to institute a new government, laying its foundation on such principles and organizing its powers in such form, as to them shall seem most likely to effect their safety and happiness. Prudence, indeed, will dictate that governments long established should not be changed for light and transient causes; and, accordingly, all experience hath shown that mankind are more disposed to suffer, while evils are sufferable, than to right themselves by abolishing the forms to which they are accustomed. But when a long train of abuses and usurpations, pursuing invariably the same object, evinces a design to reduce them under absolute despotism, it is their right, it is their duty, to throw off such government and to provide new guards for their future security. Such has been the patient sufferance of these colonies, and such is now the necessity which constrains them to alter their former systems of government. The history of the present King of Great Britain is a history of repeated injuries and usurpations, all having, in direct object, the establishment of an absolute

endowed: given **unalienable rights:** so basic that they cannot be taken away **secure:** protect **instituted:** set up **deriving:** getting **alter:** change **effect:** bring about

People set up governments to protect their basic rights. Governments get their power from the consent of the governed. If a government takes away the basic rights of the people, the people have the right to change the government.

prudence: wisdom **transient:** temporary, passing **disposed:** likely **usurpations:** taking and using powers that do not belong to a person **invariably:** always **evinces a design to reduce them under absolute despotism:** makes a clear plan to put them under complete and unjust control **sufferance:** endurance **constrains:** forces **absolute tyranny:** harsh and unjust government

DECLARATION OF INDEPENDENCE

candid: free from prejudice

People do not change governments for slight reasons. But they are forced to do so when a government becomes tyrannical. King George III has a long record of abusing his power.

assent: approval   **relinquish:** give up
inestimable: too great a value to be measured   **formidable:** causing fear

This part of the Declaration spells out three sets of wrongs that led the colonists to break with Britain.

The first set of wrongs is the king's unjust use of power. The king refused to approve laws that are needed. He has tried to control the colonial legislatures.

depository: central storehouse   **fatiguing:** tiring out   **compliance:** giving in
dissolved: broken up   **annihilation:** total destruction   **convulsions:** disturbances

The king has tried to force colonial legislatures into doing his will by wearing them out. He has dissolved legislatures (such as those of New York and Massachusetts). (See pages 149 and 153.)

endeavored: tried   **obstructing:** blocking
naturalization: process of becoming a citizen
migration: moving   **hither:** here
appropriations: grants   **obstructed the administration of justice:** prevented justice from being done   **judiciary powers:** system of law courts   **tenure:** term (of office)
erected: set up   **multitude:** large number
swarms: huge crowds   **harass:** cause trouble   **render:** make

Among other wrongs, he has refused to let settlers move west to take up new land. He has prevented justice from being done. Also, he has sent large numbers of customs officials to cause problems for the colonists.

jurisdiction: authority   **quartering:** housing
mock: false

The king has joined with others, meaning Parliament, to make laws for the colonies. The Declaration then lists the second set of wrongs—unjust acts of Parliament.

928 • Reference Section

---

tyranny over these States. To prove this, let facts be submitted to a candid world:

Wrongs Done by the King

He has refused his assent to laws the most wholesome and necessary for the public good.

He has forbidden his governors to pass laws of immediate and pressing importance, unless suspended in their operation till his assent should be obtained; and, when so suspended, he has utterly neglected to attend to them.

He has refused to pass other laws for the accommodation of the large districts of people, unless those people would relinquish the right of representation in the legislature; a right inestimable to them and formidable to tyrants only.

He has called together legislative bodies at places unusual, uncomfortable, and distant from the depository of their public records, for the sole purpose of fatiguing them into compliance with his measures.

He has dissolved representative houses, repeatedly for opposing, with manly firmness, his invasions on the rights of the people.

He has refused, for a long time after such dissolutions, to cause others to be elected: whereby the legislative powers, incapable of annihilation, have returned to the people at large for their exercise; the state remaining, in the meantime, exposed to all the danger of invasion from without and convulsions within.

He has endeavored to prevent the population of these States; for that purpose, obstructing the laws for naturalization of foreigners, refusing to pass others to encourage their migration hither, and raising the conditions of new appropriations of lands.

He has obstructed the administration of justice by refusing his assent to laws for establishing judiciary powers.

He has made judges dependent on his will alone for the tenure of their offices and the amount and payment of their salaries.

He has erected a multitude of new offices and sent hither swarms of officers to harass our people and eat out their substance.

He has kept among us, in time of peace, standing armies, without the consent of our legislatures.

He has affected to render the military independent of, and superior to, the civil power.

He has combined with others to subject us to a jurisdiction foreign to our Constitution and unacknowledged by our laws, giving his assent to their acts of pretended legislation—

For quartering large bodies of armed troops among us;

For protecting them by a mock trial from punishment for any murders which they should commit on the inhabitants of these States;

For cutting off our trade with all parts of the world;

For imposing taxes on us without our consent;

For depriving us, in many cases, of the benefit of trial by jury;

For transporting us beyond seas to be tried for pretended offences;

For abolishing the free system of English laws in a neighboring province, establishing therein an arbitrary government, and enlarging its boundaries, so as to render it at once an example and fit instrument for introducing the same absolute rule into these colonies;

For taking away our charters, abolishing our most valuable laws, and altering, fundamentally, the powers of our governments;

For suspending our own legislatures and declaring themselves invested with power to legislate for us in all cases whatsoever.

He has abdicated government here by declaring us out of his protection and waging war against us.

He has plundered our seas, ravaged our coasts, burnt out towns, and destroyed the lives of our people.

He is, at this time, transporting large armies of foreign mercenaries to complete the works of death, desolation, and tyranny already begun with circumstances of cruelty and perifidy scarcely paralleled in the most barbarous ages, and totally unworthy, the head of a civilized nation.

He has constrained our fellow citizens, taken captive on the high seas, to bear arms against their country, to become the executioners of their friends and brethren, or to fall themselves by their hands.

He has excited domestic insurrections amongst us and has endeavored to bring on the inhabitants of our frontiers, the merciless Indian savages, whose known rule of warfare is an undistinguished destruction of all ages, sexes, and conditions.

In every state of these oppressions, we have petitioned for redress in the most humble terms; our repeated petitions have been answered only by repeated injury. A prince whose character is thus marked by every act which may define a tyrant is unfit to be the ruler of a free people.

Nor have we been wanting in attention to our British brethren. We have warned them, from time to time, of attempts made by their legislature to extend an unwarrantable jurisdiction over us. We have reminded them of the circumstances of our emigration and settlement here. We have appealed to their native justice and magnanimity, and we have conjured them, by the ties of our common kindred, to disavow these usurpations, which would inevitably interrupt our connections and correspondence. They, too, have been deaf to the voice of justice and consanguinity. We must, therefore, acquiesce in the necessity which denounces our separation, and hold them, as we hold the rest of mankind, enemies in war, in peace, friends.

imposing: forcing   **depriving:** taking away **transporting us beyond seas:** sending colonists to England for trial   **neighboring province:** Quebec   **arbitrary government:** unjust rule   **fit instrument:** suitable tool **invested with power:** having the power

During the years leading up to 1776, the colonists claimed that Parliament had no right to make laws for them because they were not represented in Parliament. Here, the colonists object to recent laws of Parliament, such as the Quartering Act and the blockade of colonial ports (page 153), which cut off their trade. They also object to Parliament's claim that it had the right to tax them without their consent.

abdicated: given up   **plundered:** robbed **ravaged:** attacked   **mercenaries:** hired soldiers   **desolation:** misery   **perfidy:** falseness   **barbarous:** uncivilized **constrained:** forced   **brethren:** brothers **domestic insurrections:** internal revolts

Here, the Declaration lists the third set of wrongs—warlike acts of the king. Instead of listening to the colonists, the king has made war on them. He has hired soldiers to fight in America (page 163).

oppressions: harsh rule   **petitioned:** asked **redress:** relief   **unwarrantable jurisdiction over:** unfair authority   **magnanimity:** generosity   **conjured:** called upon **common kindred:** relatives   **disavow:** turn away from   **consanguinity:** blood relationships, kinship   **acquiesce:** agree **denounces:** speaks out against

During this time, colonists have repeatedly asked for relief. But their requests have brought only more suffering. They have appealed to the British people but received no help. So they are forced to separate.

DECLARATION OF INDEPENDENCE

Reference Section • **929**

Colonies Declare Independence

appealing: calling on **rectitude of our intentions:** moral rightness of our plans **absolved from all allegiance:** freed from loyalty **levy war:** declare war **contract alliances:** make treaties

As the representatives of the United States, they declare that the colonies are free and independent states.

The states need no longer be loyal to the British king. They are an independent nation that can make war and sign treaties.

Relying on Divine Providence, the signers of the Declaration promise their lives, money, and honor to fight for independence.

We, therefore, the representatives of the United States of America, in general Congress assembled, appealing to the Supreme Judge of the world for the rectitude of our intentions, do, in the name and by the authority of the good people of these colonies, solemnly publish and declare, that these united colonies are, and of right ought to be, free and independent states: that they are absolved from all allegiance to the British Crown, and that all political connections between them and the state of Great Britain is, and ought to be, totally dissolved; and that, as free and independent states, they have full power to levy war, conclude peace, contract alliances, establish commerce, and to do all other acts and things which independent states may of right do. And, for the support of this declaration, with a firm reliance on the protection of Divine Providence, we mutually pledge to each other our lives, our fortunes, and our sacred honor.

Signers of the Declaration of Independence

John Hancock, President
Charles Thomson, Secretary

New Hampshire
Josiah Bartlett
William Whipple
Matthew Thornton

Massachusetts
Samuel Adams
John Adams
Robert Treat Paine
Elbridge Gerry

Rhode Island
Stephen Hopkins
William Ellery

Connecticut
Roger Sherman
Samuel Huntington
William Williams
Oliver Wolcott

Delaware
Caesar Rodney
George Read
Thomas McKean

New York
William Floyd
Philip Livingston
Francis Lewis
Lewis Morris

New Jersey
Richard Stockton
John Witherspoon
Francis Hopkinson
John Hart
Abraham Clark

Georgia
Button Gwinnett
Lyman Hall
George Walton

Maryland
Samuel Chase
William Paca
Thomas Stone
Charles Carroll

North Carolina
William Hooper
Joseph Hewes
John Penn

Virginia
George Wythe
Richard Henry Lee
Thomas Jefferson
Benjamin Harrison
Thomas Nelson, Jr.
Francis Lightfoot Lee
Carter Braxton

South Carolina
Edward Rutledge
Thomas Heyward, Jr.
Thomas Lynch, Jr.
Arthur Middleton

Pennsylvania
Robert Morris
Benjamin Rush
Benjamin Franklin
John Morton
George Clymer
James Smith
George Taylor
James Wilson
George Ross

DECLARATION OF INDEPENDENCE

930 • Reference Section

The Constitution of the United States of America

The Constitution is printed in black. The titles of articles, sections, and clauses are not part of the original document. They have been added to help you find information in the Constitution. Some words or lines are crossed out because they have been changed by amendments or no longer apply. Annotations, or explanations, are on the tan side of the page. Page numbers in the annotations show where a subject is discussed in the text. Difficult words are defined.

Preamble

We the people of the United States, in order to form a more perfect Union, establish justice, insure domestic tranquillity, provide for the common defense, promote the general welfare, and secure the blessings of liberty to ourselves and our posterity, do ordain and establish this Constitution for the United States of America.

The Preamble describes the purpose of the government set up by the Constitution. Americans expect their government to defend justice and liberty and provide peace and safety from foreign enemies.

Article 1. The Legislative Branch

Section 1. A Two-House Legislature

All legislative powers herein granted shall be vested in a Congress of the United States, which shall consist of a Senate and House of Representatives.

The Constitution gives Congress the power to make laws. Congress is divided into the Senate and the House of Representatives.

Section 2. House of Representatives

1. Election of Members The House of Representatives shall be composed of members chosen every second year by the people of the several states, and the electors in each state shall have the qualifications requisite for electors of the most numerous branch of the state legislature.

Clause 1 *Electors* refers to voters. Members of the House of Representatives are elected every two years. Any citizen allowed to vote for members of the larger house of the state legislature can also vote for members of the House.

2. Qualifications No person shall be a Representative who shall not have attained to the age of twenty-five years, and been seven years a citizen of the United States, and who shall not, when elected, be an inhabitant of that state in which he shall be chosen.

Clause 2 A member of the House of Representatives must be at least 25 years old, an American citizen for 7 years, and a resident of the state he or she represents.

3. Determining Representation Representatives and direct taxes shall be apportioned among the several states which may be included within this Union, according to their respective numbers which shall be determined by adding to the whole number of free persons, including those bound to service for a term of years, and excluding Indians not taxed, three-fifths of all other persons. The actual enumeration shall be made within three years after the first meeting of the Congress of the United States, and within every subsequent term of ten years, in such manner as they shall by law direct. The number of Representatives shall not exceed one for every 30,000, but each state shall have at least one Representative; and until such enumeration shall be made, the state of New Hampshire shall be entitled to choose three; Massachusetts, eight; Rhode Island and Providence Plantations, one; Connecticut, five; New York, six; New Jersey, four; Pennsylvania, eight; Delaware, one; Maryland, six; Virginia, ten; North Carolina, five; South Carolina, five; and Georgia, three.

Clause 3 The number of representatives each state elects is based on its population. An *enumeration,* or census, must be taken every 10 years to determine population. Today, the number of representatives in the House is fixed at 435.

This is the famous Three-Fifths Compromise worked out at the Constitutional Convention (page 198). *Persons bound to service* meant indentured servants. *All other persons* meant slaves. All free people in a state were counted. However, only three fifths of the slaves were included in the population count. This three-fifths clause became meaningless when slaves were freed by the Thirteenth Amendment.

THE CONSTITUTION

Clause 4 *Executive authority* means the governor of a state. If a member of the House leaves office before his or her term ends, the governor must call a special election to fill the seat.

Clause 5 The House elects a speaker. Today, the speaker is usually chosen by the party that has a majority in the House. Also, only the House has the power to *impeach,* or accuse, a federal official of wrongdoing.

Clause 1 Each state has two senators. Senators serve for six-year terms. The Seventeenth Amendment changed the way senators were elected.

Clause 2 Every two years, one third of the senators run for reelection. Thus, the makeup of the Senate is never totally changed by any one election. The Seventeenth Amendment changed the way of filling *vacancies,* or empty seats. Today, the governor of a state must choose a senator to fill a vacancy that occurs between elections.

Clause 3 A senator must be at least 30 years old, an American citizen for 9 years, and a resident of the state he or she represents.

Clause 4 The Vice President presides over Senate meetings, but he or she can vote only to break a tie.

Clause 5 *Pro tempore* means temporary. The Senate chooses one of its members to serve as president pro tempore when the Vice President is absent.

Clause 6 The Senate acts as a jury if the House impeaches a federal official. The Chief Justice of the Supreme Court presides if the President is on trial. Two thirds of all senators present must vote for *conviction,* or finding the accused guilty. No President has ever been convicted. The House impeached President Andrew Johnson in 1868, but the Senate acquitted him of the charges (page 490). In 1974, President Richard Nixon resigned before he could be impeached.

Clause 7 If an official is found guilty by the Senate, he or she can be removed from office and barred from holding federal office in the future. These are the only punishments the Senate can impose. However, the convicted official can still be tried in a criminal court.

4. Filling Vacancies When vacancies happen in the representation from any state, the executive authority thereof shall issue writs of election to fill such vacancies.

5. Selection of Officers; Power of Impeachment The House of Representatives shall choose their Speaker and other officers; and shall have the sole power of impeachment.

Section 3. The Senate

1. Selection of Members The Senate of the United States shall be composed of two Senators from each state chosen by the legislature thereof, for six years, and each Senator shall have one vote.

2. Alternating Terms; Filling Vacancies Immediately after they shall be assembled in consequence of the first election, they shall be divided as equally as may be into three classes. The seats of the Senators of the first class shall be vacated at the expiration of the second year, of the second class at the expiration of the fourth year, and of the third class at the expiration of the sixth year, so that one-third may be chosen every second year; and if vacancies happen by resignation, or otherwise, during the recess of the legislature of any state, the executive thereof may make temporary appointments until the next meeting of the legislature, which shall then fill such vacancies.

3. Qualifications No person shall be a Senator who shall not have attained to the age of thirty years, and been nine years a citizen of the United States, and who shall not, when elected, be an inhabitant of that state for which he shall be chosen.

4. President of the Senate The Vice-President of the United States shall be president of the Senate, but shall have no vote, unless they be equally divided.

5. Election of Senate Officers The Senate shall choose their other officers, and also a president *pro tempore,* in the absence of the Vice-President, or when he shall exercise the office of the President of the United States.

6. Impeachment Trials The Senate shall have the sole power to try all impeachments. When sitting for that purpose, they shall be on oath or affirmation. When the President of the United States is tried, the Chief Justice shall preside; and no person shall be convicted without the concurrence of two-thirds of the members present.

7. Penalties Upon Conviction Judgment in cases of impeachment shall not extend further than to removal from office, and disqualification to hold and enjoy any office of honor, trust, or profit under the United States; but the party convicted shall nevertheless be liable and subject to indictment, trial, judgment, and punishment, according to law.

THE CONSTITUTION

Section 4. Elections and Meetings

1. Election of Congress The times, places, and manner of holding elections for Senators and Representatives shall be prescribed in each state by the legislature thereof; but the Congress may at any time by law make or alter such regulations, except as to the places of choosing Senators.

2. Annual Sessions The Congress shall assemble at least once in every year, and such meeting shall be on the first Monday in December, unless they shall by law appoint a different day.

Section 5. Rules for the Conduct of Business

1. Organization Each house shall be the judge of the elections, returns, and qualifications of its own members, and a majority of each shall constitute a quorum to do business; but a smaller number may adjourn from day to day, and may be authorized to compel the attendance of absent members, in such manner, and under such penalties, as each house may provide.

2. Procedures Each house may determine the rules of its proceedings, punish its members for disorderly behavior, and with the concurrence of two-thirds, expel a member.

3. A Written Record Each house shall keep a journal of its proceedings, and from time to time publish the same, excepting such parts as may in their judgment require secrecy; and the yeas and nays of the members of either house on any question shall, at the desire of one-fifth of those present, be entered on the journal.

4. Rules for Adjournment Neither house, during the session of Congress, shall, without the consent of the other, adjourn for more than three days, nor to any other place than that in which the two houses shall be sitting.

Section 6. Privileges and Restrictions

1. Salaries and Immunities The Senators and Representatives shall receive a compensation for their services, to be ascertained by law and paid out of the Treasury of the United States. They shall in all cases, except treason, felony, and breach of the peace, be privileged from arrest during their attendance at the session of their respective houses, and in going to and returning from the same; and for any speech or debate in either house, they shall not be questioned in any other place.

2. Restrictions on Other Employment No Senator or Representative shall, during the time for which he was elected, be appointed to any civil office under the authority of the United States, which shall have been created, or the emoluments whereof shall have been increased, during such time; and no person holding any office under the United States shall be a member of either house during his continuance in office.

Clause 1 Each state legislature can decide when and how congressional elections take place, but Congress can overrule these decisions. In 1842, Congress required each state to set up congressional districts with one representative elected from each district. In 1872, Congress decided that congressional elections must be held in every state on the same date in even-numbered years.

Clause 2 Congress must meet at least once a year. The Twentieth Amendment moved the opening date of Congress to January 3.

Clause 1 Each house decides whether a member has the qualifications for office set by the Constitution. A *quorum* is the smallest number of members who must be present for business to be conducted. Each house can set its own rules about absent members.

Clause 2 Each house can make rules for the conduct of members. It can only expel a member by a two-thirds vote.

Clause 3 Each house keeps a record of its meetings. *The Congressional Record* is published every day with excerpts from speeches made in each house. It also records the votes of each member.

Clause 4 Neither house can *adjourn,* or stop meeting, for more than three days unless the other house approves. Both houses of Congress must meet in the same city.

Clause 1 *Compensation* means salary. Congress decides the salary for its members. While Congress is in session, a member is free from arrest in civil cases and cannot be sued for anything he or she says on the floor of Congress. This allows for freedom of debate. However, a member can be arrested for a criminal offense.

Clause 2 *Emolument* also means salary. A member of Congress cannot hold another federal office during his or her term. A former member of Congress cannot hold an office created while he or she was in Congress. An official in another branch of government cannot serve at the same time in Congress. This strengthens the separation of powers.

THE CONSTITUTION

Clause 1 *Revenue* is money raised by the government through taxes. Tax bills must be introduced in the House. The Senate, however, can make changes in tax bills. This clause protects the principle that people can be taxed only with their consent.

Clause 2 A *bill,* or proposed law, that is passed by a majority of the House and Senate is sent to the President. If the President signs the bill, it becomes law.

A bill can also become law without the President's signature. The President can refuse to act on a bill. If Congress is in session at the time, the bill becomes law 10 days after the President receives it.

The President can *veto,* or reject, a bill by sending it back to the house where it was introduced. Or if the President refuses to act on a bill and Congress adjourns within 10 days, then the bill dies. This way of killing a bill without taking action is called the *pocket veto.*

Congress can override the President's veto if each house of Congress passes the bill again by a two-thirds vote. This clause is an important part of the system of checks and balances (page 203).

Clause 3 Congress can pass resolutions or orders that have the same force as laws. Any such resolution or order must be signed by the President (except on questions of adjournment). Thus, this clause prevents Congress from bypassing the President simply by calling a bill by another name.

Clause 1 *Duties* are tariffs. *Imposts* are taxes in general. *Excises* are taxes on the production or sale of certain goods. Congress has the power to tax and spend tax money. Taxes must be the same in all parts of the country.

Clause 2 Congress can borrow money for the United States. The government often borrows money by selling *bonds,* or certificates that promise to pay the holder a certain sum of money on a certain date (page 245).

Clause 3 Only Congress has the power to regulate foreign and *interstate trade,* or trade between states. Disagreements over interstate trade was a major problem with the Articles of Confederation (pages 190–191).

Section 7. Law-Making Process

1. Tax Bills All bills for raising revenue shall originate in the House of Representatives; but the Senate may propose or concur with amendments as on other bills.

2. How a Bill Becomes a Law Every bill which shall have passed the House of Representatives and the Senate shall, before it become a law, be presented to the President of the United States; if he approve, he shall sign it, but if not, he shall return it, with his objections, to that house in which it shall have originated, who shall enter the objections at large on their journal, and proceed to reconsider it. If after such reconsideration two-thirds of that house shall agree to pass the bill, it shall be sent, together with the objections, to the other house, by which it shall likewise be reconsidered, and, if approved by two-thirds of that house, it shall become a law. But in all such cases the votes of both houses shall be determined by yeas and nays, and the names of the persons voting for and against the bill shall be entered on the journal of each house respectively. If any bill shall not be returned by the President within ten days (Sundays excepted) after it shall have been presented to him, the same bill shall be a law, in like manner as if he had signed it, unless the Congress by their adjournment prevent its return, in which case it shall not be a law.

3. Resolutions Passed by Congress Every order, resolution, or vote to which the concurrence of the Senate and House of Representatives may be necessary (except on a question of adjournment) shall be presented to the President of the United States; and before the same shall take effect, shall be approved by him, or being disapproved by him, shall be repassed by two-thirds of the Senate and House of Representatives, according to the rules and limitations prescribed in the case of a bill.

Section 8. Powers Delegated to Congress

The Congress shall have power

1. Taxes To lay and collect taxes, duties, imposts, and excises, to pay the debts and provide for the common defense and general welfare of the United States; but all duties, imposts, and excises shall be uniform throughout the United States;

2. Borrowing To borrow money on the credit of the United States;

3. Commerce To regulate commerce with foreign nations, and among the several states, and with the Indian tribes;

4. Naturalization; Bankruptcy To establish a uniform rule of naturalization, and uniform laws on the subject of bankruptcies throughout the United States;

5. Coins; Weights; Measures To coin money, regulate the value thereof, and of foreign coin, and fix the standard of weights and measures;

6. Counterfeiting To provide for the punishment of counterfeiting the securities and current coin of the United States;

7. Post Offices To establish post offices and post roads;

8. Copyrights; Patents To promote the progress of science and useful arts by securing for limited times to authors and inventors the exclusive right to their respective writings and discoveries;

9. Federal Courts To constitute tribunals inferior to the Supreme Court;

10. Piracy To define and punish piracies and felonies committed on the high seas and offenses against the law of nations;

11. Declarations of War To declare war, ~~grant letters of marque and reprisal~~, and make rules concerning captures on land and water;

12. Army To raise and support armies, but no appropriation of money to that use shall be for a longer term than two years;

13. Navy To provide and maintain a navy;

14. Rules for the Military To make rules for the government and regulation of the land and naval forces;

15. Militia To provide for calling forth the militia to execute the laws of the Union, suppress insurrections, and repel invasions;

16. Rules for the Militia To provide for organizing, arming, and disciplining the militia, and for governing such part of them as may be employed in the service of the United States, reserving to the states, respectively, the appointment of the officers, and the authority of training the militia according to the discipline prescribed by Congress;

17. National Capital To exercise exclusive legislation in all cases whatsoever, over such district (not exceeding ten miles square) as may, by cession of particular states, and the acceptance of Congress, become the seat of government of the United States, and to exercise like authority over all places purchased by the

Clause 4 *Naturalization* is the process whereby a foreigner becomes a citizen. *Bankruptcy* is the condition in which a person or business cannot pay its debts. Congress has the power to pass laws on these two issues. The laws must be the same in all parts of the country.

Clause 5 Congress has the power to coin money and set its value. Congress has set up the National Bureau of Standards to regulate weights and measures.

Clause 6 *Counterfeiting* is the making of imitation money. *Securities* are bonds. Congress can make laws to punish counterfeiters.

Clause 7 Congress has the power to set up and control the delivery of mail.

Clause 8 Congress may pass copyright and patent laws. A *copyright* protects an author. A patent makes an inventor the sole owner of his or her work for a limited time.

Clause 9 Congress has the power to set up *inferior,* or lower, federal courts under the Supreme Court.

Clause 10 Congress can punish *piracy,* or the robbing of ships at sea.

Clause 11 Only Congress can declare war. Declarations of war are granted at the request of the President. *Letters of marque and reprisal* were documents issued by a government allowing merchant ships to arm themselves and attack ships of an enemy nation. They are no longer issued.

Clauses 12, 13, 14 These clauses place the army and navy under the control of Congress. Congress decides on the size of the armed forces and the amount of money to spend on the army and navy. It also has the power to write rules governing the armed forces.

Clauses 15, 16 The *militia* is a body of citizen soldiers. Congress can call up the militia to put down rebellions or fight foreign invaders. Each state has its own militia, today called the National Guard. Normally, the militia is under the command of a state's governor. However, it can be placed under the command of the President.

Clause 17 Congress controls the district around the national capital. In 1790, Congress made Washington, D.C., the nation's capital (page 247). In 1973, it gave residents of the District the right to elect local officials.

THE CONSTITUTION

Clause 18 Clauses 1–17 list the powers delegated to Congress. The writers of the Constitution added Clause 18 so that Congress could deal with the changing needs of the nation. It gives Congress the power to make laws as needed to carry out the first 17 clauses. Clause 18 is sometimes called the elastic clause because it lets Congress stretch the meaning of its power.

Clause 1 *Such persons* means slaves. This clause resulted from a compromise between the supporters and the opponents of the slave trade (page 198). In 1808, as soon as Congress was permitted to abolish the slave trade, it did so. The $10 import tax was never imposed.

Clause 2 A *writ of habeas corpus* is a court order requiring government officials to bring a prisoner to court and explain why he or she is being held. A writ of habeas corpus protects people from unlawful imprisonment. The government cannot suspend this right except in times of rebellion or invasion.

Clause 3 A *bill of attainder* is a law declaring that a person is guilty of a particular crime. An *ex post facto law* punishes an act which was not illegal when it was committed. Congress cannot pass a bill of attainder or ex post facto laws.

Clause 4 A *capitation tax* is a tax placed directly on each person. *Direct taxes* are taxes on people or on land. They can be passed only if they are divided among the states according to population. The Sixteenth Amendment allowed Congress to tax income without regard to the population of the states.

Clause 5 This clause forbids Congress to tax exports. In 1787, southerners insisted on this clause because their economy depended on exports.

Clause 6 Congress cannot make laws that favor one state over another in trade and commerce. Also, states cannot place tariffs on interstate trade.

Clause 7 The federal government cannot spend money unless Congress *appropriates* it, or passes a law allowing it. This clause gives Congress an important check on the President by controlling the money he or she can spend. The government must publish a statement showing how it spends public funds.

---

936 • Reference Section

consent of the legislature of the state in which the same shall be, for the erection of forts, magazines, arsenals, dock-yards, and other needful buildings; —and

18. Necessary Laws To make all laws which shall be necessary and proper for carrying into execution the foregoing powers, and all other powers vested by this Constitution in the government of the United States, or in any department or officer thereof.

Section 9. Powers Denied to the Federal Government

1. The Slave Trade ~~The migration or importation of such persons as any of the states now existing shall think proper to admit shall not be prohibited by the Congress prior to the year 1808; but a tax or duty may be imposed on such importation, not exceeding $10 for each person.~~

2. Writ of Habeas Corpus The privilege of the writ of habeas corpus shall not be suspended, unless when in cases of rebellion or invasion the public safety may require it.

3. Bills of Attainder and Ex Post Facto Laws No bill of attainder or *ex post facto* law shall be passed.

4. Apportionment of Direct Taxes ~~No capitation or other direct tax shall be laid, unless in proportion to the census or enumeration herein before directed to be taken.~~

5. Taxes on Exports No tax or duty shall be laid on articles exported from any state.

6. Special Preference for Trade No preference shall be given any regulation of commerce or revenue to the ports of one state over those of another; nor shall vessels bound to, or from, one state, be obliged to enter, clear, or pay duties in another.

7. Spending No money shall be drawn from the Treasury, but in consequence of appropriations made by law; and a regular statement and account of the receipts and expenditures of all public money shall be published from time to time.

8. Creation of Titles of Nobility No title of nobility shall be granted by the United States; and no person holding any office of profit or trust under them, shall, without the consent of the Congress, accept of any present, emolument, office, or title, of any kind whatever, from any king, prince, or foreign state.

Section 10. Powers Denied to the States

1. Unconditional Prohibitions No state shall enter into any treaty, alliance, or confederation; grant letters of marque and reprisal; coin money; emit bills of credit; make anything but gold and silver coin a tender in payment of debts; pass any bill of attainder, *ex post facto* law, or law impairing the obligation of contracts, or grant any title of nobility.

2. Powers Conditionally Denied No state shall, without the consent of the Congress, lay any imposts or duties on imports or exports, except what may be absolutely necessary for executing its inspection laws; and the net produce of all duties and imposts, laid by any state on imports or exports, shall be for the use of the Treasury of the United States; and all such laws shall be subject to the revision and control of the Congress.

3. Other Denied Powers No state shall, without the consent of Congress, lay any duty of tonnage, keep troops, or ships of war in time of peace, enter into any agreement or compact with another state, or with a foreign power, or engage in war, unless actually invaded, or in such imminent danger as will not admit of delay.

Article 2. The Executive Branch

Section 1. President and Vice-President

1. Chief Executive The executive power shall be vested in a President of the United States of America. He shall hold his office during the term of four years, and together with the Vice-President, chosen for the same term, be elected as follows:

2. Selection of Electors Each state shall appoint, in such manner as the legislature thereof may direct, a number of electors, equal to the whole number of Senators and Representatives to which the state may be entitled in the Congress; but no Senator or Representative, or person holding an office or trust or profit under the United States, shall be appointed an elector.

3. Electoral College Procedures ~~The electors shall meet in their respective states, and vote by ballot for two persons, of whom one at least shall not be an inhabitant of the same state with themselves. And they shall make a list of all the persons voted for, and of the number of votes for each; which list they shall sign and certify, and transmit sealed to the seat of the government of the United States, directed to the president of the Senate. The president of the Senate shall, in the presence of the Senate and House of Representatives, open all the certificates, and the votes shall then be counted. The person having the greatest number of votes shall be President, if such number be a majority of the whole number of electors appointed; and if there be more than one who have such majority, and have an equal number of votes, then the House of Representatives shall immediately choose by~~

Clause 8 The government cannot award titles of nobility, such as Duke or Duchess. American citizens cannot accept titles of nobility from foreign governments without the consent of Congress.

Clause 1 The writers of the Constitution did not want the states to act like separate nations. So they prohibited states from making treaties or coining money. Some powers denied to the federal government are also denied to the states. For example, states cannot pass ex post facto laws.

Clauses 2, 3 Powers listed here are forbidden to the states, but Congress can lift these prohibitions by passing laws that give these powers to the states.

Clause 2 forbids states from taxing imports and exports without the consent of Congress. States may charge inspection fees on goods entering the states. Any profit from these fees must be turned over to the United States Treasury.

Clause 3 forbids states from keeping an army or navy without the consent of Congress. States cannot make treaties or declare war unless an enemy invades or is about to invade.

Clause 1 The President is responsible for **executing,** or carrying out, laws passed by Congress.

Clauses 2, 3 Some writers of the Constitution were afraid to allow the people to elect the President directly (page 203). Therefore, the Constitutional Convention set up the electoral college. Clause 2 directs each state to choose electors, or delegates to the electoral college, to vote for President. A state's electoral vote is equal to the combined number of senators and representatives. Each state may decide how to choose its electors. Members of Congress and federal officeholders may not serve as electors. This much of the original electoral college system is still in effect.

Clause 3 called upon each elector to vote for two candidates. The candidate who received a majority of the electoral votes would become President. The runner-up would become Vice President. If no candidate won a majority, the House would choose the President. The Senate would choose the Vice President.

The election of 1800 showed a problem with the original electoral college system (page

261). Thomas Jefferson was the Republican candidate for President, and Aaron Burr was the Republican candidate for Vice President. In the electoral college, the vote ended in a tie. The election was finally decided in the House, where Jefferson was chosen President. The Twelfth Amendment changed the electoral college system so that this could not happen again.

~~ballot one of them for President; and if no person have a majority, then from the five highest on the list the said House shall in like manner choose the President. But in choosing the President the votes shall be taken by states, the representation from each state having one vote. A quorum for this purpose shall consist of a member or members from two-thirds of the states, and a majority of all the states shall be necessary to a choice. In every case, after the choice of the President, the person having the greatest number of votes of the electors shall be the Vice-President. But if there should remain two or more who have equal votes, the Senate shall choose from them by ballot the Vice-President.~~

Clause 4 Under a law passed in 1792, electors are chosen on the Tuesday following the first Monday of November every four years. Electors from each state meet to vote in December.
Today, voters in each state choose **slates**, or groups, of electors who are pledged to a candidate for President. The candidate for President who wins the popular vote in each state wins that state's electoral vote.

4. Time of Elections The Congress may determine the time of choosing the electors, and the day on which they shall give their votes; which day shall be the same throughout the United States.

Clause 5 The President must be a citizen of the United States from birth, at least 35 years old, and a resident of the country for 14 years. The first seven Presidents of the United States were born under British rule, but they were allowed to hold office because they were citizens at the time the Constitution was adopted.

5. Qualifications for President No person except a natural-born citizen ~~or a citizen of the United States, at the time of the adoption of this Constitution,~~ shall be eligible to the office of the President; neither shall any person be eligible to that office who shall not have attained to the age of thirty-five years, and been fourteen years a resident within the United States.

Clause 6 The powers of the President pass to the Vice President if the President leaves office or cannot discharge his or her duties. The wording of this clause caused confusion the first time a President died in office. When President William Henry Harrison died, it was uncertain whether Vice President John Tyler should remain Vice President and act as President or whether he should be sworn in as President. Tyler persuaded a federal judge to swear him in. So he set the precedent that the Vice President assumes the office of President when it becomes vacant. The Twenty-fifth Amendment replaced this clause.

6. Presidential Succession In case of the removal of the President from office, or of his death, resignation, or inability to discharge the powers and duties of the said office, the same shall devolve on the Vice-President, and the Congress may by law provide for the case of removal, death, resignation, or inability, both of the President and Vice-President, declaring what officer shall then act as President, and such officer shall act accordingly, until the disability be removed, or a President shall be elected.

Clause 7 The President is paid a salary. It cannot be raised or lowered during his or her term of office. The President is not allowed to hold any other federal or state position while in office. Today, the President's salary is $200,000 a year.

7. Salary The President shall, at stated times, receive for his services, a compensation, which shall neither be increased nor diminished during the period for which he shall have been elected, and he shall not receive within that period any other emolument from the United States, or any of them.

Clause 8 Before taking office, the President must promise to protect and defend the Constitution. Usually, the Chief Justice of the Supreme Court administers the oath of office to the President.

8. Oath of Office Before he enter on the execution of his office, he shall take the following oath or affirmation:—"I do solemnly swear (or affirm) that I will faithfully execute the office of President of the United States, and will to the best of my ability, preserve, protect, and defend the Constitution of the United States."

THE CONSTITUTION

Section 2. Powers of the President

1. Commander in Chief of the Armed Forces The President shall be Commander in Chief of the Army and Navy of the United States, and of the militia of the several states, when called into the actual service of the United States; he may require the opinion, in writing, of the principal officer in each of the executive departments, upon any subject relating to the duties of their respective offices, and he shall have power to grant reprieves and pardons for offenses against the United States, except in cases of impeachment.

2. Making Treaties and Nominations He shall have power, by and with the advice and consent of the Senate, to make treaties, provided two-thirds of the Senators present concur; and he shall nominate, and by and with the advice and consent of the Senate, shall appoint ambassadors, other public ministers and consuls, judges of the Supreme Court, and all other officers of the United States, whose appointments are not herein otherwise provided for, and which shall be established by law; but the Congress may by law vest the appointment of such inferior officers, as they think proper, in the President alone, in the courts of law, or in the heads of departments.

3. Temporary Appointments The President shall have power to fill up all vacancies that may happen during the recess of the Senate, by granting commissions which shall expire at the end of their next session.

Section 3. Duties

He shall from time to time give to the Congress information of the state of the Union, and recommend to their consideration such measures as he shall judge necessary and expedient; he may, on extraordinary occasions, convene both houses, or either of them, and in case of disagreement between them, with respect to the time of adjournment, he may adjourn them to such time as he shall think proper; he shall receive ambassadors and other public ministers; he shall take care that the laws be faithfully executed, and shall commission all the officers of the United States.

Section 4. Impeachment and Removal From Office

The President, Vice-President, and all civil officers of the United States, shall be removed from office on impeachment for, and conviction of, treason, bribery, or other high crimes or misdemeanors.

Article 3. The Judicial Branch

Section 1. Federal Courts

The judicial power of the United States shall be vested in one Supreme Court, and in such inferior courts as the Congress may from time to time ordain and establish. The judges, both of the Supreme and inferior courts, shall hold their offices during good

Clause 1 The President is head of the armed forces and the state militias when they are called into national service. So the military is under *civilian,* or nonmilitary, control.

The President can get advice from the heads of executive departments. In most cases, the President has the power to grant a reprieve or pardon. A *reprieve* suspends punishment ordered by law. A *pardon* prevents prosecution for a crime or overrides the judgment of a court.

Clause 2 The President has the power to make treaties with other nations. Under the system of checks and balances, all treaties must be approved by two thirds of the Senate. Today, the President also makes agreements with foreign governments. These executive agreements do not need Senate approval.

The President has the power to appoint ambassadors to foreign countries and to appoint other high officials. The Senate must *confirm,* or approve, these appointments.

Clause 3 If the Senate is in *recess,* or not meeting, the President may fill vacant government posts by making temporary appointments.

The President must give Congress a report on the condition of the nation every year. This report is now called the State of the Union Address. Since 1913, the President has given this speech in person each January.

The President can call a special session of Congress and can adjourn Congress if necessary. The President has the power to receive, or recognize, foreign ambassadors.

The President must carry out the laws. Today, many government agencies oversee the execution of laws.

Civil officers include federal judges and members of the Cabinet. *High crimes* are major crimes. *Misdemeanors* are lesser crimes. The President, Vice President, and others can be forced out of office if impeached and found guilty of certain crimes. Andrew Johnson is the only President to have been impeached.

Judicial power means the right of the courts to decide legal cases. The Constitution creates the Supreme Court but lets Congress decide on the size of the Supreme Court. Congress has the

Reference Section • **939**

power to set up inferior, or lower, courts. The Judiciary Act of 1789 (page 245) set up a system of district and circuit courts, or courts of appeal. Today, there are 95 district courts and 11 courts of appeal. All federal judges serve for life.

Clause 1 *Jurisdiction* refers to the right of a court to hear a case. Federal courts have jurisdiction over cases that involve the Constitution, federal laws, treaties, foreign ambassadors and diplomats, naval and maritime laws, disagreements between states or between citizens from different states, and disputes between a state or citizen and a foreign state or citizen.

In *Marbury* v. *Madison* (page 270), the Supreme Court established the right to judge whether a law is constitutional.

Clause 2 *Original jurisdiction* means the power of a court to hear a case where it first arises. The Supreme Court has original jurisdiction over only a few cases, such as those involving foreign diplomats. More often, the Supreme Court acts as an appellate court. An *appellate court* does not decide guilt. It decides whether the lower court trial was properly conducted and reviews the lower court's decision.

Clause 3 This clause guarantees the right to a jury trial for anyone accused of a federal crime. The only exceptions are impeachment cases. The trial must be held in the state where the crime was committed.

Clause 1 Treason is clearly defined. An *overt act* is an actual action. A person cannot be convicted of treason for what he or she thinks. A person can be convicted of treason only if he or she confesses or two witnesses testify to it.

Clause 2 Congress has the power to set the punishment for traitors. Congress may not punish the children of convicted traitors by taking away their civil rights or property.

Each state must recognize the official acts and records of any other state. For example, each state must recognize marriage certificates issued by another state. Congress can pass laws to ensure this.

940 • Reference Section

behavior, and shall, at stated times, receive for their services a compensation, which shall not be diminished during their continuance in office.

Section 2. Jurisdiction of Federal Courts

1. Scope of Judicial Power The judicial power shall extend to all cases, in law and equity, arising under this Constitution, the laws of the United States, and treaties made or which shall be made, under their authority; to all cases affecting ambassadors, other public ministers and consuls; to all cases of admiralty and maritime jurisdiction; to controversies to which the United States shall be a party; to controversies between two or more states; between a state and citizens of another state; between citizens of the same state claiming lands under grants of different states, and between a state or the citizens thereof, and foreign states, citizens, or subjects.

2. The Supreme Court In all cases affecting ambassadors, other public ministers and consuls, and those in which a state shall be a party, the Supreme Court shall have original jurisdiction. In all the other cases before mentioned, the Supreme Court shall have appellate jurisdiction, both as to law and fact, with such exceptions, and under such regulations as the Congress shall make.

3. Trial by Jury The trial of all crimes, except in cases of impeachment, shall be by jury; and such trial shall be held in the state where the said crimes shall have been committed; but when not committed within any state, the trial shall be at such place or places as the Congress may by law have directed.

Section 3. Treason

1. Definition Treason against the United States shall consist only in levying war against them, or in adhering to their enemies, giving them aid and comfort. No person shall be convicted of treason unless on the testimony of two witnesses to the same overt act, or on confession in open court.

2. Punishment The Congress shall have power to declare the punishment of treason, but no attainder of treason shall work corruption of blood or forfeiture except during the life of the person attainted.

Article 4. Relations Among the States

Section 1. Official Records and Acts

Full faith and credit shall be given in each state to the public acts, records, and judicial proceedings of every other state. And the Congress may by general laws prescribe the manner in which such acts, records, and proceedings shall be proved, and the effect thereof.

Section 2. Privileges of Citizens

1. Privileges The citizens of each state shall be entitled to all privileges and immunities of citizens in the several states.

2. Extradition A person charged in any state with treason, felony, or other crime, who shall flee from justice, and be found in another state, shall on demand of the executive authority of the state from which he fled, be delivered up, to be removed to the state having jurisdiction of the crime.

3. Return of Fugitive Slaves No person held to service or labor in one state, under the laws thereof, escaping into another, shall in consequence of any law or regulation therein, be discharged from such service or labor, but shall be delivered up on claim of the party to whom such service or labor may be due.

Section 3. New States and Territories

1. New States New states may be admitted by the Congress into this Union; but no new state shall be formed or erected within the jurisdiction of any other state; nor any state be formed by the junction of two of more states, or parts of states, without the consent of the legislatures of the states concerned as well as of the Congress.

2. Federal Lands The Congress shall have power to dispose of and make all needful rules and regulations respecting the territory or other property belonging to the United States; and nothing in this Constitution shall be so construed as to prejudice any claims of the United States, or of any particular state.

Section 4. Guarantees to the States

The United States shall guarantee to every state in this Union a republican form of government, and shall protect each of them against invasion; and on application of the legislature, or of the executive (when the legislature cannot be convened) against domestic violence.

Article 5. Amending the Constitution

The Congress, whenever two-thirds of both houses shall deem it necessary, shall propose amendments to this Constitution, or, on the application of the legislatures of two-thirds of the several states, shall call a convention for proposing amendments, which, in either case, shall be valid to all intents and purposes, as part of this Constitution, when ratified by the legislatures of three-fourths of the several states, or by conventions in three-fourths thereof, as the one or the other mode of ratification may be proposed by the Congress; provided that no amendments which may be made prior to the year 1808 shall in any manner affect the first and fourth clauses in the Ninth Section of the First Article; and that no state, without its consent, shall be deprived of its equal suffrage in the Senate.

Clause 1 All states must treat citizens of another state in the same way it treats its own citizens. However, the courts have allowed states to give residents certain privileges, such as lower tuition rates.

Clause 2 *Extradition* means the act of returning a suspected criminal or escaped prisoner to a state where he or she is wanted. State governors must return a suspect to another state. However, the Supreme Court has ruled that a governor cannot be forced to do so if he or she feels that justice will not be done.

Clause 3 *Persons held to service or labor* refers to slaves or indentured servants. This clause required states to return runaway slaves to their owners. The Thirteenth Amendment replaces this clause.

Clause 1 Congress has the power to admit new states to the Union. Existing states cannot be split up or joined together to form new states unless both Congress and the state legislatures approve. New states are equal to all other states.

Clause 2 Congress can make rules for managing and governing land owned by the United States. This includes territories not organized into states, such as Puerto Rico and Guam, and federal lands within a state.

In a *republic,* voters choose representatives to govern them. The federal government must protect the states from foreign invasion and from *domestic,* or internal, disorder if asked to do so by a state.

The Constitution can be *amended,* or changed, if necessary. An amendment can be proposed by (1) a two-thirds vote of both houses of Congress or (2) a national convention called by Congress at the request of two thirds of the state legislatures. (This second method has never been used.) An amendment must be *ratified,* or approved, by (1) three fourths of the state legislatures or (2) special conventions in three fourths of the states. Congress decides which method will be used.

THE CONSTITUTION

Reference Section • **941**

941

Article 6. National Supremacy

Section 1. Prior Public Debts

The United States government promised to pay all debts and honor all agreements made under the Articles of Confederation.

All debts contracted and engagements entered into, before the adoption of this Constitution, shall be as valid against the United States under this Constitution, as under the Confederation.

Section 2. Supreme Law of the Land

The Constitution, federal laws, and treaties that the Senate has ratified are the supreme, or highest, law of the land. Thus, they outweigh state laws. A state judge must overturn a state law that conflicts with the Constitution or with a federal law.

This Constitution, and the laws of the United States which shall be made in pursuance thereof, and all treaties made, or which shall be made, under the authority of the United States, shall be the supreme law of the land; and the judges in every state shall be bound thereby, anything in the constitution or laws of any state to the contrary notwithstanding.

Section 3. Oaths of Office

State and federal officeholders take an oath, or solemn promise, to support the Constitution. However, this clause forbids the use of religious tests for officeholders. During the colonial period, every colony except Rhode Island required a religious test for officeholders.

The Senators and Representatives before mentioned, and the members of the several state legislatures, and all executive and judicial officers, both of the United States and of the several states, shall be bound by oath or affirmation, to support this Constitution; but no religious test shall ever be required as a qualification to any office or public trust under the United States.

Article 7. Ratification

During 1787 and 1788, states held special conventions. By October 1788, the required nine states had ratified the Constitution.

The ratification of the convention of nine states shall be sufficient for the establishment of the Constitution between the states so ratifying the same.

Done in Convention, by the unanimous consent of the states present, the seventeenth day of September, in the year of our Lord one thousand seven hundred and eighty-seven, and of the independence of the United States of America the twelfth. *In Witness* whereof, we have hereunto subscribed our names.

Attest: William Jackson
Secretary

George Washington
President and Deputy from Virginia

New Hampshire
John Langdon
Nicholas Gilman

Massachusetts
Nathaniel Gorham
Rufus King

Connecticut
William Samuel Johnson
Roger Sherman

New York
Alexander Hamilton

New Jersey
William Livingston
David Brearley
William Paterson
Jonathan Dayton

Pennsylvania
Benjamin Franklin
Thomas Mifflin
Robert Morris
George Clymer
Thomas Fitzsimons
Jared Ingersoll
James Wilson
Gouverneur Morris

Delaware
George Read
Gunning Bedford, Jr.
John Dickinson
Richard Bassett
Jacob Broom

Maryland
James McHenry
Dan of St. Thomas Jennifer
Daniel Carroll

Virginia
John Blair
James Madison, Jr.

North Carolina
William Blount
Richard Dobbs Spaight
Hugh Williamson

South Carolina
John Rutledge
Charles Cotesworth Pinckney
Charles Pinckney
Pierce Butler

Georgia
William Few
Abraham Baldwin

THE CONSTITUTION

942

Amendments to the Constitution

The first ten amendments, which were added to the Constitution in 1791, are called the Bill of Rights. Originally, the Bill of Rights applied only to actions of the federal government. However, the Supreme Court has used the due process clause of the Fourteenth Amendment to extend many of the rights to protect individuals against action by the states.

Amendment 1
Freedoms of Religion, Speech, Press, Assembly, and Petition

Congress shall make no law respecting an establishment of religion, or prohibiting the free exercise thereof; or abridging the freedom of speech, or of the press; or the right of the people peaceably to assemble, and to petition the government for a redress of grievances.

The First Amendment protects five basic rights: freedom of religion, speech, the press, assembly, and petition. Congress cannot set up an established, or official, church or religion for the nation. During the colonial period, most colonies had established churches. However, the authors of the First Amendment wanted to keep government and religion separate.

Congress may not ***abridge,*** or limit, the freedom to speak and write freely. The government may not censor, or review, books and newspapers before they are printed. This amendment also protects the right to assemble, or hold public meetings. ***Petition*** means ask. ***Redress*** means to correct. ***Grievances*** are wrongs. The people have the right to ask the government for wrongs to be corrected.

Amendment 2
Right to Bear Arms

A well-regulated militia, being necessary to the security of a free state, the right of the people to keep and bear arms shall not be infringed.

State militia, such as the National Guard, have the right to bear arms, or keep weapons. Courts have generally ruled that the government can regulate the ownership of guns by private citizens.

Amendment 3
Lodging Troops in Private Homes

No soldier shall, in time of peace, be quartered in any house, without the consent of the owner; nor in time of war, but in a manner to be prescribed by law.

During the colonial period, the British quartered, or housed, soldiers in private homes without the permission of the owners (page 153). This amendment limits the government's right to use private homes to house soldiers.

Amendment 4
Search and Seizure

The right of the people to be secure in their persons, houses, papers, and effects, against unreasonable searches and seizures, shall not be violated; and no warrants shall issue but upon probable cause, supported by oath or affirmation, and particularly describing the place to be searched, and the persons or things to be seized.

This amendment protects Americans from unreasonable searches and seizures. Search and seizure are permitted only if a judge has issued a ***warrant,*** or written court order. A warrant is issued only if there is probable cause. This means an officer must show that it is probable, or likely, that the search will produce evidence of a crime. A search warrant must name the exact place to be searched and the things to be seized.

THE CONSTITUTION

In some cases, courts have ruled that searches can take place without a warrant. For example, police may search a person who is under arrest. However, evidence found during an unlawful search cannot be used in a trial.

This amendment protects the rights of the accused. **Capital crimes** are those that can be punished with death. **Infamous crimes** are those that can be punished with prison or loss of rights. The federal government must obtain an **indictment,** or formal accusation, from a grand jury to prosecute anyone for such crimes. A **grand jury** is a panel of between 12 and 23 citizens who decide if the government has enough evidence to justify a trial. This procedure prevents the government from prosecuting people with little or no evidence of guilt. (Soldiers and the militia in wartime are not covered by this rule.)

Double jeopardy is forbidden by this amendment. This means that a person cannot be tried twice for the same crime. However, if a court sets aside a conviction because of a legal error, the accused can be tried again. A person on trial cannot be forced to testify, or give evidence, against himself or herself. A person accused of a crime is entitled to **due process of law,** or a fair hearing or trial.

Finally, the government cannot seize private property for public use without paying the owner a fair price for it.

In criminal cases, the jury must be **impartial,** or not favor either side. The accused is guaranteed the right to a trial by jury. The trial must be speedy. If the government purposely postpones the trial so that it becomes hard for the person to get a fair hearing, the charge may be dismissed. The accused must be told the charges against him or her and be allowed to question prosecution witnesses. Witnesses who can help the accused can be ordered to appear in court.

The accused must be allowed a lawyer. Since 1942, the federal government has been required to provide a lawyer if the accused cannot afford one. In 1963, the Supreme Court decided that states must also provide lawyers for a defendant too poor to pay for one.

Common law refers to rules of law established by judges in past cases. This amendment guarantees the right to a jury trial in lawsuits where the sum of money at stake is more than $20. An appeals court cannot change a verdict because it disagrees with the decision of the jury. It can set aside a verdict only if legal errors made the trial unfair.

THE CONSTITUTION

Amendment 5
Rights of the Accused

No person shall be held to answer for a capital, or otherwise infamous, crime, unless on a presentment or indictment of a grand jury, except in cases arising in the land or naval forces, or in the militia, when in actual service in time of war or public danger; nor shall any person be subject for the same offense to be twice put in jeopardy of life and limb; nor shall be compelled, in any criminal case, to be a witness against himself; nor be deprived of life, liberty, or property, without due process of law; nor shall private property be taken for public use, without just compensation.

Amendment 6
Right to Speedy Trial by Jury

In all criminal prosecutions, the accused shall enjoy the right to a speedy and public trial, by an impartial jury of the state and district wherein the crime shall have been committed, which district shall have been previously ascertained by law, and to be informed of the nature and cause of the accusation; to be confronted with the witnesses against him; to have compulsory process for obtaining witnesses in his favor, and to have the assistance of counsel for his defense.

Amendment 7
Jury Trial in Civil Cases

In suits at common law, where the value in controversy shall exceed $20, the right of trial by jury shall be preserved, and no fact tried by a jury shall be otherwise re-examined in any court of the United States than according to the rules of the common law.

Amendment 8
Bail and Punishment

Excessive bail shall not be required, nor excessive fines imposed, nor cruel and unusual punishments inflicted.

Bail is money the accused leaves with the court as a pledge that he or she will appear for trial. If the accused does not appear for trial, the court keeps the money. **Excessive** means too high. This amendment forbids courts to set unreasonably high bail. The amount of bail usually depends on the seriousness of the charge and whether the accused is likely to appear for the trial. The amendment also forbids cruel and unusual punishments such as mental and physical abuse.

Amendment 9
Powers Reserved to the People

The enumeration in the Constitution, of certain rights, shall not be construed to deny or disparage others retained by the people.

The people have rights that are not listed in the Constitution. This amendment was added because some people feared that the Bill of Rights would be used to limit rights to those actually listed.

Amendment 10
Powers Reserved to the States

The powers not delegated to the United States by the Constitution, nor prohibited by it to the states, are reserved to the states respectively, or to the people.

This amendment limits the power of the federal government. Powers not given to the federal government belong to the states. The powers reserved to the states are not listed in the Constitution.

Amendment 11
Suits Against States

Passed by Congress on March 4, 1794. Ratified on January 23, 1795.

The judicial power of the United States shall not be construed to extend to any suit in law or equity, commenced or prosecuted against one of the United States, by citizens of another state, or by citizens or subjects of any foreign state.

This amendment changed part of Article 3, Section 2, Clause 1. As a result, a private citizen from one state cannot sue the government of another state in federal court. However, a citizen can sue a state government in a state court.

Amendment 12
Election of President and Vice-President

Passed by Congress on December 9, 1803. Ratified on June 15, 1804.

The electors shall meet in their respective states, and vote by ballot for President and Vice-President, one of whom, at least, shall not be an inhabitant of the same state with themselves; they shall name in their ballots the person voted for as President, and in distinct ballots the person voted for as Vice-President, and they shall make distinct lists of all persons voted for as President, and of all persons voted for as Vice-President, and of the number of votes for each, which lists they shall sign and certify, and transmit, sealed, to the seat of government of the United States, directed to the President of the Senate; the President of the Senate shall, in the presence of the Senate and House of Representatives, open all the certificates and the votes shall then be counted; the person having the greatest number of votes for President shall be the

This amendment changed the way the electoral college voted. Before the amendment was adopted, each elector simply voted for two people. The candidate with the most votes became President. The runner-up became Vice President. In the election of 1800, however, a tie vote resulted between Thomas Jefferson and Aaron Burr (page 261).

In such a case, the Constitution required the House of Representatives to elect the President. Federalists had a majority in the House. They tried to keep Jefferson out of office by voting for Burr. It took 35 ballots in the House before Jefferson was elected President.

To keep this from happening again, the Twelfth Amendment was passed and ratified in time for the election of 1804.

This amendment provides that each elector choose one candidate for President and one candidate for Vice President. If no candidate for President receives a majority of electoral votes, the House of Representatives chooses the President. If no candidate for Vice President receives a majority, the Senate elects the Vice President. The Vice President must be a person who is eligible to be President.

This system is still in use today. However, it is possible for a candidate to win the popular vote and lose in the electoral college. This happened in 1876 (pages 497–499).

The Emancipation Proclamation (1863) freed slaves only in areas controlled by the Confederacy (pages 464–465). This amendment freed all slaves. It also forbids *involuntary servitude,* or labor done against one's will. However, it does not prevent prison wardens from making prisoners work.

Congress can pass laws to carry out this amendment.

This section defines citizenship for the first time in the Constitution, and it extends citizenship to blacks. It also prohibits states from denying the rights and privileges of citizenship to any citizen. This section also forbids states to deny due process of law.

Section 1 guarantees all citizens "equal protection under the law." For a long time, however, the Fourteenth Amendment did not protect blacks from discrimination. After Reconstruction, separate facilities for blacks and whites sprang up (page 499). In 1954, the Supreme Court ruled that separate facilities for blacks and whites were by their nature unequal. This ruling, in the case of *Brown* v. *Board of Education,* made school segregation illegal.

President, if such number be a majority of the whole number of electors appointed; and if no person have such majority, then from the persons having the highest numbers not exceeding three on the list of those voted for as President, the House of Representatives shall choose immediately, by ballot, the President. But in choosing the President, the votes shall be taken by the states, the representation from each state having one vote; a quorum for this purpose shall consist of a member or members from two-thirds of the states, and a majority of all the states shall be necessary to a choice. And if the House of Representatives shall not choose a President whenever the right of choice shall devolve upon them, before the fourth day of March next following, then the Vice-President shall act as President, as in the case of the death or other constitutional disability of the President. The person having the greatest number of votes as Vice-President, shall be the Vice-President, if such number be a majority of the whole number of electors appointed, and if no person have a majority, then, from the two highest numbers on the list, the Senate shall choose the Vice-President; a quorum for the purpose shall consist of two-thirds of the whole number of Senators, and a majority of the whole number shall be necessary to a choice. But no person constitutionally ineligible to the office of President shall be eligible to that of Vice-President of the United States.

Amendment 13
Abolition of Slavery
Passed by Congress on January 31, 1865. Ratified on December 6, 1865.

Section 1. Neither slavery nor involuntary servitude, except as a punishment for crime whereof the party shall have been duly convicted, shall exist within the United States, or any place subject to their jurisdiction.

Section 2. Congress shall have power to enforce this article by appropriate legislation.

Amendment 14
Rights of Citizens
Passed by Congress on June 13, 1866. Ratified on July 9, 1868.

Section 1. Citizenship All persons born or naturalized in the United States and subject to the jurisdiction thereof, are citizens of the United States and of the state wherein they reside. No state shall make or enforce any law which shall abridge the privileges or immunities of citizens of the United States; nor shall any state deprive any person of life, liberty, or property, without due process of law; nor deny to any person within its jurisdiction the equal protection of the laws.

946 • Reference Section

Section 2. Apportionment of Representatives Representatives shall be apportioned among the several states according to their respective numbers, counting the whole number of persons in each state, excluding Indians not taxed. But when the right to vote at any election for the choice of electors for President and Vice-President of the United States, Representatives in Congress, the executive and judicial officers of a state, or the members of the legislature thereof, is denied to any of the male inhabitants of such state, being twenty-one years of age and citizens of the United States, or in any way abridged, except for participation in rebellion, or other crime, the basis of representation therein shall be reduced in the proportion which the number of such male citizens shall bear to the whole number of male citizens twenty-one years of age in such state.

Section 3. Former Confederate Officials No person shall be a Senator or Representative in Congress, or elector of President and Vice-President, or hold any office, civil or military, under the United States, or under any state, who, having previously taken an oath, as a member of Congress, or as an officer of the United States, or as a member of any state legislature, or as an executive or judicial officer of any state, to support the Constitution of the United States, shall have engaged in insurrection or rebellion against the same, or given aid or comfort to the enemies thereof. But Congress may, by vote of two-thirds of each house, remove such disability.

Section 4. Government Debt The validity of the public debt of the United States, authorized by law, including debts incurred for payment of pensions and bounties for services in suppressing insurrection or rebellion, shall not be questioned. But neither the United States nor any state shall assume or pay any debt or obligation incurred in aid of insurrection or rebellion against the United States or any claim for the loss or emancipation of any slave; but all such debts, obligations, and claims shall be held illegal and void.

Section 5. Enforcement The Congress shall have power to enforce, by appropriate legislation, the provisions of this article.

Amendment 15
Voting Rights
Passed by Congress on February 26, 1869. Ratified on February 2, 1870.

Section 1. Extending the Right to Vote The right of citizens of the United States to vote shall not be denied or abridged by the United States or any state on account of race, color, or previous condition of servitude.

Section 2. Enforcement The Congress shall have power to enforce this article by appropriate legislation.

This section replaced the three-fifths clause. It provides that representation in the House of Representatives is decided on the basis of the number of people in the state. It also provides that states which deny the vote to male citizens over age 21 will be punished by losing part of their representation in the House. This provision has never been enforced.

Despite this clause, black citizens were often prevented from voting. In the 1960s, federal laws were passed to end voting discrimination.

This section prohibited people who had been federal or state officials before the Civil War and who had joined the Confederate cause from serving again as government officials. In 1872, Congress restored the rights of former Confederate officials.

This section recognized that the United States must repay its debts from the Civil War. However, it forbade the repayment of debts of the Confederacy. This meant that people who had loaned money to the Confederacy would not be repaid. Also, states were not allowed to pay former slave owners for the loss of slaves.

Congress can pass laws to carry out this amendment.

Previous condition of servitude refers to slavery. This amendment gave blacks, both former slaves and free blacks, the right to vote. In the late 1800s, southern states used grandfather clauses, literacy tests, and poll taxes to keep blacks from voting (page 499).

Congress can pass laws to carry out this amendment. The Twenty-fourth Amendment barred the use of poll taxes in national elections. The Voting Rights Act of 1965 gave federal officials the power to register voters in places where there was voting discrimination.

THE CONSTITUTION

Amendment 16
The Income Tax
Passed by Congress on July 12, 1909. Ratified on February 3, 1913.

The Congress shall have power to lay and collect taxes on incomes, from whatever source derived, without apportionment among the several states, and without regard to any census or enumeration.

Congress has the power to collect taxes on people's income. An income tax can be collected without regard to a state's population. This amendment changed Article 1, Section 9, Clause 4.

Amendment 17
Direct Election of Senators
Passed by Congress on May 13, 1912. Ratified on April 8, 1913.

Section 1. Method of Election The Senate of the United States shall be composed of two Senators from each state, elected by the people thereof, for six years; and each Senator shall have one vote. The electors in each state shall have the qualifications requisite for electors of the most numerous branch of the state legislatures.

This amendment replaced Article 1, Section 2, Clause 1. Before it was adopted, state legislatures chose senators. This amendment provides that senators are directly elected by the people of each state.

Section 2. Vacancies When vacancies happen in the representation of any state in the Senate, the executive authority of such state shall issue writs of election to fill such vacancies: *Provided* that the legislature of any state may empower the executive thereof to make temporary appointments until the people fill the vacancies by election as the legislature may direct.

When a Senate seat becomes vacant, the governor of the state must order an election to fill the seat. The state legislature can give the governor power to fill the seat until an election is held.

Section 3. Exception ~~This amendment shall not be so construed as to affect the election or term of any Senator chosen before it becomes valid as part of the Constitution.~~

Senators who had already been elected by the state legislatures were not affected by this amendment.

Amendment 18
Prohibition of Alcoholic Beverages
Passed by Congress on December 18, 1917. Ratified on January 16, 1919.

Section 1. Ban on Alcohol ~~After one year from the ratification of this article the manufacture, sale, or transportation of intoxicating liquors within, the importation thereof into, or the exportation thereof from, the United States and all territory subject to the jurisdiction thereof for beverage purposes is hereby prohibited.~~

This amendment, known as **Prohibition,** banned the making, selling, or transporting of alcoholic beverages in the United States. Later, the Twenty-first Amendment **repealed,** or canceled, this amendment.

Section 2. Enforcement ~~The Congress and the several states shall have concurrent power to enforce this article by appropriate legislation.~~

Both the states and the federal government had the power to pass laws to enforce this amendment.

Section 3. Method of Ratification ~~This article shall be inoperative unless it shall have been ratified as an amendment to the Constitution by the legislatures of the several states, as provided in the Constitution, within seven years from the date of the submission hereof to the states by the Congress.~~

This amendment had to be approved within seven years. The Eighteenth Amendment was the first amendment to include a time limit for ratification.

Amendment 19
Women's Suffrage
Passed by Congress on June 4, 1919. Ratified on August 18, 1920.

Section 1. The Right to Vote The right of citizens of the United States to vote shall not be denied or abridged by the United States or by any state on account of sex.

Neither the federal government nor state governments can deny the right to vote on account of sex. Thus, women won *suffrage,* or the right to vote. Before 1920, some states had allowed women to vote in state elections.

Section 2. Enforcement Congress shall have power to enforce this article by appropriate legislation.

Congress can pass laws to carry out this amendment.

Amendment 20
Presidential Terms; Sessions of Congress
Passed by Congress on March 2, 1932. Ratified on January 23, 1933.

Section 1. Beginning of Term The terms of the President and Vice-President shall end at noon on the 20th day of January, and the terms of Senators and Representatives at noon on the 3rd day of January, of the years in which such terms would have ended if this article had not been ratified; and the terms of their successors shall then begin.

The date for the President and Vice President to take office is January 20. Members of Congress begin their terms of office on January 3. Before this amendment was adopted, these terms of office began on March 4.

Section 2. Congressional Sessions The Congress shall assemble at least once in every year, and such meeting shall begin at noon on the 3rd day of January, unless they shall by law appoint a different day.

Congress must meet at least once a year. The new session of Congress begins on January 3. Before this amendment, members of Congress who had been defeated in November continued to hold office until the following March. Such members were known as *lame ducks.*

Section 3. Presidential Succession If at the time fixed for the beginning of the term of the President, the President-elect shall have died, the Vice-President-elect shall become President. If a President shall not have been chosen before the time fixed for the beginning of his term, or if the President-elect shall have failed to qualify, then the Vice-President-elect shall act as President until a President shall have qualified; and the Congress may by law provide for the case wherein neither a President-elect nor a Vice-President-elect shall have qualified, declaring who shall then act as President, or the manner in which one who is to act shall be selected, and such person shall act accordingly until a President or Vice-President shall have qualified.

If the President-elect dies before taking office, the Vice President-elect becomes President. If no President has been chosen by January 20 or if the elected candidate fails to qualify for office, the Vice President-elect acts as President, but only until a qualified President is chosen.

Finally, Congress has the power to choose a person to act as President if neither the President-elect or Vice President-elect is qualified to take office.

Section 4. Elections Decided by Congress The Congress may by law provide for the case of the death of any of the persons from whom the House of Representatives may choose a President whenever the right of choice shall have devolved upon them, and for the case of the death of any of the persons from whom the Senate may choose a Vice-President whenever the right of choice shall have devolved upon them.

Congress can pass laws in cases where a presidential candidate dies while an election is being decided in the House. Congress has similar power in cases where a candidate for Vice President dies while an election is being decided in the Senate.

Section 5. Date of Implementation Sections 1 and 2 shall take effect on the 15th day of October following the ratification of this article.

Section 5 sets the date for the amendment to become effective.

Reference Section • **949**

Section 6 sets a time limit for ratification.

Section 6. Ratification Period ~~This article shall be inoperative unless it shall have been ratified as an amendment to the Constitution by the legislatures of three-fourths of the several states within seven years from the date of its submission.~~

Amendment 21
Repeal of Prohibition
Passed by Congress on February 20, 1933. Ratified on December 5, 1933.

The Eighteenth Amendment is repealed, making it legal to make and sell alcoholic beverages. Prohibition ended December 5, 1933.

Section 1. Repeal of National Prohibition The eighteenth article of amendment to the Constitution of the United States is hereby repealed.

Each state was free to ban the making and selling of alcoholic drink within its borders. This section makes bringing liquor into a "dry" state a federal offense.

Section 2. State Laws The transportation or importation into any state, territory, or possession of the United States for delivery or use therein of intoxicating liquors, in violation of the laws thereof, is hereby prohibited.

Special state conventions were called to ratify this amendment. This is the only time an amendment was ratified by state conventions rather than state legislatures.

Section 3. Ratification Period ~~This article shall be inoperative unless it shall have been ratified as an amendment to the Constitution by conventions in the several states, as provided in the Constitution, within seven years from the date of the submission hereof to the states by the Congress.~~

Amendment 22
Limit on Number of President's Terms
Passed by Congress on March 12, 1947. Ratified on March 1, 1951.

Before Franklin Roosevelt became President, no President served more than two terms in office. Roosevelt broke with this custom and was elected to four terms. This amendment provides that no President may serve more than two terms. A President who has already served more than half of someone else's term can serve only one more full term. However, the amendment did not apply to Harry Truman, who had become President after Franklin Roosevelt's death in 1945.

Section 1. Two-Term Limit No person shall be elected to the office of the President more than twice, and no person who has held the office of President, or acted as President, for more than two years of a term to which some other person was elected President shall be elected to the office of the President more than once. ~~But this Article shall not apply to any person holding the office of President when this Article was proposed by the Congress, and shall not prevent any person who may be holding the office of President, or acting as President, during the term within which this Article becomes operative from holding the office of President or acting as President during the remainder of such term.~~

A seven-year time limit is set for ratification.

Section 2. Ratification Period ~~This Article shall be inoperative unless it shall have been ratified as an amendment to the Constitution by the legislatures of three-fourths of the several states within seven years from the date of its submission to the states by the Congress.~~

Amendment 23
Presidential Electors for District of Columbia
Passed by Congress on June 16, 1960. Ratified on April 3, 1961.

Section 1. Determining the Number of Electors The District constituting the seat of Government of the United States shall appoint in such manner as the Congress may direct:
A number of electors of President and Vice-President equal to the whole number of Senators and Representatives in Congress to which the District would be entitled if it were a State, but in no event more than the least populous State; they shall be in addition to those appointed by the States, but they shall be considered, for the purposes of the election of President and Vice-President, to be electors appointed by a State; and they shall meet in the District and perform such duties as provided by the twelfth article of amendment.

This amendment gives residents of Washington, D.C., the right to vote in presidential elections. Until this amendment was adopted, people living in Washington, D.C., could not vote for President because the Constitution had made no provision for choosing electors from the nation's capital. Washington, D.C., has three electoral votes.

Section 2. Enforcement The Congress shall have power to enforce this article by appropriate legislation.

Congress can pass laws to carry out this amendment.

Amendment 24
Abolition of Poll Tax in National Elections
Passed by Congress on August 27, 1962. Ratified on January 23, 1964.

Section 1. Poll Tax Banned The right of citizens of the United States to vote in any primary or other election for President or Vice-President, for electors for President or Vice-President, or for Senator or Representative in Congress, shall not be denied or abridged by the United States or any state by reason of failure to pay any poll tax or other tax.

A **poll tax** is a tax on voters. This amendment bans poll taxes in national elections. Some states used poll taxes to keep blacks from voting. In 1966, the Supreme Court struck down poll taxes in state elections, also.

Section 2. Enforcement The Congress shall have the power to enforce this article by appropriate legislation.

Congress can pass laws to carry out this amendment.

Amendment 25
Presidential Succession and Disability
Passed by Congress on July 6, 1965. Ratified on February 11, 1967.

Section 1. President's Death or Resignation In case of the removal of the President from office or his death or resignation, the Vice-President shall become President.

If the President dies or resigns, the Vice President becomes President. This section clarifies Article 2, Section 1, Clause 6.

Section 2. Vacancies in Vice-Presidency Whenever there is a vacancy in the office of the Vice-President, the President shall nominate a Vice-President who shall take the office upon confirmation by a majority vote of both houses of Congress.

When a Vice President takes over the office of President, he or she appoints a Vice President who must be approved by a majority vote of both houses of Congress. This section was first applied after Vice President Spiro Agnew resigned in 1973. President Richard Nixon appointed Gerald Ford as Vice President.

THE CONSTITUTION

If the President declares in writing that he or she is unable to perform the duties of office, the Vice President serves as Acting President until the President recovers.

Two Presidents, Woodrow Wilson and Dwight Eisenhower, have fallen gravely ill while in office. The Constitution contained no provision for this kind of emergency.

Section 3 provided that the President can inform Congress that he or she is too sick to perform the duties of office. However, if the President is unconscious or refuses to admit to a disabling illness, Section 4 provides that the Vice President and Cabinet may declare the President disabled. The Vice President becomes Acting President until the President can return to the duties of office. In case of a disagreement between the President and the Vice President and Cabinet over the President's ability to perform the duties of office, Congress must decide the issue. A two-thirds vote of both houses is needed to find the President is disabled or unable to fulfill the duties of office.

In 1970, Congress passed a law allowing 18-year-olds to vote. However, the Supreme Court decided that Congress could not set a minimum age for state elections. So this amendment was passed and ratified.

Congress can pass laws to carry out this amendment.

If members of Congress vote themselves a pay increase, it cannot go into effect until after the next congressional election. This amendment was proposed in 1789. In 1992, Michigan became the thirty-eighth state to ratify it. Congress had placed no time limit on ratification.

Section 3. Disability of the President Whenever the President transmits to the President pro tempore of the Senate and the Speaker of the House of Representatives his written declaration that he is unable to discharge the powers and duties of his office, and until he transmits to them a written declaration to the contrary, such powers and duties shall be discharged by the Vice-President as Acting President.

Section 4. Whenever the Vice-President and a majority of either the principal officers of the executive departments or of such other body as Congress may by law provide, transmit to the President pro tempore of the Senate and the Speaker of the House of Representatives their written declaration that the President is unable to discharge the powers and duties of his office, the Vice-President shall immediately assume the powers and duties of the office as Acting President.

Thereafter, when the President transmits to the President pro tempore of the Senate and the Speaker of the House of Representatives his written declaration that no inability exists, he shall resume the powers and duties of his office unless the Vice-President and a majority of either the principal officers of the executive department or of such other body as Congress may by law provide, transmit within four days to the President pro tempore of the Senate and the Speaker of the House of Representatives their written declaration that the President is unable to discharge the powers and duties of his office. Thereupon Congress shall decide the issue, assembling within 48 hours for that purpose if not in session. If the Congress, within 21 days after receipt of the latter written declaration, or, if Congress is not in session, within 21 days after Congress is required to assemble, determines by two-thirds vote of both houses that the President is unable to discharge the powers and duties of his office, the Vice-President shall continue to discharge the same as Acting President; otherwise, the President shall assume the powers and duties of his office.

Amendment 26
Voting Age
Passed by Congress on March 23, 1971. Ratified on July 1, 1971.

Section 1. Lowering of Voting Age The right of citizens of the United States, who are 18 years of age or older, to vote shall not be denied or abridged by the United States or any state on account of age.

Section 2. Enforcement The Congress shall have the power to enforce this article by appropriate legislation.

Amendment 27
Congressional Pay Increases
Ratified on May 7, 1992.

No law varying the compensation for the services of the Senators and Representatives shall take effect, until an election of Representatives shall have intervened.

Index

Page numbers that are *italicized* refer to illustrations. An *m*, *c*, or *p* before a page number refers to a map (*m*), chart (*c*), or picture (*p*) on that page. An *n* after a page number refers to a footnote.

A

Abilene, Kan., 523, *m524*

Abolition movement, activists in, 404–405, *p404*; Dred Scott decision, 439–40; John Brown, 438; Kansas, 436–39, *p438*; Lincoln-Douglas Senate race, 441–43, *p441–42*; political parties, 440–41; religious influences, 402–403; underground railroad, 405, 407, *p421*; writers, 417–18. *See also* Antislavery movement; Slavery.

Acomas, 40

Acquired immune deficiency syndrome (AIDS), 856, *p856*

Act of Toleration, 107

Adams, Abigail, 147, 168, 328

Adams, John, 328; American Revolution, 161; Declaration of Independence, 165–66, *p166*, 927; election of 1800, 261; French Revolution, 251; on government, 189; as President, 243, 258–60, *p259*, 269, 329–30, *p922*; taxation opposition, 147, 149–50, *p152*; Treaty of Paris, 182; as Vice President, 207

Adams, John Quincy, 360, 922; Cuba and, 631; election of 1824, 328, *p328*; election of 1828, 329–30, *m329*; as Secretary of State, 319; Treaty of Ghent, 291

Adams, Samuel, 147, *p147*, 152–53, 161

Adams-Onís Treaty, 319

Addams, Jane, 572–73, *p573*, 614, 660

Adobe, 36

Adventures of Huckleberry Finn, The (Twain), 582

Affirmative action, 817

Afghanistan, 808, 831–32, *m890–91*

AFL. *See* American Federation of Labor (AFL).

Africa, *m890–91*; African trading states, 65–67, *m66*, *p67*; Barbary States, 279–80, *m280*; communism, 776; Pan-African Congress, 668; Portuguese slave trade, 67; return of African Americans, 403–404, 703; South African democracy struggle, 838, 840, *p840*; World War II, 754, *m756*; after World War II, 776, *m777*

African Americans, in American Revolution, 155, 176–77, *p176*, 182; black codes, 486; "black Seminoles," 317–18, *p318*; in Canada, 314; in cities, 570, 702–703, 816, 871–72; in Civil War, *p424–25*, 465; in colonies, 86–87, 116, 119–20, *p121*; cultural influences, 119–20, *m120*, *p247*, 871–72, *p871*; discrimination against, 386, 494, *p494*, 499, 613–15, *p614–15*, 660, 702–703, 707, 726–27, 748, 750, 789–93, *p790–93*, 814–17; education, 414, 579, 614, 615, 790–91; Exodusters, 526, *p527*; Fifteenth Amendment, 490–91; first

church, *p208*; Fourteenth Amendment, 227, 236, 487–88, 791; freedmen, 95–96, 176–77, *p176*, 189, 391, 392–93, 397, 403–404, 414, 465, 482, 483–85, *p484*, 486, *p487*, 492, *p495*; gold rush, 372; Great Depression, 726–27, *p726*; Harlem Renaissance, 694–96, *p695–96*; inventors, 546, 547–48, *p548*; Jim Crow laws, 499, 613, 791–92; Ku Klux Klan (KKK), 494, *p494*, 702, *p702*; Negro Election Day, 93; Nobel prize winners, 774, *p871*; in North, 386, p386, 570; Olympics, 739; painters, 418, 583, *p583*, *p693*, 695, *p695*; Panama Canal workers, 641, *p641*; in politics, 492, *p492*, 726, 801, 816–17, 871, *p855*; return to Africa, 403–404, 703; Roaring Twenties, *p693*, 694–96, *p696*; social equality, 871–72, *p871*; Spanish-American War, 633–34; in sports, 576, *p790*; Supreme Court Justice, 791, *791n*, *p791*, 817; unions, 552–53, 556; Vietnam War, 810; violence against, 613, 660, 703; voting rights, 86–87, 189, *c220*, 227, 330, 331, 488, 490–91, *p490*, 499, 790; War of 1812, 290; *Who Is Carrie?*, 322–33; in World War I, 658, 663–64, *p663*; in World War II, 748, 750, *p750*, 755; writers, 582, 696, *p696*, 730–31, 877, *p877*. *See also* Civil rights movement; Equality; Slavery.

Aggression, 739

Agnew, Spiro, 802

Agricultural Adjustment Act (AAA), 717, *c717*, 720

Agriculture. *See* Farming.

Aguinaldo, Emilio, 633, 637–38, *p637*

AIDS. *See* Acquired immune deficiency syndrome (AIDS).

Airplane, 550

Alabama, 57, 304, 444, *m445*, *m892–93*, *c898*

Alamo, *m357*, 358–59, *p359*

Alaska, *c16*, *m19*, *m892–93*, *c898*; land bridge of, 32, *m33*; land and climate of, 18, *m19*, 22, *m23*, 24; purchase of, 623, *623n*, *m630*

Albania, 833, *m835*, *m890–91*

Albany, N.Y., 137–38, *m170*, 171–72

Aldridge, Ira, 386

Aldrin, Buzz, 858

Algonquins, *m42*, 83, 134, 174

Alien and Sedition acts, 260, 269

Allen, Ethan, 160–61, *p160*

Allen, Richard, *p208*

Alliance for Progress, 840

Allied Powers, World War I, 650–71; World War II, 742–46, *p745*, 753–57, *m756*, 761–62. *See also* World War I; World War II.

Alvarado, Pedro de, *p71*

Amanpour, Christiane, *p743*

Amazon River, 21, 25

Amendments, constitutional, 207, *c224*, 225–27, *p226*, 941–52. *See also* specific amendment.

American Association of Retired Persons, (AARP), 875

American Colonization Society, 403–404

American Expeditionary Force (AEF), 662

American Federation of Labor (AFL), 553, 555

American Indian Movement (AIM), 820, *p820*

American Indian Religious Freedom Act, 870–71

American Protective Association, 569

American Revolution, advantages, disadvantages, both sides, 160; African Americans in, 176–77, *p176*, 182; causes and effects, *c183*; debt from, 245, 247, 269, 322–33; early battles of, 160–64, *p160*, *m163*; end of, 181, *m181*; events leading to, 143–55; France in, 172, 174, 181, *m181*, 183; independence declared, 164–67, *p165–66*; in Middle Colonies, 169–74, *m170*, *p171*; Native Americans, 175–76; peace treaty, 141, *m141*, 142–43; at sea, 176; in South, 180–81, *p180*, *m181*; in West, 175–76, *m175*; women in, 177–78, *p177–78*

American System, 313

Americans With Disabilities Act of 1990, *p 855*, 873

Americorps, 829

Amherst, Jeffrey, 139

Anarchists, 699

Anasazis, 35–36, *p36*, 40

Anderson, Marian, *p726*

Anderson, Robert, 447

Andes Mountains, 21, 25, 52, *p52*

Andropov, Yuri V., 832

Angelou, Maya, 877, *p877*

Annexation, 360

Anthony, Susan B., 409, 608

Antietam, Battle of, 459–61, *m459*, 464, 473

Antislavery movement, 408–409, *p408–409*, 435, 436. *See also* Abolition movement.

Apaches, *m42*, 361

Apalachicola River, Fla., 318

Apartheid, 837–38, *p837*

Apollo II, *p854*

Appalachian Mountains, 18–19, *m19*, *m102*

Appeal to the Colored Citizens of the World (Walker), 404

Appeasement, 741

Appomattox Courthouse, Va., *m476*, 477

Apprentice, 121–22

Appropriate, money by Congress, 230

Aquino, Corazon, 838

Arafat, Yasir, 848, *p848*

Arapahos, *m42*, 512, 515, 516, *m517*

Archaeology, 34–36, *p35*

Arctic (culture area), 37–38, *m42*

Arctic Ocean, 15, *m19*

Argentina, 25, *m315*, 317, 736, *m890–91*

Argonne Forest, Battle of, *m662*, 664–65

Arias, Oscar, 824

Aristide, Jean-Bertrand, 842–843, *p843*

Arizona, 24, 35, 40, *m42*, 75, *m75*, 133, 360, *m361*, *m892–93*, *c898*

Arkansas, 432, *c432*, 452, *m452*, *m723*, 725, *m892–93*, *c898*

Arkwright, Richard, 296

Armed forces, commander in chief, 233; Constitution, 216–17, 935; discrimination in, 614; navy expansion, 626. *See also* Arms race; Draft; specific wars.

Armistice, 665, *p667*

Arms race, 771, 782, 807–808, 832, 833

Armstrong, Louis, 694

Armstrong, Neil, 858

INDEX

INDEX

Fourteen Points, 667–68, *p671*

Fourteenth Amendment, 227, 236, 487–88, 791, 946–47

Fourth Amendment, 943

France, *m890–91*; empire in the Americas, *c64*, 132–33, *m133*; exploration, 78–79, *m80*; French and Indian War, 136–41, *p137*, *m139*, *p140*, *m141*; French Revolution, 250–52, *p251*; fur trading rivalry, 83; immigrants from, *c566*; imperialism of, 648; Louisiana Purchase, 271–76, *m273*; Native American alliances, 133–35; Vietnam, 808–809, *m809*; World War I, 649–51, *m650*, 656, 661–63, *m662*, 664–65, *c666*; World War II, *m740*, 742, *m742*, 745, 755, *m756*; XYZ Affair, 258–59, *p259*. *See also* New France.

Franklin, Benjamin, 296; Albany Congress, 137–38; American Revolution, 142, *m151*, 167; Constitutional Convention, 196, 200; Declaration of Independence, 165–66, *p166*, 927; inventions of, 122; *Poor Richard's Almanac,* 123

Franz Ferdinand, 649, *p649*

Fredericksburg, Battle of, *m459*, 472

Free enterprise system, 544

Free market economy, 834

Free Soil party, 429, 431, *p431*

Freedmen, 176–77, *p176*, 189, 391, 392–93, 397, 403–404, 414, 465; Reconstruction, 482, 483–86, *p484*, 495–96, *p495*

Freedmen's Bureau, 483–84, *p501*, 579

Freedom House, 840

Freedom Riders, 815

Freedom's Journal, 404

Frémont, John C., 366, 440–41

French and Indian War, 136–41, *p137*, *m139*, *p140*, *m141*

Freneau, Philip, 256–57

Friedan, Betty, 821

Fritz, Jean: *The Double Life of Pocahontas,* 126–27

Frontier, 142–43, *p143*, 528–29. *See also* West.

Fugitive Slave Law of 1850, 434–35, *p434*

Fuller, Margaret, 416–17

Fulton, Robert, 307, *p313*, *p321*

Fundamental Orders of Connecticut, 95

Fur trade, 80–83, 350–51, *p351*

G

Gabaldon, Guy, 750

Gadsden Purchase, 366, *m367*

Gage, Thomas, 154–55

Galarza, Ernesto: *Barrio Boy,* 880–81

Gallatin, Albert, 269

Gálvez, Bernardo de, 174

Garfield, James, 594, *p924*

Garland, Hamlin, 582

Garnet, Henry Highland, 402, 405

Garrison, William Lloyd, *p404*, 405, 406, 417

Garvey, Marcus, 703

Gaza Strip, *m845*, 847

General Court, 95

General welfare, 218

Gentlemen's Agreement, 617

Geography, 4; dictionary of terms, 26–27, *p26–27*; landforms, 16–18, *m19*; North American climates, 22–25, *m23*, *p24*, *c25*; physical regions, 18–20, *m19*, *p20*; rivers and lakes, *m19*, 20–21; South American climates, 25; South American landforms, 21; themes of, 4–7, *p5–7*; thinking geographically, 8–9, *m9*; U.S. facts, *c16. See also* Interaction of people and environment; Location; Movement; Place; Region.

Geography, Connections With: Battle of Saratoga, 173; Missouri Compromise, 430; Samoa, 629; West African music, 395

George II, King of England, 132

George III, King of England, 144, 149, 153, 161, 163–64, *p165*, 166–67, 171–72, 202, 418

Georgia, *m892–93*, *c898*; colonial, 108–109, *p108*, *m109*, *c113*, 133; Native Americans, 339–40, *m340*; secession, 444, *m445*

Germantown, Battle of, *m170*, 172

Germany, *m890–91*; in American Revolution, 163, 171; Berlin airlift, 773–75, *p774*, *m775*; Berlin Wall, 806, *p806*, 832; immigrants from, 385, *c566*; imperialism of, 648; reunification, 833; submarine warfare, 653–55, 744, 753; under Hitler, 737, *p737*, 739; World War I, 649–54, *m650*, 655, 661–62, *m662*, 664–66; World War I armistice, 665–66, 668–71; World War II, *m740*, 741, 742–45, 753–57, *m756*

Gettysburg, Address, 474–75; Battle of, *m459*, *p472–73*, 473–75

Ghost Dance, 518–19, *p519*

GI Bill of Rights, 784, *784 n*

Gingrich, Newt, 828–29, *p828*

Ginsburg, Ruth Bader, 872

Gist, Christopher, 132

Glaciers, 32–33, *m33*

Glasnost, 833

Global warming, 33, 855, 868

Globes, 8. *See also* Maps and globes.

Glorious Revolution, 116

Goddard, Mary Katherine, 167

Gold, in Africa, 66–67; in Alaska, 623; in Black Hills, 516; in California, 369, 370–71, *p372–73*, 373; in Colorado, 515; of the Incas, 53; in Spanish colonies, 70–77

Gold Rush, 369, 370–71, *p372–73*, 373

Goldwater, Barry, 799

Gompers, Samuel, 553

Good Neighbor Policy, 736, 840

Gorbachev, Mikhail, *p824*, 825, 831, 833, 834

Gore, Albert, Jr., 830

Gorgas, William, 640–41

Government: Articles of Confederation, 192–94, 196–97; branches of, 197, 201–203, *c202*, 222–24, *c223–24*, 228–30, *c229*, 234–35; developed at Constitutional Convention, 195–97; English colonies, 86–87, 112–16, *c113*, *p114*, 115–16; Iroquois, 46, 47, 199–200; limiting, 269; *m718*; separation of powers, 201–203, *c202*, 936–37; spoils system, 594, *p595. See also* Cities; Congress; Constitution: U.S.; States; specific President.

Grand Canyon, 18, 72, *m75*

Grandfather clauses, 499

Grant, Ulysses S.: as Civil War general, 461–62, *p462*, *m474*, 475–77, *p475*, *m476*; as President, 490, 496–97, *p924*

Grapes of Wrath, The (Steinbeck), 730, *p730*

Gray Panthers, 875

Great American Desert, 514

Great Awakening, 120–21

Great Basin (culture area), 39–40, *m42*

Great Britain, *m890–91*; Canada, 314–15; disarmament, 682; the French and Indian War, 136–41, *p137*, *m139*, *p140*, *m141*; French Revolution, 251–52; immigrants from, 700; imperialism of, 648; Native Americans in the West, 282, 285; Oregon Country claim, 350–51; taxation of American colonies, 143–50, *p144*; War of 1812, 286–91, *p287*, *m288*, *p289–91*; World War I, 649, *m650*, 656, 662, *c666*; World War II, 742–45, *p745*, 754–55, *m756. See also* American Revolution; England; English colonies.

Great Compromise, 197–98

Great Depression, *p676–77*; African Americans and, 726–27, *p726*; causes of, 708–12, *p709*; end of, 747; isolationism in, 736; life during, 707, 710–13, *c710*, *p712*, 722, 730–31, *p730–31*; New Deal, 714–19, *p716*, *c717*, *m718*, *c729*, 863; New Deal opposition, 719–21, *p720*; stock market crash, 708–709, *p709*; youth in, 762–63, *p762–63*

Great Gatsby, The (Fitzgerald), 694

Great Lakes, *m19*, 21, 81, 133

Great Migration, 95

Great Northern Railroad, *m524*, 537–38

Great Plains: cattle drives, 522–26, *p523*, *m524*, *p525*; climate, 23, *m23*; Dust Bowl, 723–25, *m723*, *p724*; farming, 526–29, *p527–28*, 529–31, *p530–31*, *p533*; Native Americans, 32, *m33*, 40–44, *m42*, *p43*, *p45*, 511–14, *n511*, *p513–14*, 514–21, *p515–16*, *p517*, *p519–20*; region, 7, 18; women on, 528, *p528*

Great Salt Lake, 18, 369–70, *p370*

Great Serpent Mound, 34, *p35*

Great Society, 799, 801, *p801*, 802

Great Wagon Road, 105, 110, 304

Great White Fleet, 626

Greece, 773, *m890–91*

Greeley, Horace, 350, 570

Green Mountain Boys, 160–61, *p160*, 172

Greene, Nathanael, 181, *m181*

Greenwich, England, 4, *m12*, 13

Gregg, William, 388

Grenada, *m841*, 842, *m890–91*

Grenville, George, 143, 145

Griffiths, John, 379

Grimké sisters, 405, 409

Gross domestic product (GDP), 863

Guadalcanal, 754, *m758*

Guam, *m630*, *m634*, 636, 753, *m758*

Guatemala, 48–50, *p48–49*, *m51*, *m315*, 317, 874, *m890–91*

Guerrilla warfare, 808, 809, 847

Gulf Coast, *p20*, *m42*, 44

Gulf of Mexico, 133, *m133*

Gulf Plain, *m19*, 20

Gulf of Tonkin Resolution, 809, *m809*

Gutenberg, Johannes, 63

INDEX

Latinos, 810, 817–19, *p818,* 873–74. *See also* Chicanos; Cuban Americans; Hispanics; Mexican Americans; Puerto Ricans.
Latitude, 4, 11–13, *m11*
Latvia, 742, *m742, m890–91*
Laurens, Henry, 182
Laws of the Indies, 74–76
Lazarus, Emma, 563
League of the Iroquois, 46–47, *p46,* 57, 199–200
League of Nations: condemned by Hitler, 739; Ethiopian invasion, 737; formation of, 668–69, 671, *p671;* World War II and, 745
League of Women Voters, 236, 688
Lease, Mary Elizabeth, 529, *p530*
Leaves of Grass (Whitman), 417
Lebanon, 844, *m845,* 846, *m890–91*
Lee, Richard Henry, 165
Lee, Robert E.: Civil War, 456, *p456,* 459–61, *m459,* 468, 472–74, 476–77, *m476;* Harpers Ferry, 442
Legislative branch, 197, 201–202, *c202,* 222–24, *c223,* 228–30, *c229, p230,* 931–37. *See also* Congress; House of Representatives.
Legislature, 115, 188–89
Lend-Lease Act, 744–45
Lenin, V.I., 661–62, *p661,* 682, 699, 739
Levittown, 786
Lewis, John L., 721
Lewis, Meriwether, 271, 273–76, *m273,* 277, *m277, p293,* 350
Lewis, Reginald, 871
Lewis, Sinclair, 694
Lewis and Clark expedition, 271, 273–76, *m273,* 277, *m277, p293,* 350
Lexington, Mass., 155, 160, *m163*
Liberator, The, 405, *p406*
Liberia, 403–404, *m890–91*
Liberty, 218–19
Liberty Bonds, 659
Liberty League, 720
Liliuokalani, Queen, 627, *p627*
Lincoln, Abraham, 436, *p923;* assassination, 485; Civil War, 455–58; election of 1860, 444–45, *m446;* election of 1864, 476, 744; foreign policy of, 623; Fort Sumter, 447; Gettysburg Address, 474–75; habeas corpus, 468; "House Divided Cannot Stand" speech, 427; Illinois Senate race, 441–43, *p441–42;* Reconstruction plan, 481, 482–83, *p483;* slavery issue, 463–65, *p463*
Lindbergh, Charles A., 697, *p697*
Lisa, Manuel, 352
Literacy tests, 499
Literature excerpts, *Amelia Stewart Knight's diary* (Knight), 355; *Barrio Boy* (Galarza), 880–81; *Common Sense* (Paine), 165; *The Crisis* (Paine), 170; *The Double Life of Pocahontas* (Fritz), 126–27; *A Farewell to Arms* (Hemingway), 674–75; *Farewell to Manzanar* (J.W. Houston and J.D. Houston), 766–67; *How I Found America* (Yezierska), 588–89; *Johnny Tremain* (Forbes), 212–13; *The Jungle* (Sinclair), 598; *Nightjohn* (Paulsen), 422; *The Oregon Trail* (Parkman), 349; *Paul Revere's Ride* (Longfellow), 417; *The Red Badge of Courage* (Crane), 502–503; *Who Is Carrie?* (J.L. Collier and C. Collier), 322–33

Lithuania, 742, *m742,* 833, *m835, m890–91*
Little Bighorn, Battle of, 516–18, *p516, m517*
Little Rock, Ark., 791
Livingston, Robert, 165–66, 272, 927
Lloyd George, David, 668
Location (geography theme), 4; exact location, 4; relative location, 4–5
Locke, John: *Two Treatises on Government,* 200
Lodge, Henry Cabot, 669, 671
London, Jack, 582
Lone Star Republic, 359
Long, Huey, 720
Long house, *p45,* 46
Long Island, Battle of, 169, *m170*
Longfellow, Henry Wadsworth: *Paul Revere's Ride,* 417
Longhorns, 522
Longitude, 4, 11–13, *m11*
Lopez, Jessie, 817
Los Angeles, Calif., *p75, m361,* 816
Louis XVI, King of France, 250–51
Louisbourg, 139, *m139, p140*
Louisiana, 82, *m133, m141,* 278, 304, 438, 444, *m445, m892–93, c898*
Louisiana Purchase, 272–73, *m273, m367;* Lewis and Clark expedition, 273–76, *m273, p276,* 277, *m277;* slavery and, 429, *m430*
L'Ouverture, Toussaint, 272, *p272*
Lowell, Francis Cabot, 299–300, 312, 384
Loyalists, 167, 179–81
Lumber industry, 22, 24, 604–605
Lusitania, 653–54, *p653*
Luther, Martin, 79
Lynchings, 613, 702
Lyon, Mary, 411

M

MacArthur, Douglas, 713, 753, 758, *m758,* 772, 779–80, *m780*
Madison, Dolley, 289, *p289*
Madison, James, 195–97, *p195,* 202, 205; Hamilton opposition, 247, 255–57; as President, 281, 282, *p922;* as Secretary of State, 269; states' rights, 260; War of 1812, 285, 289
Magellan, Ferdinand, *c64,* 71, 78
Magna Carta, 86, 116, 144, 200
Magnetic compass, 63
Mahan, Alfred, 626
Mail-order stores, 541, 542
Main Street (Lewis), 694
Maine, *p5, m96,* 415, 429, 430, *m892–93, c898*
Maine (battleship), 632–33, *p633*
Mainstreaming, 873
Malaria, 640–41
Malcolm X, 816, *p816*
Manchukuo, 740
Manchuria, 740, *m758*
Mandans, *m42,* 271, 274, 275
Mandela, Nelson, *p827,* 837–38
Manhattan Island, 82, 169–70
Manifest Destiny, *p324–25,* 349, 360–68, *m361, m365, m367,* 369–72
Mann, Horace, 413
Manufacturing. *See* Factories; Industry.
Mao Zedong, 778, *p779,* 807
Maps and globes, *p1,* 8–9, *m9–10;* accuracy, 13–15, *p14;* kinds, parts of, 9–11,

m9–12; latitude and longitude, 11–13, *m11;* map projections, 8, *m9;* time zones, *m12,* 13
Marbury v. Madison, 228, 270
Marcos, Ferdinand, 775, 838
Marine climate, 22, *m23, c24*
Marion, Francis, 180–81, *p180*
Marne, Battle of the, 651
Maroons, 107
Marquette, Jacques, *c64, m80,* 81–82
Marshall, George, 773
Marshall, John, 269–70, *p270,* 339
Marshall, Thurgood, 791, *p791,* 817
Marshall Plan, 773
Martí, José, 631
Marx, Karl, 661
Maryland, 120, *m892–93, c898;* Articles of Confederation, 190; Civil War, 452, *m452;* colonial, *m10,* 109–10, *c113;* free blacks, 392; Mason-Dixon Line, 106; settlement of, 106–107
Mason-Dixon Line, 106
Mass production, 549
Massachusetts, *m892–93, c898;* colonial, 94–95, *p95, m96,* 98, *c113;* Intolerable Acts, 153, *p153;* Native Americans, 98, *p98;* public schools, 121, 413; Samuel de Champlain, 8; Shays' Rebellion, 194; slavery, 177; taxation issue, 147. *See also* Boston, Mass.
Massachusetts Bay Colony, 94–95, *c113*
Massasoit, 89
Matzeliger, Jan, 546, 547, *p548, c549*
Mayas, *m42,* 48–50, *p48–49, m51*
Mayflower Compact, 89
McCarthy, Joseph, 781–82
McClellan, George, 458–59, 460–61, 476
McCormick, Cyrus, 378
McCoy, Elijah, 546, 547, *c549*
McGovern, George, 802
McKay, Claude, 695, 696
McKinley, William, 531, 601–602, 632–33, 636, 637, *p924*
McNamara, Robert, 798
Meat Inspection Act of 1906, 604
Meatpacking industry, 598, 604, *p604*
Medicaid and Medicare, 799, 863
Medicine: advances in, 855, 856, *p879;* African American contributions, 755; Civil War, 467, 471; first free clinic, 187; Incan, 53; organ transplants, 855–56; vaccines, 786, 856; women in, 411
Mediterranean climate, 22, *m23, c24*
Mellon, Andrew, 680
Melville, Herman, 416
Mentally ill, 401, 412–13, *p413*
Mercantilism, 112
Mercator map projection, 8, *m9*
Merrimack, 459, *m459, p460–61*
Mestizos, 76, 315
Metacom, 98, *p98*
Mexican Americans: in California, 371–72; cultural influences, 367, *p368;* discrimination against, 368, 617, 660, 727–28, 750, 819; farm workers, 700, 819; frontier mining, 508–509; labor strikes, 725, *p725;* vaqueros, 522–23, *p523, p525;* in World War II, 750
Mexican Cession, 366, *m367,* 429, 432–34
Mexican War, 365–66, *m365*
Mexico, *m314, m890–91;* California and, 362–63, *p362;* Díaz rebellion, 643, *p643;* financial crisis, 843; Gadsden

nial, 79, *c113*, 120–21; enslaved African Americans, 394; freedom of, 107, *p107*, 189, 207, *p208*, 209, *c217*, 943; Incan, 53; Mayan, 49; Middle Eastern, 844–48, *p846*; Mormons, 369–70, *p370*; Oregon missionaries, 352–53; Pilgrims, 87–89, *m87*; Puritans, 94–99, *p95*; slavery, 402–403; Spanish missions, *p74*, 75, *m75*, 362–63
Renaissance, 63
Rendezvous, 351, *p352*
Renewable resource, 869
Reparations, 668
Repatriation Act, 729
Republic, 199
Republican party: 1994 Congress, 828–29, *p828*; conservative revolution, 826–27, *p828*; Fifteenth Amendment, 490–91; national bank, 312; Radical Republicans, 487–88, *n487*, 496–99; Reconstruction, 485. *See also* Elections, Presidential.
Reservations, 516, *m517*, 518, 520–21, 615, 729, 819–20, 870
Revels, Hiram, 492
Revere, Paul, 148, 149, *m151*, 155
Revolutionary War. *See* American Revolution.
Rhode Island, 96–98, *m96*, *c113*, 115, 206, *m892–93*, *c898*
Richmond, Va., 457–58, *m459*, *m476*, 477
Riis, Jacob, 597
Rillieux, Norbert, 393
Rio Grande, *c16*, *m19*, 21, 40, 364, 366
Roads, 115, 304–307, *m306*
Roaring Twenties, 679, 692–97, *p693*
Roberts, Needham, 663–64
Robinson, Jackie, *p790*
Robinson map projection, 8–9, *m9*
Rochambeau, Comte de, 181, *m181*
Rock, John, 386
Rock 'n' roll, *p850*, 851, 860–61
Rockefeller, John D., 539, 544, 614, 699, 708
Rocky Mountain region, 18, *m19*, *m277*
Romania, 833, *m835*, *m890–91*
Rome-Berlin Axis, *p737*
Rommel, Erwin, 754
Roosevelt, Eleanor, 714, 725–26, 750
Roosevelt, Franklin Delano, 227–28, *p925*; Black Cabinet of, 726; 1940 election, 744; 1944 election, 755; Good Neighbor Policy of, 736, 840; Hundred Days, 715–16; labor reforms by, 721; New Deal, 714–19, *p716*, *c717*, *m718*, *c729*, *p733*; New Deal opposition, 719–22, *p720*; Social Security Act, 722; Supreme Court and, 720–21; World War II, 741–42, 743–46, *p745*, 755
Roosevelt, Theodore, *p925*; conservation, 866; foreign policy of, 639, 641–43, *m642*, 736, 840; Japanese immigration and, 617; New York governor, 602; Panama Canal and, 639; reforms as President, 601–605, *p603–605*; Spanish-American War, 602, 633–34, *p636*; Vice President, 601, 602
Roosevelt Corollary, 641
Rosenberg, Ethel and Julius, 781
Ross, Betsy, 177
Rough Riders, 621, 633, *p636*

Ruby, Jack, 798–99
Rural Electrification Administration (REA), 717–19, *c717*
Rush, Benjamin, 187
Rusk, Dean, 806
Russia, *m890–91*; immigrants from, 562, 564, 588–89; imperialism of, 648; revolutions of 1917, 655–66, *p661*; sale of Alaska, 623, *n623*, *m630*; after World War I, 649–51, *m650*, *c666*, 668, *m669*. *See also* Commonwealth of Independent States; Soviet Union.
Russian Revolution, 655–66, *p661*
Russwurm, John, 404
Ruth, "Babe," 697

S

Sacajawea, 274, 276, *p293*
Sacco and Vanzetti trial, 699, *p700*
Sachems, 46
Sadat, Anwar el, 846–47, *p846*
St. Augustine, Fla., *p74*, 75, *m75*
St. Clair, Arthur, 252
Saint-Gaudens, Augustus, *p95*
St. Lawrence River, 78, 80–81, *m80*, 82, 133, 140, *m141*, 315
St. Leger, Barry, *m170*, 172
St. Louis, Mo., 349, 593, 596
Salem, Mass., *m98*, 99
Salem, Peter, 155, 177
Salk, Jonas, 786, 856
SALT Agreement (Strategic Arms Limitation Talks), 807–808
Salt Lake City, Utah, 370
Salvation Army, 572
Samoa, 628, 629, *m629*, *m630*
Sampson, Deborah, 178
San Antonio, Tex., *m75*, 357, *m357*, 358
San Diego, Calif., *m361*, 362, 366
San Francisco, Calif., *m361*; Asian immigrants, 567–68; Chinatown, 7, *p7*, 567–68; Gold Rush, 371; Spanish mission, *m75*
San Jacinto, Battle of, *m357*, 359
San Juan Hill, Battle of, 633–34, *m634*, *p636*, *p645*
San Martín, José de, 317
Sandinistas, 841–42
Santa Anna, Antonio López de, 357–59, 366
Santa Fe, N.M., 360–61, *m361*, 366
Santa Fe Trail, *m361*, 362–63
Saratoga, Battle of, *m170*, 172, 173, *m173*
Sargent, John Singer, 583
Satellites: communications, *p859*, 860, *p879*; mapmaking, 13–15, *p14*; *Sputnik*, 782–83, *p783*
Saudi Arabia, *m845*, 849, *m890–91*
Savannah, Ga., 108, *m109*, 180, *m181*
Savings and loan crisis, 828
Scalawags, 492
Scarlet Letter, The (Hawthorne), 416
Science. *See* Technology.
Sciences, Connections With: Benjamin Franklin, 122, 123; Dust Bowl, 724; fashion and women's health, 410; Rocky Mountains, 17
Scopes trial, 701–702
Scott, Dred, 439–40, *p439*
Scott, Winfield, 366
Secession, 338, 444–45
Second Amendment, 943

Second Continental Congress, 161
Second Great Awakening, 402–403
Sectionalism, 429; election of 1824, 328–29; election of 1828, 329–30, *m329*; Mexican War, 366; Tariff of Abominations, 336–38, *p337*. *See also* North; Slavery; South; West.
Security Council, 779. *See also* United Nations.
Sedgwick, Catharine, 417
Sedition, 260
Segregation: in 1950s, 789–93, *p790–93*; apartheid, 837; Booker T. Washington and, 614; Jim Crow laws, 499, 613, 790–91; *Plessy* v. *Ferguson*, 499; in sports, *p790*; President Wilson and, 614–15; in World War I, 658; in World War II, 748, 750, *p750*
Selassie, Haile, 737
Selective Service Act, 656, *p656*, 658
Self-determination, 668
Seminole War, 341
Seminoles, *m283*, 317–18, *p318*, 338, *m340*, 341
Senate, 230, *c232*; Constitutional Convention, 197–98; organization and powers, 932; separation of powers, 201–202, 222; Seventeenth Amendment, 601, 948; slavery debate, 428–29, 432–44, *c432*, *p433*; of states, 188–89; Versailles Treaty and, 669, 671
Seneca Falls Convention, 410–11, 607
Senecas, 46, 135, 142–43, 174
Separation of powers, 200–201, *c221*, 222–23, 721
Sequoyah, 338–39, *p338*
Serbia, 649, *m650*, 835, *m835*
Serfs, 62–63
Serra, Father Junípero, 362
Service industry, *p835*, 863–64
Settlement house, 572–73, *p573*
Seventeenth Amendment, 601, 948
Seventh Amendment, 944–45
Seward, William, 444, 623–24, *m630*
Sewing machine, 378, *p558*
Shame of the Cities, The (Steffens), 593
Sharecropping, 495–9
Shawnees, *m42*, 283–85, *m283*, *p284*
Shays' Rebellion, 194, 216
Sheridan, Philip, 475–76, *m476*
Sherman, Roger, 165–66, 197–98, 927
Sherman, William Tecumseh, *m474*, 475–76
Sherman Antitrust Act, 545, 596, 603
Shiloh, Battle of, 461, *m474*
Shipbuilding, 99, 379–80
Sholes, Christopher, 548
Shoshones, 39, *m42*, 43, 274, 276, 871
Shreve, Henry, 307
Sierra Club, 866
Sierra Nevada, 18, *18n*, *m19*, 24, 508
Silent Spring (Carson), 866
Silver, 508, 530–31
Sinai Peninsula, *m845*, 847
Sinclair, Upton: *The Jungle*, 598, 604
Singapore, 753, *m758*, 776, *m864*, *m890–91*
Sioux, 271, 511, *511n*, 516–18, *p516*, *m517*, 519, 820, *p820*. *See also* Lakotas.
Sitdown strikes, 721
Sitting Bull, 514, 516–18, 519
Sixteenth Amendment, 601, 948
Sixth Amendment, 236, 944
Sketch Book, The (Irving), 416

INDEX

INDEX

Credits

Acknowledgements

Cover Illustration by Kazuhiko Sano. Concept by Michel Tcherevkoff **Editorial Services** Nancy Gilbert, Elizabeth Bostwick, Mary Aldridge, Maryellen Cancellieri, Alice Hugh Brown, McCormick Associates **Electronic Publishing** Tamara L. Newnam, Carol Richman, Paula Hartman **Visual Research** Melissa Shustyk, Maureen Raymond, Melanie Jones, Omni-Photo Communications

Text Credits

Page 126 From *The Double Life of Pocahontas* by Jean Fritz. Copyright © 1983 by Jean Fritz. Reprinted by permission of G. P. Putnam's Sons. **Page 212** From *Johnny Tremain* by Esther Forbes. Copyright © 1943 by Esther Forbes Hoskins. Copyright © renewed 1971 by Linwood M. Erskine, Jr., Executor of the Estate. Reprinted by permission of Houghton Mifflin Company. All rights reserved. **Page 322** From *Who is Carrie?* by James Lincoln Collier and Christopher Collier. Copyright © 1984 by James Lincoln Collier and Christopher Collier. Used by permission of Dell Books, a division of Bantam, Doubleday, Dell Publishing Group,

Inc. **Page 422** Delacorte Press, a division of Bantam Doubleday Dell Publishing Group, Inc. From *Nightjohn* by Gary Paulsen. Copyright © 1993 by Gary Paulsen. Used by permission of Delacorte Press, a division of Bantam Doubleday Dell Publishing Group, Inc. **Page 588** Excepts from *How I Found America: Collected Stories of Anzia Yezierska.* Copyright © 1989, 1991 by Louise Levitas Henriksen. Reprinted by permission of Persea Books, Inc. **Page 674** Reprinted with permission of Scribner, a division of Simon and Schuster, from *A Farewell to Arms* by Ernest Hemingway. Copyright © 1929 by Charles Scribner's Sons; renewal copyright © 1957 by Ernest Hemingway. **Page 766** From *Farewell to Manzanar* by James D. Houston and Jeanne Wakatsuki Houston. Copyright © 1973 by James D. Houston. Reprinted by permission of Houghton Mifflin Company. All rights reserved. **Page 812** Copyright © 1962 by Warner Bros. Music copyright © renewed 1990 by Special Rider Music. All rights reserved. International copyright secured. Reprinted by permission. **Page 877** From *On the Pulse of Morning* by Maya Angelou. Copyright © 1993 by Maya Angelou. Reprinted by permission of Random House, Inc. **Page 880** From *Barrio Boy* by Ernesto Galarza. Copyright © 1971 by the University of Notre Dame Press. Reprinted by permission of the University of Notre Dame Press.

Illustration Credits

Page v Courtesy of the Royal Ontario Museum, Toronto, Canada **vi** *t* GC; *bl* Museum of Fine Arts, Boston; *br* Courtesy of Museum of Fine Arts, Boston, Bequest of Winslow Warren **vii** *bl* *Lewis and Clark on the Lower Columbia,* Charles M. Russell, 1905, 1961.195, gouache, watercolor, and graphite on paper, Amon Carter Museum, Fort Worth; *br* M. & M. Karolik Collection, Courtesy, Museum of Fine Arts, Boston **viii** *l* The Daughters of the Republic of Texas Library at the Alamo, San Antonio, Texas; *r* Courtesy Museum of New Mexico **ix** *l* Collection of The New-York Historical Society, New York, NY **ix** *r* Chicago Historical Society, 1920.1688; *i* Chicago Historical Society, 1969.1737 **x** *l* Seaver Center for Western History Research, Museum of Natural History, Photo by Henry Grosinsky; *r* National Baseball Library and Archive, Cooperstown, NY **xi** *l* Seth Joel, Bishop Museum; *r* Culver **xii** *t* Navy Art Collection, Naval Historical Center; *bl* Stock Montage; *br* Hendrix College Gallery, Conway, Arkansas **xiv** Giraudon/AR **xv** *l* Chicago Historical Society; *r* Joan Landis Baum, Photograph courtesy of the Museum of American Folk Art, New York **xvi** *tl* LC; *tr* Reuters/Bettmann; *bl* ©Y ET P Forestier/Sygma; *bc* Tony Freeman/PhotoEdit; *br* Courtesy, Winterthur Museum **xxii–xxiii** John Lei/OPC **xxiv/xxv** *background* ©Grace Davies/OPC **xxiv** *b* John Lei/OPC; *t* Martin Kurzweil **xxix** *tl* Superstock; *tr* ©1993 Robert Mankoff and The Cartoon Bank, Inc.; *c* Grant Heilman Photography; *b* John Lei/OPC **xxv** *tl* Superstock; *tr* George Goodwin/Monkmeyer Press; *cr* ©Joyce Photographics/Photo Researchers, Inc.; *bl* John Lei/OPC; *br* ©Lenore Weber/OPC **xxvi** *t* Kathryn DePue/Binney & Smith; *b* John Lei/OPC **xxvii** *tr* Sam C. Pierson, Jr./Photo Researchers, Inc.; *tl* Conklin/Monkmeyer Press; *c* From the *Rotarian,* June 1972. By permission of the publisher; *bl* Larry Voigt/Photo Researchers, Inc.; *br* John Lei/OPC **xxviii** *t–b* Anthony Puopolo; John Lei/OPC **xxx/xxxi** *background* ©Fotopic/OPC **xxx** *l* Jennifer Hodgkins/Binney & Smith; *b* John Lei/OPC **xxxi** *tl* ©1993, Benita L. Epstein; *tr* ©92 Lightscapes/The Stock Market; *c* ©Bill Nation/Sygma; *bl* NASA/Mark Marten/Photo Researchers, Inc.; *br* John Lei/OPC **xxxii/xxxiii** *background* Superstock **xxxii** *t* Laura Rigolo; *b* John Lei/OPC **xxxiii** *tl* © Gerhard Gscheidle/Peter Arnold, Inc.; *tr* Wesley Bocxe/Photo Researchers, Inc. *bottom l–r* Vladimir Paperny/The Image Bank; Rogers/Monkmeyer Press; John Lei/OPC

UNIT 1 Page 1 The Huntington Library, San Marino, California **2** *c* Courtesy of the Wheelwright Museum of the American Indian, P12 #12; *r* Trans. no. T.I. 170 (Photo by E. Sackler), Courtesy Department of Library Services, American Museum of Natural History **3** *l* National Museum of American Art, Washington, D.C./AR; *r* Ken Karp/OPC **5** Ann Hagen Griffiths/OPC **6** Jack Parsons/OPC **7** Gary Gay/The Image Bank **12** Comstock, Inc. **14** NASA/OPC **17** Rod Walker/Mountain Stock **20** *l* Harald Sund/The Image Bank; *r* ©David Muench 1994 **24** *t* Anne Rippy/The Image Bank; *b* Stephen J. Krasemann/Photo Researchers, Inc. **29** *t, c* Photo by John Lei/OPC; *b* Buffalo Bill Historical Center, Cody, WY, Gertrude Vanderbilt Whitney Trust Fund, Purchase **30** *l* Denver Art Museum; *c* Dallas Museum of Art, Gift of Mr. and Mrs. Raymond D. Nasher; *r* Ohio Historical Society, Photo by Dirk Bakker **31** *l* The Bodleian Library, Oxford; *c* ©Loren McIntyre/Woodfin Camp & Associates; *r* Courtesy of the Royal Ontario Museum, Toronto, Canada **32** Smithsonian Institution, Photo by Chip Clark **35** *l* The Saint Louis Art Museum, Purchase, Eliza McMillan Fund; *r* Superstock **36** *l* Tom Till Photography; *r* Trans. no. 3519(2) (Photo by P. Hollembeak/J. Beckett), Courtesy Department of Library Services, American Museum of Natural History **38** Denver Art Museum **39** Trans. no. 1428(2), Courtesy Department of Library Services, American Museum of Natural History **41** Courtesy of The National Museum of the American Indian/Smithsonian Institution, 23/4131 **43** The Thomas Gilcrease Institute of Art, Tulsa, Oklahoma, 0236.10754, Photograph Courtesy of The New York State Museum **47** *t* Rochester Museum & Science Center, Rochester, New York; *b* Trans. no. K10302, Courtesy Department of Library Services, American Museum of Natural History; Cranbrook Institute of Science (inset) **48** Peabody Museum, Harvard University **50** Laurie Platt Winfrey, Inc. **52** ©Kal Muller/Woodfin Camp & Associates **56** New York Public Library **57** GC **59** ©Loren McIntyre/Woodfin Camp & Associates **60** *l* Werner Forman Archive/AR; *c* Museum Fue Volkerkunde; *r* Lee Boltin Picture Library **61** *l* Jean Loup Charmet/Science Photo Library/Photo Researchers, Inc.; *c* Courtesy of the Pilgrim Society, Plymouth, Massachusetts; *r* National Archives of Canada, Ottawa, Neg.# C-429 **62** Bridgeman/AR **65** *l* The Metropolitan Museum of Art, The Edward C. Moore Collection, Bequest of Edward C. Moore, 1891, Copyright ©1980 The Metropolitan Museum of Art; *r* Giraudon/AR **67** The Metropolitan Museum of Art, Louis V. Bell and Rogers Funds, 1972 (1972.63ab), Photograph by Stan Reis, Copyright ©1984 The Metropolitan Museum of Art **68** *l* United States Capitol Art Collection, Architect of the Capitol; *r* NASA **69** *t* Erich Lessing/AR; *c,b* GC; **71** Biblioteca Nacional Madrid **73** Arizona State Department of Library Archives and Public Records; Photo: David Barr. **74, 77** Arxiu Mas **79** Simon Wingfield Digby, Sherborne Castle, Sherborne, Dorset **81** *LaSalle Claiming Louisiana for France, April 9, 1682* (detail), George Catlin, Paul Mellon Collection, ©1993 National Gallery of Art, Washington **82** Museum of the City of New York, The J. Clarence Davies Collection **84** *l–r* Copyright British Museum; LC **85** National Portrait Gallery, Washington/AR **91** *t* Rare Books and Manuscript Division, The New York Public Library, Astor, Lenox and Tilden Foundations; *c* Courtesy of The New-York Historical Society, New York, NY; *b* National Gallery of Canada, Ottawa, Transfer from the Parliament of Canada, 1888 **92** *l* GC; *c* Rare Books and Manuscript Division, The New York Public Library, Astor, Lenox and Tilden Foundations; *r* ©Esto **93** *l* Courtesy, American Antiquarian Society; *c* Courtesy, Winterthur Museum; *r* Old Sturbridge Village, B19442 **95** The Metropolitan Museum of Art, Bequest of Jacob Ruppart, 1939 (39.65.53), Copyright ©The Metropolitan Museum of Art **97** GC **98** Shelburne Museum, Vermont, Photo by Ken Burris **99** Courtesy, Winterthur Museum; *c* Smithsonian Institution, Photo No. 72-4984; *r* Old Sturbridge Village, B11788 **101** Courtesy of the New-York Historical Society, New York, NY **103** *l* Courtesy, Museum of Fine Arts, Boston, Gift of Mrs. Maxim Karolik for the Karolik Collection of American Paintings, 1815-1865; *i* Philadelphia Museum of Art, Given by John T. Morris **104** *l* Copyright British Museum; *r* The New York Public Library **105** National Gallery of Art, Washington, Photo by Dean Beasom **106** Enoch Pratt Free Public Library **108** The New York Public Library **110** The Metropolitan Museum of Art, Gift of Edgar William & Bernice Chrysler Garbisch, 1963 (63.201.3), Copyright ©The Metropolitan Museum of Art **111** *l* National Maritime Museum, London; *i* The Peabody Museum of Salem **114** The Library Company of Philadelphia; **119** *l* GC; *r* LC **122** *t* Giraudon/AR; *bl* Copyright ©1993, The Bucks County Historical Society; *br* Erich Lessing/AR **125** *t* Courtesy, American Antiquarian Society; *c* National Gallery of Art, Washington; *b* Old Slave Mart Museum and Library, Charleston, SC **127** Ashmolean Museum, University of Oxford

UNIT 2 Page 128 Anne S. K. Brown Military Collection **130** *l–r* GC; The West Point Museum, United States Military Academy, West Point, New York, Photo by Paul Warchol; Courtesy of the Royal Ontario Museum, Toronto, Canada **131** *l–r* GC; Culver; GC **132** *l* National Archives of Canada, Ottawa; *r* Hudson Bay Company Collection, Photo by Kevin Fleming **134** National Gallery of Canada, Ottawa **137** The Thomas Gilcrease Institute of Art, Tulsa, Oklahoma, #0100-1514 **140** New Brunswick Museum **143** LC **144** *l* LC; *r* Reuters/Bettmann **146** Smithsonian Institution, Photo No. 86-4091 **147** *l* Deposited by the City of Boston, Courtesy, Museum of Fine Arts, Boston; *c* GC; *r* Courtesy of Museum of Fine Arts, Boston, Bequest of Winslow Warren. **148** Courtesy, American Antiquarian Society **152** LC **153** The Historical Society of Pennsylvania **154** *l* Scala/AR; *r* Connecticut Historical Society, Hartford, Connecticut **157** *t–b* LC; Colonial Williamsburg Foundation; Culver; The Bettmann Archive **158** *l* Courtesy Independence National Historical Park Collection; *c* Gift of Maxim Karolik, Courtesy, Museum of Fine Arts, Boston; *r* Chicago Historical Society **159** *l* Copyright Yale University Art Gallery; *r* GC **160** Fort Ticonderoga Museum **162** Gift of Mr. and Mrs. Gardner Richardson, Courtesy, Museum of Fine Arts, Boston **165** *l* *Pulling Down the Statue of George III at Bowling Green,* 1857, oil on canvas, 51 5/8" x 77 5/8", Lafayette College Art Collection **165** *r* Yale University Art Gallery; Bequest of Mrs. Katherine Rankin Wolcott Verplanck **166** *l* Yale University Art Gallery; *r* Culver **168** Massachusetts Historical Society **169** The New York Public Library, Emmett Collection **171** Nahan Galleries **173** The West Point Museum, United States Military Academy, West Point, New York, Photo by Paul Warchol **176** *l* Stockbridge Library; *r* Collection of The New-York Historical Society, New York, NY **177** Photo by John Lei/OPC **178** LC **180** *Marion Crossing the Pedee,* 1851, William T. Ranney, engraving, Amon

CREDITS

CREDITS

972 • Reference Section

chusetts Historical Society **401** *l* LC; *r* From the Collection of Boscobel Restoration, Inc., Garrison-on-Hudson, New York **403** Laurie Platt Winfrey, Inc. **404** *l* The Metropolitan Museum of Art, Gift of I.N. Phelps Stokes, Edward S. Hawes, Marion Augusta Hawes, 1937 (37.14.37), Copyright ©The Metropolitan Museum of Art; *r* National Portrait Gallery, Smithsonian Institution/AR **406** LC **408** National Portrait Gallery, Smithsonian Institution/AR **409** Sophia Smith Collection, Smith College **410** *t* Museum of the City of New York, The Harry T. Peters Collection (detail); *b* LC **413** By permission of the Houghton Library, Harvard University **414** The Saint Louis Art Museum, Museum Purchase **415** *t* The New York Public Library; *b* ©Lee Balterman/Gartman Agency **417** Stowe-Day Foundation, Hartford, CT **418** Courtesy of the Pennsylvania Academy of the Fine Arts, Philadelphia, General Fund **419** Collection of the Albany Institute of History & Art **421** *t* Sophia Smith Collection, Smith College; *c* Laurie Platt Winfrey, Inc.; *b* The Schomburg Center/Photo by John Lei/OPC; **423** Illustration from the cover of the book NIGHTJOHN copyright © 1993 by Jerry Pinkney. Written by Gary Paulsen. Published by Delacorte Press. All rights reserved. Used with permission.

UNIT 5 Page 424 *r* Avery/Stock Boston, Inc. **426** *l, r* LC; *c* The Brooklyn Museum, Gift of Miss Gwendolyn O.L. Conkling **427** *l–r Border Ruffians Invading Kansas,* F. O. C. Darley, Yale University Art Gallery, The Mabel Brady Garvan Collection; National Portrait Gallery, Smithsonian Institution/AR; The Museum of the Confederacy, Richmond, Virginia, Photography by Katherine Wetzel **428** *l–r* Courtesy of the Decorative and Industrial Arts Collection of the Chicago Historical Society, 1954.15; 1920.1274; 1920.732; 1920.6 **431** LC **433, 434** GC **438** Kansas State Historical Society **439** Missouri Historical Society **441** National Portrait Gallery, Smithsonian Institution/AR **442** *l* Courtesy of the Illinois State Historical Library; *r* ©Reuters/Brian Snyder/Archive Photos **443** The Metropolitan Museum of Art, Gift of Mr. & Mrs. Carl Stoeckel, 1897 (97.5), Copyright ©1982/1990 The Metropolitan Museum of Art **445** GC **447** *l* Fort Sumter National Monument; *r* The Museum of the Confederacy, Richmond, Virginia, Photography by Katherine Wetzel **449** *t* State Historical Society of Wisconsin; *b, c* GC **450** *l* The Museum of the Confederacy, Richmond, Virginia, Photography by Katherine Wetzel **450** *c* Collection of Michael J. McAfee; *r* LC **451** *l* Collection of The New York Historical Society, New York, NY; *r* The West Point Museum, United States Military Academy, West Point, New York **455** Museum of Fine Arts, Boston, M. and M. Karolik Collection of American Watercolors and Drawings, 1800–1875 **456** Collections of The Virginia State Historical Society, Richmond, Virginia **458** The Connecticut Historical Society, Hartford, Connecticut **461** The Collection of Jay P. Altmayer **462** Mr. and Mrs. Karolik Collection, Courtesy, Museum of Fine Arts, Boston, Mr. & Mrs. Karolik Collection **463** LC **464** Copyrighted by the White House Historical Association; Photograph by the National Geographic Society **466** The Metropolitan Museum of Art, Gift of Mrs. William F. Milton, 1923 (23.77.1), Copyright ©By The Metropolitan Museum of Art **467** LC **468** Courtesy of the Historical Society of Delaware **469** *l–r* Chicago Historical Society, 1969.1737; 1920.1688 **471** *t* LC; *b* Architect of the Capitol **472** New Hampshire Historical Society, 1921.4.2 **475** LC **479** *t* Courtesy of the Decorative and Industrial Arts Collection of the Chicago Historical Society, 1920.691; *c* The Museum of the Confederacy, Richmond, Virginia, Photography by Katherine Wetzel; *b* LC **480** *l* The Library Company of Philadelphia; *c, r* LC **481** *l, c* GC **481** *r,* The Museum of American Political Life, University of Hartford, Photo by Sally Anderson Bruce **483** Chicago Historical Society, Gift of Mr. Philip K. Wrigley, 1955.398 **484** *Sunday Morning In Virginia,* Winslow Homer, Cincinnati Art Museum, John J. Emery Fund **487** Metropolitan Museum of Art, Morris K. Jesup Fund, 1940 (40.40), Copyright ©1985/93 The Metropolitan Museum of Art **489** LC **490** GC **492** LC **494** *l* Old Court House Museum, Vicksburg, Photo by Bob Pickett; *r* Collection of State Historical Museum/Mississippi Department of Archives and History **495** Courtesy of The New York Historical Society, New York, NY **498** Hampton University Museum, Hampton, Virginia **501** *t* Courtesy, Tennessee State Museum, Tennessee Historical Society Collection, Photo By June Dorman; *c* The Children's Museum of Indianapolis; *b* LC **503** Metropolitan Museum of Art, Gift of Mrs. Frank B. Porter, 1922 (22.207), Copyright ©The Metropolitan Museum of Art

UNIT 6 Page 504 Museum of the City of New York, Gift of Mrs. William B. Miles **506** *l* Union Pacific Museum Collection; *c* Seaver Center for Western History Research, Museum of Natural History, Photo by Henry Grosinsky; *r* The Brooklyn Museum, Bequest of

Miss Charlotte R. Stillman **507** *l* LC; *r* The Homesteader's Wife, 1916, Harvey Dunn, South Dakota Art Museum Collection, Brookings **509** *l* Courtesy Levi Strauss & Co., San Francisco, California; *r* Esbin-Anderson/OPC **510** Special Collections Division, University of Washington Libraries **512** *Following the Buffalo Run,* c. 1894, Charles M. Russell, oil on canvas, Amon Carter Museum, Fort Worth, 1961.134 **513** *l* National Museum of American Art, Washington, D.C./AR; *r* Courtesy of The National Museum of the American Indian, Smithsonian Institution, 22/8539 **515** *Song of the Talking Wire* (detail), 1904, Henry Farny, oil on canvas, 22 1/16" x 40", Acc. no. 1931.466, Bequest of Mr. and Mrs. Charles Phelps Taft, Taft Museum, Cincinnati, Ohio **516** From *A Pictographic History of the Oglala Sioux,* University of Nebraska Press **519** Photograph Courtesy of The National Museum of the American Indian, Smithsonian Institution, 55299; 2/1133 **520** The National Portrait Gallery, Smithsonian Institution/AR **523** Courtesy of Luis Jimenez, Photo by Edward Fuss **525** Anshutz Collection **527** Nebraska State Historical Society **528** *The Prairie is My Garden,* Harvey Dunn, South Dakota State Art Museum Collection, Brookings, South Dakota **530** Kansas State Historical Society **533** *t* GC; *c* ©1994 Michael Freeman; *b* Solomon D. Butcher Collection, Nebraska State Historical Society **534** *l* ©1994 Michael Freeman; *c* The Bettmann Archive; *r* The George Meany Memorial Archives **535** *l* GC; *r* N. Wright/National Motor Museum **537, 538** LC **540** The Metropolitan Museum of Art, Purchase, Lyman G. Bloomingdale Gift, 1901 (01.7.1), Copyright ©The Metropolitan Museum of Art **541** The National Portrait Gallery, Smithsonian Institution, Gift of Mrs. Margaret Carnegie Miller/AR **542** *t* Culver; *b* GC **543** Culver **545** LC **547** *t* U.S. Dept. of the Interior, National Park Service, Edison National Historic Site; *b* ©1994 Michael Freeman **548** Lynn Historical Society, Lynn, Massachusetts **550, 552, 554** Culver **555** Brown Brothers **557** Culver **559** *t* GC; *bl, br, c* Culver **560** *l* Minnesota Historical Society; *c* Chinatown History Museum Archives, New York; *r* Museum of the City of New York, The J. Clarence Davies Collection **561** *l* GC; *r* Culver **563** *l, c* Photo by John Lei/OPC; *r* Lewis W. Hine, Courtesy George Eastman House **565** LC **568** Courtesy Guy Wong, Kan's Restaurant, San Francisco **572** Culver **573** *t* National Portrait Gallery, Smithsonian Institution/AR; *b* Jane Addams Memorial Collection, Special Collections, The University Library, The University of Illinois at Chicago **575** Chicago Historical Society, ICHi-01066 **577** Museum of Art, Rhode Island School of Design, Jesse Metcalf and Walter H. Kimball Funds, Photography by Cathy Carver **578** *t, c* Culver; *b* Courtesy Museum of the City of New York/Lee Boltin **580** McNaught Syndicate, Inc. **581** Laurie Platt Winfrey, Inc. **582** Culver **583** Hampton University Museum, Hampton, Virginia **584** *t* Yale University Art Gallery; *cl* Collection of The New York Historical Society, N.Y.C.; *cr Lacrosse Playing Among the Sioux Indians,* 1851, Seth Eastman, oil on canvas, 28 1/4" x 40 3/4" (71.76 x 103.51 cm), in the Collection of the Corcoran Gallery of Art, Gift of William Wilson Corcoran; *b* Cooper-Hewitt Museum **585** *t* LC; *c* Bethel Green Museum of Children, London, Photo by Pip Barnard; *b* National Baseball Library and Archive, Cooperstown, NY **587** *t* Courtesy of the Decorative and Industrial Arts Collection of the Chicago Historical Society, ICHI-25164; *bl* Courtesy of The New York Historical Society, New York, NY (detail); *br* Collection of James and Barbara Palmer, Photo Courtesy Babcock Galleries (detail) **589** The Saint Louis Art Museum, Bequest of Marie Setz Hertslet

UNIT 7 Page 590 Bequest of Edward Jackson Holmes Collection, Courtesy, Museum of Fine Arts, Boston **592** *l–r* Courtesy of The New York Historical Society, N.Y.C. **593** *l–r* Theodore Roosevelt Birthplace, Photo by John Lei, OPC; GC; The Museum of American Political Life, University of Hartford **595** *t* Chicago Historical Society, ICHI-20584; *b* Culver **597** International Museum of Photography at George Eastman House **598** *l* LC; *i* Culver **599** Toledo-Lucas County Public Library **600, 603** Culver **604** LC **605** *l* Theodore Roosevelt Collection, Harvard College Library; *r* John M. Roberts/The Stock Market **606** *Woodrow Wilson,* 1919, John Christen Johansen, National Portrait Gallery, Smithsonian/AR; *i* Collection of The New York Historical Society, New York, NY (detail) **608** GC **609** Culver **612** GC **614** *l* Schomburg Center for Research in Black Culture, Photo by John Lei/OPC; *r* Schomburg Center for Research in Black Culture, Prints and Photographs Division, The New York Public Library, Astor, Lenox and Tilden Foundations **615** LC **616** Jaune Quick-To-See Smith, Collection of Eleanor and Len Flomenhaft, Courtesy Steinbaum Krauss Gallery, NYC **619** *t* GC; *c* Museum of Connecticut History; *b* LC **620** *l* Dept. of Rare Books & Special Collections, Rush Rhees Library of the University

Reference Section • **973**

CREDITS